Handbook of Business Finance and Capital Sources

Third Edition

Dileep Rao, Ph.D.

American Management Association

First Edition
First Printing, 1979
Second Printing, 1980

Second Edition
First Printing 1982

Third Edition
First Printing 1985

Published by InterFinance Corporation
511 11th Avenue South, Minneapolis, Minnesota 55415

Library of Congress No. 84-45976

This publication is not guaranteed to be complete or error-free. Due to the large amount of data in the book, errors can occur and we do not assume responsibility for any losses due to these errors. We would appreciate it if readers would bring any errors to our attention, so that they can be corrected in future editions. Information regarding the investment criteria of the financial institutions has been given to us by the institutions themselves, and we have not verified this information independently. No responsibility is assumed for any loss or damage to anybody from the use of this publication. This book does not assume to provide legal or other advice. Such advice should be obtained from the reader's attorney, accountant, or other professional adviser. The data is published for use as a reference source only and is not intended for use in making investment decisions regarding securities of the companies listed.

International Standard Book Number 0-8144-5811-4

Printed in the United States of America

Table of Contents

BUSINESS FINANCE

PRIVATE FINANCIAL INSTITUTIONS

STATE INSTITUTIONS AND PROGRAMS

FEDERAL PROGRAMS

LIST OF FIGURES

Figure

LIST OF TABLES

Table

Business Finance

I. Introduction

The Handbook of Business Finance and Capital Sources is designed to be a comprehensive one-stop library of accurate, updated information to help businessmen, entrepreneurs, financial officers, and other professionals, such as attorneys and accountants, raise funds needed for businesses. The complex structure of the U.S. financial world makes it imperative that those attempting to raise funds know the sources most likely — and least likely — to provide financing. Entrepreneurs and businessmen, even if not in regular contact with the financial institutions and markets, should be able to use the information to raise funds efficiently and at reasonable cost. While all possible care is taken to maintain high accuracy levels, it is possible that errors do creep into the book due to the voluminous amount of data. We appreciate readers bringing any errors to our attention.

By including current information on the investment criteria of major U.S. financial institutions, as well as state and federal programs, this handbook is intended to serve as a periodic survey of U.S. financial conditions. Therefore, updated editions to record changes in this information are being planned.

How the Book is Arranged and How to Use it

The Handbook is composed of four sections:

Section One: Contains descriptive information on various aspects of business finance. Chapter one contains the introduction to the book and Table 1, which summarizes the types of financial institutions and financial instruments used for the various financial needs of businesses. Chapter two contains the fundamentals of business finance, including the financial requirements of a business, the cost of money for various types of financing, distribution of securities using private placement or public offerings, and information requirements for financial packages. Chapter three describes the various types of financial instruments and how they are used, the sources and credit criteria and the methods of raising funds using the instruments. Chapter four

TABLE 1: Financing without a Public Offering — Institutions & Instruments

BUSINESS FINANCIAL NEED / INSTITUTION	Commercial Banks	Commercial Paper Houses	Finance Companies	Industrial Banks	Insurance (Lief) Cos.	Investment Bankers	Investment (Including Closed-End) Cos.	Leasing Cos.	Mortgage Bankers	REITs & R.E. Inv. Cos.	Savings Institutions (S & Ls and MSBs)	Service Agencies of S & Ls	Venture Capital Cos. (or Sub. or Div.)	SBICs	MESBICs	Entrepreneur(s)	Sophisticated Investors
1. Equity						●	●			●			●	●	●	●	●
2. Venture Capital							●						●	●	●		●
3. Debt																	
4. Unsecured[1]																	
5. Short-Term	●	●														●	
6. Medium-Term	●					●										●	
7. Long-Term	●				●	●										●	
8. Continuous or Revolving	●	●														●	
9. Secured																	
10. Working Capital				●													
11. Seasonal	●		●														
12. Permanent/Revolving	●		●														
13. Equipment				●		●											
14. Loans or Conditional Sales Contract	●		●		●			●									
15. Leases	●		●		●			●								●	●
16. Real Estate			●	●		●			●	●	●						
17. Land Financing	●			●	●				●	●	●						
18. Construction Financing	●								●	●	●						
19. Interim Financing	●			●					●	●	●						
20. Long-Term Financing	●				●				●	●	●						
21. Lease	●				●				●	●		●				●	●
22. All Assets-Long Term	●				●	●											
23. Specialized																	
24. Import/Export	●		●														
25. Startup	●						●				●		●	●	●	●	●
26. Acquisition	●		●		●	●	●	●	●	●	●		●	●	●	●	●
27. Agriculture-Related	●				●			●			●					●	●
28. Grants																	

Footnotes

1. Unsecured loans (and even secured loans) often require personal guarantees from principal shareholders

TABLE 1. Financing Without a Public Offering — Institutions & Instruments (continued)

						U.S. GOVERNMENT AGENCIES										
	Entrepreneur's Friends, Relatives, Customers, etc	Suppliers	Employees/ESOTs/Co. Pension Fund	Local Development Corp.	Community Development Corp.	DOA/ASCS	DOA FmHA	DOA/REA	DOC/NOAA	DOC/MA	DOI/BIA	DOI/GS	SBA[3]	OPIC	DOE	INSTRUMENT & MEANS
1.	●		●		●											1,2,3,27,29,30,31
2.	●				●											1,2,26,27,31
3.																
4.															●	
5.	●	●														4,5,6,7,8,9,10
6.	●															11,12
7.	●											●				12,22
8.	●															10,11
9.																
10.															●	
11.																4,6,7,8,9,13,14,15,16,17,23,24,25,28
12.							●			●			●			12,13,14,15,16,17,23,24,25,28
13.			●	●											●	
14.	●	●		●			●		●	●			●			18,20,21,22,23,24,25
15.	●			●									●			20,21
16.			●	●	●											12,19,21,22
17.				●	●											12,19,21
18.				●	●								●			12,19,20,22
19.				●	●		●						●			12,19,20,22
20.				●	●		●						●			12,19,20,21,22
21.	●			●	●								●			20,21
22.					●		●	●			●[2]		●	●		12,22
23.																
24.		●														4,6,7,8,9,28
25.	●	●		●	●		●						●			1,2,4,6,7,11,12,13,14,15,16,17,18,19, 20,23,24,25,26,27
26.	●	●	●	●	●		●						●			1,2,4,11,12,13,14,15,16,17,18,19,20, 21,22,23,24,25,26,27,30
27.	●	●			●	●	●									7,12,16,17,18,19,20,21
28.						●				●	●					

2. Loans and grants to tribes, tribal enterprises, Indians and Alaska natives

3. SBA normally provides guarantees rather than direct loans or leases

(See next page for explanation of acronmys and listing of instruments and means.)

United States Government Agencies

DOA/ASCS:	Department of Agriculture/ Agriculture Stabilization & Conservation Service
DOA/FmHA:	Department of Agriculture/ Farmers Home Administration
DOA/REA:	Department of Agriculture/ Electrification Administration
DOC/NOAA:	Department of Commerce/ National Oceanic & Atmospheric Administration
DOC/MA:	Department of Commerce/ Maritime Administration
DOI/BIA:	Department of the Interior/ Bureau of Indian Affairs
DOI/GS:	Department of the Interior/ Geological Survey
SBA:	Small Business Administration
OPIC:	Overseas Private Investment Corporation
DOE:	Department of Energy

Instruments & Means

1. Common Stock
2. Preferred Stock
3. Retained Earnings
4. Trade Credit
5. Line of Credit
6. Transaction Loans
7. Short-term Working Capital Loans
8. Banker's Acceptance
9. Letter of Credit
10. Commercial Paper
11. Medium-term Credit-Revolving or Rollover Credit
12. Term Loans
13. Accounts Receivable Loans
14. Inventory Loans-Floating liens
15. Inventory Loans-Warehouse Receipt
16. Inventory Loans-Commodity Loans
17. Stocks & Savings Account Loans
18. Equipment Liens/ Chattel Mortgages
19. Real Estate Loans
20. Leases
21. Sale-Leaseback
22. Bonds
23. Trust Receipt
24. Floor Planning
25. Time Sales Financing
26. Convertibles
27. Warrants
28. Factoring
29. Franchising
30. Employee Stock Ownership Plans
31. Limited Partnerships

---

provides information on the different types of financial institutions, their practices, flow of funds, and types of financing. Chapter five describes topics of special interest, including some legal aspects, Eurodollars, and detailed descriptions of methods and instruments used for specialized areas of financing, such as financing for startups, acquisitions, equipment, real estate, agriculture and import/export.

Readers who are searching for specific types of financing (such as for real estate), can examine Table 1 to determine the types of institutions which provide such financing, and easily locate the institutions in Sections Two, Three or Four.

Section Two: Provides the names, addresses, contact officers and investment criteria, if available, of private (non-government) financial institutions. The institutions are arranged by type of institution (such as leasing company), by state and city, and alphabetically within the city. Each branch is given a separate listing.

Section Three : Includes information on contact officers, addresses and investment criteria of the various financial programs offered by the states to businesses located in their respective states. The chart at the beginning of the section provides the key to the specific programs offered by each state. The information on the programs is arranged in alphabetical order by state.

Section Four: Provides information on the various federal programs offering financial assistance to businessmen and farmers. The guide to federal programs at the beginning of the section separates the programs by type of beneficiary. Additional information on each of the programs can be obtained by locating its index number in the main body of the section. The programs are arranged in ascending order of these numbers.

II.
Fundamentals of Business Finance

Business Financial Requirements

Types of Assets

A business uses assets to produce and market goods and/or services to earn a profit. The common classifications of assets are:

Current Assets: including cash and other assets which are expected to be realized in cash, sold, or consumed either within one year from the date of the balance sheet or during the normal operating cycle of the business, whichever is longer. The normal operating cycle is the time taken to go from cash to cash. Current assets are listed in the balance sheet in order of decreasing liquidity, which is the average period of time required to convert the asset into cash. Normally, current assets include cash, accounts and notes receivable, inventory, temporary investments, and prepaid expenses:

Long-term Investments: including stocks and bonds of other companies which have been bought for investment;

Fixed assets: including equipment, real estate and building — that is, assets having physical substance used for producing the goods or services of the business, or held for investment;

Intangible Assets: including goodwill, patents, trademarks, copyrights, etc.

Other Assets: including long-term prepayment of expenses, fixed assets not being used, etc.

The total assets of a business are financed through funds obtained either from the owners in the form of equity or from lenders who expect to be repaid with interest. The owners of a company expect to be rewarded with an appreciation in the price of their stock or the ownership of the business, and also sometimes through a salary from the business. Lenders are looking primarily at safety of their principal, along with a return in the form of interest. They seek security in the business; security either in the form of a history of earnings adequate to satisfy creditors that future earnings will be satisfactory to repay the loan, **or** in the form of tangible — or sometimes intangible — assets, that can be liquidated to help repay the loan. Thus, liquidity of assets becomes a very important factor for lenders and, because of its implications regarding the survival of the business, for the owners of the business. Liquidity is the ability to realize the value of an asset in cash. Money is therefore the most liquid asset and has the highest degree of tradeability, which can be measured in terms of the percentage of value that can be obtained in as short a time span as possible. Thus, there are two factors associated with the liquidity of each asset — first, the time required to convert to cash and the attendant risk of not obtaining the asset's full value and, second, the percentage of value that can be obtained.

A business would be insolvent if it could not meet its obligations as they mature. Insolvency could result in the creditors taking over the business and liquidating the assets. Thus, the owners of the business should be extremely careful, by determining the proper level of debt and the appropriate kinds and maturity of debt instruments, to reduce the risk of insolvency. The terms of the debt and the method of repayment should be structured so that the business is not liquidated to repay the debts.

Changes in Asset Levels

The asset levels of a corporation can be in a trend of positive growth, negative growth, or no growth. Figure 1 shows the levels of the fixed assets, the permanent portion of the current assets less any cash reserves and the seasonal or cyclical portion of the current assets. In a positive growth trend, fixed assets usually increase at periodic intervals, with the current assets increasing with sales. Each level of fixed assets (such as buildings and equipment) can satisfy sales up to a certain level, at which time more fixed assets have to be added. In a no-growth

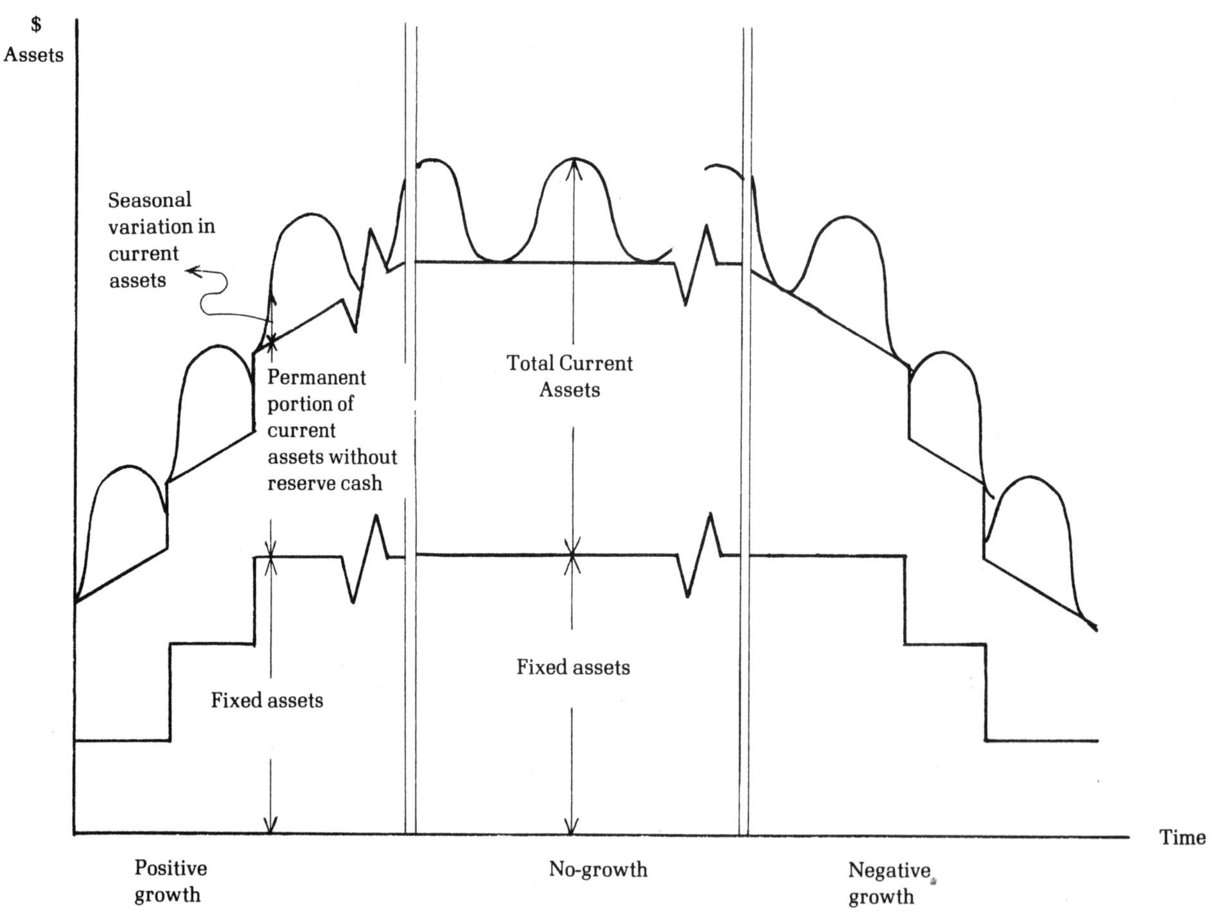

Figure 1. Asset Level Changes

situation, sales, fixed assets, and the permanent portion of current assets are approximately constant. The fluctuating portion of the current assets varies with the permanent portion as a base. Fixed assets are purchased to replace obsolete buildings or equipment. This situation exists if there is no inflation, or if the effects of inflation are the same on net revenues and the costs of fixed assets. In a case of negative growth the situation is the opposite of that during positive growth.

Financing the Assets

The assets of a company can be financed through the following:

a. Capital introduced into the business from external sources;

b. Internal generation of funds;

c. Acquisitions and mergers.

Capital from External Sources

The assets of a business can be classified into:

- Fixed or long-term or permanently installed assets, such as buildings or equipment;
- Working or circulating or current assets, such as accounts receivable, inventory, and prepaid expenses.

These assets can be financed through the following types of capital:

- Equity,
- Debt capital.

Equity capital is the permanent business capital invested by stockholders, and reflects ownership. It is the foundation stone of the financial structure and does not have to be repaid except, as in callable preferred stocks, at the company's option.

Debt capital is short or longer term. Short-term debt is usually repaid within one year from the liquidation of the assets, and is used for seasonal or cyclical buildup of inventories and accounts receivable. Longer-term debt is usually amortizing debt and is repaid from the cash flow generated from the use of the assets purchased with the funds, such as equipment, buildings, and permanent inventory and accounts receivables. Thus, debt can be classified as:

- Long-term — used for long-term assets such as buildings;
- Medium-term — used for assets such as equipment;
- Permanent working capital — used for accounts receivable and inventory financing;
- Temporary working capital — used for seasonal or cyclical buildup of accounts receivable and inventory.

Working capital is normally defined as the difference between Current Assets and Current Liabilities, i.e., "Current Assets-Current Liabilities," and is also known as Net Working Capital. The working capital of a company reflects its ability to meet its obligations as they come due, and thereby to avoid bankruptcy. Thus, the amount of working capital may influence the character and scope of the business.

Working capital requirements are the amount of current assets not financed by the suppliers through trade credit. The permanent level of working capital is financed by equity through the use of common and preferred stock and retained earnings; through medium-term and long-term loans from banks, life insurance companies, venture capital companies, etc.; and from the public through the sale of bonds and debentures. Temporary working capital is financed through the use of trade credit through extended terms, and from commercial banks with the use of short-term loans and lines of credit, in addition to any equity and internal sources. Some financing obtained with accounts receivable and inventory as collateral, such as that from commercial finance companies, can be used for longer periods of time since the collateral is revolving and hence used continuously. As the old collateral is liquidated, new collateral is created and new loans are obtained.

An optimally-financed business has enough capital at all times to meet all obligations as they come due and to take advantage of major profitable business opportunities. At the same time, the cost of capital is minimized by not having excess funds on which the cost of capital exceeds the return obtained on the funds, and by having the proper proportions of the various types of capital, which minimizes the cost of capital without jeopardizing the safety of the firm. The cost of equity is greater than the cost of debt, owing to the greater risk. This is because investors in equity instruments expect dividends and stock appreciation to be greater than interest on debt instruments as compensation for the additional risk. The dividend on equity is not tax deductible for the business, while the interest costs of debt are tax deductible. Also, the sale of stock may result in dilution of capital gains if the company succeeds, which cost may be greater than the interest rate. However, the greater the equity in the firm, the greater the firm's safety, since there are fewer lenders and fewer loans coming due. Thus, the ideal business financing package involves equity and debt in proportions which maximize the safety of the firm and maximize the rate of return on the stockholders' investment.

Since each business needs permanent capital and temporary capital — the former for permanent and long-term assets, and the latter for seasonal or cyclical assets — it needs equity and long-term debt for the permanent assets and temporary debt for temporary assets. Ideally, the total of the equity and long-term loans would equal the permanent assets, and the temporary debt would equal the temporary assets. However, since businesses operate under uncertainty, it is not possible to synchronize exactly the needs with the funds. A margin of safety with extra long-term debt or equity usually is recommended. Financing short-term needs with long-term debt or equity would mean that the business would sometimes have excess funds not in use or not earning enough return to cover costs. In addition, long-term funds generally cost more than short-term funds, thus increasing the cost of debt. Generally this cost is 0.5-1.0% higher than the cost of short-term debt. Prepayment of long-term debt is generally not allowed if it is done by borrowing from other lenders at lower interest rates. Thus, when interest rates are high, businesses usually obtain short-term financing until long-term rates have decreased.

Figure 2 contains an example of financing assets through equity, amortizing and permanent debt, retained earnings, and short-term debt. It is assumed that the company has a positive sales trend, with income after taxes being negative during the start-up phase and then increasing with sales. Initially, assets are financed through equity, and amortizing and permanent (such as trade credit) debt which is repaid from the cash flow. The short-term seasonal or cyclical needs are financed through trade credit and short-term borrowings, thus minimizing the cost of capital. The growth of the company necessitates additional fixed equipment, which can be accomplished as in 'CD', through the use of an additional offering of stock and debt instruments, or, as in 'EF', when the company is stronger and can afford more debt, through the use of debt instruments alone. The increase in permanent current assets is financed through the internal cash flow. The company borrows for short-term needs even before it has become profitable. If there are no short-term sources of credit, such as bank lines or trade credit, available to the company before it has proved its profitability, the initial financing should be increased to cover short-term needs until the company has been able to establish bank lines of credit. In this example, fixed assets and the permanent component of current assets are financed through equity and long- and medium-term debt instruments, and the needs for short-term debt are satisfied through lines of credit. The repayment schedules of the amortizing debt should be adjusted to the cash-flow generating capabilities of the business.

Figure 3 shows a company which had an initial level of equity and amortizing debt insufficient to cover the fixed assets and the permanent portion of current assets. The company could use a continuous source of financing for current assets — a revolving fund — from commercial finance companies. In effect, this would provide a permanent source of funds. Alternatively, the company could examine whether there is any equity in the fixed assets that could be used to finance current assets (examples of this are the leasing of equipment or the sale-leaseback of buildings). In the example shown in Figure 3, immediately after the company has started showing profits, a small issue of stock is sold to raise equity of the company, but not enough to dilute the stock. A later issue of stock would be priced higher than the first issue if the growth trend continued, thus preventing dilution. The additional fixed assets are financed through the sale of additional amortizing debt securities, as in 'CD' and 'GH'. After the sale of debt instruments at 'GH', the company has its permanent assets financed through the use of equity and permanent and amortizing debt. The internal cash flow generated from the net income allows the financing of the growth of permanent current assets with retained earnings.

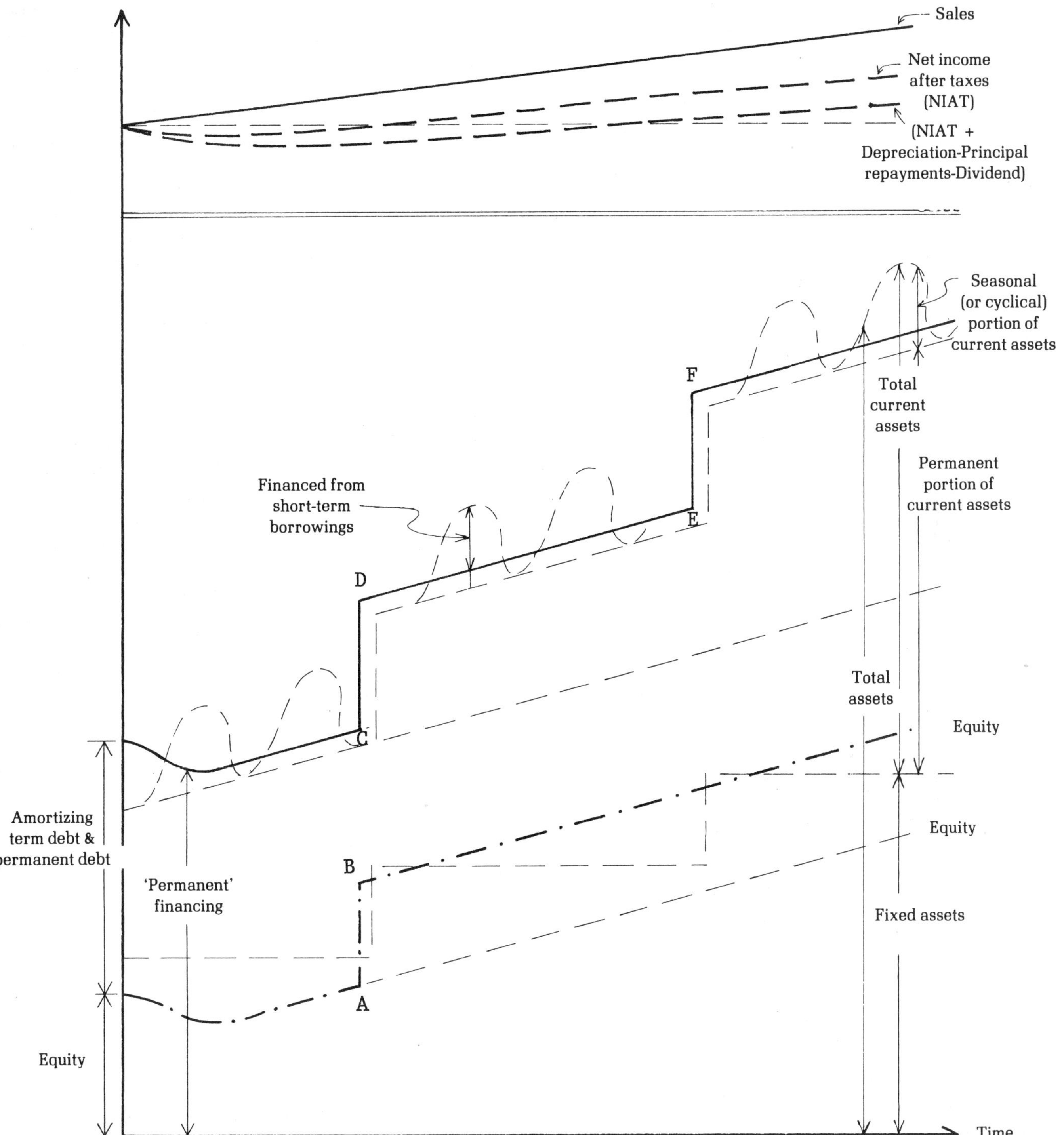
Sales
Net income after taxes (NIAT)
(NIAT + Depreciation-Principal repayments-Dividend)
Seasonal (or cyclical) portion of current assets
F
Total current assets
Permanent portion of current assets
Financed from short-term borrowings
E
D
Total assets
Equity
C
Amortizing term debt & permanent debt
Equity
B
'Permanent' financing
Fixed assets
A
Equity
Time

Figure 2. Financing Assets — Hedging

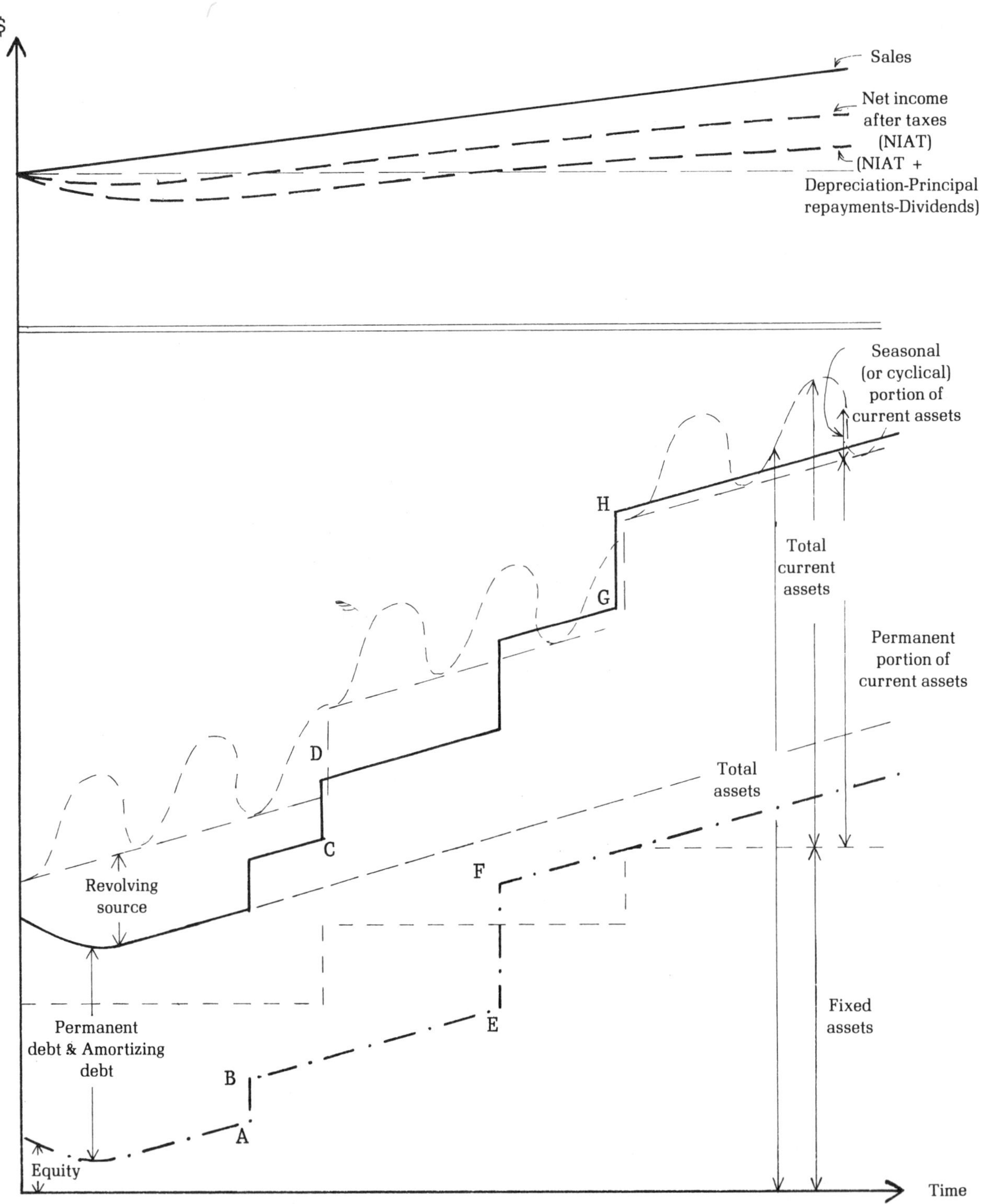
$
Sales
Net income after taxes (NIAT)
(NIAT + Depreciation-Principal repayments-Dividends)
Seasonal (or cyclical) portion of current assets
H
G
D
C
Total current assets
Permanent portion of current assets
Total assets
F
Revolving source
E
Fixed assets
Permanent debt & Amortizing debt
B
A
Equity
Time

Figure 3. Financing Assets

In a mature, profitable company which does not have growth but where sales are seasonal or cyclical, and where permanent assets are financed through equity, retained earnings, permanent debt, and amortizing debt, the proportion of equity is likely to keep increasing unless the company declares dividends; dividends reward shareholders and also keep the company's debt/equity ratio at the optimal level to reduce the cost of capital to the firm.

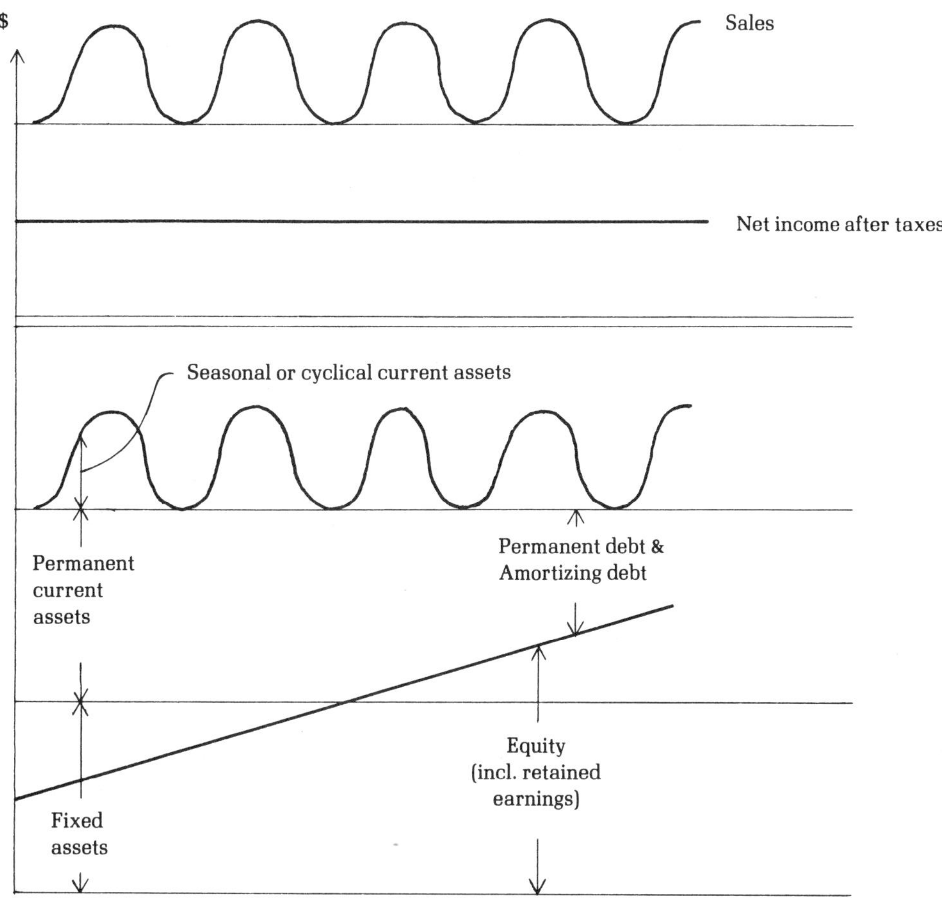

Figure 4. No-Growth Company

Financing from external sources is obtained through the sale of securities. Securities are instruments issued by corporations or other businesses and include common stock, preferred stock, bonds, and notes. The more sophisticated issues, such as classes of stock with different voting rights and preferences, convertible securities and bonds, and warrants also are securities. They can be classified as follows:

1. Equity securities which include common stock and preferred stock.
2. Debt securities which include lines of credit, transaction loans, promissory notes, secured loans, bonds, leases, etc.
3. Hybrids, which include convertibles (such as convertible notes or convertible bonds) and warrants to purchase stock.
4. Limited partnership interests, franchises, real estate interests. Limited partnerships are common with real estate financing. A limited partner cannot take an active role in the business without the risk of losing the limited liability protection. The general partner is supposed to be actively involved in the business.

(See Chapter III for more details.)

Internal Generation of Funds

Internal sources of funds include depreciation, retained after-tax earnings, increase in accounts payable, and underpayment of salaries of key officers and owner personnel. In firms where new investment is a relatively small portion of assets, depreciation and retained earnings — less principal repayments — can provide a considerable portion of cash needs. However, the replacement cost of equipment is likely to be higher owing to inflation. Therefore, if the depreciation and retained earnings, less principal repayments and dividends, are not sufficient to pay for the new equipment, the firm will have to sell securities to raise additional capital.

Depreciation

Fixed assets which have a useful life of over one year are not listed as expense in the year of purchase. The initial investment is allocated over the estimated life of the asset, and depreciation procedure provides a basis for allocating the purchase price. Depreciation reduces earnings realized in the current accounting period, and eventually affects profits and income taxes. The amount to be charged to depreciation becomes extremely important since it affects the net profits and cash flow. An amortization period smaller than the "true" life of the equipment could result in higher costs and selling price, and decreased sales and profitability. Lower than desired depreciation results in overstated assets, and possible write-offs in the future.

Methods of calculating depreciation include the following:

a. Straight-line method: This is the simplest method, with the original cost of the asset being written off in equal annual amounts over its estimated economic life. Thus if the cost is $5,000, and the residual value is estimated at $1,000 at the end of a life of 5 years, annual depreciation is (5,000-1,000)/5, or $800 per year;

b. Sum-of-the-years digits method: The original cost of the asset less the estimated residual value at the end of the economic life is multiplied by a changing fraction to determine the depreciation for each year. The fraction is the number of years remaining in the life of the asset divided by the sum of the years of the asset's economic life. Thus if the original cost is $5,000 and the residual value is estimated at $1,000 at the end of 5 years, depreciation for the third year is

$$\frac{\$(5{,}000 - 1{,}000)3}{(5 + 4 + 3 + 2 + 1)} = \$800\ ;$$

c. Diminishing value or declining balance method: The original cost less accumulated depreciation is multiplied by a fixed percentage to determine depreciation in any year. Thus if the original cost is $5,000, and the fixed percentage is 25%, then the depreciation in the first year is $5,000(0.25), or $1,250. Depreciation in the second year is (5,000-1,250)0.25, or $937.50. This method allows accelerated depreciation, whereby cash flow is increased in the first few years. The percentage should be such that the net asset value should equal the estimated residual value at the end of the economic life;

d. Sinking fund method: An equal annual payment is deposited in an interest bearing account such that at the end of the economic life, the annual payments and the interest earned will equal the original cost of the asset. The depreciation amount for each year will equal the sum of the equal annual payments and interest earned in the year. This method is not used extensively;

e. Production method: The original cost less the estimated residual value at the end of the production life (in hours) is divided by the production life to obtain the depreciation per production hour. This figure multiplied by annual usage provides the depreciation for the year. The depreciation can also be based on the number of units. Thus if the original cost is $5,000 and the residual value is $1,000 at the end of 1,000 hours of production, depreciation per production hour is $4. If the usage in any year is 250, then the depreciation charge in that year is $1,000.

The advantages of the straight-line method are that it is simple, easy to apply and flexible since the estimated life can be adjusted. The criticisms are that resale value of equipment usually depreciates faster in early years, wear is greater in years of heavy use, and repair costs are heavier in later years. The advantage of the declining balance method and the sum-of-the-years' digits method is that depreciation is accelerated resulting in a greater cash flow in the earlier years. In the declining balance method, approximately 65% can be depreciated in half the useful life, and in the sum-of-the-years'-digits method, approximately 70% can be depreciated in half the useful life. The criticism of the declining balance method is that it is quite complex.

Growth Rate Supported by Earnings and Depreciation

In many cases, the growth of the company cannot be financed entirely through internal cash flow. For example, if the company is profitable, assume that there are three levels of net income (see Figure 5). If the net income is very high, as in curve 1, the internal cash flow is sufficient not only to finance the growth in current permanent assets, but also to finance the increase in fixed assets. Management must decide what level of the debt/equity ratio will maximize the return to the stockholders while keeping the risk at

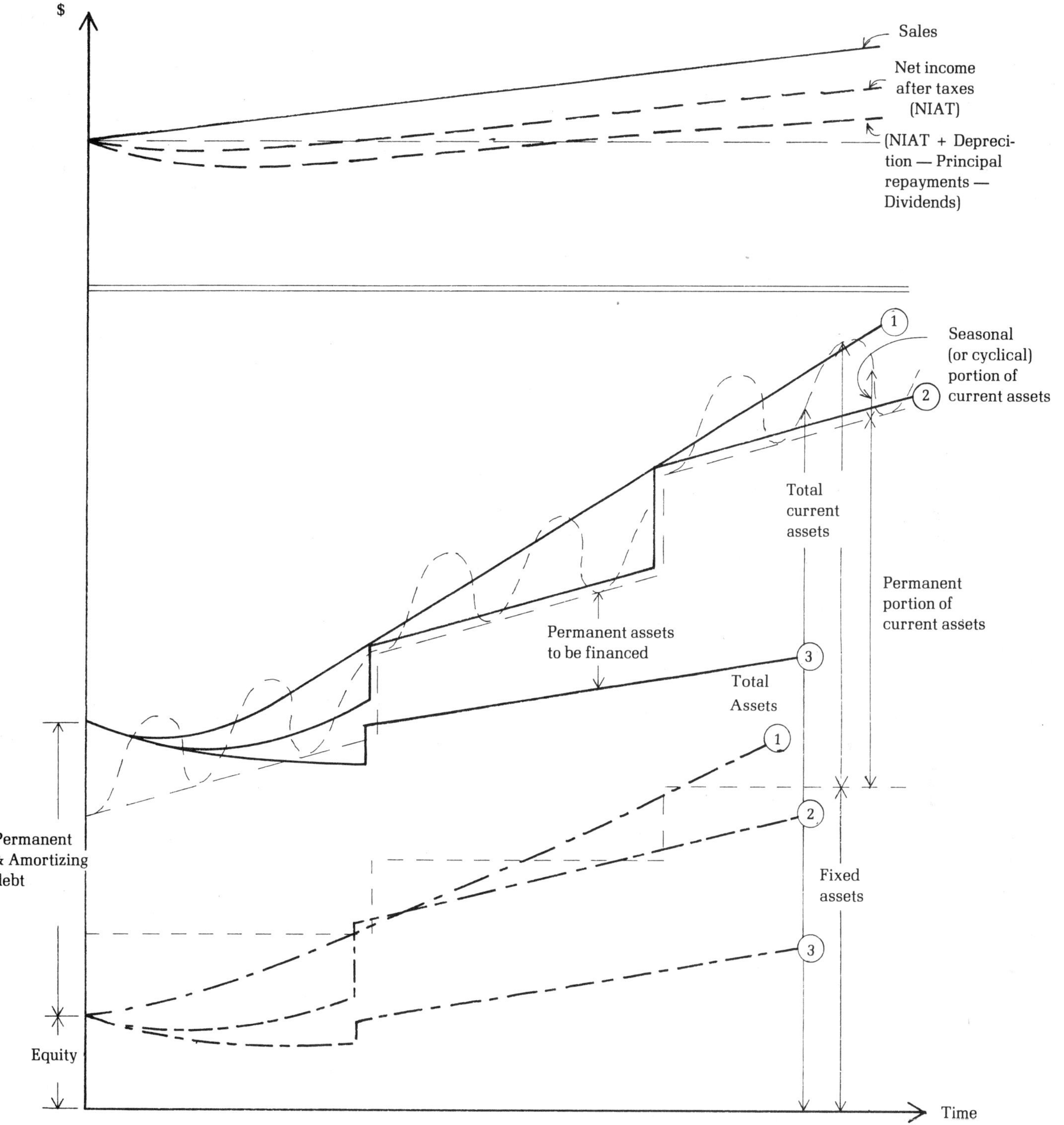

Figure 5. Growth Financed Through Internal Cash Flow.

1
2 } Various growth rates in equity
3

safe levels, and how extra cash, if any, should be used. If the growth rate is at level 2, the growth in permanent current assets is financed through the internal cash flow. However, new issues of debt and equity securities will have to be sold to finance fixed asset increases. Under growth rate 3, the net cash flow is insufficient to finance even the growth in current permanent assets. In such a case, management has to decide upon methods of raising additional cash to finance growth in permanent assets and temporary assets, or of increasing the profitability of the business and/or decreasing the growth of the business.

Growth Rate of Permanent Current Assets Possible Through Internal Cash Flow:

Within stages requiring investments in fixed assets, if earnings after taxes are x% of sales, and working capital requirements (Current Assets-Current Liabilities) are y% of sales, and if depreciation equals principal repayments, and there are no dividends, the growth rate in permanent current assets possible from internal cash flow is **100(x/y) %.** It should be noted that any increase in fixed assets may require more cash from internal sources or the sale of equity securities for the down payment required by lending institutions.

EXAMPLE:

Assuming that:

- Earnings after taxes are 5% of sales;
- (Current Assets-Current Liabilities) are 25% of sales;
- Principal repayments are equal to depreciation; and there is
- No compounding of growth rates,

Growth rate possible from internal earnings equals:

$\frac{5}{25} \times 100$, which is 20%

Acquisitions and Mergers

A firm can raise funds by acquiring a cash-rich company in return for its securities, or merging with a company which can provide it with the cash.

(See Section V for more details on Acquisitions.)

Levels of Debt and Equity

Debt in a business should be structured so that:

- The maturity of the debt instruments and interest payments can be satisfied either through the liquidation of the assets or through the normal cash flow of the business;
- The rate of return to stockholders should be maximized, subject to keeping the risk of ruptcy, through the inability to pay debts, at an acceptable level.

Many ratios can be used to determine the level of debt that a business should have. Desired ranges for these ratios vary with the kind of lender and institution, the instruments used, and the borrower's needs and degree of risk desired. The factors to be considered in deciding upon the kind of financing are:

- The return on equity to the shareholders. If the return on borrowed funds is greater than the cost of the funds, the return to stockholders is increased.
- The risk of insolvency owing to the company being unable to meet its obligations as they mature.
- The timing of the security. If interest rates are high or the equity market is not very favorable, the business may decide to float short-term securities until the markets are favorable.
- Cash flow. The growth needs of the company and the cash flow should be considered in deciding whether the security should be a debt or equity issue.
- Loss of flexibility. The stockholders should be concerned about the terms of the agreement and the loss of control of the business.
- The effect of taxes. Interest on debt issues is deductible, but dividends on equity issues are not deductible.

Some advantages of debt financing are:

- Debt securities usually cost less than equity financing because debt securities have greater security and less risk.
- Interest on debt securities is tax deductible, but dividends on equity issues are not.
- There is no dilution of equity.
- Stockholders gain the advantage of leverage;
- Often the loss of control is less; however, lenders sometimes have more voice in the affairs of the company than minority shareholders, especially if the company defaults on any terms of the agreement.
- A greater number of institutions invest mainly in debt securities — such as insurance companies, and, after the Employees Retirement Income Security Act (ERISA), pension funds.

Disadvantages of debt securities are:

- The risk of insolvency is greater if the company has a decline in earnings and is unable to meet its obligations, or defaults on any of the terms of the agreement, such as minimum working capital and net worth levels.
- Borrowing could undermine future borrowing capability since the company may be up to its

borrowing limit, leaving no options in case of problems.

- Too much debt is considered a sign of weakness in a business.
- Leverage can magnify any losses.

IF AT ANY TIME, THE COMPANY'S CASH AVAILABILITY IS LESS THAN THE CASH NEEDED, OPTIONS ARE:

TAP UNUSED DEBT CAPACITY
- Line of Credit
- Unsecured Debt
- Secured Debt

OBTAIN FUNDS THROUGH PUBLIC SALE OR PRIVATE PLACEMENT OF EQUITY OR HYBRID INSTRUMENTS
- Common Stock
- Preferred Stock
- Subordinated Convertible Notes or Debentures
- Warrants

TEMPORARILY REDUCE VOLUME AND CURRENT ASSETS

LIQUIDATE FIXED ASSETS: (PERMANENT LIQUIDATION OF UNWANTED ASSETS)

INCREASE CASH FLOW
- Increase Sales with same Margins
- Increase Net Earnings and Margins with Price Increases
- Accelerated Depreciation
- Decrease Dividends
- Reduce Variable Expenses
- Reduce Principal Payments

ACQUIRE OR MERGE WITH ANOTHER COMPANY WHICH HAS CASH

Example: Medtronic, Inc.

The example of Medtronic suggests some of the ways to finance a business in its various stages of growth. Medtronic is presently the world's largest manufacturer of cardiac pacemakers. It was started in 1949 as a partnership by Earl Bakken and Palmer Hermundslie. They formed a medical equipment repair company, called Medtronic, to repair electronic hospital equipment.

The initial plant was a 600-square-foot garage in Northeast Minneapolis. In one month in its first year of operation the company grossed $8. The company soon started representing other companies in a five-state area. Often the Medtronic engineers were asked to modify equipment or design and produce new devices needed for special tests. The company started manufacturing these items on a custom basis. In 1959, the company implanted its first electrodes for an external pacemaker in a human, and by 1960 it had established itself as an important manufacturer of cardiac pacemakers. Medtronic pacemakers had been sold in the U.S., Canada, Australia, Cuba, Europe, Africa and South America. In 1960, the first implantable pacemakers were developed by Dr. Chardack and Mr. Wilson Greatbatch. Medtronic obtained the exclusive production and marketing rights to the Chardack-Greatbatch implantable pulse generator, and production began in the same year. From that beginning, when the company had sales of $298,000 and a net loss of $53,100 (in 1960-61), the company has grown to a level of $182,201,000 in sales and income of $17,308,000 in the fiscal year ending April 30, 1978.

The following are some of the highlights on the financing sources used by Medtronic in the course of its astounding growth:

The performance and the financing of the company can be broken into three stages:

1. 1949-1959: This was the initial formative stage when the company was essentially a "craft" company performing service-type functions for low margins and low growth. Financing at this stage was primarily through partners' equity, accruals and supplier credit, and "other debt," which could be from partners or their contacts (see Table 1). The company was actively searching for a market niche, and for products which could provide the desired growth.

2. 1960-1964: These were the years when the company could be said to have been "paying dues." These years included the initial stages of product marketing and the organization of the marketing network, as well as developing customer credibility and the debugging of the various problems inherent in a company in initial stages of tremendous growth. When sales are growing at a very rapid rate, there are high costs associated with the various functions of marketing, administration, production, quality control, etc. The major financing at this stage was in the form of venture capital. It is interesting to note that the company initially made a public offering of its convertible debt, and then when it suffered severe losses in 1960-62 and was close to bankruptcy, it made another offering to private venture capitalists. Normally, the initial equity-type offering is made to the venture capitalists and the second or later ones to the public. This is due to the problems that new companies have in selling their stock or securities to the public. However, the market was very favorable for new equity-type public offerings in the Minneapolis-St. Paul area due to the tremendous success of Control Data Corporation two years earlier. Other

TABLE 2: Sources of Financing — Medtronic, Inc.**

Year end (Fiscal)	Suppliers (Payables)	Accruals	Other Debt	Long-term Secured Debt	Bank Debt	Equipment Loans	Lease-Purchase or Leases	Convertible Debentures	Eurodollar Convertible Debentures	Industrial Development Revenue Bonds	Subordinated or Unsecured Debt	Partners Equity	New Stock Issued	Stock Options Exercised	Conversion of Debt	Retained Earnings	Increase in Partners Equity or Retained Earnings
1949-1950	X	X	X									X					
1950-1951	X	X	X									X				X	$ 1,899
1951-1952	X	X	X									X				X	1,815
1952-1953	X	X	X	X								X				X	3,755
1953-1954	X	X	X	X								X					(6,300)
1954-1955	X	X	X	X								X				X	880
1955-1956	X	X	X	X								X				X	2,362
1956-1957	X	X	X	X								X				X	10,389
1957-1958*	X	X	X	X									X				(1,944)
1958-1959	X	X	X	X												X	1,521
1959-1960	X	X	X	X	1			X					X				(16,093)
1960-1961	X	X	X		1		X								X		(53,063)
1961-1962	X	X	X		1		X	X			X						(144,135)
1962-1963	X	X			(1,2)	X	X	X					X		X	X	72,923
1963-1964	X	X			1	X	X							X	X	X	151,108
1964-1965	X	X					X							X		X	199,268
1965-1966	X	X		X			X									X	307,784
1966-1967	X	X	X	X		X					X		X	X		X	469,923
1967-1968	X	X		X	X		X						X	X		X	1,073,258
1968-1969	X	X		X			X		X				X	X		X	1,314,777
1969-1970	X	X		X			X		X					X		X	2,137,613
1970-1971	X	X		X	X		X		X					X		X	2,455,984
1971-1972	X	X		X	X		X		X				X	X	X	X	3,973,077
1972-1973	X	X		X			X		X					X	X	X	5,336,449
1973-1974	X	X			X		X							X	X	X	6,371,422
1974-1975	X	X			X		X						X	X		X	9,463,000
1975-1976	X	X			X		X			X				X		X	13,325,000
1976-1977	X	X		X		X				X			X	X		X	14,607,000
1977-1978	X	X	X		X		X			X			X			X	17,308,000

1 Bank Debt secured by Accounts Receivables and Inventory
2 Demand Note secured by Equipment
* Company incorporated

** Medtronic stock is traded on the New York Stock Exchange. For purposes of this example, Medtronic financing has not changed considerably since 1978.

sources of financing at this stage were secured bank debt for current asset financing, and the building was leased, thus conserving cash for working capital. The lease allowed a long-term permanent asset to be financed through a long-term instrument.

3. 1965-onwards: In this third stage, the company has had an uninterrupted trend of impressive growth in sales and profits, resulting in the conversion of all the convertible debt. Due to the earlier public offering, the venture capitalists were assured of a public market for their stock, and hence the debt was converted in 1962-64. Since then the company has financed the bulk of its needs through internal sources, i.e., retained earnings, and through stock offerings, accruals and supplier credit. The amount of long-term debt is negligible in a company of this size, reflecting the substantial earnings and the high value placed on the company's stock. Some other types of

financing used — although in negligible amounts — have been Eurodollar financing, leases, and minimal bank debt for protection against foreign currency price fluctuations.

The company has used 16 categories of financing.

It is important to note that the public offering and the venture capital private placement were done only when the company was moving away from the craft stage to the growth situation; when it had a product which was unique, serving a large unmet market need signifying huge growth potential. The initial financing needs to capitalize on this growth potential required financing which the partners were unable to provide themselves; and the lack of mortgageable assets precluded the possibility of using long-term debt. In retrospect, the use of long-term debt instead of equity-type securities offered in 1959-60 could have bankrupted the company because the lenders might have termed themselves insecure due to the large losses suffered in the succeeding three years, and there could have been a default in principal and interest payments. Without the debt agreement, management had relatively greater autonomy to negoti-

TABLE 3: Financial Summary — Medtronic, Inc. ($1,000)

	Cash	Current Assets (less cash)	Fixed Assets	Total Assets	Current Debt	Long-Term Debt	Equity	Sales	Net Income After Taxes
1949-50	0.1 (2)	4.7 (78)	1.2 (20)	6.0 (100%)	0.6[1] (10%)	2.3[2] (38)	3.1(52)		
1950-51	0.2 (2)	9.5 (84)	1.6 (14)	11.3 (100%)	3.9[1] (34)	2.4[2] (21)	5.0 (45)		1.9
1951-52	0 (0)	10.9 (84)	2.1 (16)	13.0 (100%)	1.5[1] (11)	4.7[2] (36)	6.8 (53)		1.8
1952-53	0.1 (0)	21.9 (78)	5.9 (12)	27.9 (100%)	13.4[1] (48)	3.9 (14)	10.6 (38)		3.8
1953-54	0.1 (0)	17.1 (79)	4.4 (21)	21.6 (100%)	8.4[3] (39)	8.9 (41)	4.3 (20)		(6.3)
1954-55	0.2 (1)	15.5 (84)	2.8 (15)	18.5 (100%)	2.4 (13)	10.9 (59)	5.2 (28)		0.9
1955-56	0.6 (3)	16.6 (87)	1.9 (10)	19.1 (100%)	7.2 (38)	4.4 (23)	7.5 (39)		2.3
1956-57	2.7 (8)	23.0 (70)	7.3 (22)	33.0 (100%)	8.9 (27)	6.2 (19)	17.9 (54)		10.4
1957-58	0.1 (0)	28.2 (57)	21.4 (43)	49.7 (100%)	12.2 (25)	25.4[4] (51)	12.1 (24)		(5.8)
1958-59	0.6 (1)	42.7 (60)	27.8 (39)	71.1 (100%)	31.4 (44)	26.1 (37)	13.6 (19)	142.1	1.5
1959-60	104.5 (39)	114.0 (42)	50.4 (19)	268.9 (100%)	41.3 (15)	114.2 (42)	113.4 (43)	180.7	(16.1)
1960-61	4.1 (1)	247.2 (72)	90.7 (27)	342.0 (100%)	181.6 (53)	——	160.4 (47)	298.0	(53.1)
1961-62	1.5 (0)	359.9 (81)	84.8 (19)	446.2 (100%)	164.6 (37)	265.3 (59)	16.3 (4)	518.5	(144.1)
1962-63	11.5 (2)	513.4 (83)	95.3 (15)	620.2 (100%)	243.0 (39)	200.0 (32)	177.2 (29)	984.8	72.9
1963-64	102.5 (14)	536.1 (71)	111.8 (15)	750.4 (100%)	233.1 (31)	——	517.3 (69)	1,587.1	151.1
1964-65	40.5 (4)	788.5 (80)	155.0 (16)	984.0 (100%)	267.0 (27)	——	717.0 (73)	2,471.8	199.3
1965-66	94.7 (6)	952.2 (59)	565.7 (35)	1,612.6 (100%)	504.8 (31)	83.0 (5)	1,024.8 (64)	3,410.4	307.8
1966-67	50.9 (1)	1,762.1 (47)	1,936.6 (52)	3,749.6 (100%)	1309.3 (35)	76.4 (2)	2,363.8 (63)	5,012.8	469.9
1967-68	112.2 (2)	3,359.5 (50)	3,258.2 (48)	6,729.9 (100%)	1,797.8 (27)	60.8 (1)	4,871.2 (72)	9,946.1	1,073.3
1968-69	4,286.8 (29)	4,936.9 (33)	5,760.4 (38)	14,984.1 (100%)	2,023.2 (14)	1,785.1 (12)	11,175.8 (74)	15,322.6	1,276.8
1969-70	1623.9 (9)	7,842.4 (42)	9,081.3 (49)	18,547.6 (100%)	3,062.2 (17)	1,942.4 (10)	13,543.0 (73)	25,251.0	2,166.5
1970-71	2,261.1 (10)	11,175.0 (49)	9,307.0 (41)	22,743.1 (100%)	4,108.4 (18)	2,010.9 (9)	16,624.1 (73)	30,565.5	2,521.7
1971-72	11196.1 (30)	16,136.9 (43)	10,618.8 (27)	37,951.8 (100%)	6,886.9 (18)	1,882.0 (5)	29,182.9 (77)	41,175.7	4,045.2
1972-73	4,231.3 (9)	26,666.3 (56)	16,355.1 (35)	47,252.7 (100%)	8,877.9 (19)	1,992.8 (4)	36,382.0 (77)	54,383.4	5,336.4
1973-74	3,281.8 (5)	44,719.3 (63)	22,448.9 (32)	70,450.0 (100%)	24,390.5 (35)	1,211.7 (2)	44,847.9 (63)	78,177.7	6,371.4
1974-75	10,425.0 (11)	60,251.0 (62)	27,117 (27)	97,793 (100%)	27,471 (28)	1,586 (2)	68,736 (70)	111,996	9,463
1975-76	26,216 (22)	60,569 (51)	30,940 (27)	117,725 (100%)	30,904 (26)	3,672 (3)	83,149 (71)	129,971	13,085
1976-77	32,238 (22)	77,317 (52)	37,864 (26)	147,419 (100%)	43,432 (29)	4,429 (3)	99,558 (68)	148,278	14,607
1977-78	29,205 (17)	92,002 (54)	48,903 (29)	170,110 (100%)	49,298 (29)	5,725 (3)	115,087 (68)	182,201	17,308

[1] Including Notes and Mortgage Payable
[2] Including Other Liabilities
[3] Including Notes Payable, not Mortgage Payable
[4] Notes Payable in long-term to account for fixed asset increase

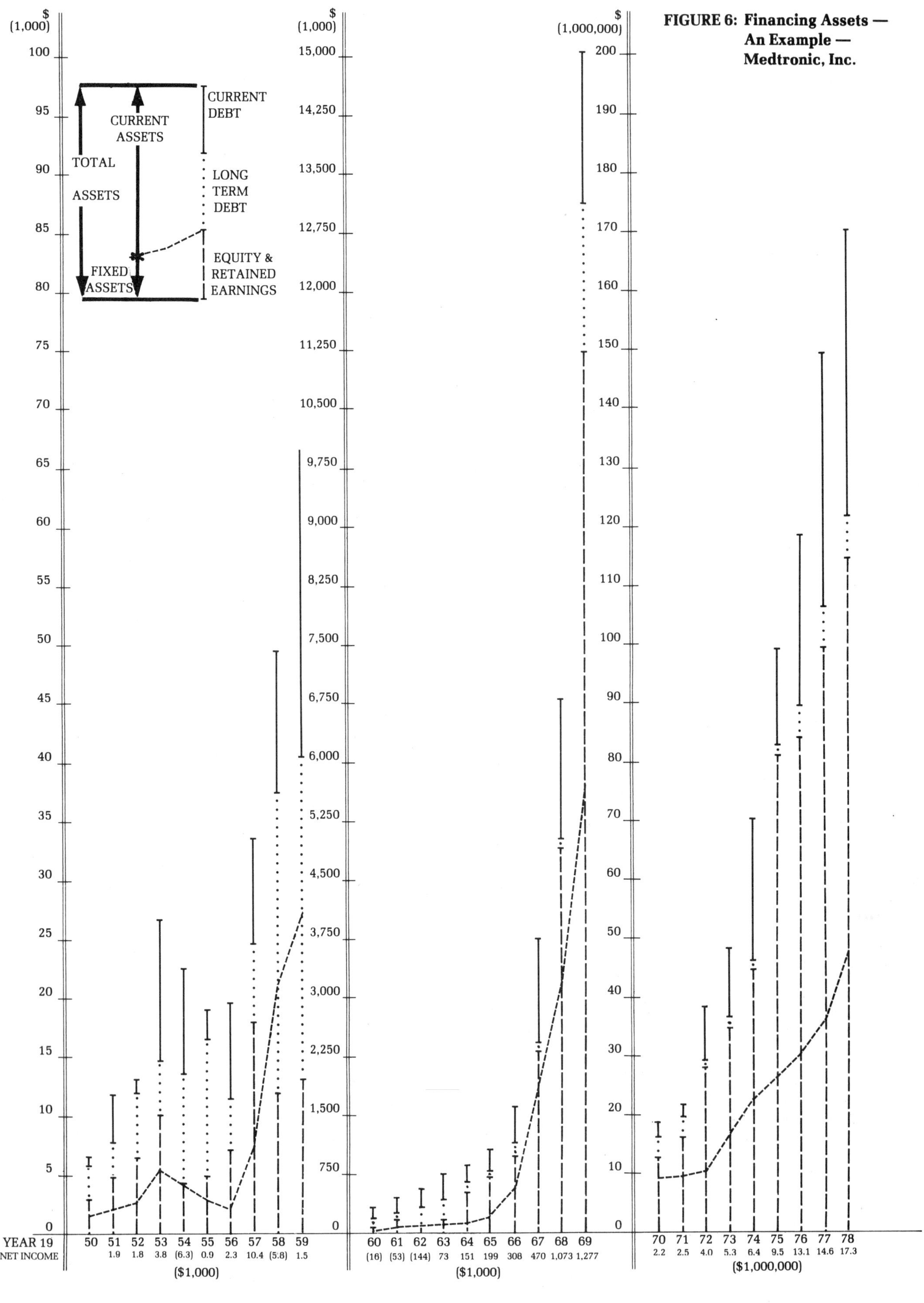

FIGURE 6: Financing Assets — An Example — Medtronic, Inc.

ate with investors who provided the venture capital needed to strengthen the company and overcome the problems.

Fixed assets have always been lower than equity and long-term debt, thus, the current ratio of the company has always been greater than 1, and in most years, fixed assets were even lower than equity. Also, the lack of seasonality or cyclicality in sales means that any increases in current assets are permanent. This permanent increase in current assets is optimally financed by long-term amortizing debt, or equity and retained earnings. Medtronic financed this increase in permanent current assets primarily through equity and equity-type securities, retained earnings, and the permanent component of current debt, such as accounts payable and accruals. Bank debt secured by current assets was used in only four years, and that was in conjunction with the use of convertible debt. Thus, permanent assets were financed with long-term funds.

The proportion of long-term debt to total assets is extremely low for the company, resulting in low leverage and a greater degree of safety to shareholders. The amount of cash in the company has been very high lately, leading to the conclusion that major cash acquisitions are possible, if the price earnings multiple of the stock is not considered adequate.

Ratio Analysis Useful for Lenders and Borrowers

The number and types of financial ratios for any institution are many; they can be categorized as balance sheet ratios, which provide clues to the firm's condition at any one point in time; as income statement ratios, which inform as to the operating efficiency of the firm over the period; and as interstatement ratios, which indicate the efficiency of usage of the assets of the firm. Satisfactory standards of various ratios vary among industries.

Balance Sheet Ratios:

Current Ratio: Current Assets/Current Liabilities. This ratio reflects the borrower's ability to meet current obligations as they mature, and hence remain solvent and avoid bankruptcy. It is among the most important ratios, and most businessmen and financiers give primary attention to this ratio, and attempt to keep it at a satisfactory level, which is usually at least 1.5:1 or 2:1.

Quick Ratio or Acid-Test Ratio: (Current Assets - Inventories)/Current Liabilities. This ratio indicates the quick convertibility of assets into cash to meet current obligations and thus remain solvent. Sometimes there might be problems in collecting accounts receivable and notes receivable on short notice.

Fixed Assets to Owners' Equity: This ratio indicates the amount of owner-contributed capital invested in fixed assets. The higher the ratio, and hence the leverage, the greater the risk for creditors.

Leverage: Borrowed Capital/Equity Capital. This ratio indicates the total amount of capital raised from creditors compared to the amount of money raised by the owners. The larger this ratio, the greater the return on equity for the shareholders if the company has a rate of return on investment larger than the interest rate. However, the larger the ratio, the weaker the financial position of the company and the higher the risk of insolvency during unprofitable years. This ratio can also be expressed in another form — Equity to Total Assets, which is called the Equity or Proprietary ratio. This ratio is usually considered as important as the current ratio. It is of special interest to long-term creditors because in difficult times, the greater the equity, the larger the probability that the company will survive. The debt should be within manageable limits so that the company can repay the principal and the interest as they come due. Stable industries can usually manage a higher debt to equity ratio.

Capitalization: This is the sum of long-term debt, capital stock, surplus, and retained earnings. An important ratio in this category is funded debt to total capitalization, which reflects the relationship between long-term debt and permanent contributed capital. Too much debt reduces the margin of safety to creditors and may result in bankruptcy in the event of a contraction in sales and income.

Investors examine the percentage of the various kinds of security issued by the company — proportions which are sometimes referred to as capitalization ratios. A higher proportion of debt increases the risk of preferred and common stock.

Other important ratios in this category are:

Bond Ratio: Face value of bonds/(Value of bonds, preferred stock, common stock, capital surplus, retained earnings, i.e., Capitalization)

Preferred Stock Ratio: Face value of preferred stock/Capitalization

Common Stock Ratio: (100 - Bond ratio - Preferred Stock ratio) %

Income Statement Ratios:

Profit Ratio: Net Income After Taxes/Net Sales. This ratio reflects the profitability and efficiency of the company especially when compared with other industries and other companies within the industry. This ratio can be altered to substitute net income before taxes, so as to reflect operating and financing efficiency, and remove the effect of taxes which can vary among and within industries.

Operating Ratio: Total Operating Expenses/Net Sales. This ratio includes all costs except financing costs and income taxes. Analysts find this ratio to be particularly important in judging the operating efficiency of the business. Operating Profit is (100-Operating Ratio %).

Number of Times Fixed Charges Earned: (Net Income After Taxes + Income Taxes + Fixed Charges) /Fixed Charges, where fixed charges include interest charges and, sometimes, rental costs. Analysts use this ratio to satisfy themselves that the business has sufficient earnings to pay fixed deductible expenses such as interest, rent, lease expenses, etc.

Interstatement Ratios:

Return on Investment: This can be measured with the use of various ratios. (Net Income After Taxes/ Stockholders Equity) is the net profitability for each dollar of investment in equity. Operating efficiency of the stockholders investment can be determined by calculating (Income before Interest and Taxes/Stockholders Equity). Net profitability and efficiency of the usage of assets can be determined by calculating the above ratios with total assets as the denominator.

Receivables Turnover: Credit Sales/Average Accounts Receivables. This ratio is sometimes expressed as the average number of days receivables are outstanding, which is equal to:

$$\frac{\text{Average accounts receivable in the period (year) X number of days in the period}}{\text{Credit sales in the period}}$$

When compared with industry averages, it reflects the quality of receivables. A comparison with sales terms for the company indicates management's collection capabilities.

Inventory Turnover: Cost of Goods Sold/Average Inventory in a period. It reflects the quality of the inventory and evaluates the merchandising capability of management to obtain maximum sales with minimum inventory. This ratio should be used carefully because variances from desired levels may be caused by many factors, such as a shortage of needed inventory, obsolete inventory kept at full value, etc.

Fixed Property Ratio: Net Sales/Fixed Assets. This ratio indicates the amount of fixed assets required for additional sales, and the efficiency with which fixed assets are used.

Cost of Borrowed Capital: Interest Paid/Borrowed Capital. This ratio gives the average cost of debt to the firm.

Coverage Ratios: These can refer to interest, dividends on preferred stock or interest and debt repayments. The coverage ratio for interest or "Times Interest Earned" is (Net Income before interest and taxes/Interest payments). Some analysts also add noncash expenses, such as depreciation, to the numerator. A prospective lender may also prefer the Debt Coverage Ratio, which can be defined as (Profits after taxes + Depreciation — Previous debt repayments)/(Principal and interest payments of new debt), at 2:1 or 3:1. There are other variations of the debt coverage ratio, including (Income before interest, depreciation and taxes/Principal and interest obligations).

Proper Use of Ratios:

Ratios should be used with care and logic. Ratios are usually compared with previous ratios of the same company, or with those of other companies; with the industry average, or with the budget or plan. Sometimes these ratios are examined without comparison. Industry standards are obtainable from Dun & Bradstreet, Robert Morris Associates, Standard & Poor's or Moody's.

Short-term creditors usually examine the current ratio, the acid-test ratio, and the turnover of receivables and inventory.

Long-term creditors are concerned with the short-term ratio, the number of times fixed charges are earned, balance sheet ratios and operating ratios.

Management concerns itself with use of all the ratios because it is concerned about all facets of the business without limiting its view. Stockholders are mainly concerned with the return and yield on their investment, the potential for capital appreciation and the amount of risk.

Cost of Money

Definitions

Interest rates: The price paid by borrowers to lenders for the use of money. Interest rates are influenced by many factors: such as the supply of and demand for money; the prime rate; the creditworthiness of the borrower; present and prospective relationship with the financial institution, and size and term of the loan. Interest rates usually fall in recessions when the demand for funds decreases, and they tend to rise during upswings in the economy. Owing to the greater liquidity, rates for short-term loans usually have been lower than those for long-term loans. Because the fixed costs of credit investigation and loan processing form a lower percentage of large loans, the size of the loan affects the rates. The interest rate is composed of the pure interest rate (the cost for the use of money without considering risk factors) and the risk premium because the loan may not be repaid when due, or because a rise in interest rates may depress prices of all except short-term obligations. Short-term borrowing from financial institutions, such as commercial banks, usually is the lowest cost method of business financing. In some cases, the funds may be used for investment in assets which are to be depreciated over the long-term. Hence, the company may be forced to borrow in the long-term market for investment in such assets, and thus increase the cost of borrowing funds.

Constant: In a long-term amortized loan, the annual payment of interest and principal expressed as a percentage of the loan amount is the constant. Thus, a 13% loan for 30 years with equal monthly payments has a 13.28% constant.

Time Value of Money

The basic concept behind interest rates is that a dollar today is worth more than a dollar sometime in the future. The rate by which the value of the money increases in a loan is the interest rate. Thus $1 today is worth $1.10 in one year at an interest rate of 10%, and $1 is worth $(1 + r)^n$ in **n** years at an annual interest rate of **r**%. Correspondingly, the present value of $1 received at the end of **n** years, where the discount (or interest) rate is **r**, equals $1/(1 + r)^n$.

The internal rate of return or the yield for an investment is the rate that equalizes the present values of the expected cash outflows and the expected cash inflows. If it is represented by **r**, then

$$\sum_{t=0}^{n} \frac{A_t}{(1+r)^t} = 0$$

where A_t is the cash flow for period **t**, when inflow or outflow exists, and **n** is the last period in which a cash flow is expected.

EXAMPLE:

If a cash investment in 1978 of $10,000 yields lump-sum after tax cash returns of $3,862.94 annually from 1979-82 (i.e., 4 years), on the anniversary of the investment, then the internal rate of return is **r**, such that

$$\frac{-10{,}000}{(1+r)^0} + \frac{3{,}862.94}{(1+r)^1} + \frac{3{,}862.94}{(1+r)^2} + \frac{3{,}862.94}{(1+r)^3} + \frac{3{,}862.94}{(1+r)^4} = 0$$

In this example, **r**, is 20%, which is the rate of return for the investment.

Stated and Actual Rates of Interest

The actual rate of interest is calculated on the basis of the amount of funds loaned for a period such as a year, with principal and interest paid at the end of the year. If the interest is collected or discounted in advance, or the loan is amortized over the period, then the effective rate is greater than the normal rate.

Thus, if interest is paid upon maturity of the note, and the interest is $1,000 paid at the end of a year on a loan of $10,000, then the interest rate is $1,000/$10,000 or 10%. This method of collecting interest is known as the collect basis. However, if the interest is deducted from the initial loan, thus advancing a sum of $9,000, then the effective rate of interest is $1,000/$9,000, or 11.1%. This method of collecting interest is known as the discount basis.

Effective rate of interest on amortized loans:

A close approximation formula for the rate of interest per year is

$$\frac{(2 \times N \times f)}{P(n+1)} \; 100\%$$

where,

N is the number of installment payments per year

f is the dollar cost of the finance charge (total paid minus total borrowed)

P is the principal

n is the number of total installment payments.

EXAMPLE:

If $1,200 is the amount borrowed, and is to be repaid in 24 monthly installments of $60 each, then

P = $1,200

f = $(60 x 24) - $1,200 = $240

n = 24

N = 12,

and the approximation of the interest rate is

$$\frac{(2 \times 12 \times 240)\,100}{1{,}200 \times 25} = 19.2\%.$$

The interest rate could be stated as

$$\frac{(240)\,100}{2 \times 1{,}200} = 10\%,$$

while the actual interest rate is 18.17%.

Methods of Computing Rates for Various Types of Financing

Cost of Debt

If **k** is the interest rate, the after-tax cost of debt to the firm is k(l-t), where **t** is the marginal tax rate. If the firm is not profitable, **t** = 0. The firm also has a cost of compensating balances deposited with commercial banks. Thus, if the interest rate is **k**%, and the requirement of the loan is that 20% of the loan be deposited as compensating balances, the effective interest rate is (k/0.8)%.

The effect of debt on the firm can be shown in this example. If capitalization alternatives are:

a. Common stock only: 100 shares @ $100 per share

b. Common stock and debt: 50 shares @ $100 per share and $5,000 debt @ 10%.

	Common stock only	**Common stock and debt**
Earnings before interest & taxes	$10,000	$10,000
Interest	0	500
Earnings before taxes	10,000	9,500
Taxes @ 50%	5,000	4,750
Earnings after taxes	5,000	4,750
Earnings per share	50	95

Cost of Common Stock

This is the most difficult to measure. Alternatives include the following:

a. Price-Earnings Multiple: The earnings divided by the price of the stock is the return from the stock to the investor. However, due to the after-tax nature of returns to stockholders, the cost of common stock should be based on the pre-tax earnings. For companies in a 40% income tax bracket, the cost according to this method is (100(Earnings/(1-0.4)))/Price. If the price of the stock is $80, and the after-tax earnings per share are $6, at a 40% tax rate, the cost of equivalent debt is (100(6/0.6))/80, or 12.5%.

b. Dividends: The dividends demanded by the shareholders can be used to determine the cost of common stock. The sum of the actual annual rate paid and the growth rate in the dividend payments is estimated to be the cost based on this method. This method is not useful when no dividends are paid.

c. In closely held companies without dividend payments, the cost of selling common stock to others can be calculated by the businessman on the basis of the loss of control or freedom, loss of future capital gains, etc.

Cost of Preferred Stock

The cost of preferred stock is the stated annual dividend (D) divided by the net proceeds of the preferred stock issue, after the costs of registration, etc., are deducted. To compare the cost of preferred stock with that of debt, the above cost should account for the tax rate of the firm, since preferred dividends are paid from after-tax income.

EXAMPLE:

Assume that the corporation's tax rate is 40%, and the annual dividend is $8 on a $100 preferred stock for which the costs of registration, etc., are $4. Then, the cost of the preferred stock to be used for comparison with debt is the following:

$$\frac{8 \times 100 \quad \%}{(1-0.4) \times (100-4)} = 13.88\%$$

Cost of Convertible Debt Securities

The cost of convertible debt securities (**r**) is obtained from the following formula:

$$M_0 = \sum_{t=1}^{n} \frac{I(1-T)}{(1+r)^t} + \frac{M_n(C.R.)}{(1+r)^n}$$

where

M_0 is the market value of convertible bond at time 0,

I is the annual interest payments,

T is the corporate tax rate,

n is the investor's horizon period, when debt is converted to stock,

M_n is the expected market price per share of stock at the end of period n,

C.R. is the conversion ratio — i.e., the number of shares into which the bond is convertible.

EXAMPLE:

If M_0 is $1,000

I is $80

T is 40%

n is 3 years, when the debt will be converted to stock,

M_n is $120

C.R. is 10

then the cost of the convertible debt securities, r, is such that

$$1{,}000 = \frac{80(0.6)}{(1+r)^1} + \frac{80(0.6)}{(1+r)^2} + \frac{80(0.6)}{(1+r)^3} + \frac{120(10)}{(1+r)^3}$$

In this example r is approximately 10.8%.

Cost of Convertible Preferred Stock

Remove (l - T) from the above formula.

Cost of Discounts on Receivables—Cash Discount

If the terms are 2% 10, net 30 days, then a $2 discount is being given for the use of $98 for 20 days, for an effective interest rate of

$$\frac{2}{98} \times \frac{360}{20} = 36.7\%$$

Cost of Capital to the Firm—The Weighted Average

The firm's cost for funds is the weighted average of the various costs of equity and debt. The categories within equity and debt have different costs; the weighted average can be calculated as follows:

Type	Amount as Capitalization	Pre-Tax Cost %	After-Tax Cost % (Assuming 50% Tax Rate)	Weighted Average Cost %
Short-term debt	20	8	4	0.8
Long-term debt	30	10	5	1.5
Preferred stock	10	8	8	0.8
Common stock	30	20	20	6.0
Retained earnings	10	20	20	2.0
Total	100%	Weighted Average Cost of Funds:		11.1%

It should be noted when making a new investment that the cost used for analysis of the investment could be for either new or incremental capital, or for total capital. There may be marginal profitability when the cost for the project investment is determined for new or incremental capital.

Distribution of Securities-Private Placements and Public Offerings

Introduction

There are various methods of distributing or selling new stock and bond issues. These can be classified into two main categories:

a. Private placements: where the issue is sold to one or a small group of investors. It includes:

- certain employee and executive purchases;
- privileged subscriptions to existing shareholders in a privately-held corporation;
- private sales to institutions or individuals, with or without the assistance of an investment banker.

b. Public offerings: where the issue is sold to the public directly or through investment bankers. These include:

- direct sales of securities without the assistance of an investment banker (mainly for small, new, and weaker issues);
- privileged subscriptions to shareholders in a publicly-held corporation, with standby underwriting;
- sale through investment bankers on an agency or best-efforts basis or with a full commitment underwriting.

Private Placements

A private placement is the sale of securities not registered with the Securities and Exchange Commission owing to its exemption from the regulations of the Securities Act of 1933. The private placement market gained importance as a funding source for corporations in the 1930s due to the purchase of corporate bonds by life insurance companies. The Securities Act of 1933 initially defined the conditions necessary for private placements. The act exempted private placements from the registration requirements necessary for public offerings because the small number of institutional investors who were to purchase the issue had the sophistication to analyze the security and the issuer before investing. The private placement market includes all kinds of securities. The private placement of new corporate securities issues reached a record level of $19 billion in 1977 (compared with public offerings of $32 billion), chiefly because the institutions involved in such financing had large sums to invest. The number of registrations and funds raised in recent years are shown in the accompanying Table 4.

TABLE 4: Sales by type of Instrument, 1980-83 ($ in millions)

			Cash Sale for Account of Issuer			
	Total		Common	Bonds, Debentures,	Preferred	
Year*	No.	Value	Stock	and Notes	Stock	Total
1980	3,402	110,583	$33,076	$42,764	$2,879	$78,719
1981	4,326	144,132	49,276	40,163	2,505	91,944
1982	4,846	164,455	50,486	63,950	3,939	118,375
1983(Prel.)	5,743	255,797	84,292	86,016	8,820	179,128

Source: See SEC Monthly Statistical Review
*Fiscal year ending Sept. 30

The estimated gross proceeds in million of dollars from primary corporate securities offered in 1975 were as follows:

	Public Sales	Private Sales	Total
Common Stock	23,398(98.4)	390(1.6)	23,788
Preferred Stock	5,050(98.7)	65(1.3)	5,115
Bonds & Notes	45,211(82.4	9,625(17.6)	54,836
Total	73,659(88)	1 0 , 0 8 0 (	83,739

Source: Statisical Abstract of the United States

Private placements are more popular for senior securities, such as mortgage bonds, debentures and notes. The estimated gross proceeds from such placements in 1975 were 25.2% as compared with 3.2% for common stock and 10.7% from preferred stock. The major reason for this is that the financial institutions involved in private placements are insurance companies and pension funds, with an investment preference for high-grade debt securities.

The Securities Act of 1933 requires that an issuing company or a person in a control relationship to such company file a registration statement with the Securities and Exchange Commission (SEC) before securities may be offered to the public. The registration statement contains prescribed financial and other information which also should be provided to potential investors in a prospectus. The basic concept underlying the Securities Act is full disclosure. The SEC has no authority to pass on the merits of the securities to be offered or the fairness of the terms of the distribution. If adequate and accurate disclosure is made, the SEC cannot deny distribution. The Securities Act exempts certain securities and transactions from the registration requirements. The "private offering" exemption from registration under the Securities Act, Section 4(2), provides that offers and sales by an issuer not involving any public offering will be exempt from registration.

The Act exempts the following classes of securities from the registration requirements:

a. A security issued by the U.S., or its territory or state or political subdivision or public instrumentality;

b. Any security issued or guaranteed by any bank or the Federal Reserve bank;

c. Interest or participation in a trust fund by banks or for the benefit of employees for qualified plans;

d. Industrial development bonds;

e. Notes, drafts, bills of exchange, or banker's acceptances with a term of less than nine months;

f. Securities issued by religious, educational, benevolent, fraternal, charitable, or reformatory non-profit organizations;

g. Securities issued by savings and loans, cooperative banks, homestead associations with some exemptions, and other organizations such as farmers' cooperative organizations;

h. Securities issued by common or contract carriers if covered by the Interstate Commerce Act;

i. Certificates issued by a receiver or by a trustee in bankruptcy, with the approval of the court;

j. Insurance or endowment policy or annuity contract or optional annuity contract supervised by an insurance or other similar commissioner;

k. Securities exchanged by the issuer with its existing security holders exclusively where no commission is paid;

l. Securities exchanged for bonafide outstanding securities, claims or property interests, or partly in such exchange and partly for cash, where certain requirements are met to allow all proposed investors a fair hearing;

m. Securities sold only to residents within a single state or territory, if the issuer is incorporated or a resident and doing business within the state, which are governed by state "blue sky" laws.

Certain transactions also are exempted from the requirements of the Act and these include:

a. Transactions by any person other than an issuer, underwriter, or dealer;

b. Transactions by an issuer not involving any public offering.

The Securities Act does not affect the jurisdiction of the securities commission of any state over any security or any persons.

Section 4(2) of the Securities Act provides that offers and sales by an issuer not involving any public offering will be exempt from registration. In April 1974, the SEC adopted Rule 146 under the Securities Act to protect investors, while at the same time providing more objective standards to curtail uncertainty about Section 4(2). The rule provides that transactions by an issuer meeting all the conditions of the rule do not involve any public offering. The major conditions to be met are the following:

a. The number of purchasers should not be more than 35, with some relatives of, as well as trusts, estates, and corporations fully owned by purchasers, being excluded, along with any persons who purchase securities of $150,000 or more. Each client of an investment adviser, each customer of a broker-dealer, and each trust administered by a bank trust department will be counted as a separate purchaser. Investment companies or pension or other trusts will be counted as one purchaser.

b. The offeree must have access to or should have been furnished with the same kind of information that registration would disclose, as well as an opportunity to acquire additional information necessary to verify that disclosure.

c. The offerees or their advisers should have the knowledge and experience to evaluate the merits and risks of the proposed investment, and the offeree should be capable of bearing the economic risk of the investment.

d. There can be no general advertising or general solicitation, including promotional seminars or meetings in connection with the offering.

e. The issuer and any person acting on its behalf must take reasonable care to assure that the purchasers are not underwriters, and that the securities will be resold only with registration or exemption, or under the conditions of Rule 144 under the Act.

f. Sales can be made only to persons the issuer reasonably believes have the requisite knowledge and experience, or who can bear the economic risk and have an advisor (meeting certain standards) who can provide the requisite knowledge and experience.

The rule is not the exclusive means for offering and selling securities. Issuers who satisfy the criteria for Section 4(2) may offer and sell without compliance to the rule. In some cases a private placement could be considered a part of a larger offering and thus the exemption could be invalidated. This could happen if:

- the offerings are part of a single plan of financing:
- the offerings involve issuance of the same class of security;
- the offerings are made at or about the same time;
- the same type of consideration is to be received; and
- the offerings are made for the same general purpose.

Public Offerings

A public offering of securities generally involves the sale of an issue to the public through public solicitation and advertisement. Some public offerings are directly from the issuer, but generally public offerings of corporate securities are handled by members of the securities industry. Public offerings can be intrastate offerings; smaller amount offerings, including Section 4 (6), Regulation A, Regulation D, Regulation F, or Form S-18 offerings; and Form S-1 offerings. A primary offering is the sale of stock by the issuing company; a secondary offering is the sale of stock owned by stockholders, not the company.

Intrastate Offerings

The Securities Act of 1933 exempts intrastate registrations from its registration requirements. The offering must be registered in the state and satisfy the state's requirements. The securities should be part of an issue offered and sold only to persons resident in a specific state by an issuer who also is a resident and doing business in that state. Rule 147, which was adopted on January 7, 1974, clarified certain conditions of the intrastate offering exemption. Each state has its own requirements, so the cost can vary. One of the major requirements of this type of offering is that each offeree must be a resident of the state, since if even a single offeree is a nonresident, the offering will not qualify for an intrastate offering. The requirements for an intrastate offering according to Rule 147 are the following:

a. The issuer must be resident and doing business within the state or territory in which the securities are offered and sold;

b. The issuer is deemed to be doing business within the state if its principal office is located within the state or territory, at least 80% of its gross revenues are derived from the state, at least 80% of its assets are within the state, and at least 80% of the net proceeds to the issuer are to be used within the state;

c. The offerees and purchasers must be resident within such state or territory;

d. Resale for a period of nine months after the last sale that is part of an issue must be made only to persons resident within the same state or territory, after which the issue is deemed to have come to rest;

e. The offering should not be part of a larger offering for a period of six months before and after the intrastate offering;

f. Persons who acquire securities from issuers in transactions complying with the rule would acquire unregistered securities that could only be reoffered and resold subject to the registration provisions of the Act;

g. The issuer should take steps to preserve the intrastate exemption by preventing resales to persons in other states or territories before the issue comes to rest by placing a legend on the certificate stating the limitations on resale, issuing stop transfer instructions to the issuer's transfer agent, and obtaining a written representation from each purchaser as to his residence.

Smaller Amount Offerings

To lower the cost of public offerings of limited character or for smaller amounts, the SEC has allowed a number of exemptions from the full registration requirements. Each of the methods has more restrictions than are noted here.

• Regulation D: The SEC replaced Rules 240, 242 and 146 with Regulation D, which includes Rules 501, 502, 503, 504, 505 and 506.

Rule 501 includes definitions, including that of "accredited investor". Accredited investors are not counted in computing the number of purchasers in offerings made under Rules 505 and 506. Accredited investors include certain institutional investors, insiders and, with certain net worth and income limitations, purchasers of securities worth at least $150,000.

Rule 502 defines the general conditions which must be satisfied for each of the exemptions to be available.

Rule 503 defines the notice of sales form.

Rule 504 exempts offerings and sales of up to $500,000 of securities during a 12 month period. The sales should be made in states which require registration of the securities, and should be made in accordance with those state regulations. It allows public resales, and public solicitation.

Rule 505 exempts offerings and sales of up to $5,000,000 of securities during a 12 month period without advertising or solicitation. Sales can be made to an unlimited number of accredited investors and to not more than 35 nonaccredited investors regardless of sophistication.

Rule 506 exempts offerings and sales of over $5,000,000 of securities without general advertising or solicitation to an unlimited number of accredited investors. The 35 nonaccredited persons must be sophisticated (alone or with a purchaser representative) and the issuer has to reasonably believe, immediately prior to making the sale, that the nonaccredited investors understand the merits and risks of the offering. Specified information has to be provided.

• Regulation F exempts sales up to $300,000 with a filing with the SEC. The SEC makes comments after examining the notice and clears it when they have no further comments.

• Section 4(6) "Accredited Investors" Exemption: This exemption allows up to $5,000,000 in sales to an unlimited number of accredited investors in an offering without general advertising or solicitation. There are slight differences in the definition of "accredited investors" as defined by section 4(6) from Regulation D.

• Regulation A Exemption: This is one of the primary methods used to offer securities publicly, short of a full registration. As of September 11, 1978, offerings that are not greater than $1,500,000 (Congress has authorized up to $2,000,000) in any 12-month period are allowed to use this exemption from registration. There is no limit on the number of offerees or purchasers. In addition to other requirements, an offering circular supplying information about the company and the securities offered must be filed with the SEC. Registration under Regulation A is frequently underwritten by smaller, regional investment bankers.

• Registration on Form S-18: Form S-18 allows small companies, which are not subject to reporting requirements under the 1934 Securities Exchange Act, to sell up to $7,500,000 in securities without restrictions on the number or nature of purchasers in the offering. Form S-18 requires less information than in full registration and may be filed with the SEC at its headquarters or regional offices.

Full S-1 Registration Offering

A full S-1 registration offering is made when the issue is to be sold for more than $1,500,000. Information to be included in a registration statement include the type and character of the business, its history, capital structure and earnings history; the names of those who manage or control the company and their backgrounds, along with their total compensation and holdings in the company; names and stockholdings of officers, directors and principal stockholders, and any material transactions they may have with the issuer; important legal agreements and any pending legal proceedings; any payments to promoters in the past two years or intended in the future; underwriters' fees and commissions; the uses for the proceeds of the offering; and financial statements that are audited and certified by independent public accountants. The preparation of this material involves the accountants and attorneys of the issuer and the attorneys of the underwriters. The information must be reviewed by the SEC, with the understanding that the registration statement becomes effective on the 20th day after filing. In practice, the SEC requires amendments to the registration statement, so that the average period before the registration statement becomes effective has been around 40 days.

Characteristics of Private Placements and Public Offerings

a. Private placements are easier and more convenient than public offerings due to dealing with a single or a limited number of investors. The time required to determine whether or not the funds will be available is relatively short, and the terms can be tailored to meet the needs of the borrowing corporation.

b. A policy of constant private placements tends to weaken contacts and credit standing which the corporation establishes with the investing public in public offerings.

c. Private placements are used to obtain cash to turnaround companies, or for takeovers or other special purposes, and to derive the financial strength to go public. Sometimes they are used because stockholders do not wish to subject their corporations and records to public scrutiny.

d. A disadvantage with private placements is that the price obtained is lower than in public offerings, resulting in greater dilution.

e. Private placements are primarily used for debt rather than equity because institutional investors have legal authority to make equity investments only on a limited scale.

f. The initial cost in a private placement is usually lower since there is no SEC registration. Both kinds of sale can involve the investment banker, adding to the cost. The interest cost in a private placement of debt may be higher than in a public offering, and might include an equity "sweetener."

g. The actual borrowing or issuing in a private placement does not have to take place immediately, but as needed.

h. Privately placed debt issues can be for small amounts allowing small companies to raise funds. Public offerings of debt issues need to be large to make them economically feasible.

i. Often, private placements of long-term debt are possible only if the applicant has or will have an unsecured bank line of credit after the placement. The long-term lender then relies on the current lender to closely monitor the company's status.

j. The private placement market is more personal and flexible than the public markets; terms of private placements frequently are negotiated and lenders often extend terms to existing borrowers during periods of tight money. The lender also may offer expert financial advice. Generally, the private placement agreement is more restrictive than that used in a public offering because the borrower is usually smaller and less secure financially. Also the public investor has a market for the securities, whereas the private lender usually is locked in, even though sometimes there is a small secondary market.

k. In private placements there usually are penalties for prepayment because lenders allocate their initial costs of analyzing the proposal over the term of the investment. With prepayment, this cost has to be amortized over a shorter period of time. Also, lenders do not want the borrower to refinance the loan at lower interest rates when general interest rates have dropped. The interest rates are higher in private placements: for the same quality of issue, the difference is about 0.05-0.5%. There might be similar prepayment penalties in public offerings, but usually the call feature is less restrictive. The public issue could be repurchased on the open market to meet sinking fund requirements.

l. The price paid for equity securities in a private placement is usually lower; the discount may be from 20% to 30% depending on various factors. The investor may insist on future registration of the stock, thus merely postponing the cost of registration. However, the state of the stock market or the company's weak financial position may preclude the public sale of securities and necessitate private placement.

m. Funds from a private placement are not dependent upon market conditions and subject to last-minute cancellations, which is sometimes the case with public financing.

n. Small and medium-sized companies usually cannot sell their debt issues in the public market because this is restricted to large corporations. However, they can sell their common stock in the public markets. For new start-up companies, the success of a public offering usually depends upon the nature of the markets and the degree of speculative issues it can absorb.

o. In public stock offerings, management may retain control of the corporation if the public will place a higher price-earnings ratio on their stock, resulting in a similar amount of funds raised for a smaller amount of stock.

p. The sale of common stock of a company to the public benefits the stockholders through the greater liquidity for their stock allowing them to retain control of the company, diversify their portfolio and to sell a portion of their holdings for a profit. It also provides a defined market value and liquidity for the stock for inheritance tax purposes. Public sale of the stock also provides additional capital to the company, increases awareness among investors and financial institutions, and helps the recruitment of talented executives through the use of stock option plans

q. Public offering is recommended if the company desires to reach a wide range of investors.

r. The timing of a public offering is influenced by the financial need of the company, the performance of the company and the attractiveness of the issue, and the general state of the market as to its acceptability of new issues.

Procedures for Raising Funds

Private Placements

A company can raise money through private placements by contacting financial institutions directly or by consulting an investment banker. Unless the company is familiar with the financial institutions and their investment criteria, the investment banker can save time. Even though the cost of the funds may not be lower, the investment banker may obtain an agreement better suited to the company and the institution (see section, "INFORMATION REQUIREMENTS").

Many private placements involve the use of **letter stock** — securities such as stock and warrants or debt securities convertible to stock, which are obtained through private placement, and not registered for public sale. Letter stock generally is purchased as an investment, and may not be resold to the public unless unforeseen events drastically change circumstances.

Investment stock held for more than three years generally is approved for resale by the SEC staff. That stock held for a period between two and three years needs to be approved with the investor filing a registration statement to justify the resale. Stock held less than two years generally is not approved for resale. Letter stock usually is sold only in companies which have, or will have, publicly traded stock, or in companies that are expected to be major growth companies due to an unusually good business idea or new technology.

Rule 144 under the Securities Act describes the conditions and the criteria for the sale of letter stock. Letter stock can be sold under the "leak-out" provisions of Rule 144 after it has been held for at least two years. As of September, 1978, Rule 144 allows holders of unregistered stock in a public company, to sell up to 1% of the number of shares issued and outstanding of the company over a three-month period, or the average weekly number of shares traded in the four weeks immediately preceding such a sale, whichever is greater.

Procedures for obtaining funds through private placement can vary depending on the nature of the company and the type of financing desired. The initial step is for the entrepreneurs to evaluate the needs of the business based on sound projections and goals. Based on these needs, the company selects the appropriate instruments and institutions. A prospectus, or feasibility study, with the required information is prepared. The amount and type of information to be included varies with the risk involved in the investment. The greater the risk, the more detailed the information requirements. The prospectus also should include the company's financial statements, preferably audited, and projections for the next 2 - 5 years, depending on the term of the investment. The use of projections is permissible in private placement, but not in public offerings. Next, selected financial institutions or private investors are contacted by the company or the investment banker. Financial institutions are chosen on the basis of their investment criteria, such as the range of investment per business, geographic area covered, type of instruments and businesses preferred, etc. Borrowing companies usually work exclusively with institutions that are seriously interested in the financing. After the institution has examined the proposal, it indicates its degree of interest. If an agreement is reached, a letter of intent describing the outline of the agreement is signed. The institution then investigates the company and, if found satisfactory, approves the investment. Often institutions ask for an investment processing fee which is refundable if the institution decides not to invest in the company.

Public Offerings

Public offerings are distributed on the basis of either a "firm commitment" or "best efforts." Under a firm commitment, the underwriters guarantee to the issuer that the issue will be sold at a specified price. Therefore, the risk of an unsuccessful offering is assumed by the investment bankers and not by the issuer. In contrast, the issuer of securities distributed on a best-efforts basis assumes the risk that they will not be sold. The issuer receives only the proceeds from the sales of securities to the public. Many issues are sold on an all-or-nothing basis, which means that if all the securities are not sold, none will be sold. Best-efforts sales also can stipulate a minimum volume of sales to fulfill the terms of the contract. The rights offering or the corporate offerings to existing shareholders before a public distribution is another kind of offering. Common stockholders have the privilege, unless waived in the original charter of the corporation or by subsequent vote of the stockholders, to purchase their pro rata share of any new issue of voting securities, or any issues convertible into voting securities being offered for sale by the corporation before it is offered to new stockholders. Often, rights offerings are made directly to the shareholders without assistance from the investment banker, and especially when the offering is priced sufficiently below the current market price. The company may have a standby contract with the investment banker whereby the latter agrees to purchase any unsubscribed shares. He is paid a standby commission based on the total number of units originally offered.

The information required by the investment banker includes the following:

a. The organization and history of the company;

b. Description of the business, market, product, marketing strategy, major customers, and competitors;

c. Five-year earnings record and balance sheet as of the end of each year (audited statements necessary in most cases);

d. Sales and profits by division and marketing arrangements;

e. Interim financial statements for the latest year and projected earnings for the current year;

f. Explanation of any unusual factors that have influenced earnings in the past;

g. Sources of raw materials;

h. Production facilities and employee relations;

i. Plans for future growth and growth potential;

j. Use of proceeds;

k. Resumes of key personnel and organization chart.

(Also see section on "Information Requirements.")

The investment banker should be selected on the basis of the size of the offering, the industry of the issuing company, the reputation of the investment banker, and his ability to maintain an after-market for the stock. After an interested investment banker is found, the deal usually is not offered to others for consideration. There are only about 350 managing underwriters in the U.S., and they usually are the larger security dealers, with capital in excess of $500,000. Firms can also be national, regional, or local with the local and regional firms being involved in smaller underwritings. Best-efforts sales are usually with one firm only, as opposed to a syndicated effort for an underwritten sale. This type of offering is thus confined to a regional or a local market. Larger underwriters are not interested in small issues (less than $1 or 2 million) or in speculative issues. Most of the larger investment bankers prefer public offerings of stock whose price is at least $10 per share, with an issue of 400,000-500,000 shares for an adequate secondary market. This means that the total offering is for $4,000,000-5,000,000. They also expect only 50% or less of the shares to be sold. Thus a reasonable valuation of the company based on industry price-earnings ratios and other comparable statistics need to be at least $8,000,000-10,000,000. These minimum figures also are greatly influenced by the speculative nature of the market. In the late 1960s, a new company with no history could raise equity capital through public offerings.

Underwritten offerings generally involve three functions:

Origination

This phase covers the policy decisions and mechanics of developing and disclosing the required information and of designing the security, the terms of the offering, and the nature of the subsequent underwriting and distribution. This phase involves only the company and the managing underwriters. After an analysis of the company and the offering, the underwriters, if interested, make an offer to the corporation. If this offer is found to be satisfactory by the corporation, a letter of intent is drawn, outlining the agreement. Even though this is not a legal contract, the parties honor the agreement unless a major problem occurs. In the underwriting contract, there is usually a "market-out" clause permitting the underwriters to cancel their obligations if some specified occurrences happen. These include any substantial change, in the financial position of the issuer or its subsidiaries or other market and economic or political conditions, before the public offering, that would, in the judgment of the underwriters, make the offering impracticable or inadvisable. The underwriter's commitment is obtained after the SEC registration takes effect. This may be 60-90 days after starting the statement; the company incurs costs (legal, accounting, etc.) in this period without a firm commitment. The underwriter obtains the certificates for cash about a week after the commitment. During this week, the underwriter may break the commitment only for catastrophic reasons.

In determining the price of the offering, the price-earnings ratio is the key. If the stock is already publicly traded, the price of the new stock is set a little lower than the market price. If it is a new issue, the price is negotiated between the underwriters and the seller. The price is negotiated by the managing underwriter(s) with the entire syndicate making the decision so as not to lose any members. The stock is priced no higher than the underwriters can sell it. If the price is too low, the clients could be dissatisfied, resulting in a loss of future business. The price per share, the earnings trend, price-earnings ratio, dividend, and the book value per share are examined for similar firms in the industry in determining price. The stock usually is priced a little lower than the prevailing market, so that it is attractive to prospective buyers, and so that the new shareholders are happy with the stock and will purchase more. It is considered favorable for the stock to have a positive trend in its market price.

Underwriting

The underwriting group — that is, the group that purchases the securities offered by the company — is larger than the origination group. This group purchases the securities from the issuer, and takes the risk of loss if the issue does not sell.

Distribution

Distribution involves the sales efforts to place the issue with investors. The distributing group includes, in addition to the underwriting syndicate, other separate dealers enlisted to augment the selling efforts of the underwriting group. The selling group members do not assume any underwriting risks and are compensated solely on the basis of the number of units sold.

Costs of Private Placements and Public Offerings

In deciding whether to have a private placement or a public offering, the borrower might minimize the sum of the cost of the nominal interest rate on the loan, the interest cost equivalent of the selling expenses, and the "cost" from loss of operating flexibility resulting from the provisions of the loan contract. However, the last cost cannot be quantified, and hence decisions are usually made on the basis of the difference between the sum of the first two costs. Thus, if the difference between the sum of the costs of the nominal interest rate and the interest cost equivalent of the selling expenses is 1% in favor of private placement, the issuer must decide whether the terms of the private placement agreement are more restrictive than the 1% worth. In the private placement of letter stock, it should be noted that most investors expect to have the right of registration within a certain defined time period either at their own expense or at company expense.

Thus, it may be that the funds obtained from the private placement of letter stock may only postpone the cost of a public offering for a few years. However, the company will have the use of the funds for the interim, and perhaps can wait until the stock obtains a more favorable price in the public market than present factors warrant.

Private Placement

In a private placement, the costs can vary depending on whether an investment banker's services are used and depending on the nature of the company and the security offered. Investment bankers usually charge from 0.25-2.0% of the amount raised, and in some cases where the amount raised is small or where the difficulty or the amount of effort required to raise the funds is large, this charge can be up to 5% of the amount raised. Terms and covenants in a private placement agreement are negotiable, but the interest rates usually are approximately 0.5% higher than in public offerings. Sometimes incentive features, called "kickers" or "sweeteners", are attached to debt issues in the form of warrants to purchase common stock of the company. This feature allows the institution to have an upside potential of gain that is not limited by the interest rate. It is usually included in the case of a relatively new company with greater potential than history, or in cases where the bonds are subordinated. The value of letter stock sold in private placements could be discounted from 20-30% from the value of the market value based on various factors, such as the history and potential of the company, the amount of trading of the stock in the secondary markets, the ease of selling the letter stock and the commitments on registration of the stock.

Public Offering

The costs of a public offering vary, depending on whether or not an investment banker is used. In practically all public offerings of any significant size, an investment banker is used. The initial cost of preparing the information and the requirements for a public offering are incurred whether or not an investment banker is used. These costs are composed of the following:

a. Executive time for collecting the information required for the prospectus;

b. Cost of corporate counsel who performs most of the work, including the preparation of the prospectus;

c. Counsel for the underwriter, who is paid by the underwriter and reviews the work of the corporate counsel on behalf of his client;

d. SEC fees;

e. Federal issue and transfer taxes, where the transfer taxes are charged for stock sold by selling shareholders;

f. Registrar and transfer fees;

g. Insurance;

h. Blue sky filing fees and the registration costs for each state in which the stock is to be sold;

i. Accounting fees;

j. The costs of printing the prospectus and the stock certificates.

In 1981, these costs ranged from $100,000 and up for some of the smaller offerings using a full S-1 registration. The costs for a Regulation A registration was approximately $65,000.

The SEC analyzed the costs of registered public offerings in 1971-72, with the following results ("Cost of Flotation of Registered Issues 1971-72," Washington, D.C., SEC, December 1974):*:

Common Stock

The average proceeds from common stock offerings was $8.4 million, with seller's compensation of 8.41% and other expenses of 4.02%, for total expenses of 12.43% of the gross proceeds. The cost of flotation is inversely proportional to the size of the issue (see Table 6). Some of the other factors influencing the costs of flotation of common stock are the following (see Table 7):

a. Issues of firms seeking equity financing for the first time tend to be relatively small, whereas issues of established firms with pre-existing trading markets tend to be larger, resulting in higher costs for firms seeking equity financing for the first time;

b. Initial public offerings are typically lower priced than those of relatively old, well-established companies, resulting in percentage spreads and other expenses of issuance varying inversely with the price of the issue;

TABLE 5: Cost of Flotation for Various Types of Securities.

Type of Security	No. of Offerings	Average Offering $000,000	Seller's Compensation %	Other Expenses %	Total Expenses %
COMMON STOCK					
To general public through securities dealers	1,599	8.4	8.41	4.02	12.43
Direct offerings to general public	23	3.2	9.24	3.47	12.71
Direct offerings to existing shareholders	22	43.1		3.59	3.59
PREFERRED STOCK					
General public through securities dealers	150	29.2	1.52	0.39	1.91
NONCONVERTIBLE DEBT					
General public through securities dealers	659	50.8	1.14	0.45	1.59
Direct to public	34	10.3	2.09	0.78	2.87
CONVERTIBLE DEBT					
General public through securities dealers	147	31.2	3.2	1.83	5.03

* This study has not been updated.

c. Where two companies of differing size sell similarly sized issues, generally the larger firm has the lower costs;

d. Rates of compensation were lowest in such industries as public utilities and highest for commercial and other industry classifications;

e. Issues that were underwritten were much larger (average offering of $9.8 million) compared with best-efforts offerings (average of $1.1 million), and the cost of underwritten offerings were approximately 9% lower than the cost of best-efforts offerings;

Direct offerings of stock to existing stockholders were much larger, with average gross proceeds of $43.1 million and an average cost of 3.59%.

Preferred Stock

The average preferred stock issue had proceeds of $29.2 million, which was about three and a half times as great as the average common stock issue. The cost was 1.9%, which was lower than the cost of distributing common stock.

TABLE 6: Cost of Flotation of Common Stock Issues Based on Size of Issue

Size of Issue $ Millions	No. of Offerings	Compensation - % of Gross Proceeds	Other Expenses - % of Gross Proceeds	Total Expenses - % of Gross Proceeds
Under 0.5	43	13.24	10.35	23.59
0.5-0.99	227	12.48	8.26	20.74
1.0-1.99	271	10.60	5.87	16.47
2.0-4.99	450	8.19	3.71	11.90
5.0-9.99	287	6.70	2.03	8.73
10.0-19.99	170	5.52	1.11	6.63
20.0-49.99	109	4.41	0.62	5.03
50.0-99.99	30	3.94	0.31	4.25
100.0-499.99	12	3.03	0.16	3.19
Over 500.0	0	—	—	—
Total/Averages	1599	8.41	4.02	12.43

f. Offerings to existing security holders through security dealers with standby contracts were three times as large on the average as those sold to the general public. The costs were about half as much.

There were only 23 direct offerings of stock to the general public, with average gross proceeds of $3.2 million. The total cost was 12.71%, where compensation of 9.24% was paid to persons authorized to distribute the issue — for example, employees of the firm, who were paid supplemental fees for their selling efforts.

Debt (Nonconvertible, Notes, and Debentures)

The average proceeds from debt offerings was $50.8 million, which was more than five times as large as the average common stock offering. The rates of compensation averaged considerably lower than common stock offerings (1.14% compared with 8.41%). The cost for debt issues was considerably lower even for issues of the same size, owing,

TABLE 7: Cost of Flotation of Common Stock to General Public Through Securities Dealers

Type of Offering	No. of Offerings	Average Offering $000,000	Compensation %	Other Expenses %	Total Expenses %
A. No existing pre-market	941	3.7	9.85		
with existing pre-market	622	15.7	6.15		
B. Underwritten	1,291	9.8	7.68	3.45	11.13
Best-efforts	212	1.1	12.77	7.19	20.02
C. Offer to general public	1,599	8.4	8.41	4.02	12.43
Offer through subscription rights	41	24.7	4.34	2.38	6.72

perhaps, to the fact that risks associated with price declines during the period of the offering were not so great, and the denominations of the debt issues were much larger, resulting in ease of distribution.

Convertible Debt

The average size of the convertible debt offering was $31.2 million compared with $50.8 million for nonconvertible debt. The total cost of flotation was 5.03% for convertible debt compared with 1.59% for nonconvertible debt. Percentage spreads and other expenses of issuance decreased in an uninterrupted fashion as the size of the issue increased. Convertible bonds are sold at higher spreads than nonconvertible bonds, perhaps owing to the heavily subordinated nature of the securities. The cost of flotation of convertible debentures is lower than the cost for common stock.

Extra Compensation

Sometimes the managing underwriter receives extra compensation in the form of warrants and options for underwriting common stock issues. These options or warrants are purchased at a nominal price and have been associated mainly with distributions of first-time public offerings. Such compensation tends to reduce spreads which would otherwise have to be obtained in their absence. Also, such arrangements are used in offerings where the risks are so high that a cash cost, which would be satisfactory to the underwriter, in relation to the risks involved, and to the issuer, in relation to the cost of the offering, cannot be agreed upon. Of all the issues which involved extra compensation, over 95% did not exceed $5 million in size; 81.4% of all issues less than $500,000, and 75.77% of all issues between $500,000 and $1,000,000 involved extra compensation. The exercise premium as a percentage of the offering price was 11.72% (range of 10.2-16.6%) and their ratio of shares exercisable to shares offered averaged 7.99% (range of 3.43-8.88%). The ratio of shares exercisable to shares offered decreased as issue size increased.

The compensation as a percentage of gross proceeds was lower for issues without extras, reflecting the lower risk of these issues. For similarly sized issues, rates of cash compensation averaged approximately two percentage points higher on issues with extras than on issues without extras.

Terms to be Negotiated

Private Placement

In addition to some of the usual terms — such as term of the loan, interest rate, etc. — the following should be discussed:

a. Registration rights for the letter stock, including piggyback registration rights and timetables for selling the investor's stock. Piggyback rights allow investors to register their stock with a company registration at a formula-determined cost or at no cost. Investors often have an agreement that allows them to register letter stock at their option. This registration can be at the investors' expense, or at the company's expense. Investors in letter stock usually demand this right because letter stocks often can be sold in the institutional secondary market only if they have registration rights. Some investors also require that registration rights be available to the initial purchaser and subsequent investors who purchase the stock;

b. Seats on the board of directors, frequency of financial statements, and right to inspection of books;

c. Financial restrictions, including additional debt and security offered, working capital, net worth, and dividend restrictions;

d. Employment and salary agreements for key personnel;

e. Call or conversion aspects of the stock or debt, including the right to call if the principal stockholders or management leave the company;

f. Key-man life insurance, property and product liability insurance, and business interruption insurance;

g. Pre-emptive rights and restrictions on sale of stock by existing stockholders to other stockholders, including the right of first refusal;

h. Payback of principal, including accelerated payments in case of better-than-anticipated profits, and deferred payments in the initial 2-3 years;

i. The amount of stock that will be sold or the amount of stock that the debt instrument can be converted to, and the conversion ratio over time;

j. A forward commitment which binds the lender to supply a stated sum of money at a designated interest rate within a specified time period. This allows the lender to match investments with the inflow of funds and to satisfy borrowers who do not have an immediate need, and it allows the borrower to formulate investment plans with greater certainty. The commitment agreement specifies the terms and provisions of the issue, and the terminal date of the commitment. There is usually a commitment fee —

usually 0.5-1.0% of the face value of the loan. The agreement does not usually commit the borrower to borrow the full amount.

k. Investors might want the company to register the restricted stock at its own expense in order to provide liquidity to their stock and a return on their investment. This registration can be done simultaneously with the company's own securities in a primary issue, or it can be done with a primary issue with a temporary delay in their offer and sale. They are normally sold less than 90 days after the sale of the primary issue and usually require an update of the registration statement at additional expense to the company. The former is called a "piggyback registration"; the latter a "shelf registration." The investor also may receive the right to register the securities in multiple stages. The agreement can specify the number of free registrations to the investor to protect the company from too many registrations at its expense. This method is called "multiple registrations." The above methods of registration can be combined.

l. If warrants are issued, the registration rights could become extremely expensive, since the registration statements would have to be updated each year until the warrants expire.

Public Offering

The following are some of the items negotiated with an investment banker in a public offering:

a. The type of security to be offered, the price of the security, the number of securities, and the timing of the offering;

b. The type of arrangement, i.e. whether the offering will be an underwritten effort or a "best-efforts" arrangement, etc.;

c. The type of registration, such as intrastate, Regulation A, etc.;

d. The cost of the underwriting, including the discount or commission, and any extra compensation; and

e. Other items, such as the indenture or the composition of the board of directors.

Institutions Involved in Private Placements

Purchasers of letter stocks include special letter stock funds, hedge funds, insurance companies, pension funds, closed-end funds, university endowment funds, trusts, wealthy individuals, nonprofit institutions, foundations, bank trust departments, investment counselors, off-share funds, open-end investment companies, private venture capital companies, and state-chartered companies. Many of the above also are involved in investing in long-term unsecured securities. Mortgage funds are obtained mainly from insurance companies, savings institutions, and commercial banks with or without Small Business Administration and Farmers Home Administration guarantees. Self-administered corporate pension funds are more aggressive in private placements. State and local government pension funds usually invest in issues of large, financially secure industrial corporations.

Information Requirements

General Principles

These general principles suggest some rules of raising funds for businesses. Some entrepreneurs have managed to raise funds even while violating the principles, because the lender or investor was sufficiently attracted by the proposal to overlook some deficiencies. Following these principles can increase the probability of success in raising funds required for the business.

a. The borrower should know the amount of funds required and for how long, and the uses to which it will be put. The uses for the funds should provide for a cash flow sufficient to repay loans to the lender or provide a market for the investors' stock, along with a rate of return, which could be the interest rate or dividend.

b. An introduction from a respected person is the best way to approach the lender or investor. When the businessman learns of a potential lender, attempts should first be made to secure an introduction through a mutual acquaintance. Such acquaintances are bankers, consultants, investment bankers, lawyers, accountants, or businessmen.

c. A carefully-drawn and well-documented written plan is an absolute necessity; the amount of information varies with the kind of financing being sought. In general, the newer the company, or the lesser the security, the greater the amount of funds required or the longer the term, the more detailed the information that will be required regarding all aspects of the business. This information package should include proforma (projected) financial statements. It is a common practice among many entrepreneurs to inflate projections to impress the lender. However, if the projections cannot be well documented by independent analysis of the markets and the company's capability and products, the effect of these overly-optimistic projections usually will be the opposite of that intended. Sometimes the lender will proceed with the loan or investment package because he considers the opportunity to be good, although not so profitable as depicted by the businessman. More often, the lender will consider the businessman's analysis to be unrealistic and unsound. It is better to be conservative and realistic in projections to convince lenders and investors that the business can do better than projected. The business plan can describe the maximum potential of the business in the "optimistic" case, i.e. if all the influential factors are favorable. Venture capital financiers like to see optimistic and pessimistic projections — i.e., best and worst possible cases.

d. The company should obtain adequate funds to operate without a deficit of working capital. No lender or investor likes to see a company returning for funds in six months when the initial projections showed that the funds would be satisfactory for three years. In exceptional cases, when the actual performance is much better than projections, there is not likely to be much problem in obtaining additional funds. But in cases where certain assumptions have not been met — such as a projected reduction in inventories not having been accomplished, or a cost overrun — the possibility of obtaining more funds becomes more remote.

e. Funds should be obtained through instruments which complement the uses for the funds. Thus, if funds are required for a long-term investment in equipment, these funds should not be raised from a line of credit which will have to be repaid within a year.

f. In new and start-up companies, lenders and investors usually will not invest in the company unless the entrepreneurial team invests substantially all of its assets in the company. The principle behind this practice is that the entrepreneurial team should have to stand to lose all its assets in case the company fails. Venture capital firms also are more likely to invest in a venture, all other things being equal, if the entrepreneurs do not budget large salaries for themselves, but are willing to risk their funds and time to obtain capital gains if the company is successful. It should be remembered that the venture capitalist makes a profit on his investment only when the company is successful.

What Financial Institutions Look For?

Although each financial institution and financial instrument may require the examination of different aspects of a business, some areas are examined for all types of financial instruments. Some typical questions raised follow:

a. Market Factors: The questions raised are those regarding the nature of the need served by the product and the product itself. Some primary considerations are whether the product is faddish or whether it is likely to have a long life. Lenders also evaluate the competitive products and firms to determine whether the company has a reasonable chance of success based on the relative merits and disadvantages of the products, the marketing organization, and the nature and size of the competition. Management should have a product plan which is growth oriented, allows adequate diversification, and reflects market needs. There should be a program for new products to replace those which are declining in sales. The company's share of the market should be increasing, or steady in an increasing market, as opposed to a declining or steady in a declining market.

b. Production Facilities: The company should have adequate and well-maintained production facilities and a satisfactory labor situation. The company should be able to meet technological change capably and profitably.

c.Caliber of Management: Management should be capable, well trained, and honest. The company should have sound long-range objectives, and realistic goals. Realistic plans should exist to achieve the goals with due consideration to available resources and manpower when formulating them. Adequate controls should be used to ensure that objectives and goals are being met. Management should be flexible enough to accept new ideas and to adapt to changing conditions.

d. Financial Characteristics: The company should have audited statements for at least 3-5 years if the company has been in existence for that long. Lenders also prefer to see the breakdown of sales by product lines and by major customers to determine whether the company is too dependent on a few customers and a few product lines. The financial position and prospects should satisfy investors or lenders of a positive return on their investment. The cash flow of the company should be able to satisfy all existing debt and any new debt that is being considered. Financial projections should be realistic and conservative and should show the income statements, balance sheets, and sources and uses of funds in reasonable detail. Above all, the lender looks to the ability to repay, and the investor looks to the potentiality of a profit through the investment.

e. Miscellaneous Factors: Lenders and investors also want to satisfy themselves that there are no existing or contemplated legal problems that could cause financial hardship to the company and hence threaten their investment. They also like to see adequate insurance coverage for unforeseen disasters and problems, such as product liability.

The Financial Package

The information requirements for a financial package depend upon the amount of funds required, the history of the company, the type of financial instrument and the degree of risk involved, the term of the loan and the collateral offered, and the financial strength of the company. In general, the larger the amount of funds required, the greater the term, the higher the risk or the lower the collateral offered, the more the amount and detail of information required in the financial package. For a small short-term loan to a company with a strong history of financial success, it is likely that the officer's signature is the only requirement. For large equity financing for a new company with no history, but only prospects, a large amount of detailed information will be required showing that the company can be successful and can provide a rate of return to the investors commensurate with the risk that they are being asked to take.

A complete financial package can contain the following information:

a. SUMMARY OF THE BUSINESS PACKAGE, FINANCIAL REQUIREMENTS AND USES;

b. THE DESCRIPTION AND HISTORY OF THE COMPANY AND THE INDUSTRY, THE BASIC BUSINESS STRATEGY IN THE PAST, AND THE ONE CONTEMPLATED IN THE FUTURE;

c. PRODUCT AND MARKETING, INCLUDING DESCRIPTION OF THE PRODUCTS, MARKETS SERVED DISTRIBUTION CHANNELS, USER CHARACTERISTICS FROM MARKET RESEARCH, AND MARKETING STRATEGY PLAN

d. PRODUCTION AND MANUFACTURING;

e. FINANCE AND ACCOUNTING;

f. MANAGEMENT AND OWNERSHIP;

g. LEGAL AND ADMINISTRATIVE;

h. MISCELLANEOUS.

Summary of the Business Package

- Short description of the company and its financial history;
- Key management;
- Financial requirements, uses, and payback.

Description of the Company and the Industry

- Company name, including its legal form, date started, and state of domicile; its telephone number, address, and contact officer;
- Where the company was started, by whom, when, original purpose, original form of the company, and evolution;
- Important changes in management and ownership of the company;
- Basic business(es), description, existing strategy, and proposed strategy;
- Subsidiaries, divisions, and major outside investments;
- Major products, including additions and deletions, with reasons and dates;
- Description of the industry, including total industry size, growth rate, major characteristics, opportunities, problems, number of companies and their sizes, and market shares, technological changes, and governmental regulations.

Products (or services) and Markets

- Description of products, including customers and consumers, uses and need satisfied; competing products, stage of development, actual and expected sales growth, proprietary positions, patents, trademarks, trade names, and brand names;
- Product line sales data, seasonality, and product mix and sales projections;
- Customer and consumer descriptions, categories, sizes, and purchasing power;
- Actual and potential market sizes, and expected rates of growth;
- Primary and secondary trade areas;
- Distribution channels;
- Major competitors including location, sales, prices, profitability, products, market share, marketing strategy, growth rates, potential, and how they compete;
- Kinds of customers and number in each category, names and history of 10-20 largest customers, and sales to each;
- Local, national, and international markets;
- Market capture strategy, including competitive advantages, advertising media and strategy, and brand image;
- New product development strategy, research and development strategy, and major technology changes expected;

- Regulations affecting product;
- Product direct costs by materials; labor, overhead, and gross margins; selling expenses; pricing policies and rationale;
- Terms of sale, including consignments, if any;
- Product guarantees, if any;
- Organization of sales program, including number of salesmen, compensation, productivity, and comparison with the industry.

Production and Manufacturing

- The major categories of raw materials and their contribution to cost;
- Names and numbers of suppliers, percentage purchased from each, and their location;
- Problems with supply, including fluctuating prices and material shortages;
- Amounts of each type of material in inventory and any associated problems, such as obsolescence, deterioration, spoilage, etc.;
- Physical facilities and equipment description and lists, including cost and appraised value, size, special equipment or buildings, space requirements for production, storage, etc., insurance, regulations and compliance with laws and codes, legal agreements (such as leases, mortgages, and sale and purchase agreements, and age and competitive aspects of equipment);
- Description of employees required, including number, job categories, skill levels, wage rates, fringe benefits, unions, work stoppages (duration and reasons), and number of shifts;
- Physical distribution methods of raw materials and finished goods from suppliers and to customers;
- Utilities required and availability problems.

Management/Ownership/Directors

- Organization chart;
- Key management and detailed resumes accounting for all periods of their life;
- Compensation of officers and directors;
- Names of directors and background;
- Stockholders and percentage of ownership;
- Legal structure of the business.

Finance and Accounting

- Audited statements for three, five, or ten years and latest unaudited statements;
- Aging of receivables and payables and their turnover;
- Credit checking procedures and policies, credit losses, and reserves;
- All supporting schedules;
- Inventory levels, turnover, and policies (LIFO or FIFO, obsolescence, subcontracting, etc.);
- Sales backlogs;
- Income tax returns;
- Projections for next three to five years showing income statements, cash flow projections, and balance sheets;
- Salaries, fringe benefits, and bonuses paid to management and officers;
- Total lease rentals and terms of lease;
- Dividends paid;
- Extraordinary gains and losses and explanation;
- Acquisitions and divestitures, and effect on financial statements;
- Pension and profit-sharing plans;
- Liabilities not shown in financial statements and reserves;
- Working capital requirements;
- Financial ratio analysis, including working capital, debt coverage, return on investment, return on sales, etc., and comparison with the industry;
- Cost accounting system description and frequency of review;
- Bank lines, term loan terms, and lenders;
- Break-even analysis in the past and with proposed changes;
- Agreements with officers and owners, such as leases, etc.;
- Use of proceeds.

Legal and Administrative

- Articles of incorporation and by-laws;
- Legal agreements;
- States in which the company does business and the states in which it is licensed to do business;
- Legal actions pending and contemplated;
- Patents, trademarks, tradenames, franchises, licensing agreements;
- Insurance including key-man, fire, extended coverage, product liability, business interruption, guarantees, hospitalization, life, workmen's compensation, unemployment, etc.;
- Contingent liabilities and resources;
- Stock and other financial instrument data, including number of shares authorized, issued, outstanding, and in treasury, their voting rights, conversion rights, offering data, stock option plans, outstanding warrants, stock repurchase agreements, market price of traded stock, and trading volume;
- Support professional groups, including bank-

ers, other lenders, attorneys, accountants, advertising agency, consultants, and trade association memberships.

Miscellaneous

- Critical risks and assumptions in the projections;
- Schedules and dates for the major aspects of the proposed plan.

III. Financial Instruments

Equity Instruments

Common Stock

Definition/Purpose

Shares of capital stock constitute the ownership of a corporation. The stock certificates held by shareholders represent ownership in the corporation, with each representing a proportion of the corporate equity. The owners' equity, or the book value of the shares, consists of the value of the assets less the liabilities. In the event of failure, stockholders usually lose only their investment or equity in the corporation, but in some states, some shareholders may be liable for wages and salaries owed to employees. There could be various classes of stock, varying in preference as to dividends and assets in case of liquidation and voting rights held. The maximum number of shares which can be sold by a corporation are stated in the articles of incorporation, and any changes in these articles require the approval of the shareholders. The shares actually sold by the corporation are called the issued stock; the shares held by the public are the outstanding stock; and the shares repurchased by the corporation from the public are treasury stock. In addition to the above, some other variations of common stock are:

a. Voting Trust Certificates are issued when a large block of common stock is entrusted to a trustee, who votes for the shareholders. The certificates are issued to the stockholders to recognize all their rights, except voting rights. Voting trust certificates are illegal in some states;

b. Guaranteed Stock: When payments, such as dividends of one company's stock, are guaranteed by another corporation or entity, the stock is guaranteed stock;

c. Deferred Stock or founders' stock is given to the promoters for organizing the company.

Sources

The major sources of funds for publicly traded corporate stock are life insurance companies, property and casualty insurance companies, pension funds, mutual savings banks, investment companies, commercial banks, foreign investors, individuals, and others. For privately held stock not traded in public markets, sources are more limited. For minority positions in privately held companies, demand is low unless the institutional investor has assurance the stock will be publicly traded in the future if the company is successful. The demand is also low unless the private investors are close associates or relatives of the entrepreneurs or are officers in the company with buy-back agreements with the company or other investors. Institutional investors, such as venture capital companies, usually lend funds to a venture but retain an option to convert their loans into stock in order to preserve their liquidity, and to obtain income in the form of interest when dividends are not paid on common stock in relatively new and young companies.

Advantages/Disadvantages — Characteristics

Some of the major advantages of common stock are:

a. Control of the corporation is vested with the common stockholders, who benefit from increases in net worth;

b. The corporation does not have fixed payments of principal or interest as in bonds or other debt;

c. The greater the equity of the corporation, the better the credit standing.

Some of the disadvantages of common stock are:

a. Some investors will not or legally cannot invest in stock, and hence stock is not always acceptable;

b. Dividends on common stock are not deductible from corporate income taxes, and hence must be paid from after-tax income;

c. No dividends may be paid common stockholders if any interest or principal is overdue on notes and debentures, or if dividends to preferred stockholders are not paid;

d Stocks cost a corporation more than other sources of funds since stockholders expect a higher return to compensate for greater risk;

e. Indiscriminate selling of common stock may result in management's losing control of the corporation;

f. Minority positions in closely held companies are not always marketable since the corporation is controlled by major stockholders who decide salaries and dividends.

How to Raise Funds (Including Data Required)

The Securities Act of 1933 and subsequent state and federal acts (see "Private Placements/Public Offerings" and "Legal Considerations") enumerate the various restrictions affecting the sale of stock to the general public. There are exemptions to these acts. The common methods of selling stock are the following:

a. Private placement;

b. Intrastate registration;

c. Smaller Amount offering; and

d. S-1 registration offering.

Private Placement

Common stock can be sold privately by the corporation or it can be sold with the assistance of an investment banker. Stock can be sold privately to existing shareholders (when the stock is not publicly traded), or to employees and officers in connection with stock option plans or savings plans. Sales to employees should be carefully scrutinized to satisfy the requirements for a private placement. Investment bankers can assist in the private placement of stock to new investors, such as individuals, venture capital companies, SBICs, etc. It is difficult to obtain the services of an investment banker if the company is new or weak. Specialized venture capital consultants can assist in such placements, especially for high technology companies. The cost for such services can be based on an hourly rate or it can range from 5 to 10 percent of the amount raised.

As noted in the section on private placement and public offerings, certain guidelines must be satisfied for an offering to qualify as a private placement. One such guideline limits the number of people (offerees) to whom the offering is made. Prospective buyers often are provided information about the kind of offering, the company, and other important aspects without disclosing the name of the corporation. Any buyer who shows no interest in the investment is then not considered an offeree.

Intrastate Registration

Intrastate registration is commonly used by small companies to avoid registration requirements of the Securities Act. The stocks must be sold only to bonafide residents of the state in which the company is incorporated and doing business. Such offerings must satisfy the state "Blue Sky" laws. The exemption sometimes can be lost if the initial purchasers resell to nonresidents (see Chapter II). Thus, the offering may have to be small and contain controls on resale of the securities. The intrastate exemption may be doubtful if the stock will be publicly traded, due to the problems of restricting resales to qualified buyers. If the intrastate offering is unsuccessful, and a later offering is made to out-of-state residents, the earlier intrastate exemption may be denied.

Smaller Amount Offering

There are a member of exemptions from the full registration requirements allowed for small offerings. These include Regulation D, Regulation F, Sec 4(6), Regulation A, and Form S-18 exemptions. (For more details, see "Private Placements/Public Offerings.") The SEC adopted these various exemptions to simplify registration requirements of the Securities Act of 1933, while the anti-fraud provisions still apply. The major advantage of these exemptions is the lower cost of the offering, although, the cost as a percentage of the amount raised might still be high. The lower cost is due to the smaller number of professionals working on the issue and to the requirements that the financial statements need not be certified, although they must be prepared in accordance with generally accepted accounting principles. Independent accountants must certify the financial statements when they are audited.

S-1 Registration Offering

For amounts above $1,500,000 which do not qualify under any of the exemptions, a full registration or "S-1" must be filed with the SEC. It requires a detailed printed prospectus, fully audited financial reports, and written documentation of the facts stated in the prospectus. Investment bankers almost always underwrite the issue. Some of the expenses involved are:

a. Special CPA audit for the prospectus;
b. Corporate counsel;
c. Underwriting expenses and counsel;
d. Prospectus and contract printing;
e. Blue Sky registration; and
f. The underwriting commission, which could vary from 6% to 15% on first issues of common stock.

In S-1 registrations, the total cost may be higher than in the other methods, but the cost as a percentage of the amount raised may be lower, depending upon the amount raised.

(See Chapter II for more details.)

Preferred Stock

Definition/Purpose

Preferred stock has preference over common stock for assets distributed upon dissolution and for the stated dividend before dividends on the common stock. Preferred stock combines features of debt and equity. If a corporation is liquidated, preferred stockholders' claim on assets comes after that of creditors and before common stockholders, but the amount of dollars paid is limited. The dividend paid on preferred stock is not tax deductible to the corporation. There is no stated term of repayment. Preferred shareholders may be denied voting rights, receiving instead compensation in the form of the preferences. Voting rights, however, may be allowed if dividends on preferred stock are not paid for a certain period of time.

A corporation may have more than one class of preferred stock, each having a different degree of preference based on benefits such as the dividend rate, etc. Preferred stock also may have the right of conversion to common stock, or some other security. This conversion right is held by the shareholder for a limited number of years, perpetually, or until the shares are repurchased by the company. The conversion ratio may vary over time, to encourage conversion within a desired period.

Retirement of Preferred Stock

Preferred stock usually is considered a temporary source of financing, and is used when it is difficult to sell common stock due to the poor condition of the company, during recessionary periods or when shareholders do not wish to dilute their holdings. It is often used to satisfy junior debt holders in reorganizing companies that have failed, with the understanding that the stock will be retired as soon as possible. It also may be used as a substitute for fixed interest debt if the earnings are erratic or if the debt-equity ratio is unsatisfactory. There is a call feature in most issues of preferred stock that allows the corporation to repurchase the preferred stock at a pre-negotiated price. If the call price is less than the market price, this call price is used; otherwise the preferred stock is repurchased in the open market. The call feature also could be used to force conversion, especially if the market value of the common stock is higher than the call price. A sinking fund can be used to repurchase preferred stock. Acquisitions using voting preferred stock are "tax-free," i.e. the acquired company or its stockholders are not liable for capital gains at the time of the acquisition, but when the stock is sold.

Sources

Preferred stocks of high-quality companies usually are sold to institutions in need of high returns — with possible gains through stock appreciation — and which enjoy the exemption on 85% of dividends from federal income taxes.

Publicly sold preferred stock is purchased mainly by life insurance companies, property and casualty insurance companies, private pension funds, investment companies, and commercial trust funds. Privately sold preferred stock is held mainly by lenders who accept it in corporate reorganizations, employees who are given preferred stock so that they may have ownership in the company without voting rights, and some investors who prefer dividends and would sacrifice voting rights. Privately held preferred stock usually can be converted to voting stock, or agreement may give the company the right to repurchase the stock from the stockholders, and the stockholders the right to sell to the company. Stockholders may be given the right to elect directors if dividends are missed.

Advantages/Disadvantages — Characteristics

Some of the advantages of preferred stock to the corporation are:

a. There is no fixed repayment on debt and interest;

b. Preferred stock can be a substitute for bonds in companies where earnings have a larger variance; and

c. It can be used for protection of control by common stockholders.

Some of the disadvantages are:

a. Preferred stock lacks the tax advantage of bonds to the issuer because the dividends are not tax deductible;

b. If there is no conversion privilege or if there is a limit on dividends, the preferred stockholders do not have the appreciation possibilities of common shareholders; and

c. It is junior to all debt.

Some of the other characteristics of preferred stock are:

a. Cumulative feature: preferred stock can be cumulative or noncumulative in its dividends. With a cumulative feature, dividends not paid are accumulated, but must be paid before common stockholders are paid dividends.

b. Voting rights: preferred shareholders sometimes have no vote unless certain things happen, such as unpaid dividends for a defined number of periods. If such events happen, the preferred shareholders are allowed to elect a prearranged number of directors on the board.

c. Participating feature: sometimes included so that preferred shareholders share in the earnings after the regular dividends are paid.

How to Raise Funds

Preferred stock is sold in a manner similar to common stock, with the exception that preferred stock often is sold at times of corporate reorganization, when junior debt holders are asked to accept preferred stock in exchange for their debt instruments. (See "Common Stock" and "Private Placement/Public Offering.")

Debt Instruments

Trade Credit

Definition/Purpose/Collateral

Trade credit is the largest form of short-term funds available to businesses. It is usually is easier to obtain credit from suppliers than from other financial institutions because of competitive pressures from other suppliers. However, most new businesses may have to pay cash for their purchases until they establish credit and negotiate credit terms with suppliers. There are three major types of trade credit:

a. Open account: the most common, where no formal debt instrument is signed for the amount owed, and only the invoice is used.

b. Notes payable: the buyer is asked to sign promissory notes instead of having an open account. It calls for payment at some specified future date. The note sometimes is used when the open account becomes overdue, and could be used when providing credit in large amounts or for extended terms.

c. Trade acceptance: the seller draws a draft on the buyer ordering payment of the draft at some future time. At maturity, the draft becomes a trade acceptance, and may be marketable if the buyer has a sound credit rating. If it is marketable, the seller can receive immediate payment for the goods by selling the draft at a discount. At final maturity, the holder of the acceptance presents it to the designated bank for collection.

Suppliers can provide credit in any of the following forms:

a. Normal credit terms (usually 10 or 30 days);

b. Special terms to account for seasonality or other circumstances;

c. Unsecured or secured loans, including installment contracts and conditional sales;

d. Leases; and

e. Consigned goods.

Terms/Payback

Terms can vary from industry to industry, but usually depend upon such factors as competition among suppliers, the life of the goods sold, kinds of customers and their credit rating, seasonality of goods sold, etc. Many industries have standard terms of "net 30," which means they expect payment in 30 days from qualified and approved customers. Often discounts are given to customers who pay within 10 days.

Sources and Credit Criteria

The sources of trade credit are the suppliers of goods. Differing criteria are used in various industries. Credit ratings from rating institutions such as Dun & Bradstreet influence the availability of trade credit. Credit criteria usually include such items as financial stature of the company (sales, net worth, current ratio, cash flow); history of the company; past payments; and any problem with other previous suppliers, including slow payment, lack of payment, bankruptcies, etc.

Advantages/Disadvantages — Characteristics

The availability of trade credit helps reduce the amount of cash that the business has to borrow from financial institutions or raise from stockholders. Since there normally is no interest charged for such credit, the cost of funds to the business is decreased. The cost of this credit is often passed on to the customer in the form of increased product costs. Many businesses would fail if there was no trade credit available.

Providing trade credit discounts to customers can be a very expensive form of financing when a cash discount is offered. If terms offered to a customer are "2% 10, net 30," the customer can deduct 2% from the cost of the goods if paid in 10 days. Thus, the supplier is offering 2% for the use of funds over 20 days, which is equivalent to an interest rate of $2 on the use of $98 over 20 days, or 36.7% annually. A customer who can afford to pay obtains the benefit of these favorable discounts.

Accounts payable can be stretched by postponing payments. The cost of doing this is the loss of the cash discount and a possible loss in credit rating, which may result in future problems with other suppliers and banks. The buyer may have to pay higher prices to those suppliers willing to do business, or pay cash on delivery (COD) of the goods.

The use of promissory notes and trade acceptances is limited in the U.S.

How to Raise Funds
(Including Data required)

See "Suppliers."

Line of Credit

Definition/Purpose/Collateral

A line of credit is established for customers who desire to borrow seasonally or for short terms. It is an understanding with a commercial bank which agrees to lend up to a maximum sum for a defined period. The bank is not legally bound to make the loan, but nearly always honors its agreement unless circumstances have changed drastically. Such drastic circumstances could include a severe change for the worse in the financial strength of the company or the nature of the economy. Lines of credit are mostly unsecured, and they often are used by businesses to satisfy temporary cyclical needs — or as "bridge" financing — and repaid through the issuance of long-term securities.

Terms/Payback

A line of credit usually is established for a one-year period and is renewable. The bank expects an annual period of about 30-60 days during which time there are no loans outstanding under the line. Some borrowers, such as finance companies, rotate their lines from one bank to another without a reduction in total bank borrowings. This is condoned by banks because they can review the decision to continue the line each year during the payout period. The notes usually are written for 90-day terms and renewed, if necessary. The amount fluctuates according to seasonal needs.

Sources and Credit Criteria

The major source of unsecured lines of credit is commercial banks. The line of credit depends on the financial strength of the corporation, and the size and lending policies of the bank. Because lines of credit are unsecured, lenders rely on a strong balance sheet and adequate short-term cash flow, either from earnings or asset liquidation. The unsecured lender has no priority over any common creditor of the borrower, and generally banks require subordination of all indebtedness of the borrowing company to its principals. Credit criteria are usually the following:

a. Working capital and current ratio: Lenders prefer the line to be less than 50% of working capital and a minimum current ratio of 1.5:1;

b. Debt-to-equity ratio: Unsecured lenders do not like high debt-to-equity ratios, usually above 2:1;

c. Earnings and cash flow: Cash flow should be adequate to repay the line within a year.

Most lenders want the loan to qualify on its own merits. However, personal guarantees will be required if the borrower is not financially sound. The principals' guarantees are able to improve the security, especially if the company is small with the principals being an inseparable part of the company.

Advantages/Disadvantages — Characteristics

A line of credit is the most attractive form of short-term financing. Borrowings under the line are decided by the company, and interest charges are based only on the amount actually borrowed. It is the simplest means of borrowing, on an unsecured basis, with minimal loan handling requirements and low cost. An open line is extended only to sound companies for short-term needs. The borrower is expected to "rest the line" by full payouts for about 30-60 days each year. Sometimes banks renew the lines for strong companies even without payouts. More often the lines are not renewed but the loan is secured and then made into a term loan, or the company is asked to obtain funds from a commercial finance company, which follows accounts more closely and is able to deal with higher-risk companies. A limitation of lines of credit is that the amount may not be enough, and it may not be available in periods of financial emergency.

Factors affecting the interest costs are:

a. The state of the economy, the prime rate and other bank borrowing costs;

b. The amount of supporting and compensating balances offered;

c. The quality of the company;

d. The costs of servicing the line, especially if it is secured;

e. The nature of the competition for the account.

The average compensating balances are around 15-20%, but they can vary based on competition, size and strength of the company, whether it deals with local or national banks, growth potential, and other benefits obtained by the bank from the relationship, such as payroll accounts, checking accounts, etc.

Since banks can purchase deposits through Certificates of Deposits and the Eurodollar market, they sometimes charge their normal rate to the borrower based on the borrower's average bank balances and the compensating balance required, and a higher rate above that amount based on the cost of purchased deposits.

Multiple Lines of Credit

A borrower can negotiate agreements with more than one bank to avoid becoming too dependent on a single bank, or to stay below each bank's limit for a single customer.

Personal Line of Credit

Loans to starting businesses for small amounts may be more easily obtained by the borrower on a personal basis. If the borrower qualifies, the bank has an opportunity to lend to growing companies without excessive exposure.

How to Raise Funds (Including Data Required)

Lenders are more impressed with borrowers who plan for their needs and who are able to provide adequate notice of future requirements. A few months advance notice is preferred.

The following information must be provided to secure a line of credit:

a. The maximum amount needed, when needed, and for how long; the time and method of repayment, i.e., periodic repayments or lump sum repayment.

b. The use for the funds (banks want to know that the money is used for purposes within bank policies and guidelines).

c. The source of repayment — whether from a seasonal drop in requirement of funds or from projected earnings.

d. The company's financial projections.

Financial statements and projections have a greater amount of credibility if done by recognized public accountants than by the company itself.

Audited statements are most desirable and often mandatory for loans above certain amounts. In many closely held companies which are not regularly audited, the statements and projections are presented on the accountant's letterhead. The accountant normally adds a disclaimer stating that the statements are not audited statements and that the projections are based on management's input. Since auditing is expensive, it should be done only after the lender has indicated an interest in the loan, and requested an audited statement.

(See "Commercial Banks" for factors to be used in selecting a bank.)

Transaction Loans

Definition/Purpose/Collateral

Transaction loans are made when a firm needs funds for a single purpose, such as a particular contract, etc. Repayment of the loan can be through obtaining permanent financing (such as for real estate mortgages), through a public offering, or from the cash flow generated by the borrower. These loans can be unsecured or secured by specific collateral, depending on the project being financed and the credit of the customer.

Terms/Payback

These loans are designed for short-term periods, although renewals are possible. Payback can be through the cash flow generated by the transaction, permanent financing, or a public offering.

Sources and Credit Criteria

The major sources of transaction loans are commercial banks. The terms and costs are negotiated separately for each new loan, and are based on the particular requirements. In addition to the credit criteria used for lines of credit, additional criteria are the nature of the collateral, its liquidation value, and ease of liquidation.

Advantages/Disadvantages — Characteristics

Transaction loans are appropriate when the amount needed is precisely known or when the bank wishes to review the situation frequently.

How to Raise Funds

Same as Line of Credit.

Short-Term Working Capital Loan

This loan can be in any of the following forms:

a. Line of credit;

b. Transaction loans;

c. Secured loans, with equipment, accounts receivable, inventory, etc.;

d. Unsecured loan.

Except for unsecured loans, these types of loans have been covered in other sections. Unsecured loans are similar to term loans (covered in a separate section), with the difference that the term is less than one year and the instrument is a promissory note — usually for 90 days — and renewable. Short-term loans typically are regarded as "self-liquidating" because the assets purchased with the proceeds generate sufficient cash flows to pay the loan in less than a year. Unsecured loans usually are available to high quality companies. The major sources are commercial banks. The interest rate is based on the size of the borrower, the size of the loan, the market rates, and the duration of the loan. It is raised with information similar to that for the line of credit.

In short-term loans, the unsecured arrangement is preferable because it is more economical for both parties. The effective use of devices for pledging conventional business assets involves high servicing costs.

Banker's Acceptances

Definition/Purpose/Collateral

A Banker's Acceptance is a draft (a request for payment) drawn by the supplier on the buyer's bank, due to its greater financial strength, rather than upon the buyer itself. The draft becomes a banker's acceptance after it is accepted by the bank. Banker's acceptances are very useful if the seller is unwilling to extend unsecured trade credit to the customer due to the large order size or in international trade. The bank looks at the purchaser's credit and collateral — which is the goods being shipped.

Terms/Payback

An acceptance confirms that a letter of credit will be paid after a reasonably short period of time, usually within 90-120 days. Acceptances are used in situations where sale of goods is possible only with the guarantee of payment to the seller by the customer's bank. The bank provides the guarantee by accepting the draft only if it is assured of payment from the buyer prior to the maturity of the acceptance. The acceptance assures the seller of payment for the goods and the buyer is given additional time for payment.

Sources & Credit Criteria

Sources of banker's acceptances are commercial banks. The bank looks at the credit of the purchaser, the liquidity of the collateral and the liquidation value, and the purchaser's cash flow.

Advantages/Disadvantages — Characteristics

The major advantage of the banker's acceptance is that it facilitates trade of large quantities of goods to be shipped over long distances when the shipper cannot or will not lend credit to the purchaser himself, but where the purchaser's bank is willing to provide this guarantee. The fee for a banker's acceptance is around 1.5% per year. The bank also charges interest if any funds are advanced, but it usually expects that amount to be paid before it must pay the draft. The vendor can sell the acceptance in the open market if he wishes to obtain the cash before the draft becomes due. If the shipper needs the funds from the sale, he can choose to discount it or borrow with the acceptance as collateral. These loans can be obtained at low interest rates due to the high quality of the collateral.

How to Raise Funds

After negotiating the purchase with the seller, the buyer arranges with his banker to accept the draft when presented to him by the seller or his banker. The buyer promises to pay the bank before it is called on to honor the draft. The bank then draws a letter of credit to the supplier with shipping instructions. After the goods are shipped, the supplier draws the draft on the buyer's bank and deposits it at his own bank along with the bill of lading and other papers. The supplier's bank sends the draft to the buyer's bank or to its correspondent in the same city, who submits it to the buyer's bank. If the draft satisfies the agreement, the buyer's bank accepts the draft, thus constituting an acceptance.

This financing method can be very helpful to firms that sell staple merchandise, especially if the goods are to be stored in warehouses or are in transit for considerable periods of time.

Letter of Credit

Definition/Purpose/Collateral

The Letter of Credit (L/C) guarantees payment of a specified amount of money to a supplier by an issuing bank if certain conditions are met by an expiration date. When the supplier or his bank calls for funds against a L/C, it is known as drafting against the L/C. If the supplier has satisfied the requirements of the L/C by the expiration date and if the L/C is irrevocable, immediate payment can be expected. L/Cs are used mainly in international trade to finance the purchases and sales of goods. When the seller cannot or will not provide unsecured credit, the L/C is used to assure the seller that he will be paid if certain specifications are met and to assure the buyer that certain pre-negotiated specifications are met. It can be used with the bankers' acceptance. The bank relies on the credit-worthiness of the buyer and the nature of the goods used in the transaction (which is also collateral). If the L/C is revocable, the lender can cancel it before shipment of goods.

Terms/Payback

In a L/C, the bank usually expects to be paid before the L/C is paid. Thus, the bank essentially guarantees to a third party (the supplier) that he will be paid if certain specifications are met. If the buyer defaults on the payment, the bank will sell the goods to recoup its loan, and expect the customer to provide additional funds to cover any losses.

Sources and Credit Criteria

The sources of L/Cs are international departments of commercial banks or the customer's bank, which would then contact their correspondent bank's international department. Some of the larger commercial finance companies also can open L/Cs. Lender criteria are the following:

a. Financial strength of the buyer: The bank would prefer to see a strong buyer for the goods, because this will assure payment to the bank and minimize its cost of being repaid.

b. Buyer's marketing ability: Importing large quantities based on a proven marketing ability or on firm purchase contracts is more preferable to bankers than importing for inventorying.

c. The types of goods: If the collateral is a commodity and easily marketable, the lender is more favorably inclined to provide an L/C for larger quantities.

d. The supplier's reputation for quality and dependability: This can be checked with other customers of the supplier and local banks or obtained from international Dun & Bradstreet reports. Buyers sometimes use a buying or inspection office in the supplier's country to inspect the goods or negotiate better terms.

e. Loan-to-value ratio: For small sums and creditworthy customers, a bank might open the L/C as a 100% contingent liability of the bank. Otherwise banks prefer that the client have an investment in the shipment, so that the lender's commitment on an L/C is equal to 75-90% of the lender's estimate of the collateral liquidation value.

Advantages/Disadvantages — Characteristics

L/Cs allow the efficient flow of international trade when the seller cannot or will not provide credit to the buyer, and the buyer wants certain specifications satisfied before payment is made. Companies which use L/Cs, such as in international trade, can obtain an additional source of funds through an L/C line.

How to Raise Funds (Including Data Required)

International trade calls for a greater degree of caution in the selection of suppliers than domestic trade, because it is more difficult to ascertain the dependability and quality of the supplier's goods and service outside the U.S. The L/C should include some of the following items to assure the supplier of the agreed upon quality and quantity of goods within desired time periods:

a. Name and address of the buyer and the supplier.

b. The amount of the credit required.

c. The type and tenor of the draft, such as a time draft, sight draft, or clean draft.

d. Documents including a commercial invoice and a bill of lading or airway bill, and a description of the merchandise, unit prices and quantities.

e. The expiration date, which is the last date on which the documents may be presented for negotiation or to the issuing bank.

f. The point of origin of the goods.

g. The trade terms, which refer to the shipping arrangements agreed to by the buyer and the seller concerning who is to incur the costs of insurance, transportation, taxes, customs, etc. Among others, the options can include F.O.B. (Free On Board: seller responsible for placing goods on location — usually vessel — named) or F.A.S. (Free Along Side: seller delivers goods along side the quoted vessel), or C.I.F. (Cost, Insurance, Freight: seller absorbs the costs of the goods, insurance, and freight costs to the destination).

The L/C also sometimes designates an inspector, such as an overseas buying agent, to protect the buyer's interests. It should state also whether partial shipments will be allowed, the method of shipment, and any changes allowed. It also lists the documents needed, including bills of lading, consular and commercial invoices, and packing lists.

Commercial Paper

Definition/Purpose/Collateral

Commercial paper is a short-term, unsecured promissory note sold in the money market by corporations for their working capital needs either to a commercial paper dealer or directly to an individual investor. Commercial paper is sold at a discount and matures at par. The secondary market for commercial paper is not so large as that for Treasury bills. Direct placers of commercial paper rely much more heavily on commercial paper and usually are larger companies who use commercial paper as an alternate source of permanent financing rather than as a substitute for interim banks loans. They sell the issue directly or through banks. To satisfy the criteria for "sophisticated investors," commercial paper is sold in minimum lots of $25,000. A round lot is $1,000,000. Paper is sold in multiples of $1,000 and many direct issuers will not sell less than $100,000 of paper. Financial institutions account for approximately 75% of outstanding commercial paper.

Terms/Payback

Commercial paper can be specifically designed with respect to maturity, which offsets the lack of a secondary market. Their maturities range from 1 to 270 days and no longer unless it is privately placed, because the Securities Act of 1933 stipulates the proceeds should be for current transactions. It is more common for paper sold through dealers to have a maturity of 30 days or greater, while directly placed paper often is issued for one day. Dealer paper normally is issued for multiples of 30 days. Payback is either through the liquidation of the assets purchased with the funds (as in seasonal needs for inventory and accounts receivables), through floating another issue of commercial paper, or through the use of the company's line of credit. Some companies, such as finance companies, use commercial paper as a permanent source of financing by selling new paper to replace maturing ones. Commercial paper also is used to meet seasonal borrowing needs, or for interim construction financing. The issuer must have lines of credit to cover 100% of the commercial paper issue.

Sources and Credit Criteria

Commercial paper is used mainly by large, well-established companies. Before World War II, commercial banks were the major investors in commercial paper. Since then, nonfinancial institutions have been the major investors. Small country banks, that have excess cash during slack periods because loan demand is of a seasonal nature, invest significantly in paper. Banks are important purchasers of commercial paper in the dealer market and the direct market, with a significant portion of their purchases being for the accounts of their correspondents and non-bank customers. Nonfinancial corporations are significant factors in the direct placement market. Insurance companies, pension funds, investment companies and trust funds temporarily place their funds in directly placed paper until they find permanent investments for their funds. Colleges and universities also buy commercial paper.

Commercial paper is rated by three companies, namely Standard & Poor's, Moody's and Fitch. All three rating systems use the 1,2,3 system, with additional ratings to denote lower quality issues. Moody's uses Prime-1, Prime-2 and Prime-3; Standard & Poor's uses A-1, A-2 and A-3. Fitch uses F-1, F-2 and F-3.

Rating 1 denotes corporations with the highest credit quality with considerable net worth. Ratings are based on subjective analysis rather than formalized criteria. Companies in this category include the largest corporations, and financial companies or their divisions, of which General Motors Acceptance Corporation is a good example.

Rating 2 is of lower quality than rating 1 companies. of cyclicality in their earnings, or may be younger cyclical, have a higher leverage and possibly a lower return on equity.

Rating 3 companies usually have a higher degree of cyclicality in their earnings, or younger companies with good growth prospects. They have sufficient bank lines to pay the commercial paper issue at maturity.

Companies can ask for nonrated paper when they disagree with the rating service on the rating given to their issue. Nonrated paper is typically not accepted as an investment vehicle by many institutions. Institutions that invest in commercial paper also consider the long-term debt rating of the issuer in addition to their commercial paper rating when evaluating the paper for investment.

Firms with short-term borrowing needs and a very high credit rating should consider commercial paper as an alternative source of funds.

Advantages/Disadvantages — Characteristics

The advantages of commercial paper are:

a. The main advantage is the lower interest cost, which may be up to 1.5-2% lower than the prime rate. The interest rate is determined by the rating of the paper. The difference in interest costs between the top rated (P1) and lower ratings (P3) can range from 0.1% to 2% depending on whether or not credit is easily available. Rates fluctuate with money market conditions, including the prime rate, rate for CDs, the discount rate, federal funds rate, etc. It reacts much faster than the prime rate. Commercial paper requires the company to have an open line of credit which requires a compensating balance. This compensating balance is lower than if the company had a direct loan (10% versus 20%);

b. Bank financing may not be available during tight money periods, but financing for companies with strong credit ratings may be available through commercial paper at rates lower than bank rates. This has caused new borrowers to enter the commercial paper market;

c. It is an additional source of financing and makes financial institutions and investors more aware of the company;

d. Bargaining power with bankers is increased;

e. Institutional investors can invest idle funds on a day-to-day basis where the term can be structured to the investors' desire.

The costs and disadvantages of commercial paper are;

a. The typical commission to the dealer is 1/8 of 1% per annum based on a 360-day basis. This cost varies with the risk in the paper and the nature of the markets;

b. The commercial paper market is maintained due to commercial banks' services and line of credit (which assure commercial paper holders of repayment). Bankers may feel they are helping their competition too much and sale of commercial paper may strain bank relations;

c. There is no real secondary market, and paper is usually purchased to be held to maturity;

d. Bank loans have greater flexibility.

How to Raise Funds (Including Data Required)

Commercial paper can be sold directly or through commercial paper dealers. Commercial paper notes generally are sold on a discount basis, but occasionally at the request of the buyer they are sold at par, with interest to be paid at maturity. To sell commercial paper, the board of directors of the company must authorize the issue, giving specific company officers authorization to sign and issue the notes. A bank is appointed as the paying and issuing agent. Numbered notes are signed by the authorized officers, and countersigned by the bank. The agency bank should be authorized to pay the notes when presented on maturity.

Medium-Term Credit — Revolving Credit Agreement or Rollover Credits

Definition/Purpose/Collateral

A revolving credit agreement is a legal commitment of the bank to provide credit up to a maximum amount for a specified length of time. The revolving credit provides funds for an intermediate term, such as for four years, rather than for a short-term. The contract specifies the maximum amount of funds which can be borrowed at any one time, using short-term notes. The loans usually are given only to quality customers, and usually with adjustable interest rates, Rollover credit has expanded the use of medium-term bank credits, introduced the system of flexible rates, and allowed syndication of bank credits among a number of banks. Medium-term credits have become more obtainable since World War II. Since the lender is committed to lend up to a certain maximum for a designated length of time, the borrower is required to pay a commitment fee on the unused portion of the revolving credit. These loans can be secured or unsecured.

Terms/Payback

These credits are for an intermediate, rather than short, term. The contractual agreements are usually for a period of 3-4 years, and only actual amounts needed are drawn. The actual notes are short-term (usually 90 days), which can be renewed through the term of the commitment. Even though rollover credits are granted for a few years, they are automatically renewed on modified terms every six months or other short period specified in the contract. Repayment of rollover credits may take place in one lump sum at the maturity date, in several installments on prespecified dates, or prepayment may be allowed as stated in the agreement, usually with advance notice.

Sources and Credit Criteria

The sources of medium-term credits are commercial banks or a syndicate of commercial banks. Credit criteria are similar to those for lines of credit.

Advantages/Disadvantages — Characteristics

The major advantage of the medium-term credit arrangement is that there is a legal commitment from the lending institutions(s) to lend a certain amount of funds for a designated time. The borrower has flexibility in borrowing and the agreement can be set up so that at maturity the borrower can convert the amount then owed into a term loans. It is also called "below the line" financing, which means that it is not treated as a current liability, thus increasing working capital.

The interest rate for the funds is higher than that for short-term funds, varying with market rates on a predetermined formula. Since the bank is legally committed to have funds, a commitment fee of approximately 0.5 - 1.0% per year usually is charged for funds not drawn down. It is easier for borrowers to obtain ordinary bank credits; rollover credits are more difficult to obtain because of possible capital shortages.

The agreement states the maximum amount, the maximum period, and the terms on which the interest rate is subject to adjustment. The interest rate charged is dependent upon the prime rates at the time of borrowing and an additional spread. The following factors could affect the spread:

a. The quality of the borrower as determined by the financial strength and credit rating;

b. The supply of medium-term credit and the demand for funds, which is affected by the economy;

c. The prime rate and the other costs of bank borrowing, along with projections for future interest rates;

d. The competition for the account; and

e. Other terms of the contract.

Term Loans

Definition/Purpose/Collateral

Term loans are those loans with maturity of more than one year. They are repaid from cash flow from operations (earnings plus depreciation) rather than from collection of receivables or sales of inventory. The funds can be used for working capital to finance growth of permanent receivables and inventory, for purchase of intermediate-term assets, and for real estate financing. The loans may be secured or unsecured, depending on the quality and size of the borrower and the size of the loan. The term loan usually has a shorter maturity and fewer holders than do bonds. The terms and provisions of the debt are in the document itself, rather than in a separate agreement (called the indenture in bonds). Term loans to small companies usually are secured, primarily with equipment and real estate. As firms become larger, the proportion of secured loans decreases.

Terms/Payback

Term loans are business loans with a maturity of more than one year and repayable on a specified schedule. Many are made for terms under 3 years, but they may be made for up to 10-12 years; the average is 3 - 5 years. Repayment often is based on the cash flow ability of the firm, on any of the following plans:

a. Equal, periodic payments over the term of the loan;

b. Periodic, unequal payments based on some formula, or dependent on earnings;

c. Equal, periodic installments with final "balloon" payment; and

d. One payment at maturity.

Term loans are made when it is reasonably certain that the assets to be financed are permanent, such as a permanent increase in receivables and inventory. If there is uncertainty about this permanency, the loan can be a "rollover" loan, and converted to a term loan when the need is ascertained. Often, term loans are refinanced at equal or larger amounts. Unless this refinancing is arranged in advance, however, this option may not be available or else the terms may be too strict. Sometimes payments on principal are not made during an initial period, such as a year, as in the case of loans for plant expansions where there will be no revenues from the asset for some time.

Sources and Credit Criteria

The sources for term loans are:

a. Commercial banks;
b. Insurance companies;
c. Trust companies;
d. Venture capital companies;
e. Savings banks;
f. Pension funds;
g. Community development corporations;
h. Investment companies;
i. Real estate investment trusts;

Businesses are evaluated for term loans on the basis of the following:

a. Financial strength and projections, including profitability, cash flow and balance sheet characteristics;

b. Quality of the management;

c. Purpose of the loan; and

d. Value of the collateral pledged.

In making a term loan, the lending institution emphasizes cash flow and security. Some lending institutions, such as insurance companies, desire evidence of an adequate cash flow over the past five years of a company's operating history. Term loan availability is based mainly on the ability to repay and the security available, with emphasis given to the balance sheet and cash flow. A major factor considered in determining the amount of term loans available to the borrower is:

Cash Flow, which is the sum of the net profits after taxes, depreciation and other noncash expenses.

Debt coverage is defined as cash flow available to service the loan — i.e., cash flow less previous loan repayment commitments. Normally, debt coverage should be more than the annual loan and interest repayment, and some institutions prefer a ratio of 2 or 3. Net worth is an important factor, with unsecured debt being around 50-100% of net worth as long as debt coverage is adequate for repayment.

A larger percentage of term loans are secured

because the risk of loss increases with the term, and higher income balances the higher costs of collateral and loan administration. Lenders obtain collateral if it is easily obtained and secured, such as collateral in the form of marketable securities from investment bankers, etc., regardless of the risk involved. Thus, lenders obtain security when it is easily available, and where the collateral has a ready market.

Advantages/Disadvantages — Characteristics

The major advantage in term loans is that, within limitations, borrowers have greater flexibility in structuring the loan to suit their needs. Fewer people are involved in the lending process, and there is greater confidentiality of information. A term loan can be closed much faster than public offerings. Also, a term loan can be a source of funds to companies that may not have access to the capital markets through public offerings. Some problems with long-term loans are the existence of restrictive provisions in the loan agreement (see "Covenants"). It should be noted that the overall purpose of covenants and guidelines is not to attempt to tell the borrower how to run his business, but to set up broad guidelines for the protection of the lender. Sometimes, in the case of a commercial bank, there may be a lending limit, which is resolved by having many banks in a syndicate. The typical long-term lender often takes equity participations, and these institutions are usually complementary to commercial banks. Thus, for example, an insurance company and a bank will participate in the loan, with the bank portion having shorter terms and insurance companies having longer maturities, thus satisfying the intermediate- and long-term needs of the borrower.

A lender cannot quote an interest rate until an analysis of the borrower has been made. Long-term loans can have variable interest rates tied to market rates. Interest rates are a function of market conditions, the size and quality of the borrower, the amount of the loan, the type of security, and the term of the loan. For high quality companies and for larger loans, the interest rates are lower because the administrative costs are proportionately lower. Where the collateral is easily marketable, and the prices are known, costs are usually reduced by eliminating extensive analysis procedures. Interest rates are higher than the rate on a short-term loan to the same borrower, and the rate may be a function of the prime rate. Additional costs could include legal expenses, a commitment fee for the amount commited but not drawn down, and compensating balances which are around 15-20% when the loan is from a commercial bank. (For special conditions, see "Covenants".)

How to Raise Funds (Including Data Required)

Some of the major information requirements are the following:

a. The amount of funds required, the uses for the funds, and a proposed repayment schedule;

b. General description of the business;

c. Description of products, and sales and profitability of each product;

d. Market description, list of important customers, and marketing strategy;

e. Description of production facilities, labor, and raw materials, including names of major suppliers;

f. Audited financial statements for the past 3-5 years;

g. Financial projections for the next 3-5 years; and

h. Resumes of executive officers.

Secured Loans

There are various forms of security for commercial loans to businesses. The security could be any of the following:

a. Personal guarantees (guaranteed by the principal shareholders);

b. Endorsement or co-maker loans requiring other guarantors;

c. Current assets, such as accounts receivable and inventories;

d. Cash value of life insurance;

e. Stocks and other securities;

f. Machinery and equipment; and

g. Real estate and any other assets.

Lenders ask for security because they then have two sources of loan payment: the cash flow of the firm and the liquidation value of the security. Even with security, lenders want the firm to have adequate expected cash flow to service debt. This is especially true when the collateral has a long life and is not expected to be liquidated to repay the loan.

Security is evidenced through the use of the lien. A lien is a priority claim on property and is defined in the Uniform Commercial Code. It is created through a legal process according to the statutes of the state under whose laws the loan is made.

Secured Loans — Accounts Receivable

Definition/Purpose/Collateral

A secured loan with accounts receivable as security is a short-term loan where the asset is liquidated to repay the loan. It provides working capital to the firm and allows it a greater sales level without a greater infusion of equity. In accounts receivable financing, the lender has recourse to the firm in case the receivables are uncollectible. This is the difference between accounts receivable financing and factoring, where the lender purchases the receivables and has no recourse to the firm. In factoring, the purchaser also notifies the customer that the account has been purchased. Accounts receivable financing can be on a notification or non-notification basis, with most borrowers choosing non-notification.

Terms/Payback

Normally, these loans are for the terms offered by the customer, usually up to 60-90 days. The loan is to be paid back when the account is paid. In practice, it is a more or less continuous form of financing.

Sources & Credit Criteria

Sources of accounts receivable financing are commercial banks and finance companies (including acceptance companies, accounts receivable companies, finance companies, and installment contract finance companies).

Accounts receivable represents one of the most liquid assets and the percentage of financing is high (usually around 70-80% of current receivables). For some accounts the advance might be as low as 50% of the face value. As collateral, lenders prefer receivables to inventory because the book values for receivables represent firm dollar claims. Difficulties for the lender are the cost of processing the collateral and the risk of fraud. Acceptable accounts must be current as shown in the aging of receivables. Accounts receivable financing is more easily obtained when the customers have a strong financial rating, when the company's sales are not dominated by a few large customers, and when there is only a minimal return of goods or delay of payments due to defective merchandise or improper shipments or billings.

Advantages/Disadvantages—Characteristics

The advantage of accounts receivable financing is that a company without a large working capital base can increase its sales, perhaps provide more liberal payment terms to its customers, and still remain competitive. If the marginal returns from the sales are higher than the costs of accounts receivable financing, the company can make a greater profit by using accounts receivable financing. Interest rates charged by commercial banks for accounts receivable financing is approximately 0.5-5% over the prime rate, with an additional service charge. Commercial finance companies charge between 12 and 25%. Commercial banks have a lower interest rate, but usually deal with the higher rated customers. Finance companies deal with the higher credit risk companies. The smaller the average size of the accounts, the higher the processing cost for the lender per loan dollar, which might cause problems in getting interested lenders. With a "bulk" assignment, the lender does not constantly monitor each individual account, but the advance against face value is lower. Commercial banks may provide loans with a security agreement covering all the assets of the company with a blanket lien which includes accounts receivable. Most lenders have a minimum on accounts receivable loans between $30,000-$150,000.

How to Raise Funds

On most receivable commitments, funds are advanced and repaid on a revolving basis. With the Uniform Commercial Code, legal requirements for establishing a receivable assignment have been simplified. The options are:

a. Limited control: Existing and future receivables are liened, but there is no continuous control over the collection of cash and replacement of the receivables. Most banks use this arrangement because they deal with high-quality accounts, and servicing costs under this arrangement are minimal.

b. Maximum control: The borrower is required to deposit cash collections in a "cash collateral account." The lender provides funds from the account when new acceptable receivables are generated. Servicing costs under this arrangement are quite high, but the lender has tighter control over cash. It is used for higher risk accounts by commercial banks, and more frequently by commercial finance companies.

Secured Loans: Inventory — Floating Liens

Definition/Purpose/Collateral

Secured loans with inventory as collateral are used to build up inventory for seasonal purposes, for international or intercontinental trade, or for permanent inventory needs through revolving loans. Arrangements for the use of inventory as collateral vary based on the nature of the inventory. Physical control of the inventory can remain with the lender or a third party on behalf of the lender, or with the borrower. Instruments used for such financing include equipment liens (or chattel mortgages), trust receipts, warehouse receipts, and continuous or floating liens.

Terms/Payback

The inventory loan is a short-term loan where the liquidation of the inventory is expected to repay the loan. Even if the inventory is not liquidated, the lender expects to be paid from the cash flow of the company. The exception is when the lender has provided a loan with a blanket lien over all assets, in which case the loan may be a term loan and amortized over a longer period.

Sources and Credit Criteria

The sources of inventory financing are mainly commercial banks and finance companies.

A secured interest in inventory can be obtained by the lender through the following means:

a. Trust receipt, floating lien or equipment lien where the inventory is in the possession of the borrower; and

b. Warehouse receipts (field or terminal) where the inventory is under the control of the lender or a third party on behalf of the lender.

The Uniform Commercial Code (UCC) allows the lender to use the "Floating Lien" whereby the lender may obtain a security interest in inventory "in general" without a specific listing of the inventory involved. Floating lien does not permit tight control, but it adds to a lender's protection by allowing a security interest in inventory and its proceeds, including future inventory, along with a lower cost of administering the loan. A security interest in inventory and proceeds can have a prior claim than a security interest in accounts receivable alone. Therefore, an accounts receivable lender will make sure that the borrower cannot secure his inventory with another lender. Security arrangements do not cover goods controlled by the lender.

Lenders advance a lower percentage against liened inventory than against warehoused goods because they have less control. However, because not all inventory can be warehoused, the lien can cover all the inventory, making the total value of the inventory higher. The lender determines a percentage advance based on the quality of the inventory, and also on the borrower's cash flow ability to service the loan. The inventory financing limits vary with the kind of inventory. Where both accounts receivable and inventory are used, loan limits are approximately 70-80% of accounts receivable and 50% of inventory. However, these limits for inventory financing vary based on the marketability of the goods. Raw material financing limits vary between 55-60% except for commodities which can have limits up to 85% due to their ease of tradeability. Finished goods' limits vary between 50% and 70%, while work-in-progress has the lowest loan-to-value ratio, usually less than 25%. The amount of inventory loans also has an upper dollar limit in order to prevent excessive accumulations of inventory which might have to be liquidated at a loss. These limits are calculated on the basis of the company's sales level, and the desired amounts of inventory (based on industry averages) to obtain the sales. These desired limits on inventory can be calculated on the basis of a percentage of receivables or inventory turnover ratios. In either case, inventory above the limits is not considered as collateral for additional inventory financing.

Advantages/Disadvantages — Characteristics

Inventory financing allows a company to increase its sales level above what would be possible with only equity financing. It also allows seasonal build-ups, and inventory purchases in international and intercontinental trade where the inventory is in transit for a long time.

As in accounts receivable financing, commercial banks lend to higher-quality accounts at a lower cost than commercial finance companies, which usually deal with higher-risk companies requiring closer monitoring and resulting in higher costs of administration. Also, commercial finance companies have a higher cost of funds because they borrow from commercial banks. The rate from commercial banks varies between 0.5-5% above prime, and that from commercial finance companies between 4-12% above prime. Minimum amounts for such loans ranges between $30,000-$100,000.

How to Raise Funds (Including Data Required)

The information required is the same as for term loans. Additional required information would be the nature of the inventory, alternate means of liquidation and liquidation values, and inventory turnover ratios.

Secured Loans: Inventory — Warehouse Receipt

Definition/Purpose/Collateral

This type of loan is similar to loans with liens, with the exception that the inventory is held in a warehouse for the lender, and the lender's approval must be obtained before it can be removed. Thus, the lender has possession of the inventory and is likely to provide a larger percentage of advance. The disadvantage is that the loan has to be paid before the goods are removed from the warehouse. It should be noted that due to fraud, lenders have lost funds in this type of lending. The warehouse can be terminal or field, in both of which the inventory to be collateralized is physically segregated under a third party warehouseman.

Terminal Warehouse Receipt Loan

A terminal warehouse receipt loan can be obtained when the inventory is stored in a public or terminal warehouse by the borrower. The borrower receives a negotiable or nonnegotiable receipt from the warehouse company establishing title to the goods. Negotiable receipts are made out to the borrower, and non-negotiable receipts in the name of the lender. Goods are released by the warehouse company only under instructions of the person named in the receipt. These receipts can be pledged as collateral for a loan. Lenders take a security interest in the goods, and require that the warehouse company release the goods only under instructions of the lender, after repayment of the loan.

Field Warehouse Loan

Borrowing through the use of a field warehouse loan requires the borrower to segregate and lease warehouse space on his own facilities to the lender for a nominal amount such as $1. This enclosed space is locked and allows the separation of goods offered as collateral from the borrower's other inventory. Access to the area is available only to an employee of the borrower who is bonded and hired by the warehousing company as field warehouse manager. The borrower is billed for the cost of the employee. Warehouse receipts are issued for goods placed in the leased area, and these receipts are used as security for loan advances and are held by the lender. When the lender is paid for certain inventory, goods are released from the area upon his instructions. Field warehouse specialists are available and have offices in most larger cities. The cost of field warehousing varies inversely with the amount of inventory in the warehouse. In addition to the cost of the employee, payroll taxes, bond and payroll processing charge, the annual cost of the warehouse can vary between 1 and 2% of the value of the inventory. Field warehousing can be used for loans ranging from $25,000 to several million dollars.

Criteria for Warehouse Loans

Some of the criteria used in a warehouse receipt loan are:

a. The financial and marketing strength of the client company;

b. The type of goods to be financed. Items which have a ready market, such as commodities, are financed more easily than specialized inventory. The ease of liquidation also influences the percentage of advance that can be obtained. The percentage could range from 40% to 85%.

c. The cost of the goods to be warehoused and the level of inventory carried by the borrower. Inventory above a certain level, dependent on the company's sales and the turnover ratio, may not be financed.

d. The borrower's profitability should be adequate to pay the costs of the loan.

Sources of such financing are commercial banks and finance companies.

Secured Loans: Inventory — Commodity Loan

Commodity loans are made to commodity dealers and brokers who acquire raw materials (mainly agricultural) for sale to manufacturers, and are advanced also to manufacturers who store and process commodities. Administering such loans requires careful monitoring and knowledge of commodity markets and fluctuations in commodity prices. This type of loan has resulted in substantial losses from fraudulent warehouse receipts, but it is very prevalent due to its convenience and necessity. Some of the information requirements are:

a. Financial and marketing strength of the borrower;

b. Insurance coverage and risk of spoilage;

c. Hedging contracts; and

d. Details of the warehousing arrangement.

The major source of financing has been commercial banks.

Secured Loans: Stock & Savings Accounts

These secured loans made to individuals and corporations are secured by stocks, bonds, cash values of life insurance and other corporate securities. These loans allow security dealers and underwriters to finance inventories of securities purchased for resale. They are easily liquidated if they can be publicly traded, and hence make good collateral. Due to lower costs of collateral administration, terms are usually better for such loans.

Loan Values: Loan-to-value ratios are influenced by credit quality, marketability, and price volatility of the securities. The maximum collateral value is assigned to short-term government securities (around 90-95%). Usually securities dealers obtain a higher loan-to-value percentage because the securities are considered a part of their inventory and they have marketing channels to liquidate the collateral fairly quickly.

Equipment Liens/ Chattel Mortgage*

Definition/Purpose/Collateral

A chattel mortgage is used when a loan is secured by inventory specified by serial number or by some other means, and when the collateral is a piece of personal property, as opposed to real property. The inventory cannot be sold unless the mortgage holder consents. Chattel mortgages can be efficiently used when the asset financed is a capital asset which is easily identified, and are not designed for inventory which turns over rapidly.

Terms/Payback

Most equipment loans range from 2 to 10 years, depending upon the life of the equipment. In most cases, the loan is amortized in equal monthly payments over the period, which is less than the useful economic life of the equipment. Loans for equipment which do not produce uniform cash flows can sometimes be amortized with lower periodic payments and a "balloon" payment at maturity. This method allows the lender to maintain the term of the loan within internally or externally imposed criteria. A new loan often can be made at maturity to cover the balloon. Equipment with seasonal cash flows sometimes can be financed with loans calling for payments during periods of adequate cash flow, so long as the annual payments are adequate to amortize the loan within the desired term.

Sources and Credit Criteria

The major source of equipment loans are commercial banks, finance companies, and finance subsidiaries of equipment manufacturers.

A chattel mortgage is a lien on personal property — i.e., property other than real estate. The borrower has control of the asset. If there is a default, the lender can repossess the equipment and sell it to recover the outstanding amount of the loan. A security agreement between the parties specifies the collateral, and the lender files a statement at the appropriate public office to secure the lien. This filing informs other lenders of the amount and nature of the liens against the asset.

The credit criteria for the loan include the following:

a. Financial and general strength of the borrower;

b. Value of the collateral;

c. Cash flow ability or source of repayment; and

d. Other general factors, such as the nature of the borrower, and whether the equipment is for special use or general purpose.

Standard equipment and machinery are generally well accepted as collateral. The value of the collateral and the cash flow (along with the financial strength) of the borrower are two principal factors

*The term 'Chattel Mortgage' has been made obsolete by the Uniform Commercial Code.

used by lenders in their evaluation. The collateral can be appraised for any of the following three values:

a. Replacement value;
b. Market value;
c. Auction or liquidation value.

These appraisals can be obtained from companies that specialize in appraisals. Lenders also often use their own appraisers. Appraisals from auction companies carry special significance because lenders can receive a guarantee that such companies will acquire the asset from them, if desired, at a stated price, which decreases over time. Loan-to-value ratios can vary from 25-75% of the market value of the equipment, and up to 150% of the auction value for operating companies.

Cash flow can be a more important barrier to raising funds through equipment liens. Lenders wish to provide funds to companies which have, or are very likely to have, the cash flow to repay the loan. The costs of repossession and auction can sometimes be very prohibitive, and lenders wish to avoid the stigma of having made a failed loan. The length of time that the borrower has to show an adequate cash flow can vary. Life insurance companies require a longer history of adequate cash flow than leasing companies or financing subsidiaries of manufacturers. If debt coverage does not exist, the borrower will have to present adequate justification for the loan. Chattel mortgages also are used in agricultural loans against livestock.

(See "Equipment Financing.")

Real Estate Mortgages

Definition/Purpose/Collateral

A mortgage is a lien on real property which is used as security for the repayment of a debt or other obligation. A mortgage has to be recorded, which means having it copied by public records. Records are usually kept in the county (or township in some states) where the property is located. If the property is located in more than one county, a record should be made in the proper public office in each county concerned. In addition to the regular mortgage described above, there are two other kinds — collective and equitable mortgages. Collective mortgages, also known as mortgage bonds, are collective because a single mortgage may be held by many beneficial owners of one mortgage. Equitable mortgages include a variety of financial arrangements which are really mortgages, such as sale with an option to repurchase.

Terms/Payback

Mortgages may be categorized on the basis of the loans which can be:

a. Land development loans;
b. Construction loans;
c. Post-construction loans.

Land development and construction loans typically are short— or intermediate-term loans depending on develop a track record proving profitability of the construction loans typically are intermediate- or long-term loans. If the permanent financing is an intermediate-term loan, the intention usually is to develop a track record providing profitability of the project and then to obtain long-term financing. These post-construction loans are usually for 5 to 30 years. Loans for less than 7 to 8 years typically are term loans with principal payment at the maturity of the loan. The long-term loans typically are amortized with equal payments on a monthly basis.

(For 'Sources and Credit Criteria', 'Advantages/Disadvantages — Characteristices' and 'How to Raise Funds', see Real Estate Financing'.)

Leases

Definition/Purpose/Collateral

A lease contract allows the lessee the use of the asset for a designated time period in return for periodic payments to the lessor. Leases can be of three main types:

- **True or operating leases:** They are usually short- or medium-term transactions where the lessee has cancellation privileges with due notice. The lessor retains the benefits and risks of ownership, including the risk of obsolescence. Operating leases are generally non-payout leases — i.e. the payments to be made by the lessee during the contractual term do not cover the cost of the equipment and the cost of financing. The lessee does not accumulate any equity in the asset, and lease payments are regarded as operating expenses and not as a capital liability. The lessor usually performs other services, such as installation, maintenance and repair, and pays taxes and insurance. It is a device for acquiring the use of equipment without the obligation of ownership.

- **Financial leases:** Usually full-payout, noncancellable leases where the lessee's payments over the life of the agreement pay for the asset and a profit to the lessor. The lessee pays for the asset and hence can obtain ownership through the payments or through a lease-purchase arrangement with an option to purchase the asset, or can renew the lease for an additional period at minimal cost. If there is no option, the lessor benefits from the residual value in the asset. In such leases, it is the lessee who usually pays for installation, maintenance and repair, and taxes and insurance.
- **Tax leases:** The Economic Recovery Tax Act of 1981 (ERTA) introduced the Tax Lease—where tax benefits (including the Investment Tax Credit (ITC) and Depreciation) are transferred from the lessee to the lessor to lower rental payments. These tax credits can be transferred from unprofitable to profitable corporations to lower costs of leasing, while allowing the lessee to maintain residual rights. The lessor must be a corporation and not a subchapter S corporation or personal holding company. In addition to other requirements (see "Leasing Companies"), the lessor's minimum investment in the leased property must not be less than 10% of the adjusted basis of the property at all times. The Tax Equity and Fiscal Responsibility Act of 1982 (TEFRA) tightened these requirements and reduced the benefits from such leases.

For some types of equipment, both operating or financial leases involve **maintenance or service leases** since the equipment frequently needs special skills for maintenance that would be too expensive for the lessee to develop. In other types of assets, such as real estate, where there are no special skills or maintenance problems, the lessee pays most of the costs of maintenance, taxes, utilities, insurance, etc. This is called a **net lease.**

Leases can cover a single piece of equipment, or might involve a **master lease plan** whereby the lessee has a leasing line of credit to acquire future equipment at a later date at the same leasing rate and under the same terms without negotiating a new lease contract.

Leases can also be **leveraged leases** where the lessor invests 10%-40% of the asset costs and borrows the balance. The lender obtains a first mortgage position on the asset, with the lessor retaining the tax benefits of accelerated depreciation and investment tax credits. Airlines used a form of leveraged leasing in equipment trust arrangements. Individuals, banks, etc. supply approximately 25% for the equity and retain the advantages of ownership, including accelerated depreciation, investment tax credits, and residual values. The balance is borrowed as straight loans with a first mortgage on the assets.

Terms/Payback

Leases can be short or longer term. In all cases, the lease period is never longer than the economic life of the asset. In short-term leases, the lessor also takes the risk of reduction in the property's value. The lessor, however, charges an "insurance premium" within the rent for this risk. Most leases call for periodic, monthly payments.

Sources and Credit Criteria

The major types of lessors are manufacturers or their finance subsidiaries, finance companies, commercial banks, independent leasing companies, special purpose leasing companies, individuals, and partnerships and profitable corporations. The lessor keeps title to the asset in a lease, thus simplifying repossession if the lessee defaults. Because of this advantage, 100% financing is obtained in most leases. The lessor might require one month's rent as a deposit for each year of the contract life. The lessor also may obtain tax advantages through accelerated depreciation and the sale of the asset at a capital gain, along with the investment tax credit. The disadvantage for the lessor is in the event of default, whereby one can claim "damage for nonperformance" and repossess the equipment. Awards for damages can depend on a judicial determination, and in the case of bankruptcy, the lessee's liabilities toward a lessor are limited.

There is a great similarity between the credit criteria for leasing and those for chattel mortgage loans. The lessor wants to avoid repossession, and hence many lessors want the lessee to have a debt coverage, even without the asset, to be greater than the leasing costs. Leasing companies seem to have easier credit criteria where the leased equipment has widespread use.

Advantages/Disadvantages — Characteristics

There are many advantages claimed for leasing. However, in some cases, these advantages may not be so important or beneficial and the disadvantages of leasing may outweigh the advantages. Each situation should be examined independently based on the company, its profitability prospects, tax rate, cash flow needs, etc. Some of the advantages claimed for leasing are:

a. Flexibility: Where the lessee can terminate the lease if the asset becomes obsolete; however, these costs are charged to the lessee through higher lease payments;

b. Lack of restrictions: Leasing does not involve indenture agreements as in bonds, and borrowing capacity is conserved for other future needs. There are no restrictive protective covenants as in loan agreements. However, lenders examine leasing agreements to determine debt coverage;

c. 100% financing: Leasing provides a greater amount of funds during the early stages of the contract, because of no down payment requirements. This conserves funds in expanding companies;

d. Off-balance sheet financing: Leasing provides a degree of "off-balance sheet" financing that allows high leverage which sometimes can be excessive. In some cases — especially in financial leases — the asset may have to be capitalized and the lease recorded as debt on the balance sheet;

e. Leasing might help to avoid stock dilution and some costs, such as underwriting fees, etc.;

f. The return on the additional cash saved from the lack of a downpayment may be greater than the increased cost of leasing.

g. Leasing usually results in the prompt acquisition of new equipment;

h. Costs are predictable;

i. Possible tax advantages, based on the tax rates of the lessee and the lessor;

j. Some special types of equipment, which need expensive and specialized maintenance, might be leased more economically since the lessor might have the trained personnel to service the leased equipment. The user of the equipment also may purchase the equipment and enter into a service contract with the manufacturer or his representative;

k. Sometimes lessors may be able to acquire the equipment by mass purchasing at lower costs and pass on these savings to the lessee;

l. Leasing companies may have better disposal means at the end of the lease, and hence be able to lower costs.

Some of the disadvantages of leasing are the following:

a. Any residual value in the asset accrues to the lessor, with high profits in some assets, such as land. The lessee could obtain an option to purchase the asset at the end of the lease for a fixed price;

b. The cost of leasing usually is higher than the cost of debt, especially when all costs are accounted for;

c. Financing improvements for buildings on leased land can transfer the benefits from the improvements to the lessor unless the lessee has an option to purchase the land.

Although no general statement can be made that leasing will be beneficial in every case, it can be very useful if the lessee needs the cash, cannot raise the cash for the downpayment, or cannot use all the tax advantages of accelerated depreciation and the investment tax credit. Leasing is a useful junior financing medium for many businesses.

How to Raise Funds (Including Data Required)

The data required for leasing is similar to data required for chattel mortgage loans.

The lease contract includes the following:

a. The basic lease period and the periodic lease payments;

b. The party responsible for payment of taxes, insurance, maintenance, repair, etc.

c. The alternatives available at the end of the lease period, such as the renewal of the lease or the purchase of the asset, and the cost of renewal or purchase.

(See "Equipment Financing" and "Leasing Companies".)

Sale - Leaseback

Definition/Purpose/Collateral

Sale-Leaseback (SL) involves the leasing of assets (equipment and real estate) already owned by the company. The asset is sold to a financial institution at a price near its market value, and it is leased back during the lease period. The type of lease is generally a full-payout financial lease. Title to the property is owned by the lessor.

Terms/Payback

The term of the agreement in SLs depends upon the nature of the asset and the remaining useful life of the property. For most automotive rolling equipment, the term is less than 3 years, and for other types of equipment, terms vary from 2 to 10 years. Real estate SLs range for a longer period of time, up to 20-40 years. After the basic lease term expires, the lessee may have an option to purchase the asset for its residual value (7-10%), or to renew the lease at a fraction of the original lease payment. Since the renewal option has better rates, it is used more often than the purchase option.

Sources & Credit Criteria

The institutions involved in SLs are insurance companies, finance companies, leasing companies, Real Estate Investment Trusts, pension funds, colleges and universities, charitable institutions, and other financial institutions. In sale-leasebacks, the lease is a financial lease, whereby the lessee is obligated to pay the lessor's investment and interest as lease payments over the lease period, and the lessor can also benefit from the residual value of the asset at the end of the lease period. The credit criteria are similar to those used in chattel mortgages and leases.

The test of investment quality in a SL is the financial stability of the lessee. Leases on retail property are usually for longer terms than those on industrial real estate.

Advantages/Disadvantages — Characteristics

SLs are very useful in the case of assets useful to the company where the depreciated book value is substantially lower than the market value. Additional cash up to 100% of the value of the asset is available immediately, and there is a tax deduction from the lease payment. SLs are used often in acquisitions, where many acquiring companies have had a leasing company buy the equipment or other fixed assets, with the assets then being leased back by the acquiring company. There are some advantages in using a trusteed pension plan of the same company in sale-leaseback transactions. The advantages, such as a high interest rate and the residual value of the asset, could accrue to the pension fund instead of another financial institution, possibly resulting in lower corporate contributions to the fund. For the investment to be considered prudent, the asset must be useful to the company, the market value of the property must be reasonable, and the lease payments sufficient to amortize the loan. In the case of a SL of real estate, the value of the property (including the land) may be deducted in rent paid, whereas land cannot be depreciated if the property is owned.

Some of the disadvantages of SLs are that the seller is tied to the lease, and the fixed charge rentals may be high for the lessee during periods of economic slowdown. Also, the seller will have to move at the end of the lease, so any increase in the value of the property will accrue to the lessor, unless the lessee has an option to renew the lease agreement at predetermined rates (usually nominal) at the end of the lease, or an option to purchase the asset at the residual value. This reacquisition has to be close to the market value to be considered a genuine rental arrangement by the Internal Revenue Service.

How to Raise Funds (Including Data Required)

Data required are similar to data for chattel and real estate mortgages and leases.

Bonds

Definition/Purpose/Collateral

Bonds are debt instruments that contain a promise to pay the principal amount of money borrowed at a fixed future date, and to pay interest periodically. Bonds are similar to promissory notes. The difference is that bonds have standard denominations and are usually negotiable. Each bond issue has a trust indenture with a trustee who holds the indenture for the benefit of all bondholders. The indenture specifies the provisions of the agreement and allows the trustee to take action in the event of default in accordance with its terms. Bonds are usually classified by the following factors:

a. The type of security offered and the seniority of the holder;

b. The reason for the issue;

c. Characteristics of interest payment; and

d. Method of repayment and terms.

Some of the definitions of terms in bonds are:

a. Coupon rate: The fixed dollar return on a bond.

b. Trustee: Represents the bondholders. Duties and responsibilities are specified in the Trust Indenture Act of 1939. The trustee has to verify the legality of the bond issue, to monitor the borrower to ensure the implementation of all the obligations in the indenture; and to take remedial action if the borrower defaults on any obligations.

c. Indenture: A separate legal agreement stating the provisions of the debt between the borrowing corporation and the trustee representing the bondholders.

d. Protective Covenants: Restrictions placed on the company by the trustee and which are enumerated in the indenture.

e. Redemption Price: The total amount that must be repaid. A bond has a definite promise to pay principal amount and interest, a definite life, a statement of the medium of exchange, the place of payment, and a reference to the indenture or other rights. Usually a bond's denomination is $1,000, but it could also be in $100, $500, or $10,000 denominations. Denominations under $1,000 are called baby bonds. Costs are higher for bonds under $1,000, and bonds of less than $500 may involve problems with acceptance. The interest rate is usually expressed as a percentage of par values — i.e., 4% is $40 on a $1,000 bond. The actual yield will depend on the actual price paid for the bond, and whether it is bought at a premium or discount. Bonds can be:

a. Bearer Bonds or Coupon Bonds: These have coupons which entitle the bearer to payment of interest if presented to the paying agent at maturity.

b. Registered Bonds: Payment is sent to the list of registered owners.

Bonds can be any of the following:

a. Unsecured: Such as debenture bonds, income bonds, receivers' certificates, convertible bonds, and participating bonds.

b. Collateral or Secured bonds: Such as nonproperty security which includes assumed, guaranteed, and joint bonds; or property security which includes personal property (collateral trust, equipment trust, sinking fund bonds) or real property security (mortgage bonds).

Unsecured Bonds

Debentures

Debentures are unsecured bonds with terms of 10-40 years. Most debentures are issued in $1,000 multiples. Debentures usually mean those bonds which are not secured by liens on any assets. Since there is no specific lien, management has greater freedom and can use secured obligations during periods of dire necessity.

Debentures are direct obligations of the issuing corporation, based on its general credit without specific liens or mortgages, with repayment depending solely on the earning ability of the corporation. A restriction in the indenture for debentures could be the negative pledge clause which restricts the corporation from pledging its assets to other creditors.

Subordinated Debentures

Subordinated debentures represent secured debt that has a lower claim on assets than senior debt. If the borrower is liquidated, subordinated debenture holders would be paid after the senior creditors were fully paid off, and ahead of preferred and common shareholders. Senior creditors regard such debt as equity, and thus it allows leveraging through further borrowing. The interest on these debentures is tax deductible, whereas the dividend on preferred shares is not.

Subordinated debentures are being used more often for long-term debt financing. They usually have a shorter maturity than mortgage bonds. The subordinated debenture is most often used by corporations with strong credit standing that lack or do not desire to pledge mortgageable assets. Corporations use subordinated debentures when they wish to keep their short-term borrowing ability intact, especially by pledging assets. Indentures for subordinated debentures usually contain restrictive covenants which are designed to protect investors by preventing financial difficulties. This might be preferable to the problems and costs associated with the liquidation of mortgaged assets recovered from the company in bankruptcy proceedings.

Subordinated debentures often have conversion privileges to common stock (see "Convertibility"). The advantage to the company is increased borrowing power, since subordinated debt can allow greater senior debt, and has a lower interest rate than subordinated debentures without conversion privileges. To sweeten the deal for the institutional investor, warrants sometimes are included with subordinated debentures along with, or instead of, convertibility. These warrants give the holder the right to buy a specified number of shares at an advantageous price within a certain period of time.

Income Bonds

A company must pay interest on income bonds only when it is earned, and hence there is no assurance of return to bondholders. There may be a cumulative feature to the interest payment, but this may be limited to a few years. The income bond is senior to preferred and common stock and subordinated debt, and the interest is tax deductible by the corporation. Income bonds (also called Adjustment Bonds) are used mainly in reorganizations to adjust fixed interest debt.

The income bond has features similar to preferred stock with regard to interest payments. However, if the issue is very similar to equity, the IRS may not allow deduction of interest rates. In older corporations, interest was not cumulative while some income bonds have provided for a minimum interest payment whether or not it is earned. The indenture may contain detailed instructions to calculate income, and the allowable deductions for depreciation, expenses, and reserves. Income bonds may be unsecured, subordinated, or senior debt. Such bonds may involve less risk for investors than preferred stock, with correspondingly lower rates, which are tax deductible to the corporation.

Reasons for the use of income bonds are:

a. Future earnings cannot be predicted with certainty;

b. Interest costs are deductible;

c. Some institutional investors, such as insurance companies, may prefer bonds with contingent interest obligations rather than stock in reorganizations because the law may require them to liquidate their stockholdings at an unfavorable time.

Receivers' Certificates

Court-appointed receivers of corporations in bankruptcy proceedings use these certificates when there is a need for short-term working capital to maintain the business as an operating entity to preserve its value until liquidation or the finalization of a satisfactory arrangement. Such certificates normally have a senior position to any previously funded debt of the corporation; however, the priority is determined by the court. Repayment of these certificates is either through the reorganization of the financial structure or through the liquidation of the assets of the business.

Convertible Bonds

Convertible bonds or bonds with warrants are used when the lenders desire income and a higher level of security than possible with common or preferred shares, but wish to share in the increased value of a growing company's stock. Such bonds usually are subordinated, and convertible to common or preferred stock for a defined time period. The interest rate is lower than it would have been without the convertible option and the conversion price is higher than the market value at the time of issuance. Bonds can have warrants that are detachable or non-detachable. Detachable warrants can be marketed separately from the bond. Bonds can be issued with both convertibility and detachable warrants, especially when the borrower has prepayment privileges. Such bonds are mainly used in high-risk or venture capital-type deals. The conversion price often increases over time. (See "Convertibility.")

Participating Bonds

Income bonds can be designed as participating bonds; holders of a participating bond receive a specified percentage of corporate earnings paid out as dividends, in addition to the stated interest rates. This clause prevents the problem in non-cumulative income bonds of adjusting corporate books to show a lack of income to pay interest on the income bonds for several years, and then paying a single year's interest on the bonds and a major dividend to stockholders.

General Obligation Bonds

General obligation bonds are sold by state and local governments backed by their credit and used for real estate, industrial buildings, etc., to encourage businesses to locate in that geographic area.

Collateral or Secured Bonds

Nonproperty Security

Assumed Bonds: These are bonds of disappearing corporations in mergers or consolidations which have been assumed by the new or surviving corporation. Usually the assumed bonds retain the existing security, in addition to being an obligation of the new corporation.

Guaranteed Bonds: Guaranteed bonds are bonds of one corporation whose terms have been guaranteed by another corporation, or by the federal, state, or local government.

Some of the reasons for the use of guaranteed bonds are:

a. A parent company or wealthy stockholders desire to help the sale of a corporation's bonds;

b. A corporation may guarantee the bonds of another corporation if it wishes to lease the property built from the proceeds;

c. The government guarantees bonds when the proceeds are used to satisfy a need considered important by the government unit.

The guarantee may be for principal and/or interest, and it may be by endorsement of each bond certificate, by a special agreement or under a lease arrangement.

Joint Bonds: If several corporations need a joint facility — such as a shipping terminal, bridge, etc. — they may form a mutually owned corporation which issues bonds to finance the new facility. Joint bonds are guaranteed jointly and individually by all the corporations in the syndicate. The investment rating of these bonds is influenced by the financial strength of the strongest corporation in the group.

Property Security / Personal Property

Collateral Trust: These are bonds secured by stocks or bonds. If there is a default, the securities are sold and the proceeds paid to the bondholders. The types of collateral are:

a. Securities of nonrelated companies held for investment;

b. Marketable securities of companies which may be partially or wholly owned;

c. Securities of companies which can profit from the financing, such as the company's customers or suppliers; and

d. Debt instruments of the borrower with a higher claim on assets than the issue being floated. Securities with the same or lower claim on assets would not add to the quality of the issue.

Equipment Trust Certificates: Equipment bonds should have a life based on the economic life of the equipment. They were originally used to purchase railroad cars. There are three variations of these bonds in actual practice:

a. Lease plan (also known as the Philadelphia plan): Which involves a trustee and an investment banker to sell equipment trust certificates to the public. The proceeds from the sale of these certificates and a down payment from the railroad are paid to the manufacturer for the equipment. The certificates are not railroad bonds, but the investor is considered to be a shareholder in a business which is leasing equipment to the railroad.

b. Conditional Sale plan (also known as the New York plan): Where the railroad or borrower makes a down payment for the equipment, and obtains a bank loan for the balance. It is similar to an ordinary bank term loan, and the bank keeps the title until all payments have been made.

c. Equipment Mortgage plan: Where the railroad or borrower makes a down payment, and bonds with a chattel mortgage are sold for the balance through an investment banker to the public or financial institutions. A trustee has title on behalf of the bondholders.

Sinking Fund Bonds: These are bonds where a sinking fund is established by the terms of the indenture, and the proceeds of this sinking fund are used to retire bonds or as security for the bonds (see "Terms/Payback").

Real Property Bonds or Mortgage Bonds

These bonds have a lien on specific assets which are described in detail in the mortgage. The assets usually are fixed assets, with a market value larger by a reasonable margin of safety than the amount of the bond issue. If the borrower defaults on any of the provisions in the indenture, the trustee takes possession of the property and liquidates it. If the proceeds are insufficient to repay all the bondholders, they become general creditors of the borrower for the balance. Mortgage bonds usually involve first lien on the property offered for security. The term is based on the useful life of the collateral, and may extend from 10-40 years. A second mortgage bond places other bondholders in a higher position. With a closed-end bond, the borrower cannot issue additional bonds under that lien with the same security. With an open-end issue, the company can issue additional bonds under an existing lien. This provides flexibility to management though usually there are limits imposed on the amount of additional debt. Restrictions could include a limit on the amount of the bonds in relation to the value of the assets that are secured and the earning capability of the company. With an after-acquired clause which is usually used with open-ended issues, the lien covers the property acquired after the bond issue and provides greater security to investors. Investors always consider the earning power of the corporation as the primary test of credit-worthiness, since the costs and inconvenience of asset liquidation are high.

Industrial Revenue Bonds

These are bonds issued with the sponsorship of a state or local government to raise funds for fixed assets with certain exceptions (country clubs, etc.). These bonds are based solely on the credit of the borrowing business. Interest from these issues is exempt from federal taxes and often from state taxes. Hence the rate is often lowered by 1.5-2.5% (or to 80% of prime in a variable rate loan). These bonds may be placed privately (banks, etc.) or through a public sale (bond underwriter). Up to $1,000,000 of revenue bonds for any one company can be issued (maximum limit of $40,000,000 per individual beneficiary). The limit may be $10,000,000 if capital expenditures at the company's location do not exceed $10,000,000 for a period of 3 years before and after the issue. There are no limits for certain projects, such as pollution control facilities (higher limits possible for UDAG projects). Existing facilities may be purchased if rehabilitation exceeds 15% of the cost of acquisition. Interest is not tax-exempt if the average length of bond maturity exceeds 120% of the average expected economic life of the facilities financed. IRB financed property cannot use Accelerated Cost Recovery System. These offerings do not have to be registered with the SEC. The rate may be lowered by obtaining bond insurance from a major insurance company. Each state has a limit on the total amount of IRBs sponsored in the state.

Terms/Payback

Most bonds are for 10-40 years. At maturity, bonds may be:

a. Paid off by selling a new issue or from cash;

b. Refunded by offering new bonds from the old writer the new bonds having greater inducements;

c. Extended in their maturity with some inducement.

The retirement of bonds may be through the following methods:

Nonsystematic Methods

a. High earnings may be used to retire some of the outstanding bonds by call or purchase on the open market, whether or not required in the indenture;

b. Bonds may be converted to common stock at the option of the holder or the borrower through a call feature, or additional stock can be sold and the proceeds used to redeem the bonds;

c. Funds may be obtained by shorter-term loans from banks or other financial institutions and used to redeem some of the outstanding bonds.

Systematic Methods

a. Sinking Fund: The indenture contains the terms of the sinking fund, and also the "call price," which is the price the trustee receives from the borrower to redeem the bonds if the market price is greater than the call price. If the call price is greater, the bonds are repurchased at the market price. The amount paid by the company can be fixed or variable and there can be a "balloon" payment.

b. Serial Bonds: These are bonds which mature serially, and have the same effect as sinking funds. The issue can be designed so that a limited number of bonds mature annually, or they can be grouped to mature in a short, medium or long term. At the maturity date, the bonds are redeemed at par. The interest rates vary with the term of the bonds. Normally the longer maturity dates carry the highest interest rates.

Sources and Credit Criteria

Most financial institutions have at least some bonds in their portfolio. More than 75% of the bonds in the U.S. are held by life insurance companies, property and casualty insurance companies, private noninsured pension funds and state and local retirement funds. The other major holders of corporate bonds are mutual savings banks, investment companies, commercial banks, foreign investors, and individuals.

Security for bonds depends upon the following:

a. Income potential — the rule of thumb is that income be twice as great as the amount needed to meet obligations;

b. Liquidation value of the security.

The mortgage can be classified according to the following characteristics:

a. According to the existence and priority of security: First, second, third, etc., or senior or junior; or unsecured;

b. According to the right of the borrower to issue additional securities: Open-end; closed-end where the borrower cannot issue bonds with a similar lien on the same asset;

c. According to the type of property covered by the mortgage: Designated property, or blanket mortgage which includes all property owned by the borrower, or blanket mortgage with an after-acquired clause to cover future purchases of property.

Advantages/Disadvantages — Characteristics

The advantages of bonds are the term for which they are available, and the rate of interest. The terms of bonds are much longer than most other forms of financing, and the interest rate usually is lower than similar loans with private placements. However, bonds are available only to the largest corporations in the country — those having certain minimum sales and earnings and a high probability of being in business for the term of the bonds. Bondholders protect themselves with strict requirements in case the company suffers adverse earnings. These requirements are detailed in the indenture, which normally contains some of the following:

a. The amount of the bond issue, including amounts to be offered in the future and conditions before future bonds may be offered;

b. The maturity dates(s) and interest rates(s);

c. The option to redeem outstanding bonds, with dates and call price, and sinking fund requirements, if any;

d. Conditions necessary for making changes in indenture;

e. Negotiability and registration of individual bonds;

f. Positive and negative covenants, and provisions in event of default;

g. Corporate seal and signature of officers.

How to Raise Funds (Including Data Required)

Bonds usually are sold with the assistance of bond underwriters, classified as investment bankers (see

Investment Bankers). Revenue bonds are distributed with the assistance of municipal bond underwriters.

Trust Receipt

The trust receipt is a financing instrument that allows a lender to maintain a certain degree of control over secured assets in the physical possession of the borrower. The lender is called the entruster; the borrower the trustee. The trust receipt documents the physical release of goods from the lender's control to the physical control of the trustee (the borrower). The assets will be held in trust by the borrower and returned to the lender upon demand, or, if assets are sold, a specified amount of cash will be paid to the lender. The trust receipt usually is used for the short-term financing of commodities released from the warehouse for sale or processing, or in the floor-planning of identifiable assets, such as machinery or automobiles. The lender usually purchases the asset from the supplier or the manufacturer on behalf of the borrower, and retains title until payment is received, even when the asset is physically controlled by the borrower.

(See "Floor Planning".)

Floor Planning

Definition/Purpose/Collateral

Dealers and distributors of certain kinds of goods use floor planning, which involves the use of the trust receipt, to finance their inventories. It is used mainly by those dealing in durable goods. The products are financed by the lending institution on behalf of the borrower, and the lender receives title to the goods. The dealer obtains possession of the assets for inventory and for sale after signing a note and the trust receipt. In a floor planning arrangement, inventory and its proceeds are held in trust by the borrower on behalf of the lender.

Terms/Payback

The loan is payable upon demand, and the proceeds of the sale are payable immediately upon sale. Lenders usually evaluate the inventory turnover of the borrower and satisfy themselves that the amount of inventory is not so excessive that the loan cannot be repaid within a reasonably short time, usually always within a year. However, the financing could be permanent, since new inventory will be purchased to replace the sold goods.

Sources & Credit Criteria

Floor planning loans are obtained from commercial banks and finance companies. They are used to finance the inventory of identifiable and high value items, which can be easily liquidated. The upper limit of the loan in floor planning is usually 90% of the cost of the financed products. Immediately after the sale of the goods in trust, the business transfers the funds to the lender to repay the loans. Some lenders loan funds for floor planning only if they can finance the purchaser's installment paper.

How to Raise Funds (Including Data Required)

The data required for floor planning are similar to data for inventory financing, with added information, such as serial numbers, to identify the product. After arranging for the required financing with the lender, the dealer orders the desired goods from the supplier. Upon shipment, the supplier requests payment from the lender. When the item is sold, the dealer repays the outstanding amount owed on the product either with cash or by assigning the required amount of the customer's paper.

Installment or Time Sales Financing

Conditional Sales Contract

Conditional Sales Contracts are promissory notes issued when the dealer of equipment sells the asset with a down payment and accepts a note for the balance. The down payment is most often between 10% and 25%, and the balance is paid over a term which is less than the useful life of the asset. Title to the equipment is retained by the seller until all the required periodic installment payments are made and the terms of the contract are satisfied. The periodic payments always keep the outstanding amount owed on the equipment less than the market value of the item. The seller may carry the note himself or he may sell it to a financial institution. The financial institution usually insists on recourse to the seller, and the dealer agrees to recourse because it is easier for him than for the financial institution to resell the equipment. Since the lender has recourse, his risk is limited; therefore, financing can be more easily obtained for equipment bought from a dealer with recourse than for a similar item bought at a lower cost from an auctioneer without recourse.

(See "Equipment Financing".)

Installment or Time Sales Financing Consumer Paper

Consumer paper is the installment note signed by a consumer in the purchase of durable goods, usually with a down payment of 10-30%. The dealer sells the paper to the consumer loan company, which services the contract and collects the periodic payments. The finance company will pay for the paper at its face value, or a higher value if the interest rate charged is attractive enough. A disadvantage with consumer paper is that the buyer may not want to borrow from a finance company unrelated to the dealer. This is because the buyer may want some leverage on the dealer, in the form of payments withheld, to obtain satisfaction if the purchased asset is defective. Sources of funds for sales of installment consumer paper are consumer finance companies, industrial banks, general finance companies, rediscount divisions of general finance companies, and commercial banks. The stability of the dealer and quality of the goods or services along with satisfactory credit of the consumer, are of major concern to the lender.

Installment or Time Sales Financing Dealer Reserve

Dealer reserve is used when the dealer wants a standardized arrangement with the finance company rather than having to obtain approval for each deal. In such an arrangement, the financing contract with the buyer can be signed at the dealer's sales offices. A customer's credit application can be supplied to the lender for credit approval. The customer pays the dealer, who pays the lender. Sometimes the customer pays the lender directly. In either case, the customer does not have to meet the lender to have the loan approved. The lender purchases the customer contracts, with or without dealer recourse, on an ongoing basis. The lender discounts to the dealer the amount paid for each note to build a dealer reserve. The factors used by lenders to evaluate such agreements are the dealers' stability and the quality of the goods or services sold.

The financing arrangement must allow the lender to make a level of profits commensurate with the risks while satisfying legal requirements. The dealer must obtain a sufficient down payment for each contract and agree to acceptable terms and repayment. The down payment required is usually between 10 and 30%, and the term is less than the useful life of the item sold. When there is no down payment, the lender might not purchase the contract until the customer has made sufficient payments to build equity. The common sources of financing are consumer finance companies, industrial banks, thrift and loan banks, and general finance companies, along with commercial banks. Because of the cost of arranging this financing, customers who pay cash for the item can usually obtain a better price than those who want terms.

Installment or Time Sales Financing Rediscounting

Rediscounting is the sale for cash of consumer installment contracts owned by one financing company to another financial institution. The seller is often a captive financing subsidiary of a manufacturer which was used to provide consistent financing packages. A finance company can recirculate its cash and receivable assets by rediscounting collateral which originally was assigned to it, and is limited by the quality of the receivables and the maximum rediscount line or the maximum amount of paper it can rediscount. This line is usually a ratio of the tangible net worth of the seller. The rediscounting advance is a percentage of the cost of the product to the seller. Thus, if the cost including overhead is $500 and the percentage of advance is decided to be 80%, then the advance would be $400 and the seller would have obtained a leverage of 4:1 by borrowing $400 with his investment of $100.

Rediscounting credit criteria includes the following:

a. The provisions of the contract and the quality of the customers must be acceptable to the purchaser;

b. The down payment and the term of the contract must be compatible with the economic life of the product;

c. The aging of receivables must be satisfactory, with bad accounts being removed from consideration.

Rediscounting permits a business to increase sales by providing standardized financial packages to customers who need this credit. The business then can recoup its cash investment in the item sold by rediscounting, which cash can be used for further sales. It may be possible to generate a profit from this financing.

A captive finance company can be started with excess cash, or by keeping some consumer paper above the cash breakeven level of the business, which then could be used as the equity.

Hybrid Instruments

Convertibles

A convertible security is a bond, note, or share of preferred stock which has conversion rights, exercisable by the holder, into common stock of the same corporation. Convertible securities appeal to speculation-oriented investors because they usually are not as secured as high-quality straight debt securities and have the potential of an upside gain through stock appreciation. They often are used for new ventures or for those of lesser-known companies. The exchange ratio between the convertible instrument and the common stock can be stated in terms of a conversion price or a conversion ratio. The price paid for the convertible instrument divided by the number of shares of common stock to which it can be converted (the conversion ratio), gives the conversion price per share. Conversion value of the security is (the conversion ratio X the market price per share of common). The conversion option can be for a fixed price throughout the conversion period, or it can be scaled upward. The escalation of the stock price serves as a conversion incentive.

The convertible security holder usually gets interest on a bond, or dividend for a preferred share, and the conversion privilege to common stock may provide capital gains. Thus the same corporation will have to pay a higher rate for securities without this conversion right.

The price of the convertible instrument is higher than its conversion value when it is issued, and this difference is known as the conversion premium. The conversion premium is usually around 10-20%. Hence, if the market price of the common is depressed, so is the offering price of the convertible. The issuing company hopes that the market price will rise to pay off the loan with stock at a higher price, so the interest rate on the convertible is lower due to the convertibility feature. For securities which can be converted to publicly traded stock the conversion price is set at a premium above the market price for the stock, while the selling price of a new issue of common stock would have to be sold at or slightly below market price to ensure its sale. Thus, convertibles are attractive to young, growing companies. If the issue meets certain criteria, dilution from additional shares does not have to be accounted for until conversion rights are exercised. The price at which the stock is converted may be adjusted downward under certain conditions, such as future issuance of common stock at a lower price.

The convertibility is at the option of the holder, and the debt would have to be repaid if the convertible debt security is not converted into common stock. Convertible securities usually have a call price allowing the corporation to repurchase the security. This move often forces conversion when the conversion value is higher than its call price, allowing the issuer to get rid of any overhang and increase equity. A new convertible issue usually is difficult to sell if the previous one is not converted, and the call option, especially for a growth company, allows the company to force conversion. The call price forces the holder to convert within a specified period (usually less than 30 days) or be paid off and lose convertibility. There could be a payment of a call premium payable by the company equal to the interest rate or dividend rate. In some issues, the company can call if certain conditions have been satisfied, such as the common stock price being a certain percentage (usually higher than 100%) of the conversion price for a defined time period. This prevents the company from denying interest and appreciation potential by calling at an inappropriate (from the investors' viewpoint) time.

Convertible securities have few of the protections normally found in high-quality debt securities or preferred stocks. They are generally subordinated to existing or future senior debt, and have no restrictions on further sales of debt securities of the same class. Preferred convertibles sometimes carry a sinking fund requirement. An antidilution clause with an adjustment of the conversion rate to maintain rights to the same proportional ownership of the company is considered extremely important and is nearly always included.

The advantages with convertibles are:

a. Interest on convertible debt is tax-deductible, and earnings are not diluted until conversion;

b. The interest rate or dividend rate is lower, and the price for the common stock is usually higher;

c. In some cases, this might be the only method of obtaining financing, as in venture capital financing where the investor wishes to obtain principal and interest, but with a potential profit based on common stock appreciation for the risk in the transaction;

d. Some financial institutions which seek income, or are prevented from investing in equity securities, can benefit from common stock appreciation through convertible securities.

The disadvantages are:

a. Conversion dilutes equity and substantial conversion can result in loss of control;

b. The overhang and the uncertainty of conversion can create problems in future offerings of securities.

Warrants

Definition/Purpose

A warrant is a right, exerciseable for a defined period, to purchase at a designated price a stated number of shares of common stock. The warrant is returned to the corporation when the holder exercises the right to buy the stock at the stated price. The exercise price can be fixed or increased with time and the periods can be perpetual. Warrants are mainly sold as 'sweeteners' with sale (often private) of debt instruments, and they may be detachable (resold separately from the security) or non-detachable. The "exercise value" of the warrant is the amount by which the stock price is greater than the warrant exercise price.

Sources

Warrants are sold to institutions as 'sweeteners' when they purchase debt securities or preferred stock and in venture capital financing. They also are used in reorganizations to provide an incentive to holders of debt instruments. Underwriters obtain warrants in the case of new companies' underwritings, since otherwise the commission charged by the underwriter would be excessive in order to compensate for the risk undertaken. Warrants also are sold to the promoters who organize the company or are offered to key employees to provide incentives.

Advantages/Disadvantages — Characteristics

The advantage of the warrant is that the corporation receives cash on the sale of the warrants and cash when the warrants are exercised.

Some disadvantages are that the warrant holder is not entitled to cash dividends, and the holder loses his investment in the warrant if the value of the common stock does not increase, making it profitable to exercise the warrant. Also, the company cannot force the exercise of the warrant, and only the expiration date limits the length of time the warrants remain outstanding and unexercised. However, a company can encourage the exercise of warrants by dropping the exercise price for a defined time period.

How to Raise Funds

(See "Private Placement/Public Offering" and Bonds.)

Miscellaneous

Factoring

Definition/Purpose/Collateral

Factoring involves the purchase of accounts receivable or a guarantee that the account will be paid by a factor, who pays the seller, on the due date of the receivables, the face amount of accounts receivable sold, less a reserve for returns and allowances. The factor performs his own credit checks and collects the guaranteed receivables and thus the seller does not have to absorb a loss from a customer's inability to pay; he can refuse certain accounts. The factor charges interest if the customer wishes to obtain funds in advance of the terms offered to the account. The receivable is sold to the factor immediately after the shipment is accepted by the customer. Commonly factoring involves notification to the client's customers that the payments are payable to the factor due to his purchase of the receivables. Factoring is very useful in business organizations with limited capital which have a large proportion of sales to credit-worthy customers.

Terms/Payback

By purchasing the accounts or notes receivable of clients, the factor assumes responsibility for their collection. Thus he guarantees to pay to his client the face value of the receivable, after certain deductions, on the due date. It is his responsibility to collect the receivables from the account. If the customer wishes an advance on the receivable sold, the factor provides him with funds, but charges interest. In any case, the factor is reimbursed from funds collected by him from the client's approved customers.

Sources and Credit Criteria

Many factoring companies are located in New York or in areas of the country where the industries which practice factoring are located. The bulk of factoring is in textiles and allied fields, and other industries such as furniture, shoes, toys, lumber, and metal products. Factoring companies are independently owned or are the subsidaries of commercial finance companies or commercial banks. Most large New York City banks have started or have acquired factoring companies and maintain such a subsidiary in order to provide a full-service package to their customers.

The general requirements for a company to be approved by a factor are the following:

a. Legitimate sales to credit-worthy customers;

b. Minimum amount of returns, because if funds are advanced against receivables that are credited due to returned merchandise, the factor has to rely upon the financial strength of the client to collect the advance.

The criteria for acceptance of accounts by the factor cannot be so strict that the customer loses accounts to competition; neither does the factor want to lose money on any account.

Advantages/Disadvantages — Characteristics

Factoring relieves the firm of credit checking, the cost of processing receivables, and collection expenses. It allows the company to concentrate on its business and sell to customers whose credit standing may be unknown to the company because of the distance between the two parties (as in international trade) or volatility in their businesses. Factoring eliminates collection of receivables, and provides credit insurance through the transfer of credit risk. It is used only by industries which accept factoring as a sound business practice. In factoring, the factor wishes to keep credit losses at 0%, whereas the company may wish to have a policy of expecting some losses so that credit losses can be kept at an "optimum" level, increasing sales to some otherwise marginal customers. The cost of factoring consists of:

a. A fee, which is usually less than 3.0% of the amount of the receivables to cover the costs of credit investigation, bookkeeping, collection, and profits. This cost varies according to the size of individual accounts, the volume of receivables sold, and the quality of accounts; and

b. Interest for any cash advance, which is often a few (1.0-2.5%) points above the commercial bank prime rate. The amount advanced could be up to the face value of receivables sold, less some reserves. The seller can also leave the funds with the factor beyond the due date and collect interest.

How to Raise Funds

Availability of factoring may depend on the following:

a. Factoring should be acceptable in the particular industry;

b. The business should be in a strong financial position, and its customers should have acceptable credit ratings;

c. The total volume of sales factored annually should be large enough — normally at least $100,000 — to make the account profitable;

d. Sales should be on open account and the average size of each account should be large;

e. Terms should be short enough to enable the factor to turn over his funds more often, resulting in higher volume and profits;

f. The product should be of good quality with minimum returns;

g. Factors prefer long-term arrangements with a one-year minimum.

Information required by the factor includes the terms of the sale, the annual volume of accounts to be factored and the size of the accounts, the names of the client's customers, the history of merchandise returns due to defects, damages, etc., and the financial statements of the company.

Franchising

Definition/Purpose

Owners (or franchisors) retail a product, service, or method through affiliated dealers (franchisees) through franchising, which is a form of licensing. Usually sales of goods or services are franchised, but it could be used for manufacturing. The franchisor control, to some degree controls the marketing of the business, which could be a product, service or process identified by a brand name. The franchisor can distribute the risks of a huge capital investment required for a national or regional distribution system among the franchisees, and benefit from their initiative without a large sales and management staff. Many franchises require some investment by the franchisor and the franchisee.

Sources of Financing

Franchisors can obtain financing from banks and other financial institutions. The financing can vary depending on whether financing is being considered on a unit-by-unit or on a wholesale basis. A franchisor could use lines of credit or medium-term revolving credits (3-4 years) to finance units individually, accumulate assets (such as completed retail units), and then arrange wholesale financing through a blanket mortgage or sale-leaseback as a private placement, or issue securities to the public. Franchisees obtain financing from commercial banks and from the franchisor, in addition to their own financing. Franchisors may supply the franchisee the inventory as his investment. From the franchisor's outlook, he may have opened a new outlet with only the investment in inventory.

Credit Criteria

Financial institutions evaluate franchisors by some of the following criteria:

a. Financial criteria: Franchisors with a long-term debt to equity ratio of 1:1 or less are favorably considered by lenders. Thus, many franchisors lease their facilities to maintain a favorable debt to equity ratio. The **coverage ratio,** which is the (recurring income before interest, principal payments and taxes)/(principal and interest obligations), is also an important criteria, with desired levels around 2:1 and higher. Lenders also want franchisors to have sufficient promotional funds, since this is the major barrier to new entries' competing with major existing franchisors.

b. Lenders also examine the basic franchise concept and its past history.

c. Franchisors should have professional management, and competent franchisees. Relations with franchisees should be good, so that franchisees continue payment of royalties.

d. Franchises should have an adequate market share, and should have favorable store locations.

Franchisors sometimes offer financial packages to the franchisees, but most often they prefer that the franchisees obtain their own financing. The financing that they do offer is more often in the form of direct investment, such as investment in inventory or ownership and sublease of the building, rather than contingent liability, such as guaranteeing loans to the franchisees. Leading institutions are more favorable towards franchises with a proven track record, than individuals with little else but a new idea.

Advantages/Disadvantages — Characteristics

Franchisors benefit from franchising because they obtain the financial and entrepreneurial resources of the franchisees, and generate revenues from the franchises in the form of an initial franchise fee, a service charge or royalties based on a percentage of sales, or sometimes purchases, rents, sales of equipment and supplies, and miscellaneous items, such as advertising charges and services for special services provided. Usually they also have the option to purchase the franchise, if it is successful. The disadvantages are that it is not always simple to maintain control over the franchisees, and it requires a great deal of sophistication to operate efficient businesses.

The franchisee benefits from franchising because he gets the experience of a proven and profitable operation, and the attached goodwill, while retaining the advantage of independent ownership. The franchisee obtains the benefit of the experience and brand name of the franchisor, and for this he pays a fee and royalty. For the franchisee, a desired arrangement is one where the initial fee pays for the franchisor's expenses, and the franchisor's profits come from the royalty payments based on sales or profits. With this type of agreement, the franchisor and franchisee have the same objective of making the franchise more profitable. Franchisors usually have an option to acquire the franchise, and they usually do acquire the more profitable ones. Franchising does not reduce the need for expansion capital, but distributes it among more individuals. Franchises have had many problems in the recent past arising from inexperienced and fraudulent franchisors.

How to Raise Funds

Franchisors have an easier time raising funds if they have an established brand name, combined with managerial assistance and audited operating statements. (For other requirements, see previous sections, and sections for Line of Credit, Revolving Credit, and Long-Term Loans.)

Employee Stock Ownership Trusts (ESOTs)

Definition/Purpose/Collateral

An Employee Stock Ownership Plan (ESOP) is an employee benefit program through which employees can acquire all or part of the stock of the corporation in which they work. The Employee Stock Ownership Trust (ESOT) is started by the corporation to purchase its own stock for the benefit of its employees. Legislation concerning ESOPs include the following:

- Regional Rail Reorganization Act of 1973 (P. L. 93-236)
- Employee Retirement Income Security Act of 1974 (P. L. 93-406)
- Trade Act of 1974 (P. L. 93-618)
- Tax Reduction Act of 1975 (P.L. 94-12)
- Tax Reform Act of 1976
- Revenue Act of 1978
- Tax Reform Act of 1984

ESOTs qualify for favored tax treatment in the Internal Revenue Code, similar to other pension and profit sharing plans. The earliest employee stock plans were started around the 1930s, with the Sears,

Roebuck plan being one of the most well-known due to the benefits that it has provided its employees. ESOPs were encouraged in the Employee Retirement Income Security Act of 1974 (ERISA), and they are becoming popular due to their ability to create capital for the corporation, and the benefits provided to the employees.

The ESOP is different from an ordinary pension fund and an employee profit-sharing system. Pension plans are not allowed to hold large blocks of employer securities in their portfolio, whereas ESOPs are designed primarily to invest in employer securities. Since the passage of the Employee Retirement Income Security Act of 1974, ESOTs are the only type of trust legally allowed to hold large blocks of employer stock. Employers can contribute cash or stock to the ESOT. ESOTs may hold up to 100% of the employer stock. ESOPs are different from profit sharing plans since, under the stock bonus type of ESOP, the company need not be profitable. ERISA defines ESOPs to be of the stock bonus type, under which benefits distributed to employees must be employer stock. This type of ESOP can borrow funds from financial institutions and invest these funds in employer securities. This is a distinguishing feature of ESOPs, since other forms of employee benefit plans are prevented from this practice. The debt is guaranteed by the employer, and the lending financial institution accepts the securities as collateral. This feature allows the employer to obtain funds from the ESOT through debt which can be repaid with pre-tax dollars. The loans should be used for the benefit of the employees and the interest rate should be reasonable. The loan is secured with the employer securities purchased with the funds. The loan has to be repaid through employer contributions to the ESOP. Employer contributions are deductible only up to 15% (or 25% to repay a loan used to purchase employer securities; in addition to interest on the loan) of compensation paid to covered employees. This limit can reach 25% if there are carryovers from previous years.

The ESOT must invest primarily in employer securities, or in other qualified assets, such as employer real estate. The assets must be purchased at fair market value. The amount of contributions to the ESOT may be on the basis of a profit-sharing principle (a fixed proportion of the profits is annually transferred to the trust), a cost principle (a fixed proportion of the cost of labor), or a fixed contribution principle (a fixed dollar amount is transferred to the trust). The stock and other securities from the ESOT are distributed to the qualified employees based on certain guidelines. Stock that is held in trust not yet vested to the employee may be forfeited if the qualifications for vesting are not satisfied, if, for example, the employee leaves the company. Employees do not have the right to sell the shares until they have been distributed. The stock can be allocated among the employees based on various factors, such as employee's wage or salary, length of service, etc. The ESOT can distribute employer stock or cash (or an annuity) based on the value of the stock, at the time of the employee's retirement. The value of the employer's securities may decline during the period they are held in the trust. Thus employees have to bear the risk of a decline in the value of their benefits through ownership of the stock.

ESOTs can be organized to satisfy a variety of objectives for the employer, such as raising new capital which can be repaid with pre-tax dollars; for financial considerations, such as the increased investment tax credit; to provide employees ownership in the company; and to enhance other pension plans.

According to ERISA, most employee benefit plans must not own more than 10% of employer stock after 1985. ESOPs, however, are exempted from this requirement.

Sources and Credit Criteria

ESOTs can obtain funds from the parent corporation or borrow them from financial institutions such as commercial banks or insurance companies that are willing to provide medium- or long-term loans with the employer stock and guarantee as collateral. Thus, the employing company will be analyzed to ensure that the stock will not lose its value and that the company can repay the loan. The credit analysis and sources are the same as for long-term loans. Eligibility for employee participation in the ESOT must be in accordance with accepted IRS criteria.

An ESOT may purchase common stock, preferred stock, convertible securities, or any other legal marketable securities. Only domestic corporations qualify for ESOTs, and they cannot be Subchapter S corporations. To benefit from the ESOT and be able to repay the loan, the corporation should be in the top income tax bracket and with good prospects of remaining at that level. SEC requirements should be checked to determine whether the sale of stock to the ESOT is considered a private placement or a public offering.

Advantages/Disadvantages — Characteristics

Some of the major benefits of ESOPs are:

a. Funds can be borrowed by the corporation so that interest and principal are tax-deductible from the corporation's income, increasing cash flow and working capital. The cash flow advantages of an ESOP can be seen in the following example:

	Profit-Sharing Trust	ESOT	No Qualified Trust
Net income before taxes	$1,000,000	1,000,000	1,000,000
Contribution to trust	200,000*	200,000**	0
Net taxable income	800,000	800,000	1,000,000
Income tax (assume 50%)	400,000	400,000	500,000
Net income after tax	400,000	400,000	500,000
Cash flow	400,000	600,000	500,000

*Cash **Stock

b. Pre-tax dollars can be used for acquisitions and divestitures;

c. Employees can obtain ownership in the company and thus share in profits, which can improve morale. In some cases when the company has been in danger of being shut down, ESOPs have been used to enable the employees to purchase the company and save the jobs;

d. Large blocks of shares can be purchased from certain shareholders who wish to sell. This provides greater liquidity, especially in closely-held companies;

e. The Tax Reform Act of 1976 allows corporations with ESOPs satisfying certain requirements a higher investment tax credit. The Economic Recovery Tax Act of 1981 replaces this tax credit with a payroll-based tax credit.

f. The Trade Act of 1974 grants preferences in federal guarantees for loans to create jobs in communities hurt by increased imports if a corporation agrees to establish an ESOP.

The disadvantages or limitations of an ESOP are:

a. The stock sales to an ESOP in a privately-held corporation can result in dilution of existing shareholders' equity. Management may lose control in the company after the stock has been distributed to the employees;

b. Expenses to administer the ESOP and satisfy the various regulations (IRS, SEC, ERISA, etc.) may be very high for small corporations;

c. The employees bear the risk of a decline in stock values if the company performs poorly. Therefore ESOPs often are used in conjunction with a pension plan using cash contributions and investing in a diversified portfolio;

d. The company will need cash to repurchase securities when employees retire and wish to sell their holdings at an inopportune time;

e. Because the amount of deductible contributions to the ESOP is tied to the covered payroll of the company, the amount of funds that can be borrowed by the ESOP is limited by the size of the payroll because the annual payments to the ESOP have to be large enough to amortize the loan.

How to Raise Funds

ESOTs can obtain funds from the parent corporation for the purchase of stock in the company, or they can borrow the funds from a financial institution to purchase stock. In the former case, the parent makes tax-deductible cash contributions annually to the ESOT, and the ESOT uses this cash to purchase stock in the parent. This returned cash is used to repay the parent company's loans. The advantage of this method in a growth company is that the ESOT purchases stock each year at a successively higher price, thus reducing dilution while keeping the cash contributions at a constant level. Alternatively, the ESOT can borrow from a financial institution, with the loan being guaranteed by the parent, and these funds are used to purchase stock. This stock is held by the lender as collateral. Annually, the parent makes tax-deductible contributions to the ESOT, and these payments are used to repay the loan.

According to the Revenue Act of 1978, some of the major requirements for an ESOP are the following:

a. Employer securities transferred to the plan or purchased by the plan should be allocated to entitled participants proportional to the participant's compensation (up to a maximum of $100,000).

b. Participants in the plan should be entitled to vote allocated shares in corporate matters.

c. Participants can demand benefit distribution in the form of employer securities or cash in lieu of securities, based upon a fair valuation formula.

d. Employers securities have been defined as tradeable common stock issued by the employer (or by a corporation which is a member of the same controlled group), or securities which have voting and dividend rights which equal or exceed that class of common stock of the issuer with the greatest voting power, and that class having the greatest dividend rights. Noncallable preferred stock may be issued if it is convertible into stock meeting the above requirements, and the conversion price is reasonable.

e. The Tax Reform Act of 1984 allows commercial lenders to exclude half the interest income received on loans made to ESOPs, where the funds are used to acquire employer securities for the ESOP.

Limited Partnerships

Definition/Purpose/Collateral

A limited partnership is normally used to raise equity capital for a business project, which equity is then leveraged with debt. The percentage of equity usually ranges between 20-30%. Typical uses include financing for real estate, oil and gas drilling, equipment leasing, research and development (R&D) of new products, etc. A limited partnership combines the tax benefits of a partnership (pass-through of profits and losses to the individual partners) with the limited liability advantages of a corporation. A partnership can either have all general partners (some of whom may be active and some passive), or have some general partners and some limited partners. The latter is a limited partnership (LP), and it requires at least one general partner and at least one limited partner. The general partner(s) can be an individual or a corporation and has management resposibility and unlimited liability. Limited partners cannot participate in management, and, hence, are passive investors whose liability is limited to their capital investment and loans for which they have committed. Limited partners are investors and an active management role can jeopardize their limited liability.

LPs are organized according to state statutes based on the Uniform Limited Partnership Act (ULPA) which was enacted in 1916 by the National Conference of Commissioners on Uniform State Laws. These have been approved by all the states except Louisiana and four states; the latter states have passed the Revised ULPA, which was enacted in 1976 to resolve ambiguities. Some of the states have passed the act with minor variations. LPs can be dissolved according to prior agreement or by court decree.

LPs are considered to be securities because it is assumed that investors expect a profit from the efforts of others, i.e., the general partners. Thus, LPs have to satisfy state and federal securities laws (see "Private Placements/Public Offerings").

The selling of LPs to investors is called syndication, which can be either through private placements or public offerings. The syndicator either markets the LP interests to the investors on a best-efforts basis for the developer (who still retains the risk that the offering may not be sold), or the syndicator may underwrite the offering, i.e., acquire the LP interests from the developer/promoter and resell it to investors. The developer can act as his own syndicator or retain an investment banker to syndicate the offering.

LPs have to be formed with great care by experienced attorneys to satisfy the IRS in form and substance. Since the statutes regarding LPs are strict, care should be taken that the LP is not considered to be an association (corporation) or a general partnership, that the LP and developer are separate and distinct entities, and that agreements are made at arms-length.

To prevent a partnership from being termed a corporation by the IRS, an LP cannot have too many corporate characteristics. Corporate characteristics include:

a. Existence of associates.
b. Operating the business at a profit.
c. Continuity of life.
d. Limited liability.
e. Free transferability of interest.
f. Centralized management.

The first two characteristics are common to both corporations and limited partnerships. Having more than two of the last four characteristics can cause a LP to be treated as a corporation.

The general partner can sometimes be a corporation, which further limits personal liability. When a corporation is a general partner, it has to satisfy the following:

• Limited partners cannot own, directly or indirectly, more than 20% of the stock of the corporate general partner.

• Net worth of the corporate general partner should be:

a. 10% of total contributions, if the total contributions to the partnership is $2.5 million or more; and

b. lower of $250,000 or 15% of total contributions, if the total contributions to the LP is less than $2.5 million.

This net worth must exist at the time of organizing, and through the life of the limited partnership. The corporate general partner's net worth has to be calculated without including the value of the corporate general partner's interest in limited partnerships.

The principle in organizing LPs is to postpone investments by the limited partners over the first few years while accelerating the tax benefits so as to increase their return on investment (ROI). In public offerings, the investments are made on a one-time basis. However, in privately placed LPs, the investments often are made in two to four installments over a period of three to five years. Along with an initial cash payment, limited partners sign a promissory note payable to the partnership or promoter. This note can be unsecured or secured with CDs, savings accounts, etc. The promoter uses this note as collateral to borrow from a short-term lender, such as a commercial bank.

Because tax benefits are a crucial reason for organizing LPs, the allocation of profits, gains and losses becomes a crucial issue in determining the attractiveness of the LP offering. Partnerships profits and losses can be allocated disproportionately if the IRS is satisfied that there is a business purpose and a financial effect to the partners. The rationale for the allocation should be included in the partnership agreement.

Thus, the agreement should specify the allocation of the profits and losses (including investment tax credits and depreciation), cash flow (or revenues) and capital (or residual) gains, if any. Thus, a general partner may get a small percentage of the profits and losses, but a larger percentage of cash flow and capital gains.

Losses from a LP offsets the partner's income from other sources. Losses can be deducted only up to the partner's adjusted basis. A partner's adjusted basis equals the original investment plus the share of liabilities for which he is personally liable plus the allocated share of profits, less cash distributions and the allocated share of losses and deductions. Prior to the introduction of the "at risk" limitation in the Tax Reform Act of 1976, a limited partner's adjusted basis was not limited to liabilities for which he was personally liable.

Types of Limited Partnerships

Real Estate Limited Partnerships (RELPs): The "at risk" limitation has one exception — real estate. In RELPs, "non-recourse" loans (i.e., loans which are not a personal liability in any form of any partner, limited or general), are divided among partners in proportion to their interest in profits and added to their basis. A lender of a non-recourse loan relies solely on the mortgage on the property for repayment and forfeits all claims from any limited or general partner.

Thus RELPs have a major advantage over other types of LPs in that the partner's deductions can exceed his investment. If the LP provides 20% of the total project and borrows the balance through a non-recourse loan, the deduction can be up to five times the investment. Through the provisions of the Tax Reform Act of 1984, the asset can be depreciated (or capital recovered") over 18 years on a straight-line or accelerated basis. This permits most of the tax losses to be concentrated in the first few years, allowing the investors a quick return on their investment. By staggering the investment over the first few years, an investor can get an attractive return and the developer can sell the LP interests. In addition, the Investment Tax Credit (ITC), allowing the deduction of a percentage of the cost of certain assets or costs of rehabilitation from an investor's tax liability, further enhances the attractiveness of the package. Use of the ITC requires the adoption of the straight-line depreciation approach.

Thus, the limited partner's profit/loss is his proportion of revenues from the project less operating expenses less interest expenses less depreciation. Through accelerated depreciation, this is normally a loss in the first few years. However, the cash flow (revenues less operating expenses less debt service less management fees) can be positive, and the general partner obtains a portion of this cash flow.

Typically, the general partner is allocated approximately 1% of the profits/losses and 5-10% of the cash flow until the limited partners have recouped their investment (or a multiple of — such as double — their investment); after this, the general partner's share of the cash flow increases to around 25-40%. Capital gains are similarly allocated. Due to the risks in the initial years, the general partners (or promoters) are asked to guarantee (for a fee) additional investment in the project, if it is required to prevent foreclosure. This investment is usually in the form of subordinated loans.

Research & Development Limited Partnerships (R&DLPs): R&DLPs have been in use since 1974 when the Supreme Court allowed the deduction of R&D expenses incurred in a taxpayer's trade or business. Even if it is not involved in marketing or selling the product(s), R&D activities by a R&DLP is considered to be a trade or business. A taxpayer can deduct paid or incurred R&D expenses in the current year or over five years (with some exceptions, such as organization/syndication expenses and capital assets owned by the R&DLP).

Usually the R&DLP is formed to raise funds from investors to finance the development of new products. The R&DLP contracts with an operating company to perform the work and develop the product for a fixed fee or a cost-plus basis. The operating company also acts as the general partner of the R&DLP and has an option to license the product to manufacture and market the product at its own expense. Often the general partner guarantees against any overruns. The R&DLP receives a royalty for the license. By properly structuring an R&DLP (such as through the use of a joint venture with the operating company to manufacture and sell the product developed and the sale of the R&DLP's interest in the joint venture to the operating company), it is possible to treat the return as capital gains.

R&DLPs allow the partners to deduct up to 80-90% of their investment in the first year. This can be a very attractive feature, since it is higher than that afforded by real estate. RELPs, however, allow a higher total write-off due to the "at risk" exception.

R&DLP's can be used to finance research or product development in new or young businesses. However, as a practical matter, the necessary requirements of a "track record" in product development and manufacturing and marketing capability makes this a tool prodominately used by existing, established firms concentrating on improvements of existing technology. Entrepreneurs with well-established reputations (such as Lear or DeLorean) also have succeeded in raising large amounts through publicly offered R&DLPs.

When the R&DLP is organized to improve and develop existing technology, the operating company sometimes transfers to the LP rights to the base technology which might have been performed prior to the organization of the R&DLP.

R&DLPs are attractive to business because there is no dilution of ownership (investors do not get stock in the operating company), there is no interest cost to be paid, and there is no obligation to repay the investment if the R&D is unsuccessful. However, the R&DLP is entitled to a royalty on sales. On a low margin product, this could cause the product to be unprofitable or uncompetitive. The royalty can be a fixed dollar amount per unit or (as is currently the practice) a percentage of sales. This royalty is high until the investment (or a multiple thereof) is recouped, and decreases thereafter. This arrangement also allows the royalties to be higher when the product is new and unique, and to decrease when the competition increases.

Oil & Gas Drilling Limited Partnerships: These LPs normally provide approximately 30% of the funds required. The general partner provides 1% with the balance being borrowed. Until payout, the general partner normally receives a smaller percentage (such as 10%) of cash flow for management fees and a higher percentage after payout.

Terms/Payback

To attract investors, an LP should be organized to allow investment in installments over a period of 1-4 years, with maximum tax benefits (in the form of tax losses which can be deducted against ordinary income) immediately, and a return (profits and gains), which is taxed as capital gains. While precise returns would be impossible to predict with certainty, investors usually expect an annual return of at least 3-4% above the inflation rate. The higher the risk, the higher should be the anticipated return.

In many LPs (such as R&DLPs), partners can deduct up to 80-90% of their investment in the first year. At a 50% tax bracket, this translates to a tax saving equal to 45% of the investment. RELPs normally have a lower first-year deduction, but, due to a non-recourse loan, have total losses equal to 4-5 times the investment.

In RELPs, the limited partners usually get 90-99% of the profits and losses and a lower percentage of cash flow and capital gains. The general partner's share increases after the limited partners recoup their investment (or a multiple of their investment).

R&DLPs normally pay the limited partners a high initial royalty (typically ranging between 7-12%) until the investment (or double the investment) is recouped, with a lower percentage for the balance of the life of the partnership. Sometimes, the general partner acquires the R&DLP's interest for a lump sum payment, which has to be at a fair market value (to satisfy the IRS) and should be high enough to satisfy the investors.

Sources & Credit Criteria

LPs are used to raise equity for a project with the balance of the funds (70%-80%) to be obtained through debt.

LPs are normally sold to investors who are attempting to reduce their taxes on ordinary income and obtain profits from the project in the form of capital gains which are taxed at a lower rate. Investors are normally at the highest tax bracket (50%), and with high taxable incomes (over $50,000).

LPs can be sold in a public offering basis or placed privately. The former is practically always done by an investment banker (snydicator), while the latter may or may not use a syndicator. Some investment bankers specialize in R&DLPs, while RELPs are also underwritten or sold by mortgage bankers. Most privately placed LPs require a minimum investment of $100,000 and more, while publicly offered LPs can be found for as little as $5,000. Financial planners can also help in the private placement of LPs.

The penalties for failed LPs can be high. An LP which has been foreclosed or sold in its first few years can cause the investment tax credit and accelerated portion of depreciation to be "recaptured" (the deductions are disallowed) and cause the limited partners to pay the extra taxes. In addition, constant losses could result in a disallowance of deductions by the IRS. Thus, LPs should be analyzed with care to ensure that they will not fold in the first few years. Normally, guarantees of additional investment are required from the general partner/promoter (for an additional fee) to prevent failure.

The most important criteria include:

a. general partners' expertise, experience and track record;

b. the feasibility of the project without accounting for tax benefits;

c. the amount of investment, financial strength, and guarantees provided by the general partner;

d. whether the project is adequately capitalized; and

e. return to the investors (including tax benefits, cash flow and internal return on investment, payback period, and cumulative cash-on-cash return, i.e., total amount of cash returned to amount of cash invested).

Each specialized form of LP also has its own criteria. These include interest rate and property appreciation rate risks in real estate; uniqueness, gross margins and market size of products in R&DLPs; oil prices in oil and gas LPs, etc.

Advantages/Disadvantages — Characteristics

The major advantages of LPs include:

a. limited liability to passive investors;

b. pass-through of profits and losses, avoiding double taxation;

c. subject to certain guidelines, a corporation can be used as a general partner, further limiting personal liability;

d. profits and losses can be allocated among partners according to prior agreement, allowing depreciation and investment tax credits to be transferred to those who can utilize them, and a higher percentage of cash flow to others (general partners);

e. unlike Subchapter S corporations, LPs can be used for all types of businesses and the number of partners is not limited;

f. limited partners cannot interfere in the management of the business without losing their limited liability status;

g. non-recourse loans (in RELPs) can enhance the attractiveness of the LP by allowing an adjusted basis much higher than the investment by the limited partner;

h. R&DLPs allow the business to raise risk funds without dilution of company ownership, with no interest costs, and no obligation to repay in case of failure;

i. R&DLPs can allow high returns because the company normally invests only 1% of the R&D costs. The company, however, has to provide start-up and operating funds.

The major disadvantages include:

a. limited partnership interests are not as easily transferred as corporate shares due to a limited secondary market;

b. if a LP is foreclosed or sold in the first few years, the limited partners could pay a "penalty" in the form of taxes due to the recapture of the investment tax credit and accelerated portion of depreciation;

c. R&DLPs, the business would have to pay a royalty which could be a problem for a product with low margins or without proprietary strengths;

d. the complexity of organizing LPs requires the use of attorneys, accountants, etc. and increases the cost of raising funds.

How to Raise Funds

LPs normally provide equity for 20-30% of the cost of the project (except for R&DLPs) with the balance being provided through debt. LPs can be sold through public offerings or private placements. The cost of syndicating LPs ranges between 6 and 10%.

The information required in a prospectus normally includes:

a. general partners' (or operating company's) history and track record in starting and managing similar projects successfully;

b. project (or product) description, showing its feasibility through independent market studies, costs and management analysis, gross margins and profitability analysis, etc.;

c. financial structure, which is influenced by total costs, investment from limited partners and timing; tax benefits; sales and profit projections; return on investment; payback period, etc. Also included should be financial requirements and sources of financing;

d. partnership agreement should mention how the profits, losses, cash flow, and residual gains will be allocated among the partners (it should satisfy IRS guidelines.);

e. guarantees, which are often needed from the general partner or promoter to reduce the risk of sale or foreclosure in the early years. Amounts provided are normally in the form of loans;

f. tax attorney's opinion should be included; and

g. benefits and risks of the offering should be noted.

IV. Capital Sources

Commercial Banks

Introduction

After the owner and his personal contact, commercial banks are usually the most important capital supplier to a business. The advice and credit supplied by the commercial banker represents the most important credit supplier relationship. Close relationships with the commercial banker also help in dealings with other capital suppliers, because most of them check with the commercial banker before providing capital.

Commercial banks provide a wide range of financing and most large banks have affiliations with other types of financial institutions which provide financing that banks do not. Traditionally, banks provided short-term funds, but presently they also provide intermediate- and long-term loans. In 1982 there were 14,963 commercial banks in the United States. Of these, 4,579 were national banks, 1,040 were state-chartered banks that were members of the Federal Reserve System, and 9,344 were state-chartered nonmember banks. The Comptroller of the Currency is responsible for approving charters for national banks, which must become members of the Federal Reserve System and the Federal Deposit Insurance Corporation (FDIC). State banking agencies approve charters for state banks, and they may choose to join the Federal Reserve System and FDIC. These banking systems have created a variety of rules and regulations among national banks and the various state banks, which affect bank policies, structure, and performance.

The major source of funds to commercial banks are demand deposits and time deposits, including Certificates of Deposits. Demand deposits usually involve working capital belonging to businesses and individuals that is withdrawable on demand. Time deposits are placed as savings or investment on which interest is paid, and which can be withdrawn at any time. Banks can make greater use of these funds and lend them for longer terms. Certificates of Deposits are funds placed for designated periods of time on which interest is paid. Demand deposits tend to fluctuate more than time deposits or Certificates of Deposits (CDs). The funds obtained by a bank are used for reserve to meet withdrawals; U.S. treasury obligations; state, county, and municipal bonds; and loans to businesses and consumers. The reserve is larger for demand deposits.

Flow of Funds

In 1982 commercial banks obtained 6.9% of their total assets from equity capital, 55.0% from time and savings deposits, 19.8% from demand deposits, 17.9% from miscellaneous liabilities, and 0.4% from subordinated notes and debentures. The assets of commercial banks include:

- Cash and other government securities 25.8%
- Federal funds sold and securities under resale agreement: 5.5%
- Real Estate Loans: 16.0%
- Loans to other financial institutions, such as REITs and mortgage companies, domestic commercial banks, banks in foreign countries, other depository institutions, other financial institutions, securities brokers, and dealers: 3.9%
- Loans to carry and purchase securities; farmers, commercial and industrial loans, and loans to individuals: 33.2%
- Other assets, including direct leases, fixed assets, and miscellaneous assets.

Types of Financing Provided

Bank provide a vast array of business financing, including:

a. Lines of credit and other working capital loans;
b. Revolving loans;
c. Transaction loans and interim construction financing;
d. Term loans with or without guarantees;
e. Accounts receivable financing;
f. Inventory loans;
g. Time sales and installment financing;
h. Equipment loans;
i. Conditional sales contracts;
j. Real estate financing;
k. Agricultural financing;
l. Government guaranteed loans;
m. Leasing;
n. Financing foreign trade through letter of credit, etc.

Bank financing does not require equity "sweeteners". However, banks do have subsidiaries or affiliates that provide risk capital which require equity participations.

Bank loans can be for the following terms:

Short — secured or unsecured loans for less than 1 year;

Intermediate — mainly secured loans for 1-10 years;

Long — loans for more than 10 years, composed mainly of real estate mortgages or those guaranteed by a government agency.

Loans may be classified based on some of the following characteristics:

a. Loans can be secured or unsecured. Unsecured loans rest solely on the credit of the borrower, whereas secured loans have a security interest in some asset which can be liquidated if the borrower defaults on payment.

b. Demand loans or time loans. Demand loans, which are also called call loans, are payable at the request of the lender or the choice of the borrower. Time loans have a fixed term and cannot be called by the lender except under certain predefined conditions, and usually cannot be repaid by the borrower before maturity, except with a prepayment penalty.

c. Loans may be single-name loans signed only by the borrower, or double-name loans guaranteed by another party. Double-name loans can be banker's acceptances, guaranteed notes, endorsed notes or drafts.

Banks also provide construction financing with permanent financing provided by a long-term lender such as a life insurance company or a savings institution. Banks also use trust receipts, warehouse receipts and bills of lading issued by common carriers as collateral. Negotiable bills of lading such as an order bill of lading, are used for loans for commodities in transit since the holder of the bill of lading can obtain possession of the goods. Securities loans are made to investment bankers to underwrite new issues, and to dealers and individuals for the purchase of securities.

Practices

The commercial bank is one of the few financial institutions which does not demand equity in the new or small business as an incentive to lend funds. Some of the other benefits obtained from a commercial bank are:

a. The bank can serve as an advisor or initiator in mergers and acquisitions by providing the names of candidates, as well as attractive introductions to either prospective buyers or sellers;

b. A commercial bank can provide credit information about suppliers and customers, and information on individuals such as new personnel, etc;

c. The commercial bank also advises other capital suppliers about the bank's relationship with the business.

Adequate notice to the banker of the businessman's need for funds is very desirable. This requires a businessman to project business needs and anticipated performance. An immediate need for a loan can result in higher cost for the funds.

Some factors involved in selecting a bank are:

Location: The bank need not be very close, but the business will be in a better position if the account is important to the bank owing either to its size or its location in the bank's prime business area.

Size: Larger banks provide more services than small banks, such as in international banking. Also a bank has a lending limit of 10% of its capital and surplus to any one customer. Most small banks have larger correspondent banks able to provide some of the services small banks cannot provide.

Adaptability: The bank should be able to adapt its lending policies to satisfy the needs of the business.

Lending policies and cost: Businesses should be concerned about the availability and cost of funds. A business benefits especially in periods of tight money if the bank is willing to lend a higher amount for the same collateral. However, this larger loan is accompanied by a higher interest rate to compensate the bank for the greater risk. If a business is profitable and can use more funds profitably, a larger loan-to-value ratio even at a moderately higher cost may be a desirable feature. A business should consider the maximum amount available; whether it is available both in easy and difficult times for the company and whether or not money is scarce or plentiful. A business also should consider the terms and security required, the loan-to-value ratio, the marginal profitability from the proceeds of the loan, and the cost.

Personality and philosophy: Mutual compatibility and trust are influential factors in obtaining bank loans. The bank also should be interested in the particular kind of business. Banks can be either conservative or liberal in their lending policies when compared to other banks.

Commercial banks usually have three major departments: commercial loans; real estate loans; and consumer loans.

Information requirements and skills for the evaluation of commercial loans often are more complex than real estate loans and consumer loans. One loan officer is assigned to each commercial account, and is responsible for account liaison and coordinating loan requirements. However, the loan officer usually cannot approve loans, especially above a predefined amount. This approval is obtained from a loan committee or a senior officer in the organization. Factors influencing loan authority limits are the type of the loan (term, collateral, etc.) and the financial strength of the borrower. Loans are repaid either through liquidation of assets, as in inventory loans, or through cash flow. Banks need to be satisfied that projections show repayment capability through one of these two sources. In addition to projections, banks also need security in the form of collateral which can be liquidated, or a strong financial statement and history of adequate earnings.

Information Requirements

Every lender or investor requires information to determine whether the application for funds should be approved. Certain information is required for all types of private placements from financial institutions, and the information requirements increase with the risk involved in the security. The information required includes:

a. Amount of the loan, uses of the proceeds, repayment capabilities, and the sources of cash for repayment. The purpose is necessary because loan requests may be disapproved due to legal or policy restrictions against the proposed uses. "Speculative" business loans without adequate collateral usually are not approved by banks.

b. History of the business and personal resumes of shareholders and management.

c. Income and cash flow statements and balance sheets for the past 5 years, or since the company began. Audited statements are always more desirable, and are required when the amount of the loan is large and/or the collateral is not adequate.

d. Major customers and suppliers, and the percentage of business done with each.

e. Sales by major product line and each line's contribution to profits.

f. Description of the markets served by the company and the distribution channels.

g. Projections of operations, especially for the next 12-24 months if the loan is short-term and longer (3-5 years) if the loan is intermediate or long-term. The banker wants to see income projections as well as cash flow forecasts.

h. Aging of accounts receivable and accounts payable, and turnover of receivables and inventory.

i. Organization chart of the company.

j. Credit and character references, which are usually required if there has been no past relationship with the banker.

Bankers use outside information sources to check applicants, such as Dun & Bradstreet, suppliers, customers, and other financial institutions with whom the company has had dealings. This investigation is discreet to prevent negative effects on the borrower. The financial statements and projections of the borrower are analyzed with the assistance of industry averages, such as those published by Robert Morris Associates. Some major ratios (see "Ratio Analysis") used are the Debt/Equity ratio and "times earned" to determine whether the company has the cash flow to repay the loan. The availability of bank credit is influenced to a remarkable degree by the bank officers' judgment of the management's character and business ability. The presentation should include a clear-cut operational plan for the use of funds and specific sources and means of payback — not vague ideas.

Some factors affecting the availability of loans are:

a. The borrower's financial rating and the bank's requirements of the borrower.

b. The bank's loan policy regarding the types of loans preferred, and its concentration in certain industries or certain sizes of companies.

c. The supply of funds as affected by deposits and the Federal Reserve Bank's policies.

d. The demand for funds, which is influenced by the state of the economy and by the sector of the economy in which the bank concentrates.

e. The effective interest rate, which is influenced by the supply of and demand for funds, and the nature of the financial markets including the prime rate, etc.

Commercial Paper Houses

Introduction

A commercial paper house is a financial institution which facilitates the sale of commercial paper by corporations that have high credit ratings, financial strength and stability. Commercial paper is the unsecured promissory notes of these corporations with maturity dates ranging from one day to nine months. Commercial paper houses can distribute these notes after purchasing them for their own account, or they can act as brokers for which they are paid a commission. The notes are purchased at a discount in lieu of interest. Issuers of commercial paper are among the nation's largest commercial, industrial and financial institutions. Less than 20 large finance companies account for approximately three-quarters of the commercial paper sold, with three companies (General Motors Acceptance Corporation, Commercial Credit Corporation, and CIT Financial Corporation) being responsible for a large portion of these sales. The total number of companies issuing commercial paper is estimated to be more than 400. There are approximately 10 American commercial paper houses and a few Canadian companies that sell paper for issuers. Most of these dealers are subsidiaries or divisions of investment banking houses. Commercial paper is distributed by the dealers through a retail sales staff to individuals, smaller commercial banks and other organizations seeking to invest funds for a short-term.

Flow of Funds

The flow of funds for commercial paper houses is similar to that of investment bankers with stockholders equity and commercial bank loans as sources.

Types of Financing Provided

The type of financing provided by commercial paper is short-term funds, for maturities up to nine months, and commonly for 90, 120, or 180 days. Commercial paper is not renewable. When necessary, new paper is sold to replace maturing notes.

Practices

The services of commercial paper dealers are utilized by practically all issuers of commercial paper. However, the largest finance companies, which account for the bulk of commercial paper sold, prefer to sell them directly to investors without the use of a dealer. The growth of direct placements is due to:

a. The ability to match the needs of the buyer with those of the seller;

b. Higher interest rates paid during tight money periods attracting funds banks cannot attract because of their restricted interest rates.

Commercial paper normally is sold in even denominations of $1,000; the minimum sold to any one purchaser being $25,000. This is because commercial paper can be sold only to sophisticated investors, and a $25,000 minimum limit is designed to prevent the sale of the paper to others. Notes are purchased at a discount, and the dealer's commission, normally 1/8%, is included in the discount. Commercial paper houses acting as both underwriters and brokers, sell commercial paper in the open market to banks, insurance companies, institutions with excess short-term cash, and private sophisticated investors. Commercial banks have been the traditional buyers of commercial paper.

Companies that sell commercial paper are large or medium-sized firms with strong financial positions reflecting a history of favorable earnings, resulting in high credit ratings. They have adequate amounts of working capital, and bank lines of credit sufficient to allow them to redeem the outstanding commercial paper, and satisfy company working capital needs.

The sale of commercial paper can be advantageous to corporations. Because it is restricted to companies with strong financial positions, sale of commercial paper lends status to a company, and increases the visibility of a company's high credit rating. In addition, it lowers the cost of funds and increases the availability of funds to the company by opening a new source of financing, often at a lower rate than from commercial banks. This could be especially valuable during tight-money periods. Also, the needs of the large finance companies are so huge when compared with bank-lending limits, that it is extremely desirable for them to have a direct link to investors for short-term funds through commercial paper.

Commercial Finance Companies

Introduction

Commercial finance companies can be classified as Discount Houses, Accounts Receivable or Acceptance Companies, Commercial Credit Companies, Installment Finance Companies, and Automobile Finance Companies. Finance companies will finance accounts receivable and inventory, or provide funds for short- or medium-term uses. There are two categories of finance companies:

a. Those that lend funds secured by pledging of accounts receivable as collateral, and;

b. Those that purchase the accounts receivable without recourse. These are called factoring companies.

Accounts receivable financing was pioneered by major commercial finance companies; presently some of the other financial institutions, such as banks, are active in this field as well. Finance companies also can be classified as companies that finance receivables from businesses and institutions (Commercial Finance Companies), and those that finance receivables from consumers (Consumer Finance Companies). The latter primarily finance the consumer through direct cash loans or through the purchase of installment sales paper. Institutions involved in this area are generally known as consumer finance companies, sales finance companies, industrial banks, and industrial loan companies.

Commercial finance companies are useful when a business needs additional funds due to undercapitalization, seasonality in the business, a temporary loss situation, inadequate internal cash flow to sustain possible growth, lack of funds from other sources such as banks, or a special situation, such as an acquisition.

Businesses often borrow from commercial finance companies when they are unable to obtain bank loans. The benefits from the availability of funds, the marginal profit from the use of the funds, and the lack of compensating balances often offsets the higher cost of funds for many businesses.

Flow of Funds

Commercial finance companies are financed primarily by equity, loans from commercial banks, earnings, and credit market instruments such as bonds and commercial paper. Funds are used for reserves, home, multi-family and commercial mortgages, consumer credit, and business loans. Many commercial finance companies also are involved in equipment leasing.

Types of Financing Provided

Some types of financing offered by commercial finance companies are:

a. Accounts receivable financing;

b. Factoring;

c. Inventory financing, such as warehouse receipt loans or inventory liens;

d. Equipment financing (and chattel mortgages);

e. Leasing;

f. Collateral loans;

g. Unsecured loans;

h. Discounting accounts receivable or sale-purchase of customers' installment contracts;

i. Time sales financing and dealer reserve financing;

j. Real estate loans;

k. Import and export financing.

Sales or Consumer Finance Companies specialize in discounting accounts receivable on installment or conditional sales contracts, and in purchasing installment paper on a retail or wholesale basis. These contracts involve durable or expensive equipment. Purchase of these contracts enables a finance company to contact a new customer who might want additional financing or a debt consolidation loan. The paper is sold by the client for its full value to the finance company if the interest charges allow the finance company to obtain an adequate return.

Practices

Commercial finance companies normally finance only the needs of businesses and industries. However, they cover a larger geographic area than commercial banks. Many commercial finance companies operate nationwide, while some operate on a regional or state basis. Commercial finance companies do not accept deposits or perform other banking functions. Even if a business' financial position is not satisfactory to obtain bank financing, CFCs will consider lending funds if a business is well managed and has good profit prospects. However, it must have a satisfactory level and quality of accounts receivable and other assets, and the earning power to ensure that it can continue to operate the business successfully.

Accounts receivable financing may be on a continuing or a temporary basis, and on notification (when customers are notified) or non-notification basis. Most businesses prefer non-notification because financing from a Commercial Finance Company sometimes can connote financial instability. Unlike commercial banks, CFCs do not require repayment of loans based on accounts receivable financing or inventory financing except on a revolving basis. Most commercial finance companies prefer a minimum loan of $50,000-$100,000. The percentage of advance varies — usually 50% for inventory financing and 75-80% for accounts receivable financing. The gross margin and type of product usually influences the percentage of advance. If the margin is low, the product is usually a commodity and easily liquidated, hence the percentage of advance may be higher. The term of the agreement is usually one year, and is automatically renewed unless the borrower gives written notice within a prespecified number of days (often 60) prior to the end of the contract period. A prepayment penalty often is charged on a term loan which is allocated over the term of the loan. Commercial finance companies have higher cost of funds than commercial banks since they do not have depositors. Therefore, since CFCs cannot enjoy future depositor relationships, the interest rate on loans is higher. Also, CFCs provide greater monitoring than do commercial banks, resulting in higher costs of operation. The stated rate is the actual rate based on daily need. There are no idle funds, compensating balances, or daily balances during line-resting periods. Rates usually vary between 1/36 - 1/20 of 1% per day, which translates to 10 - 18% per year. The loan usually is stated in cost over prime. The charge depends upon the size of the loan, since handling costs are the same, and costs for smaller loans are likely to be higher. Sometimes a risk premium is added for accounts receivable loans when the company is in poor financial condition. This results in rates up to 25%, depending upon state laws. The charge is calculated on a daily money-in-use basis.

Commercial banks and commercial finance companies have a complementary relationship. Banks bring CFCs into accounts that are marginal, and hence not completely bankable, or accounts requiring a large amount of monitoring time, or if loan requirements are larger than the bank's lending limits. Banks usually cannot devote as much time to individual accounts as do CFCs, which also possess experience and expertise in collateral analysis and dealing with marginal accounts in a wide variety of industries. This expertise can be used to closely monitor the accounts and enforce greater discipline on management, thus improving the quality of the account for the commercial bank. The bank continues to participate in the loan with the CFC, or participates in the loan after the company has managed to improve its financial condition. The bank still can continue to serve the business as an income-producing account, and can provide financing to the CFC. Banks often participate in secured loans administered by CFCs when a company becomes a greater credit risk or grows beyond its limits on unsecured borrowing. The major advantage for the borrower is that the bank's interest rate is lower, resulting in a lower average rate.

CFCs use some of the following criteria to determine the quality of the account and the collateral received:

1. If there are concentrations in sales, or if the borrower's customers do not have good credit ratings, the loan is riskier.
2. Borrowers with excessive quality problems in their shipments are considered poor accounts due to the potential of returns or offsets.
3. When a business sells to and purchases from another firm, its receivables from that firm may not be collectible in cash but deducted from the amount owed. The CFC will consider this fact when deciding whether to advance funds with the particular receivable as collateral and when determining the

percentage of advance.

4. The lender will analyze the applicant's actual experience in the areas of collection and turnover. Aging is checked to determine that a majority of the accounts are paid within the terms of sale.

The CFC also satisfies itself that the firm has good prospects for continued existence through improved profitability. Consignment sales are not eligible for accounts receivable financing.

Some advantages of using a CFC are:

1. It is an additional source of funds, especially when the credit of a business may not be strong enough for other types of borrowing.

2. Even though the interest rate is high, it is calculated on a daily money-in-use basis, and it may be low in comparison with possible profits. No compensating balances are required.

3. Accounts receivable financing may be necessary for some businesses, especially when a large part of the assets are composed of accounts receivable.

4. In factoring, there is no need for a credit and collection department.

5. CFCs provide management consulting and credit management expertise.

6. It is an alternative to permanent capital financing through sale of securities or long-term loans.

Some disadvantages of using a CFC are:

1. A higher rate of interest is charged compared with bank loans.

2. If customers are notified that their receivables are pledged or sold, they may resent it and/or discontinue relations owing to implications that the firm is in a weak financial condition.

3. Sale or pledging of receivables may make other credit difficult to obtain.

Some commercial finance companies offer many services to small business such as customer credit evaluation, and an accounting system for and collection of accounts receivable.

Factoring Companies

Introduction

Factoring companies purchase accounts receivable without recourse, and assume the loss if they are not collected. They reserve the right to approve the credit of the customer and provide credit management consulting. Factoring is useful in international trade, when a supplier is unable to perform an adequate credit analysis on new prospects or cannot keep in touch with their changing financial condition. Factoring originated when textile manufacturers in Scotland did not want to absorb the credit risk of selling in the United States. Factors guaranteed and bought accounts receivables. Factoring's predominant use has been in the textile/apparel industry, and it has been extensively used by textile firms, some wholesalers, and other small manufacturing firms.

Flow of Funds

Factoring companies have sources of funds similar to those of commercial finance companies. Their use of funds is as loans to businesses from whom they have purchased accounts receivable. Many factoring companies are subsidiaries of commercial finance companies or leasing companies, and hence they also are involved in commercial finance and leasing.

Types of Financing Provided

Basically factoring companies purchase accounts receivable from businesses with whom they have credit agreements. They reserve the right to approve the customer and the amount of credit outstanding to each. Many of the commercial finance companies also have factoring divisions, and hence these factors do the same types of financing as commercial finance companies.

A factor also can provide purchase guarantees to a supplier of a client, allowing the client to purchase on a discounted basis. Thus, the factor's client can be the seller or the buyer of goods.

Practices

After having analyzed the client's customers and sales history, factors provide them with the maximum amount of receivables that will be guaranteed for each customer at one time. Often, a majority of the client's customers may not be eligible for factoring. Due to the minimum fees charged by the factor, a large proportion of ineligible customers may make factoring undesirable. Whether or not the customer has paid, the factor guarantees to pay the client the full amount of the receivable, up to the predefined maximum, upon maturity. (It should be noted that the factor deducts a certain amount from the payment to maintain a reserve which is used to offset claims for damaged or returned goods, etc. The factor does not guarantee payment on returned or damaged goods which have been rejected by the customer.) The client can borrow against invoices that are factored. The interest rate charged is close to bank rates. Factoring is done mostly by manufacturers who are not able to know the customers' financial status on a daily basis. The seller can use the factor's guarantee to borrow from his bank.

The cost of factoring can vary between 0.5% and 3%, and usually is 1-2% of the amount factored. In addition, interest is charged on any advances. The real annual interest cost of factoring for a guarantee against losses due to uncollected accounts receivable and short-term loans can exceed 20%. However, a company that uses a factor does not need a credit and collection department.

Factors can provide three types of service:

a. Guarantee on Accounts Receivable, which is the traditional role of factoring.

b. Loan Advances, where a certain percentage of the amount of assigned invoices is advanced after assignment and before maturity.

c. Bookkeeping and Collection Service, for accounts receivables.

A factor's actual charge depends on the amount of risk and projected losses, the number of invoices and the average amount of each invoice. There can be bank participation to reduce cost on the loan service arrangement. The rate on the loans advanced is close to bank rates.

The advantage of factoring is that the cost of the credit department is transferred from the seller to the factor, allowing the seller to concentrate on his business. The disadvantage is that the factor is interested in 0% loss rather than "optimum loss."

Sales Finance Companies

Introduction

The sales finance company deals mainly with consumer financing. The companies also are involved in installment debt financing for automobiles and other business equipment, leases, accounts receivable financing and wholesale financing. The industry is dominated by a few large firms. Less than 20 firms hold approximately 80% of total consumer receivables, with the rest of the market shared by more than 1200 companies.

Flow of Funds

(Same as commercial finance companies.)

Types of Financing Provided

Some types of financing provided by sales finance companies are:

a. Retail installment credit;

b. Wholesale installment credit, discounting accounts receivable or conditional sales contracts;

c. Installment debt for automobiles and other business equipment;

d. Leases;

e. Accounts receivable financing.

Practices

Sales finance companies do not have restrictions on branch systems, nor are they regulated by state or federal organizations. Sales finance companies can be captive (like GMAC) or independent. Sales finance companies normally obtain recourse against the dealer, or may set aside a "dealers' reserve", which is used to reimburse the finance company for losses from default of installment notes purchased from the dealer. Sales finance companies specialize in buying installment receivables at a discount, and they finance durable equipment and consumer durables.

Foundations

The number of foundations is estimated at over 50,000 with the great majority being small, local, and limited in purpose. However, some large foundations have significant levels of assets. Foundations exist to provide a benevolent community service. They provide grants to charitable programs, health-related projects, education programs, scientific research, community and youth development, etc.

Grants generally are made from income obtained by investing the donated capital in diverse instruments, including bonds issued by private corporations and public bodies, common and preferred stocks, real estate and mortgages, and loans of various kinds. Based on their investment criteria, foundations may provide financing to individuals, domestic business firms and corporations, and even foreign corporations and governments.

Industrial Banks (Morris Plan Banks)

Introduction

This is a system of personal loans conceived by Arthur Morris, who founded the first "Morris Plan

Bank" (which was actually a personal loan company making co-maker loans to individuals) in 1910. This was the Fidelity Savings & Trust Company of Norfolk, Virginia. Industrial banks operate in approximately 20 states. The Morris Plan bank used a copyrighted note where repayment was guaranteed by the borrower and a co-maker(s). Such loans are used for personal use or for a small business. Late payments and other contract violations are subject to penalty, and initial investigation fees are discounted in advance. Most former industrial banks now operate under commercial bank charters. Others resemble commercial banks.

Flow of Funds

Industrial banks obtain funds from customer savings deposits and other financial sources, which include certificates of deposit, short-term loans from commercial banks, commercial paper, debentures and stock.

Types of Financing Provided

Industrial banks do some of the following types of financing:

a. Time sales financing and dealer reserve financing;
b. Consumer loans and co-maker loans;
c. Loans to small businesses.

Practices

When many states had severe usury law limits, some industrial banks sold "investment certificates" repayable monthly, resulting in an effective rate twice the stated rate. Lately they also have been providing loans to small businesses. Fundamentally, the Morris Plan provides that the maximum legal rate of interest will be charged for the term of the loan. Certain additional fees for credit investigation or for recording documents may be charged. The borrower is obligated to make uniform deposits in a savings account at regular intervals so that at the maturity date of the loan there will be on deposit an amount sufficient to pay the loan.

The highest rates charged are for single-name loans, with lower rates for co-maker and secured loans. Rates are quoted on an annual discount basis, usually 5-9%. The cost of handling and investigation is around 1-2%, charged in advance. Thus, the borrower's actual interest rate is around 15%, or higher.

Insurance Companies

Introduction

Insurance companies can be classified primarily as Life and Health companies and Property and Casualty companies. In 1983, there were about 2,100 legal reserve life insurance companies and about 3,500 property and casualty companies. Approximately 93% of life insurance companies were organized as stock companies; the balance as mutual companies. Mutuals are older and larger, and control approximately 55% of the assets. In the property and casualty area, stock companies control approximately 68% of the business and 73% of the assets in the industry. Total assets of the life insurance companies were approximately $655 billion in 1983, and assets of the property and casualty companies were approximately $231 billion. Other categories of life insurance companies are fraternal, and those owned by the savings banks in Connecticut, Massachusetts, and New York. The assets of these two groups in 1980 were $10,032 million (in the U.S. and Canada) and $942 million, respectively. The oldest life insurance company in continued existence in the world is the Presbyterian Ministers' Fund in Philadelphia, which was started in 1759.

Some characteristics of the various types of institutions are:

- Mutual companies do not issue stock but are owned by their policyholders.
- Stock companies are owned by their stockholders.
- Life insurance companies act as a form of savings institution.
- Property and casualty companies do not collect savings. (Property insurance companies sell a service and insure property for loss, etc. The contracts provide for indemnification of damage losses up to the limits of the policy.)

Casualty insurance companies (auto, workmen's compensation, etc.) primarily are concerned with losses caused by injuries to persons and by damage to property of others. Property and casualty companies cannot estimate future claims with actuarial accuracy, and so they have a greater need for liquidity.

Flow of Funds

Insurance companies obtain funds from premiums on policies, stockholders' equity, and retained earnings. Their assets are held in the form of cash; government securities; corporate securities including bonds, common stock, and preferred stock; mortgages; real estate; and other loans. They are heavily involved in the private placement market. Property and casualty insurance companies hold more of their assets in easily marketable securities (i.e., securities with a secondary market) owing to the volatility of the payments on their policies.

Types of Financing Provided

Life and Health Insurance companies differ widely from Property and Casualty companies in the types of financing they provide. Property and Casualty Insurance companies' (PCIC) investments are more liquid than Life Insurance companies' (LIC) investments because of the higher probability of large claims liability among PCICs. Hence, PCIC assets are almost exclusively in the secondary markets, with heavy emphasis on state and local government tax-exempt bonds, corporate bonds, and common stocks. PCICs are the second largest buyer of tax-exempt securities. LICs can tolerate a higher level of taxable income than PCICs due to the different income tax structures in PCICs and LICs. Also, LICs had legal restrictions on investments in common stock. Even though some of these legal restrictions no longer exist, LICs have not invested heavily in common stocks due to their preference for investments with fixed returns. PCICs seek capital gains and a lower tax rate through common stock holdings.

Since life insurance claims can be predicted with a high degree of accuracy using actuarial techniques, LICs can and do invest primarily in long-term assets. LICs invest in the following:

a. Real estate and mortgages;

b. Long-term loans to corporations through private placement;

c. Secondary market securities, including corporate and government bonds, and common and preferred stocks;

d. Short-term government and corporate securities, which is investment of temporary excess cash;

e. Policy loans, i.e., loans to policyholders with cash value as security;

f. Venture capital financing directly through the parent or a subsidiary.

Because of their relatively secure liquidity position, LICs usually hold the debenture or promissory notes or bonds to maturity; especially those with high returns. LICs are expected to invest more heavily in common stocks in the future. LICs also are significant investors in commercial real estate and mortgages on farm, commercial and industrial property, and multifamily dwellings. In the farm mortgage market, LICs are the largest private institutional lender, investing primarily in large farms. LICs use direct placement to invest a significant portion of their funds rather than acquiring publicly traded securities. LIC loans may be used for plant and equipment additions, acquisitions, or the conversion of short-term debts to longer maturities. LIC financing is not available for short-term or seasonal needs.

Practices

Differing natures of their business mean that investment practices of LICs and PCICs vary greatly. LIC assets are mainly capital-market instruments, and usually cover the entire spectrum. They emphasize long-term instruments because they have long-term contracts with policyholders. LICs do not emphasize tax-exempt securities in their portfolio because the LIC income-tax rate is lower than that for business corporations. Some other factors that affect insurance company investments are the need for diversification, safety of investments, maximization of income, and state regulation of investments.

Investments of locally generated reserves are regulated by individual states for the protection of their policyholders. In addition, companies have to satisfy requirements of their state of domicile. Regulations include limits on the percentage of total assets invested in each type of investment and in the securities of any one private borrower. Other restrictions exist on the term of the loan or leasehold, and the borrower's financial strength, such as assets and net worth. Many state laws prohibit LIC loans to unincorporated business except when secured by real estate. The loan-to-value ratios are usually 66-75%, except for FHA and VA loans. Insurance company investments usually are not geographically restricted if within the United States, and sometimes Canada.

LICs aim to obtain higher yields while maintaining a reasonable level of risk. LICs use the forward commitment process in their purchases of bonds and mortgages, and invest their cash in short-term loan instruments, such as U.S. Treasury securities and commercial paper, as a liquidity reserve to satisfy their long-term forward commitments. Forward commitments are used because insurance companies need to be fully invested. These long-term commitments are primarily in the form of corporate bonds, business loans and mortgages, lower quality bonds and unsecured debentures or notes purchased for their higher return. LICs usually expect to hold these securities until maturity. Some LICs also have been active in increasing the amount and number of loans to small businesses, directly or through venture capital subsidiaries. Prudential has a commercial and industrial loan department which makes small long-term loans to small- and medium-sized businesses. Larger insurance companies with qualified investment staffs have dominated in the supply of long-term loan funds with custom-designed terms and provisions to small, less financially secure companies. Small LICs are not predominant in the private market because they invest smaller amounts and lack the qualified staff. It is also more convenient for borrowers to deal with a smaller number of lenders than a larger consortium.

LIC long-term obligations must be secured by physical assets or by the proven earning power of the borrower. LICs usually expect the annual amortization of the proposed loan to be covered adequately by the annual cash flow of the company for the past two to three years. LICs have limits on the minimum amount invested in each company. The minimum varies among LICs, and is usually never lower than $300,000. In general, terms are greater than 10 years, and the rate of interest is slightly higher than banks. Insurance company loans complement bank loans, since insurance companies usually are interested in longer maturities than banks. They normally have a prepayment penalty because insurance companies want to invest for the long term. They usually have protective covenants similar to those of banks. LICs usually prefer that the borrower have a bank line of credit, so that they are assured of constant day-to-day monitoring of the borrower's financial condition. Loans usually are amortized over the term, and usually have a "non-callable" period because insurance companies do not want to be prepaid in a short term since they amortize the initial costs of funding and closing the loan over the term of the loan. Lenders also do not want borrowers to refinance a high interest loan when interest rates have declined. Prepayment with a penalty is usually allowed after the short term (usually five years). LICs do not usually make loans to new or young speculative companies.

Some state regulations governing insurance companies have allowed them to set aside a small portion of their assets for venture capital investment. Assets of insurance companies are so large that even a small percentage represents millions of dollars. Some insurance companies also have started Minority Enterprise Small Business Investment Companies (MESBICs).

LICS are very important in the real estate market. In the early days, they were primarily dependent upon real estate mortgages. In 1860, approximately 60% of their assets were in mortgages; in 1900 the percentage was 30%, and in 1971 it was 35%. They had about $10 billion worth of conventional real estate mortgages in 1973, mainly in office buildings and shopping centers. LICs prefer to provide permanent financing rather than construction financing (see Real Estate Financing) and to make larger loans — usually purchasing smaller residential loans in bulk. They also loan up to 100% of the value when tenants are of very high quality, and were the originators of the sale-leaseback of property. Many larger LICs are becoming very aggressive in the acquisition and development of large commercial properties as a hedge against inflation. LICs obtain referrals and investments through branch offices or independent Loan Correspondents. These correspondents can include mortgage brokers or mortgage bankers who are paid a finder's fee for their services, and often have continuing relationships with the insurance company. Mortgage bankers service the loans; finders do not. In such a case, either the insurance company or some other local correspondent services the loan.

LICs have been entering new areas of financing by acquiring other types of financial institutions, such as mutual fund management companies and mortgage banking firms, and by starting property insurance divisions.

PCIC insurance contracts are usually written for the short term (usually less than five years), and the obligations of the insurer terminate at the end of the term. There are lower cash accumulations; any large claims could reduce the assets significantly and also necessitate liquid investments. PCICs also do not have the benefits of lower income taxes enjoyed by the LICs, and hence they invest more heavily in tax-exempt bonds. Of the assets of PCICs, 75-85% are invested in government and corporate bonds and in common and preferred stocks. Less than 2.5% are invested in real estate. Thus, although they are an important factor in the secondary market, PCICs are not very important in the primary placement market or in the real estate market.

Investment Bankers

Introduction

Investment bankers are financial intermediaries in public and private placement markets for long-term funds for business. In the public markets, they distribute securities issued by corporations and public bodies to individuals or institutional investors. Their income is derived from the difference between the price paid to the issuers and the price received from investors. In private placement, they derive their income as a percentage of the amount of money raised. Thus, the major characteristics of investment bankers are their distribution capacity for selling or placing securities to be issued by a corporation and their knowledge of the securities markets. They can counsel about sources of short-term financing, mergers, and acquisitions, etc. They may act as dealers by buying and selling outstanding securities for their own account, and also as brokers by acting as agents for investors in the purchase and sale of securities. Investment bankers usually are used to obtain equity or long-term debt financing (especially unsecured debt) by businesses that may not have internal expertise in such types of financing.

Investment banking in the United States was controlled to a large extent by Europeans until American-owned firms gained prominence in the last decades of the nineteenth century. There are about 570 United States members of the Securities Industry Association; however, some of them are commercial bankers. Commercial bankers may underwrite and deal in state and local government bonds and federal government bonds, but they cannot underwrite or deal in corporate securities. Some investment bankers specialize in areas such as municipal and government securities, while others specialize in corporate securities. The precise number varies constantly due to the recent wave of mergers in the industry and economic conditions, but it is estimated approximately 300 investment bankers underwrite new security issues. Such underwritings can be done only by investment bankers who have an adequate amount of capital, and can afford to tie up large amounts of cash in single issues. Investment bankers operate on a local, regional, national or international level.

Most medium and large businesses maintain long-term relationships with their investment banker, and seek counsel regarding their financial needs and structure. This is especially true in the sale of new issues, involving the type of instrument, price and timing. In the public distribution of securities, investment bankers can act as wholesalers, purchasing from the issuer in large blocks, and selling to retail dealers in smaller lots. Wholesalers have a large asset base, while retail dealers can sell to individual investors on a local or regional level. Some investment bankers such as Merrill, Lynch & Co., can act as wholesalers and retailers.

In private placements, it is not always necessary, and sometimes not possible, to obtain the services of an investment banker. The borrower may choose to contact the lender directly, or, if the size of the loan is too small or the quality of the borrower inadequate, the investment banker may prefer not to be involved.

Flow of Funds

Investment bankers can be publicly or privately owned. In either case, the funds used are the stockholders' equity (or partners' equity). Funds borrowed from commercial banks are unsecured or use the securities as collateral.

Types of Financing Provided

Investment bankers primarily assist in raising long-term capital, whether as debt or equity issues. They also provide counseling in raising short-term funds and funds for special situations, such as mergers and acquisitions. They act as financial intermediaries, and in the case of underwritten issues, they guarantee the sale of the securities themselves. As a general rule, only corporations with a history are helped through public issues, with more lenient criteria for private placements.

Practices

There are a variety of methods used in the distribution of new security issues. Private non-regulated corporations often maintain long-term relationships with their investment banker(s), and terms for the sale of new issues usually are determined through negotiation between the company and the managing underwriter(s) negotiating for the syndicate. Syndicates are used in the distribution of large issues in order to spread the risks and achieve efficient distribution. If successful, the syndicate acquires (underwrites) the entire issue at the negotiated price and terms. Regulated companies, such as public utilities and railroads, and public bodies sell their issues to underwriters on the basis of competitive bids.

In cases where the issuer offers its new securities first to existing shareholders, such as in cases with a right of first refusal, the investment banking syndicate may commit itself to "stand-by" underwriting to acquire the securities not acquired by the shareholders. If the issue involves more risks than the investment bankers may want to absorb, such as in common stock sales of young companies, the investment bankers may agree only to a "best-efforts" offering. Usually these kinds of offerings are smaller than underwritten offerings.

Investment bankers' criteria for the selection of companies which they agree to underwrite can vary based on the size of the investment banker, the size of the company, its future prospects, the nature of the financial markets, etc. Normally, the huge international investment bankers prefer to deal with large issues and companies with earnings of at least $1,000,000. Regional and local investment bankers deal with smaller companies. Startups are considered only when the company has very attractive prospects or when the markets are favorable for such speculative issues. Investment bankers can be approached directly by the issuer, or through a respected third party, such as a commercial banker.

The costs of flotation vary by type of issue, size of issue, and industry. The range of the average commission is from approximately 1.0% for debt issues to approximately 9.0% for common stock issues, with the maximum being approximately 14.0% for some common stock issues. The expenses of preparation and registration of the issue are added costs. Although it may be possible to float an issue publicly without an investment banker, the use of the investment banker offers such advantages as:

a. Investment bankers are familiar with the nature of the financial markets, and hence can provide sound advice on the type of security, the terms, timing, etc.

b. Since it is their full-time and major function, it is usually more economical to use investment bankers to distribute an issue than to use inexperienced, internal staff.

c. An investment banker can assure the company of the availability of funds from the sale of the issue.

d. Investment bankers who underwrite issues often make markets in the stock, and hence can support the market after distribution.

e. The quality and number of investment bankers who agree to underwrite an issue can lend prestige to a company.

(For additional information see "Private Placements and Public Offerings," and "Securities Law and Registration Rights.")

Investment Companies

Introduction

The terms investment company and investment trust are used interchangeably to denote financial institutions which combine the investment funds of a few or many shareholders who have similar investment objectives. These funds are invested in a wide variety of securities by professional managers for the benefit of all the shareholders. By pooling their resources, individual shareholders are expected to benefit from skilled investment expertise and diversification in the investments. Investment companies distribute income from investments, less expenses, as dividends to shareholders.

The investment company concept was started in Belgium in the early 1820s by William I. Investment companies spread through Europe in the second half of the nineteenth century. Investment companies were founded in major American cities toward the end of the nineteenth century. These investment companies were organized either as true investment companies, with a diversified portfolio, or as holding companies to invest in a few securities for the long term, or as financing companies to hold securities for a shorter period of time.

There are many types of investment companies, such as:

a. Open-end company: Also known as a Mutual Fund. This is the most common type of investment company, accounting for approximately 90% of all investment company assets. Mutual funds do not have a fixed number of outstanding shares because they are continuously selling new shares to, and buying outstanding shares from, investors. The transaction usually is concluded at the prevailing market price. This constant trading of shares makes the mutual fund's capitalization "open" at one or both ends. Mutual funds need to maintain some liquidity due to their pledge to repurchase shares. Therefore a majority of their assets are invested in the secondary market.

b. Closed-end: Shares of these investment companies are not offered, nor does the company make a pledge to repurchase them continuously. They have a relatively fixed amount of capital stock outstanding. They are like other corporations and have few distributions. Their shares are available in the open market and are traded on the stock exchanges or over-the-counter.

c. Fixed Trust or Unit Trust: Fixed trusts were popular in the 1920s and 1930s but are not as popular today. A portfolio of securities is placed in a trust for a period of 10-25 years, and trust shares are sold by the sponsor. Securities are usually of major corporations with the highest credit ratings. Sponsors do not have major decision-making authority, and the covenants in the indenture are used to operate the trust. The disadvantage of such trusts is the extended period of time when no changes can be made in the portfolio even under changing business conditions.

Flow of Funds

Investment companies obtain their cash from the sales of capital shares. Their investments are based on the objective of the fund, and can vary among all securities that have a secondary market, such as corporate bonds and stocks; federal, state, and local government securities; and commercial paper.

Types of Financing Provided

Open-end companies only invest in securities with a secondary market because of their pledge to redeem outstanding shares at any time. Based on the type of mutual fund and its objectives, they can invest their funds in any traded security such as common stock, preferred stock, bonds, money market instruments, etc. Closed-end companies — lacking liquidity requirements — can invest in securities with limited marketability, including private placements. Closed-end companies may have a diversified portfolio similar to a mutual fund, or may invest in a few special situations, foreign securities, specific industries or groups of industries; or may include venture capital companies, Dual-Purpose funds, Small Business Investment Companies, Real Estate Investment Trusts, etc.

Practices

Investment company practices vary based on whether they are open-end or closed-end and on their investment objectives. Investment objectives could be any of the following:

a. Capital growth, with current income being a secondary consideration;

b. Maximizing current income;

c. Fine balance between growth and income;

d. Preservation of capital with stable income;

e. Venture capital investments for large, long-term growth.

Investment companies can be Load or No-Load funds. Load funds are those sold with a sales charge, and No-Load funds are sold without a sales charge. The recent trend has been toward the No-Load funds. These are bought by, rather than sold to, investors. Most are small, with assets under $100 million.

Open-end investment companies can be categorized on the basis of their investment objectives and strategies. The Investment Company Institute (ICI) has provided ten categories and definitions of open-end investment companies, along with their numbers and assets. These assets are based on 1,026 funds with $293 billion in assets reporting to the Institute at year-end 1983. The following figures are based on these funds.

a. Aggressive Growth Fund: Is a mutual fund with a capital appreciation investment objective, that invests in common stocks of higher growth potential and risk. In the ICI survey, these companies accounted for 6.4% of total assets.

b. Growth Fund: Is a mutual fund whose primary investment is long-term growth of capital, with investments mainly in common stocks with growth potential. These accounted for 8.8% of total assets.

c. Growth-Income Fund: Is a mutual fund whose aim is to provide for a degree of both income and long-term growth. Growth-Income funds accounted for 10.0% of total assets.

d. Balanced Fund: Is a mutual fund that has an investment policy of balancing its portfolio, generally by including bonds, preferred stocks and common stocks. Such funds are more conservative than common stock funds and their assets tend to fluctuate less than common stock funds. The balanced funds in the survey accounted for 1.1% of total assets.

e. Income Fund: Is a mutual fund whose primary investment objective is to maximize current income rather than seek growth of capital. It invests in stocks and bonds normally paying higher dividends and interest. This group had 3.0% of the total assets.

f. Bond Fund: Is a fund which invests primarily in bonds and other fixed-income securities, with emphasis on income rather than growth. Some funds tend to concentrate in high-grade bonds, while others may have a mixture of high, medium, and lower grade bonds. High grade bonds have less risk and income than lower grade bonds. The bond funds in the survey had 3.8% of total assets.

g. Money Market Fund: Is a fund which invests primarily in short-term instruments, such as instruments issued or guaranteed by the U.S. government, bank certificates of deposit, commercial paper, etc. Their objective is to obtain high current income while conserving capital. Approximately 320 market funds accounted for 55.5% of total assets.

h. Municipal Bond Fund: Is a fund which invests in a broad range of tax-exempt securities issued by states, cities and other governmental authorities. The interest obtained from these bonds is passed through to shareowners free of federal tax. The fund's primary objective is tax-free current income,

with the funds accounting for 5.0% of total assets.

i. Option Income Fund: Is a fund which invests in common stocks and then writes options against its portfolio holdings. Its investment objective is current income with the funds accounting for 0.6% of total assets.

j. Short-term municipal bond funds (or tax-exempt money market funds) invest in short-term municipal securities. These funds accounted for 5.7% of total assets.

In addition, there is another type of fund not included in the Investment Company Institute list: the Tax-Free Exchange fund which is organized to permit investors to postpone taxes on large capital gains in individual securities by exchanging them for a diversified portfolio of stocks, thereby lowering their risk.

Most open-end investment companies operate in secondary markets, in which they are a major factor. Some mutual fund management companies have started special funds for investment in stocks without an established and liquid market, or they invest in other venture capital companies that specialize in providing capital to small and new businesses.

Closed-end companies do not offer shares or pledge to repurchase them continuously. Their capitalization is relatively fixed, and they do not have the liquidity requirements of the open-end companies. Closed-end companies can be classified into two major types:

a. Diversified, similar to an open-end company, with a portfolio consisting of a broad array of securities, mainly common stocks;

b. Companies whose portfolios consist mostly of special situation investments, such as:

Concentration in specific industry or group of industries; companies fully or partially managed by a closed-end company; venture capital investments; small business investment companies; letter stock funds; real estate investment trusts; dual-purpose funds; foreign securities.

A Dual-Purpose Fund satisfies two different investor objectives by offering two classes of securities through one fund. The two classes are Income shares and Capital shares. Income shares have the right to collect the entire investment income, less expenses, but do not share in capital appreciation since they are callable after a stated number of years. They have a minimum cumulative dividend. Capital shares do not participate in the distribution of investment income, but they share in changes in the portfolio value. Capital shareholders sacrifice income earned on the total capital in order to obtain leverage and retain capital gains.

The specialized and non-diversified companies concentrate their investments in a particular industry(ies) or geographic area. Examples are National Aviation Corporation, which specializes in aerospace and airline companies; Petroleum Corporation, in oil and related issues; American Utility Shares and Drexel Utility Shares, in utility industries. Several specialize in convertible issues, securities of Real Estate Investment Trusts, Over-The-Counter stocks and mining companies.

The Letter Stock Funds (see "Registration" under TOPICS), are those investing in restricted securities or "letter stock." A restricted security is one that has not been registered with the SEC under the Securities Act of 1933. It cannot be distributed publicly and can be acquired or sold only through private negotiations. Funds acquire such securities directly from the issuer or from an existing shareholder. The investor in such a security signs a "letter" contract that the security is being purchased as an investment and is not for resale within a specified time. With certain exceptions and in limited quantities, the fund cannot publicly sell these restricted securities without registration. However, these securities can be sold privately with restrictions still attached. Restricted securities are purchased and sold at a discount from market values of similar registered securities.

Leasing Companies

Introduction

Equipment leasing is the rental by owners (lessors) of equipment to users (lessees), with periodic rental payments over the term of the lease. The industry is an old one — there are recorded instances of Phoenicians leasing ships. In the United States, leasing began with transportation equipment, such as railroad cars, trucks, airplanes, and then expanded to computers, automobiles, and other equipment. Lessors include equipment manufacturers, independent leasing companies, banks and their subsidiaries, insurance companies, commercial finance companies, lease brokers, and wealthy individuals. The leasing industry is expanding rapidly; estimates are that there are 1,800 leasing companies in the United States.

Types of lessors include the following:

a. Captive Leasing Companies: these are subsidiaries of equipment manufacturing companies, and primarily lease equipment manufactured by the parent. These companies are formed mainly to assist the parent in its marketing.

b. Independent Leasing Companies: these buy the equipment needed by the prospective lessee and provide finance loans.

c. Banks and Subsidiaries: estimates are that about 1,400 banks, bank-holding companies, and subsidiaries are involved in leasing or in financing leasing companies.

d. Specialized Leasing Companies: specialize in one type of equipment, such as computers, etc., and usually provide other services such as maintenance and repair, insurance, etc.

e. Lease Brokers: provide their expertise in packaging the lease and bring together lessors, investors, and lenders. Sometimes lease brokers also invest their own funds in the lease.

f. Investment Banks: who are active in the packaging and placement of leveraged tax leases.

A Commerce Department study estimated that lease-related finance methods account for approximately 33% of all new industrial and business equipment acquisitions. General equipment leasing by manufacturers or captives accounts for about half of all lease transactions, and approximately 33% is accounted for by independent finance and leasing companies, banks, and bank-holding companies. The remainder consists of auto and truck leases.

Some of the reasons for the growth in leasing are: the Comptroller of the Currency's ruling in 1963 allowing banks to lease personal property; the investment tax credit; accelerated depreciation; increasing costs of specialized equipment, its rapid obsolescence rate and high cost of maintenance and repair; cash flow problems for many companies; flexibility and speed; off-balance sheet characteristics; and often, the tax benefits. ERTA should provide leasing with additional impetus.

The major types of equipment being leased are:

a. Aircraft: Terms for these leases range from 7 to 16 years, with 100% financing provided by equity investors with leveraged leases (where the lessors borrow a portion of the funds to purchase the equipment);

b. Computers: One of the largest categories of leased items. Many computer users have preferred to lease their equipment owing to problems of obsolescence and costs of maintenance and repair;

c. Railroad cars: Can be leased under full-service contracts or under finance leases;

d. Trucks: May be leased under operating or finance leases;

e. Automobiles: Leased by banks, independent auto leasing companies, and the captive leasing companies of the auto manufacturers;

f. Medical equipment: Leased owing to the cost of equipment and problems of obsolescence;

g. Other equipment, such as electric generators, rolling stock, pollution equipment, and new manufacturing plants, energy producing equipment, machine tools, and hotel and motel furnishings.

Types of Financing

The types of leases fall into three major categories:

Operating and True Leases: A feature often found in this kind of lease is that the obsolescence risk is absorbed by the lessor, and there may not be a significant commitment by the lessee to continue to rent the equipment. These leases could be full-payout leases, where the lessee pays all the costs of the equipment plus an interest cost, but where the lessee does not want ownership because of the specialized skills required in maintaining the equipment or for some other reason; or they could be non-payout, where the lessee's payments do not repay the entire amount of the equipment. In most operating leases, the lessor performs several other functions — e.g., service, maintenance, and payment of some expenses such as taxes, insurance, etc.

Financial Leases: The lessee absorbs the risk of obsolescence in this type of lease. The lessee pays the costs of maintenance, service, insurance, legal fees, administrative and clerical costs, and the cost of arranging the financing.

Tax Leases: As allowed under ERTA and TEFRA, a marginally profitable lessee can lease allowable assets from a profitable coporation at a lower cost by transferring tax credits (Investment Tax Credit and Depreciation) to the lessor while retaining residual rights. TEFRA reduced the benefits of such leases and tightened requirements.

Operating leases are made by the manufacturers and their captive leasing companies (as in the case of computers and data processing equipment) and specialized leasing companies, such as for automobiles and other rolling equipment through dealers. Financial leases are made by practically all types of leasing companies.

Practices

Independent leasing companies have two types of clients:

a. Manufacturers of equipment and machinery who would like to use leasing as a marketing tool. The leasing company provides the contracts, trains the sales force, and in some cases, sponsors cooperative advertising.

b.The customer of the equipment who negotiates and arranges the deal with the manufacturer, at which time the leasing company purchases the equipment and leases it the lessee.

In addition to leasing companies, leases can be arranged by commercial banks and other equity investors, investment bankers, and lease packagers. Leasing companies must be licensed to do business in each state in which their leased equipment is located and are required to file reports and pay the appropriate taxes. Leasing companies can be local, regional, national, and international.

Leases for expensive equipment and plants are often leveraged, where normally the lessor invests 10-30% of the cost and borrows the balance from other financial institutions that would prefer to be lenders rather than owners, such as insurance companies, pension funds, etc. This compares with a 100% investment by the lessor in non-leveraged leases. The equipment is owned by the lessor who is normally in a high income tax bracket; and the lender has a first lien and an assignment on lease payments. The lessor benefits from the leverage, the interest and depreciation expenses, and the investment tax credit. For leveraged leases, the lessee requests lease packagers to submit lease rate bids. Lease rate is the annual payments expressed as a percentage of total equipment cost. (As an example, if the equipment cost is $100,000, and the monthly payments are $2,000, the lease rate is (2,000 x 12)/100,000, which is 24%.) Packagers submit lease rates based on the percentage of equity and debt, the expected rate of return on the equity, and the estimated interest rate on the debt. The interest rate on debt is estimated because the packager is not certain who the lenders might be or what their interest rates are. Thus, the lessee has to use judgment in selecting packagers because the one chosen may not be able to deliver the quoted lease rate. After one is chosen, the packager obtains bids on interest rates from interested lenders. This cost determines the actual cost to the lessee.

Leases offer many advantages, such as (also see "Leases"):

a. More favorable cash flow in initial years due to lack of a requirement for a down payment;

b. Lease contracts do not restrict the company's financing from other sources;

c. Lease financing is often off-balance sheet financing;

d. Leasing could be a hedge against obsolescense;

e. Leasing companies often adjust payments to the firm's cash flow needs with terms of 1-20 years, based on the life of the equipment;

f. The cost of leasing may be competitive, especially if the company cannot avail itself of the advantages of ownership, and no compensating balances are required.

Some variables affecting the costs of leases are:

a. The economic and residual value of the asset after the life of the lease, the risk of obsolescence to the lessor, and whether the lease is a full-payout or a non-payout lease;

b. The desired cash flow to the lessee and the lessor;

c. The rate of return expected by the lessor, and the cost of funds to him from the lenders in the case of a leveraged lease;

d. The costs and risks of insurance, maintenance, and types of services to be provided by the lessor;

e. Alternative sources of financing available to the lessee;

f. The extent to which leasing is used as a marketing tool by a manufacturer or a captive financing company, which may lower the expected rate of return from the lease to make the sale;

g. The tax rates of the various parties involved (the lessor and the lessee).

In large leases, the tax aspect becomes the most important factor since the lessee usually has other avenues of financing available and chooses leasing because of the tax advantages associated with it. Leasing usually is not advantageous if the potential lessee has sufficient cash for all its needs, and can use the tax benefits of ownership. Leases involving large sums usually are oriented to tax savings through the use of accelerated depreciation, investment tax credit, and interest cost deductions. If the company that needs the equipment cannot make use of the accelerated depreciation, investment tax credits, and interest cost deductions, it may be able to pass along these benefits to the lessor; in turn, the lessor, with a large amount of income from which to deduct these expenses, can return some of these benefits in the form of lower leasing costs to the lessee. Leases which are designed and negotiated for tax-benefits are submitted to the IRS for their examination and approval before the lease is finalized. Lessors' assumptions about the residual value of equipment at the end of the lease have a great effect on the cost of the lease. Lessors usually are conservative when computing the residual values; however, when there is competition, they may be more liberal with the estimate of the residual value, which decreases the lease rate.

The tax rates of the parties and the residual value of the asset affect the profitability of the lease to both parties. The lessor should be in a high tax bracket. Any future reduction in its profitability and tax rate can adversely affect the profitability of the lease. The lessee's tax rate should be low to derive tax benefits from leasing. The difference between the actual and projected residual values of the asset at the end of the lease also affects the profitability to the lessor.

The Economic Recovery Tax Act of 1981 (ERTA) has drastically altered the rules regarding leasing by liberalizing many IRS criteria for leveraged leases and by allowing the transfer of tax credits from unprofitable to profitable corporations. It should be noted, however, that final regulations from the IRS are not available yet, and Congress is reconsidering some aspects of ERTA. The major criteria for leveraged leases according to ERTA, are as follows:

a. Lessor must be a regular corporation and not a Subchapter S corporation or personal holding company;

b. Lessor's minimum investment in the leased property must not be less than 10% of the adjusted basis of the property at all times;

c. The term of the lease (including extensions) must not exceed 90% of the useful life of the property for depreciation purposes or 150% of the Asset Depreciation Range class life of the property as of January 1, 1981;

d. Property leased must be new property that qualifies for the investment credit, and the lease arrangement must be entered into within three months after the property is placed into service.

Unlike before, the lessee can help finance the property and have an option to acquire the property at the end of the lease term for less than fair market value.

Lessors also have to be concerned about the credit rating of the potential lessee. Federal laws allow lessors of real property to claim and collect only 3 years of lease payments if the lessee is declared bankrupt. Leases of personal property may be disaffirmed because leased facilities are not considered assets of the lessee, and lessors of personal property have to prove damages to collect on lease defaults.

Pension Funds

Introduction

In its simplest form, a pension is an annuity paid to retired persons as long as they live or to surviving dependents. such as spouses. Pension funds also may be designed for disability. There are more than 700,000 pension funds in the U.S. with assets greater than $930 billion. Types of pension funds include:

a. Private insured pension funds;

b. Private noninsured trusteed or self-administered funds;

c. Pension funds for state and local government employees;

d. Pension funds for federal government employees;

e. Others, such as Social Security and Railroad Retirement Fund.

In 1982, assets of private noninsured funds were approximately $344 billion; assets of government funds were approximately $358 billion. Private pension funds can be insured or noninsured (trusteed or self-administered). Insured pension plans are administered by life insurance companies, usually as a special part of their annuity programs. In general, insured pension plans are used by companies that are smaller than those that administer their own pension plans. Their funds are usually comingled with the other assets of life insurance companies. Noninsured pension funds are substantially larger than the insured funds, with total assets being more than twice as large as the insured funds. These funds can be self-administered by the employer, by the union, or by an outside financial institution, such as a trust company. Usually, if the benefits are guaranteed by the company, trustees tend to be controlled by the employer. Sometimes if the union is dominant, the fund is controlled by the union. In large funds, corporate management sometimes uses full-time professional managers and staffs.

Commercial banks — primarily a few New York City banks — dominate in the management of private pension funds. They are followed by investment advisory services and life insurance companies, which have become aggressive competitors in recent years.

The Civil Service Retirement System covers federal government employees and had accumulated assets of $97 billion at the end of 1982. The assets accummulated by this fund are considerably short of those required for discharge of benefits set by Congress.

State and Local Government Retirement Funds (SLGF) have considerably more assets than the Civil

Service Retirement System, with $260 billion in 1982. In the past, most SLGFs were managed by persons inexperienced in investment analysis. In recent years, many of the larger and more progressive funds have engaged outside investment advisory groups or banks. Usually the influence of the outside adviser tends to be limited.

Flow of Funds

Pension funds obtain their funds from contributions made by employees and employers and from retained earnings. Assets are held in the form of cash and miscellaneous assets, government securities, corporate bonds, common and preferred stock, and mortgages.

Types of Financing Provided

Since insured pension funds are managed by insurance companies, they provide financing similar to that of the insurance companies. If fully funded, whether through the contribution of the employee or the employer, the self-administered type of fund tends to have more conservative investment policies. Funds where there is a fixed contingent liability that may not be fully funded are likely to have more aggressive investment policies. Most of the assets (approximately 78%) of these funds are in corporate bonds and stocks. Less than 5% of their assets were in real estate mortgages in 1968, but this segment is growing rapidly. Real estate ownership is another rapidly growing segment of their portfolio. SLGFs place greater investment emphasis on federal, state, and local bonds than do private funds. Even in this category, mortgage loans have shown the greatest growth. Thus, the financing they provide includes:

a. Securities with a secondary market, including bonds and stocks;

b. Real estate and mortgages;

c. An increasing emphasis on private placements for long-term loans, especially among the larger pension funds.

Practices

Before 1950, pension funds were invested primarily in bonds, with the Corporate Pension Funds (CPF) investing mainly in U.S. and corporate bonds and SLFGs in federal, state, and local government bonds. Corporate stocks played a minor role for the funds. The trend has been toward common stocks for the CPFs since then, with approximately 58% of their assets being in common stock in 1982. SLGFs invest more heavily in real estate mortgages than CPFs. Since the investment income of CPFs and SLGFs are exempt from federal income taxation, the tax-exempt status of state and local government bonds is not meaningful. Hence, the CPFs are interested in higher yields. However, SLGFs invest in these bonds as a symbolic gesture. Federal pension funds invest primarily in federal securities.

Pension funds are restricted by state regulations in the types of securities they can purchase. Pension funds are often administered by officers of trust companies who minimize risk because the penalties for losses are severe, without compensating rewards for large gains. There is a propensity toward high-quality bond portfolios. Changes are likely in view of the competition from investment advisory groups and insurance companies, and also from the requirements arising from the Employee Retirement Income Security Act of 1974. In self-administered funds, all rights and responsibilities rest with the trustee — usually the employer — and are administered by officers of the corporation or by a board appointed by the corporation. Such control is with the union if it is a union-controlled fund. Large employer-administered funds are becoming more aggressive in private placements and are investing in varied types of financial instruments, including corporate debt issues with or without equity sweeteners, and common and preferred stock issues. Some bank-administered funds also are becoming more aggressive in private placements. SLGFs typically are administered by boards of trustees comprised invariably of governmental representatives and frequently including employee representatives. Pension funds are also investing in venture capital partnerships to seek capital gains.

The more aggressive bank pension departments have entered the private placement market with investment policies that are slightly more conservative than those of life insurance companies. Increasing emphasis also is being given to real estate mortgages and mutual funds. SLGFs have had an extremely limited role in the private placement market when compared with LICs and CPFs. Government officials and bodies managing public pension funds have preferred lower risk and safety of principal to higher risk and additional income. In the past, pension funds primarily have supplied funds to the secondary markets for corporate, state, and local government bonds and corporate stocks.

(See role of pension funds in real estate in "Real Estate Financing.")

Real Estate Investment Trusts (REITs)

Introduction

The earliest real estate trusts were the 19th century Massachusetts trusts. In 1960, Congress approved special income tax benefits to REITs by an amendment to the Internal Revenue Code (Sections 856-858). Under this amendment, a REIT that satisfies prescribed requirements will not be taxed on the income distributed to the shareholders or beneficiaries of the trust. Tax on this distributed income is paid only by the shareholders, thus avoiding double taxation. The 1960 law allowed the same tax treatment to REITs as that enjoyed by mutual funds. REITs can be viewed as real estate mutual funds without open-end redemption privileges. Sponsors sell shares to the public, and most REIT shares are traded on the major stock exchanges or over-the-counter. In 1969-70, REITs showed tremendous growth due to favorable conditions, such as a tight money market for real estate from other traditional sources, and the ability of REITs to raise funds through public offerings. REITs are relatively new financial institutions, with about 115 REITs having assets of approximately $8 billion in 1983.

Assets of REITs must be mainly real estate or real estate-related, with certain income restrictions, such as a minimum of 90% investment income and at least 75% from real estate. REITs qualify for corporate federal income tax benefits, such as an exemption from tax on income distributed to shareholders if certain requirements are satisfied, such as the annual distribution of at least 90% of net income to shareholders. Often REITs have been known to distribute their entire annual net income to shareholders.

Flow of Funds

REITs obtain their funds from capital stock and surplus, and from a variety of debt securities, such as commercial paper, bank term loans and revolving credits, convertible and non-convertible debt, and mortgages on real estate owned by the REIT. Because they borrow heavily from other financial institutions, such as banks and savings institutions, and because they have no access to low-cost deposits from individuals, REITs have a higher cost of capital. The uses of the funds are in real estate owned, land leasebacks, and senior and junior mortgages, including loans for land development, construction, and term loans.

Types of Financing Provided

REITs purchase real estate for their own portfolio or provide real estate construction loans and mortgages. They can and do provide some of the following types of real estate loans:

a. First mortgage loans on land;

b. First mortgage development loans, which are often made to develop land for single-family home construction;

c. First mortgage construction loans, which are short-term loans to finance the construction phase of the projects;

d. First mortgage short- and intermediate-term mortgages on completed properties, which are sometimes used as bridge financing between a REIT construction loan and long-term financing;

e. First mortgage long-term loans, usually on apartments and commercial property;

f. Junior mortgages (second and lower mortgages), which have higher risk and a greater return to the REIT. Some REITs specialize in this type of lending, but it is not a major category of investment activity for REITs.

REITs also do Land-Purchase Leasebacks, which involves a REIT purchasing the land from a real estate developer and leasing it back to him under a long-term lease. The developer increases his leverage through a land sale-leaseback by not tying up his cash in the land, while still retaining ownership of the improvements. However, most often the trust is asked to subordinate its position to that of the first mortgage holder on the improvements, in order to obtain a loan for improvements at favorable terms. If the REIT does not wish to subordinate its position, the first mortgage holder obtains an option to purchase the land at a prearranged price, or a long-term lease with renewal options, so that the loan can be repaid during the term of the lease. If the REIT subordinates its position, it obtains an equity participation, or shares in the gross receipts from the property (often above a specified minimum base amount), in addition to its lease payments on the land-lease.

Practices

REITs invest in single- and multi family residential developments, condominiums, commercial property such as motels, hotels, shopping centers, office buildings, and industrial property. At the end of 1983, 40% of REIT investments were in mortgage loans, and 60% in property ownership. REITs obtain equity interest in property through acquisitions of existing properties, or through construction of new property independently or in joint ventures with developers. Often, in joint ventures, developers construct and manage the property, and the REIT provides most of the capital. REITs are not allowed to manage properties, thus are forced to be "passive" investors. Their property is leased (mostly long-term — 10 years or more), or managed by their partners or by hired property managers. REITs have been converting to business trusts that are taxed similar to corporations, but which also have the flexibility to own and operate properties.

Of the mortgage loans, 24.5% were first mortgage construction loans, 13.4% were first mortgage land and development loans, 32.3% were first mortgage long-term loans (over 10 years), 16.2% were first mortgage short- and intermediate-term loans on completed properties, and 13.6% were junior loans. The maturity of the construction loans is designed to match the expected time of completion of the construction, and may be up to three years or longer.

REIT construction loans by type of construction in 1978 were the following:

Condominiums	19.3%
Single family homes	13.9%
Rental units	19.8%
Office buildings	9.4%
Shopping centers	16.9%
Hotels-motels	9.6%
Other commercial	6.0%
Industrial	4.8%
Mobile home parks	0.3%

(Source for all figures: National Association of REITs)

REITs are directed by a board of trustees elected by and responsible to the shareholders. Trustees generally refrain from managing daily operations of REITs, preferring instead to contract with an investment advisor who manages daily operations, monitors investments, seeks investment opportunities, packages them and seeks approval for investment from the trustees. Contracts are usually on an annual basis with rewards to the advisor on the basis of performance.

REITs can be classified as follows:

a. By type of advisor, which would be commercial banks, independent mortgage bankers, brokers or real estate oriented companies, individuals, conglomerates, life insurance companies, and others;

b. By geographic region covered in their investment activities, such as local, regional or national;

c. By types of property considered for investment;

d. By types of securities acquired, such as stock (equity trusts) or debt instruments with mortgages (mortgage trusts), or diversified (hybrid trusts). Most of the early REITs were equity trusts.

The principal types of investments of mortgage trusts are:

a. Long-term mortgages for 10-30 years, which may include equity participation;

b. Short-term mortgages for development and construction, which is for an average of 12-24 months, for about 60-70% of appraised value after development or during construction. Interest rates on interim mortgages may be 2.5-5% higher than on permanent mortgages.

Mortgage Companies

Introduction

The term Mortgage Banker or Mortgage Company may be used for all institutions that provide mortgage financing. It usually is used to denote companies that find borrowers and provide permanent financing from personal resources and bank borrowings. The company may keep the loan for its own inventory or sell the loan at the earliest opportunity to long-term lenders, and then service the loan on behalf of the lending institutions. Mortgage brokers are intermediaries; they do not maintain a continuous relationship with the borrower or lender and they do not service the loan.

Mortgage companies perform a function similar to investment bankers since their primary activity involves the acquisition and sale of new securities. Both types of firms also act as "finders" for some types of loans. They trade primarily in mortgages, and their principal activity is the origination and subsequent sale of mortgages of income and residential property. Servicing of the loan is usually retained. They originate mortgage loans in areas that need financing, and place them with institutional investors who enjoy excess funds. They act as financial intermediaries providing linkage between local real estate financing needs and large financial institutions that invest large sums on a regional or national basis. This has contributed to the development of a national mortgage market. FHA and VA guaranteed loans have tended to dominate the market because their risks and terms are relatively homogenous.

Mortgage companies usually are correspondents of financial institutions, such as life insurance companies, savings institutions, and commercial banks. Most of them are closely held, private corporations. Federal or state supervision of mortgage companies is minimal.

Flow of Funds

Due to the small margins with which they work, mortgage companies expect to have a high inventory turnover, and relatively low capital investment when compared to their business volume. Mortgage companies often obtain financing from commercial banks, and some banks also have a mortgage banking subsidiary. Bank loans can be used to carry mortgages for which prior commitment has been received from correspondent financial institutions but whose commitment will be delivered later; or for those in the mortgage banker's inventory, without advance commitment, which are to be sold at a future date. In the former type (i.e., prior commitment received), funds are used mainly for construction loans. The latter type of loans is used for warehouse operation.

Types of Financing Provided

Mortgage companies provide financing for the real estate industry through mortgage financing and construction financing. They can also assist in arranging other types of real estate financing, such as Sale-Leaseback, etc.

Practices

The main activities of mortgage bankers are originating mortgages by using their own funds, which is a retail operation; and selling them in block packages to institutional investors, with or without prior commitment. Mortgage bankers also provide or obtain construction financing for builders. The services of mortgage brokers can range from finding the loan opportunity and providing the referral to the investing institution, to packaging the loan for the financial institution, which closes the deal and provides mortgage financing. Mortgage companies deal mainly with three institutions:

- Life insurance companies
- Mutual Savings Banks, and Savings and Loan Associations
- Federal National Mortgage Association (FNMA)

Pension funds are becoming a more important source. Most of the mortgage bankers' valued customers are referrals from real estate brokers or builders. "Walk-in" customers have a poor reputation among mortgage bankers because they often are lower-quality loans being shopped around for lower interest rates, or a higher loan-to-value ratio or appraisal. Mortgage companies may provide loans to borrowers only after receiving a commitment from a "correspondent" financial institution, or they may provide uncommitted loans, using personal resources and bank credit, for future resale. They like to hold the inventory for only a short time between closing mortgage loans and delivering to ultimate investors. Whenever it makes a loan without the prior approval of some purchaser, it runs the risk of acquiring merchandise that may not be marketed at an advantageous price. Due to the costs of acquiring mortgages on a retail basis, large financial institutions prefer to pay mortgage companies a premium for a large, accumulated block of smaller mortgages. The mortgage company accumulates the mortgages at its own risk and using its own capital. The risk is due to the change in the value of the mortgages with a fluctuation in interest rates, resulting in the accumulated block possibly having to be sold at a loss, or held until the interest rates adjust.

Often the mortgage company charges the borrower a fee to process the loan and pay for expenses, whether or not the loan is made. These expenses can include appraisal fees, title insurance, title inspection fees, feasibility studies, etc. Fees charged are higher if the loan and property is of the type or quality not preferred by lenders, requiring a greater effort to find an interested lender. Mortgage bankers derive income from originating and selling mortgages in two ways:

a. A profit from a markup above the acquired cost, or an origination and closing fee of 0.25-2.5% from the borrowers, and often from the investor in the form of a premium of about 0.5% at the time of origination of the mortgage.

b. Servicing fees which range from 0.125 to 0.7%, most being 0.3-0.6%. The servicing operation has to be very efficient to earn a profit.

In contrast with the investment banking firm, the mortgage company operates primarily on the basis of continuing relationships with the institutions it serves as "correspondent." It derives income from the administration or servicing fee charged for collecting and remitting interest and principal of monthly amortized loans and by representing the investor throughout the life of the mortgage.

Government guarantees of mortgage loans, such as FHA and VA mortgages, have created a national market for mortgages with an active secondary market and increased liquidity. The Federal National Mortgage Association (FNMA) assists in maintaining liquidity by purchasing these mortgages under certain conditions. However, changing interest rates can influence and alter the immediate liquidity value of the mortgage resulting in a loss or gain to the mortgage company.

Mutual Savings Bank (MSB)

Introduction

A Mutual Savings Bank (MSB) is one kind of savings bank; the other being the S & L Association. MSBs invest primarily in capital-market instruments. There are approximately 424 mutual savings banks chartered in 16 states, with total assets of nearly $174 billion. Most of them are in the Middle Atlantic states and New England, with New York, Massachusetts, and Connecticut having approximately 312 MSBs.

MSBs are the only deposit institution chartered only by states. They are mutual institutions and owned by depositors. Earnings in excess of reserve requirements are distributed to the depositors. The MSB is managed by a board of trustees.

MSBs were originally started to provide a safe and convenient savings institution to the working poor. This need was not being satisfied by commercial banks. MSBs offered savings accounts with a high interest rate, liquidity for the consumer and safety of their funds. MSBs still operate under the same general principles even though they are financial giants today. The first MSBs in the United States were the Philadelphia Savings Fund Society and the Provident Institution for Savings in Boston, established in 1816. MSBs are strong in the Northeast, but their growth in other parts of the country where commercial banks served the need was generally weak. The Northeast also had more wage-earners who needed a safe place to save, whereas other areas had farmers and small businessmen with loan demands that could be obtained from commercial banks. Most of the MSBs were started before 1875. The MSBs are in the following states:

Alaska, Connecticut, Delaware, Indiana, Maine, Maryland, Massachusetts, Minnesota, New Hampshire, New Jersey, New York, Oregon, Pennsylvania, Rhode Island, Vermont, Washington and Wisconsin.

Flow of Funds

In 1982, deposits accounted for 89.1% of the assets of MSBs; general reserve accounts for 5.3%, and miscellaneous liabilities for the balance. These assets were held in the form of mortgages (62.1%), other loans (9.7%), securities (19.7%), with the rest being cash and other assets.

Types of Financing Provided

MSBs are involved in:

a. Real estate loans and mortgages;

b. Other capital and money market instruments;

c. Purchase and sale of mortgages from other financial institutions, including correspondents.

MSBs concentrate most heavily on real estate loans, which represent 60-75% of their assets. Their assets are similar to those of S & Ls, since both are savings institutions. Commercial and multi-family mortgages account for a major proportion of total assets. The relative importance of commercial and multi-family mortgages is growing.

Practices

Conservation of assets is a primary factor in MSB lending and investment, with earnings maximization of secondary importance. MSB investment in securities and mortgages are regulated and have to satisfy legal requirements. Some major provisions found in most laws regulating MSBs are the regulation of MSBs by a state officer — such as the Superintendent of Banks, limits on the size of individual deposits, definition of instruments and securities purchased by the bank, and regulations which prevent trustees from borrowing from their banks.

MSBs have become an important factor in interstate lending due to increased use of correspondents and relaxed regulations permitting out-of-state loans. Most of their lending is within a 25-50 mile radius. Lending territories are determined so that the loan can be properly serviced. When there is a decline in savings growth, MSBs and S & Ls tend to concentrate on in-state lending at the expense of out-of-state lending.

Due to their needs for safety of capital and the low turnover of savings accounts, MSBs find their ideal investments to be strong mortgages. Their liquidity needs are satisfied by holding short-term federal securities, amortization of real estate loans and cash flow management. MSBs traditionally have not made business loans, except loans secured by real estate and investment in marketable securities.

The ratio of loan-to-value varies and can range up to 90%, except for federally-guaranteed programs, such as FHA and GI loans. State regulations also specify maximum term for loans, and the limits on the percentage of assets or deposits invested in mortgages. Internal MSB policies may be stricter than legal restrictions.

Savings & Loan (S & L) Associations

Introduction

The S & L is one form of savings bank; the other being a Mutual Savings Bank. Both accept savings accounts only, which have a comparatively slower turnover. Thus, they primarily provide long-term loans secured by real estate and invest in capital market securities.

The first S & L was started on January 3, 1831, and there are now about 3,513 of them in the United States. The older S & Ls were organized as mutual institutions, with some of the later ones having permanent capital in the form of nonwithdrawable stock. Lately, some S & Ls have been allowed to convert from a mutual to stock status. S & Ls are organized under federal or state charters. Savings accounts of all federally chartered associations are insured up to $100,000 per account by the Federal S & L Insurance Corporation. State-chartered associations may obtain this insurance by joining the corporation. Federal and insured state associations are regulated by the Federal Home Loan Bank Board (FHLBB), and uninsured state associations by the FHLBB and state regulatory departments.

Flow of Funds

S & Ls obtain funds from savings deposits (82.1% of assets in 1983), borrowed funds from the Federal Home Loan Bank Board and others, and equity (4.0%). Of their assets, 63.1% are held in mortgages; cash and other assets account for the balance.

Types of Financing Provided

S & Ls are involved in:

a. Real estate permanent financing;

b. Construction loans;

c. Purchase and sale of mortgages from other associations, commercial banks, insurance companies, mortgage companies, and brokers.

S & Ls are the most important source of home mortgage credit. Real estate loans are approximately 64% of their total assets, with multi-family and commercial mortgages being approximately 21% of total mortgages. S & Ls are the only major financial institutions especially designed to make home mortgage loans. Almost all their investments are long-term.

S & Ls are allowed to organize service agency subsidiaries. These service agencies can provide some services that S & Ls are prevented from doing, such as purchasing and owning land and buildings for leasing and rental purposes.

Practices

S & Ls and Mutual Savings Banks specialize in real estate financing. Lending policies of S & Ls are greatly influenced by the nature of the economy. Loan screening becomes tighter with a decrease in new savings rates, and looser if real estate construction slows down. Direct placement lending by S & Ls is usually confined to an area within 100 miles from their office; but indirectly-placed loans are purchased anywhere in the country. S & Ls finance all types of real estate. Lending policies depend on government regulations (including FHA and VA), general economic conditions, and competition. S & Ls usually do not make loans with junior liens.

Loan Percentages and Terms: The loan amount has to be lower than a percentage of the lender's appraised value of the property. S & Ls normally can loan up to 75% of the value of commercial and industrial nonlivable properties and up to 80% of the value of livable properties, such as apartment buildings. The latter category includes some other categories, such as some types of nursing homes. The maximum term of the loan is 25 years for nonlivable properties and 30 years for livable properties. These loans can be amortized with equal, periodic payments so as to pay off the loan during its term, or have the amortization payments adjusted to a longer term, but including a balloon payment at the end of the term for the unpaid amount.

Federally insured S & Ls currently are allowed to purchase mortgage loan participations from other associations, commercial banks, insurance companies, and mortgage brokers. S & Ls can assist real estate developers with land acquisition and site development financing, construction financing, and permanent financing.

Trust Companies

Introduction

Trust companies and trust departments of financial institutions, such as commercial banks, are formed to manage trusts for individuals or for groups, such as employee benefit programs and pension funds. A trust is a legal device whereby assets are provided by a donor or a trustor, to be administered by the trustee for a beneficiary. In a trust, there is a transfer of ownership to the person who is trusted (the trustee). The trustee holds legal title for the beneficiary, who has the beneficial interest. The trust business serves individuals, partnerships, associations, business corporations, public, educational, social, recreational and charitable institutions, as well as units of government by settling estates, safeguarding assets, and investing them to obtain a desired rate of return. Trust services are performed mainly by trust companies, commercial banks' trust departments, and by title-guarantee companies, mortgage bankers, and safe-deposit companies.

The first trust company was the Farmers' Fire Insurance and Loan Company which was formed in 1823. However, this company did not accept its first trust until some years later. After the Civil War, the trust companies expanded steadily with the industrialization of the country. By 1900 there were about 500 trust companies, and now there are about 3,500-4,000. The trust business is concentrated, with a small percentage of institutions (approximately 4%) accounting for about 80% of the business.

Types of Financing Provided

Trust companies primarily are investors in securities with secondary markets, except where the donor provides assets which do not have a secondary market. In 1983, trust companies had invested 45.8% of their assets in common and preferred stocks, and 30.7% in corporate bonds and government debt obligations. Real estate accounts for a small portion of their assets.

Practices

Trust companies provide services that deal with the preservation and transfer of property. They provide services to individuals, corporations, or both. In most cases, a small staff handles large trust funds. Due to this lack of internal resources, trust institutions sometimes act as master trustees, and contract with investment specialists for actual management of some of the trust's assets. When trusts are managed internally, investment policies often are designed in broad terms to cover large amounts of funds in many trusts rather than providing individual attention to each small trust. Staffs of trust companies usually do not have the time to negotiate small private transactions. Therefore, trust institutions have not been a major force in private placements.

The trust agreement generally specifies the policies to be followed and the trustee's duties in trust assets management. The discretion given to the trustee may range from full control of assets, to the designation of specifics, including properties to be held, purchased or sold.

In some cases, where no provision is made, the trustee is limited by law governing trust investment. The major characteristic of trust company operations is conservation of wealth.

Venture Capital Companies

Introduction

Venture capital is the risk capital provided to new and young companies (and some special situations) through the purchase of equity or long-term debt instruments. The industry is composed of individuals, groups, or corporations placing capital into business situations with a high risk and a commensurate high potential return. Due to the high risk, the probability is large that the venture capitalist loses all or a substantial portion of the investment. However, this is offset by the extremely large profits sometimes attained on a small proportion of investments.

One of the earliest venture capital companies, started immediately after the Second World War, was American Research & Development Corporation in Boston. Some of the early, prominent venture capital companies were Rockefeller Bros., J.H. Whitney & Co., and Payson & Trask in New York. The number of venture capital companies increased rapidly after 1958, when the Small Business Investment Act was passed, providing government loans to venture capital companies organized as Small Business Investment Companies. Venture capital companies can be privately owned, limited partnerships, publicly owned, or owned by another corporation, including financial intermediaries. Some broad-based mutual funds have started special funds for investment in stocks with little or no marketability.

Venture capital is concerned with companies in initial states of development, including startups, or in special situations, such as turnarounds, mergers and acquisitions, where above-average growth is foreseen with an accompanying increase in the worth of the company's equity. A venture capital company is staffed primarily by businessmen and technologists.

Organized sources of venture capital are:

a. Private venture capital companies and limited partnerships which are independently owned and operated with the capital being provided by pension funds, corporations, wealthy individuals or families;

b. Venture capital companies which are owned by the investing public;

c. Companies which are subsidiaries of other companies, such as other financial institutions, or large corporations which have venture capital subsidiaries;

d. Venture capital companies which are owned by any of the above categories, such as individuals or families, financial institutions or large corporations, but which borrow funds from the government under the program offered by the Small Business Administration (SBA). These institutions can be either Small Business Investment Companies (SBICs), or Minority Enterprise Small Business Investment Companies (MESBICs). Both types of institutions need to obtain a license from the Small Business Administration. MESBICs invest only in companies controlled by minorities, as defined by the SBA;

e. Miscellaneous types of venture capital companies, such as Community Development Corporations (CDCs), which invest in a designated geographic area, and others such as Urban National Corporation, which is a privately owned company investing in companies controlled by minorities anywhere in the United States.

The risk involved in a venture capital investment is high because the companies in which the funds are invested may fail or not grow as expected, resulting in a worthless investment or illiquid securities.

Flow of Funds

Sources of funds to venture capital companies include the federal government, state governments, church groups, foundations, individuals, corporations, financial intermediaries, mutual funds, etc. Venture capital companies invest their funds primarily in long-term debt or equity securities of companies that have a potential for growth, thus rewarding the venture capitalist with a return commensurate with the risk. Other sources of venture capital for the entrepreneur are family, friends, and relatives; professional advisors and business acquaintances; customers and suppliers; employees and prospective employees; wealthy business people; and other private investors.

Types of Financing Provided

Venture capital companies provide four basic kinds of financing:

a. Senior debt: Which is usually for long-term financing for high-risk companies or special situations such as bridge financing. Bridge financing is designed as temporary financing in cases where the company has obtained a commitment for financing at a future date, which funds will be used to retire the debt. It is used in construction, acquisitions, anticipation of a public sale of securities, etc.;

b. Subordinated debt: Which is subordinated to financing from other financial institutions, and is usually convertible to common stock or accompanied by warrants to purchase common stock. Senior lenders consider subordinated debt as equity. This increases the amount of funds that can be borrowed, thus allowing greater leverage;

c. Preferred stock: Which is usually convertible to common stock. The venture's cash flow is helped because no fixed loan or interest payments need to be made unless the preferred stock is redeemable or dividends are mandatory. Preferred stock improves the company's debt to equity ratio. The disadvantage is that dividends are not tax deductible (see Preferred Stock);

d. Common stock: Which is usually the most expensive in terms of the percent of ownership given to the venture capital company. However, sale of common stock may be the only feasible alternative if cash flow and collateral limits the amount of debt the company can carry. The venture capital company usually reserves the right to sell its interest in the company, especially if it constitutes a minority share, to the other shareholders or to the company at a prearranged formula in the event that there is no public market for the company's shares.

Venture capital companies also may purchase warrants of the company.

Practices

Venture capital investments can be classified into three major types:

a. Startup or seed capital: Before the company has been in operation; the management team has been organized and the business plan prepared;

b. Post-startup stage: The company has been in operation for some time (e.g., 1-5 years) and consumer acceptance has been proved. Some practitioners subdivide this category further, on the basis of the number of years required for the company to achieve profitability;

c. Special situations: Capital can be obtained for acquisitions of mature companies, turnaround situations, or other situations where equity capital is needed or useful.

In tight money markets, venture capital money generally is invested in profitable companies or those which expect profits in the very near future (such as one year), and capital for other companies becomes more difficult to raise.

The first step in the process of obtaining venture capital is the selection of the appropriate venture capital company. Entrepreneurs should expend as much energy choosing a suitable venture capital company as the company spends on its choice of the venture. Some of the obvious factors in the selection process include the venture capital company's interest in the venture's industry, its stage of growth and the amount of funds required. Other factors should include its ability to raise funds from other sources to provide leverage on its "equity" financing and to satisfy future financing needs, the expertise and advice that it is capable of providing, its contacts in the business and financial community, and its experiences with other entrepreneurs, and, perhaps most importantly, the personal chemistry between the entrepreneurs and the venture capitalists. Introductions to venture capitalists from accountants, attorneys, bankers and consultants can be helpful if the venture capitalist respects the source. Direct calls are acceptable if such a referral source cannot be found.

The information that should be provided to the venture capitalists is usually broken into stages. For the initial screening, which essentially determines whether or not the nature of the company and the deal is of interest to the venture capital company, an outline of the business plan can be submitted. It should include the history and type of business; description of the product(s) and market size; management resumes; amount of funds needed and its use; and the financial projections for three to five years. Evaluation at this stage can take between a few minutes and a few weeks, with a rejection rate of approximately 90%.

If the venture capital company is satisfied with the information submitted in the preliminary proposal, a complete business plan will be requested. A well-prepared business plan should include the items listed in Chapter II under the "Information Requirements" heading.

The business plan must concisely document assertions and assumptions made by the entrepreneurs.

Information provided and omitted by the entrepreneur (such as major industry problems or risks) is used to evaluate the business and the entrepreneur. Data is obtained from discussions with trade magazine publishers and trade associations, suppliers and customers, competitors and their customers, etc., to verify and supplement information provided by the entrepreneurs. Most venture capitalists are able to obtain this information without damaging the applicant's business. This verification usually can take up to six weeks with a rejection rate at this stage of approximately 75%.

Those that pass the previous stage are analyzed in detail for company strengths and weaknesses, industry and user trends, technology, markets, and the capability, integrity and record of the management team. This function can be very tedious and time-consuming and usually takes a minimum of 8-10 weeks. Those that pass this stage are considered eligible for investment if a suitable deal can be negotiated. Approximately 2% of the deals submitted initially are approved for investment.

The items negotiated by the venture capitalists are the level of investment, the types of instruments, the terms, interest rate, and the percentage of equity given to the venture capital company. The percentage of equity required by the venture capital firm varies with many factors — including the nature of the applicant company, its growth prospects, amount of investment required, the stage of the company, the management team, etc. The amount of equity required by the venture capitalists varies in direct proportion to the risk in the investment. It could go as high as 90-95% for some companies. Other topics discussed are the form of investment, special conditions and covenants (see "Covenants"). The covenants for venture capital company debt and convertible investments are similar to those typically found in insurance company loans.

A key item negotiated by the venture capital company is the procedure to liquidate the ownership securities, which can include any of the following rights:

a. To register its stock for public distribution with the cost to be borne by the company;

b. "Piggyback" rights whereby its stock can be registered along with any other stock of the same class being registered;

c. To sell its stock to the company or the entrepreneurs at a prearranged formula;

d. To sell its stock to a third party interested in buying company stock from the entrepreneurs.

The key elements venture capitalists look for in a potential venture are:

a. The company should have a marketable product or service with competitive advantages and a long-term need.

b. The company should have major strengths, preferably in key areas.

c. The quality, integrity and energy-level of the managerial or enterpreneurial team should be very high; the team should be balanced with well-rounded business backgrounds and an achievement orientation. The entrepreneurs should be long-term oriented, and be willing to invest all their assets in the venture.

d. The business plan should be a reasoned one; it should reflect reality, and the strengths and weaknesses of the company.

e. The company should have the capability to satisfy its future financial needs through internal cash flow, or to attract outside capital at reasonable terms.

f. A projected return to the venture capitalist commensurate with the risks involved.

After the successful negotiation of a financial and working relationship between the principals, the venture capital company usually helps the small company to develop its full potential and achieve its original operating and investment objectives before the venture capitalist sells his equity in the venture to dissolve the relationship.

Due to the risks being taken, venture capitalists generally will aim for a return of approximately five times their investment in a period of 3-5 years. This return is obtained from appreciation in stock prices. The percentage of ownership of the company required by the venture capitalist varies, based on the risk. The percentage is higher — and may reach 90-95% — if the company is a startup with the venture capitalist investing all the required funds. Some venture capitalists prefer to control their investment through a majority stock position, while others prefer covenants in the debt instrument. Most venture capitalists require representation on the board of directors. In dealings with venture capitalists, it should be remembered that the typical venture capitalist loses or breaks even on his investments 80% of the time, and invests in a really solid winner 1-2% of the time. The rest are moderate successes. Thus, the entrepreneur needs to convince the venture capitalist of the probability of a good return on the investment, based on justifiable projections considering the risks involved.

Small Business Investment Companies (SBICs)

Introduction

Congress passed the Small Business Investment Act of 1958 to encourage the formation of private investment companies interested in providing long-term capital to qualified small businesses. Financing in the form of loans and equity purchases is provided to these companies, called Small Business Investment Companies (SBICs) and Minority Enterprise SBICs (MESBICs) through a program administered and licensed by the Small Business Administration (SBA). SBICs and MESBICs provide long-term financing through the use of senior or subordinated long-term loans, convertible debentures, stocks, and warrants.

SBICs are privately-owned and operated investment companies possessing a license from the SBA to provide venture capital and long-term loans to small businesses. Private sources, such as individuals, corporations and other financial institutions, provide equity to the SBIC by purchasing stock. The SBIC then can borrow funds for reinvestment directly from the government or from private institutions with government guarantees. The amount of funds that can be borrowed with government assistance is proportional to the amount of equity investment in the SBIC.

MESBICs are similar to SBICs, except that they are allowed to invest only in companies controlled and managed by socially or economically disadvantaged persons. To compensate for this restriction, MESBICs have been offered certain incentives, including the ability to borrow from the government at a lower rate and to sell preferred stock to the government.

The minimum capital required for the formation of a SBIC is $1,000,000; there is no maximum limit on the private capital that may be invested. Consideration is being given to raising the minimum capital requirements. The maximum amount of funds that can be borrowed by an SBIC with government assistance (direct loans or guaranteed) is 300 percent of combined private paid-in capital and paid-in surplus, up to a maximum of $35,000,000. An SBIC can borrow up to 400% of paid-in capital and paid-in surplus if it has 65% or more (30% for MESBICs) of its total funds available for investment invested in venture capital and if it satisfies the minimum requirements for combined private paid-in capital and paid- in surplus. Loans may be subordinated to other bonds, promissory notes or debts and obligations, and have maturity up to 15 years.

There are approximately 375 SBICs and 146 MESBICs. The majority of the SBICs are owned by relatively small groups of local investors. However, the stock of some SBICs is publicly traded, and approximately 150 are partly or wholly owned by commercial banks or major corporations.

Flow of Funds

The sources of funds to SBICs and MESBICs are

private groups or individuals, including corporations, and loans from the government or government-guaranteed loans from private institutions. These funds are invested in companies that are defined as small businesses (as defined by the SBA) in long-term loans or equity. An SBIC can obtain leverage on its equity capital by selling SBA-guaranteed subordinated debentures to the public, or selling its debentures directly to the Federal Financing Bank (FFB) on a monthly basis. The maximum amount of guarantees the SBA is allowed to provide each year is authorized by Congress. The Federal Financing Bank, which is an agency of the U.S. Government, sells debentures to investors to raise funds.

Types of Financing Provided

SBICs have invested in most kinds of instruments, depending on the company being financed and its requirements. The usual transactions are straight loans, which are usually secured and could be a second mortgage or a personal guarantee, and equity-type investments, including loans with warrants, convertible debentures, and common stock.

Practices

SBICs can invest only in small businesses — i.e., in businesses with a net worth of not more than 6.0 million, and average net income after taxes for the preceding two years of not more than $2,000,000. SBA determines the size of a business by including any affiliates; parent company, if any; and any other companies controlled by the same parent company. If a manufacturing company fails the above tests, it may still qualify as a small business if it has fewer than 250 employees. Legitimate business needs, except reinvestment or relending, can be financed by SBICs. SBICs prefer to use their funds for expansion and growth, where the company needs financing for additional working capital and fixed assets. Often SBICs are inactive for certain periods, but such inactivity is not publicized. Some SBICs also provide management consulting services to their portfolio companies.

Unlike insurance company loans, which are usually well secured by assets or a history of strong financial statements, SBIC investments are in highly risk-oriented instruments of newer companies in their initial stages of growth. Also, SBICs have a higher cost of funds than other institutions with savings or other low-cost deposits. The margin between the interest charged to the borrowers and the interest paid by the SBIC on the amount they borrow through the SBA often covers only their operating expenses. Thus, SBICs require equity participation to a much greater extent than insurance company "sweeteners," so the SBIC profits if the company grows as anticipated. SBICs are given some tax advantages, such as deducting investment losses against ordinary income and treating gains as capital gains.

MESBICs must invest in small businesses that are at least 50 percent owned and managed by individuals from certain socially and economically disadvantaged groups. They can invest up to 30 percent of paid-in capital in any one firm compared with 20 percent for SBICs. They can sell 3% cumulative preferred stock to the SBA, and obtain a subsidy on the interest rate on funds borrowed from the government. The borrowings of a MESBIC are usually below the cost of money for a comparable instrument to a SBIC.

SBIC investments can be classified as loans, stock or equity-type investments.

Loans: The interest rates on SBIC loans may be high, reflecting the high cost of money, cost of operation, and risk in the securities. SBIC loans are for at least five years (though a borrower may elect to prepay) and are usually subordinated to other financial institutions, increasing the risk of the loan. Subordinated loans usually are convertible, whereas senior loans may be straight loans.

Stock and Equity-type Investments: The most common equity-type investments are subordinated convertible loans, with or without warrants. The SBIC has the benefit of interest payments under a debt instrument and the capital gains potential of common stock through convertibility. Normally, SBICs expect to pay their operating expenses from interest and dividends, deriving capital gains from the increase in the value of the company through conversion of loans to stock, warrants or common stock. The conversion ratio for convertibility is negotiated at the time of investment, with the investment company having the option to convert. If it is not converted, the loan is repaid as designated. If the borrower has the option to prepay the loan, the investment company requires warrants to obtain capital gains. Except in certain cases, SBICs do not prefer investing in common stock due to inadequate liquidity for a minority position if there is no secondary market, and because there are no interest payments. They acquire common stock if there is a secondary market, if dividends are being paid or with a buy-back arrangement with the borrowing company or management team.

SBICs invest in all types of manufacturing and service industries, as well as in construction, retailing and wholesaling; they are not allowed to invest in agricultural businesses.

The term of SBIC loans must be within 5-15 years (with certain exceptions allowed), and may be extended for an additional 10 years. Often SBIC loans do not require principal repayments for the first two or three years, which helps the borrower's cash flow. Stock purchase warrants or convertible rights must be exercised within 10 years from the date of the investment. An SBIC may not invest more than 20 percent of its private paid-in capital and surplus in any one business. SBICs form investment syndicates when a company's needs are greater than the limit of individual SBICs. A venture capital investment for SBICs is defined as common and preferred stock, limited partnership interests, convertible debt securities and warrants to purchase stock with no repurchase requirement for five years; and other loans (whether or not convertible or having stock purchase rights) subordinated to other financial institutions, and with no principal repayments for the first three years. The maximum interest rate that can be charged is controlled by SBA regulation.

SBICs are generally prohibited from taking a controlling position in a small concern. One exception is when it is necessary to save its investment, in which case, a plan showing how the SBIC plans to divest its controlling position within seven years must be approved in writing by the SBA. An SBIC is allowed to make short-term emergency investments in a portfolio business inorder to protect its investment. SBICs do not plan to manage the company, preferring instead to act as investors with an active interest in the company.

An SBIC cannot invest more than 33 1/3 percent of its assets in real estate investments. However, loans made for reasons other than real estate investment, but which are secured by real estate mortgages are exempt from this limit.

Owing to the high cost of funds from an SBIC in interest payments, convertibility rights, and subsequent stock dilution, an SBIC should not be the sole source of money used for business. SBIC financing is most productive when it is used as equity for additional leverage from other financial institutions, such as commercial banks. SBIC financing should serve as the equity base used to raise senior debt at a lower interest rate with no dilution of equity. Small businesses should seek SBIC financing when the marginal rate of return from the extra funds, or the funds that can be leveraged with the extra funds, is greater than the marginal cost of the funds. Thus a company with fixed asset needs can borrow 70-75% of the total through long-term debt from a bank and 25-30% at a higher cost from an SBIC. There are no hard rules on the amount of equity that should be given up, but most SBICs, like venture capitalists, determine the percentage based on the risk. The higher the risk, the greater the annual return expected and the higher the percentage of the company desired. This projected return varies from 30% to 50% annually for most of the investments, based on reasonable projections. The company's expected growth influences the SBIC's decision to invest in the company, but the amount of ownership is often based on the current status of the company so that the SBIC can share in any growth. SBICs acquire stock for profitable resale, preferably to the public, to obtain higher prices due to greater liquidity, and they prefer to invest in companies where the entrepreneurs have similar goals. In the absence of a public market for the stock, a borrower may, and sometimes must, repurchase the SBIC equity, and can usually get a right of first refusal.

Because SBICs cannot control companies through stock purchases, they attempt to protect their investments by requiring financial agreements that allow them control over major strategic changes that otherwise could affect the company. Financial agreements include provisions such as future sale of stock to prevent dilution, payment of dividends, amount and kinds of borrowing, executive salaries and fringes, non-compete agreements, moonlighting, major change in company strategy including acquisitions, mergers or sale of assets, nature and quality of financial recordkeeping and information provided to the SBIC, and representation on the board of directors.

SBICs should be evaluated by the borrower on the basis of criteria similar to those used for venture capital companies so that the partnership can be mutually profitable. Some criteria include:

a. Assistance that the SBIC can provide to the borrower through management talent, expertise and contacts;
b. Previous investments in and enthusiasm for the borrower's industry;
c. Amount of equity in the SBIC, which influences the amount of funds that can be invested by the SBIC in any one borrower;
d. Restrictive provisions and nature of the financial agreement.

Customers

Introduction

Customers can sometimes provide financing for the business, but they may not be a desirable source of financing. If a small number of customers have a great deal of control over the finances of the firm, they may be able to control the firm's profitability. In some businesses, such as in construction and big ticket items, an advance from the customer is considered a necessity in order to protect the manufacturer from loss and to provide some working capital.

Types of Financing Provided

Financing from customers can be obtained in some of the following ways:

a. Cash advances;
b. Cash on delivery (COD);
c. Bankers' acceptances;
d. Letters of credit;
e. Discounts for early payment;
f. Bank draft.

Practices

Advance payments can be a substitute for Inventory and Accounts Receivable financing, while cash or COD payments makes Accounts Receivable financing unnecessary. Bank drafts also are used where the supplier needs money quickly.

Employees

Introduction

Employees are frequently a desirable source of financing for the firm, both from the viewpoint of obtaining additional financing for the firm, and of giving the employees a share of company profits. Many companies sell stock to executives under stock option and stock purchase plans. Some corporations also encourage the purchase of stock by other employees.

Types of Financing Provided

Financing could be provided through various methods by employees, such as:

a. Stock purchase by employees or employees' pension funds;
b. Sale-leaseback with pension funds;
c. Stock purchase by Employee Stock Option Trusts.

Practices

Many employers offer matching contributions to employees who wish to purchase corporate stock, often at less than the market price. There are usually restrictions on the resale of such stock for a period of time. Corporations selling stock to employees should check whether the issue will be considered a private or public offering, thus necessitating registration with the SEC (see "Private Placements and Public Offerings"). If the offerees are executive employees having access to the same information that the Securities Act of 1933 asks for in a registration statement, then the offering might be exempt from registration. Other employees are considered similar to members of the investing public, and registration rules can apply.

Funds also can be raised by having sale-leaseback agreements with the employees' pension funds. Care should be taken that the transactions are arm's length and that the agreement would benefit the fund and the company. Another form of employee financing is the Employee Stock Option Trust (ESOT) (see ESOT).

Individuals/Public

The individual investor who is financially able and willing to invest in potentially profitable ventures has been the traditional source of equity capital for most new businesses. Sources of capital can be organized or unorganized. Organized sources of capital are institutions such as banks, venture capital firms, etc. Individuals and the public are unorganized sources of capital. Most small firms usually are started with no funds from organized sources of capital; they depend upon friends, owners, officers, relatives, etc. Some ventures with prospects of extraordinary growth can obtain funds from wealthy investors or venture capital companies through private placements. They also may obtain capital from the public through public offerings with or without the aid of underwriters and investment bankers. At certain periods, when the speculative fever in the market grows, many new companies without a long history of satisfactory performance obtain funds from the public. However, at most times, firms without a satisfactory track record find it difficult to raise funds from the public. Most firms in such situations lease or rent fixed assets to allow usage of available funds for working capital, and use trade credit extensively.

Suppliers

Introduction

Trade credit from suppliers is the most commonly used source of current asset financing for businesses. As a matter of custom or convenience, suppliers usually give trade credit to be competitive, or to encourage the purchase. Because trade creditors usually expect to have a continuing sales relationship, they often take greater risks when providing credit than many types of financial institutions.

Types of Financing Provided

The types of financing provided by suppliers, which may involve bankers' guarantees or liens on inventories, are:

a. Unsecured trade credit;
b. Unsecured note;
c. Banker's acceptances;
d. Letter of credit;
e. Secured notes using inventory as collateral;
f. Time sales financing.

Practices

A trade creditor must be reasonably satisfied with the integrity and ability of management, and with the financial conditions and prospects of the business. Terms offered in trade credit usually are such that it is very profitable to pay promptly. For example, common terms are 2/10, net 30, which means that payment is expected in 30 days, but a 2% discount can be taken if payment is made in 10 days — yielding an approximate annual interest rate of 36% since a 2% discount is given for the use of money for 20 days. Companies that have the cash flow and financial expertise to understand and profit from prompt payment avail themselves of cash discounts. Some companies finance sales through their own finance companies, as does General Motors with it General Motors Acceptance Corporation.

Credit is established by businessmen through contacts with suppliers to provide information regarding the management, financial status, and credit requirements of the firm. Information also can be provided to a commercial reporting agency, such as Dun & Bradstreet for circulation to interested suppliers. However, in the case of newly formed companies without a strong financial statement, it is questionable whether or not providing credit information to credit agencies is always in the best interests of the company.

(For additional information, see "Trade Credit.")

Local Development Corporations

(Industrial Development Corporations and Industrial Foundations)

Introduction

Local Development Corporations (LDCs) are privately-sponsored community agencies serving a predefined geographic area. LDCs invest their own funds, bring enterprises in need of capital to sources of funds seeking investment, or aid in obtaining money. They can be for-profit or non-profit corporations. Many LDCs do not have a full-time staff, and time is volunteered by community leaders interested in area economic development. An LDC is a special kind of Industrial Foundation that can borrow funds from the Small Business Administration for relending to a prequalified small business. (See Small Business Administration (502/503) Program.) Some states also loan funds to LDCs in their state. The community benefits through increased payroll and other business expenditures. Though some foundations have been in operation for more than 30 years, most of them are relatively young. The group has expanded rapidly in recent years.

Flow of Funds

LDCs obtain funds by selling memberships or stock to local residents and other parties interested in economic growth in the area. They also borrow funds from other financial institutions secured by land, buildings, and equipment when they provide financing to a borrower who locates his facilities in the community. Often this loan from the financial institution is guaranteed by a government agency, such as the Small Business Administration. LDCs also obtain grants to develop industrial parks and related facilities from governmental units such as the Farmers Home Administration, Economic Development Administration, Regional Development Commissions, etc.

Types of Financing Provided

Most LDCs provide secured financing with real estate and other fixed assets, such as equipment, as collateral, but some also provide subordinated financing or purchase stock in a corporation. They are especially helpful in real estate financing, fixed equipment financing, leasing, and loans to new industry.

Practices

LDCs normally provide the following services:

a. Buying, developing, and selling or leasing industrial sites and plants;

b. Subsidizing business through donation of land, utilities or space;

c. Lending or investing funds in businesses located in the area served by the LDC;

d. Providing technical assistance to small business in management, marketing, etc.

If an LDC provides financial assistance in the form of a loan or investment, it usually requires a mortgage on land, buildings, or machinery. Some LDCs that are able to raise funds from private sources also provide working capital loans and equity-type investments. In such cases, the LDC obtains options to buy ownership in the company, and a seat(s) on the board of directors.

Community Development Corporations

Introduction

A Community Development Corporation (CDC) is a form of a Local Development Corporation. Some LDCs also are CDCs. One of the major differences is that CDCs obtain funds in the form of grants from various sources, and are able to use these funds for economic development. Practically all CDCs have a permanent full-time staff who either assist in starting new ventures owned by the CDC, or provide venture capital or secured financing to companies that locate in the area served by the CDC, if they satisfy certain requirements. These requirements or investment criteria vary among CDCs, and include such factors as number and skill levels of employees, wages, the amount of financing required, and the growth prospects for the company.

CDCs were formed with the belief that community representation in, and control of, economic development will result in greater ultimate benefits to the community than a strategy that lacks such orientation. CDCs are involved in all facets of community development — including economic development, venture financing, education, health care, job training, housing, etc. Most CDCs are non-profit.

CDCs are modeled after the Bedford-Stuyvesant Restoration Corporation, a community development corporation in the Bedford-Stuyvesant area of New York City organized by Senator Robert Kennedy in 1966. Approximately 40 CDCs on this model were funded by the Office of Economic Development. They are equally divided between urban and rural areas. Although government funding for these organizations has been drastically reduced, many CDCs have accumulated investment portfolios allowing them to continue their investment activities. There are other CDCs funded by private organizations such as foundations, church groups, and corporations.

Flow of Funds

Funds are obtained by CDCs from a variety of sources interested in economic development in high-poverty and high-unemployment areas. Such sources are federal or state governments, foundations, church groups, and corporations. CDCs usually are organized as non-profit corporations so federal or private investments will pay dividends to a community — not an individual. Funds are used in economic and community development activities.

Types of Financing Provided

Each CDC has its own practices and criteria. In general, CDCs invest either as holding or as venture capital companies. Some CDCs are interested in investing only in companies that are controlled by them. Others provide venture capital financing to new or very young companies, and usually consider deals involving greater risk than other segments of the venture capital industry. Venture capital financing is usually in the form of subordinated convertible loans. However, CDCs will consider almost any kind of financing for a sound company that promises to provide employment in the area.

Practices

No two CDCs are exactly alike, because each is tailored to reflect and solve the needs and problems of the areas it serves. They are organized by the community to obtain outside resources such as venture capital , short- and long-term loans, and technical assistance. CDCs then invest funds in for-profit corporations or subsidiaries in the form of stock or loans or convertible securities. The only inflexible requirement for a CDC investment is that the venture be located in the community being served. The programs operated by the CDCs include:

a. Economic and business development programs, including programs that provide financial and other assistance (including equity capital) to start, expand, or locate businesses in or near the areas served so as to provide employment and ownership opportunities for residents of such areas;

b. Community development and housing activities that create new training, employment and ownership opportunities and which contribute to improved living conditions; and

c. Manpower training programs for unemployed or low-income persons, which essentially subsidizes the costs of training new employees.

State Government Institutions

State government financial institutions providing funds to businesses vary from state to state. Some states have privately-owned organizations; others have state-owned organizations providing funds to businesses that can employ state residents. Privately-owned organizations usually are started by the state to promote business within the state. The variety of programs offered by these organizations is explained in detail in a following section.

U.S. Government Programs

The U.S. Government offers a wide variety of programs to businessmen and farmers through a multitude of agencies. These agencies include:

- Department of Agriculture
- Department of Commerce
- Department of Housing and Urban Development
- Department of the Interior
- Small Business Administration
- Overseas Private Investment Corporation
- Export-Import Bank of the United States

Programs offered by these agencies are explained in detail in a following section.

V.
Topics of Special Interest

Legal Considerations

Securities Law and Registration Requirements

Introduction

Sales of securities must satisfy the federal and state requirements of those states in which they will be sold. Some types of sales or securities are exempt from registration requirements. Federal law does not preempt state requirements, and therefore securities must satisfy the securities registration requirements of each state in which they are sold. If the security is sold in interstate commerce, the federal securities requirements also must be satisfied. Federal securities requirements are concerned primarily with providing all pertinent information to potential investors and offerees, and with preventing fraud. State securities laws are concerned with the above, and sometimes with the question of whether the offering is fair, just, and equitable to investors. Securities can be traded in the open market in the states in which they are registered. Unregistered securities can be traded if certain provisions are satisfied, and if company stock is traded in the public markets.

Federal Registration

A basic purpose of federal securities laws is to provide disclosure of relevant financial and other information about companies planning to obtain capital through the public offering of their securities, and about companies with publicly-held securities. These laws are not concerned with the merits of the offering or fairness to investors and offerees, but only with providing necessary information to enable investor evaluation of securities on an informed and realistic basis (1971 Annual Report, SEC).

The major federal acts regarding securities and investments are the following:

a. The Securities Act of 1933: The Securities Act prescribes the requirements that should be satisfied before securities are offered to the public by an issuing company or a person in a controlling relationship. This act is concerned with the sale of securities in the primary market;

b. The Securities Exchange Act of 1934: The Securities Exchange Act deals primarily with securities that already are outstanding, and requires issuing companies to make annual and other periodic reports, providing a public file of current material information. It deals with other facets of securities, such as solicitation of proxies for the election of directors, tender offers and other planned stock acquisitions, and insider transactions;

c. The Trust Indenture Act of 1939: This act specifies the qualifications for an indenture and the independent trustee for debt securities registered under the Securities Act of 1933. The Act enumerates the provisions which have to be included in the indenture, and those which may be considered for inclusion.

d. The Investment Company Act of 1940: The Investment Company Act and the Investment Advisers Act provide investors with information on investment companies, their securities, and their management. It is concerned with the protection of shareholders' interests in the investment company and the prevention of management fraud;

e. The Federal Investment Company Amendments Act of 1970: This act is concerned with a standard of reasonableness in respect to management fees in investment companies.

Exemptions to Registration

There are exemptions to registration under federal and state laws. The advantages of exemptions are that such offerings are less expensive, take less time, and avoid reporting requirements. Offerings may be exempt because the securities are exempt or because the transaction is exempt from the registration requirements. It should be noted that the issuer still is liable under the antifraud provisions of the securities laws. Exemptions can be lost if the exempt offering is, or appears to be, part of a coordinated financing package requiring registration. The offerings may be exempt for any of the following reasons:

a. Intrastate offerings are exempt from federal registration requirements. Care should be taken, however, that the offering is not made to out-of-state residents;

b. Private placements are exempt from registration. To qualify as a private placement the offering must be made only to sophisticated investors who can afford the risk and who have the information and the expertise to analyze the information. Such investors are assumed to have no need for federal protection under the securities laws (see Private Placements and Public Offerings for more detail);

c. Small offerings are exempt from the complete registration requirements but can be registered under a variety of alternative exemptions, which are less expensive than a full S-1 registration;

d. Securities issued by persons organized and operated exclusively for religious, educational, benevolent, fraternal, charitable, or reformatory purposes and not-for-profit organizations are exempt from the registration requirements;

e. Regulation E adopted by the SEC exempts securities issued by Small Business Investment Companies (SBICs) and Minority Enterprise SBICs (MESBICs), which are licensed by the Small Business Administration and registered under the Investment Company Act of 1940;

f. The Securities Act exempts any security exchanged by the issuer exclusively with its existing security holders where no commission or other remuneration is paid;

g. Exemptions for transactions of brokers and dealers in the secondary market;

h. Exemptions for certain kinds of securities such as short-term notes, bank drafts and bills of exchange, securities of common carriers, commercial paper, etc.;

i. Other exemptions include those for fractional undivided interests in oil or gas rights and first lien notes.

There are other rules permitting the sale of restricted securities under certain conditions. Under Rule 144, letter stock of a publicly held company can be sold through a market maker or registered brokerage firm by the investor after holding it for at least two years. The investor can sell the unregistered stock if the number of shares sold in any three-month period does not exceed the greater of 1% of the number of shares issued and outstanding of the company, or the average weekly number of shares that are publicly traded in the four weeks immediately preceding the sale.

State Blue Sky Laws

Even though securities may be exempt from the federal requirements, the various states may require registration of the security with the agency responsible for regulating the sale of securities in the state. Such compliance is required with federal registration if the securities are to be sold in the state since federal law does not preempt state regulation of securities sold. The effect of noncompliance is to void the transaction. Blue sky laws can deal with the securities, the transactions, the participants involved in the offering, and the selling effort. They are designed to protect unsophisticated investors, and hence some states have the power to rule on the fairness of the terms of the issue being offered. They also require full and fair disclosure. Blue sky laws contain antifraud provisions, as do federal laws.

Tax Aspects

There are tax considerations in every business corporation, upon which the businessman's best advisers are his attorney and his accountant. Some of the factors to be considered are the following:

Section 1244 Stock

Section 1244 of the Internal Revenue Code offers an incentive to investors in small businesses. Stock investment losses that are qualified can be written off against ordinary income, while gains are taxed at the capital gains rate if the business and investors qualify. If the stock is not Sec. 1244 stock, only $1,000 of a capital loss can be offset against ordinary income. Thus, small businesses should qualify their stock under Sec. 1244 whenever possible. To qualify for Sec. 1244, the corporation should receive not more than $1,000,000 in money and other property (and not stock and securities) for stock, as a contribution to capital and as paid-in surplus. The company must be a domestic, small business corporation, and must satisfy certain limitations on the amount of its income obtained from sources such as royalties, rents, dividends, interest, annuities, and sales or exchanges of stocks or securities. Under Sec. 1244, only original purchasers can write up to $50,000 of losses on 1244 stock off ordinary income for any taxable year.

S Corporation

An S corporation is similar to other corporations, except that the shareholders of the corporation are taxed directly for any losses or profits, with certain exceptions for passive income and capital gains. The corporation is not a separate tax-paying entity. To qualify as an S corporation, the organization must be a domestic corporation with no more than 35 shareholders, all of whom must agree to the S classification. None of the shareholders must be nonresident aliens, and the corporation must not be a member of an affiliated group. The company must have only one class of stock; however, it allows common stock with different voting rights. No more than 25% of its income can be from passive sources for three consecutive years, and all shareholders must be individuals, estates or certain trusts. An S corporation is advantageous when losses are expected, especially in a startup corporation, and when the shareholders have other income which can be written off against the losses. It is also helpful if the shareholder's tax rate is less than the corporate rate.

The shareholders of a corporation, especially a closely-held corporation in the startup stages, can realize a tax benefit by investing funds in the form of equity and loans. The loans can be repaid to the shareholder without a declaration of dividends or salary, enabling the shareholder to avoid paying income taxes on this recouped amount. Also, interest can be deducted from corporate income. However, certain complicated guidelines must be followed regarding the amount of debt and equity. The IRS and the courts require that some rules be followed to prevent debt from being considered as equity. There is a risk that the corporation may be thinly capitalized because of an excessive amount of loans to creditors for corporation debts. The debt instruments should have a maturity date and a reasonable interest rate, and interest and principal should be paid on time. Also, there should be a substantial investment in equity, equal to at least 25% of debt.

Covenants and Guidelines for Various Types of Debt Instruments

Introduction

The covenants and guidelines covered here deal primarily with debt instruments. Covenants, guidelines, and legal promises cannot assure repayment of the loan, and the credit rating of a borrower cannot be improved by a strong legal agreement. However, legal agreements can prevent management practices that could harm the company and, in turn, jeopardize the repayment of the loan; agreements also can allow the lender to control major changes, such as acquisitions, divestitures, mergers, and sale of major assets. Such control is obtained through the agreement by accelerating the repayment of the loan or by allowing the lender to control the board of directors of the corporation. Most lenders and investors prefer not to run the business, but they will do so to protect their investment.

The provisions of the loan agreement can be classified into the following:

a. The terms and conditions of the loan;
b. Covenants, positive and negative;
c. Default and remedies.

Terms and Conditions of the Loan

This section of the loan agreement includes the provisions where the respective parties agree to borrow and to lend, the amount of the loan and the terms of repayment of principal and interest, penalties for prepayment and cases where accelerated repayment is required, the interest rates and fees for commitment, the dates on which the loans will be made, the currency to be used in the transactions, the statements and guarantees made by the borrowers and the documents required and verified, the roles to be played by the borrower and the lender(s), the use of the loan proceeds, and the conditions to be satisfied for the loan to be made. Typically, most long-term lenders do not prefer prepayment, but sometimes they do allow prepayment without penalty or up to a certain amount from excess funds. The penalty is charged if the prepayment is from funds that are newly borrowed by the corporation at a lower interest rate or a shorter maturity. The penalty is highest in the early years of the loan and decreases thereafter.

Covenants

The covenants included in a loan agreement can be classified into positive covenants, whereby the borrower agrees to perform certain tasks or adhere to certain guidelines, and negative covenants, whereby the borrower agrees to refrain from certain other practices.

Positive Covenants

Some of the positive covenants found in debt agreements are the following:

a. The borrower will stay in existence;
b. The borrower will furnish the financial statements and other information as requested by the lender;
c. The borrower will maintain adequate insurance;
d. The borrower will pay all taxes and liabilities when due, except those contested in good faith;
e. The company will carry life insurance on key persons, as required by the agreement and other insurance on property and assets as required;
f. The borrower will retain key management under a management contract during the term of the loan;
g. The borrower will comply with all laws that are applicable;
h. Adequate reserves will be maintained, and sound accounting records will be kept;
i. The lender's seats on the borrower's board of directors will be maintained;
j. The borrower will satisfy all the terms of any agreement to which it is a party; and
k. The borrower will notify the lender when there is a default on any of the terms of the agreement.

Negative Covenants

Whereas positive covenants are usually standard on most agreements, negative covenants are designed for each borrower and usually are more important. Some of the important negative covenants are:

a. Negative pledge clause, prohibiting the pledging of assets to secure additional loans where the new creditor would have priority over the loan being negotiated. There are certain exceptions, such as normal tax liens, or the borrower's wanting to purchase property with a purchase money mortgage (i.e., with a mortgage already on it);

b. Covenants to ensure that the corporation has sufficient liquid assets to keep it solvent and avoid bankruptcy. These include covenants that the working capital, current assets, and net worth will not fall below a certain level; such covenants prevent excessive investment of cash in fixed assets and protect the lender against severe losses, stock repurchases, dividends, excessive salaries, etc.;

c. Limits on debt and leases, which can restrict the type and amount of debt without the prior consent of the lender, and usually above a certain dollar amount. This limit can be based on various factors, such as a percentage of assets, or an upper limit on the annual rental and repayment of principal and interest, based on the cash flow of the company. This is sometimes known as the Debt Service test, under which the borrower must have a sufficient cash flow to repay the principal and rental payments with some margin of safety;

d. Restrictions on purchase and sale of assets, repurchases of stock, dividend payments, salaries to major stockholders and management, and long-term rentals, up to a percentage of cumulative net income;

e. Restrictions on the financial activities of the subsidiaries so that they are prohibited from doing anything that the parent is prevented from doing and restricted from borrowing except from the parent;

f. Restrictions on the borrower to prevent acquisitions or a merger with another company, or the sale of the company or any portion of it, and also on investments outside the normal business of the company, so as to prevent any change in the basic nature of the company's business;

g. Restrictions on discounting accounts receivable, and sale of inventories through auctions or at distress prices;

h. Restrictions on other contingent liabilities;

i. A covenant of prior coverage and of equal coverage, which is an alternative to the negative pledge clause, and ensures that the issue is secured by a prior lien if a later mortgage is placed on the same asset, or that it is equally and ratably secured with the later liens.

Defaults and Remedies

Default occurs when any of the following events occur:

a.There is a default in the payment of any interest or principal when is becomes due and payable, and has not been satisfied within the grace period allowed;

b. There is a default in the performance of any covenant or warranty of the company in any agreement made by the company, and this default exists for more than the grace period;

c. When a court having jurisdiction judges the company to be bankrupt or insolvent, or approves a petition for reorganization, arrangement, adjustment, or composition under the Federal Bankruptcy Act;

d. The authorization by the company of proceedings to be declared bankrupt or insolvent, or the consent by the company to such proceedings;

e. The admission by the company of its inability to pay its debts as they become due, or corporate action toward such objective.

If an event of default occurs, the lender may take any of the remedies available to it, such as:

a. Calling the loan, and taking such action as may be necessary to obtain the funds;

b. Taking control of the board of directors, if the agreement so allows;

c. Such other action as may be allowed.

Practically all financial agreements contain the "boiler-plate" clause. This clause allows the financial institution to call the loan if it reasonably decides that the loan is in jeopardy. In calling the loan the lender must have reasonable, and not frivolous, grounds. This clause is inserted because no lender is a perfect forecaster — he cannot predict every possible problem that could occur to the borrower and hence cannot protect himself from all future adverse events. Even if he were able to enumerate many potential problems, the agreement would be very bulky and, sometimes, would encorach upon management's activities. This is prevented by the insertion of the boiler-plate clause, allowing the lender to call the loan if the actions of management adversely affect repayment of the loan and interest.

Specialized Financing

Startup Financing

Raising substantial funds for business startups is among the more difficult areas of financing, and with good reason. Studies show that approximately 80% of all new companies fail within five years of their startup. The major reasons for these failures are the lack of management expertise and inadequate sales.

Most businesses in a startup phase can be categorized as follows:

- Small business, or the "Ma and Pa" operation, which most likely provides jobs only to the proprietors;
- Small business of the "Ma and Pa" scope, but with a unique concept, which can be franchised in different geographic areas;
- Businesses that do not have a unique concept or a proprietary product, but can provide employment to more people than just the proprietors, are likely to have limited opportunities for growth, and limited margins and profits. Such businesses usually require large amounts of working capital, are labor intensive and have low margins;
- Businesses with an unique concept or proprietary product, which has been proven through prior sales, or which may still be in the introductory stage.

Due to the high failure rate and the low growth prospects in the first category, "Ma and Pa" businesses most often must rely on the entrepreneur, his relatives and friends, for the equity portion of the financing, and on commercial banks for the additional debt requirements. Most venture capitalists concentrate on the fourth category due to the prospects for growth and high profits. In addition, some venture capitalists consider only those companies in the fourth category that have already introduced their product in the marketplace and enjoy some sales. Community development corporations usually are interested in all of the above categories, since they consider employment prospects offered by a venture in their communities along with its prospects for growth.

To raise funds for a startup through legitimate financial institutions, an entrepreneur will need at least some of the following:

a. Personal investment;

b. A successful track record and management expertise, especially in the area of the business;

c. Assets that can be pledged for the funds;

d. Contracts with potential customers or a backlog of orders; and

e. A well-prepared investment prospectus or feasibility study showing potential profitability.

If the venture appears feasible, and is documented with a well-prepared investment package, it may be possible to attract a venture capitalist to invest in the company. Even in such cases, the venture capitalist wants to see a direct investment of funds by the entrepreneurs. An exception to this may be if the entrepreneur has developed a very significant product through the investment of his (or their) time. Investors are unlikely to consider the investment of the entrepreneurs' time as significant, unless it has resulted in a product or service.

At the startup phase, entrepreneurs may have to give up a significant portion of their company to investors, owing to the risk involved and the lack of business history. In some cases, an entrepreneur has ended up with 10% or less of the company if his sole investment is the business idea, product, or service. The balance of the company is held by the investors, and in some cases, there is a buy-back arrangement with the entrepreneur which provides opportunity to repurchase some of the stock, and sometimes majority control, based on the performance of the company.

As shown in Chapter II, the company's startup costs involve investment in plant, machinery and equipment, inventory, and other costs, such as research and development. In addition, since the company is starting with no sales, and hence no cash flow, the company will have a negative cash flow for an initial period. Thus, the business will require working capital to carry the accounts receivable and the operating expenses until the sales produce a positive cash flow. It also may happen that the sales of the company grow at a rate faster than the ability of the company to finance internally through earnings and cash flow. In this case, the company will need sufficient capital or reserve funds to enable growth at a profitable rate until it can raise additional funds through the public or private offering of securities, such as equity or debt instruments.

It is very difficult, if not impossible, to raise debt funds for a long-term investment in a startup with no collateral or equity investment in the business. Debt is available if there is sufficient equity (to provide a cushion for the debt) and collateral, along with the means of repayment. If the collateral is current assets, such as accounts receivable and inventory, a commercial finance company might carry the company until sufficient assets and reserves are built up to go to a commercial bank or other financial institutions for a term loan or a short-term loan, or even to the public markets. However, it is advisable to fund the permanent needs of the company through equity and long-term debt. The equity would be the investment by the entrepreneurs and the venture capitalists. It might be difficult for a startup to raise long-term debt unless it is in the form of a venture capital investment. Commercial banks also assist in this financing, but they prefer to see a sufficient equity base as security for their loan, and the means of repayment through cash flow or through liquidation of assets.

During the startup phase, it is advisable to keep the break-even level as low as possible so that the company has a history of profitability. This can be done by renting or leasing the plant, machinery, and equipment rather than purchasing it, and by contracting for needed services based on results rather than hiring employees. Thus, even if the dollar cost per unit of output is higher, the employees are not hired when there might not be enough work, with a corresponding increase in the breakeven level. This is the question of "Make-or-Buy" in investment decisions. Venture capitalists also prefer to see that entrepreneurs do not "bleed" the company to pay their own salaries. It is a common mistake for entrepreneurs to set their salaries at the same high levels as their previous jobs. The venture capitalist likes to see the entrepreneur obtain rewards through the long-term growth of the company with stock appreciation, since the venture capitalist will make profits only if the stock appreciates in value. In short, they prefer to see that their objectives are similar to those of the entrepreneurs and vice versa.

In raising funds for businesses, it is always desirable if not mandatory, to have a well-written investment package to present to prospective investors and lenders. Investors and lenders like to have written information about the company which they can examine in detail, along with the objectives of the entrepreneurs, the financial projections, and the marketing strategy. A written presentation conveys information accurately and completely. Also, financial information is required in written form. If the presentation or the business lacks quality, the probability of raising the funds is low. The information that should be included in a good package is described in Chapter II. Without a good written plan, the financier may not believe the entrepreneur has the dedication and ability to operate the company through its most difficult start-up period, or that the business is a feasible one.

The investment package should explain clearly the nature of the business, the amount of funds required and their uses and purposes, the financial strength of the company and the security offered, the means of repayment of the investment, the future direction and financial projections, and the integrity and expertise of the management.

Acquisition Financing

Acquisition Pricing

A company can be priced in many ways, among which are the following:

a. Market value of the company's shares;

b. Book value;

c. Book value adjusted for market value of the company's assets;

d. Valuation based on a multiplier of current earnings;

e. Valuation based on future earnings.

The market value of the company's shares can be used only if the company has an active market for its shares. Usually, book value is used only if the company does not have any profits, since otherwise the selling stockholders expect to be paid a figure for "goodwill" for an on-going business. If the assets being sold have a low book value due to depreciation, the sale price may reflect the market value of these assets. Assets which are overpriced or not needed, may be withheld by the sellers. Valuation based on a multiplier of current earnings is used most often because it reflects the quality of management and earning potential of the business. The earnings multiplier is determined by many factors, including the age of the company, its prospects for growth, its size and profitability, price earnings multiple in comparable companies, and the caliber of management. The earnings multiplier is multiplied by the earnings after taxes; and earnings are usually adjusted for changes in corporate and financial structure, principals' salaries, and extraordinary gains or losses.

The price earnings multiple paid by businesses varies from a figure as low as one, when one person is key to the organization, to between 15 and 20 for companies with growth history and potential. Established companies with average growth prospects normally sell for between 8-10 times earnings. Higher multiples have also been used for "growth companies," which have a higher rate of growth for sales and profits than the average company. A business can also be priced on the basis of future earnings. For a time horizon in which the acquirer expects to recoup his investment at a profit, projected earnings after taxes are discounted at the expected rate of return, and this present value is the price that is to be paid. Or earnings can be projected for a limited number of years in which reasonable projections can be made, and this is discounted. To this figure is added a sum for an assumed residual value, and this is the value of the business. There are many other methods of valuing a business based on combinations or variations of the above methods.

Forms of Acquisitions, Tax Aspects, and Accounting Treatment

Acquisitions: Is a general term for such forms as statutory mergers and consolidations, asset acquisitions, and stock acquisitions. A statutory merger is when two corporations are consolidated with one of them being the surviving corporation, and hence the acquirer. A statutory consolidation is the same as a statutory merger except that both merging corporations cease to exist and a new third corporation is formed, which is a combination of the two. A statutory merger and consolidation usually requires the approval of the boards of directors and the stockholders (by a required margin) of both corporations.

The transaction should satisfy the laws of the state of incorporation. In an asset acquisition, assets are purchased as individual items. The acquirer may assume selected liabilities, and accounts receivable. The cash is normally retained by the seller. Stock acquisition involves the purchase of a controlling interest in the stock of one corporation by another. This is a direct transaction between the buyer and the stockholders of the company being bought.The board of directors and the management of the company being bought may oppose the purchase of the stock by the acquiring company.

An acquisition can be a "tax-free" or a taxable

transaction. Taxes are not avoided in the sale at a profit of the assets or the stock. However, taxes can be postponed to a time when the sellers can reduce the total amount of taxes paid. An acquisition also can be partly taxable and partly tax-free. Most acquisitions are taxable to the selling shareholders if they have had a gain, unless the sale qualifies as a corporate reorganization according to the Internal Revenue Code. Some of the most common types of reorganizations are the statutory mergers and consolidations, and other acquisitions where the consideration is voting stock. In statutory mergers and consolidations, payment in cash and securities other than voting stock beyond certain limits results in a partly taxable, partly tax-free transaction. In a tax-free arrangement, taxes are paid when the stock is sold. Taxes can be deferred if the company is sold on the Installment Plan. If the seller expects his tax rate to decrease after the sale of the business, he can use this method, whereby he receives less than 30% in the calendar year in which he sells. Taxes are then paid each year on the installment received in that year.

Another concern of the seller and the buyer is the allocation of value to the assets sold in a taxable acquisition. The purchasing company would like to allocate a high value on depreciable assets (such as plant, machinery, and equipment) so as to increase the cash flow, and less on nondepreciable assets (such as inventory). They also would prefer to minimize the amount paid for goodwill because this is not deductible for tax purposes, and is deducted from after-tax income and before calculating net after-tax income of the company. In contrast, the seller wishes to allocate the maximum possible amount to goodwill, because taxes are paid at the capital gains rate, and a lower value to inventory, where the gain is taxed at the ordinary income rate. The purchaser assumes the seller's tax basis in a tax-free exchange.

The accounting treatment of an acquisition can be:

a. Pooling of interests; or

b. Purchase.

When the accounting treatment is pooling of interest, values of the assets and liabilities of buyer and seller are added to form the balance sheets of the resulting corporation. The capital surplus account is adjusted to reflect whether the purchase price is higher or lower than the book value of the selling company. There is no account for goodwill, without the resulting deductions from after-tax income.

When the acquisition is treated as a purchase, any excess of purchase price over book value of the assets is allocated to goodwill. The purchase price is allocated to the various assets based on their value, if the price is paid in stock. The goodwill must be amortized and charged against net after-tax income over its useful life, which should not exceed 40 years. If the criteria for "pooling of interests" are satisfied, the purchase must be treated as a pooling of interests; otherwise, it must be treated as a purchase.

Instruments Used in Acquisitions

The instruments used in acquisitions are the following:

a. Cash: The use of cash results in a taxable acquisition, and the accounting treatment will be a purchase or partial pooling. Cash can be obtained from borrowing, from the sale of stock, or from existing surpluses. Tax on excess accumulated earnings sometimes can be avoided by the use of cash. The use of cash does not result in a loss of control in the acquiring company;

b. Common stock: A tax-free transaction results if only voting stock is used in the acquisition, and the accounting treatment is pooling of interests. The use of common stock may result in a large block of stock in the hands of the selling stockholders. It may cause dilution in the earnings per share, and it may lead to other problems. In some cases if there are restrictions on the sale of the common stock by the seller, he retains the right to convert to debt if the purchaser does not satisfy certain performance standards;

c. Preferred stock: If the preferred stock is voting, the transaction is tax-free and pooling of interests may be used. It may have the same control and dilution problems as common stock, and the dividends paid are not tax-deductible. Nevertheless, its use is popular because it is a tax-free transaction. Control problems may be reduced by having the preferred shares convertible to a smaller number of common shares than a transaction with common stock;

d. Warrants: The use of warrants makes the transaction taxable, and the purchase accounting method is used. Warrants may have the same problems as common stock — namely, control and dilution.

e. Notes: The use of notes makes the transaction taxable, and requires the use of the purchase accounting treatment. The interest on notes is deductible from the corporation's income taxes. If the notes are convertible, dilution may occur. The notes may be secured, subordinated or unsecured.

The above instruments also can be used in combination, resulting in some transactions that are partly taxable and partly tax-free. These combinations are used where selling stockholders have different objectives — some preferring cash, others stock to postpone taxes. One method of handling this situation is for the selling corporation to repurchase the stock of the stockholders who wish to sell for cash, and then to effect a tax-free transaction with the remaining stockholders.

Financing Acquisitions Using Seller's Assets

Businesses can be acquired with the buyer making a small down payment and the seller financing the balance of the required funds. In some cases, the seller himself finances the sale, as in the Installment Sale. The other assets that can be used to obtain financing are the following:

a. Stock: The seller's stock can be used to finance the purchase of the company. In such financings, the lenders usually expect to obtain warrants or stock as sweeteners. Stock used for such financing is usually publicly traded;

b. Accounts receivable and inventory: Commercial finance companies and other financing institutions such as commercial banks, finance acquisitions with accounts receivable and inventory as security (see Accounts Receivable and Inventory Financing);

c. Machinery and equipment: These can be used to obtain financing for medium-term loans, and also can be financed through the use of sale-leaseback transactions. Sale-leaseback results in a larger cash flow, in the greater availability of working capital, and in larger tax-deductible lease expenses;

d. Real estate: This can be used in the same manner as machinery and equipment through a long-term loan or through the use of sale-leaseback transactions. Even if the real estate has a first mortgage, a second mortgage may be available if the property is important to the business, and if it has a sufficiently high market value.

Acquisitions also can be financed through the sale of unneeded assets or assets that are not producing a sufficiently high rate of return on equity, or through the use of Employee Stock Option Trusts (see ESOTs). This is done through pre-tax dollars if the acquiring corporation makes a cash and/or stock contribution to the ESOT, which is tax-deductible. The ESOT also could borrow from a financial institution — the loan being guaranteed by the parent corporation, with the parent-acquiring corporation making periodic payments on the loan. The proceeds of the loan are used to purchase the selling corporation's stock or assets.

Equipment Financing

The various types of instruments used in equipment financing are security agreements (formerly chattel mortgages), leases, lease-guarantees, sale-leasebacks, and conditional sales contracts. In financing equipment, lenders are concerned with marketability and liquidation value of the equipment. Another factor is the location of the equipment, especially in the case of heavy equipment because of the costs of transporting equipment from a less desirable liquidation area (such as a rural area). The lender must have confidence that the borrower will be profitable and have the debt coverage to meet its obligations. In some cases the borrower should have the debt coverage before the proposed equipment is added. The term of the loan or the lease is less than the useful life of the equipment so that enough value remains to protect the lender or the lessor, and is usually for more than one year. In some cases, the lessor takes the risk of obsolescence, and leases equipment for less than its useful life. However, such leases cost more, and are for general purpose rather than specialized equipment. Equipment should be easily removable from the borrower's premises if necessary for liquidation. The loan may range up to 50% of the market value for specialized equipment and is between 70-80% for general purpose equipment. Leases are written for 100% of the value of the equipment. Some sources of equipment financing are commercial banks, commercial finance companies, leasing companies, and the sellers of equipment.

The cost of the financing from commercial finance companies usually is higher than that from commercial banks. The rates from the sellers of equipment are based on the importance of leasing as a sales tool.

(Also see Equipment Liens, Leases, Sale-Leasebacks, Conditional Sales Contracts.)

Import/Export Financing

Introduction

International trade requires greater care in evaluation of credit criteria than does domestic trade because of the problems of collection across international boundaries, the distances involved, the costs of shipping and customs duties, the adequacy of credit checks, and volatility of the destination country of the goods. Important factors to consider are the credit-worthiness of the customer, the nature of the

Commercial banks and life insurance companies are the largest lenders to mortgagors of commercial property, which accounts for 20.3% of the total loans outstanding.

Real estate financing can be of various types — such as construction financing on a project; loans to contractors, which may be unsecured; lines of credit to finance mortgage bankers; land development financing; and permanent financing on residential, commercial, and industrial properties and other structures, such as churches. Almost exclusively capital market instruments with terms of 5-40 years, mortgages may be classified:

a. By method of repayment;

b. By level of priority, type of lien and type of insurance;

c. By type of financing requirements, such as new construction, permanent mortgage, or acquisition of existing property;

d. By type of property.

Repayment of the debt may be in the form of a straight term, where no payments are made during the term, with interest paid periodically. Straight term is used mainly for interim financing, for terms of 1-5 years, and usually for 50-60% of the appraised value. Amortized loans involve periodic payments (monthly, quarterly, or annually) in equal amounts so as to repay principal and interest by the end of the loan. A partially amortized loan is one where the periodic payments are not sufficient to repay the loan during its term, and where there is a balloon payment at the end of the term, which is usually refinanced. This method is used when the lending institution has limits on terms of loans.

Mortgages may be senior or junior mortgages. Senior mortgages have first claim on property upon liquidation; junior mortgages obtain funds left over after senior mortgage holders are satisfied. Mortgages can be insured by FHA, VA, and by private insurers, such as mortgage insurers. Insured mortgages have a higher loan-to-value ratio, and they are longer term.

Mortgage financing can be classified thus:

a. Land financing;

b. Construction financing;

c. Interim financing for existing buildings;

d. Long-term financing for existing buildings;

e. Miscellaneous financing, including acquisition financing.

The property may include land, residential property, commercial property, industrial property, farm property, and such other categories as churches, etc.

MORTGAGE CONSTANT: The mortgage constant is the percentage of the loan amount that is to be paid annually in principal and interest in an amortized loan to fully amortize the loan over its life. Thus, on a $10,000 loan to be amortized over 10 years at 10%, the annual payment of principal and interest based on monthly payments, is $1,585.92, or 15.86% of the loan amount, which is the mortgage constant.

Sources of Financing

Sources of financing for real estate are the following:

- Savings and loan associations
- Mutual savings banks
- Commercial banks
- Life insurance companies and other kinds of insurance companies
- Mortgage bankers and mortgage specialists
- Real estate investment trusts (REITs)
- Pension funds
- Foundations
- Trust companies
- Educational and charitable institutions
- Real estate brokers
- Private real estate syndicates and individuals
- Estates
- Second mortgage companies

S & Ls, mutual savings banks, and commercial banks lend funds secured by mortgages, and in most cases lend up to 75% of the appraised property value. The other institutions involved in real estate financing lend funds secured by mortgages and are involved in other transactions such as sale-leasebacks or purchase-leasebacks, as well as equity securities such as common stock, preferred stocks, and junior mortgages. The interest rate that can be obtained is lower if the amount of funds invested by the investor is higher — the lower the interest rate, the higher the cash flow.

The two main factors to consider in the area of real estate financing are **leverage** and **cash flow.** Leverage refers to the amount of funds raised from sources other than the investors as a ratio of the amount of funds invested by the investors. Cash flow refers to the amount that the investor obtains annually or periodically from the property after all expenses. Principal repayments are made from the cash flow. The higher the leverage, the higher the interest costs and the lower the cash flow.

Pension funds are becoming more active in real estate financing owing to the provisions in the Employee Retirement Income Security Act (ERISA) which encourage portfolio diversification to avoid risk, and owing to the liquidity offered in mortgage

buyer under the "45 days sight documents against acceptance" arrangement, whereby the buyer obtains the documents upon acceptance of the draft and obligates himself to pay upon maturity (in this case, in 45 days). The seller must wait for payment until the buyer makes payment and the dollars are transferred to his account. The seller may pay the interest on these terms himself or he may charge the buyer extra for the terms extended.

Consignment Transactions

Consignment transactions are not popular. Such shipments are made when the seller does not expect payment until the goods are sold. The risk is much greater for the seller, since he may have to dispose of the goods if they are not sold by the consignee. However, this method allows the seller to introduce and display his goods in a foreign country.

Export Guarantees

Exporters can sometimes receive guarantees of payment for disignated products from banks or the government of certain countries, when the guarantor is a bank, the exporter should satisfy himself of the bank's financial strength. This information can be obtained from international directories or international financial institutions in the seller's country.

Sources of Financing for Export Sales

Financing for export sales are obtained from approximately 350 commercial banks in the United States having their own international departments, and from local banks maintaining correspondent relationships with these banks. Factoring houses that purchase accounts receivable also might finance exports by purchasing receivables without recourse, assuring the seller of prompt payment. The cost of this service is usually higher than bank financing. Export Management Companies (EMCs), who are professional international marketers and act as export representatives, also can finance exports, absorbing the risk by assuring the seller of immediate payment. The federal government also assists exports through the Export-Import Bank, the Commodity Credit Corporation, and the Foreign Credit Insurance Association.

Export-Import Bank of the United States (Eximbank) & Foreign Credit Insurance Association (FCIA)

The Export-Import Bank of the United States (Eximbank) is an independent corporate agency of the U.S. government. Its function is to assist in financing the export trade of the United States by supplementing, not competing with, private capital.

Foreign Credit Insurance Association (FCIA) is a group of U.S property, casualty and marine insurance companies which cooperates with Eximbank to cover repayment of risks on short and medium-term export credit transactions.

More than 350 commercial banks work with Eximbank to provide funding and participate in the commercial risks of medium-term export transactions.

Export Credit Insurance Program (ECIP)

The ECIP is operated with FCIA. FCIA insures U.S. exports against commercial and political risks to provide the exporter comprehensive protection against non-payment for its foreign receivables. FCIA offers many types of policies, and policies can be tailor-made to the exporter's needs.

The Multibuyer policies include the Short-term Master, the Short-term/Medium-term Master policy. The Short-term Master policy applies to terms not exceeding 180 days to buyers in foreign countries. It includes a discretionary credit limit and a deductible amount applied to first dollar commercial losses. The Short-term/Medium-term Master policy covers short- and medium-term credits and is designed for the large volume exporter with multiple lines, some of which qualify for medium-term credits. The Medium-term Master policy is designed for the capital equipment exporter that maintains repetitive sales arrangements with dealers and distributors worldwide and needs continuous coverage.

The Single-buyer policies cover transactions between the insured and one buyer. The Medium-term single sale policy is designed for capital/quasi-capital goods shipped to an end-user. Usually there is a 90% commercial/100%political coverage on the financed portion plus coverage on interest. The Combined Short-term/Medium-term policy is designed for inventory financing of capital/quasi-capital goods to dealers/distributors. The Medium-term repetitive policy covers repetitive shipments (during one year) of (quasi) capital goods to a distributor or end-user.

The New-to-Export policy is designed for companies just beginning to export, or with limited volume. It gives 95% commercial risk protection with no deductible for two years.

Working Capital Guarantee Program (WCGP)

The WCGP provides exporters with access to working capital loans that would not otherwise be provided and without which, the exporter would not be able to export. Eximbank has to deem the exporter creditworthy, with Export Trading Companies (as defined in Sec 4 (c)(14)(f)(I) of the Bank Holding Company Act of 1956) and other exporters being eligible. The guarantee only covers loans used for export-related activities and generally will have a term of 1-12 months. The guarantee will be for 90% of the principal and interest up to a designated rate. There is a guarantee fee ranging upwards from 1%.

Commercial Bank Guarantee Program (CBGP)

Under this program, Eximbank guarantees the repayment of medium-term export obligations acquired by U.S. financial institutions from U.S. exporters. Eximbank assumes commercial and political risks from the exporters or financial institutions exporting to over 140 countries. The buyer has to make a 15% cash payment. For the financed portion, Eximbank's guarantee covers 100% of the political risk. For the commercial risk, the exporter has to retain a 10% participaiton (5% for small businesses) and the financing bank assumes a 5% or 15% participation with Eximbank covering the balance. Repayment terms should be consistent with customary international trade terms. Special coverages include floor-plan coverage, switch-cover option, bank-to-bank lines and pre-shipment coverage. Floor-plan coverage covers sales to dealers/distributors for up to 270 days, with unsold products being financed under a medium-term debt obligation. Switch-cover option allows a bank to provide guaranteed financing for sales through dealers or distributors to end-users. Bank-to-bank line covers revolving medium-term lines of credit established by a U.S. bank with a foreign bank in non-industrial countries. Pre-shipment coverage is used when the export product is specially fabricated or requires a lengthy manufacturing period.

Small Business Credit Program (SBCP)

This program allows U.S. commercial banks to extend fixed-rate, medium term export loans to small businesses (as defined by Small Business Administration) by providing standby assurance that the bank can borrow from Eximbank against the outstanding value of a medium-term foreign debt obligation. This encourages commercial banks to provide medium-term fixed rate loans to enable an exporter to obtain a foreign order. Eximbank's loan commitment covers up to 85% of the contract price of an export sale financed by the U.S. bank on terms ranging from 366 days to 5 years. Eximbank will issue advance commitments to make fixed-rate loans to eligible U.S. commercial banks when the applicant bank is not prepared to offer fixed-rate financing unless Eximbank provides a loan commitment. There is a limit of aggregate loan commitments per buyer of $10 million per year. Maximum contract value is $2.5 million per transaction.

Medium-term Credit Program (MCP)

The MCP provides fixed interest rate support for those medium-term export sales that are facing subsidized, officially supported export credit competition from abroad. Eximbank will make a fixed interest rate loan commitment to a U.S. bank that is financing the export sale and will lend its funds to the U.S. bank. Unlike the Small Business Credit Program, evidence of subsidized foreign officially supported export credit competition must accompany each request. This program is directed towards transactions normally financed on 1-5 year terms. The buyer must make a cash payment of at least 15% of the contract value.

Direct Loans and Financial Guarantee Program (DLFGP)

The DLFGP provides financing assistance for U.S. exports of heavy capital equipment and large - scale installations which are normally financed for a term of more than 5 years. Eximbank can either provide a direct loan to a public or private overseas buyer, or a financial guarantee assuring repayment of a private loan. This private credit may be in either U.S. dollars or a foreign currency acceptable to Eximbank. Eximbank often combines loans and guarantees into a single package. Eximbank will not provide credit support for transactions which will proceed without its assistance. Generally lines of credit, credit support for sales to developed or rich countries, sales of military goods or services, or credit for sales of older generation aircraft are ineligible. In each transaction, the foreign buyer has to make a cash payment of at least 15% of the export value of the U.S. purchase, and the Eximbank will provide credit for up to 65% of the U.S. export value. The balance of the financing is usually provided from private lenders, with such financing arranged by the borrower. Repayment of principal and interest is scheduled in equal semiannual installments, normally beginning six months from the date of delivery of the products or completion of the project. Eximbank usually agrees to be repaid from the later installments, with the private banks being repaid from the earlier maturities. Eximbank's interest rates are fixed for the life of the loan at the time of authorization. A credit authorization fee of 2% of the loan value is charged, along with a commitment fee of 0.5% per year on the undisbursed amount of each direct loan. A guarantee fee, generally 0.5% is charged on the outstanding balance of a guaranteed loan, and a guarantee commitment fee of 0.125% is charged on the undisbursed amount of each guaranteed loan.

Eximbank's address is 811 Vermont Avenue, N.W., Washington, D.C. 20571; telephone: (202)566-8990.

Commodity Credit Corporation (CCC)

The Export Credit Guarantee Program of the Commodity Credit Corporation (U.S.D.A.) stimulates U.S. agricultural exports of eligible commoditites by guaranteeing irrevocable letters of credit issued by the banks of foreign buyers thus encouraging U.S. bank financing. Credit terms can be up to 3 years and the guarantee must be necessary to increase or maintain U.S. exports to a foreign market. CCC does not wish to provide guarantees where commodities would be purchased for cash in absence of CCC's program. Certain countries are barred from participating in the program. The guarantee covers most of the port value (f.o.b. value) of the commodity, plus a portion of the accrued interest. CCC's guarantees may not cover martime freight or other charges arising after export.

Under the Intermediate Credit Export Sales Program (GSM-301), CCC can also finance the sale and export of U.S. agricultural exports for periods in excess of three years but not more than ten years. Information can be obtained from Foreign Agriculture Service, U.S. Department of Agriculture, Washington, D.C. 20250 (202-447-3224).

Real Estate Financing

Introduction

Real estate financing with borrowed funds is accomplished mainly through the use of the mortgage. A mortgage is used in conjunction with a debt instrument. The mortgage provides the lender security in the real estate owned or controlled by the borrower. If the borrower defaults in the payment of the loan, the lender can repossess the real estate, sell it, and apply the proceeds to the repayment of the loan. The lender becomes a general creditor against the assets of the borrower for any balance due on the loan, or the lender could be prevented from pursuing the balance from the remaining assets of the borrower. The lender is the mortgagee; the borrower the mortgagor. Mortgages are governed by the laws of the state in which the property is located.

Table 8. Mortgage Loans Outstanding by Type of Lender and Type of Property in Billions of Dollars, 1983 Year-End

	Residential Property						
Lender	1-4 Family	Multi-Family	Total	Commercial Property	Farm Property	Total Loans	%
S & Ls	389.8	42.4	432.2	61.2	—[a]	493.4	27.0
Com'l. Banks	181.7	18.0	199.7	119.8	9.3	328.9	18.0
MSBs[b]	96.6	17.8	114.4	21.7		136.1	7.4
LICs[c]	15.4	19.2	34.6	104.3	12.7	151.6	8.3
Others	531.1	53.5	584.6	44.3	87.6	716.4	39.2
TOTAL	1,214.6	150.9	1,365.5	351.3	109.6	1,826.4	100.0
Percentage	66.5	8.3	74.8	19.2	6.0	100.0	

Source: Federal Reserve Board
[a]Less than $50 million; [b]Mutual Savings Banks; [c]Life Insurance Cos.

Real Estate is an important sector of the U.S economy;total outstanding mortgages had reached $1,826 billion. As shown in table 8 the largest segment is 1-4 family dwellings, with commercial property being second.

Commercial banks and life insurance companies are the largest lenders to mortgagors of commercial property, which accounts for 19.2% of the total loans outstanding.

Real estate financing can be of various types — such as construction financing on a project; loans to contractors, which may be unsecured; lines of credit to finance mortgage bankers; land development financing; and permanent financing on residential, commercial, and industrial properties and other structures, such as churches. Almost exclusively capital market instruments with terms of 5-40 years, mortgages may be classified:

a. By method of repayment;

b. By level of priority, type of lien and type of insurance;

c. By type of financing requirements, such as new construction, permanent mortgage, or acquisition of existing property;

d. By type of property.

Repayment of the debt may be in the form of a straight term, where no payments are made during the term, with interest paid periodically. Straight term is used mainly for interim financing, for terms of 1-5 years, and usually for 50-60% of the appraised value. Amortized loans involve periodic payments (monthly, quarterly, or annually) in equal amounts so as to repay principal and interest by the end of the loan. A partially amortized loan is one where the periodic payments are not sufficient to repay the loan during its term, and where there is a balloon payment at the end of the term, which is usually refinanced. This method is used when the lending institution has limits on terms of loans.

Mortgages may be senior or junior mortgages. Senior mortgages have first claim on property upon liquidation; junior mortgages obtain funds left over after senior mortgage holders are satisfied. Mortgages can be insured by FHA, VA, and by private insurers, such as mortgage insurers. Insured mortgages have a higher loan-to-value ratio, and they are longer term.

Mortgage financing can be classified thus:

a. Land financing;

b. Construction financing;

c. Interim financing for existing buildings;

d. Long-term financing for existing buildings;

e. Miscellaneous financing, including acquisition financing.

The property may include land, residential property, commercial property, industrial property, farm property, and such other categories as churches, etc.

MORTGAGE CONSTANT: The mortgage constant is the percentage of the loan amount that is to be paid annually in principal and interest in an amortized loan to fully amortize the loan over its life. Thus, on a $10,000 loan to be amortized over 10 years at 10%, the annual payment of principal and interest based on monthly payments, is $1,585.92, or 15.86% of the loan amount, which is the mortgage constant.

Sources of Financing

Sources of financing for real estate are the following:

- Savings and loan associations
- Mutual savings banks
- Commercial banks
- Life insurance companies and other kinds of insurance companies
- Mortgage bankers and mortgage specialists
- Real estate investment trusts (REITs)
- Pension funds
- Foundations
- Trust companies
- Educational and charitable institutions
- Real estate brokers
- Private real estate syndicates and individuals
- Estates
- Second mortgage companies

S & Ls, mutual savings banks, and commercial banks lend funds secured by mortgages, and in most cases lend up to 75% of the appraised property value. The other institutions involved in real estate financing lend funds secured by mortgages and are involved in other transactions such as sale-leasebacks or purchase-leasebacks, as well as equity securities such as common stock, preferred stocks, and junior mortgages. The interest rate that can be obtained is lower if the amount of funds invested by the investor is higher — the lower the interest rate, the higher the cash flow.

The two main factors to consider in the area of real estate financing are **leverage** and **cash flow.** Leverage refers to the amount of funds raised from sources other than the investors as a ratio of the amount of funds invested by the investors. Cash flow refers to the amount that the investor obtains annually or periodically from the property after all expenses. Principal repayments are made from the cash flow. The higher the leverage, the higher the interest costs and the lower the cash flow.

Pension funds are becoming more active in real estate financing owing to the provisions in the Employee Retirement Income Security Act (ERISA) which encourage portfolio diversification to avoid risk, and owing to the liquidity offered in mortgage securities through FHA, VA, GNMA, or private mortgage insurers. The yields are high in real estate mortgages because of their specialized nature, but there is lesser marketability compared with some other securities, and there are problems and time involved in foreclosure and final settlement. Real Estate Investment Trusts (REITs) are involved in all types of real estate financing, including land development; construction financing; short-, intermediate-, and long-term financing; and junior mortgages.

Land Development Financing

Land development financing can be accomplished through the use of Land Development Loans or Land Purchase-Leasebacks or Sale-Leasebacks. Both are used by subdivision developers for the installation of necessary utilities such as sewer, water, etc.

Under a Land Development Loan or a First Mortgage Development Loan, a mortgage is designed to include the entire property; individual lots are removed from the mortgage as they are sold and the lender is paid up to a certain percentage of the purchase price of the lot. The loan is repaid before all the lots are sold. Most institutions active in real estate financing engage in this type of financing.

Land Sale-Leasebacks are negotiated with institutions which take an equity interest, such as REITs. The institution purchases the land and leases it back to the developer, giving him a greater amount of cash. If the institution doing the sale-leaseback is not the same as the one providing construction or permanent financing, the institution providing the latter kind of financing sometimes is given a first mortgage. The leasing institution then obtains an equity participation or a percentage of the gross rental in return for its greater risk.

Construction Financing

Construction financing is used for the construction of buildings and sometimes for land development. It is used until the property is refinanced through long-term permanent financing. The same institutions may not be interested in both construction and long-term financing. Life insurance companies and other similar long-term lenders are interested in permanent mortgages, and commercial banks, savings institutions, mortgage companies, REITs, and private investors are interested in construction financing and long-term financing. Construction financing can be the following types:

a. Commercial loans, secured or unsecured, to the developer which are similar to working capital loans. Established developers may have a line of credit. The loan may be in the form of one note or a series of notes which are drawn as the need arises;

b. A mortgage loan, where the developer is expected to have equity in the project and the lender has a mortgage on the property. Normally the developer's funds are used first for the project, and then the lender's.

Blanket mortgages are sometimes used in construction financing if the development consists of a number of structures (as in single-family residential construction) and individual structures are released from the mortgage as payments are made from funds obtained from sale of the units. Lenders inspect the property as construction payments are made to the contractor. They also satisfy themselves that the subcontractors are paid in order to avoid mechanic's liens on the property. The lender also wants to be satisfied that the work paid for actually is finished. At the end of the construction, about 10-15% of the funds are held back until the period for filing of mechanic's liens elapses. Since these loans are repaid from permanent mortgages, some lenders will not lend funds on certain types of projects — especially in tight-money periods — unless there is a permanent mortgage standby commitment. It is not necessary that the developer exercise the standby commitment since it is possible that other sources of funds may be available upon completion. However, a standby commitment fee is paid to the prospective lender.

Construction loans can be risky because there may be problems in completing construction on schedule — resulting in higher than anticipated costs, which may cause the project to fail. Thus, more supervision is needed for construction loans, for which lenders charge special fees of 1-3% of the principal. Construction mortgage interest rates are higher than comparable rates on completed units. The success of the project also may be affected by the nature of the economy, resulting in a lower-than-anticipated rental income.

Interim Financing

Floor Loans: These are loans given to developers of properties, usually commercial and industrial, who build without tenants to occupy the building. These loans are lower in the loan-to-value ratio than if the building were occupied. These loans could be 50% of the value of the building, and the loan could be an amortizing or non-amortizing loan. When a tenant (or tenants) are found, the developer obtains an additional loan to increase the loan to value ratio to 75% or refinances the original loan to increase the loan-to-value ratio. These loans are made after the building is constructed. Some life insurance companies and savings and loan associations participate in such loans.

Intermediate- and Long-Term Financing

With the exception of construction financing, which is temporary, most real estate financing is long-term financing. Intermediate-term financing is used when it is difficult to raise long-term funds for a project owing to the state of the economy and tight money conditions, or when there is the need to prove the profitability of a project to obtain favorable rates for long-term financing. Real estate has not been very effective in obtaining funds during tight money periods. There are various types of intermediate-term and permanent financing based on the kind of mortgages, the kind of security covered, the terms, etc. Some of them are:

Conventional Real Estate Financing

Intermediate-term financing is usually for less than 10 years and does not require amortization of the principal. Long-term financing is done for between 15 and 30 years and requires amortization of the loan. The loan limit sometimes is restricted by law to 75% of the appraised market value of the property, and the financing takes place through institutions such as life insurance companies, pension funds, REITs, S & Ls, etc.

Real Estate Bonds

Real estate bonds have been unpopular since the 1930s owing to the losses suffered by investors in such bonds. These bonds are issued with real estate as security through a mortgage. Bonds create greater participation than a private placement mortgage transaction.

Open-End Mortgage

Open-end mortgages allow the borrower to obtain funds with the same property as security at the same lien level. They are usually obtained in residential property and from the same lender so that the property owner can borrow funds to maintain or expand the property using long-term funds.

Commercial and Industrial Mortgages

The terms for commercial and industrial property are usually for 10-30 years, depending on their flexibility for other uses. Industrial property is sometimes very specialized and hence amortized in approximately 10 years.

Multi-family Mortgages

Multi-family mortgages are financed mainly through life insurance companies and savings institutions, and these loans are obtained through mortgage bankers or by direct contacts with the institutions in the national market. The institutions sometimes prefer equity participations in these income-producing properties.

Farm Mortgages (See Agricultural Financing)

The main lenders are individuals, the Federal Land Banks, commercial banks, life insurance companies, and other federal agencies such as the Farmers Home Administration, etc.

Package Financing

This type of financing is done wherever the project requires a large amount of equipment which can be financed either through the use of a chattel mortgage or along with the real estate in a package mortgage. The items of equipment included in the mortgage are designated individually in the agreement. Package financing often is useful in shopping center and apartment loans. The equipment usually has a relatively long life, thus avoiding obsolescence before the mortgage is paid and increasing the loan-to-value ratio. The advantage of this arrangement is that there is only one loan, one mortgage, and one payment — resulting sometimes in a lower cost because of lower administrative costs. The disadvantage is that a higher loan-to-value ratio can be possible by obtaining up to 100% financing through leases from the equipment manufacturers, thus raising the 75% limit.

Financing Leased Property

When the property is leased to a high credit customer with a long-term lease, the customer expects a very low cost of rental. This may be possible because lenders allow a higher loan-to-value ratio, sometimes up to 100%. It may be feasible to those who would be satisfied with a small cash flow, and would be able to use a tax loss from depreciation.

Wraparound Mortgages

Wraparound mortgages are used when the real

estate owner wants to borrow additional funds on the same property without repayment of the first mortgage. In this case, the second lender takes over the obligations to the first lender; the borrower pays the second lender, who pays the first lender. In a wraparound mortgage, the borrower pays the interest rate charged by the latter lender. Thus, if the interest rate on the first loan was lower than the rate charged on the second loan, the effective rate to the borrower from the second lender is higher than the stated rate because the second lender is paying a lower rate to the first lender. Thus, if the first rate was 7% and the second rate was 11%, the effective return to the second lender is greater than 11%.

Blanket Mortgages

If a developer owns more than two properties, the first lender on each property can be given a second position on the other property. With the greater security, the loan-to-value ratio can be increased.

Acquisition Financing by Seller

The owner can finance the sale of the property himself through the use of the following instruments:

Contract for Deed (Also called Land Contract)

The buyer makes a down payment to the seller and agrees to pay the balance in periodic installments. Title to the property is retained by the seller until all obligations are paid, at which time it is transferred to the buyer. The seller is still the owner of record in the deed, but the Land Contract restricts him from transferring title to others as long as the terms of the agreement are met by the buyer. The land contract should be signed by the seller, the buyer, and their respective spouses, or else there may be problems in the transfer of title later if the spouse refuses to relinquish title. There are other clauses to be considered — including the disposition of existing mortgages, insurance coverage, rights of any tenants, restrictions upon assignment by the buyer, penalties for prepayment, and default by buyer. Land Contracts can and should be recorded to protect the interests of all parties. A Land Contract can be converted to a regular mortgage with a transfer of title when a certain percentage of the total amount is paid. Land Contracts sometimes have very low down payments.

Purchase Money Mortgage

The Purchase Money Mortgage is similar to the Land Contract except that the seller transfers title to the buyer, but takes a mortgage, usually senior, on the property. It has the same tax advantages as the Land Contract if the sale qualifies as an Installment Sale. It is used when the down payment is higher since the problems of foreclosure in case of default are greater than in a Land Contract.

Trust Deed

In a Trust Deed, the title to the property is held by a trustee on behalf of the beneficiary, the buyer. The title is transferred to the buyer after all payments are made. In case of default, the property can be sold to pay the balance due the seller. In some states, court proceedings may not be necessary for foreclosure and a trustee's sale.

Equity Participation by Institutions

The majority of real estate financing is through mortgage loans. However, some financings are accomplished using equity and debt instruments where most, if not all, of the financing is raised from external sources with the developer lending only his expertise. Equity can be raised through incorporation and the sale of stock; and stock can be used for land, professional services, and as sweeteners to lenders. Institutions that invest in equity include life insurance companies, pension funds, service agencies of S & L, REITs and RE syndications. The regulated companies are allowed to invest a small percentage of their assets in high-risk, high-ratio loans and equity-type financing, where the loan-to-value ratio could reach 90-100%. Since the lenders are taking equity-type risks in such financings, they feel entitled to equity participations. This can be in the form of stock or in the form of an additional compensation based on the sales or income from the project in addition to a fixed payment to amortize the loan. The lenders have restrictions on their agreements, which allow them to protect their investment.

The packages used in participation agreements include the following:

a. Percentage of gross income, where the lender gets a small percentage of the gross income in addition to the regular payments, or a larger percentage above a minimum gross sales figure;

b. Percentage of net income, which is more complicated than the percentage of gross income and is used less often;

c. Stock ownership with the developer, who supplies the management and obtains a percentage of ownership in the property with minimal or no investment.

Financing Special Purpose Real Estate

Special purpose real estate is property that has limited use beyond the stated and designed one, such as hotels and theaters. Most industrial property is included in this category. Financing requirements for this type of property are similar to those for private placements. Financing is influenced by the caliber of management, the financial strength of the owner or the long-term lessee, the nature of the product and the industry, and the value of the property. The covenants in the loan agreement may cover the same items covered in private placement agreements, including restrictions on dividends and bonuses, balance sheet restrictions, and accelerated amortization of the loan based on earnings.

Sale-Leaseback

Sale-leaseback transactions involve the sale of assets, including real estate, to an institutional lender and the long-term lease of the property by the seller. The sale-leaseback arrangement has advantages to the seller:

- The seller obtains cash which can be used in the business;
- In case of depreciated property, the lease payments can be a business expense greater than the annual depreciation;
- The cost of land also can be expensed;
- The seller can obtain an option to repurchase the property at the end of or during the term of the lease;
- Some businesses such as commercial banks have further advantages, since the lending ability of the bank is determined by the amount of funds in certain assets according to their maturity and marketability. The capital freed from the ownership of the bank's real estate can be used as its lending base, thus increasing its lending ability by up to five times the sale price of the real estate, which may be higher than the book value.

Financing Leaseholds

A Leasehold is the right of a tenant to use land for a defined time period. Leaseholds are created when the owner of the land refuses to sell it but consents to lease it for a long term, such as 99 years, or when the developer sells the land to a financial institution and leases it back.

The developer, who leases the land from the owner, constructs and owns the building as long as he satisfies the terms of the lease arrangement with the landowner. It is expected that the lessee will develop the property by construction of new buildings or replacement of existing ones. In order to guarantee that development takes place, the landowner frequently requires a bond protection. If the landowner has to subordinate his security interest to the financial institution that will finance the construction and the permanent mortgage, the developer will have to make a substantial downpayment on the lease arrangement, and the lease payments may be higher than if the landowner were not to subordinate his claim. If the developer defaults, the financial institution obtains the land and improvements, but the landowner can claim it by paying the outstanding amount to the institution — resulting in the developer's losing his investment.

In a "Sale-Leaseback and Leasehold Mortgage" the land is sold to the institution, with the developer owning the building. The institution lends, for example, 75% of the value of the building, and in addition, the developer obtains funds from the sale of the land, resulting in loan-to-value ratio higher than 75% of the total property. Furthermore, since the institution owns the land, it may loan more than 75% of the value of the improvements. The developer still can depreciate the cost of the buildings and expense the lease cost of the land. Some clauses included in this agreement are renewal options, repurchase agreements, and the term of the agreement.

Types of Leases

Most long-term leases protect the lessor against the costs of operation, taxes, and maintenance. This is done either by adding these costs to the lease cost, having a provision to increase the lease costs with an increase in these costs, or making the lease a net lease where the lessee pays the expenses.

Leases can be classified on the basis of some of the following variables:

a. Term: The lease is an ordinary short-term nonamortizing lease, or a long-term amortizing lease. With the latter, the payments amortize the cost of the asset, and the lessee has the option to renew the lease at substantially reduced rates or to purchase the property at minimal cost;

b. Participation: The lessor is entitled to payments in addition to the regular periodic payments, such as a percentage of income;

c. Previous owner: The property previously was owned by the lessee or purchased by the lessor from a developer, or previous owner;

d. Gross or net leases: The lease is a gross lease if the lessor pays the expenses, such as taxes, maintenance, etc.; it is a net lease if the lessee pays;

e. Amount of payments: These could be constant, or could increase with time or as the lessee's volume or income from the asset increases.

Junior Mortgages

Junior mortgages involve more risk for the lender, and hence the cost of the funds to the borrower is likely to be higher — either in the form of a higher interest rate or an equity interest in the property. The term of junior mortgages usually is shorter than that for senior mortgages; most are for less than 5 years.

The junior mortgage should acknowledge the existing first mortgage and also allow the borrower to have future mortgages not exceeding a specified amount. This clause is known as the "lifting clause," because the mortgagor can lift the first mortgage and replace it with another one of like amount, at perhaps a lower interest rate or other favorable terms, without changing the position of the junior mortgage.

Information Requirements

Information requirements for a mortgage are similar to those for a private placement, along with other specific information about building models, specifications, blueprints and pictures, potential or signed clients and leases with them, and economic and marketing studies showing the feasibility of the project at that location.

Agriculture Financing

Introduction

Agricultural loans can be categorized into real estate loans and nonreal estate loans — i.e., loans for operating expenses, etc. Based on Table 9, real estate loans as of January 1, 1984, were 111.6 billion, and nonreal estate loans $103 billion.

TABLE 9. Balance Sheet of the Farming Sector on January 1, 1984, in Billions of Dollars

	Assets	Liabilities & Net Worth	
Financial	$ 50.1	Nonreal estate loans	$103.0
Nonreal estate	216.5	Real estate	111.6
Real estate	764.5	Total debt	214.7
Total	1,031.1	Equity & net worth	816.4

Source: **Economic Indicators of the Farm Sector, Income and Balance Sheet Statistics, 1983.** U.S. Dept. of Agriculture.

The majority of this debt was from commercial banks, with Federal Land Banks and Production Credit Associations next in order of importance. Federal Land Banks were the largest lender in real estate loans, and commercial banks were the largest lender in the nonreal estate category. Production Credit Associations were next in order of importance for nonreal estate loans, as shown in Table 10.

Table 10. Type of Farm Debt held by groups of Farm Creditors, January 1, 1984 (Preliminary)

Creditor	Real Estate Department Billions	%	Nonreal Estate Department Billions	%	Total Farm Debt Billions	%
All operating Banks	$ 9.3	8.3	39.1′	38.0	$ 48.4	22.5
Life Ins. Cos.	12.7	11.4	-	-	12.7	5.9
Fed'l Land Banks	47.9	42.9	-	-	47.9	22.3
FICBs	-	-	0.8	0.8	0.8	0.4
Prod. Cred. Assoc.	-	-	18.7	18.2	18.7	8.7
Farmers Home Admin.	9.3	8.4	14.6	14.2	23.9	11.1
Commodity Credit Corp.	-	-	10.8	10.5	10.8	5.0
Individuals & Others	32.2	28.9	18.9	18.4	51.2	23.8
	21.7	34	8.2	15	29.9	25
Total	111.6	100.0	103.0	100.0	$ 214.6	100.0

Source: **Economic Indicators of the Farm Sector, Income and Balance Sheet Statistics 1983.** Dept. of Agriculture.

The institutions involved in lending to the farm sector and the types of instruments used are the following:

Commercial Banks: These are perhaps the most important source of funds to the farm sector, accounting for 30% of the total outstanding loans, and 46% of the nonreal estate loans. Some reasons for this are bank locations, providing easy access to the farmers; their credit service, providing temporary operating credit at competitive rates; and their full range of services.

Operating loans mature annually at the end of the production cycle and can be used for livestock seed, and fertilizer.

Loans for intermediate terms are made for items such as machinery and buildings and for long terms for real estate. Balloon-type loans often are made in the farm sector, with the balloon payment usually refinanced upon maturity. Credit evaluation for farm operation loans are affected by factors such as weather, insects, disease, and prices. The major competition for banks for nonreal estate loans, where they are predominant, is from Production Credit Associations.

The Cooperative Farm Credit System: The Cooperative Farm Credit System is composed of three parts:

- The Banks for Cooperatives;
- The Federal Land Banks and Federal Land Bank Associations (FLBAs);
- The Federal Intermediate Credit Banks (FICB), Production Credit Associations (PCAs), and other financial institutions (OFLs).

There are 12 Farm Credit districts in the United States, with a Federal Land Bank, a Federal Intermediate Credit Bank, and a Bank for Cooperatives at the same location within each district. The Central Bank for Cooperatives, which participates with the districts' banks, is in Denver, Colorado. The agricultural borrowers elect the directors of the local PCAs and the FLBAs, and these directors, along with the boards of cooperatives owning stock in the Banks for Cooperatives, elect six members to the district Farm Credit Board, with a seventh member appointed by the governor of the Farm Credit Administration.

The district boards make policy for the three banks in their respective districts. The Federal Farm Credit Board is composed of one representative from each district board, who is appointed by the President of the United States, and a thirteenth member appointed by the Secretary of Agriculture. The Board appoints the governor of the Farm Credit Administration. The Farm Credit Administation (FCA) operates under federal laws, principally under the Farm Credit Act of 1971.

Figure 7. How Farmers Share in Control of the Cooperative Farm Credit System

ELIGIBLE MEMBERS ELECT BOARDS OF DIRECTORS OF LOCAL

PCAs FLBAs Banks for Cooperatives

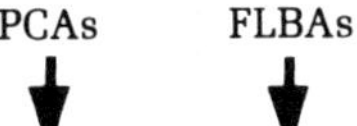

Elect Two Members each of the District Farm Credit Board, with seventh appointed by the Governor of the Farm Credit system

Each District Nominates one person to Federal Farm Credit Board, appointed by President of the U.S.

Appoints Governor of the Farm Credit System

Each of the banks can issue its own notes, bonds and debentures, and similar obligations to raise funds — subject to the supervision of the Farm Credit Administration. They can issue the instruments together with the other banks in the system. These instruments — their principal sources of funds — are sold in the money markets. They also borrow from other Farm Credit banks, commercial banks, other financial institutions, and through the sale of Farm Credit Investment Bonds to their borrowers. These obligations are not insured or guaranteed by the government.

Banks for Cooperatives

The district banks provide loans to eligible cooperatives, which may include any association of farmers, ranchers, or producers, or harvesters of aquatic products operated on a cooperative basis. A cooperative must be involved in one of the following functions:

- Storing, packing, processing, or marketing farm or aquatic products;
- Purchasing, testing, grading, processing, furnishing, or distributing farm or aquatic supplies;
- Furnishing business services to farmers, producers, harvesters of aquatic products, or other eligible cooperatives.

The Bank for Cooperatives provides:

- Short-term loans (less than 18 months), which are secured or unsecured, for current or seasonal needs;
- Secured or unsecured intermediate- and long-term loans for financing long-term assets or working capital (for land, buildings, and equipment). These loans are amortized over a number of years, with payment sometimes tied to volume, such as sales;
- Lines of credit are provided to established borrowers to handle seasonal need.

Interest rates on these loans are affected by many factors, such as the cost of money to the banks, the term and the type of loan.

Contact: District office of the Bank for Cooperatives.

The Federal Land Bank System

Loans are made through more than 500 local FLBAs. The banks are owned by the borrowers, even though they initially were capitalized by the government. Loans may be made to the following:

- Farmers or ranchers
- Rural residents
- Farm-related businesses

The Federal Land Bank makes loans — secured by first mortgages on real estate — for agricultural purposes and other credit needs. The term of the loans ranges from 5 to 40 years, and repayment plans are amortized, with the amortization schedule designed to suit the borrower's cash flow needs. The loan cannot exceed 85% of the appraised value of the real estate security, and the interest rates are variable — based on the average cost of money to the banks. The loan application is made at the local FLBA. Every borrower must purchase stock and become a member of the bank. The amount of stock purchased is between 5% and 10% of the loan amount. The stock is retired at par value when the loan is repaid. Rural residents and farm-related businesses are given certificates without voting rights in order to keep control in the hands of the farmers and ranchers.

The Production Credit System

The Production Credit System has 12 district Federal Intermediate Credit Banks (FICBs) and more than 400 Production Credit Associations (PCAs) with 1,600 full-time offices. The PCAs are the credit retail outlets with the wholesale organization being the FICB. The FICBs discount eligible paper and loans from PCAs, commercial banks, and other financial institutions. They are completely owned by the farmer borrowers. PCAs make loans to the following;

- Farmers and Ranchers
- Producers or harvesters of aquatic products
- Rural residents
- Farm-related businesses

Loans are made for working capital, equipment, or operating needs. Short-term loans include lines of credit, crop liens, and secured working capital. Intermediate-term loans include unsecured term loans, chattel mortgages, and farm improvement loans. Payback can be based on an amortization basis, or can be based on the production cycle and tied to the sale of crops or livestock. The term of the loans cannot exceed 7 years; the interest rate varies with the type and term of the loan and the cost of money to the banks. Loan criteria are the same as for the Banks for Cooperatives. PCAs also provide other services, such as credit life insurance, crop hail insurance, and farm record keeping.

The banks and associations of the Farm Credit System evaluate the loan application on the basis of the following criteria:

- Integrity of the individual or entity should be established, and there should be responsible and cooperative management, with expertise in operations and finance. This is the most important criterion.
- Financial strength and responsibility — reflecting the ability to meet obligations, to continue business operations, and to protect the lender against undue risk.
- Sufficient cash flow to repay the loan and all obligations, with a provision for contingencies.
- The loan must be constructive in amount and purpose, and must suit the repayment needs of the borrower and the lender.
- Sufficient collateral to reasonably protect the lender.

Other financial institutions which play an important role in the lending of funds to the farm sector are the following:

Life Insurance Companies

Life insurance companies are an important factor in real estate loans to farmers. However, only a few insurance companies are active in the market, with 8 companies accounting for approximately 87% of the outstanding loan amount. The loans are long-term and may range up to 25 years.

The Farmers Home Administration

The Farmers Home Administration (FmHA) is a government lending agency established in 1946 within the U.S. Department of Agriculture. FmHA credit programs to the farmer-borrower include the following:

- Operating loans made to eligible operators of family farms for livestock, equipment, feed, seed, fertilizer, or other farm and home operating needs; to refinance chattel debts; to provide operating loans to fish farmers; to carry out forestry purposes; and to develop income-producing recreational enterprises. The term of the loan usually is up to 7 years, and the interest rate varies with the cost of money to the U.S. Treasury. Maximum loan size is $100,000 for insured and $200,000 for guaranteed loans.
- Ownership loans to eligible farmers to enlarge, develop, and buy farms not larger than family farms, with the objectives mentioned above. The maximum term is 40 years.
- Emergency loans to eligible farmers in counties officially declared as disaster areas, to be used for feed, seed, fertilizer, equipment, livestock, and other purposes to restore normal operations. The term is normally less than 7 years, and the interest rate is 5-8%.

FmHA has other loans mentioned in the Government Financing Sector of the book. FmHA loans can be guaranteed or insured. In guaranteed loans, the loan funds are provided by a private lender and guaranteed to a certain limit by the FmHA. Insured loans are made by and serviced by FmHA. Even though the percentage of total farm loans made by FmHA is small, it is a very important segment because FmHA concentrates on the "high-risk" sector, which would be rejected by private lenders without some form of guarantee. FmHA also provides technical assistance and loan supervision.

Miscellaneous Sources

Other sources of credit to farm borrowers include individuals, trade credit, credit unions, savings and loan associations, finance companies, and the Small Business Administration.

Eurodollars

Introduction

Definition

The most common definition of Eurodollars is that they are dollars deposited in banks anywhere outside the United States. "Eurodollars" has become a generic term, in that dollars deposited in an Asian bank also are called Eurodollars, and the term "Eurocurrencies" has come to mean any currency deposited outside the country which originally issued such currency. In some cases, the dollars need not be deposited since dollars obtained from a citizen of France by an English investment banker become a Eurodollar offering even though they have not been routed through a commercial bank. Currencies have existed outside their native countries for a long time. However, starting in the 1950s, the amount of these currencies, in foreign control, especially dollar deposits, grew considerably and gave major importance to these dollar holdings. With the U.S. balance-of-payments deficits, U.S. investments in foreign countries, and dollar deposits by U.S. citizens in foreign banks, the Eurodollar pool has grown considerably, and it was approximately $1780 billion in 1984. The practice originated when some central banks and insurance companies kept their dollar deposits in European banks. Deposits presently are kept in foreign banks to obtain higher yields and/or lower risks. Being a free-floating pool, these funds are not regulated by any national or international organization, since most regulations are for domestic currencies.

Description

Although Eurodollars are defined as dollars deposited in foreign banks, it should be noted that the actual currency may never leave the United States. Thus, if a foreign bank obtains a deposit from the U.S. investor, it may leave the deposit in an American bank temporarily and then lend it to an American corporation for use in the United States. However, the American investor has invested his dollars in the foreign bank, which has the dollar liability and the control of the funds. U.S. banks can borrow funds from their European branches or from European banks and relend to customers in the United States. This happens during tight money periods. Most Eurodollar deposits are time deposits, ranging in term from overnight to 5 years, with most being short-term investments. The banks accepting the deposits may be anywhere in the world; the investor chooses the bank based upon the degree of commercial and political risk, and the yield on the funds. The Eurodollars may be loaned in the form of dollars or in the form of some other currency after conversion. In the latter case, either the lender or the borrower hedges the risk of changing currency fluctuation rates. Minimum deposits of Eurodollars are around $20,000, and the average maturity is around 3 months. U.S. banks that take Eurodollar deposits through their foreign branches can keep the funds safely in U.S. banks.

The major sources of Eurodollars are central banks, governments, international organizations, commercial banks, business corporations, and individuals. The major users of Eurodollars are the central banks, governments, commercial banks, and business corporations.

Instruments

The types of instruments used in the Eurodollar market fall into three major categories by term:

Short-Term

Line of Credit: Similar to the lines of credit in the United States, with maturity of less than 1 year. The rate is based on some formula, usually the interbank lending rate in London and the agreed-upon spread. This instrument is obtained from commercial banks. It should be noted that this is not a commitment and can be broken by the bank at any time, but usually, the bank does not renege unless there has been a severe change in the economy or the company.

Eurocommercial paper: Similar to commercial paper in the United States, these are promissory notes issued by commercial and industrial corporations for short-term funds, usually up to 6 months. The issuer and the investor deal directly with each other, and they are sold in multiples of $10,000 with a $50,000 minimum. The rates paid are very close to the bank rates paid to depositors.

Conventional loans: Available from the Eurocurrency market similar to those from U.S. banks, and they are for a fixed amount of money for a fixed period. The interest rates may be fixed or floating.

Medium-Term (Up to 7 years)

Eurodollar Rollover Commitment: Similar to the Revolving Credit Agreement in the U.S. The commercial bank is legally committed to provide Eurodollars up to the maximum specified amount for the period of the loan which could range up to five years. The funds can be borrowed using notes with maturities up to 12 months, which can be renewed for the term of the agreement. The interest rate paid is calculated on a base and a spread at the time the note is drawn or renewed; and the bank changes a commitment fee of approximately 1% of the unused portion of the commitment.

Term-loans: Similar to term loans or transaction loans in the United States — i.e., a fixed amount is loaned for a specified period of time. The major difference is that compensating balances are not required. The loans are amortizing, and there is sometimes a floating rate arrangement with rates being adjusted every 3-6 months with a minimum level, or they may be fixed rates. There is a growing demand for medium-term loans and roll-over credits, and these are obtained from a single institution if the amount is small (up to $10 million) and from a syndicate if the amount is larger. The medium-term notes may be publicly issued or privately placed. The private placement is similar to the public offering except that it is not formally underwritten and not generally quoted on a stock exchange. Private placement rates are about 0.5% higher than public offerings, and the amounts usually are larger for public offerings than for private placements.

Medium and Long-Term (More than 5 years)

Floating Rate Notes: May be medium-term notes and are hybrid instruments since they combine a minimum level of interest rates with fluctuations above this minimum based on market rates, thus preserving the market value of the note. These are generally listed securities. The interest rate is adjusted on the basis of the London Inter Bank Rate.

Eurobonds: Bonds sold internationally by an international syndicate of investment bankers. The currency of the bonds may be any currency other than that of at least some of the countries in which it is sold. The average Eurobond issue has a smaller term since the international investor has a smaller risk horizon than an investor purchasing debt instruments in his native country. The life of the Eurobond is usually between 12-15 years, compared with terms up to 40 years in the United States. Eurobonds are purchased mainly by private and institutional investors. The private investor was more dominant in the 1960s, but the institutional investor is becoming more important. The Eurobond secondary market has been expanding rapidly since 1974, and this has assisted the broadening of the primary market customers. Since Eurodollars are not subject to any nation's regulations and are free to move with the investor's wishes, the Eurobond market rates have been a good indicator and example of supply and demand of capital funds. Usually they have been slightly higher than U.S. domestic bond rates for the same ratings, but with the added cost of borrowing by foreign companies in the United States, the costs are competitive. Private placements have been very popular in the Eurobond market owing to the advantages of lower cost of commissions and expenses, and simplified administrative work.

Hybrids and Equity Instruments: Very large companies well known to the investor, can float equity securities. For smaller companies, hybrids may be offered in the form of convertibles or debt instruments with warrants to purchase stock. The maturity for these hybrids are about the same as straight debt instruments, but the rate is lower to account for the profit potential from the conversion or the exercise of the warrants. The conversion price is usually set at about 5-20% above the market value of the stock at the time of the issuance.

Characteristics

Advantages and Reasons for Existence of Eurodollars

Some of the advantages of and reasons for the use of Eurodollars are the following:

a. During periods of tight money in the United States, American banks can borrow Eurodollars from their foreign branches or from foreign banks for relending to clients willing to pay the price;

b. Business corporations can obtain funds offshore that can be invested or used in the United States or in foreign operations; these funds can be raised free from government restraints;

c. For some corporations and some types of securities, the cost of funds may be lower in the Eurodollar market than in any other available option;

d. The speed with which the funds can be raised is much greater in the Eurodollar market since there is no need to satisfy SEC requirements;

e. There is a withholding tax of 30% on deposit interest and dividends paid to nonresidents from their investments in the U.S. There are some treaties which allow this to be circumvented. The foreign investors cannot directly invest in U.S. corporations and banks without paying this tax, unless they use the circumventing strategies. It is easier for them to deposit in Eurodollars and let the larger institutions take advantage of the strategies. Even with precautions, there is no certainty the IRS will waive the withholding tax;

f. In some cases and in some countries, it may be cheaper to borrow in Eurodollars rather than in the local currency if there are favorable interest and forward exchange rates;

g. Eurodollars may be used if there is a lack of domestic credit at the desired terms;

h. There may be restraints on local currency, as in the United States and the United Kingdom, which do not exist with Eurocurrencies. The range of instruments may be greater than is available in the local market;

i. The type of currency that is desired may be available only in the Euromarket;

j. Some international partnerships may prefer the flexibility of the Eurodollar to the restrictions imposed if financed with the currency of each partner's native country.

Costs and Margins

The Eurodollar market is free of all government regulations and hence operates in a free market environment. Thus, the cost of the money (i.e., the rates paid to depositors) and the income, (i.e., the rates charged to borrowers) are based solely on the world supply of and demand for funds. Eurodollar rates rise when world money conditions are tight, and the difference between these rates and U.S. domestic rates increases. Generally Eurodollar lenders work with narrower margins than domestic banks owing to this free market environment. Some other factors affecting rates are:

a. There are no reserve requirements as exist in the United States, where a bank has to keep 5% of its deposits in reserve, thus having idle assets and increasing the effective cost of funds. The Eurobanker can loan all his deposits, preventing idle assets. When the U.S. banker pays 5% on time deposits, the Eurobanker can afford to pay 5.26% and have the same cost of funds;

b. The Eurobanker does not have to satisfy Regulation Q which limits the interest rates that can be paid by American banks for dollar deposits;

c. The Eurobanker does not ask for compensating balances as the U.S. banker does, and so there are no hidden costs. An 8% interest rate with a 20% compensating balance requirement from an American banker has the same cost to the borrower as a 10% cost without the compensating balance.

d. The companies borrowing in the Eurodollar market are supposed to be better credit risks than the average borrower for the U.S. bank, thus the costs can tend to be lower;

e. The deposits in Eurodollars are usually in larger amounts than in domestic banks, resulting in lower administrative costs;

f. Many Eurobanks treat the Eurodollar business as added marginal business and not the main business, and are satisfied with lower margins to keep some of the prestigious contacts and customers;

g. Eurobanks may be accustomed to lower margins of profit in their native country than the U.S. banks.

There are two margins commonly used: one is the Interbank margin, which is usually small (around 1/8%), and the other — called the "spread" — is the added margin above this rate that is applicable to nonbank customers. The interbank rate commonly used to calculate the spread is the London Interbank Rate (LIBOR). The spread is small (around ½%) for some prestigious customers such as most central banks, and is higher for others, with most being between 1-3%.

The highest quality U.S. borrowers have found better terms (up to 40 years) at lower cost for their bond issues in the U.S. market than in the Eurodollar market. However, the Eurodollar market is a means of enlarging and diversifying the sources of funds. This lower rate in long-term debt instruments in the U.S. market could be due to the limited investment time horizon among Eurodollar investors owing to political risks in addition to commercial risks. Since the bulk of the Eurodollars are short-term, the margins in this type of financing are very low and competitive with U.S. lenders.

How to Raise Funds

American corporations wishing to raise funds in the Eurodollar market should start with their U.S. investment banker or commercial banker. The customary pattern is for the U.S. corporation to borrow funds from a wholly-owned subsidiary, which, in turn, borrows the funds from the Eurodollar market. The subsidiary can be foreign or domestic depending on the use for the funds raised. The borrowings of the subsidiary are guaranteed by the parent, and there may also be warrants or convertibility into stock of the parent. The funds raised can be used in the U.S. or abroad.

The Tax Reform Act of 1984 repealed the 30% withholding tax on "Portfolio interest" paid to foreign investors for issues effective after the date of enactment. The tax is not repealed on existing obligations.

Private Financial Institutions

The institutions are listed by state, by city within state, and alphabetically within cities. The order of the states are as follows:

AK—Alaska
AL—Alabama
AR—Arkansas
AZ—Arizona
CA—California
CO—Colorado
CT—Connecticut
DC—District of Columbia
DE—Delaware
FL—Florida
GA—Georgia
HI—Hawaii
IA—Iowa
ID—Idaho
IL—Illinois
IN—Indiana
KS—Kansas
KY—Kentucky
LA—Louisiana
MA—Massachusetts
MD—Maryland
ME—Maine
MI—Michigan
MN—Minnesota
MO—Missouri
MS—Mississippi
MT—Montana
NC—North Carolina
ND—North Dakota
NE—Nebraska
NH—New Hampshire
NJ—New Jersey
NM—New Mexico
NV—Nevada
NY—New York
OH—Ohio
OK—Oklahoma
OR—Oregon
PA—Pennsylvania
RI—Rhode Island
SC—South Carolina
SD—South Dakota
TN—Tennessee
TX—Texas
UT—Utah
VA—Virginia
VT—Vermont
WA—Washington
WI—Wisconsin
WV—West Virginia
WY—Wyoming

COMMERCIAL BANKERS & FINANCE COMPANIES

(Working Capital and Equipment Loans. Also see Insurance Companies and Investment Bankers)

ALABAMA

ARIZONA

COMPANY: **Amsouth Financial Corporation**
ADDRESS: P.O. Box 2545
Birmingham, AL 35202
PHONE: (205) 326-5788
CONTACT OFFICER(S): Vernon C. Bice, Jr. Vice Pres.

COMPANY: **Greyhound Leasing & Financial Corporation**
ADDRESS: 4041 North Center Avenue
Phoenix, AZ 85012
PHONE: (602) 248-4900
CONTACT OFFICER(S): See branches
ASSETS: $1.3 billion
INVESTMENTS/LOANS MADE: In securities with a secondary market and in securities without a secondary market
INVESTMENTS/LOANS MADE: For own account; Through private placements
TYPES OF FINANCING: SECONDARY MARKET CORPORATE SECURITIES: Bonds; VENTURE CAPITAL: Later-stage expansion; LOANS: Equipment; REAL ESTATE LOANS: Long-term senior mtg.; Intermediate-term senior mtg., Land development; Construction; Standbys; Other: Equity Notes Receivables; LEASES: Single-investor; Leveraged; Tax leases; Non-tax leases; Tax-oriented lease brokerage; Lease syndications; Vendor financing programs; INTERNATIONAL; REAL ESTATE: Joint ventures; Partnerships/Syndications
GEOGRAPHIC LIMITS OF INVESTMENTS/LOANS: National
RANGE OF INV./LOAN PER BUSINESS: Min. Leases: $50,000; Loans: $250,000; Max. $—
PREFERRED TERM FOR LOANS & LEASES: Min. Leases: 1; Loans: 3 years; Max. 20 years
BUSINESS CHARACTERISTICS DESIRED-REQUIRED: Minimum number of years in business: 5; Other: Proper operating history upon which to base payment ability projections
REFERRALS ACCEPTED FROM: Investment/Mortgage Banker or Borrower/Investee
BRANCHES: John N. Henning, Donald F. Howell, Jeremiah G. Mahony, Michael J. Naughton, and William H. Vallar (V.P.-Regional Marketing Manager), 445 Park Avenue, New York, NY 10022, (212) 752-2720
Robert E. Marino, John Wm. Salyer, David A. Nielsen (V.P.-Regional Marketing Manager), Centennial Center I, 1900 East Golf Road, Suite 645, Schaumburg, IL 60195, (312) 490-9500
Bruce E. Heine, Mark Lindell, 7801 East Bush Lake Road, Suite 430, Minneapolis, MN 55435, (612) 831-7044
Joseph A. Graffagnini, Canal Place One, Suite 2510, New Orleans, LA 70130, (504) 525-1112
James M. Brown, 12400 Olive Blvd., Suite 200, St. Louis, MO 63141, (314) 469-7373
George C. Baer, 7616 LBJ Freeway, Suite 500, Dallas, TX 75251, (214) 387-3182
Dottie A. Riley, James T. Foley (V.P.-Regional Marketing Manager), 4041 North Central Avenue, Station 3504, Phoenix, AZ 85012, (602) 248-5349
Jeffrey D. Johnson, Scott D. Mayne, 5505 South 900 East, Suite 325, Salt Lake City, UT 84117, (801) 261-1311
Thomas O. Kaluza, 16400 Southcenter Parkway, Suite 203, Seattle, WA 98188, (206) 575-0246
Kenneth B. Giddes, 6400 Powers Ferry Road, Suite 300, Atlanta, GA 30339, (404) 955-3636
Patrick E. Barton, 1776 South Jackson Street, Suite 907, Denver, CO 80210, (303) 757-4973
Jack W. Quinn, Cineco Building, Suite 203, 4401 W. Tradewinds Ave., Lauderdale-by-the-Sea, FL 33308, (305) 493-8322
David C. Phillips, 600 B Street, Suite 2235, San Diego, CA 92101, (619) 231-4751
Ron W. Larson, Neil E. Leddy, Orangegate Plaza, 5455 Garden Grove Blvd., Suite 450, Westminister, CA 92683, (714) 891-2700

COMPANY: **Community First Bank, Mortgage Div.**
ADDRESS: 810 Chester
Bakersfield, CA 93301
PHONE: (805) 395-3270
TYPE OF INSTITUTION: Commercial Bank
CONTACT OFFICER(S): Grady Buck
ASSETS: $100,000,000+
TYPES OF FINANCING: VENTURE CAPITAL: Research & Development; Start-up from developed product stage; First-stage (less than 1 year); Second-stage (generally 1-3 years); Later-stage expansion; Buy-outs/Acquisitions; LOANS: Unsecured; Working capital (receivables/inventory); Equipment; REAL ESTATE LOANS: Long-term senior mtg.; Other: Short-term; REAL ESTATE: Acquisitions
GEOGRAPHIC LIMITS OF INVESTMENTS/LOANS: Local
PREFERRED TERM FOR LOANS & LEASES: Min. 1-3 years; Max. 5 years
REFERALS ACCEPTED FROM: Borrower/Investee
REMARKS: Min. of 2 years in business for loans other than venture capital

COMPANY: **General Hospital Leasing, Inc.**
ADDRESS: 20944 Sherman Way, Suite 103
Canoga Park, CA 91303
PHONE: (818) 348-9797
TYPE OF INSTITUTION: Leasing Co.
CONTACT OFFICER(S): Robert Skach, Pres.
TYPES OF FINANCING: LOANS: Sales contracts, LEASES: Operating; Tax-oriented lease brokerage
PREFERRED TYPES OF INDUSTRIES/INVESTMENTS: Hospitals; Industrial
GEOGRAPHIC LIMITS OF INVESTMENTS/LOANS: National
RANGE OF INV./LOAN PER BUSINESS: Min. $5,000
PREFERRED TERM FOR LOANS & LEASES: Min. 2; Max. 10 years

COMPANY: **Financial Guild of America**
ADDRESS: 5730 Uplander Way, Suite 103
Culver City, CA 90230
PHONE: (213) 641-9200
CONTACT OFFICER(S): Dr. Conrad Lubkay, Jr., President

COMPANY: **Pacific Lighting Leasing Company (parent)/ Pacific Lighting Commercial Loans, Inc. (subsidiary)**
ADDRESS: 6140 Bristol Parkway
Culver City, CA 90230
PHONE: (213) 642-7595
TYPE OF INSTITUTION: Wholly owned Leasing and Finance subsidiary of NYSE company
CONTACT OFFICER(S): William M. Hamburg, Vice President—Leasing & Lending
Waldo A. Rodman, Director of Leasing & Remarketing
ASSETS: $76,000,000
INVESTMENTS/LOANS MADE: For own account
INVESTMENTS/LOANS MADE: In securities with a secondary market and in securities without a secondary market
TYPES OF FINANCING: VENTURE CAPITAL; Second-stage; Later-stage; Buy-outs/Acquisitions; LOANS: Equipment; Equity-related; REAL ESTATE LOANS: Intermediateterm senior mtg.; Subordinated; Gap; Standbys; LEASES: Single-investor; Tax leases; Non-tax leases; Operating; Tax-oriented lease brokerage; Vendor financing programs
PREFERRED TYPES OF INDUSTRIES/INVESTMENTS: Office Equipment; Production Equipment; Restaurant; Medical; Air Conditioning; other
WILL NOT CONSIDER: Automobiles
GEOGRAPHIC LIMITS OF INVESTMENTS/LOANS: National
RANGE OF INV./LOAN PER BUSINESS: Min. $2,500; Max. $5,000,000
PREFERRED TERM FOR LOANS & LEASES: Min. 3 yrs; Max. 7 yrs
BUSINESS CHARACTERISTICS DESIRED/REQUIRED: Minimum number of years in business: 0; Min. annual sales $1,000,000
REFERRALS ACCEPTED FROM: Investment/Mortgage banker or Borrower/Investee

COMPANY: **Manalis Finance Company**
ADDRESS: 17141 Ventura Blvd.
Encino, CA 91316
PHONE: (213) 872-0193
CONTACT OFFICER(S): Lowell B. Delbick, Partner

COMPANY: **Pacific States Leasing, Inc.**
ADDRESS: 135 W. Shaw 105
Fresno, CA 93711
PHONE: (209) 221-6952
TYPE OF INSTITUTION: Equipment Lessor
CONTACT OFFICER(S): Al Vionnet, Exec. V.P., Director of Finance—All transactions over 100,000.
Gary Christy, V.P. Dir. of Marketing—Vendor Finance & Leasing Plans
Gary Honicutt, Asst. V.P.—Mgr. Broker Div.—Broker Transactions (Referrals, etc.)
ASSETS: $20,000,000
INVESTMENTS/LOANS MADE: For own account, managed accounts or through private placements
TYPES OF FINANCING: LOANS: Equipment; Equity-related; Commercial Contracts & Leases—All types of Equipment; LEASES: Single-investor; Leveraged; Tax leases; Non-tax leases; Operating; Tax-oriented lease brokerage; Vendor financing programs; Other; OTHER SERVICES PROVIDED: Provide funding for lease companies, for vendors desiring to be lessors; any and all activities involving equipment leasing.
PREFERRED TYPES OF INDUSTRIES/INVESTMENTS: Prefer equipment leases from $1,000 to $100,000; direct, vendor or broker plans; equipment for business use; all industries acceptable
GEOGRAPHIC LIMITS OF INVESTMENTS/LOANS: National; Other: All 50 states except Louisiana & Arkansas

RANGE OF INV./LOAN PER BUSINESS: Min. $1,000; Max. $100,000,000
PREFERRED TERM FOR LOANS & LEASES: Min. 2; Max. 7
BUSINESS CHARACTERISTICS DESIRED-REQUIRED: Minimum number of years in business: 2; Min. annual sales: no; Min. net worth $50,000; Min. annual net income $24,000;
REFERRALS ACCEPTED FROM: Investment/Mortgage banker or Borrower/Investee
BRANCHES: R.B. Klutz, Branch Mgr., Hampton E. #1, 8000 Girard Suite 418, Denver, CO 80231, (303) 368-9400

COMPANY: **Glenfed Capital Corporation**
ADDRESS: 700 North Brand Bvd.
Glendale, CA 90026
PHONE: (213) 500-2850
CONTACT OFFICER(S): Robert B. Singleton, Pres. & C.E.O.

COMPANY: **Behr Leasing & Financial Corp.**
ADDRESS: 700 S. Flower, Ste. 3200
Los Angeles, CA 90017
PHONE: (213) 627-0272
TYPE OF INSTITUTION: Leasing Co.
CONTACT OFFICER(S): Ken Goodman, Director of Marketing
Raymond B. Corob, Pres.
TYPES OF FINANCING: LOANS: Equipment; LEASES: Tax leases; Non-tax leases; Tax-oriented lease brokerage; Lease syndications, Vendor Financing Programs
GEOGRAPHIC LIMITS OF INVESTMENTS/LOANS: National
RANGE OF INV./LOAN PER BUSINESS: Min. $25,000
REMARKS: Average term: 5 years; Max 10 years

COMPANY: **Century Creditcorp**
ADDRESS: 10673 West Pico Boulevard
Los Angeles, CA 90064
PHONE: (213) 474-4003
CONTACT OFFICER(S): Michael B. Holland, Pres.

COMPANY: **Commercial Acceptance Corp.**
ADDRESS: 411 West 7th Street, Suite 700
Los Angeles, CA 90014
PHONE: (213) 626-1151
CONTACT OFFICER(S): Barry F. Gray, Pres.

COMPANY: **Professional Capital Corp.**
ADDRESS: 11726 San Vicente, Ste. 230
Los Angeles, CA 90049
PHONE: (213) 475-0304
CONTACT OFFICER(S): Bruce Hempel, Pres.
ASSETS: $1-10 million
TYPES OF FINANCING: LOANS: Unsecured; Other: Up to $50,000 to dentists and physicians

COMPANY: **State Financial Corporation**
ADDRESS: 1100 Glendon Ave.
Los Angeles, CA 90024
PHONE: (213) 208-2200
CONTACT OFFICER(S): Irving S. Reiss, President

COMPANY: **Taurus Leasing Co.**
ADDRESS: 6565 Sunset Blvd., Suite 511 (Mail: P.O. Box 108)
Los Angeles, CA 90078
PHONE: (213) 466-5144
CONTACT OFFICER(S): Roy G. Bergen, V.P. Gen. Manager
TYPES OF FINANCING: LOANS: Unsecured, Working capital, Equipment; Equity-related; LEASES: New Equipment Leases & Sale/Leaseback
PREFERRED TYPES OF INDUSTRIES/INVESTMENTS: Medical
GEOGRAPHIC LIMITS OF INVESTMENTS/LOANS: National
RANGE OF INV./LOAN PER BUSINESS: Min. $5,000.00; Max. $200,000.00
PREFERRED TERM FOR LOANS & LEASES: Min. 2 yrs; Max. 5 yrs
BUSINESS CHARACTERISTICS DESIRED-REQUIRED: Minimum number of years in business: 2; Cash Flow Lender
REFERRALS ACCEPTED FROM: Investment/Mortgage banker or Borrower/Investee
REMARKS: Sale lease-backs to physicians and dentists

COMPANY: **U. S. Bancorp Financial**
ADDRESS: 550 South Hill St. Suite 1200
Los Angeles, CA 90013
PHONE: (213) 622-3820
TYPE OF INSTITUTION: Wholly owned asset based lending institution of U.S. Bancorp, Inc.
CONTACT OFFICER(S): P. A. Yasiello, President/C.E.O.
Owen D. McGreal, Senior V.P.
ASSETS: In excess of $5 billion
INVESTMENTS/LOANS MADE: For own account
TYPES OF FINANCING: LOANS: Working capital; Equipment; Equity-related, INTERNATIONAL, OTHER SERVICES PROVIDED: To support letter of credit and other lines of credit
PREFERRED TYPES OF INDUSTRIES/INVESTMENTS: Manufacturing, distribution and service
GEOGRAPHIC LIMITS OF INVESTMENTS/LOANS: Local; State; Regional; National
RANGE OF INV./LOAN PER BUSINESS: Min. $50,000; Max. $40 million
BUSINESS CHARACTERISTICS DESIRED-REQUIRED: Minimum number of years in business: 0;
REFERRALS ACCEPTED FROM: Investment/Mortgage banker or Borrower/Investee
BRANCHES: Ed Jensen, 555 Southwest Oak, Portland, OR 97205; (503) 225-6270
Gene Drummond, Diamond Shamrock Tower, Suite 2750, 717 North Harwood, Dallas, TX 75201; (214) 651-7101
One Wilshire Building, Suite 2500, Los Angeles, CA 90017; (213) 622-3820
Orange County; (714) 834-0821
One Allen Center, Suite 1000, Houston, TX 77002; (713) 757-0038

City Center Square, 1110 Main Street, 14th Floor, Kansas City, MO 64105; (816) 221-0880

COMPANY: **Unionbanc, Leasing Division**
ADDRESS: 445 South Figueroa St.
Los Angeles, CA 90017
PHONE: (213) 687-5311
TYPE OF INSTITUTION: Leasing Co.
CONTACT OFFICER(S): Robert Casper, Dir. of Marketing
TYPES OF FINANCING: LOANS: Equipment, LEASES: Single-investor; Leveraged; Tax leases; Operating
PREFERRED TYPES OF INDUSTRIES/INVESTMENTS: Machinery
WILL NOT CONSIDER: Agricultural
GEOGRAPHIC LIMITS OF INVESTMENTS/LOANS: National
RANGE OF INV./LOAN PER BUSINESS: Min. $50,000

COMPANY: **Avco Financial Services Leasing Co.**
ADDRESS: 620 Newport Center Drive
Newport Beach, CA 92660
PHONE: (714) 640-5200
TYPE OF INSTITUTION: Leasing company
CONTACT OFFICER(S): William Dowell, Sr. V.P., Marketing
TYPES OF FINANCING: LEASES: Single-investor; Tax leases; Non-tax leases; Vendor financing programs
PREFERRED TYPES OF INDUSTRIES/INVESTMENTS: General equipment
GEOGRAPHIC LIMITS OF INVESTMENTS/LOANS: National
RANGE OF INV./LOAN PER BUSINESS: Min. $100,000; Max. $5 million
PREFERRED TERM FOR LOANS & LEASES: Min. 3 years; Max. 10 years
BUSINESS CHARACTERISTICS DESIRED-REQUIRED: Other: Balance sheet lessor
REMARKS: No start-ups; referrals from banks only; branches located in all major cities

COMPANY: **First California Business and Industrial Development Corporation**
ADDRESS: 3931 MacArthur Blvd., Suite 212
Newport Beach, CA 92660
PHONE: (714) 851-0855
TYPE OF INSTITUTION: Business Development Company/Small Business Lending
CONTACT OFFICER(S): Leslie R. Brewer, President
INVESTMENTS/LOANS MADE: For own account
TYPES OF FINANCING: VENTURE CAPITAL, First-stage (less than 1 year), Second-stage (generally 1-3 years), Later-stage expansion, Buy-outs/Acquisitions; LOANS, Working capital (receivables/inventory), Equipment; REAL ESTATE LOANS, Long-term senior mtg.; Intermediate-term senior mtg., Subordinated; INTERNATIONAL; OTHER SERVICES PROVIDED, Management consulting, Financial planning, Budgeting, Financing
PREFERRED TYPES OF INDUSTRIES/INVESTMENTS: Manufacturing; Equipment based services; Franchises
WILL NOT CONSIDER: R & D, Films, Publications
GEOGRAPHIC LIMITS OF INVESTMENTS/LOANS: State
RANGE OF INV./LOAN PER BUSINESS: Min. $50,000; Max. $550,000
PREFERRED TERM FOR LOANS & LEASES: Min. 7 years; Max. 25 years
BUSINESS CHARACTERISTICS DESIRED-REQUIRED: Minimum number of years in business: 0; Min. annual sales $500,000 Projected; Min. net worth $50,000; Min. annual net income $60,000; Min. annual cash flow $90,000
REFERRALS ACCEPTED FROM: Investment/Mortgage banker; Borrower/investee
BRANCHES: 130 Montgomery St., San Francisco, CA 94104, (415) 392-5400

COMPANY: **Winston Financial Corp**
ADDRESS: 1447 Palisades Drive
Pacific Palisades, CA 90272
PHONE: (213) 454-7030
TYPE OF INSTITUTION: Financial Services, Leasing Specialty
CONTACT OFFICER(S): Paul D. Shlensky, President
Barry G. Morganstern, V.P.
ASSETS: $10,000,000
INVESTMENTS/LOANS MADE: For own account
INVESTMENTS/LOANS MADE: In securities with a secondary market and in securities without a secondary market
TYPES OF FINANCING: SECONDARY-MARKET CORPORATE SECURITIES, VENTURE CAPITAL: Second-stage; Later-stage expansion; Buy-outs/Acquisitions, LOANS: Working capital; Equipment, LEASES: Single-investor; Leveraged; Tax leases; Operating; Vendor financing programs
PREFERRED TYPES OF INDUSTRIES/INVESTMENTS: Telecommunications, energy
GEOGRAPHIC LIMITS OF INVESTMENTS/LOANS: National
RANGE OF INV./LOAN PER BUSINESS: Min. $250,000; Max. $10,000,000
PREFERRED TERM FOR LOANS & LEASES: Min. 3 years; Max. 5 years
BUSINESS CHARACTERISTICS DESIRED-REQUIRED: Minimum number of years in business: 5 years
REFERRALS ACCEPTED FROM: Investment/Mortgage banker or Borrower/Investee

COMPANY: **CCB Business Credit, Inc.**
ADDRESS: 150 South Los Robles, Suite 800
Pasadena, CA 91101
PHONE: (818) 796-0808
TYPE OF INSTITUTION: Asset based loan company
CONTACT OFFICER(S): Mark Rosenbaum, President
Betty Hilton, Vice President-Loan Administration
Harvey Weinberger, Vice President-Marketing

ASSETS: $50 million
TYPES OF FINANCING: VENTURE CAPITAL: Buy-outs/Acquisitions; LOANS: Working capital (receivables/inventory), Equipment, Other

COMPANY: **StanChart Business Credit**
ADDRESS: 225 South Lake Avenue
Pasadena, CA 91101
PHONE: (818) 304-1798
TYPE OF INSTITUTION: Asset-Based Financing subsidiary of bank holding company
CONTACT OFFICER(S): Jack L. Meyers, President
Jerry E. Andress, Sr. Vice President & Regional Manager-Atlanta
Theodore Kompa, Vice President and Regional Manager-Pasadena
Andrew M. Conneen, Vice President & Regional Manager-Chicago
Michael J. Riley, Vice President & Regional Manager-Oakland
ASSETS: $8 Billion
INVESTMENTS/LOANS MADE: For own account
TYPES OF FINANCING: LOANS: Working capital (receivables/inventory), Equipment, Leverage Buyouts; REAL ESTATE LOANS: Intermediate-term senior mtg.; LEASES: Single-investor, Leveraged, Tax leases, Non-tax leases, Operating, Tax-oriented lease brokerage, Lease syndications, Vendor financing programs
PREFERRED TYPES OF INDUSTRIES/INVESTMENTS: Manufacturing, Distribution, Wholesaling. Prefer income-producing equipment for lease and loan transactions
GEOGRAPHIC LIMITS OF INVESTMENTS/LOANS: National
RANGE OF INV./LOAN PER BUSINESS: Min. $500,000; Max. $60,000,000
PREFERRED TERM FOR LOANS & LEASES: Min. 2 years; Max. 10 years
BUSINESS CHARACTERISTICS DESIRED-REQUIRED: Minimum number of years in business: 2; Min. annual sales $5,000,000; Min. net worth $200,000; Min. annual net income $50,000; Min annual cash flow $75,000
BRANCHES: 200 Galleria Parkway NW, Suite 1010, Atlanta, GA 30339, (404) 952-4000, Jerry Andress
33 West Monroe Street, 2nd Floor, Chicago, IL 60605, (312) 372-4755, Andrew M. Conneen
460 Hegenberger Rd., Oakland, CA 94604, (415) 577-8268, Michael J. Riley

COMPANY: **Union Bank**
ADDRESS: 225 S. Lake Avenue
Pasadena, CA 91101
PHONE: (818) 304-1700
TYPE OF INSTITUTION: Asset-Based Financing Group of Bank
CONTACT OFFICER(S): Theodore Kompa, Vice Pres. & Reg. Manager (So. Calif.) Asset Based Loans
Michael J. Riley, Vice Pres. & Reg. Manager, (No. Calif.) Asset Based Loans
Robert C. Andreasen, Vice Pres. & Manager, Equipment Finance and Leasing
ASSETS: $8 Billion
INVESTMENTS/LOANS MADE: For own account
TYPES OF FINANCING: Working capital (receivables/inventory), Equipment; REAL ESTATE LOANS: Intermediate-term senior mtg.; LEASES: Single-investor, Leveraged, Tax leases, Non-tax leases, Operating, Tax-oriented lease brokerage, Lease syndications, Vendor financing programs; OTHER SERVICES PROVIDED: Leverage Buyout Financing
PREFERRED TYPES OF INDUSTRIES/INVESTMENTS: Manufacturing, Distribution, Wholesaling. Prefer income-producing equipment for lease and loan transactions
GEOGRAPHIC LIMITS OF INVESTMENTS/LOANS: National
RANGE OF INV./LOAN PER BUSINESS: Min. $500,000; Max. $60,000,000
PREFERRED TERM FOR LOANS & LEASES: Min. 2 years; Max. 10 years
BUSINESS CHARACTERISTICS DESIRED-REQUIRED: Minimum number of years in business: 2; Min. annual sales $5,000,000; Min. net worth $200,000; Min. annual net income $50,000; Min annual cash flow $75,000
REFERRALS ACCEPTED FROM: Investment/Mortgage banker or Borrower/Investee
BRANCHES: 225 South Lake Avenue, 6th Floor, Pasadena, CA 91101, 818-304-1700, Theodore Kompa
460 Hegenberger Rd., Oakland, CA 94604, (415) 772-8158, Michael J. Riley

COMPANY: **Riviera Capital Corporation**
ADDRESS: 220 Avenue I
Redondo Beach, CA 90277
PHONE: (213) 540-9895
CONTACT OFFICER(S): Robert Bernfeld, Pres.

COMPANY: **GATX Leasing Corporation**
ADDRESS: Four Embarcadero Center, Ste. 2200
San Francisco, CA 94111
PHONE: (415) 955-3200
TYPE OF INSTITUTION: Leasing and Secured Financing-Independent
CONTACT OFFICER(S): Ronald H. Zech, Exec. V.P.-Administration & Finance
David A. Woolsey, Exec. V.P.-Marketing
Kenneth T. Gibson, V.P.-Finance
ASSETS: $651 million
INVESTMENTS/LOANS MADE: For own account, Through private placements
INVESTMENTS/LOANS MADE: Only in securities without a secondary market
TYPES OF FINANCING: LOANS: Equipment, LEASES: Single-investor; Leveraged; Operating; Tax-oriented lease brokerage; Lease syndications, OTHER SERVICES PROVIDED: Purchase of leases from other lessors (i.e. secondary lease market)
PREFERRED TYPES OF INDUSTRIES/INVESTMENTS: Aircraft, Railcars, Barges

GEOGRAPHIC LIMITS OF INVESTMENTS/LOANS: International
RANGE OF INV./LOAN PER BUSINESS: Min. $500,000; Max. $25,000,000
PREFERRED TERM FOR LOANS & LEASES: Min. 5 years; Max. 15 years
BRANCHES: Lynn E. Burgess, 6850 West Yellowstone Hwy., Casper, WY 82604; (307) 472-3298
William B. McNulty, Jr, 120 S. Riverside Plaza, Chicago, IL 60606; (312) 621-6571
Dennis R. Buchanan, Regency Center, 5th Floor, 5501 LBJ Freeway, Dallas, TX 75240; (214) 386-6684
L. Dwight Giess, 650 South Cherry St., Suite 520, Denver, CO 80222; (303)393-7700
Dennis N. Schneider, GLC Finance Corporation, P.O. Box 25727, Alburguerque, NM 86125; (505) 345-8909
Thomas P. Timmins, 8552 Katy Freeway, Suite 200, Houston, TX 77024; (713) 932-9680
Jesse V. Crewss, One Lakeway Center, Suite 1180, 3900 North Causeway Blvd., Metairie, LA 70002; (504) 838-8852
Lewis B. Everly, Gareld R. Gray II (Doc), 400 Park Avenue, 22nd Floor, New York, NY 10022; (212) 758-5200

COMPANY: **BFI - Business Finance**
ADDRESS: 900 Lafayette St., Suite 509
Santa Clara, CA 95050
PHONE: (408) 984-7122
TYPE OF INSTITUTION: Accounts Receivable financing
CONTACT OFFICER(S):David I. Lustig, President
INVESTMENTS/LOANS MADE: For own account
TYPES OF FINANCING: LOANS: Working capital, FACTORING

COMPANY: **Bay Area Financial Corporation**
ADDRESS: 606 Wilshire Blvd., Suite 604
Santa Monica, CA 90401
PHONE: (213) 451-8445
CONTACT OFFICER(S): Kenneth J. Pingree Jr., Vice Pres.

COMPANY: **Commercial Funding**
ADDRESS: P.O. Box 6429
Torrance, CA 90504
PHONE: (213) 370-3663
CONTACT OFFICER(S): Alice DeLong, Secy.-Treas.

COMPANY: **Lion Financial Inc. DBA Commercial Financing**
ADDRESS: 17291 Irvine Blvd., Suite 104
Tustin, CA 92680
PHONE: (714) 730-1313

COMPANY: **Commonwealth Financial Corporation**
ADDRESS: 2950 Buskirk Ave. P.O. Box 8100
Walnut Creek, CA 94596
PHONE: (415) 930-7550
TYPE OF INSTITUTION: Asset based lending and leasing
CONTACT OFFICERS(S): Wm. F. Plein, President
Charles Blau, V.P. and Mgr. of Leasing
ASSETS: $80,000,000
INVESTMENTS/LOANS MADE: For own (company's or principals') account
TYPES OF FINANCING: LOANS: Working capital; Equipment; REAL ESTATE LOANS: Intermediate-term senior mtg.; LEASES: Single-investor; Leveraged; Tax leases; Non-tax leases; Operating; Vendor financing programs

COMPANY: **Republic Financial Corp.**
ADDRESS: P.O. Box 22564
Denver, CO 80222
PHONE: (303) 751-3501
TYPE OF INSTITUTION: Equipment leasing
CONTACT OFFICER(S): James H. Possehl, President
Robert Jenkins, V.P. Marketing
Mike Ricks, V.P. Operations
ASSETS: $25,000,000
INVESTMENTS/LOANS MADE: For own account, Through private placements
INVESTMENTS/LOANS MADE: In Securities with a secondary market and in securities without a secondary market
TYPES OF FINANCING; LOANS: Equipment, LEASES: Single-investor; Leveraged; Tax leases; Non-tax leases; Tax-oriented lease brokerage
GEOGRAPHIC LIMITS OF INVESTMENTS/LOANS: National
RANGE OF INV./LOAN PER BUSINESS: Min. $25,000; Max. None
PREFERRED TERM FOR LOANS & LEASES: Min. 2 years; Max. 15 years
REFERRALS ACCEPTED FROM: Investment/Mortgage banker or Borrower/Investee

COMPANY: **Silverado Capital Corporation**
ADDRESS: 655 Broadway, Suite 100
Denver, CO 80203
PHONE: (303) 893-2311
TYPE OF INSTITUTION: Mortgage Banking, Business, Business Real Estate, Income Producing
CONTACT OFFICER(S): Mr. Allan H. Rouse, Senior Vice President
Mr. Steven C. Greenwald, Vice President - Loan Administration and Business Real Estate Loans
ASSETS: $6.9 million
INVESTMENTS/LOANS MADE: Through private placements
TYPES OF FINANCING: LOANS: Other: Small Business Administration (SBA) & Farmers Home Administration (FmHA); REAL ESTATE LOANS: Long-term senior mtg.; Intermediate-term senior mtg.; Subordinated; Wraparounds; Land; Land development; Construction; Gap; Standbys; Industrial revenue bonds.
PREFERRED TYPES OF INDUSTRIES/INVESTMENTS: All types of Income Producing Properties
RANGE OF INV./LOAN PER BUSINESS: Min. $100,000; Max. $ Open
PREFERRED TERM FOR LOANS & LEASES: Max. 30 years
BUSINESS CHARACTERISTICS DESIRED-REQUIRED: Minimum number of years in business; -0-

BRANCHES: Mr. Michael T. Lacy, 3225 N. Central Ave., Suite 1005, Phoenix, AZ 85012, (602) 279-2009

COMPANY: **United Agri Products Financial Services, Inc.**
ADDRESS: 1701 23rd Avenue, Suite B
Greeley, CO 80631
PHONE: (303) 356-8893
CONTACT OFFICER(S): Lloyd A. Bettis, Vice Pres.

COMPANY: **BancAmerica Commercial Corporation**
ADDRESS: 777 So. Yarrow St. Suite 101
Lakewood, CO
PHONE: (303) 988-4491
TYPE OF INSTITUTION: Equipment Finance Division
CONTACT OFFICER(S): C. L. Overson, President
George McMackin, V.P. National Credit Director
INVESTMENTS/LOANS MADE: For own account
TYPES OF FIANCING: LOANS: Working Capital; LOANS: Working capital (receivables/inventory); Equipment; LEASES: Single-investor; Non-tax leases; Vendor financing programs
GEOGRAPHIC LIMITS OF INVESTMENTS/LOANS: National

COMPANY: **Citytrust**
ADDRESS: 961 Main Street
Bridgeport, CT 06602
PHONE: (203) 384-5051
CONTACT OFFICER(S): Robert K. Streb, Asst. Vice Pres.

COMPANY: **E. F. Hutton Credit Corporation**
ADDRESS: Greenwich Office Park #1
Greenwich, CT 06830
PHONE: (203) 629-3000
TYPE OF INSTITUTION: Financing and leasing company
CONTACT OFFICER(S): Robert L. Reynolds, Sr. V.P.-Diversified Financing
Keith L. Fitch, Sr. V.P.-Corporate Financing
Charles J. French, V.P.-Commercial Financing
ASSETS: $735,890,000
INVESTMENTS/LOANS MADE: For own account
INVESTMENTS/LOANS MADE: Only in securities without a secondary market
TYPES OF FINANCING: VENTURE CAPITAL: Buy-outs/Acquisitions; LOANS: Working capital; Equipment; Other: Owner-occupied residential second mortgages; LEASES: Single-investor; Leveraged; Tax leases; Non-tax leases; Lease Syndications; Vendor financing programs; Other: Tax benefi t transfer leases; Lease syndications; Vendor financing programs
PREFERRED TYPES OF INDUSTRIES/INVESTMENTS: No preferences
GEOGRAPHIC LIMITS OF INVESTMENTS/LOANS: National
RANGE OF INV./LOAN PER BUSINESS: Min. $20,000; Max. $10,000,000
PREFERRED TERM FOR LOANS & LEASES: Min. 3 years; Max. 15 years
BUSINESS CHARACTERISTICS DESIRED-REQUIRED: Other: No specific requirements of this type
REFERRALS ACCEPTED FROM: Investment/Mortgage banker or Borrower/Investee
BRANCHES: Stratford, CT
Allentown, PA
Tampa, FL
Braintree, MA
Clifton, NJ
Pittsburgh, PA
Cleveland, OH
Atlanta, GA
Greensboro, NC
Maitland, FL
Charlotte, NC
Nashville, TN
Metairie, LA
St. Martinville, LA
Jackson, MS
Bannockburn, IL
Farmington Hills, MI
St. Paul, MN
Clayton, MO
San Francisco, CA
Dallas, TX
Houston, TX
Oklahoma City, OK
Portland, OR
Santa Monica, CA
Emeryville, CA
Salt Lake City, UT
Scottsdale, AZ
Denver, CO

COMPANY: **Xerox Credit Corporation**
ADDRESS: 2 Pickwick Plaza
Greenwich, CT 06836
PHONE: (203) 625-6700
TYPE OF INSTITUTION: Industrial Finance
CONTACT OFFICER(S): Ramiro Collazo, Sr. V.P.-General Manager-Leasing
James Reynolds, Director, Commerical Services-Vendor programs
David Roe, V.P., Planning
ASSETS: 1.6 Billion
TYPES OF FINANCING: LOANS: Equipment; Equity-related; LEASES: Single-investor; Leveraged; Tax leases; Non-tax leases; Operating; Lease syndications; Vendor financing programs
PREFERRED TYPES OF INDUSTRIES/INVESTMENTS: Any industry; any equipment
GEOGRAPHIC LIMITS OF INVESTMENTS/LOANS: National
REFERRALS ACCEPTED FROM: Investment/Mortgage banker and Borrower/Investee

COMPANY: **CBT Business Credit Corporation**
ADDRESS: 100 Constitution Plaza
Hartford, CT 06115
PHONE: (203) 244-5223
TYPE OF INSTITUTION: Commercial Finance Co.
CONTACT OFFICER(S): Mr. T. Richard Wiggins, Asset-Based Lending Division

COMPANY: **Connecticut Bank & Trust**
ADDRESS: One Constitution Plaza
Hartford, CT 06115
PHONE: (203) 244-6269
TYPE OF INSTITUTION: Construction lender, permanent lender; intermediate lender
CONTACT OFFICER(S): Oliver W. Park, President
ASSETS: $6 billion
INVESTMENTS/LOANS MADE:
TYPES OF FINANCING: SECONDARY-MARKET CORPORATE SECURITIES, LOANS: Unsecured; Working capital; Equipment; Equity-related; Other: Construction lending, Lease finaancing, REAL ESTATE LOANS: Intermediate-term senior mtg.; Wraparounds; Land; Land development; Construction; Gap; Industrial revenue bonds, FACTORING, LEASES: Single—investor; Leveraged; Non-tax leases; Operating; Vendor financing programs, INTERNATIONAL
GEOGRAPHIC LIMITS OF INVESTMENTS/LOANS: National; International
BUSINESS CHARACTERISTICS DESIRED-REQUIRED:
REFERRALS ACCEPPTED FROM: Investment/Mortgage banker or Borrower/Investee
REMARKS: 140 Branches; out on loan: $1 billion in Real Estate

COMPANY: **Connecticut Business Finance Corporation**
ADDRESS: 900 Asylum Ave.
Hartford, CT 06105
PHONE: (203) 524-1800
CONTACT OFFICER(S): Joseph J. Gillooly Jr., Pres.

COMPANY: **Mechanics Savings Bank**
ADDRESS: 100 Constitution Plaza
Hartford, CT 06115
PHONE: (203) 525-8661

COMPANY: **Pitney Bowes Credit Corporation**
ADDRESS: 201 Merritt Seven
Norwalk, CT 06851
PHONE: (203) 846-5600
TYPE OF INSTITUTION: Finance Company - wholly owned subsidiary of Pitney Bowes Inc.
CONTACT OFFICER(S): Mr. John J. Canning, Vice President - C&I Finance Division
INVESTMENTS/LOANS MADE: For own account
TYPES OF FINANCING: LOANS: Unsecured to credits above Baa; Equipment; LEASES: Single-investor; Leveraged; Tax leases; Non-tax leases; Operating; Vendor financing programs
PREFERRED TYPES OF INDUSTRIES: Equipment - Computer & Computer Peripheral Telecommunications, Medical, Construction, Farm Machinery, Test Equipment
GEOGRAPHIC LIMITS OF INVESTMENTS/LOANS: National
RANGE OF INV./LOAN PER BUSINESS: Min. $50,000; Max. $10,000,000
PREFERRED TERM FOR LOANS & LEASES: Min. 3 years; Max. 7 years
REFERRALS ACCEPTED FROM: Investment/Mortgage banker or Borrower/Investee
BRANCHES: Linda M. McAvoy, Manager-Vendor Programs, 201 Merritt Seven, Norwalk, CT 06856; (203) 846-5622

COMPANY: **General Electric Credit Corp.**
ADDRESS: 260 Long Ridge Road
Stamford, CT 06902
PHONE: (203) 357-6789
CONTACT OFFICER(S): Michael R. Dabney, V.P.

COMPANY: **First Florida Leasing Corporation**
ADDRESS: 1840 W. 49th Street, Ste. 604
Hialeah, FL 33012
PHONE: (305) 823-3022
TYPE OF INSTITUTION: Leasing Co.
CONTACT OFFICER(S): Bryan Miller, Pres.
Al Levy, Sales Manager
Lee Stanford, Sales Manager
TYPES OF FINANCING: LOANS; LEASES: Single-investor; Leveraged; Tax leases; Non-tax leases; Operating; Tax-oriented lease brokerage; Lease syndications; Vendor financing programs
PREFERRED TYPES OF INDUSTRIES/INVESTMENTS: Computers, Planes, Heavy Equipment, Trucks, Tractors, Trailers, Boats, Medical Equipment, etc.
WILL NOT CONSIDER: Autos, small ticket items
GEOGRAPHIC LIMITS OF INVESTMENTS/LOANS: International for leasing; Loans: Maine to Flordia
RANGE OF INV./LOAN PER BUSINESS: Min. $10,000; Max. None
PREFERRED TERM FOR LOANS & LEASES: Min. 3 years; Max. 7 years
BUSINESS CHARACTERISTICS DESIRED-REQUIRED; Minimum number of years in business: 2 years; Min. net worth $2½ X (times) lease amount; Other: look at each as it comes up

COMPANY: **Heritage Mortgage Corp.**
ADDRESS: 1318 N.W. 7th St.
Miami, FL 33125
PHONE: (305) 324-4000
TYPE OF INSTITUTION: Mortgage banking
CONTACT OFFICER(S): Edward Feinstein, Pres. Lending
Eric Feinstein, Sr. V. Pres. Real Estate Equities
ASSETS: 5,897,000
INVESTMENTS/LOANS MADE: For own account, For managed accounts
INVESTMENTS/LOANS MADE: In Securities with a secondary market and in securities without a secondary market
TYPES OF FINANCING: LOANS, REAL ESTATE LOANS: Long-term senior mtg.; Intermediate-term senior mtg.; Wraparounds; Land; Land development; Construction; Gap; Standbys; Industrial revenue bonds. LEASES: Single-investor. REAL ESTATE: Acquisitions; Joint ventures; Partnerships/Syndications. OTHER SERVICES PROVIDED: Title Insurance
GEOGRAPHIC LIMITS OF INVESTMENTS/LOANS: National
RANGE OF INV./LOAN PER BUSINESS: Min. $500,000; Max. None
PREFERRED TERM FOR LOANS & LEASES: Min. 1 year; Max. 30 years

COMPANY: **Southeast Bank N.A.**
ADDRESS: One Southeast Financial Center
Miami, FL 33131
PHONE: (305) 375-7150
TYPE OF INSTITUTION: Commerical Finance Unit
CONTACT OFFICER(S): Robert E. Lerch Jr., Div. Mgr.-Senior Vice President
John Gullman, Business Development Mgr.-Vice President
Gary E. Jaggard, Business Development Officer
ASSETS: Servicing volume over $9,000,000,000
INVESTMENTS/LOANS MADE: For own account
INVESTMENTS/LOANS MADE: In securities with a secondary market and in securities without a secondary market
TYPES OF FINANCING: LOANS: Working capital; Equipment
PREFERRED TYPES OF INDUSTRIES/INVESTMENTS: Citrus; Plumbing, Electrical, etc. (most wholesale/distributors in the state of Florida).
WILL NOT CONSIDER: Contractors
GEOGRAPHIC LIMITS OF INVESTMENTS/LOANS: State
RANGE OF INV./LOAN PER BUSINESS: Min. $500,000; Max. $60,000,000
PREFERRED TERM FOR LOANS & LEASES: Min. 1 year; Max. 10 years
BUSINESS CHARACTERISTICS DESIRED-REQUIRED: Minimum number of years in business: 3; Min. annual sales $2,000,000; Min. net worth $150.000;
BRANCHES: Mark Eddy, Charlie Williams, 201 N. Franklin St., Tampa, FL 33602; (813) 223-2346
Jack Gintowt, 6451 N. Federal Hwy., Ft. Lauderdale, FL 33308; (305) 472-4576
John Bearzi, 201 E. Pine St., Orlando, FL 32801; (305) 237-2148
Ed Clay, One Independence Square, Jacksonville, FL 32202; (904) 350-1730

COMPANY: **First Western SBLC, Inc.**
ADDRESS: 1380 N.E. Miami Gardens Drive
North Miami Beach, FL 33179
PHONE: (305) 949-5900
TYPE OF INSTITUTION: SBLC (90% SBA Government Guaranteed Loans)
CONTACT OFFICER(S): Lance B. Rosemore, President
Fredric M. Rosemore, Vice-president
ASSETS: $8,000,000; Loan capabilities $26,000,000
INVESTMENTS/LOANS MADE: For own account
INVESTMENTS/LOANS MADE: Only in securities without a secondary market
TYPES OF FINANCING: SECONDARY-MARKET CORPORATE SECURITIES: Business loans-commercial & manufacturing business expansion loans, VENTURE CAPITAL: Second-stage; Later-stage, LOANS: Working capital; equipment, REAL ESTATE LOANS: owner occupied ofice & warehouse condominiums-also purchases of existing businesses, REAL ESTATE: Acquisitions, OTHER SERVICES PROVIDED: Consulting and advisory
PREFERRED TYPES OF INDUSTRIES/INVESTMENTS: any type of business expansion or modernizations loan—limited in real estate to owner-occupied only. Expansion of manufacturing facilities
WILL NOT CONSIDER: Venture capital
GEOGRAPHIC LIMITS OF INVESTMENTS/LOANS: Florida, New Jersey, Georgia, Alabama
RANGE OF INV./LOAN PER BUSINESS: Min. $50,000; Max. $550,000
PREFERRED TERM FOR LOANS & LEASES: Min. 3 years; Max. 20 years
BUSINESS CHARACTERISTICS DESIRED-REQUIRED: Minimum number of years in business: 2; OTHER: all of our loans are 90% SBA guaranteed

COMPANY: **Pro-Med Capital, Inc.**
ADDRESS: 1380 N.E. Miami Gardens Drive
North Miami Beach, FL 33179
PHONE: (305) 949-5900
TYPE OF INSTITUTION: We have 2 subsidiaries: Western Financial Capital Corp (an SBIC) and First Western SBLC (an SBLC). Both are federal licensees of the Small Business Administration
CONTACT OFFICER(S): Lance B. Rosemore, Vice President
Fredric M. Rosemore, President
ASSETS: $20,000,000
INVESTMENTS/LOANS MADE: For own account
INVESTMENTS/LOANS MADE: In securities with a secondary market and in securities without a secondary market
TYPES OF FINANCING: LOANS: Equipment; business expansion loans, REAL ESTATE LOANS: SBA 90% Government guaranteed loanss for owner -occupied real estate, REAL ESTATE: Acquisitions
PREFERRED TYPES OF INDUSTRIES/INVESTMENTS: Diversified. Prefer health care and financing business expansion plans involving owner-occupied real estate (office condominiums, warehouse, etc.)
WILL NOT CONSIDER: Passive investments—no R & D
GEOGRAPHIC LIMITS OF INVESTMENTS/LOANS: National
RANGE OF INV./LOAN PER BUSINESS: Min. $25,000; Max. $550,000
PREFERRED TERM FOR LOANS & LEASES: Min. 5 years; Max. 20 years
BUSINESS CHARACTERISTICS DESIRED-REQUIRED: Minimum number of years in business: 2; OTHER: must be profitable
REFERRALS ACCEPTED FROM: Investee/Mortgage banker and Borrower/Investee

COMPANY: **Southern Leasing Services, Inc.**
ADDRESS: 618 US #One
North Palm Beach, FL 33408
PHONE: (305) 863-7900; (800) 327-3240 except Florida; (800) 432-4899 in Florida
TYPE OF INSTITUTION: Equipment Lessor
CONTACT OFFICER(S): Jean E. Miller, Asst. V.P.
John P. Little, Pres.
ASSETS: $60,000,000
INVESTMENTS/LOANS MADE: For own account, Through private placements
TYPES OF FINANCING: LOANS: Equipment, LEASES: Single-investor; Non-tax leases

PREFERRED TYPES OF INDUSTRIES/INVESTMENTS: All except aircraft
WILL NOT CONSIDER: Transactions in Arkansas (Louisiana only over $100,000)
GEOGRAPHIC LIMITS OF INVESTMENTS/LOANS: National
RANGE OF INV./LOAN PER BUSINESS: Min. $5,000; Max. No maximum
PREFERRED TERM FOR LOANS & LEASES: Min. 3 years; Max. 5 years
BUSINESS CHARACTERISTICS DESIRED-REQUIRED: Minimum number of years in business: 3
REFERRALS ACCEPTED FROM: Investment/Mortgage banker or Borrower/Investee

COMPANY: **Condor Group Holdings**
ADDRESS: 1601 Belvedere Rd.
West Palm Beach, FL 33406
PHONE: (305) 689-4906
TYPE OF INSTITUTION: Equipment leasing, Venture capital
CONTACT OFFICER(S): James A. Carpinello, Chairman of the Board
ASSETS: $24.5 mil
INVESTMENTS/LOANS MADE: For own account, For managed accounts
TYPES OF FINANCING: SECONDARY-MARKET CORPORATE SECURITIES: Common stock; Bonds, VENTURE CAPITAL: Second-stage; Buy-outs/Acquisitions, LOANS: Equipment; Equity-related, LEASES: Single-investor; Leveraged; Tax leases; Non-tax leases; Operating, Tax-oriented lease brokerage; Lease syndications; Vendor financing programs, REAL ESTATE: Acquisitions; Joint ventures; Partnerships/Syndications
PREFERRED TYPES OF INDUSTRIES/INVESTMENTS: Capital Equipment Manufacturer; Income Producing Real Estate
GEOGRAPHIC LIMITS OF INVESTMENTS/LOANS: National
RANGE OF INV./LOAN PER BUSINESS: Min. $50,000; Max. $5,000,000
PREFERRED TERM FOR LOANS & LEASES: Min. 3 years; Max. 10 years
BUSINESS CHARACTERISTICS DESIRED-REQUIRED: Minimum number of years in business: 1; Min. annual sales $500,000; Min. net worth $150,000; Min. annual net income $50,000; Min. annual cash flow $75,000
REFERRALS ACCEPTED FROM: Investment/Mortgage banker or Borrower/Investee
REMARKS: Start-ups are done

COMPANY: **Glenridge Associates, Inc.**
ADDRESS: 4501 Circle 75 Parkway, Building A Suite 1240
Atlanta, GA 30339
PHONE: (404) 955-2856
TYPE OF INSTITUTION: Equipment leasing and finance, real estate finance
CONTACT OFFICER(S): Michael L. Brown, President
ASSETS: N/A
INVESTMENTS/LOANS MADE: Through private placements
TYPES OF FINANCING: LOANS: Unsecured to credits above 'B'; Working Capital; Equipment; Equity related; Sale-Leaseback; Government guaranteed; REAL ESTATE LOANS: Long-term senior mtg.; Intermediate-term senior mtg.; Subordinated; Wraparounds; Industrial Revenue Bonds; LEASES
PREFERRED TYPES OF INDUSTRIES/INVESTMENTS: Computer oriented production/medical equipment, rolling stock, printing, all types of commercial and industrial equipment
WILL NOT CONSIDER: N/A
GEOGRAPHIC LIMITS OF INVESTMENT/LOANS: National
RANGE OF INV./LOAN PER BUSINESS: Min. $100,000; Max. None
PREFERRED TERM FOR LOANS & LEASES: Min. Two years; Max. Ten years
BUSINESS CHARACTERISTICS DESIRED/REQUIRED: Minimum number of years in business: 0; Min. annual sales $ None; Min. net worth $ N/A; Min. annual net income $ N/A; Min. annual cash flow $ N/A

COMPANY: **Citizens and Southern Commercial Corporation**
ADDRESS: 2059 Cooledge Road, (P.O. Box 4095, Atlanta 30302)
Tucker, GA 30084
PHONE: (404) 491-4839
TYPE OF INSTITUTION: Factoring, commercial finance, equipment leasing & financing (sub. of Commercial Bank)t
CONTACT OFFICER(S): Charles Mitchell, Senior V.P., Commercial Finance
Joel Chasteen, Sr. V.P. & Manager, Equipment Leasing
Bart Smith, Sr. V.P., Factoring
ASSETS: $7,620,000,000
TYPES OF FINANCING: LOANS: Working capital; Equipment, FACTORING, LEASES: Single-investor; Leveraged; Tax leases; Non-tax leases; Operating, INTERNATIONAL
PREFERRED TYPES OF INDUSTRIES/INVESTMENTS: For factoring: apparel, textiles, furniture, carpet, seafood industries; for leasing and commercial finance: manufacturers, distributors
GEOGRAPHIC LIMITS OF INVESTMENTS/LOANS: National; International
RANGE OF INV./LOAN PER BUSINESS: Max. $20,000,000
PREFERRED TERM FOR LOANS & LEASES: Min. 90 days; Max. 7 years
BUSINESS CHARACTERISTICS DESIRED-REQUIRED: Minimum number of years in business: 0; Min. annual sales $1,000,000; Min. net worth $200,000; Min. annual net income $20,000; Min. annual cash flow none; Other: Guaranties of principals with closely-held firms
REFERRALS ACCEPTED FROM: Investment/Mortgage banker or Borrower/Investee
BRANCHES: Claude McEwen, A.V.P., 300 S. Thornton Avenue, Dalton, GA 30720; (404) 278-1929
Fred Gaylord, V.P., 9841 Airport Blvd., Suite 300, Los Angeles, CA 90045; (213) 670-4772; Matthew Creo Jr., Sr. V.P., 1430 Broadway, 19th Floor, New York, NY 10018, 212-719-3700

COMPANY: **Atlanta Financial & Leasing, Inc.**
ADDRESS: 4501 Circle 75 Parkway, Suite A-1240
Atlanta, Georgia 30339
PHONE: (404) 955-2856
TYPE OF INSTITUTION: Financial and leasing brokers, mortgage loans
CONTACT OFFICERS(S): Doug Faust, Owner
Equipment leasing and financing, also act as consultants in the area of equipment purchases. Expertise in the marine (offshore) industry.
INVESTMENTS/LOANS MADE: Through private placements
INVESTMENTS/LOANS MADE: In securities with a secondary market and securities without a secondary market
TYPES OF FINANCING: LOANS: Unsecured; Working capital (receivables/inventory); Equipment; Equity-related; REAL ESTATE LOANS: Long-term senior mtg.; Intermediate-term senior mtg.; Standbys; Industrial revenue bonds; FACTORING; LEASES: Single-investor; Leveraged; Tax leases; Non-tax leases; Operating; Tax-oriented lease brokerage; Lease syndications; Vendor financing programs; REAL ESTATE: Joint ventures. OTHER: Equipment purchases, expertise in the marine industry
PREFERRED TYPES OF INDUSTRIES/INVESTMENTS: Middle market construction, medical, data processing, certain real estate transaction, equipment leasing
GEOGRAPHIC LIMITS OF INVESTMENTS/LOANS: Local; State; Regional; National; International
RANGE OF INV./LOAN PER BUSINESS: Min. $100,000; Max. $ no limit
PREFERRED TERM FOR LOANS & LEASES: Min. 3 years; Max. as pertinent
BUSINESS CHARACTERISTICS DESIRED-REQUIRED: We will look at any situation. It does need to make sense

COMPANY: **LeaseAmerica Corp.**
ADDRESS: 4333 Edgewood Rd. NE
Cedar Rapids, IA 52499
PHONE: (319) 366-5331
TYPE OF INSTITUTION: Leasing Div. of Insurance Holding Co.
CONTACT OFFICER(S): E. J. Scherrman, President
John A. Mahan, Executive Vice President
Dave Harvey, Vice President-Credit
INVESTMENTS/LOANS MADE: For own account; Through underwriting public offerings
TYPES OF FINANCING: LEASES: Single-investor; Leveraged; Tax; Non-tax; Operating; Lease syndications; Vendor financing programs
PREFERRED TYPES OF INDUSTRIES/INVESTMENTS: General Equipment Leasing Co.
GEOGRAPHIC LIMITS OF INVESTMENTS/LOANS: National
RANGE OF INV./LOAN PER BUSINESS: Min. $10,000
PREFERRED TERM FOR LOANS & LEASES: Min. 2 years; Max. 7 years
BUSINESS CHARACTERISTICS DESIRED-REQUIRED: Min. number of years in business: 2; Min. annual sales $100,000; Min. net worth $25,000
BRANCHES: LeaseAmerica Corporation, 500 Northridge Road, Suite 300, Atlanta, GA, 30338
LeaseAmerica Corporation, 8585 Stemmons Freeway, Twin Tower So. - Suite 770, Dallas, TX 75247
LeaseAmerica Corporation, 218 Harrison Street, Davenport, IA 52801
LeaseAmerica Corporation, 504 Merle Hay Tower, Des Moines, IA 50310
LeaseAmerica Corporation, 2616 South Loop West, Suite 100, Houston, TX 77054
LeaseAmerica Corporation, 2724 Commerce Tower, 911 Main Street, Kansas City, MO 64105
LeaseAmerica Corporation, The Starks Building, Suite 396, 455 South Fourth Street, Louisville, KY 40202
LeaseAmerica Corporation, 600 E. Mason St., Milwaukee, WI 53202
LeaseAmerica Corporation, Southtown Office Park, Suite 550, 8120 Penn Ave. South, Minneapolis, MN 55431
LeaseAmerica Corporation, Corporate Plaza, 11212 Davenport Street, Omaha, NE 68154
LeaseAmerica Corporation, 2000 W. Pioneer Parkway, Suite 24-B, Peoria, IL 61615

COMPANY: **The Dillon Company**
ADDRESS: 7626 Hickman Rd.
Des Moines, IA 50322
PHONE: (515) 276-7607
TYPE OF INSTITUTION: Leasing Co.
CONTACT OFFICER(S): Howard D. Hamilton, President, Lease financing, Tax partnerships between vendors and The Dillon Company
TYPES OF FINANCING: LOANS: Working capital; Equipment; Equity-related, LEASES: Single-investor; Tax leases; Non-tax leases; Tax-oriented lease brokerage; Vendor financing programs, Other: All types of equipment leasing; debt restructuring; OTHER SERVICES PROVIDED: Managing partner in partnerships created between vendors of business equipment and The Dillon Company
GEOGRAPHIC LIMITS OF INVESTMENTS/LOANS: Regional
RANGE OF INV./LOAN PER BUSINESS: Min. $15,000; Max. Unlimited
PREFERRED TERM FOR LOANS & LEASES: Min. 2 years; Max. 5 years
BUSINESS CHARACTERISTICS DESIRED-REQUIRED: Minimum number of years in business: 2 years
REMARKS: Terms on loans: 3-10 years

COMPANY: **Associates Commercial Corporation**
ADDRESS: The Associates Center, 150 North Michigan Ave.
Chicago, IL 60601
PHONE: (312) 781-5800
TYPE OF INSTITUTION: Commercial finance subsidiary of Associates Corporation of North America (The Associates), the cornerstone on the Financial Services Group of Gulf & Western Industries, Inc.
CONTACT OFFICER(S): Rocco A. Macri, Executive Vice President, Business Loans Division (Division provides accounts receivable, inventory and fixed asset loans for working capital, refinancings, acquisitions and leveraged buyouts for small annd medium-sized businesses throughout the U.S.).
ASSETS: $6.6 billion (The Associates); $3.5 billion in commerical finance recievables
INVESTMENTS/LOANS MADE: For own account

INVESTMENTS/LOANS MADE: Only in securities without a secondary market
TYPES OF FINANCING: VENTURE CAPITAL: Later-stage expansions; Buy-outs/Acquisitions, LOANS: Working capital; Equipment; Equity-related. Other: Bank participation, REAL ESTATE LOANS: Industrial plants with receivables/inventory, FACTORING, LEASES: Single-investor; Tax leases; Non-tax leases; Operating; Vendor financing programs, REAL ESTATE: Acquisitions, OTHER SERVICES PROVIDED: Retail and wholesale financing of heavy duty trucks and trailers, financing and leasing of construction and mining equipment, machine tools, business aircraft and other capital goods; fleet leasing and management services for cars and trucks
PREFERRED TYPES OF INDUSTRIES/INVESTMENTS: Heavy-duty truck and trailer financing; auto, truck and trailer fleet leasing; communications and industrial equipment financing and leasing; business loans (esp. leveraged buyout financing); and factoring
WILL NOT CONSIDER: Unsecured financing
GEOGRAPHIC LIMITS OF INVESTMENTS/LOANS: National
RANGE OF INV./LOAN PER BUSINESS: Min. $500,000; Max. $100 million or more
PREFERRED TERM FOR LOANS & LEASES: Min. two (2) years; Max. ten (10) years
BUSINESS CHARACTERISTICS DESIRED-REQUIRED: Minimum net worth $500,000
REFERRALS ACCEPTED FROM: Investment/Mortgage banker or Borrower/Investee
BRANCHES: More than 100 regional and branch offices in North America
REMARKS: Associates Commerical has six operting divisions: Business Loans, Communications, Equipment, Factoring , Fleet Leasing and Transportation

COMPANY: **Associates Commercial Corporation**
ADDRESS: The Associates Center, 150 N. Michigan Ave. Chicago, IL 60601
PHONE: (312) 781-5800
TYPE OF INSTITUTION: Commercial finance subsidiary of Associates Corporation of North America, a Gulf and Western company
CONTACT OFFICER(S): B.E. Starr, Executive V.P., Transportation Division (Retail and wholesale heavy-duty truck and trailer financing and leasing)
L.J. Pelka, Executive V.P., Equipment Division (Financing and leasing for construction, equipment, marine, aircraft and manufacturing industries)
J.D. Kines, Executive V.P., Leasing/International Divisions (Automobile/truck fleet leasing and financing)
ASSETS: $3.0 billion in net receivables
INVESTMENTS/LOANS MADE: For own account
INVESTMENTS/LOANS MADE: In securities with a secondary market and in securities without a secondary market
TYPES OF FINANCING: LOANS: Working capital (receivables/inventory); Equipment; Equity-related; Other: Bank participation, REAL ESTATE LOANS: Industrial plants with receivables/inventory, FACTORING, LEASES: Single-investor; Tax leases; Non-tax leases; Operating; Vendor financing programs, INTERNATIONAL (including import/export), REAL ESTATE: Acquisitions, OTHER SERVICES PROVIDED: Retail and wholesale financing of heavy duty trucks and trailers, construction equipment and other capital goods
PREFERRED TYPES OF INDUSTRIES/INVESTMENTS: Medium term trucking, contracting, marine and manufacturing industries
WILL NOT CONSIDER: Unsecured financing
GEOGRAPHIC LIMITS OF INVESTMENTS/LOANS: National
RANGE OF INV./LOAN PER BUSINESS: Min. $100,000; Max. $50,000,000
PREFERRED TERM FOR LOANS & LEASES: Min. 2 years; Max 10 years
BUSINESS CHARACTERISTICS DESIRED-REQUIRED: Min. net worth $500,000
REFERRALS ACCEPTED FROM: Investment/Mortgage banker or Borrower/Investee
BRANCHES: M.L. Leonard, Branch Mgr., 1895 Phoenix Blvd., Ste. 410, College Park, GA 30349; (404) 996-6700
J.F. Rowan, Branch Mgr., 3636 S. Sherwood Forest Blvd., Baton Rouge, LA 70816, P.O. Box 15389, Baton Rouge, LA 70895; (504) 292-5060
D.L. Baker, Branch Mgr., 600 Vestavia Pkwy., Ste. 300, P.O. Box 10944, Birmingham, AL 35202; (205) 979-5126
N.E. Wetzel, Branch Mgr., 1427 Thomas Dr., P.O. Box 612, Cape Girardeau, MO 63701; (314) 334-7135
F.C. Henderson, Branch Mgr., 2600 Lakeland Terrace, P.O. Box 4829, Jackson, MS 39216; (601) 982-3434
Jim Tyler, Branch Mgr., 6016 Brookvale Lane, Ste. 255, P.O. Box 11683, Knoxville, TN 37919; (615) 588-8602
J.F. Mundorff, Branch Mgr., 4232 Northern Pike, Ste. 301, P.O. Box 457, Monroeville, PA 15146; (412) 373-8050
Mike Piraino, Branch Mgr., 9602-A Palmer Hwy., Lanham, MD 20801, P.O. Box "A", College Park, MD 20740; (301) 459-8600
D.D. Shertzer, Branch Mgr., 415 Office Building, 415 Boston Turnpike, Shrewsbury, NA 01545; (617) 845-6551
K. Shrout, Branch Mgr., 2858 S. Arlington Rd., P.O. Box 2742, Akron, OH 44319; (216) 644-0045
J.D. Morrow, Branch Mgr., 800 W. Roosevelt Rd., Ste. 410,, P.O. Box 2398, Glenn Ellyn, IL 60137; (312) 790-1200
C.F. Flege, Branch Mgr., 4010 Executive Park Dr., Ste. 320, P.O. Box 41387A, Cincinnati, OH 45241; (513) 563-2211
Steve Phelps, Branch Mgr., 24011 Greenfield, P.O. Box 890, Southfield, MI 48075; (313) 557-1515
R.A. Ryan, Branch Mgr., 7007 N. Graham Rd., P.O. Box 20528, Indianapolis, IN 46220; (317) 842-5000
G.F. Schaser, Branch Mgr., 12970 W. Bluemound, Ste. 305, P.O. Box 86, Elm Grove, WI 53122; (414) 784-9030
D.R. Helvey, Branch Mgr., 7600 Parklawn Ave., Ste. 244, Edina, MN 55435; (612) 831-7208
Jack Hirsh, Branch Mgr., 5901 N. Knoxville Rd., P.O. Box 3263, Peoria, IL 61614; (309) 692-3475
Wm. Reinke, Branch Mgr., 5700 S. Quebec St., Ste. 340,, Englewood, CO 80155, P.O. Box 3478, Englewood, CO 80111; (303) 779-6111
E.D. Gray, Branch Mgr., 201 E. Abram St., Ste. 550, P.O. Box. 966, Arlington, TX 76010; (817) 640-8195
Mark Yeary, Branch Mgr., 521 N. Belt, Ste. 300, Houston, TX 77060, P.O. Box 38975, Houston, TX 77238; (713) 820-4070

R.A. Willey, Branch Mgr., 10870 Benson Dr., Ste. 2150, P.O. Box 121007,, Overland Park, KS 66212; (913) 642-7475
K.E. Fulmer, Branch Mgr., 501 N. Brookhurst, Ste. 302, P.O. Boox 3908, Anaheim, CA 92803; (714) 991-4481
D.R. Miller, Branch Mgr., 920 S. 107th Ave., Ste. 310, Omaha, NE 68114; (402) 397-4424
D. Komer, Branch Mgr., 4565 N. Channel Ave., Portland, OR 97217; (503) 289-5585
Bill Sidler, Branch Mgr., 3700 W. 2100 South, Salt Lake City, UT 84120; (801) 972-4057
W.W. Sabbagh, Branch Mgr., 777 Southland Dr., Ste. 208, Hayward, CA 94545, P.O. Box 4913, Hayward, CA 94540; (415) 783-6272
J.V. Ruddy, Branch Mgr., 13401 Bel-red Rd., Ste. A-8, Bellevue, WA 98004, P.O. Box 3702, Bellevue, WA 98009; (206) 747-4402
R. Peck, Branch Mgr., 5 200 South Yale Avenue, Suite 200, Tulsa, OK 74135, P.O. Box 35129, Tulsa, OK 74153; (918) 496-0500
G.A. Whitehurst, Branch Mgr., M.Y. Rotelli, Branch Credit Mgr., 1701 Golf Rd., Ste. 103, Rolling Meadows, IL 60008; (312) 228-0033
C. Gibson, Branch Mgr., Rick Ward, Branch Credit Mgr., 6100 Channingway Blvd., Suite 200, Columbus, OH 43227, P.O. Box 548, Regnoldsburg, OH 43068; (614) 861-2319
A.O. Bayley, Branch Mgr., M.J. Anshus, Branch Credit Mgr., 1011 North Mayfair Road, Suite 205, Wauwatosa, WI 53226; (414) 475-6070
P.J. McNelis, Branch Mgr., H.P. Huber, Branch Credit Mgr., Penn Center West One, Suite 207, Campbell's Run Rd., Pittsburgh, PA 15276; (412) 823-3970
Paul Williams, Branch Mgr., Gary Stigger, BCM, 10170 Linn Station Road, Suite 440, Louisville, KY 40223; (502) 426-0661
H.S. Hix, Branch Mgr., R.R. Navolanic, Branch Credit Mgr., 2971 Flowers Road, South, Suite 291, Atlanta, GA 30341; (404) 458-2317
J.W. Slappey, Branch Mgr., B. Brantley, Branch Credit Mgr., 8 Woodlawn Green, Suite 216, Charlotte, NC 28210; (704) 527-6150
R. Stonfer, Branch Mgr., D.A. Graetz, Branch Credit Mgr., 100 Lincoln Place, 2300 Maitland Ctr Pky., Ste. 238, Maitland, FL 32751, (305) 660-2533
R.W. Fillenwarth, Sales Office Mgr., 8120 Knue Road, Ste. 106, P.O. Box 50585, Indianapolis, IN 46250; (317) 842-7281
Paul Williams, Branch Mgr.
W.K. Cardoza, Branch Mgr., P. Cosgrove, Branch Credit Mgr., 1604 Santa Rosa Road, Suite 137, Richmond, VA 23288; (804) 285-2391
A.G. DeWall, Branch Mgr., J.K. Feinglas, Branch Credit Mgr., 13101 Preston Road at LBJ, Suite 501, P.O. Box 800297, Dallas, TX 75240; (214) 661-1413
J. Schickling, Branch Mgr., W.W. Schulz, Branch Credit Mgr., 6300 W. Loop Street South, Suite 400, P.O. Box 1102, Bellaire, TX 77401; (713) 666-0302
Ron Ort, Branch Mgr., D. Duffin, Branch Credit Mgr., 3636 S. Sherwood Forest, Suite 590, Metairie, LA 70002; P.O. Box 45550, Baton Rouge, LA 70895-4550; (504) 293-3610
H. Fowler, Branch Mgr., D. Duffin, Branch Credit Mgr., 10000 I H 10 West, Suite 324, San Antonio, TX 78230, P.O. Box 40039, San Antonio, TX 78229-290; (512) 691-1111
W.F. Goldsmith, Branch Mgr., T.R. Fanning, BCM, 5660 S. Syracuse Circle, Ste. 408, Englewood, CO 80112; (303) 770-1023
T. Marshall, Branch Mgr., M. King, Branch Credit Mgr., 4141 MacArthur Blvd., Ste. 216, Newport Beach, CA 92660, (714) 476-0515
J. Rue, Branch Mgr., D.A. Baxter, Branch Credit Mgr., 500 N.E. Multnomah, Suite 362, Portland, OR 97232; (503) 231-4000
J.W. Davis, Branch Mgr., F. Crum, Branch Credit Mgr., 4444 S. 700 E., Ste. 202, Salt Lake City, UT 84107; P.O. Box 151043 (Zip 84115); (801) 263-3518
Wes Ebner, Branch Mgr., R. Holzworth, Branch Credit Mgr., 600-108th Avenue, NE, Suite 839, Bellevue, WA 98004, P.O. Box 1705, Bellevue, WA 98009; (206) 455-1980, (509) 484-6198
W. Hull, 405 Gretna Blvd., Suite 207 "M", Gretna, LA 70053; (504) 368-9029
J. Cain, Auto, M. Phelan, Truck, L. Weidner, Truck, 2550 E. Golf Rd., Suite 206, Rolling Meadows, IL 60008; (312) 364-3700
J.J. Linden, Auto, D. Rhodes, Truck, 1297 Johnson Ferry Road, Suite 255, Marietta, GA 30067; (404) 977-8901
D. Babcock, Auto, 4445 Alpha Road, Suite 110, P.O. Box 402026, Dallas, TX 75240; (214) 661-5105
L. Pusey, Auto, 3711 Long Beach Blvd., Suite 1001, Long Beach, CA 90807; (213) 424-0701
J. Lovato, Auto, 871 Mountain Ave., Springfield, NJ

COMPANY: **BT Commercial Corporation**
ADDRESS: 233 South Wacker Drive
Chicago, IL 60606
PHONE: (212) 977-4702
CONTACT OFFICER(S): George A. Boronkay, Exec. Vice Pres.

COMPANY: **Continental Illinois Leasing Corp.**
ADDRESS: 231 S. LaSalle St.
Chicago, IL 60697
PHONE: (312) 828-7400
TYPE OF INSTITUTION: Leasing Co.
CONTACT OFFICER(S): Bernard J. McKenna, President
AnthonyJ. Cracchi olo, Senior Vice President
ASSETS: $1.1 billion
INVESTMENTS/LOANS MADE: For own account; For managed accounts; Through private placements
TYPES OF FINANCING: LOANS: Unsecured to credits above Baa; Working capital; Equipment; LEASES: Single-investor; Leveraged; Tax leases; Non-tax leases; Tax-oriented lease brokerage; Lease syndications; Vendor financing programs
GEOGRAPHIC LIMITS OF INVESTMENTS/LOANS: National; International
RANGE OF INV./LOAN PER BUSINESS: Min. $250,000; Max. None
PREFERRED TERM FOR LOANS & LEASES: Min: 5 years; Max. 10 years
BUSINESS CHARACTERISTICS DESIRED-REQUIRED: Minimum number of years in business: 3

COMPANY: **Datronic Rental Corp.**
ADDRESS: 5210 Wesley Terrace
Chicago, IL 60656

PHONE: (312) 992-0760
TYPE OF INSTITUTION: Leasing Co. & Com'l. Finance
CONTACT OFFICER(S): Edmund Lapinski, Secy/Treasurer, Lease Financing and Syndication
ASSETS: $10,000,000—100,000,000
INVESTMENTS/LOANS MADE: Through private placements
TYPES OF FINANCING: LOANS: Equipment, LEASES
GEOGRAPHIC LIMITS OF INVESTMENTS/LOANS: National
PREFERRED TERM FOR LOANS & LEASES: Min. 1-3; Max. 7-10

COMPANY: **First Chicago Credit Corp.**
ADDRESS: 20 South Clark Street, Room 220
Chicago, IL 60670
PHONE: (312) 732-0294
CONTACT OFFICER(S): Stephen C. Diamond, Chmn. of the Bd.

COMPANY: **National Acceptance Company of America**
ADDRESS: 105 West Adams Street
Chicago, IL 60603
PHONE: (312) 621-7500
CONTACT OFFICER(S): Frank R. Bergen, Sr. Vice Pres.

COMPANY: **Puritan Finance Corporation**
ADDRESS: 55 West Monroe Street, Suite 3890
Chicago, IL 60603
PHONE: (312) 372-8833
CONTACT OFFICER(S): Lawrence A. Sherman, Pres.

COMPANY: **Trans Union Leasing Corp.**
ADDRESS: 222 W. Adams
Chicago, IL 60606
PHONE: (312) 641-0233
TYPE OF INSTITUTION: Leasing Co.
CONTACT OFFICER(S): William Cox, Pres.
TYPES OF FINANCING: LOANS: Equipment; Secured Lending, LEASES: Single-investor; Non-tax leases; Lease syndications; Vendor financing programs
PREFERRED TYPES OF INDUSTRIES/INVESTMENTS: Diversified
GEOGRAPHIC LIMITS OF INVESTMENTS/LOANS: National; Canada
RANGE OF INV./LOAN PER BUSINESS: Min. $50,000; Max. $5 million
REMARKS: Term depends on equipment

COMPANY: **Walter E. Heller & Co./Commercial & Industrial Equipment Financing Group**
ADDRESS: 105 West Adams Street
Chicago, IL 60603
PHONE: (312) 621-7600
TYPE OF INSTITUTION: Equipment leasing and financing
CONTACT OFFICER(S): Samuel L. Eichenfield, President
INVESTMENTS/LOANS MADE: For own account
TYPES OF FINANCING: LOANS: Working capital; Equipment, REAL ESTATE LOANS; FACTORING, LEASES: Single-investor; Leveraged; Tax leases; Non-tax leases; Lease syndications; OTHER SERVICES PROVIDED: Floor planning
PREFERRED TYPES OF INDUSTRIES/INVESTMENTS: All types of capital equip. for businesses
GEOGRAPHIC LIMITS OF INVESTMENTS/LOANS: National
RANGE OF INV./LOAN PER BUSINESS: Min. $50,000; Max. No
PREFERRED TERM FOR LOANS & LEASES: Min. 3 years; Max. 10 years
BUSINESS CHARACTERISTICS DESIRED-REQUIRED: Minimum number of years in business: 3
REFERRALS ACCEPTED FROM: Investment/Mortgage banker or Borrower/Investee

COMPANY: **Foothill Group, Inc.**
ADDRESS: 2700 Des Plaines & River Road
Des Plaines, IL 60018
PHONE: (312) 635-6570
CONTACT OFFICER(S): Joseph J. Briganti, Sr. Vice Pres.

COMPANY: **Appleco Leasing Corporation**
ADDRESS: 850 Pratt Blvd.
Elk Grove Village, IL 60007
PHONE: (312) 593-5000
TYPE OF INSTITUTION: Captive leasing company of major plastics auxiliary equipment manufacturer
CONTACT OFFICER(S): Don Swanson, Treasurer
Michael A. Waters, Chairman of the Board
ASSETS: $1.3 million
INVESTMENTS/LOANS MADE: For own account
TYPES OF FINANCING: LOANS: Unsecured; Equipment, LEASES: Vendor financing programs; Other: Equip. leasing
PREFERRED TYPES OF INDUSTRIES/INVESTMENTS: Plastics industry, recycling-reclaiming
WILL NOT CONSIDER: Heavy machinery
GEOGRAPHIC LIMITS OF INVESTMENTS/LOANS: National
RANGE OF INV./LOAN PER BUSINESS: Min. $2,500; Max. $500,000
PREFERRED TERM FOR LOANS & LEASES: Min. 1 year; Max. 5 years
BUSINESS CHARACTERISTICS DESIRED-REQUIRED: Minimum number of years in business: 0; Other: Loose parameters; Personal financial strength
REFERRALS ACCEPTED FROM: Borrower/Investee
REMARKS: A wholly-owned subsidiary of AEC

COMPANY:**North American Capital Group, Ltd.**
ADDRESS: 7250 N. Cicero Ave., Suite 201
Lincolnwood IL 60646
PHONE: (312) 982-1010
TYPE OF INSTITUTION: Subsidiary - financial services holding company, The North American Group, Ltd.
CONTACT OFFICER(S): Gregory I. Kravitt, President
William Andersen, Associate
INVESTMENTS/LOANS MADE: For own account; Through private placements
INVESTMENTS/LOANS MADE: Only in securities without a secondary market

TYPES OF FINANCING: VENTURE CAPITAL: Second-stage; Later-stage; Buy-outs/Acquisitions; LOANS: Working capital; Equipment; Equity-related; Other: Loans with attached warrants; REAL ESTATE LOANS: Long-term senior mtg.; Intermediate-term senior mtg.; Subordinated; Wraparounds; Construction; Standbys; Other: bond guarantees; REAL ESTATE: Acquisitions; Joint ventures; OTHER SERVICES PROVIDED: Financing arranged for both qualified franchisors and qualified franchisees
PREFERRED TYPES OF INDUSTRIES/INVESTMENTS: Franchising, medium to low technology companies, Income property, Real estate (manufacturers, ditributors) leveraged buyouts, profitable service companies
WILL NOT CONSIDER: gambling casinos, entertainment
GEOGRAPHIC LIMITS OF INVESTMENTS/LOANS: Other: Midwest
RANGE OF INV./LOAN PER BUSINESS: Min. $100,000; Max. $3.0 million
PREFERRED TERM FOR LOANS & LEASES: Min. 3 years; Max. 10 years
BUSINESS CHARACTERISTICS DESIRED-REQUIRED: Minimum number of years in business: 1; Min. annual sales $500,000

COMPANY: **Affiliated Asset-Based Lending Services, Inc.**
ADDRESS: 8700 N. Waukegan Road, Suite 100, P.O. Box 98
Morton Grove, IL 60053
PHONE: (312) 965-7810
CONTACT OFFICER(S): Daniel S. Tauman, Pres.

COMPANY: **Reli Financial Corp.**
ADDRESS: 555 Skokie Blvd., P.O. Box 797
Northbrook, IL 60062
PHONE: (312) 564-6810
TYPE OF INSTITUTION: Commercial finance and leasing company
CONTACT OFFICER(S): Edward C. Latek, President
Daniel Sideman, Exec. V.P.
ASSETS: $10,000,000
INVESTMENTS/LOANS MADE: For own account
TYPES OF FINANCING: LOANS: Equipment, LEASES
PREFERRED TYPES OF INDUSTRIES/INVESTMENTS: General equipment for rental industry
GEOGRAPHIC LIMITS OF INVESTMENTS/LOANS: National
RANGE OF INV./LOAN PER BUSINESS: Min. $10,000; Max. $150,000
PREFERRED TERM FOR LOANS & LEASES: Min. 3 years; Max. 5 years
BUSINESS CHARACTERISTICS DESIRED-REQUIRED: Minimum number of years in business: 3; Min. annual sales $200,000; Min. net worth $50,000

COMPANY: **International Funding Corporation**
ADDRESS: Two Northfield Plaza, Suite 230
Northfield, IL 60093
PHONE: (312) 441-8600
TYPE OF INSTITUTION: Equipment leasing and financing
CONTACT OFFICER(S): Rudolph D. Trebels, President & Administrator, Printing and graphic equipment, machine tool and plastic molding equipment, computer and related peripheral equipment, medical and dental equipment, construction equipment
INVESTMENTS/LOANS MADE: For own account
1LOANS: Equipment; Equity-related, LEASES: Single-investor; Leveraged; Tax leases; Non-tax leases; Tax-oriented lease brokerage; Vendor financing programs
GEOGRAPHIC LIMITS OF INVESTMENTS/LOANS: National
RANGE OF INV./LOAN PER BUSINESS: Min. $50,000; Max. $50,000,000
PREFERRED TERM FOR LOANS & LEASES: Min. 3 years; Max. 15 years
BUSINESS CHARACTERISTICS DESIRED-REQUIRED: Minimum number of years in business: 3; Min. annual sales $750,000; Min. net worth $100,000; Min. annual net income $25,000; Min. annual cash flow $50,000

COMPANY: **Mellon Financial Services Corporation**
ADDRESS: 1415 West 22nd Street, Suite 1200
Oak Brook, IL 60521
PHONE: (800) 323-7338 outside IL, (312) 986-2950 inside IL
TYPE OF INSTITUTION: Asset based lending affiliate of Mellon Bank, N.A.
CONTACT OFFICER(S): Charles S. Pryce, Senior Vice President
ASSETS: $25 billion
INVESTMENTS/LOANS MADE: For own account
INVESTMENTS/LOANS MADE: In securities with a secondary market and in securities without a secondary market
TYPES OF FINANCING: LOANS: Working capital; Equipment; Equity-related; Other: intermediate term loans; LBO financing. REAL ESTATE LOANS: Intermediate-term senior mtg.; Land; Standbys; Industrial revenue bonds. LEASES: Non-tax leases. INTERNATIONAL
WILL NOT CONSIDER: Building contractors
GEOGRAPHIC LIMITS OF INVESTMENTS/LOANS: National
BUSINESS CHARACTERISTICS DESIRED-REQUIRED: Minimum number of years in business: 0 Min. annual sales $2,000,000; Min. net worth $100,000; Min. annual net income $ positive; Min. annual cash flow $ positive.
REFERRALS ACCEPTED FROM: Investment/Mortgage banker or Borrower/Investee

COMPANY: **The Financial Corporation of Illinois**
ADDRESS: 4825 North Scott Street, Suite 307
Schiller Park, IL 60176
PHONE: (312) 678-2440
TYPE OF INSTITUTION: Privately-held finance company specializing in financing and discounting of leveraged lease loans and secured loans involving equipment
CONTACT OFFICER(S): Dennis T. Roesslein, Assistant Vice President
Robert G. Roth, Chief Executive Officer
INVESTMENTS/LOANS MADE: For own account
TYPES OF FINANCING: LOANS: Equipment; Other: Leveraged lease loans, Secured equipment loans. LEASES: Single-investor; Leveraged; Tax leases

PREFERRED TYPES OF INDUSTRIES/INVESTMENTS: We will consider discounting of leveraged lease loans and direct secured equipment loans within any industry as long as the lessee/borrower is of a "BAA" or better credit quality.
WILL NOT CONSIDER: Real estate, Working capital loans
GEOGRAPHIC LIMITS OF INVESTMENTS/LOANS: National
RANGE OF INV./LOAN PER BUSINESS: Min. $200,000; Max. $2,000,000
PREFERRED TERM FOR LOANS & LEASES: Min. 3 years; Max. 5 years
BUSINESS CHARACTERISTICS DESIRED-REQUIRED: Other: Companies which are rated "BAA" or better. Non-rated companies of an equivalent size and credit quality to "BAA" or better.

COMPANY: **M.E. Hoffman Co.**
ADDRESS: 901 S. Second St., P.O. Box 1026
Springfield, IL 62705
PHONE: (217) 528-7355
TYPE OF INSTITUTION: Mortgage Banker
CONTACT OFFICER(S): M. E. Hoffman, Pres.
INVESTMENTS/LOANS MADE: For own account
INVESTMENTS/LOANS MADE: Only in securities with a secondary market
TYPES OF FINANCING: LOANS, REAL ESTATE LOANS: Long-term senior mtg.; Intermediate-term senior mtg.; Wraparounds.
PREFERRED TYPES OF INDUSTRIES/INVESTMENTS: Real Estate
GEOGRAPHIC LIMITS OF INVESTMENTS/LOANS: National
RANGE OF INV./LOAN PER BUSINESS: Min. $500,000
BUSINESS CHARACTERISTICS DESIRED-REQUIRED: Minimum number of years in business: 0

COMPANY: **Irwin Union Corporation**
ADDRESS: 500 Washington St., Box 929
Columbus, IN 47201
PHONE: (812) 372-0111
TYPE OF INSTITUTION: Bank holding company: subsidiaries; Irwin Union Bank, Inland Mortgage, white River Capital
CONTACT OFFICER(S): M. R. Ryan; Commercial Lending, President, Irwin Union Bank
S. K. Kreigh; Mortgage Lending, President, Inland Mortgage
D. J. Blair; Venture Capital, Vice President, White River Capital
ASSETS: $250 million
INVESTMENTS/LOANS MADE: For own account
INVESTMENTS/LOANS MADE: In securities with a secondary market and in securities wiithout a secondary market
TYPES OF FINANCING: SECONDARY MARKET CORPORATE SECURITIES; Industrial Revenue Bond Placements. VENTURE CAPITAL: Second-stage; Later-stage expansion. LOANS: Unsecured to credits Above BBB; Working capital; Equipment; Equity-related. REAL ESTATE LOANS: Long-term senior mtg.; Wraparounds; Construction; Industrial revenue bonds; Other: Primarily single family. OTHER SERVICES PROVIDED: Mortgage servicing, municipal finance, and pension management
PREFERRED TYPES OF INDUSTRIES/INVESTMENTS: Commercial Lending-all forms; Mortgage Banking-Single family, FHA/VA; Venture Capital-no preferences
GEOGRAPHIC LIMITS OF INVESTMENTS/LOANS: State; regional (prefer State)
RANGE OF INV./LOAN PER BUSINESS: Min. $100,000; Max. $2,000,000 (Venture $200,000)
PREFERRED TERM FOR LOANS & LEASES: Min. .25 years; Max. 20 years
BUSINESS CHARACTERISTICS DESIRED-REQUIRED: Minimum number of years in business: 1
REFERRALS ACCEPTED FROM: Investment/Mortgage banker or Borrower/Investee

COMPANY:**SCI Financial Corp.**
ADDRESS: 5610 Crawfordsville Road, Suite 1904
Indianapolis, IN 46224
PHONE: (317) 241-6370
TYPE OF INSTITUTION: Leasing consulting services to community size banks—manage their investment in equipment leasing transactions; General lease transaction brokerage; Private placement of asset based transaction
CONTACT OFFICER(S): Ray Krebs, Pres.
ASSETS: N/A
INVESTMENTS/LOANS MADE: For managed accounts; Through private placements
INVESTMENTS/LOANS MADE: Only in securities without a secondary-market
TYPES OF FINANCING: LOANS: Working capital; Equipment; LEASES: Single-investor; Leveraged; Tax leases; Non-tax leases; Operating; Tax-oriented lease brokerage; Lease syndications; Vender financing programs
PREFERRED TYPES OF INDUSTRIES/INVESTMENTS: Will consider virtually any industry. We DO NOT do Real Estate unless it is a nominal part of the transaction
WILL NOT CONSIDER: N/A
GEOGRAPHIC LIMITS OF INVESTMENTS/LOANS: Other: General leasing activity on a regional basis: larger ticket tax-oriented leases & private placements on a national basis
RANGE OF INV./LOAN PER BUSINESS: Min. $50,000; Max. $ No Limit
PREFERRED TERM FOR LOANS & LEASES: Min. 3 years; Max. 7 to 10 years
BUSINESS CHARACTERISTICS DESIRED-REQUIRED: Minimum number of years in business: 3; Min. annual sales $500,000; Min net worth $250,000; Min. annual net income $ *; Min. annual cash flow $ *; * Historical cash flow must be adequate to service new debt WITHOUT consideration to income produced by new equip. Must show stable business trends

COMPANY:**Commonwealth Financial Services Corporation/I & R Leasing, Inc.**
ADDRESS: 810 Chestnut Street
Bowling Green KY 42101
PHONE: (502) 782-2908
TYPE OF INSTITUTION: Independent

CONTACT OFFICER(S): Robert W. Wood, President of Commonwealth Financial Services Corp.
Irene H. Wood, President of I & R Leasing, Inc.
ASSETS: $5 million
INVESTMENTS/LOANS MADE: For own account
TYPES OF FINANCING: LOANS: Equipment; LEASES: Single-investor; Leveraged; Tax leases; Non-tax leases; Operating; Tax-oriented lease brokerage; Vendor financing programs; OTHER SERVICES PROVIDED: Vehicle Leasing and Financing including dealer programs
PREFERRED TYPES OF INDUSTRIES/INVESTMENTS: Will Consider All
GEOGRAPHIC LIMITS OF INVESTMENTS/LOANS: Regional
RANGE OF INV./LOAN PER BUSINESS: Max. $ None
PREFERRED TERM FOR LOANS & LEASES: Min. one year; Max. seven years
BUSINESS CHARACTERISTICS DESIRED-REQUIRED: Minimum number of years in business: 2; Other: Positive Cash Flow
REFERRALS ACCEPTED FROM: Investment/Mortgage banker only; Borrower/Investee

COMPANY: **Citizens Fidelity Leasing Corp.**
ADDRESS: 419 W. Jefferson St.
Louisville, KY 40202
PHONE: (502) 581-2686
TYPE OF INSTITUTION: Leasing Co., Subsidiary of Bank Holding Company
CONTACT OFFICER(S): A. J. Desposito, Pres.
Ted Stingwolt, Sr. V.P.
ASSETS: $100,000,000
INVESTMENTS/LOANS MADE: For own account
TYPES OF FINANCING: LOANS: Equipment; LEASES: Single-investor; Leveraged; Tax leases; Non-tax leases; Tax-oriented lease brokerage; Lease syndications
GEOGRAPHIC LIMITS OF INVESTMENTS/LOANS: National
RANGE OF INV./LOAN PER BUSINESS: Min. $200,000; Max. $10,000,000
PREFERRED TERM FOR LOANS & LEASES: Min. 3-5; Max. 10 years
BUSINESS CHARACTERISTICS DESIRED-REQUIRED: Minimum number of years in business: 5; Min. annual sales $10,000,000; Min. net worth $1,000,000; Min. annual net income $500,000; Min. annual cash flow $600,000

COMPANY: **First National Bank of Louisville**
ADDRESS: First National Tower
Louisville, KY 40202
PHONE: (502) 581-4200
TYPE OF INSTITUTION: Bank, full service including commercial finance, leasing, mergers & acquisitions & international
CONTACT OFFICER(S): Max White, S.V.P., Construction Financing
Ed Vittitoe, V.P. Corporate Finance, Mergers & Acquisitions
William Earley, S.V.P., Energy
Charles Williams, S.V.P., International
Jerry Johnston, S.V.P., National Banking
Paul Best, S.V.P., Mortgage Banking

ASSETS: $3.2 billion
INVESTMENTS/LOANS MADE: For own account
TYPES OF FINANCING: LOANS: Unsecured; Working capital (receivables/inventory); Equipment, REAL ESTATE LOANS: Intermediate-term senior mtg.; Wraparounds; Land; Construction; Standbys, LEASES: Leveraged; Tax leases; Non-tax leases; Vendor financing programs, INTERNATIONAL (including import/export)
GEOGRAPHIC LIMITS OF INVESTMENTS/LOANS: Regional; Other: Limited business nationally
RANGE OF INV./LOAN PER BUSINESS: Min. $250,000; Max. $12,000,000
PREFERRED TERM FOR LOANS & LEASES: Min. 2 years; Max. 10 years
BUSINESS CHARACTERISTICS DESIRED-REQUIRED: Minimum number of years in business: 3; Min. annual sales $5,000,000; Min. net worth $3,000,000
REFERRALS ACCEPTED FROM: Investment/Mortgage banker or Borrower/Investee
BRANCHES: Chuck Moeser, V.P., 60 E. 42nd Street, New York, NY; (212) 661-0980
John Hill, V.P., 1945 The Exchange, Suite 104, Atlanta, GA 30339; (404) 953-0930
Jim Sullivan, V.P., 625 N. Michigan Avenue, Suite 1020, Chicago, IL 60611; (312) 642-9779

COMPANY: **Atlantic Corporation**
ADDRESS: 55 Court Street, Suite 200
Boston, MA 02108
PHONE: (617) 482-1218
CONTACT OFFICER(S): Herbert Carver, Pres.

COMPANY: **The Berg Company, Inc.**
ADDRESS: Box 1961
Boston, MA 02105
PHONE: (617) 482-0290
TYPE OF INSTITUTION: Broker/Dealer
CONTACT OFFICER(S): Gordon H. Berg, Chariman-CEO
INVESTMENTS/LOANS MADE: For own account, For managed accounts, Through private placements, Through underwriting public offerings
INVESTMENTS/LOANS MADE: In securities with a secondary market and in securities without a secondary market
TYPES OF FINANCING: SECONDARY-MARKET CORPORATE SECURITIES: Bonds; Other: Priv. Plac., REAL ESTATE LOANS: Long-term senior mtg.; Intermediate-term senior mtg.; Subordinated; Wraparounds; Land; Land development; Industrial revenue bonds, LEASES: Leveraged, REAL ESTATE: Partnerships/Syndications, OTHER SERVICES PROVIDED: Pro Bono Institutions
PREFERRED TYPES OF INDUSTRIES/INVESTMENTS: Pro Bono
GEOGRAPHIC LIMITS OF INVESTMENTS/LOANS: International
RANGE OF INV./LOAN PER BUSINESS: Min. $1.5 million
REFERRALS ACCEPTED FROM: Investment/Mortgage banker or Borrower/Investee

COMPANY: **Boston Financial & Equity Corp.**

ADDRESS: 21 Burlington Ave.
Boston, MA 02215
PHONE: (617) 267-2900
TYPE OF INSTITUTION: Leasing company
CONTACT OFFICER(S): Sonny F. Monosson, President
TYPES OF FINANCING: LOANS: Equipment, LEASES: Single-investor; Leveraged; Tax leases; Non-tax leases; Operating; Tax-oriented lease brokerage; Lease syndications; Vendor financing programs
PREFERRED TYPES OF INDUSTRIES/INVESTMENTS: Strictly computers
WILL NOT CONSIDER: Any other
GEOGRAPHIC LIMITS OF INVESTMENTS/LOANS: National
REMARKS: Collateral lender

COMPANY: **John Hancock Financial Services, Inc.**
ADDRESS: John Hancock Place, P.O. Box 111
Boston, MA 02117
PHONE: (617) 421-4444
TYPE OF INSTITUTION: Equipment Leasing Subsidiary of John Hancock Mutual Life Insurance Co.
CONTACT OFFICER(S): George F. Miller, President & CEO
Joseph A. Tomlinson, V.P. Operations
Robert H. Watts, V.P. Marketing
ASSETS: $150,000,000
INVESTMENTS/LOANS MADE: For own account, For managed accounts
TYPES OF FINANCING: LOANS: Equipment, LEASES: Single-investor; Tax leases; Non-tax leases; Tax-oriented lease brokerage; Lease syndications; Vendor financing programs, OTHER SERVICES PROVIDED: Equipment Leasing Tax Shelters
PREFERRED TYPES OF INDUSTRIES/INVESTMENTS: Diversified Commercial and Agricultural (Agriculture is a specialty.)
GEOGRAPHIC LIMITS OF INVESTMENTS/LOANS: National
RANGE OF INV./LOAN PER BUSINESS: Min. $100,000; Max. $10,000,000
PREFERRED TERM FOR LOANS & LEASES: Min. 3 years; Max. 7 years
BUSINESS CHARACTERISTICS DESIRED-REQUIRED: Companies with proven ability to repay. Balance sheet lender.
BRANCHES: John Hancock Financial Services, Inc., Crossroads Bldg., Ste. 520, 1825 S. Grant St., San Mateo, CA 94402, (415) 572-0433, Leo J. Tisa, Manager-Western Regional Office
WASHINGTON, D.C.: Suite 1111, 4350 East West Highway, Bethesda, MD 20814, (301) 951-4282
SAN MATEO: Suite 520, 1825 South Grant Street, San Mateo, CA 94402, (415) 572-0401
ATLANTA: Suite 550, 6151 Powers Ferry Road, Atlanta, GA 30339, (401) 953-6872
PHOENIX: Suite 240, 11801 North Tatum Boulevard, Phoenix, AZ 85028 (602) 996-0961
SPOKANE, WA: South 176 Stevens Street, Spokane, WA 99204, (509) 747-5126
AURORA, CO: Pavilion Tower, 1-Suite 760, 2851 South Parker Road, Aurora, CO 80014, (303) 695-8770
CHAMPAIGN, IL: Robeson Buildiing, Suite 505, 206 North Randolph Street, Champaign, IL 61820, (217) 356-5518
DALLAS, TX: Suite 860, 555 Griffin Square, Dallas, TX 75202, (214) 742-9066
MEMPHIS, TN: 5710 Summer Trees Drive, Suite #1, Memphis, TN 38134, (901) 382-2720
SACRAMENTO, CA: 1900 Point West Way, Suite 188, Sacramento, CA 98515, (916) 922-6554
SIOUX CITY, IOWA: 1030 Badgerow Building, 4th & Jackson Streets, Sioux City, IA 51101, (712) 252-4323
STATESBORO, GA: Suite 101, 12 Siebald Street, Statesboro, GA 30458, (912) 764-6133

COMPANY: **Patriot Bancorporation**
ADDRESS: 57 Franklin Street
Boston, MA 02110
PHONE: (617) 451-9100
CONTACT OFFICER(S): Thomas R. Heaslip, Pres.

COMPANY: **Shawmut Bank of Boston, N.A.**
ADDRESS: 1 Federal Street
Boston, MA 02211
PHONE: (617) 292-2956
TYPE OF INSTITUTION: Equipment finance & leasing department of commercial bank
CONTACT OFFICER(S): J. L. Egenberg, V.P., Equipment Finance and Leasing
ASSETS: 7 billion
INVESTMENTS/LOANS MADE: For own account
TYPES OF FINANCING: LOANS: Equipment, LEASES: Single-investor; Leveraged; Tax leases; Tax-oriented lease brokerage; Lease syndications; Vendor financing programs, OTHER: Debt unleveraged leases; Equity notes
GEOGRAPHIC LIMITS OF INVESTMENTS/LOANS: National
RANGE OF INV./LOAN PER BUSINESS: Min. $250,000; Max. $8,000,000
PREFERRED TERM FOR LOANS & LEASES: Min. 3 years; Max. 5 years

COMPANY: **The Finance Company of America**
ADDRESS: Munsey Building
Baltimore, MD 21202
PHONE: (301) 752-8450
CONTACT OFFICER(S): Louis Eliasberg, Jr., President

COMPANY: **Suburban Bank**
ADDRESS: 6610 Rockledge Dr.
Bethesda, MD 20817
PHONE: (301) 493-7024
TYPE OF INSTITUTION: Bank's Asset Based Lending Division
CONTACT OFFICER(S): G.F. Green III, V.P.—Div. Head
Joseph E. Blythe, Assist. V.P.—Loan Admin.
David Nelson, Asset Based Lending Officer
ASSETS: $2.6 billion
TYPES OF FINANCING: REAL ESTATE LOANS: Working capital; OTHER SERVICES PROVIDED: Suburbann Bank is a full service bank with leasing and venture capital subsidiaries—information provided is for asset based lending only.

PREFERRED TYPES OF INDUSTRIES/INVESTMENTS: Wholesalers, manufacturers and government contractors
WILL NOT CONSIDER: General Construction Industry for Asset Based Lending
GEOGRAPHIC LIMITS OF INVESTMENTS/LOANS: Regional
RANGE OF INV./LOAN PER BUSINESS: Min. $400,000; Max. $10,000,000
BUSINESS CHARACTERISTICS DESIRED-REQUIRED: Minimum number of years in business: 1; Min. annual sales $3,000,000
REFERRALS ACCEPTED FROM: Investment/Mortgage banker or Borrower/Investee

COMPANY: **Maryland National Industrial Finance Corp.**
ADDRESS: Nottingham Centre, 502 Washington Ave., Suite 800
Towson, MD 21204
PHONE: (301) 821-7666
TYPE OF INSTITUTION: Commercial Finance Company
CONTACT OFFICER(S): Robert E. Stewart, Pres.
Peter S. Bird, Executive V.P./Group Head
Richard J. Baldwin, Executive V.P./Operations
TYPES OF FINANCING: LOANS: Working capital; Equipment; REAL ESTATE LOANS: Intermediate-term senior mtg.;
PREFERRED TYPES OF INDUSTRIES/INVESTMENTS: Manufacturers and wholesalers
GEOGRAPHIC LIMITS OF INVESTMENTS/LOANS: National
RANGE OF INV./LOAN PER BUSINESS: Min. $250,000
PREFERRED TERM FOR LOANS & LEASES: Min. 1 yrs.; Max. 3 years
BUSINESS CHARACTERISTICS DESIRED-REQUIRED: Minimum number of years in business: 10
BRANCHES: Baltimore Regional Office, Nottingham Centre, 502 Washington Av., Ste 700, Towson, MD 21204, Thomas E. Kane, Senior V.P. and Regional Manager; (301) 821-7666
Richmond Regional Office, P.O. Box 667, Richmond, VA 23205, Thomas E. Kane, Senior V.P. and Regional Manager; (804) 643-6781
Pittsburgh Regional Office, P.O. Box 15600 Pittsburgh, PA 15244, James A. Clemens, V.P. and Regional Manager; (412) 787-5980
Allentown Regional Office, 5100 Tilghman St., Ste 305, Allentown, PA 18104, George F. Kurteson, V.P. and Regional Manager; (215) 398-9883
Chicago Regional Office, 1315 West 22nd St., Ste 200, Oak Brook, IL 60521, Jack A. Myers, V.P. and Regional Manager; (312) 654-0602
Dallas Regional Office, Two Lincoln Center, 5420 LBJ Freeway, Ste 420, Dallas, TX 75240, Arthur R. Cordwell, Jr., V.P. and Regional Manager; (214) 239-4741
Atlanta Regional Office, 1950 Spectrum Circle, Ste A311, Marietta, GA 30067, J. Drexel Knight, V.P. and Regional Manager; (404) 953-0077

COMPANY: **Van Arnem Financial Services, Inc.**
ADDRESS: 870 Bowers
Birmingham, MI 48011
PHONE: (313) 647-3040
TYPE OF INSTITUTION: Financial Services Inc. Specializes in Tax Shelters and income programs
CONTACT OFFICER(S): Mr. H. L. Van Arnem, Chief Executive Officer
ASSETS: $400,400,000
TYPES OF FINANCING: LOANS: Working capital; Equipmment; Equity-related; LEASES: Single-investor; Leveraged; Tax leases; Non-tax leases; Lease syndications; REAL ESTATE: Partnerships/Syndications
PREFERRED TYPES OF INDUSTRIES/INVESTMENTS: Equipment Leases with Fortune 200 Companies; Equipment Lease Syndications
GEOGRAPHIC LIMITS OF INVESTMENTS/LOANS: National
RANGE OF INV./LOAN PER BUSINESS: Min. $1,000,000; Max. $10,000,000
REFERRALS ACCEPTED FROM: Investment/Mortgage banker or Borrower/Investee

COMPANY: **American Business Finance**
ADDRESS: 1190 First National Building
Detroit, MI 48226
PHONE: (313) 962-8600
TYPE OF INSTITUTION: Commercial Finance Co.
CONTACT OFFICER(S): Patrick J. Vesnaugh, Sr. V.P.
Richard J. Yates, V.P.
TYPES OF FINANCING: LOANS: Working capital (receivables/inventory); Equipment; Commercial
PREFERRED TYPES OF INDUSTRIES/INVESTMENTS: Diversified; secured
WILL NOT CONSIDER: Real Estate, Retail operations
GEOGRAPHIC LIMITS OF INVESTMENTS/LOANS: Regional; can arrange outside of region
RANGE OF INV./LOAN PER BUSINESS: Min. $250,000
PREFERRED TERM FOR LOANS & LEASES: Min. 1 year
BUSINESS CHARACTERISTICS DESIRED-REQUIRED: Min. net worth $positive; Must have some track record/do acquisitions/no venture/no equity
BRANCHES: 1030 Euclid Ave., Cleveland, OH 44115; 216-575-0510; 414 Walnut St., Cincinnati, OH 45202; 513-421-8966; 190 Monroe St. NW., Grand Rapids, MI 49503; 616-242-0232

COMPANY: **Dimmitt & Owens Financial, Inc.**
ADDRESS: 3250 West Big Beaver Road, Suite 120
Troy, MI 48084
PHONE: (313) 643-6084
CONTACT OFFICER(S): C. G. Dimmitt, Pres.

COMPANY: **F&M Marquette National Bank**
ADDRESS: 90 South Sixth Street
Minneapolis, MN 55480
PHONE: (612) 341-5611

COMPANY: **FBS Business Finance Corp.**
ADDRESS: 400 Baker Building, P.O. Box 2409
Minneapolis, MN 55402
PHONE: (612) 343-1400
CONTACT OFFICER(S): John E. McCauley, Pres.

COMPANY: **Lease Moore Equipment, Inc.**
ADDRESS: 2318 Park Ave. S.
Minneapolis, MN 55404
PHONE: (612) 872-4929
TYPE OF INSTITUTION: Financial services
CONTACT OFFICER(S): C. Moore, President
S. Braatz, Credit Mgr.
ASSETS: $10-20 million
INVESTMENTS/LOANS MADE: For own account
TYPES OF FINANCING: VENTURE CAPITAL: Buy-outs/Acquisitions, LOANS: Equipment, LEASES: Non-tax leases; Vendor financing programs
PREFERRED TYPES OF INDUSTRIES/INVESTMENTS: EDP, medical, construction and hospitality (strong operators)
GEOGRAPHIC LIMITS OF INVESTMENTS/LOANS: National
RANGE OF INV./LOAN PER BUSINESS: Min. $6,000; Max. $1,000,000
PREFERRED TERM FOR LOANS & LEASES: Min. 1 year; Max. 7 years
BUSINESS CHARACTERISTICS DESIRED-REQUIRED: Minimum number of years in business: 3

COMPANY: **Norwest Business Credit, Inc.**
ADDRESS: 780 Northstar Center
Minneapolis, MN 55402
PHONE: (612) 372-7988
CONTACT OFFICER(S): Richard F. Beckham, Pres.

COMPANY: **Norwest Leasing, Inc.**
ADDRESS: 930 Cargill Building
Minneapolis, MN 55480
PHONE: (612) 372-7617
TYPE OF INSTITUTION: Leasing & Equipment Finance
CONTACT OFFICER(S): John D. MacLeod, Pres.
John Chrum, V.P. Marketing
ASSETS: 170 million
INVESTMENTS/LOANS MADE: For own account
INVESTMENTS/LOANS MADE: Only in securities without a secondary market
TYPES OF FINANCING: LOANS: Equipment; Conditional sale contracts, LEASES: Single-investor; Leveraged; Tax leases; Non-tax leases; Tax-oriented lease brokerage; Lease syndications; Vendor financing programs; Lease purchase
PREFERRED TYPES OF INDUSTRIES/INVESTMENTS: Construction; Machine
BUSINESS CHARACTERISTICS DESIRED-REQUIRED: No startups financed;
REFERRALS ACCEPTED FROM: Investment/Mortgage banker only or Borrower/Investee
BRANCHES: John D. MacLeod, President, Norwest Leasing, Inc., Suite 930 Cargill Building, 7th Street and Marquette Avenue, Minneapolis, MN 55479; (612) 372-7819
John Chrun, Vice President, Marketing, Norwest Leasing, Inc., Suite 930 Cargill Building, 7th Street and Marquette Avenue, Minneapolis, MN 55479
Chris Hoss, Assistant Vice President, Marketing, Norwest Leasing, Inc., Norwest Center, Fourth and Main, Fargo, ND 58126, (701) 293-4273
Steve Cozzens, Assistant Vice President, Marketing, Norwest Leasing, Inc., P.O. Box 30058, 175 North 27th Street, Billings, MT 59117
Glenn Harper, Lease Marketing Officer, Norwest Equipment Leasing, Inc., P.O. Box 19070, Capital Plaza Suite 220, 9320 S.W. Barbur Boulevard, Portland, OR 97219; (503) 244-4010
Randy Wade, Lease Marketing Officer, P.O. Box 832, 701 Financial Center, Seventh and Walnut Streets, Des Moines, IA 50304
REMARKS: Prefer term of 5 years

COMPANY: **Republic Acceptance Corporation**
ADDRESS: 815 1st Bank Place W
Minneapolis, MN 55402
PHONE: (612) 333-3121
CONTACT OFFICER(S): Donald Moberg, Pres.
ASSETS: $1,000,000-10,000,000
TYPES OF FINANCING: LOANS: Working capital; Equipment
PREFERRED TYPES OF INDUSTRIES/INVESTMENTS: Manufacturing & processing; wholesaling; distribution
GEOGRAPHIC LIMITS OF INVESTMENTS/LOANS: Regional; Upper Midwest
RANGE OF INV./LOAN PER BUSINESS: Min. $50,000; Max. None
PREFERRED TERM FOR LOANS & LEASES: Min. 6 mos.; Max. no max
BUSINESS CHARACTERISTICS DESIRED-REQUIRED: No startups

COMPANY: **Industry Financial Corporation**
ADDRESS: 444 Lafayette Road
St. Paul, MN 55101
PHONE: (612) 222-7792
CONTACT OFFICER(S): Richard J. Altman, Vice Pres.

COMPANY: **ITT Commercial Finance Corp.**
ADDRESS: 8251 Maryland Avenue
St. Louis, MO 63105
PHONE: (314) 725-2525
TYPE OF INSTITUTION: Wholesale/Inventory financing or floor planning
CONTACT OFFICER(S): Melvin F. Brown, President
John W. Dobson, Senior V.P., Director of Marketing
ASSETS: In excess of $1 billion in outstandings
INVESTMENTS/LOANS MADE: For own account
TYPES OF FINANCING: SECONDARY-MARKET CORPORATE SECURITIES: Wholesale/Inventory financing or floorplanning; OTHER SERVICES PROVIDED: Floorplan financing of retail, commercial, and agricultural durable products &/or dealers of these products
PREFERRED TYPES OF INDUSTRIES/INVESTMENTS: Mobile Homes, Motorcyles, home & small business computers, TV and appliances, recreation vehicles, marine products, automobiles, agricultural equipment
1740 West Katella, Suite L, Orange, CA 92667; (714) 771-7500

1250 Winchester Parkway, Suite 101, Smynna, GA 30080, (404) 434-4801
95 Washington Street, Suite 205, Canton, MA 02021, (617) 828-7515
200 Galleria Parkway N.W., Suite 300, Atanta, GA 30339, (404) 956-1156, (800) 241-6524
Building 5600, 77 Center Drive, Charlotte, NC 28210, (704) 525-7951
One Cherry Hill Mall, Suite 217, Cherry Hill, Cherry Hill, NJ 08002, (609) 482-0930, (800) 323-5610
270 Northland Boulevard, Suite 122, Cincinnati OH 45246; (513) 771-8593
2701 N. Central Expressway, Suite 100, Richardson, TX 75080, (214) 234-0226 or (800) 527-4205
911 West Big Beaver, Suite 400, Troy, MI 48099 (313) 362-0390
10700 North Freeway, Suite 555, Houston, TX 77037 (713) 999-2020
4205 South Hocker Drive, Suite B, Independence, MO 64055, (816) 373-3808 or (800) 821-8470
11909 East Telegraph Road, Santa Fe Springs, CA 90670, (213) 949-0511
1255 "A" Lynnfield Road, Suite 143, Memphis, TN 38119 (901) 767-2750
Shoreview Building, Suite 216, 9999 N.E. Second Avenue, Miami Shores, FL 33138, (305) 754-9554
First Financial Bank, Suite 250, 3701 Williams Boulevard, Kenner, LA 70065 (504) 443-3214
77 Westport Plaza, Suite 403, St. Louis, MO 63141, (314) 434-8666 or (800) 325-9029
1225 East Fort Union Boulevard, Midvale, UT 84047, (801) 561-9211
3100 Mowry Avenue, Suite 300; Fremont, CA 94538; (415) 792-6600
1851 South Central Place, Suite 221, Kent, WA 98031, (206) 854-2050
5405 Cypress Center Drive, Suite 150, Tampa, FL 33609 (813) 875-6007

COMPANY: **Mercantile Business Credit, Inc.**
ADDRESS: One Mercantile Center
St. Louis, MO 63101
PHONE: (314) 425-8260
CONTACT OFFICER(S): Dennis B. Hirstein, Pres.

COMPANY: **BarclaysAmerican/Leasing, Inc.**
ADDRESS: 201 South Tryon Street, P.O. Box 31217
Charlotte, NC 28231
PHONE: (704) 372-5210
TYPE OF INSTITUTION: Leasing division of bank-owned finance company
CONTACT OFFICER(S): Dale D. Peters, President
Colby Burbank, III, Senior V.P., Leveraged Leasing
J.P. Lundgren, Senior V.P., Equipment Leasing and Financing
INVESTMENTS/LOANS MADE: For own account
INVESTMENTS/LOANS MADE: Only in securities without a secondary market
TYPES OF FINANCING: LOANS: Equipment, LEASES: Single-investor; Leveraged; Tax leases; Non-tax leases; Tax-oriented lease brokerage; Lease syndications
GEOGRAPHIC LIMITS OF INVESTMENTS/LOANS: National; International
RANGE OF INV./LOAN PER BUSINESS: Min. $100,000
REFERRALS ACCEPTED FROM: Borrower/Investee

COMPANY: **First Union Commercial Corporation**
ADDRESS: First Union Plaza
Charlotte, NC 28288
PHONE: (704) 374-6000
TYPE OF INSTITUTION: Asset based financing subsidiary of First Union National Bank
CONTACT OFFICER(S): Wayne F. Robinson, Vice President - Factoring
(H. Leon McGee, Vice President - Commercial Financing
Joseph J. Palisi, Vice President - Term Equipment Lending
ASSETS: $150,000,000.
INVESTMENTS/LOANS MADE: For own account
TYPES OF FINANCING: SECONDARY-MARKET CORPORATE SECURITIES: Secured lending transaction only; LOANS: Working capital; Equipment, REAL ESTATE LOANS: real estate only in conjunction with factoring, accts. receivable or equip. financing; FACTORING, LEASES: Single-investor; Leveraged; Tax leases; Non-tax leases; Tax-oriented lease brokerage; Lease syndications; Vendor financing programs; Other: Municipal leases; INTERNATIONAL
PREFERRED TYPES OF INDUSTRIES/INVESTMENTS: No preference
GEOGRAPHIC LIMITS OF INVESTMENTS/LOANS: National
RANGE OF INV./LOAN PER BUSINESS: Min. $250,000; Max. $25,000,000
PREFERRED TERM FOR LOANS & LEASES: Min. 2 years; Max. 10 years
BUSINESS CHARACTERISTICS DESIRED-REQUIRED: All variable depending on strength of collateral
REFERRALS ACCEPTED FROM: Investment/Mortgage banker or Borrower/Investee
BRANCHES: Robert Schettini, Senior Vice President, 260 Madison Avenue, New York, NY 10016; (212) 953-0123
Lewis W. Spiller, Vice President, 100 Galleria Parkway, Atlanta, GA 30339, (404) 953-4875

COMPANY: **NCNB Financial Services, Inc.**
ADDRESS: 1 NCNB Tower, P.O. Box 30533
Charlotte, NC 28230
PHONE: (704) 374-5087
CONTACT OFFICER(S): Dan J. Crowley, President

COMPANY: **Southern National Financial Corp.**
ADDRESS: P.O. Box 33849
Charlotte, NC 28233
PHONE: (704) 377-5611
CONTACT OFFICER(S): Preston L. Fowler, III, Exec. V.P.

COMPANY: **Phillips Factors Corporation**
ADDRESS: 101 West Green Drive
High Point, NC 27261
PHONE: (919) 889-3355
CONTACT OFFICER(S): Robert C. Neibauer, Pres.

COMPANY: **Summa Capital Corporation**
ADDRESS: 350 Fifth Avenue
New York, NY 10118
PHONE: (212) 244-1200
CONTACT OFFICER(S): Howard A. Schulder, Pres.

COMPANY: **Midlantic Commercial Company**
ADDRESS: 1455 Broad Street
Bloomfield, NJ 07003
PHONE: (201) 266-8385
CONTACT OFFICER(S): A. Robert Lange, Pres.

COMPANY: **Midlantic National Bank**
ADDRESS: 2 Broad St.
Bloomfield, NJ 07003
PHONE: (201) 266-6369
TYPE OF INSTITUTION: Leasing Co.
CONTACT OFFICER(S): Michael Zonghetti, Lease Admin.
TYPES OF FINANCING: LOANS: Equipment, LEASES: Single-investor; Leveraged; Tax leases; Non-tax leases; Operating; Lease syndications; Vendor financing programs; Full payout lease
PREFERRED TYPES OF INDUSTRIES/INVESTMENTS: Computer; Airline; Hospital; Printing
WILL NOT CONSIDER: Rolling Stock — Trucks, R.R., Construction
GEOGRAPHIC LIMITS OF INVESTMENTS/LOANS: Regional; NJ Basically
RANGE OF INV./LOAN PER BUSINESS: Min. $250,000; Max. $10,000,000
PREFERRED TERM FOR LOANS & LEASES: Min. 3; Max. 7 years
BUSINESS CHARACTERISTICS DESIRED-REQUIRED: Variable

COMPANY: **Heritage Bank NA**
ADDRESS: Broadway and Cooper Streets, P.O. Box 1409
Camden, NJ 08101
PHONE: (609) 964-2030
TYPE OF INSTITUTION: Wholly owned subsidiary of Heritage Bank, N.A.
CONTACT OFFICER(S): Wiliam R. Giessuebel, V.P.
Harold E. Burke, V.P.
ASSETS: $2 billion
INVESTMENTS/LOANS MADE: For own account
TYPES OF FINANCING: SECONDARY-MARKET CORPORATE SECURITIES: Other: Asset based loans, LOANS: Working capital; Equipment, LEASES: Single-investor; Non-tax leases; Vendor financing programs
PREFERRED TYPES OF INDUSTRIES/INVESTMENTS: Manufacturers and wholesalers—all types of capital equipment
GEOGRAPHIC LIMITS OF INVESTMENTS/LOANS: Regional, Tri-state: NY, PA, NJ
RANGE OF INV./LOAN PER BUSINESS: Min. $400,000; Max. $10,000,000
PREFERRED TERM FOR LOANS & LEASES: Min. 2 years; Max. 7 years
BUSINESS CHARACTERISTICS DESIRED-REQUIRED: Minimum number of years in business: 3; Min. annual sales $3,000,000
REFERRALS ACCEPTED FROM: Investment/Mortgage banker or Borrower/Investee
BRANCHES: Ray Kelly, V.P., 710 Turnpike Rd, East Brunswick, NJ 08816; (201) 390-6373

COMPANY: **Armco Commerical, Division of Armco Financial Corporation**
ADDRESS: 440 Sylvan Avenue
Englewood Cliffs, NJ 07632
PHONE: (201) 569-9200
TYPE OF INSTITUTION: Commercial Finance Company
CONTACT OFFICERS: Howard Blum, President
Irwin Berger, Vice President, Marketing
ASSETS: $125 MM
INVESTMENTS/LOANS MADE: For managed accounts
TYPES OF FINANCING: LOANS: Working capital; equipment; Other: real estate
PREFERRED TYPES OF INDUSTIRES/INVESTMENTS: Manufacturing, service and wholesale industries. Our asset-based loans are secured by A/R, M&E Inventory and RE
GEOGRAPHIC LIMITS OF INVESTMENTS/LOANS: National
RANGE OF INV./LOAN PER BUSINESS: Min. $500M
BUSINESS CHARACTERISTIS DESIRED-REQUIRED:Minimum number of years in business: 0; Min. annual sales: 4mm
REFERRALS ACCEEPTED FROM: Investment/mortgage banker and borower/investee

COMPANY: **Chase-Manhattan Leasing Co.**
ADDRESS: 560 Sylvan Avenue
Englewood Cliffs, NJ 07632
PHONE: (201) 894-4405
CONTACT OFFICER(S): Theodore Daleiden, Leasing
Frank Donahue, Loans
TYPES OF FINANCING: LOANS, LEASES
PREFERRED TYPES OF INDUSTRIES/INVESTMENTS: Electronics, Communications
GEOGRAPHIC LIMITS OF INVESTMENTS/LOANS: National
RANGE OF INV./LOAN PER BUSINESS: Min. $25,000
PREFERRED TERM FOR LOANS & LEASES: Max. 7 years
BRANCHES: Boston, MA
Atlanta, GA
Dallas, TX
Chicago, IL
Los Angeles, CA

COMPANY: **Leasetek Funding Group, Inc.**
ADDRESS: 19 Sylvan Avenue
Englewood Cliffs, NJ 07632
PHONE: (201) 224-7700
CONTACT OFFICERS: Anthony Rosato, President
ASSETS: $40,000,000
INVESTMENTS/LOANS MADE: For own account, for managed accounts, through private placements, through underwriting public offerings
INVESTMENTS/LOANS MADE: Only in securities with a secondary market
TYPES OF FINANCING: SECONDARY-MARKET CORPORATE SECURITIES, VENTURE CPAIRAL:

Start-up from developed product stage; First-stage; Second-stage; Buyouts/expansions, LOANS: Working capital, equipment, REAL ESTATE LOANS: Long-term senior mtg; intermediate-term senior mtg; wraparounds; construction, FACTORING, LEASES: Single-investor; Leveraged; Tax leases; Operating; Lease syndications; Vendor financing programs
GEOGRAPHIC LIMITS OF INVESTMENTS/LOANS: National
RANGE OF INV./LOAN PER BUSINESS: Min. $50,000; Max. $10,000,000
PREFERRED TERM FOR LOANS & LEASES: Min. 2 years; Max. 20 years

COMPANY: **First TransCapital Corporation**
ADDRESS: 2050 Center Avenue
Fort Lee, NJ 07024
PHONE: (201) 461-9700
TYPE OF INSTITUTION: Asset Based Lender
CONTACT OFFICERS: Martin Albert, President
ASSETS: over $10,000,000
INVESTMENTS/LOANS MADE: For own account
INVESTMENTS/LOANS MADE: In securities with a secondary market and in securities without a secondary market
TYPES OF FINANCING: LOANS: Working capital; equipment, REAL ESTATE LOANS: Long-erm Senior mtg.; Intermediate-term senior mtg.; Subordinated; Wraparounds
GEOGRAPHIC LIMITS OF INVESTMENTS/LOANS: Regional
RANGE OF INV./LOAN PER BUSINESS: Min. $25,000; Max. $500,000
PREFERRED TERM FOR LOANS & LEASES: Min.: One Year; Max.: 4 years
BUSINESS CHARACTERISTIS DESIRED-REQUIRED:Minimum number of years in business: 0
REFERRALS ACCEEPTED FROM: Investment/mortgage banker and borower/investee

COMPANY: **Financial Resources Group**
ADDRESS: 110 Main Street, P.O. Box 246
Hackensack, NJ 07602
PHONE: (201) 489-6123
TYPE OF INSTITUTION: Financial services (public company)
CONTACT OFFICER(S): M.L. Beer, Manager
ASSETS: $136,744,970
INVESTMENTS/LOANS MADE: For own account, For managed accounts, Through private placements, through underwriting public offerings
INVESTMENTS/LOANS MADE: In securities with a secondary market and in securities without a secondary market
TYPES OF FINANCING: LOANS: Equipment, REAL ESTATE LOANS: Long-term senior mtg.; Intermediate-term senior mtg.; Wraparounds; Construction; Gap; Standbys; Industrial revenue bonds, FACTORING, LEASES: Leveraged: Tax leases, REAL ESTATE: Acquisitions; Joint ventures; Partnerships/Syndications
PREFERRED TYPES OF INDUSTRIES/INVESTMENTS: Real estate loans
WILL NOT CONSIDER: Unsecured

GEOGRAPHIC LIMITS OF INVESTMENTS/LOANS: National
RANGE OF INV./LOAN PER BUSINESS: Min. $500,000; Max. $75,000,000
PREFERRED TERM FOR LOANS & LEASES: Min. 3 years; Max. 30 years
BUSINESS CHARACTERISTICS DESIRED-REQUIRED: Minimum number of years in business: 2; Min. annual sales None; Other: Depends on transaction
REFERRALS ACCEPTED FROM: Investment/Mortgage banker or Borrower/Investee
BRANCHES: Alan Hirsch, 935 White Plains Rd, Trumbull, CT 06611; (203) 261-8308
Ira Shapiro, P.O. Box 1306, White Plains, NY 10602 (914) 997-1976

COMPANY: **The Trust Company of New Jersey**
ADDRESS: 35 Journal Square
Jersey City, NJ 07306
PHONE: (201) 420-2810
TYPE OF INSTITUTION: Commercial bank
CONTACT OFFICER(S): Robert J. Figurski, Sr., V.P.
ASSETS: $1 Billion
INVESTMENTS/LOANS MADE: For own account
TYPES OF FINANCING: VENTURE CAPITAL: Start-up from developed product stage; First-stage; Later-stage expansions; Buy-outs/Acquisitions, LOANS: Unsecured; Working capital (receivables/inventory); Equipment; Equity related, REAL ESTATE LOANS: Long-term senior mtg.; Intermediate-term senior mtg.; Wraparounds; Land; Land development; Construction; Gap; Standbys; Industrial revenue bonds; Other: Economic Development Agency Tax Frees, INTERNATIONAL (including import/export), REAL ESTATE: Acquisitions
PREFERRED TYPES OF INDUSTRIE/INVESTMENTS: Any
RANGE OF IN./LOAN PER BUSINESS: Max. $5 Million
PREFERRED TERM FOR LOANS & LEASES: Miin. Demand; Max. 25 year payout
BUSINESS CHARACTERISTICS DESIRED-REQUIRED: Minimum number of years in business: 0
BRANCHES: 20 branches throughout New Jersey

COMPANY: **C.I.T. Corporation**
ADDRESS: 650 C.I.T. Drive
Livingston, NJ 07039
PHONE: (201) 740-5327
CONTACT OFFICER(S): Gene P. Kaplan, Pres.

COMPANY: **Raybar Leasing Corporation**
ADDRESS: 225 W. Spring Valley Ave., P.O. Box 1079
Maywood, NJ 07607
PHONE: (201) 368-2280
TYPE OF INSTITUTION: Equipment Leasing/Financing
CONTACT OFFICER(S): Patrick F. McCort, Vice President, General Manager
INVESTMENTS/LOANS MADE: For own account
TYPES OF FINANCING: LOANS: Equipment, LEASES: Single-investor; Leveraged; Tax leases; Non-tax leases; Vendor financing programs
GEOGRAPHIC LIMITS OF INVESTMENTS/LOANS: Local; State; Regional

RANGE OF INV./LOAN PER BUSINESS: Min. $20,000; Max. $1,000,000
PREFERRED TERM FOR LOANS & LEASES: Min. 3 years; Max. 7 years

COMPANY: **First National State Bank of New Jersey**
ADDRESS: 494 Broad Street
Newark, NJ 07192
PHONE: (201) 565-3336
TYPE OF INSTITUTION: Leasing division of a national bank
CONTACT OFFICER(S): Joseph F. Lynch, V.P., Senior Lease Finance Officer
Donald F. Barrett, V.P., Lease Finance Officer, Graphic Arts Equipment
Russell C. Murawski, V.P., Lease Finance Officer, Computers
Albert Bedlin, Asst. V.P., Lease Finance Officer, Transportation
James Phibbs, Asst. Cashier, Lease Finance Officer
ASSETS: $10 billion
INVESTMENTS/LOANS MADE: For own account
TYPES OF FINANCING: LOANS: Equipment, LEASES: Single-investor; Leveraged; Tax leases; Non-tax leases; Vendor financing programs
PREFERRED TYPES OF INDUSTRIES/INVESTMENTS: Graphic arts equipment; Paper & allied industries; Telecommunications, Computers and Computer peripherals
WILL NOT CONSIDER: Furniture & fixtures — private interconnect
GEOGRAPHIC LIMITS OF INVESTMENTS/LOANS: National
RANGE OF INV./LOAN PER BUSINESS: Min. $100,000; Max. Open
PREFERRED TERM FOR LOANS & LEASES: Min. 2 years; Max. 5 years
REFERRALS ACCEPTED FROM: Investment/Mortgage banker or Borrower/Investee

COMPANY: **The Howard Savings Bank**
ADDRESS: 768 Broad Street
Newark, NJ 07101
PHONE: (201) 430-2000
TYPE OF INSTITUTION: Stockholder-Owned Savings Bank
CONTACT OFFICER(S): Ralph H. Teepe, (201) 430-2075, Vice President - Commercial Lending
Richard A. Frank, (201) 430-2076, Vice President - Commercial Lending
ASSETS: $3.743 billion dollars (8/31/84)
INVESTMENTS/LOANS MADE: For own account
TYPES OF FINANCING: LOANS: Unsecured; Working capital; Equipment; Equity-related
PREFERRED TYPES OF INDUSTRIES/INVESTMENTS: Commercial and industrial
GEOGRAPHIC LIMITS OF INVESTMENTS/LOANS: National
RANGE OF INV./LOAN PER BUSINESS: Min; $25,000; Max. $15,000,000
PREFERRED TERM FOR LOANS & LEASES: Min. 6 months; Max. 7 years
BUSINESS CHARACTERISTICS DESIRED-REQUIRED: Minimum number of years in business: 3; Min. annual sales $1,000,000; Min. net worth $100,000
REFERRALS ACCEPTED FROM: Investment/Mortgage banker or Borrower/Investee
BRANCHES: We have 58 branches within the State of New Jersey

COMPANY: **Beneficial Commercial Corporation and Leasing Group (Formerly Capital Financial Services Corp)**
ADDRESS: 200 Beneficial Center
Peapack, NJ 07977
PHONE: (201) 781-3367, (800) 632-8182(Outisde NJ)
TYPE OF INSTITUTION: Commercial Finance Division of Beneficial
CONTACT OFFICER(S): Larry K. Morris, President, Andrew Rimol, V.P. Marketing
INVESTMENTS/LOANS MADE: For own account
TYPES OF FINANCING:LEASES: Leveraged
PREFERRED TYPES OF INDUSTRIES/INVESTMENTS: Airlines
GEOGRAPHIC LIMITS OF INVESTMENTS/LOANS: National
RANGE OF INV./LOAN PER BUSINESS: Min. $5,000,000; Max. None
REFERRALS ACCEPTED FROM: Investment/Mortgage banker or Borrower/Investee

COMPANY: **Armco Financial Corporation, Intermediate Term Lending Division**
ADDRESS: 104 Carnegie Center
Princeton, NJ 08540
PHONE: (609) 452-0600
TYPE OF INSTITUTION: Commerical Term Lender
CONTACT OFFICER(S): Richard S. Ballard, President
Susan M. Lamm, Vice President & Senior Loan Officer
ASSETS: $500,000,000
INVESTMENTS/LOANS MADE: For own account
INVESTMENTS/LOANS MADE: In securities with a secondary market and in securities without a secondary market
TYPES OF FINANCING: VENTURE CAPITAL: Later-stage expansion; Buy-outs/Acquisitions, LOANS: Equipment; REAL ESTATE LOANS: Intermediate-term senior mtg.; Subordinated; Wraparounds, LEASES: Non-tax leases
PREFERRED TYPES OF INDUSTRIES/INVESTMENTS: No preferences—will do all types of manufacturing compaies
WILL NOT CONSIDER: Medical Industry; Retail Businesses
GEOGRAPHIC LIMITS OF INVESTMENTS/LOANS: National
RANGE OF INV./LOAN PER BUSINESS: Min. $1,000,000; Max. $10,000,000
PREFERRED TERM FOR LOANS & LEASES: Min. 2 years
BUSINESS CHARACTERISTICS DESIRED-REQUIRED: Minimum number of years in business: 3
REFERRALS ACCEPTED FROM: Investment/Mortgage banker or Borrower/Investee

COMPANY: **Franklin State Bank**
ADDRESS: 630 Franklin Blvd.
Somerset, NJ 08873
PHONE: (201) 745-6044
CONTACT OFFICER(S): John D. Battaglia, Sr. Lending Officer/Exec. V.P.
Harvey A. Mackler, Vice President/Business Development
ASSETS: $650,000,000
INVESTMENTS/LOANS MADE: For own account
INVESTMENTS/LOANS MADE: Only in securities without a secondary market
TYPES OF FINANCING: LOANS: Unsecured; Working capital; REAL ESTATE LOANS: Long-term senior mtg.; Land; Land development; Construction; Industrial revenue bonds, LEASES: Single-investor; Leveraged; Tax leases; Non-tax leases; Vendor financing programs, OTHER SERVICES PROVIDED: Accounts receivable financing
PREFERRED TYPES OF INDUSTRIES/INVESTMENTS: Diversified
GEOGRAPHIC LIMITS OF INVESTMENTS/LOANS: State
RANGE OF INV./LOAN PER BUSINESS: Min. $100,000; Max. $6,000,000
PREFERRED TERM FOR LOANS & LEASES: Min. 1 year; Max. 15-20 years
BUSINESS CHARACTERISTICS DESIRED-REQUIRED: Minimum number of years in business: 1+; Min. annual sales $500,000; Min. net worth $100,000; Min. annual net income $50,000; Min. annual cash flow $50,000

COMPANY: **John J. McDermott Co., Inc.**
ADDRESS: 142 Riveredge Road
Tinton Falls, NJ 07724
PHONE: (201) 750-0350
CONTACT OFFICER(S): John J. McDermott, Chmn. of the Bd.

COMPANY: **Ingersoll Rand Financial Corp.**
ADDRESS: 200 Chestnut Ridge Road
Woodcliff Lake, NJ 07675
PHONE: (201) 573-3031
TYPE OF INSTITUTION: Tax Leasing and Secured Financing
CONTACT OFFICER(S): R.A. Layton, Eastern Group Manager
R.J. Rhinesmih, Western Group Manager
J.C. Colbert, National Leasing
ASSETS: $550 million
INVESTMENTS/LOANS MADE: for own account
TYPES OF FINANCING: VENTURE CAPITAL: Later-stage expansion, LOANS: Equipment, REAL ESTATE LOANS: Long-term senior mtg.; Intermediate-term senior mtg.; Standbys; Other, LEASES: Single-investor; Tax leases; Non-tax leases; Vendor financing programs
GEOGRAPHIC LIMITS OF INVESTMENTS/LOANS: National
RANGE OF INV./LOAN PER BUSINESS: Min. $100M; Max. $10,000M
PREFERRED TERM FOR LOANS & LEASES: Min. 1 year; Max. 7 years
BUSINESS CHARACTERISTICS DESIRED-REQUIRED: Minimum number of years in business: 5; Other: Each transaction will stand on merits
REFERRALS ACCEPTED FROM: Investment/Mortgage banker or Borrower/Investee
BRANCHES: Richard A. Layton, Summerfield Commons Office Park, 2585 Washington Rd., Pittsburgh, PA 15241; (412) 854-1810
Robert J. Rhinesmith, 210 Porter Drive, Suite 120, San Ramon, CA 94583; (415) 838-4606

COMPANY: **Great Western Leasing**
ADDRESS: P.O. Box 11857
Reno, NV 89510
PHONE: (702) 329-6503
TYPE OF INSTITUTION: Equipment lease financing
CONTACT OFFICER(S): John C. Deane, Chairman
Timothy R. Minor, President
Aaron P. Salloway, Senior VP, National Division Marketing
Donald Jackson, Senior VP, Middle Market
Larry Lustgarten, Senior VP, Portfolio Division
ASSETS: $180,000,000
TYPES OF FINANCING: SECONDARY-MARKET CORPORATE SECURITIES: Other: Equipment oriented straight debt financing, lease financing, acquisitions, syndications, VENTURE CAPITAL: Buy-outs/Aquisitions, LOANS: Equipment, LEASES: Single-investor; Leveraged; Tax leases; Non-tax leases; Tax-oriented lease brokerage; Lease syndications; Vendor financing programs
PREFERRED TYPES OF INDUSTRIES/INVESTMENTS: Commercial equipment such as aircraft, manufacturing, communications, graphic arts, medical, agricultural, restaurant furniture, fixtures and equipment and other equipment used for commercial enterprise
WILL NOT CONSIDER: Real Estate & Autos
GEOGRAPHIC LIMITS OF LEASES: National
RANGE OF LEASE PER BUSINESS: Min. Varies
PREFERRED TERM FOR LOANS & LEASES: Min. Varies; Max. 10 years
BUSINESS CHARACTERISTICS DESIRED-REQUIRED: Minimum number of years in business: 3; Other: cash flow coverage should be 2:1 - size of credit and company financial strength should be congruent
BRANCHES: Oakland, CA—Don Jackson, Senior Vice President, Western Regional Manager; Robert Fletcher, Vice President, Industry Services; (415) 891-9484
Portfolio Division—Larry Lustgarten, Sr. Vice President/Portfolio Manager; 520 Third St., Suite 202, Oakland, CA 94607; (415) 891-9484
Phoenix, AZ—-Theodore Pawlikowski, District Sales Manager; Tempe Executive Center; 1270 E. Broadway, Ste. 115B; Tempe, AZ 85282; (602) 968-0968
Portland, OR—Daniel Minks, District Sales Manager, 10300 S.W. Greenburg Rd., Ste. 495; Portland, OR 97223; (503) 244-5281
Reno, NV—-Mary Ganzel, District Sales Manager; 1881 S. Arlington Ave., Reno, NV 89509; (702) 329-6503
Sacramento, CA—Carol Lohmeyer, District Sales Manager; 1555 River Park Dr., Suite 205; Sacramento, CA 95815; (916) 920-3765
San Francisco, CA—Aaron P. Salloway, Senior Vice President, National Division; Bruce Dunlap, Vice

President; 350 California St., Suite 2290; San Francisco, CA 94104; (415) 989-8080

COMPANY: **HLC Leasing Co.**
ADDRESS: 7063 So. Virginia Street
Reno, NV 89511
PHONE: (702) 851-3313
TYPE OF INSTITUTION: Financial services
CONTACT OFFICER(S): Tom Gosh, Manager
ASSETS: Approx. $5 million
INVESTMENTS/LOANS MADE: For own account
TYPES OF FINANCING: SECONDARY-MARKET CORPORATE SECURITIES: Other: Equipment & vehicle leases and contracts—real estate financing (commercial and industrial) (residential/discount notes & deeds), LOANS: Equipment, REAL ESTATE LOANS: FACTORING, LEASES: Single-investor; Leveraged; Tax leases; Non-tax leases; Operating; Tax-oriented lease brokerage; Lease syndications; Vendor financing programs; Other: Mini-leases, managers of captives, and consultant underwriters to lending institutions, INTERNATIONAL (including import/export), REAL ESTATE: Acquisitions, Joint ventures, OTHER SERVICES PROVIDED: Real estate, brokerage, business brokerage, vehicle fleet leasing and sales (trucks and passenger cars—all makes and models)
PREFERRED TYPES OF INDUSTRIES/INVESTMENTS: Machinery tools; Construction; Mining; Warehousing; Aircraft; Industrial; Office equipment; Hotel; Motel; Restaurant; Computers; Telephone; Vehicles
GEOGRAPHIC LIMITS OF INVESTMENTS/LOANS: National; International
PREFERRED TERM FOR LOANS & LEASES: Min. 1 year; Max. 10-15 years
BUSINESS CHARACTERISTICS DESIRED-REQUIRED: Minimum number of years in business: 2; Min. annual sales $250,000; Min. net worth $150,000; Min. annual net income $25,000; Min. annual cash flow $25,000
REFERRALS ACCEPTED FROM: Investment/Mortgage banker or Borrower/Investee
REMARKS: We do accept bonafide broker business, and we will pay broker fees if legitimized

COMPANY: **Grumman Credit Corporation**
ADDRESS: 1111 Stewart Avenue
Bethpage, NY 11714
PHONE: (516) 575-3421
TYPE OF INSTITUTION: Captive Leasing, subsidiary of Grumman Corporation
CONTACT OFFICER(S): E. Balinsky, Persident
J. Latterner, Manager
T. Maloney, Asst. Treasurer
ASSETS: $45,000,000
INVESTMENTS/LOANS MADE: Through private placements
INVESTMENTS/LOANS MADE: In securities with a secondary market and in securities without a secondary market
TYPES OF FINANCING: LOANS: Equity-related, LEASES: Single-investor; Leveraged; Operating; Vendor financing programs, INTERNATIONAL, OTHER SERVICES PROVIDED: Municipal funding
PREFERRED TYPES OF INDUSTRIES/INVESTMENTS: Manufacturing Equips.; Municipal funding
GEOGRAPHIC LIMITS OF INVESTMENTS/LOANS: International
RANGE OF INV./LOAN PER BUSINESS: Min. $25,000; Max. $1,000,000
PREFERRED TERM FOR LOANS & LEASES: Min. 3 years; Max. 7 years
BUSINESS CHARACTERISTICS DESIRED-REQUIRED: Minimum number of years in business: 0; Min. annual sales $100,000; Min. net worth $50,000
REFERRALS ACCEPTED FROM: Investment/Mortgage banker or Borrower/Investee

COMPANY: **Goldome FSB**
ADDRESS: 1 Fountain Plaza
Buffalo, NY 14203
PHONE: (716) 847-4975
TYPE OF INSTITUTION: Bank, Investments
CONTACT OFFICER(S): R. C. Gupta, VP
ASSETS: $13 Billion (total assets of Goldome FSB)
INVESTMENTS/LOANS MADE: For own account
INVESTMENTS/LOANS MADE: In securities with a secondary market and in securities without a secondary market
TYPES OF FINANCING: SECONDARY-MARKET CORPORATE SECURITIES: Bonds. LOANS: Unsecured; REAL ESTATE LOANS: Intermediate-term senior mtg.; Subordinated. INTERNATIONAL
PREFERRED TYPES OF INDUSTRIES/INVESTMENTS: Bank, Utilities, Industrials, Mortgage bankers, etc.
WILL NOT CONSIDER: Small firms unless secured. Need some "rated" debt of the firm unless a bank
RANGE OF INV./LOAN PER BUSINESS: Max. 25 years (floating rate)
PREFERRED TERM FOR LOANS & LEASES: Min. $1 million; Max. $25 million
REFERRALS ACCEPTED FROM: Investment/Mortgage banker or Borrower/Investee
REMARKS: The basic business is to invest in fixed income securities

COMPANY:**Goldome FSB**
ADDRESS: One Fountain Plaza
Buffalo, NY 14203
PHONE: (716) 847-5879
TYPE OF INSTITUTION: Commercial Lending Division
CONTACT OFFICER(S): Charles E. Moran, Jr., Vice President—Commercial Lending
Craig I. Staley, Vice President—Commercial Lending NY Division, (212) 841-6942
ASSETS: $160 MM Commercial Lending Portfolio
INVESTMENTS/LOANS MADE: For own account
TYPES OF FINANCING: LOANS: Unsecured; Working capital; Equipment. REAL ESTATE LOANS: Land; Gap.
GEOGRAPHIC LIMITS OF INVESTMENTS/LOANS: National
RANGE OF INV./LOAN PER BUSINESS: Min. $1,000,000; Max. $15,000,000
PREFERRED TERM FOR LOANS & LEASES: Min. Lines of Credit; Max. 7 years
BUSINESS CHARACTERISTICS DESIRED-REQUIRED: No set requirements

REFERRALS ACCEPTED FROM: Investment/Mortgage banker or Borrower/Investee

COMPANY: **Lincoln First Commercial Corp.**
ADDRESS: 1325 Franklin Ave.
Garden City, NY 11530
PHONE: (516) 248-1380
CONTACT OFFICER(S): Robert E. Stark, Senior V.P.

COMPANY: **Nelson Capital Corporation**
ADDRESS: 591 Stewart Avenue
Garden City, NY 11530
PHONE: (516) 222-2555
CONTACT OFFICER(S): Irwin B. Nelson, President

COMPANY: **U.S. Capital Corporation**
ADDRESS: 525 Northern Boulevard
Great Neck, NY 11021
PHONE: (516) 466-8550
TYPE OF INSTITUTION: Asset based lender, private
CONTACT OFFICER(S): Howard Sommer, Pres.
ASSETS: $10,000,000+
INVESTMENTS/LOANS MADE: For own account
INVESTMENTS/LOANS MADE: In securities with a secondary market and in securities without a secondary market
TYPES OF FINANCING: LOANS: Working capital; Equipment. REAL ESTATE LOANS: Long-term senior mtg.; Intermediate-term senior mtg.; Subordinated; Wraparounds. OTHER SERVICES PROVIDED:: Letter of credit financing
GEOGRAPHIC LIMITS OF INVESTMENTS/LOANS: Regional
RANGE OF INV./LOAN PER BUSINESS: Min. $25,000; Max. $500,000
PREFERRED TERM FOR LOANS & LEASES: Min. 1 year; Max. 4 years
BUSINESS CHARACTERISTICS DESIRED-REQUIRED: Minimum number of years in business: 0
REFERRALS ACCEPTED FROM: Investment/Mortgage banker or Borrower/Investee

COMPANY: **Webster Factors, Inc.**
ADDRESS: 11 Middle Neck Rd.
Great Neck, NY 11021
PHONE: (516) 466-0200
TYPE OF INSTITUTION: Commercial Finance Co.
CONTACT OFFICER(S): Alter Milberg, President

COMPANY: **Zenith Financial Corporation**
ADDRESS: The Towers, 111 Great Neck Road
Great Neck, NY 11021
PHONE: (516) 487-0320
CONTACT OFFICER(S): Paul Singer, President

COMPANY: **Citicorp Industrial Credit, Inc.**
ADDRESS: 450 Mamaroneck Avenue
Harrison, NY 10528
PHONE: (914) 899-7000
TYPE OF INSTITUTION: Asset-Based Finance subsidiary of bank holding company
CONTACT OFFICER(S): John W. Dewey, President, Equipment Finance Leasing
Frederick S. Gilbert, Jr., Executive V.P., Asset-Based Lending
Robert H. Martinsen, Chrm. of the Bd.
David McCollum, E. V.P.,Corporate Asset Funding
Robert Laughlin, E. V.P., Equipment Finance
William Urban, E. V.P., Vendor Finance
J.R.A.C. Clement, V.P., Tax Leasing & Equity Syndication
ASSETS: $3.2 Billion
INVESTMENTS/LOANS MADE: For own account
TYPES OF FINANCING: VENTURE CAPITAL: Buy-outs/Acquisitions; LOANS: Working capital (receivables/inventory; Equipment; Buyouts/acquisitions, bulk purchase of receivables, FACTORING, LEASES: Leveraged; Tax leases; Non-tax leases; Operating; Tax-oriented lease brokerage; Lease syndications; Vendor financing programs
PREFERRED TYPES OF INDUSTRIES/INVESTMENTS: Manufacturers and Wholesalers
GEOGRAPHIC LIMITS OF INVESTMENTS/LOANS: National
RANGE OF INV./LOAN PER BUSINESS: Min. $50,000; Max. up to legal limit
PREFERRED TERM FOR LOANS & LEASES: Min. 2 to 5 years revolving loans, up to 10 years term loans
BRANCHES: 211 Perimeter Ctr. Parkway, Atlanta, GA, 30346; (404) 391-8500
3033 South Parker Road, Market Tower I, Suite 900, Aurora, CO, 80014; (303) 752-2530
200 South Wacker Drive, Chicago, IL, 60606; (312) 993-3230, (312) 993-3263
635 W. 7th St, Ste 400, Cincinnati, OH, 45203;
1300 East 9th Street, Cleveland, OH, 44114; (216) 696-6330/(216) 621-1383
717 North Harwood St., LB #85, Diamond Shamrock Tower, Dallas, TX, 75201; (214) 760-1829
101 Continental Boulevard, Suite 800, El Segundo, CA, 90245; (213) 640-1224
560 Sylvan Avenue, Engelwood Cliffs, NJ, 07632; (201) 657-7610
450 Mamaroneck Avenue, Harrison, NY, 10528; (914) 899-7000
Summit Tower — 11 Greenway Plaza, Houston, TX, 77046; (713) 627-8170
2 Allen Center, 1200 Smith Street, Houston, TX, 77002; (713) 654-2800
444 South Flower Street, Los Angeles, CA, 90071; (213) 745-3500
3435 Wilshire Boulevard, Los Angeles, CA, 90010
3090 Multifoods Tower, Minneapolis, MN, 55402
621 Lexington Avenue, New York, NY, 10043
44 Montgomery Street, San Francisco, CA, 94104; (415) 954-1166, (415) 954-1042
1111 Third Avenue, Suite 2700, Seattle, WA, 98101; (206) 382-6225
470 Totten Pond Road, Waltham, MA, 02154; (617) 890-1666
333 Hegenberger Rd., Ste 815, Oakland, CA 94621
One Sansome St., San Francisco, CA 94120
20 Executive Park - Ste 200, Irvine, CA 92714
1900 E. Golf, Schaumburg, IL 60195
1050 Connecticut Av., NW, Washington, DC 20036

1200 Ford Rd., Ste 270, Dallas, TX 75234

COMPANY: **Abrams & Company, Inc.**
ADDRESS: 400 Madison Avenue
New York, NY 10017
PHONE: (212) 355-4646
CONTACT OFFICER(S): Burton Abrams, President

COMPANY: **Ambassador Factors Div., Fleet Factors Corp.**
ADDRESS: 1450 Broadway
New York, NY 10018
PHONE: (212) 221-3000
TYPE OF INSTITUTION: Commercial Finance & Factoring
CONTACT OFFICER(S): William Paolillo, VP
TYPES OF FINANCING: LOANS: Working capital (receivables/inventory); Equipment, FACTORING
PREFERRED TYPES OF INDUSTRIES/INVESTMENTS: Diversified
GEOGRAPHIC LIMITS OF INVESTMENTS/LOANS: National
RANGE OF INV./LOAN PER BUSINESS: Min. $150,000

COMPANY: **American Commercial Capital Corporation**
ADDRESS: 310 Madison Avenue
New York, NY 10017
PHONE: (212) 986-3305
CONTACT OFFICER(S): Gerald J. Grossman, Pres.

COMPANY: **Amsave Credit Corporation**
ADDRESS: 1370 Ave. of the Americas
New York, NY 10019
PHONE: (212) 489-9100
CONTACT OFFICER(S): William P. Mallory, Pres.

COMPANY: **Bankers Trust Company, Asset Based Lending Group**
ADDRESS: 1775 Broadway
New York, NY 10019
PHONE: (212) 977-6123
CONTACT OFFICER(S): Richard L. Solar, V.P.

COMPANY: **Brancorp Factors**
ADDRESS: 1440 Broadway
New York, NY 10010
PHONE: (212) 840-2552
CONTACT OFFICER(S): Jack Lindner, Pres.

COMPANY: **Century Factors, Inc.**
ADDRESS: 444 Fifth Avenue
New York, NY 10018
PHONE: (212) 221-4400
CONTACT OFFICER(S): Stanley Tananbaum, Pres.

COMPANY: **The Chase Manhattan Bank, Finance Div.**
ADDRESS: 1411 Broadway
New York, NY 10018
PHONE: (212) 223-7009
TYPE OF INSTITUTION: Commercial Finance Div. of Bank
CONTACT OFFICER(S): Frank J. Donahue, V.P.
TYPES OF FINANCING: LOANS: Working capital (receivables/inventory); Equipment, LEASES
PREFERRED TYPES OF INDUSTRIES/INVESTMENTS: Diversified
GEOGRAPHIC LIMITS OF INVESTMENTS/LOANS: National
RANGE OF INV./LOAN PER BUSINESS: Min. $500,000
BRANCHES: Boston, MA
Atlanta, GA
Dallas, TX
Los Angeles, CA
Chicago, IL

COMPANY: **Commercial Credit Financial Services, Inc.**
ADDRESS: One Penn Plaza
New York, NY 10019
PHONE: (212) 502-0200
CONTACT OFFICER(S): David Goldberg, Pres.

COMPANY: **Commercial Funding, Inc.**
ADDRESS: 230 Park Avenue
New York, NY 10017
PHONE: (212) 661-4848
CONTACT OFFICER(S): Robert L. Krause, Sr. Vice Pres.

COMPANY:**Mint Factors**
ADDRESS: 215 Park Avenue South
New York, NY 10003
PHONE: (212) 254-2377
CONTACT OFFICER(S): Charlotte Mintz, Partner

COMPANY: **Congress Financial Corp.**
ADDRESS: 1133 Ave. of the Americas
New York, NY 10036
PHONE: (212) 840-3000
TYPE OF INSTITUTION: Commercial Finance Co.
CONTACT OFFICER(S): Robt. A. Miller, Exec. V.P.
Robt. Goldman, Pres.
TYPES OF FINANCING: LOANS: Working capital (receivables/inventory); Equipment, FACTORING, OTHER SERVICES PROVIDED: Finance Leverage Buy-outs; Turnaround Financing
GEOGRAPHIC LIMITS OF INVESTMENTS/LOANS: National
RANGE OF INV./LOAN PER BUSINESS: Min. $500,000; Max. $100,000,000
REMARKS: 6 operating branches: Los Angeles, Miami, New York, Minneapolis, Chicago, Puerto Rico; sales branches in other cities

COMPANY: **Credit Alliance Corporation**
ADDRESS: 770 Lexington Avenue
New York, NY 10021
PHONE: (212) 421-3600
TYPE OF INSTITUTION: Full service equipment finance company

CONTACT OFFICER(S): Daniel N. Ryan, Senior Vice President
ASSETS: $600,000,000
INVESTMENTS/LOANS MADE: For own account
TYPES OF FINANCING: LOANS: Working capital; Equipment
PREFERRED TYPES OF INDUSTRIES/INVESTMENTS: Income producing or labor saving equipment
GEOGRAPHIC LIMITS OF INVESTMENTS/LOANS: National
PREFERRED TERM FOR LOANS & LEASES: Min. 1 years; Max. 10 years
REFERRALS ACCEPTED FROM: Investment/Mortgage banker or Borrower/Investee

COMPANY: **Equilease Corporation**
ADDRESS: 750 Third Ave.
New York, NY 10017
PHONE: (212) 557-6800
CONTACT OFFICER(S): Mark Hershey, President/ Commercial Finance and Leasing
ASSETS: $700,000,000
INVESTMENTS/LOANS MADE: For own account, For managed accounts
TYPES OF FINANCING: LOANS: Equipment, LEASES: Single-investor; Leveraged; Tax leases; Non-tax leases; Operating; Tax-oriented lease brokerage; Lease syndications; Vendor financing programs; Other: International

COMPANY: **FNB Financial Co.**
ADDRESS: Two Penn. Plaza
New York, NY 10001
PHONE: (212) 613-3001
TYPE OF INSTITUTION: Commercial Finance Division—Owned by Bank of Boston
CONTACT OFFICER(S): Gabe Romeo, Senior Vice President
TYPES OF FINANCING: LOANS: Working capital; Equipment; REAL ESTATE LOANS: Land; Land development; FACTORING; INTERNATIONAL
GEOGRAPHIC LIMITS OF INVESTMENTS/LOANS: National
RANGE OF INV./LOAN PER BUSINESS: Min. $750,000
BRANCHES: All over country

COMPANY: **Gibraltar Corp. of America**
ADDRESS: 350 Fifth Ave.
New York, NY 10118
PHONE: (212) 868-4400
TYPE OF INSTITUTION: Asset-based financing sub. of bank
CONTACT OFFICER(S): Irwin Schwartz, President
Leonard Stowe, Exec. V.P.
TYPES OF FINANCING: LOANS: Working capital (receivables/inventory); Equipment
GEOGRAPHIC LIMITS OF INVESTMENTS/LOANS: Regional; Half of U.S.
RANGE OF INV./LOAN PER BUSINESS: Min. $100,000; Max. $10,000,000
PREFERRED TERM FOR LOANS & LEASES: Max. 7 years

COMPANY: **Haas Financial Corporation**
ADDRESS: 230 Park Avenue
New York, NY 10169
PHONE: (212) 490-1510
CONTACT OFFICER(S): George C. Haas Jr., President
Robert L. Cummings
Vice President
INVESTMENTS/LOANS MADE: For own account; Through private placements
INVESTMENTS/LOANS MADE: In securities with a secondary market and in securities without a secondary market
TYPES OF FINANCING: SECONDARY-MARKET CORPORATE SECURITIES: Common stock; Bonds; VENTURE CAPITAL: First-stage; Second-stage; Later-stage expansion; Buy-outs/Acquisitions; LOANS: Equipment; REAL ESTATE LOANS: Long-term senior mtg.; Intermediate-term senior mtg.; Subordinated; Wraparounds; LEASES: Single-investor; Operating; Tax-oriented lease brokerage; OTHER SERVICES PROVIDED: Merger Acquisition Divestiture Brokerage; Consulting and Valuation; Acquisition/Divestiture Financing.
PREFERRED TYPES OF INDUSTRIES/INVESTMENTS: Will look at all types of industries, firm has specialty in transportation (planes) consumer products (soft drinks)
GEOGRAPHIC LIMITS OF INVESTMENTS/LOANS: National
RANGE OF INV./LOAN PER BUSINESS: Min. $500,000
PREFERRED TERM FOR LOANS & LEASES: Min. 5 years; Max. 15 years
REFERRALS ACCEPTED FROM: Investment/Mortgage banker or Borrower/Investee

COMPANY: **Hunter, Keith, Marshall & Co., Inc.**
ADDRESS: One Penn Plaza, Ste. 1831
New York, NY 10119
PHONE: (212) 736-6140
TYPE OF INSTITUTION: Private placement investment bank
CONTACT OFFICER(S): Henry C. Marshall, Jr., Managing Director, Equipment & Real Estate
Steven I. Eisenberg, Vice President, Equipment
INVESTMENTS/LOANS MADE: For own account; Through private placements
INVESTMENTS/LOANS MADE: In securities with a secondary market and in securities without a secondary market
TYPES OF FINANCING: LOANS: Equity-related; REAL ESTATE LOANS: Long-term senior mtg.; Intermediate-term senior mtg.; LEASES: Vendor financing programs; Other: debt side of leveraged leases
GEOGRAPHIC LIMITS OF INVESTMENTS/LOANS: National; Other: Will do selected international credits
RANGE OF INV./LOAN PER BUSINESS: Min. $2 MM
PREFERRED TERM FOR LOANS & LEASES: Min. 3 years; Max. 20 years
BUSINESS CHARACTERISTICS DESIRED-REQUIRED: Min. net worth $5 MM; Min. annual net income $ 1.5MM; Min. annual cash flow: $1.5MM; Other: Will do selected startups on secured basis
REFERRALS ACCEPTED FROM: Borrower/Investee

BRANCHES: Andrew M. Hunter III, Robert J. Keith, Jr., 5100 IDS Center, Minneapolis, MN 55402, (612) 338-2799

COMPANY: **Intercontinental Credit Corp.**
ADDRESS: 2 Park Ave.
New York, NY 10016
PHONE: (212) 481-1800
TYPE OF INSTITUTION: Commercial Finance Co.
CONTACT OFFICER(S): Barry M. Weinstein, V.P.
TYPES OF FINANCING: LOANS: Working capital (receivables/inventory); Equipment
GEOGRAPHIC LIMITS OF INVESTMENTS/LOANS: National
RANGE OF INV./LOAN PER BUSINESS: Min. $100,000

COMPANY: **Investors Lease Corp.**
ADDRESS: 200 Park Ave., Ste. 228 E
New York, NY 10017
PHONE: (212) 697-4590
TYPE OF INSTITUTION: Leasing Company
CONTACT OFFICER(S): David J. Tananbaum, President
TYPES OF FINANCING: Leases.
PREFERRED TERM FOR LOANS AND LEASES: Max 3 Years

COMPANY: **Irving Trust Co.—Commercial Finance Dept.**
ADDRESS: 1290 Ave. of the Americas
New York, NY 10015
PHONE: (212) 487-2121
TYPE OF INSTITUTION: Commercial Finance Dept. of Bank
CONTACT OFFICER(S): Robert M. Grosse, V.P. & General Manager
TYPES OF FINANCING: LOANS: Working capital (receivables/inventory); Equipment, REAL ESTATE LOANS
PREFERRED TYPES OF INDUSTRIES/INVESTMENTS: Receivables
WILL NOT CONSIDER: Computers
GEOGRAPHIC LIMITS OF INVESTMENTS/LOANS: National
RANGE OF INV./LOAN PER BUSINESS: Min. $1 million
BUSINESS CHARACTERISTICS DESIRED-REQUIRED: Minimum number of years in business: 2

COMPANY: **James Talcott Inc.; James Talcott Factors Div.**
James Talcott Business Credit, Div.
ADDRESS: 1633 Broadway
New York, NY 10019
PHONE: (212) 484-0300
TYPE OF INSTITUTION: Diversified secured financial institution.
CONTACT OFFICER(S): William R. Gruttemeyer, President
Martin H. Rod, Executive V.P.
David J. Kantes, Executive V.P.
Robert W . Kramer.Executive V.P.
Phillip E. Renle, Jr., Senior V.P.
Anthony Viola, V.P.
ASSETS: Confidential
TYPES OF FINANCING: L0ANS: Working capital (receivables/inventory);Equipment; Equity-related; Leveraged buy-outs, acquisition secured by the assets of the acquired co., REAL ESTATE LOANS: Intermediate-term senior mtg.; Wraparounds; Land, FACTORING, LEASES: Single-investor; Operating; Tax-oriented lease brokerage, INTERNATIONAL (including import/export), OTHER SERVICES PROVIDED: "Boot-Strap" Acquisitions
PREFERRED TYPES OF INDUSTRIES/INVESTMENTS: We will consider all types of industries for financing and factoring loans.
WILL NOT CONSIDER: Construction and home improvement loans.
GEOGRAPHIC LIMITS OF INVESTMENTS/LOANS: National; International
RANGE OF INV./LOAN PER BUSINESS: Min. $500,000.00; Max. Unlimited
PREFERRED TERM FOR LOANS & LEASES: Min. One year; Max. Ten years
BUSINESS CHARACTERISTICS DESIRED-REQUIRED: Minimum number of years in business: 0; Min. annual sales $1,500,000; Min. net worth $250,000; Min. annual net income: open; Min. annual cash flow: open
REFERRALS ACCEPTED FROM: Investment/Mortgage banker or Borrower/Investee
BRANCHES: Donald Mintz, One Wilshire Building, Los Angeles, CA, 90017; (213) 620-9200
Vincent Panzera, 717 North Harwood Street, Suite 440, Box 36, Dallas, TX, 75201; (214) 651-8801
REMARKS: Other national offices to be opened in 1982. Parent is The Lloyds Scottish Group in Great Britain which, in turn, is controlled by The Lloyds Bank of England.

COMPANY: **Lazere Financial Corp.**
ADDRESS: 60 E. 42nd St.
New York, NY 10165
PHONE: (212) 573-9700
TYPE OF INSTITUTION: Commercial Finance Co.
CONTACT OFFICER(S): Stephen Wincott, Exec. V.P.
TYPES OF FINANCING: LOANS: Working capital (receivables/inventory); Equipment; Asset based lending
GEOGRAPHIC LIMITS OF INVESTMENTS/LOANS: National
RANGE OF INV./LOAN PER BUSINESS: Min $350,000
PREFERRED TERMS FOR LOANS & LEASES: Min. 3 years; Max. 5 years
BRANCHES: Ronald Jacobs, V.P. 444 Brickell Av., Miami, FL 33131 (305) 358-5430
Philip Kilmnick, V.P. 1801 Ave. of the Stars, Los Angeles, CA 90067 (213) 552-0920
Harry Goldson, V.P., 208 S. La Sao, Ste. 2040, Chicago, IL 60604 (312) 332-0920
REMARKS: Revolving term

COMPANY: **Manufacturers Hanover Commercial Corp.**
ADDRESS: 1211 Ave. of the Americas, 12th Floor
New York, NY 10036
PHONE: (212) 382-7000
TYPE OF INSTITUTION: Commercial Finance Co.

CONTACT OFFICER(S): Francis X. Basile, Chairman & CEO
TYPES OF FINANCING: VENTURE CAPITAL: Start-up from developed product stage; First stage (less than 1 year); Second-stage (generally 1-3 years); Later-stage expansion; Buy-outs/Acquisitions; LOANS: Equity-related; FACTORING
GEOGRAHIC LIMITS OF INVESTMENTS/LOANS: International
RANGE OF INV./LOAN PER BUSINESS: Min. $250,000

COMPANY: **Milberg Factors, Inc.**
ADDRESS: 99 Park Ave.
New York, NY 10016
PHONE: (212) 697-4200
TYPE OF INSTITUTION: Commercial Finance Co.
CONTACT OFFICER(S): Leonard L. Milberg, President
TYPES OF FINANCING: FACTORING; OTHER SERVICES PROVIDED: Commercial Financing
GEOGRAPHIC LIMITS OF INVESTMENTS/LOANS: National

COMPANY: **Natwest Commercial Services, Inc.**
ADDRESS: 600 Madison Avenue
New York, NY 10022
PHONE: (212) 980-3501
CONTACT OFFICER(S): Barry J. Essig, Exec. Vice Pres.

COMPANY: **Nordic American Bank Corporation**
ADDRESS: 600 Fifth Avennue
New York, NY 10020
PHONE: (212) 315-6500
TYPE OF INSTITUTION: Investment Banking
CONTACT OFFICER(S): Hans Eric Von der Groeben, EVP
Edward Mete, EVP
ASSESTS: $600,000,000
INVESTMENTS/LOANS MADE: For own account; Through private placements
INVESTMENTS/LOANS MADE: In securities with a secondary market and in securities without a secondary market;
TYPES OF FINANCING: SECONDARY-MARKET CORPORATE SECURITIES: Bonds; LOANS: Working Capital (receivables/inventory); Equipment; Equity-related. REAL ESTATE LOANS: Industrial revenue bonds. LEASES: Leveraged; Tax leases; Operating; Lease syndications; Vendor financing programs; INTERNATIONAL (including import/export)
PREFERRED TYPES OF INDUSTRIES/INVESTMENTS: Nordic related business in the U.S. U.S. businesses operating in the Nordic area.
GEOGRAPHIC LIMITS OF INVESTMENTS/LOANS: National; International;
BRANCHES: John A. Redding, SVP, Suite 1963, 135 So. La Salle St., Chicago, IL; (312) 855-1515

COMPANY: **Rosenthal & Rosenthal, Inc.**
ADDRESS: 1451 Broadway
New York, NY 10036
PHONE: (212) 790-1418
TYPE OF INSTITUTION: Commercial Finance Co.
CONTACT OFFICER(S): Melvin E. Rubenstein, Exec. V.P.
TYPES OF FINANCING: VENTURE CAPITAL: Startups; First stage; Second stage; Later-stage expansion; Buy-outs/Acquisitions. LOANS: Working capital (receivables/inventory); Equipment, FACTORING. INTERNATIONAL. REAL ESTATE: Acquisitions
GEOGRAPHIC LIMITS OF INVESTMENTS/LOANS: National
RANGE OF INV./LOAN PER BUSINESS: Min. $100,000; Max. $20,000,000
PREFERRED TERM FOR LOANS & LEASES: Min. 1 yr.; Max. 10 yrs.

COMPANY: **Security Pacific Finance Group**
ADDRESS: 228 East 45th Street
New York, NY 10017
PHONE: (212) 309-9300
CONTACT OFFICER(S): Martin J. Kelly, Chairman & C.E.O.

COMPANY: **The Slavenburg Corp.**
ADDRESS: One Penn Plaza
New York, NY 10119
TYPE OF INSTITUTION: Factoring & Commercial Finance
CONTACT OFFICER(S): V. P. Arminio, President
C. D. Manikas, Executive Vice President
ASSETS: Wholly owned subsidiary of Credit Lyonnais Bank Nederland N.V., The Netherlands
TYPES OF FINANCING: LOANS: Working capital (receivables/inventory); FACTORING; INTERNATIONAL (including import/export)
GEOGRAPHIC LIMITS OF INVESTMENTS/LOANS: National;
PREFERRED TERM FOR LOANS & LEASES: Under 1 year
BRANCHES: 3407 West 6th Street, Los Angeles, CA 90026 (213) 387-3629; A. Roy Saltzman, Vice President

COMPANY: **Standard Financial Corporation**
ADDRESS: 540 Madison Avenue
New York, NY 10022
PHONE: (212) 826-8000
TYPE OF INSTITUTION: Banking, financing, leasing and factoring
CONTACT OFFICER(S): Louis J. Cappelli, Executive V.P.
ASSETS: $100,000,000 and up
INVESTMENTS/LOANS MADE: For own account
TYPES OF FINANCING: LOANS, REAL ESTATE LOANS: Long-term senior mtg.; Intermediate-term senior mtg.; Wraparounds; Land; Land development; Construction; Gap; Standbys, FACTORING, LEASES: Single-investor; Leveraged; Tax leases; Non-tax leases; Operating; Tax-oriented lease brokerage; Lease syndications; Vendor financing programs, INTERNATIONAL (including import/export), REAL ESTATE
GEOGRAPHIC LIMITS OF INVESTMENTS/LOANS: International
RANGE OF INV./LOAN PER BUSINESS: Min. $100,000.00; Max. $15 million

BRANCHES: Kenneth W. Grubbs, V.P., Security Industrial Loan Association, 4th and Main St., Richmond, VA, 23219; (804) 649-1120

COMPANY: **Textile Banking Co., Inc.**
ADDRESS: 51 Madison Ave.
New York, NY 10010
PHONE: (212) 502-0200
TYPE OF INSTITUTION: Commercial Finance Co.
CONTACT OFFICER(S): Joseph Rizzo, Exec. V.P.

COMPANY: **Trefoil Capital Corporation**
810 7th Avenue
ADDRESS: New York, NY 10019
PHONE: (212) 333-7445
TYPE OF INSTITUTION: Commercial Finance Co. - Bank owned
CONTACT OFFICER(S): Gerald Blum, President
Sherwood (Jerry)Faust, Sr. Vice President, Marketing
Ronald Grist, Sr. Vice President, Credit Administration
ASSETS: $210,000,000
TYPES OF FINANCING: LOANS:Working capital; Equipment
PREFERRED TYPES INDUSTRIES/INVESTMENTS: Manufacturing and service oriented
GEOGRAPHIC LIMITS OF INVESTMENTS/LOANS: National
RANGE OF INV./LOANS PER BUSINESS: Min. $300,000; Min. $100,000,000
PREFERRED TERM FOR LOANS & LEASES: 1 year
BUSINESS CHARACTERISTICS DESIRED-REQUIRED: Min. no. of years in business; 0
REFERRALS ACCEPTED: Borrower/investee
BRANCHES:David Grende, Exec. VP, 100 Glendon Ave., Los Angeles, CA 90024, (213) 208-7600
Stuart Nectow, Exec. VP, 332 S. Michigan Ave., Chicago, IL 60604; (312) 922-1450

COMPANY: **United Credit Corporation**
ADDRESS: 10 East 40 St.
New York, NY 10016
PHONE: (212) 689-9480
TYPE OF INSTITUTION: Independent Co. Asset Based Lending Service
CONTACT OFFICER(S): Leonard R. Landis, President
ASSETS: $15 Million
INVESTMENTS/LOANS MADE: For managed accounts
TYPES OF FINANCING: LOANS: Working capital (receivables/inventory); Equipment, FACTORING
PREFERRED TYPES OF INDUSTRIES/INVESTMENTS: Mfg. & Service
WILL NOT CONSIDER: Construction, Retail
GEOGRAPHIC LIMITS OF INVESTMENTS/LOANS: Local; State; Regional; NY; NJ; Conn; New England
RANGE OF INV./LOAN PER BUSINESS: Min. $25,000; Max. $500,000
PREFERRED TERM FOR LOANS & LEASES: Revolving A/R
BUSINESS CHARACTERISTICS DESIRED-REQUIRED: Minimum number of years in business: 0;Min. annual sales $300,000; Each situation stands on its own merits

1COMPANY: **Walter E. Heller & Company**
ADDRESS: 101 Park Avenue
New York, NY 10178
PHONE: (212) 880-7062
TYPE OF INSTITUTION: Commercial Finance Company
CONTACT OFFICER(S): Robert Spitalnic, Sr. V.P.
ASSETS: $6 Billion
TYPES OF FINANCING: Asset-Based Financing, LOANS: Working capital (receivables/inventory); Equipment, FACTORING, Leveraged Buyout Financing (Asset-Based)
PREFERRED TYPES OF INDUSTRIES/INVESTMENTS: Manufacturing and Distribution
WILL NOT CONSIDER: Unsecured Financing, or Start-Ups
GEOGRAPHIC LIMITS OF INVESTMENTS/LOANS: International
RANGE OF INV./LOAN PER BUSINESS: Min. $1,000,000; Max. $50,000,000 and up
PREFERRED TERM FOR LOANS & LEASES: Min. 1; Max. 8 years
BUSINESS CHARACTERISTICS DESIRED-REQUIRED: Minimum number of years in business: 2; Min. annual sales $5 Million
REFERRALS ACCEPTED FROM: Investment/Mortgage banker or Borrower/Investee
BRANCHES: Boston, Chicago, Dallas, Los Angeles, Miami, Montreal, syracuse, Toronto

COMPANY: **William Iselin & Co., Inc.**
ADDRESS: 357 Park Ave. South
New York, NY 10010
PHONE: (212) 481-9400
TYPE OF INSTITUTION: Commercial Finance Co.

COMPANY: **Columbus National Leasing Corporation**
ADDRESS: 2570 Baird Road
Penfield, NY 14526
PHONE: (716) 385-9950
CONTACT OFFICER(S): Kenneth A. Glasgow, President
Greg Millner, V.P. (Credit Officer)
ASSETS: $25,000,000
INVESTMENTS/LOANS MADE: For own account
TYPES OF FINANCING: LOANS: Equipment, LEASES: Single-investor; Tax leases; Non-tax leases; Vendor financing programs; Other: Sale and leasebacks
PREFERRED TYPES OF INDUSTRIES/INVESTMENTS: Specialists in printing and graphic arts equipment. Also desire medical, machine tools, telephone systems, computers and most income producing equipment
WILL NOT CONSIDER: Restaurants or coin operated machinery
GEOGRAPHIC LIMITS OF INVESTMENTS/LOANS: National
RANGE OF INVESTMENT/LOAN PER BUSINESS: Min. $10,000; Max. $1,000,000
PREFERRED TERM FOR LOANS & LEASES: Min. 2 years; Max. 10 years
BUSINESS CHARACTERISTICS DESIRED-REQUIRED: Minimum number of years in business: 0; Other: Requirements are relative to the size of the lease and the nature of the equipment

REFERRALS ACCEPTED FROM: Will accept broker applications
REMARKS: We have district offices throughout the country, but initial inquiries should be made to Rochester

COMPANY: **Barrett Capital & Leasing Corporation**
ADDRESS: 707 Westchester Avenue
White Plains, NY 10604
PHONE: (914) 682-1960
TYPE OF INSTITUTION: Equipment vehicle leasing and finance company
CONTACT OFFICER(S): Barry P. Korn, President
ASSETS: $60 million
INVESTMENTS/LOANS MADE: For own account, For managed accounts
TYPES OF FINANCING: LEASES: Single-investor; Leveraged; Tax leases; Non-tax leases; Operating; Tax-oriented lease brokerage; Vendor financing programs
PREFERRED TYPES OF INDUSTRIES/INVESTMENTS: For all industries, leases of equipment and vehicles
GEOGRAPHIC LIMITS OF INVESTMENTS/LOANS: International
RANGE OF INV./LOAN PER BUSINESS: Min. $3,000; Max. $100 million
PREFERRED TERM FOR LOANS & LEASES: Min. 2 years; Max. 10 years
BUSINESS CHARACTERISTICS DESIRED-REQUIRED: Minimum number of years in business: 3
REFERRALS: Investment/Mortgage banker;Borrower/Investee

COMPANY: **Houser Financial Services, Inc.**
ADDRESS: P.O. 637
Beverly, OH 45715
PHONE: (614) 984-2393
TYPE OF INSTITUTION: Leasing and Equipment Financing
CONTACT OFFICER(S): Gary W. Warden, Executive V.P.
INVESTMENTS/LOANS MADE: Through private placements
TYPES OF FINANCING: LOANS: Working capital; Equipment; Equity-related, REAL ESTATE LOANS: Long-term senior mtg; Intermediate-term senior mtg; Construction, FACTORING, LEASES: Tax leases; Tax-oriented lease brokerage; Vendor financing programs
GEOGRAPHIC LIMITS OF INV./LOANS: National:
RANGE OF INV./LOAN PER BUSINESS: Min. $25,000; Max. No limit
BUSINESS CHARACTERISTICS DESIRED-REQUIRED: Mimimum number of years in business: 5 years
BRANCHES: 217 N. Sale St., Elletsville, IN., Phone: (812) 876-7038,OFFICER: Stephen Fisher, V.P.

COMPANY: **First Asset-Based Lending Group, Inc.**
ADDRESS: 120 North Robinson, Suite 880 C
Oklahoma City, OK 73102
PHONE: (405) 272-4500
CONTACT OFFICER(S): D. H. Pendley, Pres.

1COMPANY: **Bancorp Leasing Corp.**
ADDRESS: 700 NE Multnomah
Portland, OR 97232
PHONE: (503) 231-5206
TYPE OF INSTITUTION: Leasing Co.
CONTACT OFFICER(S): Merle K. Buck
TYPES OF FINANCING: LOANS: Term loans, LEASES: Single-investor; Leveraged; Tax leases; Non-tax leases; Tax-oriented lease brokerage; Lease syndications
GEOGRAPHIC LIMITS OF INVESTMENTS/LOANS: National
RANGE OF INV./LOAN PER BUSINESS: Min. $25,000
PREFERRED TERM FOR LOANS & LEASES: Min. 5; Max. 20 years
BUSINESS CHARACTERISTICS DESIRED-REQUIRED: Cash flow

COMPANY: **First Interstate Commercial Corporation**
ADDRESS: 1515 S.W. 5th Avenue, Suite 880
Portland, OR 97207
PHONE: (503) 277-7325
CONTACT OFFICER(S): Anthony E. Migas, Pres.

COMPANY: **BancAmerica Commercial Corporation**
ADDRESS: 1105 Hamilton Street
Allentown, PA 18101
PHONE: (215) 437-8265
TYPE OF INSTITUTION: Commercial Finance Co.
CONTACT OFFICER(S): Ronald P. Tweedy, Pres.
TYPES OF FINANCING: LOANS: Working capital (receivables/inventory); Equipment
PREFERRED TYPES OF INDUSTRIES/INVESTMENTS: Manufacturing wholesalers and distributors
GEOGRAPHIC LIMITS OF INVESTMENTS/LOANS: National
RANGE OF INV./LOAN PER BUSINESS: Min. $500,000; Max. $15,000,000
PREFERRED TERM FOR LOANS & LEASES: flexible
BRANCHES: J.E. Perotta, 1621 Cedar Crest Blvd., Ste. 101, Allentown, PA 18104; (215) 437-8174
B.N. Shear, 2809 Batterfield Rd., Ste. 370, Oak Brook, IL 60521; (312) 655-9105
B.M. Ward, 1111 W. Mockingbird Lane, Ste. 1320, Dallas, TX 75247; (214) 630-9833
J.A. MacFarlane, 230 Peachtree St. NW, Ste. 1650, Atlanta, GA 30343; (404) 65 6-1070
J.A. Jacobson, 200 S. Manchester Ave., Ste. 512, Orange, CA 92668; (714) 978-3440

COMPANY: **Westinghouse Credit Corp.**
ADDRESS: 2000 Oxford Drive Ste-202
Bethel Park PA 15102
PHONE: (412) 854-7022
TYPE OF INSTITUTION: Leasing company
CONTACT OFFICER(S): James W. Meighen, V.P., Leveraged Leasing
John McEnery, Manager, Leasing
TYPES OF FINANCING: LEASES: Single-investor; Leveraged; Tax leases; Vendor financing programs; Other: Trac leases
GEOGRAPHIC LIMITS OF INVESTMENTS/LOANS: National
RANGE OF INV./LOAN PER BUSINESS: Min. $3 million; Max. $25 million

PREFERRED TERM FOR LOANS & LEASES: Min. 3 years; Max. 18 years
BUSSINESS CHARACTERISTICS DESIRED/ REQUIRED: Other: Varies with the transaction

COMPANY: **First Valley Leasing Inc.**
ADDRESS: One Bethlehem Plaza
Bethlehem, PA 18018
PHONE: (215) 865-8713
TYPE OF INSTITUTION: Leasing subsidiary of bank holding company
CONTACT OFFICER(S): Patrick A. McGee, President
ASSETS: $5 million
INVESTMENTS/LOANS MADE: For own account
LOANS: Equipment, LEASES: Single-investor; Non-tax leases; Vendor financing programs
PREFERRED TYPES OF EQUIPMENT: We have no particular preference by industry or equipment. We intentionally look for a diversification by industry and equipment
Security, alarms, health clubss, energy management equipment dealers
GEOGRAPHIC LIMITS OF INVESTMENTS: Regional
RANGE OF INV./LOAN PER BUSINESS: Min. $5,000; Max. Unlimited
PREFERRED TERM FOR LOANS & LEASES: Min. 2 years; Max. 5 years
BUSINESS CHARACTERISTICS DESIRED-REQUIRED: Minimum number of years in business: 2; Min. annual sales $200,000; Min. net worth $50,000; Min. annual net income $10,000; Min. annual cash flow $10,000
REFERRALS ACCEPTED FROM: Investment/Mortgage banker and Borrower/Investee
REMARKS: First Valley Leasing Inc. is a bank related lessor. We write full pay-out leased based on the financial strength of the company

COMPANY: **American Business Credit Corp.**
ADDRESS: 650 Skippack Pike Blue Bell West, Suite 122
Blue Bell, PA 19422
PHONE: (215)278-8901
CONTACT OFFICER(S): Knute C. Albrecht, Pres.

COMPANY: **Industrial Valley Bank & Trust Company**
ADDRESS: 1700 Market Street
Philadelphia, PA 19103
PHONE: (215) 496-4352
CONTACT OFFICER(S): Paul A. Cottone, Vice Pres.

COMPANY: **PSFS**
ADDRESS: 12 South 12th Street
Philadelphia, PA 19107
PHONE: (215) 636-6000
TYPE OF INSTITUTION: Diversified Financial Services
CONTACT OFFICER(S): Philip A. McMunigal III, V.P., Private Placement Unit
ASSETS: $12.5 billion (June 30, 1984)
INVESTMENTS/LOANS MADE: For own account; Through private placements
INVESTMENTS/LOANS MADE: In securities with a secondary market and in securities without a secondary market
TYPES OF FINANCING: SECONDARY-MARKET CORPORATE SECURITIES: Common stock; Preferred stock; Bonds, VENTURE CAPITAL: Start-up from developed product stage, LOANS: Unsecured to credits above Baa; Working capital; Equipment; Equity-related, REAL ESTATE LOANS: Long-term senior mtg.; Intermediate-term senior mtg.; Land development; Construction; Standbys; Industrial revenue bonds, LEASES: Leveraged; Tax leases; Non-tax leases; Operating; Vendor financing programs, REAL ESTATE: Acquisitions; Joint ventures; Partnerships/ Syndications, OTHER SERVICES PROVIDED: pension fund advisory services, trade and stand-by letters of credit
PREFERRED TYPES OF INDUSTRIES/INVESTMENTS: all offerings considered
GEOGRAPHIC LIMITS OF INVESTMENTS/LOANS: Local; State; Regional; National; International
RANGE OF INV./LOAN PER BUSINESS: Min. $1,000,000; Max. depends on quality rating
PREFERRED TERM FOR LOANS & LEASES: Min. one year; Max. 10 years
BUSINESS CHARACTERISTICS DESIRED-REQUIRED: Negotiable

COMPANY: **Allegheny International Credit Corp.**
ADDRESS: One Allegheny Square, Suite 880, P.O. Box 6958
Pittsburgh, PA 15212
PHONE: (412) 562-4086
CONTACT OFFICER(S): Charles C. Maupin, President

COMPANY: **Dravo Leasing Company**
ADDRESS: One Oliver Plaza
Pittsburgh, PA 15222
PHONE: (412) 566-5186
TYPE OF INSTITUTION: Captive leasing subsidiary
CONTACT OFFICER(S): Patricia M. Rogan, General Manager & Asst. Treasurer
ASSETS: $35,000,000
TYPES OF FINANCING: LOANS: Equipment; Other: Mortgage, LEASES: Single-investor; Tax leases; Non-tax leases; Operating
PREFERRED TYPES OF INDUSTRIES/INVESTMENTS: Finance only Dravo products and services
GEOGRAPHIC LIMITS OF INVESTMENTS/LOANS: National
RANGE OF INV./LOAN PER BUSINESS: Max. $10,000,000
PREFERRED TERM FOR LOANS & LEASES: Min. 1-3 years; Max. 15-20 years
BUSINESS CHARACTERISTICS DESIRED-REQUIRED: Minimum number of years in business: 5

COMPANY: **Mellon Financial Services Leasing Group**
ADDRESS: Suite 3030 One Mellon Bank Center
Pittsburgh, PA 15258
PHONE: (412) 234-5061
TYPE OF INSTITUTION: Equipment Leasing sub. national bank
CONTACT OFFICER(S): Arthur Folsom, Jr., SVP, Andra Cochran: V.P. Marketing Division
Jerry Vaughn, V.P. Syndication Division

TOTAL ASSETS: $300,000,000
INVESTMENTS/LOANS MADE: For own account; Through private placements
INVESTMENTS/LOANS MADE: Only in securities without a secondary market
TYPES OF FINANCING: LOANS: Equipment, LEASES: Single-investor; Leveraged; Tax leases; Non-tax leases; Tax-oriented lease brokerage; Lease syndications
PREFERRED TYPES OF INDUSTRIES/INVESTMENTS: Transportation, communication, manufacturing, energy-related and communications
RANGE OF INV./LOAN PER BUSINESS: Min. $250,000; Max. $None
PREFERRED TERM FOR LOANS & LEASES: Min. 3 years; Max. 25 years
BUSINESS CHARACTERISTICS DESIRED-REQUIRED: Minimum number of years in business: 3; Min. net worth: $5,000,000
REFERRALS: Investment/Mortgage banker; Borrower/Investee
BRANCHES: John S. Ingham, One Post Office Square, Suite 3650, Boston, MA 02109, (617) 432-4151
Charles S. Wells, 2121 San Jacinto, Suite 2900, Lockbox 12, Dallas, TX 75201, (214) 760-9181
Douglas P. Williamson, 824 E. Street Rd. Warminster, PA 18974; (215) 585-4691

COMPANY: **Fleet Credit Corporation**
ADDRESS: 155 South Main St.
Providence, RI
PHONE: (401) 278-6915
TYPE OF INSTITUTION: Leasing Division/Secured Lending Division of Bank Holding Company
CONTACT OFFICER(S): Robert Merrick, Assistant Controller
ASSETS: $362 Million
INVESTMENTS/LOANS MADE: For own account
TYPES OF FINANCING: LOANS: Working capital. LEASES: Single-investor; Leveraged; Tax leases; Non-tax leases; Tax-oriented lease brokerage
PREFERRED TYPES OF INDUSTRIES/INVESTMENTS: Communication: Radio communication, Telephone Answering Service, etc. Printing: Printed circuit board, disks, HTM's
GEOGRAPHIC LIMITS OF INVESTMENTS/LOANS: National
RANGE OF INV./LOAN PER BUSINESS: Max. $20,000
PREFERRED TERM FOR LOANS & LEASES: Min. 3 years; Max. 8 years
BUSINESS CHARACTERISTICS DESIRED-REQUIRED: Minimum number of years in business: 3

COMPANY: **People's Bank, FSB**
ADDRESS: 145 Westminster Street
Providence, RI 02903
PHONE: (401) 456-5000
TYPE OF INSTITUTION: Mutual Savings Bank & Commercial Bank
CONTACT OFFICER(S): Stephen W. Palmer, President & CEO
Dag O. Johannessen, Sr. Vice Pres. & Treasurer
James B. Wolfe, Sr. Vice Pres. & Comm. Banking Div. Mgr.
Robert J. Branley, Sr. Vice Pres. & Retail Banking Div. Mgr.
ASSETS: $350 million
INVESTMENTS/LOANS MADE: For own account
INVESTMENTS/LOANS MADE: Only in securities with a secondary market
TYPES OF FINANCING: SECONDARY-MARKET CORPORATE SECURITIES. LOANS: Unsecured to credits above $25M; Working capital; Equipment; Equity-related. REAL ESTATE LOANS: Long-term senior mtg.; Intermediate-term senior mtg.; Wraparounds; Land; Land development; Construction; Standbys. REAL ESTATE: Acquisitions; Joint ventures; Partnerships/Syndications. OTHER SERVICES PROVIDED: All types of consumer lending.
GEOGRAPHIC LIMITS OF INVESTMENTS/L0ANS: Regional
RANGE OF INV./LOAN PER BUSINESS: Min. $10,000; Max $1.5 Million
PREFERRED TERM FOR LOANS & LEASES: Min. 1 year; Max. 5 years
REFERRALS ACCEPTED FROM: Investment/Mortgage banker or Borrower/Investee
REMARKS: We have 12 branches, but all corporate lending is done by the Commercial Banking Division at the main office

COMPANY: **Rhode Island Hospital Trust National Bank**
ADDRESS: 1 Hospital Trust Plaza
Providence, RI 02903
PHONE: (401) 278-8000
TYPE OF INSTITUTION: Pension area of a national bank
CONTACT OFFICER(S): Bernard N. Roth, Senior Vice President, Mezzamine financing for corporate buyouts
Celia R. Deluga, Assistant Vice President, Real estate financing, corporate buyout financing & financing for oil & gas properties
ASSETS: $80,000,000
INVESTMENTS/LOANS MADE: For managed accounts, Through private placements
INVESTMENTS/LOANS MADE: In securities with a secondary market and in securities without a secondary market
TYPES OF FINANCING: LOANS: Unsecured to credits above B, Baa; Other: all loans have equity features through the use of warrants, contingent interest, etc. REAL ESTATE LOANS: Intermediate-term senior mtg.; Subordinated; Wraparounds. OTHER SERVICES PROVIDED: Financing for oil & gas transactions
PREFERRED TYPES OF INDUSTRIES/INVESTMENTS: Financing for corporate buyouts: mature smoke stack manufacturing firms; Real estate financing: participating mortgages of office buildings, shopping centers, apartment complexes; Collateralized oil & gas loans, which provide a current return plus on equity sharing
WILL NOT CONSIDER: High tech firms
GEOGRAPHIC LIMITS OF INVESTMENTS/LOANS: National
RANGE OF INV./LOAN PER BUSINESS: Min. $2,000,000; Max. $20,000,000
PREFERRED TERM FOR LOANS & LEASES: Min. 7 years; Max. 12 years

BUSINESS CHARACTERISTICS DESIRED-REQUIRED: Minimum number of years in business: 5; Min. annual sales $25,000,000; Other: firms which have reasonable tangible asset coverage
REFERRALS ACCEPTED FROM: Investment/Mortgage banker or Borrower/Investee

COMPANY: **First Tennessee Bank National Association**
ADDRESS: 165 Madison Avenue
Memphis, TN 38103
PHONE: (901) 523-4632
TYPE OF INSTITUTION: Commercial Finance Division of National Bank
CONTACT OFFICER(S): Joseph D. Hardesty, Jr., Senior Vice President, Division Manager
Larry Allen, Vice President, Senior Loan Officer
ASSETS: $5 Billion Approximately
INVESTMENTS/LOANS MADE: For own account
TYPES OF FINANCING: LOANS: Working capital; Equipment; Other: Leveraged buy-outs and acquisitions. REAL ESTATE LOANS: Intermediate-term senior mtg.; Industrial revenue bonds. INTERNATIONAL
PREFERRED TYPES OF INDUSTRIES/INVESTMENTS: Textiles/Apparel; Leisure/Sporting Goods; Chemicals; Automative Aftermarket; Food Processors/Distributors; Industrial Supplies
GEOGRAPHIC LIMITS OF INVESTMENTS/LOANS: Other: Five hundred mile radius of Memphis, Tennessee.
RANGE OF INV./LOAN PER BUSINESS: Min. $1,000,000; Max. $25,000,000
PREFERRED TERM FOR LOANS & LEASES: Min. 2 years; Max. 7 years
BUSINESS CHARACTERISTICS DESIRED-REQUIRED: Minimum number of years in business: 2; Min. annual sales $5,000,000; Min. net worth $200,000; Min. annual net income $100,000; Min. annual cash flow $1,000,000.
REFERRALS ACCEPTED FROM: Investment/Mortgage banker or Borrower/Investee

COMPANY: **General Innkeeping Acceptance Corporation**
ADDRESS: P.O. Box 18127
Memphis, TN 38195
PHONE: (901) 362-4426
TYPE OF INSTITUTION: Finance/Leasing, Subsidiary of Holiday Inns, Inc.
CONTACT OFFICER(S): E. Tucker Dickerson, President
Bill Horne, Vice President
ASSETS: $25,000,000
INVESTMENTS/LOANS MADE: For own account
INVESTMENTS/LOANS MADE: Only in securities without a secondary market
TYPES OF FINANCING: LOANS: Equipment. REAL ESTATE LOANS: Subordinated. LEASES: Tax leases; Operating.
PREFERRED TYPES OF INDUSTRIES/INVESTMENTS: Hotel and Restaurant Furniture, Fixtures and Equipment
WILL NOT CONSIDER: Anything except above
GEOGRAPHIC LIMITS OF INVESTMENTS/LOANS: National
RANGE OF INV./LOAN PER BUSINESS: Min. $25,000; Max. $2,800,000
PREFERRED TERM FOR LOANS & LEASES: Min. 5 years; Max. 7 years
BUSINESS CHARACTERISTICS DESIRED-REQUIRED: Minimum number of years in business: 0
REFERRALS ACCEPTED FROM: Investment/Mortgage banker or Borrower/Investee

COMPANY: **First American Commercial Finance, Inc.**
ADDRESS: First American Center, 10th Floor
Nashville, TN 37237
PHONE: (615) 748-2069
TYPE OF INSTITUTION: Working Capital Lending—subsidiary of bank holding company
CONTACT OFFICER(S): Charles B. McMahan, Jr., President, Working Capital Financing
D. Michael Boyd, Assistant Vice President, Working Capital Financing
ASSETS: $40,000,000
INVESTMENTS/LOANS MADE: For own account
INVESTMENTS/LOANS MADE: In securities with or without a secondary market
TYPES OF FINANCING: LOANS: Working capital; Equipment
PREFERRED TYPES OF INDUSTRIES/INVESTMENTS: Manufacturers, Wholesalers, and Distributors
WILL NOT CONSIDER: Retail and Service Industries
GEOGRAPHIC LIMITS OF INVESTMENTS/LOANS: Regional
RANGE OF INV./LOAN PER BUSINESS: Min. $250,000; Max. $5,000,000
BUSINESS CHARACTERISTICS DESIRED-REQUIRED: Minimum number of years in business: 0; Min. annual sales $3,000,000-5,000,000

COMPANY: **C&G Covert Leasing, Inc.**
ADDRESS: 1700 W. 6th St.
Austin, TX 78703
PHONE: (512) 476-1903
CONTACT OFFICER(S): Clark Covert, General Manager
ASSETS: $2,000,000
INVESTMENTS/LOANS MADE: For own account, Through private placements, Through underwriting public offerings
TYPES OF FINANCING: VENTURE CAPITAL: Research & Development; Second-stage (generally 1-3 years); Later-stage expansion, LOANS: Equipment, LEASES: Single-investor; Leveraged; Tax leases; Non-tax leases; Operating; Tax-oriented lease brokerage; Lease syndications
PREFERRED TYPES OF INDUSTRIES/INVESTMENTS: Equipment leases low and middle market
RANGE OF INV./LOAN PER BUSINESS: Min. $7,500; Max. $1,000,000

PREFERRED TERM FOR LOANS & LEASES: Min. 3 years; Max. 7 years
BUSINESS CHARACTERISTICS DESIRED-REQUIRED: Minimum number of years in business: 3; Min. annual sales $1,000,000; Min. net worth $10X annual earnings; Min. annual net income 6 figure; Min. annual cash flow variable
REFERRALS ACCEPTED FROM: Investment/Mortgage banker or Borrower/Investee

COMPANY: **MBC Financial Services Corporation**
ADDRESS: 2501 Cedar Springs Road, Suite 400, LB 10
Dallas, TX 75201
PHONE: (214) 871-1200
TYPE OF INSTITUTION: Corporate Finance Group of Institutional Lender
CONTACT OFFICER(S): J. Michael McMahon, Senior Vice President
David S. Temin, Vice President
Lynne M. McGanity, Vice President
ASSETS: $500 million
INVESTMENTS/LOANS MADE: For own account
INVESTMENTS/LOANS MADE: In securities with a secondary market and in securities without a secondary market
TYPES OF FINANCING: SECONDARY MARKET CORPORATE SECURITIES: Bonds; Other: Subordinated loans, secured note financing; VENTURE CAPITAL: Later-stage expansion; Buy-outs/Acquisitions; LOANS: Unsecured; Working Capital; Equipment; REAL ESTATE LOANS: Intermediate-term senior mtg.; Wraparounds; Gap; Standbys; LEASES: Single-investor; Leveraged; Tax leases; Non-tax leases
GEOGRAPHIC LIMITS OF INVESTMENTS/LOANS: Regional
RANGE OF INV./LOAN PER BUSINESS: Min. $5 Million; Max. $20 Million
PREFERRED TERM FOR LOANS & LEASES: Min. 3 years; Max. 10 years
BUSINESS CHARACTERISTICS DESIRED-REQUIRED: Minimum number of years in business: 5; Min. annual sales $7 Million; Min. net worth $1 Million; Min. annual net income $1.5 Million; Min. annual cash flow $2 Million
REFERRALS ACCEPTED FROM: Investment/Mortgage banker or Borrower/Investee

COMPANY: **Mercantile Texas Credit Corp.**
ADDRESS: P.O. Box 220094
Dallas, TX 75222
PHONE: (214) 698-5719
CONTACT OFFICER(S): Ray G. Torgerson, Pres.

COMPANY: **Wells Fargo Business Credit**
ADDRESS: 12750 Merit Dr., Ste. 1300, Lock Box 9
Dallas, TX 75251
PHONE: (214) 386-5997
TYPE OF INSTITUTION: Commercial Finance Co.
CONTACT OFFICER(S): Harry Polly, First V.P., Marketing Director
TYPES OF FINANCING: LOANS: Working capital; Equipment; REAL ESTATE LOANS: Intermediate-term senior mtg.
PREFERRED TYPES OF INDUSTRIES/INVESTMENTS: Manufacturing and Wholesaling
WILL NOT CONSIDER: Construction
GEOGRAPHIC LIMITS OF INVESTMENTS/LOANS: National
RANGE OF INV./LOAN PER BUSINESS: Min. $2,000,000
PREFERRED TERM FOR LOANS & LEASES: Min. 2 years; Max. 5 years
BUSINESS CHARACTERISTICS DESIRED-REQUIRED: Minimum number of years in business: 2; Min. annual sales $5,000,000; Min. net worth $500,000; Min. annual net income $50,000; Other: Must have a tangible net worth.
REFERRALS ACCEPTED FROM: Investment/Mortgage banker or Borrower/Investee

COMPANY: **Southwestern Venture Capital of Texas, Inc.**
ADDRESS:
1250 N.E. Loop 410, Suite 700
San Antonio, TX 78209
PHONE: (512) 822-9949
TYPE OF INSTITUTION: Venture Capital and SBA Loans
CONTACT OFFICER(S): Kurt Nestman, President
TOTAL ASSETS: $5,000,000
INVESTMENTS/LOANS MADE: For own accout
INVESTMENTS/LOANS MADE: In securities with a secondary market; In securities without a secondary market
TYPES OF FINANCING: VENTURE CAPITAL: First-stage; Second-stage; Later-stage expansion; Buy-outs/Acquisitions, LOANS: Equipment, REAL ESTATE: Long-term senior mtg.; Other: Owner occupied only
GEOGRAPHIC LIMITS OF INVESTMENTS/LOANS: National
RANGE OF INV./LOANS PER BUSINESS: Min. $100,000; Max. $600,000
PREFERRED TERM FOR LOANS & LEASES: Min. 7 years; Max. 25 years
BUSINESS CHARACTERISTICS DESIRED-REQUIRED: Minimum number of years business: 2
REFERRALS: Investment/Mortgage banker; Borrower/investee
BRANCHES: Doug Hatten, Southwestern Commercial Capital, Inc., 100 Chase Stone Center, Suite 440, Colorado, Springs, CO 80903
Joe Justice, SWCC, 444 Executive Center Blvd., Suite 222, El Paso, TX 79902
Ron Kozak, SWCC, 101 Park Ave., Suite 950, Oklahoma City, OK 73102
Kurtis Nestman, SWCC, North Frost Center, 1250 N.E. Loop 410, Suite 700, San Antonio, TX 78209
Bill Murray, SWCC, 1301 Seminole Blvd., Suite 110, Largo, FL 33540
Scott Bobo, SWCC, 1717 Azurite Tr., Plano, TX 75075
REMARKS: Company makes SBA guaranteed loans in addition to venture capital investments

COMPANY: **AMVEST Capital Corporation**
ADDRESS: One Boar's Head Place, P.O. Box 5347
Charlottesville, VA 22905
PHONE: (804) 977-3350
TYPE OF INSTITUTION: Leasing and finance subsidiary of AMVEST Corp.
CONTACT OFFICER(S): Franklin M. Halsey, Executive V.P.
Kerry Garrison, V.P. & Credit Officer
ASSETS: $60,000,000
INVESTMENTS/LOANS MADE: For own account, Through private placements
INVESTMENTS/LOANS MADE: Only in securities without a secondary market
TYPES OF FINANCING: LOANS: Equipment, LEASES: Single-investor; Leveraged; Tax leases; Non-tax leases; Lease syndications; Vendor financing programs, OTHER SERVICES PROVIDED: Tax exempt lease purchase for municipalities
PREFERRED TYPES OF INDUSTRIES/INVESTMENTS: Broadcast, commercial, industrial, transportation, medical, thoroughbred horses
GEOGRAPHIC LIMITS OF INVESTMENTS/LOANS: National; International
RANGE OF INV./LOAN PER BUSINESS: Min. $100,000; Max. Open
PREFERRED TERM FOR LOANS & LEASES: Min. 3 years; Max 15 years
BUSINESS CHARACTERISTICS DESIRED-REQUIRED: Minimum number of years in business: 3; Min. annual sales $2,000,000; Min. net worth $1,000,000; Min. annual net income $100,000; Min. annual cash flow $100,000
REFERRALS ACCEPTED FROM: Investment/Mortgage banker or Borrower/Investee
BRANCHES: Edwin Ramos, V.P./Sales Admin., Pan Am Building, Suite 1203, Hato Rey, PR 00917; (809) 751-4050

COMPANY: **BVA Credit Corp.**
ADDRESS: 7 North 8th Street, P.O. Box 256412
Richmond, VA 23260
PHONE: (804) 771-7432
TYPE OF INSTITUTION: Commercial Finance
CONTACT OFFICER(S): G. J. Cannon, V.P.
Greg Sandvig, V.P.
TYPES OF FINANCING: LOANS: Working capital (receivables/inventory); Equipment, LEASES: Leveraged, OTHER SERVICES PROVIDED: Intermediate-term leveraged leasing
PREFERRED TYPES OF INDUSTRIES/INVESTMENTS: Manufacturing & Distributors
GEOGRAPHIC LIMITS OF INVESTMENTS/LOANS: Regional
RANGE OF INV./LOAN PER BUSINESS: Min. $250,000
PREFERRED TERM FOR LOANS & LEASES: Min. 2; Max. 7-10 years
BUSINESS CHARACTERISTICS DESIRED-REQUIRED: Min. no. of years in business: 0; Asset-Based Lending

COMPANY: **Rainier Leasing, Inc.**
ADDRESS: 600 University St.,, 7th Floor, Box C34028
Seattle, WA 98124
PHONE: (206) 621-5001
TYPE OF INSTITUTION: Leasing subsidiary of commercial bank
CONTACT OFFICER(S): Peter M. Jones, President
William A. Kelley, V.P., Marketing Manager
ASSETS: $125,000,000
TYPES OF FINANCING: LOANS: Equipment, LEASES: Single-investor
PREFERRED TYPES OF INDUSTRIES/INVESTMENTS: No preference
GEOGRAPHIC LIMITS OF INVESTMENTS/LOANS: National
RANGE OF INV./LOAN PER BUSINESS: Min. $150,000; Max. $5,000,000
PREFERRED TERM FOR LOANS & LEASES: Min. 3 years; Max. 10 years
BUSINESS CHARACTERISTICS DESIRED-REQUIRED: Min. net worth $2,000,000

COMPANY: **First Wisconsin Financial Corporation**
ADDRESS: 622 North Cass Street, Suite 200
Milwaukee, WI 53202
PHONE: (414) 765-4492
TYPE OF INSTITUTION: Asset-Based; Lending and Leasing
CONTACT OFFICER(S): Robert C. Smith, Pres.
Robert J. Schwaab, Exec. V.P.
ASSETS: $225,000,000.00
INVESTMENTS/LOANS MADE: Only in securities without a secondary market
TYPES OF FINANCING: LOANS: Working capital; Equipment; Other Buy-outs/Acquisitions; LEASES: Single investor; Leveraged; Tax leases; Non-tax leases; Operating; Vendor financing programs
PREFERRED TYPES OF INDUSTRIES/INVESTMENTS: Manufacturing & Distribution
GEOGRAPHIC LIMITS OF INVESTMENTS/LOANS: Regional
RANGE OF INV./LOAN PER BUSINESS: Min. $500,000; Max. $25,000,000
PREFERRED TERM FOR LOANS & LEASES: Min. 2; Max. 10
BUSINESS CHARACTERISTICS DESIRED-REQUIRED: Minimum number of years in business: 3; Min. annual sales $2,500,000
REFERRALS ACCEPTED FROM: Investment/Mortgage banker or Borrower/Investee

COMPANY: **Heritage Commercial Finance, Division of Heritage Bank**
ADDRESS: 435 East Mason Street
Milwaukee, WI 53203
PHONE: (414) 273-1000
TYPE OF INSTITUTION: Commercial Finance Division of Commercial Bank
CONTACT OFFICER(S): Trevor M. Morgan, President, Commercial Finance Division
ASSETS: $500,000,000
INVESTMENTS/LOANS MADE: For own account
INVESTMENTS/LOANS MADE: In securities with a secondary market and in securities without a secondary market
TYPES OF FINANCING: SECONDARY-MARKET CORPORATE SECURITIES: Other: Commercial Finance - Loans to privately owned businesses; LOANS: Working capital; Equipment; Other: Secured; LEASES: Non-tax leases

PREFERRED TYPES OF INDUSTRIES/INVESTMENTS: Heritage Commercial Finanace prefers accounts receivable to inventory; will do machinery and equipment and real estate with accounts receivable and inventory but not alone.
WILL NOT CONSIDER: Retailers, form products, livestock.
GEOGRAPHIC LIMITS OF INVESTMENTS/LOANS: Regional
RANGE OF INV./LOAN PER BUSINESS: Min. $20,000; Max. $5,000,000
PREFERRED TERM FOR LOANS & LEASES: Min. Revolving; Max. seven (7)
BUSINESS CHARACTERISTICS DESIRED-REQUIRED: Minimum number of years in business: 2; Min. annual sales $1,000,000; Min. annual cash flow: debt service
REFERRALS ACCEPTED FROM: Investment/Mortgage banker or Borrower/Investee

COMPANY: **Heritage Leasing Corporation**
ADDRESS: 435 East Mason Street
Milwaukee, WI 53203
PHONE: (414) 273-1000
CONTACT OFFICER(S): James P. Roemer, V.P., Heritage Leasing Corporaion
ASSETS: $500,000,000+
INVESTMENTS/LOANS MADE: For own account
INVESTMENTS/LOANS MADE: In securities with a secondary market and in securities without a secondary market
TYPES OF INVESTMENTS/LOANS MADE: LOANS: Working cpaital; Equipment; Other: Secured, LEASES: Non-tax leases
PREFERRED TYPES OF INDUSTRIES/INVESTMENTS: Heritage Leasing Corporation likes machinery and equipment
WILL NOT CONSIDER: Retailers, form products, livestock
GEOGRAPHIC LIMITS OF INVESTMENTS/LOANS: Regional
RANGE OF INV./LOAN PER BUSINESS: Min. $200,000; Max. $2,000,000
PREFERRED TERM FOR LOANS & LEASES: Min. revolving; Max. seven years
BUSINESS CHARACTERISTICS DESIRED-REQUIRED: Minimum number of years in business: 2; Min. annual sales $1,000,000; Min. net worth $0; Min. annual net income $0; Min. annual cash flow: debt service
REFERRALS ACCEPTED FROM: Investment/Mortgage banker or Borrower/Investee

COMPANY: **Lakeshore Commercial Finance Corp.**
ADDRESS: 610 North Water Street
Milwaukee, WI 53202
PHONE: (414) 273-6533
CONTACT OFFICER(S): Lawrence R. Appel, President

FACTORING COMPANIES

(Purchase Accounts Receivables)

CALIFORNIA

COMPANY: **Hindin/Owen/Engelke, Inc.**
ADDRESS: 8530 Wilshire Blvd., Ste. 205
Beverly Hills, CA 90211
PHONE: (213) 659-6611
TYPE OF INSTITUTION: Investment Bankers—Specializing in corporate finance/ institutional private placements
CONTACT OFFICER(S): Russell Hindin, LA, Managing Director
Jack Engelke, Chicago, (312) 357-1855
Robert Katcha, Dallas, (214) 788-4564
INVESTMENTS/LOANS MADE: Through private placements of debt through institutional investors
INVESTMENTS/LOANS MADE: Only in debt instruments without a secondary market
TYPES OF FINANCING: VENTURE CAPITAL: Buy-outs/Acquisitions; LOANS: Unsecured to credits below BAA; Working capital; Equipment; FACTORING; LEASES: Single-investor; Leveraged; Tax leases; Non-tax leases, Operating; OTHER SERVICES PROVIDED: Financing arranged for companies with annual sales of $3 million to $150 million, overall corporate financing of $1 million or more arranged for our clients through institutional lenders for such purposes as: refinancing and restructuring debt; expansion; acquitions/ leveraged buy-outs; additional working capital; etc.
PREFERRED TYPES OF INDUSTRIES/INVESTMENTS: We prefer to assist middle market sized companies who have a need for financing but have been turned down by their existing bank add other lenders they have approached
WILL NOT CONSIDER: Start-ups
GEOGRAPHIC LIMITS OF INVESTMENTS/LOANS: National
RANGE OF INV./LOAN PER BUSINESS: Min. $1 million; Max. open
BUSINESS CHARACTERISTICS DESIRED-REQUIRED: Minimum number of years in business: 2; Min. annual sales $3 million; Min. net worth $100,000; Min. annual net income open; Min. annual cash flow open
REFERRALS ACCEPTED FROM: Investment/Mortgage banker; Borrower/Investee
BRANCHES: Jack Engelke, 1220 Iroquois Drive, Naperville, IL 60540; (312) 357-1855
Robert Katcha, 14651 Dallas Parkway, Ste. 328, Dallas TX 25240; (214) 788-4564
REMARKS: Hindin/Owen/Engelke is the only national investment banking firm whose only business is arranging overall complete lines of credit for middle market companies

COMPANY: **BFI - Business Finance**
ADDRESS: 900 Lafayette St., Suite 509
Santa Clara, CA 95050
PHONE: (408) 984-7122
TYPE OF INSTITUTION: Accounts Receivable financing

CONTACT OFFICER(S):David I. Lustig, President
INVESTMENTS/LOANS MADE: For own account
TYPES OF FINANCING: LOANS: Working capital, FACTORING

COMPANY: **Connecticut Bank & Trust, R.E. Division**
ADDRESS: One Constitution Plaza
Hartford, CT 06115
PHONE: (203) 244-6269
TYPE OF INSTITUTION: Construction lender, permanent lender; intermediate lender
CONTACT OFFICER(S): Oliver W. Park, President
ASSETS: $6 billion
INVESTMENTS/LOANS MADE:
TYPES OF FINANCING: SECONDARY-MARKET CORPORATE SECURITIES, LOANS: Unsecured; Working capital; Equipment; Equity-related; Other: Construction lending, Lease finaancing, REAL ESTATE LOANS: Intermediate-term senior mtg.; Wraparounds; Land; Land development; Construction; Gap; Industrial revenue bonds, FACTORING, LEASES: Single—investor; Leveraged; Non-tax leases; Operating; Vendor financing programs, INTERNATIONAL
GEOGRAPHIC LIMITS OF INVESTMENTS/LOANS: National; International
BUSINESS CHARACTERISTICS DESIRED-REQUIRED:
REFERRALS ACCEPPTED FROM: Investment/Mortgage banker or Borrower/Investee
REMARKS: 140 Branches; out on loan: $1 billion in Real Estate

COMPANY: **J & D Capital Corp.**
ADDRESS: 12747 Biscayne Blvd.
North Miami, FL 33181
PHONE: (305) 893-0303
TYPE OF INSTITUTION: SBIC
CONTACT OFFICER(S): Jack Carmel, President
INVESTMENTS/LOANS MADE: For own account
TYPES OF FINANCING: VENTURE CAPITAL: Second-stage. LOANS: Equipment, REAL ESTATE LOANS: Wraparounds; FACTORING. LEASES. INTERNATIONAL
PREFERRED TYPES OF INDUSTRIES/INVESTMENTS: Small Business Investment Company
GEOGRAPHIC LIMITS OF INVESTMENTS/LOANS: Local; State
RANGE OF INV./LOAN PER BUSINESS: Min. $25,000; Max. $500,000
PREFERRED TERM FOR LOANS & LEASES: Min. 5 years; Max. 15/20 years
REFERRALS ACCEPTED FROM: Investment/Mortgage banker or Borrower/Investee

COMPANY: **Bankers Funding**
ADDRESS: P.O. Box 88472
Atlanta, GA 30356
PHONE: (404) 255-1980
TYPE OF INSTITUTION: Private Banking Company
CONTACT OFFICERS: Jim Ruska, Pres.
Wayne Staples, Admin/Operations
Wayne Fairchild, Financial
ASSETS: $3,500,000
INVESTMENTS/LOANS MADE: For own (company's or principals') account; Through private placements
INVESTMENTS/LOANS MADE: In securities with a secondary market and in securities without a secondary market
TYPES OF FINANCING: LOANS: Working capital (receivables/inventory); Equipment; Equity-related; REAL ESTATE LOANS: Long-term senior mtg.; Intermediate-term senior mtg.; Wraparounds; Land; Land development; Construction; Gap; FACTORING; LEASE: Single-investor; Leveraged; Tax leases; Non-tax leases; Operating; Tax-oriented lease brokerage; Vendor financing progams; REAL ESTATE: Acquisitions; Joint ventures; Partnerships/Syndications. OTHER SERVICES PROVIDED: Joint Venture, with original owners having a buyout amount
PREFERRED TYPES OF INDUSTRIES/INVESTMENTS: Anything
WILL NOT CONSIDER: Data Processing
GEOGRAPHIC LIMITS OF INVESTMENTS/LOANS: Local; State; Regional; National; Prefer regional, but have done many national transactions
RANGE OF INV./LOAN PER BUSINESS: Min. $50,000; Max. $50,000,000
PREFERRED TERM FOR LOANS & LEASES: Min. 6 months; Max. 10 years
BUSINESS CHARACTERISTICS DESIRED-REQUIRED; Minimum number of years in business: 1 year; Min. annual sales $100,000; Min. net worth $50,000; Min. annual net income $50,000; Min. annual cash flow $75,000

COMPANY: **The Citizens and Southern National Bank**
ADDRESS: P.O. Box 4431
Atlanta, GA 30302
PHONE: (404) 491-4188
TYPE OF INSTITUTION: Equipment Financing and Leasing Dept. of C & S National Bank
CONTACT OFFICER(S): G. Fred Costabile, V.P. and Marketing Manager
Bill G. Fite, A.V.P.
David Flanary, A.V.P.
Robert Capalbo, Leasing Officer
ASSETS: $7 billion
INVESTMENTS/LOANS MADE: For own account
TYPES OF FINANCING: LOANS: Equipment; FACTORING; LEASES: Single-investor; Tax leases; Non-tax leases; Lease syndications; OTHER SERVICES PROVIDED: Full service banking for Southeastern Equipment Distributors
PREFERRED TYPES OF INDUSTRIES/INVESTMENTS: Manufacturing; Transportation; Construction; Leasing Companies
GEOGRAPHIC LIMITS OF INVESTMENTS/LOANS: Regional
RANGE OF INV./LOAN PER BUSINESS: Min. $100,000; Max $7,000,000
PREFERRED TERM FOR LOANS & LEASES: Min. 3 years; Max. 15 years
REFERRALS ACCEPTED FROM: Investment/Mortgage banker only

COMPANY: **Citizens and Southern Commercial Corporation**

ADDRESS: 2059 Cooledge Road, (P.O. Box 4095, Atlanta 30302)
Tucker, GA 30084
PHONE: (404) 491-4839
TYPE OF INSTITUTION: Factoring, commercial finance, equipment leasing & financing (sub. of Commercial Bank)t
CONTACT OFFICER(S): Charles Mitchell, Senior V.P., Commercial Finance
Joel Chasteen, Sr. V.P. & Manager, Equipment Leasing
Bart Smith, Sr. V.P., Factoring
ASSETS: $7,620,000,000
TYPES OF FINANCING: LOANS: Working capital; Equipment, FACTORING, LEASES: Single-investor; Leveraged; Tax leases; Non-tax leases; Operating, INTERNATIONAL
PREFERRED TYPES OF INDUSTRIES/INVESTMENTS: For factoring: apparel, textiles, furniture, carpet, seafood industries; for leasing and commercial finance: manufacturers, distributors
GEOGRAPHIC LIMITS OF INVESTMENTS/LOANS: National; International
RANGE OF INV./LOAN PER BUSINESS: Max. $20,000,000
PREFERRED TERM FOR LOANS & LEASES: Min. 90 days; Max. 7 years
BUSINESS CHARACTERISTICS DESIRED-REQUIRED: Minimum number of years in business: 0; Min. annual sales $1,000,000; Min. net worth $200,000; Min. annual net income $20,000; Min. annual cash flow none; Other: Guaranties of principals with closely-held firms
REFERRALS ACCEPTED FROM: Investment/Mortgage banker or Borrower/Investee
BRANCHES: Claude McEwen, A.V.P., 300 S. Thornton Avenue, Dalton, GA 30720; (404) 278-1929
Fred Gaylord, V.P., 9841 Airport Blvd., Suite 300, Los Angeles, CA 90045; (213) 670-4772; Matthew Creo Jr., Sr. V.P., 1430 Broadway, 19th Floor, New York, NY 10018, 212-719-3700

COMPANY: **Atlanta Financial & Leasing, Inc.**
ADDRESS: 4501 Circle 75 Parkway, Suite A-1240
Atlanta, Georgia 30339
PHONE: (404) 955-2856
TYPE OF INSTITUTION: Financial and leasing brokers, mortgage loans
CONTACT OFFICERS(S): Doug Faust, Owner
Equipment leasing and financing, also act as consultants in the area of equipment purchases. Expertise in the marine (offshore) industry.
INVESTMENTS/LOANS MADE: Through private placements
INVESTMENTS/LOANS MADE: In securities with a secondary market and securities without a secondary market
TYPES OF FINANCING: LOANS: Unsecured; Working capital (receivables/inventory); Equipment; Equity-related; REAL ESTATE LOANS: Long-term senior mtg.; Intermediate-term senior mtg.; Standbys; Industrial revenue bonds; FACTORING; LEASES: Single-investor; Leveraged; Tax leases; Non-tax leases; Operating; Tax-oriented lease brokerage; Lease syndications; Vendor financing programs; REAL ESTATE: Joint ventures. OTHER: Equipment purchases, expertise in the marine industry

PREFERRED TYPES OF INDUSTRIES/INVESTMENTS: Middle market construction, medical, data processing, certain real estate transaction, equipment leasing
GEOGRAPHIC LIMITS OF INVESTMENTS/LOANS: Local; State; Regional; National; International
RANGE OF INV./LOAN PER BUSINESS: Min. $100,000; Max. $ no limit
PREFERRED TERM FOR LOANS & LEASES: Min. 3 years; Max. as pertinent
BUSINESS CHARACTERISTICS DESIRED-REQUIRED: We will look at any situation. It does need to make sense

COMPANY: **Associates Commercial Corporation**
ADDRESS: The Associates Center, 150 North Michigan Ave.
Chicago, IL 60601
PHONE: (312) 781-5800
TYPE OF INSTITUTION: Commercial finance subsidiary of Associates Corporation of North America (The Associates), the cornerstone on the Financial Services Group of Gulf & Western Industries, Inc.
CONTACT OFFICER(S): Rocco A. Macri, Executive Vice President, Business Loans Division (Division provides accounts receivable, inventory and fixed asset loans for working capital, refinancings, acquisitions and leveraged buyouts for small annd medium-sized businesses throughout the U.S.).
ASSETS: $6.6 billion (The Associates); $3.5 billion in commerical finance recievables
INVESTMENTS/LOANS MADE: For own account
INVESTMENTS/LOANS MADE: Only in securities without a secondary market
TYPES OF FINANCING: VENTURE CAPITAL: Later-stage expansions; Buy-outs/Acquisitions, LOANS: Working capital; Equipment; Equity-related. Other: Bank participation, REAL ESTATE LOANS: Industrial plants with receivables/inventory, FACTORING, LEASES: Single-investor; Tax leases; Non-tax leases; Operating; Vendor financing programs, REAL ESTATE: Acquisitions, OTHER SERVICES PROVIDED: Retail and wholesale financing of heavy duty trucks and trailers, financing and leasing of construction and mining equipment, machine tools, business aircraft and other capital goods; fleet leasing and management services for cars and trucks
PREFERRED TYPES OF INDUSTRIES/INVESTMENTS: Heavy-duty truck and trailer financing; auto, truck and trailer fleet leasing; communications and industrial equipment financing and leasing; business loans (esp. leveraged buyout financing); and factoring
WILL NOT CONSIDER: Unsecured financing
GEOGRAPHIC LIMITS OF INVESTMENTS/LOANS: National
RANGE OF INV./LOAN PER BUSINESS: Min. $500,000; Max. $100 million or more
PREFERRED TERM FOR LOANS & LEASES: Min. two (2) years; Max. ten (10) years
BUSINESS CHARACTERISTICS DESIRED-REQUIRED: Minimum net worth $500,000
REFERRALS ACCEPTED FROM: Investment/Mortgage banker or Borrower/Investee
BRANCHES: More than 100 regional and branch offices in North America

REMARKS: Associates Commerical has six operting divisions: Business Loans, Communications, Equipment, Factoring , Fleet Leasing and Transportation

COMPANY: **The Illinois Company, Inc.**
ADDRESS: 30 N. LaSalle Street
Chicago, IL 60602
PHONE: (312) 444-2100
TYPE OF INSITITION: Investment Banking
CONTACT OFFICER(S): William A. Penner, Executive Vice President, Corporate Finance
Murray R. Lessinger, Corporate Finance Associate
ASSETS: $29 million
INVESTMENT/LOANS MADE: For managed accounts; Through private placements; Through underwriting public offerings
INVESTMENT/LOANS MADE: Only in securities with a secondary market
TYPES OF FINANCING: SECONDARY-MARKET CORPORATE SECURITIES: Common stock; Preferred stock; Bonds; VENTURE CAPITAL: Reseach & Development; Start-up from developed product stage; First-stage (less than 1 year); Second-stage (generally 1-3 year); Later-stage expansion; Buy-outs/Acquistions; LOANS: Working capital; Equipment; FACTORING: REAL ESTATE
PREFERRED TYPES OF INDUSTRIES/INVESTMENTS: All
GEOGRAPHIC LIMITS OF INVESTMENTS/LOANS: National
RANGE OF INV./LOAN PER BUSINESS: Min. $500,000
BUSINESS CHARACTERISTICS DESIRED-REQUIRED: Minimum number of years in business: 0
REFERRALS ACCEPTED FROM: Investment/Mortgage banker or Borrower/Investee
BRANCHES: Patricia C. Bryan, 1902 Round Barn road, Champaign Illinois 61812; (217) 352-5201; Vice President
James Barnes, 221 West Washington, Waukegan, IL 60085; 623-0245; Branch Mgr.

COMPANY: **Walter E. Heller & Co./Commercial & Industrial Equipment Financing Group**
ADDRESS: 105 West Adams Street
Chicago, IL 60603
PHONE: (312) 621-7600
TYPE OF INSTITUTION: Equipment leasing and financing
CONTACT OFFICER(S): Samuel L. Eichenfield, President
INVESTMENTS/LOANS MADE: For own account
TYPES OF FINANCING: LOANS: Working capital; Equipment, REAL ESTATE LOANS; FACTORING, LEASES: Single-investor; Leveraged; Tax leases; Non-tax leases; Lease syndications; OTHER SERVICES PROVIDED: Floor planning
PREFERRED TYPES OF INDUSTRIES/INVESTMENTS: All types of capital equip. for businesses
GEOGRAPHIC LIMITS OF INVESTMENTS/LOANS: National
RANGE OF INV./LOAN PER BUSINESS: Min. $50,000; Max. No
PREFERRED TERM FOR LOANS & LEASES: Min. 3 years; Max. 10 years
BUSINESS CHARACTERISTICS DESIRED-REQUIRED: Minimum number of years in business: 3
REFERRALS ACCEPTED FROM: Investment/Mortgage banker or Borrower/Investee

COMPANY: **Borg-Warner Capital Services Corporation**
ADDRESS: 1355 E. Remington Rd. Suite J
Schaumburg, IL 60195
PHONE: (312) 843-6969
TYPE OF INSTITUTION: Investment Banking
CONTACT OFFICER(S): Thomas S. Ablum, Managing Director
Stephen R. Anderson, Operations Manager
INVESTMENTS/LOANS MADE: For managed accounts, Through private placements
TYPES OF FINANCING: LOANS: Working capital. REAL ESTATE LOANS: Long-term senior mtg.; Subordinated; Wraparounds; Land development; Construction; Industrial revenue bonds. LEASES: Single-investor; Leveraged; Tax leases; Non-tax leases; Tax-oriented lease brokerage; Lease syndications; Vendor financing programs. REAL ESTATE: Acquisitions. OTHER SERVICES PROVIDED: Financial Advisory Services & arrangement of above financing structures
PREFERRED TYPES OF INDUSTRIES/INVESTMENTS: No Preferences
WILL NOT CONSIDER: Land Only Acquisition & Venture Capital
RANGE OF INV./LOAN PER BUSINESS: Min. $250,000
PREFERRED TERM FOR LOANS & LEASES: Min. 1 year loan/5 leases; Max. 15 year loan/20 year lease
BUSINESS CHARACTERISTICS DESIRED-REQUIRED: Minimum number of years in business: 3; Min. annual sales $10MM; Min. net worth $500,000; Min annual net income $200,000
REFERRALS ACCEPTED FROM: Investment/Mortgage banker or Borrower/Investee

COMPANY: **First Union Commercial Corporation**
ADDRESS: First Union Plaza
Charlotte, NC 28288
PHONE: (704) 374-6000
TYPE OF INSTITUTION: Asset based financing subsidiary of First Union National Bank
CONTACT OFFICER(S): Wayne F. Robinson, Vice President - Factoring
(H. Leon McGee, Vice President - Commercial Financing
Joseph J. Palisi, Vice President - Term Equipment Lending
ASSETS: $150,000,000.
INVESTMENTS/LOANS MADE: For own account
TYPES OF FINANCING: SECONDARY-MARKET CORPORATE SECURITIES: Secured lending transaction only; LOANS: Working capital; Equipment, REAL ESTATE LOANS: real estate only in conjunction with factoring, accts. receivable or equip. financing; FACTORING, LEASES: Single-investor; Leveraged; Tax leases; Non-tax leases; Tax-oriented lease brokerage; Lease syndications; Vendor financing programs; Other: Municipal leases; INTERNATIONAL

PREFERRED TYPES OF INDUSTRIES/INVESTMENTS: No preference
GEOGRAPHIC LIMITS OF INVESTMENTS/LOANS: National
RANGE OF INV./LOAN PER BUSINESS: Min. $250,000; Max. $25,000,000
PREFERRED TERM FOR LOANS & LEASES: Min. 2 years; Max. 10 years
BUSINESS CHARACTERISTICS DESIRED-REQUIRED: All variable depending on strength of collateral
REFERRALS ACCEPTED FROM: Investment/Mortgage banker or Borrower/Investee
BRANCHES: Robert Schettini, Senior Vice President, 260 Madison Avenue, New York, NY 10016; (212) 953-0123
Lewis W. Spiller, Vice President, 100 Galleria Parkway, Atlanta, GA 30339, (404) 953-4875

COMPANY: **First Factors Corporation**
ADDRESS: 101 S. Main Street, P.O. Box 2730
High Point, NC 27261
PHONE: (919) 889-2929
TYPE OF INSTITUTION: Financial - specializing in old line factoring
CONTACT OFFICER(S): Earl N. Phillips, Jr., President
T. Lynwood Smith, Jr., Vice President-Marketing
INVESTMENTS/LOANS MADE: For own account
TYPES OF FINANCING: FACTORING
PREFERRED TYPES OF INDUSTRIES/LOANS: Textile, Furniture and Hosiery
GEOGRAPHIC LIMITS OF INVESTMENTS/LOANS: Local; State; Regional; National
RANGE OF INV./LOAN PER BUSINESS: Min. $50,000
PREFERRED TERM FOR LOANS & LEASES: Revolvers
BUSINESS CHARACTERISTICS DESIRED-REQUIRED: Min. number of years in business: 0; Min. annual sales $750,000; Min. net worth $75-100,000

COMPANY: **Chase-Manhattan Leasing Co.**
ADDRESS: 560 Sylvan Avenue
Englewood Cliffs, NJ 07632
PHONE: (201) 894-4405
CONTACT OFFICER(S): Theodore Daleiden, Leasing
Frank Donahue, Loans
TYPES OF FINANCING: LOANS, LEASES
PREFERRED TYPES OF INDUSTRIES/INVESTMENTS: Electronics, Communications
GEOGRAPHIC LIMITS OF INVESTMENTS/LOANS: National
RANGE OF INV./LOAN PER BUSINESS: Min. $25,000
PREFERRED TERM FOR LOANS & LEASES: Max. 7 years
BRANCHES: Boston, MA
Atlanta, GA
Dallas, TX
Chicago, IL
Los Angeles, CA

COMPANY: **Financial Resources Group**
ADDRESS: 110 Main Street, P.O. Box 246
Hackensack, NJ 07602
PHONE: (201) 489-6123
TYPE OF INSTITUTION: Financial services (public company)
CONTACT OFFICER(S): M.L. Beer, Manager
ASSETS: $136,744,970
INVESTMENTS/LOANS MADE: For own account, For managed accounts, Through private placements, through underwriting public offerings
INVESTMENTS/LOANS MADE: In securities with a secondary market and in securities without a secondary market
TYPES OF FINANCING: LOANS: Equipment, REAL ESTATE LOANS: Long-term senior mtg.; Intermediate-term senior mtg.; Wraparounds; Construction; Gap; Standbys; Industrial revenue bonds, FACTORING, LEASES: Leveraged: Tax leases, REAL ESTATE: Acquisitions; Joint ventures; Partnerships/Syndications
PREFERRED TYPES OF INDUSTRIES/INVESTMENTS: Real estate loans
WILL NOT CONSIDER: Unsecured
GEOGRAPHIC LIMITS OF INVESTMENTS/LOANS: National
RANGE OF INV./LOAN PER BUSINESS: Min. $500,000; Max. $75,000,000
PREFERRED TERM FOR LOANS & LEASES: Min. 3 years; Max. 30 years
BUSINESS CHARACTERISTICS DESIRED-REQUIRED: Minimum number of years in business: 2; Min. annual sales None; Other: Depends on transaction
REFERRALS ACCEPTED FROM: Investment/Mortgage banker or Borrower/Investee
BRANCHES: Alan Hirsch, 935 White Plains Rd, Trumbull, CT 06611; (203) 261-8308
Ira Shapiro, P.O. Box 1306, White Plains, NY 10602 (914) 997-1976

COMPANY: **HLC Leasing Co.**
ADDRESS: 7063 So. Virginia Street
Reno, NV 89511
PHONE: (702) 851-3313
TYPE OF INSTITUTION: Financial services
CONTACT OFFICER(S): Tom Gosh, Manager
ASSETS: Approx. $5 million
INVESTMENTS/LOANS MADE: For own account
TYPES OF FINANCING: SECONDARY-MARKET CORPORATE SECURITIES: Other: Equipment & vehicle leases and contracts—real estate financing (commercial and industrial) (residential/discount notes & deeds), LOANS: Equipment, REAL ESTATE LOANS: FACTORING, LEASES: Single-investor; Leveraged; Tax leases; Non-tax leases; Operating; Tax-oriented lease brokerage; Lease syndications; Vendor financing programs; Other: Mini-leases, managers of captives, and consultant underwriters to lending institutions, INTERNATIONAL (including import/export), REAL ESTATE: Acquisitions, Joint ventures, OTHER SERVICES PROVIDED: Real estate, brokerage, business brokerage, vehicle fleet leasing and sales (trucks and passenger cars—all makes and models)
PREFERRED TYPES OF INDUSTRIES/INVESTMENTS: Machinery tools; Construction; Mining; Warehousing; Aircraft; Industrial; Office equipment; Hotel; Motel; Restaurant; Computers; Telephone; Vehicles
GEOGRAPHIC LIMITS OF INVESTMENTS/LOANS: National; International
PREFERRED TERM FOR LOANS & LEASES: Min. 1 year; Max. 10-15 years

BUSINESS CHARACTERISTICS DESIRED-REQUIRED: Minimum number of years in business: 2; Min. annual sales $250,000; Min. net worth $150,000; Min. annual net income $25,000; Min. annual cash flow $25,000
REFERRALS ACCEPTED FROM: Investment/Mortgage banker or Borrower/Investee
REMARKS: We do accept bonafide broker business, and we will pay broker fees if legitimized

COMPANY: **Citicorp Industrial Credit, Inc.**
ADDRESS: 450 Mamaroneck Avenue
Harrison, NY 10528
PHONE: (914) 899-7000
TYPE OF INSTITUTION: Asset-Based Finance subsidiary of bank holding company
CONTACT OFFICER(S): John W. Dewey, President, Equipment Finance Leasing
Frederick S. Gilbert, Jr., Executive V.P., Asset-Based Lending
Robert H. Martinsen, Chrm. of the Bd.
David McCollum, E. V.P.,Corporate Asset Funding
Robert Laughlin, E. V.P., Equipment Finance
William Urban, E. V.P., Vendor Finance
J.R.A.C. Clement, V.P., Tax Leasing & Equity Syndication
ASSETS: $3.2 Billion
INVESTMENTS/LOANS MADE: For own account
TYPES OF FINANCING: VENTURE CAPITAL: Buy-outs/Acquisitions; LOANS: Working capital (receivables/inventory; Equipment; Buyouts/acquisitions, bulk purchase of receivables, FACTORING, LEASES: Leveraged; Tax leases; Non-tax leases; Operating; Tax-oriented lease brokerage; Lease syndications; Vendor financing programs
PREFERRED TYPES OF INDUSTRIES/INVESTMENTS: Manufacturers and Wholesalers
GEOGRAPHIC LIMITS OF INVESTMENTS/LOANS: National
RANGE OF INV./LOAN PER BUSINESS: Min. $50,000; Max. up to legal limit
PREFERRED TERM FOR LOANS & LEASES: Min. 2 to 5 years revolving loans, up to 10 years term loans
BRANCHES: 211 Perimeter Ctr. Parkway, Atlanta, GA, 30346; (404) 391-8500
3033 South Parker Road, Market Tower I, Suite 900, Aurora, CO, 80014; (303) 752-2530
200 South Wacker Drive, Chicago, IL, 60606; (312) 993-3230, (312) 993-3263
635 W. 7th St, Ste 400, Cincinnati, OH, 45203;
1300 East 9th Street, Cleveland, OH, 44114; (216) 696-6330/(216) 621-1383
717 North Harwood St., LB #85, Diamond Shamrock Tower, Dallas, TX, 75201; (214) 760-1829
101 Continental Boulevard, Suite 800, El Segundo, CA, 90245; (213) 640-1224
560 Sylvan Avenue, Engelwood Cliffs, NJ, 07632; (201) 657-7610
450 Mamaroneck Avenue, Harrison, NY, 10528; (914) 899-7000
Summit Tower — 11 Greenway Plaza, Houston, TX, 77046; (713) 627-8170
2 Allen Center, 1200 Smith Street, Houston, TX, 77002; (713) 654-2800
444 South Flower Street, Los Angeles, CA, 90071; (213) 745-3500
3435 Wilshire Boulevard, Los Angeles, CA, 90010
3090 Multifoods Tower, Minneapolis, MN, 55402
621 Lexington Avenue, New York, NY, 10043
44 Montgomery Street, San Francisco, CA, 94104; (415) 954-1166, (415) 954-1042
1111 Third Avenue, Suite 2700, Seattle, WA, 98101; (206) 382-6225
470 Totten Pond Road, Waltham, MA, 02154; (617) 890-1666
333 Hegenberger Rd., Ste 815, Oakland, CA 94621
One Sansome St., San Francisco, CA 94120
20 Executive Park - Ste 200, Irvine, CA 92714
1900 E. Golf, Schaumburg, IL 60195
1050 Connecticut Av., NW, Washington, DC 20036
1200 Ford Rd., Ste 270, Dallas, TX 75234

COMPANY: **Ambassador Factors Div., Fleet Factors Corp.**
ADDRESS: 1450 Broadway
New York, NY 10018
PHONE: (212) 221-3000
TYPE OF INSTITUTION: Commercial Finance & Factoring
CONTACT OFFICER(S): William Paolillo, VP
TYPES OF FINANCING: LOANS: Working capital (receivables/inventory); Equipment, FACTORING
PREFERRED TYPES OF INDUSTRIES/INVESTMENTS: Diversified
GEOGRAPHIC LIMITS OF INVESTMENTS/LOANS: National
RANGE OF INV./LOAN PER BUSINESS: Min. $150,000

COMPANY: **CBT Factors Corporation**
ADDRESS: 1040 Avenue of the Americas
New York, NY 10018
PHONE: (212) 944-1100
TYPE OF INSTITUTION: Commercial Finance Co.

COMPANY: **Chemical Bank — Factoring Div.**
ADDRESS: 110 E. 59th St.
New York, NY 10022
PHONE: (212) 966-8181
TYPE OF INSTITUTION: Factoring Division of Chemical Bank
CONTACT OFFICER(S): David N. Lederman, V.P. — Bus. Devel. Head
ASSETS: Excess $45 Billion (Bank)
INVESTMENTS/LOANS MADE: For own account
TYPES OF FINANCING: FACTORING
GEOGRAPHIC LIMITS OF INVESTMENTS/LOANS: National
BUSINESS CHARACTERISTICS DESIRED-REQUIRED: Minimum number of years in business: 0; Min. annual sales $1 Million Potential
REFERRALS ACCEPTED FROM: Investment/Mortgage banker or Borrower/Investee

COMPANY: **Congress Financial Corp.**
ADDRESS: 1133 Ave. of the Americas
New York, NY 10036
PHONE: (212) 840-3000
TYPE OF INSTITUTION: Commercial Finance Co.

CONTACT OFFICER(S): Robt. A. Miller, Exec. V.P.
Robt. Goldman, Pres.
TYPES OF FINANCING: LOANS: Working capital (receivables/inventory); Equipment, FACTORING, OTHER SERVICES PROVIDED: Finance Leverage Buy-outs; Turnaround Financing
GEOGRAPHIC LIMITS OF INVESTMENTS/LOANS: National
RANGE OF INV./LOAN PER BUSINESS: Min. $500,000; Max. $100,000,000
REMARKS: 6 operating branches: Los Angeles, Miami, New York, Minneapolis, Chicago, Puerto Rico; sales branches in other cities

COMPANY: **FNB Financial Co.**
ADDRESS: Two Penn. Plaza
New York, NY 10001
PHONE: (212) 613-3001
TYPE OF INSTITUTION: Commercial Finance Division—Owned by Bank of Boston
CONTACT OFFICER(S): Gabe Romeo, Senior Vice President
TYPES OF FINANCING: LOANS: Working capital; Equipment; REAL ESTATE LOANS: Land; Land development; FACTORING; INTERNATIONAL
GEOGRAPHIC LIMITS OF INVESTMENTS/LOANS: National
RANGE OF INV./LOAN PER BUSINESS: Min. $750,000
BRANCHES: All over country

COMPANY: **James Talcott Inc.; James Talcott Factors Div.**
James Talcott Business Credit, Div.
ADDRESS: 1633 Broadway
New York, NY 10019
PHONE: (212) 484-0300
TYPE OF INSTITUTION: Diversified secured financial institution.
CONTACT OFFICER(S): William R. Gruttemeyer, President
Martin H. Rod, Executive V.P.
David J. Kantes, Executive V.P.
Robert W . Kramer.Executive V.P.
Phillip E. Renle, Jr., Senior V.P.
Anthony Viola, V.P.
ASSETS: Confidential
TYPES OF FINANCING: LOANS: Working capital (receivables/inventory);Equipment; Equity-related; Leveraged buy-outs, acquisition secured by the assets of the acquired co., REAL ESTATE LOANS: Intermediate-term senior mtg.; Wraparounds; Land, FACTORING, LEASES: Single-investor; Operating; Tax-oriented lease brokerage, INTERNATIONAL (including import/export), OTHER SERVICES PROVIDED: "Boot-Strap" Acquisitions
PREFERRED TYPES OF INDUSTRIES/INVESTMENTS: We will consider all types of industries for financing and factoring loans.
WILL NOT CONSIDER: Construction and home improvement loans.
GEOGRAPHIC LIMITS OF INVESTMENTS/LOANS: National; International
RANGE OF INV./LOAN PER BUSINESS: Min. $500,000.00; Max. Unlimited
PREFERRED TERM FOR LOANS & LEASES: Min. One year; Max. Ten years
BUSINESS CHARACTERISTICS DESIRED-REQUIRED: Minimum number of years in business: 0; Min. annual sales $1,500,000; Min. net worth $250,000; Min. annual net income: open; Min. annual cash flow: open
REFERRALS ACCEPTED FROM: Investment/Mortgage banker or Borrower/Investee
BRANCHES: Donald Mintz, One Wilshire Building, Los Angeles, CA, 90017; (213) 620-9200
Vincent Panzera, 717 North Harwood Street, Suite 440, Box 36, Dallas, TX, 75201; (214) 651-8801
REMARKS: Other national offices to be opened in 1982. Parent is The Lloyds Scottish Group in Great Britain which, in turn, is controlled by The Lloyds Bank of England.

COMPANY: **Manufacturers Hanover Commercial Corp.**
ADDRESS: 1211 Ave. of the Americas, 12th Floor
New York, NY 10036
PHONE: (212) 382-7000
TYPE OF INSTITUTION: Commercial Finance Co.
CONTACT OFFICER(S): Francis X. Basile, Chairman & CEO
TYPES OF FINANCING: VENTURE CAPITAL: Start-up from developed product stage; First stage (less than 1 year); Second-stage (generally 1-3 years); Later-stage expansion; Buy-outs/Acquisitions; LOANS: Equity-related; FACTORING
GEOGRAHIC LIMITS OF INVESTMENTS/LOANS: International
RANGE OF INV./LOAN PER BUSINESS: Min. $250,000

COMPANY: **Meinhard-Commercial Corporation**
ADDRESS: 135 W. 50th St.
New York, NY 10020
PHONE: (212) 408-6000
TYPE OF INSTITUTION: Factor
CONTACT OFFICER(S): JoAnn Pesvento, AVP, New Business/Marketing
TYPES OF FINANCING: FACTORING
PREFERRED TYPES OF INDUSTRIES/INVESTMENTS: All types: Textile, Apparel, Housewares, Home Furnishings, Sporting Goods, Consumer Electronics, Plastics, Hardware, Etc. Distributors, Mfrs., Wholesalers
WILL NOT CONSIDER: Construction, Floorplanning, Venture Capital
GEOGRAPHIC LIMITS OF INVESTMENTS/LOANS: National; International
RANGE OF INV./LOAN PER BUSINESS: Min. $2,000,000
BUSINESS CHARACTERISTICS DESIRED-REQUIRED: Minimum number of years in business: 0; Min. annual sales $2,000,000; Min. net worth $150,000
REFERRALS ACCEPTED FROM: Investment/Mortgage banker or Borrower/Investee

COMPANY: **Milberg Factors, Inc.**
ADDRESS: 99 Park Ave.
New York, NY 10016
PHONE: (212) 697-4200
TYPE OF INSTITUTION: Commercial Finance Co.

CONTACT OFFICER(S): Leonard L. Milberg, President
TYPES OF FINANCING: FACTORING; OTHER SERVICES PROVIDED: Commercial Financing
GEOGRAPHIC LIMITS OF INVESTMENTS/LOANS: National

COMPANY: **Regulus International Capital Company, Inc.**
ADDRESS: 10 Rockefeller Plaza
New York, NY 10020
PHONE: (212) 582-7715
TYPE OF INSTITUTION: Venture Capital Company
CONTACT OFFICER(S): Lee H. Miller, President
INVESTMENTS/LOANS MADE: For own account, For managed accounts, Through private placements
TYPES OF FINANCING: VENTURE CAPITAL: Research & Development; Start-up from developed product stage; Second-stage (generally 1-3 years); Buy-outs/Acquisitions, FACTORING, INTERNATIONAL (including import/export), REAL ESTATE
PREFERRED TYPES OF INDUSTRIES/INVESTMENTS: Printing, Packaging & Converting, Plastics
GEOGRAPHIC LIMITS OF INVESTMENTS/LOANS: Regional
RANGE OF INV./LOAN PER BUSINESS: Min. $200,000; Max. $2,000,000

COMPANY: **Republic Factors Corp.**
ADDRESS: 355 Lexington Avenue
New York, NY 10017
PHONE: (212) 573-5500
TYPE OF INSTITUTION: Factor
CONTACT OFFICER(S): Robert S. Sandler, Executive V.P.
Saul Langer, Executive V.P.
Morton Leader, Sr. V.P.
TYPES OF FINANCING: FACTORING
GEOGRAPHIC LIMITS OF INVESTMENTS/LOANS: National; International;F18REFERRALS ACCEPTED FROM: Borrower/investee;
BRANCHES: Samuel Ehrlich, Exec. V.P., 1605 West Olympic Blvd., Los Angeles, CA 90015; (213) 383-9355

COMPANY: **Rosenthal & Rosenthal, Inc.**
ADDRESS: 1451 Broadway
New York, NY 10036
PHONE: (212) 790-1418
TYPE OF INSTITUTION: Commercial Finance Co.
CONTACT OFFICER(S): Melvin E. Rubenstein, Exec. V.P.
TYPES OF FINANCING: VENTURE CAPITAL: Startups; First stage; Second stage; Later-stage expansion; Buy-outs/Acquisitions. LOANS: Working capital (receivables/inventory); Equipment, FACTORING. INTERNATIONAL. REAL ESTATE: Acquisitions
GEOGRAPHIC LIMITS OF INVESTMENTS/LOANS: National
RANGE OF INV./LOAN PER BUSINESS: Min. $100,000; Max. $20,000,000
PREFERRED TERM FOR LOANS & LEASES: Min. 1 yr.; Max. 10 yrs.

COMPANY: **The Slavenburg Corp.**
ADDRESS: One Penn Plaza
New York, NY 10119
TYPE OF INSTITUTION: Factoring & Commercial Finance
CONTACT OFFICER(S): V. P. Arminio, President
C. D. Manikas, Executive Vice President
ASSETS: Wholly owned subsidiary of Credit Lyonnais Bank Nederland N.V., The Netherlands
TYPES OF FINANCING: LOANS: Working capital (receivables/inventory); FACTORING; INTERNATIONAL (including import/export)
GEOGRAPHIC LIMITS OF INVESTMENTS/LOANS: National;
PREFERRED TERM FOR LOANS & LEASES: Under 1 year
BRANCHES: 3407 West 6th Street, Los Angeles, CA 90026 (213) 387-3629; A. Roy Saltzman, Vice President

COMPANY: **Standard Financial Corporation**
ADDRESS: 540 Madison Avenue
New York, NY 10022
PHONE: (212) 826-8000
TYPE OF INSTITUTION: Banking, financing, leasing and factoring
CONTACT OFFICER(S): Louis J. Cappelli, Executive V.P.
ASSETS: $100,000,000 and up
INVESTMENTS/LOANS MADE: For own account
TYPES OF FINANCING: LOANS, REAL ESTATE LOANS: Long-term senior mtg.; Intermediate-term senior mtg.; Wraparounds; Land; Land development; Construction; Gap; Standbys, FACTORING, LEASES: Single-investor; Leveraged; Tax leases; Non-tax leases; Operating; Tax-oriented lease brokerage; Lease syndications; Vendor financing programs, INTERNATIONAL (including import/export), REAL ESTATE
GEOGRAPHIC LIMITS OF INVESTMENTS/LOANS: International
RANGE OF INV./LOAN PER BUSINESS: Min. $100,000.00; Max. $15 million
BRANCHES: Kenneth W. Grubbs, V.P., Security Industrial Loan Association, 4th and Main St., Richmond, VA, 23219; (804) 649-1120

COMPANY: **United Credit Corporation**
ADDRESS: 10 East 40 St.
New York, NY 10016
PHONE: (212) 689-9480
TYPE OF INSTITUTION: Independent Co. Asset Based Lending Service
CONTACT OFFICER(S): Leonard R. Landis, President
ASSETS: $15 Million
INVESTMENTS/LOANS MADE: For managed accounts
TYPES OF FINANCING: LOANS: Working capital (receivables/inventory); Equipment, FACTORING
PREFERRED TYPES OF INDUSTRIES/INVESTMENTS: Mfg. & Service
WILL NOT CONSIDER: Construction, Retail
GEOGRAPHIC LIMITS OF INVESTMENTS/LOANS: Local; State; Regional; NY; NJ; Conn; New England
RANGE OF INV./LOAN PER BUSINESS: Min. $25,000; Max. $500,000

PREFERRED TERM FOR LOANS & LEASES: Revolving A/R
BUSINESS CHARACTERISTICS DESIRED-REQUIRED: Minimum number of years in business: 0;Min. annual sales $300,000; Each situation stands on its own merits

COMPANY: **Walter E. Heller & Company**
ADDRESS: 101 Park Avenue
New York, NY 10178
PHONE: (212) 880-7062
TYPE OF INSTITUTION: Commercial Finance Company
CONTACT OFFICER(S): Robert Spitalnic, Sr. V.P.
ASSETS: $6 Billion
TYPES OF FINANCING: Asset-Based Financing, LOANS: Working capital (receivables/inventory); Equipment, FACTORING, Leveraged Buyout Financing (Asset-Based)
PREFERRED TYPES OF INDUSTRIES/INVESTMENTS: Manufacturing and Distribution
WILL NOT CONSIDER: Unsecured Financing, or Start-Ups
GEOGRAPHIC LIMITS OF INVESTMENTS/LOANS: International
RANGE OF INV./LOAN PER BUSINESS: Min. $1,000,000; Max. $50,000,000 and up
PREFERRED TERM FOR LOANS & LEASES: Min. 1; Max. 8 years
BUSINESS CHARACTERISTICS DESIRED-REQUIRED: Minimum number of years in business: 2; Min. annual sales $5 Million
REFERRALS ACCEPTED FROM: Investment/Mortgage banker or Borrower/Investee
BRANCHES: Boston, Chicago, Dallas, Los Angeles, Miami, Montreal, syracuse, Toronto

COMPANY: **Houser Financial Services, Inc.**
ADDRESS: P.O. 637
Beverly, OH 45715
PHONE: (614) 984-2393
TYPE OF INSTITUTION: Leasing and Equipment Financing
CONTACT OFFICER(S): Gary W. Warden, Executive V.P.
INVESTMENTS/LOANS MADE: Through private placements
TYPES OF FINANCING: LOANS: Working capital; Equipment; Equity-related, REAL ESTATE LOANS: Long-term senior mtg; Intermediate-term senior mtg; Construction, FACTORING, LEASES: Tax leases; Tax-oriented lease brokerage; Vendor financing programs
GEOGRAPHIC LIMITS OF INV./LOANS: National:
RANGE OF INV./LOAN PER BUSINESS: Min. $25,000; Max. No limit
BUSINESS CHARACTERISTICS DESIRED-REQUIRED: Mimimum number of years in business: 5 years
BRANCHES: 217 N. Sale St., Elletsville, IN., Phone: (812) 876-7038,OFFICER: Stephen Fisher, V.P.

COMPANY: **Cromwell & Kyle**
ADDRESS: 234 Fountainville Center
Fountainville, PA 18923
PHONE: (215) 249-3583
TYPE OF INSTITUTION: Consulting Investment Bankers
CONTACT OFFICER(S): Alec B. Kyle
Roger J.K. Cromwell
INVESTMENTS/LOANS MADE: Through private placements
INVESTMENTS/LOANS MADE: In securities without a secondary market
TYPES OF FINANCING: SECONDARY-MARKET CORPORATE SECURITIES: Common stock; Preferred stock; Bonds, VENTURE CAPITAL: Research & Development; Start-up from developed product stage; First-stage (less than 1 year); Second-stage (generally 1-3 years); Later-stage expansion; Buy-outs/ Acquisitions, LOANS: Unsecured; Working capital (receivables/inventory); Equipment; Equity-related; Other: Mezzanine financing in leveraged buy-outs. Loans against receivables from Mexican government entities, REAL ESTATE LOANS: Long-term senior mtg.; Intermediate-term senior mtg.; Subordinated; Wraparounds; Land; Land development; Construction; Gap; Standbys; Industrial revenue bonds, FACTORING, INTERNATIONAL (including import/ export), REAL ESTATE: Acquisitions; Joint ventures; Partnerships/Syndications, OTHER SERVICES PROVIDED: Restructuring financings to command low-interest Swiss funding
PREFERRED TYPES OF INDUSTRIES/INVESTMENTS: No preference
GEOGRAPHIC LIMITS OF INVESTMENTS/LOANS: National; International
RANGE OF INV./LOAN PER BUSINESS: Min. $500,000; Max. $75,000,000
REFERRALS ACCEPTED FROM: Investment/Mortgage banker or Borrower/Investee
BRANCHES: 1960 Bronson Rd., Fairfield, CT 06430; (203) 259-3269

COMPANY: **Universal Financial Corporation**
ADDRESS: 56 Broad Street, P.O. Box 1014
Charleston, SC 29402
PHONE: (803) 577-4324
TYPE OF INSTITUTION: Business and financial broker
CONTACT OFFICER(S): William E. Craver, Jr., President
INVESTMENTS/LOANS MADE: For own account, Through private placements, Through underwriting public offerings
INVESTMENTS/LOANS MADE: In securities with a secondary market and in securities without a secondary market
TYPES OF FINANCING: VENTURE CAPITAL: Start-up from developed product stage; First-stage (less than 1 year); Second-stage (generally 1-3 years); Later-stage expansion; Buy-outs/Acquisitions, LOANS: Working capital (receivables/inventory); Equipment, Equity-related, REAL ESTATE LOANS: Intermediate-term senior mtg., FACTORING, LEASES: Single-investor; Operating; Tax-oriented lease brokerage; Vendor financing programs, REAL ESTATE: Acquisitions; Joint ventures, OTHER SERVICES PROVIDED: Financial consulting
GEOGRAPHIC LIMITS OF INVESTMENTS/LOANS: Regional; National
RANGE OF INV./LOAN PER BUSINESS: Min. $250,000; Max. Open
PREFERRED TERM FOR LOANS & LEASES: Min. Open; Max. Open

BUSINESS CHARACTERISTICS DESIRED-REQUIRED: Minimum number of years in business: 0
REFERRALS ACCEPTED FROM: Investment/Mortgage banker or Borrower/Investee

COMPANY: **Juig U.S. Management, Inc.**
ADDRESS: 1008 N. Bowen Road
Arlington, TX 76012
PHONE: (817) 860-5222
TYPE OF INSTITUTION: Financial Management Division Of Merchant/Investment Banking Firm
CONTACT OFFICER(S): John Ross, Chief Executive Officer
Byron K. Devine, C.P.A. Executive Vice President
P.J. Clark, Asst. Vice President
ASSETS: $50,000,000 (Approx.)
INVESTMENTS/LOANS MADE: For own account, For managed accounts
INVESTMENTS/LOANS MADE: In securities with or without a secondary market
TYPES OF FINANCING: SECONDARY-MARKET CORPORATE SECURITIES: Bonds; Other: Certain capital notes, warrants & debentures. VENTURE CAPITAL: Second-stage; Later-stage expansion; Buy-outs/Acquisitions. LOANS: Working capital; Equipment; Other: Secured credits (4-10 yr. term). REAL ESTATE LOANS: Long-term senior mtg.; Land; Standbys; Industrial revenue bonds. FACTORING. LEASES: Vendor financing programs. INTERNATIONAL. REAL ESTATE: Acquisitions. OTHER SERVICES PROVIDED: Various domestic/ international financial services for selected clients.
PREFERRED TYPES OF INDUSTRIES/INVESTMENTS: Investments in ongoing companies; Income producing real estate
WILL NOT CONSIDER: Industries, Equipment
GEOGRAPHIC LIMITS OF INVESTMENTS/LOANS: International
RANGE OF INV./LOAN PER BUSINESS: Min. $250,000; Max. $5,000,000 (Normally)
PREFERRED TERM FOR LOANS & LEASES: Min. 4 years; Max. 10 years domestically, 20 years internationally
BUSINESS CHARACTERISTICS DESIRED-REQUIRED: Min. annual sales $1,000,000; Min. annual cash flow $250,000
REFERRALS ACCEPTED FROM: Investment/Mortgage banker or Borrower/Investee
REMARKS: Any submissions must demonstrate annual minimum internal rate on return on cash of 25%, after infusion and before debt service.

COMPANY: **Miller, Martin & Co.**
ADDRESS: Box 328
Dallas, TX 75221
PHONE: (214) 922-0029
TYPE OF INSTITUTION: Commercial Finance Co.
CONTACT OFFICER(S): Richard Miller, Pres.
Bill MaHaley V.P.
TYPES OF FINANCING: FACTORING
PREFERRED TYPES OF INDUSTRIES/INVESTMENTS: Service Related Industries
GEOGRAPHIC LIMITS OF INVESTMENTS/LOANS: National
BUSINESS CHARACTERISTICS DESIRED-REQUIRED: Varies

COMPANY: **KBK Financial Inc.**
ADDRESS: P.O Box 61487, 1320 Niels Esperson Bldg.
Houston, TX 77208
PHONE: (713) 224-4791
TYPE OF INSTITUTION: Commercial Finance Co.
CONTACT OFFICER(S): R. Doyle Kelley, Pres.
TYPES OF FINANCING: FACTORING
PREFERRED TYPES OF INDUSTRIES/INVESTMENTS: Oil related/accounts receivable
WILL NOT CONSIDER: Retail financing or real estate financing
GEOGRAPHIC LIMITS OF INVESTMENTS/LOANS: State; Regional; Other: Texas & Louisiana, Oklahoma and New Mexico
RANGE OF INV./LOAN PER BUSINESS: Min. $50,000; Max. $1,000,000

INDUSTRIAL REVENUE BOND UNDERWRITERS

(Acquire/place/guarantee IRBs)

ALABAMA

COMPANY: **Hendrix, Mohr & Yardley, Inc.**
ADDRESS: 2020 First National-Southern Natural Building
Birmingham, AL 35203
PHONE: (205) 328-2980
TYPE OF INSTITUTION: IRB & Mun. bond dealer
CONTACT OFFICER(S): James R. Hendrix
Robert H. Cochrane
Dorothy Noyes
ASSETS: Approx. $2 million
TYPES OF FINANCING: SECONDARY-MARKET CORPORATE SECURITIES: Common stock; Preferred stock; Bonds; REAL ESTATE LOANS: Industrial revenue bonds
GEOGRAPHIC LIMITS OF INVESTMENTS/LOANS: National
RANGE OF INV./LOAN PER BUSINESS: Min. no; Max. no
REFERRALS ACCEPTED FROM: Borrower/Investee

COMPANY: **Sterne, Agee & Leach, Inc.**
ADDRESS: First National-Southern Natural Bldg.
Birmingham, AL 35203
PHONE: (205) 252-5900
CONTACT OFFICER(S): William K. McHenry, Jr.
Henry Elinn Jr.
Linda Daniel, Real Est. Syndication
ASSETS: $6,650,000
TYPES OF FINANCING: SECONDARY-MARKET CORPORATE SECURITIES: Common stock; Bonds, Other: Tax-exempt bonds; REAL ESTATE LOANS: Industrial revenue bonds, REAL ESTATE: Partnerships/Syndications
PREFERRED TYPES OF INDUSTRIES/INVESTMENTS: Diversified
GEOGRAPHIC LIMITS OF INVESTMENTS/LOANS: Regional
BUSINESS CHARACTERISTICS DESIRED-REQUIRED: Financially strong
BRANCES: Will Hill Tankersley, P.O. Box 750, Montgomery, AL 36102; (205) 263-3892
Frank B. Frazer, 2515 1st National Bank Bld., Mobile, AL 36602; (205) 432-8886
Thomas Boyd, P.O. Box 998; Selma, AL 36702; (205) 872-6241

CALIFORNIA

COMPANY: **Bateman Eichler, Hill Richards, Inc.**
ADDRESS: 700 So. Flower St., P.O. 759 (90053)
Los Angeles, CA 90017
PHONE: (213) 625-2525
TYPE OF INSTITUTION: Mun. bond dealer
CONTACT OFFICER(S): Alexis Jackson, V.P., Public Finance
TYPES OF FINANCING: Industrial revenue bonds; Other: Residential, mtg. financing, certificates of participation
PREFERRED TYPES OF INDUSTRIES/INVESTMENTS: Diversified

GEOGRAPHIC LIMITS OF INVESTMENTS/LOANS: NationalREMARKS: 30 branches in California, 33 altogether

COMPANY: **Bangert, Dawes, Reade, Davis & Thom Incorporated**
ADDRESS: 1138 Taylor St.
San Francisco, CA 94108
PHONE: (415) 441-6161
TYPE OF INSTITUTION: Investment Bankers
CONTACT OFFICER(S): Dexter B. Dawes, Chairman
K. Deane Reade, Pres., New York, N.Y. Office
INVESTMENTS/LOANS MADE: Through private placements
INVESTMENTS/LOANS MADE: Only in securities without a secondary market
TYPES OF FINANCING: VENTURE CAPITAL: Research and Development; Buy-outs/Acquisitions, LOANS: Unsecured; Working capital; Equipment; Equity-related, Government guaranteed (FMHA, EDA, UDAG); Leveraged Buy-outs Other: Subordinated with equity features; REAL ESTATE: only plant expansions; OTHER SERVICES PROVIDED: Merger, Acquisitions & Divestitures ESOP (Employee Stock Ownersip Plans); Leveraged Buyouts
PREFERRED TYPES OF INDUSTRIES/INVESTMENTS: Will consider all
WILL NOT CONSIDER: Real Estate except Industrial Plant Expansions
GEOGRAPHIC LIMITS OF INVESTMENTS/LOANS: National; International
RANGE OF INV./LOAN PER BUSINESS: Min. $1.0 Million; Max. $100.0 Million
PREFERRED TERM FOR LOANS & LEASES: Min. 2; Max. 15 years
BUSINESS CHARACTERISTICS DESIRED-REQUIRED: Min. annual sales $3.0 Mil.; Min. net worth $0.5 Mil.; Min. annual net income $0.3 Mil
REFERRALS ACCEPTED FROM: Investment/Mortgage banker or Borrower/Investee
BRANCHES: K. Deane Reade, 3 Park Ave., New York, NY 10017; (212) 689-7404

COMPANY: **Birr, Wilson & Co. Inc.**
ADDRESS: 155 Sansome St.
San Francisco, CA 94104
PHONE: (415) 983-7700
TYPE OF INSTITUTION: Investment Bank
CONTACT OFFICER(S): H. Michael Richardson, Exec. V.P. & Mgr.; 983-7967
Ted Birr III, Chairman
Don Wetmore, Pres.
TYPES OF FINANCING: SECONDARY MARKET CORPORATE SECURITIES: Common Stock; Preferred Stock; Bonds; REAL ESTATE LOANS: Long-Term senior mtg.; intermediate term senior mtg.; industrial revenue bonds; Other: all kinds; LEASES: all kinds
GEOGRAPHIC LIMITS OF INVESTMENTS/LOANS: Western U.S.
RANGE OF INV./LOAN PER BUSINESS: Min.$500,000
PREFERRED TERM FOR LOANS & LEASES: Min. Varies

BUSINESS CHARACTERISTICS DESIRED-REQUIRED: Other: Varies
REMARKS: 23 branches

COMPANY: **Stone & Youngberg**
ADDRESS: One California Street
San Francisco, CA 94111
PHONE: (415) 981-1314
TYPE OF INSTITUTION: Investment Banker
CONTACT OFFICER(S): Scott Sollers, Partner
William Huck, Partner
Ken Williams, Partner
TYPES OF FINANCING: REAL ESTATE LOANS: Long-term senior mtg.; Industrial revenue bonds. OTHER SERVICES PROVIDED: Tax exempt municipal financing, Capital programs for municipalities, Development infrastructure, Underwrite municipal bonds
PREFERRED TYPES OF INDUSTRIES/INVESTMENTS: RE developers, Industrial park developers, Municipalities
GEOGRAPHIC LIMITS OF INVESTMENTS/LOANS: State
RANGE OF INV./LOAN PER BUSINESS: Min. $500,000; Max. $100,000,000

COMPANY: **Coughlin and Company, Inc.**
ADDRESS: 621 17th St., 19th fl.
Denver, CO 80202
PHONE: (303) 295-3000
TYPE OF INSTITUTION: Investment Banker; Municipal & CorporateFinance
CONTACT OFFICER(S): George F. Coughlin, Sr. V.P., Syndicate & Trading
James M. Coughlin, President
Dennis F. Coughlin, Sr. V.P.
TYPES OF FINANCING: REAL ESTATE LOANS: Industrial revenue bonds; OTHER SERVICES PROVIDED: Corporate finance; tax exempt municipal bonds
GEOGRAPHIC LIMITS OF INVESTMENTS/LOANS: National

COMPANY: **Hanifen Imhoff, Inc.**
ADDRESS: 1125 17th Street, Suite 1700
Denver, CO 80202
PHONE: (303) 296-2300
TYPE OF INSTITUTION: Investment Banker, Municipal Bond Underwriting and Financial Advisors
CONTACT OFFICER(S): Ned Chapman, S.V.P. Municipal Syndication
Tom Bishop, E.V.P. Public Finance Dept.
TYPES OF FINANCING: REAL ESTATE LOANS: Industrial revenue bonds
GEOGRAPHIC LIMITS OF INVESTMENTS/LOANS: Regional; Other: CO, KS, NM, UT, WY
RANGE OF INV./LOAN PER BUSINESS: Max. Limit
BUSINESS CHARACTERISTICS DESIRED-REQUIRED: Other: Depending on situation

COMPANY: **Kirchner, Moore & Co.**
ADDRESS: 717 17th Street, Ste. 2700
Denver, CO 80202
PHONE: (303) 292-1600
CONTACT OFFICER(S): Charles J. Canepa, V.P.
Robert K. Dalton, Manager & V.P.
PREFERRED TYPES OF INDUSTRIES/INVESTMENTS: Housing Bonds
GEOGRAPHIC LIMITS OF INVESTMENTS/LOANS: National

COMPANY: **American Heritage Life Insurance Company**
ADDRESS: 11 E. Forsyth St.
Jacksonville, FL 32202
PHONE: (904) 354-1776
CONTACT OFFICER(S): C. A. Verlander, V.P. Securities-Investments
Wm. L. Kluessner, Asst. V.P. & Treasurer-Mortgages
ASSETS: $100 million and up
INVESTMENTS/LOANS MADE: In securities with a secondary market and in securities without a secondary market
TYPES OF FINANCING: SECONDARY-MARKET CORPORATE SECURITIES: Common Stock; Preferred Stock; Bonds; REAL ESTATE LOANS: Intermediate term senior mortgage; Subordinated; Land; Land development; Gap; Industrial Revenue bonds
PREFERRED TYPES OF INDUSTRIES/INVESTMENTS: R. E. professional office buildings; shopping centers
GEOGRAPHIC LIMITS OF INVESTMENTS/LOANS: National
PREFERRED TERM FOR LOANS & LEASES: Min. 5-7 years (R.E.)
BUSINESS CHARACTERISTICS DESIRED-REQUIRED: Min. annual net income loan amount (R.E.)
REFERRALS ACCEPTED FROM: Investment/Mortgage banker or Borrower/Investee
REMARKS: Range for investments: $250,000-1,000,000; Range for R.E. loans: $25,000-500,000

COMPANY: **Raymond, James & Associates, Inc.**
ADDRESS: 1400 66th St. N.
St. Petersburg, FL 33710-5579
PHONE: (813) 381-3800
TYPE OF INSTITUTION: Full Line Securities Firm
CONTACT OFFICER(S): Francis S. Godbold , Exec. V.P. Corp. Finance
John Hardy, Asst. V.P., Municipal Finance Industrial Revenue Bonds
ASSETS: $79,500,000
INVESTMENTS/LOANS MADE: Through private placements, Underwriting public offerings
INVESTMENTS/LOANS MADE: In securities with a secondary market and in securities without a secondary market
TYPES OF FINANCING: SECONDARY-MARKET CORPORATE SECURITIES: Common stock; Preferred stock; Bonds; Partnerships, VENTURE CAPITAL: Buy-outs/Acquisitions; REAL ESTATE LOANS: Industrial revenue bonds, LEASES: Single-investor; Leveraged; Tax leases; Non-tax leases; Operating; Tax-oriented lease brokerage, REAL ESTATE: Partnerships/ Syndications
GEOGRAPHIC LIMITS OF INVESTMENTS/LOANS: National
REFERRALS ACCEPTED FROM: Investment/Mortgage banker or Borrower/Investee
REMARKS: 182 branches

COMPANY: **Robinson-Humphrey /American Express Inc.**
ADDRESS: 3333 Peachtree Rd., N.E.
Atlanta, GA 30326
PHONE: (404) 581-7188
TYPE OF INSTITUTION: Investment Bankers
CONTACT OFFICER(S): Thomas A. Avery, V.P., Corporate Finance
Deborah Reel
David Smith, Asst. V.P., Corporate Finance
ASSETS: $100,000,000+
INVESTMENTS/LOANS MADE: Through private placements; Through underwriting public offerings
INVESTMENTS/LOANS MADE: In securities with a secondary market and in securities without a secondary market
TYPES OF FINANCING: SECONDARY-MARKET CORPORATE SECURITIES: Common stock; Preferred stock; Bonds, VENTURE CAPITAL: Second-stage (generally 1-3 years); Later-stage expansion; Buy-outs/ Acquisitions, LOANS: Unsecured to credits above B; Working capital (receivables/inventory); Equipment, REAL ESTATE LOANS: Long-term senior mtg.; Intermediate-term senior mtg.; Land; Industrial revenue bonds, OTHER SERVICES PROVIDED: Valuations o f securities for a variety of different situations
GEOGRAPHIC LIMITS OF INVESTMENTS/LOANS: Southeast orientation, but will work with companies on a selective basis located elsewhere.
RANGE OF INV./LOAN PER BUSINESS: Min. $1,000,000; Max. None
BUSINESS CHARACTERISTICS DESIRED-REQUIRED: Minimum number of years in business: 1; Management must be in place and experienced in the business
REFERRALS ACCEPTED FROM: Investment/Mortgage banker or Borrower/Investee

COMPANY: **R. G. Dickinson & Co.**
ADDRESS: 200 Des Moines Building
Des Moines, IA 50309
PHONE: (515) 247-8100
CONTACT OFFICER(S): Robert C. Gibb, V.P., Manager, Municipal Finance Dept.
ASSETS: $30 million
BRANCHES: Chicago, IL
Los Angeles, CA
Wichita, KS
Omaha, NE
Colorado Springs, CO
INVESTMENTS/LOANS MADE: In securities with a secondary market and in securities without a secondary market
TYPES OF FINANCING: SECONDARY-MARKET CORPORATE SECURITIES: Common stock; Preferred stock; Bonds, VENTURE CAPITAL: Research & Development; Start-up from developed product stage; First-stage (less than 1 year); Second-stage (generally

1-3 years); Later-stage expansion; Buy-outs/ Acquisitions, REAL ESTATE LOANS: Industrial revenue bonds, REAL ESTATE: Acquisitions; Joint ventures; Partnerships/Syndications
GEOGRAPHIC LIMITS OF INVESTMENTS/LOANS: Primarily regional
BUSINESS CHARACTERISTICS DESIRED-REQUIRED: Minimum number of years in business; 0

COMPANY: **Clayton Brown & Associates, Inc.**
ADDRESS: 300 W. Washington St.
Chicago, IL 60606
PHONE: (312) 641-3300
TYPE OF INSTITUTION: Investment Bank, Municipal Finance
CONTACT OFFICER(S): Ed Maloney, Senior Vice President, Municipal Finance Dept.
ASSETS: $20,000,000 capital
INVESTMENTS/LOANS MADE: For own acccount (tax-exempt & IDR Bonds); Through private placements; Through underwriting public offerings
INVESTMENTS/LOANS MADE: Only in municipal securities and IR Bonds
TYPES OF FINANCING: SECONDARY-MARKET CORPORATE SECURITIES: Bonds; Tax-exempt, REAL ESTATE LOANS: Industrial revenue bonds, LEASES: Non-tax leases; Other Services Provided: Underwriting, selling, trading of tax-exempt securities
GEOGRAPHIC LIMITS OF INVESTMENTS/LOANS: National
BRANCHES: 70 Pine Street, New York, NY 10270, 212-425-9170
330 East Kilbourn Avenue, Milwaukee, WI 53202, 414-276-2236
1515 Ringling Boulevard, Sarasota, FL 33577

COMPANY: **Irwin Union Corporation**
ADDRESS: 500 Washington St., Box 929
Columbus, IN 47201
PHONE: (812) 372-0111
TYPE OF INSTITUTION: Bank holding company: subsidiaries; Irwin Union Bank, Inland Mortgage, white River Capital
CONTACT OFFICER(S): M. R. Ryan; Commercial Lending, President, Irwin Union Bank
S. K. Kreigh; Mortgage Lending, President, Inland Mortgage
D. J. Blair; Venture Capital, Vice President, White River Capital
ASSETS: $250 million
INVESTMENTS/LOANS MADE: For own account
INVESTMENTS/LOANS MADE: In securities with a secondary market and in securities wiithout a secondary market
TYPES OF FINANCING: SECONDARY MARKET CORPORATE SECURITIES; Industrial Revenue Bond Placements. VENTURE CAPITAL: Second-stage; Later-stage expansion. LOANS: Unsecured to credits Above BBB; Working capital; Equipment; Equity-related. REAL ESTATE LOANS: Long-term senior mtg.; Wraparounds; Construction; Industrial revenue bonds; Other: Primarily single family. OTHER SERVICES PROVIDED: Mortgage servicing, municipal finance, and pension management

PREFERRED TYPES OF INDUSTRIES/INVESTMENTS: Commercial Lending-all forms; Mortgage Banking-Single family, FHA/VA; Venture Capital-no preferences
GEOGRAPHIC LIMITS OF INVESTMENTS/LOANS: State; regional (prefer State)
RANGE OF INV./LOAN PER BUSINESS: Min. $100,000; Max. $2,000,000 (Venture $200,000)
PREFERRED TERM FOR LOANS & LEASES: Min. .25 years; Max. 20 years
BUSINESS CHARACTERISTICS DESIRED-REQUIRED: Minimum number of years in business: 1
REFERRALS ACCEPTED FROM: Investment/Mortgage banker or Borrower/Investee

COMPANY: **The Lincoln National Inv. Management Co.**
ADDRESS: 1300 South Clinton St.
Ft. Wayne, IN 46801
PHONE: (219) 427-2000
CONTACT OFFICER(S): Patrick E. Falconio, Sr. V.P.
Robert Stewart, 2nd V.P.
Pat Chasey, 2nd V.P.
Jim Rogers, 2nd V.P.
Barbara S. Kowalczyk, 2nd V.P.
Ann L. Warner, 2nd V.P.
TYPES OF FINANCING: LOANS: Unsecured; Equipment; Equity-related; REAL ESTATE LOANS: Intermediate term senior mtg.; Subordinated; Land development; Standbys; Bond guarantees; OHTER: Industrial Revenue Bond Guarantees; REAL ESTATE: Acquisitions; OTHER SERVICES PROVIDED: Joint ventures on proposed properties; (R.E.) partnerships (R.E.)
WILL NOT CONSIDER: Retail, automotive
GEOGRAPHIC LIMITS OF INVESTMENTS/LOANS: National; International; Other: Western Europe
RANGE OF INV./LOAN PER BUSINESS: Min. $2 million; Max. $15 million; $25 million (R.E.)
PREFERRED TERM FOR LOANS & LEASES: Min. 3 years; Max. 7 years, 10 years (R.E.)

COMPANY: **Hattier, Sanford & Reynoir**
ADDRESS: 1310 Whitney Bank Building
New Orleans, LA 70130
PHONE: (504) 525-4171
TYPE OF INSTITUTION: Mun. bond dealer
CONTACT OFFICER(S): Ronald J. Levy, Dealer-Municipal Bonds
Gus Reynoir, Partner
TYPES OF FINANCING: REAL ESTATE LOANS: Industrial revenue bonds
GEOGRAPHIC LIMITS OF INVESTMENTS/LOANS: Regional

COMPANY:**Miller & Schroeder Municipals Inc.**
ADDRESS: 7900 Xerxes Av. S. Suite 2400
Bloomington MN 55431
PHONE: (612) 831-1500; 333-2626
TYPE OF INSTITUTION: Investment Bank
CONTACT OFFICER(S): F. Warren Preeshl
TYPES OF FINANCING: REAL ESTATE LOANS: Industrial revenue bonds

COMPANY: **George K. Baum & Company**
ADDRESS: 1004 Baltimore Avenue
Kansas City, MO 64105
PHONE: (816) 474-1100
TYPE OF INSTITUTION: Corporate Finance Department—Investment Banker
CONTACT OFFICER(S): William D. Thomas, V.P., Dept. Head. Corp. Fin.
INVESTMENTS/LOANS MADE: For own account; For managed accounts; Through private placements; Through underwriting public offerings
INVESTMENTS/LOANS MADE: In securities with a secondary market and in securities without a secondary market
TYPES OF FINANCING: SECONDARY-MARKET CORPORATE SECURITIES: Common stock; Preferred stock; Bonds, VENTURE CAPITAL: Research & Development; Start-up from developed product stage; First-stage (less than 1 year); Second-stage (generally 1-3 years); Later-stage expansion; Buy-outs/Acquisitions, LOANS: Unsecured to credits above B; Working capital (receivables/inventory); Equipment; Equity-related. OTHER SERVICES PROVIDED: Merger/Aquisition/Divestiture/Leveraged Buy-out/Other Investment Banking as needed
PREFERRED TYPES OF INDUSTRIES/INVESTMENTS: No Preference
GEOGRAPHIC LIMITS OF INVESTMENTS/LOANS: National
RANGE OF INV./LOAN PER BUSINESS: Min. $1,000,000; Max. No Limit
REFERRALS ACCEPTED FROM: Investment/Mortgage banker or Borrower/Investee

COMPANY: **D. A. Davidson & Co., Inc.**
ADDRESS: Davidson Building
Great Falls, MT 59401
PHONE: (406) 727-4200
TYPE OF INSTITUTION: Investment Securities
CONTACT OFFICER(S): Eugene Hufford, Sr. V.P., Corporate and Municipal Finance
ASSETS: $33,366,826
INVESTMENTS/LOANS MADE: Through private placements; Through underwriting public offerings
INVESTMENTS/LOANS MADE: In securities with a secondary market and in securities without a secondary market
TYPES OF FINANCING: SECONDARY-MARKET CORPORATE SECURITIES: Common stock; Preferred stock; Bonds, VENTURE CAPITAL: Second-stage (generally 1-3 years); Later-stage expansion, LOANS: Unsecured to credits above BAA; REAL ESTATE LOANS: Industrial revenue bonds, LEASES: Tax-oriented lease brokerage; REAL ESTATE: Partnerships/Syndications
GEOGRAPHIC LIMITS OF INVESTMENTS/LOANS: Regional

COMPANY: **Interstate Securities Corp.**
ADDRESS: 2700 NCNB Plaza
Charlotte, NC 28280
PHONE: (704) 379-9156
TYPE OF INSTITUTION: Mun. bond dealer
CONTACT OFFICER(S): George Ivey Woodall, Jr., V.P., Pub. Finance
TYPES OF FINANCING: REAL ESTATE LOANS: Industrial revenue bonds
RANGE OF INV./LOAN PER BUSINESS: Min. $250,000; Max. Limit
BUSINESS CHARACTERISTICS DESIRED-REQUIRED: Other: Extremely variable
REMARKS: Prefer long-term bonds

COMPANY: **Financial Resources Group**
ADDRESS: 110 Main Street, P.O. Box 246
Hackensack, NJ 07602
PHONE: (201) 489-6123
TYPE OF INSTITUTION: Financial services (public company)
CONTACT OFFICER(S): M.L. Beer, Manager
ASSETS: $136,744,970
INVESTMENTS/LOANS MADE: For own account, For managed accounts, Through private placements, through underwriting public offerings
INVESTMENTS/LOANS MADE: In securities with a secondary market and in securities without a secondary market
TYPES OF FINANCING: LOANS: Equipment, REAL ESTATE LOANS: Long-term senior mtg.; Intermediate-term senior mtg.; Wraparounds; Construction; Gap; Standbys; Industrial revenue bonds, FACTORING, LEASES: Leveraged: Tax leases, REAL ESTATE: Acquisitions; Joint ventures; Partnerships/Syndications
PREFERRED TYPES OF INDUSTRIES/INVESTMENTS: Real estate loans
WILL NOT CONSIDER: Unsecured
GEOGRAPHIC LIMITS OF INVESTMENTS/LOANS: National
RANGE OF INV./LOAN PER BUSINESS: Min. $500,000; Max. $75,000,000
PREFERRED TERM FOR LOANS & LEASES: Min. 3 years; Max. 30 years
BUSINESS CHARACTERISTICS DESIRED-REQUIRED: Minimum number of years in business: 2; Min. annual sales None; Other: Depends on transaction
REFERRALS ACCEPTED FROM: Investment/Mortgage banker or Borrower/Investee
BRANCHES: Alan Hirsch, 935 White Plains Rd, Trumbull, CT 06611; (203) 261-8308
Ira Shapiro, P.O. Box 1306, White Plains, NY 10602 (914) 997-1976

COMPANY: **Kious and Company, Inc.**
ADDRESS: 900 First Interstate Bldg., P.O. Drawer L
Albuquerque, NM 87103
PHONE: (505) 243-3703
TYPE OF INSTITUTION: Mun. bond dealer
CONTACT OFFICER(S): Harold Kious, President
Mike Kious, V.P.
TYPES OF FINANCING: REAL ESTATE LOANS: Industrial revenue bonds
GEOGRAPHIC LIMITS OF INVESTMENTS/LOANS: State

COMPANY: **Hotel Investment Group, Inc.**
ADDRESS: 333 Sylvan Av.
Englewood Cliffs NY 07632
PHONE: (201) 568-2525
TYPE OF INSTITUTION: Mortgage bankers, equity investors, development consultants
CONTACT OFFICER(S): Jeffrey D. Wolfert, President
ASSETS: $6,000,000
INVESTMENTS/LOANS MADE: For own account, For managed accounts, Through private placements, Through underwriting public offerings
TYPES OF FINANCING: SECONDARY-MARKET CORPORATE SECURITIES: Hotels and motels, LOANS: Real estate, REAL ESTATE LOANS: Long-term senior mtg.; Intermediate-term senior mtg.; Subordinated; Wraparounds; Construction; Gap; Standbys; Industrial revenue bonds; Other: Any hotel related financing including JVs and acquisitions, REAL ESTATE: Acquisitions; Joint ventures; Partnerships/ Syndications, OTHER SERVICES PROVIDED: Development consulting
PREFERRED TYPES OF INDUSTRIES/INVESTMENTS: Hotels and motels only
GEOGRAPHIC LIMITS OF INVESTMENTS/LOANS: National
RANGE OF INV./LOAN PER BUSINESS: Min. $7.5 million
PREFERRED TERM FOR LOANS & LEASES: Min. 1 year; Max. 30 years
BUSINESS CHARACTERISTICS DESIRED-REQUIRED: Minimum number of years in business: 0
REFERRALS ACCEPTED FROM: Investment/Mortgage banker or Borrower/Investee

COMPANY: **Allen & Company, Inc.**
ADDRESS: 711 Fifth Ave.
New York, NY 10022
PHONE: (212) 832-8000
TYPE OF INSTITUTION: Investment Banker
CONTACT OFFICER(S): James S. Abrams, Exec. V.P.
TYPES OF FINANCING: REAL ESTATE LOANS: Industrial revenue bonds
PREFERRED TYPES OF INDUSTRIES/INVESTMENTS: Very diversified
GEOGRAPHIC LIMITS OF INVESTMENTS/LOANS: National

COMPANY: **Barr Brothers & Co., Inc.**
ADDRESS: 40 Wall St., 57th Floor
New York, NY 10005
PHONE: (212) 269-4500
TYPE OF INSTITUTION: Mun. bond dealer
CONTACT OFFICER(S): Robert F. Derry, President
TYPES OF FINANCING: SECONDARY MRKET CORPORATE SECURITIES: Common stock; Bonds; Other: Strictly tax exempt. REAL ESTATE LOANS: Industrial revenue bonds
PREFERRED TYPES OF INDUSTRIES/INVESTMENTS: Diversified
GEOGRAPHIC LIMITS OF INVESTMENTS/LOANS: National
REMARKS: Will look at most deals; A lot of older bonds; Tax-exempt municipal bonds

NEW YORK

COMPANY: **Brislin & Woram**
ADDRESS: 30 Broad Street
New York, NY 10004
PHONE: (212) 344-6370
TYPE OF INSTITUTION: Mun. bond dealer
CONTACT OFFICER(S): Andrew B. Brislin, Principal
Charles G. Woram, Principal
TYPES OF FINANCING: REAL ESTATE LOANS: Industrial revenue bonds
PREFERRED TYPES OF INDUSTRIES/INVESTMENTS: Diversified
WILL NOT CONSIDER: None
GEOGRAPHIC LIMITS OF INVESTMENTS/LOANS: National
BUSINESS CHARACTERISTICS DESIRED-REQUIRED: Dealt with on an individual basis

COMPANY: **Chapdelaine & Co.**
ADDRESS: 20 Exchange Place
New York, NY 10005
PHONE: (212) 208-2600
CONTACT OFFICER(S): Richard G. McDermott, Jr., Pres.
TYPES OF FINANCING: SECONDARY MARKET CORPORATE SECURITIES: Municipal bonds
GEOGRAPHIC LIMITS OF INVESTMENTS/LOANS: National

COMPANY: **The Drexel Burnham Lambert Group Inc.**
ADDRESS: 55 Broad St.
New York, NY 10004
PHONE: (212) 480-6000
CONTACT OFFICER(S): Frederick Joseph, Sr. Exec. V.P., Corp. Finance, Private Placements, Leasing
Joel Meszik, Industrial Revenue Bonds
Richard E. Bruce, Syndicate Dept.

COMPANY: **Herbert J. Sims & Co., Inc.**
ADDRESS: 77 Water Street
New York, NY 10005
PHONE: (212) 248-5600
TYPE OF INSTITUTION: Investment Banker and Tax-Exempt Bond Underwriter
CONTACT OFFICER(S): Herbert J. Sims, Chairman
William B. Sims, President
Jonathan R. Banton, V.P.
ASSETS: Have managed underwritings of over $2 billion
INVESTMENTS/LOANS MADE: Through private placements; Through underwriting public offerings
INVESTMENTS/LOANS MADE: In securities with a secondary market and in securities without a secondary market
TYPES OF FINANCING: REAL ESTATE LOANS: Industrial revenue bonds, OTHER SERVICES PROVIDED: Long-term financing for continuing and start-up projects with tax-exempt revenue bonds Housing for the elderly, Health Care, CATV, Recreation
GEOGRAPHIC LIMITS OF INVESTMENTS/LOANS: National
RANGE OF INV./LOAN PER BUSINESS: Min. $1,000,000
PREFERRED TERM FOR LOANS & LEASES: Min. 10; Max. 30 years

BUSINESS CHARACTERISTICS DESIRED-REQUIRED: Min. no. of years in business: 0; Cash flow coverage of debt service = 1.4 times
REFERRALS ACCEPTED FROM: Investment/Mortgage banker or Borrower/Investee

COMPANY: **Matthews & Wright, Inc.**
ADDRESS: 14 Wall Street
New York, NY 10005
PHONE: (212) 267-4470
CONTACT OFFICER(S): George W. Benoit, Chairman
William Marlin, Pres.
ASSETS: $15-20 million
TYPES OF FINANCING: REAL ESTATE LOANS: Industrial revenue bonds
GEOGRAPHIC LIMITS OF INVESTMENTS/LOANS: National

COMPANY: **Nordic American Bank Corporation**
ADDRESS: 600 Fifth Avenue
New York, NY 10020
PHONE: (212) 315-6500
TYPE OF INSTITUTION: Investment Banking
CONTACT OFFICER(S): Hans Eric Von der Groeben, EVP
Edward Mete, EVP
ASSESTS: $600,000,000
INVESTMENTS/LOANS MADE: For own account; Through private placements
INVESTMENTS/LOANS MADE: In securities with a secondary market and in securities without a secondary market;
TYPES OF FINANCING: SECONDARY-MARKET CORPORATE SECURITIES: Bonds; LOANS: Working Capital (receivables/inventory); Equipment; Equity-related. REAL ESTATE LOANS: Industrial revenue bonds. LEASES: Leveraged; Tax leases; Operating; Lease syndications; Vendor financing programs; INTERNATIONAL (including import/export)
PREFERRED TYPES OF INDUSTRIES/INVESTMENTS: Nordic related business in the U.S. U.S. businesses operating in the Nordic area.
GEOGRAPHIC LIMITS OF INVESTMENTS/LOANS: National; International;
BRANCHES: John A. Redding, SVP, Suite 1963, 135 So. La Salle St., Chicago, IL; (312) 855-1515

COMPANY: **Prudential Bache Securities Inc.**
ADDRESS: 100 Gold Street
New York, NY 10292
PHONE: (212) 791-1000
TYPE OF INSTITUTION: Investment Banker
TYPES OF FINANCING: REAL ESTATE LOANS: Industrial revenue bonds

COMPANY: **Thomson McKinnon Securities Inc.—Public Finance Department**
ADDRESS: One New York Plaza
New York, NY 10004
PHONE: (212) 482-7252
TYPE OF INSTITUTION: Public Finance Department of Investment Banking Firm
CONTACT OFFICER(S): Jay Booth, Manager and Senior V.P., Public Finance Dept. Specializing in Housing, Healthcare, Water and Sewer, Industrial Revenue Bonds, and Power-Negotiated Municipal bond issues
ASSETS: $1,315,148,000 (up to June 26, 1981)
INVESTMENTS/LOANS MADE: For own account, For managed accounts, Through private placements, Through underwriting public offerings
INVESTMENTS/LOANS MADE: In securities with a secondary market and in securities without a secondary market
TYPES OF FINANCING: SECONDARY-MARKET CORPORATE SECURITIES: Bonds; REAL ESTATE LOANS: Industrial revenue bonds

COMPANY: **Prescott, Ball & Turben**
ADDRESS: 1331 Euclid Avenue
Cleveland, OH 44115
PHONE: (216) 574-7300
TYPE OF INSTITUTION: Investment banking firm - public underwritings , private placements, leasing
CONTACT OFFICER(S): Richard Howe, Public Underwriting
Norman E. Reed, Public Financing
Herbert R. Martens, Jr., Lease Financing
John L. Kalmbach (NY), Energy Financing
J. Jeffrey Eakin, Hospital Financing
Donald Chadwick, Housing Financing
Donald R. Chadwick, Industrial Revenue & Pollution Control Financing
Albert L. Nelson, III, Mergers, Acquisitions & Divestitures
Richard Zappala, Real Estate Financing
Richard Howe, Venture Capital & Private Placements
ASSETS: $1.3 billion
INVESTMENTS/LOANS MADE: For own account, For managed accounts, Through private placements, underwriting public offerings
TYPES OF FINANCING: SECONDARY-MARKET CORPORATE SECURITIES: Common stock; Preferred stock; Bonds; Other: Convertible debentures, VENTURE CAPITAL: Research & Development; Start-up from developed product stage; First-stage; Second-stage; Later-stage expansion; Buy-outs/Acquisitions, REAL ESTATE LOANS: Wraparounds; Land development; Industrial revenue bonds, LEASES: Single-investor; Leveraged; Tax leases; Non-tax leases; Tax-oriented lease brokerage; Lease syndications; Vendor financing programs, OTHER SERVICES PROVIDED: Divestitures
GEOGRAPHIC LIMITS OF INVESTMENTS/LOANS: National
RANGE OF INV./LOAN PER BUSINESS: Min. $2 million; Max. None
BUSINESS CHARACTERISTICS DESIRED-REQUIRED: Minimum number of years in business: 0
REFERRALS ACCEPTED FROM: Investment/Mortgage banker or Borrower/Investee
REMARKS: 35 branches

COMPANY: **Boenning & Scattergood, Inc.**
ADDRESS: 1809 Walnut St.
Philadelphia, PA 19103
PHONE: (215) 568-7325

TYPE OF INSTITUTION: Securities Brokerage
CONTACT OFFICER(S): Michael B. Bell, V.P., Manager, Fixed Income Dept.
Francis W. Kelly, E.V.P., Manager, Equity Dept.
TYPES OF FINANCING: SECONDARY-MARKET CORPORATE SECURITIES: Common stock; Preferred stock; Bonds, REAL ESTATE LOANS: Industrial revenue bonds
PREFERRED TYPES OF INDUSTRIES/INVESTMENTS: Diversified
GEOGRAPHIC LIMITS OF INVESTMENTS/LOANS: Regional

COMPANY: **Butcher & Singer, Inc.**
ADDRESS: 211 S. Broad St., 9th Floor
Philadelphia, PA 19107
PHONE: (215) 985-5571
TYPE OF INSTITUTION: Investment Banker
CONTACT OFFICER(S): John H. Foote, 1st V.P., Pub. Finance
TYPES OF FINANCING: REAL ESTATE LOANS: Industrial revenue bonds

COMPANY: **First Tennessee Bank National Association**
ADDRESS: 165 Madison Avenue
Memphis, TN 38103
PHONE: (901) 523-4632
TYPE OF INSTITUTION: Commercial Finance Division of National Bank
CONTACT OFFICER(S): Joseph D. Hardesty, Jr., Senior Vice President, Division Manager
Larry Allen, Vice President, Senior Loan Officer
ASSETS: $5 Billion Approximately
INVESTMENTS/LOANS MADE: For own account
TYPES OF FINANCING: LOANS: Working capital; Equipment; Other: Leveraged buy-outs and acquisitions. REAL ESTATE LOANS: Intermediate-term senior mtg.; Industrial revenue bonds. INTERNATIONAL
PREFERRED TYPES OF INDUSTRIES/INVESTMENTS: Textiles/Apparel; Leisure/Sporting Goods; Chemicals; Automative Aftermarket; Food Processors/Distributors; Industrial Supplies
GEOGRAPHIC LIMITS OF INVESTMENTS/LOANS: Other: Five hundred mile radius of Memphis, Tennessee.
RANGE OF INV./LOAN PER BUSINESS: Min. $1,000,000; Max. $25,000,000
PREFERRED TERM FOR LOANS & LEASES: Min. 2 years; Max. 7 years
BUSINESS CHARACTERISTICS DESIRED-REQUIRED: Minimum number of years in business: 2; Min. annual sales $5,000,000; Min. net worth $200,000; Min. annual net income $100,000; Min. annual cash flow $1,000,000.
REFERRALS ACCEPTED FROM: Investment/Mortgage banker or Borrower/Investee

COMPANY: **Morgan, Keegan & Co., Inc.**
ADDRESS: One Commerce Square
Memphis, TN 38103
PHONE: (901) 524-4100
TYPE OF INSTITUTION: Brokerage and investment banking firm
CONTACT OFFICER(S): Robert A. Baird, 1st Vice President, Investment Banking
Richard McStay, Sr. Vice President, Investment Banking
ASSETS: $26,000,000+
INVESTMENTS/LOANS MADE: Through private placement, Through underwriting public offerings
INVESTMENTS/LOANS MADE: In securities with or without a secondary market
TYPES OF FINANCING: SECONDARY-MARKET CORPORATE SECURITIES: Common stock; Preferred stock; Bonds; Other: Mergers/Acquisitions, Industrial Revenue & Pollution Control Financings. VENTURE CAPITAL: Second-stage; Later-stage expansion; Buy-outs/Acquisitons. LOANS: Unsecured to credits above Baa; Equipment; Equity-related. Other: Loans are placed with institutional investors. REAL ESTATE LOANS: Long-term senior mtg.; Intermediate-term senior mtg.; Subordinated; Industrial revenue bonds. LEASES: Single-investor; Leveraged; Tax leases. REAL ESTATE: Partnerships/Syndications.
GEOGRAPHIC LIMITS OF INVESTMENTS/LOANS: National
RANGE OF INV./LOAN PER BUSINESS: Min. $3,000,000
BUSINESS CHARACTERISTICS DESIRED-REQUIRED: Min. annual sales $20 million; Min. net worth $10 million; Min. annual net income $500,000
BRANCHES: Memphis, TN
Nashville, TN
Knoxville, TN
Jackson, Miss.
New Orleana, LA
Ft Lauderdale, FL.
Palm Beach, FL.
Atlanta, GA
Montgomery, AL
Boston, MA
New York, NY

COMPANY: **Juig U.S. Management, Inc.**
ADDRESS: 1008 N. Bowen Road
Arlington, TX 76012
PHONE: (817) 860-5222
TYPE OF INSTITUTION: Financial Management Division Of Merchant/Investment Banking Firm
CONTACT OFFICER(S): John Ross, Chief Executive Officer
Byron K. Devine, C.P.A. Executive Vice President
P.J. Clark, Asst. Vice President
ASSETS: $50,000,000 (Approx.)
INVESTMENTS/LOANS MADE: For own account, For managed accounts
INVESTMENTS/LOANS MADE: In securities with or without a secondary market
TYPES OF FINANCING: SECONDARY-MARKET CORPORATE SECURITIES: Bonds; Other: Certain capital notes, warrants & debentures. VENTURE CAPITAL: Second-stage; Later-stage expansion; Buy-outs/Acquisitions. LOANS: Working capital; Equipment; Other: Secured credits (4-10 yr. term). REAL ESTATE LOANS: Long-term senior mtg.; Land; Standbys; Industrial revenue bonds. FACTORING.

LEASES: Vendor financing programs.
INTERNATIONAL. REAL ESTATE: Acquisitions.
OTHER SERVICES PROVIDED: Various domestic/international financial services for selected clients.
PREFERRED TYPES OF INDUSTRIES/INVESTMENTS: Investments in ongoing companies; Income producing real estate
WILL NOT CONSIDER: Industries, Equipment
GEOGRAPHIC LIMITS OF INVESTMENTS/LOANS: International
RANGE OF INV./LOAN PER BUSINESS: Min. $250,000; Max. $5,000,000 (Normally)
PREFERRED TERM FOR LOANS & LEASES: Min. 4 years; Max. 10 years domestically, 20 years internationally
BUSINESS CHARACTERISTICS DESIRED-REQUIRED: Min. annual sales $1,000,000; Min. annual cash flow $250,000
REFERRALS ACCEPTED FROM: Investment/Mortgage banker or Borrower/Investee
REMARKS: Any submissions must demonstrate annual minimum internal rate on return on cash of 25%, after infusion and before debt service.

COMPANY: **Underwood, Neuhaus & Co., Incorporated**
ADDRESS: 724 Travis
Houston, TX 77002
PHONE: (713) 221-2413
TYPE OF INSTITUTION: Full Service Regional Investment Banking Firm
CONTACT OFFICER(S): Robert S. Moore 2nd, Corporate Finance
J. Randall Brlansky, Corporate Finance
Ben F. Ederer, Corporate Finance
ASSETS: More than $15,000,000 of equity capital; more than $60,000,000 of assets
INVESTMENTS/LOANS MADE: For own account; Through private placements; Through underwriting public offerings
INVESTMENTS/LOANS MADE: In securities with a secondary market and in securities without a secondary market
TYPES OF FINANCING: SECONDARY-MARKET CORPORATE SECURITIES: Common stock; Preferred stock; Bonds; Convertibles and Units of Common with Warrants, Bonds with Warrants, etc., VENTURE CAPITAL: Research & Development; Second-stage (generally 1-3 years); Later-stage expansion; Buy-outs/Acquisitions, LOANS: Unsecured to credits above B; Equipment; Equity-related, REAL ESTATE LOANS: Long-term senior mtg.; Intermediate-term senior mtg.; Subordinated, LEASES: Single-investor; Leveraged; Tax leases, OTHER SERVICES PROVIDED: Direct Participations—i.e. limited partnership financing of equipment of all types
GEOGRAPHIC LIMITS OF INVESTMENTS/LOANS: National
RANGE OF INV./LOAN PER BUSINESS: Min. $2,000,000; Max. $100,000,000
PREFERRED TERM FOR LOANS & LEASES: Min. 5; Max. 20 years
BUSINESS CHARACTERISTICS DESIRED-REQUIRED: Minimum number of years in business: 1; Min. annual net income $500,000
REMARKS: The Corporate Finance part of Underwood, Neuhaus includes almost 30 professionals who in 1981 completed more than 80 different transactions.

COMPANY: **Craigie Inc.**
ADDRESS: P.O. Box 1854—814 E. Main
Richmond, VA 23215
PHONE: (804) 649-3946
CONTACT OFFICER(S): William B. Reynolds, Sr. V.P.
TYPES OF FINANCING: SECONDARY-MARKET CORPORATE SECURITIES: Bonds; Secondary market bonds, REAL ESTATE LOANS: Industrial revenue bonds
PREFERRED TYPES OF INDUSTRIES/INVESTMENTS: Debt Securities; Gov't. Agencies; Gov't. Bonds
GEOGRAPHIC LIMITS OF INVESTMENTS/LOANS: National
BUSINESS CHARACTERISTICS DESIRED-REQUIRED: Not specifically

COMPANY: **Baird & Co., Inc.**
ADDRESS: 777 East Wisconsin Ave.
Milwaukee, WI 53202
PHONE: (414) 765-3730
CONTACT OFFICER(S): J. Jay Cavanaugh, 1st V.P. & Manager, Fixed Income
Al Bathrick, Sr. V.P.
Nick Wilson
TYPES OF FINANCING: SECONDARY-MARKET CORPORATE SECURITIES, REAL ESTATE LOANS: Industrial revenue bonds, OTHER SERVICES PROVIDED: Underwriters of any Secondary market; Primary market: Fixed Income
PREFERRED TYPES OF INDUSTRIES/INVESTMENTS: Retail; Institutional
WILL NOT CONSIDER: Trading Commodities
GEOGRAPHIC LIMITS OF INVESTMENTS/LOANS: Regional

INSURANCE (LIFE) COMPANIES

(Diversified Medium-term and Long-term Financing)

ALABAMA

COMPANY: **Liberty National Life Insurance Company**
ADDRESS: P.O. Box 2612
Birmingham, AL 35202
PHONE: (205) 325-2048
CONTACT OFFICER(S): W. H. Ray, Exec. V.P. Investment Division
William G. Byars, V.P. Real Estate
Michael J. Klice, V.P. Securities
ASSETS: $2.1 billion
TYPES OF FINANCING: SECONDARY-MARKET CORPORATE SECURITIES: Common stock; Preferred stock; Bonds, REAL ESTATE LOANS: Other: Mortgages REAL ESTATE: Acquisitions
GEOGRAPHIC LIMITS OF INVESTMENTS/LOANS: National
RANGE OF INV./LOAN PER BUSINESS: Min. $2 million; Max. $14 million (R.E.), $5 million (Private Placement)
REFERRALS ACCEPTED FROM: Investment/Mortgage Banker or Borrower/Investee

COMPANY: **Protective Corporation**
ADDRESS: P.O. Box 2606
Birmingham, AL 35202
PHONE: (205) 879-9230
TYPE OF INSTITUTION: Life insurance holding company
CONTACT OFFICER(S): Roland V. Lee, 2nd V.P., Mortgage Loans
Troy Mohon, 2nd V.P. Securities
ASSETS: $700,000,000
INVESTMENTS/LOANS MADE: For own account
INVESTMENTS/LOANS MADE: In securities with a secondary market and in securities without a secondary market
TYPES OF FINANCING: SECONDARY-MARKET CORPORATE SECURITIES: Preferred stock; Bonds, REAL ESTATE LOANS: Long-term senior mtg.; Industrial revenue bonds REAL ESTATE: Joint ventures
PREFERRED TYPES OF INDUSTRIES/INVESTMENTS: Shopping centers, office, warehouse
GEOGRAPHIC LIMITS OF INVESTMENTS/LOANS: National
RANGE OF INV./LOAN PER BUSINESS: Min. $500,000; Max. $2,000,000
REFERRALS ACCEPTED FROM: Investment/Mortgage banker or Borrower/Investee

COMPANY: **Southern Life and Health Insurance Company**
ADDRESS: 2101 Highland Av., P.O. Box 671
Birmingham, AL 35201
PHONE: (205) 933-1160
CONTACT OFFICER(S): James G. Tatum, V.P., Investments
John Shepherd, Sec. Treasurer

ASSETS: $100 million and up
INVESTMENTS/LOANS MADE: In securities with a secondary market and in securities without a secondary market
TYPES OF FINANCING: SECONDARY-MARKET CORPORATE SECURITIES: Bonds
GEOGRAPHIC LIMITS OF INVESTMENTS/LOANS: Bonds Nationally
RANGE OF INV./LOAN PER BUSINESS: Min. $100,000; Max. $600,000
PREFERRED TERM FOR LOANS & LEASES: Min. 10-15; Max. 15-20 years
REFERRALS ACCEPTED FROM: Investment/Mortgage banker or Borrower/Investee

COMPANY: **Legacy Life Insurance Company**
ADDRESS: Box 10380
Phoenix, AZ
PHONE: (602) 957-8781
TYPE OF INSTITUTION: Insurance company
CONTACT OFFICER(S): R. Kent Fielder, CPA, Asst. V.P.-Finance/Treasurer
Wayne A. Schreck, FSA
V. Pres.-Finance
Richard C. Eiler, President
George S. Ashley, Exec. Vice President
ASSETS: Excess of $6,000,000 (Dec. 31, 1983)
INVESTMENTS/LOANS MADE: For managed accounts; Through private placements
INVESTMENTS/LOANS MADE: In securities with a secondary market and in securities without a secondary market
TYPES OF FINANCING: SECONDARY-MARKET CORPORATE SECURITIES: Common Stock, Preferred Stock, Bonds; REAL ESTATE LOANS: Long-term senior mtg.; Intermediate-term senior mtg., Industrial Revenue Bonds; REAL ESTATE: Acquisitions; Partnerships/Syndications
PREFERRED TYPES OF INDUSTRIES/INVESTMENTS: Senior mtges; T-Bills; C.D.'s; Commercial paper; Repos; Money Market Accounts; T-Notes; Stocks & Bonds
RANGE OF INV./LOAN PER BUSINESS: Min. $10,000.00; Max. $250,000.00
PREFERRED TERM FOR LOANS & LEASES: Min. 6 months; Max. 30 years

COMPANY: **E. F. Hutton Life Insurance Co.**
ADDRESS: 11011 N. Torrey Pines
La Jolla, CA 92038
PHONE: (619) 452-9060
CONTACT OFFICER(S): Alan Richards, Pres.

COMPANY: **Beneficial Standard Life Insurance Company**
ADDRESS: 3700 Wilshire Blvd., Suite 250
Los Angeles, CA 90010
PHONE: (213) 381-8291
TYPE OF INSTITUTION: Life Insurance Company
CONTACT OFFICER(S): Peter H. Ulrich, Director, Mortgage Investments
James C. Whitten, Ass't. Dir., Mortgage Investments
Tina K. Kelly, Ass't. Dir., Mortgage Investments
INVESTMENTS/LOANS MADE: For own account

TYPES OF FINANCING: REAL ESTATE LOANS: OTHER: First mortgages only
PREFERRED TYPES OF INDUSTRIES/INVESTMENTS: Mortgages on Income producing Real Estate — Apartments, Office Buildings, and Shopping Centers
WILL NOT CONSIDER: Single purpose income producing properties
GEOGRAPHIC LIMITS OF INVESTMENTS/LOANS: Prefer western states, Texas and Oklahoma
RANGE OF INV./LOAN PER BUSINESS: Min. $200,000; Max. $2,000,000
PREFERRED TERM FOR LOANS & LEASES: Min. 5; Max. 25 years
BUSINESS CHARACTERISTICS DESIRED-REQUIRED: Min. number of years in business: 0
REFERRALS ACCEPTED FROM: Investment/Mortgage banker

COMPANY: **Golden State Mutual Life Insurance Co.**
ADDRESS: 1999 W. Adams Blvd.
Los Angeles, CA 90018
PHONE: (213) 731-1131
CONTACT OFFICER(S): Thaddieus McCray, Dir. of Administrative Services

COMPANY: **Transamerica Occidental Life Insurance Co.**
ADDRESS: 1150 South Olive St., Ste. 2700
Los Angeles, CA 90015
PHONE: (213) 742-3555
CONTACT OFFICER(S): Charles R. Drake, V.P.
Walter Kirkbride, V.P.
TYPES OF FINANCING: SECONDARY-MARKET CORPORATE SECURITIES: Common stock; Preferred stock; Bonds, REAL ESTATE: Acquisitions; Joint ventures; Partnerships/Syndications, SERVICES PROVIDED: Not a lender, just an investor
PREFERRED TYPES OF INDUSTRIES/INVESTMENTS: Diversified
GEOGRAPHIC LIMITS OF INVESTMENTS/LOANS: National; International; Other: Canada, Australia
RANGE OF INV./LOAN PER BUSINESS: Min. $2 million; Max. $10 million

COMPANY: **Pacific Mutual Life Insurance Company**
ADDRESS: 700 Newport Center Drive
Newport Beach, CA 92663
PHONE: (714) 640-3770
CONTACT OFFICER(S): John T. Chapple, Sr. V.P., Realty Investment

COMPANY: **Pacific Standard Life Insurance Company**
ADDRESS: 3820 Chiles Rd., P.O. Box 1796
Sacramento, CA 95808
PHONE: (916) 756-3030
TYPE OF INSTITUTION: Management company for oil and gas and venture capital investments
CONTACT OFFICER(S): Exec. V.P., Finance
ASSETS: Over $3,000,000
INVESTMENTS/LOANS MADE: For managed accounts; Through private placements

INVESTMENTS/LOANS MADE: In securities with a secondary market and in securities without a secondary market
TYPES OF FINANCING: VENTURE CAPITAL: Research & Development, Start-up from developed product stage, First-stage, Second-stage, Later-stage expansion; OTHER SERVICES PROVIDED: Management company/general partner for oil and gas drilling
PREFERRED TYPES OF INDUSTRIES/INVESTMENTS: Electronics, Finance and Financial Services, Oil and Gas, Newspapers, magazines, television,
WILL NOT CONSIDER: construction, consumer products, hotels, motels, restaurants, leasing, motion pictures, real estate
GEOGRAPHIC LIMITS OF INVESTMENTS/LOANS: National
RANGE OF INV./LOAN PER BUSINESS: Min. $100,000; Max. $500,000
BUSINESS CHARACTERISTICS DESIRED-REQUIRED: Minimum number of years in business: 0; Min. annual sales $0; Min. net worth $0; Min. annual net income $0; Min. annual cash flow $0
REFERRALS ACCEPTED FROM: Investment/Mortgage banker and Borrower/InvesteeE

COMPANY: **Capitol Life Insurance Co.**
ADDRESS: P.O. Box 1200
Denver, CO 80201
PHONE: (303) 861-4065
CONTACT OFFICER(S): Kenneth Peterson, Sr. V.P.
Paul K. Moyer Sr.V.P.
ASSETS: 2.4 Billion
INVESTMENTS/LOANS MADE: Only in securities without a secondary market
TYPES OF FINANCING: LOANS: Equity-related; REAL ESTATE LOANS: Long-term senior mtg.; Intermediate-term senior mtg; Short term mtg
GEOGRAPHIIC LIMITS OF INVESTMENTS/LOANS: National
RANGE OF INV./LOAN PER BUSINESS: Min. $2 million; Max. $10 million
PREFERRED TERM FOR LOANS & LEASES: Min. 7 years; Max. 10 years
BUSINESS CHARACTERISITICS DESIRED-REQUIRED: Minimum number of years in business: 0; Must have a business plan

COMPANY: **National Farmers Union Life Insurance Company**
ADDRESS: 12025 E. 45th Avenue
Denver, CO 80239
PHONE: (303) 371-1760
TYPE OF INSTITUTION: Insurance Company
CONTACT OFFICER(S): L. C. Ellis, Asst. V.P., Stocks & Bonds
Deborah Birdwhistell, Mortgage Investment Supervisor, Commercial Real Estate
ASSETS: $10,000,000 - $100,000,000
INVESTMENTS/LOANS MADE: For own account
INVESTMENTS/LOANS MADE: In securities with a secondary market and in securities without a secondary market
TYPES OF FINANCING: SECONDARY-MARKET CORPORATE SECURITIES: Common stock; Preferred stock; Bonds, REAL ESTATE LOANS: Long-term senior mtg.; Intermediate-term senior mtg.; Industrial revenue bonds
PREFERRED TYPES OF INDUSTRIES/INVESTMENTS: Real Estate, Commercial, 75% of appraised value by a qualified appraiser.
GEOGRAPHIC LIMITS OF INVESTMENTS/LOANS: Regional
RANGE OF INV./LOAN PER BUSINESS: Min. $300,000; Max. $1,000,000
PREFERRED TERM FOR LOANS & LEASES: Min. 10-15; Max. 20 years & up
BUSINESS CHARACTERISTICS DESIRED-REQUIRED: Minimum number of years in business 7;Min. net worth 2 x loan; Min. annual net income 1.3 x loan
REFERRALS ACCEPTED FROM: Investment/Mortgage banker or Borrower/Investee

COMPANY: **Security Life of Denver**
ADDRESS: Security Life Bldg.
Denver, CO 80202
PHONE: (303) 534-1861
CONTACT OFFICER(S): B. J. Muller, Asst. V.P.

COMPANY: **The Paul Revere Investment Management Corporation**
ADDRESS: 1275 King St.
Greenwich, CT 06830
PHONE: (203) 531-2800
CONTACT OFFICER(S): Charles Y. Brush, President
John J. Delucca, Treasurer
ASSETS: $100 million and up
TYPES OF FINANCING: Secondary Market Corporate Securities: Bonds; REAL ESTATE LOANS: Intermediate term senior mortgage; Other: private placements
GEOGRAPHIC LIMITS OF INVESTMENTS/LOANS: National; Other: Canada
RANGE OF INV./LOAN PER BUSINESS: Min. 1 million Max. 5 million
PREFERRED TERM FOR LOANS & LEASES: Min. 2-3 years; Max. 15-20 years
REFERRALS ACCEPTED FROM: Investment/Mortgage banker or Borrower/Investee

COMPANY: **Aetna Life & Casualty**
ADDRESS: 151 Farmington Ave.
Hartford, CT 06156
PHONE: (203) 273-0123
CONTACT OFFICER(S): Peter G. Russell, V.P., Bond Investment Dept, 203-275-2701
James Richmond, V.P. Aetna Realty Investors, 205-275-3247
ASSETS: 48 billion
INVESTMENTS/LOANS MADE: In securities with a secondary market and in securities without a secondary market
TYPES OF FINANCING: SECONDARY-MARKET CORPORATE SECURITIES, LOANS: REAL ESTATE LOANS: Long-term senior mtg.; Intermediate-term

senior mtg.; Construction, REAL ESTATE: Other: Equity purchases
PREFERRED TYPES OF INDUSTRIES/INVESTMENTS: R.E.: Agriculture related; construction & development; shopping centers; industrial; warehousing, office buildings, hotels
GEOGRAPHIC LIMITS OF INVESTMENTS/LOANS: National
RANGE OF INV./LOAN PER BUSINESS: Min. $5 million (R.E.); $5 million (P.P.); Max. None
PREFERRED TERM FOR LOANS & LEASES: Max. 15+ (R.E.) years
REFERRALS ACCEPTED FROM: Investment/Mortgage banker or Borrower/Investee

COMPANY: **CIGNA CORPORATION**
ADDRESS: South Bldg. S-306
Hartford, CT 06152
PHONE: (203) 726-6000
TYPE OF INSTITUTION: Insurance Co.
CONTACT OFFICER(S): Richard W. Maine, Pres.
CIGNA Capital Advisors, 726-6131
David P. Marks, Sr. V.P.
Philip Ward Sr. V.P. RE Production
Thomas J. Watt Sr. V.P. Agricultural RE.
Richard Caupchunos, Sr. V.P. Asset Management
Arthurn C. Reeds, Sr. V.P. Portfolio Management
TYPES OF FINANCING: SECONDARY-MARKET CORPORATE SECURITIES: Common stock; Preferred stock; Bonds, VENTURE CAPITAL, LOANS: Unsecured; Working capital (receivables/inventory); Equipment; Equity-related; REAL ESTATE LOANS: Long-term senior mtg.; Intermediate-term senior mtg.; Subordinated Land; Land development; Standbys; Industrial revenue bonds; Other: Pure development equity, REAL ESTATE: Acquisitions; Joint ventures; Partnerships/Syndications
PREFERRED TYPES OF INDUSTRIES/INVESTMENTS: Mortgage; Communications; Manufacturing and technology; Retail; Foreign
WILL NOT CONSIDER: Gaming industry
RANGE OF INV./LOAN PER BUSINESS: Min. $3 million; Max $40 million
PREFERRED TERM FOR LOANS & LEASSES: Min. 1 year; Max. 20 years

COMPANY: **Connecticut Mutual Life Insurance Co.**
ADDRESS: 140 Garden St.
Hartford, CT 06154
PHONE: (203) 727-6500
CONTACT OFFICER(S): Raymond J. Houworth, Second V.P.
John Weber V.P. Marketable Securities
Robert Hunter, V.P., Urban R.E.
George Schwab, V.P., Agriculture R.E.
ASSETS: $7 billion
TYPES OF FINANCING: SECONDARY-MARKET CORPORATE SECURITIES: Common stock; Preferred stock; Bonds, LOANS: Equipment, Equity-related REAL ESTATE LOANS: Long-term senior mtg.; Subordinated; Wraparounds; Construction, REAL ESTATE: Joint ventures
PREFERRED TYPES OF INDUSTRIES/INVESTMENTS: Office Buildings
GEOGRAPHIC LIMITS OF INVESTMENTS/LOANS: National
RANGE OF INV./LOAN PER BUSINESS: Min. $500,000; Max. $15 million
PREFERRED TERM FOR LOANS & LEASES: Max. 10 years
BUSINESS CHARACTERISTICS DESIRED-REQUIRED: minimum number of years in business: 0
REFERRALS ACCEPTED FROM: Investment/Mortgage banker or Borrower/Investee

COMPANY: **Hartford Insurance Group**
ADDRESS: Hartford Plaza
Hartford, CT 06115
PHONE: (203) 547-5000
CONTACT OFFICER(S): Bernard F. Wilbur, Jr., V.P., R.E. Mortgages
Dick Hamilton, R.E. Investment
ASSETS: $14 billion
TYPES OF FINANCING: Seondary market corporate securites: bonds; real estate loans; REAL ESTATE: Acquisitions
PREFERRED TYPES OF INDUSTRIES/ INVESTMENTS/EQUIPMENT/REAL ESTATE: Real Estate; suburban offices
GEOGRAPHIC LIMITS OF INVESTMENTS/LOANS: National
RANGE OF INV./LOAN PER BUSINESS: Min $2 million; Max.: $50 million

COMPANY: **Phoenix Mutual Life Insurance Company**
ADDRESS: 1 American Row
Hartford, CT 06115
PHONE: (203) 275-5439
CONTACT OFFICER(S): Norman W. Douglass, Vice President
ASSETS: $4,000,000,000
INVESTMENTS/LOANS MADE: For own account; For managed accounts; Through private placements; Through underwriting publicc offerings
INVESTMENTS/LOANS MADE: In securities with a secondary market and in securities without a secondary market
TYPES OF FINANCING: SECONDARY-MARKET CORPORATE SECURITIES: Common stock; Bonds; LOANS: Unsecured to credits above Ba; Working capital (receivables/inventory); Equipment; Equity-related; REAL ESTATE: Acquisitions; Joint ventures; Partnerships/Syndications
GEOGRAPHIC LIMITS OF INVESTMENTS/LOANS: National
RANGE OF INV./LOAN PER BUSINESS: Min. $1,000,000; Max. $10,000,000
PREFERRED TERM FOR LOANS & LEASES: Min. 2 years; Max. 10 years
BUSINESS CHARACTERISTICS DESIRED-REQUIRED: Minimum number of years in business: 5
REFERRALS ACCEPTED FROM: Investment/Mortgage banker or Borrower/Investee

COMPANY: **The Union Labor Life Insurance Co.**
ADDRESS: 1 Masssachusetts Ave. NW
Washington, D.C. 20001

CONTACT OFFICER(S): Herbert C. Canapary, V.P., Investments
E. R. Saatchoff, V.P., Mortgages
ASSETS: $100 million and up
TYPES OF FINANCING: LOANS, REAL ESTATE LOANS: Long-term senior mtg.
GEOGRAPHIC LIMITS OF INVESTMENTS/LOANS: National
RANGE OF INV./LOAN PER BUSINESS: Min. $500,000 (R.E.); Max. $3,000,000 (R.E.)
PREFERRED TERM FOR LOANS & LEASES: Min. 15-20 years (Investments); Max. 20+ years
BUSINESS CHARACTERISTICS DESIRED-REQUIRED: Other: R.E.: Union labor for construction to provide jobs and attract labor union moneys
REMARKS: No range limits for Investments

COMPANY: **Acacia Mutual Life Insurance Company**
ADDRESS: 51 Louisiana Ave., N.W.
Washington, DC 20001
PHONE: (202) 628-4506
CONTACT OFFICER(S): Joseph A. Clorety, Sr. V.P., Investments
Andrew S. White, 2nd V.P. Securities
Patricia D. Hevner, Asst. V.P. Equities
Albert H. Kroening, Jr., V.P., R.E.
Jean O. Brinks, Treasurer
INVESTMENT/LOANS MADE OR ARRANGED: In securities with a secondary market and in securities without a secondary market
TYPES OF FINANCING: SECONDARY-MARKET CORPORATE SECURITIES: Common stock; Preferred stock; Bonds; REAL ESTATE: Joint ventures; Partnerships/Syndications. OTHER SERVICES PROVIDED: private placements; certificates of deposit; R.E. Equities
PREFERRED TYPES OF INDUSTRIES/INVESTMENTS: low rise office parks
GEOGRAPHIC LIMITS OF INVESTMENTS/LOANS: National
RANGE OF INV./LOAN PER BUSINESS: Max. $4 million
REFERRALS ACCEPTED FROM: Investment/Mortgage banker or Borrower/Investee

COMPANY: **USLICO Corporation**
ADDRESS: 1701 Pennsylvania Ave., N.W.
Washington, DC 20006
PHONE: (202) 298-6235
CONTACT OFFICER(S): Leslie P. Schultz, Chairman
W. Alan Aument, Sr. V.P. & Treasurer (Inv.)
J. Rodman Myers, V.P., Mortgage R.E.,
J.M. Schultz, V.P. Securities
ASSETS: $100,000,000 and up
INVESTMENTS/LOANS MADE: In securities with a secondary market and in securities without a secondary market
TYPES OF FINANCING: LOANS: Equipment, REAL ESTATE LOANS
PREFERRED TYPES OF INDUSTRIES/INVESTMENTS: Diversified
GEOGRAPHIC LIMITS OF INVESTMENTS/LOANS: National
RANGE OF INV./LOAN PER BUSINESS: Min. None; Max. $2,000,000
REFERRALS ACCEPTED FROM: Investment/Mortgage banker or Borrower/Investee
REMARKS: Maximum amount for bonds is $1,000,000

COMPANY: **Continental American Life Insurance Co.**
ADDRESS: 300 Continental Dr.
Newark, DE 19713
PHONE: (302) 454-5000
CONTACT OFFICER(S): Michael Greenleaf, V.P.
Thomas Ryan, Asst. V.P.
TYPES OF FINANCING: SECONDARY-MARKET CORPORATE SECURITIES: Common stock; Preferred stock; Bonds, VENTURE CAPITAL: Buy-outs/Acquisitions, LOANS: Working capital (receivables/inventory); Equipment; Other: Secured, REAL ESTATE LOANS: Land; Land development; Other: Land purchase lease-back (short-term 5-7 yrs), REAL ESTATE: Joint ventures
PREFERRED TYPES OF INDUSTRIES/INVESTMENTS: Diversified
WILL NOT CONSIDER: Fast foods
GEOGRAPHIC LIMITS OF INVESTMENTS/LOANS: National
RANGE OF INV./LOAN PER BUSINESS: Min. $500,000; Max. $2-3 million
PREFERRED TERM FOR LOANS & LEASES: Min. 3 years; Max. 10 years
BUSINESS CHARACTERISTICS DESIRED-REQUIRED:Minimum number of years in business: 3

COMPANY: **American Heritage Life Insurance Company**
ADDRESS: 11 E. Forsyth St.
Jacksonville, FL 32202
PHONE: (904) 354-1776
CONTACT OFFICER(S): C. A. Verlander, V.P. Securities-Investments
Wm. L. Kluessner, Asst. V.P. & Treasurer-Mortgages
ASSETS: $100 million and up
INVESTMENTS/LOANS MADE: In securities with a secondary market and in securities without a secondary market
TYPES OF FINANCING: SECONDARY-MARKET CORPORATE SECURITIES: Common Stock; Preferred Stock; Bonds; REAL ESTATE LOANS: Intermediate term senior mortgage; Subordinated; Land; Land development; Gap; Industrial Revenue bonds
PREFERRED TYPES OF INDUSTRIES/INVESTMENTS: R. E. professional office buildings; shopping centers
GEOGRAPHIC LIMITS OF INVESTMENTS/LOANS: National
PREFERRED TERM FOR LOANS & LEASES: Min. 5-7 years (R.E.)
BUSINESS CHARACTERISTICS DESIRED-REQUIRED: Min. annual net income loan amount (R.E.)
REFERRALS ACCEPTED FROM: Investment/Mortgage banker or Borrower/Investee
REMARKS: Range for investments: $250,000-1,000,000; Range for R.E. loans: $25,000-500,000

COMPANY: **Gulfco Capital Mgmt. Inc.**
ADDRESS: Gulf Life Tower
Jacksonville, FL 32207
PHONE: (904) 390-7800
CONTACT OFFICER(S): Robert L. Collins, Ex. V.P., mortgages
ASSETS: $100 million and up
TYPES OF FINANCING: REAL ESTATE LOANS: Intermediate-term senior mtg.
PREFERRED TYPES OF INDUSTRIES/INVESTMENTS: Income properties: office buildings; shopping centers; medical office buildings; warehouses
GEOGRAPHIC LIMITS OF INVESTMENTS/LOANS: Regional; Other: 49 states with emphasis on SE U.S.; all states except Texas
RANGE OF INV./LOAN PER BUSINESS: Min. 1 mil.; Max. 10 mil.
PREFERRED TERM FOR LOANS & LEASES: Min. 5 yrs; Max. 10 yrs
REFERRALS ACCEPTED FROM: Investment/Mortgage banker or Borrower/Investee
REMARKS: Preferred term: 5-10 years

COMPANY: **Central Life Insurance Company of Florida**
ADDRESS: 1400 N. Blvd.
Tampa, FL 33607
PHONE: (813) 251-1897
CONTACT OFFICER(S): Bettye F. Stanford, Sec., Treasurer
ASSETS: $1,000,000 - 10,000,000
TYPES OF FINANCING: REAL ESTATE LOANS
GEOGRAPHIC LIMITS OF INVESTMENTS/LOANS: State
RANGE OF INV./LOAN PER BUSINESS: Max. $50,000
PREFERRED TERM FOR LOANS & LEASES: Max. 20+ years
REFERRALS ACCEPTED FROM: Investment/Mortgage banker or Borrower/Investee

COMPANY: **LeaseAmerica Corp.**
ADDRESS: 4333 Edgewood Rd. NE
Cedar Rapids, IA 52499
PHONE: (319) 366-5331
TYPE OF INSTITUTION: Leasing Div. of Insurance Holding Co.
CONTACT OFFICER(S): E. J. Scherrman, President
John A. Mahan, Executive Vice President
Dave Harvey, Vice President-Credit
INVESTMENTS/LOANS MADE: For own account; Through underwriting public offerings
TYPES OF FINANCING: LEASES: Single-investor; Leveraged; Tax; Non-tax; Operating; Lease syndications; Vendor financing programs
PREFERRED TYPES OF INDUSTRIES/INVESTMENTS: General Equipment Leasing Co.
GEOGRAPHIC LIMITS OF INVESTMENTS/LOANS: National
RANGE OF INV./LOAN PER BUSINESS: Min. $10,000
PREFERRED TERM FOR LOANS & LEASES: Min. 2 years; Max. 7 years
BUSINESS CHARACTERISTICS DESIRED-REQUIRED: Min. number of years in business: 2; Min. annual sales $100,000; Min. net worth $25,000
BRANCHES: LeaseAmerica Corporation, 500 Northridge Road, Suite 300, Atlanta, GA, 30338
LeaseAmerica Corporation, 8585 Stemmons Freeway, Twin Tower So. - Suite 770, Dallas, TX 75247
LeaseAmerica Corporation, 218 Harrison Street, Davenport, IA 52801
LeaseAmerica Corporation, 504 Merle Hay Tower, Des Moines, IA 50310
LeaseAmerica Corporation, 2616 South Loop West, Suite 100, Houston, TX 77054
LeaseAmerica Corporation, 2724 Commerce Tower, 911 Main Street, Kansas City, MO 64105
LeaseAmerica Corporation, The Starks Building, Suite 396, 455 South Fourth Street, Louisville, KY 40202
LeaseAmerica Corporation, 600 E. Mason St., Milwaukee, WI 53202
LeaseAmerica Corporation, Southtown Office Park, Suite 550, 8120 Penn Ave. South, Minneapolis, MN 55431
LeaseAmerica Corporation, Corporate Plaza, 11212 Davenport Street, Omaha, NE 68154
LeaseAmerica Corporation, 2000 W. Pioneer Parkway, Suite 24-B, Peoria, IL 61615

COMPANY: **Bankers Life Company**
ADDRESS: 711 High St.
Des Moines, IA 50307
PHONE: (515) 247-5111
TYPE OF INSTITUTION: Mutual Insurance Company
CONTACT OFFICER(S): Bob Wilkins, V.P., Fixed Income Securities
ASSETS: $12 Billion
INVESTMENTS/LOANS MADE: For own account; For managed accounts; Through private placements
INVESTMENTS/LOANS MADE: In securities with a secondary market and in securities without a secondary market
TYPES OF FINANCING: SECONDARY-MARKET CORPORATE SECURITIES: Common stock; Bonds, LOANS: Unsecured to credits above Baa; Equipment; Equity-related,REAL ESTATE LOANS: Long-term senior mtg., Land, LEASES
WILL NOT CONSIDER: Land development, Bank Holding Companies
GEOGRAPHIC LIMITS OF INVESTMENTS/LOANS: International
RANGE OF INV./LOAN PER BUSINESS: Min. $2,000,000; Max. $40,000,000
PREFERRED TERM FOR LOANS & LEASES: Min. 2; Max. 15 years
BUSINESS CHARACTERISTICS DESIRED-REQUIRED: Other: Min. assets: $15 million
REFERRALS ACCEPTED FROM: Investment/Mortgage banker and Borrower/Investee
REMARKS: Average term: 10.5 years

COMPANY: **Central Life Assurance Company**
ADDRESS: 611 Fifth Avenue
Des Moines, IA 50306
PHONE: (515) 283-2371
CONTACT OFFICER(S): Lance S. Nelson, Securities V.P.
ASSETS: $1.1 Billion

INVESTMENTS/LOANS MADE: For own account; Through private placements; through underwriting public offerings
INVESTMENTS/LOANS MADE: In securities with a secondary market and in securities without a secondary market
TYPES OF FINANCING: SECONDARY-MARKET CORPORATE SECURITIES: Bonds, LOANS: Unsecured to credits above Baa; Equipment; REAL ESTATE LOANS: Intermediate-term senior mtg., REAL ESTATE: Joint ventures
GEOGRAPHIC LIMITS OF INVESTMENTS/LOANS: National
RANGE OF INV./LOAN PER BUSINESS: Min. $1,000,000; Max. $5,000,000
PREFERRED TERM FOR LOANS & LEASES: Min. 3; Max. 10 years
BUSINESS CHARACTERISTICS DESIRED-REQUIRED: Minimum number of years in business: 5; Min. annual sales $100 million; Min. net worth $25 million, Min. annual net income $5 million
REFERRALS ACCEPTED FROM: Investment/Mortgage banker or Borrower/Investee

COMPANY: **Pacific Empire Life Insurance Company**
ADDRESS: 815 Park Blvd.
Boise, ID 83705
PHONE: (208) 345-4000
CONTACT OFFICER(S): Keith Boudreau, V.P., Treasurer
Yvonne Gaundry, Acctg.
ASSETS: $1,000,000 - 10,000,000
INVESTMENTS/LOANS MADE: In securities with a secondary market and in securities without a secondary market
TYPES OF FINANCING: SECONDARY-MARKET CORPORATE SECURITIES
GEOGRAPHIC LIMITS OF INVESTMENTS/LOANS: Limited by statute of Idaho
RANGE OF INV./LOAN PER BUSINESS: Min. None; Max. 7% of total admitted assets
PREFERRED TERM FOR LOANS & LEASES: Min. 10-15; Max. 20+ years

COMPANY: **Country Life Insurance Company**
ADDRESS: P.O. Box 2646
Bloomington, IL 61701
PHONE: (309) 557-3236
CONTACT OFFICER(S): Wayne A. Brown, V.P., Fixed Income Dept.
Bernard R. Dorneden, Investment Officer, Equity Inv.
ASSETS: $1.3 billion
INVESTMENTS/LOANS MADE: For own account; Through private placements,underwriting public offerings
INVESTMENTS/LOANS MADE: In securities with a secondary market and in securities without a secondary market
TYPES OF FINANCING: SECONDARY-MARKET CORPORATE SECURITIES: Common stock; Preferred stock; Bonds; Mortgages, REAL ESTATE LOANS: Long-term senior mtg.; Intermediate-term senior mtg.; Industrial revenue bonds, LEASES
PREFERRED TYPES OF INDUSTRIES/INVESTMENTS: Open
GEOGRAPHIC LIMITS OF INVESTMENTS/LOANS: National
RANGE OF INV./LOAN PER BUSINESS: Min. $750,000; Max. $5,000,000
PREFERRED TERM FOR LOANS & LEASES: Min. 5; Max. 30 years
BUSINESS CHARACTERISTICS DESIRED-REQUIRED: Minimum number of years in business: 5
REFERRALS ACCEPTED FROM: Investment/Mortgage banker or Borrower/Investee

COMPANY: **State Farm Life Insurance Company**
ADDRESS: One State Farm Plaza
Bloomington, IL 61701
PHONE: (309) 662-2361
CONTACT OFFICER(S): Rex J. Bates, V.P. Finance
William C. Gale, East Territory
Neil Brown, West Territory

COMPANY: **Bankers Life & Casualty Co.**
ADDRESS: 4444 W. Lawrence Ave.
Chicago, IL 60630
PHONE: (312) 777-7000
TYPE OF INSTITUTION: Insurance Co.
CONTACT OFFICER(S): Jerry Hitpas

COMPANY:**Continental Assurance**
ADDRESS: CNA Plaza
Chicago, IL 60685
PHONE: (312) 822-5000
TYPE OF INSTITUTION: Insurance Co.
CONTACT OFFICER(S): Warren L. Murry, Dir. Private Placements, (312) 822-4919
Oscar Chavarria, Associate, (312) 822-4156
INVESTMENTS/LOANS MADE: In securities with a secondary market; In securities without a secondary market
TYPES OF FINANCING: SECNDARY-MARKET CORPORATE SECURITIES: Preferred stock; Bonds; Other: Private placement
PREFERRED TYPES OF INDUSTRIES/INVESTMENTS: Industrials
GEOGRAPHIC LIMITS OF INVESTMENTS/LOANS: National
RANGE OF INV./LOAN PER BUSINESS: Min. 2-3 million; Max. 10 million
BUSINESS CHARACTERISTICS DESIRED-REQUIRED: Minimum number of years in business: 5; Min. annual sales: $250,000,000
REFERRALS ACCEPTED FROM: Investment/Mortgage banker

COMPANY: **Kemper Investors Life Insurance Co.**
ADDRESS: 120 S. LaSalle Street
Chicago, IL 60603
PHONE: (312) 781-1121
TYPE OF INSTITUTION: Life Insurance Co.
CONTACT OFFICER(S): William Bueking, V.P.
Ken Urbaszewski, V.P.

COMPANY: **Federal Life Insurance Company (Mutual)**
ADDRESS: 3750 W. Deerfield Rd.
Riverwoods, IL 60015
PHONE: (312) 520-1900
CONTACT OFFICER(S): James J. Breen, Exec. V.P. & Sec. General Counsel
ASSETS: $100 million and up
INVESTMENTS/LOANS MADE: In securities with a secondary market and in securities without a secondary market
TYPES OF FINANCING: SECONDARY-MARKET CORPORATE SECURITIES: Preferred stock
GEOGRAPHIC LIMITS OF INVESTMENTS/LOANS: National
RANGE OF INV./LOAN PER BUSINESS: Min. None; Max. $500,000
REFERRALS ACCEPTED FROM: Investment/Mortgage banker or Borrower/Investee

COMPANY: **Montgomery Ward Life Ins. Co.**
ADDRESS: 200 N. Martingale Rd.
Schaumburg, IL 60194
PHONE: (312) 490-5510
CONTACT OFFICER(S): Robert S. Bartlow, V.P. & Treasurer
ASSETS: $200 million
INVESTMENTS/LOANS MADE: Securities with a public market only
GEOGRAPHIC LIMITS OF INVESTMENTS/LOANS: National
RAGE OF INV./LOAN PER BUSINESS: Min.: $1 million; Max. $3 million
REFERRALS ACCEPTED FROM: Investment/Mortgage banker only

COMPANY: **The Franklin Life Insurance Company**
ADDRESS: Franklin Square
Springfield, IL 62713
PHONE: (217) 528-2011
CONTACT OFFICER(S): John Akers, C.F.A., Treasurer—Corporate Public Offerings
Stanley G. Howard, V.P.—Commercial Mortgage Loans
William D. Ward, C.F.A., V.P.—Corporate Private Placement Common Stocks
ASSETS: $2,459,650,584
INVESTMENTS/LOANS MADE: For own account; Through private placements,underwriting public offerings
INVESTMENTS/LOANS MADE: In securities with a secondary market and in securities without a secondary market
TYPES OF FINANCING: SECONDARY-MARKET CORPORATE SECURITIES: Common stock; Preferred stock; Bonds, REAL ESTATE LOANS: Long-term senior mtg., LEASES: Single-investor; Leveraged; Tax leases; Non-tax leases; Operating
GEOGRAPHIC LIMITS OF INVESTMENTS/LOANS: National
RANGE OF INV./LOAN PER BUSINESS: Min. $1,000,000; Max. $12,000,000
PREFERRED TERM FOR LOANS & LEASES: Min. 5; Max. 12-15 years
BUSINESS CHARACTERISTICS DESIRED-REQUIRED: Minimum number of years in business: 10; Min. net worth $25,000,000
REFERRALS ACCEPTED FROM: Investment/Mortgage banker

COMPANY: **Horace Mann Life Insurance Company**
ADDRESS: 1 Horace Mann Plaza
Springfield, IL 62715
PHONE: (217) 789-2500
CONTACT OFFICER(S): Milton Wiggers, Secretary/ Director, Mtg. & R.E.
ASSETS: $100 million and up
TYPES OF FINANCING: REAL ESTATE LOANS: Long-term senior mtg. OTHER: Commercial and residential
PREFERRED TYPES OF INDUSTRIES/INVESTMENTS: No single purpose structures
GEOGRAPHIC LIMITS OF INVESTMENTS/LOANS: National
RANGE OF INV./LOAN PER BUSINESS: Min. $400,000; Max. $5 million
PREFERRED TERM FOR LOANS & LEASES: Min. 7 years; Max. 10 years
REFERRALS ACCEPTED FROM: Investment/Mortgage banker only
REMARKS: Preferred term for loans and leases subject to change

COMPANY: **The Lincoln National Inv. Management Co.**
ADDRESS: 1300 South Clinton St.
Ft. Wayne, IN 46801
PHONE: (219) 427-2000
CONTACT OFFICER(S): Patrick E. Falconio, Sr. V.P.
Robert Stewart, 2nd V.P.
Pat Chasey, 2nd V.P.
Jim Rogers, 2nd V.P.
Barbara S. Kowalczyk, 2nd V.P.
Ann L. Warner, 2nd V.P.
TYPES OF FINANCING: LOANS: Unsecured; Equipment; Equity-related; REAL ESTATE LOANS: Intermediate term senior mtg.; Subordinated; Land development; Standbys; Bond guarantees; OHTER: Industrial Revenue Bond Guarantees; REAL ESTATE: Acquisitions; OTHER SERVICES PROVIDED: Joint ventures on proposed properties; (R.E.) partnerships (R.E.)
WILL NOT CONSIDER: Retail, automotive
GEOGRAPHIC LIMITS OF INVESTMENTS/LOANS: National; International; Other: Western Europe
RANGE OF INV./LOAN PER BUSINESS: Min. $2 million; Max. $15 million; $25 million (R.E.)
PREFERRED TERM FOR LOANS & LEASES: Min. 3 years; Max. 7 years, 10 years (R.E.)

COMPANY: **American United Life Insurance Company**
ADDRESS: 1 American Square
Indianapolis, IN 46204
PHONE: (317) 263-1877
TYPE OF INSTITUTION: Life Insurance
CONTACT OFFICER(S): Leonard Schutt, Sr. V.P.,
David Sapp, V.P., Securities
Edmund W. Genier, V.P., Mtg. Loans
ASSETS: $2.0 billion

INVESTMENTS/LOANS MADE: For own account
INVESTMENTS/LOANS MADE: In securities with a secondary market and in securities without a secondary market
TYPES OF FINANCING: SECONDARY-MARKET CORPORATE SECURITIES: Common stock; Preferred stock; Bonds; LOANS: Unsecured to credits above BA; Working capital; Equipment; REAL ESTATE LOANS: Long-term senior mtg.; Intermediate-term senior mtg.

COMPANY: **The College Life Insurance Company of America**
ADDRESS: P.O. Box 68181
Indianapolis, IN 46268
PHONE: (317) 871-4200
CONTACT OFFICER(S): David Bollinger
ASSETS: $207,757,800
INVESTMENTS/LOANS MADE: In securities with a secondary market and in securities without a secondary market
TYPES OF FINANCING: SECONDARY-MARKET CORPORATE SECURITIES: Bonds; REAL ESTATE LOANS: Long-term senior mtg.; Intermediate-term senior mtg.;
GEOGRAPHIC LIMITS OF INVESTMENTS/LOANS: National
RANGE OF INV./LOAN PER BUSINESS: Min. $500,000; $2 million
PREFERRED TERM FOR LOANS & LEASES: Min. 5 yrs; Max. 10 yrs.
BUSINESS CHARACTERISTICS DESIRED-REQUIRED: Minimum number of years in business: 0

COMPANY: **Indianapolis Life Insurance Company**
ADDRESS: P.O. Box 1230
Indianapolis, IN 46206
PHONE: (317) 927-6522
CONTACT OFFICER(S): Donald S. Lawhorn, Sr. V.P. & Chief Investment office
ASSETS: $700 million
INVESTMENTS/LOANS MADE: For own account; For managed accounts; Through private placements; Through underwriting public offerings
INVESTMENTS/LOANS MADE: In securities with a secondary market and in securities without a secondary marketing
TYPES OF FINANCING: SECONDARY-MARKET CORPORATE SECURITIES: Bonds, VENTURE CAPITAL: Later-stage expansion; LOANS: Unsecured to credits above Baa; Working capital; Equipment; REAL ESTATE LOANS: Long-term senior mtg.; Intermediate-term senior mtg.
GEOGRAPHIC LIMITS OF INVESTMENTS/LOANS: National
RANGE OF INV./LOAN PER BUSINESS: Min. $200,000; Max. $2.5 million
PREFERRED TERM FOR LOANS & LEASES: Min. 5 years.; Max. 20 years
BUSINESS CHARACTERISTICS DESIRED-REQUIRED: Min. net worth $50 Million
REFERRALS ACCEPTED FROM: Investment/Mortgage banker or Borrower/Investee

COMPANY: **The State Life Insurance Company**
ADDRESS: P.O. Box 406, 141 E. Washington St.
Indianapolis, IN 46206
PHONE: (317) 632-3551
TYPE OF INSTITUTION: Life and Health Insurance
CONTACT OFFICER(S): David A. Martin, Private Placement, Bonds, Public Bonds, Mtg. Loans
ASSETS: $150 million
INVESTMENTS/LOANS MADE: For own account; Through private placements,underwriting public offerings
TYPES OF FINANCING: SECONDARY-MARKET CORPORATE SECURITIES: Bonds, LOANS: Unsecured to credits above A, REAL ESTATE LOANS: Long-term senior mtg.; Intermediate-term senior mtg.
WILL NOT CONSIDER: Finance
GEOGRAPHIC LIMITS OF INVESTMENTS/LOANS: National
REFERRALS ACCEPTED FROM: Investment/Mortgage banker

COMPANY: **Security Benefit Group of Companies**
ADDRESS: 700 Harrison
Topeka, KS 66636
PHONE: (913) 295-3000
CONTACT OFFICER(S): Jack W. Carolan, V.P.
ASSETS: $1.4 billion
TYPES OF FINANCING: REAL ESTATE LOANS: Intermediate-term senior mtg.
GEOGRAPHIC LIMITS OF INVESTMENTS/LOANS: National
RANGE OF INV./LOAN PER BUSINESS: Min. $800,000; Max. $4 million
PREFERRED TERM FOR LOANS & LEASES: Min. 5 years; Max. 15 years
REFERRALS ACCEPTED FROM: Investment/mortgage banker or Borrower/Investee

COMPANY: **Kentucky Central Insurance Cos.**
ADDRESS: Kincaid Towers
Lexington, KY 40508
PHONE: (606) 253-5293
TYPE OF INSTITUTION: Life, Property & Casualty Insurance Companies
CONTACT OFFICER(S): Clifton H. Forbush, Jr., V.P. — Investments
John F. Rampulla, III, V.P. — Mortgage Loans
ASSETS: $700 million
INVESTMENTS/LOANS MADE: For own account; Through private placements,underwriting public offerings
INVESTMENTS/LOANS MADE: In securities with a secondary market and in securities without a secondary market
TYPES OF FINANCING: SECONDARY-MARKET CORPORATE SECURITIES: Common stock; Preferred stock; Bonds, LOANS: Unsecured to credits above Ba; Equipment; REAL ESTATE LOANS: Long-term senior mtg., Land, LEASES: Single-investor; Leveraged; Vendor financing programs; OTHER SERVICES PROVIDED: no longer do tax-exempt
PREFERRED TYPES OF INDUSTRIES/INVESTMENTS: Finance & Insurance; Manufacturing & Processing;

Medical & Other Health Services; Natural Resources; Services; Transportation, Utilities; Diversified
GEOGRAPHIC LIMITS OF INVESTMENTS/LOANS: National
RANGE OF INV./LOAN PER BUSINESS: Min. $500,000; Max. $1,000,000
PREFERRED TERM FOR LOANS & LEASES: Min. 5-10; Max. 10-15 years
BUSINESS CHARACTERISTICS DESIRED-REQUIRED: Min. annual sales $75-100 million; Min. net worth $15 million; Min. annual net income $2 million
REFERRALS ACCEPTED FROM: Investment/Mortgage banker

COMPANY: **Pan American Life**
ADDRESS: Pan American Life Center
New Orleans, LA 70130
PHONE: (504) 566-1300
TYPE OF INSTITUTION: Mutual life insurance company
CONTACT OFFICER(S): Luis Ingles, V.P., Securities
Larry Dupuy, V.P., Mortgage Loans & Real Estate
Mayo Emory, Senior Securities Analyst
John Herrington, Second V.P., Mortgage Loans
ASSETS: $875 million
INVESTMENTS/LOANS MADE: For own account, Through private placements
INVESTMENTS/LOANS MADE: In securities with a secondary market and in securities without a secondary market
TYPES OF FINANCING: SECONDARY-MARKET CORPORATE SECURITIES: Common stock; Bonds, LOANS: Unsecured to credits above, BA; Equipment; Equity-related, REAL ESTATE LOANS: Intermediate-term senior mtg.; Other: Short-term senior mtg.; Intermediate-term senior mtg. with participation only, LEASES: Leveraged, REAL ESTATE: Acquisitions; Joint ventures
PREFERRED TYPES OF INDUSTRIES/INVESTMENTS: Securities: Generally open on all types; Mortgages
GEOGRAPHIC LIMITS OF INVESTMENTS/LOANS: National
RANGE OF INV./LOAN PER BUSINESS: Min. $500,000; Max. 5 million
PREFERRED TERM FOR LOANS & LEASES: Min. 5 years, amortized; Max. 10-15 years amortized
REFERRALS ACCEPTED FROM: Investment/Mortgage banker or Borrower/Investee

COMPANY: **John Hancock Mutual Life Insurance Co.**
ADDRESS: John Hancock Place, P.O. Box 111
Boston, MA 02117
PHONE: (617) 421-6000
TYPE OF INSTITUTION: Life insurance co.
CONTACT OFFICER(S): Stephen L. Brown, Executive V.P., Investment Operations; John Q. Adams, Private Placements
ASSETS: Approximately $30 billion
INVESTMENTS/LOANS MADE: For own account, For managed accounts, Through private placements, Through underwriting public offerings
INVESTMENTS/LOANS MADE: In securities with a secondary market and in securities without a secondary market
TYPES OF FINANCING: SECONDARY-MARKET CORPORATE SECURITIES: Common stock; Preferred stock; Bonds; Other: R. estate, VENTURE CAPITAL: Later-stage expansion, LOANS: Unsecured; Working capital; Equipment; Equity-related, REAL ESTATE LOANS: Long-term senior mtg., Intermediate-term senior mtg.; Land; Land development; Industrial revenue bonds, LEASES: Leveraged; Tax leases; Non-tax leases; Operating; Vendor financing programs, REAL ESTATE: Acquisitions; Joint ventures; Partnerships/Syndications
PREFERRED TYPES OF INDUSTRIES/INVESTMENTS: Agriculture
GEOGRAPHIC LIMITS OF INVESTMENTS/LOANS: National; International
RANGE OF INV./LOAN PER BUSINESS: Min. variable
PREFERRED TERM FOR LOANS & LEASES: Min. variable
BUSINESS CHARACTERISTICS DESIRED-REQUIRED: Minimum number of years in business: 10;
REFERRALS ACCEPTED FROM: Investment/Mortgage banker or Borrower/Investee

COMPANY: **New England Mutual Life Insurance Co.**
ADDRESS: 501 Boylston Street
Boston, MA 02117
PHONE: (617) 266-3700
CONTACT OFFICER(S): John Rodgers, Sr. V.P. Securities
Hamilton Coolidge, Sr. V.P. Mortgage
ASSETS: 21,479,000,000 (& subs)
INVESTMENTS/LOANS MADE: For own account
INVESTMENTS/LOANS MADE: In securities with a secondary market and in securities without a secondary market
TYPES OF FINANCING: SECONDARY-MARKET CORPORATE SECURITIES: Common stock; Preferred stock; Bonds; Other: Convertibles. VENTURE CAPITAL: Research & Development; First-stage (less than 1 year); Second-stage (generally 1-3 years) Later-stage expansion; LOANS; Unsecured; Working capital (receivables/inventory); Equipment; Equity-related; REAL ESTATE LOANS: Intermediate-term senior mtg.; Wraparounds; Land; Land development; Construction; Industrial revenue bonds; Other: 2nd mtg. & blanket; LEASES: Single-investor; Leveraged; Tax leases; Non-tax leases; Operating; Lease syndications; REAL ESTATE: Acquisitions; Joint ventures; Partnerships/Syndications; OTHER SERVICES PROVIDED: discount brokerage tax shelter deals thru NESCO
GEOGRAPHIC LIMITS OF INVESTMENTS/LOANS: National
RANGE OF INV./LOAN PER BUSINESS: Min. $1 million; Max. $30 million
BUSINESS CHARACTERISTICS DESIRED-REQUIRED: Min. no. of years in business: 0
REFERRALS ACCEPTED FROM: Investment/Mortgage banker or Borrower/Investee
BRANCHES: Loomis, Sayles, & Co. Inc., 225 Franklin St., Boston, MA 02110; does own investing and all equity for parent

COMPANY: **Boston Mutual Life Insurance Company**
ADDRESS: 120 Royall St.
Canton, MA 02021
PHONE: (617) 828-7000
CONTACT OFFICER(S): Robert McNally, V.P., R.E. & Mtg.
Howard Neff, Mtg. Officer
ASSETS: $175 million
TYPES OF FINANCING: REAL ESTATE LOANS
GEOGRAPHIC LIMITS OF INVESTMENTS/LOANS: National
RANGE OF INV./LOAN PER BUSINESS: Min. $500,000; Max. $1,500,000
PREFERRED TYPES OF INDUSTRIES/INVESTMENTS: Real Estate: apartment houses, shopping centers, office buildings
BUSINESS CHARACTERISTICS DESIRED-REQUIRED: Minimum number of years in business: 7; Min. annual net income positive; Other: Minimum net worth should exceed mortgage request
REFERRALS ACCEPTED FROM: Investment/Mortgage banker or Borrower/Investee

COMPANY: **Berkshire Life Insurance Co.**
ADDRESS: 700 South Street
Pittsfield, MA 01201
PHONE: (413) 499-4321
CONTACT OFFICER(S): Colin MacFadyen, V.P., Securities
ASSETS: $500 million
INVESTMENTS/LOANS MADE: In securities with a secondary market and in securities without a secondary market
TYPES OF FINANCING: SECONDARY-MARKET CORPORATE SECURITIES: Common stock; Bonds, REAL ESTATE LOANS: Intermediate-term senior mtg., REAL ESTATE: Limited Partnerships
PREFERRED TYPES OF INDUSTRIES/INVESTMENTS: Varied
WILL NOT CONSIDER: Vary
GEOGRAPHIC LIMITS OF INVESTMENTS/LOANS: National
RANGE OF INV./LOAN PER BUSINESS: Min. $250,000; Max. $1.5 million
PREFERRED TERM FOR LOANS & LEASES: Min. 5 years; Max. 20 years
BUSINESS CHARACTERISTICS DESIRED-REQUIRED: BAA quality credit mtgs; prime features: location, good economy in area, bonds, AA or higher
REFERRALS ACCEPTED FROM: Investment/Mortgage banker or Borower/Investee
REMARKS: Desired level of investment: $500,000-$1,000,000; desired term: 10-15 years

COMPANY: **Massachusetts Mutual Life Insurance Co.**
ADDRESS: 1295 State St.
Springfield, MA 01111
PHONE: (413) 788-8411
CONTACT OFFICER(S): Scott C. Noble, Sr. V.P. R.E.
Gary E. Wendlandt, Private Placements
ASSETS: $12.5 billion
INVESTMENTS/LOANS MADE: In securities with a secondary market and in securities without a secondary market
TYPES OF FINANCING: LOANS: Equity-related, REAL ESTATE LOANS
GEOGRAPHIC LIMITS OF INVESTMENTS/LOANS: National
RANGE OF INV./LOAN PER BUSINESS: Min. $2 mil.; Max. 30 mil.
PREFERRED TERM FOR LOANS & LEASES: Min. 3 years; Max. 15 years
REFERRALS ACCEPTED FROM: Investment/Mortgage banker or Borrower/Investee
BRANCHES: RE: 6 branches, originate new investments—Atlanta, Chicago, Dallas, LA, Wash. D.C., NE Springfield

COMPANY: **State Mutual Life Assurance Co. of America**
ADDRESS: 440 Lincoln St.
Worcester, MA 01541
PHONE: (617) 852-1000
TYPE OF INSTITUTION: Insurance Co.
CONTACT OFFICER(S): Dix F. Davis, Vice. Pres.
Jon Austad, Asst. Vice Pres.-Securities
John W. Nunley, Second Vice Pres.-Mortgages
ASSETS: 4 Billion
INVESTMENTS/LOANS MADE: For own account, For managed accounts, Through private placements, Through underwriting public offerings
INVESTMENTS/LOANS MADE: In securities with a secondary market and in securities without a secondary market
TYPES OF FINANCING: SECONDARY-MARKET CORPORATE SECURITIES: Bonds, LOANS: Unsecured to credits above B, REAL ESTATE LOANS: Long-term senior mtg.; Intermediate-term senior mtg.; Wraparounds, REAL ESTATE: Joint ventures
GEOGRAPHIC LIMITS OF INVESTMENTS/LOANS: National
RANGE OF INV./LOAN PER BUSINESS: Min. $2,000,000; Max. $5,000,000
PREFERRED TERM FOR LOANS & LEASES: Min. 2 years: Max. 10 years
REFERRALS ACCEPTED FROM: Investment/Mortgage banker or Borrower/Investee

COMPANY: **Maccabees Mutual Life Insurance Co.**
ADDRESS: 25800 Northwestern Highway
Southfield, MI 48037
PHONE: (313) 357-4800
CONTACT OFFICER(S): John McCormick, V.P. Treasurer
Mark Maisonneuve, Inv. Analyst
TYPES OF FINANCING: SECONDARY-MARKET CORPORATE SECURITIES: Bonds
WILL NOT CONSIDER: Tobacco, liquor, industries, real estate
GEOGRAPHIC LIMITS OF INVESTMENTS/LOANS: National
RANGE OF INV./LOAN PER BUSINESS: Min. $1 Million; Max. $2.5 million
BUSINESS CHARACTERISTICS DESIRED-REQUIRED: Minimum number of years in business: 1

COMPANY:**Midwest Family Mutual**
ADDRESS: 10601 Wayzata Blvd.
Hopkins, MN 55343
PHONE: (612) 545-6000

MINNESOTA

TYPE OF INSTITUTION: Life Insurance Co.
CONTACT OFFICER(S): William Laidlaw, Pres.
ASSETS: $11.7 million

COMPANY: **Congress Life Ins. Co.**
ADDRESS: 1200 2nd Ave.
Minneapolis, MN 55403
PHONE: (612) 333-1295
TYPE OF INSTITUTION: (A wholly-owned subsidiary of Security Life Ins. Co. of Am. Mpls., MN)
CONTACT OFFICER(S): Alan M. Strathers, V.P. Investments
ASSETS: $8 million
INVESTMENTS/LOANS MADE: Only in securities with a secondary market
TYPES OF FINANCING: SECONDARY-MARKET CORPORATE SECURITIES: Common Stock; Bonds

COMPANY: **IDS American Express**
ADDRESS: IDS Tower
Minneapolis, MN 55402
PHONE: (612) 372-3131
TYPE OF INSTITUTION: Life Ins. Co.
CONTACT OFFICER(S): Richard Latzer; V.P. Certificate insurance and investments
ASSETS: 18.5 billion
INVESTMENTS/LOANS MADE: SECONDARY-MARKET CORPORATE SECURITIES: Common stock; Preferred stock; Bonds; Other; LOANS: Unsecured; Equipment; REAL ESTATE LOANS: Intermediate-term senior mtg.; Subordinated; Wraparounds; Standbys, Industrial Revenue Bonds; REAL ESTATE: Joint ventures; Partnerships/ Syndications; OTHER SERVICES PROVIDED
RANGE OF INV./LOAN PER BUSINESS: $2 million
REFERRALS ACCEPTED FROM: Investment/Mortgage banker or Borrower/Investee

COMPANY: **Lutheran Brotherhood**
ADDRESS: 625 Fourth Avenue South
Minneapolis, MN 55415
PHONE: (612) 340-7000
TYPE OF INSTITUTION: Insurance Co.
CONTACT OFFICER(S): James Walline, A.V.P.; Roy Bjelland, E.V.P.
ASSETS: $2.5 billion
INVESTMENTS/LOANS MADE: In securities with a secondary market; In securities without a secondary market
TYPES OF FINANCING: SECONDARY-MARKET CORPORATE SECURITIES: Common stock; Bonds, REAL ESTATE LOANS: Long-term senior mtg.; Intermediate-term senior mtg.; Subordinated, REAL ESTATE: Acquisitions; Joint ventures; Partnerships/ Syndiciations
PREFERRED TYPES OF INDUSTRIES/INVESTMENTS: Private placement bonds; Commercial loans
GEOGRAPHIC LIMITS OF INVESTMENTS/LOANS: National
REFERRALS ACCEPTED FROM: Investment/Mortgage banker; Borrower/Investee

COMPANY: **Ministers Life — A Mutual Life Insurance Company**
ADDRESS: 3100 West Lake Street
Minneapolis, MN 55416
PHONE: (612) 927-7131
CONTACT OFFICER(S): Bruce Nicholson, V.P.-Finance Investments
INVESTMENTS/LOANS MADE: For own account
TYPES OF FINANCING: REAL ESTATE LOANS: Intermediate-term senior mtg.
PREFERRED TYPES OF INDUSTRIES/INVESTMENTS: Multi purpose buildings
GEOGRAPHIC LIMITS OF INVESTMENTS/LOANS: National
RANGE OF INV./LOAN PER BUSINESS: Min. $300,000; Max. $800,000
REFERRALS ACCEPTED FROM: Investment/Mortgage banker
REMARKS: Investing is handled through Washington Square Advisors Mike Eidem (612) 372-1820

COMPANY: **Security Life Insurance Co. of America**
ADDRESS: 1200 Second Ave., So.
Minneapolis, MN 55403
PHONE: (612) 333-1295
CONTACT OFFICER(S): Alan M. Struthers, V.P. — Investments
ASSETS: $20,000,000
INVESTMENTS/LOANS MADE: For own account
INVESTMENTS/LOANS MADE: Only in securities with a secondary market
TYPES OF FINANCING: SECONDARY-MARKET CORPORATE SECURITIES: Common stock; Bonds
PREFERRED TYPES OF INDUSTRIES/INVESTMENTS: No Preferences

COMPANY: **Washington Square Capital, Inc.**
ADDRESS: 100 Washington Square, Box 20
Minneapolis, MN 55440
PHONE: (612) 375-7541
TYPE OF INSTITUTION: Investment Advisory Firm
CONTACT OFFICER(S): Donald M. Feroe, V.P., Corporate Securities
Harold W. Leiferman, V.P., Mortgage Loans
Gary J. Kallsen, V.P., Real Estate
ASSETS: $2,800,000,000
INVESTMENTS/LOANS MADE: For managed accounts; Through private placements
INVESTMENTS/LOANS MADE: In securities with a secondary market and in securities without a secondary market
TYPES OF FINANCING: SECONDARY-MARKET CORPORATE SECURITIES: Bonds, VENTURE CAPITAL: Later-stage expansion; Buy-outs/ Acquisitions, LOANS: Unsecured to credits above Baa; Working capital (receivables/inventory); Equipment; Equity-related, REAL ESTATE LOANS: Intermediate-term senior mtg.; Wraparounds; Construction; Standbys; Loan Guarantees, LEASES: Leveraged; Non-tax leases; Vendor financing programs, REAL ESTATE: Acquisitions; Joint ventures
PREFERRED TYPES OF INDUSTRIES/INVESTMENTS: Any

GEOGRAPHIC LIMITS OF INVESTMENTS/LOANS: U.S. and Canada
RANGE OF INV./LOAN PER BUSINESS: Min. $2,000,000; Max. $25,000,000
PREFERRED TERM FOR LOANS & LEASES: Min. 1; Max. 10 years
BUSINESS CHARACTERISTICS DESIRED-REQUIRED: Minimum number of years in business: 5
REFERRALS ACCEPTED FROM: Investment/Mortgage banker or Borrower/Investee

COMPANY:**Minnesota Mutual Fire Casualty Co.**
ADDRESS: 10225 Yellow Cr. Dr.
Minneapolis MN 55343
PHONE: (612) 933-5033
CONTACT OFFICER: Jim Jordan, Exec. V.P.
ASSETS: $35 million
INVESTMENTS/LOANS MADE: In securities with a secondary market or without a secondary market
TYPES OF FINANCING: SECONDARY-MARKET CORPORATE SECURITIES: Common stock; Preferred stock; Bonds; REAL ESTATE LOANS: Other: pools of mortgages—no indv. mtgs.
PREFERRED TYPES OF INDUSTRIES/INVESTMENTS: Gov't. guarantees, municipalities
GEOGRAPHIC LIMITS OF INVESTMENTS/LOANS: National

COMPANY: **Midwest Life Ins. Co.**
ADDRESS: 100 Dain Tower
Minneapolis MN 55402
PHONE: (612) 371-7774
CONTACT OFFICER(S): Bonnie Russ, Sr. V.P. in charge of Administration
ASSETS: $70 million
INVESTMENTS/LOANS MADE: In securities with a secondary market and in securities without a secondary market
TYPES OF FINANCING: SECONDARY-MARKET CORPORATE SECURITIES: Bonds; REAL ESTATE LOANS: Long-term senior mtg.; Intermediate-term senior mtg.
GEOGRAPHIC LIMITS OF INVESTMENTS/LOANS: National
RANGE OF INV./LOAN PER BUSINESS: Min. —; Max. $1 mil.
PREFERRED TERM FOR LOANS & LEASES: Min. — years; Max. 30 years
REFERRALS ACCEPTED FROM: Investment/Mortgage banker or Borrower/Investee

COMPANY: **All Nation Insurance Co.**
ADDRESS: 155 Aurora Ave.
St. Paul, MN 55103
PHONE: (612) 224-5765
TYPE OF INSTITUTION: Casualty Ins. Co.
CONTACT OFFICER(S): Darryl Durum, President
ASSETS: $17 million
INVESTMENTS/LOANS MADE: In securities with a secondary market
TYPES OF FINANCING: SECONDARY-MARKET CORPORATE: Common stock; Bonds; Other: Municipal & gov't. bonds
GEOGRAPHIC LIMITS OF INVESTMENTS/LOANS: National

COMPANY: **MIMLIC Asset Management Co.**
ADDRESS: 400 North Robert
St. Paul, MN 55101
PHONE: (612) 298-3844
TYPE OF INSTITUTION: Registered investment advisor for MN Mutual Life and its subsidiaries
CONTACT OFFICER(S): Fritz Feuerherm, Sr. Inv. Off., Bonds, Fixed Income
John Clymer, Sr. Inv. Officer, Mortgage & RE
Tim Kasper, Sr. Inv. Officer, Equity
ASSETS: $2.8 billion
INVESTMENTS/LOANS MADE: In securities with a secondary market and in securities without a secondary market
TYPES OF FINANCING: SECONDARY-MARKET CORPORATE SECURITIES: Common stock; Preferred stock; Bonds; Other: Limited partnerships. VENTURE CAPITAL: Later-stage expansion; Oil exploration. LOANS: Unsecured; Working capital; Equipment; Equity-related. REAL ESTATE LOANS: Long-term senior mtg.; Intermediate-term senior mtg.; Subordinated; Wraparounds; Land; Land development. LEASES: Leveraged; Non-tax leases; Operating; Other: equipment. REAL ESTATE: Acquisitions; Joint ventures; Partnerships/Syndications.
PREFERRED TYPES OF INDUSTRIES/INVESTMENTS: Mostly fixed incomes
GEOGRAPHIC LIMITS OF INVESTMENTS/LOANS: National
RANGE OF INV./LOAN PER BUSINESS: Min. $1 million
BUSINESS CHARACTERISTICS DESIRED-REQUIRED: Minimum number of years in business: 5
REFERRALS ACCEPTED FROM: Investment/Mortgage banker or Borrower/Investee

COMPANY: **The Minnesota Mutuual Life Insurance Co.**
ADDRESS: 400 North Robert
St. Paul, MN 55101
PHONE: (612) 298-3500
CONTACT OFFICER(S): Fritz Feuerherm, Inv. Off.
TYPES OF FINANCING: SECONDARY-MARKET CORPORATE SECURITIES: Bonds. LOANS: Equipment, Equity-related. REAL ESTATE LOANS: Long-term senior mtg.; Subordinated
PREFERRED TYPES OF INDUSTRIES/INVESTMENTS: Corporate loans
WILL NO CONSIDER: Banks
GEOGRAPHIC LIMITS OF INVESTMENTS/LOANS: National
RANGE OF INV./LOAN PER BUSINESS: Min. $2 million; Max. $8 million
PREFERRED TERM FOR LOANS & LEASES: Min. 2 years; Max. 15 years
BUSINESS CHARACTERISTICS DESIRED-REQUIRED: Minimum number of years in business: 5; Other: Operating profits within last 5 years
REFERRALS ACCEPTED FROM: Investment/Mortgage banker or Borrower/Investee

COMPANY: **Mutual Service Life Insurance Co.**
ADDRESS: Two Pine Tree Dr.
St. Paul, MN 55112
PHONE: (612) 631-7000
CONTACT OFFICER(S): Loren A. Haugland, VP Investments
INVESTMENTS/LOANS MADE: In securities with a secondary market and in securities without a secondary market
TYPES OF FINANCING: SECONDARY-MARKET CORPORATE SECURITIES: Common stock; Preferred stock; Bonds. VENTURE CAPITAL. REAL ESTATE LOANS: Intermediate-term senior mtg.; Wraparounds; Other: will do second mortgages. LEASES: Single-investor; Leveraged. REAL ESTATE: Acquisitions. OTHER SERVICES PROVIDED: Participate in most phases of venture capital through pooling
GEOGRAPHIC LIMITS OF INVESTMENTS/LOANS: National
RANGE OF INV./LOAN PER BUSINESS: Min. $250,000; Max. $3 million
PREFERRED TERM FOR LOANS & LEASES: Min. 3 years
REFERRALS ACCEPTED FROM: Investment/Mortgage banker or Borrower/Investee

COMPANY: **North Central Life Insurance Company**
ADDRESS: 445 Minnesota Street
St. Paul, MN 55101
PHONE: (612) 227-8001
CONTACT OFFICER(S): John Drake
ASSETS: $10 million — 100 million
INVESTMENTS/LOANS MADE: Only in securities with a secondary market

COMPANY: **Employees Mutual Benefit Assoc.**
ADDRESS: 1457 Grand Ave.
St. Paul MN 55105
PHONE: (612) 698-3539
TYPE OF INSTITUION: Life Insurance Co.
CONTACT OFFICER(S): Joel Pearson, Pres.
ASSETS: 12 million
INVESTMENTS/LOANS MADE: Only in securities with a secondary market
TYPES OF INVESTMENTS/LOANS MADE: Mainly corporate bonds, treasury issues

COMPANY: **Business Mens Assurance Co.**
ADDRESS: Box 458
Kansas City, MO 64141
PHONE: (816) 753-8000
TYPE OF INSTITUTION: Life insurance company
CONTACT OFFICER(S): Tony Jacobs, Sr. V.P. & Sr. Sec. Off.
Robert Sawyer, Securities V.P.
Connie Troutman
Charles D. Durbin, Asst. V.P.
TYPES OF FINANCING: SECONDARY-MARKET CORPORATE SECURITIES: Common stock; Preferred stock; Bonds, VENTURE CAPITAL: Research & Development, REAL ESTATE LOANS: Land development, OTHER SERVICES PROVIDED: Purchases through BMA Properties — R.E. & Mortgaging
PREFERRED TYPES OF INDUSTRIES/INVESTMENTS: Diversified
GEOGRAPHIC LIMITS OF INVESTMENTS/LOANS: National
RANGE OF INV./LOAN PER BUSINESS: Min. None; Max. $3 million
PREFERRED TERM FOR LOANS & LEASES: Min. Varies

COMPANY: **Kansas City Life Insurance Company**
ADDRESS: 3520 Broadway, P.O. Box 139
Kansas City, MO 64141-0139
PHONE: (816) 753-7000
CONTACT OFFICER(S): Richard L. Finn, Sr. V.P. Financial
ASSETS: $100 million and up
TYPES OF FINANCING: REAL ESTATE LOANS: Long-term senior mtg.; Intermediate-term senior mtg.
PREFERRED TYPES OF INDUSTRIES/INVESTMENTS: Industrial and Retail
GEOGRAPHIC LIMITS OF INVESTMENTS/LOANS: National; Primarily South, Southwest & West Coast
RANGE OF INV./LOAN PER BUSINESS: Min. $400,000; Max. $4,000,000
PREFERRED TERM FOR LOANS & LEASES: Min. 5; Max. 7-10 years
REFERRALS ACCEPTED FROM: Investment/Mortgage banker or Borrower/Investee

COMPANY: **General American Life Insurance Co.**
ADDRESS: 700 Market St.
St. Louis, MO 63101
PHONE: (314) 444-0624
TYPE OF INSTITUTION: Insurance Company
CONTACT OFFICER(S): Leonard M. Rubenstein
Bruce C. Fernandez
Kathy R. Lange
ASSETS: $2 Billion +
INVESTMENTS/LOANS MADE: For own account; for managed accounts; through private placements; through underwriting public offerings
INVESTMENTS/LOANS MADE: In securities with a secondary market and in securities without a secondary market
TYPES OF FINANCING: SECONDARY-MARKET CORPORATE SECURITIES: Bonds; LOANS: Unsecured to credits above Baa; Equipment, LEASES: Single-investor; Leveraged; Tax leases
PREFERRED TYPES OF INDUSTRIES/INVESTMENTS: No Preference
GEOGRAPHIC LIMITS OF INVESTMENTS/LOANS: National/No Foreign Loans
RANGE OF INV./LOAN PER BUSINESS: Min. 3 million; Max. 10 million
PREFERRED TERM FOR LOANS & LEASES: Min. 5; Max. 15 years
BUSINESS CHARACTERISTICS DESIRED-REQUIRED: Minimum number of years in business: 5; Min. net worth $50 mil.
REFERRALS ACCEPTED FROM: Investment/Mortgage banker or Borrower/Investee

MISSOURI

COMPANY: **The Reliable Life Insurance Company**
ADDRESS: 231 W. Lockwood
Webster Groves, MO 63119
PHONE: (314) 968-4900
CONTACT OFFICER(S): Lisa Luehrman, V.P.
ASSETS: $260 million
INVESTMENTS/LOANS MADE: In securities with a secondary market and in securities without a secondary-market
TYPES OF FINANCING: SECONDARY-MARKET CORPORATE SECURITIES: Common stock; Preferred stock; Bonds; VENTURE CAPITAL: First-stage; Second-stage; Buy-outs/Acquisitions; LOANS: Equity-related; REAL ESTATE LOANS: Long-term senior mtg.; Intermediate-term senior mtg.; Land; Land development; Construction; Standbys; REAL ESTATE: Acquisitions; Partnerships/Syndications
GEOGRAPHIC LIMITS OF INVESTMENTS/LOANS: Regional; Midwest; South; Southwest
RANGE OF INV./LOAN PER BUSINESS: Max. 10 years
PREFERRED TERM FOR LOANS & LEASES: Max. 10 years
REFERRALS ACCEPTED FROM: Investment/Mortgage banker only
REMARKS: Have a number of wholly-owned subsidiaries through the Midwest; 50 locations —insurance; all investing done through this office

COMPANY: **Southern Farm Bureau Life Insurance Company**
ADDRESS: 1401 Livingston Lane, P.O. Box 78
Jackson, MS 39213
PHONE: (601) 981-7422
CONTACT OFFICER(S): Walter J. Olson, III Portfolio Mgr.
Joel M. Melton, Manager, Mortgage Loans and Real Estate Department
Jerry Betterson, Investment Analyst
ASSETS: $1,300,000,000.00
INVESTMENTS/LOANS MADE: For own account
INVESTMENTS/LOANS MADE: In securities with a secondary market and in securities without a secondary market
TYPES OF FINANCING: LOANS: SECONDARY-MARKET CORPORATE SECURITIES: Common stock; Bonds; VENTURE CAPITAL: Later-stage expansion; Buy-outs/Acquisitions; LOANS: Unsecured to credits above BAA; Equipment; Equity-related; REAL ESTATE LOANS: Intermediate-term senior mtg.; Wraparounds; Construction; Standbys; Industrial revenue bonds; REAL ESTATE: Acquisitions; Joint ventures; OTHER SERVICES PROVIDED: Mortgage Banking
PREFERRED TYPES OF INDUSTRIES/INVESTMENTS: Will consider most types.
WILL NOT CONSIDER: Some S & L and Finance
GEOGRAPHIC LIMITS OF INVESTMENTS/LOANS: National
RANGE OF INV./LOAN PER BUSINESS: Min. $500,000; Max. $5,000,000
PREFERRED TERM FOR LOANS & LEASES: Min. 1; Max. 10 years
BUSINESS CHARACTERISTICS DESIRED-REQUIRED: A rated or equivalent

NORTH CAROLINA

COMPANY: **North Carolina Mutual Life Insurance Co.**
ADDRESS: Mutual Plaza
Durham, NC 27701
PHONE: (919) 682-9201
CONTACT OFFICER(S): Milan R. Pakaski, R.E.
M. K. Sloan, Treasurer, Equities
ASSETS: $200 million
TYPES OF FINANCING: SECONDARY-MARKET CORPORATE SECURITIES: Bonds, LOANS, REAL ESTATE LOANS
GEOGRAPHIC LIMITS OF INVESTMENTS/LOANS: Regional; Other: East Coast exclusive of NY
RANGE OF INV./LOAN PER BUSINESS: Min. None; Max. $2 mil. for R.E.
PREFERRED TERM FOR LOANS & LEASES: Min. 10-15 years; Max. 15-20 years
BUSINESS CHARACTERISTICS DESIRED-REQUIRED: Other: A, AA, AAA rated on provisional rated; not actively seeking industrial revenues and municipals
REFERRALS ACCEPTED FROM: Investment/Mortgage banker or Borrower/Investee
BRANCHES: 44 branches-district office; 14 states & D.C.

COMPANY: **Jefferson-Pilot Investments, Inc.**
ADDRESS: P.O. Box 20407
Greensboro, NC 27420
PHONE: (919) 378-2387
TYPE OF INSTITUTION: Investment Management Subsidiary of Jefferson-Pilot Corporation
CONTACT OFFICER(S): George Garey, Jr., Senior Vice President-Securities
Hugh B. North, Jr., Senior Vice President-Mortgage Loan
ASSETS: $2.5 Billion
INVESTMENTS/LOANS MADE: For own account; For managed accounts; Through private placements; Through underwriting public offerings
INVESTMENTS/LOANS MADE: In securities with a secondary market and in securities without a secondary market
TYPES OF FINANCING: SECONDARY-MARKET CORPORATE SECURITIES: Common stock; Preferred stock; Bonds; LOANS: Unsecured to credits above BAA; Working capital; Equipment; REAL ESTATE LOANS: Long-term senior mtg.; Intermediate-term senior mtg.; Industrial revenue bonds; LEASES: Single-investor; Leveraged; REAL ESTATE: Acquisitions; Joint Ventures
GEOGRAPHIC LIMITS OF INVESTMENTS/LOANS: National
RANGE OF INV./LOAN PER BUSINESS: Min. $500,000; Max. $10,000,000
PREFERRED TERM FOR LOANS & LEASES: Varies
REFERRALS ACCEPTED FROM: Investment/Mortgage banker or Borrower/Investee

COMPANY: **Southern Life Insurance Company**
ADDRESS: One Southern Life Center, P.O. Box 21887
Greensboro, NC 27420
PHONE: (919) 275-9681
CONTACT OFFICER(S): W. Lee Carter, III, V.P., Investments

ASSETS: $180 million and up
INVESTMENTS/LOANS MADE: In securities with a secondary market and in securities without a secondary market
TYPES OF FINANCING: SECONDARY-MARKET CORPORATE SECURITIES, LOANS:, REAL ESTATE LOANS
GEOGRAPHIC LIMITS OF INVESTMENTS/LOANS: National; Canada
RANGE OF INV./LOAN PER BUSINESS: Min. $100,000; Max. $1,000,000
REFERRALS ACCEPTED FROM: Investment/Mortgage banker or Borrower/Investee

COMPANY: **Durham Life Insurance Company**
ADDRESS: 2610 Wycliff Road, P.O. Box 27807
Raleigh, NC 27611
PHONE: (919) 782-6110
TYPE OF INSTITUTION: Insurance Co.
CONTACT OFFICER(S): F.P. Coley — Executive V.P. & Treasurer-Finance
F. E. Skipper, V.P & Sec.
ASSETS: $400,000,000+
INVESTMENTS/LOANS MADE: For own account; For managed accounts; Through private placements, underwriting public offerings
INVESTMENTS/LOANS MADE: In securities with a secondary market and in securities without a secondary market
TYPES OF FINANCING: SECONDARY-MARKET CORPORATE SECURITIES: Common stock; Preferred stock; Bonds, LOANS: Unsecured to credits above "A" or better, REAL ESTATE LOANS: Long-term senior mtg.; Intermediate-term senior mtg., REAL ESTATE: Acquisitions
PREFERRED TYPES OF INDUSTRIES/INVESTMENTS: Diversified
GEOGRAPHIC LIMITS OF INVESTMENTS/LOANS: Regional; National; Real Estate — Regional; Securities — National
RANGE OF INV./LOAN PER BUSINESS: Min. $200,000; Max. $3,000,000
BUSINESS CHARACTERISTICS DESIRED-REQUIRED: AAA Paper
REFERRALS ACCEPTED FROM: Investment/Mortgage banker and Borrower/Investee
BRANCHES: NC, SC, VA

COMPANY: **McM Corporation**
ADDRESS: P.O. Box 12317
Raleigh, NC 27605
PHONE: (919) 821-0364
TYPE OF INSTITUTION: Insurance holding company, parent of Occidental Life Insurance Co. of N.C.
CONTACT OFFICER(S): Stephen L. Stephano, Chief Financial & Invest. Officer
ASSETS: $500,000,000+
INVESTMENTS/LOANS MADE: For own account
INVESTMENTS/LOANS MADE: Only in securities with a secondary market
TYPES OF FINANCING: SECONDARY-MARKET CORPORATE SECURITIES: Bonds—Corp., Govt., Municipals

COMPANY: **Bankers Life Insurance Company of Nebraska**
ADDRESS: 5900 "O" St.
Lincoln, NE 68510
PHONE: (402) 467-1122
CONTACT OFFICER(S): Jon C. Headrick, V.P. Securities
ASSETS: $950 million
INVESTMENTS/LOANS MADE: For own account; For managed accounts; Through private placements; Through underwriting public offerings
INVESTMENTS/LOANS MADE: In securities with a secondary market and in securities without a secondary market
TYPES OF FINANCING: SECONDARY-MARKET: Common stock; Preferred stock; Bonds; VENTURE CAPITAL: Start-up from developed product stage; LOANS: Unsecured to credits above BAA; Equipment; Equity related; REAL ESTATE LOANS: Long-term senior mtg.; Intermediate-term senior mtg.; LEASES: Single-Investor; Leveraged; Tax leases; REAL ESTATE: Acquisitions; Joint ventures; Partnerships/Syndications.
GEOGRAPHIC LIMITS OF INVESTMENTS/LOANS: National
RANGE OF INV./LOAN PER BUSINESS: Min. $1,000,000; Max. $5,000,000
PREFERRED TERM FOR LOANS & LEASES: Min. 3 years; Max. 15 years
REFERRALS ACCEPTED FROM: Investment/Mortgage banker; Borrower/Investee

COMPANY: **The Security Mutual Life Insurance Company**
ADDRESS: 200 Centennial Mall N., P.O. Box 82248
Lincoln, NE 68501
PHONE: (402) 477-4141
CONTACT OFFICER(S): Fred Gottchalk, V.P., Investments
ASSETS: $100 million and up
INVESTMENTS/LOANS MADE: In securities with a secondary market and in securities without a secondary market
TYPES OF FINANCING: SECONDARY-MARKET CORPORATE SECURITIES: Bonds, REAL ESTATE LOANS: Long-term senior mtg.
GEOGRAPHIC LIMITS OF INVESTMENTS/LOANS: Regional; Generally West of Mississippi
PREFERRED TERM FOR LOANS & LEASES: Min. 10-15; Max. 20+ years
BUSINESS CHARACTERISTICS DESIRED-REQUIRED: Securities qualify under Nebraska investment statutes
REFERRALS ACCEPTED FROM: Investment/Mortgage banker
REMARKS: Maximum amount is $500,000 for bonds and $850,000 for mortgages.

COMPANY: **Guarantee Mutual Life Company**
ADDRESS: 8721 Indian Hills Drive
Omaha, NE 68114
PHONE: (402) 391-2121
TYPE OF INSTITUTION: Life Ins. Co.
CONTACT OFFICER(S): Don Schaneberg, V.P. Ass't. Treasurer

ASSETS: $450 million
INVESTMENTS/LOANS MADE: Through private placements; Through underwriting public offerings
INVESTMENTS/LOANS MADE: In securities with a secondary market and in securities without a secondary market
TYPES OF FINANCING: SECONDARY-MARKET CORPORATE SECURITIES: Common stock; Bonds; Other: Govt., Corp., Municipal; REAL ESTATE LOANS: Long-term senior mtg., Intermediate term senior mortgages; Land developments; Other: First mtgs. only; REAL ESTATE: Joint ventures
WILL NOT CONSIDER: Bank holding companies, electric utilities with nuclear exposures
GEOGRAPHIC LIMITS OF INVESTMENTS/LOANS: National; Other: States where the Co. is licensed to sell ins—Real Estate
RANGE OF INV./LOAN PER BUSINESS: Min. $500,000; Max. $2.4 million R.E.
PREFERRED TERM FOR LOANS & LEASES: Min. 5 years; Max. 10 years
BUSINESS CHARACTERISTICS DESIRED-REQUIRED: 5 year track record, flexible
REFERRALS ACCEPTED FROM: Investment/Mortgage banker or Borrower/Investee

COMPANY: **United of Omaha Life Insurance Co.**
ADDRESS: Mutual of Omaha Plaza
Omaha, NE 68175
PHONE: (402) 342-7600
CONTACT OFFICER(S): Bill Arnold, 2nd V.P.
Tom Schmit, 2nd V.P., Securities
ASSETS: $2.25 billion
TYPES OF FINANCING: REAL ESTATE LOANS: Long-term senior mtg.; REAL ESTATE: Joint ventures, Equity Purchase
PREFERRED TYPES OF INDUSTRIES/INVESTMENTS: Diversified
GEOGRAPHIC LIMITS OF INVESTMENTS/LOANS: National
RANGE OF INV./LOAN PER BUSINESS: Min.$500,000; Max. $5,000,000
PREFERRED TERM FOR LOANS & LEASES: Max. 10 years
REFERRALS ACCEPTED FROM: Investment/Mortgage banker

COMPANY: **Woodman of the World Life Insurance Society**
ADDRESS: Woodman Tower, 1700 Farnam Street
Omaha, NE 68102
PHONE: (402) 342-1890
CONTACT OFFICER(S): Stephen W. Mellor, Asst. V.P., Mtg. Loans
Donald Miller, Asst. V.P., Securities
ASSETS: $100 million and up
TYPES OF FINANCING: LOANS: Unsecured; Working Capital; Equipment, REAL ESTATE LOANS: Long-term senior mtg.; Intermediate-term senior mtg.; REAL ESTATE: Joint Ventures
PREFERRED TYPES OF INDUSTRIES/INVESTMENTS: R.E.: Shopping Centers, Office Bldgs., Warehouses, Industrial
GEOGRAPHIC LIMITS OF INVESTMENTS/LOANS: National; Prefer Southeast & Southwest for R.E.
RANGE OF INV./LOAN PER BUSINESS: Min. $1,000,000; Max. $10 million (R.E.), $2 million (other)
PREFERRED TERM FOR LOANS & LEASES: Min. 5-10; Max. 7-15 years
BUSINESS CHARACTERISTICS DESIRED-REQUIRED: Non-Real Estate Loans: BBA, AA Credit Rating
REFERRALS ACCEPTED FROM: Investment/Mortgage banker or Borrower/Investee

COMPANY: **The Mutual Benefit Life Insurance Co.**
ADDRESS: 520 Broad Street
Newark, NJ 07101
PHONE: (201) 481-8000
CONTACT OFFICER(S): Donald Hagemann, V.P., Fixed income securities
Robert W. Kopchins, Sr. V.P., RE investments
ASSETS: $8.4 billion
INVESTMENTS/LOANS MADE: In securities with a secondary market and in securities without a secondary market
TYPES OF FINANCING: SECONDARY-MARKEET CORPORATE SECURITIES: Common Stock; Preferred stock; Bonds; Fixed income, LOANS: Unsecured; Working capital; Equipment, REAL ESTATE LOANS: Long-term senior mtg.; Intermediate-term senior mtg.; Subordinated; Gap; Standbys, REAL ESTATE: Acquisitions; Joint ventures, OTHER SERVICES PROVIDED: generally do venture capital in partnerships
GEOGRAPHIC LIMITS OF INVESTMENTS/LOANS: National: Mexico, Canada, Europe
RANGE OF INV./LOAN PER BUSINESS: Min. $1 mil.; Max. $35 mil.
PREFERRED TERM FOR LOANS & LEASES: Min. 3-10 years
BUSINESS CHARACTERISTICS DESIRED-REQUIRED: Minimum number of years in business: 5; Other: 3-10 mil. generally
REFFERALS ACCEPTED FROM: Investment/Mortgage banker or Borrower/Investee
BRANCHES: Lots of subsidiaries: do investing for all of them.

COMPANY: **The Equitable Life Assurance Society of the United States**
ADDRESS: 1285 Avenue of the Americas
New York, NY 10019
PHONE: (212) 554-1234
TYPE OF INSTITUTION: Mutual Insurance Company with extensive pension management operations and leasing subsidiary
CONTACT OFFICER(S): John Miller, V.P.
Harold S. Woolley, V.P. — Public Bonds
George R. Peacock, Senior V.P. — Real Estate
Roderic Eaton, Senior V.P. — Equico Lessors
ASSETS: $44 billion
INVESTMENTS/LOANS MADE: For own account; For managed accounts; Through private placements
INVESTMENTS/LOANS MADE: In securities with a secondary market and in securities without a secondary market

TYPES OF FINANCING: SECONDARY-MARKET CORPORATE SECURITIES: Common stock; Preferred stock; Bonds; Private placements, LOANS: Unsecured to credits above mid BA; Equipment; Equity-related, REAL ESTATE LOANS: Long-term senior mtg.; Intermediate-term senior mtg.; Wraparounds; Land; Land development; Construction; Standbys, LEASES: Single-investor; Leveraged; Tax leases; Non-tax leases; Vendor financing programs, REAL ESTATE: Acquisitions; Joint ventures; Partnerships/Syndications
PREFERRED TYPES OF INDUSTRIES/INVESTMENTS: Private Placements — BAA industrial, financial and utility credits; Real Estate — commercial mortgages with kickers or outright purchases of commercial properties.
WILL NOT CONSIDER: Fast-food, start-up venture capital situations
GEOGRAPHIC LIMITS OF INVESTMENTS/LOANS: International
RANGE OF INV./LOAN PER BUSINESS: Min. $3 Million; Max. $100 Million
PREFERRED TERM FOR LOANS & LEASES: Min. 3; Max. 15 years
BUSINESS CHARACTERISTICS DESIRED-REQUIRED: Minimum number of years in business: 5; Min. annual sales $100 million; Min. net worth $20 million; Min. annual net income $3 million; Min. annual cash flow $4 million
REFERRALS ACCEPTED FROM: Investment/Mortgage banker or Borrower/Investee
BRANCHES: National Real Estate Headquarters: Monarch Plaza 3414 Peachtree Road N.E., Atlanta, GA 30326
Field Offices: C.J. Harwood, Regional Vice President, 60 State Street-Suite 1720, Boston, MA 02109, (617) 723-7183
John T. Quartuccio, Regional Vice President, 1350 Avenue of the Americas, 20th Fl., New York, NY 10019, (212) 541-5830
Warren G. Bevan, Regional Vice President, 8 Penn Center-Suite 1900, Philadelphia, PA 19103, (215) 569-0554
Robert L. Blakeman, Regional Vice President, 1875 "Eye" Street, N.W.-Suite 1140, Washington, D.C. 20006, (202) 775-8340
Donald L. Batson, Regional Vice President, Peachtree-Dunwoody Pavillion, 5775-E Peachtree-Dunwoody Road-Suite 500, Atlanta, GA 30342, (404) 256-1020
Joseph W. Kellum, Regional Vice President, 1 Lincoln Place-Suite 451, 1900 Glades Rd., Boca Raton, FL 33431, (305) 392-3902
Edward G. Smith, Regional Vice President, 401 No. Michigan Avenue-Rm. 3350, Chicago, IL 60611, (312) 321-4720
Jerome W. Fruin, Regional Manager, One Centerre Plaza-Suite 2100, St. Louis, MO 63101, (314) 421-5900
Douglas A. Tibbetts, Regional Vice President, Park Central VII-Suite 1100, 12750 Merit Drive, Dallas, TX 75251, (214) 239-1850
Daniel C. Gardner, Regional Vice President, 1140 First National Bank Building, 621 17th St., Denver, CO 80293, (303) 292-3600
Jack Kueneman, Regional Vice President, One Market Plaza, Steuart Street Tower-Suite 1900, San Francisco, CA 94105, (415) 541-5130
John J. Wilhelm III, Regional Vice President, 4100 Wells Fargo Building, 444 South Flower Street, Los Angeles, CA 90071, (213) 689-1900

COMPANY: **Guardian Life Insurance Co.**
ADDRESS: 201 Park Ave. So.
New York, NY 10003
PHONE: (212) 598-8000
CONTACT OFFICER(S): Charles E. Albers, V.P. Equities & Securities, 598-8420
Henry Spencer, 2nd V.P., Investments
George Keim, Consultant
ASSETS: 2,254,000,000
TYPES OF FINANCING: SECONDARY-MARKET CORPORATE SECURITIES: Common stock; Preferred stock; Bonds, LOANS: Unsecured, REAL ESTATE LOANS: Long-term senior mtg.; Industrial revenue bonds
PREFERRED TYPES OF INDUSTRIES/INVESTMENTS: Real Estate; Commercial properties
GEOGRAPHIC LIMITS OF INVESTMENTS/LOANS: National
RANGE OF INV./LOAN PER BUSINESS: Min. $500,000; Max. $12 million
PREFERRED TERM FOR LOANS & LEASES: Max. 10 years

COMPANY: **Home Life Insurance Company**
ADDRESS: 253 Broadway
New York, NY 10007
PHONE: (212) 306-2060
TYPE OF INSTITUTION: Investment department—Securities section of life insurance company
CONTACT OFFICER(S): Jerry D. Cohen, V.P. , manages Securities Sec.
ASSETS: $2.5 billion and up
INVESTMENTS/LOANS MADE: For own account; Through private placements; Through underwriting public offerings
INVESTMENTS/LOANS MADE: In securities with a secondary market and in securities without a secondary market
TYPES OF FINANCING: SECONDARY-MARKET CORPORATE SECURITIES: Common stock; Preferred stock; Bonds; LOANS: Unsecured; Equipment; Equity-related. LEASES: Other; Debt portion of leveraged lease
WILL NOT CONSIDER: Finance, leasing or foreign companies
GEOGRAPHIC LIMITS OF INVESTMENTS/LOANS: National; Other: Canada
RANGE OF INV./LOAN PER BUSINESS: Min. $1,000,000; Max. $10,000,000
PREFERRED TERM FOR LOANS & LEASES: Min. 7-10 years; Max. 15 years
BUSINESS CHARACTERISTICS DESIRED-REQUIRED: Min. net worth $5,000,000; Min. annual net income Positive

COMPANY: **The Manhattan Life Insurance Company**
ADDRESS: 111 W. 57th St.
New York, NY 10019

PHONE: (212) 484-9300
CONTACT OFFICER(S): Tony Miller, Dir. of R&D
James M. Creedon, V.P., Securities
L. John Achenback, II, Sr. V.P., Investments
David Smith, V.P. Mortgages
ASSETS: $1 billion
INVESTMENTS/LOANS MADE: In securities with a secondary market and in securities without a secondary market
TYPES OF FINANCING: SECONDARY-MARKET CORPORATE SECURITIES, LOANS, REAL ESTATE LOANS: Other: Senior mortgages
GEOGRAPHIC LIMITS OF INVESTMENTS/LOANS: National
RANGE OF INV./LOAN PER BUSINESS: Min. $1,000,000; Max. $5,000,000 (R.E.)
BUSINESS CHARACTERISTICS DESIRED-REQUIRED: Min. net worth $20 million
REFERRALS ACCEPTED FROM: Investment/Mortgage banker only
REMARKS: Referrals accepted from brokers

COMPANY: **Metropolitan Life Insurance Company**
ADDRESS: One Madison Avenue
New York, NY 10010
PHONE: (212) 578-2211
TYPE OF INSTITUTION: Real Estate Investments Department of insurance company
CONTACT OFFICER(S): Mr. E. A. Stoudt, V.P.
Mr. T. Bates Westerberg, V.P.
INVESTMENTS/LOANS MADE: For own account, For managed accounts
TYPES OF FINANCING: LOANS: Equity-related, REAL ESTATE: Acquisitions; Joint ventures
PREFERRED TYPES OF INDUSTRIES/INVESTMENTS: Office buildings, hotels, retail, industrial
GEOGRAPHIC LIMITS OF INVESTMENTS/LOANS: National; Other: Canada
RANGE OF INV./LOAN PER BUSINESS: Min. $5,000,000
REFERRALS ACCEPTED FROM: Investment/Mortgage banker or Borrower/Investee
BRANCHES: John Powell, Midwestern Office, Oak Brook, IL; (312) 920-7100
Tom Garesche, Northeastern Office, New York, NY; (212) 578-2211
Charles Sayres, Southeastern Office, Atlanta, GA; (404) 393-0630
Fred Arnholt, Southwestern Office, Houston, TX; (713) 931-4486
William Ripberger, Western Office, Foster City, CA; (415) 574-8181
Andre Vauclair, Canadian Office, Montreal, Canada; (514) 861-0923

COMPANY: **The Mutual Life Insurance Company of New York**
ADDRESS: 1740 Broadway
New York, NY 10019
PHONE: (212) 708-2000
TYPE OF INSTITUTION: Insurance Co.
CONTACT OFFICER(S): Michael J. Drabb, S.V.P.-Securities Invest. Dept.
ASSETS: $10.5 billion
INVESTMENTS/LOANS MADE: For own account, For managed accounts, Through private placements, Through underwriting public offerings
INVESTMENTS/LOANS MADE: In securities with a secondary market and in securities without a secondary market
TYPES OF FINANCING: SECONDARY-MARKET CORPORATE SECURITIES: Bonds. LOANS: Unsecured to credits above Ba. REAL ESTATE LOANS: Intermediate-term senior mtg. INTERNATIONAL. REAL ESTATE: Acquisitions; Joint ventures.
GEOGRAPHIC LIMITS OF INVESTMENTS/LOANS: International
RANGE OF INV./LOAN PER BUSINESS: Min. $3,000,000; Max. $20,000,000
PREFERRED TERM FOR LOANS & LEASES: Min. 3 years; Max. 12 years
BUSINESS CHARACTERISTICS DESIRED-REQUIRED: No startups
REFERRALS ACCEPTED FROM: Investment/Mortgage banker or Borrower/Investee

COMPANY: **New York Life Insurance Company**
ADDRESS: 51 Madison Ave., Room 904
New York, NY 10010
PHONE: (212) 576-7000
CONTACT OFFICER(S): Harold K. Herzog, Sr.V.P., Direct Supervision of the company's real estate & mortgage loan operations
ASSETS: $6,698,063,000
INVESTMENTS/LOANS MADE: For own account
TYPES OF FINANCING: REAL ESTATE LOANS: Intermediate-term senior mtg. REAL ESTATE: Acquisitions; Joint ventures; Partnerships/Syndications
PREFERRED TYPES OF INDUSTRIES/INVESTMENTS: Office buildings; Shopping centers; Apartments; Industrial buildings; Warehouses
GEOGRAPHIC LIMITS OF INVESTMENTS/LOANS: National
PREFERRED TERM FOR LOANS & LEASES: Min. 3 years; Max. 15 years

COMPANY: **Teachers Insurance & Annuity Association**
ADDRESS: 730 Third Ave.
New York, NY 10017
PHONE: (212) 490-9000
CONTACT OFFICER(S): Frank J. Pados, Securities
John Somers, V.P., Mtg. & R.E.
ASSETS: $100 million and up
TYPES OF FINANCING: SECONDARY-MARKET CORPORATE SECURITIES, LOANS: Equity-related, REAL ESTATE LOANS, LEASES, REAL ESTATE
GEOGRAPHIC LIMITS OF INVESTMENTS/LOANS: National; Other: Canada
RANGE OF INV./LOAN PER BUSINESS: Min. $1,000,000; Max. None
PREFERRED TERM FOR LOANS & LEASES: Min. 7-10 years (Securities); 15-20 years (R.E.); Max. 20+ years
BUSINESS CHARACTERISTICS DESIRED-REQUIRED: Minimum number of years in business: 3-5; Min. annual sales $100 million (Securities)
REFERRALS ACCEPTED FROM: Investment/Mortgage banker or Borrower/Investee

REMARKS: Provide equity; active in buyouts and acquisitions

COMPANY: **Venture Capital Management, Inc. (sub. of Prudential Ins. Co. of America**
ADDRESS: 717 5th Avenue, Suite 1600
New York, NY 10022
PHONE: (201) 877-6000
CONTACT OFFICER(S): William Field, Chairman
John Childs, Sr. V.P.
ASSETS: $100 million and up
INVESTMENTS/LOANS MADE: In securities with a secondary market and in securities without a secondary market
TYPES OF FINANCING: LOANS: Equity-related; Other: Guarantees, REAL ESTATE LOANS: Long-term senior mtg.; Intermediate-term senior mtg.; Subordinated, LEASES, REAL ESTATE: Acquisitions; Joint ventures, OTHER SERVICES PROVIDED: Equity financing
GEOGRAPHIC LIMITS OF INVESTMENTS/LOANS: International
RANGE OF INV./LOAN PER BUSINESS: Min. $500,000; Max. Over $100,000,000
PREFERRED TERM FOR LOANS & LEASES: Min. 10-15 years; Max. 15-20 years

COMPANY: **American Financial Corp.**
ADDRESS: 1 East Fourth Street
Cincinnati, OH 45202
PHONE: (513) 579-2489
TYPE OF INSTITUTION: Financial Holding Co.
CONTACT OFFICER(S): Fred Runk, V.P. & Controller
Robert Lintz, V.P., 579-2548
TYPES OF FINANCING: SECONDARY-MARKET CORPORATE SECURITIES: Common stock; Preferred stock; Bonds, LOANS: Working capital (receivables/inventory); Equipment; Equity-related; Other: Secured
PREFERRED TYPES OF INDUSTRIES/INVESTMENTS: Diversified
GEOGRAPHIC LIMITS OF INVESTMENTS/LOANS: National
RANGE OF INV./LOAN PER BUSINESS: Min. $4 million
PREFERRED TERM FOR LOANS & LEASES: Short-term

COMPANY: **The Ohio National Life Insurance Company**
ADDRESS: 237 William Howard Taft Rd., P.O. Box 237
Cincinnati, OH 45201
PHONE: (513) 861-3600
CONTACT OFFICER(S): Joseph Brom, V.P., Securities
Steve Williams (Equities), Portfolio Manager
Steve Sauten (Public Fixed Income), Portfolio Manager
Delores Miller (Private Placements), Portfolio Manager
ASSETS: $1,200,000,000
INVESTMENTS/LOANS MADE: For own account; Through private placement
INVESTMENTS/LOANS MADE: In securities with a secondary market and in securities without a secondary market
TYPES OF FINANCING: SECONDARY-MARKET CORPORATE SECURITIES: Common stock; Preferred stock; Bonds; Lease Transactions; LOANS; Unsecured; Working capital; Equipment; Equity-related; REAL ESTATE LOANS: Intermediate-term senior mtg.; LEASES; Leveraged; Tax leases; Non-tax leases
PREFERRED TYPES OF INDUSTRIES/INVESTMENTS: Diversified
GEOGRAPHIC LIMITS OF INVESTMENTS/LOANS: National
RANGE OF INV./LOAN PER BUSINESS: Min. $500,000; Max. $4,000,000
BUSINESS CHARACTERISTICS DESIRED-REQUIRED: Min. net worth $3-5 million
REFERRALS ACCEPTED FROM: Investment/Mortgage banker or Borrower/Investee

COMPANY: **The Union Central Life Insurance Company**
ADDRESS: P.O. Box 179
Cincinnati, OH 45201
PHONE: (513) 595-2200
CONTACT OFFICER(S): Michael Conway, Sr. V.P., CEO
John A. Cooney, V.P., Mortgage
Ronald Killinger, V.P., Corp. Finance Inv.
ASSETS: $1.3 billion
TYPES OF FINANCING: LOANS, REAL ESTATE LOANS: Long-term senior mtg.; Subordinated, LEASES
PREFERRED TYPES OF INDUSTRIES/INVESTMENTS: Diversified
GEOGRAPHIC LIMITS OF INVESTMENTS/LOANS: National
REFERRALS ACCEPTED FROM: Investment/Mortgage banker or Borrower/Investee
REMARKS: Range for R.E.: $500,000-2,500,000; Range for Private Placement: $200,000-5,000,000

COMPANY: **The Western and Southern Life Insurance Company**
ADDRESS: 400 Broadway
Cincinnati, OH 45202
PHONE: (513) 629-1800
CONTACT OFFICER(S): William F. Ledwin, V.P., Finance Department
Richard L. Siegel, V.P., Finance Department
ASSETS: $3.2 Billion
INVESTMENTS/LOANS MADE: For own account
INVESTMENTS/LOANS MADE: In securities with a secondary market and in securities without a secondary market
TYPES OF FINANCING: SECONDARY-MARKET CORPORATE SECURITIES: Common stock; Preferred stock; Bonds; Government Guaranteed Loans, LOANS: Unsecured to credits above A; Equity-related; Equity-Related Mortgage, REAL ESTATE LOANS: Land, LEASES: Leveraged, REAL ESTATE: Joint ventures
PREFERRED TYPES OF INDUSTRIES/INVESTMENTS: Flexible, however, prefer stable industries for bond related financings. Mortgage and real estate preferences are office buildings, etc. as opposed to small retail financings.
GEOGRAPHIC LIMITS OF INVESTMENTS/LOANS: National
RANGE OF INV./LOAN PER BUSINESS: Min. $250,000; Max. 10-20 million

PREFERRED TERM FOR LOANS & LEASES: Min. 2; Max. 15 years
BUSINESS CHARACTERISTICS DESIRED-REQUIRED: Minimum numbers of years in business: 3; Assets: $100MM
REFERRALS ACCEPTED FROM: Investment/Mortgage banker or Borrower/Investee

COMPANY: **The Columbus Mutual Life Insurance Company**
ADDRESS: 303 East Broad St.
Columbus, OH 43215
PHONE: (614) 221-5875
CONTACT OFFICER(S): James Barton, V.P. & Chief Investment Officer
J. Gill, Admin. Assistant Mortgage Loans
ASSETS: $500,000,000 & up
INVESTMENTS/LOANS MADE: For own account; Through private placements,underwriting public offerings
INVESTMENTS/LOANS MADE: In securities with a secondary market and in securities without a secondary market
TYPES OF FINANCING: SECONDARY-MARKET CORPORATE SECURITIES, LOANS, REAL ESTATE LOANS, REAL ESTATE: Joint ventures; Partnerships/ Syndications
WILL NOT CONSIDER: Specialty Type Real Estate (Fast Foods, etc.)
GEOGRAPHIC LIMITS OF INVESTMENTS/LOANS: National
RANGE OF INV./LOAN PER BUSINESS: Min. $500,000; Max. $1,500,000
PREFERRED TERM FOR LOANS & LEASES: varies depending on real estate
REFERRALS ACCEPTED FROM: Investment/Mortgage banker

COMPANY: **The Midland Mutual Life Insurance Co.**
ADDRESS: 250 E. Broad St.
Columbus, OH 43215
PHONE: (614) 228-2001
CONTACT OFFICER(S): Mr. Dyer, V.P., Mtg. & Real Estate
ASSETS: $100 million and up
TYPES OF FINANCING: REAL ESTATE LOANS: Long-term senior mtg.; Intermediate-term senior mtg; Wraparounds, REAL ESTATE: Acquisitions; Joint ventures
GEOGRAPHIC LIMITS OF INVESTMENTS/LOANS: National
RANGE OF INV./LOAN PER BUSINESS: Min. $500,000; Max $1,500,000
PREFERRED TERM FOR LOANS & LEASES: Max. 7 years
REMARKS: Referrals accepted from Correspondent. Maximum amounts: $1.5 million for mortgages & $1 million for private placements; amounts in bonds are percent of assets

COMPANY: **Nationwide Life Insurance Company**
ADDRESS: One Nationwide Plaza
Columbus, OH 43216
PHONE: (614) 227-7696
CONTACT OFFICER(S): Robert J. Woodward, V.P., R.E. Investment
ASSETS: $100 million and up
TYPES OF FINANCING: LOANS, REAL ESTATE LOANS: Senior Mortgages
PREFERRED TYPES OF INDUSTRIES/INVESTMENTS: Diversified
GEOGRAPHIC LIMITS OF INVESTMENTS/LOANS: National
RANGE OF INV./LOAN PER BUSINESS: Min. $1,000,000 (R.E.); $2,000,000 (P.P.); Max. $5,000,000
PREFERRED TERM FOR LOANS & LEASES: Min. 15-20; Max. 20+ years
BUSINESS CHARACTERISTICS DESIRED-REQUIRED: Minimum number of years in business: 5
REFERRALS ACCEPTED FROM: Investment/Mortgage banker or Borrower/Investee

COMPANY: **Mid-Continent Life Insurance Company**
ADDRESS: 1400 Classen Drive, P.O. Box 60269
Oklahoma City, OK 73106
PHONE: (405) 524-8444
CONTACT OFFICER(S): Daniel D. Adams, Jr. V.P.

COMPANY: **Standard Insurance Co.**
ADDRESS: P.O. Box 711
Portland, OR 97207
PHONE: (503) 248-2836
TYPE OF INSTITUTION: Life insurance company
CONTACT OFFICER(S): Vicky Chase, Asst. V.P.
Wayne Atterberry, V.P., Mortgage Loans
TYPES OF FINANCING: SECONDARY-MARKET CORPORATE SECURITIES: Bonds, LOANS: Equity-related, REAL ESTATE: Acquisitions
PREFERRED TYPES OF INDUSTRIES/INVESTMENTS: Commercial
GEOGRAPHIC LIMITS OF INVESTMENTS/LOANS: Real estate Regional; Bonds : National
RANGE OF INV./LOAN PER BUSINESS: Min. $250,000; Max. $2 million
PREFERRED TERM FOR LOANS & LEASES: Min. 5 years; Max. 12 years
BUSINESS CHARACTERISTICS DESIRED-REQUIRED: Minimum number of years in business: 5 for bonds; Other: Quality Baa or equivalent

COMPANY: **Provident Mutual Life Insurance Company of Philadelphia**
ADDRESS: 1600 Market Street, P.O. Box 7378
Philadelphia, PA 19103
PHONE: (215) 636-5000
CONTACT OFFICER(S): Mr. Craig Snyder, V.P. Mtg. & R.E.
ASSETS: 2.2 billion
INVESTMENTS/LOANS MADE: In securities with a secondary market and in securities without a secondary market
TYPES OF FINANCING: SECONDARY-MARKET CORPORATE SECURITIES: Common stock; Preferred stock; Bonds, REAL ESTATE LOANS: Intermediate-term senior mtg., REAL ESTATE: Acquisitions; Joint ventures

PREFERRED TYPES OF INDUSTRIES/INVESTMENTS: shopping centers, office buildings, industrial warehouse space
WILL NOT CONSIDER: Special purpose buildings: hotels, recreational facilities
GEOGRAPHIC LIMITS OF INVESTMENTS/LOANS: National
RANGE OF INV/LOAN PER BUSINESS: Min. $1 million; Max. $8 million
PREFERRED TERM FOR LOANS & LEASES: Min. 3 years; Max. 10 years
REFERRALS ACCEPTED FROM: Investment/Mortgage banker or Borrower/Investee

COMPANY: **Provident Life and Accident Insurance Company**
ADDRESS: Fountain Square
Chattanooga, TN 37402
PHONE: (615) 755-1564
CONTACT OFFICER(S): Sam E. Miles, V.P.
John Van Wickler, Sr. V.P.,
A. V. Keyes, V.P., Equity
David Fussell, V.P., Securities & P.P.
Jack R. McNutt V.P. Mtg. Loan & R.E.
ASSETS: $3,194,000,000
TYPES OF FINANCING: LOANS, REAL ESTATE LOANS: Intermediate-term senior mtg., OTHER SERVICES PROVIDED: Equity financing in joint ventures
PREFERRED TYPES OF INDUSTRIES/INVESTMENTS: Shopping centers; medical office buildings
WILL NOT CONSIDER: Farm; Industrial (except distribution); Manufacturing
GEOGRAPHIC LIMITS OF INVESTMENTS/LOANS: National
RANGE OF INV./LOAN PER BUSINESS: Min. $1 million; Max. $24 million
PREFERRED TERM FOR LOANS & LEASES: Max. 10+ years

COMPANY: **Life and Casualty Insurance Company of Tennessee**
ADDRESS: American General Center
Nashville, TN 37250
PHONE: (615) 749-2000
CONTACT OFFICER(S): J. P. Ellis, Jr., V.P.
ASSETS: $100 million and up
TYPES OF FINANCING: REAL ESTATE LOANS: Long-term senior mtg.; Intermediate-term senior mtg.
PREFERRED TYPES OF INDUSTRIES/INVESTMENTS: Shopping centers; industrial buildings
GEOGRAPHIC LIMITS OF INVESTMENTS/LOANS: Regional
RANGE OF INV./LOAN PER BUSINESS: Min. $500,000; Max. $2,000,000
PREFERRED TERM FOR LOANS & LEASES: Min. 15-20 years; Max. 20+ years
REFERRALS ACCEPTED FROM: Investment/Mortgage banker or Borrower/Investee
REMARKS: Sub. of American General Life, Houston, TX

COMPANY: **National Western Life Insurance Co.**
ADDRESS: Hwy. 183 at I.H. 35, 850 E. Anderson
Austin, TX 78776
PHONE: (512) 836-1010
CONTACT OFFICER(S): Lee Posey, V.P., Public Relations
ASSETS: $100 million and up
TYPES OF FINANCING: LOANS: Working capital (receivables/inventory); Equipment; Equity-related; Loan guarantees, REAL ESTATE LOANS
PREFERRED TYPES OF INDUSTRIES/INVESTMENTS: Diversified
GEOGRAPHIC LIMITS OF INVESTMENTS/LOANS: National
PREFERRED TERM FOR LOANS & LEASES: Max. 20 + years
REFERRALS ACCEPTED FROM: Investment/Mortgage banker or Borrower/Investee

COMPANY: **Alliance Investment Corporation**
ADDRESS: 1201 Elm St., Ste. 5200
Dallas, TX 75270
CONTACT OFFICER(S): J. K. Lanyon, Sr. V.P., Securities — (214) 653-4242
Ken Peugh, Assoc. V.P., Mtg. Loans — (214) 653-2753
ASSETS: $100 million and up
INVESTMENTS/LOANS MADE: In securities with a secondary market and in securities without a secondary market
TYPES OF FINANCING: LOANS, REAL ESTATE LOANS: Long-term senior mtg.; Intermediate-term senior mtg.
GEOGRAPHIC LIMITS OF INVESTMENTS/LOANS: National
PREFERRED TERM FOR LOANS & LEASES: Min. 10-15; Max. 20+ years
BUSINESS CHARACTERISTICS DESIRED-REQUIRED: Minimum number of years in business: 5; Min. net worth of $10 million for R.E. loans & $50 million for other loans; No payment default for prior 5 years
REFERRALS ACCEPTED FROM: Investment/Mortgage banker or Borrower/Investee
REMARKS: Range of $1. million — 5 million for Loans; $750,000-3,000,000 for R. E. Loans

COMPANY: **American General Corp.**
ADDRESS: 2727 Allen Pkwy, P.O. Box 3247
Houston, TX 77253
PHONE: (713) 522-1111
TYPE OF INSTITUTION: Insurance Co.
CONTACT OFFICER(S): Julia Tucker, VP
Nick Rasmussen, EVP
ASSETS: $19,000,000,000
INVESTMENTS/LOANS MADE: For own account; Through private placements; Through underwriting public offerings
INVESTMENTS/LOANS MADE: In securities with a secondary market; In securities without a secondary market
TYPES OF FINANCING: SECONDARY-MARKET CORPORATE SECURITIES: Common stock; Preferred stock; Bonds, VENTURE CAPITAL, LOANS: Unsecured, Equipment, Equity-related; REAL ESTATE LOANS: Long-term senior mtg.; Intermediate-term senior mtg., REAL ESTAE: Acquisitions; Joint ventures,

OTHER SERVICES PROVIDED: Government industries
GEOGRAPHIC LIMITS OF INVESTMENTS/LOANS: National
RANGE OF INV./LOAN PER BUSINESS: Min. $3,000,000
PREFERRED TERM FOR LOANS & LEASES: Min. 3 years; Max. 12 years
BUSINESS CHARACTERISTICS DESIRED-REQUIRED: Minimum number of years in business: 5

COMPANY: **Beneficial Life Insurance Co.**
ADDRESS: 36 South State St.
Salt Lake City, UT 84136
PHONE: (801) 531-7979
CONTACT OFFICER(S): Reed L. Reeve, V.P., Securities, Investment Officer
TOTAL ASSETS: $600,000,000
INVESTMENTS/LOANS MADE: For own account
INVESTMENTS/LOANS MADE: Only in securities with a secondary market
TYPES OF FINANCING: SECONDARY-MARKET CORPORATE SECURITIES: Common stock; Preferred stock; Bonds

COMPANY: **Surety Life Insurance Company**
ADDRESS: 200 East South Temple
Salt Lake City, UT 84111
PHONE: (801) 355-3000
TYPE OF INSTITUTION: Insurance Company (Mortgage Banking and lending)
CONTACT OFFICER(S): Hoyt S. Wimer, Assistant V.P. — Mortgage Loans
ASSETS: $125,000,000 and up
INVESTMENTS/LOANS MADE: For own account; For managed accounts
INVESTMENTS/LOANS MADE: In securities with a secondary market and in securities without a secondary market
TYPES OF FINANCING: REAL ESTATE LOANS: Long-term senior mtg.; Wraparounds, OTHER SERVICES PROVIDED: Presently originating and servicing mortgages in Utah and other surrounding western states.
PREFERRED TYPES OF INDUSTRIES/INVESTMENTS: Real Estate
WILL NOT CONSIDER: Loan not secured by Real Estate
GEOGRAPHIC LIMITS OF INVESTMENTS/LOANS: Regional; Western Regional and some International on larger loans.
RANGE OF INV./LOAN PER BUSINESS: Min. $500,000.00; Max. open
PREFERRED TERM FOR LOANS & LEASES: Min. 5; Max. 10 years
BUSINESS CHARACTERISTICS DESIRED-REQUIRED: Minimum number of years in business: 5; Prefer 25 to 1 net worth minimum
REFERRALS ACCEPTED FROM: Investment/Mortgage banker or Borrower/Investee

COMPANY: **Fidelity Bankers Life Insurance Company**
ADDRESS: P.O. Box 2368
Richmond, VA 23218
PHONE: (804) 649-8411
CONTACT OFFICER(S): Donald M. Davis, Sr. V.P., Investments
ASSETS: $200 million and up
INVESTMENTS/LOANS MADE: In securities with a secondary market and in securities without a secondary market
TYPES OF FINANCING: REAL ESTATE LOANS: Long-term senior mtg.; Intermediate-term senior mtg.
GEOGRAPHIC LIMITS OF INVESTMENTS/LOANS: National
RANGE OF INV./LOAN PER BUSINESS: Min. $250,000; Max. $1,000,000
PREFERRED TERM FOR LOANS & LEASES: Min. 5-8; Max. 10 years
REFERRALS ACCEPTED FROM: Investment/Mortgage Banker only

COMPANY: **Home Beneficial Life Insurance Company**
ADDRESS: P.O. Box 27572
Richmond, VA 23261
PHONE: (804) 358-8431
CONTACT OFFICER(S): R. W. Wiltshire, Jr., V.P. Securities Dept.
ASSETS: $880,000,000
INVESTMENTS/LOANS MADE: For own account
INVESTMENTS/LOANS MADE: In securities with a secondary market and in securities without a secondary market
TYPES OF FINANCING: SECONDARY-MARKET CORPORATE SECURITIES: Common stock; Preferred stock; Bonds; Other: Mtg. Loans. LOANS: Unsecured to credits above Baa. REAL ESTATE LOANS: Intermediate-term senior mtg.

COMPANY: **The Life Insurance Company of Virginia**
ADDRESS: P.O. Box 27424
Richmond, VA 23235
PHONE: (804) 281-6595
TYPE OF INSTITUTION: Life Insurance Company
CONTACT OFFICER(S): Daniel B. Belcore, Assistant V.P., Private Placement Portfolio Manager
Ron McRoberts V.P., Real Estate & Mtg.
ASSETS: $1.6 Billion
INVESTMENTS/LOANS MADE: For own account; For managed accounts; Through private placements
INVESTMENTS/LOANS MADE: In securities with a secondary market and in securities without a secondary market
TYPES OF FINANCING: SECONDARY-MARKET CORPORATE SECURITIES: Common stock; Preferred stock; Bonds, LOANS: Unsecured; Equipment; Equity-related; REAL ESTATE LOANS: Long-term senior mtg.; Industrial revenue bonds, LEASES: Single-investor; Leveraged; Tax leases, REAL ESTATE: Acquisitions
GEOGRAPHIC LIMITS OF INVESTMENTS/LOANS: National
RANGE OF INV./LOAN PER BUSINESS: Min. $500,000; Max. $5,000,000
PREFERRED TERM FOR LOANS & LEASES: Min. 3; Max. 12 years

BUSINESS CHARACTERISTICS DESIRED-REQUIRED: Minimum number of years in business: 10; Min. annual sales $30 million; Min. net worth $10 million
REFERRALS ACCEPTED FROM: Investment/Mortgage banker or Borrower/Investee

COMPANY: **Shenandoah Life Insurance Co.**
ADDRESS: 2301 Brambleton Av., S.W., P.O. Box 12847
Roanoke, VA 24029
PHONE: (703) 345-6711
CONTACT OFFICER(S): William A. Magee, V.P. Investments
ASSETS: $100 million and up
TYPES OF FINANCING: REAL ESTATE LOANS: Long-term senior mtg.; Intermediate-term senior mtg.
PREFERRED TYPES OF INDUSTRIES/INVESTMENTS: Diversified
GEOGRAPHIC LIMITS OF INVESTMENTS/LOANS: Regional
RANGE OF INV./LOAN PER BUSINESS: Min. $150,000; Max. $800,000
PREFERRED TERM FOR LOANS & LEASES: Min. 10-15; Max. 20+ years
REFERRALS ACCEPTED FROM: Investment/Mortgage banker or Borrower/Investee

COMPANY: **National Life Insurance Co.**
ADDRESS: National Life Drive
Montpelier, VT 05602
PHONE: (802) 229-3333
TYPE OF INSTITUTION: Life insurance company
CONTACT OFFICER(S): Edward S. Blackwell, V.P., Fixed Income
Ralph T. Heath, V.P., R.E. & Mortgages
George C. Coquillard, Exec. V.P., Investment
TYPES OF FINANCING: SECONDARY-MARKET CORPORATE SECURITIES: Common stock; Preferred stock; Bonds, LOANS: Unsecured; Equipment; Equity-related; OTHER: Secured, REAL ESTATE LOANS: Construction, REAL ESTATE: Acquisitions; Joint ventures; Partnerships/Syndications
PREFERRED TYPES OF INDUSTRIES/INVESTMENTS: Bonds; Oil, gas; R.E.; Industrial
WILL NOT CONSIDER: Specialty buildings
GEOGRAPHIC LIMITS OF INVESTMENTS/LOANS: National; International; Other: Canada
RANGE OF INV./LOAN PER BUSINESS: Min. $1 million; Max. $5 million
PREFERRED TERM FOR LOANS & LEASES: Min. 1 year; Max. 10 years
REMARKS: Average investment $2-3 million

COMPANY: **Aid Association for Lutherans**
ADDRESS: 4321 North Ballard Road
Appleton, WI 54919
PHONE: (414) 734-5721
TYPE OF INSTITUTION: Insurance Co.
CONTACT OFFICER(S): James Abitz, Second V.P.—Securities
Roy B. Glazier, V.P.—Real Estate
ASSETS: $3.3 billion
INVESTMENTS/LOANS MADE: For own account; Through private placements
INVESTMENTS/LOANS MADE: In securities with a secondary market and in securities without a secondary market
TYPES OF FINANCING: SECONDARY-MARKET CORPORATE SECURITIES: Common stock; Bonds; LOANS: Unsecured to credits above Baa; Working capital; Equipment; REAL ESTATE LOANS: Intermediate-term senior mtg.; LEASES: Leveraged
PREFERRED TYPES OF INDUSTRIES/INVESTMENTS: Open to a broad mix
WILL NOT CONSIDER: Bank holding company paper
GEOGRAPHIC LIMITS OF INVESTMENTS/LOANS: National
RANGE OF INV./LOAN PER BUSINESS: Min. 1 million; Max. $10-15 million
PREFERRED TERM FOR LOANS & LEASES: Min. 2½ years; Max. 7-10 years
BUSINESS CHARACTERISTICS DESIRED-REQUIRED: Minimum number of years in business: 0; Other: Min. # years in business—if it is a new subsidiary of a larger, proven company
REFERRALS ACCEPTED FROM: Investment/Mortgage banker or Borrower/Investee

COMPANY: **CUNA Mutual Insurance Co.**
ADDRESS: 5910 Mineral Pointe Road, P.O. 391
Madison, WI 53701
PHONE: (608) 238-5851
CONTACT OFFICER(S): Lyle T. Ibeling, V.P., Secur. Mngr.
William W. Sayles, Sec. Analyst
Alan Hembel, Asst. V.P., R.E. Manager
TYPES OF FINANCING: SECONDARY-MARKET CORPORATE SECURITIES: Common stock; Preferred stock; Bonds, LOANS: Secured, REAL ESTATE LOANS: 3 yr. notes, REAL ESTATE: Acquisitions; Joint Ventures
PREFERRED TYPES OF INDUSTRIES/INVESTMENTS: Diversified
GEOGRAPHIC LIMITS OF INVESTMENTS/LOANS: National
RANGE OF INV./LOAN PER BUSINESS: Min. $2 million; Max. $5 million
PREFERRED TERM FOR LOANS & LEASES: Max. 3 years
BUSINESS CHARACTERISTICS DESIRED-REQUIRED: Other: Credit-union related financial institutions
BRANCHES: Pomona, CA

COMPANY: **The Northwestern Mutual Life Insurance Company**
ADDRESS: 720 E. Wisconsin Av.
Milwaukee, WI 53202
PHONE: (414) 271-1444
CONTACT OFFICER(S): James D. Ericson, Sr. V.P., Investments
ASSETS: $14.6 billion
INVESTMENTS/LOANS MADE: In securities with a secondary market and in securities without a secondary market
TYPES OF FINANCING: SECONDARY-MARKET CORPORATE SECURITIES: Common stock; Bonds, LOANS, REAL ESTATE LOANS: Long-term senior mtg.; Intermediate-term senior mtg.

WISCONSIN

GEOGRAPHIC LIMITS OF INVESTMENTS/LOANS: National
RANGE OF INV./LOAN PER BUSINESS: Min. $10 million; Max. None
PREFERRED TERM FOR LOANS & LEASES: Min. 10; Max. 20 + years
REFERRALS ACCEPTED FROM: Investment/Mortgage banker or Borrower/Investee
REMARKS: 15 Real Estate production offices throughout the country

COMPANY: **Wisconsin National Life Insurance Company**
ADDRESS: 220 Washington Ave., Box 740
Oshkosh, WI 54902
PHONE: (414) 235-0800
CONTACT OFFICER(S): David Diercks, Financial V.P.
ASSETS: $141,000,000
INVESTMENTS/LOANS MADE: In securities with a secondary market and in securities without a secondary market
TYPES OF FINANCING: REAL ESTATE LOANS
GEOGRAPHIC LIMITS OF INVESTMENTS/LOANS: Regional; Midwest
RANGE OF INV./LOAN PER BUSINESS: Min. $200,000; Max. $500,000
REFERRALS ACCEPTED FROM: Investment/Mortgage banker

INVESTMENT BANKERS

(Diversified Financing)

ALABAMA

COMPANY: **Sterne, Agee & Leach, Inc.**
ADDRESS: First National-Southern Natural Bldg.
Birmingham, AL 35203
PHONE: (205) 252-5900
CONTACT OFFICER(S): William K. McHenry, Jr.
Henry Elinn Jr.
Linda Daniel, Real Est. Syndication
ASSETS: $6,650,000
TYPES OF FINANCING: SECONDARY-MARKET CORPORATE SECURITIES: Common stock; Bonds, Other: Tax-exempt bonds; REAL ESTATE LOANS: Industrial revenue bonds, REAL ESTATE: Partnerships/Syndications
PREFERRED TYPES OF INDUSTRIES/INVESTMENTS: Diversified
GEOGRAPHIC LIMITS OF INVESTMENTS/LOANS: Regional
BUSINESS CHARACTERISTICS DESIRED-REQUIRED: Financially strong
BRANCES: Will Hill Tankersley, P.O. Box 750, Montgomery, AL 36102; (205) 263-3892
Frank B. Frazer, 2515 1st National Bank Bld., Mobile, AL 36602; (205) 432-8886
Thomas Boyd, P.O. Box 998; Selma, AL 36702; (205) 872-6241

CALIFORNIA

COMPANY: **Hindin/Owen/Engelke, Inc.**
ADDRESS: 8530 Wilshire Blvd., Ste. 205
Beverly Hills, CA 90211
PHONE: (213) 659-6611
TYPE OF INSTITUTION: Investment Bankers—Specializing in corporate finance/ institutional private placements
CONTACT OFFICER(S): Russell Hindin, LA, Managing Director
Jack Engelke, Chicago, (312) 357-1855
Robert Katcha, Dallas, (214) 788-4564
INVESTMENTS/LOANS MADE: Through private placements of debt through institutional investors
INVESTMENTS/LOANS MADE: Only in debt instruments without a secondary market
TYPES OF FINANCING: VENTURE CAPITAL: Buy-outs/Acquisitions; LOANS: Unsecured to credits below BAA; Working capital; Equipment; FACTORING; LEASES: Single-investor; Leveraged; Tax leases; Non-tax leases, Operating; OTHER SERVICES PROVIDED: Financing arranged for companies with annual sales of $3 million to $150 million, overall corporate financing of $1 million or more arranged for our clients through institutional lenders for such purposes as: refinancing and restructuring debt; expansion; acquitions/ leveraged buy-outs; additional working capital; etc.
PREFERRED TYPES OF INDUSTRIES/INVESTMENTS: We prefer to assist middle market sized companies

who have a need for financing but have been turned down by their existing bank add other lenders they have approached
WILL NOT CONSIDER: Start-ups
GEOGRAPHIC LIMITS OF INVESTMENTS/LOANS: National
RANGE OF INV./LOAN PER BUSINESS: Min. $1 million; Max. open
BUSINESS CHARACTERISTICS DESIRED-REQUIRED: Minimum number of years in business: 2; Min. annual sales $3 million; Min. net worth $100,000; Min. annual net income open; Min. annual cash flow open
REFERRALS ACCEPTED FROM: Investment/Mortgage banker; Borrower/Investee
BRANCHES: Jack Engelke, 1220 Iroquois Drive, Naperville, IL 60540; (312) 357-1855
Robert Katcha, 14651 Dallas Parkway, Ste. 328, Dallas TX 25240; (214) 788-4564
REMARKS: Hindin/Owen/Engelke is the only national investment banking firm whose only business is arranging overall complete lines of credit for middle market companies

COMPANY: **Ventana Group, Inc.**
ADDRESS: 19600 Fairchild, Ste. 150
Irvine, CA 92715
PHONE: (714) 476-2204
TYPE OF INSTITUTION: Venture capital, investment banking, syndication
CONTACT OFFICER(S): Thomas O. Gephart, Chairman and Sr. General Partner
ASSETS: $30 million
INVESTMENTS/LOANS MADE: Through private placements
INVESTMENTS/LOANS MADE: In securities with a secondary market and in securities without a secondary market
TYPES OF FINANCING: VENTURE CAPITAL: Research & Development; Later-stage expansion; Buy-outs/Acquisitions
PREFERRED TYPES OF INDUSTRIES/INVESTMENTS: Medical/bio technology; Electronics/computing; energy management and conservation
GEOGRAPHIC LIMITS OF INVESTMENTS/LOANS: International
RANGE OF INV./LOAN PER BUSINESS: Min. $500,000; Max. $5 million
PREFERRED TERM FOR LOANS & LEASES: Min. 2 years; Max. 10 years
BUSINESS CHARACTERISTICS DESIRED-REQUIRED: Min. annual sales $1 million; Min. net worth $200,000; Min. annual cash flow can be negotiated
REFERRALS ACCEPTED FROM: Investment/Mortgage banker or Borrower/Investee
BRACHES: Duane Townsend, 1660 Hotel Circle N., Ste. 502, San Diego, CA 92108; (619) 291-2757
REMARKS: Equity investors

COMPANY: **EMC II Venture Partners**
ADDRESS: 8950 Villa La Jolla Dr., Suite 2132
La Jolla, CA 92037
PHONE: (619) 455-0362
TYPE OF INSTITUTION: Private venture capital firm affiliated with McKewon Securities, Investment Banker and Broker-Dealer
CONTACT OFFICER(S): Ray W. McKewon, General Partner
Bradley B. Gordon, General Partner– Alan J. Grant, General Partner
Hans W. Schoepflin, General Partner
ASSETS: In excess of $20,000,000
INVESTMENTS/LOANS MADE: For own account and through private placements
INVESTMENTS/LOANS MADE: In securities with a secondary market and in securities without a secondary market
TYPES OF FINANCING: SECONDARY-MARKET CORPORATE SECURITIES; VENTURE CAPITAL: Research & Development; Start-up; First-stage; Second-stage; Buy-outs/Acquisitions; LOANS: Equity-related; INTERNATIONAL; OTHER SERVICES PROVIDED: International joint ventures
PREFERRED TYPES OF INDUSTRIES/INVESTMENTS: Communications; computer related; distribution; manufacturing; medical; energy resources & technologies; retail (specialty) and real estate and financial services
GEOGRAPHIC LIMITS OF INVESTMENTS/LOANS: National, International
RANGE OF INV./LOAN PER BUSINESS: Min. $250,000; Max. $3,000,000
BUSINESS CHARACTERISTICS DESIRED-REQUIRED: Min. number of years in business: 0; Min. annual sales: $15 million by year 5; Other: request business plan detailing product/service concept, market opportunity, qualifications of management team, and 3-5 years projected profit and loss and cash flow
REFERRALS ACCEPTED FROM: Investment/Mortgage banker or Borrower/Investee

COMPANY: **McKewon Securities**
ADDRESS: 8950 Villa La Jolla Dr., Ste. 2131
La Jolla, CA 92037
PHONE: (619) 455-7860
TYPE OF INSTITUTION: Investment Bank
CONTACT OFFICER(S): James D. Timmins, Managing Partner
INVESTMENTS/LOANS MADE: For own account; for managed accounts; through private placements; through underwriting public offerings
INVESTMENTS/LOANS MADE: In securities with a secondary market and in securities without a secondary market
TYPES OF FINANCING: SECONDARY-MARKET CORPORATE SECURITIES: Common stock; Preferred stock; Bonds; VENTURE CAPITAL: Research & Development; Second-stage; Later-stage expansion; Buy-outs/Acquisitions; LOANS: LEASES: Single-investor; Leveraged; Tax leases; Non-tax leases, Operating; Lease Syndications; REAL ESTATE LOANS: Industrial revenue bonds; REAL ESTATE: Acquisitions; Joint ventures; Partnerships/Syndications; OTHER SERVICES PROVIDED: Merger and Acquisitions; valuations; corporate finance advisory; acquisitions; divestitures; leveraged buy-outs

COMPANY: **Bateman Eichler, Hill Richards, Inc.**
ADDRESS: 700 S. Flower Street
Los Angeles, CA 90017
PHONE: (213) 625-3545
TYPE OF INSTITUTION: Investment Banker
CONTACT OFFICER(S): James Lewis, Corp. Finance
ASSETS: $100,000,000 and up
GEOGRAPHIC LIMITS OF INVESTMENTS/LOANS: International
RANGE OF INV./LOAN PER BUSINESS: Min. $1,000,000
BUSINESS CHARACTERISTIVS DESIRED-REQUIRED: Minimum number of years in business: 3-5; Minimum annual sales: $10-15 million; Minimum net worth: $1 million (after taxes)
REMARKS: Interested in public issues, private placement, mergers and acquisitions, no venture capital

CO9MPANY: **Wedbush, Noble, & Cooke, Inc.**
ADDRESS: 615 South Flower St.
Los Angeles, CA 90017
PHONE: (213) 687-7000
TYPE OF INSTITUTION: Investment Bank
CONTACT OFFICER(S): Donald Royce Jr., S.V.P.
Bart Gurewitz
Charlie F. Fullerton, (Venture Capital)
ASSETS: $234,000,000
PREFERRED TYPES OF INDUSTRIES/ INVESTEMENTS: Emerging growth companies on the west coast
GEOGRAPHIC LIMITS OF INVESTMENTS/LOANS: Regional
BUSINESS CHARACTERISTICS DESIRED-REQUIRED: Minimum number of years in business: 0; Other: Middle market; Experienced management
REMARKS: Over 100 correspondents

COMPANY:**Wedbush, Noble, Cooke, Inc.**
ADDRESS: 615 South Flower St.
Los Angeles, CA 90017
PHONE: (213) 687-7000
TYPE OF INSTITUTION: Venture capital arm of investment banker
CONTACT OFFICER(S): Charlie F. Fullerton
ASSETS: $234,000,000
TYPES OF FINANCING: VENTURE CAPITAL: Start-up from developed product stage; Second-stage; Later-stage expansion; Buy-outs/Acquisitions, OTHER: Mezzanine financing & leveraged buyouts
GEOGRAPHIC LIMITS OF INVESTMENTS/LOANS: Regional; Other: Western states
RANGE OF INV./LOAN PER BUSINESS: Min. $250,000 - $500,000; Max. $1,000,000
REMARKS: Balanced, diversified portfolio

COMPANY: **Crowell, Weedon & Co.**
ADDRESS: One Wilshire Blvd., 28th floor
Los Angeles, CA 90017
PHONE: (213) 620-1850
TYPE OF INSTITUTION: Investment Banker
CONTACT OFFICER(S): Harold Harrigian, Director of Corporate Finance
James W. Fox, Associate Director of Corporate Finance, Public Underwriting, Mergers & Acquisitions, Venture Captial, Private Placements
TOTAL ORGANIZATION ASSETS: $75,000,000
INVESTMENTS/LOANS MADE: Through private placements; Through underwriting public offerings
INVESTMENTS/LOANS MADE: In securities with a secondary market and in securities without a secondary market
TYPES OF FINANCING: SEONDARY-MARKET CORPORATE SECURITIES: Common stock; Preferred stock; Bonds; Venture Capital Leverage BuyoutsVENTURE CAPITAL: Research & Development; Start-up from developed product stage; First-stage (less than 1 year); Second-stage (generally 1-3 years); Later-stage expansion; Buy-outs/ AcquisitionsLOANS: Unsecured to credits above BBB; Working capital (receivables/inventory); EquipmentOTHER SERVICES PROVIDED: Mergers & Acquisitions; Leveraged Buyouts
PREFERRED TYPES OF INDUSTRIES/INVESTMENTS: No preference in industries or investments; Will do selected real estate syndications
GEOGRAPHIC LIMITS OF INVESTMENTS/LOANS: Regional
RANGE OF INV./LOAN PER BUSINESS: Min. $3,000,000; Max. $20,000,000
BUSINESS CHARACTERISITCS DESIRED-REQUIRED: Minimum number of years in business: 0; Min. annual sales $5,000,000; Min. net worth $2,000,000; Min. annual net income $500,000; Min. annual cash flow $ 500,000
REFERRALS ACCEPTED FROM: Borrower/Investee
BRANCHES: Main Office, One Wilshire Blvd., Los Angeles, CA 90017; (213) 620-1850
Carlsbad Office, 2584A El Camino Real, Carlsbad, CA 92008; (619 729-9141
Long Beach Office, 249 E. Ocean Blvd., Long Beach, CA 90802; (213) 432-8733
Anaheim Office, 300 South Harbor Blvd., Anaheim, CA 92805; (714) 956-0110
Laguna Hills Office, 23521 Paseo de Valencia, Laguna Hills, CA 92653; (714) 837-8900
Newport Center, 567 San Nicolas Dr., Newport Beach, CA 92660; (714) 644-1890
Encino Office, 16130 Ventura Blvd., Encino, CA 91436; (818) 783-1200
Covina Office, 100 E. Badillo St., Covina, CA 91722; (818) 966-0551
Pasadena Office, 95 S. Lake Ave., Pasadena, CA 91101; (818) 449-0330

COMPANY: **James A. Matzdorff & Company**
ADDRESS: 249 S. Lafayette Park Place, Suite 132
Los Angeles, CA 90057
PHONE: (213) 384-4449
TYPE OF INSTITUTION: Investment banking/mortgage banking and brokering, business intermediary
CONTACT OFFICERS(S): James A. Matzdorff, Managing Partner
INVESTMENTS/LOANS MADE: For own account; For managed accounts; Through private placements
INVESTMENTS/LOANS MADE: In securities with a secondary market and in securities without a secondary market

TYPES OF FINANCING: VENTURE CAPITAL: Second-stage (generally 1-3 years); Later-stage expansion; Buy-outs/Acquisitions; LOANS: Unsecured; Working capital (receivables/inventory); Equipment; Equity-related; REAL ESTATE LOANS: Long-term senior mtg.; Intermediate-term senior mtg.; Subordinated; Wraparounds; Land; Construction; Standbys; Other: Hard money seconds, raw lands loans; REAL ESTATE: Acquisitions; Joint ventures; Partnershhips/ Syndications. OTHER SERVICES PROVIDED: Arranging corporate financings for mid-market companies with sales of between $2 million to $20 million annually.
PREFERRED TYPES OF INDUSTRIES/INVESTMENTS: Wholesale distributors, industrial, manufacturing, real estate development, motion picture industry
GEOGRAPHIC LIMITS OF INVESTMENTS/LOANS: National
RANGE OF INV./LOAN PER BUSINESS: Min. $250,000; Max. $25,000,000
REFERRALS ACCEPTED FROM: Investment/Mortgage banker; Borrower/Investee
BRANCHES: Capital Development Group, 9903 Santa Monica Boulevard St. 264, Beverly Hills, CA 90212, (213) 383-3268

COMPANY: **Seidler Amdec Securities**
ADDRESS: 515 South Figueroa Street, 6th floor
Los Angeles, CA 90017-3396
PHONE: (213) 624-4232
TYPE OF INSTITUTION: Investment Banker
CONTACT OFFICER(S): Bruce Emmeluth, S.V.P.
Robert W. Campbell, Asst. V.P.
GEOGRAPHIC LIMITS OF INVESTMENTS/LOANS: Regional; Other: Southwest; West Coast & Rocky Mountain
RANGE OF INV./LOAN PER BUSINESS: Min. $100,000; Max. $400,000

COMPANY: **Diehl, Speyer & Brown**
ADDRESS: 1201 Dave Street
Newport Beach, CA 92660
PHONE: (714) 955-2000
TYPE OF INSTITUTION: Investment Banking
CONTACT OFFICER(S): Russell R. Diehl, Mng. Partner
Michael Henton
GEOGRAPHIC LIMITS OF INVESTMENTS/LOANS: Regional
RANGE OF INV./LOAN PER BUSINESS: Min. $200,000; Max. $500,000
BUSINESS CHARACTERISTICS DESIRED-REQUIRED: Min. annual sales $2 million; Other: Near to or at profitability
REFERRALS ACCEPTED FROM: Investment/Mortgage banker or Borrower/Investee

COMPANY: **First Affiliated Securities, Inc.**
ADDRESS: 6970 Miramar Road
San Diego, CA 92121
PHONE: (619 578-9030
TYPE OF INSTITUTION: Investment Banking; Discount Brokerage
CONTACT OFFICER(S): Jack A. Alexander, Chrmn. CEO
Kenneth W. Elsberry, President
Richard P. Woltman, Exec. V.P.
William J. Patton, Sr. V.P.
Jay Donald Hill, Sr. V.P., Syndicate Mgr. in N.Y.
INVESTMENTS/LOANS MADE: For own account; For managed accounts; Through private placements; Through underwriting public offerings
INVESTMENTS/LOANS MADE: In securities with a secondary market and in securities without a secondary market
TYPES OF FINANCING: SECONDARY-MARKET CORPORATE SECURITIES: Common stock; Preferred stock; Bonds; VENTURE CAPITAL: Second-stage; Later-stage expansion; Buy-outs/Acquisitions (middle); REAL ESTATE: Partnerships; OTHER SERVICES PROVIDED: Venture Capital done in participation with other firms
PREFERRED TYPES OF INDUSTRIES/INVESTMENTS: High-tech; Diversified
GEOGRAPHIC LIMITS OF INVESTMENTS/LOANS: National
BUSINESS CHARACTERISTICS DESIRED-REQUIRED: Minimum number of years in business: 3; Other: Depends on individual company
REFERRALS ACCEPTED FROM: Investment/Mortgage banker or Borrower/Investee

COMPANY: **Vista Capital Corporation/Vista partners, Inc.**
ADDRESS: 701 "B" Street, Suite 760
San Diego, CA 92101
PHONE: (619) 236-1800
TYPE OF INSTITUTION: Small business Investment Company/Investment Banking
CONTACT OFFICER(S): Fred J. Howden, Jr, Chairman
Leslie S. Buck, President
Gregory D. Howard, Vice President
ASSETS: $5 million
INVESTMENTS/LOANS MADE: For own account, through private placements
INVESTMENTS/LOANS MADE: In securities with a secondary market and securities without a secondary market
TYPES OF FINANCING: SECONDARY MARKET CORPORATE SECURITIES: Common stock; Preferred stock; Bonds; VENTURE CAPITAL: Research & Development; start-up from developed product stage; Second-stage; Later-stage expans ion; Buy-outs/ Acquisitions, LOANS: Equity-related; LEASES: Leveraged; Tax leases, Non-tax leases, Operating
PREFERRED TYPES OF INDUSTRIES/INVESTMENTS: Diversified; Computer related, Biotechnology
GEOGRAPHIC LIMITS OF INVESTMENTS/LOANS: Regional
RANGE OF INV./LOAN PER BUSINESS: Min. $300,000
BUSINESS CHARACTERISTICS DESIRED-REQUIRED: Minimum number of years in business 3; Min. annual sales $3,000,000

COMPANY: **Bangert, Dawes, Reade, Davis & Thom Incorporated**
ADDRESS: 1138 Taylor St.
San Francisco, CA 94108
PHONE: (415) 441-6161

TYPE OF INSTITUTION: Investment Bankers
CONTACT OFFICER(S): Dexter B. Dawes, Chairman
K. Deane Reade, Pres., New York, N.Y. Office
INVESTMENTS/LOANS MADE: Through private placements
INVESTMENTS/LOANS MADE: Only in securities without a secondary market
TYPES OF FINANCING: VENTURE CAPITAL: Research and Development; Buy-outs/Acquisitions, LOANS: Unsecured; Working capital; Equipment; Equity-related, Government guaranteed (FMHA, EDA, UDAG); Leveraged Buy-outs Other: Subordinated with equity features; REAL ESTATE: only plant expansions; OTHER SERVICES PROVIDED: Merger, Acquisitions & Divestitures ESOP (Employee Stock Ownersip Plans); Leveraged Buyouts
PREFERRED TYPES OF INDUSTRIES/INVESTMENTS: Will consider all
WILL NOT CONSIDER: Real Estate except Industrial Plant Expansions
GEOGRAPHIC LIMITS OF INVESTMENTS/LOANS: National; International
RANGE OF INV./LOAN PER BUSINESS: Min. $1.0 Million; Max. $100.0 Million
PREFERRED TERM FOR LOANS & LEASES: Min. 2; Max. 15 years
BUSINESS CHARACTERISTICS DESIRED-REQUIRED: Min. annual sales $3.0 Mil.; Min. net worth $0.5 Mil.; Min. annual net income $0.3 Mil
REFERRALS ACCEPTED FROM: Investment/Mortgage banker or Borrower/Investee
BRANCHES: K. Deane Reade, 3 Park Ave., New York, NY 10017; (212) 689-7404

COMPANY: **Birr, Wilson & Co. Inc.**
ADDRESS: 155 Sansome St.
San Francisco, CA 94104
PHONE: (415) 983-7700
TYPE OF INSTITUTION: Investment Bank
CONTACT OFFICER(S): H. Michael Richardson, Exec. V.P. & Mgr.; 983-7967
Ted Birr III, Chairman
Don Wetmore, Pres.
TYPES OF FINANCING: SECONDARY MARKET CORPORATE SECURITIES: Common Stock; Preferred Stock; Bonds; REAL ESTATE LOANS: Long-Term senior mtg.; intermediate term senior mtg.; industrial revenue bonds; Other: all kinds; LEASES: all kinds
GEOGRAPHIC LIMITS OF INVESTMENTS/LOANS: Western U.S.
RANGE OF INV./LOAN PER BUSINESS: Min.$500,000
PREFERRED TERM FOR LOANS & LEASES: Min. Varies
BUSINESS CHARACTERISTICS DESIRED-REQUIRED: Other: Varies
REMARKS: 23 branches

COMPANY: **Chappell & Company**
ADDRESS: One Lombard Street
San Francisco, CA 94111
PHONE: (415) 397-5094
CONTACT OFFICER(S): Robert H. Chappell, President
N. Colin Lind, V.P.
C. Steven Chapman, V.P. (LBO)
Richard J. Sanduli, V.P. (LBO)
Michael T. Hsieh, Asst. V.P.
R. Craig Lind, Asst. V.P.
INVESTMENTS/LOANS MADE: For managed accounts, through private placements
INVESTMENTS/LOANS MADE: In securities with a secondary market and in securities without a secondary market
TYPES OF FINANCING: SECONDARY-MARKET CORPORATE SECURITIES: Common tock; VENTURE CAPITAL: Start-up from developed product stage; First-stage; Buy-outs/Acquisitions
RANGE OF INV./LOAN PER BUSINESS: Min. $100,000
BUSINESS CHARACTERISTICS DESIRED-REQUIRED: Minimum number of years in business: 0
REFERRALS ACCEPTED FROM: Investment/Mortgage banker or Borrower/Investee
BRANCHES: Richard J. Sanduli, Wall Street Plaza, 88 Pine Street, New York, NY 10005; (212) 269-5180

COMPANY: **Davis Skaggs Capital**
ADDRESS: 160 Sansome Street
San Francisco, CA 94104
PHONE: (415) 392-7700
TYPE OF INSTITUTION: Venture capital and investment banking
CONTACT OFFICER(S): Charles P. Stetson, Jr., 393-0274, President
Robert S. Miller, Chairman
INVESTMENTS/LOANS MADE: For own account, through private placements
TYPES OF FINANCING: VENTURE CAPITAL: First-stage; Second-stage; Later-stage expansion; Buy-outs/Acquisitions, OTHER SERVICES PROVIDED: financial consulting service w/investment
REMARKS: Now owned by Shearson-Lehman Am. Express

COMPANY: **Hambrecht & Quist**
ADDRESS: 235 Montgomery Street
San Francisco, CA 94104
PHONE: (415) 576-3300
TYPE OF INSTITUTION: Investment banker
CONTACT OFFICER(S): Thomas S. Volpe, Chief Operating Officer
William R. Hambrecht, President
ASSETS: more than $50 million
INVESTMENTS/LOANS MADE: For own account, For managed accounts, Through private placements, underwriting public offerings
INVESTMENTS/LOANS MADE: In securities with a secondary market and in securities without a secondary market
TYPES OF FINANCING: SECONDARY-MARKET CORPORATE SECURITIES: Common stock; Preferred stock; Bonds, VENTURE CAPITAL: Research & Development; Start-up from developed product stage; First-stage; Second-stage; Later-stage expansion; Buy-outs/Acquisitions, OTHER SERVICES PROVIDED: Corporate Partnering/Mergers & Acquisitions
PREFERRED TYPES OF INDUSTRIES/INVESTMENTS: High technology, medical technology, defense electronics

GEOGRAPHIC LIMITS OF INVESTMENTS/LOANS: National
REFERRALS ACCEPTED FROM: Investment/Mortgage banker or Borrower/Investee
BRANCHES: Thomas Greig, 277 Park Avenue, New York, NY 10172; (212) 207-1400
Robert Morrill/Robert Whelan, 45 Milk Street, Boston, MA 02181; (617) 338-4339
Thomas Turney, 700 S. Flower St., #3310, Los Angeles, CA 90017; (213) 617-3101
REMARKS: Hambrecht & Quist does not provide loans to companies.

COMPANY: **Montgomery Securities**
ADDRESS: 600 Montgomery St.
San Francisco, CA 94111
PHONE: (415) 627-2000
TYPE OF INSTITUTION: Investment Bankers
CONTACT OFFICER(S): Alan L. Stein, Director of Corporate Finance
Thom Weisel, Senior Partner
ASSETS: Over $100,000,000
INVESTMENTS/LOANS MADE: For own account, For managed accounts, Through private placements, Through underwriting public offerings
INVESTMENTS/LOANS MADE: In securities with a secondary market and in securities without a secondary market
TYPES OF FINANCING: SECONDARY-MARKET CORPORATE SECURITIES: Common stock; Convertible Securities; VENTURE CAPITAL: Start-up from developed product stage; First-stage; Second-stage; Later-stage expansion; Buy-outs/Acquisitions. LOANS: Equity-related.
PREFERRED TYPES OF INDUSTRIES/INVESTMENTS: Technology, Medical, Consumer Services
WILL NOT CONSIDER: Real Estate, Natural Resources
GEOGRAPHIC LIMITS OF INVESTMENTS/LOANS: None
RANGE OF INV./LOAN PER BUSINESS: Min. $250,000; Max. $1,500,000
PREFERRED TERM FOR LOANS & LEASES: Min. N/A
BUSINESS CHARACTERISTICS DESIRED-REQUIRED: Minimum number of years in businss: 0 ('0' if startups financed)
REFERRALS ACCEPTED FROM: Investment/Mortgage banker or Borrower/Investee

COMPANY: **Robertson, Colman & Stephens**
ADDRESS: One Embarcadero Center
San Francisco, CA 94111
PHONE: (415) 781-9700
TYPE OF INSTITUTION: Investment Bank
CONTACT OFFICER(S): Sanford R. Robertson, Partner
Robert S. Colman, Partner
Paul H. Stephens, Partner
Christopher H. Covington, Partner
INVESTMENTS/LOANS MADE: Through private placements, Through underwriting public offerings
INVESTMENTS/LOANS MADE: In securities with a secondary market and in securities without a secondary market
TYPES OF FINANCING: SECONDARY-MARKET CORPORATE SECURITIES: Common stock; Preferred stock; Convertible Debt. VENTURE CAPITAL: Start-up from developed product stage; First-stage; Second-stage; Later-stage expansion; Buy-outs/acquisitions. OTHER SERVICES PROVIDED: Mergers and Acquisitions
PREFERRED TYPES OF INDUSTRIES/INVESTMENTS: Fast growing companies, Industries, Telecommunications, Information processing, Semiconductor, Micro computers, Peripherals, Defense electronics, software, Medical instrumentation, Health care
GEOGRAPHIC LIMITS OF INVESTMENTS/LOANS: International
REMARKS: Investment bank specializing in emerging growth, high technology companies

COMPANY: **Stone & Youngberg**
ADDRESS: One California Street
San Francisco, CA 94111
PHONE: (415) 981-1314
TYPE OF INSTITUTION: Investment Banker
CONTACT OFFICER(S): Scott Sollers, Partner
William Huck, Partner
Ken Williams, Partner
TYPES OF FINANCING: REAL ESTATE LOANS: Long-term senior mtg.; Industrial revenue bonds. OTHER SERVICES PROVIDED: Tax exempt municipal financing, Capital programs for municipalities, Development infrastructure, Underwrite municipal bonds
PREFERRED TYPES OF INDUSTRIES/INVESTMENTS: RE developers, Industrial park developers, Municipalities
GEOGRAPHIC LIMITS OF INVESTMENTS/LOANS: State
RANGE OF INV./LOAN PER BUSINESS: Min. $500,000; Max. $100,000,000

COMPANY: **Sutro & Co. Incorporated**
ADDRESS: 201 California Street
San Francisco, CA 94111
PHONE: (415) 445-8500
TYPE OF INSTITUTION: Investment Bankers
CONTACT OFFICER(S): Thomas E. Bertelson, Jr. Exec. V.P.
ASSETS: $120 million
INVESTMENTS/LOANS MADE: For own account; For managed accounts; Through private placements; Through underwriting public offerings
INVESTMENTS/LOANS MADE: In securities with a secondary market and in securities without a secondary market
TYPES OF FINANCING: SECONDARY-MARKET CORPORATE SECURITIES: Common stock; Preferred stock; Bonds, VENTURE CAPITAL: Research & Development; Start-up from developed product stage; First-stage (less than 1 year); Second-stage (generally 1-3 years); Later-stage expansion; Buy-outs/Acquisitions, LOANS: Unsecured to credits above Ba, LEASES: Single-investor; Leveraged; Tax leases; Non-tax leases; Tax-oriented lease brokerage; Lease syndications; Vendor financing programs, REAL ESTATE: Joint ventures; Partnerships/Syndications, OTHER SERVICES PROVIDED: Financial advisory

PREFERRED TYPES OF INDUSTRIES/INVESTMENTS: Telecommunications, Health Care, Communications, Financial Services
GEOGRAPHIC LIMITS OF INVESTMENTS/LOANS: Regional
RANGE OF INV./LOAN PER BUSINESS: Min. $1 million
BUSINESS CHARACTERISTICS DESIRED-REQUIRED: Minimum number of years in business: 0
REFERRALS ACCEPTED FROM; Investment/mortgage Banker or Borrower/Investee

COMPANY: **Alta Investment Company**
ADDRESS: 518 Seventeenth St., #610
Denver, CO 80202
PHONE: (303) 573-7244
TYPE OF INSTITUTION: Investment Banker; Stock Broker/Dealer
CONTACT OFFICER(S): Robert W. Sneed, President
ASSETS: $ 70,000,000
INVESTMENTS/LOANS MADE: For own (company's or principals') account
Through underwriting public offerings
INVESTMENTS/LOANS MADE: Only in securities with a secondary market
TYPES OF FINANCING: SECONDARY-MARKET CORPORATE SECURITIES: Common stock; Oil and Gas Production; VENTURE CAPITAL: Start-up from developed product stage; First-stage (less than 1 year)
PREFERRED TYPES OF INDUSTRIES/INVESTMENTS: Oil & Gas Production
GEOGRAPHIC LIMITS OF INVESTMENTS/LOANS: Regional
RANGE OF INV./LOAN PER BUSINESS: Min. $no minimum; Max. $no maximum
PREFERRED TERMS FOR LOANS & LEASES: Min. 6 months; Max. 30 years
REFERRALS ACCEPTED FROM: Investment/Mortgage banker and Borrower/Investee

COMPANY: **Hanifen, Imhoff, Inc.**
ADDRESS: 1125 17th St., Suite 1700
Denver, CO 80202
PHONE: 8303) 296-2300
CONTACT OFFICER(S): John Crum, Sr. V.P., Corporate Underwriting
Richard Gunderson, V.P., Municipal Leasings
ASSETS: $15 Million
INVESTMENTS/LOANS MADE: Through private placements, Underwriting public offerings
TYPES OF FINANCING: SECONDARY-MARKET CORPORATE SECURITIES: Common stock Preferred stock; Bonds
PREFERRED TYPES OF INDUSTRIES/INVESTMENTS: Energy Related; High Technology; Medical Products
GEOGRAPHIC LIMITS OF INVESTMENTS/LOANS: Rocky Mountains Region

COMPANY: **E.J. Pittock Inc.**
ADDRESS: 7951 E. Maplewood Suite 230
Englewood, CO 80111
PHONE: (303) 740-7272
TYPE OF INSTITUTION: Investment Banking - Regional Brokerage Firm
CONTACT OFFICER(S): George S. Yochmowitz, Esq, Corporate Counsel
Mark F. Burgeson, Director Corporate Finance
Andrea K. Ferguson, Syndication Manager
ASSETS: N/A
INVESTMENTS/LOANS MADE: Through underwriting public offerings
BRANCHES: Ft. Colins, CO
Greeley, CO
Grand Junction, CO
Colorado Spgs., CO
Buffalo, NY
TYPES OF FINANCING: SECONDARY-MARKET CORPORATE SECURITIES: Common stock; Preferred stock; Bonds; VENTURE CAPITAL: Start-up from developed product stage; Later-stage expansion; Buy-outs/Acquisitions
PREFERRED TYPES OF INDUSTRIES/INVESTMENTS: Primarily an investment banker for the I.P.O.'s of energy or technology related companies over the last 10 years. Recent expansion plans include bond division and merger/acquisition dept.
GEOGRAPHIC LIMITS OF INVESTMENTS/LOANS: No geographic limitations
RANGE OF INV./LOAN PER BUSINESS: Min.: $250,000; Max. $20,000,000
BUSINESS CHARACTERISTICS DESIRED-REQUIRED: Minimum number of years in business 1+; Other: Qualified management, progressive industry, large market potential

COMPANY: **Parker Benjamin, Inc.**
ADDRESS: 120 Mountain Avenue
Bloomfield, CT 06002
PHONE: (203) 242-7277
TYPE OF INSTITUTION: Private Investment Bank serving primarily middle market companies and real estate developers
CONTACT OFFICER(S): Paul M. Ruby, President, Mergers and Acquisitions, Venture Capital
Thomas A. D'Avanzo, Executive Vice President, Private Placement of Debt, Real Estate Financing, Industrial Revenue Bonds Apprisals
INVESTMENTS/LOANS MADE: Through private placements
INVESTMENTS/LOANS MADE: VENTURE CAPITAL: Research & Development; Start-up from developed product stage; First-stage (less than 1 year); Second-stage (generally 1-3 years); Later-stage expansion; Buy-outs/Acquistions; LOANS: Unsecured to credits above Baa; Working capital (receivables/inventory); Equipment; Equity-related; Other: Industrial Revenue Bonds; REAL ESTATE LOANS: Long-term senior mtg.; Intermediate-term senior mtg.; Subordinated; Wraparounds; Land; Land development; Construction; Gap; Standbys; Industrial revenue bonds; LEASES: Single-Investor; Leveraged; Tax leases; Non-tax leases; Operating; Tax-oriented lease brokerage; vendor financing programs; REAL ESTATE: Acquisitions; Joint ventures; OTHER SERVICES PROVIDED: Appraisal of privately owned businesses
PREFERRED TYPES OF INDUSTRIES/INVESTMENTS: All

GEOGRAPHIC LIMITS OF INVESTMENTS/LOANS: International
RANGE OF INV./LOAN PER BUSINESS: Min. $500,000
REMARKS: The firm represents pension fund money for prime real estate development projects.

COMPANY: **Advest, Inc.**
ADDRESS: 6 Central Row
Hartford, CT 06103
PHONE: (203) 525-1421
TYPE OF INSTITUTION: Investment banking, mortgage banking, equity syndication
CONTACT OFFICER(S): John Everetts, Corporate Finance
ASSETS: $384,483,000
INVESTMENTS/LOANS MADE: For own account, Through private placements, Through underwriting public offerings
INVESTMENTS/LOANS MADE: In securities with a secondary market and in securities without a secondary market
TYPES OF FINANCING: SECONDARY-MARKET CORPORATE SECURITIES: Common stock; Preferred stock; Bonds, VENTURE CAPITAL: Research & Development; First-stage (less than 1 year), LOANS: Equity-related, REAL ESTATE LOANS: Long-term senior mtg.; Intermediate-term senior mtg.; Subordinated; Wraparounds; Land; Land development; Gap; Standbys; Industrial revenue bonds, LEASES: Non-tax leases; Operating; Tax-oriented lease brokerage, REAL ESTATE: Acquisitions; Joint ventures; Partnerships/Syndications
GEOGRAPHIC LIMITS OF INVESTMENTS/LOANS: National
RANGE OF INV./LOAN PER BUSINESS: Min. $500,000 Max. $25 million
BRANCHES: 87 offices throughout Northeastern US

COMPANY: **B. L. McTeague & Co., Inc.**
ADDRESS: 37 Lewis Street
Hartford, CT 06103
PHONE: (203) 247-6741
TYPE OF INSTITUTION: Private Investment Banking Firm
CONTACT OFFICER(S): Bertrand L. McTeague, President
Robert E. Darling, Jr., Sr. V.P.
Andre Daniel-Dreyfus, V.P. Senior Associate
Sheldon J. Hoffman, V.P. Senior Associate
Mark Breen, Sr. V.P., Real Estate Syndication, 203-241-0140
INVESTMENTS/LOANS MADE: Through private placements; Through underwriting public offerings
INVESTMENTS/LOANS MADE: In securities with a secondary market and in securities without a secondary market
TYPES OF FINANCING: SECONDARY-MARKET CORPORATE SECURITIES: Common stock; Preferred stock; Bonds; Government Agency Guaranteed Securities, VENTURE CAPITAL, LOANS, REAL ESTATE LOANS; LEASES: All kinds; REAL ESTATE: Partnerships/Syndications; OTHER SERVICES PROVIDED: Appraisals of securities of privately-held businesses

GEOGRAPHIC LIMITS OF INVESTMENTS/LOANS: Local; State; Regional; National
RANGE OF INV./LOAN PER BUSINESS: Min. $1.5 million
BUSINESS CHARACTERISTICS DESIRED-REQUIRED: Minimum number of years in business: 0
REFERRALS ACCEPTED FROM: Investment/Mortgage Banker or Borrow/Investee
BRANCHES: Andre Daniel-Dreyfus, V.P., Frederick B. Barclay, Asst. V.P., 50 Milk St., Ste. 1500, Boston, MA 02109; 617-357-5395

COMPANY: **Memhard Investment Bankers**
ADDRESS: 22 Fifth Street, Suite 204
Stamford, CT 06905
PHONE: (203) 348-6802
TYPE OF INSTITUTION: Investment banking firm investing own funds or those of partners and clients.
CONTACT OFFICER(S): Richard C. Memhard, President
INVESTMENTS/LOANS MADE: For own account; Through private placements
INVESTMENTS/LOANS MADE: Only in securities without a secondary market
TYPES OF FINANCING: VENTURE CAPITAL: Research & Development; Start-up from developed product stage; First-stage (less than 1 year); Second-stage (generally 1-3 years); Later-stage expansion; Buy-outs/Acquisitions
PREFERRED TYPES OF INDUSTRIES/INVESTMENTS: Manufacturing, Technology, Computer Related, Medical, Natural Resources, Retail, Services.
GEOGRAPHIC LIMITS OF INVESTMENTS/LOANS: National
RANGE OF INV./LOAN PER BUSINESS: Min. $600,000; Max. No limit
BUSINESS CHARACTERISTICS DESIRED-REQUIRED: Min. annual sales $500,000

COMPANY: **Greenwich Investors Corp.**
ADDRESS: 155 Post Road East
Westport, CT 06880
PHONE: (203) 227-0856
TYPE OF INSTITUTION: Private investment banking firm
CONTACT OFFICER(S): George Artope, President
ASSETS: $5,000,000
INVESTMENTS/LOANS MADE: For own account; For managed accounts; Through private placement
INVESTMENTS/LOANS MADE: In securities with a secondary market and in securities without a secondary market
TYPES OF FINANCING: SECONDARY-MARKET CORPORATE SECURITIES: Common stock; Preferred stock; Bonds; VENTURE CAPITAL: Start-up from developed product stage; First-stage (less than 1 year); Buy-outs/Acquisitions; LOANS: Working capital (receivables/inventory); Equipment; Equity-related; REAL ESTATE: Acquisitions; Joint ventures; Partnerships/Syndications

COMPANY: **Ewing Capital, Inc.**
ADDRESS: 1016-16th Street, NW, Ste. 650
Washington, DC 20036

PHONE: (202) 463-8787
TYPE OF INSTITUTION: Consulting or Investment Banking firm evaluating and analyzing venture projects and arranging private placements.
CONTACT OFFICER(S): Samuel D. Ewing, President
INVESTMENTS/LOANS MADE: Through private placements
TYPES OF FINANCING: SECONDARY-MARKET CORPORATE SECURITIES: Common stock; Preferred stock; Bonds; Debt with warrants; VENTURE CAPITAL: First-stage; Second-stage Later-stage expansion; Buy-outs/Aquisitions; LOANS: Unsecured, Working capital; Equipment; Equity-related; REAL ESTATE LOANS: Long-term Senior Mtg; Intermediate Term Senior Mtg; Subordinated; Wraparounds; LandFACTORING; REAL ESTATE: Acquistions; Joint ventures
PREFERRED TYPES OF INDUSTRIES/INVESTMENTS: Broadcasting; Commercial Communications; Consumer Products; Communications Equipment; Computer Equipment; Electronic Components
GEOGRAPHIC LIMITS OF INVESTMENTS/LOANS: National; No geographical preference
RANGE OF INV./LOAN PER BUSINESS: Min. $500,000
BUSINESS CHARACTERISTICS DESIRED-REQUIRED: Profitable within 18-24 mos. Early stage co. show potential $30 mil. sales in 5 yrs.
REMARKS: ECI functions as an investment banking firm

COMPANY: **First Washington Securities Corp.**
ADDRESS: 1735 I Street, NW, Ste. 605
Washington, DC 20006
PHONE: (202) 296-2394
CONTACT OFFICER(S): Sherwood J. Pierce, V.P., Private Placement
INVESTMENTS/LOANS MADE: Through private placements
TYPES OF FINANCING: REAL ESTATE

COMPANY: **Wachtel & Co., Inc.**
ADDRESS: 1101 14th St., N.W.
Washington, DC 20005-5680
PHONE: (202) 898-1144
TYPE OF INSTITUTION: Investment Banking; Securities Brokerage; Venture Capital
CONTACT OFFICER(S): Sidney B. Wachtel, President
John D. Sanders, V.P.
Wendie L. Wachtel, V.P.
Bonnie K. Wachtel, V.P. & General Counsel
ASSETS: 5-10 million
INVESTMENTS/LOANS MADE: For own account;Through private placements; Through underwriting public offerings
INVESTMENTS/LOANS MADE: In securities with a secondary market and in securities without a secondary market
TYPES OF FINANCING: SECONDARY-MARKET CORPORATE SECURITIES: Common stock; VENTURE CAPITAL: Start-up from developed product stage; First-stage (less than 1 year); Second-stage (generally 1-3 years); Later-stage expansion; LOANS: Equity-related, OTHER SERVICES PROVIDED: Financial Advisory to small emerging companies

PREFERRED TYPES OF INDUSTRIES/INVESTMENTS: We prefer equity situations in data processing and electronics (high technology), but will consider any situation showing merit, particularly if the seeker has invested, or is prepared to invest a significant portion of the funds desired.
WILL NOT CONSIDER: anything relating directly or indirectly to real estate, or any other operation involving leveraging. Also capital intensive industries.
GEOGRAPHIC LIMITS OF INVESTMENTS/LOANS: Regional
RANGE OF INV./LOAN PER BUSINESS: Min. $500,000 (public); no minimum (private); Max. $10 million (public); $200,000 (private)
BUSINESS CHARACTERISTICS DESIRED-REQUIRED: Min. no. of years in business: 0; Other: As just noted, we do startups, but prefer companies that have been in business at least 6 months to one year.
REFERRALS ACCEPTED FROM: Investment/Mortgage banker or Borrower/Investee
REMARKS: Please note that we have been in business since 1961, and that we are strictly equity-oriented re our own as well as our client's investments.

COMPANY: **Raymond, James & Associates, Inc.**
ADDRESS: 1400 66th St. N.
St. Petersburg, FL 33710-5579
PHONE: (813) 381-3800
TYPE OF INSTITUTION: Full Line Securities Firm
CONTACT OFFICER(S): Francis S. Godbold , Exec. V.P. Corp. Finance
John Hardy, Asst. V.P., Municipal Finance Industrial Revenue Bonds
ASSETS: $79,500,000
INVESTMENTS/LOANS MADE: Through private placements, Underwriting public offerings
INVESTMENTS/LOANS MADE: In securities with a secondary market and in securities without a secondary market
TYPES OF FINANCING: SECONDARY-MARKET CORPORATE SECURITIES: Common stock; Preferred stock; Bonds; Partnerships, VENTURE CAPITAL: Buy-outs/Acquisitions; REAL ESTATE LOANS: Industrial revenue bonds, LEASES: Single-investor; Leveraged; Tax leases; Non-tax leases; Operating; Tax-oriented lease brokerage, REAL ESTATE: Partnerships/ Syndications
GEOGRAPHIC LIMITS OF INVESTMENTS/LOANS: National
REFERRALS ACCEPTED FROM: Investment/Mortgage banker or Borrower/Investee
REMARKS: 182 branches

COMPANY: **Communications Equity Associates**
ADDRESS: 851 Lincoln Center, 5401 W. Kennedy Blvd.
Tampa, FL 33609
PHONE: (813) 877-8844
TYPE OF INSTITUTION: Investment banking/brokerage firm for cable communications
CONTACT OFFICER(S): J. Patrick Michaels, Jr., Chairman
Harold D. Ewen, President
H. Gene Gawthrop, Sr. Vice President/Chief Financial Officer

INVESTMENTS/LOANS MADE: Through private placements
TYPES OF FINANCING: VENTURE CAPITAL: First-stage; Second-stage; Buy-outs/Acquisitions, LOANS: Unsecured to credits above; Working capital; . Equipment; Equity-related
PREFERRED TYPES OF INDUSTRIES/INVESTMENTS: Communications related specializing in cable television
GEOGRAPHIC LIMITS OF INVESTMENTS/LOANS: International
RANGE OF INV./LOAN PER BUSINESS: Min. $1,000,000
BUSINESS CHARACTERISTICS DESIRED-REQUIRED: Minimum number of years in business: 0

COMPANY: **Bankers Funding**
ADDRESS: P.O. Box 88472
Atlanta, GA 30356
PHONE: (404) 255-1980
TYPE OF INSTITUTION: Private Banking Company
CONTACT OFFICERS: Jim Ruska, Pres.
Wayne Staples, Admin/Operations
Wayne Fairchild, Financial
ASSETS: $3,500,000
INVESTMENTS/LOANS MADE: For own (company's or principals') account; Through private placements
INVESTMENTS/LOANS MADE: In securities with a secondary market and in securities without a secondary market
TYPES OF FINANCING: LOANS: Working capital (receivables/inventory); Equipment; Equity-related; REAL ESTATE LOANS: Long-term senior mtg.; Intermediate-term senior mtg.; Wraparounds; Land; Land development; Construction; Gap; FACTORING; LEASE: Single-investor; Leveraged; Tax leases; Non-tax leases; Operating; Tax-oriented lease brokerage; Vendor financing progams; REAL ESTATE: Acquisitions; Joint ventures; Partnerships/Syndications. OTHER SERVICES PROVIDED: Joint Venture, with original owners having a buyout amount
PREFERRED TYPES OF INDUSTRIES/INVESTMENTS: Anything
WILL NOT CONSIDER: Data Processing
GEOGRAPHIC LIMITS OF INVESTMENTS/LOANS: Local; State; Regional; National; Prefer regional, but have done many national transactions
RANGE OF INV./LOAN PER BUSINESS: Min. $50,000; Max. $50,000,000
PREFERRED TERM FOR LOANS & LEASES: Min. 6 months; Max. 10 years
BUSINESS CHARACTERISTICS DESIRED-REQUIRED; Minimum number of years in business: 1 year; Min. annual sales $100,000; Min. net worth $50,000; Min. annual net income $50,000; Min. annual cash flow $75,000

COMPANY: **Grubb & Company**
ADDRESS: 1500 Tower Place, 3340 Peachtree Rd.
Atlanta, GA 30026
PHONE: (404) 237-6222
TYPE OF INSTITUTION: Investment Bank
CONTACT OFFICER(S): Stephen B. Grubb, Managing Director
David E. Thomas, Director
INVESTMENTS/LOANS MADE: Through private placements
INVESTMENTS/LOANS MADE: Only in Securities without a secondary market
TYPES OF FINANCING: VENTURE CAPITAL: Research & Development; Start-up from developed product stage; First-stage; Second-stage; Later-stage; Buy-outs/Acquisitions
PREFERRED TYPES OF INDUSTRIES/INVESTMENTS: Corporate finance only
GEOGRAPHIC LIMITS OF INVESTMENT/LOANS: Regional
RANGE OF INV./LOAN PER BUSINESS: Min. $250,000
BUSINESS CHARACTERISTICS DESIRED/REQUIRED: Minimum number of years in business: 0; Min. annual sales $0; Min. net worth $0; Min. annual net income $0; Min. annual cash flow $0
REFERRALS ACCEPTED FROM: Investment/Mortgage banker only; Borrower/Investee

COMPANY: **Philipps J. Hook & Assoc., Inc.**
ADDRESS: 5600 Roswell Rd. NE Suite 300, Prodo North
Atlanta, GA 30342
PHONE: (404) 252-1994
TYPE OF INSTITUTION: Investment Bankers, Corporate Finance Advisor's
CONTACT OFFICER(S): P. J. Hook, Pres.
INVESTMENTS/LOANS MADE: In securities with a secondary market and in securities without a secondary market
TYPES OF FINANCING: SECONDARY-MARKET CORPORATE SECURITIES: Common stock; Preferred stock; Bonds, VENTURE CAPITAL: Research & Development; Start-up from developed product stage; First-stage (less than 1 year); Second-stage (generally 1-3 years); Later-stage expansion; Buy-outs/Acquisitions, LOANS: Unsecured; Equity-related, OTHER SERVICES PROVIDED: Corporate Director
WILL NOT CONSIDER: Real Estate
GEOGRAPHIC LIMITS OF INVESTMENTS/LOANS: National
RANGE OF INV./LOAN PER BUSINESS: Min. $750,000; Max. $20 million
BUSINESS CHARACTERISTICS DESIRED-REQUIRED: Min. no. of years in business: 0
REFERRALS ACCEPTED FROM: Investment/Mortgage banker or Borrower/Investee

COMPANY: **Robinson-Humphrey /American Express Inc.**
ADDRESS: 3333 Peachtree Rd., N.E.
Atlanta, GA 30326
PHONE: (404) 581-7188
TYPE OF INSTITUTION: Investment Bankers
CONTACT OFFICER(S): Thomas A. Avery, V.P., Corporate Finance
Deborah Reel
David Smith, Asst. V.P., Corporate Finance
ASSETS: $100,000,000+
INVESTMENTS/LOANS MADE: Through private placements; Through underwriting public offerings
INVESTMENTS/LOANS MADE: In securities with a secondary market and in securities without a secondary market

TYPES OF FINANCING: SECONDARY-MARKET CORPORATE SECURITIES: Common stock; Preferred stock; Bonds, VENTURE CAPITAL: Second-stage (generally 1-3 years); Later-stage expansion; Buy-outs/Acquisitions, LOANS: Unsecured to credits above B; Working capital (receivables/inventory); Equipment, REAL ESTATE LOANS: Long-term senior mtg.; Intermediate-term senior mtg.; Land; Industrial revenue bonds, OTHER SERVICES PROVIDED: Valuations o f securities for a variety of different situations
GEOGRAPHIC LIMITS OF INVESTMENTS/LOANS: Southeast orientation, but will work with companies on a selective basis located elsewhere.
RANGE OF INV./LOAN PER BUSINESS: Min. $1,000,000; Max. None
BUSINESS CHARACTERISTICS DESIRED-REQUIRED: Minimum number of years in business: 1; Management must be in place and experienced in the business
REFERRALS ACCEPTED FROM: Investment/Mortgage banker or Borrower/Investee

COMPANY: **Merit Capital Corporation**
ADDRESS: 1110 Financial Center
Des Moines, IA 50309
PHONE: (515) 280-8363
CONTACT OFFICER(S): James T. Munro, President
PREFERRED TYPES OF INDUSTRIES/INVESTMENTS: RE limited partnerships
WILL NOT CONSIDER: Public offerings
GEOGRAPHIC LIMITS OF INVESTMENTS/LOANS: National
RANGE OF INV./LOAN PER BUSINESS: Min. $100,000; Max. $600,000

COMPANY: **R. G. Dickinson & Co.**
ADDRESS: 200 Des Moines Building
Des Moines, IA 50309
PHONE: (515) 247-8100
CONTACT OFFICER(S): Robert C. Gibb, V.P., Manager, Municipal Finance Dept.
ASSETS: $30 million
BRANCHES: Chicago, IL
Los Angeles, CA
Wichita, KS
Omaha, NE
Colorado Springs, CO
INVESTMENTS/LOANS MADE: In securities with a secondary market and in securities without a secondary market
TYPES OF FINANCING: SECONDARY-MARKET CORPORATE SECURITIES: Common stock; Preferred stock; Bonds, VENTURE CAPITAL: Research & Development; Start-up from developed product stage; First-stage (less than 1 year); Second-stage (generally 1-3 years); Later-stage expansion; Buy-outs/Acquisitions, REAL ESTATE LOANS: Industrial revenue bonds, REAL ESTATE: Acquisitions; Joint ventures; Partnerships/Syndications
GEOGRAPHIC LIMITS OF INVESTMENTS/LOANS: Primarily regional
BUSINESS CHARACTERISTICS DESIRED-REQUIRED: Minimum number of years in business; 0

COMPANY: **Clayton Brown & Associates, Inc.**
ADDRESS: 300 W. Washington St.
Chicago, IL 60606
PHONE: (312) 641-3300
TYPE OF INSTITUTION: Investment Bank, Municipal Finance
CONTACT OFFICER(S): Ed Maloney, Senior Vice President, Municipal Finance Dept.
ASSETS: $20,000,000 capital
INVESTMENTS/LOANS MADE: For own acccount (tax-exempt & IDR Bonds); Through private placements; Through underwriting public offerings
INVESTMENTS/LOANS MADE: Only in municipal securities and IR Bonds
TYPES OF FINANCING: SECONDARY-MARKET CORPORATE SECURITIES: Bonds; Tax-exempt, REAL ESTATE LOANS: Industrial revenue bonds, LEASES: Non-tax leases; Other Services Provided: Underwriting, selling, trading of tax-exempt securities
GEOGRAPHIC LIMITS OF INVESTMENTS/LOANS: National
BRANCHES: 70 Pine Street, New York, NY 10270, 212-425-9170
330 East Kilbourn Avenue, Milwaukee, WI 53202, 414-276-2236
1515 Ringling Boulevard, Sarasota, FL 33577

COMPANY: **Capital B Corporation**
ADDRESS: 303 East Wacker Drive, Ste. 940
Chicago, IL 60601
PHONE: (312) 565-0850
TYPE OF INSTITUTION: Investment Banking
CONTACT OFFICER(S): Bernard Filler, President
INVESTMENTS/LOANS MADE: For own account, For managed accounts, Through private placements
INVESTMENTS/LOANS MADE: In securities with a secondary market and in securities without a secondary market
TYPES OF FINANCING: SECONDARY-MARKET CORPORATE SECURITIES: Common stock; Preferred stock; VENTURE CAPTIAL: Start-up from developed product stage; First-stage (less than 1 year); Second-stage (generally 1-3 years); Later-stage expansion; Buy-outs/Acquisitions; REAL ESTATE: Acquisition; Joint ventures; Partnerships/Syndication; OTHER SERVICES PROVIDED: Leverage Buyouts and Corporate Acquisitions
RANGE OF INV./LOAN PER BUSINESS: Min. $1 million

COMPANY: **Mesirow Venture Capital**
ADDRESS: 135 S. LaSalle
Chicago, IL
PHONE: (312) 443-5757
TYPE OF INSTITUTION: Venture Capital Division of Investment Banker
CONTACT OFFICER(S): James C. Tyree, Executive Vice President
INVESTMENTS/LOANS/MADE: For own account; For managed accounts; Through private placements; Through underwriting public offerings

INVESTMENTS/LOANS MADE: In securities with a secondary market and in securities without a secondary market
TYPES OF FINANCING: SECONDARY-MARKET CORPORATE SECURITIES: Common stock; Preferred stock; Bonds; VENTURE CAPITAL: Second-stage (generally 1-3 years); Later-stage expansion; Buy-outs/ Acquisitions
PREFERRED TYPES OF INDUSTRIES/INVESTMENTS: All
GEOGRAPHIC LIMITS OF INVESTMENTS/LOANS: National
RANGE OF INV./LOAN PER BUSINESS: Min. $250,000; Max. $20,000,000
PREFERRED TERM FOR LOANS & LEASES: Min. 2 years; Max. 10 years
BUSINESS CHARACTERISTICS DESIRED-REQUIRED: Minimum number of years in business: 1; Min. annual sales $1,000,000;
REFERRALS ACCEPTED FROM: Investment/Mortgage banker or Borrower/Investee

COMPANY: **The Luken Company**
ADDRESS: 135 S. LaSalle St., Suite 711
Chicago, IL 60603
PHONE: (312) 263-4015
TYPE OF INSTITUTION: Investment Banking & Consulting
CONTACT OFFICER(S): Donald J. Luken, President
INVESTMENTS/LOANS/MADE: For own account; Through private placements
INVESTMENTS/LOANS/MADE: Only in securities without a secondary market
TYPES OF FINANCING: VENTURE CAPITAL: Research & Development; Start-up from developed product stage; First-stage (less than 1 year); Second-stage (generally 1 to 3 years); Later-stage expansion; Buy-outs/Acquisitions; LOANS: Equity-related; OTHER SERVICES PROVIDED: Financial Consulting/ Management
PREFERRED TYPES OF INDUSTRIES/INVESTMENTS: Medium Technology; Service Industries
GEOGRAPHIC LIMITS OF INVESTMENTS/LOANS: Regional
RANGE OF INV./LOAN PER BUSINESS: Min. $250,000; Max. $3,000,000
BUSINESS CHARACTERISTICS DESIRED-REQUIRED: Minimum number of years in business: 0 Other: Must have demonstrable technology

COMPANY: **The Illinois Company, Inc.**
ADDRESS: 30 N. LaSalle Street
Chicago, IL 60602
PHONE: (312) 444-2100
TYPE OF INSITITION: Investment Banking
CONTACT OFFICER(S): William A. Penner, Executive Vice President, Corporate Finance
Murray R. Lessinger, Corporate Finance Associate
ASSETS: $29 million
INVESTMENT/LOANS MADE: For managed accounts; Through private placements; Through underwriting public offerings
INVESTMENT/LOANS MADE: Only in securities with a secondary market
TYPES OF FINANCING: SECONDARY-MARKET CORPORATE SECURITIES: Common stock; Preferred stock; Bonds; VENTURE CAPITAL: Reseach & Development; Start-up from developed product stage; First-stage (less than 1 year); Second-stage (generally 1-3 year); Later-stage expansion; Buy-outs/Acquistions; LOANS: Working capital; Equipment; FACTORING: REAL ESTATE
PREFERRED TYPES OF INDUSTRIES/INVESTMENTS: All
GEOGRAPHIC LIMITS OF INVESTMENTS/LOANS: National
RANGE OF INV./LOAN PER BUSINESS: Min. $500,000
BUSINESS CHARACTERISTICS DESIRED-REQUIRED: Minimum number of years in business: 0
REFERRALS ACCEPTED FROM: Investment/Mortgage banker or Borrower/Investee
BRANCHES: Patricia C. Bryan, 1902 Round Barn road, Champaign Illinois 61812; (217) 352-5201; Vice President
James Barnes, 221 West Washington, Waukegan, IL 60085; 623-0245; Branch Mgr.

COMPANY: **The December Group, Ltd.**
ADDRESS: Suite 1119, 135 So. La Salle Street
Chicago, IL 60603
PHONE: (312) 372-7733
TYPE OF INSTITUTION: Private Investment Banking
CONTACT OFFICER(S): Gerald K. Neavolls, President
INVESTMENTS/LOANS MADE: For own account; Through private placements
TYPES OF FINANCING: VENTURE CAPITAL: Later-stage expansion; Buy-outs/Acquisitions, LOANS: Equity-related, OTHER SERVICES PROVIDED: Resource Development—Primarily Oil & Gas
PREFERRED TYPES OF INDUSTRIES/INVESTMENTS: Oil & Gas, Coal, Other n atural resources
GEOGRAPHIC LIMITS OF INVESTMENTS/LOANS: National
RANGE OF INV./LOAN PER BUSINESS: Min. $750,000; Max. $3,500,000

COMPANY: **Residual Based Finance Corp.**
ADDRESS: Three First National Plaza, Suite 1400
Chicago, IL
PHONE: (312) 726-0693
TYPE OF INSTITUTION: Investment Bank
CONTACT OFFICER(S): Vincent A. Kolber, President
Charles H. Kolber, Executive Vice President
ASSETS: Not Available
INVESTMENTS/LOANS/MADE: For own account; Through private placements
TYPES OF FINANCING: VENTURE CAPITAL; LOANS: Equipment; LEASES: Single-investor; Leveraged; Tax leases; Non-tax leases; Operating; Tax-oriented lease brokerage; Lease syndications; Vendor financing programs; Other: Residual purchases; OTHER SERVICES PROVIDED: Financial Insurance including Asset Value Insurance
PREFERRED TYPES OF INDUSTRIES/INVESTMENTS: We seek investments and loan opportunities in assets which have a long useful life and a low probability of market and/or technological obsolescense

GEOGRAPHIC LIMITS OF INVESTMENTS/LOANS: International
RANGE OF INV./LOAN PER BUSINESS: Min. $1,000,000;
PREFERRED TERM FOR LOANS & LEASES: Min. 1 year; Max. 10 years
BUSINESS CHARACTERISTICS DESIRED-REQUIRED: Minimum number of years in business: 2
REFERRALS ACCEPTED FROM: Investment/Mortgage banker or Borrower/Investee
BRANCHES: 575 Madison Ave., New York, NY 10022, 212-605-0130, Charles Kolber

COMPANY: **Sucsy, Fischer & Co.**
ADDRESS: 135 S. LaSalle St.
Chicago, IL 60603
PHONE: (312) 346-4545
TYPE OF INSTITUTION: Investment Banking Firm
CONTACT OFFICER(S): Lawrence G. Sucsy
Paul F. Fischer
INVESTMENTS/LOANS MADE: For own account; Through private placements
INVESTMENTS/LOANS MADE: In securities with a secondary market and in securities without a secondary market
TYPES OF FINANCING: SECONDARY-MARKET CORPORATE SECURITIES: Common stock; Preferred stock, VENTURE CAPITAL: Start-up from developed product stage; First-stage (less than 1 year); Second-stage (generally 1-3 years); Later-stage expansion; Buy-outs/Acquisitions
PREFERRED TYPES OF INDUSTRIES/INVESTMENTS: Technology, Manufacturing, Medical, Computer, Related Graphic Arts
GEOGRAPHIC LIMITS OF INVESTMENTS/LOANS: National
RANGE OF INV./LOAN PER BUSINESS: Min. $200,000; Max. $600,000
BUSINESS CHARACTERISTICS DESIRED-REQUIRED: Minimum number of years in business: 0
REFERRALS ACCEPTED FROM: Investment/Mortgage banker or Borrower/Investee

COMPANY: **William Blair & Company**
ADDRESS: 135 S. LaSalle St., Suite 2900
Chicago, IL 60603
PHONE: (312) 236-1600
TYPE OF INSTITUTION: Investment Bank
CONTACT OFFICER(S): E. David Coolidge III, Partner in Charge, Corporate Finance Dept.
Richard P. Kiphard, Partner
INVESTMENTS/LOANS MADE: For own account; For managed accounts; Through private placements; Through underwriting public offerings
INVESTMENTS/LOANS MADE: In securities with a secondary market and in securities without a secondary market
TYPES OF FINANCING: SECONDARY-MARKET CORPORATE SECURITIES: Common stock; Preferred stock; Bonds; Initial Public Offerings, VENTURE CAPITAL: First-stage (less than 1 year); Second-stage (generally 1-3 years); Later-stage expansion; Buy-outs/Acquisitions

GEOGRAPHIC LIMITS OF INVESTMENTS/LOANS: National
RANGE OF INV./LOAN PER BUSINESS: Min. $250,000
BUSINESS CHARACTERISTICS DESIRED-REQUIRED: Other: Looking for profitable growth potential
BRANCHES: James M. Corboy, 1225 17th St., Denver, CO 80202, (303) 825-1600
Michael D. Easterly, 3414 Peachtree Rd., NE, Atlanta, GA 30326, (404) 577-1600

COMPANY: **Circle Business Credit, Inc.**
ADDRESS: 20 E. 91st Street, Suite 200
Indianapolis, IN 46240
PHONE: (317) 257-7321
TYPE OF INSTITUTION: Middle ticket leasing & financing subsidiary of Xerox Credit Corporation
CONTACT OFFICER(S): Stanley K. Paulson, Chairman & C.E.O.; Ronald E. Reehling, President & C.O.O.; Laird W. Shick, National Credit Manager
ASSETS: $100,000.000.00
INVESTMENTS/LOANS MADE: For own account
TYPES OF FINANCING: LOANS: Working Capital, Equipment; LEASES: Single-investor; Tax leases; Non-tax leases; Operating; Vendor financing programs
PREFERRED TYPES OF INDUSTRIES/INVESTMENTS: Sanitation Construction; Machine Tool; Refuse Cryogenic; Office Machine; Food Service Production & Fabricating; Transportation
GEOGRAPHIC LIMITS OF INVESTMENTS/LOANS: National
RANGE OF INV./LOAN PER BUSINESS: Min. $25,000; Max. $2,500,000.00
PREFERRED TERM FOR LOANS & LEASES: Min. 3 yrs; Max. 7 yrs.
BUSINESS CHARACTERISTICS DESIRED-REQUIRED: Min. yrs. in business: 3; Min. annual sales $1,100,000; Min. net worth $100,000;
REMARKS: Regional Service Centers are located in Indianapolis, IN; Orange County, CA; Atlanta, GA; and Whippany, NJ

COMPANY: **City Securities Corp.**
ADDRESS: 400 Circle Tower
Indianapolis, IN 46204
PHONE: (317) 634-4400
CONTACT OFFICER(S): Cecil M. Fritz, Pres.
ASSETS: $16 million
INVESTMENTS/LOANS MADE: Through private placements, underwriting public offerings
TYPES OF FINANCING: SECONDARY-MARKET CORPORATE SECURITIES: Common stock; Bonds; Tax-exempt bond issues
PREFERRED TYPES OF INDUSTRIES/INVESTMENTS: Diversified
GEOGRAPHIC LIMITS OF INVESTMENTS/LOANS: Regional; IN
RANGE OF INV./LOAN PER BUSINESS: Min. $500,000
BUSINESS CHARACTERISTICS DESIRED-REQUIRED: Minimum number of years in business: 5; varies
REFERRALS ACCEPTED FROM: Investment/Mortgage banker or Borrower/Investee
BRANCHES: Lafayette, IN
South Bend, IN
Anderson, IN

COMPANY: **Raffensperger, Hughes & Co., Inc.**
ADDRESS: 20 N. Meridian St.
Indianapolis, IN 46204
PHONE: (317) 635-4551
TYPE OF INSTITUTION: Investment Banker
CONTACT OFFICER(S): Charles L. Rees, V.P., Private Placements, South Bend
Jack Wodock, V.P., Industrial
Russell Breeden III, V.P., Leasing
ASSETS: $1-10 million
INVESTMENTS/LOANS MADE: For own account, Through private placements, Under writing public offerings
INVESTMENTS/LOANS MADE: In securities with a secondary market and in securities without a secondary market
TYPES OF FINANCING: SECONDARY-MARKET CORPORATE SECURITIES: Common stock; Bonds, OTHER SERVICES PROVIDED: Private Placements
PREFERRED TYPES OF INDUSTRIES/INVESTMENTS: Diversified
GEOGRAPHIC LIMITS OF INVESTMENTS/LOANS: Regional; IN
REFERRALS ACCEPTED FROM: Investment/Mortgage banker or Borrower/Investee
BRANCHES: South Bend, IN
Evansville, IN

COMPANY: **K. J. Brown & Co., Inc.**
ADDRESS: 122 East Main St.
Muncie, IN 47305
PHONE: (317) 284-9791
CONTACT OFFICER(S): Kenneth J. Brown, Pres.
Dante Raggio, V.P.
F. Scott Brown, V.P.
INVESTMENTS/LOANS MADE: Through private placements, Underwriting public offerings
INVESTMENTS/LOANS MADE: In securities with a secondary market and in securities without a secondary market
TYPES OF FINANCING: SECONDARY-MARKET CORPORATE SECURITIES: Bonds
GEOGRAPHIC LIMITS OF INVESTMENTS/LOANS: Regional

COMPANY: **Beecroft, Cole & Company**
ADDRESS: No. 1 Townsite Plaza
Topeka, KS 66603
PHONE: (913) 234-5671
TYPE OF INSTITUTION: Investment Banker
CONTACT OFFICER(S): Walter I. Cole, Jr., Partner, Bonds
Joseph L. Pierce, Partner
Dennis Nelson, partner
Dennis Campbell, Partner
INVESTMENTS/LOANS MADE: Through private placements, Underwriting public offerings
TYPES OF FINANCING: SECONDARY-MARKET CORPORATE SECURITIES: Common stock; Preferred stock; Bonds; Municipal bonds, specifically
PREFERRED TYPES OF INDUSTRIES/INVESTMENTS: Muncipals and general corporate financing
GEOGRAPHIC LIMITS OF INVESTMENTS/LOANS: National
RANGE OF INV./LOAN PER BUSINESS: Min. $500,000
BUSINESS CHARACTERISTICS DESIRED-REQUIRED: Minimum number of years in business: 5
REFERRALS ACCEPTED FROM: Investment/Mortgage banker or Borrower/Investee
REMARKS: do occasional start-ups

COMPANY: **J.J.B. Hilliard, W.L. Lyons, Inc.**
ADDRESS: 545 South Third Street
Louisville, KY 40202
PHONE: (502) 588-8400
TYPE OF INSTITUTION: Investment Bank
CONTACT OFFICER(S): E. Halsey Sandford, Senior V.P.
Gerald R. Martin, Senior V.P.
ASSETS: $500 Million
INVESTMENTS/LOANS MADE: Through private placements; Through underwriting public offerings
INVESTMENTS/LOANS MADE: In securities with a secondary market and in securities without a secondary market
TYPES OF FINANCING: SECONDARY-MARKET CORPORATE SECURITIES: Common stock; Preferred stock; Bonds, VENTURE CAPITAL: Research & Development; Second-stage; Later-stage expansion; Buy-outs/Acquisitions, LOANS: Unsecured to credits above C, REAL ESTATE: Partnerships/Syndications
PREFERRED TYPES OF INDUSTRIES/INVESTMENTS: None
WILL NOT CONSIDER: All
GEOGRAPHIC LIMITS OF INVESTMENTS/LOANS: National
RANGE OF INV./LOAN PER BUSINESS: Min. $ None
PREFERRED TERM FOR LAONS & LEASES: Min. None
BUSINESS CHARACTERISTICS DESIRED-REQUIRED: Minimum number of years in business: 0
REFERRALS ACCEPTED FROM: Investment/Mortgage banker or Borrower/Investee
REMARKS: 35 Branches in KY, IND, OH, W VA, VA, TN, IL

COMPANY:**Howard, Weil, Labouisse Friedricks Inc.**
ADDRESS: 211 Carondelet St.
New Orleans LA 70130
PHONE: (504) 588-2942
TYPE OF INSTITUTION: Regional brokerage firm
CONTACT OFFICER(S): A. Pike Howard, Executive V.P.
INVESTMENTS/LOANS MADE: Through private placements, Through underwriting public offerings
INVESTMENTS/LOANS MADE: In securities with a secondary market and in securities without a secondary market
TYPES OF FINANCING: SECONDARY-MARKET CORPORATE SECURITIES: Common stock; Preferred stock; Bonds; VENTURE CAPITAL: Second-stage; LOANS: Unscured to credits above BAA; Working capital; Equipment; Equity-related; LEASES: Single-investor; Leveraged; Operating
GEOGRAPHIC LIMITS OF INVESTMENTS/LOANS: Regional; Other: LA, Miss., Ala., Fla.
RANGE OF INV./LOAN PER BUSINESS: Min. $5,000,000
BRANCHES: 25 branches—Ala., LA, Miss., Fla.

COMPANY: **First New England Securities Corporation**
ADDRESS: 225 Franklin Street
Boston, MA 02110
PHONE: (617) 482-6640
TYPE OF INSTITUTION: Investment Banker
CONTACT OFFICER(S): Gregory P. Plunkett, President

COMPANY: **Gordon Berg Company Incorporated**
ADDRESS: 1 Liberty Square Box 6802
Boston, MA 02102
PHONE: (617) 482-0290
TYPE OF INSTITUTION: Investment banking firm
CONTACT OFFICER(S): Gordon Berg, Chairman
PREFERRED TYPES OF INDUSTRIES/INVESTMENTS: The projects must have redeeming social value, that is, to develop housing for the low or moderate income or elderly; to create opportunities for employment or urban revitalization, to finance health care activities; or to find education or cultural purposes
GEOGRAPHIC LIMITS OF INVESTMENTS/LOANS: National
RANGE OF INV./LOAN PER BUSINESS: Min. $350,000 Equity, $1 Mil. Debt

COMPANY: **Harbour Financial Company**
ADDRESS: 45 Milk Street
Boston, MA 01209
PHONE: (617) 426-8106
TYPE OF INSTITUTION: Investment Banking Firm/ Venture Capital
CONTACT OFFICER(S): John R. Schwanbeck, President
INVESTMENTS/LOANS MADE: For own account; Through private placements
INVESTMENTS/LOANS MADE: Only in securities without a secondary market
TYPES OF FINANCING: VENTURE CAPITAL: Research & Development; Start-up from developed product stage; First-stage (less than 1 year); Second-stage (generally 1-3 years); Later-stage expansion; Buy-outs/Acquisitions, LOANS: Unsecured; Equipment, LEASES: Leveraged, OTHER SERVICES PROVIDED: Financial consulting
GEOGRAPHIC LIMITS OF INVESTMENTS/LOANS: Regional, New England
RANGE OF INV./LOAN PER BUSINESS: Min. $500,000
BUSINESS CHARACTERISTICS DESIRED-REQUIRED: Minimum number of years in business: 0; Other: Must show strong management

COMPANY: **The Peckham Boston Company**
ADDRESS: Four Longfellow Place
Boston, MA 02114
PHONE: (617) 523-4440
TYPE OF INSTITUTION: Investment Banker
CONTACT OFFICER(S): John M. Peckham III, President
ASSETS: Approx. $200 million
INVESTMENTS/LOANS MADE: For own account; For managed accounts
INVESTMENTS/LOANS MADE: Only in securities without a secondary market
TYPES OF FINANCING: VENTURE CAPITAL: Buy-outs/Acquisitions; REAL ESTATE LOANS: Long-term senior mtg.; Intermediate-term senior mtg.; Subordinated; Wraparounds; Land; Land development; Construction; Gap, Standbys; Other: Condominium/ Cooperative Conversion or Development Loans; REAL ESTATE: Acquisitions; Joint ventures; Partnerships/ Syndications
PREFERRED TYPES OF INDUSTRIES/INVESTMENTS: Real Estate
GEOGRAPHIC LIMITS OF INVESTMENTS/LOANS: National; International
RANGE OF INV./LOAN PER BUSINESS: Min. $2,000,000; Max. $100,000,000
PREFERRED TERM FOR LOANS & LEASES: Min. 3 years; Max. 10 years
REFERRALS ACCEPTED FROM: Investment/Mortgage banker or Borrower/Investee

COMPANY: **Peter A. Ulin**
ADDRESS: 1 Boston Place
Boston, MA 02108
PHONE: (617) 227-0760
TYPE OF INSTITUTION: Investment Bank
CONTACT OFFICER(S): Peter A. Ulin, Director, Mergers & Acquisitions
INVESTMENTS/LOANS MADE: Through private placements
INVESTMENTS/LOANS MADE: In securities with a secondary market and in securities without a secondary market
TYPES OF FINANCING: SECONDARY-MARKET CORPORATE SECURITIES: Common stock; Equity-related, OTHER SERVICES PROVIDED: Mergers & acquisitions for sellers of established companies or divisions
GEOGRAPHIC LIMITS OF INVESTMENTS/LOANS: National
RANGE OF INV./LOAN PER BUSINESS: Min. $5 Million; Max. None
BUSINESS CHARACTERISTICS DESIRED-REQUIRED: Min. annual sales $10 Million; Min. net worth $5 Million; Min. annual net income $1 Million

COMPANY: **Alex Brown & Sons, Inc.**
ADDRESS: 135 E. Baltimore St.
Baltimore, MD 21202
PHONE: (301) 727-1700
TYPE OF INSTITUTION: Investment Banker
CONTACT OFFICER(S): Donald Hebb, Managing director & Pres.
F. Barton Harvey, Mg. Dir. & Chairman
Joseph R. Hardiman, Mg. Dir. & COO
ASSETS: $100,000,000 and up
INVESTMENTS/LOANS MADE: For own account, For managed accounts, Through private placements, Through underwriting public offerings
INVESTMENTS/LOANS MADE: In securities with a secondary market and in securities without a secondary market
TYPES OF FINANCING: SECONDARY-MARKET CORPORATE SECURITIES: Common stock; Preferred stock; Bonds. VENTURE CAPITAL: Start-up from developed product stage; First-stage; Second-stage;

Later-stage expansion. REAL ESTATE LOANS: Long-term senior mtg.; Intermediate-term senior mtg.; Subordinated; Wraparounds; Land development; Industrial revenue bonds. LEASES. REAL ESTATE: Acquisitions; Partnerships/Syndications. OTHER SERVICES PROVIDED: Corporate finance & public finance
PREFERRED TYPES OF INDUSTRIES/INVESTMENTS:
WILL NOT CONSIDER:
GEOGRAPHIC LIMITS OF INVESTMENTS/LOANS: National
RANGE OF INV./LOAN PER BUSINESS:
PREFERRED TERM FOR LOANS & LEASES:
BUSINESS CHARACTERISTICS DESIRED-REQUIRED:
REFERRALS ACCEPTED FROM: Investment/Mortgage banker or Borrower/Investee
BRANCHES:
REMARKS:

COMPANY: **Baker, Watts & Co.**
ADDRESS: 100 Light Street
Baltimore, MD 21202
PHONE: (301) 685-2600
TYPE OF INSTITUTION: Investment Bank
CONTACT OFFICER(S): E. Roger Novak, Jr.

COMPANY: **Legg Mason Wood Walker Inc.**
ADDRESS: 7 East Redwood St.
Baltimore, MD 21203
PHONE: (202) 452-4096
TYPE OF INSTITUTION: Investment Banker
CONTACT OFFICER(S): Walter Rye, V.P. (301) 539-3400
Doug Petty, V.P. Corp. Finance (202) 452-4096
ASSETS: $39 million
GEOGRAPHIC LIMITS OF INVESTMENTS/LOANS: Regional
BRANCHES: 37 Branches

COMPANY: **First of Michigan Corp.**
ADDRESS: 100 Renaissance Center, 26th Floor
Detroit, MI 48243
PHONE: (313) 259-2600
TYPE OF INSTITUTION: Investment banker
CONTACT OFFICER(S): Frederick J. Schroeder, Jr. E.V.P. Corporate Finance
ASSETS: 40 million
GEOGRAPHIC LIMITS OF INVESTMENTS/LOANS: Regional; Some National
RANGE OF INV./LOAN PER BUSINESS: Min. $5 million (equity) varies (private); $10 million (debt)
BUSINESS CHARACTERISTICS DESIRED-REQUIRED: Look at each case individually

COMPANY: **The Bancorp Group, Inc.**
ADDRESS: 3000 Town Center, Suite 3220
Southfield, MI 48075
PHONE: (313) 354-8160
TYPE OF INSTITUTION: Independent lessor and investment banker
CONTACT OFFICERS: Herman J. Drazick, Chairman
James T. Pawlak, V. P. Tax Leasing
Thomas X. Dunigan, Vice President, Medical Equipment Financing
ASSETS: $25 million
INVESTMENTS/LOANS MADE: For own account; For managed accounts
INVESTMENTS/LOANS MADE: only in securities without a secondary market
TYPES OF FINANCING: VENTURE CAPITAL: Buy-outs/Acquisitions; LOANS: Equity-related; LEASES: Single-investor; Leveraged; Tax leases; Non-tax leases; Operating; Tax-oriented lease brokerage; Vendor financing programs; Other: Develop and manage portfolios for corporate lessors
PREFERRED TYPES OF INDUSTRIES/INVESTMENTS: No preferences
GEOGRAPHIC LIMITS OF INVESTMENTS/LOANS: National
RANGE OF INV./LOAN PER BUSINESS: Min. $25,000 in equity; Max. $1 million in equity
PREFERRED TERM FOR LOANS & LEASES: Min. 3 years; Max. 10 years
BUSINESS CHARACTERISTICS DESIRED-REQUIRED: Minimum number of years in business: 2; Min. annual sales $ 1 million; Min. net worth $ 100,000; Min. annual net income positive; Min. annual cash flow positive
REFERRALS ACCEPTED FROM: Investment/Mortgage banker or Borrower/Investee
BRANCHES: 4056 Plainfield, N.E., Suite L-2, Grand Rapids, MI 49505; (616) 361-1311; William Zahradnick
5050 Excelsior Boulevard, Suite 415, Minneapolis, MN 55416; (612) 925-2886; Scott Whipple
760 U.S. Highway 1, Suite 201, North Palm Beach, FL 33408; (305) 694-1477; Thomas Vaughan

COMPANY: **Robert S.C. Peterson, Inc.**
ADDRESS: 28 Water Street
Excelsior, MN 55331
PHONE: (612) 474-8801
TYPE OF INSTITUTION: Investment Bank
CONTACT OFFICER(S): Robert S.C. Peterson, President
Dennis Driggers, Vice President
GEOGRAPHIC LIMITS OF INVESTMENTS/LOANS: Regional
RANGE OF INV./LOAN PER BUSINESS: Min. $500,000; Max. $5,000,000
BUSINESS CHARACTERISTICS DESIRED-REQUIRED: Other: Case by case
REFERRALS ACCEPTED FROM: Investment/Mortgage banker; Borrower/Investee

COMPANY: **Craig-Hallum, Inc.**
ADDRESS: 133 South Seventh Street
Minneapolis, MN 55402
PHONE: (612) 332-1212
TYPE OF INSTITUTION: Corporate Finance Dept.—Investment Securities Firm
CONTACT OFFICER(S): William B. Adams, V.P.
Thomas Martinson, Sr. V.P.
Mary Weingart, V.P.
ASSETS: $50 million and up
INVESTMENTS/LOANS MADE: For managed accounts; Thro ugh private placements; Through underwriting public offerings

INVESTMENTS/LOANS MADE: In securities with a secondary market and in securities without a secondary market
TYPES OF FINANCING: SECONDARY-MARKET CORPORATE SECURITIES: Common stock; Preferred stock; Bonds, VENTURE CAPITAL: Research & Development; Start-up from developed product stage; First-stage (less than 1 year); Second-stage (generally 1-3 years); Later-stage expansion; Buy-outs/ Acquisitions, OTHER: Public offerings (Venture Capital); Corporate strategic consulting
PREFERRED TYPES OF INDUSTRIES/INVESTMENTS: We provide the following corporate finance services: 1) Private Placements, 2) Public Underwriting, 3) Mergers, 4) Acquisitions, 5) Divestitures, 6) Real Estate Brokerage, Underwritings are typically emerging High Tech
GEOGRAPHIC LIMITS OF INVESTMENTS/LOANS: National
BUSINESS CHARACTERISTICS DESIRED-REQUIRED: We will consult with a start-up situation w/strong management, exceptional growth potential
REFERRALS ACCEPTED FROM: Investment/Mortgage banker or Borrower/Investee
REMARKS: Range of Underwriting: $2½ to 10 mil.

COMPANY: **Dain Bosworth Incorporated**
ADDRESS: 100 Dain Tower
Minneapolis, MN 55402
PHONE: (612) 371-2711
TYPE OF INSTITUTION: Corporate Finance Department of Investment Banking Firm
CONTACT OFFICER(S): Douglas R. Coleman, Jr., Senior V.P., Corporate Finance Department
Peter A. Randall, 1st V.P., Minneapolis Corporate Finance
INVESTMENTS/LOANS MADE: Through private placements; Through underwriting public offerings
INVESTMENTS/LOANS MADE: In securities with a secondary market and in securities without a secondary market
TYPES OF FINANCING: SECONDARY-MARKET CORPORATE SECURITIES: Common stock; Preferred stock; Bonds, VENTURE CAPITAL: Research & Development; Start-up from developed product stage; First-stage (less than 1 year); Second-stage (generally 1-3 years); Later-stage expansion; Buy-out/Acquisitions, LOANS: Unsecured to credits above Baa, Equity-related, LEASES: Leveraged; Tax-oriented lease brokerage
GEOGRAPHIC LIMITS OF INVESTMENTS/LOANS: Regional: Upper Midwest; Rocky Mountains; Pacific North West
RANGE OF INV./LOAN PER BUSINESS: Min. $1,000,000
BUSINESS CHARACTERISTICS DESIRED-REQUIRED: Minimum number of years in business: 2
REFERRALS ACCEPTED FROM: Borrower/Investee
BRANCHES: Robert Weisman, 1225 17th Street, Suite 1800; Denver, CO 80202; (303) 294-7223
Wayne Hester, 112 S. Dubuque Plaza, Iowa City, IA 52240; (319) 354-7800
James Sterns, 999 3rd Ave., Ste. 1500, Seattle, WA 98104; (206) 621-3112
Wayne Hester, 112 S. Dubugue Plaza, Iowa City, ID 52240; (319) 354-7800
REMARKS: Investment banking services include public offerings, private placement of debt and equity, merger/acquisition/divestiture, tax shelter, valuations; Venture capital

COMPANY: **Engler & Budd Company**
ADDRESS: Midwest Plaza Building
Minneapolis, MN 55402
PHONE: (612) 333-1161
TYPE OF INSTITUTION: Investment Banker
CONTACT OFFICER(S): Mike Engler, President
Steven Engler, Vice President
Richard Heise, Corporate Finance
GEOGRAPHIC LIMITS OF INVESTMENTS/LOANS: National
REMARKS: Three branches in Colorado

COMPANY: **Midwest Discount Securities**
ADDRESS: 13 South Ninth Street
Minneapolis, MN 55402
PHONE: (612) 375-1660
TYPE OF INSTITUTION: Investment Banker
CONTACT OFFICER(S): Ben B. Reuben, President
Lyman Cole, Vice President
GEOGRAPHIC LIMITS OF INVESTMENTS/LOANS: Regional
BRANCHES: William Metcalf, Las Vegas, NV

COMPANY: **Offerman & Co., Inc.**
ADDRESS: 5831 Cedar Lake Rd.
Minneapolis, MN 55416
PHONE: (612) 541-8900
TYPE OF INSTITUTION: Investment Banker
CONTACT OFFICER(S): Joseph H. Offerman, President
Scott J. Offerman, V.P.
ASSETS: $10,000,000
GEOGRAPHIC LIMITS OF INVESTMENTS/LOANS: National
RANGE OF INV./LOAN PER BUSINESS: Min. $1,500,000; Max. None
BUSINESS CHARACTERISTICS DESIRED-REQUIRED: Minimum number of years in business: 5; Min. net worth $2,000,000; Other: Profitable
REFERRALS ACCEPTED FROM: Investment/Mortgage banker; Borrower/Investee

COMPANY: **Piper Jaffray & Hopwood, Inc.**
ADDRESS: 733 Marquette Ave., Suite 800
Minneapolis, MN 55402
PHONE: (612) 371-6111
TYPE OF INSTITUTION: Investment bank
CONTACT OFFICER(S): Hunt Greene, V.P.
INVESTMENTS/LOANS MADE: For own account, Through private placements, Through underwriting public offerings
INVESTMENTS/LOANS MADE: In securities with a secondary market and in securities without a secondary market
TYPES OF FINANCING: VENTURE CAPITAL: Research & Development; Start-up from developed

product stage; First-stage; Second-stage; Later-stage expansion; Buy-outs/Acquisitons, LOANS: Equity-related; Other: Leverage buy-outs, REAL ESTATE LOANS: Long-term senior mtg.; Intermediate-term senior mtg.; Subordinated; Wraparounds; Industrial revenue bonds, OTHER SERVICES PROVIDED: Tax incentives
PREFERRED TYPES OF INDUSTRIES/INVESTMENTS: High-technology; Medical; Electronics
WILL NOT CONSIDER: Land per se
GEOGRAPHIC LIMITS OF INVESTMENTS/LOANS: Regional; National
BUSINESS CHARACTERISTICS DESIRED-REQUIRED: Minimum number of years in business: 0; Min. annual sales 0; Min. net worth 0; Min. annual net income 0; Min. annual cash flow 0
REMARKS: 42 branches (sales offices)

COMPANY: **Summit Investment Corporation**
ADDRESS: 500 International Centre, Ninth & 2nd Ave.
Minneapolis, MN 55402
PHONE: (612) 338-1400
TYPE OF INSTITUTION: Investment Bank
CONTACT OFFICER(S): G. James Spinner, President
Robert Abrams, Syndication
ASSETS: 2.8 million
INVESTMENTS/LOANS MADE: For own account; Through private placements; Through underwriting public offerings
INVESTMENTS/LOANS MADE: In securities with a secondary market; In securities without a secondary market
TYPES OF FINANCING: SECONDARY-MARKET CORPORATE SECURITIES: Common stock; Bonds, VENTURE CAPITAL: Research & Development; Start-up from developed products stage; First-stage; Second-stage; Later-stage; Buy-outs/Acquisitions, REAL ESTATE: Partnerships/Syndications
PREFERRED TYPES OF INDUSTRIES/INVESTMENTS: Oil and gas, Real estate
GEOGRAPHIC LIMITS OF INVESTMENTS/LOANS: Local; National
RANGE OF INV./LOAN PER BUSINESS: Min. $400,000 private placement, $5,000,000 public underwriting
BUSINESS CHARACTERISTICS DESIRED-REQUIRED: Other: Varies
REFERRALS ACCEPTED FROM: Investment/Mortgage banker; Borrower/Investee

COMPANY: **George K. Baum & Company**
ADDRESS: 1004 Baltimore Avenue
Kansas City, MO 64105
PHONE: (816) 474-1100
TYPE OF INSTITUTION: Corporate Finance Department—Investment Banker
CONTACT OFFICER(S): William D. Thomas, V.P., Dept. Head. Corp. Fin.
INVESTMENTS/LOANS MADE: For own account; For managed accounts; Through private placements; Through underwriting public offerings
INVESTMENTS/LOANS MADE: In securities with a secondary market and in securities without a secondary market

TYPES OF FINANCING: SECONDARY-MARKET CORPORATE SECURITIES: Common stock; Preferred stock; Bonds, VENTURE CAPITAL: Research & Development; Start-up from developed product stage; First-stage (less than 1 year); Second-stage (generally 1-3 years); Later-stage expansion; Buy-outs/Acquisitions, LOANS: Unsecured to credits above B; Working capital (receivables/inventory); Equipment; Equity-related. OTHER SERVICES PROVIDED: Merger/Aquisition/Divestiture/Leveraged Buy-out/Other Investment Banking as needed
PREFERRED TYPES OF INDUSTRIES/INVESTMENTS: No Preference
GEOGRAPHIC LIMITS OF INVESTMENTS/LOANS: National
RANGE OF INV./LOAN PER BUSINESS: Min. $1,000,000; Max. No Limit
REFERRALS ACCEPTED FROM: Investment/Mortgage banker or Borrower/Investee

COMPANY: **A. G. Edwards & Sons, Inc.**
ADDRESS: One North Jefferson Avenue
St. Louis, MO 63103
PHONE: (314) 289-3000
TYPE OF INSTITUTION: Securities Brokerage and Investment Banking
CONTACT OFFICER(S): Charles F. Fay, Corporate V.P., Manager of Investment Banking
ASSETS: $575,000,000+
INVESTMENTS/LOANS MADE: Through private placements; Through underwriting public offerings
TYPES OF FINANCING: SECONDARY-MARKET CORPORATE SECURITIES: Common stock. LOANS: Unsecured to credits above Baa; Equity-related
WILL NOT CONSIDER: Start-up companies
GEOGRAPHIC LIMITS OF INVESTMENTS/LOANS: National
RANGE OF INV./LOAN PER BUSINESS: Min. $3,000,000
BUSINESS CHARACTERISTICS DESIRED-REQUIRED: Min. annual net income $750,000
REFERRALS ACCEPTED FROM: Investment/Mortgage banker or Borrower/Investee
REMARKS: We have 245 branches and over 2,200 brokers throughout the U.S.

COMPANY:**Stifel, Nicolaus & Co., Inc.**
ADDRESS: 500 North Broadway
St. Louis, MO 63102
PHONE: (312) 782-3100
TYPE OF INSTITUTION: Investment banker
CONTACT OFFICER(S): Lyle Dickes

COMPANY: **D. A. Davidson & Co., Inc.**
ADDRESS: Davidson Building
Great Falls, MT 59401
PHONE: (406) 727-4200
TYPE OF INSTITUTION: Investment Securities
CONTACT OFFICER(S): Eugene Hufford, Sr. V.P., Corporate and Municipal Finance
ASSETS: $33,366,826
INVESTMENTS/LOANS MADE: Through private placements; Through underwriting public offerings

INVESTMENTS/LOANS MADE: In securities with a secondary market and in securities without a secondary market
TYPES OF FINANCING: SECONDARY-MARKET CORPORATE SECURITIES: Common stock; Preferred stock; Bonds, VENTURE CAPITAL: Second-stage (generally 1-3 years); Later-stage expansion, LOANS: Unsecured to credits above BAA; REAL ESTATE LOANS: Industrial revenue bonds, LEASES: Tax-oriented lease brokerage; REAL ESTATE: Partnerships/Syndications
GEOGRAPHIC LIMITS OF INVESTMENTS/LOANS: Regional

COMPANY:**Carolina Securities Corp**
ADDRESS: 127 W. Hargett St.
Raleigh, NC 27601
PHONE: (919) 832-3711
TYPE OF INSTITUTION: Investment Banker
CONTACT OFFICER(S): Bennett Love, A.V.P., Corporate Finance
ASSETS: $8-10 Million
GEOGRAPHIC LIMITS OF INVESTMENTS/LOANS: National
RANGE OF INV./LOAN PER BUSINESS: $1,000,000 (private placement); $3,000,000 (public placement)
BUSINESS CHARACTERISTICS DESIRED-REQUIRED: OTHER: Minimum number of years in business: 3; Min. annual net income: $500,000 - $600,000; $1,000,000 next year

COMPANY: **Chiles, Heider & Co., Inc./American Express Inc.**
ADDRESS: 1300 Woodmen Tower
Omaha, NE 68102
PHONE: (402) 346-6677
TYPE OF INSTITUTION: Mortgage Banker
CONTACT OFFICER(S): Lawrence J. Kremla, V.P. Corporate Finance
INVESTMENTS/LOANS MADE: Through private placements; Through underwriting public offerings
INVESTMENTS/LOANS MADE: In securities with a secondary market; In securities without a secondary market
TYPES OF FINANCING: SECONDARY-MARKET CORPORATE SECURITIES: Common stock; Preferred stock; Bonds, VENTURE CAPITAL: Start-up from developed product stage; Buy-outs/Acquisitions, LOANS: REAL ESTATE LOANS: REAL ESTATE: Partnerships/Syndications
PREFERRED TYPES OF INDUSTRIES/INVESTMENTS: All types
GEOGRAPHIC LIMITS OF INVESTMENTS/LOANS: Regional; Other: Midwest
RANGE OF INV./LOAN PER BUSINESS: Min. $200,000; Max. None
BUSINESS CHARACTERISTICS DESIRED-REQUIRED: Minimum number of years in business: 0
BRANCHES: Michael Sparks, Liberty Bldg. Des Moines, IA, (515) 243-0833

COMPANY: **Bourgeois Fils & Co., Inc.**
ADDRESS: Gorham Hall, P.O. Box 990
Exeter, NH 03833
PHONE: (603) 778-1020
TYPE OF INSTITUTION: Investment banking/venture capital
CONTACT OFFICER(S): William J. Nyhan, V.P. Corporate Finance
Carlyle H. Singer, V.P., Corporate Finance
Thed Melas-Kyriazi, Manager, Corporate Finance
ASSETS: $30,000,000
INVESTMENTS/LOANS MADE: For own account, For managed accounts, Through private placements10INVESTMENTS/LOANS MADE: Only in securities without a secondary market
TYPES OF FINANCING: LEASES: VENTURE CAPITAL: Start-up from developedd product stage: First-stage; Buy-outs/Acquisitions, LOANS: Working capital; Equpment; Equity-related, LEASES: Single-investor; Leveraged; Operating; Vendor fnancing programs, REAL ESTATE: Acquisitions; Joint ventres: Partnerships/Syndications, OTHER SERVICES PROVIDED: Project financings in energy, etc.
GEOGRAPHIC LIMITS OF INVESTMENTS/LOANS: National
RANGE OF INV./LOAN PER BUSINESS: Min. $1,000,000; Max. $50,000,000
PREFERRED TERM FOR LOANS & LEASES: Min. 2 years; Max. None
BUSINESS CHARACTERISTIS DESIRED-REQUIRED:Minimum number of years in business: 0
REFERRALS ACCEPTED FROM: Investment/Mortgage banker and Borrower/Investee

COMPANY: **Jersey Capital Markets Group Inc.**
ADDRESS: Gateway one, Suite 100
Newark, NJ 07102
PHONE: (201) 623-6500
TYPE OF INSTITUTION: Investment Banking; NEW ISSUE FINANCINGS:
CONTACT OFFICER(S): John T. Booth, President
Francis X. Fleischmann, Vice Pres.
Rudolph J.. Ozol, Director of Operations
Virginia C. DaVeiga, Assistant Vice President
INVESTMENTS/LOANS MADE: Through private placements; Through underwriting public offerings
TYPES OF FINANCING: Bonds; LOANS: Unsecured; REAL ESTATE: Long-term senior mtg.; Intermediate-term senior mtg., REAL ESTATE: Acquisitions; Joint ventures; Partnersips/Syndications
PREFERRED TYPES OF INDUSTRIES/INVESTMENTS: Tax exempt Issues (to structure and Finance), Housing, Healthcare, Industrial Development Bonds, Utility Bonds, Electric, School Bonds, Refunding Bonds
GEOGRAPHIC LIMITS OF INVESTMENTS/LOANS: National
REFERRALS ACCEPTED FROM Investment/Mortgage banker or Borrower/Investee

COMPANY: **Buffalo Capital Corporation**
ADDRESS: Mount Morris Road
Geneseo, NY 14454
PHONE: (716) 243-4310
TYPE OF INSTITUTION: Merchant Banker
CONTACT OFFICER(S): John H. Hickman, Chairman
ASSETS: $5,000,000+

INVESTMENTS/LOANS MADE: For own account, For managed accounts, Through private placements
INVESTMENTS/LOANS MADE: In securities with a secondary market and in securities without a secondary market
TYPES OF FINANCING: SECONDARY-MARKET CORPORATE SECURITIES: Common stock; Preferred stock; Bonds. VENTURE CAPITAL: Second-stage. LOANS: Equity-related. REAL ESTATE: Acquisitions;; Partnerships/Syndications. OTHER SERVICES PROVIDED: Management buy-outs; strategic planning, management and financial counsel.
PREFERRED TYPES OF INDUSTRIES/INVESTMENTS: Electronics, Health Care, Financial Services, Specialty Retailing, Consumer Products, General Manufacturing
GEOGRAPHIC LIMITS OF INVESTMENTS/LOANS: Upstate New York; Florida
RANGE OF INV./LOAN PER BUSINESS: Min. $250,000; Max. $2,500,000
PREFERRED TERM FOR LOANS & LEASES: Min. 2 years; Max. 5 years
BUSINESS CHARACTERISTICS DESIRED-REQUIRED: Minimum number of years in business: 2; Min. annual sales $1,000,000; Min. net worth $500,000; Min. annual net income $50,000
REFERRALS ACCEPTED FROM: Investment/mortgage banker or Borrower/Investee

COMPANY: **A. T. Brod & Co., Inc.**
ADDRESS: 17 Battery Place Suite #1043
New York, NY 10005
PHONE: (212) 422-5900
CONTACT OFFICER(S): Albert T. Brod, Pres.
Michael Brod, V.P., Corp. Syndicate
INVESTMENTS/LOANS MADE: For own account, Through private placements, Through underwriting public offerings
INVESTMENTS/LOANS MADE: In securities with a secondary market and in securities without a secondary market
TYPES OF FINANCING: SECONDARY-MARKET CORPORATE SECURITIES: Common stock
GEOGRAPHIC LIMITS OF INVESTMENTS/LOANS: National
REFERRALS ACCEPTED FROM: Investment/Mortgage banker or Borrower/Investee

COMPANY: **Allen & Company, Incorporated**
ADDRESS: 711 Fifth Avenue
New York, NY 10022
PHONE: (212)832-8000
TYPE OF INSTITUTION: Investment bankers and investors
CONTACT OFFICER(S): Harold M. Wit, Executive V.P. & Managing Director
ASSETS: Have available sufficient funds to do whatever we wish to do.
INVESTMENTS/LOANS MADE: For own account; Through private placements; Through underwriting public offerings
INVESTMENTS/LOANS MADE: In securities with a secondary market and in securities without a secondary market
TYPES OF FINANCING: SECONDARY-MARKET CORPORATE SECURITIES: Common stock; Preferred stock; Bonds, VENTURE CAPITAL: Research & Development; Start-up from developed product stage; First-stage (less than 1 year); Second-stage (generally 1-3 years); Later-stage expansion; Buy-outs/ Acquisitions, OTHER SERVICES PROVIDED: We are interested as principals in all types of investments involving equity participation.
PREFERRED TYPES OF INDUSTRIES/INVESTMENTS: None preferred. Open to considering any industry. We are interested only in investments involving equity.
BUSINESS CHARACTERISTICS DESIRED-REQUIRED: Each deal to stand on its own merits

COMPANY: **Bank Julius Baer & Co. Ltd.-New York Branch**
ADDRESS: 330 Madison Avenue
New York, NY 10017
PHONE: (212) 949-9044
TYPE OF INSTITUTION: Investment Banking
CONTACT OFFICER(S): Richard D. Bruns, Senior Vice President Portfolio Management
Martin P. Egli, Senior Vice President Trading & Credits
ASSETS: Several billion dollars
INVESTMENTS/LOANS MADE: For managed accounts
TYPES OF FINANCING: SECONDARY-MARKET CORPORATE SECURITIES: Common stock; Preferred stock; Bonds; Other: International Securities. LOANS: Unsecured; Working capital. INTERNATIONAL: OTHER SERVICES PROVIDED: Foreign Exchange/ Precious Metals

COMPANY: **Broadchild Securities Corp.**
ADDRESS: 1 Whitehall Street
New York, NY 10004
PHONE: (212) 248-0300
TYPE OF INSTITUTION: Stock, Bond Brokers & Investment Bankers
CONTACT OFFICER(S): Josephine Arcano, Vice Chairman of Board
ASSETS: $3 million
INVESTMENTS/LOANS MADE: Through underwriting public offerings
INVESTMENTS/LOANS MADE: In securities with a secondary market and securities without a secondary market
TYPES OF FINANCING: SECONDARY-MARKET CORPORATE SECURITIES: Common stock; Preferred stock; Bonds. VENTURE CAPITAL: Research & Development; Start-up from developed product stage; Second-stage
PREFERRED TYPES OF INDUSTRIES/INVESTMENTS: Health care; Movie distributors; Specialty
GEOGRAPHIC LIMITS OF INVESTMENTS/LOANS: Local; State; Regional; National; International
RANGE OF INV./LOAN PER BUSINESS: Min. $2,000,000; Maax. $6,000,000
REFERRALS ACCEPTED FROM: Investment/Mortgage banker or Borrower/Investee
BRANCHES: Los Angeles, CA

COMPANY: **Butler Capital**
ADDRESS: 767 Fifth Ave.
New York, NY 10025
PHONE: (212) 980-0606
TYPE OF INSTITUTION: Merchant bank
CONTACT OFFICER(S): Charles Sukenik, Managing director
ASSETS: $300 million
INVESTMENTS/LOANS MADE: For own account; Through private placements
INVESTMENTS/LOANS MADE: Only in securities without a secondary market
TYPES OF FINANCING: VENTURE CAPITAL: Later-stage expansion; Buy-outs/Acquisitions
PREFERRED TYPES OF INDUSTRIES/INVESTMENTS: Management buyouts, expansion and acquisition financing; All industries
WILL NOT CONSIDER: Start-up, High tech
GEOGRAPHIC LIMITS OF INVESTMENTS/LOANS: National
RANGE OF INV./LOAN PER BUSINESS: Min. $2 million; Max. $50 million
PREFERRED TERM FOR LOANS & LEASES: Min. 5 years; Max. 12 years
BUSINESS CHARACTERISTICS DESIRED-REQUIRED: Minimum number of years in business: 5; Min. annual sales $10 million; Min net worth $3 million; Min. annual net income $1 million; Other: 2 million pre-tax
REFERRALS ACCEPTED FROM: Investment/Mortgage banker or Borrower/Investee

COMPANY: **Carl Marks & Co., Inc.**
ADDRESS: 77 Water St.
New York, NY 10005
PHONE: (212) 437-7078
CONTACT OFFICER(S): Kenner, V.P., Private Placements
ASSETS: $100 million +
INVESTMENTS/LOANS MADE: In securities with a secondary market and in securities without a secondary market
TYPES OF FINANCING: VENTURE CAPITAL: Second-stage (generally 1-3 years); Buy-outs/Acquisitions, OTHER SERVICES PROVIDED: Leverage Buy-outs; General
PREFERRED TYPES OF INDUSTRIES/INVESTMENTS: Diversified
GEOGRAPHIC LIMITS OF INVESTMENTS/LOANS: National
RANGE OF INV./LOAN PER BUSINESS: Min. $500,000
BUSINESS CHARACTERISTICS DESIRED-REQUIRED: Minimum number of years in business: 5; Min. annual sales $10,000,000; Min. net worth $2,000,000; Min. annual net income $500,000; Min. annual cash flow $500,000
REFERRALS ACCEPTED FROM: Investment/Mortgage banker or Borrower/Investee

COMPANY:**Herzfeld & Stern Inc.**
ADDRESS: 30 Broad Street
New York, NY 10004
PHONE: (212) 480-1800
TYPE OF INSTITUTION: Investment banker
CONTACT OFFICER(S): Richard Leursohn, S.V.P. Corporate Finance
BUSINESS CHARACTERISTICS DESIRED-REQUIRED: OTHER: Profitable history of operations

COMPANY:**Bear, Stearns, & Co.**
ADDRESS: 55 Water Street
New York, NY 10041
PHONE: (212) 952-5000
TYPE OF INSTITUTION: Investment banker
CONTACT OFFICER(S): John Rosenwald, Partner Corp. Finance
ASSETS: $15,000,000,000
GEOGRAPHIC LIMITS OF INVESTMENTS/LOANS: National
BRANCHES: Marshall Geller, Chicago, IL; (312) 580-4000
Fred Kayne, Los Angeles, CA; (213) 201-2600
Gary Schumano, San Francisco, CA; (415) 442-6700
Hill Feinberg, Dallas, TX; (214) 741-8100
Keigh Kretschmer, Atlanta, GA; (404) 262-3070

COMPANY: **Daiwa Securities**
ADDRESS: One Liberty Plaza
New York, NY 10006
PHONE: (212) 732-6600
CONTACT OFFICER(S): Jeff Tanaka, Exec. V.P., Corp. Finance
INVESTMENTS/LOANS MADE: Through private placements, Through underwriting public offerings
INVESTMENTS/LOANS MADE: Only in securities with a secondary market
TYPES OF FINANCING: SECONDARY-MARKET CORPORATE SECURITIES: Common stock; Bonds, REAL ESTATE: Partnerships/Syndications
GEOGRAPHIC LIMITS OF INVESTMENTS/LOANS: International; Mostly Japanese Market
BRANCHES: Los Angeles, CA
Chicago, IL

COMPANY: **Donaldson, Lufkin & Jenrette, Inc.**
ADDRESS: 140 Broadway
New York, NY 10005
PHONE: (212) 902-2000

COMPANY: **The Drexel Burnham Lambert Group Inc.**
ADDRESS: 55 Broad St.
New York, NY 10004
PHONE: (212) 480-6000
CONTACT OFFICER(S): Frederick Joseph, Sr. Exec. V.P., Corp. Finance, Private Placements, Leasing
Joel Meszik, Industrial Revenue Bonds
Richard E. Bruce, Syndicate Dept.

COMPANY: **EuroPartners Securities Corporation**
ADDRESS: 1 World Trade Center, Suite 3411
New York, NY 10048
PHONE: (212) 466-6100
TYPE OF INSTITUTION: Investment Bank
CONTACT OFFICER(S): Pierre Gerard Misrahi, President
Jon Einsidler, V.P., Corporate Finance
Kevin Nord Clowe
Assistant V.P.-Mergers ad Acquisitions

INVESTMENTS/LOANS MADE: For managed accounts; Through private placements; Through underwriting public offerings
INVESTMENTS/LOANS MADE: In securities with a secondary market and in securities without a secondary market
TYPES OF FINANCING: REAL ESTATE LOANS: Long-term senior mtg.; Intermediate-term senior mtg.; Subordinated; Industrial revenue bonds, LEASES: Single-investor; Leveraged; Tax leases; Non-tax leases; Operating; Tax-oriented lease brokerage; Vendor financing programs, REAL ESTATE: Acquisitions; OTHER SERVICES PROVIDED: Public offerings

COMPANY: **FINAMERICA, INC.**
ADDRESS: 4 West 58th Street
New York, NY 10019
PHONE: (212) 888-9190
TYPE OF INSTITUTION: Investment Bank
CONTACT OFFICER(S): Edward C. Von Saher, MANAGING DIRECTOR
James R. Bechtel, Vice President
ASSETS: Confidential
INVESTMENTS/LOANS MADE: For own account; For managed accounts; Through private placements
Only in securities without a secondary market
TYPES OF FINANCING: VENTURE CAPITAL: Second-stage; Later-stage expansion; Buy-outs/Acquisitions INTERNATIONAL : Ventures in Mideast; REAL ESTATE: Acquisitions; Joint ventures; OTHER SERVICES PROVIDED: Mergers & Acquisitions; Strategic Planning; Management Consulting
PREFERRED TYPES OF INDUSTRIES/ INVESTMENTS:Represent investment group seeking leveraged buyouts and real estate development opportunites. Financial advisory and management services for wealthy individuals and private companies. (Through affiliates: investment management; real estate development; insurance brokerage; appraisal, technical and engineering services.)
WILL NOT CONSIDER: Passive Limited-Partner Funds
GEOGRAPHIC LIMITS OF INVESTMENTS/LOANS: International
RANGE OF INV./LOAN PER BUSINESS: Min. $500,000; Max. $50,000,000
BUSINESS CHARACTERISTICS DESIRED-REQUIRED: Minimum number of years in business: 3-5; Min. annual sales $1 Million; Min. annual net income $100,000; Min. annual cash flow $100,000; Other: Strong management team; liquidity within five years

COMPANY: **Herbert J. Sims & Co., Inc.**
ADDRESS: 77 Water Street
New York, NY 10005
PHONE: (212) 248-5600
TYPE OF INSTITUTION: Investment Banker and Tax-Exempt Bond Underwriter
CONTACT OFFICER(S): Herbert J. Sims, Chairman
William B. Sims, President
Jonathan R. Banton, V.P.
ASSETS: Have managed underwritings of over $2 billion
INVESTMENTS/LOANS MADE: Through private placements; Through underwriting public offerings
INVESTMENTS/LOANS MADE: In securities with a secondary market and in securities without a secondary market
TYPES OF FINANCING: REAL ESTATE LOANS: Industrial revenue bonds, OTHER SERVICES PROVIDED: Long-term financing for continuing and start-up projects with tax-exempt revenue bonds Housing for the elderly, Health Care, CATV, Recreation
GEOGRAPHIC LIMITS OF INVESTMENTS/LOANS: National
RANGE OF INV./LOAN PER BUSINESS: Min. $1,000,000
PREFERRED TERM FOR LOANS & LEASES: Min. 10; Max. 30 years
BUSINESS CHARACTERISTICS DESIRED-REQUIRED: Min. no. of years in business: 0; Cash flow coverage of debt service = 1.4 times
REFERRALS ACCEPTED FROM: Investment/Mortgage banker or Borrower/Investee

COMPANY: **Ingham, Becker & Co., Inc.**
ADDRESS: 202 E. 39th St.
New York, NY 10016
PHONE: (212) 697-6644
TYPE OF INSTITUTION: Investment Bank, Brokerage, Money Management
CONTACT OFFICER(S): Jonathan Ingham, Chairman
John A. Becker, President
ASSETS: 10 million +
INVESTMENTS/LOANS MADE: For own account; For managed accounts; Through private placements; Through underwriting public offerings
INVESTMENTS/LOANS MADE: In securities with a secondary market and in securities without a secondary market
TYPES OF FINANCING: Common stock; Preferred stock; Bonds; VENTURE CAPITAL: Research & Development; Start-up from developed product stage; First-stage; Second-stage; Later-stage expansion; Buy-outs/Acquisitions; LOANS: Unsecured; Working capital; Equipment; Equity-related; Other: Private placements; LEASES
PREFERRED TYPES OF INDUSTRIES/INVESTMENTS: Robotics; Automation; Publishing; Manufacturing
REFERRALS ACCEPTED FROM: Investment/Mortgage banker or Borrower/Investee

COMPANY: **Laidlaw Ansbacher Inc.**
ADDRESS: 275 Madison Avenue
New York, NY 10016
PHONE: (212) 210-5600
TYPE OF INSTITUTION: Investment Banking Firm
CONTACT OFFICER(S): James N. Cooke III, Managing Director, Corporate Finance
Dale F. Bizily, Mg. Dir., Mergers & Acquisitions
Bruce Bromberg, V.P., Corporate Finance
Bart C. Gutekunst, V.P., Corporate Finance
Gary Fine, V.P., Director of Private Placements
INVESTMENTS/LOANS MADE: For own account, For managed accounts, Through private placements, Through underwriting public offerings

INVESTMENTS/LOANS MADE: In securities with a secondary market and in securities without a secondary market
TYPES OF FINANCING: SECONDARY-MARKET CORPORATE SECURITIES: Common stock; Preferred stock; Bonds; All forms of public securities and private financings, VENTURE CAPITAL: Second-stage (generally 1-3 years); Later-stage expansion; Buy-outs/Acquisitions, OTHER SERVICES PROVIDED: Mergers and Acquisitions, valuations and appraisals, Financial consulting, fairness opinions.
PREFERRED TYPES OF INDUSTRIES/INVESTMENTS: Computer Related; Telecommunications; Medical Products; Distribution; Energy Related; Technology Related; Manufacturing
GEOGRAPHIC LIMITS OF INVESTMENTS/LOANS: National
RANGE OF INV./LOAN PER BUSINESS: Min. $3,000,000
BUSINESS CHARACTERISTICS DESIRED-REQUIRED: Minimum number of years in business: 1-3
REFERRALS ACCEPTED FROM: Investment/Mortgage banker or Borrower/Investee
BRANCHES: Robert H. Clayton, Chmn. & CEO
James N. Cooke, President, 40 Rector Street, New York, NY 10006 (Syndicate, Brokerage & Operations); (212) 306-6100
REMARKS: Eight other branches in the U.S.

COMPANY: **Lehman Brothers Kuhn Loeb, Incorporated**
ADDRESS: 55 Water Street, 44th floor.
New York, NY 10041
PHONE: (212) 558-1500
CONTACT OFFICER(S): Henry S. Miller

COMPANY: **M. Rimson & Company., Inc.**
ADDRESS: 150 Broadway
New York, NY 10022
PHONE: (212) 964-2626 (800) 722-7211
TYPE OF INSTITUTION: Investment Bankers
CONTACT OFFICER(S): George R. Hebert, Director Corporate Research & Finance.
ASSETS: $10,000,000
INVESTMENTS/LOANS MADE: For own account, For managed accounts, Through private placements, Through underwriting public offerings
TYPES OF FINANCING: SECONDARY-MARKET CORPORATE SECURITIES: Common stock; Preferred stock; VENTURE CAPITAL: Research & Development; Start-up from developed product stage; First-stage (less than 1 year); Second-stage (generally 1-3 years); Later-stage expansion; Buy-outs/Acquisitions;LEASES:
GEOGRAPHIC LIMITS OF INVESTMENTS/LOANS: National
RANGE OF INV./LOAN PER BUSINESS: Min. $10,000; Max. $1,000,000
PREFERRED TERM FOR LOANS & LEASES: Min. 30 days; Max. 2 years
BUSINESS CHARACTERISTICS DESIRED-REQUIRED: Min. annual sales $100,000
REFERRALS ACCEPTED FROM: Either of the above

COMPANY: **Merrill Lynch Leasing**
ADDRESS: 165 Broadway, 48th Floor
New York, NY 10080
PHONE: (212) 766-6074
CONTACT OFFICER(S): Lester Schoenfeld

COMPANY: **Morgan Stanley & Company, Inc.**
ADDRESS: 1251 Avenue of the Americas
New York, NY 10020
PHONE: (212) 974-4000
CONTACT OFFICER(S): Gregory Joseph

COMPANY: **Moseley, Hallgarten, Estabrook & Weeden, Inc.**
ADDRESS: One New York Plaza
New York, NY 10004
PHONE: (212) 363-6900
TYPE OF INSTITUTION: Investment Bank
CONTACT OFFICER(S): Bruce G. Miller, Vice President, Corporate Finance
Win Fitzpatrick, Vice President, Tax Advantaged Investments
William Crow, Vice President, Municipal Finance
ASSETS: Capital $45 million
INVESTMENTS/LOANS MADE: Through private placements; Through underwriting public offerings
INVESTMENTS/LOANS MADE: in both of the above
TYPES OF FINANCING: SECONDARY MARKET: Common stock; Preferred stock, Bonds. VENTURE CAPITAL: Buy-outs/AcquisitionsREAL ESTATE LOANS: Industrial revenue bonds; LEASES: Leveraged; Tax leases; Non-tax leases; Lease syndications; REAL ESTATE: Partnerships/Syndications
PREFERRED TYPES OF INDUSTRIES/INVESTMENTS: Initial Public Offerings, Other Equity Public Offerings-No Industry or Geographical preference, Preferred size $5 to $15 million
WILL NOT CONSIDER: start ups
BUSINESS CHARACTERISTICS DESIRED-REQUIRED: Minimum number of years in business: 3-5; Min. annual net income $15-1MM

COMPANY: **Oppenheimer Properties, Inc.**
ADDRESS: One New York Plaza
New York, NY 10004
PHONE: (212) 825-8180
TYPE OF INSTITUTION: Real estate investment affiliate of investment bank
CONTACT OFFICER(S): James H. Levi, President
Arnold Adlin, Senior V.P.
ASSETS: More than $1,000,000,000
INVESTMENTS/LOANS MADE: For own account, For managed accounts,
TYPES OF FINANCING: LEASES: Single-investor; Leveraged; Tax leases; Non-tax leases; Tax-oriented lease brokerage; Lease syndications, REAL ESTATE: Acquisitions; Joint ventures; Partnerships/Syndications, OTHER SERVICES PROVIDED: Hotel investments and financing
PREFERRED TYPES OF INDUSTRIES/INVESTMENTS: Existing income producing real estate including shopping centers, apartments, hotels, office buildings, industrial properties

GEOGRAPHIC LIMITS OF INVESTMENTS/LOANS: National
REFERRALS ACCEPTED FROM: Investment/Mortgage banker or Borrower/Investee

COMPANY: **Paine Webber, Inc.**
ADDRESS: 1221 Avenue of the Americas
New York, NY 10020
PHONE: (212) 730-8500
TYPE OF INSTITUTION: Investment bankers
CONTACT OFFICER(S): W. Gibson Harris, II, Managing Director
ASSETS: $100,000,000
TYPES OF FINANCING: VENTURE CAPITAL: Research & Development; Start-up from developed product stage; First-stage; Second-stage; Later-stage expansion; Buy-outs/Acquisitions
PREFERRED TYPES OF INDUSTRIES/INVESTMENTS: Equity-related; High technology
GEOGRAPHIC LIMITS OF INVESTMENTS/LOANS: National: Continental U.S.
RANGE OF INV./LOAN PER BUSINESS: Min. $750,000; Max. $5 million
BUSINESS CHARACTERISTICS DESIRED-REQUIRED: Minimum number of years in business: 0; Other: No limits
REFERRALS ACCEPTED FROM: Investment/Mortgage banker or Borrower/Investee
BRANCHES: Neill Brownstein, 300 Sand Hill Rd., Mento Park, CA 94025 (415) 854-2200
G. Felda Hardymon, 83 Walnut St. Wellesley Hills, MA 02181, (617) 237-6050

COMPANY: **Salomon Brothers**
ADDRESS: 1 New York Plaza
New York, NY 10004
PHONE: (212) 747-7115
CONTACT OFFICER(S): C.D. Tyree

COMPANY: **Shearson-Lehman American Express, Inc.**
ADDRESS: Two World Trade Center, 105th Floor
New York, NY 10048
PHONE: (212) 321-6000
TYPE OF INSTITUTION: Leasing & Asset Based Financing Group — Corporate Finance Department of an Investment Bank
CONTACT OFFICER(S): Bruce B. Clark, First V.P.
INVESTMENTS/LOANS MADE: Through private placements, underwriting public offerings
INVESTMENTS/LOANS MADE: In securities with a secondary market and in securities without a secondary market
TYPES OF FINANCING: Privately Placed Debt & Equity for Leverage Leases, LEASES: Leveraged; Tax leases
PREFERRED TYPES OF INDUSTRIES/INVESTMENTS: Personal Property about $10mm in Equipment Cost
GEOGRAPHIC LIMITS OF INVESTMENTS/LOANS: International
RANGE OF INV./LOAN PER BUSINESS: Min. $10,000,000
PREFERRED TERM FOR LOANS & LEASES: Min. 8 yrs; Max. 30 yrs.
REFERRALS ACCEPTED FROM: Borrower/Investee

COMPANY: **Shelby Cullom Davis & Co.**
ADDRESS: 70 Pine Street
New York, NY 10270
PHONE: (212) 425-3212
TYPE OF INSTITUTION: Member N.Y. Stock Exchange
CONTACT OFFICER(S): Shelby Cullom Davis, Chmn.
ASSETS: $310 million
INVESTMENTS/LOANS MADE: For own account, For managed clients accounts
INVESTMENTS/LOANS MADE: Only in securities with a secondary market

COMPANY: **Smith Barney Harris Upham & Company, Inc.**
ADDRESS: 1345 Avenue of the Americas
New York, NY 10019
PHONE: (212) 399-6056
CONTACT OFFICER(S): Vincent Cannaliato Jr.

COMPANY: **The Sprout Group**
ADDRESS: 140 Broadway
New York, NY 10005
PHONE: (212) 902-2492
CONTACT OFFICER(S): Richard E. Kroon, Managing Partner
Peter T. Grauer, General Partner
David L. Mordy, General Partner
Lloyd D. Ruth, General Partner
ASSETS: $200 million
INVESTMENTS/LOANS MADE: For own account
INVESTMENTS/LOANS MADE: In securities with a secondary market and in securities without a secondary market;
TYPES OF FINANCING: SECONDARY-MARKET CORPORATE SECURITIES: Common stock; Preferred stock; VENTURE CAPITAL: Research & Development; Start-up from developed product stage; First-stage; Second-stage; Buy-outs/Acquisitions; LOANS: Working capital (receivables/inventory); Equity-related.
PREFERRED TYPES OF INDUSTRIES/INVESTMENTS: Computer related; Electronic components and instrumentation; Data communication; Genetic engineering; Medical/Health related; Industrial automation; Robotics; Finance and insurance
WILL NOT CONSIDER: Entertainment
GEOGRAPHIC LIMITS OF INVESTMENTS/LOANS: National
RANGE OF INV./LOAN PER BUSINESS: Min. $500,000; Max. $6,000,000
BUSINESS CHARACTERISTICS DESIRED-REQUIRED: Minimum number of years in business: 0;
REFERRALS ACCEPTED FROM: Investment/Mortgage banker or Borrower/Investee
BRANCHES: Gary W. Kalbach, General Partner, 5300 Stevens Creek Blvd., Suite 320, San Jose, CA 95129, (408) 554-1515
Larry E. Reeder, General Partner 100 Summer Street, Boston, MA 02110, (617) 451-2954

COMPANY: **Sutton Place Securities, Inc.**
ADDRESS: 77 Water St.
New York, NY 10017
PHONE: (212) 248-3800
TYPE OF INSTITUTION: Brokerage Firm
CONTACT OFFICER(S): Mali Eisenman, Corporate Secretary
Herman R. Garcia, President
Randy Block, Trader
INVESTMENTS/LOANS MADE: Through underwriting public offerings
GEOGRAPHIC LIMITS OF INVESTMENTS;LOANS: Local; State; Regional; National;

COMPANY: L.F. Rothschild, Unterberg, Towbin
ADDRESS: 55 Water Street
New York, NY 10036
PHONE: (212) 425-3300
TYPE OF INSTITUTION: Investment Banking and Securities Brokerage
CONTACT OFFICER: Norman J. Levy, Administrative Managing Director.
INVESTMENTS/LOANS MADE: For own account; Through private placements; Through underwriting public offerings.
TYPES OF FINANCING: SECONDARY-MARKET CORPORATE SECURITIES: Common Stock; Preferred stock; Bonds; VENTURE CAPITAL. INTERNATIONAL. REAL ESTATE: Partnerships/ Syndications.
PREFERRED TYPES OF INDUSTRIES/INVESTMENTS: High technology and non-technology growth industries.
BUSINESS CHARACTERITIS DESIRES-REQUIRED: Min. annual net income $1,000,000.
Bruce A. Mann, Administrative Managing Director. Four Embarcadero Center, Ste. 1670, San Francisco, CA 94111, (415) 984-5657.

COMPANY: **Thomson McKinnon Securities Inc.—Public Finance Department**
ADDRESS: One New York Plaza
New York, NY 10004
PHONE: (212) 482-7252
TYPE OF INSTITUTION: Public Finance Department of Investment Banking Firm
CONTACT OFFICER(S): Jay Booth, Manager and Senior V.P., Public Finance Dept. Specializing in Housing, Healthcare, Water and Sewer, Industrial Revenue Bonds, and Power-Negotiated Municipal bond issues
ASSETS: $1,315,148,000 (up to June 26, 1981)
INVESTMENTS/LOANS MADE: For own account, For managed accounts, Through private placements, Through underwriting public offerings
INVESTMENTS/LOANS MADE: In securities with a secondary market and in securities without a secondary market
TYPES OF FINANCING: SECONDARY-MARKET CORPORATE SECURITIES: Bonds; REAL ESTATE LOANS: Industrial revenue bonds

COMPANY: **Wertheim & Co.**
ADDRESS: 200 Park Avenue
New York, NY 10166
PHONE: (212) 578-0200
TYPES OF INSTITUTION: Investment Bank
CONTACT OFFICERS: Stephen L. Schechter, General Partner, Leasing and Private Placements
Mark L. Shapiro, Special Partner, General Corp. Fin. - H&A
Stephen F. Oakes, Vice President, Leasing and Private Placements
INVESTMENTS/LOANS ARRANGED: For own account; Through private placements; Through underwriting public offerings
INVESTMENTS/LOANS ARRANGED: In securities with a secondary market; In securities without a secondary market
TYPES OF FINANCING ARRANGED: SECONDARY-MARKET CORPORATE SECURITIES:Common stock; Preferred stock; Bonds, VENTURE CAPITAL: Research & Development; Start-up from developed product stage; First-stage; Second-stage; Later-stage; Buy-outs/Acquisitions, LOANS: Unsecured to credits above Ba; Working capital; Equipment; Equity-related, LEASES: Single-investor; Leverage; Tax leases; Non-tax leases; Operating; Vendor financing programs, INTERNATIONAL
PREFERRED TYPES OF INDUSTRIES/INVESTMENTS: All
GEOGRAPHIC LIMITS OF INVESTMENTS/LOANS: International
RANGE OF INV./LOANS PER BUSINESS: Min. $500,000;
PREFERRED TERM FOR LOANS & LEASES: Min. 1 year; Max 30 years
BUSINESS CHARACTERISTICS DESIRES-REQUIRED: Interested in looking at all situations

COMPANY: **Winthrop Ventures**
ADDRESS: 74 Trinity Place
New York, NY 10006
PHONE: (212) 422-0100
TYPE OF INSTITUTION: Private investment bank; registered investment advisor, Computer consultants
CONTACT OFFICER(S): C. Brown
INVESTMENTS/LOANS MADE: For own account, Through private placements
INVESTMENTS/LOANS MADE: In securities with a secondary market and in securities without a secondary market
TYPES OF FINANCING: SECONDARY-MARKET CORPORATE SECURITIES: Common stock; Preferred stock; Bonds; Other: Subordinated debt, VENTURE CAPITAL: Start-up from developed product stage; First-stage (less than 1 year); Second-stage (generally 1-3 years); Later-stage expansion; Buy-outs/ Acquisitions, LOANS: Unsecured; Working capital (receivables/inventory); Equipment; Equity-related, OTHER SERVICES PROVIDED: Portfolio management, computer consulting
PREFERRED TYPES OF INDUSTRIES/INVESTMENTS: Proprietary manufacturing, technology-related, aviation, and other industries with high returns on invested capital
WILL NOT CONSIDER: Real estate, extractive industries
GEOGRAPHIC LIMITS OF INVESTMENTS/LOANS: International
RANGE OF INV./LOAN PER BUSINESS: Min. $500,000; Max. $10,000,000

PREFERRED TERM FOR LOANS & LEASES: Max. 15 years
BUSINESS CHARACTERISTICS DESIRED-REQUIRED: Minimum number of years in business: 0; Other: Track record and financial participation of principals
REFERRALS ACCEPTED FROM: Borrower/Investee

COMPANY: **McDonald & Company**
ADDRESS: 2100 Central National Bank Building
Cleveland, OH 44114
PHONE: (216) 443-2300
TYPE OF INSTITUTION: Investment Bank
CONTACT OFFICER(S): Paul H. Carleton, Public Offerings
Norman W. Hadsell, Private Placements
Thomas W. Weiden, Lease Financing
Rudolph H. Garfield, Mergers and Acquisitions
Frank B. Carr, Mergers and Acquisitions
Thomas M. O'Donnell, Exchange and Tender Offers
Philip M. Mantey, Valuations
Charles J. Kilroy, Pollution Control Financing, Industrial Revenue Bonds
John C. Conner, Hospital Revenue Bonds
Thomas M. O'Donnell, Real Estate Financing
INVESTMENTS/LOANS MADE: Through private placements, Underwriting public offerings
TYPES OF FINANCING: SECONDARY-MARKET CORPORATE SECURITIES: Common stock; Preferred stock; Bonds, VENTURE CAPITAL: First-stage (less than 1 year); Second-stage (generally 1-3 years); Later-stage expansion; Buy-outs/Acquisitions, LOANS: Unsecured to credits above Baa; Equity-related, LEASES
BRANCHES: Martin J. Rastatter, 2460 Winters Bank Tower; Dayton, OH 45423; (513) 223-3195

COMPANY: **McDonald & Company Securities Inc.**
ADDRESS: 2100 Central National Bank Bldg.
Cleveland, OH 44114
PHONE: (216) 623-2708
CONTACT OFFICER(S): Thomas W. Weiden

COMPANY: **Prescott, Ball & Turben**
ADDRESS: 1331 Euclid Avenue
Cleveland, OH 44115
PHONE: (216) 574-7300
TYPE OF INSTITUTION: Investment banking firm - public underwritings , private placements, leasing
CONTACT OFFICER(S): Richard Howe, Public Underwriting
Norman E. Reed, Public Financing
Herbert R. Martens, Jr., Lease Financing
John L. Kalmbach (NY), Energy Financing
J. Jeffrey Eakin, Hospital Financing
Donald Chadwick, Housing Financing
Donald R. Chadwick, Industrial Revenue & Pollution Control Financing
Albert L. Nelson, III, Mergers, Acquisitions & Divestitures
Richard Zappala, Real Estate Financing
Richard Howe, Venture Capital & Private Placements
ASSETS: $1.3 billion
INVESTMENTS/LOANS MADE: For own account, For managed accounts, Through private placements, underwriting public offerings
TYPES OF FINANCING: SECONDARY-MARKET CORPORATE SECURITIES: Common stock; Preferred stock; Bonds; Other: Convertible debentures, VENTURE CAPITAL: Research & Development; Start-up from developed product stage; First-stage; Second-stage; Later-stage expansion; Buy-outs/Acquisitions, REAL ESTATE LOANS: Wraparounds; Land development; Industrial revenue bonds, LEASES: Single-investor; Leveraged; Tax leases; Non-tax leases; Tax-oriented lease brokerage; Lease syndications; Vendor financing programs, OTHER SERVICES PROVIDED: Divestitures
GEOGRAPHIC LIMITS OF INVESTMENTS/LOANS: National
RANGE OF INV./LOAN PER BUSINESS: Min. $2 million; Max. None
BUSINESS CHARACTERISTICS DESIRED-REQUIRED: Minimum number of years in business: 0
REFERRALS ACCEPTED FROM: Investment/Mortgage banker or Borrower/Investee
REMARKS: 35 branches

COMPANY: **The Ohio Company**
ADDRESS: 155 E. Broad Street
Columbus, OH 43215
PHONE: (614) 464-6849
TYPE OF INSTITUTION: Investment Banking
CONTACT OFFICER(S): Martin Vogtsberger, V.P. Public Finance
Curtis Milner, V.P., Corporate Finance
Thomas Walker, Pres., Venture Capital
ASSETS: 35 million — 500 million under mgt.
INVESTMENTS/LOANS MADE: Through private placements; through underwriting public offerings
INVESTMENTS/LOANS MADE: SECONDARY-MARKET CORPORATE SECURITIES: Common stock; Preferred stock; Bonds, VENTURE CAPITAL: Second-stage, Later-stage, LOANS, REAL ESTATE LOANS: Intermediate-term senior mtg, Subordinated; Industrial revenue bonds
GEOGRAPHIC LIMITS OF INVESTMENTS/LOANS: Local; State; Regional
BUSINESS CHARACTERISTICS DESIRED-REQUIRED: Min. annual sales $25 million
REFERRALS ACCEPTED FROM: Investment/Mortgage banker or Borrower/Investee

COMPANY: **Rosenfeld & Co.**
ADDRESS: 625 S.W. Washington Street
Portland, OR 97205
PHONE: (503) 228-7686
TYPE OF INSTUITUTION: Private investment banking firm
CONTACT OFFICER(S): William W. Rosenfeld, Jr., Managing partner
ASSETS: in excess of $1,000,000
INVESTMENTS/LOANS MADE: For own account; Through private placements
INVESTMENTS/LOANS MADE: In securities with a secondary market and in securities without a secondary market

TYPES OF FINANCING: SECONDARY-MARKET CORPORATE SECURITIES; Bonds; Other: Particularly interest in gtd portion of FmHA and BA loans, VENTURE CAPITAL: Second-stage; Later-stage expansion; Buy-outs/Acquisitions, LOANS: Working capital; Equipment, REAL ESTATE LOANS: Long-term senior mtg.; Intermediate-term senior mtg; Subordinated, Industrial Revenue Bonds; OTHER SERVICES PROVIDED: Merger and acquisition and divestiture related services
PREFERRED TYPES OF INDUSTRIES/INVESTMENTS: Manufacturing, natural resources related, agribusiness, distribution, medical equipment and services, health care.
WILL NOT CONSIDER: Residential real estate, fast food, retail businesses
GEOGRAPHIC LIMITS OF INVESTMENTS/LOANS: Regional; Pacific Northwest emphasis
RANGE OF INVESTMENT/LOAN PER BUSINESS: Min. $500,000; Max. $50,000,000
PREFERRED TERM FOR LOANS & LEASES: Max. 15 years
BUSINESS CHARACTERISTICS DESIRED-REQUIRED: Minimum number of ears in business: 2-3; Min. annual sales $1,000,000; Min. net worth $250,000; Min. annual net income $100,000; Min. annual cash flow $100,000
REFERRALS ACCEPTED FROM: Investment/Mortgage banker

COMPANY: **Chemical Markets & Investments Co.**
ADDRESS: 3078 Glendon Road
Bethlehem, PA 18017
PHONE: (215) 691-1179
TYPE OF INSTITUTION: Investment banking, Mergers & Acquisitions and financing of businesses (start-up and established)
CONTACT OFFICER(S): Myron Curtis Gackenbach, President
ASSETS: $10 million
VENTURE CAPITAL: Research & Development; Start-up from deveoped product stage; First-stage; Seconnd-stage; Later-stage; Buy-outs/Acquisitions, LOANS: Equity-related; Other: Public and private issues, REAL ESTATE LOANS: Long-term senior mtg; Intermediate-term senior mtg.; Subordinated; Wraparounds; Land; Land deveopment; Industrial revenue bonds, LEASES: Single-investor; Leveraged; Tax leases; Non-tax leases, Operating; Tax-oriented lease brokerage, INTERNATIONAL, REAL ESTATE: Acquisitions; Joint Ventures; Partnerships/Syndications, OTHER SERVIVES PROVIDED: Market research and private placements, also corporate legal service
PREFERRED TYPES OF INDUSTRIES/ INVVESTMENTS: specialty, commodity and industrial chemicals, proprietary and ethical pharmaceuticals, health care aids and devices, medical electronics and bio-engineering
GEOGRAPHIC LIMITS OF INVESTMENTS/LOANS: International
RANGE OF INVESTMENT/LOAN PER BUSINESS: Min. $500,000; Max. $50 million
PREFERRED TERM FOR LOANS & LEASES: Max. 30 years
BUSINESS CHARACTERISTICS DESIRED-REQUIRED: Minimum number of years in business: 12; Min. net worth: $1 million; Min. annual net income $50,000; Min. annual cash flow $100,000
REFERRALS ACCEPTED FROM: Investment/Mortgage banker and Borrower/Investee

COMPANY: **Advest**
ADDRESS: 518 McKean Avenue
Charleroi PA 15022
PHONE: (412) 416-1233
CONTACT OFFICER(S): Robert C. Arthurs, Sr. V.P., Corp. Finance
INVESTMENTS/LOANS MADE: Through private placements, Through underwriting public offerings
INVESTMENTS/LOANS MADE: In securities with a secondary market and in securities without a secondary market
TYPES OF FINANCING: SECONDARY-MARKET CORPORATE SECURITIES: Common stock; Preferred stock; Bonds, REAL ESTATE: Acquisitions; Joint ventures; Partnerships/Syndications
PREFERRED TYPES OF INDUSTRIES/INVESTMENTS: Diversified
GEOGRAPHIC LIMITS OF INVESTMENTS/LOANS: Regional
BRANCHES: Beaver, PA
Beaver Falls, PA
Charleroi, PA
Indiana, PA
Mt. Lebanon, PA
St. Mary's, PA
Warren, PA

COMPANY: **Boenning & Scattergood, Inc.**
ADDRESS: 1809 Walnut St.
Philadelphia, PA 19103
PHONE: (215) 568-7325
TYPE OF INSTITUTION: Securities Brokerage
CONTACT OFFICER(S): Michael B. Bell, V.P., Manager, Fixed Income Dept.
Francis W. Kelly, E.V.P., Manager, Equity Dept.
TYPES OF FINANCING: SECONDARY-MARKET CORPORATE SECURITIES: Common stock; Preferred stock; Bonds, REAL ESTATE LOANS: Industrial revenue bonds
PREFERRED TYPES OF INDUSTRIES/INVESTMENTS: Diversified
GEOGRAPHIC LIMITS OF INVESTMENTS/LOANS: Regional

COMPANY: **Butcher & Singer Inc.**
ADDRESS: 211 So. Broad St.
Philadelphia, PA 19107
PHONE: (215) 985-5000
TYPE OF INSTITUTION: Investment Banking
CONTACT OFFICER(S): Gary G. Takessian, Senior V.P.
ASSETS: $1 Billion—managing clients investments
INVESTMENTS/LOANS MADE: Through private placements, Through underwriting public offerings
INVESTMENTS/LOANS MADE: In securities with a secondary market and in securities without a secondary market
TYPES OF FINANCING: VENTURE CAPITAL: Second-stage (generally 1-3 years); Later-stage expansion; Buy-

outs/Acquisitions, LOANS: Equity-related, REAL ESTATE LOANS: Industrial revenue bonds
PREFERRED TYPES OF INDUSTRIES/INVESTMENTS: Energy, Technology, Industrial & Service
WILL NOT CONSIDER: Cyclical or Start-up
GEOGRAPHIC LIMITS OF INVESTMENTS/LOANS: National
RANGE OF INV./LOAN PER BUSINESS: Min. $500,000; Max. $25,000,000
PREFERRED TERM FOR LOANS & LEASES: Min. 5; Max. 10 years
BUSINESS CHARACTERISTICS DESIRED-REQUIRED: Minimum number of years in business: 5-7; Min. annual sales $5-10 million; Min. net worth $1 million; Min. annual net income $250,000
REFERRALS ACCEPTED FROM: Investment/Mortgage banker or Borrower/Investee

COMPANY: **Cunningham, Schmertz & Co., Inc.**
ADDRESS: Dollar Bank Bldg., 309 Smithfield St., Ste. 3000
Pittsburgh, PA 15222
PHONE: (412) 434-8750
CONTACT OFFICER(S): Thomas L. Barr, V.P., Private Placements, Ind. Rev. Bonds
Kirkwood B. Cunningham, Pres. & Director
James J. Anfang, Exec. V.P. & Director
INVESTMENTS/LOANS MADE: Through private placements, Underwriting public offerings
INVESTMENTS/LOANS MADE: In securities with a secondary market and in securities without a secondary market
TYPES OF FINANCING: SECONDARY-MARKET CORPORATE SECURITIES: Common stock; Preferred stock; Bonds; Mutual funds; Tax shelters; Options, OTHER SERVICES PROVIDED: Tax-exempt Municipals
GEOGRAPHIC LIMITS OF INVESTMENTS/LOANS: Regional; Other: Pennsylvania, W. Virginia

COMPANY: **Benton & Company**
ADDRESS: 5731 Lyons View Drive, P.O. Box 19803
Knoxville, TN 37939-2803
PHONE: (615) 584-4123
TYPE OF INSTITUTION: Investment banker & Mortgage banker: Municipal bonds; Housing specialists
CONTACT OFFICER(S): Edward E. Lee, Vice President
Donald L. Turner, Vice President
Robert K. Trent, Vice President
INVESTMENTS/LOANS MADE: For own account, Through private placements, Through underwriting public offerings
INVESTMENTS/LOANS MADE: In securities with or without a secondary market
TYPES OF FINANCING: SECONDARY-MARKET CORPORATE SECURITIES: Municipal bonds. REAL ESTATE LOANS: Other: multifamily housing loans. REAL ESTATE: Acquisitions; Partnerships/ Ssyndications. OTHER SERVICES PROVIDED: Real Estate Syndications
PREFERRED TYPES OF INDUSTRIES/ INVESTMENTS:Ql
WILL NOT CONSIDER:
GEOGRAPHIC LIMITS OF INVESTMENTS/LOANS: National
BUSINESS CHARACTERISTICS DESIRED-REQUIRED: Other: Multi-family housing over $1 million
REFERRALS ACCEPTED FROM: Investment/Mortgage banker or Borrower/Investee
BRANCHES: 625 N. Michigan Avenue, Suite 500; Chicago, IL 60611, (312) 642-6124, Joe K. Hawkins
206 Heritage Building, Corner of Congress & Capitol; Jackson, MS, 39201, (601) 354-0007, Steven Patterson

COMPANY: **Morgan, Keegan & Co., Inc.**
ADDRESS: One Commerce Square
Memphis, TN 38103
PHONE: (901) 524-4100
TYPE OF INSTITUTION: Brokerage and investment banking firm
CONTACT OFFICER(S): Robert A. Baird, 1st Vice President, Investment Banking
Richard McStay, Sr. Vice President, Investment Banking
ASSETS: $26,000,000+
INVESTMENTS/LOANS MADE: Through private placement, Through underwriting public offerings
INVESTMENTS/LOANS MADE: In securities with or without a secondary market
TYPES OF FINANCING: SECONDARY-MARKET CORPORATE SECURITIES: Common stock; Preferred stock; Bonds; Other: Mergers/Acquisitions, Industrial Revenue & Pollution Control Financings. VENTURE CAPITAL: Second-stage; Later-stage expansion; Buy-outs/Acquisitons. LOANS: Unsecured to credits above Baa; Equipment; Equity-related. Other: Loans are placed with institutional investors. REAL ESTATE LOANS: Long-term senior mtg.; Intermediate-term senior mtg.; Subordinated; Industrial revenue bonds. LEASES: Single-investor; Leveraged; Tax leases. REAL ESTATE: Partnerships/Syndications.
GEOGRAPHIC LIMITS OF INVESTMENTS/LOANS: National
RANGE OF INV./LOAN PER BUSINESS: Min. $3,000,000
BUSINESS CHARACTERISTICS DESIRED-REQUIRED: Min. annual sales $20 million; Min. net worth $10 million; Min. annual net income $500,000
BRANCHES: Memphis, TN
Nashville, TN
Knoxville, TN
Jackson, Miss.
New Orleana, LA
Ft Lauderdale, FL.
Palm Beach, FL.
Atlanta, GA
Montgomery, AL
Boston, MA
New York, NY

COMPANY: **Equitable Securities Corp.**
ADDRESS: First American Center
Nashville, TN 37238
PHONE: (615) 244-9420
TYPE OF INSTITUTION: Investment Bank
CONTACT OFFICER(S): William H. Cammack, Corporate Finance
ASSETS: $3,700,000

GEOGRAPHIC LIMITS OF INVESTMENTS/LOANS: Regional

COMPANY: **J. C. Bradford & Co.**
ADDRESS: 170 4th Ave. No.
Nashville, TN 37219
PHONE: (800) 251-1060
CONTACT OFFICER(S): Mike Shea, Managing Partner, Corp. Finance
Luke Simons, Partner
Bob Doolittle, Partner
INVESTMENTS/LOANS MADE: Through private placements, Underwriting public offerings
INVESTMENTS/LOANS MADE: In securities with a secondary market and in securities without a secondary market
TYPES OF FINANCING: SECONDARY-MARKET CORPORATE SECURITIES: Common stock; Preferred stock; Bonds, VENTURE CAPITAL, REAL ESTATE: Acquisitions; Joint ventures; Partnerships/Syndications
GEOGRAPHIC LIMITS OF INVESTMENTS/LOANS: Regional; S.E. to N.E., also CA
REFERRALS ACCEPTED FROM: Investment/Mortgage banker or Borrower/Investee

COMPANY: **Juig U.S. Management, Inc.**
ADDRESS: 1008 N. Bowen Road
Arlington, TX 76012
PHONE: (817) 860-5222
TYPE OF INSTITUTION: Financial Management Division Of Merchant/Investment Banking Firm
CONTACT OFFICER(S): John Ross, Chief Executive Officer
Byron K. Devine, C.P.A. Executive Vice President
P.J. Clark, Asst. Vice President
ASSETS: $50,000,000 (Approx.)
INVESTMENTS/LOANS MADE: For own account, For managed accounts
INVESTMENTS/LOANS MADE: In securities with or without a secondary market
TYPES OF FINANCING: SECONDARY-MARKET CORPORATE SECURITIES: Bonds; Other: Certain capital notes, warrants & debentures. VENTURE CAPITAL: Second-stage; Later-stage expansion; Buy-outs/Acquisitions. LOANS: Working capital; Equipment; Other: Secured credits (4-10 yr. term). REAL ESTATE LOANS: Long-term senior mtg.; Land; Standbys; Industrial revenue bonds. FACTORING. LEASES: Vendor financing programs. INTERNATIONAL. REAL ESTATE: Acquisitions. OTHER SERVICES PROVIDED: Various domestic/ international financial services for selected clients.
PREFERRED TYPES OF INDUSTRIES/INVESTMENTS: Investments in ongoing companies; Income producing real estate
WILL NOT CONSIDER: Industries, Equipment
GEOGRAPHIC LIMITS OF INVESTMENTS/LOANS: International
RANGE OF INV./LOAN PER BUSINESS: Min. $250,000; Max. $5,000,000 (Normally)
PREFERRED TERM FOR LOANS & LEASES: Min. 4 years; Max. 10 years domestically, 20 years internationally

BUSINESS CHARACTERISTICS DESIRED-REQUIRED: Min. annual sales $1,000,000; Min. annual cash flow $250,000
REFERRALS ACCEPTED FROM: Investment/Mortgage banker or Borrower/Investee
REMARKS: Any submissions must demonstrate annual minimum internal rate on return on cash of 25%, after infusion and before debt service.

COMPANY: **Financial Services-Austin Inc.**
ADDRESS: 301 West 6th Street
Austin, TX 78701
PHONE: (512) 472-7171
TYPE OF INSTITUTION: Investment Bank with Venture Fund
CONTACT OFFICER(S): H.A. Abshier, Jr., Chairman of the Board
Ward Greenwood, Senior Vice President
Rex Gwinn, Senior Vice President
ASSETS: $15,000,000 plus
INVESTMENTS/LOANS MADE: For own account, For managed accounts, Through private placements
INVESTMENTS/LOANS MADE: Only in securities without a secondary market
TYPES OF FINANCING: VENTURE CAPITAL: Start-up from developed product stage; First-stage; Second-stage. REAL ESTATE LOANS: Long-term senior mtg. REAL ESTATE: Acquisitions
GEOGRAPHIC LIMITS OF INVESTMENTS/LOANS: State
RANGE OF INV./LOAN PER BUSINESS: Min. $500,000; Max. 5,000,000
BUSINESS CHARACTERISTICS DESIRED-REQUIRED: Minimum number of years in business: 0

COMPANY: **Eppler, Guerin & Turner, Inc.**
ADDRESS: 2001 Bryan Street, Suite 2300
Dallas, TX 75201
PHONE: (214) 880-9000
TYPE OF INSTITUTION: Investment Banker
CONTACT OFFICER(S): Thomas F. O'Toole, Exec. Vice President
Frank T. Lavinger, Managing Director
ASSETS: $70 million
GEOGRAPHIC LIMITS OF INVESTMENTS/LOANS: National; Other: Primarily in the southwest
BUSINESS CHARACTERISTICS DESIRED-REQUIRED: Other: Case by case
REFERRALS ACCEPTED FROM: Investment/Mortgage banker; Borrower/Investee

COMPANY: **First Dallas Financial Company**
ADDRESS: 3302 Southland Center
Dallas, TX 75201
PHONE: (214) 922-0070
TYPE OF INSTITUTION: Investment Bank
CONTACT OFFICER(S): John T. McGuire, President
INVESTMENTS/LOANS MADE: Through private placements
TYPES OF FINANCING: VENTURE CAPITAL: Second-stage (generally 1-3 years); Buy-outs/Acquisitions, LOANS: Equity-related

PREFERRED TYPES OF INDUSTRIES/INVESTMENTS: Oil & Gas, Energy Related, High Technology; Industrial
WILL NOT CONSIDER: Real Estate
GEOGRAPHIC LIMITS OF INVESTMENTS/LOANS: Regional (Southwest)

COMPANY: **Rauscher Pierce Refsnes, Inc.**
ADDRESS: Plaza of the Americas, 2500 North Tower
Dallas, TX 75201
PHONE: (214) 748 0111
TYPE OF INSTITUTION: Investment Banking
CONTACT OFFICER(S): Barry B. Conrad
Senior Vice President - Manager
INVESTMENTS/LOANS MADE: Through private placements; Through underwriting public offerings
INVESTMENTS/LOANS MADE: In securities with a secondary market and in securities without a secondary market
TYPES OF FINANCING: SECONDARY-MARKET CORPORATE SECURITIES: Common stock; Preferred stock; Bonds; VENTURE CAPITAL: Second-stage; Later-stage expansion; Buy-outs/Acquisitions
PREFERRED TYPES OF INDUSTRIES/INVESTMENTS: Energy; Health Care; Technology; Consumer/Retail; Financial Services
WILL NOT CONSIDER: Real Estate
GEOGRAPHIC LIMITS OF INVESTMENTS/LOANS: Regional; Other: Southwest
RANGE OF INV./LOAN PER BUSINESS: Min. $1,000,000
BUSINESS CHARACTERISTICS DESIRED-REQUIRED: Minimum number of years in business: 2-3
BRANCHES: G. Clyde Buck, 3400 Two Houston Center, Houston, TX 77010, (713) 652-3033

COMPANY: **Schneider Bernet & Hickman, Inc.**
ADDRESS: 2400 Interfirst Two
Dallas, TX 75270
PHONE: (214) 761-5100
TYPE OF INSTITUTION: Investment Banking
CONTACT OFFICER(S): William B. Madden, Pres.
INVESTMENTS/LOANS MADE: Through private placements; Through underwriting public offerings
INVESTMENTS/LOANS MADE: In securities with a secondary market and in securities without a secondary market
TYPES OF FINANCING: SECONDARY-MARKET CORPORATE SECURITIES: Common stock; Preferred stock; Bonds; Convertible Debentures; OTHER SERVICES PROVIDED: Mergers & Acquisitions

COMPANY: **Southwest Securities**
ADDRESS: 500 Texas National Bank Building
Dallas, TX 75225
PHONE: (214) 739-8888
TYPE OF INSTITUTION: Investment Banker
CONTACT OFFICER(S): Don Buchholz, C.O.O.
ASSETS: $13,000,00014Regional
REFERRALS ACCEPTED FROM: Investment/Mortgage banker; Borrower/Investee
REMARKS: Member NYSE

COMPANY: **Weber, Hall, Sale & Associates, Inc.**
ADDRESS: 1800 LTV Tower Bldg.
Dallas, TX 75201
PHONE: (214) 954-9412
TYPE OF INSTITUTION: Investment Bank

COMPANY: **Moncrief, Smith & Co.**
ADDRESS: 11 Greenway Plaza, Ste 2620
Houston, TX 77046
PHONE: (713) 622-0622
TYPE OF INSTITUTION: Investment Bank
CONTACT OFFICER(S): Lee P. Moncrief, Pres.

COMPANY: **Rotan-Mosle**
ADDRESS: 3800 Republic Bank Center
Houston, TX 77002
PHONE: (713) 236-3000
TYPE OF INSTITUTION: Investment Banker
CONTACT OFFICER(S): Jake Taylor
David Frishkorn
George Kelly
Jeff Hertel
ASSETS: $30,000,000 (equity)
INVESTMENTS/LOANS MADE: Regional; Southwest
BRANCHES: Brucee Swenson, 2600 First International Bank Bldg., Dallas, TX 75270, (214) 651-6919
REMARKS: Subsidiary of Paine-Weber

COMPANY: **Underwood, Neuhaus & Co., Incorporated**
ADDRESS: 724 Travis
Houston, TX 77002
PHONE: (713) 221-2413
TYPE OF INSTITUTION: Full Service Regional Investment Banking Firm
CONTACT OFFICER(S): Robert S. Moore 2nd, Corporate Finance
J. Randall Brlansky, Corporate Finance
Ben F. Ederer, Corporate Finance
ASSETS: More than $15,000,000 of equity capital; more than $60,000,000 of assets
INVESTMENTS/LOANS MADE: For own account; Through private placements; Through underwriting public offerings
INVESTMENTS/LOANS MADE: In securities with a secondary market and in securities without a secondary market
TYPES OF FINANCING: SECONDARY-MARKET CORPORATE SECURITIES: Common stock; Preferred stock; Bonds; Convertibles and Units of Common with Warrants, Bonds with Warrants, etc., VENTURE CAPITAL: Research & Development; Second-stage (generally 1-3 years); Later-stage expansion; Buy-outs/ Acquisitions, LOANS: Unsecured to credits above B; Equipment; Equity-related, REAL ESTATE LOANS: Long-term senior mtg.; Intermediate-term senior mtg.; Subordinated, LEASES: Single-investor; Leveraged; Tax leases, OTHER SERVICES PROVIDED: Direct Participations—i.e. limited partnership financing of equipment of all types
GEOGRAPHIC LIMITS OF INVESTMENTS/LOANS: National

RANGE OF INV./LOAN PER BUSINESS: Min. $2,000,000; Max. $100,000,000
PREFERRED TERM FOR LOANS & LEASES: Min. 5; Max. 20 years
BUSINESS CHARACTERISTICS DESIRED-REQUIRED: Minimum number of years in business: 1; Min. annual net income $500,000
REMARKS: The Corporate Finance part of Underwood, Neuhaus includes almost 30 professionals who in 1981 completed more than 80 different transactions.

COMPANY: **DeRand Corporation**
ADDRESS: 2201 Wilson Blvd.
Arlington, VA 22201
PHONE: (703) 527-3827
TYPE OF INSTITUTION: Investment Banking, Syndications, Securities Brokerage
CONTACT OFFICER(S): William A. Conway, President-International Stock Brokerage
Randall N. Smith, Chairman of Board-Real Estate
W. David Powell, Vice President-Municipal bonds
ASSETS: $100,000,000+
INVESTMENTS/LOANS MADE: For own account, Through private placements, Through underwriting public offerings
TYPES OF FINANCING: SECONDARY-MARKET CORPORATE SECURITIES: Common stock; Preferred stock; Bonds; Other: Real Estate, Oil and Gas, Telecommunications private placements, municipal bond financing. REAL ESTATE LOANS: Long-term senior mtg.; Intermediate-term senior mtg.; Subordinated; Wraparounds; Industrial revenue bonds. REAL ESTATE: Partnerships/Syndications.
REFERRALS ACCEPTED FROM: Investment/Mortgage banker or Borrower/Investee

COMPANY: **Craigie Inc.**
ADDRESS: P.O. Box 1854—814 E. Main
Richmond, VA 23215
PHONE: (804) 649-3946
CONTACT OFFICER(S): William B. Reynolds, Sr. V.P.
TYPES OF FINANCING: SECONDARY-MARKET CORPORATE SECURITIES: Bonds; Secondary market bonds, REAL ESTATE LOANS: Industrial revenue bonds
PREFERRED TYPES OF INDUSTRIES/INVESTMENTS: Debt Securities; Gov't. Agencies; Gov't. Bonds
GEOGRAPHIC LIMITS OF INVESTMENTS/LOANS: National
BUSINESS CHARACTERISTICS DESIRED-REQUIRED: Not specifically

COMPANY: **Interpacific Investors Services, Inc.**
ADDRESS: 1111 Norton Bldg.
Seattle, WA 98104
PHONE: (206) 623-2784
TYPE OF INSTITUTION: General securities broker dealer
CONTACT OFFICER(S): Ralph Stuart, C.E.O.
ASSETS: $4,200,000
GEOGRAPHIC LIMITS OF INVESTMENTS/LOANS: National

COMPANY: **Bozarth & Turner Securities, Inc.**
ADDRESS: Suite 1130, Seafirst Financial Center
Spokane, WA 99201
CONTACT OFFICER(S): G. David Bozarth, Pres.
TYPES OF FINANCING: SECONDARY-MARKET CORPORATE SECURITIES: Common stock; Preferred stock; Bonds; Other: Tax Free Securities
PREFERRED TYPES OF INDUSTRIES/INVESTMENTS: Well-known Companies
GEOGRAPHIC LIMITS OF INVESTMENTS/LOANS: Regional
BUSINESS CHARACTERISTICS DESIRED-REQUIRED: Established
REFERRALS ACCEPTED FROM: Investment/Mortgage banker or Borrower/Investee

COMPANY: **Robert W. Baird & Co., Inc.**
ADDRESS: 777 E. Wisconsin Ave.
Milwaukee, WI 53201
PHONE: (414) 765-3750
TYPE OF INSTITUTION: Corporate Finance Department of Investment Banker
CONTACT OFFICER(S): Ralph C. Inbusch, Vice Chairman
Robert M. Leonhardt, First V.P., Corporate Finance
Nicholas C. Wilson, First V.P., Corporate Finance
John D. Emory, V.P., Corporate Finance
INVESTMENTS/LOANS MADE: For own account; Through private placements; Through underwriting public offerings
INVESTMENTS/LOANS MADE: In securities with a secondary market and in securities without a secondary market
TYPES OF FINANCING: SECONDARY-MARKET CORPORATE SECURITIES: Common stock; Preferred stock; Bonds; VENTURE CAPITAL: Research & Development; Start-up from developed product stage; First-stage; Second-stage; Later-stage expansion; Buy-outs/Acquisitions; LOANS: Working capital (receivables/inventory); Equipment; Other; REAL ESTATE LOANS: Industrial revenue bonds
GEOGRAPHIC LIMITS OF INVESTMENTS/LOANS: National
RANGE OF INV./LOAN PER BUSINESS: Min. $250,000 million; Max. $5,000,000
BUSINESS CHARACTERISTICS DESIRED-REQUIRED: Minimum number of years in business: 1; Positive cash flow and/or earnings
REFERRALS ACCEPTED FROM: Investment/Mortgage banker or Borrower/Investee

COMPANY: **B.C. Ziegler and Company**
ADDRESS: 215 North Main Street
West Bend, WI 53095
PHONE: (414) 334-5521
TYPE OF INSTITUTION: Broker Dealer, Investment Broker
CONTACT OFFICER(S): Eugene H. Rudnicki, All Corporate Financing
James R. Wyatt, Health-Care Financing
John J. Becker, Leasing
ASSETS: $47,000,000

WISCONSIN

INVESTMENTS/LOANS MADE: Through underwriting public offerings
INVESTMENTS/LOANS MADE: In securities with a secondary market and in securities without a secondary market
TYPES OF FINANCING: SECONDARY-MARKET CORPORATE SECURITIES: Bonds; LEASES: Single investor; Leveraged; Tax leases; Vendor financing programs
PREFERRED TYPES OF INDUSTRIES/INVESTMENTS: Health-care, churches and any corporate issuers of debt securities
GEOGRAPHIC LIMITS OF INVESTMENTS/LOANS: International
RANGE OF INV./LOAN PER BUSINESS: Min. $1,000,000; Max. None
PREFERRED TERM FOR LOANS & LEASES: Min. 5 years; Max. 15 years

INVESTMENT COMPANIES

(Mainly Secondary Market Securities)

ARIZONA

COMPANY: **H.R. Company**
ADDRESS: 25 E. Eva St.
Phoenix, AZ
PHONE: (602) 944-1049
CONTACT OFFICER(S): R.G. Starsman, Sole Owner
ASSETS: $250,000 to 1,000,000
INVESTMENTS/LOANS MADE: For own account
INVESTMENTS/LOANS MADE: Only in securities with a secondary market
TYPES OF FINANCING: SECONDARY-MARKET CORPORATE SECURITIES: Common stock; Bonds; Other: Real estate
GEOGRAPHIC LIMITS OF INVESTMENTS/LOANS: National
PREFERRED TERM FOR LOANS & LEASES: Min. 0-1 year; Max. 1-3 years
REFERRALS ACCEPTED FROM: Investment/Mortgage banker only

COMPANY: **The Acorn Fund, Inc.**
ADDRESS: 120 S. LaSalle St.
Chicago, IL 60603
PHONE: (312) 621-0630
TYPE OF INSTITUTION: Mutual fund
CONTACT OFFICER(S): Maxine Ziv, Director of Marketing
ASSETS: $199.9 million
INVESTMENTS/LOANS MADE: For own account
INVESTMENTS/LOANS MADE: Only in securities with a secondary market
TYPES OF FINANCING: SECONDARY-MARKET CORPORATE SECURITIES: Common stock; Preferred stock; Bonds

MASSACHUSETTS

COMPANY: **MassMutual Corporate Investors, Inc.**
ADDRESS: 1295 State St.
Springfield, MA 01095
PHONE: (413) 788-8411
TYPE OF INSTITUTION: Closed-end direct placement fund
CONTACT OFFICER(S): Guy C. Roberts, V.P.
ASSETS: $100 million
INVESTMENTS/LOANS MADE: For own account; Through private placements
INVESTMENTS/LOANS MADE: In securities with a secondary market and in securities without a secondary market
TYPES OF FINANCING: LOANS: Unsecured to credits above B
PREFERRED TYPES OF INDUSTRIES/INVESTMENTS: No preference
GEOGRAPHIC LIMITS OF INVESTMENTS/LOANS: National
RANGE OF INV./LOAN PER BUSINESS: Min. $1 million; Max. $10 million

PREFERRED TERM FOR LOANS & LEASES: Min. 5 years; Max. 15 years
REFERRALS ACCEPTED FROM: Investment/Mortgage banker or Borrower/Investee

COMPANY:**Goldome, FSB**
ADDRESS: One Fountain Plaza
Buffalo, NY 14203
PHONE: (716) 845-5240
TYPE OF INSTITUTION: Investment Division
CONTACT OFFICER(S): Richard L. Marshall, V.P.-Investment
ASSETS: $13 Billion (total assets of Goldome, FSB)
INVESTMENTS/LOANS MADE: For own account
INVESTMENTS/LOANS MADE: Only in securities with a secondary market
TYPES OF FINANCING: SECONDARY-MARKET CORPORATE SECURITIES: Common stock; Preferred stock; Bonds
PREFERRED TYPES OF INDUSTRIES/INVESTMENTS: Equity investments in consumer and technological industries
RANGE OF INV./LOAN PER BUSINESS: Min. $50,000; Max. $5,000,000
BUSINESS CHARACTERISTICS DESIRED-REQUIRED: Minimum number of years in business: 5 Min. annual sales $100 MM; Min. net worth $25,000,000

COMPANY: **Tucker Leasing Corporation**
ADDRESS: /301 Madison Avenue
New York, NY, 10017
PHONE: (212) 867-5670
CONTACT OFFICER(S): Ken Williams

COMPANY: **General American Investors Company, Inc.**
ADDRESS: 330 Madison Avenue
New York, NY 10017
PHONE: (212) 916-8400
TYPE OF INSTITUTION: Regulated investment company (closed-end) and registered investment adviser
CONTACT OFFICER(S): Eugene L. DeStaebler, Jr., V.P., Administration
ASSETS: $1.2 billion
INVESTMENTS/LOANS MADE: For own account, For managed accounts
INVESTMENTS/LOANS MADE: Only in securities with a secondary market
TYPES OF FINANCING: SECONDARY-MARKET CORPORATE SECURITIES: Common stock; VENTURE CAPITAL: 2nd and later stage to a very limited extent—under 5% in nonmarketable equity securities
PREFERRED TYPES OF INDUSTRIES/INVESTMENTS: Equity securities with public marketability

COMPANY: **Tri-Continental Corporation**
ADDRESS: One Bankers Trust Plaza
New York, NY 10006
PHONE: (212) 488-0200
TYPE OF INSTITUTION: Closed-end investment company
CONTACT OFFICER(S): Ronald T. Schroeder, President
ASSETS: $869,795,000
INVESTMENTS MADE: For own account

COMPANY: **Valley Forge Fund Inc.**
ADDRESS: Box 262
Valley Forge, PA 9990
PHONE: (215) 688-6839
TYPE OF INSTITUTION: No-load growth oriented mutual fund
CONTACT OFFICER(S): Bernard B. Klawans, President
ASSETS: $6,200,000
INVESTMENTS/LOANS MADE: For own account
INVESTMENTS/LOANS MADE: Only in securities with a secondary market
TYPES OF FINANCING: SECONDARY-MARKET CORPORATE SECURITIES: Common stock; Preferred stock; Bonds; Other: Short-term corporate paper and Euro $
PREFERRED TYPES OF INDUSTRIES/INVESTMENTS: Low multiple listed stocks with a good track record
GEOGRAPHIC LIMITS OF INVESTMENTS/LOANS: International
RANGE OF INV./LOAN PER BUSINESS: Min. $10,000; Max. $3,000,000
BUSINESS CHARACTERISTICS DESIRED-REQUIRED: Listed Stocks

LEASING COMPANIES

(Lessors. Also see Commercial Bankers and Finance Companies, Insurance Companies and Investment Bankers)

ALASKA

COMPANY: **Alaska Pacific Leasing Inc., Alaska Pacific Bancorporation**
ADDRESS: P.O. Box 3200
Anchorage, AK 99510
PHONE: (907) 276-0003
CONTACT OFFICER(S): Gary Ratzlaff

COMPANY: **Amsouth Financial Corp.**
ADDRESS: P.O. Box 2545
Birmingham, AL 35202
PHONE: (205) 326-5780
CONTACT OFFICER(S): Jack G. Hays

COMPANY: **N & V Leasing Company, Inc.**
ADDRESS: 1020 Downtowner Blvd, Suite 135 B
Mobile, AL 36609
PHONE: (205) 342-1001
TYPE OF INSTITUTION: Equipment Leasing
CONTACT OFFICER(S): Brasher V. Miller, President
ASSETS: $603,258.48
INVESTMENT/LOANS MADE: For own account
TYPES OF FINANCING: LOANS: LEASES: Tax-leases; Tax-oriented lease brokerage
PREFERRED TYPES OF INDUSTRIES/INVESTMENTS: Office Equipment
WILL NOT CONSIDER: Telephone Systems and Cash Registers

COMPANY: **First Alabama Leasing, Inc.**
ADDRESS: P.O. Box 1203
Montgomery, AL 36102
PHONE: (205) 832-8550
CONTACT OFFICER(S): Jerry L. Wynne

COMPANY: **First Arkansas Leasing Corp., First Arkansas Bankstock Corp.**
ADDRESS: P.O. Box 1681, Worthen Bank Building
Little Rock, AR 72203
PHONE: (501) 378-1656
CONTACT OFFICER(S): Thomas L. Geis

ARIZONA

COMPANY: **Greyhound Computer Corporation**
ADDRESS: Greyhound Tower, Suite 1407
Phoenix, AZ 85077
PHONE: (602) 248-2596
CONTACT OFFICER(S): Wayne U. Smith

COMPANY: **Greyhound Leasing & Financial Corporation**
ADDRESS: 4041 North Center Avenue
Phoenix, AZ 85012
PHONE: (602) 248-4900
CONTACT OFFICER(S): See branches
ASSETS: $1.3 billion

INVESTMENTS/LOANS MADE: In securities with a secondary market and in securities without a secondary market
INVESTMENTS/LOANS MADE: For own account; Through private placements
TYPES OF FINANCING: SECONDARY MARKET CORPORATE SECURITIES: Bonds; VENTURE CAPITAL: Later-stage expansion; LOANS: Equipment; REAL ESTATE LOANS: Long-term senior mtg.; Intermediate-term senior mtg., Land development; Construction; Standbys; Other: Equity Notes Receivables; LEASES: Single-investor; Leveraged; Tax leases; Non-tax leases; Tax-oriented lease brokerage; Lease syndications; Vendor financing programs; INTERNATIONAL; REAL ESTATE: Joint ventures; Partnerships/Syndications
GEOGRAPHIC LIMITS OF INVESTMENTS/LOANS: National
RANGE OF INV./LOAN PER BUSINESS: Min. Leases: $50,000; Loans: $250,000; Max. $—
PREFERRED TERM FOR LOANS & LEASES: Min. Leases: 1; Loans: 3 years; Max. 20 years
BUSINESS CHARACTERISTICS DESIRED-REQUIRED: Minimum number of years in business: 5; Other: Proper operating history upon which to base payment ability projections
REFERRALS ACCEPTED FROM: Investment/Mortgage Banker or Borrower/Investee
BRANCHES: John N. Henning, Donald F. Howell, Jeremiah G. Mahony, Michael J. Naughton, and William H. Vallar (V.P.-Regional Marketing Manager), 445 Park Avenue, New York, NY 10022, (212) 752-2720
Robert E. Marino, John Wm. Salyer, David A. Nielsen (V.P.-Regional Marketing Manager), Centennial Center I, 1900 East Golf Road, Suite 645, Schaumburg, IL 60195, (312) 490-9500
Bruce E. Heine, Mark Lindell, 7801 East Bush Lake Road, Suite 430, Minneapolis, MN 55435, (612) 831-7044
Joseph A. Graffagnini, Canal Place One, Suite 2510, New Orleans, LA 70130, (504) 525-1112
James M. Brown, 12400 Olive Blvd., Suite 200, St. Louis, MO 63141, (314) 469-7373
George C. Baer, 7616 LBJ Freeway, Suite 500, Dallas, TX 75251, (214) 387-3182
Dottie A. Riley, James T. Foley (V.P.-Regional Marketing Manager), 4041 North Central Avenue, Station 3504, Phoenix, AZ 85012, (602) 248-5349
Jeffrey D. Johnson, Scott D. Mayne, 5505 South 900 East, Suite 325, Salt Lake City, UT 84117, (801) 261-1311
Thomas O. Kaluza, 16400 Southcenter Parkway, Suite 203, Seattle, WA 98188, (206) 575-0246
Kenneth B. Giddes, 6400 Powers Ferry Road, Suite 300, Atlanta, GA 30339, (404) 955-3636
Patrick E. Barton, 1776 South Jackson Street, Suite 907, Denver, CO 80210, (303) 757-4973
Jack W. Quinn, Cineco Building, Suite 203, 4401 W. Tradewinds Ave., Lauderdale-by-the-Sea, FL 33308, (305) 493-8322
David C. Phillips, 600 B Street, Suite 2235, San Diego, CA 92101, (619) 231-4751
Ron W. Larson, Neil E. Leddy, Orangegate Plaza, 5455 Garden Grove Blvd., Suite 450, Westminister, CA 92683, (714) 891-2700

COMPANY: **Manufacturers Lease Plans, Inc., MLPI Newcorp, Inc.**
ADDRESS: 2525 W. Beryl Avenue
Phoenix, AZ 85021
PHONE: (602) 944-4411
CONTACT OFFICER(S): Gary L. DeSeelhorst

COMPANY: **Metlease, Inc.**
ADDRESS: P.O. Box 16628
Phoenix, AZ 85014
PHONE: (602) 264-0016
CONTACT OFFICER(S): Sheridan Kevin Towers

COMPANY: **Railroad Holding Enterprises**
ADDRESS: 2211 East Highland Avenue
Phoenix, AZ 85016
PHONE: (602) 956-0310
CONTACT OFFICER(S): Charles R. Newman

COMPANY: **United Security Corporation**
ADDRESS: 3408 North Central Avenue, Leasing Division
Phoenix, AZ 85012
PHONE: (602) 248-2433
CONTACT OFFICER(S): Thomas R. Purcell

COMPANY: **Valley Bank Leasing, Inc., The Valley National Bank of AZ**
ADDRESS: 234 N. Central Ave., Suite 522
Phoenix, AZ 85004
PHONE: (602) 261-2223
CONTACT OFFICER(S): Allen E. Wilson

COMPANY: **Park Financial Corp.**
ADDRESS: 9808 Wilshire Blvd., Ste. 203
Beverly Hills, CA 90212
PHONE: (213) 550-1345
TYPE OF INSTITUTION: Leasing Co.
CONTACT OFFICER(S): Albert A. Peskin, V.P.
TYPES OF FINANCING: LEASES: Equipment
PREFERRED TYPES OF INDUSTRIES/INVESTMENTS: Refuse Business
WILL NOT CONSIDER: Autos
GEOGRAPHIC LIMITS OF INVESTMENTS/LOANS: State
RANGE OF INV./LOAN PER BUSINESS: Min. $5,000
PREFERRED TERM FOR LOANS & LEASES: Min. 1.5; Max. 5 years
BUSINESS CHARACTERISTICS DESIRED-REQUIRED: Minimum number of years in business: 2; Personal guarantees

COMPANY: **The Westminster Group**
ADDRESS: 9601 Wilshire Boulevard Mezzanine
Beverly Hills, CA 90210
PHONE: (213) 271-5187
CONTACT OFFICER(S): Gary P. Flyer

COMPANY: **All Type Equipment Leasing Inc.**
ADDRESS: 1350 Old Bayshore Highway, Suite 360

Burlingame, CA 94010
PHONE: (415) 342-2100
CONTACT OFFICER(S): A.J. Batt

COMPANY: **Simmons Company**
ADDRESS: 1201 Howard Avenue, Suite 305
Burlingame, CA 94010
PHONE: (415) 342-7600
CONTACT OFFICER(S): Carol Simmons

COMPANY: **General Hospital Leasing, Inc.**
ADDRESS: 20944 Sherman Way, Suite 103
Canoga Park, CA 91303
PHONE: (818) 348-9797
TYPE OF INSTITUTION: Leasing Co.
CONTACT OFFICER(S): Robert Skach, Pres.
TYPES OF FINANCING: LOANS: Sales contracts, LEASES: Operating; Tax-oriented lease brokerage
PREFERRED TYPES OF INDUSTRIES/INVESTMENTS: Hospitals; Industrial
GEOGRAPHIC LIMITS OF INVESTMENTS/LOANS: National
RANGE OF INV./LOAN PER BUSINESS: Min. $5,000
PREFERRED TERM FOR LOANS & LEASES: Min. 2; Max. 10 years

COMPANY: **Ericsson Inc./Ericsson Leasing**
ADDRESS: 20660 Nordhoff Street
Chatsworth, CA 91311
PHONE: (213) 709-7790
CONTACT OFFICER(S): Henry Y. Tileston

COMPANY: **Pacific Lighting Leasing Company (parent)/ Pacific Lighting Commercial Loans, Inc. (subsidiary)**
ADDRESS: 6140 Bristol Parkway
Culver City, CA 90230
PHONE: (213) 642-7595
Wholly owned Leasing and Finance subsidiary of NYSE company
CONTACT OFFICER(S): William M. Hamburg, Vice President—Leasing & Lending
Waldo A. Rodman, Director of Leasing & Remarketing
ASSETS: $76,000,000
INVESTMENTS/LOANS MADE: For own account
INVESTMENTS/LOANS MADE: In securities with a secondary market and in securities without a secondary market
TYPES OF FINANCING: VENTURE CAPITAL; Second-stage; Later-stage; Buy-outs/Acquisitions; LOANS: Equipment; Equity-related; REAL ESTATE LOANS: Intermediateterm senior mtg.; Subordinated; Gap; Standbys; LEASES: Single-investor; Tax leases; Non-tax leases; Operating; Tax-oriented lease brokerage; Vendor financing programs
PREFERRED TYPES OF INDUSTRIES/INVESTMENTS: Office Equipment; Production Equipment; Restaurant; Medical; Air Conditioning; other
WILL NOT CONSIDER: Automobiles
GEOGRAPHIC LIMITS OF INVESTMENTS/LOANS: National
RANGE OF INV./LOAN PER BUSINESS: Min. $2,500; Max. $5,000,000
PREFERRED TERM FOR LOANS & LEASES: Min. 3 yrs; Max. 7 yrs
BUSINESS CHARACTERISTICS DESIRED/REQUIRED: Minimum number of years in business: 0; Min. annual sales $1,000,000
REFERRALS ACCEPTED FROM: Investment/Mortgage banker or Borrower/Investee

COMPANY: **Leasametric, Inc.**
ADDRESS: 1164 Triton Drive
Foster City, CA 94404
PHONE: (415) 574-4410
CONTACT OFFICER(S): R.D. Ringe

COMPANY: **Liberty Equipment Leasing Co., Inc.**
ADDRESS: P.O. Box 9572
Fresno, CA 93793
PHONE: (209) 226-6046
CONTACT OFFICER(S): Henry L. Wheeler

COMPANY: **Pacific States Leasing, Inc.**
ADDRESS: 135 W. Shaw 105
Fresno, CA 93711
PHONE: (209) 221-6952
TYPE OF INSTITUTION: Equipment Lessor
CONTACT OFFICER(S): Al Vionnet, Exec. V.P., Director of Finance—All transactions over 100,000.
Gary Christy, V.P. Dir. of Marketing—Vendor Finance & Leasing Plans
Gary Honicutt, Asst. V.P.—Mgr. Broker Div.—Broker Transactions (Referrals, etc.)
ASSETS: $20,000,000
INVESTMENTS/LOANS MADE: For own account, managed accounts or through private placements
TYPES OF FINANCING: LOANS: Equipment; Equity-related; Commercial Contracts & Leases—All types of Equipment; LEASES: Single-investor; Leveraged; Tax leases; Non-tax leases; Operating; Tax-oriented lease brokerage; Vendor financing programs; Other; OTHER SERVICES PROVIDED: Provide funding for lease companies, for vendors desiring to be lessors; any and all activities involving equipment leasing.
PREFERRED TYPES OF INDUSTRIES/INVESTMENTS: Prefer equipment leases from $1,000 to $100,000; direct, vendor or broker plans; equipment for business use; all industries acceptable
GEOGRAPHIC LIMITS OF INVESTMENTS/LOANS: National; Other: All 50 states except Louisiana & Arkansas
RANGE OF INV./LOAN PER BUSINESS: Min. $1,000; Max. $100,000,000
PREFERRED TERM FOR LOANS & LEASES: Min. 2; Max. 7
BUSINESS CHARACTERISTICS DESIRED-REQUIRED: Minimum number of years in business: 2; Min. annual sales: no; Min. net worth $50,000; Min. annual net income $24,000;
REFERRALS ACCEPTED FROM: Investment/Mortgage banker or Borrower/Investee
BRANCHES: R.B. Klutz, Branch Mgr., Hampton E. #1, 8000 Girard Suite 418, Denver, CO 80231, (303) 368-9400

LEASING COMPANIES

(Lessors. Also see Commercial Bankers and Finance Companies, Insurance Companies and Investment Bankers)

COMPANY: **National Funding Corporation**
ADDRESS: 16168 Beach Blvd., Suite 232
Huntington Beach, CA 92647
PHONE: (714) 848-0644
CONTACT OFFICER(S): T. Paul Buchanan, Pres.
John D. Jackson, V. P.
Glenn A. Cassens, V.P.
ASSETS: In excess of $250,000
INVESTMENTS/LOANS MADE: For own account
TYPES OF FINANCING: LEASES: Single-investor; Leveraged; Tax leases; Operating; Lease syndications; Vendor financing programs;
PREFERRED TYPES OF INDUSTRIES/INVESTMENTS: Rated commercial and industrial leases; Medical equipment
GEOGRAPHIC LIMITS OF INVESTMENTS/LOANS: National
RANGE OF INV./LOAN PER BUSINESS: Min. $25,000; Max. $30,000,000
PREFERRED TERM FOR LOANS & LEASES: Min. 3 yrs.; Max. 20 yrs.
BRANCHES: The Barn Office Center, 2 Village Road, Suite 5, Horsham, PA 19044, (215) 659-7878, Chris Adams, Regional Manager
2191 Northlake Pkwy., Suite 32, Tucker, GA 30084; (404) 939-1973, Mardee Small, Regional Manager, 1701 E. Woodfield Dr., Suite 521, Schaumburg, IL 60195; (312) 843-0005, Ronald J. Guimon, District Manager
9071 Metcalf Ave., Suite 141, Overland Park, KS 66212; (913) 764-0033, Ann Harms, District Manager
4212F Knob Oak Lane, Charlotte, NC 28211; (704) 364-7065, Michael DuPree, District Manager
1700 Westlake Avenue North, Seattle, WA 98109; (206) 285-1235, John Wilkinson, District Manager
5019 McKinney Ave., Suite 155, Dallas, TX 75205; (214) 528-3950, Pat Desmond, District Manager
16168 Beach Blvd., Suite 232, Huntington Beach, CA 92647; (714) 848-0644, Virginia Johnson, District Manager, Mary Marcho, District Manager
5776 Stoneridge Mall Road #225, Pleasanton, CA 94566, (415) 463-1840, Gayle Wainwright, District Manager
50 Tremont Street, Suite 205B, Melrose, MA 02176; (617) 662-4885, Maureen Crowther, District Manager
1212 Sycamore Street, Suite 21D, Cincinnati, Ohio 45210; (513) 751-4646, Hank Davis, District Manager
P.O. Box 593, Sebring, FL 33870; (813) 385-3381, Bill Perin, District Manager

COMPANY: **Century Financial Services Inc.**
ADDRESS: 17748 Skypark Blvd, Ste. 200
Irvine, CA 92714
PHONE: (714) 966-1800
CONTACT OFFICER(S): Paul Bent

COMPANY: **McDonnell Douglas Finance Corporation**
ADDRESS: 100 Oceangate
Long Beach, CA 90802
PHONE: (213) 593-8471
CONTACT OFFICER(S): Donald V. Black

COMPANY: **Behr Leasing & Financial Corp.**
ADDRESS: 700 S. Flower, Ste. 3200
Los Angeles, CA 90017
PHONE: (213) 627-0272
TYPE OF INSTITUTION: Leasing Co.
CONTACT OFFICER(S): Ken Goodman, Director of Marketing
Raymond B. Corob, Pres.
TYPES OF FINANCING: LOANS: Equipment; LEASES: Tax leases; Non-tax leases; Tax-oriented lease brokerage; Lease syndications, Vendor Financing Programs
GEOGRAPHIC LIMITS OF INVESTMENTS/LOANS: National
RANGE OF INV./LOAN PER BUSINESS: Min. $25,000
REMARKS: Average term: 5 years; Max 10 years

COMPANY: **East Land Leasing Co.**
ADDRESS: 5400 E. Olympic Blvd. Suite 300
Los Angeles, CA 90022
PHONE: (213) 721-1655
CONTACT OFFICER(S): Anthony Souza V.P.
TYPES OF FINANCING: OTHER SERVICES PROVIDED: Strictly auto equipment lease financing
GEOGRAPHIC LIMITS OF INVESTMENTS/LOANS: Local; State
RANGE OF INV./LOAN PER BUSINESS: Min. $10,000; Max. $100,000
PREFERRED TERM FOR LOANS & LEASES: Min. 36 mos.; Max. 60 months
BUSINESS CHARACTERISTICS DESIRED-REQUIRED: Minimum number of years in business: 3 years; Other: look at financial statement; currently healthy; potenial growth

COMPANY: **Hempel Financial Services**
ADDRESS: 11726 San Vicente, Ste. 230
Los Angeles, CA 90049
PHONE: (213) 475-0304
TYPE OF INSTITUTION: Medical leasing, also has a division that buys mortgages and trust deeds
CONTACT OFFICERS(S): Bruce Hemple, Pres.
Heidi Elliot, V.P.
ASSETS: $ 1-10 million
TYPES OF FINANCING: LEASES; Other: Sale leasebacksOTHER SERVICES PROVIDES: buys mortgages and trust deeds which are not necessarily medical; all other investments are medical
PREFERRED TYPES OF INDUSTRIES/INVESTMENTS: Medical and other health services/medical and dental equipment and furnishings
GEOGRAPHIC LIMITS OF INVESTMENTS/LOANS: National
RANGE OF INV./LOAN PER BUSINESS: Min. $10,000
PREFERRED TERM FOR LOANS & LEASES: Min. 5 years
BUSINESS CHARACTERISTICS DESIRED-REQUIRED: Client must be a practicing physician or dentist
REFERRALS ACCEPTED FROM: Investment/Mortgage banker; Borrower/Investee

COMPANY: **Hydril Company**
ADDRESS: 714 West Olympic Boulevard
Los Angeles, CA 90015
PHONE: (213) 680-1910

LEASING COMPANIES

(Lessors. Also see Commercial Bankers and Finance Companies, Insurance Companies and Investment Bankers)

CONTACT OFFICER(S): Eugene P. Adams

COMPANY: **Taurus Leasing Co.**
ADDRESS: 6565 Sunset Blvd., Suite 511 (Mail: P.O. Box 108)
Los Angeles, CA 90078
PHONE: (213) 466-5144
CONTACT OFFICER(S): Roy G. Bergen, V.P. Gen. Manager
TYPES OF FINANCING: LOANS: Unsecured, Working capital, Equipment; Equity-related; LEASES: New Equipment Leases & Sale/Leaseback
PREFERRED TYPES OF INDUSTRIES/INVESTMENTS: Medical
GEOGRAPHIC LIMITS OF INVESTMENTS/LOANS: National
RANGE OF INV./LOAN PER BUSINESS: Min. $5,000.00; Max. $200,000.00
PREFERRED TERM FOR LOANS & LEASES: Min. 2 yrs; Max. 5 yrs
BUSINESS CHARACTERISTICS DESIRED-REQUIRED: Minimum number of years in business: 2; Cash Flow Lender
REFERRALS ACCEPTED FROM: Investment/Mortgage banker or Borrower/Investee
REMARKS: Sale lease-backs to physicians and dentists

COMPANY: **Unionbanc, Leasing Division**
ADDRESS: 445 South Figueroa St.
Los Angeles, CA 90017
PHONE: (213) 687-5311
TYPE OF INSTITUTION: Leasing Co.
CONTACT OFFICER(S): Robert Casper, Dir. of Marketing
TYPES OF FINANCING: LOANS: Equipment, LEASES: Single-investor; Leveraged; Tax leases; Operating
PREFERRED TYPES OF INDUSTRIES/INVESTMENTS: Machinery
WILL NOT CONSIDER: Agricultural
GEOGRAPHIC LIMITS OF INVESTMENTS/LOANS: National
RANGE OF INV./LOAN PER BUSINESS: Min. $50,000

COMPANY: **FNS Corporate Funding**
ADDRESS: 100 Tiburon Boulevard
Mill Valley, CA 94941
PHONE: (415) 381-3590
CONTACT OFFICER(S): Ronald L. Berg

COMPANY: **International Marketing & Finance Group, Inc.**
ADDRESS: 655 Redwood Highway
Mill Valley, CA
PHONE: (415) 492-9300
TYPE OF INSTITUTION: Financial services and equipment leasing
CONTACT OFFICER(S): President, International and Domestic Computer Transactions, Tax Shelter Programs
Carol A. McCollister, Executive V.P., All types of general leasing
ASSETS: $15 million
INVESTMENTS/LOANS MADE: For own account, Through private placements
TYPES OF FINANCING: LEASES: Single-investor; Leveraged; Tax leases; Non-tax leases; Operating; Tax-oriented lease brokerage; Lease syndications; Vendor financing programs, INTERNATIONAL lease/conditional sales, OTHER SERVICES PROVIDED: Tax shelter programs, corporate and individual
PREFERRED TYPES OF INDUSTRIES/INVESTMENTS: All types
WILL NOT CONSIDER: Start up restaurants, unless backed by real estate
GEOGRAPHIC LIMITS OF INVESTMENTS/LOANS: National; International
RANGE OF INV./LOAN PER BUSINESS: Min. $50,000; Max. $10,000,000
PREFERRED TERM FOR LOANS & LEASES: Min. 3 years; Max. 7 years
BUSINESS CHARACTERISTICS DESIRED-REQUIRED: Minimum number of years in business: 3; Min. annual sales $1.0 Million; Min. net worth $200,000; Min. annual net income $100,000; Min. annual cash flow open
BRANCHES: Peter A. Jackson, Executive V.P., 285 Washington, Marblehead, MA 01945; (617) 631-3955

COMPANY: **National Advanced Systems Corporation**
ADDRESS: 800 E. Middlefield Road
Mountain View, CA 94043
PHONE: (415) 962-6000
CONTACT OFFICER(S): David Roberson

COMPANY: **Avco Financial Services Leasing Co.**
ADDRESS: 620 Newport Center Drive
Newport Beach, CA 92660
PHONE: (714) 640-5200
TYPE OF INSTITUTION: Leasing company
CONTACT OFFICER(S): William Dowell, Sr. V.P., Marketing
TYPES OF FINANCING: LEASES: Single-investor; Tax leases; Non-tax leases; Vendor financing programs
PREFERRED TYPES OF INDUSTRIES/INVESTMENTS: General equipment
GEOGRAPHIC LIMITS OF INVESTMENTS/LOANS: National
RANGE OF INV./LOAN PER BUSINESS: Min. $100,000; Max. $5 million
PREFERRED TERM FOR LOANS & LEASES: Min. 3 years; Max. 10 years
BUSINESS CHARACTERISTICS DESIRED-REQUIRED: Other: Balance sheet lessor
REMARKS: No start-ups; referrals from banks only; branches located in all major cities

COMPANY: **Concour Corporation**
ADDRESS: 49 Pacheco Creek Drive
Novato, CA 94947
PHONE: (415) 461-8600
CONTACT OFFICER(S): Dennis T. Flynn

COMPANY: **Winston Financial Corp**
ADDRESS: 1447 Palisades Drive

Pacific Palisades, CA 90272
PHONE: (213) 454-7030
TYPE OF INSTITUTION: Financial Services, Leasing Specialty
CONTACT OFFICER(S): Paul D. Shlensky, President
Barry G. Morganstern, V.P.
ASSETS: $10,000,000
INVESTMENTS/LOANS MADE: For own account
INVESTMENTS/LOANS MADE: In securities with a secondary market and in securities without a secondary market
TYPES OF FINANCING: SECONDARY-MARKET CORPORATE SECURITIES, VENTURE CAPITAL: Second-stage; Later-stage expansion; Buy-outs/ Acquisitions, LOANS: Working capital; Equipment, LEASES: Single-investor; Leveraged; Tax leases; Operating; Vendor financing programs
PREFERRED TYPES OF INDUSTRIES/INVESTMENTS: Telecommunications, energy
GEOGRAPHIC LIMITS OF INVESTMENTS/LOANS: National
RANGE OF INV./LOAN PER BUSINESS: Min. $250,000; Max. $10,000,000
PREFERRED TERM FOR LOANS & LEASES: Min. 3 years; Max. 5 years
BUSINESS CHARACTERISTICS DESIRED-REQUIRED: Minimum number of years in business: 5 years
REFERRALS ACCEPTED FROM: Investment/Mortgage banker or Borrower/Investee

COMPANY: **Garnett & Company**
ADDRESS: 170 N. Fair Oaks Ave.
Pasadena, CA 91103
PHONE: (213) 681-4619
TYPE OF INSTITUTION: Leasing Co.
CONTACT OFFICER(S): William J. Garnett III, President
Richard Londgren, V.P.
TYPES OF FINANCING: LOANS, LEASES: Single-investor, Leveraged, Tax leases; Non-tax leases, Tax-oriented lease brokerage, Lease syndications, Vendor financing programs
GEOGRAPHIC LIMITS OF INVESTMENTS/LOANS: National, International
RANGE OF INV./LOAN PER BUSINESS: Min. $10,000; Max. No
PREFERRED TERM FOR LOANS & LEASES: Min. 3; Max. 7 years
BUSINESS CHARACTERISTICS DESIRED-REQUIRED: Minimum number of years in business: 0
REFERRALS ACCEPTED FROM: Investment/Mortgage banker and Borrower/Investee
REMARKS: Start-ups financed if credit is good; must give financial statements

COMPANY: **Union Bank**
ADDRESS: 225 S. Lake Avenue
Pasadena, CA 91101
PHONE: (818) 304-1700
TYPE OF INSTITUTION: Asset-Based Financing Group of Bank
CONTACT OFFICER(S): Theodore Kompa, Vice Pres. & Reg. Manager (So. Calif.) Asset Based Loans
Michael J. Riley, Vice Pres. & Reg. Manager, (No. Calif.) Asset Based Loans
Robert C. Andreasen, Vice Pres. & Manager, Equipment Finance and Leasing
ASSETS: $8 Billion
INVESTMENTS/LOANS MADE: For own account
TYPES OF FINANCING: Working capital (receivables/ inventory), Equipment; REAL ESTATE LOANS: Intermediate-term senior mtg.; LEASES: Single-investor, Leveraged, Tax leases, Non-tax leases, Operating, Tax-oriented lease brokerage, Lease syndications, Vendor financing programs; OTHER SERVICES PROVIDED: Leverage Buyout Financing
PREFERRED TYPES OF INDUSTRIES/INVESTMENTS: Manufacturing, Distribution, Wholesaling. Prefer income-producing equipment for lease and loan transactions
GEOGRAPHIC LIMITS OF INVESTMENTS/LOANS: National
RANGE OF INV./LOAN PER BUSINESS: Min. $500,000; Max. $60,000,000
PREFERRED TERM FOR LOANS & LEASES: Min. 2 years; Max. 10 years
BUSINESS CHARACTERISTICS DESIRED-REQUIRED: Minimum number of years in business: 2; Min. annual sales $5,000,000; Min. net worth $200,000; Min. annual net income $50,000; Min annual cash flow $75,000
REFERRALS ACCEPTED FROM: Investment/Mortgage banker or Borrower/Investee
BRANCHES: 225 South Lake Avenue, 6th Floor, Pasadena, CA 91101, 818-304-1700, Theodore Kompa
460 Hegenberger Rd., Oakland, CA 94604, (415) 772-8158, Michael J. Riley

COMPANY: **Unionbanc Leasing Corporation**
ADDRESS: 225 S. Lake Ave., 6th Floor
Pasadena, CA 91101
PHONE: (213) 304-1807
CONTACT OFFICER(S): Karen Harter

COMPANY: **United Medical Leasing Co., Inc.**
ADDRESS: 225 S. Lake Ave.
Pasadena, CA 91101
PHONE: (213) 796-0376
CONTACT OFFICER(S): W.M. Eddington

COMPANY: **The Dowdell Corporation**
ADDRESS: 555 Capitol Mall, Suite 640
Sacramento, CA 95814
PHONE: (916) 444-0494
CONTACT OFFICER(S): John L. Dowdell

COMPANY: **American States Leasing Corp.**
ADDRESS: 2442 4th Avenue, P.O. Box 82357
San Diego, CA 92138
PHONE: (619) 231-3942
CONTACT OFFICER(S): Armon E. Kamesar

COMPANY: **Equitable Life Leasing Corporation**
ADDRESS: 10251 Vista Sorrento Parkway, Suite 300
San Diego, CA 92121
PHONE: (619) 458-4400

TYPE OF INSTITUTION: Leasing subsidiary of The Equitable Life Assurance Society of the U.S.
CONTACT OFFICER(S):Edward R. Herman, President & CEO
Roderic L. Eaton, Sr. V.P., Manufacturer Partnerhips
Donald J. Kovacs, V.P. National Vendor Programs
Michael F. Herman, V.P., Operating Lease
ASSETS: $615,986 (thousand)
TYPES OF FINANCING: LEASES: Single-investor; Leveraged; Tax leases; Operating; Vendor financing programs; Leasing partnerships
PREFERRED TYPES OF INDUSTRIES/INVESTMENTS: Industry: electronicsss, banking, Fortune 2000, technological & service oriented; Equipment: computers, CAD/CAM equipment, banking automation, electronic-test & measurement & ATE
GEOGRAPHIC LIMITS OF INVESTMENTS/LOANS: National
RANGE OF LEASE PER BUSINESS: Min. $$100,000
PREFERRED TERM FOR LOANS & LEASES: Min. 1-3 years
BRANCHES: EASTERN* Christopher Morell, 1777 Walton Road, Suite 101, Merion Towle Building, Blue Bell, PA 19422; (215) 646-6300
Richard Bowman, 40 William Street, Wellesley, MA 02181; (617) 237-3660
Charles LaChiusa*, 107 Delaware Avenue, Statler Bldg., Suite 540, Buffalo, NY 14202
John McEwen, One Metro Plaza 505 Thornall Street, Edison, NJ 08817; (201) 494-0300
Walter Steimel, 1777 Walton Road, Suite 201, Merion Towle Building, Blue Bell, PA 19422; (215) 628-0350
James Mignogna, Manor Oak One, Suite 540, 1910 Cochran Road Pittsburgh, PA 15220; (412) 343-8122
Al Juliano*, 2 Soundview Drive Greenwich, CT 06830
Shelby Francis, 1350 Piccard Drive, Suite 105, Rockville, MD 20850; (301) 258-7878
CENTRAL: Mark Gullett, P.O Box 2538, Des Plaines, IL 60018; (312) 296-6030
Robert Ernst* Lookout Corporate Center, Suite 410, 1717 Dixie Highway, Fort Wright, KY 41011
Steve Buckley, 6100 Rockside Woods Blvd., Suite 440, Cleveland, OH 44131; (216) 524-0780
Patrick Curran*, P.0. Box 1138, Birmingham, MI 48012; (313) 646-9333
Michael Rose, P.O. Box 35699, Minneapolis, MN 55435, (612) 944-8740
SOUTHERN: Robert Golden, 8302 Dunwoody Place, Suite 207, Atlanta, GA 30338, (404) 922-2217
James Cody, 8302 Dunwoody Place, Suite 207, Atlanta, GA 30338; (404) 992-2217
4401 Colwick Road, Suite 310, Charlotte, N.C. 28222
Ronald Hogue, 1320 Greenway Drive, Suite 225, Irving, TX 75038; (214) 659-9730
Ronald Hogue (Dallas office) 6200 Savoy Drive, Suite 440, Houston, TX 77036; (713) 977-5761
Roger Innes*, P.O. Box 12525, Overland Park, KS 66212, (913) 642-8450
Stephen Lundergan, 12125 Woodcrest Executive Drive, Suite 110, St. Louis, MO 63141; (314) 878-0075
Mark Souers, P.O. Box 21167, Tampa, Florida 33622-1167 (813) 876-1090
WESTERN: Richard Viviano, P.O. Box 81224, San Diego, CA 92138-1224, (619) 458-4400
Gregory Vye, P.O. Box 24002, Denver, CO 80224; (303) 761-3290
Robert Stanley, P.O. Box 33 361, Long B each, CA 90801; (213) 493-5431
Dale Trimble*, 3020 East Camelback Road, Suite 300, Phoenix, AZ 85016; (602) 954-8766
David Murray*, 6950 S.W. Hampton Street, Suite 108, Tigard, OR 97223; (503) 684-1828
Gary Atkins*, P.O. Box 81224, San Diego, CA 92138-1224; (619) 458-4400
50 West Broadway, Suite 900, Salt Lake City, UT 84101; (801) 531-0303
2000 Alameda de Las Pulgas, Suite 156, San Mateo, CA 94403; (415) 571-8881
P.O. Box 396, Bellevue, WA 98009, (206) 455-3723

COMPANY: **Equitable/Omnilease Corp.**
ADDRESS: 10251 Vista Sorrento Parkway, Suite 300, P.O. Box 81224
San Diego, CA 92138
PHONE: (619) 453-0881
CONTACT OFFICER(S): Edward R. Herman

COMPANY: **Heritage Leasing Corporation**
ADDRESS: 4379 30th Street
San Diego, CA 92104
PHONE: (619) 280-8822
TYPE OF INSTITUTION: Equipment Leasing
CONTACT OFFICER(S): Ronald Wagner, Exec. V.P.-Marketing
ASSETS: $20 million
INVESTMENTS/LOANS MADE: For own account, for managed accounts
INVESTMENTS/LOANS MADE: Only in securities without a secondary market
TYPES OF FINANCING: LEASES: Tax leases; Non-tax leases; Tax-oriented lease brokerage; Vendor financing programs
PREFERRED TYPES OF INDUSTRIES/INVESTMENTS: Residential, apartments, office buildings, industrials and research and development
GEOGRAPHIC LIMITS OF INVESTMENTS/LOANS: Regional, Western U.S.
RANGE OF INV./LOAN PER BUSINESS: Min. $5,000; Max. $5,000,000
PREFERRED TERM FOR LOANS & LEASES: Min. 3 years; Max. 30 years
BUSINESS CHARACTERISTICS DESIRED-REQUIRED: Minimum number of years in business: 3; Min. net worth $100,000
REFERRALS ACCEPTED FROM: Borrower/Investee
BRANCHES: Orange County Office: 2915 Red Hill Avenue, Suite G-104, Costa Mesa, CA 92626; (714) 546-6916
Fresno Office: P.O. Box 65001, Pinedale, CA 93650-5001; (209) 435-9220
Sacramento Office: 11050 Coloma Road, Suite R, Rancho Cordova, CA 95670; (916) 638-4411
Bellevue Office: 1050 140th Ave., N.E., Suite D, Bellevue, Washington 98005; (206) 746-6700
Billings Office: Metro Park, 1148 1st Ave. N., Suite 112, Billings, MT 59103; (406) 252-5846
Walla Walla Office: 3301 East Isaacs Avenue, Walla Walla, WA 99362; (509) 529-7186
REMARKS: all contacts should be made through the corporate office in San Diego, CA.

LEASING COMPANIES

(Lessors. Also see Commercial Bankers and Finance Companies, Insurance Companies and Investment Bankers)

COMPANY: **PHD Corporation**
ADDRESS: 4285 Camino Del Rio S.
San Diego, CA 92120
PHONE: (619) 283-7161
TYPE OF INSTITUTION: Leasing Co.
CONTACT OFFICER(S): Jerome B. LaDow
TYPES OF FINANCING: LEASES: Operating
PREFERRED TYPES OF INDUSTRIES/INVESTMENTS: Cars, Trucks
GEOGRAPHIC LIMITS OF INVESTMENTS/LOANS: National
RANGE OF INV./LOAN PER BUSINESS: Min. $5,000
PREFERRED TERM FOR LOANS & LEASES: Min. 2; Max. 5 years
BRANCHES: 5 Branches all in San Diego

COMPANY: **Security Pacific Finance Corp.**
ADDRESS: 10089 Willow Creek Road
San Diego, CA 92131
PHONE: (619) 578-6150
CONTACT OFFICER(S): David G. Balk

COMPANY: **Associates Venture Capital Corp.**
ADDRESS: 425 California Street
San Francisco, CA 94104
PHONE: (415) 956-1444
TYPE OF INSTITUTION: Venture Capital
CONTACT OFFICER(S): Walter P. Strycker, President
ASSETS: $3,000,000
INVESTMENTS/LOANS MADE: For own account, through private placements
INVESTMENTS/LOANS MADE: In securities with a secondary market and in securities without a secondary market
TYPES OF FINANCING: SECONDARY MARKET CORPORATE SECURITIES: Preferred stock; VENTURE CAPITAL: Start-up from developed product stage; First-stage; Second-stage; Buy-outs/Acquisitions, LEASES: Leveraged, Lease syndications
PREFERRED TYPES OF INDUSTRIES/INVESTMENTS: Energy, electronics, medical, communications, computer terminals
WILL NOT CONSIDER: Real estate
GEOGRAPHIC LIMITS OF INVESTMENTS/LOANS: National
RANGE OF INV./LOAN PER BUSINESS: Min. $150,000; Max. $1,000,000
PREFERRED TERM FOR LOANS & LEASES: Min. 1 year; Max. 5 years
BUSINESS CHARACTERISTICS DESIRED-REQUIRED: Minimum number of years in business 0
BRANCHES: Harold McCormick, Vice Pres., Signal Technology, 30 Grosner Hill, London, W1 England; 011-44-499-8292

COMPANY: **BankAmeriLease Group**
ADDRESS: 2 Embarcadero Center, 28th Floor
San Francisco, CA 94111
PHONE: (415) 622-6280
TYPE OF INSTITUTION: Leasing company
CONTACT OFFICER(S): Peter Nevitt
TYPES OF FINANCING: LEASES: Single-investor; Leveraged; Tax leases; Non-tax leases; Operating; Tax-oriented lease brokerage; Lease syndications; Vendor financing programs
WILL NOT CONSIDER: Restaurant equipment; Store fixtures
GEOGRAPHIC LIMITS OF INVESTMENTS/LOANS: National
RANGE OF INV./LOAN PER BUSINESS: Min. $300,000
BUSINESS CHARACTERISTICS DESIRED-REQUIRED: Minimum years in business: 0
REMARKS: Minimum lease amount per business for California: $50,000; Preferred range of term: 3-10 for direct leases and 5-25 for leveraged leases

COMPANY: **Belvedere Equipment Finance**
ADDRESS: 675 California Street
San Francisco, CA 94108
PHONE: (415) 392-4950
CONTACT OFFICER(S): Richard Leask

COMPANY: **Caravan Leasing Inc.**
ADDRESS: 44 Montgomery Street, Ste. 800
San Francisco, CA 94104
PHONE: (415) 981-8394
CONTACT OFFICER(S): Gordon E. Inouye

COMPANY: **CIS Equipment Leasing Corp.**
ADDRESS: 445 Washington Street
San Francisco, CA 94111
PHONE: (415) 989-7420
CONTACT OFFICER(S): Stephen R. Harwood

COMPANY:**Pacesetter Leasing Corporation**
ADDRESS: 601 California St., Suite 601
San Francisco, CA 94108
PHONE: (415) 397-8246
TYPE OF INSTITUTION: Equipment Leasing Company
CONTACT OFFICER(S): Max E. La Counte, President
ASSETS: $5,000,000
INVESTMENTS/LOANS MADE: For own account, For managed accounts, Through private placements
TYPES OF FINANCING: LEASES: Operating; Vendor financing programs
PREFERRED TYPES OF INDUSTRIES/INVESTMENTS: Manufacturers and vendors of high tech computer peripheral products. Typically terminals, disk & tape drives, word processing, office automation products.
GEOGRAPHIC LIMITS OF INVESTMENTS/LOANS: National
RANGE OF INV./LOAN PER BUSINESS: Min. $5,000,000; Max. $50,000,000
PREFERRED TERM FOR LOANS & LEASES: Min. 1 year; Max. 5 years.
BUSINESS CHARACTERISTICS DESIRED-REQUIRED: Minimum number of years in business: 5; Min. annual sales $10,000,000

COMPANY: **Crocker Equipment Leasing**
ADDRESS: 201 Third Street, 5th Floor
San Francisco, CA 94103

CALIFORNIA

PHONE: (415) 477-1283
CONTACT OFFICER(S): Allen L. Meier

COMPANY: **D'Accord Inc.**
ADDRESS: 300 Montgomery Street
San Francisco, CA 94104
PHONE: (415) 981-3812
CONTACT OFFICER(S): Donald W. Smiegiel

COMPANY: **GATX Leasing Corporation**
ADDRESS: Four Embarcadero Center, Ste. 2200
San Francisco, CA 94111
PHONE: (415) 955-3200
TYPE OF INSTITUTION: Leasing and Secured Financing-Independent
CONTACT OFFICER(S): Ronald H. Zech, Exec. V.P.-Administration & Finance
David A. Woolsey, Exec. V.P.-Marketing
Kenneth T. Gibson, V.P.-Finance
ASSETS: $651 million
INVESTMENTS/LOANS MADE: For own account, Through private placements
INVESTMENTS/LOANS MADE: Only in securities without a secondary market
TYPES OF FINANCING: LOANS: Equipment, LEASES: Single-investor; Leveraged; Operating; Tax-oriented lease brokerage; Lease syndications, OTHER SERVICES PROVIDED: Purchase of leases from other lessors (i.e. secondary lease market)
PREFERRED TYPES OF INDUSTRIES/INVESTMENTS: Aircraft, Railcars, Barges
GEOGRAPHIC LIMITS OF INVESTMENTS/LOANS: International
RANGE OF INV./LOAN PER BUSINESS: Min. $500,000; Max. $25,000,000
PREFERRED TERM FOR LOANS & LEASES: Min. 5 years; Max. 15 years
BRANCHES: Lynn E. Burgess, 6850 West Yellowstone Hwy., Casper, WY 82604; (307) 472-3298
William B. McNulty, Jr, 120 S. Riverside Plaza, Chicago, IL 60606; (312) 621-6571
Dennis R. Buchanan, Regency Center, 5th Floor, 5501 LBJ Freeway, Dallas, TX 75240; (214) 386-6684
L. Dwight Giess, 650 South Cherry St., Suite 520, Denver, CO 80222; (303)393-7700
Dennis N. Schneider, GLC Finance Corporation, P.O. Box 25727, Alburguerque, NM 86125; (505) 345-8909
Thomas P. Timmins, 8552 Katy Freeway, Suite 200, Houston, TX 77024; (713) 932-9680
Jesse V. Crewss, One Lakeway Center, Suite 1180, 3900 North Causeway Blvd., Metairie, LA 70002; (504) 838-8852
Lewis B. Everly, Gareld R. Gray II (Doc), 400 Park Avenue, 22nd Floor, New York, NY 10022; (212) 758-5200

COMPANY: **Helm Financial Corporation**
ADDRESS: One Embarcadero Center, Suite 3320
San Francisco, CA 94111
PHONE: (415) 398-4510
CONTACT OFFICER(S): Robert L. Hoverson

COMPANY: **Itel Corp., Portfolio Mgmt. Div.**
ADDRESS: 55 Francisco Street
San Francisco, CA 94133
PHONE: (415) 955-0000
CONTACT OFFICER(S): Gay V. Weake

COMPANY: **Matrix Leasing International, Inc.**
ADDRESS: 555 California Street, Suite 5190
San Francisco, CA 94104
PHONE: (415) 398-0300
TYPE OF INSTITUTION: Wholly owned subsidiary of flagship bank of major multibank holding company
CONTACT OFFICER(S): Harold K. Criswell, President
Joseph Lapeglia, Senior V.P.
Joseph Ebnor, V.P.
ASSETS: $15 billion
INVESTMENTS/LOANS MADE: For own account, Through private placements, underwriting public offerings
TYPES OF FINANCING: LEASES: Single-investor; Leveraged; Tax leases; Non-tax leases; Tax-oriented lease brokerage; Lease syndications, INTERNATIONAL, OTHER SERVICES PROVIDED: Lease analysis/advisors
PREFERRED TYPES OF INDUSTRIES/INVESTMENTS: Prefer ships, plants, airplanes, etc.
GEOGRAPHIC LIMITS OF INVESTMENTS/LOANS: International
RANGE OF INV./LOAN PER BUSINESS: Min. $5,000,000; Max. $150,000,000
PREFERRED TERM FOR LOANS & LEASES: Min. 3-5 years; Max. 20+ years
BUSINESS CHARACTERISTICS DESIRED-REQUIRED: Other: Borrowers must be substantial, established, rated Ba or better or its equivalent
BRANCHES: Stephen Hirsch, 122 E. 42nd St., New York, NY 10017; (212) 867-4690
Joseph LaPaglia, 210 W. Main st., Suite 202, Tutson, CA 92680; (714) 544-0496
Joseph Ebner, 8600 W. Bryn Mawr Ave., Suite 200N, Chicago, IL 60631; (312) 298-7600
Charles M. Tilden, 120 Ss. 6th Street, Minneapolis, MN 55402; (612) 370-4340

COMPANY: **Polaris Aircraft Leasing Corporation**
ADDRESS: 600 Montgomery Street
San Francisco, CA 94111
PHONE: (415) 362-0333
TYPE OF INSTITUTION: Leasing Company
CONTACT OFFICER(S): Peter G. Pfendler, President
Marc P. Desautels, Executive Vice President
Marian M. Jung, Controller
TYPES OF FINANCING: LEASES: Leveraged; Tax leases; Non-tax leases; Operating; Lease syndications
PREFERRED TYPES OF INDUSTRIES/INVESTMENTS: Aircraft
GEOGRAPHIC LIMITS OF INVESTMENTS/LOANS: National
PREFERRED TERM FOR LOANS & LEASES: Max. 15 years

COMPANY: **Savance Corporation**
ADDRESS: 45 Belden Street

San Francisco, CA 94104
PHONE: (415) 956-6000
CONTACT OFFICER(S): Walter J. Cummings, III

COMPANY: **Security Pacific Leasing Corp.**
ADDRESS: Four Embarcadero Center, Suite 1200
San Francisco, CA 94111
PHONE: (415) 445-4461
CONTACT OFFICER(S): Norman L. Chapman

COMPANY: **Steiner Financial Corporation**
ADDRESS: One Market Plaza, Suite 2510
San Francisco, CA 94105
PHONE: (415) 777-4600
CONTACT OFFICER(S): Paul C. Kepler

COMPANY: **Transamerica Equipment Leasing Company**
ADDRESS: 600 Montgomery Street, P.O. Box 7994
San Francisco, CA 94120
PHONE: (415) 983-5000
CONTACT OFFICER(S): James G. Mangan

COMPANY: **TXL Corporation**
ADDRESS: One Embarcadero Center, Suite 3800
San Francisco, CA 94111
PHONE: (415) 434-0850
CONTACT OFFICER(S): Jay Stevens

COMPANY: **U.S. Leasing International**
ADDRESS: 633 Battery Street
San Francisco, CA 94111
PHONE: (415) 445-7512
CONTACT OFFICER(S): John H. Giddens

COMPANY: **Wells Fargo Leasing Corporation**
ADDRESS: 101 California Street, Suite 2800
San Francisco, CA 94111
PHONE: (415) 989-8730
TYPE OF INSTITUTION: Leasing Subsidiary of Wells Fargo & Company
CONTACT OFFICER(S): David A. Brown, Senior V.P. & Chief Marketing Officer
Richard V. Harris, V.P. & National Sales Manager
ASSETS: $1 billion (approx.)
INVESTMENTS/LOANS MADE: For own account & syndication
TYPES OF FINANCING: LEASES: Single-investor; Leveraged; Lease syndications; Vendor financing programs
PREFERRED TYPES OF INDUSTRIES/INVESTMENTS: Profitable private sector business enterprises
GEOGRAPHIC LIMITS OF INVESTMENTS/LOANS: National; International
RANGE OF INV./LOAN PER BUSINESS: Min. $5,000,000; Max. $50,000,000 (Vendor minimum $50,000)
PREFERRED TERM FOR LOANS & LEASES: Min. 3 years; Max. 20 years
BUSINESS CHARACTERISTICS DESIRED-REQUIRED: Minimum number of years in business: 5
REFERRALS ACCEPTED FROM: All sources
BRANCHES: William A. Sellier, Regional Manager, 101 California Street, Suite 2800, San Francisco, CA 94111; (415) 399-5896
Glen P. Davis, Regional Manager, 55 West Monroe Street, Suite 1100, Chicago, IL 60603; (312) 782-0881
Richard Vogt, Regional Manager, Chrysler Building, 405 Lexington Ave., New York, NY 10174; (212) 697-7377

COMPANY: **Commercial & Industrial Leasing Company**
ADDRESS: 1777 Hamilton Avenue, Suite 204
San Jose, CA 95125
PHONE: (408) 448-2400
CONTACT OFFICER(S): Thomas C. Evans

COMPANY: **Western Technology Investment**
ADDRESS: 1792 Technology Drive
San Jose, CA 95110
PHONE: (408) 298-8577
CONTACT OFFICER(S): Ronald W. Swenson

COMPANY: **Bankers Leasing & Financial Corporation**
ADDRESS: 2655 Campus Drive
San Mateo, CA 94403
PHONE: (415) 573-1200
CONTACT OFFICER(S): Bernard Goldman

COMPANY: **Intercoastal Leasing**
ADDRESS: P.O. Box 3535
San Rafael, CA 94912
PHONE: (415) 457-5100
CONTACT OFFICER(S): Michael Sabarese

COMPANY: **Phoenix Leasing, Inc.**
ADDRESS: 2401 Kerner Blvd.
San Rafael, CA 94901-5527
PHONE: (415) 485-4500
TYPE OF INSTITUTION: Leasing Co.
CONTACT OFFICER(S): Paritosh Choksi
TYPES OF FINANCING: LEASES: Single-investor; Leveraged; Tax leases; Non-tax leases; Operating; Tax-oriented lease brokerage; Lease syndications; Vendor financing programs
PREFERRED TYPES OF INDUSTRIES/INVESTMENTS: Prefer Computers
GEOGRAPHIC LIMITS OF INVESTMENTS/LOANS: National
RANGE OF INVESTMENT/LOAN: Min $35.000
PREFERRED TERM FOR LOANS & LEASES: Min. 1 year; Max. 5 years

COMPANY: **Triple C. Leasing, Inc.**
ADDRESS: 68 Mitchell Blvd., Ste. 270
San Rafael, CA 94903
PHONE: (415) 472-7464
TYPE OF INSTITUTION: Leasing Co.
CONTACT OFFICER(S): Harold McAfee, Pres.
ASSETS: 26 million
TYPES OF FINANCING: LEASES: Straight financing; OTHER: Will be doing tax leases

PREFERRED TYPES OF INDUSTRIES/INVESTMENTS: Computers; Heavy Machinery; Medical Leasing; Agricultural
WILL NOT CONSIDER: Aircraft, vehicles, boats
GEOGRAPHIC LIMITS OF INVESTMENTS/LOANS: 11 Western states
RANGE OF INV./LOAN PER BUSINESS: Min. $25,000
PREFERRED TERM FOR LOANS & LEASES: Min. 3 years; Max. 7 years
BUSINESS CHARACTERISTICS DESIRED-REQUIRED: Minimum number of years in business: 3; Other: depends on size of lease request
REFERRALS ACCEPTED FROM: Investment/Mortgage banker; Borrower/Investee
BRANCHES: Dave Johnson, Los Angeles, CA; (714) 624-9649
Ken Nielson, Spokane, WA; (509) 926-2650

COMPANY: **Amplicon, Inc.**
ADDRESS: 2130 E. Fourth Street, Suite 250
Santa Ana, CA 92705
PHONE: (714) 854-0217
CONTACT OFFICER(S): Patrick E. Paddon

COMPANY: **Puritan Leasing Co.**
ADDRESS: 1600 Anacapa St.
Santa Barbara, CA 93102
PHONE: (805) 966-3187
TYPE OF INSTITUTION: Leasing Co.
CONTACT OFFICER(S): Paul Menzel, V.P., General Manager
TYPES OF FINANCING: LEASES: Single-investor; Tax leases; Tax-oriented lease brokerage
GEOGRAPHIC LIMITS OF INVESTMENTS/LOANS: Regional
RANGE OF INV./LOAN PER BUSINESS: Min. $50,000; Max. $3 million
PREFERRED TERM FOR LOANS & LEASES: variable
REMARKS: Credit Lessor

COMPANY: **Rolm Credit Corporation**
ADDRESS: 4900 Old Ironsides Drive
Santa Clara, CA 95050
PHONE: (408) 988-2900

COMPANY: **HB Enterprises**
ADDRESS: 3231 Ocean Park Boulevard, Suite 109
Santa Monica, CA 90405
PHONE: (213) 870-3735
CONTACT OFFICER(S): L. H. Bennett

COMPANY: **MNC-Western Leasing & Capital**
ADDRESS: Three Harbor Drive, Suite 111
Sausalito, CA 94965
PHONE: (415) 331-7321
CONTACT OFFICER(S): J. Leslie Riddel

COMPANY: **Unicom Computer Corporation**
ADDRESS: 2829 Bridgeway Boulevard
Sausalito, CA 94965
PHONE: (415) 332-2585
CONTACT OFFICER(S): Peter Dooley

COMPANY: **Utilities Leasing Corporation**
ADDRESS: 24 Varda Landing Road
Sausalito, CA 94965
PHONE: (415) 332-6450
CONTACT OFFICER(S): Joseph G. Veit, Jr.

COMPANY: **Memorex Finance Company**
ADDRESS: 1153 Bordeaux Drive, Suite 201
Sunnyvale, CA 94089
PHONE: (408) 734-2261
CONTACT OFFICER(S): Clyge J. Johnston

COMPANY: **TSC Leasing Corporation**
ADDRESS: 1252 Orleans Drive
Sunnyvale, CA 94088
PHONE: (408) 734-9720
TYPE OF INSTITUTION: Venture Capital Firm
CONTACT OFFICER(S): Stanley Marquis
ASSETS: 3.5 Million
INVESTMENTS/LOANS MADE: Through private placement
INVESTMENTS/LOANS MADE: Only in securities without a secondary market (9b-9h)
TYPES OF FINANCING: VENTURE CAPITAL: Research & Development; Start-up from developed product stage; First-stage (less than 1 year); Second-stage (generally 1-3 years); REAL ESTATE: Partnerships/Syndications.
PREFERRED TYPES OF INDUSTRIES/INVESTMENTS: Low Technology, Real Estate
WILL NOT CONSIDER: Biotechnology
GEOGRAPHIC LIMITS OF INVESTMENTS/LOANS: Local
RANGE OF INV./LOAN PER BUSINESS: Min. $ None; Max. $1 MM
BUSINESS CHARACTERISICS DESIRED: Minimum number of years in business; 3; Min. annual sales $1 MM; Min net worth $positive; Min. annual net income $positive; Min. annual cash flow $positive

COMPANY: **California Group Services**
ADDRESS: P.O. Box 8012
Walnut Creek, CA 94596
PHONE: (415) 945-0660
CONTACT OFFICER(S): Fred Shieman

COMPANY: **First Industrial Financial**
ADDRESS: 791 Chambers Road, Suite 412
Aurora, CO 80011
CONTACT OFFICER(S): Paul R. Sandquist

COMPANY: **Municipal Funding Corp.**
ADDRESS: 3151 S. Vaughn Way, Suite #510
Aurora, CO 80014
PHONE: (303) 696-6600
TYPE OF INSTITUTION: Leasing Co.

CONTACT OFFICER(S): John Blanton, Chairman of the board
Dan Grotle, President
TYPES OF FINANCING: LEASES: Single-investor; Other: Municipal leasing, OTHER SERVICES PROVIDED: Lease strictly political subdivisions; Installment sale leases
PREFERRED TYPES OF INDUSTRIES/INVESTMENTS: Tax-exempt entity
GEOGRAPHIC LIMITS OF INVESTMENTS/LOANS: National
RANGE OF INV./LOAN PER BUSINESS: Min. $15,000
PREFERRED TERM FOR LOANS & LEASES: Max. 5 years

COMPANY: **Capital Associates International Inc.**
ADDRESS: 3393 Iris Avenue
Boulder, CO 80301
PHONE: (303) 442-0100
CONTACT OFFICER(S): Gary M. Jacobs

COMPANY: **Leasetec Corporation**
ADDRESS: 1426 Pearl Street
Boulder, CO 80302
PHONE: (303) 443-8064
CONTACT OFFICER(S): Richard Barrett

COMPANY: **Storage Technology Leasing Corporation**
ADDRESS: 2945 Center Green Court South
Boulder, CO 80301
PHONE: (303) 440-4600
TYPE OF INSTITUTION: Leasing subsidiary of manufacturing company
CONTACT OFFICER(S): N.D. Bernt; President
Jeffery J. Hiller; Manager of Operation
Ann Ergenbright; Equity Sales
ASSETS: $35,000,000
INVESTMENTS/LOANS MADE: For own (company's or principals') account
For managed accounts
Through private placements
Through underwriting public offerings
TYPES OF FINANCING: LEASES: Single-investor; Leveraged; Tax leases; Non-tax leases; Operating; Tax-oriented lease brokerage; Lease syndications; Vendor financing programs; Other unique leasing opportunities
PREFERRED TYPES OF INDUSTRIES/INVESTMENTS: Computers and Computer Peripheral Equipment
GEOGRAPHIC LIMITS OF INVESTMENTS/LOANS: National
RANGE OF INV./LOAN PER BUSINESS: Min. $250,000; Max. $ no maximum
PREFERRED TERM FOR LOANS & LEASES: Min. 3 years; Max. 5 years
REFERRALS ACCEPTED FROM: Investment/Mortgage banker and Borrower/Investee

COMPANY: **Imperial Municipal Services Group, Inc.**
ADDRESS: 7800 East Union Avenue, Suite 400
Denver, CO 80237
PHONE: (303) 694-1700
CONTACT OFFICER(S): Donovan Stevens

COMPANY: **IntraWest Leasing Company**
ADDRESS: 633 17th St., Suite 1970
Denver, CO 80202
PHONE: (303) 292-0515
TYPE OF INSTITUTION: Leasing Co.
CONTACT OFFICER(S): Robert S. McRae, President
Kirk D. Reed, Sr. Vice President
William G. Loeber, Vice President
ASSETS: $67,000,000 managed
INVESTMENTS/LOANS MADE: In securities with a secondary market and in securities without a secondary market
TYPES OF FINANCING: LEASES: Single-investor; Tax leases; Non-tax leases
PREFERRED TYPES OF INDUSTRIES/INVESTMENTS: Varied
WILL NOT CONSIDER: Municipal and automobile leases
GEOGRAPHIC LIMITS OF INVESTMENTS/LOANS: National
RANGE OF INV./LOAN PER BUSINESS: Min. $50,000
PREFERRED TERM FOR LOANS & LEASES: Min. 3; Max. 7 years
BUSINESS CHARACTERISTICS DESIRED-REQUIRED: Variable

COMPANY: **Lease Finance, Inc.**
ADDRESS: 600 S. Cherry St., Suite 314
Denver, CO 80222
PHONE: (303) 321-0400
TYPE OF INSTITUTION: Leasing company
CONTACT OFFICER(S): William R. Jones, President
D.K. Stemsrud, V.P. & Secretary
TYPES OF FINANCING: LEASES: Tax leases; Non-tax leases; Other: Finance lease, OTHER SERVICES PROVIDED: Full pay-out financing
PREFERRED TYPES OF INDUSTRIES/INVESTMENTS: Diversified
GEOGRAPHIC LIMITS OF INVESTMENTS/LOANS: Regional
RANGE OF INV./LOAN PER BUSINESS: Min. $2,000; Max. $100,000
PREFERRED TERM FOR LOANS & LEASES: Min. 2 years; Max. 5 years
BUSINESS CHARACTERISTICS DESIRED-REQUIRED: Minimum number of years in business: 0
REMARKS: Broker ability up to 1,000,000

COMPANY: **Republic Financial Corp.**
ADDRESS: P.O. Box 22564
Denver, CO 80222
PHONE: (303) 751-3501
TYPE OF INSTITUTION: Equipment leasing
CONTACT OFFICER(S): James H. Possehl, President
Robert Jenkins, V.P. Marketing
Mike Ricks, V.P. Operations

ASSETS: $25,000,000
INVESTMENTS/LOANS MADE: For own account, Through private placements
INVESTMENTS/LOANS MADE: In Securities with a secondary market and in securities without a secondary market
TYPES OF FINANCING; LOANS: Equipment, LEASES: Single-investor; Leveraged; Tax leases; Non-tax leases; Tax-oriented lease brokerage
GEOGRAPHIC LIMITS OF INVESTMENTS/LOANS: National
RANGE OF INV./LOAN PER BUSINESS: Min. $25,000; Max. None
PREFERRED TERM FOR LOANS & LEASES: Min. 2 years; Max. 15 years
REFERRALS ACCEPTED FROM: Investment/Mortgage banker or Borrower/Investee

COMPANY: **Timpte Inc.**
ADDRESS: 5990 N. Washington Street
Denver, CO 80216
PHONE: (303) 893-3366
CONTACT OFFICER(S): Rick Stifel

COMPANY: **Uniwest Financial Corp.**
ADDRESS: 7979 E. Tufts Ave. Parkway, Suite #110
Denver, CO
PHONE: (303) 694-9777
TYPE OF INSTITUTION: Financial Services, Savings and Loan Holdings Co.
CONTACT OFFICER(S): Chuck McKelvey, Executive Vice President Real Estate; James R. Newman, National Credit Manager Leasing; John Holzman, Vice President Securities
ASSETS: $250,000,000
INVESTMENTS/LOANS MADE: For own account; Through private placements
INVESTMENTS/LOANS MADE: In securities with a secondary market and in securities without a secondary market
TYPES OF FINANCING: VENTURE CAPITAL: First-stage (less than 1 year); Second-stage (generally 1-3 years); REAL ESTATE LOANS: Construction; LEASES; REAL ESTATE: Acquisitions; Joint ventures; Partnerships/Syndications
PREFERRED TYPES OF INDUSTRIES/INVESTMENTS: Real Estate, Leasing
GEOGRAPHIC LIMITS OF INVESTMENTS/LOANS: Sun Belt States
RANGE OF INV./LOAN PER BUSINESS: Min. $250,000; Max. $10,000,000
PREFERRED TERM FOR LOANS & LEASES: Min. One-Three years; Max. Thirty years

COMPANY: **First Municipal Leasing Corporation**
ADDRESS: 7840 East Berry Place
Englewood, CO 80111
PHONE: (303) 773-6992
TYPE OF INSTITUTION: Tax-exempt Leasing Corporation
CONTACT OFFICER(S): James D. Colfer, Senior Vice President
John O. Lohre, President
L. Robert Bauers, Executive Vice President
ASSETS: $1,500,000.00
INVESTMENTS/LOANS MADE: For own account; For managed accounts; Through private placements; Through underwriting public offerings
INVESTMENTS/LOANS MADE: In securities with a secondary market and in securities without a secondary market
TYPES OF FINANCING: Tax-exempt Municipal Leases
PREFERRED TYPES OF INDUSTRIES/INVESTMENTS: Equipment leases to political subdivision
WILL NOT CONSIDER: Commercial of Federal Government Leases
GEOGRAPHIC LIMITS OF INVESTMENTS/LOANS: National
RANGE OF INV./LOAN PER BUSINESS: Min. $50,000.00; Max. $ No maximum
PREFERRED TERM FOR LOANS & LEASES: Min. Three years; Max. Ten years
BUSINESS CHARACTERISTICS DESIRED-REQUIRED: Must be a political subdivision
REFERRALS ACCEPTED FROM: Investment/Mortgage banker; Borrower/Investee
BRANCHES: Chester Blakemore, Lewis State Bank Building, Suite 632, 215 South Monroe, Tallahassee, FL 32301, (904) 224-2950
Steven D. Grotewold, 208 South LaSalle Street, Room 2059, Chicago, IL 60604, (312) 726-2945
Jack Young, 140 Mayhew Way, Suite 100, Pleasant Hills, CA 94523, (415) 945-0122.

COMPANY: **BancAmerica Commercial Corporation**
ADDRESS: 777 So. Yarrow St. Suite 101
Lakewood, CO
PHONE: (303) 988-4491
TYPE OF INSTITUTION: Equipment Finance Division
CONTACT OFFICER(S): C. L. Overson, President
George McMackin, V.P. National Credit Director
INVESTMENTS/LOANS MADE: For own account
TYPES OF FIANCING: LOANS: Working Capital; LOANS: Working capital (receivables/inventory); Equipment; LEASES: Single-investor; Non-tax leases; Vendor financing programs
GEOGRAPHIC LIMITS OF INVESTMENTS/LOANS: National

COMPANY: **Mentor Capital Corporation**
ADDRESS: 1457 Ammons Street
Lakewood, CO 80215
PHONE: (303) 234-1717
CONTACT OFFICER(S): Earl Friedman

COMPANY: **Mountain Medical Leasing**
ADDRESS: 10488 W. Centennial Road
Littleton, CO 80127
PHONE: (303) 973-1200
CONTACT OFFICER(S): Jon P. Jung

COMPANY: **Parker Benjamin, Inc.**
ADDRESS: 120 Mountain Avenue
Bloomfield, CT 06002
PHONE: (203) 242-7277

LEASING COMPANIES

(Lessors. Also see Commercial Bankers and Finance Companies, Insurance Companies and Investment Bankers)

TYPE OF INSTITUTION: Private Investment Bank serving primarily middle market companies and real estate developers
CONTACT OFFICER(S): Paul M. Ruby, President, Mergers and Acquisitions, Venture Capital
Thomas A. D'Avanzo, Executive Vice President, Private Placement of Debt, Real Estate Financing, Industrial Revenue Bonds Apprisals
INVESTMENTS/LOANS MADE: Through private placements
INVESTMENTS/LOANS MADE: VENTURE CAPITAL: Research & Development; Start-up from developed product stage; First-stage (less than 1 year); Second-stage (generally 1-3 years); Later-stage expansion; Buy-outs/Acquistions; LOANS: Unsecured to credits above Baa; Working capital (receivables/inventory); Equipment; Equity-related; Other: Industrial Revenue Bonds; REAL ESTATE LOANS: Long-term senior mtg.; Intermediate-term senior mtg.; Subordinated; Wraparounds; Land; Land development; Construction; Gap; Standbys; Industrial revenue bonds; LEASES: Single-Investor; Leveraged; Tax leases; Non-tax leases; Operating; Tax-oriented lease brokerage; vendor financing programs; REAL ESTATE: Acquisitions; Joint ventures; OTHER SERVICES PROVIDED: Appraisal of privately owned businesses
PREFERRED TYPES OF INDUSTRIES/INVESTMENTS: All
GEOGRAPHIC LIMITS OF INVESTMENTS/LOANS: International
RANGE OF INV./LOAN PER BUSINESS: Min. $500,000
REMARKS: The firm represents pension fund money for prime real estate development projects.

COMPANY: **Scientific Leasing Inc.**
ADDRESS: 790 Farmington Ave.
Farmington, CT 06032
PHONE: (203) 677-8700
TYPE OF INSTITUTION: Independent Equipment Lessors
CONTACT OFFICER(S): Barry R. Bronfin, Chairman & President; Leonard S. Cohen, Exec. V.P.
W. Barry Tanner, V.P.-Finance
Vincent T. Jazwinski, Sales and Marketing
David J. Spiegel, V.P. and Gen. Counsel
Robert P. Medwid, V.P., Financial Analysis & Reporting
ASSETS: $149,000,000 at 6/30/84
INVESTMENTS/LOANS MADE: For own account
TYPES OF FINANCING: LEASES: Finance leases, operating leases; Vendor financing programs
PREFERRED TYPES OF INDUSTRIES/INVESTMENTS: Technology-oriented industries; health care providers; research & development equipment, medical systems, communications, data processing, other hi-tech equipment
GEOGRAPHIC LIMITS OF INVESTMENTS/LOANS: National
REFERRALS ACCEPTED FROM: Brokers

COMPANY: **The Bi-Modal Corporation**
ADDRESS: 200 Railroad Avenue, P.O. Box 935
Greenwich, CT 06830
PHONE: (203) 629-4692
CONTACT OFFICER(S): James Louney

COMPANY: **Connecticcut Bank & Trust, R.E. Division**
ADDRESS: One Constitution Plaza
Hartford, CT 06115
PHONE: (203) 244-6269
TYPE OF INSTITUTION: Construction lender, permanent lender; intermediate lender
CONTACT OFFICER(S): Oliver W. Park, President
ASSETS: $6 billion
INVESTMENTS/LOANS MADE:
TYPES OF FINANCING: SECONDARY-MARKET CORPORATE SECURITIES, LOANS: Unsecured; Working capital; Equipment; Equity-related; Other: Construction lending, Lease finaancing, REAL ESTATE LOANS: Intermediate-term senior mtg.; Wraparounds; Land; Land development; Construction; Gap; Industrial revenue bonds, FACTORING, LEASES: Single—investor; Leveraged; Non-tax leases; Operating; Vendor financing programs, INTERNATIONAL
GEOGRAPHIC LIMITS OF INVESTMENTS/LOANS: National; International
BUSINESS CHARACTERISTICS DESIRED-REQUIRED:
REFERRALS ACCEPPTED FROM: Investment/Mortgage banker or Borrower/Investee
REMARKS: 140 Branches; out on loan: $1 billion in Real Estate

COMPANY: **Sonecor Credit Corporation**
ADDRESS: 142 Temple Street
New Haven, CT 06510
PHONE: (203) 624-1596
CONTACT OFFICER(S): Michael J. Marchese

COMPANY: **Leasing Associates Corporation**
ADDRESS: P.O. Box 272, 177 Sound Beach Avenue
Old Greenwich, CT 06870
PHONE: (203) 637-8500
CONTACT OFFICER(S): Joseph H. Rice

COMPANY: **General Electric Credit Corp.**
ADDRESS: P.O. Box 8300, 260 Long Ridge Road
Stamford, CT 06902
PHONE: (203) 357-4460
CONTACT OFFICER(S): Gary C. Wendt

COMPANY: **Intech Leasing Corporation**
ADDRESS: The Intech Building, 10 Signal Road
Stamford, CT 06902
PHONE: (203) 324-1300
CONTACT OFFICER(S): Donald A. Bernard

COMPANY: **Litton Financial Services**
ADDRESS: Ten Stamford Forum, P.O. Box 6011
Stamford, CT 06904
PHONE: (203) 328-2700
TYPE OF INSTITUTION: Leasing Co.
CONTACT OFFICER(S): Robert L. Burke, Senior Vice President, Leaveraged Leasing

Douglas D. Perez, Senior Vice President, Vendor Finance Programs
John F. Spain, Jr., Senior Vice President, Single Investor Tax Leases
ASSETS: $900 million
TYPES OF FINANCING: LOANS: Equipment; LEASES: Single-investor; Leveraged; Tax leases; Non-tax leases; Tax-oriented lease brokerage; Lease syndications; Vendor financing programs
PREFERRED TYPES OF INDUSTRIES/INVESTMENTS: Investment decisions are based on current financial position of customer and type of equipment
WILL NOT CONSIDER: Real Estate
GEOGRAPHIC LIMITS OF INVESTMENTS/LOANS: International
RANGE OF INV./LOAN PER BUSINESS: Min. $1,000; Max. $50,000,000
PREFERRED TERMS FOR LOANS & LEASES: Min. 2 (Middle Market); Max. 10 (Middle Market) years
BUSINESS CHARACTERISTICS DESIRED-REQUIRED: Minimum number of years in business: 3; Min. net worth $300,000 unless supported by vendor program
REFFERALS ACCEPTED FROM: Investment/Mortgage banker or Borrower/Investee

COMPANY: **Somerset Investment Services**
ADDRESS: 274 Riverside Avenue
Westport, CT 06880
PHONE: (203) 226-1279
CONTACT OFFICER(S): Joseph A. Pallone

COMPANY: **Technology Finance Group, Inc.**
ADDRESS: 315 Post Road W.
Westport, CT 06880
PHONE: (203) 226-7501
TYPE OF INSTITUTION: Leasing Co.
CONTACT OFFICER(S): Jerry Minsky, Pres.
TYPES OF FINANCING: LEASES: Single-investor; Leveraged; Tax leases; Non-tax leases; Tax-oriented lease brokerage; Lease syndications; Vendor financing programs
GEOGRAPHIC LIMITS OF INVESTMENTS/LOANS: Regional
RANGE OF INV./LOAN PER BUSINESS: Min. $250,000
BUSINESS CHARACTERISTICS DESIRED-REQUIRED: Minimum number of years in business: 3 yrs. financial statements
REFERRALS ACCEPTED FROM: Investment/Mortgage banker; Borrower/Investee

COMPANY: **The Trend Group LTD.**
ADDRESS: 90 Post Road East
Westport, CT 06880
PHONE: (203) 226-7468
CONTACT OFFICER(S): D. C. Wehrly

COMPANY: **North American Bank & Trust Company**
ADDRESS: 1776 Meriden Road
Wolcott, CT 06716
PHONE: (203) 879-2577
TYPE OF INSTITUTION: Commercial Bank
CONTACT OFFICER(S): Kenneth G. Brennan, V.P., Leasing Dept.
ASSETS: $120,000.000.
INVESTMENT/LOANS MADE: For own account; Through private placements
TYPES OF FINANCING: LEASES: Single-investor; Tax leases; Non-tax leases; Vendor financing programs; Municipal
PREFERRED TYPES OF INDUSTRIES/INVESTMENTS: Any type
GEOGRAPHIC LIMITS OF INVESTMENTS/LOANS: State
RANGE OF INV./LOAN PER BUSINESS: Min. $10,000; Max. $1,000,000
PREFERRED TERM FOR LOANS & LEASES: Min. 12 mos.; Max. 60 mos.
BUSINESS CHARACTERISTICS DESIRED-REQUIRED: Minimum number of years in business: 3
REFERRALS ACCEPTED FROM: Investment/Mortgage banker; Borrower/Investor

COMPANY: **Leasing Systems, Inc.**
ADDRESS: 1413 K St., N.W. Ste., 1200
Washington, DC 20005
PHONE: (202) 872-0333
TYPE OF INSTITUTION: Long Term Vehicle & Equipment Leasing Corporation
CONTACT OFFICER(S): Lee E. Nathanson, President (CEO)
ASSETS: over 20 mil.
INVESTMENTS/LOANS MADE: For own account
TYPES OF FINANCING: Asset Based financing, LEASES: Single-investor; Tax leases; Non-tax leases; Operating; Vendor financing programs, OTHER SERVICES PROVIDED: Vehicle Leasing (Long Term) Third party lease transactions
PREFERRED TYPES OF INDUSTRIES/INVESTMENTS: Commercial clients only; Any industrial, medical, aviation or commercial capital equipment
WILL NOT CONSIDER: Life support equipment
GEOGRAPHIC LIMITS OF INVESTMENTS/LOANS: National
RANGE OF INV./LOAN PER BUSINESS: Min. $100,000-$300,000; Max. Several million
PREFERRED TERM FOR LOANS & LEASES: Min. 1 year; Max. 5-7 years
BUSINESS CHARACTERISTICS DESIRED-REQUIRED: Minimum number of years in business: 0; Other: Will consider any reasonable credit
REFERRALS ACCEPTED FROM: Investment/Mortgage banker or Borrower/Investee
BRANCHES: Edward Hutman, 11634 Boiling Brook Place, Rockville, MD 20852; (301) 770-1811

LEASING COMPANIES

(Lessors. Also see Commercial Bankers and Finance Companies, Insurance Companies and Investment Bankers)

DISTRICT OF COLUMBIA

COMPANY: **MTV Leasing Corporation**
ADDRESS: 2033 M. St., N.W., Suite 402
Washington, DC 20036
PHONE: (202) 293-7047
TYPE OF INSTITUTION: Equipment Leasing Company
CONTACT OFFICER(S): John M. Jacquemin, President
INVESTMENTS/LOANS MADE: For own account; Through private placements
INVESTMENTS/LOANS MADE: Only in securities without a secondary market
TYPES OF FINANCING: LEASES: Single-investor; Leveraged; Tax leases; Operating; Tax-oriented lease brokerage
PREFERRED TYPES OF INDUSTRIES/INVESTMENTS: BAA or equivalent credit; no industry preference; all types of equipment (computers, major medical, telephone systems, construction, rail and others)
GEOGRAPHIC LIMITS OF INVESTMENTS/LOANS: National
RANGE OF INV./LOAN PER BUSINESS: Min. $200,000; Max. $5,000,000
PREFERRED TERM FOR LOANS & LEASES: Min. 3; Max. 7 years
BUSINESS CHARACTERISTICS DESIRED-REQUIRED: Minimum number of years in business: 10; Min. annual sales $100 MM Min. net worth $30 MM; Min. annual net income $5MM
REFERRALS ACCEPTED FROM: Investment/Mortgage banker; Borrower/Investee

COMPANY: **National Cooperative Services Corporation**
ADDRESS: 1115 - 30th Street N.W.
Washington, DC 20007
PHONE: (202) 337-6700
CONTACT OFFICER(S): Richard B. Bulman

FLORIDA

COMPANY: **American Capital Group, Inc.**
ADDRESS: 3040 Gulf to Bay
Clearwater, FL 33519
PHONE: (813) 797-2090
CONTACT OFFICER(S): Richard D. Chandler

COMPANY: **Financial Industries Leasing Corporation**
ADDRESS: 1307 U.S. Hwy 19 South, Suite 408
Clearwater, FL 33546
PHONE: (404) 396-1390
CONTACT OFFICER(S): Richard L. Moore

COMPANY: **Caribank Leasing Corporation**
ADDRESS: 255 E. Dania Beach Boulevard
Dania, FL 33004
PHONE: (305) 925-2211
CONTACT OFFICER(S): Michael Chaney

COMPANY: **Capital Group, Inc.**
ADDRESS: 701 W. Cypress Creek Rd.
Ft. Lauderdale, FL 33309
PHONE: (305) 772-1954
TYPE OF INSTITUTION: Leasing Co.
CONTACT OFFICER(S): Clifford W. Buck, President
TYPES OF FINANCING: LEASES: Single-investor; Leveraged; Tax leases; Non-tax leases; Operating; Tax-oriented lease brokerage; Lease syndications; Vendor financing programs
PREFERRED TYPES OF INDUSTRIES/INVESTMENTS: Diversified
GEOGRAPHIC LIMITS OF INVESTMENTS/LOANS: National
RANGE OF INV./LOAN PER BUSINESS: Min. $5,000; Max. $5,000,000
PREFERRED TERM FOR LOANS & LEASES: Min. 1; Max. 10 years
BUSINESS CHARACTERISTICS DESIRED-REQUIRED: Good Credit

COMPANY: **Sterling Financial Corporation**
ADDRESS: Suite 506, International Bldg., 2455 East Sunrise Boulevard
Ft. Lauderdale, FL 33304
PHONE: (305) 563-7774
CONTACT OFFICER(S): David W. Steketee

COMPANY: **Sunbelt Financial Systems Inc.**
ADDRESS: 2711 NW 6th Street, Suite C
Gainesville, FL 32602
PHONE: (904) 375-3285
CONTACT OFFICER(S): David S. Cook

COMPANY: **Coulter Leasing Corporation**
ADDRESS: 601 West 20th Street
Hialeah, FL 33010
PHONE: (305) 885-0131
CONTACT OFFICER(S): Barry Friedman

COMPANY: **First Florida Leasing Corporation**
ADDRESS: 1840 W. 49th Street, Ste. 604
Hialeah, FL 33012
PHONE: (305) 823-3022
TYPE OF INSTITUTION: Leasing Co.
CONTACT OFFICER(S): Bryan Miller, Pres.
Al Levy, Sales Manager
Lee Stanford, Sales Manager
TYPES OF FINANCING: LOANS; LEASES: Single-investor; Leveraged; Tax leases; Non-tax leases; Operating; Tax-oriented lease brokerage; Lease syndications; Vendor financing programs
PREFERRED TYPES OF INDUSTRIES/INVESTMENTS: Computers, Planes, Heavy Equipment, Trucks, Tractors, Trailers, Boats, Medical Equipment, etc.
WILL NOT CONSIDER: Autos, small ticket items
GEOGRAPHIC LIMITS OF INVESTMENTS/LOANS: International for leasing; Loans: Maine to Flordia
RANGE OF INV./LOAN PER BUSINESS: Min. $10,000; Max. None
PREFERRED TERM FOR LOANS & LEASES: Min. 3 years; Max. 7 years
BUSINESS CHARACTERISTICS DESIRED-REQUIRED; Minimum number of years in business: 2 years; Min. net worth $2½ X (times) lease amount; Other: look at each as it comes up

COMPANY: **EMIDC Associates Inc.**
ADDRESS: 409 Palm Springs Blvd.
Indian Harbour Beach, FL 33293
PHONE: (305) 777-2271
CONTACT OFFICER(S): Ron Proffitt

COMPANY: **Harris Corporation**
ADDRESS: 1025 NASA Blvd.
Melbourne, FL 32919
PHONE: (305) 727-9104
CONTACT OFFICER(S): L.G. Smith

COMPANY: **American Bankers Leasing Inc.**
ADDRESS: P.O. Box 1139, 3 Grove Isle Dr., Penthouse 6
Miami, FL 33233
PHONE: (305) 285-0023
CONTACT OFFICER(S): Angelo G. Mannarino

COMPANY: **Columbia Commercial Leasing Corporation**
ADDRESS: 8798 N.W. 15th Street
Miami, FL 33172
PHONE: (305) 591-8800
CONTACT OFFICER(S): Raymond Kreger

COMPANY: **Compuquip Leasing Corporation**
ADDRESS: P.O. Box 55-7219
Miami, FL 33255
PHONE: (305) 856-4021
CONTACT OFFICER(S): Alberto Dosal

COMPANY: **Denrich Leasing Inc.**
ADDRESS: 1401 Brickell Avenue, Suite 204
Miami, FL 33131
PHONE: (305) 358-1094
CONTACT OFFICER(S): Richard Steele

COMPANY: **Ryder System Inc.**
ADDRESS: 3600 NW 82 Avenue
Miami, FL 33166
PHONE: (305) 593-3241
CONTACT OFFICER(S): C. Phillip Alexander

COMPANY: **Southeast Bank N.A.**
ADDRESS: One Southeast Financial Center
Miami, FL 33131
PHONE: (305) 375-7335
TYPE OF INSTITUTION: Southeast Bank Leasing Company
CONTACT OFFICER(S): Robert E. Lerch Jr., President-Senior Vice President
John F. McCarthy, Vice President-General Manager
Gary E. Jaggard, Leasing Officer-Marketing
ASSETS: Servicing volume over $9,000,000,000+
INVESTMENTS/LOANS MADE: For own account
INVESTMENTS/LOANS MADE: In securities with a secondary market and in securities without a secondary market
TYPES OF FINANCING: LOANS: Equipment, LEASES: Single-investor; Leveraged; Tax leases; Operating; Tax-oriented lease brokerage; Lease syndications
PREFERRED TYPES OF INDUSTRIES/INVESTMENTS: All types of industries, emphasis on transportation, heavy equipment, computer, and telecommunications
WILL NOT CONSIDER: Restaurant industries
GEOGRAPHIC LIMITS OF INVESTMENTS/LOANS: State; Regional
RANGE OF INV./LOAN PER BUSINESS: Min. $50,000; Max. $60,000,000
PREFERRED TERM FOR LOANS & LEASES: Min. 3 years; Max. 10 years
BUSINESS CHARACTERISTICS DESIRED-REQUIRED: Minimum number of years in business: 3; Min. annual sales $1,000,000; Min. net worth $100,000
BRANCHES: Mark Eddy, 201 N. Franklin St., Tampa, FL 33602; (813) 223-2346
Jack Gintowt, 6451 N. Federal Hwy., Ft. Lauderdale, FL 33308; (305) 492-4576
John Bearzi, 201 E. Pine St., Orlando, FL 32801; (305) 237-2148
Ed Clay, One Independence Square, Jacksonville, FL 32202; (904) 350-1730

COMPANY: **Quincy Midwest Leasing, Inc.**
ADDRESS: Box 487
Mt. Dora, FL 32757
CONTACT OFFICER(S): W.E. Chapin

COMPANY: **J & D Capital Corp.**
ADDRESS: 12747 Biscayne Blvd.
North Miami, FL 33181
PHONE: (305) 893-0303
TYPE OF INSTITUTION: SBIC
CONTACT OFFICER(S): Jack Carmel, President
INVESTMENTS/LOANS MADE: For own account
TYPES OF FINANCING: VENTURE CAPITAL: Second-stage. LOANS: Equipment, REAL ESTATE LOANS:

Wraparounds; FACTORING. LEASES. INTERNATIONAL
PREFERRED TYPES OF INDUSTRIES/INVESTMENTS: Small Business Investment Company
GEOGRAPHIC LIMITS OF INVESTMENTS/LOANS: Local; State
RANGE OF INV./LOAN PER BUSINESS: Min. $25,000; Max. $500,000
PREFERRED TERM FOR LOANS & LEASES: Min. 5 years; Max. 15/20 years
REFERRALS ACCEPTED FROM: Investment/Mortgage banker or Borrower/Investee

COMPANY: **Southern Leasing Services, Inc.**
ADDRESS: 618 US #One
North Palm Beach, FL 33408
PHONE: (305) 863-7900; (800) 327-3240 except Florida; (800) 432-4899 in Florida
TYPE OF INSTITUTION: Equipment Lessor
CONTACT OFFICER(S): Jean E. Miller, Asst. V.P.
John P. Little, Pres.
ASSETS: $60,000,000
INVESTMENTS/LOANS MADE: For own account, Through private placements
TYPES OF FINANCING: LOANS: Equipment, LEASES: Single-investor; Non-tax leases
PREFERRED TYPES OF INDUSTRIES/INVESTMENTS: All except aircraft
WILL NOT CONSIDER: Transactions in Arkansas (Louisiana only over $100,000)
GEOGRAPHIC LIMITS OF INVESTMENTS/LOANS: National
RANGE OF INV./LOAN PER BUSINESS: Min. $5,000; Max. No maximum
PREFERRED TERM FOR LOANS & LEASES: Min. 3 years; Max. 5 years
BUSINESS CHARACTERISTICS DESIRED-REQUIRED: Minimum number of years in business: 3
REFERRALS ACCEPTED FROM: Investment/Mortgage banker or Borrower/Investee

COMPANY: **Florida Leasing and Capital Corporation**
ADDRESS: 1001 Executive Center Dr., Suite 251,
Enterprise Bldg.
Orlando, FL 32803
PHONE: (305) 896-3531
CONTACT OFFICER(S): Albert F. Schroeder

COMPANY: **Growth Leasing LTD.**
ADDRESS: 1801 N. Westshore Blvd., Suite 29
Tampa, FL 33607
PHONE: (813) 879-8196
CONTACT OFFICER(S): George Lerner

COMPANY: **GTE Leasing Corporation**
ADDRESS: One Tampa City Center, Suite 1840, 201 N.
Franklin Street
Tampa, FL 33602
PHONE: (813) 229-6000
CONTACT OFFICER(S): Raymond A. Beahn

COMPANY: **Condor Group Holdings**
ADDRESS: 1601 Belvedere Rd.
West Palm Beach, FL 33406
PHONE: (305) 689-4906
TYPE OF INSTITUTION: Equipment leasing, Venture capital
CONTACT OFFICER(S): James A. Carpinello, Chairman of the Board
ASSETS: $24.5 mil
INVESTMENTS/LOANS MADE: For own account, For managed accounts
TYPES OF FINANCING: SECONDARY-MARKET CORPORATE SECURITIES: Common stock; Bonds, VENTURE CAPITAL: Second-stage; Buy-outs/ Acquisitions, LOANS: Equipment; Equity-related, LEASES: Single-investor; Leveraged; Tax leases; Non-tax leases; Operating, Tax-oriented lease brokerage; Lease syndications; Vendor financing programs, REAL ESTATE: Acquisitions; Joint ventures; Partnerships/ Syndications
PREFERRED TYPES OF INDUSTRIES/INVESTMENTS: Capital Equipment Manufacturer; Income Producing Real Estate
GEOGRAPHIC LIMITS OF INVESTMENTS/LOANS: National
RANGE OF INV./LOAN PER BUSINESS: Min. $50,000; Max. $5,000,000
PREFERRED TERM FOR LOANS & LEASES: Min. 3 years; Max. 10 years
BUSINESS CHARACTERISTICS DESIRED-REQUIRED: Minimum number of years in business: 1; Min. annual sales $500,000; Min. net worth $150,000; Min. annual net income $50,000; Min. annual cash flow $75,000
REFERRALS ACCEPTED FROM: Investment/Mortgage banker or Borrower/Investee
REMARKS: Start-ups are done

COMPANY: **CFC International**
ADDRESS: 41 Perimeter Center East, Suite 250
Atlanta, GA 30346
PHONE: (404) 394-3040
CONTACT OFFICERS:: G. Huxley Nixon, Jr, EVP
Kenneth V. Madren, Pres.
Eugene N. Martini, EVP
ASSETS: 20,000,000
INVESTMENTS/LOANS MADE: For own (company's or principals') account; Through private placements
TYPES OF FINANCING: LEASES: Single-investor; Leveraged; Tax leases; Tax-oriented lease brokerage; Lease syndications; INTERNATIONAL (including import/exporting)
PREFERRED TYPES OF INDUSTRIES/INVESTMENTS: No preference
BUSINESS CHARACTERISTICS DESIRED/REQUIRED: Minimum number of years in business: 5; Min. annual sales $100,000,000; Min. net worth $10,000,000
REFERRALS ACCEPTED FROM: Investment/Mortgage banker or Borrower/Investee
BRANCHES: Ross Romary, 5050 Quorum Drive, Suite 420, Dallas TX 75240; (214) 387-9204
Rick Firman, 601 Ewing St., Suite B-7, Princeton, NJ 08540; (609) 921-8025

GEORGIA

COMPANY: **Charter Financial Company**
ADDRESS: 41 Perimeter Center East, Suite 250
Atlanta, GA 30346
PHONE: (404) 394-3040
CONTACT OFFICER(S): Huxley Nixon

COMPANY: **The Citizens and Southern National Bank**
ADDRESS: P.O. Box 4431
Atlanta, GA 30302
PHONE: (404) 491-4188
TYPE OF INSTITUTION: Equipment Financing and Leasing Dept. of C & S National Bank
CONTACT OFFICER(S): G. Fred Costabile, V.P. and Marketing Manager
Bill G. Fite, A.V.P.
David Flanary, A.V.P.
Robert Capalbo, Leasing Officer
ASSETS: $7 billion
INVESTMENTS/LOANS MADE: For own account
TYPES OF FINANCING: LOANS: Equipment; FACTORING; LEASES: Single-investor; Tax leases; Non-tax leases; Lease syndications; OTHER SERVICES PROVIDED: Full service banking for Southeastern Equipment Distributors
PREFERRED TYPES OF INDUSTRIES/INVESTMENTS: Manufacturing; Transportation; Construction; Leasing Companies
GEOGRAPHIC LIMITS OF INVESTMENTS/LOANS: Regional
RANGE OF INV./LOAN PER BUSINESS: Min. $100,000; Max $7,000,000
PREFERRED TERM FOR LOANS & LEASES: Min. 3 years; Max. 15 years
REFERRALS ACCEPTED FROM: Investment/Mortgage banker only

COMPANY: **Equifax Services Inc.**
ADDRESS: 1600 Peachtree N.W.
Atlanta, GA 30302
PHONE: (404) 885-8440
CONTACT OFFICER(S): James G. Brannan Jr.

COMPANY: **Jon R. Cleveland & Associates**
ADDRESS: Suite 444, 3340 Peachtree Rd. N.E.
Atlanta, GA 30326
PHONE: (404) 231-8575
TYPE OF INSTITUTION: Lease Broker
CONTACT OFFICER(S): Jon R. Cleveland, President
TYPES OF FINANCING: LEASES: Single-investor; Leveraged; Tax leases; Non-tax Leases, Operating Leases, Tax-oriented lease brokerage; Lease syndications; Vendor financing programs
PREFERRED TYPES OF INDUSTRIES/INVESTMENTS: Vendor programs
GEOGRAPHIC LIMITS OF INVESTMENTS/LOANS: National
RANGE OF INV./LOAN PER BUSINESS: Min. $50,000; Max. None
PREFERRED TERM FOR LOANS & LEASES: Min. 3 years; Max. None
BUSINESS CHARACTERISTICS DESIRED-REQUIRED: Minimum number of years in business: 3
REFERRALS ACCEPTED FROM: Investment/Mortgage banker or Borrower/Investee

COMPANY: **Leasco Equipment Co.**
ADDRESS: P.O. Box 19797
Atlanta, GA 30318
PHONE: (404) 355-1651
CONTACT OFFICER(S): Brooks Schoen

COMPANY: **Leasetech, Inc.**
ADDRESS: 1370 Center Drive, S-106
Atlanta, GA 30338
PHONE: (404) 393-4800
CONTACT OFFICER(S): Gary Barnes

COMPANY: **PLC Leasing Inc.**
ADDRESS: 340 Interstate North, Suite 170
Atlanta, GA 30339
PHONE: (404) 955-2856
CONTACT OFFICER(S): D. Keith Bates

COMPANY: **Source Analysis Inc.**
ADDRESS: 5780 Peachtree Dunwoody NE, Suite 195
Atlanta, GA 30342
PHONE: (404) 256-0030
CONTACT OFFICER(S): James B. Ward

COMPANY: **Citizens and Southern Commercial Corporation**
ADDRESS: 2059 Cooledge Road, (P.O. Box 4095, Atlanta 30302)
Tucker, GA 30084
PHONE: (404) 491-4839
TYPE OF INSTITUTION: Factoring, commercial finance, equipment leasing & financing (sub. of Commercial Bank)t
CONTACT OFFICER(S): Charles Mitchell, Senior V.P., Commercial Finance
Joel Chasteen, Sr. V.P. & Manager, Equipment Leasing
Bart Smith, Sr. V.P., Factoring
ASSETS: $7,620,000,000
TYPES OF FINANCING: LOANS: Working capital; Equipment, FACTORING, LEASES: Single-investor; Leveraged; Tax leases; Non-tax leases; Operating, INTERNATIONAL
PREFERRED TYPES OF INDUSTRIES/INVESTMENTS: For factoring: apparel, textiles, furniture, carpet, seafood industries; for leasing and commercial finance: manufacturers, distributors
GEOGRAPHIC LIMITS OF INVESTMENTS/LOANS: National; International
RANGE OF INV./LOAN PER BUSINESS: Max. $20,000,000
PREFERRED TERM FOR LOANS & LEASES: Min. 90 days; Max. 7 years
BUSINESS CHARACTERISTICS DESIRED-REQUIRED: Minimum number of years in business: 0; Min. annual sales $1,000,000; Min. net worth $200,000; Min. annual net income $20,000; Min. annual cash flow none; Other: Guaranties of principals with closely-held firms
REFERRALS ACCEPTED FROM: Investment/Mortgage banker or Borrower/Investee

BRANCHES: Claude McEwen, A.V.P., 300 S. Thornton Avenue, Dalton, GA 30720; (404) 278-1929
Fred Gaylord, V.P., 9841 Airport Blvd., Suite 300, Los Angeles, CA 90045; (213) 670-4772; Matthew Creo Jr., Sr. V.P., 1430 Broadway, 19th Floor, New York, NY 10018, 212-719-3700

COMPANY: **Lanier Financial Services, Inc.**
ADDRESS: 2501 Tucker Stone Pkwy.
Tucker, GA 30084
PHONE: (404) 493-2300
CONTACT OFFICER(S): A.D. Odom, Jr.

COMPANY: **Bancorp Leasing of Hawaii Inc., Bancorp Hawaii Inc.**
ADDRESS: P.O. Box 2900
Honolulu, HI 96846
PHONE: (808) 537-8811
CONTACT OFFICER(S): Gary G. Osterman

COMPANY: **First Hawaiian Leasing Inc.**
ADDRESS: 165 South King Street, Suite 1600
Honolulu, HI 96813
PHONE: (808) 525-7035
TYPE OF INSTITUTION: Full service leasing activities
CONTACT OFFICER(S): Donald G. Horner, Executive Vice President & Manager
Stephen J. Marcuccilli, Vice President
ASSETS: Holding company total assets $2.5+ billion.
INVESTMENTS/LOANS MADE: For own account
INVESTMENTS/LOANS MADE: N/A
TYPES OF FINANCING: LEASES: Single-investor; Leveraged; Tax leases; Non-tax leases; Tax-oriented lease brokerage; Vendor financing programs
GEOGRAPHIC LMITS OF INVESTMENTS/LOANS: International
RANGE OF INV./LOAN PER BUSINESS: Min. $250,000; Max. $75,000,000
PREFERRED TERM FOR LOANS & LEASES: Min. 3 years; Max. 15 years

COMPANY: **GECC Hawaii Leasing**
ADDRESS: 700 Bishop St., Suite 902
Honolulu, HI 96813
PHONE: (808) 945-8333
CONTACT OFFICER(S): John C. Walker, Jr.

COMPANY: **Agri Industries Leasing Company**
ADDRESS: P.O. Box 4887
Des Moines, IA 50306
PHONE: (515) 223-3700
CONTACT OFFICER(S): Robert S. Miller

COMPANY: **The Dillon Company**
ADDRESS: 7626 Hickman Rd.
Des Moines, IA 50322
PHONE: (515) 276-7607
TYPE OF INSTITUTION: Leasing Co.
CONTACT OFFICER(S): Howard D. Hamilton, President, Lease financing, Tax partnerships between vendors and The Dillon Company
TYPES OF FINANCING: LOANS: Working capital; Equipment; Equity-related, LEASES: Single-investor; Tax leases; Non-tax leases; Tax-oriented lease brokerage; Vendor financing programs, Other: All types of equipment leasing; debt restructuring; OTHER SERVICES PROVIDED: Managing partner in partnerships created between vendors of business equipment and The Dillon Company
GEOGRAPHIC LIMITS OF INVESTMENTS/LOANS: Regional
RANGE OF INV./LOAN PER BUSINESS: Min. $15,000; Max. Unlimited
PREFERRED TERM FOR LOANS & LEASES: Min. 2 years; Max. 5 years
BUSINESS CHARACTERISTICS DESIRED-REQUIRED: Minimum number of years in business: 2 years
REMARKS: Terms on loans: 3-10 years

COMPANY: **Norwest Financial Leasing Inc.**
ADDRESS: 336 S.W. 8th
Des Moines, IA 50309
PHONE: (515) 286-4750
CONTACT OFFICER(S): Harold H. Ritchie

COMPANY: **Park Leasing Company**
ADDRESS: 1290 Financial Center
Des Moines, IA 50309
PHONE: (515) 288-1023
CONTACT OFFICER(S): Robert W. Arnold

COMPANY: **UCB Leasing Corporation**
ADDRESS: 900 United Central Bank Bldg.
Des Moines, IA 50309
PHONE: (515) 245-7222
CONTACT OFFICER(S): Douglas R. Hawkins

COMPANY: **MIC Leasing Co., Mahaska Investment Co.**
ADDRESS: First Ave. E. P.O. Box 133
Oskaloosa, IA 52577
PHONE: (515) 673-8448
TYPE OF INSTITUTION: Leasing
CONTACT OFFICER(S): Steve J. Posovich
TYPES OF FINANCING: LEASES: Other: Full payout; REAL ESTATE
PREFERRED TYPES OF INDUSTRIES/INVESTMENTS: Farm
RANGE OF INV./LOAN PER BUSINESS: Min. $10,000; Max. $1,400,000
REMARKS: Lease Term 3-5 yrs.; Loan Term: Variable

COMPANY: **Silopress Financial Corp.**
ADDRESS: P.O. Box 1314
Sioux City, IA 51102
PHONE: (712) 255-4569
CONTACT OFFICER(S): Richard J. Salem

COMPANY: **Asset Leasing**
ADDRESS: P.O. Box 1856
Waterloo, IA 50704
PHONE: (319) 235-1818
CONTACT OFFICER(S): William J. Taylor

COMPANY: **Control O Fax Management Inc.**
ADDRESS: 3070 West Airline Highway
Waterloo, IA 50704
PHONE: (319) 234-4651
CONTACT OFFICER(S): T. W. Davis

COMPANY: **Moore Leasing**
ADDRESS: P.O. Box 8247
Boise, ID 83733
PHONE: (208) 383-7336
CONTACT OFFICER(S): David A. Cook

COMPANY: **Power Equipment Leasing Company, Inc.**
ADDRESS: P.O. Box 329
Brookfield, IL 60513
PHONE: (312) 485-0995
CONTACT OFFICER(S): Ken G. Wettour

COMPANY: **Asset Leasing Corporation**
ADDRESS: 20 North Wacker Drive, Suite 550
Chicago, IL 60606
PHONE: (312) 346-1580
CONTACT OFFICER(S): Milton G. Lefton
TYPES OF FINANCING: LEASES
PREFERRED TYPES OF INDUSTRIES/INVESTMENTS: Manufacturing equipment
GEOGRAPHIC LIMITS OF INVESTMENTS/LOANS: Local; North IL
RANGE OF INV./LOAN PER BUSINESS: Max.: under $50,000.

COMPANY: **Bell & Howell Acceptance Corp.**
ADDRESS: 7100 N McCormick Rd.
Chicago, IL 60645
PHONE: (312) 262-1600
CONTACT OFFICER(S): N. L. Dennis

COMPANY: **Colonial Leasing, Colonial Bank & Trust Co.**
ADDRESS: 5850 W. Belmont Ave.
Chicago, IL 60634
PHONE: (312) 283-3700
CONTACT OFFICER(S): William A. Hense

COMPANY: **Continental Illinois Leasing Corp.**
ADDRESS: 231 S. LaSalle St.
Chicago, IL 60697
PHONE: (312) 828-7400
TYPE OF INSTITUTION: Leasing Co.
CONTACT OFFICER(S): Bernard J. McKenna, President
AnthonyJ. Cracchi olo, Senior Vice President
ASSETS: $1.1 billion
INVESTMENTS/LOANS MADE: For own account; For managed accounts; Through private placements
TYPES OF FINANCING: LOANS: Unsecured to credits above Baa; Working capital; Equipment; LEASES: Single-investor; Leveraged; Tax leases; Non-tax leases; Tax-oriented lease brokerage; Lease syndications; Vendor financing programs
GEOGRAPHIC LIMITS OF INVESTMENTS/LOANS: National; International
RANGE OF INV./LOAN PER BUSINESS: Min. $250,000; Max. None
PREFERRED TERM FOR LOANS & LEASES: Min: 5 years; Max. 10 years
BUSINESS CHARACTERISTICS DESIRED-REQUIRED: Minimum number of years in business: 3

COMPANY: **The Corporate Capital Group**
ADDRESS: 222 West Adams, Suite 1098
Chicago, IL 60606
PHONE: (312) 781-0960
CONTACT OFFICER(S): Morley M. Mathewson

COMPANY: **Datronic Rental Corp.**
ADDRESS: 5210 Wesley Terrace
Chicago, IL 60656
PHONE: (312) 992-0760
TYPE OF INSTITUTION: Leasing Co. & Com'l. Finance
CONTACT OFFICER(S): Edmund Lapinski, Secy/Treasurer, Lease Financing and Syndication
ASSETS: $10,000,000—100,000,000
INVESTMENTS/LOANS MADE: Through private placements
TYPES OF FINANCING: LOANS: Equipment, LEASES
GEOGRAPHIC LIMITS OF INVESTMENTS/LOANS: National
PREFERRED TERM FOR LOANS & LEASES: Min. 1-3; Max. 7-10

COMPANY: **DSA Capital Funding**
ADDRESS: 33 West Monroe Street
Chicago, IL 60603
PHONE: (312) 853-5533
CONTACT OFFICER(S): Robert D. Endacott

COMPANY: **First Chicago Credit Corp.**
ADDRESS: 20 South Clark Street, Suite 0163
Chicago, IL 60670
PHONE: (312) 732-4000
CONTACT OFFICER(S): William T. Zadrozny

COMPANY: **First Chicago Leasing Corp.**
ADDRESS: Two First National Plaza
Chicago, IL 60670
PHONE: (312) 732-8917
TYPE OF INSTITUTION: Venture Capital Subsidiaries of a National Bank Holding Company (First Chicago Corporation)
CONTACT OFFICER(S): Geoffrey L. Stringer
ASSETS: $300 Million
INVESTMENTS/LOANS MADE: For own account; Through private placements

INVESTMENTS/LOANS MADE: In securities with a secondary market and in securities without a secondary market
TYPES OF FINANCING: VENTURE CAPITAL: Start-up from developed product stage; First-stage (less than 1 year); Second-stage (generally 1-3 years); Later-stage expansion; Buy-outs/Acquisitions
PREFERRED TYPES OF INDUSTRIES/INVESTMENTS: No Preference
GEOGRAPHIC LIMITS OF INVESTMENTS/LOANS: National
RANGE OF INV./LOAN PER BUSINESS: Min. $1,000,000; Max. $15,000,000
BUSINESS CHARACTERISTICS DESIRED-REQUIRED: Min. no. of years in business: 0
REFERRALS ACCEPTED FROM: Investment Mortgage banker or Borrower/Investee
BRANCHES: 133 Federal St., 6th Fl., Boston, MA 02110, (617) 542-9195E

COMPANY: **FMC Finance Corporation**
ADDRESS: 200 East Randolph Drive
Chicago, IL 60601
PHONE: (312) 861-6250
CONTACT OFFICER(S): Richard K. Loan

COMPANY: **Harco Leasing Company Inc.**
ADDRESS: 600 Woodfield, 5th floor
Chicago, IL 60196
PHONE: (312) 836-2000
CONTACT OFFICER(S): C.L. Masten

COMPANY: **International Capital Equipment, Inc.**
ADDRESS: 401 N. Michigan Avenue, Suite 2540
Chicago, IL 60611
PHONE: (312) 329-9800
CONTACT OFFICER(S): M.J. Mulvihill

COMPANY: **Lease Investment Corp.**
ADDRESS: 3 Illinois Center, 303 E. Wacker Dr., Ste. 1300
Chicago, IL 60601
PHONE: (312) 467-5500
TYPE OF INSTITUTION: Leasing Investment Banking
CONTACT OFFICER(S): Martin E. Zimmerman/President
Philip Schneck/V.P.
TYPES OF FINANCING: LEASES: Single-investor; Leveraged
PREFERRED TYPES OF INDUSTRIES/INVESTMENTS: Medical; Telecommunications
WILL NOT CONSIDER: Hotel/Motel
GEOGRAPHIC LIMITS OF INVESTMENTS/LOANS: National
RANGE OF INV./LOAN PER BUSINESS: Min. $100,000; Max. $10,000,000
BRANCHES: P.O. Box 1147, Cashiers, NC 28717; (704) 743-2422; Mr. Butch Warren
Equipment Analytics, Inc. 4501 Indian School Road, N.E., Suite G, Albuquerque, NM 87110; (505) 268-0600; Bob Maier
Bill King, LINC Medical Equipment, Inc., 31 Marquardt Dr., Wheeling, IL 60090; (312) 459-9340
Luc Pols, Lease Investment Corporation, 4676 Admiralty Way, Suite 401, Marina Del Rey, CA 90291; (213) 306-1022
Mr. Chuck Mooney, 5996 Wilderness Lane, Parma Heights, OH 44130; (216) 886-6300

COMPANY: **Lease Management Corporation**
ADDRESS: 1 IBM Plaza, Suite 3230
Chicago, IL 60611
PHONE: (312) 467-4570
CONTACT OFFICER(S): Robert T. DePree

COMPANY: **Medical Investors Fund**
ADDRESS: 6315 North Milwaukee Ave.
Chicago, IL 60646
PHONE: (312) 775-7566
CONTACT OFFICER(S): David E. Gross

COMPANY: **Norlease, Inc., The Northern Trust Co.**
ADDRESS: 50 South LaSalle Street
Chicago, IL 60675
PHONE: (312) 630-6000
CONTACT OFFICER(S): William G. Brannen

COMPANY: **Northbrook Leasing**
ADDRESS: 1000 West North Avenue
Chicago, IL 60622
PHONE: (312) 951-0150
CONTACT OFFICER(S): Kenneth D. Goodman

COMPANY: **NSCC Leasing Corp.**
ADDRESS: 1737 West Howard Street, Suite 315
Chicago, IL 60626
PHONE: (312) 743-2112
CONTACT OFFICER(S): Lawrence E. Gilford

COMPANY: **Prudential Bache Securities, Equipment Leasing Division**
ADDRESS: Suite 340, 135 S. LaSalle Street
Chicago, IL 60603
PHONE: (312) 630-7318
CONTACT OFFICER(S): Lawrence R. Grant

COMPANY: **Trailmobile Finance Company**
ADDRESS: 200 East Randolph Drive
Chicago, IL 60601
PHONE: (312) 322-7770
CONTACT OFFICER(S): W. Clayton Stephens

COMPANY: **Trans Union Leasing Corp.**
ADDRESS: 222 W. Adams
Chicago, IL 60606
PHONE: (312) 641-0233
TYPE OF INSTITUTION: Leasing Co.
CONTACT OFFICER(S): William Cox, Pres.
TYPES OF FINANCING: LOANS: Equipment; Secured Lending, LEASES: Single-investor; Non-tax leases; Lease syndications; Vendor financing programs

PREFERRED TYPES OF INDUSTRIES/INVESTMENTS: Diversified
GEOGRAPHIC LIMITS OF INVESTMENTS/LOANS: National; Canada
RANGE OF INV./LOAN PER BUSINESS: Min. $50,000; Max. $5 million
REMARKS: Term depends on equipment

COMPANY: **Walter E. Heller & Co./Commercial & Industrial Equipment Financing Group**
ADDRESS: 105 West Adams Street
Chicago, IL 60603
PHONE: (312) 621-7600
TYPE OF INSTITUTION: Equipment leasing and financing
CONTACT OFFICER(S): Samuel L. Eichenfield, President
INVESTMENTS/LOANS MADE: For own account
TYPES OF FINANCING: LOANS: Working capital; Equipment, REAL ESTATE LOANS; FACTORING, LEASES: Single-investor; Leveraged; Tax leases; Non-tax leases; Lease syndications; OTHER SERVICES PROVIDED: Floor planning
PREFERRED TYPES OF INDUSTRIES/INVESTMENTS: All types of capital equip. for businesses
GEOGRAPHIC LIMITS OF INVESTMENTS/LOANS: National
RANGE OF INV./LOAN PER BUSINESS: Min. $50,000; Max. No
PREFERRED TERM FOR LOANS & LEASES: Min. 3 years; Max. 10 years
BUSINESS CHARACTERISTICS DESIRED-REQUIRED: Minimum number of years in business: 3
REFERRALS ACCEPTED FROM: Investment/Mortgage banker or Borrower/Investee

COMPANY: **SECC Financial Services, Inc.**
ADDRESS: P.O. Box 796
Crystal Lake, IL 60014
PHONE: (815) 459-7700
CONTACT OFFICER(S): Lee E. Johnson

COMPANY: **Deutsche Credit Corporation**
ADDRESS: 2333 Waukegan Road
Deerfield, IL 60015
PHONE: (312) 948-7272
CONTACT OFFICER(S): Jim Colbert

COMPANY: **Appleco Leasing Corporation**
ADDRESS: 850 Pratt Blvd.
Elk Grove Village, IL 60007
PHONE: (312) 593-5000
TYPE OF INSTITUTION: Captive leasing company of major plastics auxiliary equipment manufacturer
CONTACT OFFICER(S): Don Swanson, Treasurer
Michael A. Waters, Chairman of the Board
ASSETS: $1.3 million
INVESTMENTS/LOANS MADE: For own account
TYPES OF FINANCING: LOANS: Unsecured; Equipment, LEASES: Vendor financing programs; Other: Equip. leasing
PREFERRED TYPES OF INDUSTRIES/INVESTMENTS: Plastics industry, recycling-reclaiming
WILL NOT CONSIDER: Heavy machinery
GEOGRAPHIC LIMITS OF INVESTMENTS/LOANS: National
RANGE OF INV./LOAN PER BUSINESS: Min. $2,500; Max. $500,000
PREFERRED TERM FOR LOANS & LEASES: Min. 1 year; Max. 5 years
BUSINESS CHARACTERISTICS DESIRED-REQUIRED: Minimum number of years in business: 0; Other: Loose parameters; Personal financial strength
REFERRALS ACCEPTED FROM: Borrower/Investee
REMARKS: A wholly-owned subsidiary of AEC

COMPANY: **Nationwide Funding, Inc.**
ADDRESS: 1550 Higgins Road, Suite 132
Elk Grove Village, IL 60007
PHONE: (312) 981-9898
CONTACT OFFICER(S): Ron Winicour

COMPANY: **Dekalb Equipment Leasing Corp.**
ADDRESS: P.O. Box 385
Geneva, IL 60134
PHONE: (312) 232-9222
CONTACT OFFICER(S): William R. Mondi

COMPANY: **International Financial Services Corporation**
ADDRESS: 1701 Lake Avenue, Suite 365
Glenview, IL 60025
PHONE: (312) 729-7820
CONTACT OFFICER(S): Robert G. Seeds

COMPANY: **John Deere Leasing Company, Deere & Company**
ADDRESS: John Deere Road
Moline, IL 61265
PHONE: (309) 752-5639
CONTACT OFFICER(S): M. B. Orr

COMPANY: **Haven Leasing Corporation**
ADDRESS: Abbott Park, D-312
North Chicago, IL 60064
CONTACT OFFICER(S): S. E. Bradt

COMPANY: **Dart & Kraft Financial Corporation**
ADDRESS: 2211 Sanders Rod
Northbrook, IL 60062
PHONE: (312) 498-8181
CONTACT OFFICER(S): Paul I. Gaumnitz

COMPANY: **Financial Management Ventures**
ADDRESS: 824 Sunset Ridge Road
Northbrook, IL 60062
PHONE: (312) 480-4747
CONTACT OFFICER(S): Joe Nachbin

LEASING COMPANIES

(Lessors. Also see Commercial Bankers and Finance Companies, Insurance Companies and Investment Bankers)

ILLINOIS

COMPANY: **Reli Financial Corp.**
ADDRESS: 555 Skokie Blvd., P.O. Box 797
Northbrook, IL 60062
PHONE: (312) 564-6810
TYPE OF INSTITUTION: Commercial finance and leasing company
CONTACT OFFICER(S): Edward C. Latek, President
Daniel Sideman, Exec. V.P.
ASSETS: $10,000,000
INVESTMENTS/LOANS MADE: For own account
TYPES OF FINANCING: LOANS: Equipment, LEASES
PREFERRED TYPES OF INDUSTRIES/INVESTMENTS: General equipment for rental industry
GEOGRAPHIC LIMITS OF INVESTMENTS/LOANS: National
RANGE OF INV./LOAN PER BUSINESS: Min. $10,000; Max. $150,000
PREFERRED TERM FOR LOANS & LEASES: Min. 3 years; Max. 5 years
BUSINESS CHARACTERISTICS DESIRED-REQUIRED: Minimum number of years in business: 3; Min. annual sales $200,000; Min. net worth $50,000

COMPANY: **Stratford Leasing Company**
ADDRESS: 255 Revere Drive, Suite 101
Northbrook, IL 60062
PHONE: (312) 564-0606
CONTACT OFFICER(S): Burton B. Schwartz

COMPANY: **Trans Leasing International**
ADDRESS: 3000 Dundee Road
Northbrook, IL 60062
PHONE: (800) 323-1180
TYPES OF INSTITUTION: Independent Medical Equipment Leasing Company
CONTACT OFFICER(S): Richard Grossman
TYPES OF FINANCING: LEASES: Tax leases; Non-tax leases; Vendor financing programs; OTHER SERVICES PROVIDED: Lease Card - credit card for leasing medical equipment
PREFERRED TYPES OF INDUSTRIES/INVESTMENTS: Medical Equipment
GEOGRAPHIC LIMITS OF INVESTMENTS/LOANS: National
RANGE OF INV./LOAN PER BUSINESS: Min. $500; Max. $ None
PREFERRED TERM FOR LOANS & LEASES: Min. One year; Max. Seven years
BUSINESS CHARACTERISTICS DESIRED-REQUIRED: All Medical Professionals

COMPANY: **International Funding Corporation**
ADDRESS: Two Northfield Plaza, Suite 230
Northfield, IL 60093
PHONE: (312) 441-8600
TYPE OF INSTITUTION: Equipment leasing and financing
CONTACT OFFICER(S): Rudolph D. Trebels, President & Administrator, Printing and graphic equipment, machine tool and plastic molding equipment, computer and related peripheral equipment, medical and dental equipment, construction equipment
INVESTMENTS/LOANS MADE: For own account
1LOANS: Equipment; Equity-related, LEASES: Single-investor; Leveraged; Tax leases; Non-tax leases; Tax-oriented lease brokerage; Vendor financing programs
GEOGRAPHIC LIMITS OF INVESTMENTS/LOANS: National
RANGE OF INV./LOAN PER BUSINESS: Min. $50,000; Max. $50,000,000
PREFERRED TERM FOR LOANS & LEASES: Min. 3 years; Max. 15 years
BUSINESS CHARACTERISTICS DESIRED-REQUIRED: Minimum number of years in business: 3; Min. annual sales $750,000; Min. net worth $100,000; Min. annual net income $25,000; Min. annual cash flow $50,000

COMPANY: **Indiana Michigan Corporation**
ADDRESS: 1301 22nd Street
Oak Brook, IL 60521
PHONE: (312) 277-9300
CONTACT OFFICER(S): Anthony Jablonsky

COMPANY: **Mellon Financial Services Corporation**
ADDRESS: 1415 West 22nd Street, Suite 1200
Oak Brook, IL 60521
PHONE: (800) 323-7338 outside IL, (312) 986-2950 inside IL
TYPE OF INSTITUTION: Asset based lending affiliate of Mellon Bank, N.A.
CONTACT OFFICER(S): Charles S. Pryce, Senior Vice President
ASSETS: $25 billion
INVESTMENTS/LOANS MADE: For own account
INVESTMENTS/LOANS MADE: In securities with a secondary market and in securities without a secondary market
TYPES OF FINANCING: LOANS: Working capital; Equipment; Equity-related; Other: intermediate term loans; LBO financing. REAL ESTATE LOANS: Intermediate-term senior mtg.; Land; Standbys; Industrial revenue bonds. LEASES: Non-tax leases. INTERNATIONAL
WILL NOT CONSIDER: Building contractors
GEOGRAPHIC LIMITS OF INVESTMENTS/LOANS: National
BUSINESS CHARACTERISTICS DESIRED-REQUIRED: Minimum number of years in business: 0 Min. annual sales $2,000,000; Min. net worth $100,000; Min. annual net income $ positive; Min. annual cash flow $ positive.
REFERRALS ACCEPTED FROM: Investment/Mortgage banker or Borrower/Investee

COMPANY: **Portec Lease Corp., Portec Inc.**
ADDRESS: 300 Windsor Drive
Oak Brook, IL 60521
PHONE: (312) 920-4600
CONTACT OFFICER(S): W.W. Farnsworth

COMPANY: **Charter Leasing Corporation**
ADDRESS: 800 E. Northwest Highway
Palatine, IL 60067
PHONE: (312) 359-7800
TYPE OF INSTITUTION: Private Corporation

CONTACT OFFICER(S): David F. Wyatt, President & Chief Executive Officer
INVESTMENTS/LOANS MADE: For own account; For managed accounts
TYPES OF FINANCING: LEASES: Single-investor; Non-tax leases; Operating; Vendor financing programs
PREFERRED TYPES OF INDUSTRIES/INVESTMENTS: We lease all types of income producing capital equipment for industry.
GEOGRAPHIC LIMITS OF INVESTMENTS/LOANS: National, International
RANGE OF INV./LOAN PER BUSINESS: Min. $5,000
PREFERRED TERM FOR LOANS & LEASES: Min. 6 months; Max. 7 years
BUSINESS CHARACTERISTICS DESIRED-REQUIRED: Minimum number of years in business: 2; Min. annual sales $300,000; Min. net worth $50,000; Min. annual net income $10,000.

COMPANY: **Commercial National Bank of Peoria**
ADDRESS: 301 S.W. Adams Street
Peoria, IL 61631
PHONE: (309) 655-5479
CONTACT OFFICER(S): Philip A. Polonus

COMPANY: **HFC Leasing Inc., Household Finance Corp.**
ADDRESS: 2700 Sanders Road
Prospect Heights, IL 60070
PHONE: (312) 564-5000
CONTACT OFFICER(S): Hugh J. Zick, President
Carl W. Giessel, Sr. V.P.
ASSETS: $1,079,000,000
INVESTMENTS/LOANS MADE: For own account, For managed accounts
INVESTMENTS/LOANS MADE: Only in securities without a secondary market
TYPES OF FINANCING: LEASES: Single-investor; Leveraged; Tax leases; Lease syndications; REAL ESTATE: Partnership/Syndications
PREFERRED TYPES OF INDUSTRIES/INVESTMENTS: All capital intensive industries
GEOGRAPHIC LIMITS OF INVESTMENTS/LOANS: National
RANGE OF INV./LOAN PER BUSINESS: Min. $2 million
PREFERRED TERM FOR LOANS & LEASES: Min. 4 years; Max. 35 years
BUSINESS CHARACTERISTICS DESIRED-REQUIRED: Minimum number of years in business: 5
REFERRALS ACCEPTED FROM: Investment/Mortgage banker or Borrower/Investee

COMPANY: **Evans Railcar Leasing Company**
ADDRESS: 2550 Golf Road East Tower, Suite 900
Rolling Meadows, IL 60008
PHONE: (312) 640-7000
CONTACT OFFICER(S): William M. Peyton

COMPANY: **Comdisco Inc.**
ADDRESS: 6400 Shafer Ct.
Rosemont, IL 60018
PHONE: (312) 698-3000
CONTACT OFFICER(S): Frank D. Trznadel Jr.

COMPANY: **G I C Financial Services Corp.**
ADDRESS: 9701 W. Higgins Rd., Suite 420
Rosemont, IL 60018
PHONE: (312) 823-6976
CONTACT OFFICER(S): Walter L. Crowley

COMPANY: **Borg-Warner Capital Services Corporation**
ADDRESS: 1355 E. Remington Rd. Suite J
Schaumburg, IL 60195
PHONE: (312) 843-6969
TYPE OF INSTITUTION: Investment Banking
CONTACT OFFICER(S): Thomas S. Ablum, Managing Director
Stephen R. Anderson, Operations Manager
INVESTMENTS/LOANS MADE: For managed accounts, Through private placements
TYPES OF FINANCING: LOANS: Working capital. REAL ESTATE LOANS: Long-term senior mtg.; Subordinated; Wraparounds; Land development; Construction; Industrial revenue bonds. LEASES: Single-investor; Leveraged; Tax leases; Non-tax leases; Tax-oriented lease brokerage; Lease syndications; Vendor financing programs. REAL ESTATE: Acquisitions. OTHER SERVICES PROVIDED: Financial Advisory Services & arrangement of above financing structures
PREFERRED TYPES OF INDUSTRIES/INVESTMENTS: No Preferences
WILL NOT CONSIDER: Land Only Acquisition & Venture Capital
RANGE OF INV./LOAN PER BUSINESS: Min. $250,000
PREFERRED TERM FOR LOANS & LEASES: Min. 1 year loan/5 leases; Max. 15 year loan/20 year lease
BUSINESS CHARACTERISTICS DESIRED-REQUIRED: Minimum number of years in business: 3; Min. annual sales $10MM; Min. net worth $500,000; Min annual net income $200,000
REFERRALS ACCEPTED FROM: Investment/Mortgage banker or Borrower/Investee

COMPANY: **Mid-States Financial Corp.**
ADDRESS: 2385 Hammond Dr., Suite 10
Schaumburg, IL 60195
PHONE: (312) 397-0063
TYPE OF INSTITUTION: Leasing Company
CONTACT OFFICER(S): James Bailey, V.P.
TYPES OF FINANCING: LEASES: Tax leases; Vendor financing programs
PREFERRED TYPES OF INDUSTRIES/INVESTMENTS: Machine Tools; Computers; Telephones; Production
GEOGRAPHIC LIMITS OF INVESTMENTS/LOANS: Regional
RANGE OF INV./LOAN PER BUSINESS: Min. $5,000

PREFERRED TERM FOR LOANS & LEASES: Min. 3; Max. 7 years

COMPANY: **Prime Leasing Inc.**
ADDRESS: 1701 Woodfield Drive
Schaumburg, IL 60195
PHONE: (312) 843-1818
CONTACT OFFICER(S): James A. Friedman

COMPANY: **The Financial Corporation of Illinois**
ADDRESS: 4825 North Scott Street, Suite 307
Schiller Park, IL 60176
PHONE: (312) 678-2440
TYPE OF INSTITUTION: Privately-held finance company specializing in financing and discounting of leveraged lease loans and secured loans involving equipment
CONTACT OFFICER(S): Dennis T. Roesslein, Assistant Vice President
Robert G. Roth, Chief Executive Officer
INVESTMENTS/LOANS MADE: For own account
TYPES OF FINANCING: LOANS: Equipment; Other: Leveraged lease loans, Secured equipment loans. LEASES: Single-investor; Leveraged; Tax leases
PREFERRED TYPES OF INDUSTRIES/INVESTMENTS: We will consider discounting of leveraged lease loans and direct secured equipment loans within any industry as long as the lessee/borrower is of a "BAA" or better credit quality.
WILL NOT CONSIDER: Real estate, Working capital loans
GEOGRAPHIC LIMITS OF INVESTMENTS/LOANS: National
RANGE OF INV./LOAN PER BUSINESS: Min. $200,000; Max. $2,000,000
PREFERRED TERM FOR LOANS & LEASES: Min. 3 years; Max. 5 years
BUSINESS CHARACTERISTICS DESIRED-REQUIRED: Other: Companies which are rated "BAA" or better. Non-rated companies of an equivalent size and credit quality to "BAA" or better.

COMPANY: **Knowles Leasing Corporation**
ADDRESS: 4825 North Scott Street
Schiller Park, IL 60176
PHONE: (312) 678-2440
CONTACT OFFICER(S): Dennis T. Roesslein

COMPANY: **Wilson Leasing Company**
ADDRESS: 7840 Lincoln Avenue
Skokie, IL 60077
PHONE: (312) 673-5858
CONTACT OFFICER(S): Lawrence S. Wilson

COMPANY: **Custom Leasing Company**
ADDRESS: 2401 Meyer Rd.
Ft. Wayne, IN 46803
PHONE: (219) 422-4676
TYPE OF INSTITUTION: Partnership
CONTACT OFFICER(S): W.E. Doetsch, Ptr.
ASSETS: $5,000,000
INVESTMENTS/LOANS MADE: For own account
TYPES OF FINANCING: SECONDARY MARKET CORPORATE SECURITIES: Leases LEASES
PREFERRED TYPES OF INDUSTRIES/INVESTMENTS: Medical Equipment; Commercial Equipment; Office Equipment; Shop Equipment
GEOGRAPHIC LIMITS OF INVESTMENTS/LOANS: Mid West
RANGE OF INV./LOAN PER BUSINESS: Min. $3,000; Max. $50000.00
PREFERRED TERM FOR LOANS & LEASES: Min. 3 years; Max. 5 years
BUSINESS CHARACTERISTICS DESIRED-REQUIRED: Min. yrs. in business: 2; Net Worth 4 to 1 of Loan or Lease

COMPANY: **Waterfield Mortgage Co., Inc.**
ADDRESS: 333 E. Washington Blvd.
Ft. Wayne, IN 46802
PHONE: (219) 425-8393
TYPE OF INSTITUTION: Mortgage Banker
CONTACT OFFICER(S): Thomas A. Gauldin, V.P., Manager, C.M.B.—Commercial loans
ASSETS: $3 billion
INVESTMENTS/LOANS MADE: For own account; for managed accounts and through private placements
INVESTMENTS/LOANS MADE: In securities with a secondary market and in securities without a secondary market
TYPES OF FINANCING: REAL ESTATE LOANS: SECONDARY-MARKET CORPORATE SECURITIES: Private placements; VENTURE CAPITAL: Start-up from developed product stage; LOANS: Equipment; Equity-related; REAL ESTATE LOANS: Long-term senior mtg.; Intermediate-term senior mtg.; Subordinated; Wraparounds; Land; Land development; Construction; Gap; Standbys; Industrial revenue bonds; LEASES: Single-investor; Leveraged; Tax leases; Non-tax leases; Operating; Tax-oriented lease brokerage; Lease syndications; REAL ESTATE: Acquisitions; Joint ventures; Partnerships/Syndications
PREFERRED TYPES OF INDUSTRIES/INVESTMENTS: Office; Warehouse, Shopping; Retail; Apartments; Motel/hotels
GEOGRAPHIC LIMITS OF INVESTMENTS/LOANS: National
RANGE OF INV./LOAN PER BUSINESS: Min. $200,000; Max. Unlimited
PREFERRED TERM FOR LOANS & LEASES: Min. Flexible
BUSINESS CHARACTERISTICS DESIRED-REQUIRED: Min. yrs. in business: 5
BRANCHES: 35 Nationwide

COMPANY: **American Fletcher Leasing Corp., American Fletcher Corp.**
ADDRESS: 111 Monument Circle, Suite 510
Indianapolis, IN 46277
PHONE: (317) 639-8036
CONTACT OFFICER(S): James F. Donahue

COMPANY: **Sullair Finance Corporation**
ADDRESS: 3700 East Michigan Blvd.
Michigan City, IN 46360

PHONE: (219) 879-5451
CONTACT OFFICER(S): W.S. Carlisle, Jr.

COMPANY: **SLC Of North America, Inc.**
5822 Reeds Road KS 66202
PHONE: (913) 677-5700
CONTACT OFFICER(S): Ronald E. Sexton

COMPANY: **Polaris Leasing**
ADDRESS: One Polaris Plaza, P.O. Box 1488
Hutchinson, KS 67501
PHONE: (316) 662-6401
CONTACT OFFICER(S): Mike Chapin

COMPANY: **North Supply Company, Inc.**
ADDRESS: 600 Industrial Parkway
Industrial Airport KS 66031
PHONE: (913) 791-7000
CONTACT OFFICER(S): Roy F. Lee

COMPANY: **Unimark Inc.**
ADDRESS: 8400 West 110th Street, Suite 200
Overland Park, KS 66210
PHONE: (91 649-2424
CONTACT OFFICER(S): D.W. Lawrence

COMPANY: **Southern Leasing Of Kansas City Inc.**
ADDRESS: 4200 W. 83rd Street
Shawnee Mission, KS 66208
PHONE: (913) 649-5445
CONTACT OFFICER(S): Marshall H. Dean

COMPANY: **Celco Inc. of America, The Farmers Alliance Mutual Insurance Co.**
ADDRESS: 101 S. Main St., P.O. Box 160
Stafford, KS 67578
PHONE: (316) 234-5211
CONTACT OFFICER(S): John R. Edsall

COMPANY: **Misco Leasing, Inc.**
ADDRESS: 257 N. Broadway
Wichita, KS 67202
PHONE: (316) 265-6641
CONTACT OFFICER(S): Larry Guhr, President
John Peyton, Credit Manager
TYPES OF FINANCING: LEASES
GEOGRAPHIC LIMITS OF INVESTMENTS/LOANS: Regional; Midwest
RANGE OF INV./LOAN PER BUSINESS: Min. $2,500
PREFERRED TERM FOR LOANS & LEASES: Min. 3-5 yrs; Max. 5-7 yrs
BUSINESS CHARACTERISTICS DESIRED-REQUIRED: Minimum number of years in business: 1
REMARKS: All information subject to change as company may be changing hands

COMPANY: **I & R Leasing Inc.**
ADDRESS: P.O. Box 2550
Bowling Green, KY 42101
PHONE: (502) 842-7245
CONTACT OFFICER(S): Robert W. Wood

COMPANY:**Commonwealth Financial Services Corporation/I & R Leasing, Inc.**
ADDRESS: 810 Chestnut Street
Bowling Green KY 42101
PHONE: (502) 782-2908
TYPE OF INSTITUTION: Independent
CONTACT OFFICER(S): Robert W. Wood, President of Commonwealth Financial Services Corp.
Irene H. Wood, President of I & R Leasing, Inc.
ASSETS: $5 million
INVESTMENTS/LOANS MADE: For own account
TYPES OF FINANCING: LOANS: Equipment; LEASES: Single-investor; Leveraged; Tax leases; Non-tax leases; Operating; Tax-oriented lease brokerage; Vendor financing programs; OTHER SERVICES PROVIDED: Vehicle Leasing and Financing including dealer programs
PREFERRED TYPES OF INDUSTRIES/INVESTMENTS: Will Consider All
GEOGRAPHIC LIMITS OF INVESTMENTS/LOANS: Regional
RANGE OF INV./LOAN PER BUSINESS: Max. $ None
PREFERRED TERM FOR LOANS & LEASES: Min. one year; Max. seven years
BUSINESS CHARACTERISTICS DESIRED-REQUIRED: Minimum number of years in business: 2; Other: Positive Cash Flow
REFERRALS ACCEPTED FROM: Investment/Mortgage banker only; Borrower/Investee

COMPANY: **Leasepac Corporation**
ADDRESS: 1200 South Broadway
Lexington, KY 40504
PHONE: (606) 233-0906
CONTACT OFFICER(S): James J. Levenson

COMPANY: **Citizens Fidelity Leasing Corp.**
ADDRESS: 419 W. Jefferson St.
Louisville, KY 40202
PHONE: (502) 581-2686
TYPE OF INSTITUTION: Leasing Co., Subsidiary of Bank Holding Company
CONTACT OFFICER(S): A. J. Desposito, Pres.
Ted Stingwolt, Sr. V.P.
ASSETS: $100,000,000
INVESTMENTS/LOANS MADE: For own account
TYPES OF FINANCING: LOANS: Equipment; LEASES: Single-investor; Leveraged; Tax leases; Non-tax leases; Tax-oriented lease brokerage; Lease syndications
GEOGRAPHIC LIMITS OF INVESTMENTS/LOANS: National
RANGE OF INV./LOAN PER BUSINESS: Min. $200,000; Max. $10,000,000
PREFERRED TERM FOR LOANS & LEASES: Min. 3-5; Max. 10 years
BUSINESS CHARACTERISTICS DESIRED-REQUIRED: Minimum number of years in business: 5; Min. annual sales $10,000,000; Min. net worth $1,000,000; Min.

annual net income $500,000; Min. annual cash flow $600,000

COMPANY:**First Lease & Equipment Consulting Corp.**
ADDRESS: 420 Hurstbourne Lane
Louisville, KY 40222
PHONE: (502) 423-7730
TYPE OF INSTITUTION: Lease consulting (back office activities for leasing at banks)
CONTACT OFFICER(S): Terry J. Winders, President
ASSETS: $15,000,000
TYPES OF FINANCING: LEASES: Single-investor; Leveraged; Tax leases; Non-tax leases; Operating; Tax-oriented lease brokerage; Lease syndications; Vendor financing programs; Other: Training seminars; OTHER SERVICES PROVIDED: Equipment disposal & evaluation
PREFERRED TYPES OF INDUSTRIES/INVESTMENTS: Banks and Savings & Loans
GEOGRAPHIC LIMITS OF INVESTMENTS/LOANS: National
RANGE OF INV./LOAN PER BUSINESS: Min. $ N/A
PREFERRED TERM FOR LOANS & LEASES: Min. $ N/A
REFERRALS ACCEPTED FROM: Investment/Mortgage banker or Borrower/Investee
BRANCHES: LaCrosse, WI
Chicago, IL

COMPANY: **First Lease & Equipment Consulting Corporation**
ADDRESS: 420 Hurstbourne La., Suite 202
Louisville, KY 40222
PHONE: (502) 423-7730
CONTACT OFFICER(S): Terry J. Winders

COMPANY: **First National Bank of Louisville**
ADDRESS: First National Tower
Louisville, KY 40202
PHONE: (502) 581-4200
TYPE OF INSTITUTION: Bank, full service including commercial finance, leasing, mergers & acquisitions & international
CONTACT OFFICER(S): Max White, S.V.P., Construction Financing
Ed Vittitoe, V.P. Corporate Finance, Mergers & Acquisitions
William Earley, S.V.P., Energy
Charles Williams, S.V.P., International
Jerry Johnston, S.V.P., National Banking
Paul Best, S.V.P., Mortgage Banking
ASSETS: $3.2 billion
INVESTMENTS/LOANS MADE: For own account
TYPES OF FINANCING: LOANS: Unsecured; Working capital (receivables/inventory); Equipment, REAL ESTATE LOANS: Intermediate-term senior mtg.; Wraparounds; Land; Construction; Standbys, LEASES: Leveraged; Tax leases; Non-tax leases; Vendor financing programs, INTERNATIONAL (including import/export)
GEOGRAPHIC LIMITS OF INVESTMENTS/LOANS: Regional; Other: Limited business nationally
RANGE OF INV./LOAN PER BUSINESS: Min. $250,000; Max. $12,000,000
PREFERRED TERM FOR LOANS & LEASES: Min. 2 years; Max. 10 years
BUSINESS CHARACTERISTICS DESIRED-REQUIRED: Minimum number of years in business: 3; Min. annual sales $5,000,000; Min. net worth $3,000,000
REFERRALS ACCEPTED FROM: Investment/Mortgage banker or Borrower/Investee
BRANCHES: Chuck Moeser, V.P., 60 E. 42nd Street, New York, NY; (212) 661-0980
John Hill, V.P., 1945 The Exchange, Suite 104, Atlanta, GA 30339; (404) 953-0930
Jim Sullivan, V.P., 625 N. Michigan Avenue, Suite 1020, Chicago, IL 60611; (312) 642-9779

COMPANY: **Liberty National Leasing Co., Liberty National Bank**
ADDRESS: 416 West Jefferson Street, P.O. Box 32500
Louisville, KY 40232
PHONE: (502) 566-2249
CONTACT OFFICER(S): Hugh M. Shwab, III

COMPANY: **United Leaseshares Inc.**
ADDRESS: 734 S. First Street
Louisville, KY 40202
PHONE: (502) 589-7000
CONTACT OFFICER(S): Robert L. Callander

COMPANY: **CAPBANC Leasing Corporation**
ADDRESS: P.O. Box 2710
Baton Rouge, LA 70821
PHONE: (504) 927-3730
CONTACT OFFICER(S): W. G. Powell Jr.

COMPANY: **Leasing Services, Inc.**
ADDRESS: 619 Jefferson Hwy. Box 586
Baton Rouge, LA 70821
PHONE: (504) 923-1555
CONTACT OFFICER(S): Galen F. Meyers

COMPANY: **Louisiana National Leasing Corp.**
ADDRESS: P.O. Box 451, 451 Florida Street
Baton Rouge, LA 70821
PHONE: (504) 389-4531
CONTACT OFFICER(S): George D. Hollingsworth

COMPANY: **Adams Financial Co. Inc.**
ADDRESS: P.O. Box 747
Metairie, LA 70004
PHONE: (504) 831-4600
CONTACT OFFICER(S): Thomas A. Agnew

COMPANY: **Household Research Corporation**
ADDRESS: 76 Rowe Street
Auburndale, MA 02166
PHONE: (617) 969-4200
CONTACT OFFICER(S): Richard L. Weinberg

COMPANY: **Continental Resources, Inc.**
ADDRESS: 175 Middlesex Turnpike
Bedford, MA 01730
PHONE: (617) 275-0850
TYPE OF INSTITUTION: Leasing Co.
CONTACT OFFICER(S): Robert L. Hahn, V.P.
TYPES OF FINANCING: LEASES: Operating; Vendor financing programs
PREFERRED TYPES OF INDUSTRIES/INVESTMENTS: High Technology
GEOGRAPHIC LIMITS OF INVESTMENTS/LOANS: National
PREFERRED TERM FOR LOANS & LEASES: Min. 1; Max. 3 years

COMPANY: **American Finance Group Inc.**
ADDRESS: 1 Liberty Square, 5th Floor
Boston, MA 02109
PHONE: (617) 720-1200
CONTACT OFFICER(S): Max Makaitis

COMPANY: **Boston Financial & Equity Corp.**
ADDRESS: 21 Burlington Ave.
Boston, MA 02215
PHONE: (617) 267-2900
TYPE OF INSTITUTION: Leasing company
CONTACT OFFICER(S): Sonny F. Monosson, President
TYPES OF FINANCING: LOANS: Equipment, LEASES: Single-investor; Leveraged; Tax leases; Non-tax leases; Operating; Tax-oriented lease brokerage; Lease syndications; Vendor financing programs
PREFERRED TYPES OF INDUSTRIES/INVESTMENTS: Strictly computers
WILL NOT CONSIDER: Any other
GEOGRAPHIC LIMITS OF INVESTMENTS/LOANS: National
REMARKS: Collateral lender

COMPANY: **Boston Leasing Group, Inc.**
ADDRESS: 286 Congress Street
Boston, MA 02110
PHONE: (617) 542-7600
CONTACT OFFICER(S): Stephen G. Morison

COMPANY: **CBT Leasing Corporation**
ADDRESS: 60 State Street
Boston, MA 02109
PHONE: (617) 227-0903
TYPE OF INSTITUTION: Leasing Co.
CONTACT OFFICER(S):J. Peter Yankowski, President
Ingo K. Kozak, Executive Vice President
Hensey A. Fenton, Assistant Vice President
ASSETS: 200MM+
INVESTMENTS/LOANS MADE: For own account, Through private placements
TYPES OF FINANCING: LEASES: Leveraged; Tax leases; Non-tax leases; Lease syndications; Vendor financing programs
PREFERRED TYPES OF INDUSTRIES/INVESTMENTS: Equipment leasing and financing based on credit evaluation of lesee/borrower
GEOGRAPHIC LIMITS OF INVESTMENTS/LOANS: International
RANGE OF INV./LOAN PER BUSINESS: Min. $100M; Max. $40MM
PREFERRED TERM FOR LOANS & LEASES: Max. 10 years
BUSINESS CHARACTERISTICS DESIRED-REQUIRED: Minimum number of years in business: 5; Min. annual sales $10MM; Min net worth $2MM
REFERRALS ACCEPTED FROM: Investment/Mortgage banker or Borrower/Investee

COMPANY: **Chancellor Corporation**
ADDRESS: Federal Reserve Plaza
Boston, MA 02210
PHONE: (617) 723-3500
CONTACT OFFICER(S): John J. Flynn, Sr. Vice Pres. Lease Origination
V. W. Garrett, Pres.
ASSETS: $300,000,000
INVESTMENTS/LOANS MADE: For own account, For managed accounts, Through private placements
INVESTMENTS/LOANS MADE: In securities without a secondary market
TYPES OF FINANCING: LEASES: Single-investor; Leveraged; Tax leases; Operating; Tax-oriented lease brokerage; Lease syndications; Vendor financing programs
PREFERRED TYPES OF INDUSTRIES/INVESTMENTS: Transportation Equipment, Materials, Handling Equipment, Production/Manufacturing Equipment
GEOGRAPHIC LIMITS OF INVESTMENTS/LOANS: National
RANGE OF INV./LOAN PER BUSINESS: Min. $500,000; Max. $15,000,000
PREFERRED TERM FOR LOANS & LEASES: Min. 3 years; Max. 10 years
BUSINESS CHARACTERISTICS DESIRED-REQUIRED: Minimum number of years in business: 5; Min. net worth $15.0M
REFERRALS ACCEPTED FROM: Investment/Mortgage banker or Borrower/Investee

COMPANY: **CSA Financial Corp.**
ADDRESS: 2 Oliver Street
Boston, MA 02109
PHONE: (617) 482-4671
TYPE OF INSTITUTION: Leasing Co.
CONTACT OFFICER(S): Edward Harnett, V.P., Marketing
TYPES OF FINANCING: LEASES: Leveraged; Tax leases; Non-tax leases; Operating; Tax-oriented lease brokerage; Lease syndications; Vendor financing programs
PREFERRED TYPES OF INDUSTRIES/INVESTMENTS: Computer Systems (Large Companies); Truck Fleets; Aircraft; Heavy Equipment; Medical Equipment
GEOGRAPHIC LIMITS OF INVESTMENTS/LOANS: National; International

COMPANY: **Firstbank Financial Corp.**
ADDRESS: 100 Federal Street
Boston, MA 02110

PHONE: (617) 434-4042
CONTACT OFFICER(S): Peter J. Manning

COMPANY: **Funding Resources, Inc.**
ADDRESS: 262 Beacon Street
Boston, MA 02116
PHONE: (617) 267-1176
TYPE OF INSTITUTION: Equipment leasing & finance
CONTACT OFFICER(S): Don O. Crawford, President
Marcia Richmond, Leasing Mgr.
TYPES OF FINANCING: LEASES: Single-investor; Leveraged; Tax leases; Non-tax leases; Operating; Tax-oriented lease brokerage
GEOGRAPHIC LIMITS OF INVESTMENTS/LOANS: National
RANGE OF INV./LOAN PER BUSINESS: Min. $50,000; Max. None
PREFERRED TERM FOR LOANS & LEASES: Min. 3 years; Max. 15 years
BUSINESS CHARACTERISTICS DESIRED-REQUIRED: Minimum number of years in business: 0
REFERRALS ACCEPTED FROM: Investment/Mortgage banker or Borrower/Investee

COMPANY: **Healthco Professional Services Corp.**
ADDRESS: 25 Stuart Street
Boston, MA 02116
PHONE: (617) 423-6045
CONTACT OFFICER(S): Joseph Sands

COMPANY: **John Hancock Financial Services, Inc.**
ADDRESS: John Hancock Place, P.O. Box 111
Boston, MA 02117
PHONE: (617) 421-4444
TYPE OF INSTITUTION: Equipment Leasing Subsidiary of John Hancock Mutual Life Insurance Co.
CONTACT OFFICER(S): George F. Miller, President & CEO
Joseph A. Tomlinson, V.P. Operations
Robert H. Watts, V.P. Marketing
ASSETS: $150,000,000
INVESTMENTS/LOANS MADE: For own account, For managed accounts
TYPES OF FINANCING: LOANS: Equipment, LEASES: Single-investor; Tax leases; Non-tax leases; Tax-oriented lease brokerage; Lease syndications; Vendor financing programs, OTHER SERVICES PROVIDED: Equipment Leasing Tax Shelters
PREFERRED TYPES OF INDUSTRIES/INVESTMENTS: Diversified Commercial and Agricultural (Agriculture is a specialty.)
GEOGRAPHIC LIMITS OF INVESTMENTS/LOANS: National
RANGE OF INV./LOAN PER BUSINESS: Min. $100,000; Max. $10,000,000
PREFERRED TERM FOR LOANS & LEASES: Min. 3 years; Max. 7 years
BUSINESS CHARACTERISTICS DESIRED-REQUIRED: Companies with proven ability to repay. Balance sheet lender.
BRANCHES: John Hancock Financial Services, Inc., Crossroads Bldg., Ste. 520, 1825 S. Grant St., San Mateo, CA 94402, (415) 572-0433, Leo J. Tisa, Manager-Western Regional Office
WASHINGTON, D.C.: Suite 1111, 4350 East West Highway, Bethesda, MD 20814, (301) 951-4282
SAN MATEO: Suite 520, 1825 South Grant Street, San Mateo, CA 94402, (415) 572-0401
ATLANTA: Suite 550, 6151 Powers Ferry Road, Atlanta, GA 30339, (401) 953-6872
PHOENIX: Suite 240, 11801 North Tatum Boulevard, Phoenix, AZ 85028 (602) 996-0961
SPOKANE, WA: South 176 Stevens Street, Spokane, WA 99204, (509) 747-5126
AURORA, CO: Pavilion Tower, 1-Suite 760, 2851 South Parker Road, Aurora, CO 80014, (303) 695-8770
CHAMPAIGN, IL: Robeson Buildiing, Suite 505, 206 North Randolph Street, Champaign, IL 61820, (217) 356-5518
DALLAS, TX: Suite 860, 555 Griffin Square, Dallas, TX 75202, (214) 742-9066
MEMPHIS, TN: 5710 Summer Trees Drive, Suite #1, Memphis, TN 38134, (901) 382-2720
SACRAMENTO, CA: 1900 Point West Way, Suite 188, Sacramento, CA 98515, (916) 922-6554
SIOUX CITY, IOWA: 1030 Badgerow Building, 4th & Jackson Streets, Sioux City, IA 51101, (712) 252-4323
STATESBORO, GA: Suite 101, 12 Siebald Street, Statesboro, GA 30458, (912) 764-6133

COMPANY: **Leasing Services, Inc.**
ADDRESS: 134 Beech St.
Boston, MA 02111
PHONE: (617) 542-4200
CONTACT OFFICER(S): Bud Holbert, Gen. Sales Mgr.
Dick Coveney, Pres.
ASSETS: $85 million approx.
TYPES OF FINANCING: LOANS; LEASES: Single-investor; Leveraged; Tax leases; Non-tax leases; operating; Tax-oriented lease brokerage; Lease Syndications; Vendor financial programs; Municipal; REAL ESTATE: Partnerships/Syndications
PREFERRED TYPES OF INDUSTRIES/INVESTMENTS: Diversified
WILL NOT CONSIDER: IBM mainframes (Large computers)
GEOGRAPHIC LIMITS OF INVESTMENTS/LOANS: National
PREFERRED TERM FOR LOANS & LEASES: Min. 1 year; Max. 12 years
REFERRALS ACCEPTED FROM: Investment/Mortgage banker or Borrower/Investee

COMPANY: **New England Merchants Leasing Corp.**
ADDRESS: 50 Milk Street
Boston, MA 02107
PHONE: (617) 338-2100
CONTACT OFFICER(S): E.F. McCulloch, Jr.

COMPANY: **Shawmut Bank of Boston, N.A.**
ADDRESS: 1 Federal Street
Boston, MA 02211
PHONE: (617) 292-2956
TYPE OF INSTITUTION: Equipment finance & leasing department of commercial bank

MASSACHUSETTS

CONTACT OFFICER(S): J. L. Egenberg, V.P., Equipment Finance and Leasing
ASSETS: 7 billion
INVESTMENTS/LOANS MADE: For own account
TYPES OF FINANCING: LOANS: Equipment, LEASES: Single-investor; Leveraged; Tax leases; Tax-oriented lease brokerage; Lease syndications; Vendor financing programs, OTHER: Debt unleveraged leases; Equity notes
GEOGRAPHIC LIMITS OF INVESTMENTS/LOANS: National
RANGE OF INV./LOAN PER BUSINESS: Min. $250,000; Max. $8,000,000
PREFERRED TERM FOR LOANS & LEASES: Min. 3 years; Max. 5 years

COMPANY: **State Street Boston Leasing Co., Inc.**
ADDRESS: 225 Franklin Street
Boston, MA 02101
PHONE: (617) 786-3087
CONTACT OFFICER(S): John D. Rusher, III

COMPANY: **Baybanks Finance & Leasing Co. Inc.**
ADDRESS: 7 New England Executive Park, 10th Floor
Burlington, MA 01803
PHONE: (617) 273-1700
CONTACT OFFICER(S): Harold C. Foley

COMPANY: **Financial Architects Inc.**
ADDRESS: 865 Providence Highway
Dedham, MA 02026
PHONE: (617) 326-4650
CONTACT OFFICER(S): James E. Hogan

COMPANY: **Compulease Inc.**
ADDRESS: 10 Speen Street
Framingham, MA 01701
PHONE: (617) 872-4004
CONTACT OFFICER(S): Peter C. Zeytoonjian

COMPANY: **Eaton Financial Corporation**
ADDRESS: 27 Hollis Street
Framingham, MA 01701
PHONE: (617) 620-0099
TYPE OF INSTITUTION: Leasing-Independent
CONTACT OFFICER(S): Paul S. Gass, President
John P. Colton, Senior Vice President, (Primary Contact)
Rene A. Lefebvre, Vice President/Treasurer
ASSETS: $41,000,000
INVESTMENTS/LOANS MADE: For own account
TYPES OF FINANCING: LEASES: Vendor financing programs; Other: general equipment
PREFERRED TYPES OF INDUSTRIES/INVESTMENTS: General equipment related to "small ticket" under $50,000 leasing
GEOGRAPHIC LIMITS OF INVESTMENTS/LOANS: National
RANGE OF INV./LOAN PER BUSINESS: Min. $1,000; Max. $100,000
PREFERRED TERM FOR LOANS & LEASES: Min. 6 months; Max. 8 years
BUSINESS CHARACTERISTICS DESIRED-REQUIRED: Minimum number of years in business: 0
REFERRALS ACCEPTED FROM: Investment/Mortgage banker or Borrower/Investee
BRANCHES: 1002-A Greentree Campus, Marlton, NJ 08053, (609) 596-0990
4902 Eisenhower Boulevard, Tampa, FL 33614, (813) 888-5888
Lookout Corporation Center, 1717 Dixie Highway, Fort Wright, KY 41011, (606) 341-6010
The Plum Creek Commons, 405 S. Wilcox Street, Suite 103, Castle Rock, CO 80104, (303) 688-6990, 6500 Village Parkway, Dublin, CA 95568, (415) 833-1852

COMPANY: **Integrated Resources Equip. Group**
ADDRESS: 394 Lowell St., Suite #4
Lexington, MA 02173
PHONE: (617) 861-1411
TYPE OF INSTITUTION: Leasing Co.
CONTACT OFFICER(S): Bill Adair, Pres. in NY, (212) 949-7800
TYPES OF FINANCING: LEASES

COMPANY: **R. T. Whitney & Co. Inc.**
ADDRESS: 8 Tucker Street
Marblehead, MA 01945
PHONE: (617) 631-3833
CONTACT OFFICER(S): Richard T. Whitney

COMPANY: **Enterprise Leasing**
ADDRESS: 103 Wilkins Glen
Medfield, MA 02052
PHONE: (617) 359-7356
TYPE OF INSTITUTION: Third Party equipment lessor
CONTACT OFFICER(S): Robert S. Welling, President
ASSETS: $3,500,000-7,500,000
TYPES OF FINANCING: LEASES: Single investor; True Full Payout Leases; Leveraged; Tax leases
PREFERRED TYPES OF INDUSTRIES/INVESTMENTS: Computery Industry (Computer mfgs., computer DEM's, computer dealers, computer retailers); Communications; Research and development; High technology
WILL NOT CONSIDER: Restaurants, food establishments
GEOGRAPHIC LIMITS OF INVESTMENTS/LOANS: Other: Northeast-New England, New York, New Jersey, Washingtn, DC, Pennsylvania
RANGE OF INV./LOAN PER BUSINESS: Min. $3,000; Max. $150,000
PREFERRED TERM FOR LOANS & LEASES: Min. 1-3 years; Max. 5-8 years
BUSINESS CHARACTERISTICS DESIRED-REQUIRED: Minimum number of years in business: 2-3; Other: Net worth should be 4-6 times amount to be leased; sales trend up; net income-trend up; positive cash flows; profits latest 2 years
REFERRALS ACCEPTED FROM: Investment/Mortgage bankers or Bankers/Vendors of Products

COMPANY: **Prime Leasing, Prime Computer, Inc.**
ADDRESS: Prime Park MS 15-29
Natick, MA 01760
PHONE: (617) 655-8000
CONTACT OFFICER(S): Ron Swanson

COMPANY: **First Equipment Leasing Co. (FELCO)**
ADDRESS: 381 Elliot St.
Newton Upper Falls, MA 02164
PHONE: (617) 332-7900
TYPE OF INSTITUTION: General Equipment Leasing
CONTACT OFFICER(S): Richard E. Sands, V. Pres.
INVESTMENTS/LOANS MADE: For own account, Through private placements
TYPES OF FINANCING: LEASES: tax leases; Tax-oriented lease brokerage; Vendor financing programs
WILL NOT CONSIDER: Vehicles, aircraft
GEOGRAPHIC LIMITS OF INVESTMENTS/LOANS: National
PREFERRED TERM FOR LOANS & LEASES: Max. 5 years
REFERRALS ACCEPTED FROM: Investment/Mortgage banker or Borrower/Investee

COMPANY: **Multibank Leasing Company**
ADDRESS: 1400 Hancock Street
Quincy, MA 02169
PHONE: (617) 471-6404
CONTACT OFFICER(S): Christopher Shannon

COMPANY: **Plymouth Savings Bank**
ADDRESS: 226 Main Street, P.O. Box 431
Wareham, MA 02571
PHONE: (617) 295-3800
TYPE OF INSTITUTION: Bank—Mortgage banking, commercial lending
CONTACT OFFICER(S): Frank D. Fantasia, Sr. Vice President—Sr. Lending Officer
ASSETS: $270,000,000
TYPES OF FINANCING: VENTURE CAPITAL: Second-stage; Later-stage expansion, LOANS: Working capiital; Equipment; Equity-related, REAL ESTATE LOANS: Long-term senior mtg.; Intermediate-term senior mtg.; Wraparounds; Land; Land development; Construction; Standbys; Industrial revenue bonds, LEASES: Single-investor; Leveraged; Non-tax leases; Operating; Vendor financing programs, REAL ESTATE: Acquisitions; Joint ventures; Partnerships/Syndications
WILL NOT CONSIDER: Restaurants, motels
GEOGRAPHIC LIMITS OF INVESTMENTS/LOANS: Regional
RANGE OF INV./LOAN PER BUSINESS: Min. $25,000; Max. $500,000
REFERRALS ACCEPTED FROM: Investment/Mortgage banker or Borrower/Investee

COMPANY: **Encore Leasing**
ADDRESS: 15 Walnut Street
Wellesley Hills, MA 02181
PHONE: (617) 875-1606
CONTACT OFFICER(S): Paul A. Renner

COMPANY: **Key Capital Corp.**
ADDRESS: 57 River Street
Wellesley Hills, MA 02181
PHONE: (617) 431-7770
TYPE OF INSTITUTION: Leasing Company
CONTACT OFFICER(S):Richard A. Molyneux, Executive Vice President
PREFERRED TYPES OF INDUSTRIES/INVESTMENTS: Loans: Aircraft & Yachts, Leases: Automobiles
WILL NOT CONSIDER: General Equipment
GEOGRAPHIC LIMITS OF INVESTMENTS/LOANS: National
RANGE OF INV./LOAN PER BUSINESS: Min. $50,000
PREFERRED TERM FOR LOANS & LEASES: Min. Tailored

COMPANY: **Leasemakers**
ADDRESS: 572 Washington St.
Wellesley, MA 02181
PHONE: (617) 237-4850
TYPE OF INSTITUTION: Lease broker, consultant
CONTACT OFFICER(S): G. Stewart Baird, Jr., President
INVESTMENTS/LOANS MADE: For managed accounts, Through private placements
INVESTMENTS/LOANS MADE: Only in securities without a secondary market
TYPES OF FINANCING: VENTURE CAPITAL: Start-up from developed product stage; First-stage, LOANS: Equipment; Equity-related, LEASES: Single-investor; Leveraged; Tax leases; Non-tax leases; Operating; Tax-oriented lease brokerage; Vendor financing programs, OTHER SERVICES PROVIDED: Direct marketing programs developed and piloted, including micro-computer based sales management systems, for products and services
PREFERRED TYPES OF INDUSTRIES/INVESTMENTS: Any tax-qualified types
GEOGRAPHIC LIMITS OF INVESTMENTS/LOANS: State
RANGE OF INV./LOAN PER BUSINESS: Min. $200,000; Max. $2,000,000
PREFERRED TERM FOR LOANS & LEASES: Min. 3 years; Max. 10 years
BUSINESS CHARACTERISTICS DESIRED-REQUIRED: Minimum number of years in business: 0 for venture capital; 1 year for leasing
REFERRALS ACCEPTED FROM: Borrower/Investee

COMPANY: **LFC Lessors, Inc.**
ADDRESS: #4A Henshaw St.
Woburn, MA 01801
PHONE: (617) 935-5911
TYPE OF INSTITUTION: Leasing Co.
CONTACT OFFICER(S): Edgar E. Jackson, Pres. Harry Frandsen, V.P.
TYPES OF FINANCING: LEASES: Operating; Tax-oriented lease brokerage; Vendor financing programs
PREFERRED TYPES OF INDUSTRIES/INVESTMENTS: Office & Photo Typesetting
GEOGRAPHIC LIMITS OF INVESTMENTS/LOANS: National
RANGE OF INV./LOAN PER BUSINESS: Min. $10,000; Max. $100,000

PREFERRED TERM FOR LOANS & LEASES: Min. 2; Max. 5 years

COMPANY: **National Surety Leasing, Inc.**
ADDRESS: 672 Greenbriar Lane
Annapolis, MD 21401
PHONE: (301) 269-0354
CONTACT OFFICER(S): Patrick E. O'Malley

COMPANY: **Phillips Leasing**
ADDRESS: 114 Forbes Street
Annapolis, MD 21401
PHONE: (301) 263-1330
CONTACT OFFICER(S): Ralph E. Meloy

COMPANY: **FCA Leasing Corporation**
ADDRESS: Munsey Building, P.O. Box 508
Baltimore, MD 21203
PHONE: (301) 752-8450
CONTACT OFFICER(S): Louis Eliasberg Jr.

COMPANY: **The Savers Leasing Group**
ADDRESS: 1 N. Charles St., Suite 207
Baltimore, MD 21201
PHONE: (301) 539-0108
CONTACT OFFICER(S): Larry D. Unger, President
Arnold E. Greene
Sr. Vice President
ASSETS: $1,000,000
INVESTMENTS/LOANS MADE: For own account; Through private placements
TYPES OF FINANCING: LEASES: Single-investor; Leveraged; Tax leases; Non-tax leases; Tax-oriented lease brokerage; Lease syndications
RANGE OF INV./LOAN PER BUSINESS: Min. $100,000; Max. $10,000,000
PREFERRED TERM FOR LOANS & LEASES: Min. 2 years: Max. 10 years
BUSINESS CHARACTERISTICS DESIRED-REQUIRED: Minimum number of years in business: 3

COMPANY: **Union-Tidewater Financial**
ADDRESS: 10 East Baltimore Street, P.O. Box 2373
Baltimore, MD 21203
PHONE: (301) 539-2250
CONTACT OFFICER(S): Thomas B. Howard, Jr.

COMPANY: **Financial Funding Systems Inc.**
ADDRESS: 4810 Auburn Avenue
Bethesda, MD 20814
CONTACT OFFICER(S): Joe Goldberg

COMPANY: **Suburban Funding Corporation**
ADDRESS: 6610 Rockledge Dr.
Bethesda, MD 20817
PHONE: (301) 493-2950
CONTACT OFFICER(S): Clarence M. Wilcox

COMPANY: **Capital Sources, Inc.**
ADDRESS: P.O. Box 1151
Columbia, MD 21044
PHONE: (301) 995-6666
CONTACT OFFICER(S): Michael M. Flax

COMPANY: **Kidde Credit Corporation**
ADDRESS: 30 Washington Center
Hagerstown, MD 21740
PHONE: (301) 791-7600
CONTACT OFFICER(S): Robert E. Duncan

COMPANY: **The Equipment Leasing Company**
ADDRESS: Ruxton Towers, P.O. Box 307
Riderwood, MD 21139
PHONE: (301) 828-1746
CONTACT OFFICER(S): G. A. Kaufman

COMPANY: **Maryland National Leasing Corp.**
ADDRESS: Nottingham Centre, 502 Washington Ave.
Towson, MD 21204
PHONE: (301) 321-1100
TYPE OF INSTITUTION: Equipment leasing subsidiary of Bank Holding Co.
CONTACT OFFICER(S): Milton M. Harris, Chrm.
Edward A. Dahlka, Pres.
ASSETS: $200 MM
INVESTMENTS/LOANS MADE: For own account; For managed accounts; Through private placements
INVESTMENTS/LOANS MADE: Only in securities without a secondary market
TYPES OF FINANCING: SECONDARY-MARKET CORPPOARATE SECURITIES: Other: Loans & Leases; LOANS: Equipment; LEASES: Single-investor; Leveraged; Tax leases; Non-tax leases; Operating; Tax-oriented lease brokerage; Lease syndications; Vendor financing programs; Other: Municipal leases
PREFERRED TYPES OF INDUSTRIES/INVESTMENTS: Open
GEOGRAPHIC LIMITS OF INVESTMENTS/LOANS: National
RANGE OF INV./LOAN PER BUSINESS: Min. $500,000
PREFERRED TERM FOR LOANS & LEASES: Min. 2-3 yrs.; Max. 10-15
REFERRALS ACCEPTED FROM: Investment/Mortgage banker or Borrower/Investee

COMPANY: **Ann Arbor Leasing Company**
ADDRESS: 3135 South State, Suite 101
Ann Arbor, MI 48104
PHONE: (313) 663-6666
CONTACT OFFICER(S): Michael R. Levine

COMPANY: **Captec Leasing Company**
ADDRESS: 325 E. Eisenhower Ste. 204
Ann Arbor, MI 48104
PHONE: (313) 994-5505
CONTACT OFFICER(S): Patrick L. Beach

COMPANY: **CPHA Financial Services**
ADDRESS: 1968 Green Road, P.O. Box 1809
Ann Arbor, MI 48106
PHONE: (313) 769-6511
CONTACT OFFICER(S): Robert A Shaw

COMPANY: **Ervin Leasing, A Division of Ervin Industries, Inc.**
ADDRESS: 3893 Research Pk, Dr., P.O. Box 1168
Ann Arbor, MI 48106
PHONE: (313) 769-4600
TYPE OF INSTITUTION: Leasing division of manufacturing company
CONTACT OFFICER(S): D.B. Gaffney, Divisional V.P.
ASSETS: $11,000,000
TYPES OF FINANCING: LEASES: Single-investor; Tax leases; Non-tax leases; Vendor financing programs
WILL NOT CONSIDER: Rolling stock
GEOGRAPHIC LIMITS OF INVESTMENTS/LOANS: National
RANGE OF INV./LOAN PER BUSINESS: Min. $3,000.00; Max. $300,000.00
PREFERRED TERM FOR LOANS & LEASES: Min. 36 mos.; Max. 60 mos.
BUSINESS CHARACTERISTICS DESIRED-REQUIRED: Minimum number of years in business: 2
BRANCHES: Doug Jones, 161 Ottawa N.W., Ste. 502-C, Grand Rapids, MI 49503, 614-431-1625
Mike Pendy, 2021 E. Dublin-Granville Rd., Ste. 135, Columbus, OH 43229, 616-458-5395

COMPANY: **Appliance Buyers Credit Corporation**
ADDRESS: 553 Benson Road
Benton Harbor, MI 49022
PHONE: (616) 926-5528
CONTACT OFFICER(S): Phillip Harrison

COMPANY: **ESC Funding Inc.**
ADDRESS: 950 E. Maple Road, Suite L1
Birmingham, MI 48011
PHONE: (313) 642-0577
CONTACT OFFICER(S): Michael N. Day

COMPANY: **First National Capital**
ADDRESS: 1100 N. Woodward Ave., Suite 214
Birmingham, MI 48013
PHONE: (313) 540-4740
TYPE OF INSTITUTION: Capital Equipment Leasing
CONTACT OFFICER(S): Alan M. Forrester, Pres.
Thomas F. Husband, V. P.
ASSETS: $40,000,000
INVESTMENTS/LOANS MADE: For own account; Through private placements
INVESTMENTS/LOANS MADE: Only in securities without a secondary market
TYPES OF FINANCING: VENTURE CAPITAL: LEASES: Single-investor; Leveraged; Tax leases; Non-tax leases; Operating; Tax-oriented lease brokerage; Lease syndications
PREFERRED TYPES OF INDUSTRIES/INVESTMENTS: Lessees are BBB or better credits; Equipment: computer peripherals; transporation; heavy manufacturing
WILL NOT CONSIDER: No CPU's over $1 million in cost; No cars
GEOGRAPHIC LIMITS OF INVESTMENTS/LOANS: National
RANGE OF INV./LOAN PER BUSINESS: Min. $200,000; Max. $5,000,000
PREFERRED TERM FOR LOANS & LEASES: Min. 2 yrs; Max. 10 yrs.
BUSINESS CHARACTERISTICS DESIRED-REQUIRED: Other: Public or private with BBB or better bond equivalent rating
REFERRALS ACCEPTED FROM: Investment/Mortgage banker or Borrower/Investee

COMPANY: **Van Arnem Financial Services, Inc.**
ADDRESS: 870 Bowers
Birmingham, MI 48011
PHONE: (313) 647-3040
TYPE OF INSTITUTION: Financial Services Inc. Specializes in Tax Shelters and income programs
CONTACT OFFICER(S): Mr. H. L. Van Arnem, Chief Executive Officer
ASSETS: $400,400,000
TYPES OF FINANCING: LOANS: Working capital; Equipmment; Equity-related; LEASES: Single-investor; Leveraged; Tax leases; Non-tax leases; Lease syndications; REAL ESTATE: Partnerships/Syndications
PREFERRED TYPES OF INDUSTRIES/INVESTMENTS: Equipment Leases with Fortune 200 Companies; Equipment Lease Syndications
GEOGRAPHIC LIMITS OF INVESTMENTS/LOANS: National
RANGE OF INV./LOAN PER BUSINESS: Min. $1,000,000; Max. $10,000,000
REFERRALS ACCEPTED FROM: Investment/Mortgage banker or Borrower/Investee

COMPANY: **General Funding Corporation**
ADDRESS: 525 N. Woodward Avenue, Suite 2150
Bloomfield Hills, MI 48013
PHONE: (313) 540-2444
CONTACT OFFICER(S): Burke Fossee III

COMPANY: **North American Computer Equipment, Inc.**
ADDRESS: 1145 W. Long Lake Road
Bloomfield Hills, MI 48013
PHONE: (313) 540-6900
CONTACT OFFICER(S): Larry G. Johnson

COMPANY: **Sun Financial Inc.**
ADDRESS: 4190 Telegraph Road, Suite 101
Bloomfield Hills, MI 48013
PHONE: (313) 540-6155
CONTACT OFFICER(S): Clay M. Biddinger

COMPANY: **Clark Equipment Credit Corp.**
ADDRESS: 128 East Front Street
Buchanan, MI 49107
PHONE: (616) 697-4211
CONTACT OFFICER(S): T. R. Morton

LEASING COMPANIES

(Lessors. Also see Commercial Bankers and Finance Companies, Insurance Companies and Investment Bankers)

COMPANY: **Comerica Financial Services**
ADDRESS: 243 West Congress, P.O. Box 59
Detroit, MI 48231
PHONE: (313) 222-9356
CONTACT OFFICER(S): J. Patrick Godfrey

COMPANY: **Manubank Leasing Corporation, Manufacturers Natl Bank of Detroit**
ADDRESS: 100 Renaissance Center
Detroit, MI 48243
PHONE: (313) 222-9730
CONTACT OFFICER(S): Timothy V. Talbert

COMPANY: **Roney Capital Corporation**
ADDRESS: 542 BuhlBuilding
Detroit, MI 48226
PHONE: (313) 961-7270
CONTACT OFFICER(S): David W. Harris

COMPANY: **VMS Financial, Inc., American Int'l Resources**
ADDRESS: 1100 Buhl Building
Detroit, MI 48226
PHONE: (313) 225-5500
CONTACT OFFICER(S): Bob Dorr

COMPANY: **Michigan National Leasing Corp.**
ADDRESS: 38200 West Ten Mile Road
Farmington Hills, MI 48024
PHONE: (313) 478-4130
CONTACT OFFICER(S): John C. Verdon

COMPANY: **The Hawthorne Financial Group, Inc.**
ADDRESS: 31555 W. 14 Mile Rd.
Farmington Hills MI 48018
PHONE: (313) 855-4683
CONTACT OFFICER(S): Charles F. Barnes

COMPANY: **Corporate Funding Inc.**
ADDRESS: 401 B Waters Building
Grand Rapids, MI 49503
PHONE: (616) 459-0266
CONTACT OFFICER(S): John S. Edison

COMPANY: **Old Kent Leasing Corp.**
ADDRESS: One Vandenberg Center
Grand Rapids, MI 49503
PHONE: (616) 774-5252
TYPE OF INSTITUTION: Leasing Co.
CONTACT OFFICER(S): Steve Potter, Asst. V.P.
ASSETS: 5.5 million
TYPES OF FINANCING: LEASES: Single-investor; Leveraged; Tax leases; Non-tax leases; Tax-oriented lease brokerage; Vendor financing programs
WILL NOT CONSIDER: Computers, rolling stock
GEOGRAPHIC LIMITS OF INVESTMENTS/LOANS: National
RANGE OF INV./LOAN PER BUSINESS: Min. $100,000; Max. $none
PREFERRED TERM FOR LOANS & LEASES: Min. 5 years; Max. 10 years

COMPANY: **Master Lease Corp.**
ADDRESS: 26125 Woodward Av.
Huntington Wood, MI 48070
PHONE: (313) 399-9800
TYPE OF INSTITUTION: Leasing Co.
TYPES OF FINANCING: LEASES: Tax leases
GEOGRAPHIC LIMITS OF INVESTMENTS/LOANS: Regional; National
RANGE OF INV./LOAN PER BUSINESS: Max. $100,000
PREFERRED TERM FOR LOANS & LEASES: Min. 3; Max. 4 years

COMPANY: **The Allen Group Leasing Corp.**
ADDRESS: 12921 Stark Rd.
Livonia, MI 48150
PHONE: (313) 427-4930
CONTACT OFFICER(S): Jack L. Eichelbaum

COMPANY: **First Macomb Leasing Corporation**
ADDRESS: 1 North Gratiot
Mount Clemens, MI 48043
PHONE: (313) 469-6111
CONTACT OFFICER(S): M. A. Deitrich

COMPANY: **Brannigan's, Ltd.**
ADDRESS: 5688 S. Lake Shore Dr.
Remus, MI 49340
PHONE: (517) 561-2494
TYPE OF INSTITUTION: Privately held leasing corporation
CONTACT OFFICER(S): Patricia L. Welgs, President, General Management, Sales & Credit
N. G. Burmeister, Chairman, General Management, Sales & Credit
ASSETS: $5,000,000
INVESTMENTS/LOANS MADE: For own account
TYPES OF FINANCING: LEASES: Single-investor; Leveraged; Tax leases; Non-tax leases; Tax-oriented lease brokerage; Vendor financing programs; OTHER: On site sales units with prospects
PREFERRED TYPES OF INDUSTRIES/INVESTMENTS: Specializing in Computers, machine tools, medical equipment to profitable entities
WILL NOT CONSIDER: Non-income producing assets
GEOGRAPHIC LIMITS OF INVESTMENTS/LOANS: State,
RANGE OF INV./LOAN PER BUSINESS: Min. $5,000.00; Max. $ none
PREFERRED TERM FOR LOANS & LEASES: Min. 3 years; Max. 5 years
BUSINESS CHARACTERISTICS DESIRED-REQUIRED: Minimum number of years in business: 3; Min. net worth $50,000; Min. annual net income $100,000
REFERRALS ACCEPTED FROM: Borrower/Investee

COMPANY: **The Bancorp Group Inc.**
ADDRESS: 3000 Town Center, Suite 3220
Southfield, MI 48075
PHONE: (313) 354-8160
CONTACT OFFICER(S): Steven M. Kirkpatrick

COMPANY: **The Bancorp Group, Inc.**
ADDRESS: 3000 Town Center, Suite 3220
Southfield, MI 48075
PHONE: (313) 354-8160
TYPE OF INSTITUTION: Independent lessor and investment banker
CONTACT OFFICERS: Herman J. Drazick, Chairman
James T. Pawlak, V. P. Tax Leasing
Thomas X. Dunigan, Vice President, Medical Equipment Financing
ASSETS: $25 million
INVESTMENTS/LOANS MADE: For own account; For managed accounts
INVESTMENTS/LOANS MADE: only in securities without a secondary market
TYPES OF FINANCING: VENTURE CAPITAL: Buy-outs/Acquisitions; LOANS: Equity-related; LEASES: Single-investor; Leveraged; Tax leases; Non-tax leases; Operating; Tax-oriented lease brokerage; Vendor financing programs; Other: Develop and manage portfolios for corporate lessors
PREFERRED TYPES OF INDUSTRIES/INVESTMENTS: No preferences
GEOGRAPHIC LIMITS OF INVESTMENTS/LOANS: National
RANGE OF INV./LOAN PER BUSINESS: Min. $25,000 in equity; Max. $1 million in equity
PREFERRED TERM FOR LOANS & LEASES: Min. 3 years; Max. 10 years
BUSINESS CHARACTERISTICS DESIRED-REQUIRED: Minimum number of years in business: 2; Min. annual sales $ 1 million; Min. net worth $ 100,000; Min. annual net income positive; Min. annual cash flow positive
REFERRALS ACCEPTED FROM: Investment/Mortgage banker or Borrower/Investee
BRANCHES: 4056 Plainfield, N.E., Suite L-2, Grand Rapids, MI 49505; (616) 361-1311; William Zahradnick
5050 Excelsior Boulevard, Suite 415, Minneapolis, MN 55416; (612) 925-2886; Scott Whipple
760 U.S. Highway 1, Suite 201, North Palm Beach, FL 33408; (305) 694-1477; Thomas Vaughan

COMPANY: **Bankers Leasing Services, Inc.-subsidiary of UnionBancorp-Grand Rapids**
ADDRESS: 28575 Greenfield Road, Suite 208
Southfield, MI 48034
PHONE: (313) 353-9630
TYPE OF INSTITUTION: Sub. of Bank Holding Co.
ASSETS: over $900 million
TYPES OF FINANCING: LEASES
GEOGRAPHIC LIMITS OF INVESTMENTS/LOANS: National
RANGE OF INV./LOAN PER BUSINESS: Min. $5,000; Max. $5,000,000
PREFERRED TERM FOR LOANS & LEASES: Max. 5 years
BUSINESS CHARACTERISTICS DESIRED-REQUIRED: Minimum number of years in business: 0; Other: ability of customer to make payments
REFERRALS ACCEPTED FROM: Investment/Mortgage banker or Borrower/Investtee

COMPANY: **Federated Financial Reserve Corporation**
ADDRESS: 20000 West 12 Mile Road
Southfield, MI 48076
PHONE: (313) 557-9100
CONTACT OFFICER(S): Louis P. Ferris Jr.

COMPANY: **National Computer Equipment Corporation**
ADDRESS: 27557 Harper Ave.
St. Clair Shores MI 48081
PHONE: (313) 774-7400
CONTACT OFFICER(S): John Mills, President
James Carleton, Vice President
Joseph Romeo, V.P. Marketing
John Billotti
V.P. Finance
ASSETS: 8,000,000
INVESTMENTS/LOANS MADE: For own account; Through private placements
INVESTMENTS/LOANS MADE: LEASES: Single-investor; Leverage; Tax leases; Non-tax leases; Operating; Tax-oriented lease brokerage; Lease syndications
PREFERRED TYPES OF INDUSTRIES/INVESTMENTS: Capital equipment concentration on computer equipment
GEOGRAPHIC LIMITS OF INVESTMENTS/LOANS: National
RANGE OF INV./LOAN PER BUSINESS: Min. $100,000; Max. $10,000,000
PREFERRED TERM FOR LOANS & LEASES: Min. No Minimum years; Max. 7 years
REFERRALS ACCEPTED FROM: Investment/Mortgage banker or Borrower/Investee
BRANCHES: 6465 Monroe, Suite 1, P.O. Box 801, Sylvonia, 0H 43560; 419-885-4620; Acct. Mgr.: George Owen Jr.
Suite 305, Manor Oak 1, 1910 Cochron Rd., Pittsburgh, PA 15220; 412-341-2522; Acct. Mgr.: Gus Sandonnas
Westgate Tower, 20525 Center Ridge, Suite 136, Rocky River, OH 44116: 216-356-1213

COMPANY: **American Business Funding, Inc.**
ADDRESS: P.O. Box 1468
Troy, MI 48099
PHONE: (313) 689-2525
CONTACT OFFICER(S): Gerald W. Dana

COMPANY: **CMI Corporation**
ADDRESS: 755 West Big Beaver Road, Suite 1900
Troy, MI 48084
PHONE: (313) 362-1000
CONTACT OFFICER(S): Frank Chartier

COMPANY: **EX-CELL-O Credit Corporation**
ADDRESS: 2855 Collidge
Troy, MI 48084
PHONE: (313) 637-1000
CONTACT OFFICER(S): Robert L. Russell

COMPANY:**CHR Equipment Financing, Inc.**
ADDRESS: 7525 Mitchell Road, Suite 300
Eden Prairie, MN 55344
PHONE: (612) 937-9150
TYPE OF INSTITUTION: General Equipment Lessor
CONTACT OFFICER(S): Stephen T. Grundahl, Vice President-Marketing
INVESTMENTS/LOANS MADE: For own account
TYPES OF FINANCING: LEASES: Leveraged; Tax leases; Vendor financing programs
PREFERRED TYPES OF INDUSTRIES/INVESTMENTS: Machine Tools, Production Equipment, Hospital/Medical, EDP, Tractors and Trailers, Phone Systems
GEOGRAPHIC LIMITS OF INVESTMENTS/LOANS: National
RANGE OF INV./LOAN PER BUSINESS: Min. $50,000.00; Max. $5,000,000.00
PREFERRED TERM FOR LOANS & LEASES: Min. Three (3) years; Max. Seven (7) years
BRANCHES: Roy A. Jackson, 13999 Goldmark Drive, Suite 350, Dallas, TX 75240; (214) 680-1014
Thomas J. Esch, Woodfield Grove Business Center, 890 E. Higgins Road, Suite 150C, Chicago, IL 60195; (312) 885-3301

COMPANY: **Gelco Equipment Leasing Co., Gelco Corporation**
ADDRESS: 3 Gelco Drive
Eden Prairie, MN 55344
PHONE: (612) 828-1001
CONTACT OFFICER(S): Jerome W. Gormley

COMPANY: **Winthrop Financial Corp.**
ADDRESS: 6400 Flying Cloud Drive
Eden Prairie, MN 55344
PHONE: (612) 941-0510
CONTACT OFFICER(S): Kirk A. MacKenzie

COMPANY: **Flexi-Lease Corporation, Polar Manufacturing Co.**
ADDRESS: RR 1
Holdingford, MN 56340
PHONE: (612) 746-2555
CONTACT OFFICER(S): John Viere

COMPANY: **Dataserv Equipment Inc.**
ADDRESS: 509 2nd Avenue, P.O. Box 3003
Hopkins, MN 55343
PHONE: (612) 933-2575
CONTACT OFFICER(S): Ronald G. Olson

COMPANY: **Hubbard Leasing Company**
ADDRESS: 424 North Front Street
Mankato, MN 56001
PHONE: (507) 345-2417
CONTACT OFFICER(S): Joseph M. Keenan, General Manager
INVESTMENTS/LOANS MADE: For own account
INVESTMENTS/LOANS MADE: Only in securities without a secondary market
TYPES OF FINANCING: VENTURE CAPITAL: Later-stage expansion; LEASES: Single-investor; Tax leases; Vendor financing programs
GEOGRAPHIC LIMITS OF INVESTMENTS/LOANS: Regional
RANGE OF INV./LOAN PER BUSINESS: Min. $5,000.00; Max. $600,000.00
PREFERRED TERM FOR LOANS & LEASES: Min. 3 years; Max. 5 years
BUSINESS CHARACTERISTICS DESIRED-REQUIRED: Min. number of years in business: 3; Other: Depends on amount of equipment

COMPANY: **Business Credit Leasing**
ADDRESS: 115 W. College Dr.
Marshall, MN 56258
PHONE: (507) 532-3274
CONTACT OFFICER(S): Floyd Robinson

COMPANY: **Cargill Leasing Corp.**
ADDRESS: P.O. Box 5627
Minneapolis, MN
PHONE: (612) 475-7611
TYPE OF INSTITUTION: Leasing subsidiary of industrial company
CONTACT OFFICER(S): Perry B. Mead, Regional Mgr.-lev. leasing
ASSETS: Over $100 Million
INVESTMENTS/LOANS MADE: For own account
TYPES OF FINANCING: LEASES: Single-investor; Leveraged; Operating
PREFERRED TYPES OF INDUSTRIES/INVESTMENTS: None
GEOGRAPHIC LIMITS OF INVESTMENTS/LOANS: National
RANGE OF INV./LOAN PER BUSINESS: Min. $100,000; Max. $100 Million
PREFERRED TERM FOR LOANS & LEASES: Min. 2 years; Max. 12 years
BUSINESS CHARACTERISTICS DESIRED-REQUIRED: Minimum number of years in business: 3; Min. net worth $500M
REFERRALS ACCEPTED FROM: Investment/Mortgage banker or Borrower/Investee
BRANCHES: 44 Union Boulevard, Lakewood, CO 80228; (303) 989-5900
Woodfield Executive Plaza, 650 Woodfield Dr., Suite 205, Schaumburg, IL 60195; (312) 843-1310
5525 High Point Dr., Suite 110, Irving, TX 75062; (214) 257-3672
5800 Foxridge Drive, Suite 150, Mission, KS 66202; (913) 722-3162

COMPANY: **Centron Financial Services Company**
ADDRESS: 7480 W. 78th Street
Minneapolis, MN 55435

PHONE: (612) 994-9161
CONTACT OFFICER(S): Errol Carlstrom

COMPANY: **Clayton Management Inc.**
ADDRESS: 510 Margrette Ave., SB
Minneapolis, MN 55402
PHONE: (612) 333-0025
CONTACT OFFICER(S): John C. Henrikson

COMPANY: **Lease Moore Equipment, Inc.**
ADDRESS: 2318 Park Ave. S.
Minneapolis, MN 55404
PHONE: (612) 872-4929
TYPE OF INSTITUTION: Financial services
CONTACT OFFICER(S): C. Moore, President
S. Braatz, Credit Mgr.
ASSETS: $10-20 million
INVESTMENTS/LOANS MADE: For own account
TYPES OF FINANCING: VENTURE CAPITAL: Buy-outs/Acquisitions, LOANS: Equipment, LEASES: Non-tax leases; Vendor financing programs
PREFERRED TYPES OF INDUSTRIES/INVESTMENTS: EDP, medical, construction and hospitality (strong operators)
GEOGRAPHIC LIMITS OF INVESTMENTS/LOANS: National
RANGE OF INV./LOAN PER BUSINESS: Min. $6,000; Max. $1,000,000
PREFERRED TERM FOR LOANS & LEASES: Min. 1 year; Max. 7 years
BUSINESS CHARACTERISTICS DESIRED-REQUIRED: Minimum number of years in business: 3

COMPANY: **Marquette Lease Services, Inc.**
ADDRESS: Sixth and Marquette
Minneapolis, MN 55480
PHONE: (612) 341-5610
CONTACT OFFICER(S): J. Michael Maxwell

COMPANY: **Norwest Business Credit, Inc.**
ADDRESS: 780 Northstar Ctr.
Minneapolis, MN 55402
PHONE: (612) 372-7988
TYPE OF INSTITUTION: Commercial Finance Company
CONTACT OFFICER(S): Richard F. Beckham, President
Robert L. Olson, SVP/Marketing
Mark A. Morley, Sr. New Bus. Exec.
Rob C. Severson, Sr. New Bus. Exec.
Greg J. Schwarck, Sr. New Bus. Exec.
TYPES OF FINANCING: LOANS: Working capital; Equipment; OTHER SERVICES PROVIDED: Equipment; Installment loans
PREFERRED TYPES OF INDUSTRIES/INVESTMENTS: Manufacturing, Wholesale, Distributors, Food Processors, Related Industries.
WILL NOT CONSIDER: Small loans
GEOGRAPHIC LIMITS OF INVESTMENTS/LOANS: National
RANGE OF INV./LOAN PER BUSINESS: Min. $200,000
BUSINESS CHARACTERISTICS DESIRED-REQUIRED: Other: Corporations and partnerships

COMPANY: **Norwest Leasing, Inc.**
ADDRESS: 930 Cargill Building
Minneapolis, MN 55480
PHONE: (612) 372-7617
TYPE OF INSTITUTION: Leasing & Equipment Finance
CONTACT OFFICER(S): John D. MacLeod, Pres.
John Chrum, V.P. Marketing
ASSETS: 170 million
INVESTMENTS/LOANS MADE: For own account
INVESTMENTS/LOANS MADE: Only in securities without a secondary market
TYPES OF FINANCING: LOANS: Equipment; Conditional sale contracts, LEASES: Single-investor; Leveraged; Tax leases; Non-tax leases; Tax-oriented lease brokerage; Lease syndications; Vendor financing programs; Lease purchase
PREFERRED TYPES OF INDUSTRIES/INVESTMENTS: Construction; Machine
BUSINESS CHARACTERISTICS DESIRED-REQUIRED: No startups financed;
REFERRALS ACCEPTED FROM: Investment/Mortgage banker only or Borrower/Investee
BRANCHES: John D. MacLeod, President, Norwest Leasing, Inc., Suite 930 Cargill Building, 7th Street and Marquette Avenue, Minneapolis, MN 55479; (612) 372-7819
John Chrun, Vice President, Marketing, Norwest Leasing, Inc., Suite 930 Cargill Building, 7th Street and Marquette Avenue, Minneapolis, MN 55479
Chris Hoss, Assistant Vice President, Marketing, Norwest Leasing, Inc., Norwest Center, Fourth and Main, Fargo, ND 58126, (701) 293-4273
Steve Cozzens, Assistant Vice President, Marketing, Norwest Leasing, Inc., P.O. Box 30058, 175 North 27th Street, Billings, MT 59117
Glenn Harper, Lease Marketing Officer, Norwest Equipment Leasing, Inc., P.O. Box 19070, Capital Plaza Suite 220, 9320 S.W. Barbur Boulevard, Portland, OR 97219; (503) 244-4010
Randy Wade, Lease Marketing Officer, P.O. Box 832, 701 Financial Center, Seventh and Walnut Streets, Des Moines, IA 50304
REMARKS: Prefer term of 5 years

COMPANY: **Commonwealth Leasing Corp.**
ADDRESS: Opus Center, Suite 1000, 9900 Bren Road
Minnetonka, MN 55343
PHONE: (612) 938-9400
CONTACT OFFICER(S): Howard Boyer

COMPANY: **Advance Acceptance Corporation**
ADDRESS: P.O. Box 888
Spring Park, MN 55384
PHONE: (612) 471-9335
TYPE OF INSTITUTION: Equipment leasing
CONTACT OFFICER(S): Robert W. Amis, President and CEO
Raymond C. Norum, V.P.-Leasing Officr
Barbara Aspholm, V.P., Office Manager
ASSETS: $7,000,000
INVESTMENTS/LOANS MADE: For own account

TYPES OF FINANCING: LEASES: Single-investor; Vendor leasing programs
PREFERRED TYPES OF INDUSTRIES/INVESTMENTS: All types of small ticket industrial/commercial equipment leasing for vendors or directly to user
GEOGRAPHIC LIMITS OF INVESTMENTS/LOANS: National
RANGE OF INV./LOAN PER BUSINESS: Min. $2,000; Max. $75,000
PREFERRED TERM FOR LOANS & LEASES: Min. 1 year; Max. 5 years
BUSINESS CHARACTERISTICS DESIRED-REQUIRED: Minimum number of years in business: 3; Other: Net worth three times amount of lease

COMPANY: **Total Equipment Leasing Corp.**
ADDRESS: 111 1/2 S 7th Avenue
St. Cloud, MN 56301
PHONE: (612) 253-3131
CONTACT OFFICER(S): Pat Makovec

COMPANY: **Industry Financial Corporation**
ADDRESS: 444 Lafayette Road
St. Paul, MN 55101
PHONE: (612) 222-7792
CONTACT OFFICER(S): R. J. Altman

COMPANY: **ITT Capital Resources Group, Incorporated**
ADDRESS: 1400 North Central Life Tower, P.O. Box 43777
St. Paul, MN 55164
PHONE: (612) 227-2932
CONTACT OFFICER(S): Pete Smith

COMPANY: **John H. Pence Co., Inc.**
ADDRESS: 200 S. Winthrop, P.O. Box 3421
St. Paul, MN 55165
PHONE: (612) 738-6648
CONTACT OFFICER(S): John H. Pence

COMPANY: **Chesterfield Financial Corp.**
ADDRESS: 1415 Eldbridge Payne Road, Suite 210, P.O. Box 421
Chesterfield, MO 63017
PHONE: (314) 532-2827
CONTACT OFFICER(S): Alex M. Nowicki

COMPANY: **Computer Sales International**
ADDRESS: 222 S. Central, Suite 702
Clayton, MO 63105
PHONE: (314) 727-7010
CONTACT OFFICER(S): Kenneth B. Steinback

COMPANY: **Christopher Capital Corp.**
ADDRESS: 4800 Main
Kansas City, MO 64112
PHONE: (816) 241-0030
CONTACT OFFICER(S): Robert C. Neptune

COMPANY: **Third Century, Inc.**
ADDRESS: 63 North Morley, P.O. Box 601
Moberly, MO 65270
PHONE: (816) 263-7924
TYPE OF INSTITUTION: Leasing Company
CONTACT OFFICER(S): W.L. (Barry) Orscheln, President
ASSETS: $31,000,000
INVESTMENTS/LOANS MADE: For own account
INVESTMENTS/LOANS MADE: Only in securities without a secondary market
TYPES OF FINANCING: LEASES: Tax leases; Vendor financing programs
PREFERRED TYPES OF INDUSTRIES/INVESTMENTS: Office Equipment; Medical Equipment
GEOGRAPHIC LIMITS OF INVESTMENTS/LOANS: National
RANGE OF INV./LOAN PER BUSINESS: Min. $1,000; Max. $50,000
PREFERRED TERM FOR LOANS & LEASES: Min. 1 year; Max. 5 years
BUSINESS CHARACTERISTICS DESIRED-REQUIRED: Minimum number of years in business: 3
REFERRALS ACCEPTED FROM: Borrower/Investee

COMPANY: **Transwestern Leasing Company, Inc.**
ADDRESS: 1722 RR, South Glenstone
Springfield, MO 65804
PHONE: (417) 883-5830
CONTACT OFFICER(S): William Max Lathrom

COMPANY: **Computer Sales International, Inc.**
ADDRESS: 222 S. Central, 7th Floor
St. Louis, MO 63105
PHONE: (314) 727-7010
TYPE OF INSTITUTION: Computer Dealer/Lessor
CONTACT OFFICER(S): Kenneth B. Steinback, President
ASSETS: $16,000,000
INVESTMENTS/LOANS MADE: For own account, For managed accounts
INVESTMENTS/LOANS MADE: Only in securities without a secondary market
TYPES OF FINANCING: LEASES: Single-investor; Leveraged; Tax leases; Non-tax leases; Operating; Tax-oriented lease brokerage.
BRANCHES: 14511 Falling Creek Drive, Suite 507, Houston, TX 77014, (713) 444-0246
14009 North Dale Mabry Highway, Suite 1C, Tampa, FL 33618, (813) 963-5556

COMPANY: **General Dynamics Credit Corp.**
ADDRESS: 12101 Woodcrest Executive Dr.
St. Louis, MO 63141
PHONE: (314) 434-6100
CONTACT OFFICER(S): Edward J. Hornung

COMPANY: **HBE Leasing Corporation**
ADDRESS: 1330 Olive Street Rd.
St. Louis, MO 63141
PHONE: (314) 567-9000
CONTACT OFFICER(S): Bruce Horton

COMPANY: **Mark Twain Leasing Company, Mark Twain Bancshares, Inc.**
ADDRESS: 8820 Ladue Road
St. Louis, MO 63124
PHONE: (314) 727-1000
CONTACT OFFICER(S): E.W. Gillula

COMPANY: **Beach Leasing Company**
ADDRESS: P.O. Box 6098
Gulfport, MS 39503
PHONE: (601) 832-3885
CONTACT OFFICER(S): Glenn Whorton

COMPANY: **Continental Leasing Corp.**
ADDRESS: 1102 Highway 49 North, P.O. Box 2036
Hattiesburg, MS 39401
PHONE: (601) 264-4705
CONTACT OFFICER(S): Joseph J. Tucker

COMPANY: **Leasing Group, Inc.**
ADDRESS: 53 Market St., P.O. Box 2137
Asheville, NC 28802
PHONE: (704) 255-8336
CONTACT OFFICER(S): Richard G. Hageman

COMPANY: **First Union Commercial Corporation**
ADDRESS: First Union Plaza
Charlotte, NC 28288
PHONE: (704) 374-6000
TYPE OF INSTITUTION: Asset based financing subsidiary of First Union National Bank
CONTACT OFFICER(S): Wayne F. Robinson, Vice President - Factoring
(H. Leon McGee, Vice President - Commercial Financing
Joseph J. Palisi, Vice President - Term Equipment Lending
ASSETS: $150,000,000.
INVESTMENTS/LOANS MADE: For own account
TYPES OF FINANCING: SECONDARY-MARKET CORPORATE SECURITIES: Secured lending transaction only; LOANS: Working capital; Equipment, REAL ESTATE LOANS: real estate only in conjunction with factoring, accts. receivable or equip. financing; FACTORING, LEASES: Single-investor; Leveraged; Tax leases; Non-tax leases; Tax-oriented lease brokerage; Lease syndications; Vendor financing programs; Other: Municipal leases; INTERNATIONAL
PREFERRED TYPES OF INDUSTRIES/INVESTMENTS: No preference
GEOGRAPHIC LIMITS OF INVESTMENTS/LOANS: National
RANGE OF INV./LOAN PER BUSINESS: Min. $250,000; Max. $25,000,000
PREFERRED TERM FOR LOANS & LEASES: Min. 2 years; Max. 10 years
BUSINESS CHARACTERISTICS DESIRED-REQUIRED: All variable depending on strength of collateral
REFERRALS ACCEPTED FROM: Investment/Mortgage banker or Borrower/Investee

BRANCHES: Robert Schettini, Senior Vice President, 260 Madison Avenue, New York, NY 10016; (212) 953-0123
Lewis W. Spiller, Vice President, 100 Galleria Parkway, Atlanta, GA 30339, (404) 953-4875

COMPANY: **Guaranty National Corporation**
ADDRESS: 6616 Yateswood Drive, Suite I
Charlotte, NC 28212
PHONE: (704) 536-7660
CONTACT OFFICER(S): James L. Thompson

COMPANY: **NCNB Leasing Corporation, North Carolina Natl Bank**
ADDRESS: One NCNB Plaza, Suite T18-3
Charlotte, NC 28255
PHONE: (704) 374-8975
CONTACT OFFICER(S): Donald E. Howell

COMPANY: **Southern National Leasing Corp.**
ADDRESS: P.O. Box 31273
Charlotte, NC 28231
PHONE: (704) 333-1181
CONTACT OFFICER(S): Thomas Peacock

COMPANY: **Coastal Leasing Corp.**
ADDRESS: P.O. Box 647
Greenville, NC 27834
PHONE: (919) 752-3850
TYPE OF INSTITUTION: Leasing Co.
CONTACT OFFICER(S): J. Carlton Taylor, General Manager
ASSETS: $5 million
TYPES OF FINANCING: LEASES: Vendor financing programs; Small Ticket Leases/Straight Finance—Type Leases
PREFERRED TYPES OF INDUSTRIES/INVESTMENTS: Office Equipment, Industrial Equipment
WILL NOT CONSIDER: Video Games
GEOGRAPHIC LIMITS OF INVESTMENTS/LOANS: Regional
RANGE OF INV./LOAN PER BUSINESS: Min. $1,000; Max. $50,000
PREFERRED TERM FOR LOANS & LEASES: Min. 2; Max. 5 years
BUSINESS CHARACTERISTICS DESIRED-REQUIRED: Minimum number of years in business: 2;

COMPANY: **Northwestern Leasing Corp.**
ADDRESS: P.O. Box 310
North Wilkesboro, NC 28674
PHONE: (919) 667-2111
CONTACT OFFICER(S): Bob Kennelly

COMPANY: **Telerent Leasing Corp.**
ADDRESS: 4209 Fayetteville Rd., P.O. 26627
Raleigh, NC 27611
PHONE: (919) 772-8600
TYPE OF INSTITUTION: Leasing Co.
CONTACT OFFICER(S): James R. Maynard, Pres.
E. Eugene Whitmire, V.P., Finance & Treas.

TYPES OF FINANCING: LEASES
PREFERRED TYPES OF INDUSTRIES/INVESTMENTS: Motels, Hotels, Hospitals
GEOGRAPHIC LIMITS OF INVESTMENTS/LOANS: National
RANGE OF INV./LOAN PER BUSINESS: Min. $10,000
PREFERRED TERM FOR LOANS & LEASES: Min. 5; Max. 7 years
REMARKS: Purchase Option Leases — television equipment — sell, install and lease own equipment to motels, hotels and hospitals

COMPANY: **UCB Leasing Corporation**
ADDRESS: 2906 Brentwood Road, P.O. Box 20145
Raleigh, NC 27619
PHONE: (919) 872-1290
CONTACT OFFICER(S): Ed Ziegler

COMPANY: **Wachovia Leasing Corporation**
ADDRESS: P.O. Box 3099
Winston-Salem, NC 27102
PHONE: (919) 748-6662
CONTACT OFFICER(S): R. Bruce Heye

COMPANY: **Wallwork Lease & Rental Co., Inc.**
ADDRESS: Box 143
Fargo, ND 58102
PHONE: (701) 282-2324
CONTACT OFFICER(S): Tom Jennings

COMPANY: **Affiliated Midwest Bancs Leasing Inc.**
ADDRESS: 100 American Plaza
Bellevue, NE 68005
PHONE: (402) 292-5600
CONTACT OFFICER(S): Allen E. Peithman Sr.

COMPANY: **Lindsay Credit Corporation, Dekalb AG Research**
ADDRESS: P.O. Box 1159
Columbus, NE 68601
PHONE: (402) 564-1251
CONTACT OFFICER(S): C.A. Garrett

COMPANY: **Cen/Lease, Inc.**
ADDRESS: Box 467
Norfolk, NE 68701
PHONE: (402) 371-2123
CONTACT OFFICER(S): Robert W. Adkins

COMPANY: **First National Leasing, Inc.**
ADDRESS: One First National Center
Omaha, NE 68103
PHONE: (402) 341-0500
TYPE OF INSTITUTION: Leasing Co.
CONTACT OFFICER(S): V. E. Summerlin, V.P.
W. Scott Morris, 2nd V.P.
TYPES OF FINANCING: LEASES: Single-investor; Leveraged; Tax leases; Tax-oriented lease brokerage; Lease syndications; Vendor financing programs

PREFERRED TYPES OF INDUSTRIES/INVESTMENTS: Agriculture
WILL NOT CONSIDER: Airline
GEOGRAPHIC LIMITS OF INVESTMENTS/LOANS: National
RANGE OF INV./LOAN PER BUSINESS: Min. $25,000
PREFERRED TERM FOR LOANS & LEASES: Min. 5; Max. 10 years
BUSINESS CHARACTERISTICS DESIRED-REQUIRED: Individual evaluation

COMPANY: **Metro Leasing Company**
ADDRESS: 202 South 71st Street, Suite E
Omaha, NE 68132
PHONE: (402) 391-8600
CONTACT OFFICER(S): Jerry J. Boulay

COMPANY: **Omnabanc Leasing Company**
ADDRESS: 17th and Farnam Streets
Omaha, NE 68102
PHONE: (402) 348-6483
CONTACT OFFICER(S): Michael L. Dahir

COMPANY: **Valmont Financial Corporation**
ADDRESS: Hwy 275
Valley, NE 68064
PHONE: (402) 359-2201
TYPE OF INSTITUTION: Leasing subsidiary of manufacturer
CONTACT OFFICER(S): F. W. Stevens; President
Gregory C. McAllister,Vice President-Administration
Dennis M. Dickinson, Vice President-Marketing
ASSETS: $65,000,000
INVESTMENTS/LOANS MADE: Through private placements
TYPES OF FINANCING: LEASES: Leveraged; Tax leases; Tax-oriented lease brokerage, OTHER SERVICES PROVIDED: Insurance
PREFERRED TYPES OF INDUSTRIES/INVESTMENTS: Agriculture—automated irrigation equipment/personal computer/cellular communication towers and related items.
GEOGRAPHIC LIMITS OF INVESTMENTS/LOANS: National
PREFERRED TERM FOR LOANS & LEASES: Min. 0.5 years; Max. 10.0 years

COMPANY: **Signal Capital Corporation**
ADDRESS: Liberty Lane
Hampton, NH 03842
PHONE: (603) 926-5911
CONTACT OFFICER(S): Michael C. Regan

COMPANY: **Emerald Leasing Corporation**
ADDRESS: P.O. Drawer E, 85 Emerald Street
Keene, NH 03431
PHONE: (603) 352-1505
CONTACT OFFICER(S): Emerson H. O'Brien, Jr.

NEW JERSEY

COMPANY: **Midlantic National Bank**
ADDRESS: 2 Broad St.
Bloomfield, NJ 07003
PHONE: (201) 266-6369
TYPE OF INSTITUTION: Leasing Co.
CONTACT OFFICER(S): Michael Zonghetti, Lease Admin.
TYPES OF FINANCING: LOANS: Equipment, LEASES: Single-investor; Leveraged; Tax leases; Non-tax leases; Operating; Lease syndications; Vendor financing programs; Full payout lease
PREFERRED TYPES OF INDUSTRIES/INVESTMENTS: Computer; Airline; Hospital; Printing
WILL NOT CONSIDER: Rolling Stock — Trucks, R.R., Construction
GEOGRAPHIC LIMITS OF INVESTMENTS/LOANS: Regional; NJ Basically
RANGE OF INV./LOAN PER BUSINESS: Min. $250,000; Max. $10,000,000
PREFERRED TERM FOR LOANS & LEASES: Min. 3; Max. 7 years
BUSINESS CHARACTERISTICS DESIRED-REQUIRED: Variable

COMPANY: **Heritage Bank NA**
ADDRESS: Broadway and Cooper Streets, P.O. Box 1409
Camden, NJ 08101
PHONE: (609) 964-2030
TYPE OF INSTITUTION: Wholly owned subsidiary of Heritage Bank, N.A.
CONTACT OFFICER(S): Wiliam R. Giessuebel, V.P.
Harold E. Burke, V.P.
ASSETS: $2 billion
INVESTMENTS/LOANS MADE: For own account
TYPES OF FINANCING: SECONDARY-MARKET CORPORATE SECURITIES: Other: Asset based loans, LOANS: Working capital; Equipment, LEASES: Single-investor; Non-tax leases; Vendor financing programs
PREFERRED TYPES OF INDUSTRIES/INVESTMENTS: Manufacturers and wholesalers—all types of capital equipment
GEOGRAPHIC LIMITS OF INVESTMENTS/LOANS: Regional, Tri-state: NY, PA, NJ
RANGE OF INV./LOAN PER BUSINESS: Min. $400,000; Max. $10,000,000
PREFERRED TERM FOR LOANS & LEASES: Min. 2 years; Max. 7 years
BUSINESS CHARACTERISTICS DESIRED-REQUIRED: Minimum number of years in business: 3; Min. annual sales $3,000,000
REFERRALS ACCEPTED FROM: Investment/Mortgage banker or Borrower/Investee
BRANCHES: Ray Kelly, V.P., 710 Turnpike Rd, East Brunswick, NJ 08816; (201) 390-6373

COMPANY: **Clearview Leasing Corporation**
ADDRESS: 560 Sylvan Avenue
Englewood Cliffs, NJ 07632
PHONE: (201) 567-6112
CONTACT OFFICER(S): A. Dale Mayo

COMPANY: **Leasetek Funding Group, Inc.**
ADDRESS: 19 Sylvan Avenue
Englewood Cliffs, NJ 07632
PHONE: (201) 224-7700
CONTACT OFFICERS: Anthony Rosato, President
ASSETS: $40,000,000
INVESTMENTS/LOANS MADE: For own account, for managed accounts, through private placements, through underwriting public offerings
INVESTMENTS/LOANS MADE: Only in securities with a secondary market
TYPES OF FINANCING: SECONDARY-MARKET CORPORATE SECURITIES, VENTURE CPAIRAL: Start-up from developed product stage; First-stage; Second-stage; Buyouts/expansions, LOANS: Working capital, equipment, REAL ESTATE LOANS: Long-term senior mtg; intermediate-term senior mtg; wraparounds; construction, FACTORING, LEASES: Single-investor; Leveraged; Tax leases; Operating; Lease syndications; Vendor financing programs
GEOGRAPHIC LIMITS OF INVESTMENTS/LOANS: National
RANGE OF INV./LOAN PER BUSINESS: Min. $50,000; Max. $10,000,000
PREFERRED TERM FOR LOANS & LEASES: Min. 2 years; Max. 20 years

COMPANY: **American Capital Resources Inc.**
ADDRESS: Fort Lee Executive Park, One Executive Drive
Fort Lee, NJ 07024
PHONE: (201) 592-7620
CONTACT OFFICER(S): Guy Ferrante

COMPANY: **Computer Financial Inc.**
ADDRESS: One University Plaza
Hackensack, NJ 07601
PHONE: (201) 489-2600
CONTACT OFFICER(S): Tom Martin

COMPANY: **Computer Leasing Inc.**
ADDRESS: Two University Plaza
Hackensack, NJ 07601
PHONE: (201) 646-9300
CONTACT OFFICER(S): Michael P. McCormick

COMPANY: **Summit Leasing & Capital Corp.**
ADDRESS: Heights Plaza, 777 Terrace Avenue
Hasbrouck Heights, NJ 07604
PHONE: (201) 288-8180
CONTACT OFFICER(S): James Jenco

COMPANY: **Federal Leasing Corp.**
ADDRESS: 66 West Mt. Pleasant Avenue
Livingston, NJ 07039
PHONE: (201) 533-0500
TYPE OF INSTITUTION: Leasing Co.
CONTACT OFFICER(S): Stan L. Furst, Pres.
TYPES OF FINANCING: LEASES: Leveraged; Tax leases; Non-tax leases; Operating; Tax-oriented lease brokerage; Vendor financing programs
PREFERRED TYPES OF INDUSTRIES/INVESTMENTS: Medical Fields
GEOGRAPHIC LIMITS OF INVESTMENTS/LOANS: National

RANGE OF INV./LOAN PER BUSINESS: Min. $10,000
PREFERRED TERM FOR LOANS & LEASES: Max. 10 years

COMPANY: **Delta Leasing Inc.**
ADDRESS: 1 Eves Dr., Ste. 101, Evesham Corp. Center
Marlton, NJ 08053
PHONE: (609) 596-4500
TYPE OF INSTITUTION: Leasing Co.
CONTACT OFFICER(S): Dorothy Troutman, President
TYPES OF FINANCING: LEASES
PREFERRED TYPES OF INDUSTRIES/INVESTMENTS: General Equipment
GEOGRAPHIC LIMITS OF INVESTMENTS/LOANS: National
PREFERRED TERM FOR LOANS & LEASES: Max. 7-8 years

COMPANY: **Raybar Leasing Corporation**
ADDRESS: 225 W. Spring Valley Ave., P.O. Box 1079
Maywood, NJ 07607
PHONE: (201) 368-2280
TYPE OF INSTITUTION: Equipment Leasing/Financing
CONTACT OFFICER(S): Patrick F. McCort, Vice President, General Manager
INVESTMENTS/LOANS MADE: For own account
TYPES OF FINANCING: LOANS: Equipment, LEASES: Single-investor; Leveraged; Tax leases; Non-tax leases; Vendor financing programs
GEOGRAPHIC LIMITS OF INVESTMENTS/LOANS: Local; State; Regional
RANGE OF INV./LOAN PER BUSINESS: Min. $20,000; Max. $1,000,000
PREFERRED TERM FOR LOANS & LEASES: Min. 3 years; Max. 7 years

COMPANY:**Amlease Systems Incorporated**
ADDRESS: Box 537
Montvale, NJ 07645
PHONE: (914) 623-0500
CONTACT OFFICER(S): Duane P. Howell

COMPANY: **The Morris County Savings Bank**
ADDRESS: 21 South Street
Morristown, NJ 07960
PHONE: (201) 539-0500
TYPE OF INSTITUTION: Savings Bank
CONTACT OFFICER(S): Charles W. Frost, Chief Executive Officer
Jerry F. Smith, Real Estate Financing
Robert W. Freund, Commerical Lending, Leasing
Michael Allison, Investments
ASSETS: $867,500,000
INVESTMENTS/LOANS MADE: For own account
INVESTMENTS/LOANS MADE: Only in securities with a secondary market
TYPES OF FINANCING: SECONDARY-MARKET CORPORATE SECURITIES: Bonds; Other: Commerical Paper, B.A.'s, etc., LOANS: Unsecured; Working capital; Equipment, REAL ESTATE LOANS: Long-term senior mtg; Intermediate-term senior mtg; Subordinated; Construction, LEASES: Operating, REAL ESTATE: Joint Ventures
PREFERRED TYPES OF INDUSTRIES/INVESTMENTS: Not restricted as to industry, interested in developing full relationships with quality credit
GEOGRAPHIC LIMITS OF INVESTMENTS/LOANS: State; National
RANGE OF INV./LOAN PER BUSINESS: Min. $250,000; Max. $4,250,000
PREFERRED TERM FOR LOANS & LEASES: Min. 1/2 year; Max. 3 years
BUSINESS CHARACTERISTICS DESIRED-REQUIRED: Minimum number of years in business: 3; Min. annual sales $1MM; Min. net worth $200M; Min. annual net income $100M; Min. annual cash fow $150M
REFERRALS ACCEPTED FROM Investment/Mortgage banker or Borrower/Investee
REMARKS: All branches within Northwest New Jersey

COMPANY: **First National State Bank of New Jersey**
ADDRESS: 494 Broad Street
Newark, NJ 07192
PHONE: (201) 565-3336
TYPE OF INSTITUTION: Leasing division of a national bank
CONTACT OFFICER(S): Joseph F. Lynch, V.P., Senior Lease Finance Officer
Donald F. Barrett, V.P., Lease Finance Officer, Graphic Arts Equipment
Russell C. Murawski, V.P., Lease Finance Officer, Computers
Albert Bedlin, Asst. V.P., Lease Finance Officer, Transportation
James Phibbs, Asst. Cashier, Lease Finance Officer
ASSETS: $10 billion
INVESTMENTS/LOANS MADE: For own account
TYPES OF FINANCING: LOANS: Equipment, LEASES: Single-investor; Leveraged; Tax leases; Non-tax leases; Vendor financing programs
PREFERRED TYPES OF INDUSTRIES/INVESTMENTS: Graphic arts equipment; Paper & allied industries; Telecommunications, Computers and Computer peripherals
WILL NOT CONSIDER: Furniture & fixtures — private interconnect
GEOGRAPHIC LIMITS OF INVESTMENTS/LOANS: National
RANGE OF INV./LOAN PER BUSINESS: Min. $100,000; Max. Open
PREFERRED TERM FOR LOANS & LEASES: Min. 2 years; Max. 5 years
REFERRALS ACCEPTED FROM: Investment/Mortgage banker or Borrower/Investee

COMPANY: **FNSB Leasing Company**
ADDRESS: First Natl State Bank, 550 Broad Street, Leasing Department
Newark, NJ 07192
PHONE: (201) 565-3336
CONTACT OFFICER(S): Joseph F. Lynch

COMPANY: **Prucapital, Inc.**
ADDRESS: 153 Halsey Street
Newark, NJ 07101
PHONE: (201) 877-7623
CONTACT OFFICER(S): Pamela Easton Flynn

COMPANY: **IPS Computer Marketing Corp.**
ADDRESS: Mack Centre III, 140 E. Ridgewood Avenue
Paramus, NJ 07652
PHONE: (201) 262-9500
CONTACT OFFICER(S): George Heilborn

COMPANY: **Tri-Continental Leasing Corp., Yegen Associates, Inc.**
ADDRESS: Mack Centre Drive
Paramus, NJ 07652
PHONE: (201) 262-9300
CONTACT OFFICER(S): Robert W. Stubbs

COMPANY: **Hertz Commercial Leasing**
ADDRESS: 7 Entin Road
Parsippany, NJ 07054
PHONE: (201) 428-6131
CONTACT OFFICER(S): Alan W. Quinn

COMPANY: **Copelco Financial Services Group**
ADDRESS: One Mediq Plaza
Pennsauken, NJ 08110
PHONE: (609) 665-6400
CONTACT OFFICER(S): Ian J. Berg

COMPANY: **Armco Financial Corporation, Intermediate Term Lending Division**
ADDRESS: 104 Carnegie Center
Princeton, NJ 08540
PHONE: (609) 452-0600
TYPE OF INSTITUTION: Commerical Term Lender
CONTACT OFFICER(S): Richard S. Ballard, President
Susan M. Lamm, Vice President & Senior Loan Officer
ASSETS: $500,000,000
INVESTMENTS/LOANS MADE: For own account
INVESTMENTS/LOANS MADE: In securities with a secondary market and in securities without a secondary market
TYPES OF FINANCING: VENTURE CAPITAL: Later-stage expansion; Buy-outs/Acquisitions, LOANS: Equipment; REAL ESTATE LOANS: Intermediate-term senior mtg.; Subordinated; Wraparounds, LEASES: Non-tax leases
PREFERRED TYPES OF INDUSTRIES/INVESTMENTS: No preferences—will do all types of manufacturing compaies
WILL NOT CONSIDER: Medical Industry; Retail Businesses
GEOGRAPHIC LIMITS OF INVESTMENTS/LOANS: National
RANGE OF INV./LOAN PER BUSINESS: Min. $1,000,000; Max. $10,000,000
PREFERRED TERM FOR LOANS & LEASES: Min. 2 years
BUSINESS CHARACTERISTICS DESIRED-REQUIRED: Minimum number of years in business: 3
REFERRALS ACCEPTED FROM: Investment/Mortgage banker or Borrower/Investee

COMPANY: **Princeton Equipment Corp.**
ADDRESS: P.O. Box 1304
Princeton, NJ 08542
PHONE: (609) 586-5996
CONTACT OFFICER(S): Eric R. Keller

COMPANY: **World Leasing Corporation**
ADDRESS: 124 Prospect Street
Ridgewood, NJ 07450
PHONE: 201) 444-3222
CONTACT OFFICER(S): Thomas W. Burke, President
Derek W. Morrison, Treasurer
ASSETS: 35,000,000
INVESTMENTS/LOANS MADE: For own account
TYPES OF FINANCING: LEASES: Single-investor; Operating
PREFERRED TYPES OF INDUSTRIES/INVESTMENTS: Equipment—Computer Peripherals
WILL NOT CONSIDER: Investments & Real Estate
GEOGRAPHIC LIMITS OF LEASES: International
RANGE OF LEASE PER BUSINESS: Min. $50,000; Max. None
BUSINESS CHARACTERISTICS DESIRED-REQUIRED: Other: S&P Credit Rating "A"

COMPANY: **Franklin State Bank**
ADDRESS: 630 Franklin Blvd.
Somerset, NJ 08873
PHONE: (201) 745-6044
CONTACT OFFICER(S): John D. Battaglia, Sr. Lending Officer/Exec. V.P.
Harvey A. Mackler, Vice President/Business Development
ASSETS: $650,000,000
INVESTMENTS/LOANS MADE: For own account
INVESTMENTS/LOANS MADE: Only in securities without a secondary market
TYPES OF FINANCING: LOANS: Unsecured; Working capital; REAL ESTATE LOANS: Long-term senior mtg.; Land; Land development; Construction; Industrial revenue bonds, LEASES: Single-investor; Leveraged; Tax leases; Non-tax leases; Vendor financing programs, OTHER SERVICES PROVIDED: Accounts receivable financing
PREFERRED TYPES OF INDUSTRIES/INVESTMENTS: Diversified
GEOGRAPHIC LIMITS OF INVESTMENTS/LOANS: State
RANGE OF INV./LOAN PER BUSINESS: Min. $100,000; Max. $6,000,000
PREFERRED TERM FOR LOANS & LEASES: Min. 1 year; Max. 15-20 years
BUSINESS CHARACTERISTICS DESIRED-REQUIRED: Minimum number of years in business: 1+; Min. annual salès $500,000; Min. net worth $100,000; Min. annual net income $50,000; Min. annual cash flow $50,000

COMPANY: **Landmark Leasing Inc.**
ADDRESS: 114 East Oak Road, P.O. Box 705
Vineland, NJ 08360
PHONE: (609) 696-0400
CONTACT OFFICER(S): Robert A. Rudolph

COMPANY: **Ingersoll Rand Financial Corp.**
ADDRESS: 200 Chestnut Ridge Road
Woodcliff Lake, NJ 07675
PHONE: (201) 573-3031
TYPE OF INSTITUTION: Tax Leasing and Secured Financing
CONTACT OFFICER(S): R.A. Layton, Eastern Group Manager
R.J. Rhinesmih, Western Group Manager
J.C. Colbert, National Leasing
ASSETS: $550 million
INVESTMENTS/LOANS MADE: for own account
TYPES OF FINANCING: VENTURE CAPITAL: Later-stage expansion, LOANS: Equipment, REAL ESTATE LOANS: Long-term senior mtg.; Intermediate-term senior mtg.; Standbys; Other, LEASES: Single-investor; Tax leases; Non-tax leases; Vendor financing programs
GEOGRAPHIC LIMITS OF INVESTMENTS/LOANS: National
RANGE OF INV./LOAN PER BUSINESS: Min. $100M; Max. $10,000M
PREFERRED TERM FOR LOANS & LEASES: Min. 1 year; Max. 7 years
BUSINESS CHARACTERISTICS DESIRED-REQUIRED: Minimum number of years in business: 5; Other: Each transaction will stand on merits
REFERRALS ACCEPTED FROM: Investment/Mortgage banker or Borrower/Investee
BRANCHES: Richard A. Layton, Summerfield Commons Office Park, 2585 Washington Rd., Pittsburgh, PA 15241; (412) 854-1810
Robert J. Rhinesmith, 210 Porter Drive, Suite 120, San Ramon, CA 94583; (415) 838-4606

COMPANY: **Bankers Leasing Association**
ADDRESS: 155 Revere Drive
Northbrook, IL 60062 PHONE: (312) 564-5353
CONTACT OFFICER(S): Maurice Gross

COMPANY: **First Nevada Financial Serv.**
ADDRESS: 3160 S. Valley View Blvd., Suite 206
Las Vegas, NV 89102
PHONE: (702) 367-0364
CONTACT OFFICER(S): Ronald Johnson

COMPANY: **Great Western Leasing**
ADDRESS: P.O. Box 11857
Reno, NV 89510
PHONE: (702) 329-6503
TYPE OF INSTITUTION: Equipment lease financing
CONTACT OFFICER(S): John C. Deane, Chairman
Timothy R. Minor, President
Aaron P. Salloway, Senior VP, National Division Marketing
Donald Jackson, Senior VP, Middle Market
Larry Lustgarten, Senior VP, Portfolio Division
ASSETS: $180,000,000
TYPES OF FINANCING: SECONDARY-MARKET CORPORATE SECURITIES: Other: Equipment oriented straight debt financing, lease financing, acquisitions, syndications, VENTURE CAPITAL: Buy-outs/Aquisitions, LOANS: Equipment, LEASES: Single-investor; Leveraged; Tax leases; Non-tax leases; Tax-oriented lease brokerage; Lease syndications; Vendor financing programs
PREFERRED TYPES OF INDUSTRIES/INVESTMENTS: Commercial equipment such as aircraft, manufacturing, communications, graphic arts, medical, agricultural, restaurant furniture, fixtures and equipment and other equipment used for commercial enterprise
WILL NOT CONSIDER: Real Estate & Autos
GEOGRAPHIC LIMITS OF LEASES: National
RANGE OF LEASE PER BUSINESS: Min. Varies
PREFERRED TERM FOR LOANS & LEASES: Min. Varies; Max. 10 years
BUSINESS CHARACTERISTICS DESIRED-REQUIRED: Minimum number of years in business: 3; Other: cash flow coverage should be 2:1 - size of credit and company financial strength should be congruent
BRANCHES: Oakland, CA—Don Jackson, Senior Vice President, Western Regional Manager; Robert Fletcher, Vice President, Industry Services; (415) 891-9484
Portfolio Division—Larry Lustgarten, Sr. Vice President/Portfolio Manager; 520 Third St., Suite 202, Oakland, CA 94607; (415) 891-9484
Phoenix, AZ—-Theodore Pawlikowski, District Sales Manager; Tempe Executive Center; 1270 E. Braodway, Ste. 115B; Tempe, AZ 85282; (602) 968-0968
Portland, OR—Daniel Minks, District Sales Manager, 10300 S.W. Greenburg Rd., Ste. 495; Portland, OR 97223; (503) 244-5281
Reno, NV—-Mary Ganzel, District Sales Manager; 1881 S. Arlington Ave., Reno, NV 89509; (702) 329-6503
Sacramento, CA—Carol Lohmeyer, District Sales Manager; 1555 River Park Dr., Suite 205; Sacramento, CA 95815; (916) 920-3765
San Francisco, CA—Aaron P. Salloway, Senior Vice President, National Division; Bruce Dunlap, Vice President; 350 California St., Suite 2290; San Francisco, CA 94104; (415) 989-8080

COMPANY: **HLC Leasing Co.**
ADDRESS: 7063 So. Virginia Street
Reno, NV 89511
PHONE: (702) 851-3313
TYPE OF INSTITUTION: Financial services
CONTACT OFFICER(S): Tom Gosh, Manager
ASSETS: Approx. $5 million
INVESTMENTS/LOANS MADE: For own account
TYPES OF FINANCING: SECONDARY-MARKET CORPORATE SECURITIES: Other: Equipment & vehicle leases and contracts—real estate financing (commercial and industrial) (residential/discount notes & deeds), LOANS: Equipment, REAL ESTATE LOANS: FACTORING, LEASES: Single-investor; Leveraged; Tax leases; Non-tax leases; Operating; Tax-oriented lease brokerage; Lease syndications; Vendor financing programs; Other: Mini-leases, managers of captives, and consultant underwriters to lending institutions, INTERNATIONAL (including import/export), REAL ESTATE: Acquisitions, Joint ventures,

OTHER SERVICES PROVIDED: Real estate, brokerage, business brokerage, vehicle fleet leasing and sales (trucks and passenger cars—all makes and models)
PREFERRED TYPES OF INDUSTRIES/INVESTMENTS: Machinery tools; Construction; Mining; Warehousing; Aircraft; Industrial; Office equipment; Hotel; Motel; Restaurant; Computers; Telephone; Vehicles
GEOGRAPHIC LIMITS OF INVESTMENTS/LOANS: National; International
PREFERRED TERM FOR LOANS & LEASES: Min. 1 year; Max. 10-15 years
BUSINESS CHARACTERISTICS DESIRED-REQUIRED: Minimum number of years in business: 2; Min. annual sales $250,000; Min. net worth $150,000; Min. annual net income $25,000; Min. annual cash flow $25,000
REFERRALS ACCEPTED FROM: Investment/Mortgage banker or Borrower/Investee
REMARKS: We do accept bonafide broker business, and we will pay broker fees if legitimized

COMPANY: **Norstar Leasing Services, Inc., Norstar Bancorp**
ADDRESS: 1450 Western Avenue, P.O. Box 1769
Albany, NY 12201
PHONE: (518) 447-4003
CONTACT OFFICER(S): James Andi

COMPANY: **Grumman Credit Corporation**
ADDRESS: 1111 Stewart Avenue
Bethpage, NY 11714
PHONE: (516) 575-3421
TYPE OF INSTITUTION: Captive Leasing, subsidiary of Grumman Corporation
CONTACT OFFICER(S): E. Balinsky, Persident
J. Latterner, Manager
T. Maloney, Asst. Treasurer
ASSETS: $45,000,000
INVESTMENTS/LOANS MADE: Through private placements
INVESTMENTS/LOANS MADE: In securities with a secondary market and in securities without a secondary market
TYPES OF FINANCING: LOANS: Equity-related, LEASES: Single-investor; Leveraged; Operating; Vendor financing programs, INTERNATIONAL, OTHER SERVICES PROVIDED: Municipal funding
PREFERRED TYPES OF INDUSTRIES/INVESTMENTS: Manufacturing Equips.; Municipal funding
GEOGRAPHIC LIMITS OF INVESTMENTS/LOANS: International
RANGE OF INV./LOAN PER BUSINESS: Min. $25,000; Max. $1,000,000
PREFERRED TERM FOR LOANS & LEASES: Min. 3 years; Max. 7 years
BUSINESS CHARACTERISTICS DESIRED-REQUIRED: Minimum number of years in business: 0; Min. annual sales $100,000; Min. net worth $50,000
REFERRALS ACCEPTED FROM: Investment/Mortgage banker or Borrower/Investee

COMPANY:**Goldome FSB**
ADDRESS: One Fountain Plaza
Buffalo, NY 14203
PHONE: (716) 847-5974
TYPE OF INSTITUTION: Leveraged Lease Securities
CONTACT OFFICER(S): Hans J. Parker, Vice President & Manager
ASSETS: $550,000,000 (leveraged leasing area)
INVESTMENTS/LOANS MADE: For own account
INVESTMENTS/LOANS MADE: Only in securities with a secondary market
TYPES OF FINANCING: LEASES: Leveraged, Lease syndications
PREFERRED TYPES OF INDUSTRIES/INVESTMENTS: Computers, Peripheral equipment, Corporate aircrafts
GEOGRAPHIC LIMITS OF INVESTMENTS/LOANS: National
RANGE OF INV./LOAN PER BUSINESS: Min. $1,000,000; Max. $10,000,000
PREFERRED TERM FOR LOANS & LEASES: Min. 24 mos.; Max. 60 mos.
BUSINESS CHARACTERISTICS DESIRED-REQUIRED: BAA/A S&P Moody's or equivalent
REFERRALS ACCEPTED FROM: Borrower/Investee

COMPANY: **Firstmark Leasing Corporation**
ADDRESS: First Building, 135 Delaware Avenue
Buffalo, NY 14202
PHONE: (716) 854-2480
CONTACT OFFICER(S): Leonard Rochwarger

COMPANY: **Manufacturers and Traders Trust Company, Equip. Finance & Leasing**
ADDRESS: P.O. Box 767-B
Buffalo, NY 14240
PHONE: (716) 626-3468
CONTACT OFFICER(S): Michael Weis

COMPANY: **Marine Midland Leasing Corp.**
ADDRESS: One Marine Midland Center, 16th Floor
Buffalo, NY 14240
PHONE: (716) 843-4157
CONTACT OFFICER(S): Paul M. Sciandra

COMPANY: **Vendor Funding Co., Inc.**
ADDRESS: 108-18 Queens Blvd.
Forest Hills, NY 11375
PHONE: (212) 459-8400
TYPE OF INSTITUTION: Equipment Lease Financing
CONTACT OFFICER(S): Douglas W. Baena, Chairman, CEO
Joseph J. Messina, President
Joseph F.X. O'Sullivan, Exec. Vice President
INVESTMENTS/LOANS MADE: For own account
TYPES OF FINANCING: LEASES: Single-investor; Leveraged; Tax leases; Non-tax leases; Operating; Tax-oriented lease brokerage; Lease syndications;; Vendor financing programs
PREFERRED TYPES OF INDUSTRIES/INVESTMENTS: Data Processing, Telecommunication, High Tech
GEOGRAPHIC LIMITS OF INVESTMENTS/LOANS: National
RANGE OF INV./LOAN PER BUSINESS: Min. $1000; Max. $50,000,000

PREFERRED TERM FOR LOANS & LEASES: Min. 1 year; Max. 10 years
BUSINESS CHARACTERISTICS DESIRED-REQUIRED: Minimum number of years in business: 2 years
REFERRALS ACCEPTED FROM: Investment/Mortgage banker or Borrower/Investee
BRANCHES: 409 Mulberry Street, Coraopolis, PA 15108, (412) 269-6275
One Jocoma Blvd., Old Bridge, NJ 08857, (201) 591-0400
120 South Olive Ave. Suite 200, West Palm Beach, FL 33402, (305) 655-3307

COMPANY: **Sussex Leasing Corp.**
ADDRESS: 175 Great Neck Road
Great Neck, NY 11021
PHONE: (516) 482-7373
CONTACT OFFICER(S): Harvey Granat

COMPANY: **Citicorp Industrial Credit, Inc.**
ADDRESS: 450 Mamaroneck Avenue
Harrison, NY 10528
PHONE: (914) 899-7000
TYPE OF INSTITUTION: Asset-Based Finance subsidiary of bank holding company
CONTACT OFFICER(S): John W. Dewey, President, Equipment Finance Leasing
Frederick S. Gilbert, Jr., Executive V.P., Asset-Based Lending
Robert H. Martinsen, Chrm. of the Bd.
David McCollum, E. V.P., Corporate Asset Funding
Robert Laughlin, E. V.P., Equipment Finance
William Urban, E. V.P., Vendor Finance
J.R.A.C. Clement, V.P., Tax Leasing & Equity Syndication
ASSETS: $3.2 Billion
INVESTMENTS/LOANS MADE: For own account
TYPES OF FINANCING: VENTURE CAPITAL: Buy-outs/Acquisitions; LOANS: Working capital (receivables/inventory; Equipment; Buyouts/acquisitions, bulk purchase of receivables, FACTORING, LEASES: Leveraged; Tax leases; Non-tax leases; Operating; Tax-oriented lease brokerage; Lease syndications; Vendor financing programs
PREFERRED TYPES OF INDUSTRIES/INVESTMENTS: Manufacturers and Wholesalers
GEOGRAPHIC LIMITS OF INVESTMENTS/LOANS: National
RANGE OF INV./LOAN PER BUSINESS: Min. $50,000; Max. up to legal limit
PREFERRED TERM FOR LOANS & LEASES: Min. 2 to 5 years revolving loans, up to 10 years term loans
BRANCHES: 211 Perimeter Ctr. Parkway, Atlanta, GA, 30346; (404) 391-8500
3033 South Parker Road, Market Tower I, Suite 900, Aurora, CO, 80014; (303) 752-2530
200 South Wacker Drive, Chicago, IL, 60606; (312) 993-3230, (312) 993-3263
635 W. 7th St, Ste 400, Cincinnati, OH, 45203;
1300 East 9th Street, Cleveland, OH, 44114; (216) 696-6330/(216) 621-1383
717 North Harwood St., LB #85, Diamond Shamrock Tower, Dallas, TX, 75201; (214) 760-1829
101 Continental Boulevard, Suite 800, El Segundo, CA, 90245; (213) 640-1224
560 Sylvan Avenue, Engelwood Cliffs, NJ, 07632; (201) 657-7610
450 Mamaroneck Avenue, Harrison, NY, 10528; (914) 899-7000
Summit Tower — 11 Greenway Plaza, Houston, TX, 77046; (713) 627-8170
2 Allen Center, 1200 Smith Street, Houston, TX, 77002; (713) 654-2800
444 South Flower Street, Los Angeles, CA, 90071; (213) 745-3500
3435 Wilshire Boulevard, Los Angeles, CA, 90010
3090 Multifoods Tower, Minneapolis, MN, 55402
621 Lexington Avenue, New York, NY, 10043
44 Montgomery Street, San Francisco, CA, 94104; (415) 954-1166, (415) 954-1042
1111 Third Avenue, Suite 2700, Seattle, WA, 98101; (206) 382-6225
470 Totten Pond Road, Waltham, MA, 02154; (617) 890-1666
333 Hegenberger Rd., Ste 815, Oakland, CA 94621
One Sansome St., San Francisco, CA 94120
20 Executive Park - Ste 200, Irvine, CA 92714
1900 E. Golf, Schaumburg, IL 60195
1050 Connecticut Av., NW, Washington, DC 20036
1200 Ford Rd., Ste 270, Dallas, TX 75234

COMPANY: **DPF, Computer Leasing**
ADDRESS: 141 Central Park Ave. So.
Hartsdale, NY 10530
PHONE: (914) 428-5000
TYPE OF INSTITUTION: Leasing Co.
CONTACT OFFICER(S): Martin Goldstein, Pres.
TYPES OF FINANCING: LEASES
PREFERRED TYPES OF INDUSTRIES/INVESTMENTS: Computer
GEOGRAPHIC LIMITS OF INVESTMENTS/LOANS: National
REMARKS: Preferred term: 4-5 years

COMPANY: **A.I.N. Leasing Corporation**
ADDRESS: 501 Burnside Avenue
Inwood, NY 11696
PHONE: (516) 239-1503
CONTACT OFFICER(S): Joseph D. Castano

COMPANY: **Diversified Commercial Services Corp.**
ADDRESS: Two Jericho Plaza, P.O. Box 343
Jericho, NY 11753
PHONE: (516) 499-0822
CONTACT OFFICER(S): Paul M. Finfer

COMPANY: **Macrolease International Corp.**
ADDRESS: 50 Jericho Turnpike
Jericho, NY 11753
PHONE: (516) 997-9000
CONTACT OFFICER(S): Daniel West

COMPANY: **Parimist Funding Corporation**
ADDRESS: 50 Jericho Turnpike
Jericho, NY 11753
PHONE: (516) 334-3300
CONTACT OFFICER(S): Paul Eidelkind

LEASING COMPANIES

(Lessors. Also see Commercial Bankers and Finance Companies, Insurance Companies and Investment Bankers)

COMPANY: **Studebaker Worthington Leasing**
ADDRESS: 100 Jericho Quadrangle
Jericho, NY 11753
PHONE: (516) 938-5460
CONTACT OFFICER(S): Kenneth M. Paston

COMPANY: **U.S. Concord Inc.**
ADDRESS: 1890 Palmer Avenue
Larchmont, NY 10538
PHONE: (914) 834-9500
CONTACT OFFICER(S): Robert B. Frank

COMPANY: **E. L. S. Leasing Corporation**
ADDRESS: P.O. Box 504, 20 West Park Avenue
Long Beach, NY 11561
PHONE: (516) 432-1300; 800-645-3342
CONTACT OFFICER(S): Daniel E. Joffe

COMPANY: **American Express Leasing Corp.**
ADDRESS: American Express Plaza, 18th Floor
New York, NY 10004
PHONE: (212) 480-3909
CONTACT OFFICER(S): Runy M. Sarda, Jr.

COMPANY: **Americom Leasing Group Inc.**
ADDRESS: 40 East 49th Street
New York, NY 10017
PHONE: (212) 689-7051
CONTACT OFFICER(S): Harry A. Ault

COMPANY: **Amsave Credit Corporation**
ADDRESS: 1370 Avenue of the Americas
New York, NY 10019
PHONE: (212) 489-9111
CONTACT OFFICER(S): William P. Mallory

COMPANY: **Arlon Capital & Leasing Corp.**
ADDRESS: 277 Park Avenue
New York, NY 10172
PHONE: (212) 826-5412
CONTACT OFFICER(S): David G. Bullock

COMPANY: **Atlantic Capital Corp.**
ADDRESS: 40 Wall St.
New York, NY 10005
PHONE: (212) 363-5600
CONTACT OFFICER(S): Harold Phaumgarten, Sr. V.P.
TYPES OF FINANCING: VENTURE CAPITAL, REAL ESTATE LOANS, LEASES, REAL ESTATE, OTHER SERVICES PROVIDED: private placements, corporate financing, mergers and acquisitions
RANGE OF INV./LOAN PER BUSINESS: Min. $1 million
REMARKS: Transaction oriented house; no start-ups

COMPANY: **C.I.T. Leasing Corporation**
ADDRESS: 650 Madison Avenue
New York, NY 10022
PHONE: (212) 977-9500
TYPE OF INSTITUTION: Leasing Co.

COMPANY: **Canadian Imperial Leasing Inc.**
ADDRESS: 237 Park Avenue
New York, NY 10017
PHONE: (212) 309-8850
CONTACT OFFICER(S): Anthony M. Minard

COMPANY: **Ceres Capital Corporation**
ADDRESS: 350 Fifth Avenue, Suite 3424
New York, NY 10118
PHONE: (212) 279-4467
CONTACT OFFICER(S): James H. Hooker

COMPANY: **The Chase Manhattan Bank, Finance Div.**
ADDRESS: 1411 Broadway
New York, NY 10018
PHONE: (212) 223-7009
TYPE OF INSTITUTION: Commercial Finance Div. of Bank
CONTACT OFFICER(S): Frank J. Donahue, V.P.
TYPES OF FINANCING: LOANS: Working capital (receivables/inventory); Equipment, LEASES
PREFERRED TYPES OF INDUSTRIES/INVESTMENTS: Diversified
GEOGRAPHIC LIMITS OF INVESTMENTS/LOANS: National
RANGE OF INV./LOAN PER BUSINESS: Min. $500,000
BRANCHES: Boston, MA
Atlanta, GA
Dallas, TX
Los Angeles, CA
Chicago, IL

COMPANY: **Chemco Financial Services LTD.**
ADDRESS: 1 World Trade Center, Suite 8321
New York, NY 10048
PHONE: (212) 820-5916
CONTACT OFFICER(S): T.J. Harrington

COMPANY: **Colt Industries Credit Corp.**
ADDRESS: 430 Park Avenue
New York, NY 10022
PHONE: (212) 940-0503
CONTACT OFFICER(S): Harvey H. Starr

COMPANY: **Commercial Union Capital Corp.**
ADDRESS: 115 E. 57th Street
New York, NY 10022
PHONE: (212) 644-0920
CONTACT OFFICER(S): Mark S. Comora

COMPANY: **Commercial Funding Inc.**
ADDRESS: 230 Park Avenue, Suite 3410
New York, NY 10169

PHONE: (212) 661-4848
CONTACT OFFICER(S): Alan A. Fischer

COMPANY:**Integrated Resources Equipment Group**
ADDRESS: 733 3rd Ave. 5th Floor
New York, NY 10017
PHONE: (212) 949-7800
CONTACT OFFICER(S): Bill Adair, President
TYPES OF FINANCING:LEASES: Single-investor; Leveraged; Tax leases; Operating; Tax-oriented lease brokerage; Lease syndications; Vendor financing programs; Other: Full payout leases
PREFERRED TYPES OF INDUSTRIES/INVESTMENTS: Fortune 1000 companies
GEOGRAPHIC LIMITS OF INVESTMENTS/LOANS: National
RANGE OF INV./LOAN PER BUSINESS: Min. $500,000; Max. $100 million
BRANCHES: Joseph Din, 394 Lowell St., Ste. 4, Lexington, MA 02173, (617) 861-1411
Steve Hannash, 601 California St., Ste. 1801, San Francisco, CA 94108-2849, (415) 392-0511
Jack Moran,, 100 S. Wacker Dr., Ste. 1950, Chicago, IL 60606, (312) 346-7606
Richard Barret, 2350 Valley View Lane, Dallas TX 75234, (214) 620-9200

COMPANY: **Creditleasing International Corporation**
ADDRESS: 95 Wall Street
New York, NY 10005
PHONE: (212) 344-1915
TYPE OF INSTITUTION: Leasing Sub of Bank
CONTACT OFFICER(S): Patrick Bastin, Exec. V.P. & Manager
TYPES OF FINANCING: LEASES: Single-investor; Leveraged; Non-tax leases; Tax-oriented lease brokerage; Vendor financing programs

COMPANY: **Dean Witter Reynolds, Inc.**
ADDRESS: 130 Liberty Street
New York, NY 10006
PHONE: (212) 524-2222
CONTACT OFFICER(S): James E. Swigart

COMPANY: **Dexel Leasing Corporation**
ADDRESS: 1250 Broadway
New York, NY 10001
PHONE: (212) 279-1717
CONTACT OFFICER(S): Prem K. Bhandari

COMPANY: **Equilease Corporation**
ADDRESS: 750 Third Ave.
New York, NY 10017
PHONE: (212) 557-6800
CONTACT OFFICER(S): Mark Hershey, President/ Commercial Finance and Leasing
ASSETS: $700,000,000
INVESTMENTS/LOANS MADE: For own account, For managed accounts
TYPES OF FINANCING: LOANS: Equipment, LEASES: Single-investor; Leveraged; Tax leases; Non-tax leases; Operating; Tax-oriented lease brokerage; Lease syndications; Vendor financing programs; Other: International

COMPANY: **Euramlease Inc.**
ADDRESS: 10 Hanover Square
New York, NY 10015
PHONE: (212) 437-2397
CONTACT OFFICER(S): Richard W. Moskwa

COMPANY: **Goldman Sachs & Co.**
ADDRESS: 85 Broad Street, 21st Floor
New York, NY 10004
PHONE: (212) 902-1000
CONTACT OFFICER(S): David A. George

COMPANY: **Haas Financial Corporation**
ADDRESS: 230 Park Avenue
New York, NY 10169
PHONE: (212) 490-1510
CONTACT OFFICER(S): George C. Haas Jr., President
Robert L. Cummings
Vice President
INVESTMENTS/LOANS MADE: For own account; Through private placements
INVESTMENTS/LOANS MADE: In securities with a secondary market and in securities without a secondary market
TYPES OF FINANCING: SECONDARY-MARKET CORPORATE SECURITIES: Common stock; Bonds; VENTURE CAPITAL: First-stage; Second-stage; Later-stage expansion; Buy-outs/Acquisitions; LOANS: Equipment; REAL ESTATE LOANS: Long-term senior mtg.; Intermediate-term senior mtg.; Subordinated; Wraparounds; LEASES: Single-investor; Operating; Tax-oriented lease brokerage; OTHER SERVICES PROVIDED: Merger Acquisition Divestiture Brokerage; Consulting and Valuation; Acquisition/Divestiture Financing.
PREFERRED TYPES OF INDUSTRIES/INVESTMENTS: Will look at all types of industries, firm has specialty in transportation (planes) consumer products (soft drinks)
GEOGRAPHIC LIMITS OF INVESTMENTS/LOANS: National
RANGE OF INV./LOAN PER BUSINESS: Min. $500,000
PREFERRED TERM FOR LOANS & LEASES: Min. 5 years; Max. 15 years
REFERRALS ACCEPTED FROM: Investment/Mortgage banker or Borrower/Investee

COMPANY: **Harper Leasing Limited**
ADDRESS: P.O. Box 392
New York, NY 10011
PHONE: (212) 242-2279
CONTACT OFFICER(S): Craig S. Harper

COMPANY: **Heather Leasing Company**
ADDRESS: 1 World Trade Center, Suite 86047
New York, NY 10048
PHONE: (212) 524-9707
CONTACT OFFICER(S): Robert Whitehead

COMPANY: **Hundred East Credit Corp.**
ADDRESS: 100 East 42nd Street
New York, NY 10017
PHONE: (212) 697-3600
CONTACT OFFICER(S): J. W. Corcoran

COMPANY: **Hunter, Keith, Marshall & Co., Inc.**
ADDRESS: One Penn Plaza, Ste. 1831
New York, NY 10119
PHONE: (212) 736-6140
TYPE OF INSTITUTION: Private placement investment bank
CONTACT OFFICER(S): Henry C. Marshall, Jr., Managing Director, Equipment & Real Estate
Steven I. Eisenberg, Vice President, Equipment
INVESTMENTS/LOANS MADE: For own account; Through private placements
INVESTMENTS/LOANS MADE: In securities with a secondary market and in securities without a secondary market
TYPES OF FINANCING: LOANS: Equity-related; REAL ESTATE LOANS: Long-term senior mtg.; Intermediate-term senior mtg.; LEASES: Vendor financing programs; Other: debt side of leveraged leases
GEOGRAPHIC LIMITS OF INVESTMENTS/LOANS: National; Other: Will do selected international credits
RANGE OF INV./LOAN PER BUSINESS: Min. $2 MM
PREFERRED TERM FOR LOANS & LEASES: Min. 3 years; Max. 20 years
BUSINESS CHARACTERISTICS DESIRED-REQUIRED: Min. net worth $5 MM; Min. annual net income $ 1.5MM; Min. annual cash flow: $1.5MM; Other: Will do selected startups on secured basis
REFERRALS ACCEPTED FROM: Borrower/Investee
BRANCHES: Andrew M. Hunter III, Robert J. Keith, Jr., 5100 IDS Center, Minneapolis, MN 55402, (612) 338-2799

COMPANY: **Integrated Resources Equipment Group Inc.**
ADDRESS: 666 Third Avenue
New York, NY 10017
PHONE: (212) 878-0659
CONTACT OFFICER(S): Frank A. Savage

COMPANY: **Interet Corporation**
ADDRESS: 733 Third Avenue
New York, NY 10017
PHONE: (212) 687-9411
CONTACT OFFICER(S): James Ahlstrom

COMPANY: **Japan Leasing (USA), Inc.**
ADDRESS: 1133 Ave. of the Americas
New York, NY 10036
PHONE: (212) 921-1844
TYPE OF INSTITUTION: Leasing firm
CONTACT OFFICER(S): Mr. Minoru Imokawa, President
Mr. Jun Ogihara, V.P.

COMPANY: **Kendall & Company Inc.**
ADDRESS: 405 W. 44 Street
New York, NY 10036
PHONE: (212) 307-6560
CONTACT OFFICER(S): Donald R. Kendall Jr.

COMPANY: **Kidder Peabody & Co, Inc., Project & Lease Finance Group**
ADDRESS: Corporate Finance Department, 10 Hanover Square
New York, NY 10005
PHONE: (212) 747-2335
CONTACT OFFICER(S): Edward P. Brennan

COMPANY: **Leasing Service Corporation**
ADDRESS: 770 Lexington Avenue
New York, NY 10017
PHONE: (212) 421-3600
TYPE OF INSTITUTION: Full service leasing company.
CONTACT OFFICER(S): Daniel N. Ryan, Senior Vice President
INVESTMENTS/LOANS MADE: For own account.
TYPES OF FINANCING: LEASES: Single-Investor; Leveraged; Tax leases; Non-tax leases; Vendor financing programms.
PREFERRED TYPES OF INDUSTRIES/INVESTMENTS: Income producing or labor saving equipment.
GEOGRAPHIC LIMITS OF INVESTMENTS/LOANS: National.
PREFERRED TERMS FOR LOANS & LEASES: Min. 1 year; Max. 10 years.

COMPANY: **Manufacturers Hanover Leasing**
ADDRESS: 270 Park Avenue
New York, NY 10017
PHONE: (212) 286-5500
CONTACT OFFICER(S): Karl M. Parrish

COMPANY: **Merrill Lynch Industrial Resources**
ADDRESS: 4 World Trade Center, 6th Floor
New York, NY 10048
PHONE: (212) 766-6114
CONTACT OFFICER(S): Richard A. Hanson

COMPANY: **MGC Leasing Corporation**
ADDRESS: 666 Fifth Avenue
New York, NY 10103
PHONE: (212) 581-2400
CONTACT OFFICER(S): Jerome Butkow

COMPANY: **Mitsui Leasing Development LTD.**
ADDRESS: 200 Park Avenue
New York, NY 10166
PHONE: (212) 878-6784
CONTACT OFFICER(S): Hiroshi Aoki

COMPANY: **Morgan Grenfell Incorporated**
ADDRESS: 520 Madison Avenue
New York, NY 10022

PHONE: (212) 715-1700
CONTACT OFFICER(S): C. Wendell Tewell

COMPANY: **Nordic American Bank Corporation**
ADDRESS: 600 Fifth Avennue
New York, NY 10020
PHONE: (212) 315-6500
TYPE OF INSTITUTION: Investment Banking
CONTACT OFFICER(S): Hans Eric Von der Groeben, EVP
Edward Mete, EVP
ASSESTS: $600,000,000
INVESTMENTS/LOANS MADE: For own account; Through private placements
INVESTMENTS/LOANS MADE: In securities with a secondary market and in securities without a secondary market;
TYPES OF FINANCING: SECONDARY-MARKET CORPORATE SECURITIES: Bonds; LOANS: Working Capital (receivables/inventory); Equipment; Equity-related. REAL ESTATE LOANS: Industrial revenue bonds. LEASES: Leveraged; Tax leases; Operating; Lease syndications; Vendor financing programs; INTERNATIONAL (including import/export)
PREFERRED TYPES OF INDUSTRIES/INVESTMENTS: Nordic related business in the U.S. U.S. businesses operating in the Nordic area.
GEOGRAPHIC LIMITS OF INVESTMENTS/LOANS: National; International;
BRANCHES: John A. Redding, SVP, Suite 1963, 135 So. La Salle St., Chicago, IL; (312) 855-1515

COMPANY: **P C Leasing Corporation**
ADDRESS: 630 Third Avenue
New York, NY 10017
PHONE: (212) 687-2121
CONTACT OFFICER(S): James A. Youngling

COMPANY: **RTS Capital Corporation**
ADDRESS: 39 Broadway, 21st Floor
New York, NY 10006
PHONE: (212) 742-2224
CONTACT OFFICER(S): William C. Richy

COMPANY: **Schroder Leasing Corporation**
ADDRESS: One State Street
New York, NY 10004
PHONE: (212) 269-6500
CONTACT OFFICER(S): J.J. MacIsaac

COMPANY: **Sogelease Corporation**
ADDRESS: 50 Rockefeller Plaza
New York, NY 10021
PHONE: (212) 397-5050
CONTACT OFFICER(S): Alan P. Plusquellec

COMPANY: **Sonic Leasing Corporation**
ADDRESS: 420 Lexington Avenue
New York, NY 10017
PHONE: (212) 986-5115
CONTACT OFFICER(S): Ernest Reichard

COMPANY: **Sperry Financial Corporation**
ADDRESS: 1290 Avenue of the Americas
New York, NY 10104
PHONE: (212) 484-4444
CONTACT OFFICER(S): Robert H. Faje

COMPANY: **Sumitomo Corporation Of America**
ADDRESS: 345 Park Avenue
New York, NY 10154
PHONE: (212) 935-8497
CONTACT OFFICER(S): T. Ohrui

COMPANY: **Thomson/McKinnon Leasing Inc.**
ADDRESS: One State Street Plaza, 35th Floor
New York, NY 10004
PHONE: (212) 421-1400
CONTACT OFFICER(S): Alan M. Arsht

COMPANY: **Wasco Funding Corp.**
ADDRESS: 950 Third Avenue
New York, NY 10022
PHONE: (212) 751-3673
CONTACT OFFICER(S): Ira P. Wasserman

COMPANY: **Residual Valve Management Corporation**
ADDRESS: P.O. Box 820C, New King Street
North White Plains, NY 10603
PHONE: (914) 428-1717
CONTACT OFFICER(S): Aaron B. Stern

COMPANY: **Columbus National Leasing Corporation**
ADDRESS: 2570 Baird Road
Penfield, NY 14526
PHONE: (716) 385-9950
CONTACT OFFICER(S): Kenneth A. Glasgow, President
Greg Millner, V.P. (Credit Officer)
ASSETS: $25,000,000
INVESTMENTS/LOANS MADE: For own account
TYPES OF FINANCING: LOANS: Equipment, LEASES: Single-investor; Tax leases; Non-tax leases; Vendor financing programs; Other: Sale and leasebacks
PREFERRED TYPES OF INDUSTRIES/INVESTMENTS: Specialists in printing and graphic arts equipment. Also desire medical, machine tools, telephone systems, computers and most income producing equipment
WILL NOT CONSIDER: Restaurants or coin operated machinery
GEOGRAPHIC LIMITS OF INVESTMENTS/LOANS: National
RANGE OF INVESTMENT/LOAN PER BUSINESS: Min. $10,000; Max. $1,000,000
PREFERRED TERM FOR LOANS & LEASES: Min. 2 years; Max. 10 years
BUSINESS CHARACTERISTICS DESIRED-REQUIRED: Minimum number of years in business: 0; Other: Requirements are relative to the size of the lease and the nature of the equipment

LEASING COMPANIES

(Lessors. Also see Commercial Bankers and Finance Companies, Insurance Companies and Investment Bankers)

REFERRALS ACCEPTED FROM: Will accept broker applications
REMARKS: We have district offices throughout the country, but initial inquiries should be made to Rochester

COMPANY: **Genesee Capital Inc.**
ADDRESS: 183 E. Main Street, Suite 1450, Alliance Building
Rochester, NY 14604
PHONE: (716) 262-4716
CONTACT OFFICER(S): A. Keene Bolton

COMPANY: **Lincoln Lease/Way Inc., Lincoln First Bank NA**
ADDRESS: One Lincoln First Square
Rochester, NY 14643
PHONE: (716) 258-6477
CONTACT OFFICER(S): James F. Taylor

COMPANY: **Xerox Corporation**
ADDRESS: Xerox Square
Rochester, NY 14644
PHONE: (716) 423-6585
CONTACT OFFICER(S): D. F. Harringson

COMPANY: **Tilden Financial Corp.**
ADDRESS: 2 Lambert Street
Roslyn Heights, NY 11577
PHONE: (516) 484-4600
CONTACT OFFICER(S): Milton Rudin

COMPANY: **Multi-State Leasing Corp.**
ADDRESS: 500 South Salina Street, Suite 218
Syracuse, NY 13202
PHONE: (315) 471-9194
CONTACT OFFICER(S): Jim Mattern

COMPANY: **Syracuse Supply Leasing Co.**
ADDRESS: P.O. Box 4814
Syracuse, NY 13221
PHONE: (315) 463-9511
CONTACT OFFICER(S): Philip J. Addabbo

COMPANY: **Telmark, Incorporated, Agway, Inc.**
ADDRESS: Box 4943
Syracuse, NY 13221
PHONE: (315) 477-6439
CONTACT OFFICER(S): A.J. Llewellyn

COMPANY: **Computer Affiliates Co. Inc.**
ADDRESS: 1085 Rockaway Avenue
Valley Stream, NY 11581
PHONE: (516) 568-1300
TYPE OF INSTITUTION: Dealer/Lessor of IBM Equipment
CONTACT OFFICERS: Paul C. Schwartz, President
Francis McCarroll, Vice President
INVESTMENTS/LOANS MADE: For own account
TYPES OF FINANCING: LEASES: Single-investor; Tax leases; Operating

COMPANY: **GB Leasing Corporation**
ADDRESS: 300 Hempstead Turnpike
W. Hempstead, NY 11552
PHONE: (516) 486-3304
CONTACT OFFICER(S): Robert T. Schutte

COMPANY: **Barrett Capital & Leasing Corporation**
ADDRESS: 707 Westchester Avenue
White Plains, NY 10604
PHONE: (914) 682-1960
TYPE OF INSTITUTION: Equipment vehicle leasing and finance company
CONTACT OFFICER(S): Barry P. Korn, President
ASSETS: $60 million
INVESTMENTS/LOANS MADE: For own account, For managed accounts
TYPES OF FINANCING: LEASES: Single-investor; Leveraged; Tax leases; Non-tax leases; Operating; Tax-oriented lease brokerage; Vendor financing programs
PREFERRED TYPES OF INDUSTRIES/INVESTMENTS: For all industries, leases of equipment and vehicles
GEOGRAPHIC LIMITS OF INVESTMENTS/LOANS: International
RANGE OF INV./LOAN PER BUSINESS: Min. $3,000; Max. $100 million
PREFERRED TERM FOR LOANS & LEASES: Min. 2 years; Max. 10 years
BUSINESS CHARACTERISTICS DESIRED-REQUIRED: Minimum number of years in business: 3
REFERRALS: Investment/Mortgage banker;Borrower/Investee

COMPANY: **ICON Group Inc.**
ADDRESS: 204 Martine Avenue
White Plains, NY 10601
PHONE: (914) 997-0063
CONTACT OFFICER(S): Peter D. Beekman

COMPANY: **National Industrial Services**
ADDRESS: 34 South Broadway
White Plains, NY 10601
PHONE: (914) 428-8600
CONTACT OFFICER(S): Howard D. Blank

COMPANY: **Techlease, Inc.**
ADDRESS: 1025 Westchester Avenue
White Plains, NY 10604
PHONE: (914) 682-8770
TYPE OF INSTITUTION: Leasing Company - Privately Owned
CONTACT OFFICER(S): Fredric B. Heilman, President
Bernard Finkiel, Vice President - C.E.O.
TOTAL ASSETS: $100,000,000
INVESTMENTS/LOANS MADE: For own account; Through private placements
TYPES OF FINANCING: VENTURE CAPITAL: Start-up from developed product stage; Buy-outs/Acquisitions,

LOANS: Equipment, LEASES: Single-leveraged; Leveraged; Tax leases; Non-tax leases; Operating; Tax-oriented lease brokerage; Lease syndication; Vendor financing programs

COMPANY: **Winfield Capital Corp.**
ADDRESS: 237 Mamaroneck Av.
White Plains, NY 10605
PHONE: (914) 949-2600
TYPE OF INSTITUTION: SBIC
CONTACT OFFICER(S): Stanley Pechman, Pres.
TYPES OF FINANCING: LOANS: Working capital (receivables/inventory); Equipment, LEASES
PREFERRED TYPES OF INDUSTRIES/INVESTMENTS: Manufacturers & Wholesale Trades
GEOGRAPHIC LIMITS OF INVESTMENTS/LOANS: Regional
RANGE OF INV./LOAN PER BUSINESS: Min. $100,000
PREFERRED TERM FOR LOANS & LEASES: Min. 5 years
BUSINESS CHARACTERISTICS DESIRED-REQUIRED: No start-ups

COMPANY: **Neptune Computer Group, Inc.**
ADDRESS: 1616 Whitestone Expressway
Whitestone, NY 11357
PHONE: (212) 767-5100
CONTACT OFFICER(S): Jacques G. Pomeranz

COMPANY: **American Cascade Leasing Co., Inc.**
ADDRESS: 3250 W. Market Street, P.O. Box 5480
Akron, OH 44313
PHONE: (216) 836-9557
CONTACT OFFICER(S): Robert W. Hall

COMPANY: **First Ohio Leasing Corp.**
ADDRESS: P.O. Box 5317
Akron, OH 44313
PHONE: (216) 864-2108
CONTACT OFFICER(S): H. S. Blythe

COMPANY: **Houser Financial Services**
ADDRESS: Dietz Shopping Center, P.O. Box 637
Beverly, OH 45715
PHONE: (614) 984-2393
CONTACT OFFICER(S): Jeffrey L. Weihl

COMPANY:**Gradison Leasing Inc.**
ADDRESS: 580 Bldg. Suite 120
Cincinnati, OH 45202
PHONE: (513) 579-8980, 800-543-5522 (outside OH); 800-582-8866 (In Oh)
CONTACT OFFICER: I. Dumont Gouge, President

COMPANY: **Great American Management Services**
ADDRESS: 1 East 4th Street, Suite 800, P.O. Box 1906
Cincinnati, OH 45202
PHONE: (513) 369-5602
CONTACT OFFICER(S): Allen L. Davis

COMPANY: **Omni Funding Corporation**
ADDRESS: One Triangle Park
Cincinnati, OH 45246
PHONE: (513) 772-8989
CONTACT OFFICER(S): Raymond H. Coger

COMPANY: **AFI Financial Corporation — AFI Leasing**
ADDRESS: 1668 Hanna Building, 1422 Euclid Avenue
Cleveland, OH 44115
PHONE: (216) 621-4455
CONTACT OFFICER(S): Otto Lombardo
Ms. Laureen S. Himes, V.P.

COMPANY: **Eaton Credit Corporation**
ADDRESS: 100 Erieview Plaza
Cleveland, OH 44114
PHONE: (216) 523-4200
CONTACT OFFICER(S): Elmer P. Gates

COMPANY: **Leaseway Transportation Leasing Company**
ADDRESS: 3700 East Park Drive
Cleveland, OH 44122
PHONE: (216) 464-3300
CONTACT OFFICER(S): James M. Peterson

COMPANY: **Leasing Dynamics Inc.**
ADDRESS: 1717 East Ninth Street, Suite 915
Cleveland, OH 44114
PHONE: (216) 687-0100
CONTACT OFFICER(S): Robert S. Kendall

COMPANY: **Technicare Corporation**
ADDRESS: P.O. Box 5130
Cleveland, OH 44139
PHONE: (216) 248-1800
CONTACT OFFICER(S): H.R. Chakford

COMPANY: **Banc One Leasing Corporation**
ADDRESS: Department 0385
Columbus, OH 43271
PHONE: (614) 895-4499
CONTACT OFFICER(S): Robert L. Paulson

COMPANY: **Bancohio Leasing Company**
ADDRESS: 155 E. Broad Street
Columbus, OH 43265
PHONE: (614) 463-8010
CONTACT OFFICER(S): Len Hibbard

COMPANY: **The Huntington Leasing Co., Huntington National Bank**
ADDRESS: P.O. Box 1558
Columbus, OH 43260
PHONE: (614) 469-7087
CONTACT OFFICER(S): Robert W. Lucas

COMPANY: **Park Leasing Corporation**
ADDRESS: 150 East Broad Street
Columbus, OH 43215
PHONE: (614) 228-0063
CONTACT OFFICER(S): George S. Hoster, Jr.

COMPANY: **Stone Leasing Co.**
ADDRESS: 1215 W. Mound Street, P.O. Box 23063
Columbus, OH 43223
PHONE: (614) 461-9080
CONTACT OFFICER(S): Dana H. Stone

COMPANY: **Worthington Leasing Corp.**
ADDRESS: P.O. Box 29186, 1050 Dearborn Drive
Columbus, OH 43229
PHONE: (614) 438-5898
CONTACT OFFICER(S): Stephen M. Polk

COMPANY: **Reyna Financial Corporation, Reynolds & Reynolds Company**
ADDRESS: P.O. Box 1005
Dayton, OH 45401
PHONE: (513) 443-2018
CONTACT OFFICER(S): Dale L. Medford

COMPANY: **Potomac Leasing Company**
ADDRESS: 1300 Indian Wood Circle
Maumee, OH 43537
PHONE: (419) 893-7420
CONTACT OFFICER(S): Edward J. Schultz

COMPANY: **Miami Citizens Financial Corp.**
ADDRESS: 326 N. Main St., P.O. Boxx 739
Piqua, OH 45356
PHONE: (513) 778-0698
CONTACT OFFICER(S): James C. Siegel

COMPANY: **LTW Leasing International, Inc.**
ADDRESS: 339 Highgate Avenue
Worthington, OH 43085
PHONE: (614) 846-5327
CONTACT OFFICER(S): Laurence J. Mily

COMPANY: **Central Leasing Corporation**
ADDRESS: P.O. Box 18243
Oklahoma City, OK 73118
PHONE: (405) 848-4840
CONTACT OFFICER(S): J.C. Hammond

COMPANY: **FNB Leasing Company Inc., First National Bank & Trust**
ADDRESS: 120 North Robinson, Ste. 880C
Oklahoma City, OK 73102
PHONE: (405) 272-4712
CONTACT OFFICER(S): Robert Radford

COMPANY: **Kerr-McGee Leasing Corporation**
ADDRESS: P.O. Box 25861
Oklahoma City, OK 73125
PHONE: (405) 270-1313
CONTACT OFFICER(S): Thomas B. Stephens

COMPANY: **TII Lease, Inc.**
ADDRESS: 320 South Boston, Suite 1501
Tulsa, OK 74103
PHONE: (918) 587-5000
TYPE OF INSTITUTION: Independent Leasing Company
CONTACT OFFICER(S): Grant G. Goodman, Pres.
ASSETS: $5 million plus
INVESTMENTS/LOANS MADE: For own account; For managed accounts
TYPES OF FINANCING: LEASES: Operating; Vendor financing programs
PREFERRED TYPES OF INDUSTRIES/INVESTMENTS: Computer peripheral equipment
GEOGRAPHIC LIMITS OF INVESTMENTS/LOANS: National
RANGE OF INV./LOAN PER BUSINESS: Min. $5,000; Max. $500,000
PREFERRED TERM FOR LOANS & LEASES: Min. One year; Max. Three years
BUSINESS CHARACTERISITCS DESIRED-REQUIRED: Minimum net worth, $250,000

COMPANY: **Toronto Dominion Leasing LTD.**
ADDRESS: P.O. Box 149, Toronto-Dominion Centre
Toronto, Ontario M5K 1A2
PHONE: (416) 866-8880
TYPE OF INSTITUTION: Equipment Leasing Co. - Sub. of the Toronto - Dominion Bank
CONTACT OFFICER(S): S.J. Wilson, President
T.S. Czegel, Vice Pres. & Treasurer, P. Gauthier, Vice Pres. Marketing
ASSETS: $120 million
INVESTMENTS/LOANS MADE: For own account
INVESTMENTS/LOANS MADE: In securities with a secondary market and in securities without a secondary market
TYPES OF FINANCING: LEASES: Single investor; Leveraged; Tax leases; Non-tax leases; Operating; Lease syndications; Vendor financing programs
PREFERRED TYPES OF INDUSTRIES/INVESTMENTS: All kinds of equipment - prefer higher capital cost allowance assets
GEOGRAPHIC LIMITS OF INVESTMENTS/LOANS: National; Other: Canada
RANGE OF INV./LOAN PER BUSINESS: Min. $10,000
PREFERRED TERM FOR LOANS & LEASES: Min. 3 years; Max. 15 years
BUSINESS CHARACTERISTICS DESIRED-REQUIRED: Minimum number of years in business: 3
REFERRALS ACCEPTED FROM: Investment/Mortgage banker or Borrower/Investee

COMPANY: **Colonial Pacific Leasing Co.**
ADDRESS: P.O. Box 646
Clackamas, OR 97015
PHONE: (503) 655-7760
TYPE OF INSTITUTION: Leasing Co.

CONTACT OFFICER(S): Joe Woodley
Mike Burns
William Grater
ASSETS: $80 million
TYPES OF FINANCING: LEASES: Tax leases; Non-tax leases; Tax-oriented lease brokerage; Vendor financing programs
PREFERRED TYPES OF INDUSTRIES/INVESTMENTS: General Equipment
WILL NOT CONSIDER: Airplanes
GEOGRAPHIC LIMITS OF INVESTMENTS/LOANS: Regional; Anything west of Mississippi
RANGE OF INV./LOAN PER BUSINESS: Min. $5,000
PREFERRED TERM FOR LOANS & LEASES: Min. 3 years; Max. 5 years
BRANCHES: Terry Maher, 6209 Hendricks NE, Albuquerque, NM 87110; (505) 881-1135

COMPANY: **Bancorp Leasing Corp.**
ADDRESS: 700 NE Multnomah
Portland, OR 97232
PHONE: (503) 231-5206
TYPE OF INSTITUTION: Leasing Co.
CONTACT OFFICER(S): Merle K. Buck
TYPES OF FINANCING: LOANS: Term loans, LEASES: Single-investor; Leveraged; Tax leases; Non-tax leases; Tax-oriented lease brokerage; Lease syndications
GEOGRAPHIC LIMITS OF INVESTMENTS/LOANS: National
RANGE OF INV./LOAN PER BUSINESS: Min. $25,000
PREFERRED TERM FOR LOANS & LEASES: Min. 5; Max. 20 years
BUSINESS CHARACTERISTICS DESIRED-REQUIRED: Cash flow

COMPANY: **The Benjamin Franklin Leasing Company**
ADDRESS: 2611 S.W. 3rd, Suite 303
Portland, OR 97201
PHONE: (503) 243-1470
CONTACT OFFICER(S): Claire M. Gray

COMPANY: **Industrial Leasing Corporation**
ADDRESS: 2300 S W Sixth Avenue
Portland, OR 97201
PHONE: (503) 228-2111
CONTACT OFFICER(S): Howard Freedman

COMPANY: **Northwest Acceptance Corporation**
ADDRESS: 1001 SW Fifth Avenue
Portland, OR 97204
PHONE: (503) 222-7920
CONTACT OFFICER(S): James E. LeBlanc, Exec. V.P./Marketing & Operatons
Lawrence R. Appel, Sr. V.P./Vendor Leasing Programs
Gary V. Hayward, Sr. V.P./Receivables & Inventory
H.O. Koenig, Exec. V.P./Heavy Equipment Financing
ASSETS: $260 million
INVESTMENTS/LOANS MADE: For own account
TYPES OF FINANCING: VENTURE CAPITAL: Buyouts/Acquisitions LOANS: Working capital; Equipment, LEASES: Single-investor; Non-tax leases; Vendor financing programs
PREFERRED TYPES OF INDUSTRIES/INVESTMENTS: Business equipment; Construction; Receivable loans to manufacturers and distributors
GEOGRAPHIC LIMITS OF INVESTMENTS/LOANS: National
PREFERRED TERM FOR LOANS & LEASES: Min. 2 years; Max. 7 years

COMPANY: **R.F.S. Leasing Company**
ADDRESS: 1800 S.W. First Avenue, Suite 180
Portland, OR 97201
PHONE: (503) 295-7793
CONTACT OFFICER(S): Gordon Boorse

COMPANY: **US Bancorp Financial, Inc., US Bancorporation**
ADDRESS: Lloyd 700 Building, Suite 600, 700 N.E. Multnomah
Portland, OR 97232
PHONE: (503) 231-5206
CONTACT OFFICER(S): Merle K. Buck

COMPANY: **Public Leasing Company**
ADDRESS: 100 Presidential Blvd. N., P.O. Box 5
Bala Cynwyd, PA 19004
PHONE: (215) 839-0225
CONTACT OFFICER(S): Stephen H. Gatter

COMPANY: **Westinghouse Credit Corp.**
ADDRESS: 2000 Oxford Drive Ste-202
Bethel Park PA 15102
PHONE: (412) 854-7022
TYPE OF INSTITUTION: Leasing company
CONTACT OFFICER(S): James W. Meighen, V.P., Leveraged Leasing
John McEnery, Manager, Leasing
TYPES OF FINANCING: LEASES: Single-investor; Leveraged; Tax leases; Vendor financing programs; Other: Trac leases
GEOGRAPHIC LIMITS OF INVESTMENTS/LOANS: National
RANGE OF INV./LOAN PER BUSINESS: Min. $3 million; Max. $25 million
PREFERRED TERM FOR LOANS & LEASES: Min. 3 years; Max. 18 years
BUSSINESS CHARACTERISTICS DESIRED/REQUIRED: Other: Varies with the transaction

COMPANY: **First Valley Leasing Inc.**
ADDRESS: One Bethlehem Plaza
Bethlehem, PA 18018
PHONE: (215) 865-8713
TYPE OF INSTITUTION: Leasing subsidiary of bank holding company
CONTACT OFFICER(S): Patrick A. McGee, President
ASSETS: $5 million
INVESTMENTS/LOANS MADE: For own account
LOANS: Equipment, LEASES: Single-investor; Non-tax leases; Vendor financing programs
PREFERRED TYPES OF EQUIPMENT: We have no particular preference by industry or equipment. We

intentionally look for a diversification by industry and equipment
Security, alarms, health clubss, energy management equipment dealers
GEOGRAPHIC LIMITS OF INVESTMENTS: Regional
RANGE OF INV./LOAN PER BUSINESS: Min. $5,000; Max. Unlimited
PREFERRED TERM FOR LOANS & LEASES: Min. 2 years; Max. 5 years
BUSINESS CHARACTERISTICS DESIRED-REQUIRED: Minimum number of years in business: 2; Min. annual sales $200,000; Min. net worth $50,000; Min. annual net income $10,000; Min. annual cash flow $10,000
REFERRALS ACCEPTED FROM: Investment/Mortgage banker and Borrower/Investee
REMARKS: First Valley Leasing Inc. is a bank related lessor. We write full pay-out leased based on the financial strength of the company

COMPANY: **Equitable Financial Management Inc.**
ADDRESS: 1100 Washington Avenue
Carnegie, PA 15106
PHONE: (412) 279—9250
CONTACT OFFICER(S): C. L. Dixon

COMPANY: **Financial Institutional Funding**
ADDRESS: 600 North Bell Avenue, Suite 119
Carnegie, PA 15106
PHONE: (412) 276-3454
CONTACT OFFICER(S): Richard J. Santucci

COMPANY: **Superior Financial Corporation**
ADDRESS: 600 North Bell Ave., Suite 212, Bldg. 100
Carnegie, PA 15106
PHONE: (412) 279-7454
CONTACT OFFICER(S): Thomas L. Park

COMPANY: **Fulcrum Financial Services Inc.**
ADDRESS: 1100 Ridge Pike
Conshohocken, PA 19428
PHONE: (215) 825-5445
CONTACT OFFICER(S): Al Marland

COMPANY: **Lease Group, Inc.**
ADDRESS: 715 Twining Road, Suite 113
Dresher, PA 19025
PHONE: (215) 572-0678
CONTACT OFFICER(S): Ronald A. Coruzzi

COMPANY: **Triumphe Leasing Company**
ADDRESS: 550 Pinetown Road, Suite 250
Fort Washington, PA 19034
PHONE: (215) 641-0120
CONTACT OFFICER(S): Harvey I. Kantor, President
Stephen B. Fischer, V.P.
ASSETS: $5,000,000
INVESTMENTS/LOANS MADE: For own account
INVESTMENTS/LOANS MADE: Only in securities without a secondary market
LEASES: Vendor financing programs
PREFERRED TYPES OF INDUSTRIES/INVESTMENTS: Telecommunications; Data processing; Medical; Industrial
GEOGRAPHIC LIMITS OF INVESTMENTS/LOANS: Local
RANGE OF INV./LOAN PER BUSINESS: Min. $2,000; Max. $250,000
PREFERRED TERM FOR LOANS & LEASES: Min. 2 years; Max. 5 years
BUSINESS CHARACTERISTICS DESIRED-REQUIRED: Minimum number of years in business: 2; Min. annual sales $150,000; Min. net worth $25,000; Min. annual net income $10,000; Min. annual cash flow $20,000
REFERRALS ACCEPTED FROM: Borrower/Investee only

COMPANY: **Dala Co. Inc.**
ADDRESS: 14 Greenfield Road
Lancaster, PA 17602
PHONE: (717) 392-0641
CONTACT OFFICER(S): Paul Derstine

COMPANY: **Hilliard-Lyons Leasing Corp.**
ADDRESS: The Lafayette Bldg, Chesley Dr.
Media, PA 19063
PHONE: (215) 565-8330
CONTACT OFFICER(S): Michael D. Vulpio

COMPANY: **First Pennsylvania Leasing Inc.**
ADDRESS: 1600 Market St., 19th Floor
Philadelphia, PA 19101
PHONE: (215) 786-7700
TYPE OF INSTITUTION: Leasing Division of a Commercial Bank
CONTACT OFFICER(S): Michael J. Hassett, V.P.
Joseph C. Metz, Asst. V.P.
Anthony J. Kupcinski, Commercial Officer
ASSETS: $5,000,000,000
INVESTMENTS/LOANS MADE: For own account
TYPES OF FINANCING: LEASES: Lease Syndications
PREFERRED TYPES OF INDUSTRIES/INVESTMENTS: Maufacturing Equipment, Computer Equipment, Hospital and Medical Equipment, etc.
WILL NOT CONSIDER: Oil Drilling Rigs, Off-The-Road Vehicles
GEOGRAPHIC LIMITS OF INVESTMENTS/LOANS: Regional
RANGE OF INV./LOAN PER BUSINESS: Min. $100,000; Max. $5,000,000
PREFERRED TERM FOR LOANS & LEASES: Min. one year; Max. six years
BUSINESS CHARACTERISTICS DESIRED-REQUIRED: Minimum number of years in business: 3
REFERRALS ACCEPTED FROM: Borrower/Broker/ Vendor only
REMARKS: Referrals only accepted at address shown in #2

COMPANY: **Innovest Group, Inc.**
ADDRESS: 1700 Market Street, Ste. 1228
Philadelphia, PA 19103
PHONE: (215) 564-3960

TYPE OF INSTITUTION: Private Venture Capital Company
CONTACT OFFICER(S): Richard E. Woosnam, President
Nila K. Sendzik, V.P.
ASSETS: $10 Million
INVESTMENTS/LOANS MADE: For own account; Through private placements
INVESTMENTS/LOANS MADE: Only in securities without a secondary market
TYPES OF FINANCING: VENTURE CAPITAL: Start-up from developed product stage; First-stage; Second-stage; Later-stage expansion, LEASES: Single-investor; Leveraged; Tax leases; Vendor financing programs, REAL ESTATE
PREFERRED TYPES OF INDUSTRIES/INVESTMENTS: Communications — cable TV, commercial communication, data comm, satellite & miicrowave comm., telephone related; Computer Related —- computer graphics & CAD/CAM, computer services, memory devices, micro 7 mini computers, software systems; Electronics Equipment — medical products, laser related, analytical and scientific instrumentation, optics technology, semiconduction; Medical — diagnostic equipment, therapeutic equipment; Other — education related, real estate
GEOGRAPHIC LIMITS OF INVESTMENTS/LOANS: Regional
RANGE OF INV./LOAN PER BUSINESS: Min. $250,000; Max. $1,000,000
BUSINESS CHARACTERISTICS DESIRED-REQUIRED: Minimum number of years in business: 0
REFERRALS ACCEPTED FROM: Investment banker or Borrower/Investee

COMPANY: **The Philadelphia National Bank**
ADDRESS: Leasing Department, P.O. Box 8377, Broad & Chestnut Streets
Philadelphia, PA 19101
PHONE: (215) 629-4537
CONTACT OFFICER(S): C. Rogers Childs, Jr., Vice President
ASSETS: $9,275,857,000 as of June 30, 1984
INVESTMENTS/LOANS MADE: For own account
TYPES OF FINANCING: LOANS: Equipment, LEASES: Single-investor; Leveraged; Tax leases; Non-tax leases; Tax-oriented lease brokerage; Lease syndications; Vendor finanging programs, OTHER SERVICES PROVIDED: Debt side of leveraged lease transactions
GEOGRAPHIC LIMITS OF INVESTMENTS/LOANS: Local; State; Regional; National; International
RANGE OF INV./LOAN PER BUSINESS: Min. $250,000; Max. legal limit
PREFERRED TERM FOR LOANS & LEASES: Min. 3 to 8 years; Max. 10 to 15 years
BUSINESS CHARACTERISTICS DESIRED-REQUIRED: Minimum number of years in business: 5
REFERRALS ACCEPTED FROM: Investment/Mortgage banker or Borrower/Investee

COMPANY: **Provident National Leasing Corporation**
ADDRESS: Broad and Chestnut Streets
Philadelphia, PA 19101
PHONE: (215) 585-5260
CONTACT OFFICER(S): Theodore S. Radomile

COMPANY: **PSFS**
ADDRESS: 12 South 12th Street
Philadelphia, PA 19107
PHONE: (215) 636-6000
TYPE OF INSTITUTION: Diversified Financial Services
CONTACT OFFICER(S): Philip A. McMunigal III, V.P., Private Placement Unit
ASSETS: $12.5 billion (June 30, 1984)
INVESTMENTS/LOANS MADE: For own account; Through private placements
INVESTMENTS/LOANS MADE: In securities with a secondary market and in securities without a secondary market
TYPES OF FINANCING: SECONDARY-MARKET CORPORATE SECURITIES: Common stock; Preferred stock; Bonds, VENTURE CAPITAL: Start-up from developed product stage, LOANS: Unsecured to credits above Baa; Working capital; Equipment; Equity-related, REAL ESTATE LOANS: Long-term senior mtg.; Intermediate-term senior mtg.; Land development; Construction; Standbys; Industrial revenue bonds, LEASES: Leveraged; Tax leases; Non-tax leases; Operating; Vendor financing programs, REAL ESTATE: Acquisitions; Joint ventures; Partnerships/ Syndications, OTHER SERVICES PROVIDED: pension fund advisory services, trade and stand-by letters of credit
PREFERRED TYPES OF INDUSTRIES/INVESTMENTS: all offerings considered
GEOGRAPHIC LIMITS OF INVESTMENTS/LOANS: Local; State; Regional; National; International
RANGE OF INV./LOAN PER BUSINESS: Min. $1,000,000; Max. depends on quality rating
PREFERRED TERM FOR LOANS & LEASES: Min. one year; Max. 10 years
BUSINESS CHARACTERISTICS DESIRED-REQUIRED: Negotiable

COMPANY: **Anchor Leasing Corp.**
ADDRESS: Seven Wood St.
Pittsburgh, PA 15222
PHONE: (412) 765-0690
TYPE OF INSTITUTION: Leasing Co.
CONTACT OFFICER(S): James H. Rich
TOTAL ASSETS: $10,000,000
TYPES OF FINANCING: LEASES: Non-tax leases; Vendor financing programs; Other start-ups in exchange for equity
PREFERRED TYPES OF INDUSTRIES/INVESTMENTS: Broadcast Equipment
WILL NOT CONSIDER: Restaurants, Vending Machines
GEOGRAPHIC LIMITS OF INVESTMENTS/LOANS: National
RANGE OF INV./LOAN PER BUSINESS: Min. $25,000; Max. $300,000
PREFERRED TERM FOR LOANS & LEASES: Min. 3; Max. 5 years

COMPANY: **Chapel Equipment Services, Inc., or Funding Systems Asset Management Corp.**
ADDRESS: 1000 RIDC Plaza
Pittsburgh, PA 15238

PHONE: (412) 963-9870
TYPE OF INSTITUTION: Financial Services
CONTACT OFFICER(S): Jeff Auslander, Sr. VP
Harold L. Lehman, VP andTreasurer
Michael Daniel, VP Operations
Mark T. Ruane, Manager
INVESTMENTS/LOANS MADE: For own account; For managed accounts; through private placements
TYPES OF FINANCES: LEASES: Single-investor; Leveraged; Tax leases; Non-tax leases; Operating; Tax-oriented lease brokerage; Lease syndication; Vendor financing programs, OTHER SERVICES PROVIDED: Portfolio Management systems for lessors and investors of/in equipment leases
GEOGRAPHIC LIMITS OF INV./LOANS: National; International
RANGE OF INVESTMENT/LOAN PER BUSINESS: Min. $250,000; Max. No limit
PREFERRED TERM FOR LOANS & LEASES: Min. 2 years; Max. 25 years
BUSINESS CHARACTERISTICS DESIRED-REQUIRED: Minimum number of years in business: 0
REFERRALS:Investment/Mortgage banker; Borrower/ Investee

COMPANY: **Dravo Leasing Company**
ADDRESS: One Oliver Plaza
Pittsburgh, PA 15222
PHONE: (412) 566-5186
TYPE OF INSTITUTION: Captive leasing subsidiary
CONTACT OFFICER(S): Patricia M. Rogan, General Manager & Asst. Treasurer
ASSETS: $35,000,000
TYPES OF FINANCING: LOANS: Equipment; Other: Mortgage, LEASES: Single-investor; Tax leases; Non-tax leases; Operating
PREFERRED TYPES OF INDUSTRIES/INVESTMENTS: Finance only Dravo products and services
GEOGRAPHIC LIMITS OF INVESTMENTS/LOANS: National
RANGE OF INV./LOAN PER BUSINESS: Max. $10,000,000
PREFERRED TERM FOR LOANS & LEASES: Min. 1-3 years; Max. 15-20 years
BUSINESS CHARACTERISTICS DESIRED-REQUIRED: Minimum number of years in business: 5

COMPANY: **Dresser Leasing Corp.**
ADDRESS: Three Gateway Center, Suite 300
Pittsburgh, PA 15222
PHONE: (412) 562-7700
CONTACT OFFICER(S): John W. Salzer
TOTAL ASSETS: $200,000,000
TYPES OF FINANCING: LEASES: Single-investor; Tax leases; Non-tax leases; Operating
PREFERRED TYPES OF INDUSTRIES/INVESTMENTS: General Equipment, Vehicles
WILL NOT CONSIDER: Restaurant Equipment
GEOGRAPHIC LIMITS OF INVESTMENTS/LOANS: National
RANGE OF INV./LOAN PER BUSINESS: Min. $20,000; Max. $5,000,000
PREFERRED TERM FOR LOANS & LEASES: Min. 3; Max. 10 years

BUSINESS CHARACTERISTICS DESIRED/REQUIRED: Minimum number of years in business: 3

COMPANY: **F/S Asset Management Corp.**
ADDRESS: 1000 RIDC Plaza, Suite 404
Pittsburgh, PA 15238
PHONE: (412) 963-9870
CONTACT OFFICER(S): Mark T. Ruane

COMPANY: **First Westmoreland Corporation**
ADDRESS: P.O. Box 8718
Pittsburgh, PA 15221
PHONE: (412) 327-1300
CONTACT OFFICER(S): Fred A. Holcomb

COMPANY: **Joy Finance Company**
ADDRESS: 301 Grant Street
Pittsburgh, PA 15219
PHONE: (412) 562-4732
CONTACT OFFICER(S): Lawrence G. Hofmann, Jr.

COMPANY: **LMV Leasing Inc.**
ADDRESS: 121 Freeport Road
Pittsburgh, PA 15238
PHONE: (412) 782-6200
CONTACT OFFICER(S): Andrew A. Strauss

COMPANY: **Mellon Financial Services Leasing Group**
ADDRESS: Suite 3030 One Mellon Bank Center
Pittsburgh, PA 15258
PHONE: (412) 234-5061
TYPE OF INSTITUTION: Equipment Leasing sub. national bank
CONTACT OFFICER(S): Arthur Folsom, Jr., SVP, Andra Cochran: V.P. Marketing Division
Jerry Vaughn, V.P. Syndication Division
TOTAL ASSETS: $300,000,000
INVESTMENTS/LOANS MADE: For own account; Through private placements
INVESTMENTS/LOANS MADE: Only in securities without a secondary market
TYPES OF FINANCING: LOANS: Equipment, LEASES: Single-investor; Leveraged; Tax leases; Non-tax leases; Tax-oriented lease brokerage; Lease syndications
PREFERRED TYPES OF INDUSTRIES/INVESTMENTS: Transportation, communication, manufacturing, energy-related and communications
RANGE OF INV./LOAN PER BUSINESS: Min. $250,000; Max. $None
PREFERRED TERM FOR LOANS & LEASES: Min. 3 years; Max. 25 years
BUSINESS CHARACTERISTICS DESIRED-REQUIRED: Minimum number of years in business: 3; Min. net worth: $5,000,000
REFERRALS: Investment/Mortgage banker; Borrower/ Investee
BRANCHES: John S. Ingham, One Post Office Square, Suite 3650, Boston, MA 02109, (617) 432-4151
Charles S. Wells, 2121 San Jacinto, Suite 2900, Lockbox 12, Dallas, TX 75201, (214) 760-9181

Douglas P. Williamson, 824 E. Street Rd. Warminster, PA 18974; (215) 585-4691

COMPANY: **National Financial Services Corporation**
ADDRESS: Manor Oak II, Suite 362
Pittsburgh, PA 15220
PHONE: (412) 343-8841
CONTACT OFFICER(S): Kevin M. Vaughn

COMPANY: **National Leasing Corp.**
ADDRESS: 150 Beta Drive, P.O. Box 11464
Pittsburgh, PA 15238
PHONE: (412) 963-1100
TYPE OF INSTITUTION: Leasing Co.
CONTACT OFFICER(S): Aubrey W. Gladstone
Thomas A. Evans
Gregor Thompson
TYPES OF FINANCING: Leases; Single-investor; Leveraged; Tax leases; Non-tax leases; Operating; Tax-oriented lease brokerage; Vendor financing programs
PREFERRED TYPES OF INDUSTRIES/INVESTMENTS: Corporate aircraft; Diversified
GEOGRAPHIC LIMITS OF INVESTMENTS/LOANS: National
RANGE OF INVESTMENTS/LOAN PER BUSINESS: Min. $500,000; Max. $7,000,000
PREFERRED TERMS FOR LOANS & LEASES: Min. 2 years; Max. 10 years

COMPANY: **Helios Capital Corporation**
ADDRESS: Two Radnor Corporate Ctr, Suite 320, 100 Matsonford Rd.
Radnor, PA 19087
PHONE: (215) 293-6822
CONTACT OFFICER(S): R. A. Pew

COMPANY: **Anchor Leasing Corp.**
ADDRESS: Seven Wood St.
Pittsburgh, PA 15222

COMPANY: **Lease Financing Corporation**
ADDRESS: #3 Radnor Corporate Center
Radnor, PA 19087
PHONE: (215) 964-2000
TYPE OF INSTITUTION: Leasing Company
CONTACT OFFICER(S): Frank P. Slattery, President
Richard E. Caruso, Senior Vice President
Richard W. Stewart, Vice President
TOTAL ASSETS: $600,000,000
INVESTMENTS/LOANS MADE: For own account
TYPES OF FINANCING: LEASES: Single-investor; Leveraged; Tax leases; Non-tax leases; Operating; Vendor financing programs
GEOGRAPHIC LIMITS OF INVESTMENTS/LOANS: National; International

COMPANY: **Radnor Associates Ltd.**
ADDRESS: P.O. Box 124
Radnor, PA 19807
PHONE: (215) 687-4801
CONTACT OFFICER(S): Louis A. Zehner

COMPANY: **American Equipment Leasing Co., Inc.**
ADDRESS: P.O. Box 1258, 142 Pearl Street
Reading, PA 19603
PHONE: (215) 375-4267
CONTACT OFFICER(S): A. A. Haberberger

COMPANY: **Norbanc Lease, Inc.**
ADDRESS: Penn Avenue & Spruce Street
Scranton, PA 18503
PHONE: (717) 961-7222
CONTACT OFFICER(S): Joseph P. Durkin

COMPANY: **Servilease Corp.**
ADDRESS: 1015 N. Main Ave.
Scranton, PA 18504
PHONE: (717) 346-7708
TYPE OF INSTITUTION: Leasing Co.
CONTACT OFFICER(S): Thomas F. Fitzpatrick, Pres.
ASSETS: $150,000—1,000,000
TYPES OF FINANCING: LEASES: Sale-leaseback
GEOGRAPHIC LIMITS OF INVESTMENTS/LOANS: Regional
RANGE OF INV./LOAN PER BUSINESS: Min. $2,000
PREFERRED TERM FOR LOANS & LEASES: Min. 1-3; Max. 5-7

COMPANY: **The Devilbiss Leasing Company**
ADDRESS: P.O. Box 635, East Main Street
Somerset, PA 15501
PHONE: (814) 443-4881
CONTACT OFFICER(S): Larry E. Price

COMPANY: **Development Leasing Corp.**
ADDRESS: P.O. Box 858
Valley Forge, PA 19482
PHONE: (215) 337-1000
CONTACT OFFICER(S): Anthony J. Mendicino

COMPANY: **Triumphe Leasing Co., Inc.**
ADDRESS: P.O. Box 235
Warrington, PA 18976
PHONE: (215) 296-9419
CONTACT OFFICER(S): Harvey I. Kantor

COMPANY: **Lease Programs Inc.**
ADDRESS: Two Glenhardie Corp. Center, 1285 Drummers Lane
Wayne, PA 19087
PHONE: (215) 687-4434
CONTACT OFFICER(S): Mark S. Bazrod

COMPANY: **Century Equipment Leasing Corp.**
ADDRESS: 905 North York Road
Willow Grove, PA 19090
PHONE: (215) 657-5707
CONTACT OFFICER(S): Howard J. Moses

LEASING COMPANIES

(Lessors. Also see Commercial Bankers and Finance Companies, Insurance Companies and Investment Bankers)

COMPANY: **Emons Leasing Co. Inc., Emons Industries Inc.**
ADDRESS: 1 W. Market Street
York, PA 17401
PHONE: (717) 848-5959
CONTACT OFFICER(S): Joseph W. Marino

COMPANY: **Medical Technical Equipment Leasing Company**
ADDRESS: Banco Popular Center, Suite 909
Hato Rey, PR 00918
PHONE: (809) 753-8165
CONTACT OFFICER(S): Mr. Oscar Martinez

COMPANY: **Cameleglo Leasing, A Division of Camaleglo Corp.**
ADDRESS: G.P.O. Box 2222
San Juan, PR 00936
PHONE: (809) 784-8000
CONTACT OFFICER(S): Claudio L. Lloreda

COMPANY: **Safe Lease Company**
ADDRESS: 815 Reservoir Avenue, P.O. Box 3567
Cranston, RI 02910
PHONE: (401) 943-1600
CONTACT OFFICER(S): N.B. Baker

COMPANY: **Citizens Leasing Corporation**
ADDRESS: 870 Westminster Street
Providence, RI 02903
PHONE: (401) 456-7571
CONTACT OFFICER(S): Robert S. Nelson, President
Mary Beth Corrente, Assistant Treasurer
Laurel L. Bowerman, Leasing Representative
INVESTMENTS/LOANS MADE: For own account; Through private placements
TYPES OF FINANCING: LEASES: Single-investor; Leveraged; Tax leases; Non-tax leases; Vendor financing programs
PREFERRED TYPES OF INDUSTRIES/INVESTMENTS: Production Equipment
WILL NOT CONSIDER: Rolling Stock - Vehicles
GEOGRAPHIC LIMITS OF INVESTMENTS/LOANS: Regional; National
RANGE OF INV./LEASES, SINGLE INVESTOR: Min. $25,000; Max. $1,000,000
PREEFERRRED TERM FOR LOANS & LEASES: Min. 3 years; Max. 5 years
BUSINESS CHARACTERISTICSS DESIRED-REQUIRED: Minimum numbr of years in business: 12

COMPANY: **Fleet Credit Corporation**
ADDRESS: 155 South Main St.
Providence, RI
PHONE: (401) 278-6915
TYPE OF INSTITUTION: Leasing Division/Secured Lending Division of Bank Holding Company
CONTACT OFFICER(S): Robert Merrick, Assistant Controller
ASSETS: $362 Million
INVESTMENTS/LOANS MADE: For own account
TYPES OF FINANCING: LOANS: Working capital. LEASES: Single-investor; Leveraged; Tax leases; Non-tax leases; Tax-oriented lease brokerage
PREFERRED TYPES OF INDUSTRIES/INVESTMENTS: Communication: Radio communication, Telephone Answering Service, etc. Printing: Printed circuit board, disks, HTM's
GEOGRAPHIC LIMITS OF INVESTMENTS/LOANS: National
RANGE OF INV./LOAN PER BUSINESS: Max. $20,000
PREFERRED TERM FOR LOANS & LEASES: Min. 3 years; Max. 8 years
BUSINESS CHARACTERISTICS DESIRED-REQUIRED: Minimum number of years in business: 3

COMPANY: **Home Loan & Investment Bank, HLIB Leasing Division**
ADDRESS: 84 Weybosset Street
Providence, RI 02903
PHONE: (401) 272-5100
CONTACT OFFICER(S): Vincent J. Allesandro

COMPANY: **In Leasing Corp.**
ADDRESS: 155 S. Main St.
Providence, RI 02903
PHONE: (401) 278-6913
TYPE OF INSTITUTION: Leasing Co.
CONTACT OFFICER(S): Fred Robinson, National Sales
TYPES OF FINANCING: LOANS, LEASES: Single-investor; Leveraged; Tax leases; Non-tax leases; Tax-oriented lease brokerage; Lease syndications; Vendor financing programs
PREFERRED TYPES OF INDUSTRIES/INVESTMENTS: Middle market lessor
WILL NOT CONSIDER: Corp Aircraft, School bus fleets, Auto
GEOGRAPHIC LIMITS OF INVESTMENTS/LOANS: National
RANGE OF INV./LOAN PER BUSINESS: Min. $50,000
PREFERRED TERM FOR LOANS & LEASES: Min. 3 years
BRANCHES: Atlanta, GA; Boston, MA; Cincnnati, OH; Cleveland, OH; Dallas, TX; Minneapolis, MN; Pittsburgh, PA; Tulsa, OK

COMPANY: **Universal Financial Corporation**
ADDRESS: 56 Broad Street, P.O. Box 1014
Charleston, SC 29402
PHONE: (803) 577-4324
TYPE OF INSTITUTION: Business and financial broker
CONTACT OFFICER(S): William E. Craver, Jr., President
INVESTMENTS/LOANS MADE: For own account, Through private placements, Through underwriting public offerings
INVESTMENTS/LOANS MADE: In securities with a secondary market and in securities without a secondary market
TYPES OF FINANCING: VENTURE CAPITAL: Start-up from developed product stage; First-stage (less than 1 year); Second-stage (generally 1-3 years); Later-stage expansion; Buy-outs/Acquisitions, LOANS: Working capital (receivables/inventory); Equipment, Equity-related, REAL ESTATE LOANS: Intermediate-term

senior mtg., FACTORING, LEASES: Single-investor; Operating; Tax-oriented lease brokerage; Vendor financing programs, REAL ESTATE: Acquisitions; Joint ventures, OTHER SERVICES PROVIDED: Financial consulting
GEOGRAPHIC LIMITS OF INVESTMENTS/LOANS: Regional; National
RANGE OF INV./LOAN PER BUSINESS: Min. $250,000; Max. Open
PREFERRED TERM FOR LOANS & LEASES: Min. Open; Max. Open
BUSINESS CHARACTERISTICS DESIRED-REQUIRED: Minimum number of years in business: 0
REFERRALS ACCEPTED FROM: Investment/Mortgage banker or Borrower/Investee

COMPANY:**Liberty Life Insurance Company**
ADDRESS: P.O. Box 789
Greenville, SC 29602
PHONE: (803) 268-8111
CONTACT OFFICER(S): Paul L. Van Kampen, V.P.—Securities (Private Placements)
Douglas W. Kroske, Assistant V.P. (Private Plaements)
ASSETS: $635 million
INVESTMENTS/LOANS MADE: For own account, Through private placements, underwriting public offerings
INVESTMENTS/LOANS MADE: In securities with a secondary market and in securities without a secondary market
TYPES OF FINANCING: SECONDARY-MARKET CORPORATE SECURITIES: Common stock; Bonds, LOANS: Unsecured to credits above Ba; Equipment, REAL ESTATE LOANS: Long-term senior mtg.; Intermediate-term senior mtg.; LEASES: Leveraged, REAL ESTATE: Acquisitions, OTHER SERVICES PROVIDED: Finance debt portion of leveraged lease transactions
GEOGRAPHIC LIMITS OF INVESTMENTS/LOANS: National; Mortgage loans in Southeast only
RANGE OF INV./LOAN PER BUSINESS: Min. $500,000; Max. $3,000,000
PREFERRED TERM FOR LOANS & LEASES: Min. 2 years; Max. 7 years
BUSINESS CHARACTERISTICS DESIRED-REQUIRED: Minimum number of years in business: 10; Min. annual sales $50 million; Min. net worth $10 million; Min. annual net income $1.5 million; Min. annual cash flow $2.5 million
REFERRALS ACCEPTED FROM: Investment/Mortgage banker or Borrower/Investee

COMPANY: **Equipment Leasing Corp.**
ADDRESS: 1930 Augusta Rd., P.O. 8457
Greenville, SC 29604
PHONE: (803) 242-6994
TYPE OF INSTITUTION: Leasing Co.
CONTACT OFFICER(S): Harold A. Carey, Jr., Sr. V.P.

COMPANY: **First National Lease Corp.**
ADDRESS: 1306 S. Church Street, P.O. Box 9058
Greenville, SC 29604
PHONE: (803) 271-6512
CONTACT OFFICER(S): Gerald T. Cavan

COMPANY: **Fiduciary Leasco, Inc.**
ADDRESS: P.O. Drawer 5208
Hilton Head Island, SC 29938
PHONE: (803) 785-7730
CONTACT OFFICER(S): Kenneth W. Pavia

COMPANY: **Mid America Leasing Company**
ADDRESS: 101 N. Main Avenue, Box 1326
Sioux Falls, SD 57101
PHONE: (605) 336-9473
CONTACT OFFICER(S): Larry Bierman

COMPANY: **Garrett Financial Services, Inc.**
ADDRESS: 210 N. Main St.
Goodlettsville, TN 37072
PHONE: (615) 859-1138
TYPE OF INSTITUTION: Equipment Leasing
CONTACT OFFICER(S): John Winchester, Exec. Vice-President
ASSETS: $50,000,000
TYPES OF FINANCING: LEASES: Single-investor; Leveraged; Tax leases; Non-tax leases; Operating; Tax-oriented lease brokerage; Lease syndications; Vendor financing programs
PREFERRED TYPES OF INDUSTRIES/INVESTMENTS: Equipment leases—commercial
GEOGRAPHIC LIMITS OF INVESTMENTS/LOANS: Regional
RANGE OF INV./LOAN PER BUSINESS: Min. $10,000; Max. $5,000,000
PREFERRED TERM FOR LOANS & LEASES: Min. 3 years; Max. 7 years
BUSINESS CHARACTERISTICS DESIRED-REQUIRED: Minimum number of years in business: 5; Min. annual sales $40,000,000; Min. net worth $800,000; Min. annual net income $150,000
REFERRALS ACCEPTED FROM: Investment/Mortgage banker or Borrower/Investee
BRANCHES: 1841 Monclaire Lane, Suite 103, Birmingham, AL 35216, (205) 822-8282, Warren Hawkins (Regional Agent)
801 Executive Park Drive, Suite 102, Mobile, AL 36606, (205) 473-1800, John Hitson
3564 C West, Fairfield Drive, Pensacola, FL 32505, (904) 456-6623, Myrna Nations
P.O. Box 940215, Atlanta, GA 30362, (404) 478-1603 or 1606, Jim Ladd (Regional Agent)
P.O. Box 7227, Huntsville, AL 35807, (205) 533-1454, Bo Bohannon
P.O. Box 2204, Muscle Shoals, AL 35662, (205) 381-8695, Ed Inman
P.O. Box 20619, St. Petersburg, FL 33742, (813) 527-3449, Joe E. Anderson

Suite 325, 501 Broad Street, Rome, GA 30161, (404) 232-4488, Tom Caldwell
P.O. Box 5771, Evansville, IN 47715, (812) 479-9741, Brian Fulkerson
1719 Ashley Circle, P.O. Box 1779, Bowling Green, KY 42102-1779, (502) 781-2020, Rodney Perkins (Regional Agent)
P.O. Box 7212, Columbia, MO 65205, (314) 442-5214, Jim Hendren
P.O. Box 1333, Hixon, TN 37343, (615) 877-4414, Tommy Marlin (Regional Agent)
P.O. Box 307, Elizabethton, TN 37643, (615) 543-4398, Jerry Vandyke
1200 S. Broadway, Lexington, KY 40504, (606) 233-0906, Jim Levenson, Sr. (Regional Agent)
P.O. Box 902, 731 N. Main, Sikeston, MO 63801, (314) 471-6000, Hense Winchesther (Regional Agent),
508 N. Dixie, Cookeville, TN 38501, (615) 526-5700, Hill Carlen
238 Peters Road, Suite 201, Knoxville, TN 37923, (615) 690-2195, Tim Pearson (Regional Agent)
Republic Foods Bldg., 2633 Swiss Avenue, Dallas, TX, 75204, (214) 823-7560, Bill Farris (Regional Agent)
P.O. Box 123, Lexington, TN 38351, (901) 968-7078, Lee McCollum

COMPANY: **United American Financial Corp.**
ADDRESS: 800 Gay Street, UAB Plaza
Knoxville, TN 37929
PHONE: (615) 971-2267
CONTACT OFFICER(S): Bobby H. Wright

COMPANY: **Craddock Leasing Company**
ADDRESS: 1407 Union Avenue
Memphis, TN 38104
PHONE: (901) 726-5160
CONTACT OFFICER(S): John E. Webb

COMPANY: **Economic Computer Sales, Inc.**
ADDRESS: 845 Crossover Lane, Suite 140, P.O. Box 240297
Memphis, TN 38124
PHONE: (901) 767-9130
CONTACT OFFICER(S): Kenneth A. Bouldin

COMPANY: **GIAC Leasing Corporation**
ADDRESS: 3779 Lamar Avenue
Memphis, TN 38195
PHONE: (901) 362-4429
CONTACT OFFICER(S): E. Tucker Dickerson

COMPANY: **Home Federal Leasing**
ADDRESS: 4700 Poplar, Suite 333
Memphis, TN 38117
PHONE: (901) 761-5602
CONTACT OFFICER(S): Charles Y. Bancroft

COMPANY: **U C Leasing Inc.**
ADDRESS: P.O. Box 3410
Memphis, TN 38103
PHONE: (901) 527-0761
CONTACT OFFICER(S): Dan H. Waters

COMPANY: **Union Planters National**
ADDRESS: 67 Madison Avenue, Suite 804, P.O. Box 387
Memphis, TN 38147
PHONE: (901) 523-6570
CONTACT OFFICER(S): Jerry L. Parker

COMPANY: **Coble Equipment Leasing, Cobel Systems**
ADDRESS: 214 Hermitage Avenue, P.O. Box 1104
Nashville, TN 37202
PHONE: (615) 259-2121
CONTACT OFFICER(S): S. L. Boord

COMPANY: **Machinery Leasing Company, North America, Inc.**
ADDRESS: 4717 Centennial Blvd., P.O. Box 24026
Nashville, TN 37202
PHONE: (615) 383-8747
CONTACT OFFICER(S): Richard Baruzzini

COMPANY: **Northern Telecom Finance Corp.**
ADDRESS: Nashville House, One Vantage Way
Nashville, TN 37228
PHONE: (615) 366-4440
CONTACT OFFICER(S): George Fargis Jr.

COMPANY: **Third Lease Corporation**
ADDRESS: Drawer 1100
Nashville, TN 37244
PHONE: (615) 748-4291
CONTACT OFFICER(S): William L. Rockholz

COMPANY: **Incline Leasing Inc.**
ADDRESS: P.O. Box 6228
Arlington, TX 76011
PHONE: (817) 640-0410
CONTACT OFFICER(S): Robert J. Glovitz

COMPANY: **Applied Financial Associates Incorporated**
ADDRESS: 8701 Shoal Creek Blvd., Suite 102, P.O. Box 9374
Austin, TX 78766
PHONE: (512) 452-7653
CONTACT OFFICER(S): John Jantzen
TYPES OF FINANCING: LEASES: Tax leases; Non-tax leases; Vendor financing programs.
PREFERRED TYPES OF INDUSTRIES/INVESTMENTS: Any type of equipment, basically a credit oriented lessor
GEOGRAPHIC LIMITS OF INVESTMENTS/LOANS: National
RANGE OF INV./LOAN PER BUSINESS: Min. $2,500; Max. $10,000,000
PREFERRED TERM FOR LOANS & LEASES: Min. 2 years; Max. 7 years

BUSINESS CHARACTERISTICS DESIRED-REQUIRED: Minimum number of years in business: 2; Other: Cash flow to service debt
REFERRALS ACCEPTED FROM: Investment/Mortgage banker or Borrower/Investee

COMPANY: **C&G Covert Leasing, Inc.**
ADDRESS: 1700 W. 6th St.
Austin, TX 78703
PHONE: (512) 476-1903
CONTACT OFFICER(S): Clark Covert, General Manager
ASSETS: $2,000,000
INVESTMENTS/LOANS MADE: For own account, Through private placements, Through underwriting public offerings
TYPES OF FINANCING: VENTURE CAPITAL: Resarch & Development; Second-stage (generally 1-3 years); Later-stage expansion, LOANS: Equipment, LEASES: Single-investor; Leveraged; Tax leases; Non-tax leases; Operating; Tax-oriented lease brokerage; Lease syndications
PREFERRED TYPES OF INDUSTRIES/INVESTMENTS: Equipment leases low and middle market
RANGE OF INV./LOAN PER BUSINESS: Min. $7,500; Max. $1,000,000
PREFERRED TERM FOR LOANS & LEASES: Min. 3 years; Max. 7 years
BUSINESS CHARACTERISTICS DESIRED-REQUIRED: Minimum number of years in business: 3; Min. annual sales $1,000,000; Min. net worth $10X annual earnings; Min. annual net income 6 figure; Min. annual cash flow variable
REFERRALS ACCEPTED FROM: Investment/Mortgage banker or Borrower/Investee

COMPANY: **Trans-Texas Leasing Inc.**
ADDRESS: 8301 Balcones Drive, Suite 218
Austin, TX 78759
PHONE: (512) 346-4286
CONTACT OFFICER(S): Charles Smith

COMPANY: **EDS Financial Corporation**
ADDRESS: 7171 Forest Lane
Dallas, TX 75230
PHONE: (214) 661-6164
CONTACT OFFICER(S): Don W. Ulm

COMPANY: **First Continental Leasing Corporation**
ADDRESS: 810 Capital Bank Building, 5307 E. Mockingbird Lane
Dallas, TX 75206
PHONE: (214) 826-5000
CONTACT OFFICER(S): Dick Rochetti

COMPANY: **GFH Financial Services Corp.**
ADDRESS: P.O. Box 47127
Dallas, TX 75247
PHONE: (214) 258-7369
CONTACT OFFICER(S): Richard L. Eastman

COMPANY: **MBC Financial Services Corporation**
ADDRESS: 2501 Cedar Springs Road, Suite 400, LB 10
Dallas, TX 75201
PHONE: (214) 871-1200
TYPE OF INSTITUTION: Corporate Finance Group of Institutional Lender
CONTACT OFFICER(S): J. Michael McMahon, Senior Vice President
David S. Temin, Vice President
Lynne M. McGanity, Vice President
ASSETS: $500 million
INVESTMENTS/LOANS MADE: For own account
INVESTMENTS/LOANS MADE: In securities with a secondary market and in securities without a secondary market
TYPES OF FINANCING: SECONDARY MARKET CORPORATE SECURITIES: Bonds; Other: Subordinated loans, secured note financing; VENTURE CAPITAL: Later-stage expansion; Buy-outs/Acquisitions; LOANS: Unsecured; Working Capital; Equipment; REAL ESTATE LOANS: Intermediate-term senior mtg.; Wraparounds; Gap; Standbys; LEASES: Single-investor; Leveraged; Tax leases; Non-tax leases
GEOGRAPHIC LIMITS OF INVESTMENTS/LOANS: Regional
RANGE OF INV./LOAN PER BUSINESS: Min. $5 Million; Max. $20 Million
PREFERRED TERM FOR LOANS & LEASES: Min. 3 years; Max. 10 years
BUSINESS CHARACTERISTICS DESIRED-REQUIRED: Minimum number of years in business: 5; Min. annual sales $7 Million; Min. net worth $1 Million; Min. annual net income $1.5 Million; Min. annual cash flow $2 Million
REFERRALS ACCEPTED FROM: Investment/Mortgage banker or Borrower/Investee

COMPANY: **Mercantile Texas Capital Corporation**
ADDRESS: P.O. Box 225415
Dallas, TX 75265
PHONE: (214) 698-6323
CONTACT OFFICER(S): Charles V. Lemmon III

COMPANY: **Republic National Leasing Corp., Republic Bank Dallas N.A.**
ADDRESS: P.O. Box 146
Dallas, TX 75221
PHONE: (214) 922-4149
CONTACT OFFICER(S): Harold C. Hunter, Jr.

COMPANY: **Trans-National Leasing, Inc.**
ADDRESS: P.O. Box 802615
Dallas, TX 75380
PHONE: (214) 233-6806
CONTACT OFFICER(S): Louis J. Maher

COMPANY: **Universal Leasing Corporation**
ADDRESS: Gateway I, 8131 LBJ Freeway, Suite 275
Dallas, TX 75251
PHONE: (214) 644-1911
CONTACT OFFICER(S): Richard J. Bennett

COMPANY: **Financial Leasing Co.**
ADDRESS: 1202 Ridglea Bank Bldg.
Ft. Worth, TX 76116
PHONE: (817) 737-9482
TYPE OF INSTITUTION: Leasing Co.
CONTACT OFFICER(S): O. W. Garner
TYPES OF FINANCING: LEASES: Single-investor; Tax leases; Tax-oriented lease brokerage; Vendor financing programs
PREFERRED TYPES OF INDUSTRIES/INVESTMENTS: Office Equipment (small ticket)
WILL NOT CONSIDER: Autos, Planes
GEOGRAPHIC LIMITS OF INVESTMENTS/LOANS: State
RANGE OF INV./LOAN PER BUSINESS: Min. $5,000
PREFERRED TERM FOR LOANS & LEASES: Min 2; Max. 7 years

COMPANY: **Affiliated Commercial Services Inc.**
ADDRESS: 10190 Old Katy Road, Suite 250
Houston, TX 77043
PHONE: (713) 461-4454
CONTACT OFFICER(S): Richard A. Galtelli

COMPANY: **Elder Leasing Company**
ADDRESS: 2500 East T.C. Jester
Houston, TX 77008
PHONE: (713) 466-4353
CONTACT OFFICER(S): Charles Graham

COMPANY: **First City Leasing Corporation**
ADDRESS: P.O. Box 4517, 1111 Fannin, Ste. 1000
Houston, TX 77210
PHONE: (713) 658-7774
CONTACT OFFICER(S): J. L. Williams

COMPANY: **Glesby-Marks Corporation**
ADDRESS: P.O. Box 56727
Houston, TX 77256
PHONE: (713) 627-1700
CONTACT OFFICER(S): Morris Glesby

COMPANY: **KBK Financial Inc.**
ADDRESS: P.O Box 61487, 1320 Niels Esperson Bldg.
Houston, TX 77208
PHONE: (713) 224-4791
TYPE OF INSTITUTION: Commercial Finance Co.
CONTACT OFFICER(S): R. Doyle Kelley, Pres.
TYPES OF FINANCING: FACTORING
PREFERRED TYPES OF INDUSTRIES/INVESTMENTS: Oil related/accounts receivable
WILL NOT CONSIDER: Retail financing or real estate financing
GEOGRAPHIC LIMITS OF INVESTMENTS/LOANS: State; Regional; Other: Texas & Louisiana, Oklahoma and New Mexico
RANGE OF INV./LOAN PER BUSINESS: Min. $50,000; Max. $1,000,000

COMPANY: **Leasing Associates, Inc.**
ADDRESS: 3101 Smith Street, P.O. Box 243
Houston, TX 77001
PHONE: (713) 522-9771
CONTACT OFFICER(S): George O. Gillespie

COMPANY: **Rockwell International Corp.**
ADDRESS: 1200 N. Alma Rd., Mail Station 420-115
Richardson TX 75081
PHONE: (214) 996-7467
CONTACT OFFICER(S): Ron Hicks

COMPANY: **Commercial Equipment Leasing Co.**
ADDRESS: 118 Broadway
San Antonio, TX 78205
PHONE: (512) 223-5525
TYPE OF INSTITUTION: Leasing Co.
CONTACT OFFICER(S): Jim Scott, Vice President
TOTAL ASSETS: $15,000,000
INVESTMENTS/LOANS MADE: For own account
TYPES OF FINANCING: VENTURE CAPITAL: Reasearch & Development; Start-up from developed product stage; First-stage; Second-stage; Later-stage expansion; Buy-outs/Acquisitions, LEASES: Single-investor; Leveraged; Tax leases; Non-tax leases; Vendor financing programs
PREFERRED TYPES OF INDUSTRIES/INVESTMENTS: Equipment leases
GEOGRAPHIC LIMITS OF INVESTMENTS/LOANS: Regional
RANGE OF INV./LOAN PER BUSINESS: Min. $10,000; Max. $250,000
PREFERRED TERMS FOR LOANS & LEASES: Min. 2 years; Max. 7 years
BUSINESS CHARACTERISTICS DESIRED-REQUIRED: Minimum number of years in business: 3

COMPANY: **Marcway Financial Corporation**
ADDRESS: 754 Isom Road
San Antonio, TX 78216
PHONE: (512) 341-4431
CONTACT OFFICER(S): Wayne E. Marcy, Jr.

COMPANY: **Miller Leasing Company**
ADDRESS: P.O. Box 5410
San Antonio, TX 78201
PHONE: (512) 732-2295
CONTACT OFFICER(S): Stephen C. Miller

COMPANY: **Bennett Leasing Company**
ADDRESS: 221 W. 2100 South St.
Salt Lake City, UT 84115
PHONE: (801) 486-1861
TYPE OF INSTITUTION: Leasing Co.
CONTACT OFFICER(S): John H. Bennett, Pres.
TYPES OF FINANCING: LEASES: Single-investor; Tax leases; Non-tax leases; Operating; Tax-oriented lease brokerage; Vehicle leasing
PREFERRED TYPES OF INDUSTRIES/INVESTMENTS: Vehicles —Equipment Leases

GEOGRAPHIC LIMITS OF INVESTMENTS/LOANS: Regional; CO, NM, NV
RANGE OF INV./LOAN PER BUSINESS: Min. $3,000; Max. $300,000
PREFERRED TERM FOR LOANS & LEASES: Min. 2 years
BUSINESS CHARACTERISTICS DESIRED-REQUIRED: Variable

COMPANY: **Commercial Security Bank, Leasing Division**
ADDRESS: CSB Tower, Suite 2000, 50 South Main
Salt Lake City, UT 84144
PHONE: (801) 535-1000
CONTACT OFFICER(S): David F. Klomp, Manager, Leasing Department

COMPANY: **First Security Leasing Company**
ADDRESS: P.O. Box 25357
Salt Lake City, UT 84125
PHONE: (801) 350-5801
CONTACT OFFICER(S): C. S. Cummings

COMPANY: **MFT Leasing**
ADDRESS: 135 S. Main St.
Salt Lake City, UT 84111
PHONE: (801) 350-3000
TYPE OF INSTITUTION: Leasing Co.
CONTACT OFFICER(S): Glen F. Groo, Ex. V.P. and General Manager
Ray Russell, V.P.
Robert Barr, V.P.
TYPES OF FINANCING: LEASES: Single-investor; General Equipment
PREFERRED TYPES OF INDUSTRIES/INVESTMENTS: Dentists, Doctors, Chiropractors, Office Furniture, Machine Tool, Manufacturing, Printing, Photography
WILL NOT CONSIDER: Autos, Truck
GEOGRAPHIC LIMITS OF INVESTMENTS/LOANS: Regional; Inter-mountain area
RANGE OF INV./LOAN PER BUSINESS: Min. $5,000; Max. $250,000
PREFERRED TERM FOR LOANS & LEASES: Min. 3; Max. 7 years
BUSINESS CHARACTERISTICS DESIRED-REQUIRED: Minimum number of years in business: 3

COMPANY: **Moore Leasing Company**
ADDRESS: 2450 East 7000 South, P.O. Box 21368
Salt Lake City, UT 84121
PHONE: (801) 584-1600
CONTACT OFFICER(S): Larry R. Stevens

COMPANY: **Prudential Leasing Co.**
ADDRESS: P.O. Box 15500, 155 East 3300 South
Salt Lake City, UT 84115
PHONE: (801) 487-8951
CONTACT OFFICER(S): Larry R. Stevens

COMPANY: **Valley Leasing**
ADDRESS: P.O. Box 1567
Salt Lake City, UT 84110
PHONE: (801) 973-5378
CONTACT OFFICER(S): Verdi C. Schill

COMPANY: **Vestigrowth 2000**
ADDRESS: 1406 South 1100 East
Salt Lake City, UT 84105
PHONE: (801) 467-3211
CONTACT OFFICER(S): Terry A. Isom

COMPANY: **Zions Leasing Company**
ADDRESS: 310 South Main Street, P.O. Box 2324
Salt Lake City, UT 84110
PHONE: (801) 364-1906
TYPE OF INSTITUTION: Leasing Co.
CONTACT OFFICER(S): Don E. Timpson, Vice President
M. Scott Newbold, Assistant Vice President
TYPES OF FINANCING: LEASES: SECONDARY-MARKET CORPORATE SECURITIES: Other: General Equipment Leasing. LEASES: Leveraged; Non-tax leases
WILL NOT CONSIDER: Non-commercial
GEOGRAPHIC LIMITS OF INVESTMENTS/LOANS: National
RANGE OF INV./LOAN PER BUSINESS: Min. $2,000; Max. $1,000,000
PREFERRED TERM FOR LOANS & LEASES: Max. 5 years
BRANCHES: 1109 West Littleton Blvd., Littleton, CO, (303) 794-3103, Earnest Perry, Sales Representative
161 Main Avenue West, Twin Falls, ID 83301, (208) 733-9456, Kerry Collins, Lease Representative

COMPANY: **AMVEST Capital Corporation**
ADDRESS: One Boar's Head Place, P.O. Box 5347
Charlottesville, VA 22905
PHONE: (804) 977-3350
TYPE OF INSTITUTION: Leasing and finance subsidiary of AMVEST Corp.
CONTACT OFFICER(S): Franklin M. Halsey, Executive V.P.
Kerry Garrison, V.P. & Credit Officer
ASSETS: $60,000,000
INVESTMENTS/LOANS MADE: For own account, Through private placements
INVESTMENTS/LOANS MADE: Only in securities without a secondary market
TYPES OF FINANCING: LOANS: Equipment, LEASES: Single-investor; Leveraged; Tax leases; Non-tax leases; Lease syndications; Vendor financing programs, OTHER SERVICES PROVIDED: Tax exempt lease purchase for municipalities
PREFERRED TYPES OF INDUSTRIES/INVESTMENTS: Broadcast, commercial, industrial, transportation, medical, thoroughbred horses
GEOGRAPHIC LIMITS OF INVESTMENTS/LOANS: National; International
RANGE OF INV./LOAN PER BUSINESS: Min. $100,000; Max. Open
PREFERRED TERM FOR LOANS & LEASES: Min. 3 years; Max 15 years

BUSINESS CHARACTERISTICS DESIRED-REQUIRED: Minimum number of years in business: 3; Min. annual sales $2,000,000; Min. net worth $1,000,000; Min. annual net income $100,000; Min. annual cash flow $100,000
REFERRALS ACCEPTED FROM: Investment/Mortgage banker or Borrower/Investee
BRANCHES: Edwin Ramos, V.P./Sales Admin., Pan Am Building, Suite 1203, Hato Rey, PR 00917; (809) 751-4050

COMPANY: **Spectrum Leasing Corporation**
ADDRESS: 11781 Lee Jackson Mem. Hwy.
Fairfax, VA 22033
PHONE: (703) 821-0910
CONTACT OFFICER(S): M. J. Wueste

COMPANY: **SMS Leasing Incorporated**
ADDRESS: 7777 Leesburg Pike, Suite 218
Falls Church, VA 22043
PHONE: (703) 827-0640
CONTACT OFFICER(S): Albert F. Rosecan

COMPANY: **Charter Leasing Corp.**
ADDRESS: 4222 Cox Rd.
Glenallen, VA 23060
PHONE: (804) 747-1430
TYPE OF INSTITUTION: Leasing Co.
CONTACT OFFICER(S): Jean Martin, V.P.
TYPES OF FINANCING: LEASES
PREFERRED TYPES OF INDUSTRIES/INVESTMENTS: Only Telephone Systems
GEOGRAPHIC LIMITS OF INVESTMENTS/LOANS: Regional; Other: FL, GA, SC, VA, MD
RANGE OF INV./LOAN PER BUSINESS: Min. $3,000
PREFERRED TERM FOR LOANS & LEASES: Min. 3 years; Max. 6 years
BUSINESS CHARACTERISTICS DESIRED-REQUIRED: Minimum number of years in business: 4; Other: must have excellent credit standing
REMARKS: Subsidiary of Jarvis Corp.

COMPANY: **Finalco Financial Services, Inc.**
ADDRESS: 8200 Greensboro Drive
McLean, VA 22102
PHONE: (703) 790-0970
CONTACT OFFICER(S): James H. Manvell, V.P. & General Manager
Josh O. Wout, Assistant V.P.
Sutton S. Stroup, Assistant V.P.
Don L. Viohl, Assistant V.P.
INVESTMENTS/LOANS MADE: For managed accounts, Through private placements
INVESTMENTS/LOANS MADE: In securities with a secondary market and in securities without a secondary market
TYPES OF FINANCING: LOANS: Equipment; Equity-related, LEASES: Single-investor; Leveraged; Tax leases; Operating; Tax-oriented lease brokerage; Lease syndications; Vendor financing programs
PREFERRED TYPES OF INDUSTRIES/INVESTMENTS: Primarily tax leases provided to Ba or better credits (or equivalents) for all types of equipment
GEOGRAPHIC LIMITS OF INVESTMENTS/LOANS: National
RANGE OF INV./LOAN PER BUSINESS: Min. $250,000; Max. No limit
PREFERRED TERM FOR LOANS & LEASES: Min. 3 years; Max. No limit
BUSINESS CHARACTERISTICS DESIRED-REQUIRED: Investment/Mortgage banker or Borrower/Investee

COMPANY: **Finalco Inc.**
ADDRESS: 8200 Greensboro Drive
McLean, VA 22102
PHONE: (703) 790-0970
CONTACT OFFICER(S): Terry J. Billingsley, President, Finalco, Inc.
ASSETS: $988,000,000
INVESTMENTS/LOANS MADE: For own account, Through private placements, Through private placements
TYPES OF FINANCING: LOANS: Equipment. LEASES: Single-investor; Leveraged; Tax leases; Non-tax leases; Operating; Tax-oriented lease brokerage; Lease syndications; Vendor financing programs. REAL ESTATE: Partnerships/Syndications
PREFERRED TYPES OF INDUSTRIES/INVESTMENTS: General equipment
GEOGRAPHIC LIMITS OF INVESTMENTS/LOANS: National
RANGE OF INV./LOAN PER BUSINESS: Min. $200,000; Max. No limit
PREFERRED TERM FOR LOANS & LEASES: Min. 1 year; Max. No limit
BRANCHES: 1553 Little Willeo Road,Marietta, GA 30067
Baldwin Office Park 12 Alfred Street, Woburn, MA 01801
221 N. LaSalle Street, Ste. 1038, Chicago, IL 60601
10999 Reed Highway, Suite 237-239, Cincinnati, OH 45242
Lincoln Center II, 5420 LBJ Freeway, Ste. 1100, Dallas, TX 75240
3333 S. Wadsworth Blvd. Lakewood, CO 80227
30800 Telegraph Road, #3875, Birmingham, MI 48010
12 Greenway Plaza, Ste. 1148, Houston, TX 77046
120 South 6th Street, 1908 First Bank Place West, Minneapolis, MN 55402
4350 Von Karman Ave., Ste. 370, Newport Beach, CA 92660
747 3rd Avenue, 32nd Floor, N.Y.C., NY 10017
5104 N. Orange Blossom Trail, Suite 114, Orlando, FL 32804
1107 Goffle Road, Hawthorne, NJ 07506
8603 E. Royal Palms Rd., Scottsdale, AZ 85258
345 Mt. Lebanon Blvd. Pittsburgh, PA 15234
3470 Mt. Diablo Blvd., Ste. 150, Lafayette, CA 94549
500 Summer Street, Ste. 502, Stamford, CT 06901
5130 Eisenhower Blvd., Tampa. FL 33614

COMPANY: **Finalco Municipal Leasing, Inc.**
ADDRESS: P.O. Box 3606
McLean, VA 22103
PHONE: (703) 790-0970

TYPE OF INSTITUTION: Leasing company
CONTACT OFFICER(S): Mitzi Trivisani, Regional Manager
INVESTMENTS/LOANS MADE: Through private placements
TYPES OF FINANCING: SECONDARY-MARKET CORPORATE SECURITIES: Tax-exempt, LEASES: Non-tax leases
RANGE OF INV./LOAN PER BUSINESS: Min. $100,000; Max. $10,000,000
PREFERRED TERM FOR LOANS & LEASES: Min. 3 years; Max. 5 years
BUSINESS CHARACTERISTICS DESIRED-REQUIRED: Other: Municipal tax-exempt

COMPANY: **Municipal Leasing Corporation**
ADDRESS: 8260 Greensboro Drive
McLean, VA 22102
PHONE: (703) 893-2460
TYPE OF INSTITUTION: Independent Leasing Company
CONTACT OFFICER(S): Phillip G. Norton, President-Marketing
Bruce M. Bowen, Director of Finance
ASSETS: $100,000,000
INVESTMENTS/LOANS MADE: For own account, Through private placements, Through underwriting public offerings
INVESTMENTS/LOANS MADE: In securities with or without a secondary market
TYPES OF FINANCING: LEASES: Leveraged; Tax leases; Non-tax leases; Operating; Tax-oriented lease brokerage. OTHER SERVICES PROVIDED: Government financing—equipment for federal, state & local government
PREFERRED TYPES OF INDUSTRIES/INVESTMENTS: All types of real and personal property—principally computers, telephone and high tech equipment
GEOGRAPHIC LIMITS OF INVESTMENTS/LOANS: National
RANGE OF INV./LOAN PER BUSINESS: Min. $50,000; Max. $100,000,000
PREFERRED TERM FOR LOANS & LEASES: Min. 1 year; Max. 15 years
BUSINESS CHARACTERISTICS DESIRED-REQUIRED:
REFERRALS ACCEPTED FROM: Investment/Mortgage banker or Borrower/Investee

COMPANY: **United Leasing Corp.**
ADDRESS: 5960 Chamberlayne, Suite 104, P.O. Box 1022
Mechanicsville, VA 23111
PHONE: (804) 730-9500
TYPE OF INSTITUTION: Leasing company
CONTACT OFFICER(S): Edward H. Shield, President
Walter Johnson, Secretary-Treasurer
TYPES OF FINANCING: LEASES: Single-investor; Leveraged; Tax leases; Non-tax leases; Operating; Tax-oriented lease brokerage; Lease syndications; Vendor financing programs; Other: Tailored financing, Some accounts receivable, Some mortgages
PREFERRED TYPES OF INDUSTRIES/INVESTMENTS: Diversified
WILL NOT CONSIDER: Restaurants, auto
GEOGRAPHIC LIMITS OF INVESTMENTS/LOANS: National
RANGE OF INV./LOAN PER BUSINESS: Min. $5,000 (local); Max. $25,000 (outside)
PREFERRED TERM FOR LOANS & LEASES: Min. 3 years; Max. 5 years
BUSINESS CHARACTERISTICS DESIRED-REQUIRED: Minimum number of years in business: 3; Other: Good paying history, good cash flow

COMPANY: **Allstate Leasing Corporation**
ADDRESS: 1609 First Virginia Bank Tower
Norfolk, VA 23510
PHONE: (804) 627-0431
CONTACT OFFICER(S): William M. Manrov

COMPANY: **BVA Credit Corp.**
ADDRESS: 7 North 8th Street, P.O. Box 256412
Richmond, VA 23260
PHONE: (804) 771-7432
TYPE OF INSTITUTION: Commercial Finance
CONTACT OFFICER(S): G. J. Cannon, V.P.
Greg Sandvig, V.P.
TYPES OF FINANCING: LOANS: Working capital (receivables/inventory); Equipment, LEASES: Leveraged, OTHER SERVICES PROVIDED: Intermediate-term leveraged leasing
PREFERRED TYPES OF INDUSTRIES/INVESTMENTS: Manufacturing & Distributors
GEOGRAPHIC LIMITS OF INVESTMENTS/LOANS: Regional
RANGE OF INV./LOAN PER BUSINESS: Min. $250,000
PREFERRED TERM FOR LOANS & LEASES: Min. 2; Max. 7-10 years
BUSINESS CHARACTERISTICS DESIRED-REQUIRED: Min. no. of years in business: 0; Asset-Based Lending

COMPANY: **ELC Leasing Company**
ADDRESS: P.O. Box 8765
Richmond, VA 23226
PHONE: (804) 282-6522
CONTACT OFFICER(S): W. N. Smith Jr.

COMPANY: **Federal Leasing Inc.**
ADDRESS: 2070 Chain Bridge Road, Suite 490
Vienna, VA 22180
PHONE: (703) 821-8770

COMPANY: **Transcapital Corporation**
ADDRESS: 8150 Leesburg Pike, Suite 1114
Vienna, VA 22180
PHONE: (703) 790-8210
CONTACT OFFICER(S): Joseph F. Campagna

COMPANY: **North Star Leasing Company**
ADDRESS: P.O. Box 621
Burlington, VT 05401
PHONE: (802) 862-6084
CONTACT OFFICER(S): Phil Goldman

COMPANY: **Paccar Leasing Corporation**
ADDRESS: P.O. Box 1518
Bellevue, WA 98009
PHONE: (206) 445-7400
CONTACT OFFICER(S): Edward D. Wallace

COMPANY: **Simlog Leasing Company**
ADDRESS: 1715 114th Avenue, S.E., Suite 128, P.O. Box 3028
Bellevue, WA 98004
PHONE: (206) 455-9790
CONTACT OFFICER(S): Bruce Woodruff

COMPANY: **Rainier Leasing, Inc.**
ADDRESS: 600 University St.,, 7th Floor, Box C34028
Seattle, WA 98124
PHONE: (206) 621-5001
TYPE OF INSTITUTION: Leasing subsidiary of commercial bank
CONTACT OFFICER(S): Peter M. Jones, President
William A. Kelley, V.P., Marketing Manager
ASSETS: $125,000,000
TYPES OF FINANCING: LOANS: Equipment, LEASES: Single-investor
PREFERRED TYPES OF INDUSTRIES/INVESTMENTS: No preference
GEOGRAPHIC LIMITS OF INVESTMENTS/LOANS: National
RANGE OF INV./LOAN PER BUSINESS: Min. $150,000; Max. $5,000,000
PREFERRED TERM FOR LOANS & LEASES: Min. 3 years; Max. 10 years
BUSINESS CHARACTERISTICS DESIRED-REQUIRED: Min. net worth $2,000,000

COMPANY: **SAFECO Credit Company, Inc.,**
ADDRESS: SAFECO Plaza (T-9)
Seattle, WA 98185
PHONE: (206) 545-5140
TYPE OF INSTITUTION: Commercial/Industrial Finance & Leasing
CONTACT OFFICER(S): C. C. Sims, A.V.P. - Marketing Manager
ASSETS: $3.4 billion
INVESTMENTS/LOANS MADE: For own account
TYPES OF FINANCING: LOANS: Working capital; Equipment; LEASES: Single-investor; Tax leases; Vendor financing programs

COMPANY: **Empire Lease Co., Inc.**
ADDRESS: 715 W. Second Av.
Spokane, WA 99204
PHONE: (509) 747-3085
TYPE OF INSTITUTION: Leasing Co.
CONTACT OFFICER(S): John E. Bradley, Pres.
TYPES OF FINANCING: LEASES: Capital Equipment
PREFERRED TYPES OF INDUSTRIES/INVESTMENTS: Diversified
GEOGRAPHIC LIMITS OF INVESTMENTS/LOANS: Regional
RANGE OF INV./LOAN PER BUSINESS: Min. $2,000
PREFERRED TERM FOR LOANS & LEASES: Min. 1 year; Max. 6 years
REFERRALS ACCEPTED FROM: Investment/Mortgage banker or Borrower/Investee

COMPANY: **Old National Leasing Co.**
ADDRESS: P.O. Box 3247
Spokane, WA 99220
PHONE: (509) 456-6709
TYPE OF INSTITUTION: Leasing Co.
CONTACT OFFICER(S): William Gabrio, Pres.
TYPES OF FINANCING: LEASES: Single-investor; Tax leases; Non-tax leases; Vendor financing programs
PREFERRED TYPES OF INDUSTRIES/INVESTMENTS: Computer; Medical; Transportation
GEOGRAPHIC LIMITS OF INVESTMENTS/LOANS: Regional
RANGE OF INV./LOAN PER BUSINESS: Min. $10,000
BUSINESS CHARACTERISTICS DESIRED-REQUIRED: Minimum number of years in business: 3
BRANCHES: Donald Courter, P.O. Box 3782, Bellevue, WA 98009 (206) 455-6680
REMARKS: Average term: 5 years

COMPANY: **American Industrial Leasing Co.**
ADDRESS: 1305 N. Barker Rd.; P.O. Box 683
Brookfield, WI 53005
PHONE: (414) 784-6230
TYPE OF INSTITUTION: Leasing Co.
CONTACT OFFICER(S): L. L. Lyons Jr., Pres.
TYPES OF FINANCING: LEASES
PREFERRED TYPES OF INDUSTRIES/INVESTMENTS: All types of equipment
GEOGRAPHIC LIMITS OF INVESTMENTS/LOANS: Regional
PREFERRED TERM FOR LOANS & LEASES: Min. 30 months; Max. 60 mos.

COMPANY: **Agristor Credit Corporation**
ADDRESS: 250 Bishops Way, P.O. Box 2000
Elm Grove, WI 53122
PHONE: (414) 784-5420
CONTACT OFFICER(S): Jon C. Bruss

COMPANY: **Valley Bank Lease Corporation**
ADDRESS: P.O. Box 2427, 201 S. Military Avenue
Green Bay, WI 54306
PHONE: (414) 432-1222
CONTACT OFFICER(S): James C. Deuster

COMPANY: **Anchor Financial Corporation**
ADDRESS: P.O. Box 7933
Madison, WI 53707
PHONE: (608) 252-8820
CONTACT OFFICER(S): Karl Solberg

COMPANY: **First Leasing & Investment Corporation**
ADDRESS: 6025 Monona Drive
Madison, WI 53716
PHONE: (608) 221-9245
CONTACT OFFICER(S): A. E. Falk

COMPANY: **Madison Leasing Co., Inc.**
ADDRESS: P.O. Box 2713, 2101 West Beltline Highway
Madison, WI 53701
PHONE: (608) 271-2100
CONTACT OFFICER(S): Robert C. Wilson

COMPANY: **Allis Chalmers Credit Corp., Allis Chalmers Corporation**
ADDRESS: P.O. Box 512
Milwaukee, WI 53201
PHONE: (414) 475-2723
CONTACT OFFICER(S): Leslie J. Wilson

COMPANY: **First National Leasing Corp.**
ADDRESS: 161 W. Wisconsin Ave., Ste. 7182
Milwaukee, WI 53203
PHONE: (414) 272-2374
TYPE OF INSTITUTION: Leasing Co.
CONTACT OFFICER(S): Norton McLean, Chairman of the Board
Ron Orndorff, Pres.
Casey Kolp, Exec. V.P.
TYPES OF FINANCING: LEASES: Single investor; Tax leases; Non-tax leases; Operating; Tax-oriented lease brokerage; Vendor financing programs
PREFERRED TYPES OF INDUSTRIES/INVESTMENTS: General equipment
GEOGRAPHIC LIMITS OF INVESTMENTS/LOANS: National
RANGE OF INV./LOAN PER BUSINESS: Min. $25,000; Max. $2,000,000
PREFERRED TERM FOR LOANS & LEASES: Min. 3 years; Max. 5 years
BUSINESS CHARACTERISTICS DESIRED-REQUIRED: Minimum number of years in business: 5; Other: Flexible
BRANCHES: Grand Rapids, MI
Cleveland, OH
Oak Brook, IL
St. Louis, MO
Indianapolis, IN
Detroit, MI

COMPANY: **First Savings Leasing Corp.**
ADDRESS: 700 North Water Street
Milwaukee, WI 53202
PHONE: (414) 278-1777
CONTACT OFFICER(S): Dan F. Hovendick

COMPANY: **First Wisconsin Financial Corporation**
ADDRESS: 622 North Cass Street, Suite 200
Milwaukee, WI 53202
PHONE: (414) 765-4492
TYPE OF INSTITUTION: Asset-Based; Lending and Leasing
CONTACT OFFICER(S): Robert C. Smith, Pres.
Robert J. Schwaab, Exec. V.P.
ASSETS: $225,000,000.00
INVESTMENTS/LOANS MADE: Only in securities without a secondary market
TYPES OF FINANCING: LOANS: Working capital; Equipment; Other Buy-outs/Acquisitions; LEASES: Single investor; Leveraged; Tax leases; Non-tax leases; Operating; Vendor financing programs
PREFERRED TYPES OF INDUSTRIES/INVESTMENTS: Manufacturing & Distribution
GEOGRAPHIC LIMITS OF INVESTMENTS/LOANS: Regional
RANGE OF INV./LOAN PER BUSINESS: Min. $500,000; Max. $25,000,000
PREFERRED TERM FOR LOANS & LEASES: Min. 2; Max. 10
BUSINESS CHARACTERISTICS DESIRED-REQUIRED: Minimum number of years in business: 3; Min. annual sales $2,500,000
REFERRALS ACCEPTED FROM: Investment/Mortgage banker or Borrower/Investee

COMPANY: **First Wisconsin Leasing Corp.**
ADDRESS: 622 North Cass Street
Milwaukee, WI 53202
PHONE: (414) 765-4706
TYPE OF INSTITUTION: Bank Subsidiary
CONTACT OFFICER(S): Richard S. Leslie, Senior Vice President
Greg Schulte, Vice President
INVESTMENTS/LOANS MADE: For own account
TYPES OF FINANCING: LEASES: Single investor; Leveraged; Tax leases; Non-tax leases; Operating; Tax-oriented lease brokerage; Vendor financing programs
GEOGRAPHIC LIMITS OF INVESTMENTS/LOANS: Regional; Other: Wisconsin, Michigan, Illinois
RANGE OF INV./LOAN PER BUSINESS: Min. $50,000; Max. $5,000,000
PREFERRED TERM FOR LOANS & LEASES: Min. Three (3); Max. Ten (10)
BUSINESS CHARACTERISTICS DESIRED-REQUIRED: Minimum number of years in business: 3
REFERRALS ACCEPTED FROM: Investment/Mortgage banker or Borrower/Investee
REMARKS: Work with nineteen banks in holding company, correspondent banks, brokers, other leasing companies

COMPANY: **Heritage Commercial Finance, Division of Heritage Bank**
ADDRESS: 435 East Mason Street
Milwaukee, WI 53203
PHONE: (414) 273-1000
TYPE OF INSTITUTION: Commercial Finance Division of Commercial Bank
CONTACT OFFICER(S): Trevor M. Morgan, President, Commercial Finance Division
ASSETS: $500,000,000
INVESTMENTS/LOANS MADE: For own account
INVESTMENTS/LOANS MADE: In securities with a secondary market and in securities without a secondary market
TYPES OF FINANCING: SECONDARY-MARKET CORPORATE SECURITIES: Other: Commercial Finance - Loans to privately owned businesses; LOANS: Working capital; Equipment; Other: Secured; LEASES: Non-tax leases

PREFERRED TYPES OF INDUSTRIES/INVESTMENTS: Heritage Commercial Finanace prefers accounts receivable to inventory; will do machinery and equipment and real estate with accounts receivable and inventory but not alone.
WILL NOT CONSIDER: Retailers, form products, livestock.
GEOGRAPHIC LIMITS OF INVESTMENTS/LOANS: Regional
RANGE OF INV./LOAN PER BUSINESS: Min. $20,000; Max. $5,000,000
PREFERRED TERM FOR LOANS & LEASES: Min. Revolving; Max. seven (7)
BUSINESS CHARACTERISTICS DESIRED-REQUIRED: Minimum number of years in business: 2; Min. annual sales $1,000,000; Min. annual cash flow: debt service
REFERRALS ACCEPTED FROM: Investment/Mortgage banker or Borrower/Investee

COMPANY: **Heritage Leasing Corporation**
ADDRESS: 435 East Mason Street
Milwaukee, WI 53203
PHONE: (414) 273-1000
CONTACT OFFICER(S): James P. Roemer, V.P., Heritage Leasing Corporaion
ASSETS: $500,000,000+
INVESTMENTS/LOANS MADE: For own account
INVESTMENTS/LOANS MADE: In securities with a secondary market and in securities without a secondary market
TYPES OF INVESTMENTS/LOANS MADE: LOANS: Working cpaital; Equipment; Other: Secured, LEASES: Non-tax leases
PREFERRED TYPES OF INDUSTRIES/INVESTMENTS: Heritage Leasing Corporation likes machinery and equipment
WILL NOT CONSIDER: Retailers, form products, livestock
GEOGRAPHIC LIMITS OF INVESTMENTS/LOANS: Regional
RANGE OF INV./LOAN PER BUSINESS: Min. $200,000; Max. $2,000,000
PREFERRED TERM FOR LOANS & LEASES: Min. revolving; Max. seven years
BUSINESS CHARACTERISTICS DESIRED-REQUIRED: Minimum number of years in business: 2; Min. annual sales $1,000,000; Min. net worth $0; Min. annual net income $0; Min. annual cash flow: debt service
REFERRALS ACCEPTED FROM: Investment/Mortgage banker or Borrower/Investee

COMPANY: **Marinebanc Leasing Co., Inc., Marine Corporation**
ADDRESS: P.O. Box 1475
Milwaukee, WI 53201
PHONE: (414) 765-2971
CONTACT OFFICER(S): W.D. Olson

COMPANY: **Michels Financial Corporation**
ADDRESS: 3289 North Mayfair Road
Milwaukee, WI 53222
PHONE: (414) 258-3838
TYPE OF INSTITUTION: Independent
CONTACT OFFICER(S): Brian P. Johnson, Executive Vice President
James J. Michel, Secretary
ASSETS: $8,000,000
INVESTMENTS/LOANS MADE: For own account; For managed accounts
TYPES OF FINANCING: LEASES: Single investor; Leveraged; Tax leases; Tax-oriented lease brokerage; Lease syndications
GEOGRAPHIC LIMITS OF INVESTMENTS/LOANS: National
RANGE OF INV./LOAN PER BUSINESS: Min. $25,000; Max. $1,000,000
PREFERRED TERM FOR LOANS & LEASES: Min. 5; Max. 7
BUSINESS CHARACTERISTICS DESIRED-REQUIRED: Minimum number of years in business: 3

COMPANY: **J I Case Credit Corporation**
ADDRESS: 700 State Street
Racine, WI 53404
PHONE: (414) 636-6973
CONTACT OFFICER(S): T. J. Gilbreath

COMPANY: **Citizens Equipment Financing Corporation**
ADDRESS: P.O. Box 171
Sheboygan, WI 53081
CONTACT OFFICER(S): G. T. Rogers

COMPANY: **Sentry Financial Services Corporation**
ADDRESS: 1800 North Point Drive
Stevens Point, WI 54481
PHONE: (715) 346-6820
CONTACT OFFICER(S): William F. Dachel

COMPANY: **Ziegler Leasing Corporation, The Ziegler Company, Inc.**
ADDRESS: 215 North Main Street
West Bend, WI 53095
PHONE: (414) 334-5521
CONTACT OFFICER(S): John J. Becker

MINORITY ENTERPRISE SMALL BUSINESS INVESTMENT COMPANIES (MESBICs)

(Venture Capital to Minority Firms. Also see Venture Capital Companies & Small Business Investment Companies)

ALABAMA

COMPANY: **Alabama Capital Corporation**
ADDRESS: 16 Midtown Park East
Mobile, AL 36606
PHONE: (205) 476-0700
TYPE OF INSTITUTION: Minority Enterprise small business investment company
CONTACT OFFICER(S): David C. Delaney, President
INVESTMENTS/LOANS MADE: For own account
INVESTMENTS/LOANS MADE: Only in securities without a secondary market
TYPES OF FINANCING: LOANS: Working capital; Equipment; Equity-related; Other: Real Estate secured; REAL ESTATE LOANS: Long-term senior mtg.; intermediate-term senior mtg.; Subordinate; Wraparounds; Land; Land development; Construction
GEOGRAPHIC LIMITS OF INVESTMENTS/LOANS: Local; State
RANGE OF INV./LOAN PER BUSINESS: Min. $5,000.00; Max. $500,000.00
PREFERRED TERM FOR LOANS & LEASES: Min. 5 years; Max. 10 years
BUSINESS CHARACTERISTICS DESIRED-REQUIRED: Minimum number of years in business: 0

COMPANY: **Tuskegee Capital Corporation**
ADDRESS: P.O. Drawer GG
Tuskegee Institute, AL 36088
PHONE: (205) 727-2550
CONTACT OFFICER(S): E. Taylor Harmon, Jr., President
REMARKS: Private capital of $500,000

ARKANSAS

COMPANY: **Capital Management Services, Inc.**
ADDRESS: 1910 North Grant Street, Suite 200
Little Rock, AR 72207
PHONE: (501) 664-8613
CONTACT OFFICER(S): David L. Hale, President
REMARKS: Private Capital of $500,500

COMPANY: **Kar-Mal Venture Capital, Inc.**
ADDRESS: Suite 610, Plaza West Office Bldg.
Little Rock, AR 72205
PHONE: (501) 661-0010
CONTACT OFFICER(S): Thomas Karam, President
REMARKS: Private Capital of $500,000

COMPANY: **Lippo Finance and Investment, Inc.**
ADDRESS: 801 Scott Street, Suite 200
Little Rock, AR 72201
PHONE: (501) 372-0060
CONTACT OFFICER(S): Mr. Rust B. Deacon, President
REMARKS: Private capital of $3,010,000

COMPANY: **Power Ventures Inc.**
ADDRESS: 829 Highway 270 North
Malvern, AR 72104
PHONE: (501) 332-3695
CONTACT OFFICER(S): Dorsey D. Glover, President
REMARKS: Private Capital of $500,000

MESBICs

(Venture Capital to Minority Firms. Also see Venture Capital Companies & Small Business Investment Companies)

COMPANY: **Ally Finance Corporation**
ADDRESS: 9100 Wilshire Blvd., Suite 408
Beverly Hills, CA 90212
PHONE: (213) 550-8100
CONTACT OFFICER(S): Percy P. Lin, President
REMARKS: Private capital of $625,000

COMPANY: **Bay Area Western Venture Group**
ADDRESS: 383 Diablo Road, Suite 100
Danville, CA 94526
PHONE: (415) 820-8079
CONTACT OFFICER(S): Samuel Burford, President
REMARKS: Private Capital of $742,900

COMPANY: **Telacu Investment Co., Inc.**
ADDRESS: 5400 E. Olympic Blvd. Ste. 300
E. Los Angeles, CA 90022
PHONE: (213) 721-1655
CONTACT OFFICER(S): Jess Garcia, President
ASSETS: $3 million
INVESTMENTS/LOANS MADE: For own account
TYPES OF FINANCING: VENTURE CAPITAL: Second-stage (generally 1-3 years), LOANS: Equipment
PREFERRED TYPES OF INDUSTRIES/INVESTMENTS: Minority owned, labor intensive
GEOGRAPHIC LIMITS OF INVESTMENTS/LOANS: National
RANGE OF INV./LOAN PER BUSINESS: Min. $50,000; Max. $200,000
PREFERRED TERM FOR LOANS & LEASES: Min. 36 months; Max. 10 years
BUSINESS CHARACTERISTICS DESIRED-REQUIRED: Min. annual sales $100,000

COMPANY: **Pacific Capital Fund Incorporated**
ADDRESS: 3420 East Third Avenue
Foster City, CA 94404
PHONE: (415) 571-5441
CONTACT OFFICER(S): Benedicto Yujuico, Chairman
REMARKS: Private capital of $1,000,000

COMPANY: **Yosemite Capital Inv. Company**
ADDRESS: 448 Fresno Street
Fresno, CA 93706
PHONE: (209) 485-2431
CONTACT OFFICER(S): J. Horace Hampton, President
REMARKS: Private Capital of $305,300

COMPANY: **Asian American Capital Corporation**
ADDRESS: 1191 West Tennyson Road, Suite #5
Hayward, CA 94545
PHONE: (415) 887-6888
TYPE OF INSTITUTION: Small business investment corporation
CONTACT OFFICER(S): George Wong, M.D., Chairman
David Der, M.D., Pres.
INVESTMENTS/LOANS MADE: For own account, managed accounts or through private placements
INVESTMENTS/LOANS MADE: In securities with a secondary market and in securities without a secondary market
TYPES OF FINANCING: SECONDARY-MARKET CORPORATE SECURITIES: Common stock; Preferred stock; Bonds; VENTURE CAPITAL: First-stage; Second-stage; Later-stage expansion; LOANS: Unsecured; Working capital; Equipment; INTERNATIONAL
WILL NOT CONSIDER: Real estate
GEOGRAPHIC LIMITS OF INVESTMENTS/LOANS: Local; State
RANGE OF INV./LOAN PER BUSINESS: Min. $10,000; Max. $150,000
PREFERRED TERM FOR LOANS & LEASES: Min. 4 yrs.; Max. 7 yrs.
BUSINESS CHARACTERISTICS DESIRED-REQUIRED: Min. number of years in business: 1; Min. annual sales $200,000
REFERRALS ACCEPTED FROM: Investment/Mortgage banker or Borrower/Investee

COMPANY: **Continental Investors, Incorporated**
ADDRESS: 8781 Seaspray Drive
Huntington Beach CA 92646
PHONE: (714) 964-5207
CONTACT OFFICER(S): Lae Thantrong, President
REMARKS: Private capital of $2,000,000

COMPANY: **First American Capital Funding, Inc.**
ADDRESS: 18662 MacArthur Boulevard, Suite 400
Irvine, CA 92715
PHONE: (714) 833-8100
CONTACT OFFICER(S): Luu Trankiem, President
REMARKS: Private capital of $564,000

COMPANY: **Business Equity & Dev. Corp.**
ADDRESS: 1411 West Olympic Blvd., Suite 200
Los Angeles, CA 90015
PHONE: (213) 385-0351
TYPE OF INSTITUTION: Venture Capital limited partnership
CONTACT OFFICER(S): Richardo J. Olivarez, President
ASSETS: $250,000,000
INVESTMENTS/LOANS MADE: For own account, through private placement
INVESTMENTS/LOANS MADE: In securities with a secondary market and in securities without a secondary market
TYPES OF FINANCING: VENTURE CAPITAL: Start-up from developed product stage; First-stage; Second-stage; Buy-outs/Acquisitions
PREFERRED TYPES OF INDUSTRIES/INVESTMENTS: High technology including data processing, communications, medical equipment, and energy related.
WILL NOT CONSIDER: Consumer retail products, real estate
RANGE OF INV./LOAN PER BUSINESS: Min. $500,000; Max. $5,000,000 (est.)
BUSINESS CHARACTERISTICS DESIRED-REQUIRED: Minimum number of years in business: 0
REFERRALS ACCEPTED FROM: Investment/Mortgage banker or Borrower/Investee

BRANCHES: Toby Schreiber, 601 California Street, Suite 450, San Francisco, CA 94108; (415) 788-4893
REMARKS: Private Capital of $1,873,034

COMPANY: **Charterway Investment Corporation**
ADDRESS: 222 South Hill Street, Suite 800
Los Angeles, CA 90012
PHONE: (213) 687-8539
CONTACT OFFICER(S): Harold H. M. Chuang, President
REMARKS: Private capital of $1,000,000

COMPANY: **Dime Investment Corp.**
ADDRESS: 2772 West Eighth Street
Los Angeles, CA 90005
PHONE: (213) 739-1847
CONTACT OFFICER(S): Chun Y. Lee, President
REMARKS: Private capital of $500,000

COMPANY: **Lailai Capital Corp.**
ADDRESS: 1545 Wilshire Blvd., Suite 510
Los Angeles, CA 90017
PHONE: (213) 484-5085
CONTACT OFFICER(S): Hsing-Jong Duan, Pres. & General Manager
REMARKS: Private capital of $700,000

COMPANY: **Lasung Investment & Finance Co.**
ADDRESS: 3600 Wilshire Blvd., Suite 1410
Los Angeles, CA 90010
PHONE: (213) 384-7548
CONTACT OFFICER(S): Mr. Jung Su Lee, President
REMARKS: Private Capital of $1,307,000

COMPANY: **Los Angeles Capital Corporation**
ADDRESS: 606 North Larchmont Blvd., Suite 309
Los Angeles, CA 90004
PHONE: (213) 460-4646
CONTACT OFFICER(S): Mr. Kuytae Hwang, President
REMARKS: Private capital of $506,500

COMPANY: **Myriad Capital, Inc.**
ADDRESS: 8820 S. Sepulveda Blvd., Suite 204
Los Angeles, CA 90045
PHONE: (213) 641-7936
TYPE OF INSTITUTION: MESBIC (Minority Enterprise Small Business Investment Company)
CONTACT OFFICER(S): Mr. Chuang-I Lin, President
Kuo-Hung Chen, Secretary
ASSETS: $5,300,000
INVESTMENTS/LOANS MADE: For own account
TYPES OF FINANCING: VENTURE CAPITAL: Research & Development; Second-stage (generally 1-3 years); Later-stage expansion; LOANS: Working capital (receivables/inventory); Equipment; Equity-related; REAL ESTATE: Joint ventures; Partnership/ Syndications
PREFERRED TYPE OF INDUSTRIES/INVESTMENT: High tech manufacturing, Real estate hotel motel and construction
GEOGRAPHIC LIMITS OF INVESTMENTS/LOANS: Local; State; We don't invest in foreign country. We prefer local opportunity but not limited to local businesses
RANGE OF INV./LOAN PER BUSINESS: $50,000; Max. $400,000
PREFERRED TERM FOR LOANS & LEASES: Min. 5 years; Max. 7 years
BUSINESS CHARACTERISTICS DESIRED-REQUIRED: Minimum number of years in business: 3; Min annual sales $ 0; Min. net worth $1,000,000; Min. annual net income $ 0; Min. annual cash flow $ 0
REFERRALS ACCEPTED FROM: Investment/Mortgage banker; Borrower/Investee

COMPANY: **Allied Business Investors, Inc.**
ADDRESS: 428 South Atlantic Blvd., Suite 201
Monterey Park, CA 91754
PHONE: (213) 289-0186
CONTACT OFFICER(S): Jack Hong, President
REMARKS: Private capital of $600,000

COMPANY: **United Business Ventures, Inc.**
ADDRESS: 3931 MacArthur, Ste. 212
Newport Beach, CA 92660
PHONE: (714) 851-0855
CONTACT OFFICER(S): Leslie R. Brewer, President
ASSETS: $3.5 million
INVESTMENTS/LOANS MADE: For own account
INVESTMENTS/LOANS MADE: Only in securities without a secondary market
TYPES OF FINANCING: VENTURE CAPITAL: Start-up from developed product stage; First-stage; Second-stage; Later-stage expansions; Buy-outs/Acquisitions; LOANS: Working capital; equipment; equity related; REAL ESTATE LOANS: Subordinated; Land deveolpment; Construction; Gap; INTERNATIONAL; REAL ESTATE: Acquisitions; Joint ventures; OTHER SERVICES PROVIDED: Management consulting—financial planning, budgeting, financing
PREFERRED TYPE OF INDUSTRIES/INVESTMENTS: Manufacturing; Equipment based services; franchises
WILL NOT CONSIDER: R & D, Films, Publications
GEOGRAPHIC LIMITS OF INVESTMENTS/LOANS: State
RANGE OF INV./LOAN PER BUSINESS: Min. $50,000; Max. 300,000
PREFERRED TERM FOR LOANS & LEASES: Min. 5 years; Max. 10 years
BUSINESS CHARACTERISTICS DESIRED-REQUIRED: Minimum number of years in business: 0; Min. annual sales $500,000 projected; Min. net worth $50,000; Min. Annual net income $60,000; Min. annual cash flow $90,000
REFERRALS ACCEPTED FROM: Investment/Mortgage banker or Borrower/Investee
BRANCHES: 130 Montgomery St., San Francisco, CA 94104; (415) 392-5400

COMPANY: **Unity Capital Corp.**
ADDRESS: 4343 Morena Blvd., Suite 3A
San Diego, CA 92117
PHONE: (619) 275-6030

MESBICs

(Venture Capital to Minority Firms. Also see Venture Capital Companies & Small Business Investment Companies)

CALIFORNIA

TYPE OF INSTITUTION: MESBIC
CONTACT OFFICER(S): Frank Owen, President
ASSETS: $500,000
INVESTMENTS/LOANS MADE: For own account
TYPES OF FINANCING: VENTURE CAPITAL: Research & Development; Second-stage (generally 1-3 years); Later-stage expansion; Buy-outs/Acquisitions, LOANS: Working capital (receivables/inventory); Equipment; Equity-related
PREFERRED TYPES OF INDUSTRIES/INVESTMENTS: No preference
GEOGRAPHIC LIMITS OF INVESTMENTS/LOANS: State
RANGE OF INV./LOAN PER BUSINESS: Min. $16,000; Max. $90,000
PREFERRED TERM FOR LOANS & LEASES: Min. 3; Max. 8 years
BUSINESS CHARACTERISTICS DESIRED-REQUIRED: Must be qualified as SBA small business, qualified for MESBIC
REFERRALS ACCEPTED FROM: Borrower/Investee
REMARKS: no start-ups

COMPANY: **Associates Venture Capital Corp.**
ADDRESS: 425 California Street
San Francisco, CA 94104
PHONE: (415) 956-1444
TYPE OF INSTITUTION: Venture Capital
CONTACT OFFICER(S): Walter P. Strycker, President
ASSETS: $3,000,000
INVESTMENTS/LOANS MADE: For own account, through private placements
INVESTMENTS/LOANS MADE: In securities with a secondary market and in securities without a secondary market
TYPES OF FINANCING: SECONDARY MARKET CORPORATE SECURITIES: Preferred stock; VENTURE CAPITAL: Start-up from developed product stage; First-stage; Second-stage; Buy-outs/Acquisitions, LEASES: Leveraged, Lease syndications
PREFERRED TYPES OF INDUSTRIES/INVESTMENTS: Energy, electronics, medical, communications, computer terminals
WILL NOT CONSIDER: Real estate
GEOGRAPHIC LIMITS OF INVESTMENTS/LOANS: National
RANGE OF INV./LOAN PER BUSINESS: Min. $150,000; Max. $1,000,000
PREFERRED TERM FOR LOANS & LEASES: Min. 1 year; Max. 5 years
BUSINESS CHARACTERISTICS DESIRED-REQUIRED: Minimum number of years in business 0
BRANCHES: Harold McCormick, Vice Pres., Signal Technology, 30 Grosner Hill, London, W1 England; 011-44-499-8292

COMPANY: **Equitable Capital Corporation**
ADDRESS: 855 Sansome Street
San Francisco, CA 94111
PHONE: (415) 434-4114
CONTACT OFFICER(S): John C. Lee, President
REMARKS: Private Capital of $500,000

COLORADO

COMPANY: **Opportunity Capital Corporation**
ADDRESS: 50 California St., Suite 205
San Francisco, CA 94111
PHONE: (415) 421-5935
CONTACT OFFICER(S): J. Peter Thompson, President
REMARKS: Private Capital of $2,910,849

COMPANY: **Positive Enterprises, Incorporated**
ADDRESS: 399 Arguello Street
San Francisco, CA 94118
PHONE: (415) 386-6600
CONTACT OFFICER(S): Mr. Kwok Szeto, President
REMARKS: Private Capital of $505,000

COMPANY: **RSC Financial Corp.**
ADDRESS: 223 East Thousand Oaks Blvd., Suite 310
Thousand Oaks, CA 91360
PHONE: (805) 496-2955
CONTACT OFFICER(S): Frederick K. Bae, President

COMPANY: **MCA New Ventures, Inc.**
ADDRESS: 100 Universal City Plaza
Universal City, CA 91608
PHONE: (818) 508-2937
TYPE OF INSTITUTION: MESBIC
CONTACT OFFICER(S): W. Roderick Hamilton, President
ASSETS: $6,000,000 to $9,000,000
INVESTMENTS/LOANS MADE: For own account
INVESTMENTS/LOANS MADE: In securities with a secondary market and in securities without a secondary market
TYPES OF FINANCING: SECONDARY-MARKET CORPORATE SECURITIES: Common stock; Preferred stock; Bonds, VENTURE CAPITAL: First-stage (less than 1 year); Second-stage (generally 1-3 years); Later-stage expansion; Buy-outs/Acquisitions, LOANS: Working capital (receivables/inventory); Equipment; Equity-related
PREFERRED TYPES OF INDUSTRIES/INVESTMENTS: Communications, Leisure-related & Entertainment
WILL NOT CONSIDER: Films or Music
GEOGRAPHIC LIMITS OF INVESTMENTS/LOANS: National
RANGE OF INV./LOAN PER BUSINESS: Min. $150,000; Max. $500,000
PREFERRED TERM FOR LOANS & LEASES: Min. 3; Max. 10 years
REFERRALS ACCEPTED FROM: Investment/Mortgage banker or Borrower/Investee

COMPANY: **Mile Hi Small Business Investment Company**
ADDRESS: 1355 South Colorado Boulevard
Denver, CO 80222
PHONE: (303) 830-0087
CONTACT OFFICER(S): E. Preston Sumner, Vice-President
REMARKS: Private capital of $550,000

COMPANY: **Broadcast Capital Inc.**
ADDRESS: 1771 N Street, N.W.
Washington, DC 20036
PHONE: (202) 293-3575
CONTACT OFFICER(S): John E. Oxendine, President
REMARKS: Private Capital of $2,000,000

COMPANY: **Fulcrum Venture Capital Corporation**
ADDRESS: 2021 K Street, N.W. Suite 301
Washington, DC 20006-1085
PHONE: (202) 833-9590
TYPE OF INSTITUTION: MESBIC
CONTACT OFFICER(S): Divakar Kamath, President
Renate K. Todd, Portfolio Manager
ASSETS: $7 million
INVESTMENTS/LOANS MADE: For own account; Through private placements
INVESTMENTS/LOANS MADE: Only in securities without a secondary market
TYPES OF FINANCING: VENTURE CAPITAL: Second-stage (generally 1-3 years); Later-stage expansion; Buy-outs/Acquisitions, LOANS: Working capital (receivables/inventory)
PREFERRED TYPES OF INDUSTRIES/INVESTMENTS: technology-oriented
WILL NOT CONSIDER: leisure, real estate sports, consulting/service companies
GEOGRAPHIC LIMITS OF INVESTMENTS/LOANS: National
RANGE OF INV./LOAN PER BUSINESS: Min. $100,000; Max. $500,000
PREFERRED TERM FOR LOANS & LEASES: Min. 5; Max. 10 years
BUSINESS CHARACTERISTICS DESIRED-REQUIRED: Min. annual sales $1,0000,000; Other: pre-tax margin of 10%
REFERRALS ACCEPTED FROM: Investment/Mortgage banker or Borrower/Investee
REMARKS: Actively seeking investment opportunities in transportation related and technology based businesses principally owned by socially and/or economically business persons.

COMPANY: **Minority Broadcast Investment Corporation**
ADDRESS: 1220 19th Street, N.W., Suite 501
Washington, DC 20036
PHONE: (202) 293-1166
TYPE OF INSTITUTION: MESBIC
CONTACT OFFICER(S): Larry Edler, President
Minta D. Branham, Assistant V.P.
ASSETS: $3,300,000
INVESTMENTS/LOANS MADE: Through private placements
INVESTMENTS/LOANS MADE: In securities with a secondary market and in securities without a secondary market
TYPES OF FINANCING: VENTURE CAPITAL: Start-up from developed product stage; First-stage; Second-stage; Buy-outs/Acquisitions
PREFERRED TYPES OF INDUSTRIES/INVESTMENTS: Communications; including radio, TV, cable TV, MDS, DBS, LPTV as well as related technology applications and programming
GEOGRAPHIC LIMITS OF INVESTMENTS/LOANS: National
RANGE OF INV./LOAN PER BUSINESS: Min. $100,000; Max. $300,000
PREFERRED TERM FOR LOANS & LEASES: Min. 5; Max. 10 years
BUSINESS CHARACTERISTICS DESIRED-REQUIRED: Parameters set on an individual basis
REFERRALS ACCEPTED FROM: Borrower/Investee

COMPANY: **Syncom Capital Corporation**
ADDRESS: 1625 I Street, N.W., Suite 414
Washington, DC 20006
PHONE: (202) 293-9428
CONTACT OFFICER(S): Herbert P. Wilkins, President
REMARKS: Private Capital of $2,250,000

COMPANY: **Washington Finance and Investment Corp.**
ADDRESS: 2600 Virginia Avenue, N.W., 515
Washington, DC 20037
PHONE: (202) 338-2900
CONTACT OFFICER(S): Chang H. Lie, President
REMARKS: Private capital of $505,000

COMPANY: **Trans Florida Capital Corporation**
ADDRESS: 1450 Madruga Avenue
Coral Gables, FL 33134
PHONE: (305) 665-5489
CONTACT OFFICER(S): Antonio A. Bechily, President
REMARKS: Private capital of $500,000

COMPANY: **First B.D.J. Financial Service, Inc.**
ADDRESS: 4747 North Ocean Blvd., Suite 215
Ft. Lauderdale, FL 33308
PHONE: (305) 782-9494
CONTACT OFFICER(S): John Rhodes, President
REMARKS: Private Capital of $500,000

COMPANY: **Venture Group, Inc.**
ADDRESS: 5433 Buffalo Avenue
Jacksonville, FL 32208
PHONE: (904) 353-7313
CONTACT OFFICER(S): Ellis W. Hitzing, President
REMARKS: Private capital of $500,000

COMPANY: **Cubico Ltd., Inc.**
ADDRESS: 7425 N.W. 79th Street
Miami, FL 33166
PHONE: (305) 885-8881
CONTACT OFFICER(S): Anthony G. Marina, President
REMARKS: Private Capital of $500,000

COMPANY: **Ideal Financial Corporation**
ADDRESS: 780 N.W. 42nd Avenue, Suite 304
Miami, FL 33126
PHONE: (305) 442-4665
CONTACT OFFICER(S): Mario O. Pineda, General Manager
REMARKS: Private capital of $500,000

COMPANY: **Safeco Capital, Inc.**
ADDRESS: 835 S.W. 37th Avenue
Miami, FL 33135
PHONE: (305) 443-7953
CONTACT OFFICER(S): Rene J. Leonard, President

COMPANY: **Universal Financial Services, Inc.**
ADDRESS: 225 N.E. 35th Street
Miami, FL 33137
PHONE: (305) 573-7496
CONTACT OFFICER(S): Norman Zipkin, President
REMARKS: Private Capital of $500,000

COMPANY: **Venture Opportunities Corporation**
ADDRESS: 444 Brickell Avenue
Miami, FL 33131
PHONE: (305) 358-0359
TYPE OF INSTITUTION: MESBIC
CONTACT OFFICER(S): A. Fred March, Pres. & C.E.O.
ASSETS: $3.5 million
INVESTMENTS/LOANS MADE: For own account
TYPES OF FINANCING: SECONDARY-MARKET CORPORATE SECURITIES: Common stock; Preferred stock; Bonds; Combination, VENTURE CAPITAL: Second stage; Later-Stage Expansion; Buy-Outs/Acquisitions; LOANS: Working capital (receivables/inventory); Equipment, INTERNATIONAL (including import/export), OTHER SERVICES PROVIDED: Mgt. & Financial Consulting, Construction
WILL NOT CONSIDER: Real Estate Mortgages. Short term loans — start-ups
GEOGRAPHIC LIMITS OF INVESTMENTS/LOANS: National; Prefer S.E. and entire Atlantic Coast
RANGE OF INV./LOAN PER BUSINESS: Min. $100,000; Max. $175,000
PREFERRED TERM FOR LOANS & LEASES: Min. 5; Max. 10 years
BUSINESS CHARACTERISTICS DESIRED-REQUIRED: Minimum number of years in business: 3; Min. annual sales $2,000,000; Min. net worth $350,000; Min. annual net income $250,000; Min. annual cash flow $350,000
REFERRALS ACCEPTED FROM: Investment/Mortgage banker or Borrower/Investee
REMARKS: Can go into syndication for higher maximum investment

COMPANY: **First American Lending Corp. (The)**
ADDRESS: 401 Northlake Blvd.
N. Palm Beach FL 33408
PHONE: (305) 863-9826
CONTACT OFFICER(S): Roy W. Talmo, Chairman
REMARKS: Private Capital of $500,000

COMPANY: **Progressive Funding, Incorporated**
ADDRESS: 920 South Ocean Boulevard
Palm Beach, FL 33480
CONTACT OFFICER(S): James V. Sullivan, President
REMARKS: Private capital of $505,000

COMPANY: **Broward Venture Capital Corp.**
ADDRESS: Plantation, FL 33322

COMPANY: **Broadcast Capital Inc.**
PHONE: (305) 474-4449
CONTACT OFFICER(S): William H. Lackey, President
REMARKS: Private Capital of $1,936,282

COMPANY: **Verde Capital Corp.**
ADDRESS: 6701 Sunset Drive
South Miami, FL 33143
PHONE: (305) 666-8789
CONTACT OFFICER(S): Jose Dearing, President
REMARKS: Private Capital of $1,438,000

COMPANY: **Central Georgia Cap. Funding Corp.**
ADDRESS: Panola Road & Fairview Road, P.O. Box 218
Ellenwood, GA 30049
PHONE: (404) 474-8726
CONTACT OFFICER(S): H. Edward Downey, President
REMARKS: Private capital of $500,000

COMPANY: **Sunbelt Funding Corp.**
ADDRESS: 3590 Riverside Drive, P.O. Box 7006
Macon, GA 31298
PHONE: (912) 474-5137
CONTACT OFFICER(S): Charles H. Jones, President
REMARKS: Private Capital of $2,001,200

COMPANY: **Pacific Venture Capital, Ltd.**
ADDRESS: Ste. 302, Waiakanilo Square, 1405 N. King St.,
Honolulu, HI 96817
PHONE: (808) 847-6502
CONTACT OFFICER(S): Dexter J. Taniguchi, President
REMARKS: Private Capital of $721,000

COMPANY: **Cedco Capital Corp.**
ADDRESS: 180 North Michigan Avenue
Chicago, IL 60601
PHONE: (312) 984-5950
CONTACT OFFICER(S): Frank B. Brooks, President
REMARKS: Private Capital of $668,800

COMPANY: **Chicago Community Ventures, Inc.**
ADDRESS: 108 North State Street, Ste. 902
Chicago, IL 60603
PHONE: (312) 726-6084
CONTACT OFFICER(S): Phyllis George, President
REMARKS: Private Capital of $1,005,000

COMPANY: **Combined Opportunities Incorporated**
ADDRESS: 1525 E. 53rd St.
Chicago, IL 60615
PHONE: (312) 752-5355
CONTACT OFFICER(S): Wallace Buya, President
REMARKS: Private Capital of $500,000

COMPANY: **Neighborhood Fund, Inc. (The)**
ADDRESS: 1950 East 71st Street
Chicago, IL 60649
PHONE: (312) 684-8074
CONTACT OFFICER(S): James Fletcher, President
ASSETS: $950,000

TYPES OF FINANCING: VENTURE CAPITAL; LOANS: Equity-related; Equity financing
PREFERRED TYPES OF INDUSTRIES/INVESTMENTS: Minority businesses
GEOGRAPHIC LIMITS OF INVESTMENTS/LOANS: Other: Primary-Chicago-south side
RANGE OF INV./LOAN PER BUSINESS: Min. $10,000; Max. $150,000
REMARKS: Term structured to fit

COMPANY: **Peterson Finance and Investment Company**
ADDRESS: 3300 West Peterson Avenue, Suite A
Chicago, IL 60659
PHONE: (312) 583-6300
CONTACT OFFICER(S): Thomas Lhee, President

COMPANY: **Tower Ventures, Inc.**
ADDRESS: Sears Tower, BSC 43-50
Chicago, IL 60684
PHONE: (312) 875-0571
CONTACT OFFICER(S): James M. Troka, President
REMARKS: Private Capital of $4,000,000

COMPANY: **Urban Fund of Illinois Inc., The**
ADDRESS: 1525 E. 53rd Street
Chicago, IL 60615
PHONE: (312) 266-3050
CONTACT OFFICER(S): E. Patric Jones, President
REMARKS: Private Capital of $650,000

COMPANY: **Equal Opportunity Finance, Inc.**
ADDRESS: 420 Hurstbourne Lane, Ste. 201
Louisville, KY 40201
PHONE: (502) 423-1943
CONTACT OFFICER(S): Franklin Justice, Jr., V.P. & Mgr.
REMARKS: Private Capital of $1,107,262

COMPANY: **SCDF Investment Corp.**
ADDRESS: 1006 Surrey Street
Lafayette, LA 70501
PHONE: (318) 232-3769
CONTACT OFFICER(S): Rev. Albert J. McKnight, President
REMARKS: Private Capital of $2,000,010

COMPANY: **Edict Investment Corp.**
ADDRESS: 2908 S. Carrollton Ave.
New Orleans, LA 70118
PHONE: (504) 861-2364
CONTACT OFFICER(S): Rev. Robert P. Morin, President
REMARKS: Private Capital of $218,500

COMPANY: **Massachusetts Venture Capital Co.**
ADDRESS: 59 Temple Place
Boston, MA 02111
PHONE: (617) 426-0208
CONTACT OFFICER(S): President
ASSETS: $1,000,000—10,000,000

TYPES OF FINANCING: VENTURE CAPITAL, LOANS: Equity-related
RANGE OF INV./LOAN PER BUSINESS: Min. $50,000; Max. $210,000
PREFERRED TERM FOR LOANS & LEASES: Min. 3-5; Max. 7-10 years

COMPANY: **New England MESBIC**
ADDRESS: 50 Kearney Rd., Suite #3
Needham, MA 02194
PHONE: (617) 449-2066
TYPE OF INSTITUTION: Minority Enterprise Small Business Investment Company
CONTACT OFFICER(S): Chris Chen, Manager
ASSETS: $1,000,000
INVESTMENTS/LOANS MADE: For own account
INVESTMENTS/LOANS MADE: In securities with a secondary market or in securities without a secondary market
TYPES OF FINANCING: SECONDARY-MARKET CORPORATE SECURITIES: Common stock, VENTURE CAPITAL: Research & Development; Start-up from developed product stage, LOANS: Equity-related
GEOGRAPHIC LIMITS OF INVESTMENTS/LOANS: National
RANGE OF INV./LOAN PER BUSINESS: Min. $50,000; Max. $150,000
PREFERRED TERM FOR LOANS & LEASES: Min. 4 years; Max. 10 years
BUSINESS CHARACTERISTICS DESIRED-REQUIRED: Minimum number of years in business: 0
REFERRALS ACCEPTED FROM: Investment/Mortgage banker or Borrower/Investee

COMPANY: **W.C.C.I. Capital Corporation**
ADDRESS: 340 Main Street, Suite 836
Worcester, MA 01608
PHONE: (617) 791-0941
TYPE OF INSTITUTION: Non-profit—restricted to lending only in the city of Worcester
CONTACT OFFICER(S): Gerald Garrity, V.P. & Gen. manager
Peter Brennan, Clerk
ASSETS: $300,000
TYPES OF FINANCING: VENTURE CAPITAL: OTHER SERVICES PROVIDED: Debt & Equity
PREFERRED TYPES OF INDUSTRIES/INVESTMENTS: Must be in Worcester
GEOGRAPHIC LIMITS OF INVESTMENTS/LOANS: Local, Worcester
BUSINESS CHARACTERISTICS DESIRED-REQUIRED: Minimum number of years in business: 0;

COMPANY: **Albright Venture Capital, Inc.**
ADDRESS: 8005 Rappahannock Ave.
Jessup, MD 20794
PHONE: (301) 799-7935
CONTACT OFFICER(S): John R. Laughlin, Financial Analyst
INVESTMENTS/LOANS MADE: For own account

TYPES OF FINANCING: VENTURE CAPITAL: First-stage; LOANS: Working capital; Eqity-related; INTERNATIONAL
PREFERRED TYPES OF INDUSTRIES/INVESTMENTS: Diversified. Prefer collateralized situations that are not suitable for usual financing institutions due to lack of equity input, type of collateral, etc.
WILL NOT CONSIDER: Uncollateralized startups
GEOGRAPHIC LIMITS OF INVESTMENTS/LOANS: Regional
RANGE OF INV./LOAN PER BUSINESS: Min. $50,000; Max. $150,000
PREFERRED TERM FOR LOANS & LEASES: Min. 5 yrs.; Max. 8
BUSINESS CHARACTERISTICS DESIRED-REQUIRED: Minimum number of years in business: 1
REFERRALS ACCEPTED FROM: Investment/Mortgage banker or Borrower/Investee

COMPANY: **S.L.C. Investment Corporation**
ADDRESS: 152 Rollins Avenue, Suite 208
Rockville, MD 20852
PHONE: (301) 984-9177
CONTACT OFFICER(S): Jack Sun, President
REMARKS: Private capital of $500,000

COMPANY: **Security Financial and Investment Corp.**
ADDRESS: 8757 Georgia Avenue, Suite 504
Silver Spring, MD 20910
PHONE: (301) 589-5502
CONTACT OFFICER(S): Mr. Han Y. Cho, President
REMARKS: Private capital of $510,000

COMPANY: **Dearborn Capital Corp.**
ADDRESS: P.O. Box 1729
Dearborn, MI 48121
PHONE: (313) 337-8577
TYPE OF INSTITUTION: MESBIC, subsidiary of Ford Motor Company
CONTACT OFFICER(S): Stephen M. Aronson, President
Michael L. LaManes, V.P.
INVESTMENTS/LOANS MADE: For own account
INVESTMENTS/LOANS MADE: Only in securities without a secondary market
TYPES OF FINANCING: VENTURE CAPITAL: Second-stage (generally 1-3 years); Later-stage expansion; Buy-outs/Acquisitions, LOANS: Working capital (receivables/inventory); Equipment; Equity-related
PREFERRED TYPES OF INDUSTRIES/INVESTMENTS: Must be related to automotive industry - manufacturing or services
GEOGRAPHIC LIMITS OF INVESTMENTS/LOANS: National
RANGE OF INV./LOAN PER BUSINESS: Min. $50,000; Max. $350,000
PREFERRED TERM FOR LOANS & LEASES: Min. 4 yrs; Max. 10 yrs.
BUSINESS CHARACTERISTICS DESIRED-REQUIRED: Other: Business must be owned, operated and controlled by minority(ies)

ADDRESS: 1505 Woodward, Suite 700
Detroit, MI 48226
PHONE: (313) 961-2470
CONTACT OFFICER(S): Walter M. McMurtry, Jr., President
REMARKS: Private Capital of $2,619,293

COMPANY: **Motor Enterprises, Incorporated**
ADDRESS: 3044 West Grand Blvd.
Detroit, MI 48202
PHONE: (313) 556-4273
CONTACT OFFICER(S): James Kobus, Manager
REMARKS: Private Capital of $1,250,000

COMPANY: **Metro-Detroit Inv. Co.**
ADDRESS: 30777 Northwestern Hwy., Ste. 300
Farmington Hills MI 48018
PHONE: (313) 851-6300
CONTACT OFFICER(S): William J. Fowler, President
REMARKS: Private Capital of $2,000,000

COMPANY: **Mutual Investment Co. Incorporated**
ADDRESS: 21415 Civic Center Drive, Mark Plaza Bldg., Ste. 217
Southfield, MI 48076
PHONE: (313) 559-5210
CONTACT OFFICER(S): Jack Najor, President
REMARKS: Private Capital of $1,100,060

COMPANY: **Control Data Community Ventures Fund, Inc.**
ADDRESS: 3601 West 77th Street
Minneapolis, MN 55435
PHONE: (612) 921-4352
TYPE OF INSTITUTION: MESBIC
CONTACT OFFICER(S): Thomas Hunt, President
ASSETS: $2,000,000 private capital
TYPES OF FINANCING: VENTURE CAPITAL: Start-up from developed product stage; First-stage; Second-stage; Later-stage; Buy-outs/Acquisitions
PREFERRED TYPES OF INDUSTRIES/INVESTMENTS: Diversified
WILL NOT CONSIDER: Restaurants, Mineral deals, Franchises
GEOGRAPHIC LIMITS OF INVESTMENTS/LOANS: National
RANGE OF INV./LOAN PER BUSINESS: Min. $150,000; Max. $600,000
PREFERRED TERM FOR LOANS & LEASES: Min. 5 years; Max. 10 years
BUSINESS CHARACTERISTICS DESIRED-REQUIRED: Minimum number of years in business: 0; Other: Potential for rapid and substantial growth
REFERRALS ACCEPTED FROM: Investment/Mortgage banker; Borrower/Investee

COMPANY: **Sun-Delta Cap. Access Center, Inc.**
ADDRESS: 819 Main Street
Greenville, MS 38701
PHONE: (601) 335-5291
CONTACT OFFICER(S): Charles Bannerman, President

REMARKS: Private Capital of $1,258,100

COMPANY: **Vanguard Investment Company, Inc.**
ADDRESS: 308-A South Elm Street
Greensboro, NC
PHONE: (919) 864-4447
CONTACT OFFICER(S): Marion "Rex" Harris
REMARKS: Private Capital of $900,053

COMPANY: **Community Equity Corp. of Nebraska**
ADDRESS: 6421 Ames Ave.,
Omaha, NE 68104
PHONE: (402) 455-7722
CONTACT OFFICER(S): William C. Moore, President
REMARKS: Private Capital of $775,000

COMPANY: **Rutgers Minority Inv. Co.**
ADDRESS: 180 University Avenue
Newark, NJ 07102
PHONE: (201) 648-5627
CONTACT OFFICER(S): Oscar Figueroa, President
ASSETS: Private Capital $1.3 million
INVESTMENTS/LOANS MADE: For own account
TYPES OF FINANCING: VENTURE CAPITAL, LOANS
GEOGRAPHIC LIMITS OF INVESTMENTS/LOANS: Regional
REFERRALS ACCEPTED FROM: Investment/Mortgage banker or Borrower/Investee

COMPANY: **Associated Southwest Investors, Inc.**
ADDRESS: 2425 Alamo S.E.
Albuquerque, NM 87106
PHONE: (505) 842-5955
TYPE OF INSTITUTION: MESBIC
CONTACT OFFICER(S): John R. Rice, President
INVESTMENTS/LOANS MADE: For own account; Through private placements
INVESTMENTS/LOANS MADE: In securities with a secondary market and in securities without a secondary market
TYPES OF FINANCING: VENTURE CAPITAL: Start-up from developed product stage; First-stage (less than 1 year); Second-stage (generally 1-3 years); Later-stage expansion, LOANS: Working capital (receivables/ inventory); Equipment; Equity-related
PREFERRED TYPES OF INDUSTRIES/INVESTMENTS: Communications sought, but every industry is reviewed (Portfolio is 25% communications)
WILL NOT CONSIDER: Real Estate, Restaurants
GEOGRAPHIC LIMITS OF INVESTMENTS/LOANS: Prefer Southwest, will work nationally
RANGE OF INV./LOAN PER BUSINESS: Min. $50,000
PREFERRED TERM FOR LOANS & LEASES: Min. 5; Max. 10 years
BUSINESS CHARACTERISTICS DESIRED-REQUIRED: Minimum number of years in business: 0

COMPANY: **Triad Capital Corp. of New York**
ADDRESS: 7 Hugh Grant Circle
Bronx, NY 10462
CONTACT OFFICER(S): Lorenzo J. Barrera, President
REMARKS: Private capital of $500,000

COMPANY: **ODA Capital Corp.**
ADDRESS: 82 Lee Avenue
Brooklyn, NY 11211
PHONE: (212) 963-9270
CONTACT OFFICER(S): Philip Klein, Executive Director
REMARKS: Private Capital of $801,500

COMPANY: **Situation Ventures Corp.**
ADDRESS: 502 Flushing Ave.
Brooklyn, NY 11205
PHONE: (212) 855-1835
CONTACT OFFICER(S): Sam Hollander, Pres.
ASSETS: $2,500,000
TYPES OF FINANCING: VENTURE CAPITAL, LOANS: Equity-related
GEOGRAPHIC LIMITS OF INVESTMENTS/LOANS: National
RANGE OF INV./LOAN PER BUSINESS: Min. $50,000; Max. $200,000

COMPANY: **Medallion Funding Corporation**
ADDRESS: 86 Glen Cove Road
East Hills, NY 11577
PHONE: (212) 682-3300
REMARKS: Main office: New York, NY

COMPANY:**Korean Capital Corp.**
ADDRESS: 144-43 25th Rd.
Flushing, NY 11354
PHONE: (212) 762-8866
CONTACT OFFICER(S): Min Ja Oh, President
REMARKS: Private Capital of $516,000

COMPANY: **Roedal Associates, Ltd.**
ADDRESS: 77-51 141st Street
Flushing, NY 11367
PHONE: (212) 591-2838
CONTACT OFFICER(S): Robert Cohen, President
REMARKS: Private capital of $500,000

COMPANY: **Yang Capital Corp.**
ADDRESS: 41-40 Kissena Boulevard
Flushing, NY 11355
PHONE: (516) 482-1578
CONTACT OFFICER(S): Ms. Maysing Yang, President
REMARKS: Private capital of $500,000

COMPANY: **Square Deal Venture Capital Corp.**
ADDRESS: 135-56 39th Avenue, Suite 440
Flushing NY 11354
PHONE: (212) 939-9802
CONTACT OFFICER(S): Mordechai Z. Fledman, President
REMARKS: Private Capital of $546,000

COMPANY: **Pierre Funding Corp.**
ADDRESS: 141 South Central Avenue
Hartsdale, NY 10530
PHONE: (914) 683-1144
CONTACT OFFICER(S): Elias Debbas, President
REMARKS: Private capital of $921,000

COMPANY: **CEDC Mesbic, Inc.**
ADDRESS: 106 Main Street
Hempstead, NY 11550
PHONE: (516) 292-9710
CONTACT OFFICER(S): John L. Kearse, President
REMARKS: Private Capital of $500,000

COMPANY: **American Asian Capital Corporation**
ADDRESS: 130 Water Street, Suite 6-L
New York, NY 10005
PHONE: (212) 422-6880
CONTACT OFFICER(S): Howard H. Lin, President
REMARKS: Private Capital of $503,000

COMPANY: **Amistad Dot Venture Capital, Inc.**
ADDRESS: 805 Second Avenue, Suite 303
New York, NY 10017
PHONE: (212) 537-6600
CONTACT OFFICER(S): Percy E. Sutton, President
REMARKS: Private Capital of $3,500,000

COMPANY: **Avdon Capital Corp.**
ADDRESS: 576 Fifth Avenue
New York, NY 10036
PHONE: (212) 391-1119
CONTACT OFFICER(S): A. M. Donner, President
REMARKS: Private capital of $500,000

COMPANY: **Bancap Corporation**
ADDRESS: 155 East 42nd Street, Suite 305
New York, NY 10017
PHONE: (212) 687-6470
CONTACT OFFICER(S): William L. Whitely, President
REMARKS: Private Capital of $1,000,000

COMPANY: **Capital Investors & Management Corp.**
ADDRESS: 3 Pell Street, Suite 3
New York, NY 10013
PHONE: (212) 964-2480
TYPE OF INSTITUTION: SBIC/MESBIC
CONTACT OFFICER(S): Rose Chao, Manager
ASSETS: $8,000,000
INVESTMENTS/LOANS MADE: For own account
INVESTMENTS/LOANS MADE: Only in securities without a secondary market
TYPES OF FINANCING: VENTURE CAPITAL: First-stage; Buy-outs/Acquisitions, LOANS
PREFERRED TYPES OF INDUSTRIES/INVESTMENTS: Communications industry (radio, TV), related media, print media
GEOGRAPHIC LIMITS OF INVESTMENTS/LOANS: National
RANGE OF INV./LOAN PER BUSINESS: Min. $500,000; Max. $900,000
BUSINESS CHARACTERISTICS DESIRED-REQUIRED: Minimum number of years in business: 0
REMARKS: Private Capital of $500,000

COMPANY: **Cohen Capital Corp.**
ADDRESS: 163 East 36th Street, Ste. 2A
New York, NY 10016
PHONE: (212) 689-9030
CONTACT OFFICER(S): Edward H. Cohen, President
REMARKS: Private Capital of $500,000

COMPANY: **Columbia Capital Corporation**
ADDRESS: 419 Park Avenue South
New York, NY 10016
PHONE: (212) 696-4688
CONTACT OFFICER(S): Mark Scharfman, President
REMARKS: Private capital of $500,000

COMPANY: **CVC Capital Corp.**
ADDRESS: 666 Fifth Avenue
New York, NY 10019
PHONE: (212) 246-1980
CONTACT OFFICER(S): Joerg G. Klebe, President
REMARKS: Private capital of $2,005,000

COMPANY: **Elk Associates Funding Corp.**
ADDRESS: 277 Park Avenue, Suite 4300
New York, NY 10172
PHONE: (212) 888-7574
CONTACT OFFICER(S): Gary C. Granoff, President
REMARKS: Private Capital of $1,885,001

COMPANY: **Equico Capital Corp.**
ADDRESS: 1290 Avenue of the Americas, Suite 3400
New York, NY 10019
PHONE: (212) 554-8413
CONTACT OFFICER(S): Duane Hill, President
REMARKS: Private Capital of $10,550,000

COMPANY: **Exim Capital Corp.**
ADDRESS: 290 Madison Avenue
New York, NY 10017
PHONE: (212) 683-3200
CONTACT OFFICER(S): Victor K. Chun, President
REMARKS: Private Capital of $510,000

COMPANY: **Fair Capital Corp.**
ADDRESS: 514 Broadway, Mezzanine Floor
New York, NY 10012
PHONE: (212) 334-8199
CONTACT OFFICER(S): Robert Yet Sen Chen, President
REMARKS: Private capital of $508,000

COMPANY: **Freshstart Venture Capital Corp.**
ADDRESS: 250 West 7th Street, Suite 612
New York, NY 10017
PHONE: (212) 265-2249

CONTACT OFFICER(S): Zindel Zelmanovich, President
REMARKS: Private capital of $500,000

COMPANY: **H.B.R. Capital Corp.**
ADDRESS: 1775 Broadway, Suite 417
New York, NY 10019
PHONE: (212) 247-8040
CONTACT OFFICER(S): Manny Zissar, Manager
REMARKS: Private Capital of $505,000

COMPANY: **Hop Chung Capital Investors Inc.**
ADDRESS: 74A Mott Street
New York, NY 10013
PHONE: (212) 219-1777
CONTACT OFFICER(S): You Hon Lee, President
Peter Wong, Secretary-Treasurer
ASSETS: $1,000,000.00
INVESTMENTS/LOANS MADE: For own account; Through private placements
INVESTMENTS/LOANS MADE: In securities with a secondary market and in securities without a secondary market
TYPES OF FINANCING: VENTURE CAPITAL: Start-up from developed product stage; Second-stage; LOANS: Working capital; Equipment; REAL ESTATE: Joint ventures
PREFERRED TYPES OF INDUSTRIES/INVESTMENTS: Restaurant & Garment
GEOGRAPHIC LIMITS OF INVESTMENTS/LOANS: Local; Regional

RANGE OF INV./LOAN PER BUSINESS: Min. $50,000; Max. $150,000
PREFERRED TERM FOR LOANS & LEASES: Min. 4 years
BUSINESS CHARACTERISTICS DESIRED-REQUIRED: Min. no. of years in business: 0;

COMPANY: **Intercontinental Capital Funding Corp.**
ADDRESS: 80 Mott Street
New York, NY 10013
PHONE: (212) 431-8790
CONTACT OFFICER(S): James S. Yu, President
REMARKS: Private capital of $500,000

COMPANY: **Intergroup Funding Corporation**
ADDRESS: 230 Park Avenue
New York, NY 10017
PHONE: (212) 661-5428
CONTACT OFFICER(S): Ben Hauben, President
REMARKS: Private Capital of $510,000

COMPANY: **International Paper Cap. Formation, Inc.**
ADDRESS: 77 West 45th Street
New York, NY 10036
PHONE: (212) 536-6000
CONTACT OFFICER(S): Bernard L. Riley, President
REMARKS: Private capital of $1,000,000

COMPANY: **Japanese American Cap. Corporation**
ADDRESS: 120 Broadway
New York, NY 10005
PHONE: (212) 964-4077
CONTACT OFFICER(S): Stephen C. Huang, President
REMARKS: Private Capital of $525,000

COMPANY: **Medallion Funding Corporation**
ADDRESS: 205 E. 42nd St., Suite 2020
New York, NY 10017
PHONE: (212) 682-3300
CONTACT OFFICER(S): Alvin Murstein, President
REMARKS: Private Capital of $1,993,600

COMPANY: **Merit Funding, Inc.**
ADDRESS: One Battery Park Plaza
New York, NY 10004
PHONE: (212) 344-6254
CONTACT OFFICER(S): Roger L. Cohen, President
REMARKS: Private Capital of $500,000

COMPANY: **Minority Equity Cap. Co., Inc.**
ADDRESS: 275 Madison Avenue
New York, NY 10016
PHONE: (212) 686-9710
CONTACT OFFICER(S): Patrick O. Burns, General Manager
REMARKS: Private Capital of $2,204,047

COMPANY: **New Oasis Capital Corporation**
ADDRESS: 114 Liberty Street, Suite 404
New York, NY 10006
PHONE: (212) 349-2804
CONTACT OFFICER(S): James Haung, President
REMARKS: Private Capital of $500,000

COMPANY: **North American Funding Corporation**
ADDRESS: 177 Canal Street
New York, NY 10013
PHONE: (212) 226-0080
CONTACT OFFICER(S): Franklin F.Y. Wong, V.P. & Gen. Mgr.
REMARKS: Private Capital of $500,000

COMPANY: **Pan Pac Capital Corp.**
ADDRESS: 19 Rector St., 35th floor
New York, NY 10006
PHONE: (212) 344-9295
CONTACT OFFICER(S): Dr. In Ping Jack Lee, President
REMARKS: Private Capital of $503,000

COMPANY: **Pierre Funding Corp.**
ADDRESS: 270 Madison Avenue, Suite 1608
New York, NY 10017
PHONE: (212) 597-5522
REMARKS: Main office - White Plains, NY

COMPANY: **Rainbow Bridge Capital Corporation**
ADDRESS: 170 Canal Street, 3rd floor
New York, NY 10013

PHONE: (212) 219-0707
CONTACT OFFICER(S): Nai-Ching Sun, President
REMARKS: Private Capital of $500,000

COMPANY: **Taroco Capital Corp.**
ADDRESS: 19 Rector St., 35th Floor
New York, NY 10006
PHONE: (212) 964-6877
CONTACT OFFICER(S): David R.C. Chang, President
REMARKS: Private Capital of $505,000

COMPANY: **Transportation SBIC, Incorporated**
ADDRESS: 60 East 42nd Street, Suite 3126
New York, NY 10168
PHONE: (212) 697-4885
CONTACT OFFICER(S): Melvin L. Hirsh, Pres.
Robert Silver, V.P.
Dorothy T. Hirsch, Treas.
ASSETS: $10,000,000
INVESTMENTS/LOANS MADE: For own account
INVESTMENTS/LOANS MADE: only in securities without a secondary market;
TYPES OF FINANCING: SECONDARY-MARKET CORPORATE SECURITIES: Notes VENTURE CAPITAL: Start-up from developed product stage; First-stage (less than 1 year); Second-stage (generally 1-3 years); LOANS: Working capital (receivables/ inventory); Equipment; Equity-related.
PREFERRED TYPES OF INDUSTRIES/INVESTMENTS: TSBIC only makes investments in the taxicab and radio car service industries in New York City, Philadelphia & Boston.
WILL NOT CONSIDER: see above.
RANGE OF INV./LOAN PER BUSINESS: Min. $30,000; Max. $750,000
PREFERRED TERM FOR LOANS & LEASES: Min. four years; Max. seven years
BUSINESS CHARACTERISTICS DESIRED-REQUIRED: Min. no. of years in buisness: 0

COMPANY: **Watchung Capital Corp.**
ADDRESS: 431 Fifth Avenue, Fifth Floor
New York, NY 10016
PHONE: (212) 889-3466
CONTACT OFFICER(S): S.T. Jeng, President
REMARKS: Private Capital of $500,000

COMPANY: **Ibero American Investors Corp.**
ADDRESS: 55 St. Paul Street
Rochester, NY 14604
PHONE: (716) 544-0450
CONTACT OFFICER(S): Emilio Serrano, President
REMARKS: Private Capital of $929,786

COMPANY: **North Street Capital Corp.**
ADDRESS: 250 North Street —RA-6S
White Plains, NY 10625
PHONE: (914) 335-7901
TYPE OF INSTITUTION: MESBIC
CONTACT OFFICER(S): Ralph L. McNeal, Sr., President
INVESTMENTS/LOANS MADE: For own account
INVESTMENTS/LOANS MADE: Only in securities without a secondary market
TYPES OF FINANCING: Common stock; Convertible Debentures, VENTURE CAPITAL: Buy-outs/ Acquisitions, LOANS
PREFERRED TYPES OF INDUSTRIES/INVESTMENTS: Diversified
WILL NOT CONSIDER: Consulting, Single Franchises
GEOGRAPHIC LIMITS OF INVESTMENTS/LOANS: National
RANGE OF INV./LOAN PER BUSINESS: Min. $100,000; Max. $360,000
PREFERRED TERM FOR LOANS & LEASES: Min. 3-5; Max. 10 years
BUSINESS CHARACTERISTICS DESIRED-REQUIRED: Min. annual sales $1 million
REFERRALS ACCEPTED FROM: Borrower/Investee

COMPANY: **Center City MESBIC**
ADDRESS: Centre City Office Building, Suite 762, 40 South Main Street
Dayton, OH 45402
PHONE: (513) 461-6164
CONTACT OFFICER(S): Micheal A. Robinson, President
REMARKS: Private Capital of $500,000

COMPANY: **Salween Financial Services Inc.**
ADDRESS: 228 North Pottstown Pike
Exton, PA 19341
PHONE: (215) 524-1880
CONTACT OFFICER(S): Dr. Ramarao Naidu, President
REMARKS: Private capital of $800,000

COMPANY: **Alliance Enterprise Corp.**
ADDRESS: 1801 Market St., 3rd Floor
Philadelphia, PA 19103
PHONE: (215) 972-4230
CONTACT OFFICER(S): Duane McKnight, V.P.
ASSETS: $1,000,000—10,000,000
TYPES OF FINANCING: VENTURE CAPITAL, LOANS: Equity-related
WILL NOT CONSIDER: Entertainment, Real estate
GEOGRAPHIC LIMITS OF INVESTMENTS/LOANS: Eastern & Southwestern U.S.
RANGE OF INV./LOAN PER BUSINESS: Min. $150,000; Max. 1 million
BUSINESS CHARACTERISTICS DESIRED-REQUIRED: Min. number of years in business: 0; Other: Start-ups must have 15% of funds needed

COMPANY: **Greater Phila. Venture Cap. Corp. Inc.**
ADDRESS: 920 Lewis Tower Bldg., 225 South Fifteenth St.
Philadelphia, PA 19102
PHONE: (215) 732-3415
CONTACT OFFICER(S): Wilson D. DeWald, President
REMARKS: Private Capital of $756,583

COMPANY: **North America Inv. Corp.**
ADDRESS: Banco Ctr. #1710, M Rivera Av. Stop 34
Hato Rey, PR 00936

PHONE: (809) 751-6178
CONTACT OFFICER(S): Santigo Ruz Betacourt, President
REMARKS: Private Capital of $750,000

COMPANY: **Venture Capital P.R., Incorporated**
ADDRESS: Executive Building, Suite 1204, Ponce De Leon Avenue, #623
Hato Rey, PR 00918
PHONE: (809) 751-8040
CONTACT OFFICER(S): Manuel L. Prats, President
REMARKS: Private Capital of $1,150,000

COMPANY: **First Puerto Rico Capital, Inc.**
ADDRESS: 54 W. McKinley Street
Mayaguez, PR 00708
PHONE: (809) 833-2929
CONTACT OFFICER(S): Eliseo E. Font, President
REMARKS: Private Capital of $500,000

COMPANY: **Valley Capital Corporation**
ADDRESS: Suite 806, Krystal Bldg., 100 M. L. King Blvd.
Chattanooga, TN 37402
PHONE: (615) 265-1557
TYPE OF INSTITUTION: MESBIC
CONTACT OFFICER(S): Lamar J. Partridge, President
ASSETS: $2,000,000
INVESTMENTS/LOANS MADE: For own account
TYPES OF FINANCING: VENTURE CAPITAL: Later-stage expansion; Buy-outs/Acquisitions. LOANS: Working capital; Equipment; Equity-related.
PREFERRED TYPES OF INDUSTRIES/INVESTMENTS: Radio, lower power television; All types distribution and various types retail
WILL NOT CONSIDER: Motion pictures, promotion companies
GEOGRAPHIC LIMITS OF INVESTMENTS/LOANS: Regional
RANGE OF INV./LOAN PER BUSINESS: Min. $100,000; Max. $250,000
PREFERRED TERM FOR LOANS & LEASES: Min. 7 years; Max. 10 years
BUSINESS CHARACTERISTICS DESIRED-REQUIRED: Minimum number of years in business: 3; Min. annual sales $500,000; Min. net worth $100,000; Min. annual net income $50,000; Min. annual cash flow $50,000.
REFERRALS ACCEPTED FROM: Investment/Mortgage banker or Borrower/Investee

COMPANY: **Chickasaw Capital Corporation**
ADDRESS: 60 North Third St.
Memphis, TN 38103
PHONE: (901) 523-6404
TYPE OF INSTITUTION: MESBIC
CONTACT OFFICER(S): H. Morgan Brookfield III, President
INVESTMENTS/LOANS MADE: For own account, For managed accounts, Through private placements
TYPES OF FINANCING: VENTURE CAPITAL: Second-stage; Later-stage; Buy-outs/Acquisitions. LOANS: Working capital; Equipment; Equity-related. REAL ESTATE LOANS: Intermediate-term senior mtg.; Subordinated; Wraparounds; Standbys; Industrial revenue bonds. REAL ESTATE: Acquisitions; Joint ventures; Partnerships/Syndications.
WILL NOT CONSIDER: without business plan being submitted
GEOGRAPHIC LIMITS OF INVESTMENTS/LOANS: Regional
REFERRALS ACCEPTED FROM: Investment/Mortgage banker or Borrower/Investee
REMARKS: Private Capital of $500,000

COMPANY: **Tennessee Equity Capital Corp.**
ADDRESS: 4515 Poplar Ave.
Memphis, TN 38117
PHONE: (901) 761-3410
TYPE OF INSTITUTION: 301 (D) SBIC
CONTACT OFFICER(S): Richard Kantor, Pres., (Memphis)
Walter Coher, Treasurer/Sec., (Nashville)

COMPANY: **West Tennessee Venture Capital Corporation**
ADDRESS: 152 Beale Street, P.O. Box 300
Memphis, TN 38101
PHONE: (901) 527-6091
TYPE OF INSTITUTION: MESBIC
CONTACT OFFICER(S): Bennie L. Marshall, Manager/Venture Capital Financing
ASSETS: $1.3 million
INVESTMENTS/LOANS MADE: For own account, Through private placements
INVESTMENTS/LOANS MADE: Only in securities without a secondary market
TYPES OF FINANCING: VENTURE CAPITAL: Start-up from developed product stage; First-stage; Second-stage; Later-stage expansion; Buy-outs/Acquisitions. LOANS: Working capital; Equipment; Equity-related
WILL NOT CONSIDER: Passive real estate deals
GEOGRAPHIC LIMITS OF INVESTMENTS/LOANS: National
RANGE OF INV./LOAN PER BUSINESS: Min. $50,000; Max. $350,000
PREFERRED TERM FOR LOANS & LEASES: Min. 4 years; Max. 10 years
BUSINESS CHARACTERISTICS DESIRED-REQUIRED: Minimum number of years in business: 0
REFERRALS ACCEPTED FROM: Investment/Mortgage banker or Borrower/Investee

COMPANY: **Tennessee Equity Cap. Corp.**
ADDRESS: 1102 Stonewall Jackson Court
Nashville, TN 37220
PHONE: (615) 373-4502

COMPANY: **Tennessee Venture Capital Corp.**
ADDRESS: 162 Fourth Avenue North, Suite 125
Nashville, TN 37219
PHONE: (615) 244-6935
CONTACT OFFICER(S): Wendell P. Knox, President
REMARKS: Private Capital of $500,000

COMPANY: **MESBIC Financial Corporation of Dallas**
ADDRESS: 7701 N. Stemmons Freeway, Suite 836
Dallas, TX 75247
PHONE: (214) 637-0445
TYPE OF INSTITUTION: MESBIC (owned by 100 banks and corporations)
CONTACT OFFICER(S): W. W. Durham, Chairman
N. D. Campbell, V.P.
T. G. Gerron, V.P. — Comptroller
ASSETS: $4.3 million
INVESTMENTS/LOANS MADE: For own account; Through private placements
INVESTMENTS/LOANS MADE: In securities with a secondary market and in securities without a secondary market
TYPES OF FINANCING: Common stock; Preferred stock, VENTURE CAPITAL: Second-stage (generally 1-3 years); Later-stage expansion; Buy-outs/Acquisitions, LOANS: Working capital (receivables/inventory); Equipment; Equity-related, OTHER SERVICES PROVIDED: Management Services, i.e., accounting, planning, etc.
PREFERRED TYPES OF INDUSTRIES/INVESTMENTS: On-going, profitable growth oriented businesses owned by minorities, females or other socially or economically disadvantaged individuals
GEOGRAPHIC LIMITS OF INVESTMENTS/LOANS: State; Prefer Texas — will consider participating in other areas of U.S.
RANGE OF INV./LOAN PER BUSINESS: Min. $25,000; Max. $500,000
PREFERRED TERM FOR LOANS & LEASES: Min. 3; Max. 8 years
BUSINESS CHARACTERISTICS DESIRED-REQUIRED: Minimum number of years in business: 2; Min. annual sales $500,000; Min. net worth $50,000; Min. annual net income $50,000; Min. annual cash flow $50,000
REFERRALS ACCEPTED FROM: Investment/Mortgage banker or Borrower/Investee

COMPANY: **Chen's Financial Group, Inc.**
ADDRESS: 1616 West Loop South, Suite 200
Houston, TX 77027
PHONE: (713) 850-0879
CONTACT OFFICER(S): Samuel S. C. Chen, President
REMARKS: Private capital of $1,000,000

COMPANY: **Evergreen Capital Company, Inc.**
ADDRESS: 8502 Tybor, 201
Houston, TX 77074
PHONE: (713) 778-9889
TYPE OF INSTITUTION: MESBIC
CONTACT OFFICER(S): Richard Shenlim Lin, Chariman and President
ASSETS: $700,000
INVESTMENTS/LOANS MADE: For own account
TYPES OF FINANCING: VENTURE CAPITAL: Start-up from developed product stage; Later-stage expansion; Buy-outs/Acquisitions, OTHER SERVICES PROVIDED: Prefer start-ups
PREFERRED TYPES OF INDUSTRIES/INVESTMENTS: Diversified
WILL NOT CONSIDER: Real estate
GEOGRAPHIC LIMITS OF INVESTMENTS/LOANS: National
RANGE OF INV./LOAN PER BUSINESS: Min. $100,000; Max. $200,000

COMPANY: **Evergreen Capital Company, Inc.**
ADDRESS: 8502 Tybor Drive, Suite 201
Houston, TX 77074
PHONE: (713) 778-9770
CONTACT OFFICER(S): Shen-Lim Lin, Chairman & President
REMARKS: Private capital of $701,000

COMPANY: **MESBIC Financial Corporation of Houston**
ADDRESS: 1801 Main St., Ste. 320
Houston, TX 77002
PHONE: (713) 228-8321
TYPE OF INSTITUTION: M.E.S.B.I.C.
CONTACT OFFICER(S): Richard Rothfeld, President
TYPES OF FINANCING: VENTURE CAPITAL: First-stage (less than 1 year); Second-stage (generally 1-3 years); Later-stage expansion; Buy-outs/Acquisitions, LOANS: Working capital (receivables/inventory); Equipment
PREFERRED TYPES OF INDUSTRIES/INVESTMENTS: Minority owned and operated; manufacturing, distribution, service
WILL NOT CONSIDER: Professionals, re-investment
GEOGRAPHIC LIMITS OF INVESTMENTS/LOANS: Local
RANGE OF INV./LOAN PER BUSINESS: Min. $25,000; Max. $250,000
PREFERRED TERM FOR LOANS & LEASES: Min. 4; Max. 7 years
BUSINESS CHARACTERISTICS DESIRED-REQUIRED: Minimum number of years in business: 1; Min. annual sales $100,000; Min. net worth $25,000; Min. annual net income $10,000
REFERRALS ACCEPTED FROM: Borrower/Investee

COMPANY: **Minority Enterprise Funding, Inc.**
ADDRESS: Space Center Inn, 2020 Nasa Road One,
Building A, Suite D
Houston, TX 77058
PHONE: (713) 332-3551
CONTACT OFFICER(S): Frederick C. Chang, President
REMARKS: Private capital of $550,000

COMPANY: **Southern Orient Cap. Corporation**
ADDRESS: 2419 Fannin, Suite 200
Houston, TX 77002
PHONE: (713) 225-3369
CONTACT OFFICER(S): Min H. Liang, President
REMARKS: Private Capital of $550,000

COMPANY: **United Oriental Cap. Corporation**
ADDRESS: 13432 Hempsted Highway
Houston, TX 77040
PHONE: (713) 462-0937
CONTACT OFFICER(S): Don J. Wang, President
REMARKS: Private capital of $500,000

COMPANY: **MESBIC of San Antonio Incorporated**
ADDRESS: 2300 West Commerce
San Antonio, TX 78207
PHONE: (512) 224-0909
TYPE OF INSTITUTION: MESBIC Subsidiary of Community Development Corp.
CONTACT OFFICER(S): Ruben M. Saenz, VP
TYPES OF FINANCING: VENTURE CAPITAL: Second-stage, LOANS: Working capital; Equipment
PREFERRED TYPES OF INDUSTRIES/INVESTMENTS: Diversified
GEOGRAPHIC LIMITS OF INVESTMENTS/LOANS: Local
RANGE OF INVESTMENT/LOAN PER BUSINESS: Min. $50,000; Max. $200,000
PREFERRED TERM FOR LOANS & LEASES: Max. 7 years
BUSINESS CHARACTERISTICS DESIRED-REQUIRED: Minimum number of years in business: 2

COMPANY: **Basic Investment Corp.**
ADDRESS: 6723 Whittier Avenue
McLean, VA 22101
PHONE: (703) 356-4300
CONTACT OFFICER(S): Ridgway B. Espy, Jr., General Manager
REMARKS: Private capital of $500,000

COMPANY: **East West United Inv. Co.**
ADDRESS: 6723 Whittier Ave., Suite 205B
McLean, VA 22101
PHONE: (703) 821-6616
CONTACT OFFICER(S): Bui Trac, Chairman
REMARKS: Private Capital of $500,000

COMPANY: **Norfolk Investment Company, Inc.**
ADDRESS: Plume Ctr. West, 100 W. Plume St., Ste 208
Norfolk, VA 23510
PHONE: (804) 623-1042
CONTACT OFFICER(S): Kirk W. Saunders, General Manager
REMARKS: Private Capital of $700,000

COMPANY: **Eastpac, Inc.**
ADDRESS: 1940 - 116th Avenue, N.E., Suite B
Bellevue, WA 98004
PHONE: (206) 455-2823
CONTACT OFFICER(S): Charles Ying, President
REMARKS: Private capital of $1,050,000

COMPANY: **SC Opportunities, Inc.**
ADDRESS: 1112 Seventh Avenue
Monroe, WI 53566
PHONE: (608) 328-8400
CONTACT OFFICER(S): Robert L. Ableman, Secretary
REMARKS: Private Capital of $300,000

MUTUAL SAVINGS BANKS

(Primarily Real Estate Financing)

ARKANSAS

COMPANY: **Alaska Mutual Savings Bank**
ADDRESS: P.O. Box 10-1120
Anchorage, AK 99510
PHONE: (907) 274-3561

COMPANY: **Mt. McKinley Mutual Savings Bank**
ADDRESS: 531 Third Avenue
Fairbanks, AK 99701
PHONE: (907) 452-1751

COMPANY: **Mechanics & Farmers Savings Bank**
ADDRESS: 930 Main Street
Bridgeport, CT 06601
PHONE: (203) 382-6363

COMPANY: **People's Savings Bank—Bridegport**
ADDRESS: 899 Main Street
Bridgeport, CT 06601
PHONE: (203) 579-7171

COMPANY: **Bristol Savings Bank**
ADDRESS: 150 Main Street
Bristol, CT 06010
PHONE: (203) 582-8181

CONNECTICUT

COMPANY: **The Derby Savings Bank**
ADDRESS: 1 Elizabeth Street
Derby, CT 06418
PHONE: (203) 736-9921

COMPANY: **Society For Savings**
ADDRESS: 31 Pratt Street
Hartford, CT 06103
PHONE: (203) 727-5000

COMPANY: **The Central Bank For Savings**
ADDRESS: Central Plaza, 43 East Main Street
Meriden, CT 06450
PHONE: (203) 238-2300
TYPE OF INSTITUTION: Mutual Savings Bank
CONTACT OFFICER(S): James H. Doak, Jr., President
BRANCHES: Lee Nordstrom, Asst. Treasurer, P.O. Box 417, Storrs, CT06268; (203) 429-6487
Francis E. Smith, Jr., Assistant V.P., Central Plaza, 138 Weymouth Road, Enfield, CT 06082; (203) 623-3476
Ronald York, Jr., Asst. Treas., 820 East Main Street, Meriden, CT 06450; (203) 238-2300
Theresa Grimaldi, Asst. Treasurer, Centennial Plaza, West Main Street, Meriden, CT 06450; (203) 238-2300

COMPANY: **Liberty Bank For Savings**
ADDRESS: 315 Main Street
Middletown, CT 06457
PHONE: (203) 344-7200

COMPANY: **Connecticut Savings Bank**
ADDRESS: 47 Church Street
New Haven, CT 06510
PHONE: (203) 773-4200

MUTUAL SAVINGS BANKS

(Primarily Real Estate Financing)

DELAWARE

COMPANY: **Artisans' Savings Bank**
ADDRESS: 9th and Tatnall Streets
Wilmington, DE 19899
PHONE: (302) 658-6881

COMPANY: **Wilmington Savings Fund Society**
ADDRESS: 838 Market Street
Wilmington, DE 19899
PHONE: (302) 571-7000

MASSACHUSETTS

COMPANY: **Andover Savings Bank**
ADDRESS: 61 Main Street
Andover, MA 01810
PHONE: (617) 475-6103

COMPANY: **Arlington Five Cents Savings Bank**
ADDRESS: 626 Massachusetts Avenue
Arlington, MA 02174
PHONE: (617) 643-0011

COMPANY: **Belmont Savings Bank**
ADDRESS: 2 Leonard Street, P.O. Box 146
Belmont, MA 02178
PHONE: (617) 484-6700

COMPANY: **The Boston Five Cents Savings Bank**
ADDRESS: 10 School Street
Boston, MA 02104
PHONE: (617) 742-6000

COMPANY: **Home Savings Bank**
ADDRESS: 69 Tremont Street
Boston, MA 02108
PHONE: (617) 723-1600

COMPANY: **Hyde Park Savings Bank**
ADDRESS: 1196 River Street
Boston, MA 02136
PHONE: (617) 361-6900

COMPANY: **Mutual Bank For Savings**
ADDRESS: 45 Franklin Street
Boston, MA 02110
PHONE: (617) 482-7530

COMPANY: **New World Savings Bank**
ADDRESS: 55 Summer Street
Boston, MA 02110
PHONE: (617) 482-2600

COMPANY: **The Provident Institution for Savings in the Town of Boston**
ADDRESS: 30 Winter Street
Boston, MA 02108
PHONE: (617) 423-9600

COMPANY: **South Boston Savings Bank**
ADDRESS: 460 West Broadway
Boston, MA 02127
PHONE: (617) 268-2500

COMPANY: **Union Warren Savings Bank**
ADDRESS: 133 Federal Street
Boston, MA 02110
PHONE: (617) 482-4590

COMPANY: **Cambridge Savings Bank**
ADDRESS: 1374 Massachusetts Avenue
Cambridge, MA 02238
PHONE: (617) 864-8700

COMPANY: **Boston Five Cents Savings Bank**
ADDRESS: 385 Broadway
Chelsea, MA 02151
PHONE: (617) 289-9000

COMPANY: **Middlesex Institution For Savings**
ADDRESS: 64 Main Street
Concord, MA 01742
PHONE: (617) 369-8112

COMPANY: **Dedham Institution For Savings**
ADDRESS: 55 Elm Street
Dedham, MA 02026
PHONE: (617) 329-6700

COMPANY: **East Boston Savings Bank**
ADDRESS: 10 Meridian Street
East Boston, MA 02128
PHONE: (617) 567-1500

COMPANY: **Fitchburg Savings Bank**
ADDRESS: 780 Main Street
Fitchburg, MA 01420
PHONE: (617) 345-1061

COMPANY: **Florence Savings Bank**
ADDRESS: 85 Main Street
Florence, MA 01060
PHONE: (413) 586-1300

COMPANY: **The Cape Cod Five Cents Savings Bank**
ADDRESS: 532 Main Street
Harwich Port, MA 02646
PHONE: (617) 432-1030

MUTUAL SAVINGS BANKS

(Primarily Real Estate Financing)

COMPANY: **The Family Mutual Savings Bank**
ADDRESS: 153 Merrimack Street
Haverhill, MA 01830
PHONE: (617) 374-1911

COMPANY: **Community Savings Bank**
ADDRESS: 200 Main Street
Holyoke, MA 01040
PHONE: (413) 536-7220

COMPANY: **Vanguard Savings Bank**
ADDRESS: 143 Chestnut Street
Holyoke, MA 01040
PHONE: (413) 533-7121

COMPANY: **First Essex Savings Bank**
ADDRESS: 296 Essex Street
Lawrence, MA 01840
PHONE: (617) 681-7500

COMPANY: **First Service Bank**
ADDRESS: 15 Monument Square
Loeminster, MA 01453
PHONE: (617) 342-8741

COMPANY: **The Lowell Five Cent Savings Bank**
ADDRESS: 34 John Street
Lowell, MA 01852
PHONE: (617) 459-2361

COMPANY: **Lowell Institution For Savings**
ADDRESS: 18 Shattuck Street
Lowell, MA 01852
PHONE: (617) 454-2500

COMPANY: **Lynn Five Cents Savings Bank**
ADDRESS: 112 Market Street
Lynn, MA 01901
PHONE: (617) 599-5555

COMPANY: **The Bank For Savings**
ADDRESS: 399 Main Street
Malden, MA 02148
PHONE: (617) 322-0720

COMPANY: **Marlborough Savings Bank**
ADDRESS: 166 Main Street
Marlborough, MA 01752
PHONE: (617) 481-8300

COMPANY: **Assabet Institution For Savings**
ADDRESS: 17 Nason Street, P.O. Box 309
Maynard, MA 01754
PHONE: (617) 897-3232

COMPANY: **Medford Savings Bank**
ADDRESS: 29 High Street
Medford, MA 02155
PHONE: (617) 395-7700

COMPANY: **New Bedford Five Cents Savings Bank**
ADDRESS: 791 Purchase Street
New Bedford, MA 02740
PHONE: (617) 994-5000

COMPANY: **Institution for Savings in Newburyport and its Vicinity**
ADDRESS: 93 State Street
Newburyport, MA 01950
PHONE: (617) 462-3106

COMPANY: **North Adams Hoosac Savings Bank**
ADDRESS: 93 Main Street
North Adams, MA 01247
PHONE: (413) 633-5353

COMPANY: **Northampton Institution For Savings**
ADDRESS: 109 Main Street
Northampton, MA 01060
PHONE: (413) 584-0997

COMPANY: **City Savings Bank of Pittsfield**
ADDRESS: 116 North Street
Pittsfield, MA 01201
PHONE: (413) 443-4421

COMPANY: **Plymouth Five Cents Savings Bank**
ADDRESS: 20 North Park Avenue, Box 1079
Plymouth, MA 02360
PHONE: (617) 746-4600

COMPANY: **Quincy Savings Bank**
ADDRESS: 1200 Hancock St.
Quincy, MA 02169
PHONE: (617) 471-3500

COMPANY: **Massachusetts Bank**
ADDRESS: 123 Haven St.
Reading, MA 01867
PHONE: (617) 662-0100

COMPANY: **Salem Five Cents Savings Bank**
ADDRESS: 210 Essex Street
Salem, MA 01970
PHONE: (617) 745-5555

COMPANY: **New World Savings Bank**
ADDRESS: 307 Main Street
South Yarmouth, MA 02664
PHONE: (617) 398-0321

COMPANY: **Springfield Institution For Savings**
ADDRESS: 1441 Main Street
Springfield, MA 01103
PHONE: (413) 781-8000

COMPANY: **Plymouth Savings Bank**
ADDRESS: 226 Main Street, P.O. Box 431
Wareham, MA 02571
PHONE: (617) 295-3800
TYPE OF INSTITUTION: Bank—Mortgage banking, commercial lending
CONTACT OFFICER(S): Frank D. Fantasia, Sr. Vice President—Sr. Lending Officer
ASSETS: $270,000,000
TYPES OF FINANCING: VENTURE CAPITAL: Second-stage; Later-stage expansion, LOANS: Working capiital; Equipment; Equity-related, REAL ESTATE LOANS: Long-term senior mtg.; Intermediate-term senior mtg.; Wraparounds; Land; Land development; Construction; Standbys; Industrial revenue bonds, LEASES: Single-investor; Leveraged; Non-tax leases; Operating; Vendor financing programs, REAL ESTATE: Acquisitions; Joint ventures; Partnerships/Syndications
WILL NOT CONSIDER: Restaurants, motels
GEOGRAPHIC LIMITS OF INVESTMENTS/LOANS: Regional
RANGE OF INV./LOAN PER BUSINESS: Min. $25,000; Max. $500,000
REFERRALS ACCEPTED FROM: Investment/Mortgage banker or Borrower/Investee

COMPANY: **Westfield Savings Bank**
ADDRESS: 141 Elm Street
Westfield, MA 01086
PHONE: (413) 568-1911

COMPANY: **Woburn Five Cents Savings Bank**
ADDRESS: 19 Pleasant Street
Woburn, MA 01801
PHONE: (617) 933-0040

COMPANY: **Consumers Savings Bank**
ADDRESS: 50 Front Street
Worcester, MA 01608
PHONE: (617) 754-2653

COMPANY: **Peoples Bank**
ADDRESS: 120 Front St.
Worcester, MA 01608
PHONE: (617) 791-3861

COMPANY: **Central Savings Bank**
ADDRESS: 201 North Charles, P.O. Box 1316
Baltimore, MD 21201
PHONE: (301) 539-1636

COMPANY: **Provident Savings Bank of Baltimore**
ADDRESS: 114 E. Lexington St., P.O. Box 1661
Baltimore, MD 21020-1661
PHONE: (301) 547-7000

COMPANY: **The Savings Bank of Baltimore**
ADDRESS: Charles and Baltimore Streets
Baltimore, MD 21203
PHONE: (301) 244-3360

COMPANY: **Peoples Savings Bank**
ADDRESS: 481 Congress Street
Portland, ME 04104
PHONE: (207) 774-5643

COMPANY: **New Hampshire Savings Bank**
ADDRESS: 27 North State Street
Concord, NH 03301
PHONE: (603) 224-7711

COMPANY: **Cheshire County Savings Bank**
ADDRESS: 194 West Street
Keene, NH 03431
PHONE: (603) 352-2502

COMPANY: **Amoskeag Savings Bank**
ADDRESS: 875 Elm Street
Manchester, NH 03105
PHONE: (603) 624-3200

COMPANY: **The Merchants Savings Bank of Manchester**
ADDRESS: One Hampshire Plaza
Manchester, NH 03101
PHONE: (603) 624-2424

COMPANY: **Harmonia Savings Bank**
ADDRESS: 1 Union Square
Elizabeth, NJ 07207
PHONE: (201) 289-0800

COMPANY: **Hudson City Savings Bank**
ADDRESS: 587 Summit Avenue
Jersey City, NJ 07306
PHONE: (201) 653-8950

COMPANY: **Provident Savings Bank**
ADDRESS: 239 Washington Street
Jersey City, NJ 07302
PHONE: (201) 795-5600
CONTACT OFFICERS: James K. Feely, President
ASSETS: 1.2 Billion

COMPANY: **The Morris County Savings Bank**
ADDRESS: 21 South Street
Morristown, NJ 07960
PHONE: (201) 539-0500
TYPE OF INSTITUTION: Savings Bank
CONTACT OFFICER(S): Charles W. Frost, Chief Executive Officer

Jerry F. Smith, Real Estate Financing
Robert W. Freund, Commerical Lending, Leasing
Michael Allison, Investments
ASSETS: $867,500,000
INVESTMENTS/LOANS MADE: For own account
INVESTMENTS/LOANS MADE: Only in securities with a secondary market
TYPES OF FINANCING: SECONDARY-MARKET CORPORATE SECURITIES: Bonds; Other: Commerical Paper, B.A.'s, etc., LOANS: Unsecured; Working capital; Equipment, REAL ESTATE LOANS: Long-term senior mtg; Intermediate-term senior mtg; Subordinated; Construction, LEASES: Operating, REAL ESTATE: Joint Ventures
PREFERRED TYPES OF INDUSTRIES/INVESTMENTS: Not restricted as to industry, interested in developing full relationships with quality credit
GEOGRAPHIC LIMITS OF INVESTMENTS/LOANS: State; National
RANGE OF INV./LOAN PER BUSINESS: Min. $250,000; Max. $4,250,000
PREFERRED TERM FOR LOANS & LEASES: Min. 1/2 year; Max. 3 years
BUSINESS CHARACTERISTICS DESIRED-REQUIRED: Minimum number of years in business: 3; Min. annual sales $1MM; Min. net worth $200M; Min. annual net income $100M; Min. annual cash fow $150M
REFERRALS ACCEPTED FROM Investment/Mortgage banker or Borrower/Investee
REMARKS: All branches within Northwest New Jersey

COMPANY: **New Brunswick Savings Bank**
ADDRESS: 70 Bayard Street
New Brunswick, NJ 08903
PHONE: (201) 247-1100

COMPANY: **The Howard Savings Bank**
ADDRESS: 768 Broad Street
Newark, NJ 07101
PHONE: (201) 430-2000
TYPE OF INSTITUTION: Stockholder-Owned Savings Bank
CONTACT OFFICER(S): Anthony P. Meli, Jr. (201) 533-7721, Vice President - Mortgage Administration
ASSETS: $3.743 billion dollars (8/31/84)
INVESTMENTS/LOANS MADE: For own account
INVESTMENTS/LOANS MADE: Only in securities with a secondary market
TYPES OF FINANCING: SECONDARY-MARKET CORPORATE SECURITIES: Common stock; Preferred stock; Bonds; LOANS: Unsecured; Working capital; Equipment; Equity-related; Other: Warehouse credit lines to mortgage bankers; REAL ESTATE LOANS: Intermediate-term senior mtg.; Land development; Construction; REAL ESTATE
PREFERRED TYPES OF INDUSTRIES/INVESTMENTS: Financial services industries
GEOGRAPHIC LIMITS OF INVESTMENTS/LOANS: National
PREFERRED TERM FOR LOANS & LEASES: Min. 1/4 year; Max. 10 years
REFERRALS ACCEPTED FROM: Investment/Mortgage banker or Borrower/Investee
BRANCHES: We have 58 branches within the State of New Jersey

COMPANY: **The Howard Savings Bank**
ADDRESS: 768 Broad Street
Newark, NJ 07101
PHONE: (201) 430-2000
TYPE OF INSTITUTION: Stockholder-Owned Savings Bank
CONTACT OFFICER(S): Richard K. Donnelly, (201) 533-7836, Vice President - Investments
ASSETS: $3.743 billion dollars (8/31/84)
INVESTMENTS/LOANS MADE: For own account
INVESTMENTS/LOANS MADE: Only in securities with a secondary market
TYPES OF FINANCING: SECONDARY-MARKET CORPORATE SECURITIES: Common stock; Preferred stock; Bonds
BRANCHES: We have 58 branches within the State of New Jersey

COMPANY: **Hudson City Savings Bank**
ADDRESS: West 80 Century Road
Paramus, NJ 07652
PHONE: (201) 967-1900

COMPANY: **Perth Amboy Savings Institution**
ADDRESS: 210 Smith Street
Perth Amboy, NJ 08861
PHONE: (201) 442-4100

COMPANY: **Home & City Savings Bank**
ADDRESS: 100 State Street
Albany, NY 12201
PHONE: (518) 447-5000

COMPANY: **Albany Savings Bank**
ADDRESS: State & North Pearl Streets
Albany, NY 12207
PHONE: (518) 445-2000

COMPANY: **Dime Savings Bank**
ADDRESS: 111 Washington Avenue
Albany, NY 12201
PHONE: (518) 436-0811

COMPANY: **The Binghamton Savings Bank**
ADDRESS: 66 Exchange Street
Binghamton, NY 13902
PHONE: (607) 773-2525

COMPANY: **Dry Dock Savings Bank**
ADDRESS: 2530 Grand Concourse
Bronx, NY 10458
PHONE: (212) 584-6000

MUTUAL SAVINGS BANKS
(Primarily Real Estate Financing)

COMPANY: **The Metropolitan Savings Bank**
ADDRESS: 211 Montague
Brooklyn, NY 11202
PHONE: (212) 522-0030

COMPANY: **Empire of America, FSB**
ADDRESS: One Main Place
Buffalo, NY 14202
PHONE: (716) 845-7000

COMPANY: **Citizens Savings Bank**
ADDRESS: 118 North Tioga Street, P.O. Box 400
Ithaca, NY 14850
PHONE: (607) 273-7111

COMPANY: **American Savings Bank**
ADDRESS: 380 Madison Avenue
New York, NY 10036
PHONE: (212) 219-7500

COMPANY: **Apple Bank for Savings**
ADDRESS: 666 Third Ave.
New York, NY 10017
PHONE: (212) 787-4500

COMPANY: **The Bowery Savings Bank**
ADDRESS: 110 East 42nd Street
New York, NY 10017
PHONE: (212) 953-8000

COMPANY: **East River Savings Bank**
ADDRESS: 26 Cortlandt Street
New York, NY 10007
PHONE: (212) 553-9611
TYPE OF INSTITUTION: Savings Bank
CONTACT OFFICER(S): Joseph Charla Jr., E.V.P.
Frank Magilligan, E.V.P.
ASSETS: $1.9 Billion
INVESTMENTS/LOANS MADE: For own account; Through private placements
INVESTMENTS/LOANS MADE: In securities with a secondary market and in securities without a secondary market
TYPES OF FINANCING: REAL ESTATE LOANS: Intermediate-term senior mtg.; Wraparounds; Land; Land development; Construction; Standbys. REAL ESTATE: Joint ventures
GEOGRAPHIC LIMITS OF INVESTMENTS/LOANS: Local; State; Regional; National

COMPANY: **Emigrant Savings Bank**
ADDRESS: 5 East 42 Street
New York, NY 10017
PHONE: (212) 883-5800

COMPANY: **Goldome**
ADDRESS: 1230 Avenue of the Americas
New York, NY 10020
PHONE: (212) 841-7000

COMPANY: **The Greater New York Savings Bank**
ADDRESS: 1 Penn Plaza
New York, NY 10119
PHONE: (212) 613-4000

COMPANY: **The Lincoln Savings Bank**
ADDRESS: 200 Park Ave.
New York, NY 10166
PHONE: (212) 972-9500

COMPANY: **The Manhattan Savings Bank**
ADDRESS: 385 Madison Avenue
New York, NY 10017
PHONE: (212) 688-3000

COMPANY: **The Seamen's Bank for Savings**
ADDRESS: 30 Wall Street
New York, NY 10005
PHONE: (212) 797-5000

COMPANY: **Poughkeepsie Savings Bank**
ADDRESS: 21 Market Street, P.O. Box 31
Poughkeepsie, NY 12602
PHONE: (914) 454-1100

COMPANY: **Monroe Savings Bank**
ADDRESS: 300 Main Street East
Rochester, NY 14604
PHONE: (716) 325-3250

COMPANY: **Rochester Community Savings Bank**
ADDRESS: 40 Franklin Street
Rochester, NY 14604
PHONE: (716) 263-4400

COMPANY: **Eastern Savings Bank**
ADDRESS: 1075 Central Park Avenue
Scarsdale, NY 10583
PHONE: (914) 725-5600

COMPANY: **Onondaga Savings Bank**
ADDRESS: 101 So. Salina Street, P.O. Box 4983
Syracuse, NY 13221
PHONE: (315) 424-4400

COMPANY: **Syracuse Savings Bank**
ADDRESS: One Clinton Square, P.O. Box 4821
Syracuse, NY 13221
PHONE: (315) 471-7101

COMPANY: **Pioneer Savings Bank**
ADDRESS: 21 Second Street
Troy, NY 12180
PHONE: (518) 274-4800

COMPANY: **The Troy Savings Bank**
ADDRESS: 32 Second Street
Troy, NY 12180
PHONE: (518) 270-3200

COMPANY: **The Savings Bank of Utica**
ADDRESS: 233 Genesee Street
Utica, NY 13501
PHONE: (315) 797-9200
TYPE OF INSTITUTION: Mutual Savings Bank
CONTACT OFFICER(S): William L. Schrauth, President
Robert A. Drew, Jr., Vice President, Loan Off.
TOTAL ASSETS: $704,000,000
INVESTMENT/LOANS MADE: For own account
INVESTMENT/LOANS MADE: Only in securities with a secondary market
TYPES OF FINANCING: SECONDARY-MARKET CORPORATE SECURITIES: Bonds; Other: Mortgage loans, Mobile home loans, Student loans, REAL ESATE LOANS
PREFERRED TYPES OF INDUSTRIES/INVESTMENTS: Real Estate
GEOGRAPHIC LIMITS OF INV./LOANS: National
RANGE OF INV./LOAN PER BUSINESS: Min.$500,000.00; Max. $1,500,000.00
PREFERRED TERM FOR LOANS & LEASES: Min. 7-10 years, repricing inone to three year invtervals

COMPANY: **The Home Savings Bank**
ADDRESS: 170 Hamilton Avenue
White Plains, NY 10601
PHONE: (914) 681-5800
TYPE OF INSITUTION: Mutual Savings Bank
CONTACT OFFICER(S): Walter J. Dianis, President & Chief Executive Officer
TOTAL ASSETS: $435,000,000
INVESTMENTS/LOANS: For own account
INVESTMENTS/LOANS MADE: Only in securities with a secondary market
TYPES OF FINANCING: SECONDARY-MARKET CORPORATE SECURITIES: Bonds; LOANS: REAL ESTATE LOANS: Land, Land development
PREFERRED TYPES OF INDUSTRIES/INVESTMENTS: Residential mortgages
GEOGRAPHIC LIMITS OF INVESTMENTS/LOANS: Local
RANGE OF INV./LOANS: Min. $25,000; Max. $250,000

COMPANY: **Oregon First Bank**
ADDRESS: 234 Southwest Broadway (97205), P.O. Box 2882 (97208)
Portland, OR
PHONE: (503) 248-6612

COMPANY: **Germantown Savings Bank**
ADDRESS: City Line and Belmont Avenues, GSB Bldg.
Bala-Cynwyd, PA 19004
PHONE: (215) 667-9300

COMPANY: **Beneficial Savings Bank**
ADDRESS: 1200 Chestnut Street
Philadelphia, PA 19107
PHONE: (215) 864-6000

COMPANY: **Dollar Savings Bank**
ADDRESS: 533 Smithfield Street
Pittsburgh, PA 15222
PHONE: (412) 261-4900

COMPANY: **The Savings Bank of Newport**
ADDRESS: 10 Washington Square, P.O. Box 450
Newport, RI 02840
PHONE: (401) 846-3400

COMPANY: **People's Bank, FSB**
ADDRESS: 145 Westminster Street
Providence, RI 02903
PHONE: (401) 456-5000
TYPE OF INSTITUTION: Mutual Savings Bank & Commercial Bank
CONTACT OFFICER(S): Stephen W. Palmer, President & CEO
Dag O. Johannessen, Sr. Vice Pres. & Treasurer
James B. Wolfe, Sr. Vice Pres. & Comm. Banking Div. Mgr.
Robert J. Branley, Sr. Vice Pres. & Retail Banking Div. Mgr.
ASSETS: $350 million
INVESTMENTS/LOANS MADE: For own account
INVESTMENTS/LOANS MADE: Only in securities with a secondary market
TYPES OF FINANCING: SECONDARY-MARKET CORPORATE SECURITIES. LOANS: Unsecured to credits above $25M; Working capital; Equipment; Equity-related. REAL ESTATE LOANS: Long-term senior mtg.; Intermediate-term senior mtg.; Wraparounds; Land; Land development; Construction; Standbys. REAL ESTATE: Acquisitions; Joint ventures; Partnerships/Syndications. OTHER SERVICES PROVIDED: All types of consumer lending.
GEOGRAPHIC LIMITS OF INVESTMENTS/L0ANS: Regional
RANGE OF INV./LOAN PER BUSINESS: Min. $10,000; Max $1.5 Million
PREFERRED TERM FOR LOANS & LEASES: Min. 1 year; Max. 5 years
REFERRALS ACCEPTED FROM: Investment/Mortgage banker or Borrower/Investee
REMARKS: We have 12 branches, but all corporate lending is done by the Commercial Banking Division at the main office

COMPANY: **Woonsocket Institution for Savings**
ADDRESS: 25 Cummings Way, P.O. Box B
Woonsocket, RI 02895
PHONE: (401) 767-3900

COMPANY: **First Mutual Savings Bank**
ADDRESS: 10430 N.E. 8th
Bellevue, WA 98004

PHONE: (206) 455-7300

COMPANY: **Prudential Mutual Savings Bank, FSB**
ADDRESS: 1100 Third Avenue
Seattle, WA 98101
PHONE: (206) 382-7500

COMPANY: **Savings Bank of Puget Sound**
ADDRESS: 815 Second Avenue
Seattle, WA 98104
PHONE: (206) 447-5700

REAL ESTATE LENDERS & INVESTORS

(Real Estate Financing—Loans, Partnerships, Joint Ventures and Acquisitions. Also see Investment Bankers, Mutual Savings Bankers & Finance Companies)

COMPANY: **Camp & Company**
ADDRESS: 3940 Montclair Road, Suite 502
Birmingham, AL
PHONE: (205) 871-8146
TYPE OF INSTITUTION: Mortgage banker
CONTACT OFFICER(S): Ehney A. Camp, III, President
INVESTMENTS/LOANS MADE: For managed accounts
TYPES OF FINANCING: REAL ESTATE LOANS: Long-term senior mtg., Intermediate Term Sr. Mortgage; Subordinated; Wraparounds; Construction; Standbys; Industrial Revenue Bonds; REAL ESTATE: Acquisitions; Joint ventures; Partnerships/Syndications
PREFERRED TYPES OF INDUSTRIES/INVESTMENTS: Real estate development and management
GEOGRAPHIC LIMITS OF INVESTMENTS/LOANS: Regional
RANGE OF INV./LOAN PER BUSINESS: Min. $1,000,000; Max. None
PREFERRED TERM FOR LOANS & LEASES: Min. Variable; Max. None
REFERRALS ACCEPTED FROM: Investment/Mortgage banker or Borrower/Investee
BRANCHES: Richard Brinson, 2866 Dolphin Street, Suite "W," Mobile, AL 36606 (205) 473-1831

COMPANY: **Collateral Investment Company**
ADDRESS: 2100 First Avenue North
Birmingham, AL 35203
PHONE: 205) 252-1000
TYPE OF INSTITUTION: Mortgage banker
CONTACT OFFICER(S): J. K. V. Ratliff, Jr., V.P.—Income Property Loans
ASSETS: $83,000,000
INVESTMENTS/LOANS MADE: For own account, Through private placements
INVESTMENTS/LOANS MADE: Only in securities with a secondary market
TYPES OF FINANCING: LOANS: Working capital; Equipment, REAL ESTATE LOANS: Long-term senior mtg.; Intermediate-term senior mtg.; Subordinated; Wraparounds, Land; Land development; Construction; Gap. Standbys
PREFERRED TYPES OF INDUSTRIES/INVESTMENTS: No preference
GEOGRAPHIC LIMITS OF INVESTMENTS/LOANS: Regional
RANGE OF INV./LOAN PER BUSINESS: Min. $100,000; Max. None
PREFERRED TERM FOR LOANS & LEASES: Min. 10 years; Max. 30 years
REFERRALS ACCEPTED FROM: Investment/Mortgage banker or Borrower/Investee
REMARKS: Branches located over Southeast

COMPANY:**Goldome Credit Corporation (A Subsidiary of Goldome, FSB)**
ADDRESS: 3125 Independence Drive
Birmingham, Al
PHONE: (205) 870-4400
TYPE OF INSTITUTION: Consumer & Mortgage lending subsidiary of Goldome, FSB
CONTACT OFFICER(S): Robert Brannon, President-Ben G. McDaniel, EVP
ASSETS: $5,331,000 (Assets under Goldome Credit Corp.)

INVESTMENTS/LOANS MADE: For managed accounts
INVESTMENTS/LOANS MADE: Only in securities without a secondary market
TYPES OF FINANCING: REAL ESTATE LOANS: Other: Home Improvement Secured by Real Estate, 1st Mortgages. OTHER SERVICES PROVIDED: Commercial loans secured by 1st and 2nd mortgages on real estate
PREFERRED TYPES OF INDUSTRIES/INVESTMENTS: Real estate exclusively
GEOGRAPHIC LIMITS OF INVESTMENTS/LOANS: Regional (East coast & Southeast U.S.)
RANGE OF INV./LOAN PER BUSINESS: Min. $2,500; Max. 80/20 loan to value
PREFERRED TERM FOR LOANS & LEASES: Min. 5 years; Max. 20 years
BUSINESS CHARACTERISTICS DESIRED-REQUIRED: Min. annual cash flow $1.2 debt service coverage; Other: Adequate real estate collateral; net worth, liquidity, and expertise of principals
BRANCHES: John Meehan, 1800 Chapel Ave., W., Commerce Center, Suite 124, Cherry Hill, NJ 08002, (609) 665-6353
REMARKS: Aggressively seeking 1st & 2nd mortgage income property loans from $200,000 to $1.5 million

COMPANY: **Goldome Credit Corporation**
ADDRESS: 3125 Independence Drive
Birmingham, AL 35209
PHONE: 205) 870-4400
TYPE OF INSTITUTION: A mutual savings bank
CONTACT OFFICER(S): David A. Roberts, Vice President
W. Richard Anthony, II, Asst. Vice President
Steven G. Waite, Commercial Loan Officer
ASSETS: $11 billion
INVESTMENTS/LOANS MADE: For own account
INVESTMENTS/LOANS MADE: In securities with a secondary market and in securities without a secondary market
TYPES OF FINANCING: LOANS: REAL ESTATE LOANS: Intermediate-term senior mtg.; Subordinated; Wraparounds, Construction; Gap. Standbys
PREFERRED TYPES OF INDUSTRIES/INVESTMENTS: Apartments, Office Buildings, Shopping Centers, Multi-tenant Industrials
GEOGRAPHIC LIMITS OF INVESTMENT/LOANS: National
RANGE OF INV./LOAN PER BUSINESS: Min. $250,000; Max. $15 million
PREFERRED TERM FOR LOANS & LEASED: Min. 2 years; Max. 7 years
REFERRALS ACCEPTED FROM: Investment/Mortgage Banker or Borrower/Investee

COMPANY: **Liberty National Life Insurance Company**
ADDRESS: P.O. Box 2612
Birmingham, AL 35202
PHONE: (205) 325-2048
CONTACT OFFICER(S): W. H. Ray, Exec. V.P. Investment Division
William G. Byars, V.P. Real Estate
Michael J. Klice, V.P. Securities
ASSETS: $2.1 billion
TYPES OF FINANCING: SECONDARY-MARKET CORPORATE SECURITIES: Common stock; Preferred stock; Bonds, REAL ESTATE LOANS: Other: Mortgages REAL ESTATE: Acquisitions
GEOGRAPHIC LIMITS OF INVESTMENTS/LOANS: National
RANGE OF INV./LOAN PER BUSINESS: Min. $2 million; Max. $14 million (R.E.), $5 million (Private Placement)
REFERRALS ACCEPTED FROM: Investment/Mortgage Banker or Borrower/Investee

COMPANY: **Protective Corporation**
ADDRESS: P.O. Box 2606
Birmingham, AL 35202
PHONE: (205) 879-9230
TYPE OF INSTITUTION: Life insurance holding company
CONTACT OFFICER(S): Roland V. Lee, 2nd V.P., Mortgage Loans
Troy Mohon, 2nd V.P. Securities
ASSETS: $700,000,000
INVESTMENTS/LOANS MADE: For own account
INVESTMENTS/LOANS MADE: In securities with a secondary market and in securities without a secondary market
TYPES OF FINANCING: SECONDARY-MARKET CORPORATE SECURITIES: Preferred stock; Bonds, REAL ESTATE LOANS: Long-term senior mtg.; Industrial revenue bonds REAL ESTATE: Joint ventures
PREFERRED TYPES OF INDUSTRIES/INVESTMENTS: Shopping centers, office, warehouse
GEOGRAPHIC LIMITS OF INVESTMENTS/LOANS: National
RANGE OF INV./LOAN PER BUSINESS: Min. $500,000; Max. $2,000,000
REFERRALS ACCEPTED FROM: Investment/Mortgage banker or Borrower/Investee

COMPANY:**Alabama Capital Corporation**
ADDRESS: 16 Midtown Park East
Mobile, AL 36606
PHONE: (205) 476-0700
TYPE OF INSTITUTION: Minority Enterprise small business investment company
CONTACT OFFICER(S): David C. Delaney, President
INVESTMENTS/LOANS MADE: For own account
INVESTMENTS/LOANS MADE: Only in securities without a secondary market
TYPES OF FINANCING: LOANS: Working capital; Equipment; Equity-related; Other: Real Estate secured; REAL ESTATE LOANS: Long-term senior mtg.; intermediate-term senior mtg.; Subordinate; Wraparounds; Land; Land development; Construction
GEOGRAPHIC LIMITS OF INVESTMENTS/LOANS: Local; State
RANGE OF INV./LOAN PER BUSINESS: Min. $5,000.00; Max. $500,000.00
PREFERRED TERM FOR LOANS & LEASES: Min. 5 years; Max. 10 years
BUSINESS CHARACTERISTICS DESIRED-REQUIRED: Minimum number of years in business: 0

REAL ESTATE LENDERS & INVESTORS

(Real Estate Financing—Loans, Partnerships, Joint Ventures and Acquisitions. Also see Investment Bankers, Mutual Savings Bankers & Finance Companies)

ARKANSAS

COMPANY: **Colonial Mortgage Comp.**
ADDRESS: 250 Commerce
Montgomery, AL 36142
PHONE: (205) 263-4483
TYPE OF INSTITUTION: Mortgage Banker
CONTACT OFFICER(S): Ronnie F. Wynn, Pres.
ASSETS: Servicing Volume over $1.1 billion
TYPES OF FINANCING: LOANS: Equity-related, REAL ESTATE LOANS: Long-term senior mtg.; Intermediate-term senior mtg.; Subordinated; Sale-Leaseback; OTHER: Second mtgs. or income producing R.E.
PREFERRED TYPES OF INDUSTRIES/INVESTMENTS: Real Estate; Retailing, Wholesaling & Distribution
GEOGRAPHIC LIMITS OF INVESTMENTS/LOANS: Regional
RANGE OF INV./LOAN PER BUSINESS: Min. $300,000; Max. None
PREFERRED TERM FOR LOANS & LEASES: Min. 15-20; Max. 20+ years
REMARKS: Branches throughout the Southeast

COMPANY: **Block Mortgage Co., Inc.**
ADDRESS: Markham and State Streets
Little Rock, AR 72203
PHONE: (501) 372-7700
TYPE OF INSTITUTION: Mortgage Banker
CONTACT OFFICER(S): A. S. Rosen, Chairman of the Board
James R. Carroll, President
TYPES OF FINANCING: R.E. LOANS: Long-term senior mortgage; Intermediate term senior mortgage
PREFERRED TYPES OF INDUSTRIES/INVESTMENTS: National Firms
GEOGRAPHIC LIMITS OF INVESTMENTS/LOANS: State
RANGE OF INV./LOAN PER BUSINESS: Min. $30,000.00
PREFERRED TERM FOR LOANS & LEASES: Min. 20 & up
REFERRALS ACCEPTED FROM: Investment/Mortgage banker or Borrower/Investee

COMPANY: **First Commercial Mortgage Co.**
ADDRESS: Capitol and Broadway Streets, P.O. Box 626
Little Rock, AR 72203
PHONE: (501) 371-7361
TYPE OF INSTITUTION: Mortgage Banker
CONTACT OFFICER(S): Dale Taylor, Exec. V.P.
Patt Greenlee Sr. V.P
ASSETS: 600 million in servicing
TYPES OF FINANCING: REAL ESTATE LOANS: Long-term senior mortgage; Intermediate-term senior mortgage; Land development; Standbys; Other: Land development only in conjunction with a project; REAL ESTATE: Acquisitions; Partnerships/Syndications
GEOGRAPHIC LIMITS OF INVESTMENTS/LOANS: National
RANGE OF INV./LOAN PER BUSINESS: Min. $500,000
PREFERRED TERM FOR LOANS & LEASES: Max. 30 years
BUSINESS CHARACTERISTICS DESIRED-REQUIRED: Minimum number of years in business: 0
BRANCHES: Springdale, AR
Longview, TX

ARIZONA

COMPANY: **Bancwest Mortgage Corporation**
ADDRESS: 2035 N. Central Ave.
Phoenix, AZ 85004
PHONE: (602) 252-7321
TYPE OF INSTITUTION: Mortgage Banker (a wholly owned subsidiary of The Arizona Bank)
CONTACT OFFICER(S): James F. McCormick, Sr. V.P. and Manager, Income Property Finance Div.
TOTAL ORGANIZATION ASSETS; $850,000,000 in servicing
INVESTMENTS/LOANS MADE: for managed accounts; through private placements
TYPES OF FINANCING: REAL ESTATE LOANS
PREFERRED TYPES OF INVESTMENTS: Multi-Family, office, Industrial, Retail, and other income producing properties
GEOGRAPHIC LIMITS OF INVESTMENTS/LOANS: Regional; AZ, NV, NM
RANGE OF INV./LOAN PER BUSINESS: Min. $1,000,000

COMPANY: **Greyhound Leasing & Financial Corporation**
ADDRESS: 4041 North Center Avenue
Phoenix, AZ 85012
PHONE: (602) 248-4900
CONTACT OFFICER(S): See branches
ASSETS: $1.3 billion
INVESTMENTS/LOANS MADE: In securities with a secondary market and in securities without a secondary market
INVESTMENTS/LOANS MADE: For own account; Through private placements
TYPES OF FINANCING: SECONDARY MARKET CORPORATE SECURITIES: Bonds; VENTURE CAPITAL: Later-stage expansion; LOANS: Equipment; REAL ESTATE LOANS: Long-term senior mtg.; Intermediate-term senior mtg., Land development; Construction; Standbys; Other: Equity Notes Receivables; LEASES: Single-investor; Leveraged; Tax leases; Non-tax leases; Tax-oriented lease brokerage; Lease syndications; Vendor financing programs; INTERNATIONAL; REAL ESTATE: Joint ventures; Partnerships/Syndications
GEOGRAPHIC LIMITS OF INVESTMENTS/LOANS: National
RANGE OF INV./LOAN PER BUSINESS: Min. Leases: $50,000; Loans: $250,000; Max. $—
PREFERRED TERM FOR LOANS & LEASES: Min. Leases: 1; Loans: 3 years; Max. 20 years
BUSINESS CHARACTERISTICS DESIRED-REQUIRED: Minimum number of years in business: 5; Other: Proper operating history upon which to base payment ability projections
REFERRALS ACCEPTED FROM: Investment/Mortgage Banker or Borrower/Investee
BRANCHES: John N. Henning, Donald F. Howell, Jeremiah G. Mahony, Michael J. Naughton, and William H. Vallar (V.P.-Regional Marketing Manager), 445 Park Avenue, New York, NY 10022, (212) 752-2720
Robert E. Marino, John Wm. Salyer, David A. Nielsen (V.P.-Regional Marketing Manager), Centennial Center

I, 1900 East Golf Road, Suite 645, Schaumburg, IL 60195, (312) 490-9500
Bruce E. Heine, Mark Lindell, 7801 East Bush Lake Road, Suite 430, Minneapolis, MN 55435, (612) 831-7044
Joseph A. Graffagnini, Canal Place One, Suite 2510, New Orleans, LA 70130, (504) 525-1112
James M. Brown, 12400 Olive Blvd., Suite 200, St. Louis, MO 63141, (314) 469-7373
George C. Baer, 7616 LBJ Freeway, Suite 500, Dallas, TX 75251, (214) 387-3182
Dottie A. Riley, James T. Foley (V.P.-Regional Marketing Manager), 4041 North Central Avenue, Station 3504, Phoenix, AZ 85012, (602) 248-5349
Jeffrey D. Johnson, Scott D. Mayne, 5505 South 900 East, Suite 325, Salt Lake City, UT 84117, (801) 261-1311
Thomas O. Kaluza, 16400 Southcenter Parkway, Suite 203, Seattle, WA 98188, (206) 575-0246
Kenneth B. Giddes, 6400 Powers Ferry Road, Suite 300, Atlanta, GA 30339, (404) 955-3636
Patrick E. Barton, 1776 South Jackson Street, Suite 907, Denver, CO 80210, (303) 757-4973
Jack W. Quinn, Cineco Building, Suite 203, 4401 W. Tradewinds Ave., Lauderdale-by-the-Sea, FL 33308, (305) 493-8322
David C. Phillips, 600 B Street, Suite 2235, San Diego, CA 92101, (619) 231-4751
Ron W. Larson, Neil E. Leddy, Orangegate Plaza, 5455 Garden Grove Blvd., Suite 450, Westminister, CA 92683, (714) 891-2700

COMPANY: **H.S. Pickrell Company**
ADDRESS: 3300 N. Central Avenue, #2400
Phoenix, AZ 85012
PHONE: (602) 264-8600
CONTACT OFFICER(S): George O'Connell, Vice President, Mgr. Commercial Real Estate Loans
Paul Sargent, Loan Officer
Rocco Mandala, Loan Officer
ASSETS: $1.5 Billion
TYPES OF FINANCING: REAL ESTATE LOANS: Long-term senior mtg.; Intermediate-term senior mtg., Construction; Standbys; Other: Joint Venture Financing; REAL ESTATE: Acquisitions; Joint ventures; Partnerships/Syndications
PREFERRED TYPE OF INDUSTRIES/INVESTMENTS: Shopping Center, Office, Warehouse, incubater office/whse, apartments
GEOGRAPHIC LIMITS OF INVESTMENTS/LOANS: Local; State; Regional; Other: Western U.S.
RANGE OF INV./LOAN PER BUSINESS: Min. $500,000; Max. $46,500,000

COMPANY: **Hebbard & Webb**
ADDRESS: 5001 East Washington
Phoenix, AZ 85034
PHONE: (602) 275-5715
TYPE OF INSTITUTION: Agricultural Mortgage Loan Correspondent
CONTACT OFFICER(S): Milton Webb
ASSETS: $50,000,000
INVESTMENTS/LOANS MADE: Strictly Agricultural R.E. loans arranged
GEOGRAPHIC LIMITS OF INVESTMENTS/LOANS: Arizona & New Mexico
RANGE OF INV./LOAN PER BUSINESS: Minimum $500,000

COMPANY: **Legacy Life Insurance Company**
ADDRESS: Box 10380
Phoenix, AZ
PHONE: (602) 957-8781
TYPE OF INSTITUTION: Insurance company
CONTACT OFFICER(S): R. Kent Fielder, CPA, Asst. V.P.-Finance/Treasurer
Wayne A. Schreck, FSA
V. Pres.-Finance
Richard C. Eiler, President
George S. Ashley, Exec. Vice President
ASSETS: Excess of $6,000,000 (Dec. 31, 1983)
INVESTMENTS/LOANS MADE: For managed accounts; Through private placements
INVESTMENTS/LOANS MADE: In securities with a secondary market and in securities without a secondary market
TYPES OF FINANCING: SECONDARY-MARKET CORPORATE SECURITIES: Common Stock, Preferred Stock, Bonds; REAL ESTATE LOANS: Long-term senior mtg.; Intermediate-term senior mtg., Industrial Revenue Bonds; REAL ESTATE: Acquisitions; Partnerships/Syndications
PREFERRED TYPES OF INDUSTRIES/INVESTMENTS: Senior mtges; T-Bills; C.D.'s; Commercial paper; Repos; Money Market Accounts; T-Notes; Stocks & Bonds
RANGE OF INV./LOAN PER BUSINESS: Min. $10,000.00; Max. $250,000.00
PREFERRED TERM FOR LOANS & LEASES: Min. 6 months; Max. 30 years

COMPANY: **Security Mortgage Co., Inc.**
ADDRESS: 3507 N. Central Av.
Phoenix, AZ 85012
PHONE: (602) 277-1416
TYPE OF INSTITUTION: Mortgage Banker
CONTACT OFFICER(S): Arv Yancher, Pres.
ASSETS: Servicing Volume $10 million — $100 million
TYPES OF FINANCING: REAL ESTATE LOANS: Long-term senior mtg.; Intermediate-term senior mtg.
PREFERRED TYPES OF INDUSTRIES/INVESTMENTS: Office Bldgs.; Industrial & Commercial
WILL NOT CONSIDER: Single Family
GEOGRAPHIC LIMITS OF INVESTMENTS/LOANS: State
RANGE OF INV./LOAN PER BUSINESS: Min. $25,000; Max. None
PREFERRED TERM FOR LOANS & LEASES: Min. 10-15; Max. 20+ years

COMPANY: **Territorial Mortgage and Investment Company**
ADDRESS: 3033 North Central Avenue, Suite 108
Phoenix, AZ 85012
PHONE: (602) 277-1514
CONTACT OFFICER(S): James L. Lafler, CMB, President/Chief Executive Officer
N. Lawrence Kuhlmann, Jr.

Vice President/Loan Officer
Larry A. Bull
Asst. Vice President/Loan Officer
INVESTMENTS/LOANS MADE: For own account; For managed accounts; Through private placements; Through underwriting public offerings
INVESTMENTS/LOANS MADE: In securities with a secondary market and in securities without a secondary market
TYPES OF FINANCING: REAL ESTATE LOANS: Long-term senior mtg.; Intermediate-term senior mtg.; Subordinated; Wraparounds; Land; Land development; Construction; Gap; Standbys; Industrial revenue bonds; REAL ESTATE: Acquisitions; Joint ventures; Partnerships/Syndications
PREFERRED TYPES OF INDUSTRIES/INVESTMENTS: Income Real Estate
WILL NOT CONSIDER: Home loans
GEOGRAPHIC LIMITS OF INVESTMENTS/LOANS: National
RANGE OF INV./LOAN PER BUSINESS: Min. $500,000
PREFERRED TERM FOR LONAS & LEASES: Min. 3-5 years; Max. 30 years
BUSINESS CHARACTERISTICS DESIRED-REQUIRED: Depends on Borrower

COMPANY: **Community First Bank, Mortgage Div.**
ADDRESS: 810 Chester
Bakersfield, CA 93301
PHONE: (805) 395-3270
TYPE OF INSTITUTION: Commercial Bank
CONTACT OFFICER(S): Grady Buck
ASSETS: $100,000,000+
TYPES OF FINANCING: VENTURE CAPITAL: Research & Development; Start-up from developed product stage; First-stage (less than 1 year); Second-stage (generally 1-3 years); Later-stage expansion; Buy-outs/Acquisitions; LOANS: Unsecured; Working capital (receivables/inventory); Equipment; REAL ESTATE LOANS: Long-term senior mtg.; Other: Short-term; REAL ESTATE: Acquisitions
GEOGRAPHIC LIMITS OF INVESTMENTS/LOANS: Local
PREFERRED TERM FOR LOANS & LEASES: Min. 1-3 years; Max. 5 years
REFERALS ACCEPTED FROM: Borrower/Investee
REMARKS: Min. of 2 years in business for loans other than venture capital

COMPANY: **C. A. Larson Investment Company**
ADDRESS: 8929 Wilshire Blvd., Suite 115
Beverly Hills, CA 90211
PHONE: (213) 657-8311
TYPE OF INSTITUTION: Mortgage Bankers
CONTACT OFFICER(S): W. V. Watts, President
J. E. Settles, Vice President
Hal D. Richmond, Ass't Vice President
ASSETS: $500 million
INVESTMENTS/LOANS MADE: for own (company's or principals') account
INVESTMENTS/LOANS MADE: Only in securities with a secondary market
TYPES OF FINANCING: REAL ESTATE LOANS: Long-term senior mtg.; Intermediate-term senior mtg.; Subordinated, Wraparounds; Land; Standbys; Second T. D.'s; REAL ESTATE: Acquisitions; Joint ventures
GEOGRAPHIC LIMITS OF INVESTMENTS/LOANS: State
RANGE OF INV./LOAN PER BUSINESS: Min. $500,000; Max. $70,000,000
PREFERRED TERM FOR LOANS & LEASES: Min. 3 years; Max. 30 years

COMPANY: **George Elkins Co.**
ADDRESS: 499 N. Canon Drive
Beverly Hills, CA 90210
PHONE: (213) 272-3456
TYPE OF INSTITUTION: Mortgage bank; R.E. Management; Commercial/Res. Broker
CONTACT OFFICER(S): Ron Robbins, Sr. V.P.
ASSETS: $100 million
INVESTMENTS/LOANS MADE: For own (company's or principals') account
TYPES OF FINANCING: REAL ESTATE LOANS: Long-term senior mtg.; Intermeediate-term senior mtf.; Subordinated; Land; Land development; Construction; Subordinated to leasehold; REAL ESTATE:: Acquisitions; Joint ventures; Partnerships
GEOGRAPHIIC LIMITS OF INVESTMENTS/LOANS: National; mostly West Coast
RANGE OF INV./LOAN PER BUSINESS: Min. $500,000

COMPANY: **Hollingsworth & Lord, Inc.**
ADDRESS: 9301 Wilshire Blvd., P.O. Box 5358
Beverly Hills, CA 90210
PHONE: (213) 272-5800
TYPE OF INSTITUTION: Mortgage Banker
CONTACT OFFICER(S): Clifford W. Lord, Chairman
TYPES OF FINANCING: REAL ESTATE LOANS: Long-term senior mtg.; Intermediate-term senior mtg.; Income producing loans; Subordinated; Wraparounds; Land; Land development; Construction; Gap; Standbys; 1st and 2nd mortgages
GEOGRAPHIC LIMITS OF INVESTMENTS/LOANS: Regional; Western U.S.; HI; Alaska
RANGE OF INV./LOAN PER BUSINESS: Min. $500,000; Max. $50,000,000
PREFERRED TERM FOR LOANS & LEASES: Min. 3 years; Max. 30+ years

COMPANY: **Metropolitan Venture Company, Inc.**
ADDRESS: 8383 Wilshire Boulevard, Suite 360
Beverly Hills, CA 90211-2410
PHONE: (213) 651-2171
CONTACT OFFICER(S): Esther Lowy, President
ASSETS: $1,000,000
INVESTMENTS/LOANS MADE: In securities with a secondary market; Securities without a secondary market
TYPES OF FINANCING: VENTURE CAPITAL: Second-stage; Buy-outs; Acquisitions; LOANS; Working capital; Equipment; REAL ESTATE
PREFERRED TYPES OF INDUSTRIES/INVESTMENTS: Real Estate
GEOGRAPHIC LIMITS OF INVESTMENTS/LOANS: State (CA)

RANGE OF INV./LOAN PER BUSINESS: Min. $50,000; Max. $200,000
PREFERRED TERM FOR LOANS & LEASES: Min. 5 years; Max. 10 years
REFERRALS ACCEPTED FROM: Investment/Mortgage Banker or Borrower/Investee

COMPANY: **Wallace Moir Co.**
ADDRESS: 9595 Wilshire Blvd.
Beverly Hills, CA 90212
PHONE: (213) 273-7300
TYPE OF INSTITUTION: Mortgage Banker
CONTACT OFFICER(S): Wayne R. Knickmeyer, Exec. V.P.
TYPES OF FINANCING: REAL ESTATE LOANS: Long-term senior mtg.
PREFERRED TYPES OF INDUSTRIES/INVESTMENTS: Hotels, Motels & Restaurants; Medical & Other Health Services; Retailing, Wholesaling & Distribution
GEOGRAPHIC LIMITS OF INVESTMENTS/LOANS: National
RANGE OF INV./LOAN PER BUSINESS: Min. $1,000,000
PREFERRED TERM FOR LOANS & LEASES: Min. 5 years; Max. 30 years

COMPANY: **Glen Fed Corp.**
ADDRESS: P.O. Box 7712
Burbank, CA 91510
PHONE: (818) 507-5000
TYPE OF INSTITUTION: Mortgage Banker
CONTACT OFFICER(S): Hnery Mattel, President
ASSETS: Servicing Volume over $100,000,000
INVESTMENTS/LOANS MADE: for managed accounts
INVESTMENTS/LOANS MADE: Only in securities with a secondary market
TYPES OF FINANCING: REAL ESTATE LOANS: Long-term senior mtg.; Intermediate-term senior mtg.
GEOGRAPHIC LIMITS OF INVESTMENTS/LOANS: Regional
RANGE OF INV./LOAN PER BUSINESS: Min. $500,000; Max. $7,000,000
PREFERRED TERM FOR LOANS & LEASES: Min. 15-20; Max. 20+ years
BRANCHES: Mike Madlock, 13931 S. Hawthorne Blvd., Hawthorne, CA 90250; (213) 644-2266
Harvey Ricin, 521 W. Channel Islands Blvd., #6, Port Hueneme, CA 93041; (805) 984-8080
Bill Swailes, 229 E. Badillo St., Covina, CA 91723; (818) 331-0691
Wade Andrews, 11021 Winners Circle #206, Los Alamitos, CA 90720; (213) 636-7950
Carole McCormack, 1900 E. 4th St., #140, Santa Ana, CA 92705; (213) 746-2144
Phil Hamilton, 438 Camino del Rio South, #211, San Diego, CA 92108; (619) 294-4500
Earl & Cheryl Hamilton, 2828 Shadelands Dr., #115, Walnut Creek, CA 94598; (415) 938—6490
Sam Jiron, 1405 N. San Fernando Blvd., Burbank, CA 91504; (818) 841-9911
Kris Clark, 16310 E. Whittier Blvd., Whittier, CA 90603; (213) 947-9481

COMPANY: **Wm. Stanwell Co.**
ADDRESS: 1140 Galaxy Way, Suite 100
Concord, CA 94520
PHONE: (415) 825-2250
TYPE OF INSTITUTION: Mortgage banker
CONTACT OFFICER(S): Tim Mulholland, P.O. Box 15025, Las Vegas, NV 89114; (702) 873-3940
ASSETS: Servicing volume over $300,000,000
TYPES OF FINANCING: REAL ESTATE LOANS: Long-term senior mtg.; Wraparounds; Land; Standbys
GEOGRAPHIC LIMITS OF INVESTMENTS/LOANS: National
RANGE OF INV./LOAN PER BUSINESS: Min. $500,000; Max. None
BRANCHES: Tim Mulholland, P.O. Box 15025, Las Vegas, NV 89114; (702) 873-3940
Hiroshi Imanura, 567 So. King St., Suite 328, Honolulu, HI 96813; (808) 523-8691
Bill Delange, 1112 Cole Rd., Box 4546, Boise, ID 83704; (208) 322-8868
Bonnie Cornelius, 1755 E. Plumb Lane, Suite 249, Reno, NV 89502; (702) 786-6335

COMPANY: **Pacific Lighting Leasing Company (parent)/ Pacific Lighting Commercial Loans, Inc. (subsidiary)**
ADDRESS: 6140 Bristol Parkway
Culver City, CA 90230
PHONE: (213) 642-7595
Wholly owned Leasing and Finance subsidiary of NYSE company
CONTACT OFFICER(S): William M. Hamburg, Vice President—Leasing & Lending
Waldo A. Rodman, Director of Leasing & Remarketing
ASSETS: $76,000,000
INVESTMENTS/LOANS MADE: For own account
INVESTMENTS/LOANS MADE: In securities with a secondary market and in securities without a secondary market
TYPES OF FINANCING: VENTURE CAPITAL; Second-stage; Later-stage; Buy-outs/Acquisitions; LOANS: Equipment; Equity-related; REAL ESTATE LOANS: Intermediateterm senior mtg.; Subordinated; Gap; Standbys; LEASES: Single-investor; Tax leases; Non-tax leases; Operating; Tax-oriented lease brokerage; Vendor financing programs
PREFERRED TYPES OF INDUSTRIES/INVESTMENTS: Office Equipment; Production Equipment; Restaurant; Medical; Air Conditioning; other
WILL NOT CONSIDER: Automobiles
GEOGRAPHIC LIMITS OF INVESTMENTS/LOANS: National
RANGE OF INV./LOAN PER BUSINESS: Min. $2,500; Max. $5,000,000
PREFERRED TERM FOR LOANS & LEASES: Min. 3 yrs; Max. 7 yrs
BUSINESS CHARACTERISTICS DESIRED/REQUIRED: Minimum number of years in business: 0; Min. annual sales $1,000,000
REFERRALS ACCEPTED FROM: Investment/Mortgage banker or Borrower/Investee

CALIFORNIA

COMPANY: **Genstar Mortgage Corp.**
ADDRESS: 700 N. Central Ave.
Glendale, CA 91203
PHONE: (818) 956-5600
TYPE OF INSTITUTION: Mortgage banker
CONTACT OFFICER(S): Arthur F. Collins, Sr. V.P., Finance
ASSETS: 168 million
INVESTMENTS/LOANS MADE: For own account
INVESTMENTS/LOANS MADE: Only in securities with a secondary market
TYPES OF FINANCING: REAL ESTATE LOANS: Long-term mtg.;
PREFERRED TYPES OF INDUSTRIES/INVESTMENTS: FHA/VA loans
GEOGRAPHIC LIMITS OF INVESTMENTS/LOANS: National;

COMPANY: **STM Mortgage Co.**
ADDRESS: 10741 Los Alamitos Blvd., P.O. Box 458
Los Alamitos, CA 90720
PHONE: (213) 594-8871
TYPE OF INSTITUTION: Mortgage banker
CONTACT OFFICER(S): John Hood, Branch Manager
TYPES OF FINANCING: REAL ESTATE LOANS: Long-term senior mtg.
BRANCHES: 2355 Stemmons Frwy., Dallas, TX 75207; (214) 637-4950

COMPANY: **American Consolidated Equities**
ADDRESS: 2029 Century Park E, #960
Los Angeles, CA 90067
PHONE: (213) 277-6318
CONTACT OFFICER(S): Tony Sarno, Controller

COMPANY: **Bank of Palm Springs**
ADDRESS: 444 S. Flower Street, Ste 2220
Los Angeles, CA 90071
PHONE: (213) 488-9951
TYPE OF INSTITUTION: R. E. Lender
CONTACT OFFICER(S): Alan P. Livadas, V.P.

COMPANY: **Beneficial Standard Life Insurance Company**
ADDRESS: 3700 Wilshire Blvd., Suite 250
Los Angeles, CA 90010
PHONE: (213) 381-8291
TYPE OF INSTITUTION: Life Insurance Company
CONTACT OFFICER(S): Peter H. Ulrich, Director, Mortgage Investments
James C. Whitten, Ass't. Dir., Mortgage Investments
Tina K. Kelly, Ass't. Dir., Mortgage Investments
INVESTMENTS/LOANS MADE: For own account
TYPES OF FINANCING: REAL ESTATE LOANS: OTHER: First mortgages only
PREFERRED TYPES OF INDUSTRIES/INVESTMENTS: Mortgages on Income producing Real Estate — Apartments, Office Buildings, and Shopping Centers
WILL NOT CONSIDER: Single purpose income producing properties
GEOGRAPHIC LIMITS OF INVESTMENTS/LOANS: Prefer western states, Texas and Oklahoma
RANGE OF INV./LOAN PER BUSINESS: Min. $200,000; Max. $2,000,000
PREFERRED TERM FOR LOANS & LEASES: Min. 5; Max. 25 years
BUSINESS CHARACTERISTICS DESIRED-REQUIRED: Min. number of years in business: 0
REFERRALS ACCEPTED FROM: Investment/Mortgage banker

COMPANY: **Charterhouse Investment Company**
ADDRESS: 1801 Ave of the Stars, Ste 525
Los Angeles, CA 90067
PHONE: (213) 277-2100
CONTACT OFFICER(S): Ronald G. Cox, President

COMPANY: **Coldwell Banker Real Estate Finance Services—Division of Coldwell Banker Commercial Group, Incorporated**
ADDRESS: 533 Fremont Avenue
Los Angeles, CA 90071
PHONE: (213) 613-3331
TYPE OF INSTITUTION: Debt and Equity—Mortgage banking
CONTACT OFFICER(S): Robert Morgan, Pres/General Manager
TYPES OF FINANCING: REAL ESTATE LOANS: Long-term senior mtg.; Intermediate-term senior mtg.; Wraparounds; Gap; Standbys; Industrial revenue bonds, REAL ESTATE: Acquisitions; Joint ventures
PREFERRED TYPES OF INDUSTRIES/INVESTMENTS: All types of income producing property
GEOGRAPHIC LIMITS OF INVESTMENTS/LOANS: National
RANGE OF INV./LOAN PER BUSINESS: Min. $300,000; Max. $50 million +
PREFERRED TERM FOR LOANS & LEASES: Max. 15 years
REFERRALS ACCEPTED FROM: Borrower/Investee
REMARKS: 20 branches

COMPANY: **Dwyer-Curlet Co.**
ADDRESS: 6336 Wilshire Blvd.
Los Angeles, CA 90048
PHONE: (213) 653-8300
TYPE OF INSTITUTION: Mortgage banker
CONTACT OFFICER(S): Robert McCarter, Exec. V.P.
TYPES OF FINANCING: REAL ESTATE LOANS: Long-term senior mtg.; Intermediate-term senior mtg.
PREFERRED TYPES OF INDUSTRIES/INVESTMENTS: Industrial buildings; Medical and other health services
GEOGRAPHIC LIMITS OF INVESTMENTS/LOANS: Local
RANGE OF INV./LOAN PER BUSINESS: Min. $500,000; Max. $5,000,000
PREFERRED TERM FOR LOANS & LEASES: Min. 10 years; Max. 15 years
BRANCHES: Richard K.C. Lau, Dwyer-Curlet-Pacific, Inc., Suite 1610, 841 Bishop St., Davies Pacific Center, Honolulu, HI 96813; (808) 524-4166

COMPANY: **Farmers New World Life Insurance Co.**
ADDRESS: 4680 Wilshire Blvd.
Los Angeles, CA 90010
PHONE: (213) 932-3275

TYPE OF INSTITUTION: Insurance Co.
CONTACT OFFICER(S): Harold F. Gingrich, V.P.

COMPANY: **Growth Realty Companies**
ADDRESS: 2029 Century Park East, Suite 2000
Los Angeles, CA 90067
PHONE: (213) 277-3110
CONTACT OFFICER(S): Robert D. Saunders, Exec. V.P. and C.O.O.
Lewis W. Dolson, Chairman, Growth Realty Financial
Robert Riley, V.P.
ASSETS: $100,000,000
INVESTMENTS/LOANS MADE: For own account, For managed accounts
TYPES OF FINANCING: REAL ESTATE LOANS: Long-term senior mtg.; Land development; Construction; Other: Mortgage-lending area, REAL ESTATE: Acquisitions; Joint ventures; Partnerships/Syndications
PREFERRED TYPES OF INDUSTRIES/INVESTMENTS: Commerical properties
GEOGRAPHIC LIMITS OF INVESTMENTS/LOANS: National; International; Other: England, P.R., Nova Scotia
RANGE OF INV./LOAN PER BUSINESS: Min. $1-20 million

COMPANY: **Key Stone Mortgage Co.**
ADDRESS: Suite 300, 11340 W. Olympic Blvd.
Los Angeles, CA 90064
PHONE: (213) 479-4121
TYPE OF INSTITUTION: Mortgage banker
CONTACT OFFICER(S): Ron Buchanan, V.P.
Christopher E. Turner, Exec. V.P.
TYPES OF FINANCING: REAL ESTATE LOANS: Long-term senior mtg.
GEOGRAPHIC LIMITS OF INVESTMENTS/LOANS: Local/Southern California
RANGE OF INV./LOAN PER BUSINESS: Min. $300,000; Max. None

COMPANY: **Lloyds Bank California**
ADDRESS: 612 S. Flower Street
Los Angeles, CA 90017
PHONE: (213) 613-2673
TYPE OF INSTITUTION: R. E. Lender
CONTACT OFFICER(S): Kenneth A. Haydis, 613-2682

COMPANY: **Mitsui Manufacturers Bank**
ADDRESS: 135 East 9th Street
Los Angeles, CA 90015
PHONE: (213 688-8100
CONTACT OFFICER(S): Price Scott, S.V.P.
Alan Naiman, V.P.
TYPES OF FINANCING: REAL ESTATE LOANS: Interim Construction Financing
PREFERRED TYPES OF INDUSTRIES/INVESTMENTS: Office Buildings; Shopping Centers; Industrial Buildings
GEOGRAPHIC LIMITS OF INVESTMENTS/LOANS: State: CADon Dolreis, Mitsui Manufacturers Bldg., 9701 Wilshire Blvd, Beverly Hills, CA 90212, (213) 205-3700
Ira Morrison, Mitsui Manufacturers Bldg. #13, 16255 Ventura blvd., Encino, CA 91436, (213) 716-4500
Miles Wittie, Mitsui Manufacturers Bldg. #20, One Newport Plaza, Newport Beach, CA 92610, (714) 752-0600
REMARKS:

COMPANY: **Molton/Cooper Mortgage Investors, Inc.**
ADDRESS: 9800 S. Sepulveda Blvd., Suite 520
Los Angeles, CA 90045
PHONE: (213) 822-3011
TYPE OF INSTITUTION: Mortgage Banking Corporation
CONTACT OFFICERS(S): Robert B. Cooper, President
INVESTMENTS/LOANS MADE: Through private placements
TYPES OF FINANCING: LOANS: Equity-related; REAL ESTATE LOANS: Long-term senior mtg.; Intermediate-term senior mtg.; Subordinated; Wraparounds; Land development; Construction; Gap; Standbys; Industrial revenue bonds; REAL ESTATE: Acquisitions; Joint ventures;
GEOGRAPHIC LIMITS OF INVESTMENTS/LOANS: Local; State; Regional; National
RANGE OF INV./LOAN PER BUSINESS: Min. $500,000; Max. $ None
PREFERRED TERM FOR LOANS & LEASES: Min. 3 years; Max. 30 years
REFERRALS ACCEPTED FROM: Investment/Mortgage banker;Borrower/Investee

COMPANY: **Santa Anita Realty Enterprises, Inc.**
ADDRESS: One Wilshire Bldg., #2303
Los Angeles, CA 90017
PHONE: (213) 485-9220
TYPE OF INSTITUTION: REIT
CONTACT OFFICER(S): Glen Carpenter, V.P., Finance (714) 990-8964
Royce B. McKinley, Pres.

COMPANY: **Security Pacific National Bank**
ADDRESS: 333 South Hope Street
Los Angeles, CA 90051
PHONE: (213) 631-6211
TYPE OF INSTITUTION: Mortgage Banker
CONTACT OFFICER(S): Robert Hamaguchi
ASSETS: $43,000,000,000
TYPES OF FINANCING: REAL ESTATE LOANS: Long-term senior mtg.; Intermediate-term senior mtg.; Subordinated; Wraparounds; Land; Land development; construction; Gap; Standbys; Industrial revenue bonds, REAL ESTATE: Joint ventures; Partnerships/ Syndications
GEOGRAPHIC LIMITS OF INVESTMENTS/LOANS: Max. $20-25 Million
RANGE OF INV./LOAN PER BUSINESS: Min. 3 years; Max. 5 years
REMARKS: Branches all over California and U.S.

COMPANY: **Transamerica Realty Services**
ADDRESS: Hill and Olive at 12th St.
Los Angeles, CA 90015
PHONE: (213) 742-3141

TYPE OF INSTITUTION: Subsidiary of Trans America Corporation
CONTACT OFFICER(S): Kelly Stevens, Corporate & Mortgage Financing
ASSETS: $1 billion and up
TYPES OF FINANCING: REAL ESTATE LOANS: Intermediate-term senior mtg.; Wraparounds; Land; Land development; Gap; Standbys; REAL ESTATE: Acquisitions; Joint ventures
PREFERRED TYPES OF INDUSTRIES/INVESTMENTS: Apartments, R&D, Offices, Shopping centers
GEOGRAPHIC LIMITS OF INVESTMENTS/LOANS: National
RANGE OF INV./LOAN PER BUSINESS: Min. $1 million; Max. $20 million

COMPANY: **Transamerica Occidental Life Insurance Co.**
ADDRESS: 1150 South Olive St., Ste. 2700
Los Angeles, CA 90015
PHONE: (213) 742-3555
CONTACT OFFICER(S): Charles R. Drake, V.P.
Walter Kirkbride, V.P.
TYPES OF FINANCING: SECONDARY-MARKET CORPORATE SECURITIES: Common stock; Preferred stock; Bonds, REAL ESTATE: Acquisitions; Joint ventures; Partnerships/Syndications, SERVICES PROVIDED: Not a lender, just an investor
PREFERRED TYPES OF INDUSTRIES/INVESTMENTS: Diversified
GEOGRAPHIC LIMITS OF INVESTMENTS/LOANS: National; International; Other: Canada, Australia
RANGE OF INV./LOAN PER BUSINESS: Min. $2 million; Max. $10 million

COMPANY: **Wells Fargo Mortgage and Equity Trust**
ADDRESS: P.O. Box 30015
Los Angeles, CA 90030
PHONE: (213) 822-2032
TYPE OF INSTITUTION: REIT
CONTACT OFFICER(S): Frederick W. Petri, Pres.
A. Larry Chapman, E.V.P.
Dale Bentz, S.V.P.
TYPES OF FINANCING: LOANS, REAL ESTATE LOANS: Construction; REAL ESTATE: Acquisitions; Joint ventures; Partnerships/Syndications
PREFERRED TYPES OF INDUSTRIES/INVESTMENTS: Non-Residential; Conventional
GEOGRAPHIC LIMITS OF INVESTMENTS/LOANS: National
RANGE OF INV./LOAN PER BUSINESS: Min. $1 million; Max. $30 million
BUSINESS CHARACTERISTICS DESIRED-REQUIRED: Financial strength
REMARKS: Managed by Wells Fargo Realty Advisors

COMPANY: **Wells Fargo Realty Advisors**
ADDRESS: 330 Washington St.
Marina Del Rey, CA
PHONE: (213) 822-2032
TYPE OF INSTITUTION: Real estate subsidiary of Bank Holding Co. (Wells Fargo & Co.)
CONTACT OFFICER(S): Fred Petri, President
A. Larry Chapman, Exec. Vice President
Dale Bentz, Sr. Vice President
ASSETS: $1.7 billion (Wells Fargo Realty Adv.); $28 Billion (Wells Fargo & Co.)
INVESTMENTS/LOANS MADE: For own account; for managed accounts; through private placements
TYPES OF FINANCING: LOANS: Unsecured; REAL ESTATE LOANS: Intermediate-term senior mtg.; Subordinated (seconds); Land; Land deveopment; Construction; Secured & unsecured lines of credit; REAL ESTATE: Acquisitions; Joint ventures; In addition to managing its own "Loan Portfolio", WFRA manages 3 separate entities (1) "Wells Fargo Mortgage and Equity Trust" (REIT); (2) "Wells Fargo Real Estate Equity Fund" (Domestic Co-Mingled Pension Fund; (3) "Wells Fargo Property Unit Trust" (U.K. Pension Fund)
PREFERRED TYPES OF INDUSTRIES/INVESTMENTS: Make real estate loans to national & regional developers; invest funds of entities we manage for joint ventures, real estate investments (completed properties); Participating mortgages. Will make contingent interest loans for WFRA.
WILL NOT CONSIDER: Long term mortgages
GEOGRAPHIC LIMITS OF INVESTMENTS/LOANS: National
RANGE OF INV./LOAN PER BUSINESS: Min. $1 million; Max. $100 million
PREFERRED TERM FOR LOANS & LEASES: Min. 1 year; Max. 7 years
BUSINESS CHARACTERISTICS DESIRED-REQUIRED: Experienced, professional R/E developers with proven track record and strong financial condition
REFERRALS ACCEPTED FROM: Borrower/Investee

COMPANY: **Pacific Real Estate Investment Trust**
ADDRESS: 750 Menlo Ave.
Menlo Park, CA 94025
PHONE: (415) 327-7147
TYPE OF INSTITUTION: REIT
CONTACT OFFICER(S): Harry E. Kellogg, Pres.

COMPANY: **Coldwell Banker Real Estate Services**
ADDRESS: 4440 Von Karman
Newport Beach, CA 92660
PHONE: (714) 955-4006
CONTACT OFFICER(S): Robert Morgan, President
TYPES OF FINANCING: REAL ESTATE LOANS: Long-term senior mtg.; Intermediate-term senior mtg.; Wraparounds; Other: Equity Participation; REAL ESTATE: Acquisitions; Joint ventures
PREFERRED TYPES OF INDUSTRIES/INVESTMENTS: Office Buildings; Medical; Light Industrial/Office
GEOGRAPHIC LIMITS OF INVESTMENTS/LOANS: National
RANGE OF INV./LOAN PER BUSINESS: Min. $5 million
PREFERRED TERM FOR LOANS & LEASES: Min. 3 years; Max. 15 years

COMPANY: **United Business Ventures, Inc.**
ADDRESS: 3931 MacArthur, Ste. 212
Newport Beach, CA 92660

PHONE: (714) 851-0855
CONTACT OFFICER(S): Leslie R. Brewer, President
ASSETS: $3.5 million
INVESTMENTS/LOANS MADE: For own account
INVESTMENTS/LOANS MADE: Only in securities without a secondary market
TYPES OF FINANCING: VENTURE CAPITAL: Start-up from developed product stage; First-stage; Second-stage; Later-stage expansions; Buy-outs/Acquisitions; LOANS: Working capital; equipment; equity related; REAL ESTATE LOANS: Subordinated; Land deveolpment; Construction; Gap; INTERNATIONAL; REAL ESTATE: Acquisitions; Joint ventures; OTHER SERVICES PROVIDED: Management consulting—financial planning, budgeting, financing
PREFERRED TYPE OF INDUSTRIES/INVESTMENTS: Manufacturing; Equipment based services; franchises
WILL NOT CONSIDER: R & D, Films, Publications
GEOGRAPHIC LIMITS OF INVESTMENTS/LOANS: State
RANGE OF INV./LOAN PER BUSINESS: Min. $50,000; Max. 300,000
PREFERRED TERM FOR LOANS & LEASES: Min. 5 years; Max. 10 years
BUSINESS CHARACTERISTICS DESIRED-REQUIRED: Minimum number of years in business: 0; Min. annual sales $500,000 projected; Min. net worth $50,000; Min. Annual net income $60,000; Min. annual cash flow $90,000
REFERRALS ACCEPTED FROM: Investment/Mortgage banker or Borrower/Investee
BRANCHES: 130 Montgomery St., San Francisco, CA 94104; (415) 392-5400

COMPANY: **First California Business and Industrial Development Corporation**
ADDRESS: 3931 MacArthur Blvd., Suite 212
Newport Beach, CA 92660
PHONE: (714) 851-0855
TYPE OF INSTITUTION: Business Development Company/Small Business Lending
CONTACT OFFICER(S): Leslie R. Brewer, President
INVESTMENTS/LOANS MADE: For own account
TYPES OF FINANCING: VENTURE CAPITAL, First-stage (less than 1 year), Second-stage (generally 1-3 years), Later-stage expansion, Buy-outs/Acquisitions; LOANS, Working capital (receivables/inventory), Equipment; REAL ESTATE LOANS, Long-term senior mtg.; Intermediate-term senior mtg., Subordinated; INTERNATIONAL; OTHER SERVICES PROVIDED, Management consulting, Financial planning, Budgeting, Financing
PREFERRED TYPES OF INDUSTRIES/INVESTMENTS: Manufacturing; Equipment based services; Franchises
WILL NOT CONSIDER: R & D, Films, Publications
GEOGRAPHIC LIMITS OF INVESTMENTS/LOANS: State
RANGE OF INV./LOAN PER BUSINESS: Min. $50,000; Max. $550,000
PREFERRED TERM FOR LOANS & LEASES: Min. 7 years; Max. 25 years
BUSINESS CHARACTERISTICS DESIRED-REQUIRED: Minimum number of years in business: 0; Min. annual sales $500,000 Projected; Min. net worth $50,000; Min. annual net income $60,000; Min. annual cash flow $90,000
REFERRALS ACCEPTED FROM: Investment/Mortgage banker; Borrower/investee
BRANCHES: 130 Montgomery St., San Francisco, CA 94104, (415) 392-5400

COMPANY: **Am Cal Company**
ADDRESS: 4737 Lankershim Blvd.
North Hollywood, CA
PHONE: (818) 763-6206
TYPE OF INSTITUTION: Real Estate Investment Adviser
CONTACT OFFICER(S): S. Q. DellaGrotta, Executive Vice President, Marketing
ASSETS: $325 million
INVESTMENTS/LOANS MADE: For managed accounts
TYPES OF FINANCING: REAL ESTATE LOANS: Long-term senior mtg.; Intermediate-term senior mtg.; REAL ESTATE: Acquisitions; OTHER SERVICES PROVIDED: Real Estate "workouts" of distressed properties; writing Real Estate Investment guidelines for Pension Funds.
PREFERRED TYPES OF INDUSTRIES/INVESTMENTS: Income producing Real Estate (office and professional buildings; industrial parks; mini-warehouses; shopping centers; apartment complex, etc.).
WILL NOT CONSIDER: Land Banking
GEOGRAPHIC LIMITS OF INVESTMENTS/LOANS: National
PREFERRED TERM FOR LOANS & LEASES: Min. Leases: 3-5 years; loans: 7 years; Max. Loans: 12-15 years
BUSINESS CHARACTERISTICS DESIRED-REQUIRED: Case-by-case basis

COMPANY: **Equitec Properties Company**
ADDRESS: 7677 Oakport St.
Oakland, CA 94614
PHONE: (415) 430-9900
TYPE OF INSTITUTION: Financial Services
CONTACT OFFICER: Duane Barney, V.P., Mortgage (Oakland)
Jim Keene, Senior Analyst—Mortgage (Oakland)
ASSETS: Total corporate assets: $2 billion; Mortgage assets: $150 million
INVESTMENTS/LOANS MADE: For managed accounts
INVESTMENTS/LOANS MADE: In securities with a secondary market and in securities without a secondary market
TYPES OF FINANCING: REAL ESTATE LOANS: Long-term senior mtg.; wraparounds; REAL ESTATE: Acquisitions; Partnerships/Syndications
PREFERRED TYPES OF INDUSTRIES/INVESTMENTS: Income producing real estate acquisitions and loans for shopping centers, light industrial office, office buiding, and apartments.
WILL NOT CONSIDER: Special purpose properties
GEOGRAPHIC LIMITS OF INVESTMENTS/LOANS: National; Metropolitan areas
BRANCHES: Alan Jones, 200 West Monroe, Ste 1504, Chicago, IL 60606; (312) 899-1934
Dave Freeman, 5501 LBJ Freeway, Ste 301 , Dallas, TX 75250; (214) 385-2393

REAL ESTATE LENDERS & INVESTORS

(Real Estate Financing—Loans, Partnerships, Joint Ventures and Acquisitions. Also see Investment Bankers, Mutual Savings Bankers & Finance Companies)

COMPANY: **Mason-McDuffie Financial Corporation**
ADDRESS: 4 Orinda Way, Ste. 240D
Orinda, CA 94563
PHONE: (415) 254-9060
TYPE OF INSTITUTION: Mortgage Banker
CONTACT OFFICER(S): Michael W. Davis, President
ASSETS: Servicing volume over $550,000,000
TYPES OF FINANCING: REAL ESTATE LOANS: Long-term senior mtg.; Intermediate-term senior mtg.; Subordinated; Land; Construction; Sale-Leaseback, REAL ESTATE: Acquisitions; Joint ventures
GEOGRAPHIC LIMITS OF INVESTMENTS/LOANS: Regional
RANGE OF INV./LOAN PER BUSINESS: Min. $1 million; Max. over $40,000,000
PREFERRED TERM FOR LOANS & LEASES: Min. 5-20 years; Max. 20+ years

COMPANY: **First Interstate Mortgage Co.**
ADDRESS: 245 S. Los Robles Ave.
Pasadena, CA 91109
PHONE: (818) 356-7600
TYPE OF INSTITUTION: Mortgage banker
CONTACT OFFICER(S): Norman R. Richards, Exec. V.P.
INVESTMENTS/LOANS MADE: REAL ESTATE LOANS: Long-term senior mtg., intermediate-term senior mtg., Standbys, Bullet loans, Tax exempt mtgs., Mtgs. with income participation; REAL ESTATE: Joint ventures; OTHER SERVICES PROVIDED: Corp. finance, Land sale lease-back, Interest-accrual loans, Equity purchases, Standby eq. purchases
PREFERRED TYPE OF INDUSTRIES/INVESTMENTS: Medical, Retail, Offices, Shopping Centers, R&D, Industrial Buildings & Parks, Hotels, Motels, Retirement facilities
GEOGRAPHIC LIMITS OF INVESTMENTS/LOANS: National
RANGE OF INV./LOAN PER BUSINESS: Min. 1 million
BUSINESS CHARACTERISTICS DESIRED-REQUIRED: Minimum number of years in business: 0
REFERRALS ACCEPTED FROM: Investment/Mortgage banker or Borrower/Investee
BRANCHES: Bill S. Hamilton, S.V.P., 17291 Irvine Blvd., Tustin, CA 92680; (714) 558-5432
George Boynton, S.V.P., 123 Camino de la Reina, San Diego, CA 92108; (714) 293-7115
Neil Nostrand, Exec. V.P., Suite 2401, One Embarcadero Center, San Francisco, CA 94111; (415) 544-5907

COMPANY: **Union Bank**
ADDRESS: 225 S. Lake Avenue
Pasadena, CA 91101
PHONE: (818) 304-1700
TYPE OF INSTITUTION: Asset-Based Financing Group of Bank
CONTACT OFFICER(S): Theodore Kompa, Vice Pres. & Reg. Manager (So. Calif.) Asset Based Loans
Michael J. Riley, Vice Pres. & Reg. Manager, (No. Calif.) Asset Based Loans
Robert C. Andreasen, Vice Pres. & Manager, Equipment Finance and Leasing
ASSETS: $8 Billion
INVESTMENTS/LOANS MADE: For own account
TYPES OF FINANCING: Working capital (receivables/inventory), Equipment; REAL ESTATE LOANS: Intermediate-term senior mtg.; LEASES: Single-investor, Leveraged, Tax leases, Non-tax leases, Operating, Tax-oriented lease brokerage, Lease syndications, Vendor financing programs; OTHER SERVICES PROVIDED: Leverage Buyout Financing
PREFERRED TYPES OF INDUSTRIES/INVESTMENTS: Manufacturing, Distribution, Wholesaling. Prefer income-producing equipment for lease and loan transactions
GEOGRAPHIC LIMITS OF INVESTMENTS/LOANS: National
RANGE OF INV./LOAN PER BUSINESS: Min. $500,000; Max. $60,000,000
PREFERRED TERM FOR LOANS & LEASES: Min. 2 years; Max. 10 years
BUSINESS CHARACTERISTICS DESIRED-REQUIRED: Minimum number of years in business: 2; Min. annual sales $5,000,000; Min. net worth $200,000; Min. annual net income $50,000; Min annual cash flow $75,000
REFERRALS ACCEPTED FROM: Investment/Mortgage banker or Borrower/Investee
BRANCHES: 225 South Lake Avenue, 6th Floor, Pasadena, CA 91101, 818-304-1700, Theodore Kompa
460 Hegenberger Rd., Oakland, CA 94604, (415) 772-8158, Michael J. Riley

COMPANY: **The Whittle Investment Company**
ADDRESS: 234 East Colorado Boulevard, Suite 514
Pasadena, CA 91101
PHONE: (818) 795-5123
TYPE OF INSTITUTION: Mortgage banker
CONTACT OFFICER(S): Merril J. Ostler, Vice President
ASSETS: Over $100,000,000
INVESTMENTS/LOANS MADE: For own account; For managed accounts; Through private placements
TYPES OF FINANCING: REAL ESTATE LOAN: Long-term senior mtg., Intermediate-term senior mtg., Wraparound; REAL ESTATE: Joint ventures, Partnerships/Syndications
PREFERRED TYPES OF INDUSTRIES/INVESTMENTS: General purpose commercial and industrial properties
GEOGRAPHIC LIMITS OF INVESTMENTS/LOANS: Local; Southern California
RANGE OF INV./LOAN PER BUSINESS: Min. $250,000
PREFERRED TERM FOR LOANS & LEASES: Min. 3-15 years; Max. 20+ years
REFERRALS ACCEPTED FROM: Investment/Mortgage banker or Borrower/Investee

COMPANY: **Westland Mortgage Service Co.**
ADDRESS: P.O. Box 254978
Sacramento, CA 95825
PHONE: (916) 488-5500
TYPE OF INSTITUTION: Mortgage banker
CONTACT OFFICER(S): Charles Barnaby, Asst.V.P.
Brian Lyttle, Exec. V.P.
TYPES OF FINANCING: REAL ESTATE LOANS: Long-term senior mtg., OTHER SERVICES PROVIDED: Tax exempt bond financing for multi-family projects
WILL NOT CONSIDER: Commercial financing

GEOGRAPHIC LIMITS OF INVESTMENTS/LOANS: National
RANGE OF INV./LOAN PER BUSINESS: Min. $500,000
PREFERRED TERM FOR LOANS & LEASES: Min. 10 years
BRANCHES: Gary Zellmer, 574 Manzanita Ave., Chico, CA 95926; (916) 891-5966
Tim Dalske, 1007 Live Oak Blvd., Yuba City, CA 95991; (916) 671-4710
Priscilla Taylor, 5651 No. Pershing, Stockton, CA; (209) 957-5961
Byron Cook, 3100 Mill St., Reno, NV; (702) 329-6591
Roger Linhart, 2501 Catlin St., Missoula, MT 59801; (406) 549-4191

COMPANY: **Central Savings & Loan Assn.**
ADDRESS: 225 Broadway
San Diego, CA 92138
PHONE: (619) 236-8725
CONTACT OFFICER(S): James Broome, Mgr.

COMPANY: **John Burnham & Co.**
ADDRESS: 1555 Sixth Ave.
San Diego, CA 92101
PHONE: (619) 236-1555
TYPE OF INSTITUTION: R. E. Lender
CONTACT OFFICER(S): Steven Quinn, S. V.P.

COMPANY: **Pacific Southwest Mortgage**
ADDRESS: 3333 Camino Del Rio S., Ste 420
San Diego, CA 92108
PHONE: (619) 280-1600
TYPE OF INSTITUTION: Mortgage Banker
CONTACT OFFICER(S): D. R. 'Randy' Schwartz, V.P.

COMPANY: **San Diego Trust and Savings Bank**
ADDRESS: 530 Broadway
San Diego, CA
PHONE: (619) 238-4647
TYPE OF INSTITUTION: R.E. Lender
CONTACT OFFICER(S): Richard Yven, Corporate, (619) 238-5028
Phil Wilson, Loan Administration, (619) 238-4649
ASSETS: $922,080,000
TYPES OF FINANCING: REAL ESTATE LOANS: Construction
PREFERRED TYPES OF INDUSTRIES/INVESTMENTS: Commercial construction of all types
GEOGRAPHIC LIMITS OF INVESTMENTS/LOANS: Local; Other: San Diego County
RANGE OF INV./LOAN PER BUSINESS: Max. under $10,000,000

COMPANY: **BA Mortgage and International Realty Corp.**
ADDRESS: 500 Waslington St., 4th Floor
San Francisco, CA 94111
PHONE: (415) 622-8363
TYPE OF INSTITUTION: Mortgage banker/Investment Co.
CONTACT OFFICER(S): Jerry South, President
TYPES OF FINANCING: REAL ESTATE LOANS: Intermediate-term senior mtg.; Subordinated; Wraparounds; Land; Land development; Construction; Standbys; Industrial Revenue Bonds; Other: Sale-leaseback, REAL ESTATE: Joint Ventures; Partnerships
BUSINESS CHARACTERISTICS DESIRED-REQUIRED: Minimum number of years in business: 0; Min. annual sales $1,500,000; Min. net worth $1,000,000; Min. annual net income $150,000; Min. annual cash flow $200,000
BRANCHES: Donald Gianone, Division Pres., BA Mortgage Company of Chicago, 55 W. Monroe, Ste. 2330 Chicago, IL 60603; (312) 876-7290
Peter Asch, V. P., BA Mortgage Company of Dallas, 8150 N. Central Expressway, St. 875, Dallas, TX 75206; (214) 696-6953
Gerry Thomas, BA Mortgage Company of Denver, 4700 S. Syracuse Parkway, Ste. 804, Denver, CO 80237; (303) 770-3883
Herb Hedley, BA Mortgage Company of Houston, 6750 West Loop South, Suite 770, Bellaire, TX 77401; (713) 667-3000
Floyd Rush, President, BA Mortgage Company of Georgia, 57 Executive Park South, Suite 495, Atlanta, GA 30329; (404) 321-5600
Lee Lannoye, Division President, BA Mortgage Company of Washington, 11058 Main St., Bellevue, WA 98004; (206) 451-8120
James Clendening, Division President, BA Mortgage Company of Tampa, 5201 W. Kennedy Blvd., Lincoln Center, Suite 601, Tampa, FL 33609; (813) 877-8191
John McIntosh, Peninsula Branch of BA Mortgage Co., 530 Litton Ave., Suite 308, Palo Alto, CA 94305; (415) 328-2860
Greg Grandchamp, Century City branch of BA Mortgage Co., 2049 Century Park East, Suite 3060, Los Angeles, CA 90067; (213) 550-3557
Gib Gorman, BA Mortgage of Arizona, 777 E. Missouri, Suite 119, Phoenix, AZ 85014; (602) 274-3161

COMPANY: **The Bank of California, N.A.**
ADDRESS: 400 California Street
San Francisco, CA 94104
PHONE: (415) 765-0400
TYPE OF INSTITUTION: R. E. Lender
CONTACT OFFICER(S): David A. Bryant, Ext. 2281

COMPANY: **Bankamerica Realty Investors**
ADDRESS: Suite 4275, 555 California Street
San Francisco, CA 94104
PHONE: (415) 622-6530
TYPE OF INSTITUTION: Real estate investment trust
CONTACT OFFICER(S): Howard E. Mason, Jr., Senior V.P., Finance
ASSETS: $197,000,000
INVESTMENTS/LOANS MADE: For own account
TYPES OF FINANCING: LOANS: Equity-related, REAL ESTATE LOANS: Long-term senior mtg.; Intermediate-term senior mtg.; Subordinated; Wraparounds, REAL ESTATE: Acquisitions
PREFERRED TYPES OF INDUSTRIES/INVESTMENTS: Office and light industrial buildings, apartments, shopping centers

GEOGRAPHIC LIMITS OF INVESTMENTS/LOANS: National
RANGE OF INV./LOAN PER BUSINESS: Min. $1,000,000; Max. $5,000,000

COMPANY: **Barry S. Slatt Mortgage Co.**
ADDRESS: 50 California Street, Ste 770
San Francisco, CA 94111
PHONE: (415) 392-2467
TYPE OF INSTITUTION: Mortgage Banker
CONTACT OFFICER(S): Barry S. Slatt
Terance O'Mahoney

COMPANY: **California Real Estate Investment Trust**
ADDRESS: 601 Montgomery St., Suite 800
San Francisco, CA 94111
PHONE: (415) 433-1805
TYPE OF INSTITUTION: REIT
CONTACT OFFICER(S): E. Samuel Wheeler, President
ASSETS: $34 million
TYPES OF FINANCING: REAL ESTATE LOANS: Other: Equity-related; REAL ESTATE: Acquisitions; Joint ventures; Partnerships/Syndications
PREFERRED TYPES OF INDUSTRIES/INVESTMENTS: Office Buildings; Shopping Centers; Apartments; R&D; Light Industrial
WILL NOT CONSIDER: Special Purpose
GEOGRAPHIC LIMITS OF INVESTMENTS/LOANS: Other: CA; TX
RANGE OF INV./LOAN PER BUSINESS: Min. $4 million (purchase price) 2 million (cash investment); Max. $10 million (purchase price) 4 million (cash investment)
PREFERRED TERM FOR LOANS & LEASES: Min. 5 years
BUSINESS CHARACTERISTICS DESIRED-REQUIRED: Minimum number of years in business: 1
REFERRALS ACCEPTED FROM: Investment/Mortgage banker or Borrower/Investee
BRANCHES: Gary L. Marsh, 10830 N. Central Expressway Suite 300, (214) 691-7171, Dallas, TX 75231

COMPANY: **Crocker Mortgage Company, Inc.**
ADDRESS: One Montgomery Street West Tower 18th fl.
San Francisco, CA 94105
PHONE: (415) 984-2307
TYPE OF INSTITUTION: Mortgage Banker
CONTACT OFFICER(S): James D. MacKinnon
ASSETS: $5 billion in servicing
TYPES OF FINANCING: REAL ESTATE LOANS: Long-term senior mtg.; Intermediate-term senior mtg.; Subordinated; Wraparounds; Construction; Gap; Standbys; Industrial revenue bonds; REAL ESTATE: Joint ventures
PREFERRED TYPES OF INDUSTRIES/INVESTMENTS: Income Properties
GEOGRAPHIC LIMITS OF INVESTMENTS/LOANS: National
RANGE OF INV./LOAN PER BUSINESS: Min. $1 million
PREFERRED TERM FOR LOANS & LEASES: Min. 3 years; Max. 30 years
REMARKS: Branches in: Los Angeles CA; San Francisco CA; Irvine CA; Dallas TX

COMPANY: **Davis Skaggs Capital**
ADDRESS: 160 Sansome Street
San Francisco, CA 94104
PHONE: (415) 392-7700
TYPE OF INSTITUTION: Venture capital and investment banking
CONTACT OFFICER(S): Charles P. Stetson, Jr., 393-0274, President
Robert S. Miller, Chairman
INVESTMENTS/LOANS MADE: For own account, through private placements
TYPES OF FINANCING: VENTURE CAPITAL: First-stage; Second-stage; Later-stage expansion; Buy-outs/Acquisitions, OTHER SERVICES PROVIDED: financial consulting service w/investment
REMARKS: Now owned by Shearson-Lehman Am. Express

COMPANY: **E.S. Merriman & Sons**
ADDRESS: 3200 Crocker Plaza, Suite 3200
San Francisco, CA 94104
PHONE: (415) 397-2200
TYPE OF INSTITUTION: Mortgage banker
CONTACT OFFICER(S): James A. Walker, President
Ronald Rankin, V. P.
TYPES OF FINANCING: REAL ESTATE LOANS, REAL ESTATE: Acquisitions
GEOGRAPHIC LIMITS OF INVESTMENTS/LOANS: Regional
RANGE OF INV./LOAN PER BUSINESS: Min. $500,000; Max. $30,000,000
PREFERRED TERM FOR LOANS & LEASES: Min. 10-15 years; Max. 20+ years

COMPANY: **First Nationwide Savings/Mortgage Banking Department**
ADDRESS: 700 Market Street
San Francisco, CA 94102
PHONE: (415) 772-1532
CONTACT OFFICER(S): Don Cootz, S.V.P. Secondary Marketing
ASSETS: $10,000,000,000+
TYPES OF FINANCING: REAL ESTATE: Long-term senior mtg.; Intermediate-term senior mtg; Subordinated; Waraparoundss; Land; Land development; Construction; Gap; Standbys; Industrial revenue bonds, REAL ESTATE: Acquuisitions; Joint ventures; Partnerships/Syndications
PREFERRED TYPES OF INDUSTRIES/INVESTMENTS: Medium income range housing lending
GEOGRAPHIC LIMITS OF INVESTMENTS/LOANS: National
RANGE OF INV./LOAN PER BUSINESS: Min. $20,000; Max. $20,000,000
PREFERRED TERM FOR LOANS & LEASES: Max. $30 years
REMARKS: Main lending offices: CA, FL, NY

CALIFORNIA

COMPANY: **The Hibernia Bank**
ADDRESS: 201 California Street
San Francisco, CA 94111
PHONE: (415) 565-7320
TYPE OF INSTITUTION: R.E. Lender
CONTACT OFFICER(S): Larry Smith, Construction Lending, (415) 565-7416 John Weingartner, Permanent Financing, (415) 565-7573
Len Saver, General, (415) 565-7571
ASSETS: $1,280,317,000
TYPES OF FINANCING: REAL ESTATE: Long-term senior mtg.; Intermediate-term senior mtg.; Ssubordinated; Wraparounds; Land; Land development; Construction; Gap; Standbys; Industrial revenue bonds, REAL ESTATE: Acquisitions; Joint ventures; Partnerships/Syndications, OTHER: In the future will be able to do joint ventures; Real estate investment advisory
PREFERRED TYPES OF INDUSTRIES/INVESTMENTS: General Commercial
WILL NOT CONSIDER: Condominium
GEOGRAPHIC LIMITS OF INVESTMENTS/LOANS: Regional; Other: West Coast
RANGE OF INV./LOAN PER BUSINESS: Min. $2,000,000 (construction), $5,000,000 (permanent); Max. $25,000,000 and up
PREFERRED TERM FOR LOANS & LEASES: Varies

COMPANY: **Norris, Beggs & Simpson**
ADDRESS: 243 Kearny St.
San Francisco, CA 94108
PHONE: (415) 362-5660
TYPE OF INSTITUTION: Mortgage Banker/R.E. Investment/Lessor
CONTACT OFFICER(S): Michael Corsetti, V.P.
ASSETS: Servicing Volume over $100,000,000
TYPES OF FINANCING: REAL ESTATE LOANS: Long-term senior mtg.; Intermediate-term senior mtg.; Subordinated; Wraparounds. LEASING: Single investor; Lease brokerage. REAL ESTATE: Acquisitions; Joint Ventures; Partnerships/ Syndications.
GEOGRAPHIC LIMITS OF INVESTMENTS/LOANS: Regional; WA, OR, CA, HI
RANGE OF INV./LOAN PER BUSINESS: Min. $200,000; Max. $100,000,000

COMPANY: **Redwood Bank**
ADDRESS: 735 Montgomery Street
San Francisco, CA 94111
PHONE: (415) 788-3700
TYPE OF INSTITUTION: R. E. Lender
CONTACT OFFICER(S): Tom Moulton

COMPANY: **The RREEF Funds, Inc.**
ADDRESS: 650 California Street
San Francisco, CA 94108
PHONE: (415) 781-3300
CONTACT OFFICER(S): Richard Bertero
Martin L. Cannon

COMPANY: **The Sierra Capital Companies**
ADDRESS: 300 Montgomery St., Suite 525
San Francisco, CA 94104
PHONE: (415) 391-0129
TYPE OF INSTITUTION: Real Estate Investment-Advisor to the Sierra Real Estate Equity Trusts
CONTACT OFFICER(S): Thomas B. Swartz, Chr. & CEO
Robert R. Walker, Jr., Pres.-Acquisitions
Wm. B. Stevenson, Sr. V-Pres.-Acquisitions
ASSETS: $100+M
INVESTMENTS/LOANS MADE: For own account
TYPES OF FINANCING: REAL ESTATE: Acquisitions; Joint ventures; Partnerships/Syndications
PREFERRED TYPES OF INDUSTRIES/INVESTMENTS: Commercial and industrial; Retail; Office; Residential for private offering only
WILL NOT CONSIDER: Raw land
GEOGRAPHIC LIMITS OF INVESTMENTS/LOANS: Regional; Sunbelt; Mountain & Western States; Other metropolitan growth areas
RANGE OF INV./LOAN PER BUSINESS: Min. $5M; Max. $15M

COMPANY: **T.W. Richardson & Co., Inc.**
ADDRESS: 601 California Street, Suite 301
San Francisco, CA
PHONE: (415) 391-2880
TYPE OF INSTITUTION: Investment manager, real estate developer, investor
CONTACT OFFICER(S):Thomas W. Richardson, President
ASSETS: $10,000,000
INVESTMENTS/LOANS MADE: For own account and for managed accounts
INVESTMENTS/LOANS MADE: In securities with a secondary market and in securities without a secondary market
TYPES OF FINANCING: SECONDARY-MARKET CORPORATE SECURITIES: Common stock; Preferred stock, VENTURE CAPITAL: Buy-outs/Acquisitions, REAL ESTATE: Acquisitions; Joint ventures; Partnerships/Syndications
PREFERRED TYPES OF INDUSTRIES/INVESTMENTS: Real estate investment companies with office-industrial portfolios and/or undeveloped land assets; operating companies with same.
WILL NOT CONSIDER: Limited partner positions, loans, passive investments, real estate service businesses
GEOGRAPHIC LIMITS OF INVESTMENTS/LOANS: Regional; Western and southern states
RANGE OF INV./LOAN PER BUSINESS: Min. $500,000; Max. $3,000,000
BUSINESS CHARACTERISTICS DESIRED-REQUIRED: Min. number of years in business: 3
REFERRALS ACCEPTED FROM: Investment/Mortgage banker or Investee

CALIFORNIA

COMPANY: **Trans America Realty Investors**
ADDRESS: 600 Montgomery St.
San Francisco, CA 94111
PHONE: (415) 983-5420; 5400
TYPE OF INSTITUTION: Real Estate Co.
CONTACT OFFICER(S): Kent L. Colwell, President
John Benzie, V.P. Finance
ASSETS: $46.7 million
INVESTMENTS/LOANS MADE: For own account
TYPES OF FINANCING: REAL ESTATE: Acquisitions; Joint ventures; Partnerships
PREFERRED TYPES OF INDUSTRIES/INVESTMENTS: Institutional Grade Real Estate
GEOGRAPHIC LIMITS OF INVESTMENTS/LOANS: Regional; Other: West Coast
RANGE OF INV./LOAN PER BUSINESS: Min. $2 million; Max. $8 million
BRANCHES: Kelly Stevens, 1150 S. Olive, Los Angeles, CA (213) 742-3141

COMPANY: **Wells Fargo Realty Finance**
ADDRESS: 600 Montgomery St.
San Francisco, CA 94111
PHONE: (415) 396-5111
TYPE OF INSTITUTION: Mortgage Banker
CONTACT OFFICER(S): George Tillotson, President
ASSETS: 150,000,000
TYPES OF FINANCING: REAL ESTATE LOANS: Long-term senior mtg.; Gap; Long-term Arranged; Short-term made directly; REAL ESTATE: Acquisitions; Joint ventures; R.E. Acquisitions and Jt. ventures arranged
GEOGRAPHIC LIMITS OF INVESTMENTS/LOANS: Regional; Southern & Western states
BRANCHES: 226 W. Brokaw, Suite 630, San Jose, CA 95110; (408) 277-6270
3420 Ocean Park Blvd., Suite 3030, Santa Monica CA 90405; (213) 450-8811
1600 Dove Street, Newport Beach, CA 92660

COMPANY: **Western Investment R.E. Trust**
ADDRESS: P.O. Box 18277
San Francisco, CA 94118
PHONE: (415) 755-1411
TYPE OF INSTITUTION: REIT
CONTACT OFFICER(S): Bernard Etcheverry, Secretary
O.A. Talmage, V. Chairman (415) 221-2032
Chester R. MacPhee, Jr., C.F.O. (415) 668-6606
ASSETS: $24 million (share holder's equity)
TYPES OF FINANCING: REAL ESTATE: Acquisitions, OTHER SERVICES PROVIDED: Developer has property and tenants—needs some buyer
PREFERRED TYPES OF INDUSTRIES/INVESTMENTS: Commercial
WILL NOT CONSIDER: Residential
GEOGRAPHIC LIMITS OF INVESTMENTS/LOANS: Regional; Other: CA, NV
RANGE OF INV./LOAN PER BUSINESS: Min. 1 million Max. 6 million
REMARKS: American Stock Exchange Co.

COMPANY: **First California Mortgage Co.**
ADDRESS: 1401 Los Gamos Drive
San Rasale, CA 94939
PHONE: (415) 492-1008
TYPE OF INSTITUTION: Mortgage Banking
CONTACT OFFICER(S): Bob Williams, V.P.
ASSETS: $200,000,000
INVESTMENTS/LOANS MADE: For own account
TYPES OF FINANCING: REAL ESTATE LOANS: Long-term senior mtg.; Intermediate-term senior mtg.; Subordinated, REAL ESTATE: Partnerships/ Syndications, OTHER SERVICES PROVIDED: Insurance Services
PREFERRED TYPES OF INDUSTRIES/INVESTMENTS: Residential Developments in Calif., Nevada, Arizona
RANGE OF INV./LOAN PER BUSINESS: Min. $1,000,000; Max. $10,000,000
BRANCHES: James C. Munson, 1031 15th St.,Suite 3, P.O. Box 3443, Modesto, CA, 95354; (209) 527-2500
Margaret Garcia, 2750 North Texas St. #300, P.O. Box 732, Fairfield, CA, 94533; (707) 429-5210
Anne Ray, V.P., 7700 College Town Drive #216, P.O. Box 25-5394, Sacramento, CA, 95865; (916) 381-4050
Marlene McEvoy, 2129 Fourth Street, P.O. Box 532, Santa Rosa, CA, 95402; (707) 525-8362
Diana Pinner, 2001 North 3rd St., Suite 108, Phoenix, AZ, 85004; (602) 252-5900
Jim LaBranch, 230 Mt. Herman Road #209, P.O. Box 66869, Scotts Valley, CA, 95066; (408) 438-5666

COMPANY: **Butterfield Capital Corporation**
ADDRESS: 200 E. Sandpointe Ave.
Santa Ana, CA 92707
PHONE: (714) 241-4600; (800) 221-2562
TYPE OF INSTITUTION: Real Estate Syndication
CONTACT OFFICER(S): David W. Endresen, Chairman and Chief Acquisitions Officer
David A. Foley, Vice President/Acquisitions
Charles W. Wadell Jr., Vice President/Acquisitions
INVESTMENTS/LOANS MADE: Through private placements
TYPES OF FINANCING: REAL ESTATE: Acquisitions; Joint ventures; Partnerships/Syndications
PREFERRED TYPES OF INDUSTRIES/INVESTMENTS: Multi-family Residential; Office Buildings; Shopping Centers
WILL NOT CONSIDER: Special purpose situations

GEOGRAPHIC LIMITS OF INVESTMENTS/LOANS: National
RANGE OF INV./LOAN PER BUSINESS: Min. $2500,000; Max. $15,000,000
REFERRALS ACCEPTED FROM: Investment/Mortgage banker or Borrower/Investee

COMPANY: **Real Estate Investment Trust of California**
ADDRESS: 2444 Wilshire Blvd., Suite 300
Santa Monica, CA 90403
PHONE: (213) 829-6892
TYPE OF INSTITUTION: REIT
CONTACT OFFICER(S): William Walters, Jr., Pres.
LeRoy Carlson, C.F.O.
ASSETS: $40 million (under management)
TYPES OF FINANCING: REAL ESTATE LOANS: Other: First trust deed RE loans; REAL ESTATE: Acquisitions; Joint ventures; Partnerships/Syndications; OTHER SERVICES PROVIDED: Considering RE Loans
PREFERRED TYPES OF INDUSTRIES/INVESTMENTS: Commercial Complexes; Shopping Centers; Apartments
GEOGRAPHIC LIMITS OF INVESTMENTS/LOANS: State; Other: Primarily Southern CA—Ventura County
RANGE OF INV./LOAN PER BUSINESS: Min. $500,000; Max. $10 million
BUSINESS CHARACTERISTICS DESIRED-REQUIRED: Min. annual cash flow Immediate positive; Other: Must be able to make 10% return to shareholders

COMPANY: **States Realty Co.**
ADDRESS: 3032-B Exposition Blvd.
Santa Monica, CA 90404
PHONE: (213) 829-2132; 479-1525
TYPE OF INSTITUTION: Real estate construcion/take-out loans (all types)
CONTACT OFFICER(S): Stephen A. Gianni, President
INVESTMENTS/LOANS MADE: Through private placements
TYPES OF FINANCING: REAL ESTATE LOANS: Construction; StandbysREAL ESTATE: Partnerships/Syndications.OTHER SERVICES PROVIDED: Financing for R.E. Construction listing & sales income producing properties (all types)
GEOGRAPHIC LIMITS OF INVESTMENTS/LOANS: Local; State; Regional; National
RANGE OF INV./LOAN PER BUSINESS: Min. $100,000; Max. $40,000,000
PREFERRED TERM FOR LOANS & LEASES: Min. 10-40 years
BUSINESS CHARACTERISTICS DESIRED-REQUIRED: Minimum number of years in business: 25 ('0' if startups financed);

COMPANY: **Real Estate Investment Properties**
ADDRESS: 21031 Ventura Blvd., Ste 315
Woodland Hills, CA 91364
PHONE: (818) 883-9510
TYPE OF INSTITUTION: Real Estate Investment Trust
CONTACT OFFICER(S): Glenn A. Ellis, Treasurer
Brian J. Farrell, Director of Operations
ASSETS: $48,000,000
INVESTMENTS/LOANS MADE: For own account
TYPES OF FINANCING: REAL ESTATE: Acquisitions
PREFERRED TYPES OF INDUSTRIES/INVESTMENTS: Hotel investments—direct ownership
GEOGRAPHIC LIMITS OF INVESTMENTS/LOANS: National
RANGE OF INV./LOAN PER BUSINESS: Min. $3,000.000; Max. $20,000.000
REFERRALS ACCEPTED FROM: Investment/Mortgage banker or Borrower/Investee

COMPANY: **Boettcher & Company, Inc.**
ADDRESS: 828 17th St.
Denver, CO 80202
PHONE: (303) 628-8000
TYPE OF INSTITUTION: Investment Banker
CONTACT OFFICER(S): Stanley Fallis, Chief Financial Officer, 303-628-8294
Robert Manning, Stephen G. McConahey
ASSETS: $80 million
INVESTMENTS/LOANS MADE: Through private placements, Underwriting public offerings
INVESTMENTS/LOANS MADE: In securities with a secondary market and in securities without a secondary market
TYPES OF FINANCING: SECONDARY-MARKET CORPORATE SECURITIES: Common stock; Preferred stock; Bonds; R. Estate, REAL ESTATE LOANS, REAL ESTATE
PREFERRED TYPES OF INDUSTRIES/INVESTMENTS: Diversified
GEOGRAPHIC LIMITS OF INVESTMENTS/LOANS: Regional; Rocky Mountain region
REFERRALS ACCEPTED FROM: Investment/Mortgage banker or Borrower/Investee

COMPANY: **Cambridge Venture Partners**
ADDRESS: 88 Steele Street, Suite 200
Denver, CO 80206
PHONE: (303) 393-1111
TYPE OF INSTITUTION: Private venture capital fund
CONTACT OFFICER(S): Bruce B. Paul, Managing Partner - all areas
Jack Snyder General Partner - Medical technology
ASSETS: $12,200,000
INVESTMENTS/LOANS MADE: For own account; Through private placements
INVESTMENTS/LOANS MADE: In securities with a secondary market and only in securities without a secondary market
TYPES OF FINANCING: VENTURE CAPITAL: Research & Development; Start-up from developed product stage; First-stage (less than 1 year); Second-stage (generally 1-3 years); Later-stage expansion; Buy-out/Acqusitions; LOANS: Working Capital; REAL ESTATE: Acqusitions
PREFERRED TYPES OF INDUSTRIES/INVESTMENTS: Advanced communications, computer and medical technology
GEOGRAPHIC LIMITS OF INVESTMENTS/LOANS: Regional; prefer Rocky Mountain region and West Coast region
RANGE OF INV./LOAN PER BUSINESS: Min. $100,000; Max. $500,000
BUSINESS CHARACTERISTICS DESIRED-REQUIRED: Minimum number of years in business: 0

BRANCHES: Jack Snyder, 18610 Bernardo Trails Drive, San Diego, CA 92128; (619) 485-9692; Jack Snyder

COMPANY: **Capitol Life Insurance Co.**
ADDRESS: P.O. Box 1200
Denver, CO 80201
PHONE: (303) 861-4065
CONTACT OFFICER(S): Kenneth Peterson, Sr. V.P.
Paul K. Moyer Sr.V.P.
ASSETS: 2.4 Billion
INVESTMENTS/LOANS MADE: Only in securities without a secondary market
TYPES OF FINANCING: LOANS: Equity-related; REAL ESTATE LOANS: Long-term senior mtg.; Intermediate-term senior mtg; Short term mtg
GEOGRAPHIIC LIMITS OF INVESTMENTS/LOANS: National
RANGE OF INV./LOAN PER BUSINESS: Min. $2 million; Max. $10 million
PREFERRED TERM FOR LOANS & LEASES: Min. 7 years; Max. 10 years
BUSINESS CHARACTERISITICS DESIRED-REQUIRED: Minimum number of years in business: 0; Must have a business plan

COMPANY: **Colorado National Mortgage Co.**
ADDRESS: 950 17th St., Ste. 100
Denver, CO 80202
PHONE: (303) 893-1913
TYPE OF INSTITUTION: Mortgage Banker
CONTACT OFFICER(S): Ray Yostin, V.P.
TYPES OF FINANCING: REAL ESTATE LOANS: Long-term senior mtg; Other: Commerical and residential
GEOGRAPHIC LIMITS OF INVESTMENTS/LOANS: Regional; CO, WY
PREFERRED TERM FOR LOANS & LEASES: Max. 30 years

COMPANY: **Cowperthwaite & Co.**
ADDRESS: 3575 Cherry Creek Dr. N., Ste. 200
Denver, CO 80209
PHONE: (303) 399-2962
TYPE OF INSTITUTION: Mortgage Banker
CONTACT OFFICER(S): Ginny Howe, Loan Officer
Stephen Cowperthwaite, Loan Officer
ASSETS: Servicing Volume $10,000,000-100,000,000
TYPES OF FINANCING: LOANS, REAL ESTATE LOANS:
PREFERRED TYPES OF INDUSTRIES/INVESTMENTS: Shopping Centers; Warehouses; Office Buildings
GEOGRAPHIC LIMITS OF INVESTMENTS/LOANS: Regional
RANGE OF INV./LOAN PER BUSINESS: Min. $600,000
REMARKS: Average term of loans is 30 years

COMPANY: **IntraWest Mortgage Company**
ADDRESS: 14th Fl, 633 17th St.
Denver, CO 80270
PHONE: (303) 292-2900
TYPE OF INSTITUTION: Mortgage Banker
CONTACT OFFICER(S): L. Cleve Brown, V.P.
ASSETS: Servicing Volume over $1.4 billion
TYPES OF FINANCING: REAL ESTATE LOANS: Long-term senior mtg.; Intermediate-term senior mtg.; Wraparounds; OTHER: Land sale-leasebacks; Equity placements
GEOGRAPHIC LIMITS OF INVESTMENTS/LOANS: Regional, CO; NM; WY
RANGE OF INV./LOAN PER BUSINESS: Min. $300,000
REMARKS: Will be opening a branch in Colorado Springs

COMPANY: **Mellon Financial Services Corporation #9**
ADDRESS: 2300 Mellon Financial Center
Denver, CO 80203
PHONE: (303) 837-2000
TYPE OF INSTITUTION: Mortgage banker
CONTACT OFFICER(S): Robert E. Skolout, President
ASSETS: $10,000,000-100,000,000
TYPES OF FINANCING: REAL ESTATE LOANS: Long-term senior mtg.; Construction; OTHER: Participation Loans
GEOGRAPHIC LIMITS OF INVESTMENTS/LOANS: Regional
RANGE OF INV./LOAN PER BUSINESS: Min. $250,000
PREFERRED TERM FOR LOANS & LEASES: Max. 20+ years
BRANCHES: Henry Saldana, Asst. V.P., 3225 N. Central Ave., Suite 102, Phoenix, AZ 85012; (602) 277-5521
Bill Fanning, Asst. V.P., 1311 S. College Ave. #1, Ft. Collins, CO 80521; (303) 482-2914
REMARKS: Branches to be opened December 1984: N.W. Denver, Gary Garten; S.E. Denver, Mike Laveo; Colorado Springs, Bernie Alberter

COMPANY: **Moore Mortgage Co.**
ADDRESS: 300 Speer Boulevard
Denver, CO 80203
PHONE: (303) 778-1800
TYPE OF INSTITUTION: Mortgage bankers
CONTACT OFFICER(S): T. K. Jones, Pres.
D.L. Franz, S.V.P. Residential Loan; Kennth A. Portz, S.V.P. Marketing; Rod Johnson, V.P. Finance
ASSETS: $230,000,000 under service
INVESTMENTS/LOANS MADE: For own account, For managed accounts, Through private placements
TYPES OF FINANCING: REAL ESTATE LOANS: Long-term senior mtg.; Intermediate-term senior mtg.; Subordinated; Wraparounds; Land; Land development; Standbys; Industrial revenue bonds
PREFERRED TYPES OF INDUSTRIES/INVESTMENTS: Medical & other health services; real estate, apartments, office buildings, office-warehouses; industrial
WILL NOT CONSIDER: Motel/hotels, restaurants, recreational facilities, single-purpose buildings
GEOGRAPHIC LIMITS OF INVESTMENTS/LOANS: State
RANGE OF INV./LOAN PER BUSINESS: Min. $250,000; Max. None
PREFERRED TERM FOR LOANS & LEASES: Min. 5 years; Max. 30 years
BUSINESS CHARACTERISTICS DESIRED-REQUIRED: Minimum number of years in business: 0; Other: All things in proper relationship to loan requested

REFERRALS ACCEPTED FROM: Investment/Mortgage banker or Borrower/Investee

COMPANY: **National Farmers Union Life Insurance Company**
ADDRESS: 12025 E. 45th Avenue
Denver, CO 80239
PHONE: (303) 371-1760
TYPE OF INSTITUTION: Insurance Company
CONTACT OFFICER(S): L. C. Ellis, Asst. V.P., Stocks & Bonds
Deborah Birdwhistell, Mortgage Investment Supervisor, Commercial Real Estate
ASSETS: $10,000,000 - $100,000,000
INVESTMENTS/LOANS MADE: For own account
INVESTMENTS/LOANS MADE: In securities with a secondary market and in securities without a secondary market
TYPES OF FINANCING: SECONDARY-MARKET CORPORATE SECURITIES: Common stock; Preferred stock; Bonds, REAL ESTATE LOANS: Long-term senior mtg.; Intermediate-term senior mtg.; Industrial revenue bonds
PREFERRED TYPES OF INDUSTRIES/INVESTMENTS: Real Estate, Commercial, 75% of appraised value by a qualified appraiser.
GEOGRAPHIC LIMITS OF INVESTMENTS/LOANS: Regional
RANGE OF INV./LOAN PER BUSINESS: Min. $300,000; Max. $1,000,000
PREFERRED TERM FOR LOANS & LEASES: Min. 10-15; Max. 20 years & up
BUSINESS CHARACTERISTICS DESIRED-REQUIRED: Minimum number of years in business 7;Min. net worth 2 x loan; Min. annual net income 1.3 x loan
REFERRALS ACCEPTED FROM: Investment/Mortgage banker or Borrower/Investee

COMPANY: **National Mortgage Co.**
ADDRESS: 1550 E. 17th Av., P.O. Box 18309
Denver, CO 80218
PHONE: (303) 832-9500
TYPE OF INSTITUTION: Mortgage Banker
CONTACT OFFICER(S): Zelie Berenbaum, Pres.
ASSETS: Servicing Volume over $100,000,000
TYPES OF FINANCING: REAL ESTATE LOANS: Long-term senior mtg.
PREFERRED TYPES OF INDUSTRIES/INVESTMENTS: Apartments; Shopping Centers; Warehouses; Offices
GEOGRAPHIC LIMITS OF INVESTMENTS/LOANS: Regional
RANGE OF INV./LOAN PER BUSINESS: Min. $250,000
PREFERRED TERM FOR LOANS & LEASES: Max. 20+ years

COMPANY: **Silverado Capital Corporation**
ADDRESS: 655 Broadway, Suite 100
Denver, CO 80203
PHONE: (303) 893-2311
TYPE OF INSTITUTION: Mortgage Banking, Business, Business Real Estate, Income Producing
CONTACT OFFICER(S): Mr. Allan H. Rouse, Senior Vice President
Mr. Steven C. Greenwald, Vice President - Loan Administration and Business Real Estate Loans
ASSETS: $6.9 million
INVESTMENTS/LOANS MADE: Through private placements
TYPES OF FINANCING: LOANS: Other: Small Business Administration (SBA) & Farmers Home Administration (FmHA); REAL ESTATE LOANS: Long-term senior mtg.; Intermediate-term senior mtg.; Subordinated; Wraparounds; Land; Land development; Construction; Gap; Standbys; Industrial revenue bonds.
PREFERRED TYPES OF INDUSTRIES/INVESTMENTS: All types of Income Producing Properties
RANGE OF INV./LOAN PER BUSINESS: Min. $100,000; Max. $ Open
PREFERRED TERM FOR LOANS & LEASES: Max. 30 years
BUSINESS CHARACTERISTICS DESIRED-REQUIRED: Minimum number of years in business; -0-
BRANCHES: Mr. Michael T. Lacy, 3225 N. Central Ave., Suite 1005, Phoenix, AZ 85012, (602) 279-2009

COMPANY: **Uniwest Financial Corp.**
ADDRESS: 7979 E. Tufts Ave. Parkway, Suite #110
Denver, CO
PHONE: (303) 694-9777
TYPE OF INSTITUTION: Financial Services, Savings and Loan Holdings Co.
CONTACT OFFICER(S): Chuck McKelvey, Executive Vice President Real Estate; James R. Newman, National Credit Manager Leasing; John Holzman, Vice President Securities
ASSETS: $250,000,000
INVESTMENTS/LOANS MADE: For own account; Through private placements
INVESTMENTS/LOANS MADE: In securities with a secondary market and in securities without a secondary market
TYPES OF FINANCING: VENTURE CAPITAL: First-stage (less than 1 year); Second-stage (generally 1-3 years); REAL ESTATE LOANS: Construction; LEASES; REAL ESTATE: Acquisitions; Joint ventures; Partnerships/Syndications
PREFERRED TYPES OF INDUSTRIES/INVESTMENTS: Real Estate, Leasing
GEOGRAPHIC LIMITS OF INVESTMENTS/LOANS: Sun Belt States
RANGE OF INV./LOAN PER BUSINESS: Min. $250,000; Max. $10,000,000
PREFERRED TERM FOR LOANS & LEASES: Min. One-Three years; Max. Thirty years

COMPANY: **Van Schaack & Co.**
ADDRESS: 950 - 17th St., S 1100
Denver, CO 80202
PHONE: (303) 572-5307
TYPE OF INSTITUTION: Mortgage Banker
CONTACT OFFICER(S): Scott Morris, Director Jack Timpe V.P. Marketing
ASSETS: Servicing Volume over $400,000,000
TYPES OF FINANCING: REAL ESTATE LOANS: Long-term senior mtg.; Intermediate-term senior mtg.; Construction; Other: Commercial

GEOGRAPHIC LIMITS OF INVESTMENTS/LOANS: Regional
RANGE OF INV./LOAN PER BUSINESS: Min. $350,000; Max. $100,000,000
PREFERRED TERM FOR LOANS & LEASES: Min. 1 year; Max. 30 years

COMPANY: **Parker Benjamin, Inc.**
ADDRESS: 120 Mountain Avenue
Bloomfield, CT 06002
PHONE: (203) 242-7277
TYPE OF INSTITUTION: Private Investment Bank serving primarily middle market companies and real estate developers
CONTACT OFFICER(S): Paul M. Ruby, President, Mergers and Acquisitions, Venture Capital
Thomas A. D'Avanzo, Executive Vice President, Private Placement of Debt, Real Estate Financing, Industrial Revenue Bonds Apprisals
INVESTMENTS/LOANS MADE: Through private placements
INVESTMENTS/LOANS MADE: VENTURE CAPITAL: Research & Development; Start-up from developed product stage; First-stage (less than 1 year); Second-stage (generally 1-3 years); Later-stage expansion; Buy-outs/Acquistions; LOANS: Unsecured to credits above Baa; Working capital (receivables/inventory); Equipment; Equity-related; Other: Industrial Revenue Bonds; REAL ESTATE LOANS: Long-term senior mtg.; Intermediate-term senior mtg.; Subordinated; Wraparounds; Land; Land development; Construction; Gap; Standbys; Industrial revenue bonds; LEASES: Single-Investor; Leveraged; Tax leases; Non-tax leases; Operating; Tax-oriented lease brokerage; vendor financing programs; REAL ESTATE: Acquisitions; Joint ventures; OTHER SERVICES PROVIDED: Appraisal of privately owned businesses
PREFERRED TYPES OF INDUSTRIES/INVESTMENTS: All
GEOGRAPHIC LIMITS OF INVESTMENTS/LOANS: International
RANGE OF INV./LOAN PER BUSINESS: Min. $500,000
REMARKS: The firm represents pension fund money for prime real estate development projects.

COMPANY: **The Paul Revere Investment Management Corporation**
ADDRESS: 1275 King St.
Greenwich, CT 06830
PHONE: (203) 531-2800
CONTACT OFFICER(S): Charles Y. Brush, President
John J. Delucca, Treasurer
ASSETS: $100 million and up
TYPES OF FINANCING: Secondary Market Corporate Securities: Bonds; REAL ESTATE LOANS: Intermediate term senior mortgage; Other: private placements
GEOGRAPHIC LIMITS OF INVESTMENTS/LOANS: National; Other: Canada
RANGE OF INV./LOAN PER BUSINESS: Min. 1 million Max. 5 million
PREFERRED TERM FOR LOANS & LEASES: Min. 2-3 years; Max. 15-20 years
REFERRALS ACCEPTED FROM: Investment/Mortgage banker or Borrower/Investee

COMPANY: **Xerox Credit Corporation**
ADDRESS: 2 Pickwick Plaza
Greenwich, CT 06836
PHONE: (203) 625-6700
TYPE OF INSTITUTION: Industrial Finance
CONTACT OFFICER(S): Ramiro Collazo, Sr. V.P.-General Manager-Leasing
James Reynolds, Director, Commerical Services-Vendor programs
David Roe, V.P., Planning
ASSETS: 1.6 Billion
TYPES OF FINANCING: LOANS: Equipment; Equity-related; LEASES: Single-investor; Leveraged; Tax leases; Non-tax leases; Operating; Lease syndications; Vendor financing programs
PREFERRED TYPES OF INDUSTRIES/INVESTMENTS: Any industry; any equipment
GEOGRAPHIC LIMITS OF INVESTMENTS/LOANS: National
REFERRALS ACCEPTED FROM: Investment/Mortgage banker and Borrower/Investee

COMPANY: **Aetna Life & Casualty**
ADDRESS: 151 Farmington Ave.
Hartford, CT 06156
PHONE: (203) 273-0123
CONTACT OFFICER(S): Peter G. Russell, V.P., Bond Investment Dept, 203-275-2701
James Richmond, V.P. Aetna Realty Investors, 205-275-3247
ASSETS: 48 billion
INVESTMENTS/LOANS MADE: In securities with a secondary market and in securities without a secondary market
TYPES OF FINANCING: SECONDARY-MARKET CORPORATE SECURITIES, LOANS: REAL ESTATE LOANS: Long-term senior mtg.; Intermediate-term senior mtg.; Construction, REAL ESTATE: Other: Equity purchases
PREFERRED TYPES OF INDUSTRIES/INVESTMENTS: R.E.: Agriculture related; construction & development; shopping centers; industrial; warehousing, office buildings, hotels
GEOGRAPHIC LIMITS OF INVESTMENTS/LOANS: National
RANGE OF INV./LOAN PER BUSINESS: Min. $5 million (R.E.); $5 million (P.P.); Max. None
PREFERRED TERM FOR LOANS & LEASES: Max. 15+ (R.E.) years
REFERRALS ACCEPTED FROM: Investment/Mortgage banker or Borrower/Investee

COMPANY: **CIGNA Corporation**
ADDRESS: South Bbldg. S-306
Hartford, CT 06152
PHONE: (203) 726-6000
TYPE OF INSTITUTION: Insurance Co.
CONTACT OFFICER(S): Richard W. Maine, Pres. CIGNA Capital Advisors, 726-6131
David P. Marks, Sr. V.P.

Philip Ward Sr. V.P. RE Production
Thomas J. Watt Sr. V.P. Agricultural RE.
Richard Caupchunos, Sr. V.P. Asset Management
Arthurn C. Reeds, Sr. V.P. Portfolio Management
TYPES OF FINANCING: SECONDARY-MARKET CORPORATE SECURITIES: Common stock; Preferred stock; Bonds, VENTURE CAPITAL, LOANS: Unsecured; Working capital (receivables/inventory); Equipment; Equity-related; REAL ESTATE LOANS: Long-term senior mtg.; Intermediate-term senior mtg.; Subordinated Land; Land development; Standbys; Industrial revenue bonds; Other: Pure development equity, REAL ESTATE: Acquisitions; Joint ventures; Partnerships/Syndications
PREFERRED TYPES OF INDUSTRIES/INVESTMENTS: Mortgage; Communications; Manufacturing and technology; Retail; Foreign
WILL NOT CONSIDER: Gaming industry
RANGE OF INV./LOAN PER BUSINESS: Min. $3 million; Max $40 million
PREFERRED TERM FOR LOANS & LEASSES: Min. 1 year; Max. 20 years

COMPANY: **Connecticut Bank & Trust, R.E. Division**
ADDRESS: One Constitution Plaza
Hartford, CT 06115
PHONE: (203) 244-6269
TYPE OF INSTITUTION: Construction lender, permanent lender; intermediate lender
CONTACT OFFICER(S): Oliver W. Park, President
ASSETS: $6 billion
INVESTMENTS/LOANS MADE:
TYPES OF FINANCING: SECONDARY-MARKET CORPORATE SECURITIES, LOANS: Unsecured; Working capital; Equipment; Equity-related; Other: Construction lending, Lease finaancing, REAL ESTATE LOANS: Intermediate-term senior mtg.; Wraparounds; Land; Land development; Construction; Gap; Industrial revenue bonds, FACTORING, LEASES: Single—investor; Leveraged; Non-tax leases; Operating; Vendor financing programs, INTERNATIONAL
GEOGRAPHIC LIMITS OF INVESTMENTS/LOANS: National; International
BUSINESS CHARACTERISTICS DESIRED-REQUIRED:
REFERRALS ACCEPPTED FROM: Investment/Mortgage banker or Borrower/Investee
REMARKS: 140 Branches; out on loan: $1 billion in Real Estate

COMPANY: **Connecticut Mutual Life Insurance Co.**
ADDRESS: 140 Garden St.
Hartford, CT 06154
PHONE: (203) 727-6500
CONTACT OFFICER(S): Raymond J. Houworth, Second V.P.
John Weber V.P. Marketable Securities
Robert Hunter, V.P., Urban R.E.
George Schwab, V.P., Agriculture R.E.
ASSETS: $7 billion
TYPES OF FINANCING: SECONDARY-MARKET CORPORATE SECURITIES: Common stock; Preferred stock; Bonds, LOANS: Equipment, Equity-related REAL ESTATE LOANS: Long-term senior mtg.; Subordinated; Wraparounds; Construction, REAL ESTATE: Joint ventures
PREFERRED TYPES OF INDUSTRIES/INVESTMENTS: Office buildings
GEOGRAPHIC LIMITS OF INVESTMENTS/LOANS: National
RANGE OF INV./LOAN PER BUSINESS: Min. $500,000; Max. $15 million
PREFERRED TERM FOR LOANS & LEASES: Max. 10 years Business characteristics desired-required: minimum number of yers in business: 0 REFERRALS ACCEPTED FROM: Investment/mortgage banker or Borrower/Investee

COMPANY: **Hartford Insurance Group**
ADDRESS: Hartford Plaza
Hartford, CT 06115
PHONE: (203) 547-5000
CONTACT OFFICER(S): Bernard F. Wilbur, Jr., V.P., R.E. Mortgages
Dick Hamilton, R.E. Investment
ASSETS: $14 billion
TYPES OF FINANCING: Seondary market corporate securites: bonds; real estate loans; REAL ESTATE: Acquisitions
PREFERRED TYPES OF INDUSTRIES/ INVESTMENTS/EQUIPMENT/REAL ESTATE: Real Estate; suburban offices
GEOGRAPHIC LIMITS OF INVESTMENTS/LOANS: National
RANGE OF INV./LOAN PER BUSINESS: Min $2 million; Max.: $50 million

COMPANY: **Phoenix Mutual Life Insurance Company**
ADDRESS: 1 American Row
Hartford, CT 06115
PHONE: (203) 275-5439
CONTACT OFFICER(S): Norman W. Douglass, Vice President
ASSETS: $4,000,000,000
INVESTMENTS/LOANS MADE: For own account; For managed accounts; Through private placements; Through underwriting publicc offerings
INVESTMENTS/LOANS MADE: In securities with a secondary market and in securities without a secondary market
TYPES OF FINANCING: SECONDARY-MARKET CORPORATE SECURITIES: Common stock; Bonds; LOANS: Unsecured to credits above Ba; Working capital (receivables/inventory); Equipment; Equity-related; REAL ESTATE: Acquisitions; Joint ventures; Partnerships/Syndications
GEOGRAPHIC LIMITS OF INVESTMENTS/LOANS: National
RANGE OF INV./LOAN PER BUSINESS: Min. $1,000,000; Max. $10,000,000
PREFERRED TERM FOR LOANS & LEASES: Min. 2 years; Max. 10 years
BUSINESS CHARACTERISTICS DESIRED-REQUIRED: Minimum number of years in business: 5
REFERRALS ACCEPTED FROM: Investment/Mortgage banker or Borrower/Investee

COMPANY: **Daseke & Co., Inc.**
ADDRESS: One Glendening Place
Westport, CT 06880
PHONE: (203) 222-5800
CONTACT OFFICER(S): William Hillemeyer, Exec. V.P.
ASSETS: Real estate portfolio of income projects valued at over $1.4 billion
INVESTMENTS/LOANS MADE: For own account, Through private placements
TYPES OF FINANCING: REAL ESTATE: Acquisitions; Joint ventures; Partnerships/Syndications
PREFERRED TYPES OF INDUSTRIES/INVESTMENTS: Office buildings, 100,000 square feet +; Apartment projects, 200 units +
WILL NOT CONSIDER: Condos
GEOGRAPHIC LIMITS OF INVESTMENTS/LOANS: National
RANGE OF INV./LOAN PER BUSINESS: Min. $1,500,000; Max. $15,000,000
REFERRALS ACCEPTED FROM: Investment/Mortgage banker or Borrower/Investee
BRANCHES: Bruce G. McCauley, 4780 Bank of America Building, 555 California St., San Francisco, CA; (415) 788-4850
Marshall Edwards, 555 Two Lincoln Center, LB-82; 5420 LBJ Freeway, Dallas TX 75240;
Victor MacFarlane, Jr. Denver Technological Center, Ste. 820, Englewood, CO 80111; (303) 793-3150
George Cornwell, Powers Ferry Landing, 6250 Powers Ferry Ste. 200, Atlanta, GA 30339; (404) 951-2081

COMPANY: **The Union Labor Life Insurance Co.**
ADDRESS: 1 Masssachusetts Ave. NW
Washington, D.C. 20001
CONTACT OFFICER(S): Herbert C. Canapary, V.P., Investments
E. R. Saatchoff, V.P., Mortgages
ASSETS: $100 million and up
TYPES OF FINANCING: LOANS, REAL ESTATE LOANS: Long-term senior mtg.
GEOGRAPHIC LIMITS OF INVESTMENTS/LOANS: National
RANGE OF INV./LOAN PER BUSINESS: Min. $500,000 (R.E.); Max. $3,000,000 (R.E.)
PREFERRED TERM FOR LOANS & LEASES: Min. 15-20 years (Investments); Max. 20+ years
BUSINESS CHARACTERISTICS DESIRED-REQUIRED: Other: R.E.: Union labor for construction to provide jobs and attract labor union moneys
REMARKS: No range limits for Investments

COMPANY: **Acacia Mutual Life Insurance Company**
ADDRESS: 51 Louisiana Ave., N.W.
Washington, DC 20001
PHONE: (202) 628-4506
CONTACT OFFICER(S): Joseph A. Clorety, Sr. V.P., Investments
Andrew S. White, 2nd V.P. Securities
Patricia D. Hevner, Asst. V.P. Equities
Albert H. Kroening, Jr., V.P., R.E.
Jean O. Brinks, Treasurer
INVESTMENT/LOANS MADE OR ARRANGED: In securities with a secondary market and in securities without a secondary market
TYPES OF FINANCING: SECONDARY-MARKET CORPORATE SECURITIES: Common stock; Preferred stock; Bonds; REAL ESTATE: Joint ventures; Partnerships/Syndications. OTHER SERVICES PROVIDED: private placements; certificates of deposit; R.E. Equities
PREFERRED TYPES OF INDUSTRIES/INVESTMENTS: low rise office parks
GEOGRAPHIC LIMITS OF INVESTMENTS/LOANS: National
RANGE OF INV./LOAN PER BUSINESS: Max. $4 million
REFERRALS ACCEPTED FROM: Investment/Mortgage banker or Borrower/Investee

COMPANY: **Anacostia Economic Development Corporation**
ADDRESS: 2041 Martin Luther King Jr. Ave., S.E.
Washington, DC 20020
PHONE: (202) 889-9507
TYPE OF INSTITUTION: Community economic development corporation
CONTACT OFFICER(S): Albert R. Hopkins, Jr., President
Augustus Palmer, V.P.ASSETS: $2,000,000
INVESTMENTS/LOANS MADE: For own account; through private placements
INVESTMENTS/LOANS MADE: Only in securities without a secondary market
TYPES OF FINANCING: VENTURE CAPITAL: Second-stage (generally 1-3 years); Buy-outs/Acquisitions, LOANS: Working capital (receivables/inventory); Equipment, REAL ESTATE LOANS: Long-term senior mtg.; Subordinated; Construction; Gap, REAL ESTATE: Acquisitions; Joint ventures; Partnerships/Syndications
PREFERRED TYPES OF INDUSTRIES/INVESTMENTS: Labor intensive, low skill; commercial RE development
WILL NOT CONSIDER: Single family housing
GEOGRAPHIC LIMITS OF INVESTMENTS/LOANS: Local
RANGE OF INV./LOAN PER BUSINESS: Min. $10,000; Max. $150,000
PREFERRED TERM FOR LOANS & LEASES: Min. 2 years
BUSINESS CHARACTERISTICS DESIRED-REQUIRED: Minimum number of years in business: 1
REMARKS: Interested primarily in development projects in S.E. Washington, DC; Terms for loans: can do 5 year amitization

COMPANY: **D.R.G. Financial**
ADDRESS: 1099 30th N.W.
Washington, DC 20007
PHONE: (202) 965-7000
TYPE OF INSTITUTION: Mortgage bank
CONTACT OFFICER(S): Donald M. DeFranceaux, President,
Patrick Nolan , E.V.P.,
James L. Latta, E.V.P.,
Eugene Ford, V.P.,
Steve Wolt, V.P.,
Michael Sullivan, V.P.,
Alan Maddox, V.P.
John Sweazey, S.V.P

INVESTMENTS/LOANS MADE: For own account; For managed accounts; Through private placements
TYPES OF FINANCING: REAL ESTATE LOANS: Long-term senior mtg.; Construction; Industrial revenue bonds, REAL ESTATE: Acquisitions; Joint ventures; Partnerships/Syndications
PREFERRED TYPES OF INDUSTRIES/INVESTMENTS: Apartment houses; Office buildings; Shopping centers, Industrials, hotels & motels
GEOGRAPHIC LIMITS OF INVESTMENTS/LOANS: National
RANGE OF INV./LOAN PER BUSINESS: Min. $3,000,000; Max. None
PREFERRED TERM FOR LOANS & LEASES: Min. 5 years; Max. 35 years
REMARKS: Average term of loans are 35 yearsBRANCHES: 147 E. Layman Av., Ste. 100, Winter Park, FL 32789, (305) 629-1800 Alan Maddox, V.P.
650 California St., 32nd fl, San Francisco, CA 94108; (415) 397-9900 John Sweazey, SVP.

COMPANY: **USLICO Corporation**
ADDRESS: 1701 Pennsylvania Ave., N.W.
Washington, DC 20006
PHONE: (202) 298-6235
CONTACT OFFICER(S): Leslie P. Schultz, Chairman
W. Alan Aument, Sr. V.P. & Treasurer (Inv.)
J. Rodman Myers, V.P., Mortgage R.E.,
J.M. Schultz, V.P. Securities
ASSETS: $100,000,000 and up
INVESTMENTS/LOANS MADE: In securities with a secondary market and in securities without a secondary market
TYPES OF FINANCING: LOANS: Equipment, REAL ESTATE LOANS
PREFERRED TYPES OF INDUSTRIES/INVESTMENTS: Diversified
GEOGRAPHIC LIMITS OF INVESTMENTS/LOANS: National
RANGE OF INV./LOAN PER BUSINESS: Min. None; Max. $2,000,000
REFERRALS ACCEPTED FROM: Investment/Mortgage banker or Borrower/Investee
REMARKS: Maximum amount for bonds is $1,000,000

COMPANY: **Walker & Dunlop, Inc.**
ADDRESS: 1156 15th Street, N.W.
Washington, DC 20005
PHONE: (202) 872-5500
CONTACT OFFICER(S): W. W. Smyth, V.P.
Merrill A. Yavinsky, Sr. V.P.
ASSETS: Servicing $920,000,000 in mortgage loans
INVESTMENTS/LOANS MADE: Through private placements
INVESTMENTS/LOANS MADE: In securities with a secondary market and in securities without a secondary market
TYPES OF FINANCING: REAL ESTATE LOANS: Long-term senior mtg.; Intermediate-term senior mtg.; Wraparounds; Construction; Industrial revenue bonds, OTHER SERVICES PROVIDED: Sales-leasing; property management
PREFERRED TYPES OF INDUSTRIES/INVESTMENTS: Commercial real estate secured by first deed of trust
GEOGRAPHIC LIMITS OF INVESTMENTS/LOANS: Other: Mid east coast
RANGE OF INV./LOAN PER BUSINESS: Min. $500,000; Max. None
BUSINESS CHARACTERISTICS DESIRED-REQUIRED: Other: Prefer experienced developer
REFERRALS ACCEPTED FROM: Investment/Mortgage banker or Borrower/Investee

COMPANY: **Continental American Life Insurance Co.**
ADDRESS: 300 Continental Dr.
Newark, DE 19713
PHONE: (302) 454-5000
CONTACT OFFICER(S): Michael Greenleaf, V.P.
Thomas Ryan, Asst. V.P.
TYPES OF FINANCING: SECONDARY-MARKET CORPORATE SECURITIES: Common stock; Preferred stock; Bonds, VENTURE CAPITAL: Buy-outs/Acquisitions, LOANS: Working capital (receivables/inventory); Equipment; Other: Secured, REAL ESTATE LOANS: Land; Land development; Other: Land purchase lease-back (short-term 5-7 yrs), REAL ESTATE: Joint ventures
PREFERRED TYPES OF INDUSTRIES/INVESTMENTS: Diversified
WILL NOT CONSIDER: Fast foods
GEOGRAPHIC LIMITS OF INVESTMENTS/LOANS: National
RANGE OF INV./LOAN PER BUSINESS: Min. $500,000; Max. $2-3 million
PREFERRED TERM FOR LOANS & LEASES: Min. 3 years; Max. 10 years
BUSINESS CHARACTERISTICS DESIRED-REQUIRED:Minimum number of years in business: 3

COMPANY: **Gilpin, Van Trump and Montgomery, Inc.**
ADDRESS: One Customs House Square, One Customs House Plaza
Wilmington, DE 19801
PHONE: (302) 656-5400
CONTACT OFFICER(S): Robert F. McCann, Sr. V.P.
ASSETS: $146,000,000
INVESTMENTS/LOANS MADE: For own account, For managed accounts
INVESTMENTS/LOANS MADE: In securities with a secondary market and in securities without a secondary market
TYPES OF FINANCING: SECONDARY-MARKET CORPORATE SECURITIES: Bonds; REAL ESTATE LOANS: Long-term senior mtg.; Intermediate-term senior mtg.; Subordinated; Wraparounds; Land; Land development; Construction; Gap; Standbys, Industrial revenue bonds, REAL ESTATE: Acquisitions; Joint ventures; Partnerships/Syndications
PREFERRED TYPES OF INDUSTRIES/INVESTMENTS: Real estate, shopping centers, office buildings, hotels and land
WILL NOT CONSIDER: Recreational properties, motels
GEOGRAPHIC LIMITS OF INVESTMENTS/LOANS: National
RANGE OF INV./LOAN PER BUSINESS: Min. $1,000,000
REFERRALS ACCEPTED FROM: Investment/Mortgage banker or Borrower/Investee

COMPANY: **CSB Commercial Mortgage**
ADDRESS: 1840 W. 49th Street, Ste. 604
Hialeah, FL 33012
PHONE: (305) 823-3022
CONTACT OFFICER(S): Jerry Weisman, President
TYPES OF FINANCING: REAL ESTATE LOANS: Construction
REMARKS: Subsidiary of First Florida Leasing Corp.

COMPANY: **Alliance Mortgage Co.**
ADDRESS: 25 W. Forsyth
Jacksonville, FL 32202
PHONE: (904) 798-6000
TYPE OF INSTITUTION: Mortgage banker
CONTACT OFFICER(S): William H. Dukelow, Exec. V.P.
ASSETS: Servicing volume over 5 billion
TYPES OF FINANCING: REAL ESTATE LOANS: Long-term senior mtg.; Intermediate-term senior mtg.; Land development; Construction; Industrial revenue bonds; REAL ESTATE: Acquisitions; Joint Ventures, Partnerships/Syndications
PREFERRED TYPES OF INDUSTRIES/INVESTMENTS: Shopping centers, Office complexes, apartments, warehouses, nursing homes
GEOGRAPHIC LIMITS OF INVESTMENTS/LOANS: State; Regional; Other: Commercial in state
RANGE OF INV./LOAN PER BUSINESS: Min. 1 million; Max. none
PREFERRED TERM FOR LOANS & LEASES: Min. 1 yr. Max. 30 yrs.
REMARKS: Alliance is a wholly-owned subsidiary of Florida National Bank which will do some additional types of financing.

COMPANY: **American Heritage Life Insurance Company**
ADDRESS: 11 E. Forsyth St.
Jacksonville, FL 32202
PHONE: (904) 354-1776
CONTACT OFFICER(S): C. A. Verlander, V.P. Securities-Investments
Wm. L. Kluessner, Asst. V.P. & Treasurer-Mortgages
ASSETS: $100 million and up
INVESTMENTS/LOANS MADE: In securities with a secondary market and in securities without a secondary market
TYPES OF FINANCING: SECONDARY-MARKET CORPORATE SECURITIES: Common Stock; Preferred Stock; Bonds; REAL ESTATE LOANS: Intermediate term senior mortgage; Subordinated; Land; Land development; Gap; Industrial Revenue bonds
PREFERRED TYPES OF INDUSTRIES/INVESTMENTS: R. E. professional office buildings; shopping centers
GEOGRAPHIC LIMITS OF INVESTMENTS/LOANS: National
PREFERRED TERM FOR LOANS & LEASES: Min. 5-7 years (R.E.)
BUSINESS CHARACTERISTICS DESIRED-REQUIRED: Min. annual net income loan amount (R.E.)
REFERRALS ACCEPTED FROM: Investment/Mortgage banker or Borrower/Investee
REMARKS: Range for investments: $250,000-1,000,000; Range for R.E. loans: $25,000-500,000

COMPANY: **Gulfco Capital Mgmt. Inc.**
ADDRESS: Gulf Life Tower
Jacksonville, FL 32207
PHONE: (904) 390-7800
CONTACT OFFICER(S): Robert L. Collins, Ex. V.P., mortgages
ASSETS: $100 million and up
TYPES OF FINANCING: REAL ESTATE LOANS: Intermediate-term senior mtg.
PREFERRED TYPES OF INDUSTRIES/INVESTMENTS: Income properties: office buildings; shopping centers; medical office buildings; warehouses
GEOGRAPHIC LIMITS OF INVESTMENTS/LOANS: Regional; Other: 49 states with emphasis on SE U.S.; all states except Texas
RANGE OF INV./LOAN PER BUSINESS: Min. 1 mil.; Max. 10 mil.
PREFERRED TERM FOR LOANS & LEASES: Min. 5 yrs; Max. 10 yrs
REFERRALS ACCEPTED FROM: Investment/Mortgage banker or Borrower/Invested
REMARKS: Preferred term: 5-10 years

COMPANY: **William H. Hill Associates Inc.**
ADDRESS: 3100 University Blvd. S. S201
Jacksonville, FL 32216
PHONE: (904) 721-8956
TYPE OF INSTITUTION: Mergers Acquisitions, Appraisals & Consulting
CONTACT OFFICER(S): William H. Hill, President
INVESTMENTS/LOANS MADE: For own account
TYPES OF FINANCING: REAL ESTATE: Acquisitions; OTHER SERVICES PROVIDED: Acqquisitions Mergers; Appraisals; Consulting; Divesturers
WILL NOT CONSIDER: Banks, Insurance Co. Franchises
RANGE OF INV./LOAN PER BUSINESS: Min. $500,000; Max. $20,000,000
BUSINESS CHARACTERISTICS DESIRED-REQUIRED: Minimum number of years in business: 5; Min. annual sales $1,000,000; Min. net worth $500,000; Min. annual net income $100,000; Min. annual cash flow $250,000
REFERRALS ACCEPTED FROM: Investment/Mortgage banker or Borrower/Investee

COMPANY: **Gold Coast Capital Corporation**
ADDRESS: 3550 Biscayne Blvd., Room 601
Miami, FL 33137
PHONE: (305) 576-2012
TYPE OF INSTITUTION: Small Business Investment Corp. (S.B.I.C)
CONTACT OFFICER(S): William I. Gold, President
ASSETS: $3,000,000
INVESTMENTS/LOANS MADE: For own account
TYPES OF FINANCING: VENTURE CAPITAL: Second-stage; LOANS: Equipment; REAL ESTATE LOANS: Land development; Construction; REAL ESTATE: Acquisitions; Joint ventures OTHER SERVICES PROVIDED: Loans to all businesses secured by property

GEOGRAPHIC LIMITS OF INVESTMENTS/LOANS: Local; State
RANGE OF INV./LOAN PER BUSINESS: Min. $25,000
PREFERRED TERM FOR LOANS & LEASES: 5 yrs.

COMPANY: **Heritage Mortgage Corp.**
ADDRESS: 1318 N.W. 7th St.
Miami, FL 33125
PHONE: (305) 324-4000
TYPE OF INSTITUTION: Mortgage banking
CONTACT OFFICER(S): Edward Feinstein, Pres. Lending
Eric Feinstein, Sr. V. Pres. Real Estate Equities
ASSETS: 5,897,000
INVESTMENTS/LOANS MADE: For own account, For managed accounts
INVESTMENTS/LOANS MADE: In Securities with a secondary market and in securities without a secondary market
TYPES OF FINANCING: LOANS, REAL ESTATE LOANS: Long-term senior mtg.; Intermediate-term senior mtg.; Wraparounds; Land; Land development; Construction; Gap; Standbys; Industrial revenue bonds. LEASES: Single-investor. REAL ESTATE: Acquisitions; Joint ventures; Partnerships/Syndications. OTHER SERVICES PROVIDED: Title Insurance
GEOGRAPHIC LIMITS OF INVESTMENTS/LOANS: National
RANGE OF INV./LOAN PER BUSINESS: Min. $500,000; Max. None
PREFERRED TERM FOR LOANS & LEASES: Min. 1 year; Max. 30 years

COMPANY: **Pan-American Mortgage Corporation**
ADDRESS: 150 S.E. 3rd Ave., P.O. Box 013131 (33101)
Miami, FL 33131
PHONE: (305) 577-5711
TYPE OF INSTITUTION: Mortgage banker
CONTACT OFFICER(S): Winthrop Davis, Pres.
ASSETS: Servicing volume over $100,000,000
TYPES OF FINANCING: REAL ESTATE LOANS: Long-term senior mtg; Intermediate-term senior mtg; Subordinated; Wraparounds; Land; Land development; construction; Standbys; Industrial revenue bonds, REAL ESTATE: Acquisitions; Joint ventures, Partnerships/syndications
GEOGRAPHIC LIMITS OF INVESTMENTS/LOANS: National
RANGE OF INV./LOAN PER BUSINESS: Min. $500,000; Max. None
PREFERRED TERM FOR LOANS & LEASES: Min. 15-20 years; Max. 20+ years
BRANCHES: A. R. Jorr, 250 N. Orange Ave., Orlando, FL 32801; (305) 841-8871

COMPANY: **United Trust Fund**
ADDRESS: 4770 Biscayne Blvd.
Miami, FL 33137
PHONE: (305) 576-7711
CONTACT OFFICER(S): James Nolan, Exec. Vice President
Fred Berliner, Sr. Vice President
ASSETS: 100,000,000
INVESTMENTS/LOANS MADE: For own account
TYPES OF FINANCING: LEASES: Single-investor; Non-tax leases; Net lease credit tenants only
PREFERRED TYPES OF INDUSTRIES/INVESTMENTS: Single tenant corporate real estate
GEOGRAPHIC LIMITS OF INVESTMENTS/LOANS: National
RANGE OF INV./LOAN PER BUSINESS: Min. $5,000,000; Max. $50,000,000
PREFERRED TERM FOR LOANS & LEASES: Min. 10 years; Max. 20 years
BUSINESS CHARACTERISTICS DESIRED-REQUIRED: Baa credit or better
REFERRALS ACCEPTED FROM: Investment/Mortgage banker or Borrower/Investee

COMPANY: **First Western SBLC, Inc.**
ADDRESS: 1380 N.E. Miami Gardens Drive
North Miami Beach, FL 33179
PHONE: (305) 949-5900
TYPE OF INSTITUTION: SBLC (90% SBA Government Guaranteed Loans)
CONTACT OFFICER(S): Lance B. Rosemore, President
Fredric M. Rosemore, Vice-president
ASSETS: $8,000,000; Loan capabilities $26,000,000
INVESTMENTS/LOANS MADE: For own account
INVESTMENTS/LOANS MADE: Only in securities without a secondary market
TYPES OF FINANCING: SECONDARY-MARKET CORPORATE SECURITIES: Business loans-commercial & manufacturing business expansion loans, VENTURE CAPITAL: Second-stage; Later-stage, LOANS: Working capital; equipment, REAL ESTATE LOANS: owner occupied ofice & warehouse condominiums-also purchases of existing businesses, REAL ESTATE: Acquisitions, OTHER SERVICES PROVIDED: Consulting and advisory
PREFERRED TYPES OF INDUSTRIES/INVESTMENTS: any type of business expansion or modernizations loan—limited in real estate to owner-occupied only. Expansion of manufacturing facilities
WILL NOT CONSIDER: Venture capital
GEOGRAPHIC LIMITS OF INVESTMENTS/LOANS: Florida, New Jersey, Georgia, Alabama
RANGE OF INV./LOAN PER BUSINESS: Min. $50,000; Max. $550,000
PREFERRED TERM FOR LOANS & LEASES: Min. 3 years; Max. 20 years
BUSINESS CHARACTERISTICS DESIRED-REQUIRED: Minimum number of years in business: 2; OTHER: all of our loans are 90% SBA guaranteed

COMPANY: **Pro-Med Capital, Inc.**
ADDRESS: 1380 N.E. Miami Gardens Drive
North Miami Beach, FL 33179
PHONE: (305) 949-5900
TYPE OF INSTITUTION: We have 2 subsidiaries: Western Financial Capital Corp (an SBIC) and First Western SBLC (an SBLC). Both are federal licensees of the Small Business Administration
CONTACT OFFICER(S): Lance B. Rosemore, Vice President
Fredric M. Rosemore, President
ASSETS: $20,000,000
INVESTMENTS/LOANS MADE: For own account

INVESTMENTS/LOANS MADE: In securities with a secondary market and in securities without a secondary market
TYPES OF FINANCING: LOANS: Equipment; business expansion loans, REAL ESTATE LOANS: SBA 90% Government guaranteed loanss for owner -occupied real estate, REAL ESTATE: Acquisitions
PREFERRED TYPES OF INDUSTRIES/INVESTMENTS: Diversified. Prefer health care and financing business expansion plans involving owner-occupied real estate (office condominiums, warehouse, etc.)
WILL NOT CONSIDER: Passive investments—no R & D
GEOGRAPHIC LIMITS OF INVESTMENTS/LOANS: National
RANGE OF INV./LOAN PER BUSINESS: Min. $25,000; Max. $550,000
PREFERRED TERM FOR LOANS & LEASES: Min. 5 years; Max. 20 years
BUSINESS CHARACTERISTICS DESIRED-REQUIRED: Minimum number of years in business: 2; OTHER: must be profitable
REFERRALS ACCEPTED FROM: Investee/Mortgage banker and Borrower/Investee

COMPANY: **Western Financial Capital Corp.**
ADDRESS: 1380 N.E. Miami Gardens Drive
North Miami Beach, FL 33179
PHONE: (305) 949-5900
TYPE OF INSTITUTION: SBIC (Small business Investment Corp.)
CONTACT OFFICER(S): Fredric M. Rosemore, President
Lance B. Rosemore, Vice-President
ASSETS: $7,000,000
INVESTMENTS/LOANS MADE: For own account
INVESTMENTS/LOANS MADE: Only in securities without a secondary market
TYPES OF FINANCING: VENTURE CAPITAL: Second-stage; Later-stage, LOANS: Working capital; Equipment; Equity related; purchases of health care practices and business; REAL ESTATE LOANS: Owner occupied-commercial only, LEASES: Vendor financing programs, REAL ESTATE: Acquisitions, OTHER SERVICES PROVIDED: cnnsulting and advisory
PREFERRED TYPES OF INDUSTRIES/INVESTMENTS: Financing doctors, dentists, optometrists, veterinarians, podiatrists for start-ups and business expansion/ modernization
WILL NOT CONSIDER: Equity investments only—Debt and Equity O.K.
GEOGRAPHIC LIMITS OF INVESTMENTS/LOANS: National
RANGE OF INV./LOAN PER BUSINESS: Min. $20,000; Max. $700,000
PREFERRED TERM FOR LOANS & LEASES: Min. 5 years; Max. 20 years

COMPANY: **Sunbank Mortgage Co.**
ADDRESS: 200 S. Orange, P.O. Box 1480
Orlando, FL 32802
PHONE: (305) 237-4560
TYPE OF INSTITUTION: Mortgage Banker
CONTACT OFFICER(S): Carl E. Nimnicht, Pres.
ASSETS: $700 million + in servicing volume
TYPES OF FINANCING: REAL ESTATE LOANS: Long-term senior mtg; Intermediate-term senior mtg; Wraparounds; Land develoment; Construction; Industrial revenue bonds, REAL ESTATE: Acquisitions; Joint ventures
PREFERRED TYPES OF INDUSTRIES/INVESTMENTS: Office bldgs., warehouse spaces, professional bldgs.
WILL NOT CONSIDER: hotels
GEOGRAPHIC LIMITS OF INVESTMENTS/LOANS: State
PREFERRED TERM FOR LOANS & LEASES: Max. 25 years
REFERRALS ACCEPTED FROM: Investment/Mortgage banker or Borrower/Investee

COMPANY: **Business Research Company**
ADDRESS: 205 Worth Ave. P.O. 2137
Palm Beach, FL 33480
PHONE: (305) 832-2155
CONTACT OFFICER(S): George B. Kilborne, Managing Director
A. Donald Grosset, Jr., Managing Director
INVESTMENTS/LOANS MADE: For own account, Through private placements
INVESTMENTS/LOANS MADE: In securities with a secondary market and in securities without a secondary market
TYPES OF FINANCING: VENTURE CAPITAL: Later-stage; Buy-outs/Acquisitions, REAL ESTATE: Acquisitions, OTHER SERVICES PROVIDED: Solutions to ownership problems in private/closely held corporation
PREFERRED TYPES OF INDUSTRIES/INVESTMENTS: Engineered hard goods, General manufacturing, Distribution
WILL NOT CONSIDER: Retailing, High tech, Startups
GEOGRAPHIC LIMITS OF INVESTMENTS/LOANS: Other: Prefer east coast and near midwest
RANGE OF INV./LOAN PER BUSINESS: Min. $500,000
BUSINESS CHARACTERISTICS DESIRED-REQUIRED: Minimum number of years in business: 3; Min. net worth $5,000,000
REMARKS: Specialty is working with family controlled corporations where certain family members are seeking partial or total liquidity.

COMPANY: **Venture Capital Management Corporation**
ADDRESS: P.O. Box 2626
Satellite Beach, FL 32937
TYPE OF INSTITUTION: Private venture capital company
CONTACT OFFICER(S): Dr. Robert A. Adams, President
INVESTMENTS/LOANS MADE: For own account, Through private placements
INVESTMENTS/LOANS MADE: Only in securities without a secondary market
TYPES OF FINANCING: VENTURE CAPITAL: Second-stage; Buy-outs/Acquisitions, LOANS: Equity-related, INTERNATIONAL, REAL ESTATE: Acquisitions; Joint ventures; Partnerships/Syndications, OTHER SERVICES PROVIDED: Financial consulting, Private placement packaging, Chapter 11 bankruptcy reorganization

GEOGRAPHIC LIMITS OF INVESTMENTS/LOANS: State
RANGE OF INV./LOAN PER BUSINESS: Min. $100,000
PREFERRED TERM FOR LOANS & LEASES: Min. 3 years; Max. 5 years
BUSINESS CHARACTERISTICS DESIRED-REQUIRED: Minimum number of years in business: 2; Min. annual sales $500,000; Min. annual net income $Break even
REFERRALS ACCEPTED FROM: Borrower/Investee

COMPANY: **Central Life Insurance Company of Florida**
ADDRESS: 1400 N. Blvd.
Tampa, FL 33607
PHONE: (813) 251-1897
CONTACT OFFICER(S): Bettye F. Stanford, Sec., Treasurer
ASSETS: $1,000,000 - 10,000,000
TYPES OF FINANCING: REAL ESTATE LOANS
GEOGRAPHIC LIMITS OF INVESTMENTS/LOANS: State
RANGE OF INV./LOAN PER BUSINESS: Max. $50,000
PREFERRED TERM FOR LOANS & LEASES: Max. 20+ years
REFERRALS ACCEPTED FROM: Investment/Mortgage banker or Borrower/Investee

COMPANY: **Cenvill Investors, Inc.**
ADDRESS: East Drive, Century Village
West Palm Beach, FL 33409
PHONE: (305) 686-2577
TYPE OF INSTITUTION: Real Estate Investment Trust
CONTACT OFFICER(S): Alvin Wilensky, President
Joseph Weingard, Advisor
ASSETS: $125 million
INVESTMENTS/LOANS MADE: For own account
INVESTMENTS/LOANS MADE: In securities with a secondary market and in securities without a secondary market
TYPES OF FINANCING: REAL ESTATE LOANS: Intermediate-term senior mtg.; Subordinated; Wraparounds; Land; Land development; Construction REAL ESTATE: Acquisitions; Joint ventures
PREFERRED TYPES OF INDUSTRIES/INVESTMENTS: Real Estate - Residential and Commercial
GEOGRAPHIC LIMITS OF INVESTMENTS/LOANS: Regional
RANGE OF INV./LOAN PER BUSINESS: Min. $1 million; Max. $20 million
PREFERRED TERM FOR LOANS & LEASES: Min. One year; Max. Five years

COMPANY: **Condor Group Holdings**
ADDRESS: 1601 Belvedere Rd.
West Palm Beach, FL 33406
PHONE: (305) 689-4906
TYPE OF INSTITUTION: Equipment leasing, Venture capital
CONTACT OFFICER(S): James A. Carpinello, Chairman of the Board
ASSETS: $24.5 mil
INVESTMENTS/LOANS MADE: For own account, For managed accounts
TYPES OF FINANCING: SECONDARY-MARKET CORPORATE SECURITIES: Common stock; Bonds, VENTURE CAPITAL: Second-stage; Buy-outs/Acquisitions, LOANS: Equipment; Equity-related, LEASES: Single-investor; Leveraged; Tax leases; Non-tax leases; Operating, Tax-oriented lease brokerage; Lease syndications; Vendor financing programs, REAL ESTATE: Acquisitions; Joint ventures; Partnerships/Syndications
PREFERRED TYPES OF INDUSTRIES/INVESTMENTS: Capital Equipment Manufacturer; Income Producing Real Estate
GEOGRAPHIC LIMITS OF INVESTMENTS/LOANS: National
RANGE OF INV./LOAN PER BUSINESS: Min. $50,000; Max. $5,000,000
PREFERRED TERM FOR LOANS & LEASES: Min. 3 years; Max. 10 years
BUSINESS CHARACTERISTICS DESIRED-REQUIRED: Minimum number of years in business: 1; Min. annual sales $500,000; Min. net worth $150,000; Min. annual net income $50,000; Min. annual cash flow $75,000
REFERRALS ACCEPTED FROM: Investment/Mortgage banker or Borrower/Investee
REMARKS: Start-ups are done

COMPANY: **Bank South Mortgage Inc.**
ADDRESS: 875 Johnson Ferry Rd., NE, Ste 100
Atlanta, GA 30342
PHONE: (404) 257-5800
CONTACT OFFICER(S): E. Metz Bissell, Pres.

COMPANY: **Cauble & Company**
ADDRESS: 233 Peachtree Street Northeast
Atlanta, GA 30303
PHONE: (404) 577-7332
TYPE OF INSTITUTION: Mortgage Banker
CONTACT OFFICER(S): Bick Cardwell
ASSETS: $350 million
TYPES OF FINANCING: REAL ESTATE LOANS: Long-term senior mtg.; Intermediate-term senior mtg.; Subordinated; Wraparounds; Land; Land development; Construction; Gap; Standbys; Industrial revenue bonds REAL ESTATE: Acquisitions; Joint ventures
WILL NOT CONSIDER: No Residential
GEOGRAPHIC LIMITS OF INVESTMENTS/LOANS: Regional; Other: Southeast
RANGE OF INV./LOAN PER BUSINESS: Min. $500,000
PREFERRED TERM FOR LOANS & LEASES: Max. 20 years

COMPANY: **Citizens & Southern Financial Corp.**
ADDRESS: P.O. Box 4065
Atlanta, GA 30302
PHONE: (404) 491-4475
TYPE OF INSTITUTION: Mortgage Banker
CONTACT OFFICER(S): Gus Connelly, Exec. V.P.
ASSETS: $7 billion
TYPES OF FINANCING: REAL ESTATE LOANS: Long-term senior mtg.; Intermediate-term senior mtg.; Wraparounds; Land development; Construction; Industrial revenue bonds; REAL ESTATE: Joint ventures

PREFERRED TYPES OF INDUSTRIES/INVESTMENTS: Construction
GEOGRAPHIC LIMITS OF INVESTMENTS/LOANS: Regional; Southeastern U.S.
RANGE ON INV./LOAN PER BUSINESS: Min. $ —; Max. $25 million
BUSINESS CHARACTERISICS: Minimum number of years in business: 2
REMARKS: 5 branches including Tallahasse, Memphis, Tampa

COMPANY: **Consumers Ventures/ American Reserves, Inc.**
ADDRESS: 35 Glenlake Parkway, Suite 110
Atlanta, GA 30328
PHONE: (404) 396-4000
TYPE OF INSTITUTION: Private Venture Captial
CONTACT OFFICER(S): H. Friedman, Director
A. Moro, Director
A. Gooodwin, Director
INVESTMENTS/LOANS MADE: For own account; For managed accounts; Through private placments
INVESTMENTS/LOANS MADE: In securities with a secondary market and in securities without a secondary market
TYPES OF FINANCING: SECONDARY-MARKET CORPORATE SECURITIES: Common stock; Preferred stock; VENTURE CAPITAL: Start-up from developed product stage; First-stage (less than 1 year); Second-stage (generally 1-3 years); Later-stage expansion; Buy-outs/Acquisitions; LOANS: Working capital; Equity-related; REAL ESTATE LOANS: Land; Land development; REAL ESTATE: Joint ventures; Partnerships/Syndications
PREFERRED TYPES OF INDUSTRIES/INVESTMENTS: Consumer Product/Service
GEOGRAPHIC LIMITS OF INVESTMENTS/LOANS: Local; State; Regional; National
RANGE OF INV./LOAN PER BUSINESS: Min. $250,000; Max. $1,000,000
PREFERRED TERM FOR LOANS & LEASES: Min. 2 years; Max. 5 years
BUSINESS CHARACTERISITICS DESIRED-REQUIRED: Minimum number of years in business: 0
REFERRALS ACCEPTED FROM: Investment/Mortgage banker or Borrower/Investee

COMPANY: **Ensign Mortgage Corp.**
ADDRESS: 2100 Powers Ferry Rd. Ste. 300
Atlanta, GA 30339
PHONE: (404) 953-0500; (800) 241-4346
TYPE OF INSTITUTION: Mortgage Banker
CONTACT OFFICER(S): Jerry A. Shaifer, Pres.
ASSETS: $5,000,000 and up
TYPES OF FINANCING: REAL ESTATE LOANS: Long-term senior mtg.; Intermediate-term senior mtg.; land development; construction;
GEOGRAPHIC LIMITS OF INVESTMENT/LOANS: State; Other: Service National
RANGE OF INV./LOAN PER BUSINESS: Min. $200,000; Max. $7,000,000
PREFERRED TERM FOR LOANS & LEASES: Min. 15-20 years

COMPANY: **Equitable Real Estate Investment Management, Inc.**
ADDRESS: 3414 Peachtree Road NE, Suite 1400
Atlanta, GA 30326-1162
PHONE: (404) 239-5000
TYPE OF INSTITUTION: R.E. Investment subsidiary of Equitable Life Assurance Society
CONTACT OFFICER(S): Bruce Moulthrop, E.V.P.
TYPES OF FINANCING: REAL ESTATE LOANS: Long-term senior mtg.; Intermediate-term senior mtg.; Subordinated; Wraparounds; Land; Land development; Construction; Gap; Standbys; Industrial revenue bonds REAL ESTATE: Acquisitions; Joint ventures; Partnerships/Syndications
PREFERRED TYPES OF INDUSTRIES/INVESTMENTS: Diversified
GEOGRAPHIC LIMITS OF INVESTMENTS/LOANS: National; Other: Canada
BUSINESS CHARACTERISTICS DESIRED-REQUIRED: Other: Established businesses

COMPANY: **First Atlanta Mortgage Corp.**
ADDRESS: 615 Peachtree St., N.E.
Atlanta, GA 30308
PHONE: (404) 875-3070
TYPE OF INSTITUTION: Mortgage Banker
CONTACT OFFICER(S): Robert J. Grote, V.P.
ASSETS: $100,000,000 and up
TYPES OF FINANCING: REAL ESTATE LOANS: Long-term senior mtg.; Intermediate-term senior mtg.; Subordinated; Construction; Standbys
GEOGRAPHIC LIMITS OF INVESTMENTS/LOANS: National
RANGE OF INV./LOAN PER BUSINESS: Min. $200,000; Max. None
PREFERRED TERM FOR LOANS & LEASES: Min. 3-5 years; Max. 10 years

COMPANY: **First Capital Financial Corp.**
ADDRESS: 5775 Peachtree Dunwoodie Rd., Bldg. D. Ste. 650
Atlanta, GA 30343
PHONE: (404) 255-3698
TYPE OF INSTITUTION: Public syndicator
CONTACT OFFICER(S): William R. Johnson, V.P. Acquisitions
ASSETS: 750 million
INVESTMENTS/LOANS MADE: For own account
TYPES OF FINANCING: REAL ESTATE: Acquisitions; Joint ventures; Partnerships/Syndications
PREFERRED TYPES OF INDUSTRIES/INVESTMENTS: Commercial real estate (shopping centers, warehouses, office buildings) throughout southeast United States only
GEOGRAPHIC LIMITS OF INVESTMENTS/LOANS: National
RANGE OF INV./LOAN PER BUSINESS: Min. $10 million; Max. $60 million
REMARKS: H.Q. to be located in Chicago

COMPANY: **The First National Bank of Atlanta**
ADDRESS: 2 Peachtree Street
Atlanta, GA 30302
PHONE: (404) 588-5426
TYPE OF INSTITUTION: R. E. Lender
CONTACT OFFICER(S): Patrick Tolleson, Group V.P.

COMPANY: **Georgia Federal Bank, FSB**
ADDRESS: 20 Marietta Street NW; P.O. Box 1723 (Zip: 30301)
Atlanta, GA 30303
PHONE: (404) 588-2600
TYPE OF INSTITUTION: Mortgage Banker
CONTACT OFFICER(S): Wyatt E. Johnson, Vice President
ASSETS: $2,131,179.00
TYPES OF FINANCING: REAL ESTATE LOANS: Construction REAL ESTATE: Acquisitions; Joint ventures; Partnerships/Syndications
GEOGRAPHIC LIMITS OF INVESTMENTS/LOANS: State; Regional
PREFERRED TERM FOR LOANS & LEASES: Min. Varies
BRANCHES: 72 branches in GA.

COMPANY: **Glenridge Associates, Inc.**
ADDRESS: 4501 Circle 75 Parkway, Building A Suite 1240
Atlanta, GA 30339
PHONE: (404) 955-2856
TYPE OF INSTITUTION: Equipment leasing and finance, real estate finance
CONTACT OFFICER(S): Michael L. Brown, President
ASSETS: N/A
INVESTMENTS/LOANS MADE: Through private placements
TYPES OF FINANCING: LOANS: Unsecured to credits above 'B'; Working Capital; Equipment; Equity related; Sale-Leaseback; Government guaranteed; REAL ESTATE LOANS: Long-term senior mtg.; Intermediate-term senior mtg.; Subordinated; Wraparounds; Industrial Revenue Bonds; LEASES
PREFERRED TYPES OF INDUSTRIES/INVESTMENTS: Computer oriented production/medical equipment, rolling stock, printing, all types of commercial and industrial equipment
WILL NOT CONSIDER: N/A
GEOGRAPHIC LIMITS OF INVESTMENT/LOANS: National
RANGE OF INV./LOAN PER BUSINESS: Min. $100,000; Max. None
PREFERRED TERM FOR LOANS & LEASES: Min. Two years; Max. Ten years
BUSINESS CHARACTERISTICS DESIRED/REQUIRED: Minimum number of years in business: 0; Min. annual sales $ None; Min. net worth $ N/A; Min. annual net income $ N/A; Min. annual cash flow $ N/A

COMPANY: **Gulf States Mortgage Co., Inc.**
ADDRESS: 2781 Whitley Rd. N.W.
Atlanta, GA 30339
PHONE: (404) 952-8933
TYPE OF INSTITUTION: Mortgage Banker
CONTACT OFFICER(S): Howard Wilensky, Vice President Commercial
ASSETS: $185,000,000
INVESTMENTS/LOANS MADE: Through private placements
TYPES OF FINANCING: REAL ESTATE LOANS: Long-term senior mtg.; Intermediate-term senior mtg.; Subordinated; Wraparounds; Standbys; REAL ESTATE: Acquisitions; Partnerships/Syndications
PREFERRED TYPES OF INDUSTRIES/INVESTMENTS: Commercial mortgages; office buildings; shopping centers; apartments
GEOGRAPHIC LIMITS OF INVESTMENTS/LOANS: Regional
RANGE OF INV./LOAN PER BUSINESS: Min. $500,000; Max. $50,000,000
REFERRALS ACCEPTED FROM: Investment/Mortgage banker only; Borrower/Investee
BRANCHES: Commercial Division—Atlanta Office Only

COMPANY: **Home Federal Savings & Loan Assn. of Atlanta**
ADDRESS: 79 W. Paces Ferry Rd., NW
Atlanta, GA 30305
PHONE: (406) 266-2255
TYPE OF INSTITUTION: R. E. Lender
CONTACT OFFICER(S): Rick Richard
William B. Pendleton, S. V.P.

COMPANY: **Horizon Mortgage & Investment Company**
ADDRESS: 10 Corporate Square Suite 130
Atlanta, GA 30329
PHONE: (404 634-9361
TYPE OF INSTITUTION: Mortgage Banker
CONTACT OFFICER(S): Gilbert M. Lovenz, President
TYPES OF FINANCING: REAL ESTATE LOANS: Long-term senior mtg.; Intermediate-term senior mtg.; Subordinated; Wraparounds; Construction; Gap; Standbys; Industrial revenue bondsREAL ESTATE: Joint ventures
PREFERRED TYPES OF INDUSTRIES/INVESTMENTS: Shopping Centers; Apartment Buildings; Office buildings; Warehouses; Industries
WILL NOT CONSIDER: Special purpose properties
GEOGRAPHIC LIMITS OF INVESTMENTS/LOANS: Regional; Other: Southeast
RANGE OF INV./LOAN PER BUSINESS: Min. $1 million

COMPANY: **Johnstown American Companies**
ADDRESS: 5775 A Peachtree Dunwoody Rd.
Atlanta GA 30342
PHONE: (404) 252-8780
CONTACT OFFICER(S): David V. John, S. V.P.

COMPANY: **Johnstown Mortgage Company**
ADDRESS: 5775-B Peachtree Dunwoody Road, Suite 110
Atlanta, GA 30342
PHONE: (404) 256-4352
TYPE OF INSTITUTION: Mortgage Banker
CONTACT OFFICER(S): Syd Rosenberg, Mgr. Commercial Lending
Scott Douglas, V.P. Marketing
ASSETS: $275 million in servicing
TYPES OF FINANCING: REAL ESTATE LOANS: Long-term senior mtg.; Intermediate-term senior mtg.; Subordinated; Wraparounds; Land; Land development; Construction; Gap; Standbys; Industrial revenue bonds REAL ESTATE: Acquisitions; Joint ventures; Partnerships/Syndications; OTHER SERVICES PROVIDED: Permanent take-out
PREFERRED TYPES OF INDUSTRIES/INVESTMENTS: Multi family, Medical Bldgs; Retail
GEOGRAPHIC LIMITS OF INVESTMENTS/LOANS: National
RANGE OF INV./LOAN PER BUSINESS: Min. $1 million
PREFERRED TERM FOR LOANS & LEASES: Max. 30 years
BRANCHES: Branches in: Canoga Park, CA
Newport Beach, CA
Austin, TX
Houston, TX
Tampa, FL
Boston, MA

COMPANY: **Standard Mortgage Corporation of Georgia**
ADDRESS: 1845 The Exchange
Atlanta, GA 30339
PHONE: (404) 955-0075
TYPE OF INSTITUTION: Mortgage Banker
CONTACT OFFICER(S): Dennis H. James, E. V.P.
Thomas Browning, V.P.
ASSETS: $1-10 million
TYPES OF FINANCING: REAL ESTATE LOANS: Long-term senior mtg.; Intermediate-term senior mtg.; Subordinated; Wraparounds; Construction; Gap; Standbys; Industrial revenue bonds 1-15 yrs; REAL ESTATE: Acquisitions; Joint ventures
PREFERRED TYPES OF INDUSTRIES/INVESTMENTS: Income producing properties: Office; Industrial; Retails
WILL NOT CONSIDER: Special purpose
GEOGRAPHIC LIMITS OF INVESTMENTS/LOANS: Regional
RANGE OF INV./LOAN PER BUSINESS: Min. $250,000; Max. $25 million
PREFERRED TERM FOR LOANS & LEASES: Min. 3 years; Max. 10 years
BRANCHES: Tom Johnson, Suite 100, Omni Pointe, 3444 Memorial Hwy., Tampa, FL 33609; (813) 872-8671

COMPANY: **Trust Company Mortgage**
ADDRESS: 1945 The Exchange, Suite 400, P.O. Box 4333
Atlanta, GA 30339
PHONE: (404) 955-9456
TYPE OF INSTITUTION: Mortgage Banker
CONTACT OFFICER(S): Barry C. Graham
ASSETS: $1,000,000,000+ in servicing
TYPES OF FINANCING: REAL ESTATE LOANS: Long-term senior mtg.; Intermediate-term senior mtg.; Subordinated; Wraparounds; Land; Land development; Construction; Gap; Standbys; Industrial revenue bonds, REAL ESTATE: Joint ventures, OTHER SERVICES PROVIDED: 100% equity financing
PREFERRED TYPES OF INDUSTRIES/INVESTMENTS: Varies with client
GEOGRAPHIC LIMITS OF INVESTMENTS/LOANS: Regional; Other: Southeast
RANGE OF INV./LOAN PER BUSINESS: Min. $1,000,000; Max. None
PREFERRED TERM FOR LOANS & LEASES: Min. 3 years; Max. 15 years
BUSINESS CHARACTERISTICS DESIRED-REQUIRED: Other: Case by case; Experienced developers/owners
BRANCHES: McCord Fraser, Mgr. & VP, Horizon at Tampa Bay Park, 4511 N. Hines Avenue, Suite 145, Tampa, FL 33614, (813) 877-6726

COMPANY: **Weinberg/Matheson, Inc.**
ADDRESS: 1934-B North Druid Hills Road
Atlanta, GA 30319
PHONE: (404) 634-4700
TYPE OF INSTITUTION: Mortgage Banker
CONTACT OFFICER(S): Laurence Weinberg
ASSETS: $150,000,000 annual servicing volume
TYPES OF FINANCING: REAL ESTATE LOANS: Long-term senior mtg.; Intermediate-term senior mtg.; Subordinated; Wraparounds; Land; Land development; Construction; Gap; Standbys; Industrial revenue bonds; REAL ESTATE: Acquisitions; Joint venutures; Partnerships/Syndications
RANGE OF INV./LOAN PER BUSINESS: Regional; National
PREFERRED TERM FOR LOANS & LEASES: Min. $100,000; Max. None

COMPANY: **Atlanta Financial & Leasing, Inc.**
ADDRESS: 4501 Circle 75 Parkway, Suite A-1240
Atlanta, Georgia 30339
PHONE: (404) 955-2856
TYPE OF INSTITUTION: Financial and leasing brokers, mortgage loans
CONTACT OFFICERS(S): Doug Faust, Owner
Equipment leasing and financing, also act as consultants in the area of equipment purchases. Expertise in the marine (offshore) industry.
INVESTMENTS/LOANS MADE: Through private placements
INVESTMENTS/LOANS MADE: In securities with a secondary market and securities without a secondary market
TYPES OF FINANCING: LOANS: Unsecured; Working capital (receivables/inventory); Equipment; Equity-related; REAL ESTATE LOANS: Long-term senior mtg.; Intermediate-term senior mtg.; Standbys;

Industrial revenue bonds; FACTORING; LEASES: Single-investor; Leveraged; Tax leases; Non-tax leases; Operating; Tax-oriented lease brokerage; Lease syndications; Vendor financing programs; REAL ESTATE: Joint ventures. OTHER: Equipment purchases, expertise in the marine industry
PREFERRED TYPES OF INDUSTRIES/INVESTMENTS: Middle market construction, medical, data processing, certain real estate transaction, equipment leasing
GEOGRAPHIC LIMITS OF INVESTMENTS/LOANS: Local; State; Regional; National; International
RANGE OF INV./LOAN PER BUSINESS: Min. $100,000; Max. $ no limit
PREFERRED TERM FOR LOANS & LEASES: Min. 3 years; Max. as pertinent
BUSINESS CHARACTERISTICS DESIRED-REQUIRED: We will look at any situation. It does need to make sense

COMPANY: **Bell Investment Co.**
ADDRESS: Front & Valley St., P.O. Box 576
Burlington, IA 52601
PHONE: (319) 752-5426
TYPE OF INSTITUTION: Mortgage Banker
CONTACT OFFICER(S): James O. Melton, Pres.
ASSETS: Servicing Volume over $300,000,000
TYPES OF FINANCING: REAL ESTATE LOANS
PREFERRED TYPES OF INDUSTRIES/INVESTMENTS: Agriculture
GEOGRAPHIC LIMITS OF INVESTMENTS/LOANS: Regional; Corn Belt
RANGE OF INV./LOAN PER BUSINESS: Min. $500,000; Max. None
PREFERRED TERM FOR LOANS & LEASES: Min. 3-5; Max. 10-15 years
BUSINESS CHARACTERISTICS DESIRED-REQUIRED: 320 Acres Tillable Land
BRANCHES: Ronald Wilson, Bell Investment Co. East, 207A W. State St., Pendleton, IN 46064
Larry Bishop, 916 Tandy, Columbia, MO 65201

COMPANY: **Bankers Life Company**
ADDRESS: 711 High St.
Des Moines, IA 50307
PHONE: (515) 247-5111
TYPE OF INSTITUTION: Mutual Insurance Company
CONTACT OFFICER(S): Bob Wilkins, V.P., Fixed Income Securities
ASSETS: $12 Billion
INVESTMENTS/LOANS MADE: For own account; For managed accounts; Through private placements
INVESTMENTS/LOANS MADE: In securities with a secondary market and in securities without a secondary market
TYPES OF FINANCING: SECONDARY-MARKET CORPORATE SECURITIES: Common stock; Bonds, LOANS: Unsecured to credits above Baa; Equipment; Equity-related,REAL ESTATE LOANS: Long-term senior mtg., Land, LEASES
WILL NOT CONSIDER: Land development, Bank Holding Companies
GEOGRAPHIC LIMITS OF INVESTMENTS/LOANS: International
RANGE OF INV./LOAN PER BUSINESS: Min. $2,000,000; Max. $40,000,000
PREFERRED TERM FOR LOANS & LEASES: Min. 2; Max. 15 years
BUSINESS CHARACTERISTICS DESIRED-REQUIRED: Other: Min. assets: $15 million
REFERRALS ACCEPTED FROM: Investment/Mortgage banker and Borrower/Investee
REMARKS: Average term: 10.5 years

COMPANY: **Brenton Mortgages, Inc.**
ADDRESS: P.O. Box 5005
Des Moines, IA 50306
PHONE: (515) 282-8155
CONTACT OFFICER(S): Jerry L. Hietbrink, V.P. Acting Manager
ASSETS: Servicing Volume over $100,000,000
TYPES OF FINANCING: REAL ESTATE LOANS: Long-term senior mtg.; Intermediate-term senior mtg.; Subordinated; Construction; Industrial Revenue Bonds
PREFERRED TYPES OF INDUSTRIES/INVESTMENTS: Office Bldgs.; Commercial; Apartments
GEOGRAPHIC LIMITS OF INVESTMENTS/LOANS: Regional
RANGE OF INV./LOAN PER BUSINESS: Min. $350,000; Max. $7,000,000
PREFERRED TERM FOR LOANS & LEASES: Min. 1-3; Max. 20+ years
BUSINESS CHARACTERISTICS DESIRED-REQUIRED: Minimum number of years in business: 0

COMPANY: **Central Life Assurance Company**
ADDRESS: 611 Fifth Avenue
Des Moines, IA 50306
PHONE: (515) 283-2371
CONTACT OFFICER(S): Lance S. Nelson, Securities V.P.
ASSETS: $1.1 Billion
INVESTMENTS/LOANS MADE: For own account; Through private placements; through underwriting public offerings
INVESTMENTS/LOANS MADE: In securities with a secondary market and in securities without a secondary market
TYPES OF FINANCING: SECONDARY-MARKET CORPORATE SECURITIES: Bonds, LOANS: Unsecured to credits above Baa; Equipment; REAL ESTATE LOANS: Intermediate-term senior mtg., REAL ESTATE: Joint ventures
GEOGRAPHIC LIMITS OF INVESTMENTS/LOANS: National
RANGE OF INV./LOAN PER BUSINESS: Min. $1,000,000; Max. $5,000,000
PREFERRED TERM FOR LOANS & LEASES: Min. 3; Max. 10 years
BUSINESS CHARACTERISTICS DESIRED-REQUIRED: Minimum number of years in business: 5; Min. annual sales $100 million; Min. net worth $25 million, Min. annual net income $5 million
REFERRALS ACCEPTED FROM: Investment/Mortgage banker or Borrower/Investee

COMPANY: **MIC Leasing Co., Mahaska Investment Co.**
ADDRESS: First Ave. E. P.O. Box 133
Oskaloosa, IA 52577

PHONE: (515) 673-8448
TYPE OF INSTITUTION: Leasing
CONTACT OFFICER(S): Steve J. Posovich
TYPES OF FINANCING: LEASES: Other: Full payout; REAL ESTATE
PREFERRED TYPES OF INDUSTRIES/INVESTMENTS: Farm
RANGE OF INV./LOAN PER BUSINESS: Min. $10,000; Max. $1,400,000
REMARKS: Lease Term 3-5 yrs.; Loan Term: Variable

COMPANY: **Control O Fax Management Inc.**
ADDRESS: 3070 West Airline Highway
Waterloo, IA 50704
PHONE: (319) 234-4651
CONTACT OFFICER(S): T. W. Davis

COMPANY: **Century Life of America**
ADDRESS: Heritage Way
Waverly, IA 50677
PHONE: (319) 352-4090
CONTACT OFFICER(S): Donald Heltner, V.P. Mtg. & R.E.
Charlie Knudsen, Sr. Investment Analyst RE & Mtg.
ASSETS: $850 million
TYPES OF FINANCING: REAL ESTATE: Aquisitions
GEOGRAPHIC LIMITS OF INVESTMENTS/LOANS: National; Other: Targeted SMSA's Chicago, Dallas, Denver, Los Angeles, Minneapolis, San Francisco, Seattle
RANGE OF INV./LOAN PER BUSINESS: Min. $2 Mil.; Max. 4 mil.
REFERRALS ACCEPTED FROM: Investment/Mortgage banker or Borrower/Investee

COMPANY: **Country Life Insurance Company**
ADDRESS: P.O. Box 2646
Bloomington, IL 61701
PHONE: (309) 557-3236
CONTACT OFFICER(S): Wayne A. Brown, V.P., Fixed Income Dept.
Bernard R. Dorneden, Investment Officer, Equity Inv.
ASSETS: $1.3 billion
INVESTMENTS/LOANS MADE: For own account; Through private placements,underwriting public offerings
INVESTMENTS/LOANS MADE: In securities with a secondary market and in securities without a secondary market
TYPES OF FINANCING: SECONDARY-MARKET CORPORATE SECURITIES: Common stock; Preferred stock; Bonds; Mortgages, REAL ESTATE LOANS: Long-term senior mtg.; Intermediate-term senior mtg.; Industrial revenue bonds, LEASES
PREFERRED TYPES OF INDUSTRIES/INVESTMENTS: Open
GEOGRAPHIC LIMITS OF INVESTMENTS/LOANS: National
RANGE OF INV./LOAN PER BUSINESS: Min. $750,000; Max. $5,000,000
PREFERRED TERM FOR LOANS & LEASES: Min. 5; Max. 30 years
BUSINESS CHARACTERISTICS DESIRED-REQUIRED: Minimum number of years in business: 5
REFERRALS ACCEPTED FROM: Investment/Mortgage banker or Borrower/Investee

COMPANY: **Associates Commercial Corporation**
ADDRESS: The Associates Center, 150 North Michigan Ave.
Chicago, IL 60601
PHONE: (312) 781-5800
TYPE OF INSTITUTION: Commercial finance subsidiary of Associates Corporation of North America (The Associates), the cornerstone on the Financial Services Group of Gulf & Western Industries, Inc.
CONTACT OFFICER(S): Rocco A. Macri, Executive Vice President, Business Loans Division (Division provides accounts receivable, inventory and fixed asset loans for working capital, refinancings, acquisitions and leveraged buyouts for small annd medium-sized businesses throughout the U.S.).
ASSETS: $6.6 billion (The Associates); $3.5 billion in commerical finance recievables
INVESTMENTS/LOANS MADE: For own account
INVESTMENTS/LOANS MADE: Only in securities without a secondary market
TYPES OF FINANCING: VENTURE CAPITAL: Later-stage expansions; Buy-outs/Acquisitions, LOANS: Working capital; Equipment; Equity-related. Other: Bank participation, REAL ESTATE LOANS: Industrial plants with receivables/inventory, FACTORING, LEASES: Single-investor; Tax leases; Non-tax leases; Operating; Vendor financing programs, REAL ESTATE: Acquisitions, OTHER SERVICES PROVIDED: Retail and wholesale financing of heavy duty trucks and trailers, financing and leasing of construction and mining equipment, machine tools, business aircraft and other capital goods; fleet leasing and management services for cars and trucks
PREFERRED TYPES OF INDUSTRIES/INVESTMENTS: Heavy-duty truck and trailer financing; auto, truck and trailer fleet leasing; communications and industrial equipment financing and leasing; business loans (esp. leveraged buyout financing); and factoring
WILL NOT CONSIDER: Unsecured financing
GEOGRAPHIC LIMITS OF INVESTMENTS/LOANS: National
RANGE OF INV./LOAN PER BUSINESS: Min. $500,000; Max. $100 million or more
PREFERRED TERM FOR LOANS & LEASES: Min. two (2) years; Max. ten (10) years
BUSINESS CHARACTERISTICS DESIRED-REQUIRED: Minimum net worth $500,000
REFERRALS ACCEPTED FROM: Investment/Mortgage banker or Borrower/Investee
BRANCHES: More than 100 regional and branch offices in North America
REMARKS: Associates Commerical has six operting divisions: Business Loans, Communications, Equipment, Factoring , Fleet Leasing and Transportation

COMPANY: **Baird & Warner, Inc.**
ADDRESS: 115 S. Lasalle St.
Chicago, IL 60603

PHONE: (312) 368-1855
TYPE OF INSTITUTION: Mortgage banker
CONTACT OFFICER(S): Richard T. Palmisano, V.P., R.E. Finance Group
ASSETS: Servicing volume over $500,000,000
INVESTMENTS/LOANS MADE: Through private placements
TYPES OF FINANCING: REAL ESTATE LOANS: Long-term senior mtg.; Intermediate-term senior mtg.; Subordinated; Wraparounds; Land; Land development; Construction; Gap; Standbys; Industrial revenue bonds; REAL ESTATE: Acquisitions; Joint ventures; Partnerships/Syndications
PREFERRED TYPES OF INDUSTRIES/INVESTMENTS: Investment type real estate
WILL NOT CONSIDER: Single family loans
RANGE OF INV./LOAN PER BUSINESS: Min. $500,000
PREFERRED TERM FOR LOANS & LEASES: Min. 5 years; Max. 15 years
REFERRALS ACCEPTED FROM: Borrower/Investee
BRANCHES: Earl S. Belopsky, V.P., 730 17th Street, Denver, CO 80202; (303) 571-1855
Paul S. Gardner, Mgr., 170 S. Main St., Ste 650, Salt Lake City, UT; (801) 531-1855

COMPANY: **The Chicago Dock and Canal Trust**
ADDRESS: 401 N. Michigan Ave., #3145
Chicago, IL 60611
PHONE: (312) 467-1870
TYPE OF INSTITUTION: REIT
CONTACT OFFICER(S): Charles R. Gardner

COMPANY: **Cohen Financial Corp.**
ADDRESS: Two N. LaSalle Street
Chicago, IL 60602
PHONE: (312) 346-5680
CONTACT OFFICER(S): Jack M. Cohen, V.P.
Skip Weiss

COMPANY: Focus Real Estate Finance Co.
ADDRESS: 200 W. Madison St.
Chicago, IL 60606
(312) 726-9400
TYPE OF INSTITUTION: Commercial Mortgage Banker, Real Estate Finance Company
CONTACT OFFICER(S): Stuart L. Greenberg C.M.B., Exec. Vice President
ASSETS: Services in excess of $500 million in loans, only income properties.
INVESTMENT/LOANS MADE: For own account; For managed accounts; Through private placements
TYPES OF FINANCING: REAL ESTATE LOANS: Long-term senior mtg.; Intermediate-term senior mtg.; Subordinated; Wraparounds; Land; Land development; Construction; Gap; Industrial revenue bonds; Other; Only income properties, provides equity placement, new construction; REAL ESTATE; Acquistions; Joint ventures; Partnerships/Syndications; OTHER SERVICES PROVIDED: Construction services and management services in headquarters office, limited forms of syndications.
PREFERRED TYPES OF INDUSTRIES/INVESTMENTS: All types of income properties; no residential single family, not looking for sports facilities, racquet clubs, tennis courts; Will do office buildings, shopping centers, light industries, national chain hotels and motels, service centers apartment projects, and various other types of income properties.
WILL NOT CONSIDER: See above (single family residential, racquet clubs, tennis courts)
GEOGRAPHIC LIMITS OF INVESTMENTS/LOANS: Regional; National; Midwest United States, Midnorth, Southwest, and Southeast
RANGE OF INV./LOAN PER BUSINESS: Min. $1,500,000; Max. $50 million
PREFERRED TERM FOR LOANS & LEASES: Min. For direct deals: 1 to 5 years; For longterm: 7 to 12 years
BUSINESS CHARACTERISTICS DESIRED-REQUIRED: Minimum number of years in business: 2-3; Min. net worth $1 million; Other; should have some development or investing experience
REFERRALS ACCEPTED FROM: Investment/Mortgage banker or Borrower/Investee; but will not pay fees to referree's
BRANCHES: Focus Finance of Colorado, 400 S. Colorado Blvd., Denver, CO; 303-355-3480; John Ehrhardt, President, Denver, CO

COMPANY: **Talman Home Mortgage Corporation**
ADDRESS: 4242 North Harlem Avenue
Chicago, IL 60634
PHONE: (312) 456-0400
TYPE OF INSTITUTION: Mortgage Banker
CONTACT OFFICER(S): Charles Goetze, A.V.P.; (312) 641-1404
ASSETS: $90 million
TYPES OF FINANCING: REAL ESTATE LOANS: Long-term senior mtg.; Intermediate-term senior mtg.; Subordinated; Wraparounds; Land; Land development; Construction; Gap; Standbys
GEOGRAPHIC LIMITS OF INVESTMENTS/LOANS: National
REFERRALS ACCEPTED FROM: Investment/Mortgage banker or Borrower/Investee

COMPANY: **Northern Trust Bank/O'Hare N.A.**
ADDRESS: 8501 West Higgins Road
Chicago, IL 60631
PHONE: (312) 693-5555
TYPE OF INSTITUTION: R.E. Lending
CONTACT OFFICER(S): Thomas O. Leigh, S.V.P
ASSETS: $250 million
TYPES OF FINANCING: REAL ESTATE LOANS: Intermediate-term senior mtg.; Construction; Industrial revenue bonds; REAL ESTATE: Acquisitons
PREFERRED TYPES OF INDUSTRIES/INVESTMENTS: Small Industrial
GEOGRAPHIC LIMITS OF INVESTMENTS/LOANS: Local; Metropolitan
RANGE OF INV./LOAN PER BUSINESS: Min. $200,000; Max. $1 million
PREFERRED TERM FOR LOANS & LEASES: Min. 5 years; Max. 20 years
REFERRALS ACCEPTED FROM: Borrower/Investee

COMPANY: **National Boulevard Bank of Chicago**
ADDRESS: 400-410 North Michigan Avenue
Chicago, IL 60611
PHONE: (312) 836-6500
TYPE OF INSTITUTION: Commercial Bank
CONTACT OFFICER(S): Carl Jansen, V.P.
ASSETS: $500 million
TYPES OF FINANCING: REAL ESTATE LOANS: Long-term senior mtg.; Intermediate-term senior mtg.; Construction; Industrial Revenue Bonds; REAL ESTATE: Acquisitions
PREFERRED TYPES OF INDUSTRIES/INVESTMENTS: Commercial; Industrial office
GEOGRAPHIC LIMITS OF INVESTMENTS/LOANS: Local
RANGE OF INV./LOAN PER BUSINESS: Min. $1 million; Max. $7.5 million
PREFERRED TERM FOR LOANS & LEASES: Max. 15 years
REFERRALS ACCEPTED FROM: Investment/Mortgage banker or Borrower/Investee

COMPANY: **LaSalle National Bank**
ADDRESS: 135 South LaSalle Street
Chicago, IL 60690
PHONE: (312) 443-2000
TYPE OF INSTITUTION: Commercial Real Estate Lenders
CONTACT OFFICER(S): Bruce Duncan, V.P. Division Manager
ASSETS: $1.4 billion
TYPES OF FINANCING: REAL ESTATE LOANS: Intermediate-term senior mtg.; Subordinated; Wraparounds; Construction; OTHER SERVICES PROVIDED: Bank does not do R.E. acqusitions but has another division that advises on them.
PREFERRED TYPES OF INDUSTRIES/INVESTMENTS: Income producing properties
WILL NOT CONSIDER: Special use properties
GEOGRAPHIC LIMITS OF INVESTMENTS/LOANS: Regional
RANGE OF INV./LOAN PER BUSINESS: Min. $500,000
PREFERRED TERM FOR LOANS & LEASES: Max. 3 years
REFERRALS ACCEPTED FROM: Borrower/Investee
REMARKS: Subsidiary of Algemene Bank Nederland, Amsterdam, Holland

COMPANY: **ILCO Properties, Inc.**
ADDRESS: 30 North LaSalle Street, Ste. 263
Chicago, IL 60602
PHONE: (312) 444-2100
TYPE OF INSTITUTION: Investment Real Estate Syndication for Limited Partnerships
CONTACT OFFICER(S): Richard R. Wood, President
Richard Johnson, Vice President
ASSETS: $60,000,000
INVESTMENTS/LOANS MADE: Through private placements
INVESTMENT/LOANS MADE: Only in securities without a secondary market
TYPES OF FINANCING: SECONDARY-MARKET CORPORATE SECURITIES: Real Estate Limited Partnership Equity; REAL ESTATE: Acqusitions; Joint ventures; Partnerships/Syndications
PREFERRED TYPES OF INDUSTRIES/INVESTMENTS: Shopping Centers, Office Buildings & Apt. Buildings
WILL NOT CONSIDER: Real Estate, Oil & Gas
GEOGRAPHIC LIMITS OF INVESTMENTS/LOANS: National
RANGE OF INV./LOAN PER BUSINESS: Min. $1,000,000; Max. $3,000,000
PREFERRED TERM FOR LOANS & LEASES: Min. Fifteen (15) years; Max. Fifty (50) years
BUSINESS CHARACTERISTICS DESIRED-REQUIRED: Minimum number of years in business: 0
REFERRALS ACCEPTED FROM: Investment/Mortgage or Borrow/Investee

COMPANY:**The Canadian Imperial bank of Commerce/ Corporate Finance Group USA**
ADDRESS: 30 North LaSalle Street, Ste. 2726
Chicago, IL 60602
PHONE: (312) 368-1165
TYPE OF INSTITUTION: Real estate specialty group of bank
CONTACT OFFICER(S): Robert Snell, Sr. Manager—Real estate
ASSETS: $55 billion
TYPES OF FINANCING: REAL ESTATE LOANS: Intermediate-term senior mtg.; Land; Land development; Construction; Gap; Standbys
PREFERRED TYPES OF INDUSTRIES/ INVESTMENTS:offices; business parks; shopping centers; industrial loans
WILL NOT CONSIDER: Residential developments; Condominiums
GEOGRAPHIC LIMITS OF INVESTMENTS/LOANS: National
RANGE OF INV./LOAN PER BUSINESS: Min. $10 million
PREFERRED TERM FOR LOANS & LEASES: Min. 2 years; Max. 10 years

COMPANY:**Bernard Cohen & Company, Inc.**
ADDRESS: 135 South LaSalle Street, Ste. 1018
Chicago, IL 60603
PHONE: (312) 236-0786
TYPE OF INSTITUTION: R.E. Lender
CONTACT OFFICER(S):Bernard Cohen, President
TYPES OF FINANCINC: REAL ESTATE LOANS: Long-term senior mtg.; Intermediate-term senior mtg.; Wraparounds; Construction; Gap; Standbys; Industrial revenue bonds, REAL ESTATE: Acquisitions; Joint ventures
PREFERRED TYPES OF INDUSTRIES/INVESTMENTS: office; industrial; regional shopping centers
GEOGRAPHIC LIMITS OF INVESTMENTS/LOANS: National
RANGE OF INV./LOAN PER BUSINESS: Min. $500,000
PREFERRED TERM FOR LOANS & LEASES: Min. 3 years; Max. 10 years

COMPANY: **Draper & Kramer, Inc.**
ADDRESS: 33 W. Monroe St.
Chicago, IL 60603
PHONE: (312) 346-8600
TYPE OF INSTITUTION: Mortgage Banker

CONTACT OFFICER(S): David Tomfordy, V.P.
TYPES OF FINANCING: REAL ESTATE LOANS
GEOGRAPHIC LIMITS OF INVESTMENTS/LOANS: National
PREFERRED TERM FOR LOANS & LEASES: Max. 20+ years

COMPANY: **First City Mortgage Corp.**
ADDRESS: 55 W. Monroe St., Ste 910
Chicago, IL 60603
PHONE: (312) 332-6200
TYPE OF INSTITUTION: Mortgage Bank
CONTACT OFFICER(S): Jan C. Faulkner, President

COMPANY: **The First National Bank of Chicago**
ADDRESS: One First National Plaza
Chicago, IL 60670
PHONE: (312) 732-4000
TYPE OF INSTITUTION: R. E. Lender
CONTACT OFFICER(S): Daniel A. Lupiani, S. V.P.

COMPANY: **JMB Realty Trust**
ADDRESS: 875 N. Michigan Ave.
Chicago, IL 60611
PHONE: (312) 440-4800
CONTACT OFFICER(S): Burton E. Glazov, V.P.

COMPANY: **Lake Michigan Financial Group**
ADDRESS: 69 W. Washington St.
Chicago, IL 60602
PHONE: (312) 236-2545
TYPE OF INSTITUTION: Mortgage banker and real estate consulting/sales
CONTACT OFFICER(S): Robert S. Julian, Pres.
David A. Downey, V.P.
INVESTMENTS/LOANS MADE: For own account, Through private placements
INVESTMENTS/LOANS MADE: Only in securities without a secondary market
TYPES OF FINANCING: REAL ESTATE LOANS: Long-term senior mtg.; Intermediate-term senior mtg.; Subordinated; Wraparounds; Construction; Industrial revenue bonds, REAL ESTATE: Acquisitions; Joint ventures; Pre-sales
PREFERRED TYPES OF INDUSTRIES/INVESTMENTS: Real estate only
GEOGRAPHIC LIMITS OF INVESTMENTS/LOANS: National
RANGE OF INV./LOAN PER BUSINESS: Min. $2,500,000
REFERRALS ACCEPTED FROM: Investment/Mortgage banker or Borrower/Investee

COMPANY: **Liberty Mortgage & Development Co.**
ADDRESS: 180 N. LaSalle Street
Chicago, IL 60601
PHONE: (312) 782-7878
TYPE OF INSTITUTION: Mortgage Bank
CONTACT OFFICER(S): Alf G. McConnell, President

COMPANY: **The Philipsborn Company**
ADDRESS: 115 S. LaSalle St., Ste 2800
Chicago, IL 60603
PHONE: (312) 781-8800
CONTACT OFFICER(S): Don C. Trossman, S. V.P.

COMPANY: **Republic Realty Mortgage Corp.**
ADDRESS: 111 W. Washington Street, Ste 1737
Chicago IL 60602
PHONE: (312) 558-8282
TYPE OF INSTITUTION: Mortgage Bank
CONTACT OFFICER(S): Jerome R. Prassas, Exec. V.P.

COMPANY: **Salk, Ward & Salk, Inc.**
ADDRESS: 55 E. Monroe St., Ste 4607
Chicago, IL 60603
PHONE: (312) 236-0825
TYPE OF INSTITUTION: Mortgage Bank
CONTACT OFFICER(S): Erwin A. Falk, President
Albert K. Berkson, S. V.P.

COMPANY: **Dwinn-Shaffer and Company**
ADDRESS: 55 West Monroe Street, Ste. 790
Chicago IL 60603
PHONE: (312) 346-9191
TYPE OF INSTITUTION: Mortgage Banking
CONTACT OFFICER(S): Arnold H. Dwinn, Chairman of the Board
TYPES OF FINANCING: REAL ESTATE LOANS: Long-term senior mtg.; Intermediate-term senior mtg.; Subordinated; Wraparounds; Land; Land development; Construction; Gap; Standbys; Industrial revenue bonds; REAL ESTATE: Acquistions; Joint ventures
PREFERRED TYPES OF INDUSTRIES/INVESTMENTS: All types income producing Real Estate
GEOGRAPHIC LIMITS OF INVESTMENTS/LOANS: National
RANGE OF INV./LOAN PER BUSINESS: Min. $500,000
PREFERRED TERM FOR LOANS & LEASES: Min. 3 years; Max. 30 years

COMPANY:**North American Capital Group, Ltd.**
ADDRESS: 7250 N. Cicero Ave., Suite 201
Lincolnwood IL 60646
PHONE: (312) 982-1010
TYPE OF INSTITUTION: Subsidiary - financial services holding company, The North American Group, Ltd.
CONTACT OFFICER(S): Gregory I. Kravitt, President
William Andersen, Associate
INVESTMENTS/LOANS MADE: For own account; Through private placements
INVESTMENTS/LOANS MADE: Only in securities without a secondary market
TYPES OF FINANCING: VENTURE CAPITAL: Second-stage; Later-stage; Buy-outs/Acquisitions; LOANS: Working capital; Equipment; Equity-related; Other: Loans with attached warrants; REAL ESTATE LOANS: Long-term senior mtg.; Intermediate-term senior mtg.; Subordinated; Wraparounds; Construction; Standbys; Other: bond guarantees; REAL ESTATE: Acquisitions; Joint ventures; OTHER SERVICES PROVIDED:

Financing arranged for both qualified franchisors and qualified franchisees
PREFERRED TYPES OF INDUSTRIES/INVESTMENTS: Franchising, medium to low technology companies, Income property, Real estate (manufacturers, ditributors) leveraged buyouts, profitable service companies
WILL NOT CONSIDER: gambling casinos, entertainment
GEOGRAPHIC LIMITS OF INVESTMENTS/LOANS: Other: Midwest
RANGE OF INV./LOAN PER BUSINESS: Min. $100,000; Max. $3.0 million
PREFERRED TERM FOR LOANS & LEASES: Min. 3 years; Max. 10 years
BUSINESS CHARACTERISTICS DESIRED-REQUIRED: Minimum number of years in business: 1; Min. annual sales $500,000

COMPANY: **Mellon Financial Services Corporation**
ADDRESS: 1415 West 22nd Street, Suite 1200
Oak Brook, IL 60521
PHONE: (800) 323-7338 outside IL, (312) 986-2950 inside IL
TYPE OF INSTITUTION: Asset based lending affiliate of Mellon Bank, N.A.
CONTACT OFFICER(S): Charles S. Pryce, Senior Vice President
ASSETS: $25 billion
INVESTMENTS/LOANS MADE: For own account
INVESTMENTS/LOANS MADE: In securities with a secondary market and in securities without a secondary market
TYPES OF FINANCING: LOANS: Working capital; Equipment; Equity-related; Other: intermediate term loans; LBO financing. REAL ESTATE LOANS: Intermediate-term senior mtg.; Land; Standbys; Industrial revenue bonds. LEASES: Non-tax leases. INTERNATIONAL
WILL NOT CONSIDER: Building contractors
GEOGRAPHIC LIMITS OF INVESTMENTS/LOANS: National
BUSINESS CHARACTERISTICS DESIRED-REQUIRED: Minimum number of years in business: 0 Min. annual sales $2,000,000; Min. net worth $100,000; Min. annual net income $ positive; Min. annual cash flow $ positive.
REFERRALS ACCEPTED FROM: Investment/Mortgage banker or Borrower/Investee

COMPANY: **Borg-Warner Capital Services Corporation**
ADDRESS: 1355 E. Remington Rd. Suite J
Schaumburg, IL 60195
PHONE: (312) 843-6969
TYPE OF INSTITUTION: Investment Banking
CONTACT OFFICER(S): Thomas S. Ablum, Managing Director
Stephen R. Anderson, Operations Manager
INVESTMENTS/LOANS MADE: For managed accounts, Through private placements
TYPES OF FINANCING: LOANS: Working capital. REAL ESTATE LOANS: Long-term senior mtg.; Subordinated; Wraparounds; Land development; Construction; Industrial revenue bonds. LEASES: Single-investor; Leveraged; Tax leases; Non-tax leases; Tax-oriented lease brokerage; Lease syndications; Vendor financing programs. REAL ESTATE: Acquisitions. OTHER SERVICES PROVIDED: Financial Advisory Services & arrangement of above financing structures
PREFERRED TYPES OF INDUSTRIES/INVESTMENTS: No Preferences
WILL NOT CONSIDER: Land Only Acquisition & Venture Capital
RANGE OF INV./LOAN PER BUSINESS: Min. $250,000
PREFERRED TERM FOR LOANS & LEASES: Min. 1 year loan/5 leases; Max. 15 year loan/20 year lease
BUSINESS CHARACTERISTICS DESIRED-REQUIRED: Minimum number of years in business: 3; Min. annual sales $10MM; Min. net worth $500,000; Min annual net income $200,000
REFERRALS ACCEPTED FROM: Investment/Mortgage banker or Borrower/Investee

COMPANY: **Balcor Mortgage Advisors**
ADDRESS: 4849 Golf Road
Skokie, IL 60077
PHONE: (312) 677-2900
TYPE OF INSTITUTION: Lending division of area real estate investment.
CONTACT OFFICER(S): Paul Gottwald, Brian Nagle, Tony Raimondi, Carol Reynolds, Connie Graham, Jay Rosen. All Loan Officers are nationwide
ASSETS: $1,200,000,000
INVESTMENTS/LOANS MADE: Through public pension offerings, underwriting
TYPES OF FINANCING: REAL ESTATE LOANS: Long-term senior mtg.
PREFERRED TYPES OF INDUSTRIES/INVESTMENTS: Apartment Complexes
WILL NOT CONSIDER: Single purpose buildings
RANGE OF INV./LOAN PER BUSINESS: Min. $1,000,000; Max. $26,000,000
PREFERRED TERM FOR LOANS & LEASES: Min. 8; Max. 15 years
BUSINESS CHARACTERISTICS DESIRED-REQUIRED: Other: wraps — existing with proven history of success, firsts — constructed and pre-leased
REMARKS: All of our loan officers are nationwide

COMPANY: **The Franklin Life Insurance Company**
ADDRESS: Franklin Square
Springfield, IL 62713
PHONE: (217) 528-2011
CONTACT OFFICER(S): John Akers, C.F.A., Treasurer—Corporate Public Offerings
Stanley G. Howard, V.P.—Commercial Mortgage Loans
William D. Ward, C.F.A., V.P.—Corporate Private Placement Common Stocks
ASSETS: $2,459,650,584
INVESTMENTS/LOANS MADE: For own account; Through private placements,underwriting public offerings
INVESTMENTS/LOANS MADE: In securities with a secondary market and in securities without a secondary market
TYPES OF FINANCING: SECONDARY-MARKET CORPORATE SECURITIES: Common stock; Preferred stock; Bonds, REAL ESTATE LOANS: Long-term

senior mtg., LEASES: Single-investor; Leveraged; Tax leases; Non-tax leases; Operating
GEOGRAPHIC LIMITS OF INVESTMENTS/LOANS: National
RANGE OF INV./LOAN PER BUSINESS: Min. $1,000,000; Max. $12,000,000
PREFERRED TERM FOR LOANS & LEASES: Min. 5; Max. 12-15 years
BUSINESS CHARACTERISTICS DESIRED-REQUIRED: Minimum number of years in business: 10; Min. net worth $25,000,000
REFERRALS ACCEPTED FROM: Investment/Mortgage banker

COMPANY: **Horace Mann Life Insurance Company**
ADDRESS: 1 Horace Mann Plaza
Springfield, IL 62715
PHONE: (217) 789-2500
CONTACT OFFICER(S): Milton Wiggers, Secretary/ Director, Mtg. & R.E.
ASSETS: $100 million and up
TYPES OF FINANCING: REAL ESTATE LOANS: Long-term senior mtg. OTHER: Commercial and residential
PREFERRED TYPES OF INDUSTRIES/INVESTMENTS: No single purpose structures
GEOGRAPHIC LIMITS OF INVESTMENTS/LOANS: National
RANGE OF INV./LOAN PER BUSINESS: Min. $400,000; Max. $5 million
PREFERRED TERM FOR LOANS & LEASES: Min. 7 years; Max. 10 years
REFERRALS ACCEPTED FROM: Investment/Mortgage banker only
REMARKS: Preferred term for loans and leases subject to change

COMPANY: **M.E. Hoffman Co.**
ADDRESS: 901 S. Second St., P.O. Box 1026
Springfield, IL 62705
PHONE: (217) 528-7355
TYPE OF INSTITUTION: Mortgage Banker
CONTACT OFFICER(S): M. E. Hoffman, Pres.
INVESTMENTS/LOANS MADE: For own account
INVESTMENTS/LOANS MADE: Only in securities with a secondary market
TYPES OF FINANCING: LOANS, REAL ESTATE LOANS: Long-term senior mtg.; Intermediate-term senior mtg.; Wraparounds.
PREFERRED TYPES OF INDUSTRIES/INVESTMENTS: Real Estate
GEOGRAPHIC LIMITS OF INVESTMENTS/LOANS: National
RANGE OF INV./LOAN PER BUSINESS: Min. $500,000
BUSINESS CHARACTERISTICS DESIRED-REQUIRED: Minimum number of years in business: 0

COMPANY: **Irwin Union Corporation**
ADDRESS: 500 Washington St., Box 929
Columbus, IN 47201
PHONE: (812) 372-0111
TYPE OF INSTITUTION: Bank holding company: subsidiaries; Irwin Union Bank, Inland Mortgage, white River Capital
CONTACT OFFICER(S): M. R. Ryan; Commercial Lending, President, Irwin Union Bank
S. K. Kreigh; Mortgage Lending, President, Inland Mortgage
D. J. Blair; Venture Capital, Vice President, White River Capital
ASSETS: $250 million
INVESTMENTS/LOANS MADE: For own account
INVESTMENTS/LOANS MADE: In securities with a secondary market and in securities wiithout a secondary market
TYPES OF FINANCING: SECONDARY MARKET CORPORATE SECURITIES; Industrial Revenue Bond Placements. VENTURE CAPITAL: Second-stage; Later-stage expansion. LOANS: Unsecured to credits Above BBB; Working capital; Equipment; Equity-related. REAL ESTATE LOANS: Long-term senior mtg.; Wraparounds; Construction; Industrial revenue bonds; Other: Primarily single family. OTHER SERVICES PROVIDED: Mortgage servicing, municipal finance, and pension management
PREFERRED TYPES OF INDUSTRIES/INVESTMENTS: Commercial Lending-all forms; Mortgage Banking-Single family, FHA/VA; Venture Capital-no preferences
GEOGRAPHIC LIMITS OF INVESTMENTS/LOANS: State; regional (prefer State)
RANGE OF INV./LOAN PER BUSINESS: Min. $100,000; Max. $2,000,000 (Venture $200,000)
PREFERRED TERM FOR LOANS & LEASES: Min. .25 years; Max. 20 years
BUSINESS CHARACTERISTICS DESIRED-REQUIRED: Minimum number of years in business: 1
REFERRALS ACCEPTED FROM: Investment/Mortgage banker or Borrower/Investee

COMPANY: **The Lincoln National Inv. Management Co.**
ADDRESS: 1300 South Clinton St.
Ft. Wayne, IN 46801
PHONE: (219) 427-2000
CONTACT OFFICER(S): Patrick E. Falconio, Sr. V.P.
Robert Stewart, 2nd V.P.
Pat Chasey, 2nd V.P.
Jim Rogers, 2nd V.P.
Barbara S. Kowalczyk, 2nd V.P.
Ann L. Warner, 2nd V.P.
TYPES OF FINANCING: LOANS: Unsecured; Equipment; Equity-related; REAL ESTATE LOANS: Intermediate term senior mtg.; Subordinated; Land development; Standbys; Bond guarantees; OHTER: Industrial Revenue Bond Guarantees; REAL ESTATE: Acquisitions; OTHER SERVICES PROVIDED: Joint ventures on proposed properties; (R.E.) partnerships (R.E.)
WILL NOT CONSIDER: Retail, automotive
GEOGRAPHIC LIMITS OF INVESTMENTS/LOANS: National; International; Other: Western Europe
RANGE OF INV./LOAN PER BUSINESS: Min. $2 million; Max. $15 million; $25 million (R.E.)
PREFERRED TERM FOR LOANS & LEASES: Min. 3 years; Max. 7 years, 10 years (R.E.)

COMPANY: **Waterfield Mortgage Co., Inc.**
ADDRESS: 333 E. Washington Blvd.
Ft. Wayne, IN 46802
PHONE: (219) 425-8393
TYPE OF INSTITUTION: Mortgage Banker
CONTACT OFFICER(S): Thomas A. Gauldin, V.P., Manager, C.M.B.—Commercial loans
ASSETS: $3 billion
INVESTMENTS/LOANS MADE: For own account; for managed accounts and through private placements
INVESTMENTS/LOANS MADE: In securities with a secondary market and in securities without a secondary market
TYPES OF FINANCING: REAL ESTATE LOANS: SECONDARY-MARKET CORPORATE SECURITIES: Private placements; VENTURE CAPITAL: Start-up from developed product stage; LOANS: Equipment; Equity-related; REAL ESTATE LOANS: Long-term senior mtg.; Intermediate-term senior mtg.; Subordinated; Wraparounds; Land; Land development; Construction; Gap; Standbys; Industrial revenue bonds; LEASES: Single-investor; Leveraged; Tax leases; Non-tax leases; Operating; Tax-oriented lease brokerage; Lease syndications; REAL ESTATE: Acquisitions; Joint ventures; Partnerships/Syndications
PREFERRED TYPES OF INDUSTRIES/INVESTMENTS: Office; Warehouse, Shopping; Retail; Apartments; Motel/hotels
GEOGRAPHIC LIMITS OF INVESTMENTS/LOANS: National
RANGE OF INV./LOAN PER BUSINESS: Min. $200,000; Max. Unlimited
PREFERRED TERM FOR LOANS & LEASES: Min. Flexible
BUSINESS CHARACTERISTICS DESIRED-REQUIRED: Min. yrs. in business: 5
BRANCHES: 35 Nationwide

COMPANY: **American United Life Insurance Company**
ADDRESS: 1 American Square
Indianapolis, IN 46204
PHONE: (317) 263-1877
TYPE OF INSTITUTION: Life Insurance
CONTACT OFFICER(S): Leonard Schutt, Sr. V.P.,
David Sapp, V.P., Securities
Edmund W. Genier, V.P., Mtg. Loans
ASSETS: $2.0 billion
INVESTMENTS/LOANS MADE: For own account
INVESTMENTS/LOANS MADE: In securities with a secondary market and in securities without a secondary market
TYPES OF FINANCING: SECONDARY-MARKET CORPORATE SECURITIES: Common stock; Preferred stock; Bonds; LOANS: Unsecured to credits above BA; Working capital; Equipment; REAL ESTATE LOANS: Long-term senior mtg.; Intermediate-term senior mtg.
INVESTMENTS/LOANS MADE: In securities with a secondary market and in securities without a secondary market
TYPES OF FINANCING: SECONDARY-MARKET CORPORATE SECURITIES: Bonds; REAL ESTATE LOANS: Long-term senior mtg.; Intermediate-term senior mtg.;
GEOGRAPHIC LIMITS OF INVESTMENTS/LOANS: National
RANGE OF INV./LOAN PER BUSINESS: Min. $500,000; $2 million
PREFERRED TERM FOR LOANS & LEASES: Min. 5 yrs; Max. 10 yrs.
BUSINESS CHARACTERISTICS DESIRED-REQUIRED: Minimum number of years in business: 0

COMPANY: **Indiana Mortgage Corp.**
ADDRESS: Ste. M-960, 151 N. Delaware St.
Indianapolis, IN 46266
PHONE: (317) 266-5169
TYPE OF INSTITUTION: Mortgage banker
CONTACT OFFICER(S): Gerald L. Rush, Sr. V.P.
TYPES OF FINANCING: REAL ESTATE LOANS: Long-term senior mtg.; Intermediate-term senior mtg, REAL ESTATE: Joint ventures
GEOGRAPHIC LIMITS OF INVESTMENTS/LOANS: Midwest
RANGE OF INV./LOAN PER BUSINESS: Min. $500,000; Max. None
PREFERRED TERM FOR LOANS & LEASES: Min. 3-5 years; Max. 20 years & up
BRANCHES: Michael Montgomery; 11311 Cornell Park Dr. Cinncinati, OH 45242 (513) 489-1840

COMPANY: **Indianapolis Life Insurance Company**
ADDRESS: P.O. Box 1230
Indianapolis, IN 46206
PHONE: (317) 927-6522
CONTACT OFFICER(S): Donald S. Lawhorn, Sr. V.P. & Chief Investment office
ASSETS: $700 million
INVESTMENTS/LOANS MADE: For own account; For managed accounts; Through private placements; Through underwriting public offerings
INVESTMENTS/LOANS MADE: In securities with a secondary market and in securities without a secondary marketing
TYPES OF FINANCING: SECONDARY-MARKET CORPORATE SECURITIES: Bonds, VENTURE CAPITAL: Later-stage expansion; LOANS: Unsecured to credits above Baa; Working capital; Equipment; REAL ESTATE LOANS: Long-term senior mtg.; Intermediate-term senior mtg.
GEOGRAPHIC LIMITS OF INVESTMENTS/LOANS: National
RANGE OF INV./LOAN PER BUSINESS: Min. $200,000; Max. $2.5 million
PREFERRED TERM FOR LOANS & LEASES: Min. 5 years.; Max. 20 years
BUSINESS CHARACTERISTICS DESIRED-REQUIRED: Min. net worth $50 Million
REFERRALS ACCEPTED FROM: Investment/Mortgage banker or Borrower/Investee

COMPANY: **The State Life Insurance Company**
ADDRESS: P.O. Box 406, 141 E. Washington St.
Indianapolis, IN 46206
PHONE: (317) 632-3551
TYPE OF INSTITUTION: Life and Health Insurance
CONTACT OFFICER(S): David A. Martin, Private Placement, Bonds, Public Bonds, Mtg. Loans
ASSETS: $150 million
INVESTMENTS/LOANS MADE: For own account; Through private placements,underwriting public offerings
TYPES OF FINANCING: SECONDARY-MARKET CORPORATE SECURITIES: Bonds, LOANS: Unsecured to credits above A, REAL ESTATE LOANS: Long-term senior mtg.; Intermediate-term senior mtg.
WILL NOT CONSIDER: Finance
GEOGRAPHIC LIMITS OF INVESTMENTS/LOANS: National
REFERRALS ACCEPTED FROM: Investment/Mortgage banker

COMPANY: **Security Benefit Group of Companies**
ADDRESS: 700 Harrison
Topeka, KS 66636
PHONE: (913) 295-3000
CONTACT OFFICER(S): Jack W. Carolan, V.P.
ASSETS: $1.4 billion
TYPES OF FINANCING: REAL ESTATE LOANS: Intermediate-term senior mtg.
GEOGRAPHIC LIMITS OF INVESTMENTS/LOANS: National
RANGE OF INV./LOAN PER BUSINESS: Min. $800,000; Max. $4 million
PREFERRED TERM FOR LOANS & LEASES: Min. 5 years; Max. 15 years
REFERRALS ACCEPTED FROM: Investment/mortgage banker or Borrower/Investee

COMPANY: **Fidelity Investment Co.**
ADDRESS: 229 S. Market
Wichita, KS 67202
PHONE: (316) 265-2261
TYPE OF INSTITUTION: Mortgage Banker
CONTACT OFFICER(S): Clark Bastian, V.P.
ASSETS: Servicing Volume over $200,000,000
INVESTMENTS/LOANS MADE: For own account; Through private placements
TYPES OF FINANCING: REAL ESTATE LOANS: Long-term senior mtg.; Intermediate-term senior mtg.; Wraparounds; Construction; Gap, REAL ESTATE: Joint ventures; Partnerships/Syndications
PREFERRED TYPES OF INDUSTRIES/INVESTMENTS: Apartments
WILL NOT CONSIDER: Motels—Hotels; Special Purpose Property
GEOGRAPHIC LIMITS OF INVESTMENTS/LOANS: State
RANGE OF INV./LOAN PER BUSINESS: Min. $100,000; Max. $10,000,000
REFERRALS ACCEPTED FROM: Investment/Mortgage banker or Borrower/Investee

COMPANY: **Kentucky Central Insurance Cos.**
ADDRESS: Kincaid Towers
Lexington, KY 40508
PHONE: (606) 253-5293
TYPE OF INSTITUTION: Life, Property & Casualty Insurance Companies
CONTACT OFFICER(S): Clifton H. Forbush, Jr., V.P. — Investments
John F. Rampulla, III, V.P. — Mortgage Loans
ASSETS: $700 million
INVESTMENTS/LOANS MADE: For own account; Through private placements,underwriting public offerings
INVESTMENTS/LOANS MADE: In securities with a secondary market and in securities without a secondary market
TYPES OF FINANCING: SECONDARY-MARKET CORPORATE SECURITIES: Common stock; Preferred stock; Bonds, LOANS: Unsecured to credits above Ba; Equipment; REAL ESTATE LOANS: Long-term senior mtg., Land, LEASES: Single-investor; Leveraged; Vendor financing programs; OTHER SERVICES PROVIDED: no longer do tax-exempt
PREFERRED TYPES OF INDUSTRIES/INVESTMENTS: Finance & Insurance; Manufacturing & Processing; Medical & Other Health Services; Natural Resources; Services; Transportation, Utilities; Diversified
GEOGRAPHIC LIMITS OF INVESTMENTS/LOANS: National
RANGE OF INV./LOAN PER BUSINESS: Min. $500,000; Max. $1,000,000
PREFERRED TERM FOR LOANS & LEASES: Min. 5-10; Max. 10-15 years
BUSINESS CHARACTERISTICS DESIRED-REQUIRED: Min. annual sales $75-100 million; Min. net worth $15 million; Min. annual net income $2 million
REFERRALS ACCEPTED FROM: Investment/Mortgage banker

COMPANY: **Kentucky Mortgage Co.**
ADDRESS: P.O. Box 13013
Lexington, KY 40512
PHONE: (606) 276-4322
TYPE OF INSTITUTION: Mortgage banker
CONTACT OFFICER(S): Halmer Hail, Pres.
K. Darwin Akins, Sr. V.P.
ASSETS: $100,000,000 and up
TYPES OF FINANCING: REAL ESTATE LOANS: Long-term senior mtg.; intermediate-term senior mtg.; wraparounds; Land development; Construction; REAL ESTATE: Acquisitions
GEOGRAPHIC LIMITS OF INVESTMENTS/LOANS: Regional
RANGE OF INV./LOAN PER BUSINESS: Min. $1 million; Max. $ None
PREFERRED TERM FOR LOANS & LEASES: Min. 15 years; Max. 30 years
BRANCHES: Janice Fowlken, 410 Osborne Office Ct., Chattanooga, TN 37411; (615) 894-6530
Burt Gill, 8044 Ray Mears Blvd., Ste. 100, Knoxville, TN 37919; (615) 691-1991
Sally Gant, 287 Plus Park Blvd., Ste. C, Nashville, TN 37217; (615) 361-6715

Jack Rottgering, Marla Pruitt, P.O. Box 7544, Paducah, KY 42011, (502) 443-7373
Larry Hall, 1001 Linn Station Rd., Ste. 405, Louisville, KY 40223 (502) 423-1500

COMPANY: **Citizens Fidelity Mortgage Co.**
ADDRESS: 437 W. Jefferson
Louisville, KY 40296
PHONE: (502) 581-2120
TYPE OF INSTITUTION: Mortgage Banker
CONTACT OFFICER(S): Geret Foy, Pres. & CEO
ASSETS: $800 million in servicing volume
TYPES OF FINANCING: REAL ESTATE LOANS: Long-term senior mtg.; Intermediate-term senior mtg.; Wraparounds; Land; Land development; Construction; Gap; Standbys; Industrial revenue bonds; REAL ESTATE: Acquisitions; Joint ventures; Partnerships/Syndications
PREFERRED TYPES OF INDUSTRIES/INVESTMENTS: office buildings, shopping centers
GEOGRAPHIC LIMITS OF INVESTMENTS/LOANS: Regional: Other: S.E. quadrant United States
RANGE OF INV./LOAN PER BUSINESS: Min. $700,000
BUSINESS CHARACTERISTICS DESIRED-REQUIRED: Other: Income producing, well established professional
REFERRALS ACCEPTED FROM: Investment/Mortgage banker or Borrower/Investee
BRANCHES: Orlando, FL
Indianapolis, IN

COMPANY:**Colwell Financial Corp.**
ADDRESS: 700 West Liberty, P.O. Box 353
Louisville, KY 40203
PHONE: (502) 566-5100
TYPE OF INSTITUTION: Mortgage banker
CONTACT OFFICER(S): Kevin D. Cogan, Sr. V.P.
Linda Jackson, V.P., 566-5195
Gary Janeway, S.V.P., 566-5190
TYPES OF FINANCING: REAL ESTATE LOANS: Long-term senior mtg.; Construction; Gap; Industrial revenue bonds; Other: Short term mortgages; REAL ESTATE: Acquisitions; Joint ventures
PREFERRED TYPES OF INDUSTRIES/INVESTMENTS: Multi-family units, hotels, office, retail
GEOGRAPHIC LIMITS OF INVESTMENTS/LOANS: National
RANGE OF INV./LOAN PER BUSINESS: Min. $ 2 million
BUSINESS CHARACTERISTICS DESIRED-REQUIRED: Minimum number of years in business: 0
BRANCHES: Most major cities

COMPANY: **First National Bank of Louisville**
ADDRESS: First National Tower
Louisville, KY 40202
PHONE: (502) 581-4200
TYPE OF INSTITUTION: Bank, full service including commercial finance, leasing, mergers & acquisitions & international
CONTACT OFFICER(S): Max White, S.V.P., Construction Financing
Ed Vittitoe, V.P. Corporate Finance, Mergers & Acquisitions
William Earley, S.V.P., Energy
Charles Williams, S.V.P., International
Jerry Johnston, S.V.P., National Banking
Paul Best, S.V.P., Mortgage Banking
ASSETS: $3.2 billion
INVESTMENTS/LOANS MADE: For own account
TYPES OF FINANCING: LOANS: Unsecured; Working capital (receivables/inventory); Equipment, REAL ESTATE LOANS: Intermediate-term senior mtg.; Wraparounds; Land; Construction; Standbys, LEASES: Leveraged; Tax leases; Non-tax leases; Vendor financing programs, INTERNATIONAL (including import/export)
GEOGRAPHIC LIMITS OF INVESTMENTS/LOANS: Regional; Other: Limited business nationally
RANGE OF INV./LOAN PER BUSINESS: Min. $250,000; Max. $12,000,000
PREFERRED TERM FOR LOANS & LEASES: Min. 2 years; Max. 10 years
BUSINESS CHARACTERISTICS DESIRED-REQUIRED: Minimum number of years in business: 3; Min. annual sales $5,000,000; Min. net worth $3,000,000
REFERRALS ACCEPTED FROM: Investment/Mortgage banker or Borrower/Investee
BRANCHES: Chuck Moeser, V.P., 60 E. 42nd Street, New York, NY; (212) 661-0980
John Hill, V.P., 1945 The Exchange, Suite 104, Atlanta, GA 30339; (404) 953-0930
Jim Sullivan, V.P., 625 N. Michigan Avenue, Suite 1020, Chicago, IL 60611; (312) 642-9779

COMPANY:**Mellon Financial Services Corporation #7**
ADDRESS: 3850 North Causeway Boulevard, Suite 1800
Metairie, LA 70002
PHONE: (504) 831-4811
TYPE OF INSTITUTION: Mortgage Banker
CONTACT OFFICER(S): Julian O. Hecker, Jr., President
Donna J. Pillard, Senior Vice President
Vincent J. Balsamo, Jr., Senior Vice President
ASSETS: $160 Million
TYPES OF FINANCING: REAL ESTATE LOANS: Long-term senior mtg.; Intermediate-term senior mtg.; Land; Land development; Construction; Other: Land Participation
PREFERRED TYPES OF INDUSTRIES/INVESTMENTS: Land Acquisition, Land Development, Construction Loans, Residential Permanent LoansGEOGRAPHIC LIMITS OF INVESTMENTS/LOANS: Regional
BRANCHES: Jimmie L. Raymond, Mellon Financial Services, 3601 I-10 Service Road, Metairie, LA 70002, (504) 885-4811
Ronald L. Simmons, Mellon Financial Services, 3842 Independece Drive, Suite A, Alexandria, LA 71303, (318) 473-9529
Marjorie F. Thompson, Mellon Financial Services, 4334 S. Sherwood Forest Boulevard, Baton Rouge, LA 70816, (504) 292-9590
Mackie A. Olmstead, Mellon Financial Services, 825 Kaliste Saloom, Suite 104, Brandywine I, Lafayette, LA 70508, (318) 235-4805
Jo Ann C. Bland, Mellon Financial Services, 300 East McNeese Street, Suite 1A, Lake Charles, LA 70605, (318) 474-9534
Marlyne C. Malley, Mellon Financial Services, 100 Ormond Boulevard, Suite B, LaPlace, LA 70068, (504) 652-1443

Steven P. Accardo, Mellon Financial Services, 6600 Plaza Drive, Suite 110, New Orleans, LA 70127, (504) 246-3011
Mellon Financial Services, 4348 Youree Drive, Suite A, Shreveport, LA 71105, (318) 868-3682
William L. Folse, Jr., Mellon Financial Services, 1415 Corporate Square Boulevard, Slidell, LA 70458, (504) 641-0711
Patricia R. Mader, Mellon Financial Services, 537 Holmes Boulevard, Gretna, LA 70053; (504) 368-5411
Margaret W. Anderson, Mellon Financial Services, 1408 N. Westshore Boulevard, Suite 508, Tampa, FL 33607, (813) 876-5047

COMPANY: **Pan American Life**
ADDRESS: Pan American Life Center
New Orleans, LA 70130
PHONE: (504) 566-1300
TYPE OF INSTITUTION: Mutual life insurance company
CONTACT OFFICER(S): Luis Ingles, V.P., Securities
Larry Dupuy, V.P., Mortgage Loans & Real Estate
Mayo Emory, Senior Securities Analyst
John Herrington, Second V.P., Mortgage Loans
ASSETS: $875 million
INVESTMENTS/LOANS MADE: For own account, Through private placements
INVESTMENTS/LOANS MADE: In securities with a secondary market and in securities without a secondary market
TYPES OF FINANCING: SECONDARY-MARKET CORPORATE SECURITIES: Common stock; Bonds, LOANS: Unsecured to credits above, BA; Equipment; Equity-related, REAL ESTATE LOANS: Intermediate-term senior mtg.; Other: Short-term senior mtg.; Intermediate-term senior mtg. with participation only, LEASES: Leveraged, REAL ESTATE: Acquisitions; Joint ventures
PREFERRED TYPES OF INDUSTRIES/INVESTMENTS: Securities: Generally open on all types; Mortgages
GEOGRAPHIC LIMITS OF INVESTMENTS/LOANS: National
RANGE OF INV./LOAN PER BUSINESS: Min. $500,000; Max. 5 million
PREFERRED TERM FOR LOANS & LEASES: Min. 5 years, amortized; Max. 10-15 years amortized
REFERRALS ACCEPTED FROM: Investment/Mortgage banker or Borrower/Investee

COMPANY: **Standard Mortgage Corp.**
ADDRESS: 300 Plaza, One Shell Square
New Orleans, LA 70139
PHONE: (504) 581-3383
TYPE OF INSTITUTION: Mortgage banker
CONTACT OFFICER(S): E. A. Bright Jr., Pres.
Anthony Camento, Residential
Larry Smith, Commercial Loans
ASSETS: $4.3 million (net worth)
TYPES OF FINANCING: REAL ESTATE LOANS: Long-term senior mtg,; Intermediate-term senior mtg.; Wraparounds; Construction; Industrial revenue bonds; REAL ESTATE: Joint ventures
PREFERRED TYPES OF INDUSTRIES/INVESTMENTS: Real Estate: Office buildings, Hospitals, Office condos, Shopping centers, Hotels, Motels, Industrial warehousing
GEOGRAPHIC LIMITS OF INVESTMENTS/LOANS: Regional
RANGE OF INV./LOAN PER BUSINESS: Min. $1 Million
PREFERRED TERM FOR LOANS & LEASES: Min. 1 year; Max. 10-15 years
BUSINESS CHARACTERISTICS DESIRED-REQUIRED: Min. number of years in business: 0

COMPANY:**Crossland Capital Corp.**
ADDRESS: 4050 Wilshire Boulevard
Los Angeles
TYPE OF INSTITUTION: Real Estate Investment Banking
CONTACT OFFICER(S): John G. Collins, Sr. Vice President & Division Manager
Peter A. Kehoe, Sr. Vice President - Residential Property
James H. Alexander
Clifford F. Bourland, First Vice President
Eric C. Salveson, First Vice President
ASSETS: $5.6 Billion
INVESTMENTS/LOANS MADE: For own account, Through private placements
INVESTMENTS/LOANS MADE: In securities with a secondary market and in securities without a secondary market
TYPES OF FINANCING: SECONDARY-MARKET CORPORATE SECURITIES: Other: G.N.M.A.; REAL ESTATE LOANS: Long-term senior mtg.; Intermediate-term senior mtg.; Subordinated; Wraparounds; Land; Land development; Construction; Gap; Standbys; Industrial revenue bonds; Other: Convertible Mortgages, Participating Mortgages; REAL ESTATE: Acquisitions; Joint ventures; Partnerships/Syndications; OTHER SERVICE PROVIDED: Property Management, Insurance
PREFERRED TYPES OF INDUSTRIES/INVESTMENTS: General Purpose Real Estate
GEOGRAPHIC LIMITS OF INVESTMENTS/LOANS: International
RANGE OF INV./LOAN PER BUSINESS: Min. $500,000; Max. $ None
PREFERRED TERM FOR LOANS & LEASES: Min. 0-1 years; Max.30-35 years
REFERRALS ACCEPTED FROM: Investment/Mortgage banker or Borrower/Investee
BRANCHES: Louis T. Moore, AVP, 4665 MacArthur Ct., #250, Newport Beach, CA 92660
Michael G. Lindsley, V.P., 1601 N. California Blvd., Walnut Creek, CA 94596, (415) 930-8388
W. Gardiner Champlin, Jr., Vice President
John Fierst, Vice President, 989 Avenue of the Americas, New York, NY 10018
Warren O. Sutton, 500 Cooper N.W., #300A, Albuquerque, NM 87102, (505) 247-0103
Churchill G. Carey, International Charter Bldg., Hato Rey, PR, 00917, (809) 753-0245
REMARKS: Name changed from Ralph C. Sutro Co. on October 1, 1984

COMPANY: **Bank of Boston**
ADDRESS: 100 Federal Street, 19th Floor

Boston, MA 02110
PHONE: (617) 434-2200
TYPE OF INSTITUTION: Real Estate Division of Bank
CONTACT OFFICER(S): Garlan Morse, Jr., S.V.P.
Raymond H. Weaving, V.P.
ASSETS: $22,000,000,000
TYPES OF FINANCING: REAL ESTATE LOANS: Land Developments; Construction, OTHER: Collateral loans to mtg. companies, REAL ESTATE: Acquisitions
PREFERRED TYPES OF INDUSTRIES/INVESTMENTS: Shopping centers; Office buildings; Apartments; Industrial buildings
WILL NOT CONSIDER: Special purpose
GEOGRAPHIC LIMITS OF INVESTMENTS/LOANS: National
RANGE OF INV./LOAN PER BUSINESS: Min. 1 year; Max. 5 years
BRANCHES: Windsor Aylesworth, V.P., 1499 West Palmetto Parkway, Boca Raton, FL 33432, (305) 392-8255
Dennis Kemper, V.P. 211 Perimeter Center Parkway, Suite 910, Atlanta, GA 30346, (404) 393-4676
Derek Cavanaugh, V.P., 700 N. Pearl St., Suite 1840, Plaza of the Americas, Dallas, TX 75201, (214) 754-7071

COMPANY: **Bank of New England, N.A.**
ADDRESS: 28 State Street
Boston, MA 02109
PHONE: (617) 724-4000
CONTACT OFFICER(S): Robert S. Swain, S.V.P.
James M. Sweeney, V.P.
ASSETS: $6,000,000,000
TYPES OF FINANCING: REAL ESTATE LOANS: Long-term senior mtg; Intermediate-term senior mtg; Wraparounds; Land; Land development; Construction; Gap; Standbys; Industrial revenue bonds, REAL ESTATE: Acquisitions; Joint ventures; Partnerships/ Syndications
PREFERRED TYPES OF INDUSTRIES/INVESTMENTS: Construction, Office and R&D space
GEOGRAPHIC LIMITS OF INVESTMENTS/LOANS: National
RANGE OF INV./LOAN PER BUSINESS: Min. $250,000; Max. $20,000,000
PREFERRED TERM FOR LOANS & LEASES: Max. 5 years
BRANCHES: Joseph L. Carboni, V.P., 1900 Market St. Suite 52, Philadelphia, PA 19103

COMPANY: **Bay Financial Corp.**
ADDRESS: Two Faneuil Hall Marketplace
Boston, MA 02109
PHONE: (617) 742-7550
TYPE OF INSTITUTION: RE Developers
CONTACT OFFICER(S): R. Douglas Hall III, President
ASSETS: $200,000,000
TYPES OF FINANCING: REAL ESTATE: Acquisitions; Joint ventures, OTHER SERVICES PROVIDED: R.E. development with institution
PREFERRED TYPES OF INDUSTRIES/INVESTMENTS: Suburban office buildings R. & D. Industrial Properties
WILL NOT CONSIDER: Retail, Special purpose buildings
GEOGRAPHIC LIMITS OF INVESTMENTS/LOANS: National
RANGE OF INV./LOAN PER BUSINESS: Min. $2,000,000; Max. $30,000,000

COMPANY: **The Berg Company, Inc.**
ADDRESS: Box 1961
Boston, MA 02105
PHONE: (617) 482-0290
TYPE OF INSTITUTION: Broker/Dealer
CONTACT OFFICER(S): Gordon H. Berg, Chariman-CEO
INVESTMENTS/LOANS MADE: For own account, For managed accounts, Through private placements, Through underwriting public offerings
INVESTMENTS/LOANS MADE: In securities with a secondary market and in securities without a secondary market
TYPES OF FINANCING: SECONDARY-MARKET CORPORATE SECURITIES: Bonds; Other: Priv. Plac., REAL ESTATE LOANS: Long-term senior mtg.; Intermediate-term senior mtg.; Subordinated; Wraparounds; Land; Land development; Industrial revenue bonds, LEASES: Leveraged, REAL ESTATE: Partnerships/Syndications, OTHER SERVICES PROVIDED: Pro Bono Institutions
PREFERRED TYPES OF INDUSTRIES/INVESTMENTS: Pro Bono
GEOGRAPHIC LIMITS OF INVESTMENTS/LOANS: International
RANGE OF INV./LOAN PER BUSINESS: Min. $1.5 million
REFERRALS ACCEPTED FROM: Investment/Mortgage banker or Borrower/Investee

COMPANY: **Boston Financial Technology Group, Inc.**
ADDRESS: One Post Office Square
Boston, MA 02109
PHONE: (617) 482-9790
CONTACT OFFICER(S): James S. Hughes
Fred N. Pratt
George J. Fantini
ASSETS: $200 Million equity
INVESTMENTS/LOANS MADE: Through private placements
INVESTMENTS/LOANS MADE: In securities without a secondary market
TYPES OF FINANCING: REAL ESTATE LOANS: Long-term senior mtg.; Intermediate-term senior mtg.; Subordinated; Wraparounds, REAL ESTATE: Acquisitions; Joint ventures; Partnerships/Syndications
PREFERRED TYPES OF INDUSTRIES/INVESTMENTS: Real estate: equity placements, mortgage placements
GEOGRAPHIC LIMITS OF INVESTMENTS/LOANS: National
RANGE OF INV./LOAN PER BUSINESS: Min. $3 million; Max. $50 million

COMPANY: **The Boston Five Cents Savings Bank**
ADDRESS: 10 School Street
Boston, MA 02108
PHONE: (617) 742-6000
CONTACT OFFICER(S): John Hosmer, V.P.

REAL ESTATE LENDERS & INVESTORS

(Real Estate Financing—Loans, Partnerships, Joint Ventures and Acquisitions. Also see Investment Bankers, Mutual Savings Bankers & Finance Companies)

COMPANY: **Boston Mortgage Company, Inc.**
ADDRESS: One Milk Street
Boston, MA 02109
PHONE: (617) 423-1989
TYPE OF INSTITUTION: Mortgage Banker; Real Estate Consultant
CONTACT OFFICER(S): Harold McKennna, Chairman
Richard Quinn, Pres.
Thomas Rowland, Sr. V.P.
INVESTMENTS/LOANS MADE: For own account, For managed accounts, Through private placements
INVESTMENTS/LOANS MADE: Only in securities without a secondary market
TYPES OF FINANCING: REAL ESTATE LOANS: Long-term senior mtg.; Intermediate-term senior mtg.; Subordinated; Wraparounds; Land; Land development; Construction; Gap; Standbys; Industrial revenue bonds. REAL ESTATE: Acquisitionns; Joint ventures; Partnerships/Syndications.
PREFERRED TYPES OF INDUSTRIES/INVESTMENTS: Commercial Real Estate exceeding $2,000,000 value, no maximum
WILL NOT CONSIDER: Special Purpose Real Estate
GEOGRAPHIC LIMITS OF INVESTMENTS/LOANS: Regional
RANGE OF INV./LOAN PER BUSINESS: Min. $1,500,000
BUSINESS CHARACTERISTICS DESIRED-REQUIRED: Varies with real estate
REFERRALS ACCEPTED FROM: Investment/Mortgage banker or Borrower/Investee
BRANCHES: Thomas Rowland, 47 Clapboard Hill Rd., Guilford, CT 06437, (203) 453-0808

COMPANY: **Bradley R.E. Trust**
ADDRESS: 250 Boylston St.
Boston, MA 02116
PHONE: (617) 421-0675
TYPE OF INSTITUTION: REIT
CONTACT OFFICER(S): Lawrence Miller, V.P.
TYPES OF FINANCING: REAL ESTATE LOANS, REAL ESTATE: Acquisitions, Joint Ventures, OTHER SERVICES PROVIDED: Strictly equity-related lending
PREFERRED TYPES OF INDUSTRIES/INVESTMENTS: Commercial, Office buildings, Shopping Centers
GEOGRAPHIC LIMITS OF INVESTMENTS/LOANS: National
RANGE OF INV./LOAN PER BUSINESS: Max. 25-30 Million
REMARKS: No preference on term, depends on deal

COMPANY: **Commonwealth Mortgage Company, Inc.**
ADDRESS: 120 Tremont Street
Boston, MA 02108
PHONE: (617) 423-9300
TYPE OF INSTITUTION: Mortgage Banker
CONTACT OFFICER(S): Vincent E. Hayes, Jr., E.V.P.
ASSETS: $900,000,000 in servicing portfolio
TYPES OF FINANCING: REAL ESTATE LOANS: Long-term senior mtg.; Intermediate-term senior mtg.; Land; Land development; Construction; Standbys, REAL ESTATE: Joint ventures
PREFERRED TYPES OF INDUSTRIES/INVESTMENTS: Commercial & Industrial Brokerage
GEOGRAPHIC LIMITS OF INVESTMENTS/LOANS: Regional; Other: New England
PREFERRED TERM FOR LOANS & LEASES: Min. 15 years; Max. 30 years

COMPANY: **Hubbard Real Estate Investments**
ADDRESS: 125 High St.
Boston, MA 02110
PHONE: (617) 426-6158
TYPE OF INSTITUTION: REIT
CONTACT OFFICER(S): William F. Murdoch, Jr., President, 2 Broadway, N.Y., NY (212) 908-8478
Stephen C. Hagen, V.P., 2 Broadway, N.Y., NY (212) 908-8483
ASSETS: $158,000,000
INVESTMENTS/LOANS MADE: For own account
TYPES OF FINANCING: REAL ESTATE LOANS: Intermediate-term senior mtg.; Land; Land development; Construction, LEASES: Single-investor; Operating, REAL ESTATE: Acquisitions; Joint ventures
PREFERRED TYPES OF INDUSTRIES/INVESTMENTS: Real estate
GEOGRAPHIC LIMITS OF INVESTMENTS/LOANS: National
RANGE OF INV./LOAN PER BUSINESS: Min. $1,000,000; Max. $20,000,000
PREFERRED TERM FOR LOANS & LEASES: Min. Varies
REFERRALS ACCEPTED FROM: Investment/Mortgage banker or Borrower/Investee

COMPANY: **John Hancock Mutual Life Insurance Co.**
ADDRESS: John Hancock Place, P.O. Box 111
Boston, MA 02117
PHONE: (617) 421-6000
TYPE OF INSTITUTION: Life insurance co.
CONTACT OFFICER(S): Stephen L. Brown, Executive V.P., Investment Operations; John Q. Adams, Private Placements
ASSETS: Approximately $30 billion
INVESTMENTS/LOANS MADE: For own account, For managed accounts, Through private placements, Through underwriting public offerings
INVESTMENTS/LOANS MADE: In securities with a secondary market and in securities without a secondary market
TYPES OF FINANCING: SECONDARY-MARKET CORPORATE SECURITIES: Common stock; Preferred stock; Bonds; Other: R. estate, VENTURE CAPITAL: Later-stage expansion, LOANS: Unsecured; Working capital; Equipment; Equity-related, REAL ESTATE LOANS: Long-term senior mtg., Intermediate-term senior mtg.; Land; Land development; Industrial revenue bonds, LEASES: Leveraged; Tax leases; Non-tax leases; Operating; Vendor financing programs, REAL ESTATE: Acquisitions; Joint ventures; Partnerships/Syndications
PREFERRED TYPES OF INDUSTRIES/INVESTMENTS: Agriculture
GEOGRAPHIC LIMITS OF INVESTMENTS/LOANS: National; International
RANGE OF INV./LOAN PER BUSINESS: Min. variable
PREFERRED TERM FOR LOANS & LEASES: Min. variable

BUSINESS CHARACTERISTICS DESIRED-REQUIRED: Minimum number of years in business: 10;
REFERRALS ACCEPTED FROM: Investment/Mortgage banker or Borrower/Investee

COMPANY: **Korff Associates, Berman, Lewenberg, Redstone & Korff,**
ADDRESS: 211 Congress Street
Boston, MA 02110
PHONE: (617) 426-9300
TYPE OF INSTITUTION: Private investment of family capital
CONTACT OFFICER(S): Ira A. Korff
INVESTMENTS/LOANS MADE: For own account
TYPES OF FINANCING: VENTURE CAPITAL: Buy-outs/Acquisitions, REAL ESTATE LOANS: Intermediate-term senior mtg.; INTERNATIONAL (including import/export), REAL ESTATE: Acquisitions
WILL NOT CONSIDER: Services

COMPANY: **Meredith and Grew, Inc.**
ADDRESS: 125 High St.
Boston, MA 02110
PHONE: (617) 482-5330
TYPE OF INSTITUTION: Mortgage Banker
CONTACT OFFICER(S): George M. Lovejoy Jr., Pres.
Kevin C. Phelan, Sr. V.P.
TYPES OF FINANCING: REAL ESTATE LOANS: Long-term senior mtg.; Intermediate-term senior mtg.; Subordinated; Wraparounds; Land development; Construction; Gap; Standbys; Industrial revenue bonds, REAL ESTATE: Acquisitions; Joint ventures; Partnerships/Syndications
PREFERRED TYPES OF INDUSTRIES/INVESTMENTS: Diversified
GEOGRAPHIC LIMITS OF INVESTMENTS/LOANS: National, International, Specialize N.E. United States
RANGE OF INV./LOAN PER BUSINESS: Min. $1 million; Max. None

COMPANY: **Mortgage Growth Investors**
ADDRESS: One P.O. Square
Boston, MA 02109
PHONE: (617) 423-4747
TYPE OF INSTITUTION: REIT
CONTACT OFFICER(S): W. Pearce Coues

COMPANY: **New England Mutual Life Insurance Co.**
ADDRESS: 501 Boylston Street
Boston, MA 02117
PHONE: (617) 266-3700
CONTACT OFFICER(S): John Rodgers, Sr. V.P. Securities
Hamilton Coolidge, Sr. V.P. Mortgage
ASSETS: 21,479,000,000 (& subs)
INVESTMENTS/LOANS MADE: For own account
INVESTMENTS/LOANS MADE: In securities with a secondary market and in securities without a secondary market
TYPES OF FINANCING: SECONDARY-MARKET CORPORATE SECURITIES: Common stock; Preferred stock; Bonds; Other: Convertibles. VENTURE CAPITAL: Research & Development; First-stage (less than 1 year); Second-stage (generally 1-3 years) Later-stage expansion; LOANS; Unsecured; Working capital (receivables/inventory); Equipment; Equity-related; REAL ESTATE LOANS: Intermediate-term senior mtg.; Wraparounds; Land; Land development; Construction; Industrial revenue bonds; Other: 2nd mtg. & blanket; LEASES: Single-investor; Leveraged; Tax leases; Non-tax leases; Operating; Lease syndications; REAL ESTATE: Acquisitions; Joint ventures; Partnerships/Syndications; OTHER SERVICES PROVIDED: discount brokerage tax shelter deals thru NESCO
GEOGRAPHIC LIMITS OF INVESTMENTS/LOANS: National
RANGE OF INV./LOAN PER BUSINESS: Min. $1 million; Max. $30 million
BUSINESS CHARACTERISTICS DESIRED-REQUIRED: Min. no. of years in business: 0
REFERRALS ACCEPTED FROM: Investment/Mortgage banker or Borrower/Investee
BRANCHES: Loomis, Sayles, & Co. Inc., 225 Franklin St., Boston, MA 02110; does own investing and all equity for parent

COMPANY: **Regent Financial Corp.**
ADDRESS: 10 Commercial Wharf West, Suite 502
Boston, MA 02110
PHONE: (617) 723-4820
CONTACT OFFICER(S): Jason S. Rosenberg, President
INVESTMENTS/LOANS MADE: For own account
INVESTMENTS/LOANS MADE: In securities with a secondary market and in securities without a secondary market
TYPES OF FINANCING: VENTURE CAPITAL: First-stage; Second-stage; Later-stage; Buy-outs/Acquisitions, LOANS: Working capital; Equipment; Equity-related, REAL ESTATE LOANS: Long-term senior mtg.; Intermediate-term senior mtg.; Subordinated; Wraparounds, REAL ESTATE: Acquisitions; Joint ventures; Partnerships/Syndications
PREFERRED TYPES OF INDUSTRIES/INVESTMENTS: Commercial real estate; General
GEOGRAPHIC LIMITS OF INVESTMENTS/LOANS: New England
RANGE OF INV./LOAN PER BUSINESS: Min. $50,000; Max. $500,000
PREFERRED TERM FOR LOANS & LEASES: Min. 1 year
REFERRALS ACCEPTED FROM: Investment/Mortgage banker or Borrower/Investee

COMPANY: **Shawmut Bank of Boston, N.A.**
ADDRESS: One Federal Street
Boston, MA 02211
PHONE: (617) 292-2000
CONTACT OFFICER(S): Elizabeth Conahan, Vice President
ASSETS: $3.1 billion bank; $6 billion holding company
TYPES OF FINANCING: REAL ESTATE: Subordinated; Wraparounds; Land development; Construction; Gap; Other: Mini-perms, relatively short term, 3-5 years
GEOGRAPHIC LIMITS OF INVESTMENTS/LOANS: Regional; National; Other: Regional—direct; national—participating

RANGE OF INV./LOAN PER BUSINESS: Min. $1,000,000; Max. $15,000,000
PREFERRED TERM FOR LOANS & LEASES: Max. 5 years

COMPANY: **State Street Bank & Trust Company**
ADDRESS: 225 Franklin Street
Boston MA 02110
PHONE: (617) 654-3692
CONTACT OFFICER(S): Andrew L. Ala, S. V.P.

COMPANY: **Union Warren Savings Bank**
ADDRESS: 133 Federal Street
Boston, MA 02110
PHONE: (617) 482-4590
ASSETS: $641,000,000
TYPES OF FINANCING: REAL ESTATE LOANS: Intermediate-term senior mtg.; Construction
GEOGRAPHIC LIMITS OF INVESTMENTS/LOANS: Regional; Other: New England
PREFERRED TERM FOR LOANS & LEASES: Min. 3 years; Max. 5 years

COMPANY: **UST Capital Corporation**
ADDRESS: 40 Court St.
Boston, MA 02108
PHONE: (617) 726-7000
TYPE OF INSTITUTION: SBIC
CONTACT OFFICER(S): Stephen R. Lewinstein, President
Rick Kohn, V.P.
ASSETS: Approx. $2,000,000
INVESTMENTS/LOANS MADE: For own account; Through private placements
INVESTMENTS/LOANS MADE: In securities with a secondary market and in securities without a secondary market
TYPES OF FINANCING: VENTURE CAPITAL: First-stage (less than 1 year); Second-stage (generally 1-3 years); Later-stage expansion; Buy-outs/Acquisitions, LOANS: Working capital (receivables/inventory); Equipment; Equity-related, REAL ESTATE LOANS: Subordinated; Land; Land development; Construction; Standbys, REAL ESTATE: Acquisitions; Joint ventures; Partnerships/Syndications
PREFERRED TYPES OF INDUSTRIES/INVESTMENTS: General opportunities
WILL NOT CONSIDER: R & D or start-ups
GEOGRAPHIC LIMITS OF INVESTMENTS/LOANS: National
RANGE OF INV./LOAN PER BUSINESS: Our personal SBIC limit is approx. $300,000, but we syndicate up to $5,000,000
PREFERRED TERM FOR LOANS & LEASES: Max. 10 years
BUSINESS CHARACTERISTICS DESIRED-REQUIRED: Minimum number of years in business: 1; Min. annual sales None—prefer positive net worth
REFERRALS ACCEPTED FROM: Investment/Mortgage banker or Borrower/Investee

COMPANY: **Malmart Mortgage Company, Inc.**
ADDRESS: 111 Washington Street
Brookline, MA 02146
PHONE: (617) 738-4646
TYPE OF INSTITUTION: Mortgage Banking
CONTACT OFFICER(S): James E. Cofield, Jr., President
Kathleen A. Devine, Commercial-Chairman, Investment Committee
ASSETS: Approx. $0.5 billion
INVESTMENTS/LOANS MADE: For own account; For managed accounts; Through private placements
INVESTMENTS/LOANS MADE: In securities with a secondary market or in securities without a secondary market
TYPES OF FINANCING: REAL ESTATE LOANS: Long-term senior mtg.; Intermediate-term senior mtg.; Wraparounds; Land development; Construction; Gap; Standbys; Industrial revenue bonds; REAL ESTATE: Acquisitions; Joint ventures; Partnerships/Syndications
REMARKS: Malmart Mortgage Company, Inc. is one of the few full service mortgage banking firms in New England. The company provides permanent mortgage financing to both residential and commercial real estate markets and it arranges construction loans for insured project mortgages and conventional developments. In the area of commercial loans, it seeks office buildings, shopping centers, apartment buildings, industrial buildings and hotels and motels. (also provides conventional, FHA and VA residential mortgages)

COMPANY: **Memorial Drive Trust**
ADDRESS: 20 Acorn Park
Cambridge, MA 02140
PHONE: (617) 864-5770
TYPE OF INSTITUTION: Diversified investment trust
CONTACT OFFICER(S): Jean deValpine, Chief Exec. Officer-Art, Intelligence, Robotics & Electronics
Jan Senerchia, Telecomm. Computer R.E.
Paul Shanwal, Energy related chem., Gen. mfg., Semi-conductors
Schorr Berman, Computers, CadCam, Artificial intelligence, Consumer related, Bio-tech
ASSETS: $280,000,000
INVESTMENTS/LOANS MADE: For own account
INVESTMENTS/LOANS MADE: In securities with a secondary market and in securities without a secondary market
TYPES OF FINANCING: SECONDARY-MARKET CORPORATE SECURITIES: Common stock; Preferred stock; Other: Convertible notes, options, etc., VENTURE CAPITAL: First-stage (less than 1 year); Second-stage (generally 1-3 years); Later-stage expansion; Buy-outs/Acquisitions, REAL ESTATE: Partnerships/Syndications, OTHER SERVICES PROVIDED: Publicly traded bonds, direct investment, parcel developing
PREFERRED TYPES OF INDUSTRIES/INVESTMENTS: Telecommunications, micro-electronics, computer related, advanced materials, other "high-technology", artificial intelligence
GEOGRAPHIC LIMITS OF INVESTMENTS/LOANS: National, prefer regional
REFERRALS ACCEPTED FROM: Investment/Mortgage banker or Borrower/Investee

COMPANY: **Boston Mutual Life Insurance Company**
ADDRESS: 120 Royall St.
Canton, MA 02021
PHONE: (617) 828-7000
CONTACT OFFICER(S): Robert McNally, V.P., R.E. & Mtg.
Howard Neff, Mtg. Officer
ASSETS: $175 million
TYPES OF FINANCING: REAL ESTATE LOANS
GEOGRAPHIC LIMITS OF INVESTMENTS/LOANS: National
RANGE OF INV./LOAN PER BUSINESS: Min. $500,000; Max. $1,500,000
PREFERRED TYPES OF INDUSTRIES/INVESTMENTS: Real Estate: apartment houses, shopping centers, office buildings
BUSINESS CHARACTERISTICS DESIRED-REQUIRED: Minimum number of years in business: 7; Min. annual net income positive; Other: Minimum net worth should exceed mortgage request
REFERRALS ACCEPTED FROM: Investment/Mortgage banker or Borrower/Investee

COMPANY: **Wedgestone Realty Investors Trust**
ADDRESS: 181 Wells Ave.
Newton, MA 02159
PHONE: (617) 965-8330
TYPE OF INSTITUTION: REIT
CONTACT OFFICER(S): John McGovern, E.V.P.
ASSETS: $13,000,000
TYPES OF FINANCING: REAL ESTATE LOANS: Subordinated; Wraparounds; Land; Land development; Construction; Gap; Standbys; Other: All short term, REAL ESTATE: Joint ventures
GEOGRAPHIC LIMITS OF INVESTMENTS/LOANS: Regional; Other: Northeast
RANGE OF INV./LOAN PER BUSINESS: Min. $200,000; Max. $2,000,000
BUSINESS CHARACTERISTICS DESIRED-REQUIRED: Real estate equity

COMPANY: **Berkshire Life Insurance Co.**
ADDRESS: 700 South Street
Pittsfield, MA 01201
PHONE: (413) 499-4321
CONTACT OFFICER(S): Colin MacFadyen, V.P., Securities
ASSETS: $500 million
INVESTMENTS/LOANS MADE: In securities with a secondary market and in securities without a secondary market
TYPES OF FINANCING: SECONDARY-MARKET CORPORATE SECURITIES: Common stock; Bonds, REAL ESTATE LOANS: Intermediate-term senior mtg., REAL ESTATE: Limited Partnerships
PREFERRED TYPES OF INDUSTRIES/INVESTMENTS: Varied
WILL NOT CONSIDER: Vary
GEOGRAPHIC LIMITS OF INVESTMENTS/LOANS: National
RANGE OF INV./LOAN PER BUSINESS: Min. $250,000; Max. $1.5 million
PREFERRED TERM FOR LOANS & LEASES: Min. 5 years; Max. 20 years
BUSINESS CHARACTERISTICS DESIRED-REQUIRED: BAA quality credit mtgs; prime features: location, good economy in area, bonds, AA or higher
REFERRALS ACCEPTED FROM: Investment/Mortgage banker or Borower/Investee
REMARKS: Desired level of investment: $500,000-$1,000,000; desired term: 10-15 years

COMPANY: **Massachusetts Mutual Life Insurance Co.**
ADDRESS: 1295 State St.
Springfield, MA 01111
PHONE: (413) 788-8411
CONTACT OFFICER(S): Scott C. Noble, Sr. V.P. R.E.
Gary E. Wendlandt, Private Placements
ASSETS: $12.5 billion
INVESTMENTS/LOANS MADE: In securities with a secondary market and in securities without a secondary market
TYPES OF FINANCING: LOANS: Equity-related, REAL ESTATE LOANS
GEOGRAPHIC LIMITS OF INVESTMENTS/LOANS: National
RANGE OF INV./LOAN PER BUSINESS: Min. $2 mil.; Max. 30 mil.
PREFERRED TERM FOR LOANS & LEASES: Min. 3 years; Max. 15 years
REFERRALS ACCEPTED FROM: Investment/Mortgage banker or Borrower/Investee
BRANCHES: RE: 6 branches, originate new investments—Atlanta, Chicago, Dallas, LA, Wash. D.C., NE Springfield

COMPANY: **MASSMUTUAL MORTGAGE AND REALTY INVESTORS**
ADDRESS: 1295 State Street
Springfield, MA 01111
PHONE: (413) 788-8411
TYPE OF INSTITUTION: REIT
CONTACT OFFICER(S): Charles J. Lavoie, Vice President & Treasurer
ASSETS: $200 Million
INVESTMENTS/LOANS MADE: For own account
INVESTMENTS/LOANS MADE: Only in securities without a secondary market
TYPES OF FINANCING: REAL ESTATE LOANS: Construction, REAL ESTATE: Acquisitions; Joint ventures; Partnerships/Syndications
PREFERRED TYPES OF INDUSTRIES/INVESTMENTS: R.E. equity investments in office buildings, Shopping Centers, Industrial/Warehouse, Apartments, Land purchase-leasebacks
WILL NOT CONSIDER: Hotels
GEOGRAPHIC LIMITS OF INVESTMENTS/LOANS: National
RANGE OF INV./LOAN PER BUSINESS: Min. $2 million; Max. $10 million
REFERRALS ACCEPTED FROM: Investment/Mortgage banker or Borrower/Investee
REMARKS: Advised by Massachusetts Mutual Life Ins. Co.

COMPANY: **Plymouth Savings Bank**
ADDRESS: 226 Main Street, P.O. Box 431
Wareham, MA 02571
PHONE: (617) 295-3800
TYPE OF INSTITUTION: Bank—Mortgage banking, commercial lending
CONTACT OFFICER(S): Frank D. Fantasia, Sr. Vice President—Sr. Lending Officer
ASSETS: $270,000,000
TYPES OF FINANCING: VENTURE CAPITAL: Second-stage; Later-stage expansion, LOANS: Working capiital; Equipment; Equity-related, REAL ESTATE LOANS: Long-term senior mtg.; Intermediate-term senior mtg.; Wraparounds; Land; Land development; Construction; Standbys; Industrial revenue bonds, LEASES: Single-investor; Leveraged; Non-tax leases; Operating; Vendor financing programs, REAL ESTATE: Acquisitions; Joint ventures; Partnerships/Syndications
WILL NOT CONSIDER: Restaurants, motels
GEOGRAPHIC LIMITS OF INVESTMENTS/LOANS: Regional
RANGE OF INV./LOAN PER BUSINESS: Min. $25,000; Max. $500,000
REFERRALS ACCEPTED FROM: Investment/Mortgage banker or Borrower/Investee

COMPANY: **State Mutual Life Assurance Co. of America**
ADDRESS: 440 Lincoln St.
Worcester, MA 01541
PHONE: (617) 852-1000
TYPE OF INSTITUTION: Insurance Co.
CONTACT OFFICER(S): Dix F. Davis, Vice. Pres.
Jon Austad, Asst. Vice Pres.-Securities
John W. Nunley, Second Vice Pres.-Mortgages
ASSETS: 4 Billion
INVESTMENTS/LOANS MADE: For own account, For managed accounts, Through private placements, Through underwriting public offerings
INVESTMENTS/LOANS MADE: In securities with a secondary market and in securities without a secondary market
TYPES OF FINANCING: SECONDARY-MARKET CORPORATE SECURITIES: Bonds, LOANS: Unsecured to credits above B, REAL ESTATE LOANS: Long-term senior mtg.; Intermediate-term senior mtg.; Wraparounds, REAL ESTATE: Joint ventures
GEOGRAPHIC LIMITS OF INVESTMENTS/LOANS: National
RANGE OF INV./LOAN PER BUSINESS: Min. $2,000,000; Max. $5,000,000
PREFERRED TERM FOR LOANS & LEASES: Min. 2 years: Max. 10 years
REFERRALS ACCEPTED FROM: Investment/Mortgage banker or Borrower/Investee

COMPANY: **Commercial Credit Development Corporation**
ADDRESS: 300 St. Paul Place
Baltimore, MD 21202
PHONE: (301) 332-3881
TYPE OF INSTITUTION: Commercial real estate subsidiary of non bank financial institution
CONTACT OFFICER(S): Donald A. Gabriel, Acct.-executive
ASSETS: Commercial Credit Company $6 billion
INVESTMENTS/LOANS MADE: Only in securities without a secondary market
TYPES OF FINANCING: REAL ESTATE: Joint Ventures
PREFERRED TYPES OF INDUSTRIES/INVESTMENTS: General purpose, Real Estate: office buildings, apartments, industrial, shopping centers
WILL NOT CONSIDER: Speculative land loans
GEOGRAPHIC LIMITS OF INVESTMENTS/LOANS: National
RANGE OF INV./LOAN PER BUSINESS: Min. $2 million
BUSINESS CHARACTERISTICS DESIRED-REQUIRED: Must be experienced commercial real estate operators

COMPANY: **Mercantile Mortgage Corp.**
ADDRESS: P.O. Box 17027
Baltimore, MD 21203
PHONE: (301) 237-5656
TYPE OF INSTITUTION: Mortgage Banker
CONTACT OFFICER(S): Richard A. Wriggelsworth, Jr., Pres.
ASSETS: 17 million
TYPES OF FINANCING: REAL ESTATE LOANS: Long-term senior mtg.; Intermediate-term senior mtg.; Subordinated; Wraparounds; Land; Land development; Construction; Industrial Revenue bonds
GEOGRAPHIC LIIMITS OF INVESTMENTS/LOANS: Regional
RANGE OF INV./LOAN PER BUSINESS: Min. $250,000; Max. $30 million
BRANCHES: Wilmington, DE

COMPANY: **Wye Investment Corp.**
ADDRESS: 7801 York Road
Baltimore, MD 21204
PHONE: (301) 296-3700
TYPE OF INSTITUTION: Investment Company
CONTACT OFFICER(S): William R. Alborn, Pres.
Michael D. Quinn, Chairman of the Board
INVESTMENTS/LOANS MADE: Through private placements
TYPES OF FINANCING: REAL ESTATE: Acquisitions; Joint ventures; Partnerships/Syndications
PREFERRED TYPES OF INDUSTRIES/INVESTMENTS: Apartments; Office buildings; Hotel/motel; Warehouse
WILL NOT CONSIDER: Land
GEOGRAPHIC LIMITS OF INVESTMENTS/LOANS: Regional; Mid Atlantic States
RANGE OF INV./LOAN PER BUSINESS: Min. $100,000; Max. None
REFERRALS ACCEPTED FROM: Investment/Mortgage banker or Borrower/Investee

COMPANY: **WYE Mortgage Corp.**
ADDRESS: 7801 York Road
Baltimore, MD 21204
PHONE: (301) 296-3700
TYPE OF INSTITUTION: Mortgage Banker
CONTACT OFFICER(S): Joseph T. Burke, Pres.
Richard W. Hall, Ex. V.P.

Andrew J. Hundertmark, Jr., Ex. V.P.
E. Philip Brady, Ex. V.P.
INVESTMENTS/LOANS MADE: Through private placements
TYPES OF FINANCING: REAL ESTATE LOANS: Long-term senior mtg.
GEOGRAPHIC LIMITS OF INVESTMENTS/LOANS: Regional; Mid Atlantic
REFERRALS ACCEPTED FROM: Investment/Mortgage banker or Borrower/Investee

COMPANY: **The Carey Winston Co.**
ADDRESS: 4350 East-West Hwy.
Bethesda, MD 20814
PHONE: (301) 656-4212
TYPE OF INSTITUTION: Mortgage banker
CONTACT OFFICER(S): Michael Winston, Pres.
Jerry Romberg, V.P.
TYPES OF FINANCING: REAL ESTATE LOANS: Long-term senior mtg.; Intermediate-term senior mtg.; Subordinated; Wraparounds; Land; Land development; Construction; Standbys; Industrial revenue bonds. REAL ESTATE: Acquisitions; Joint ventures;
PREFERRED TYPES OF INDUSTRIES/INVESTMENTS: Office buildings; Office warehouse bldgs.; Shopping centers; Motels; Mobile home parks; Medical offices
WILL NOT CONSIDER: Fast food
GEOGRAPHIC LIMITS OF INVESTMENTS/LOANS: Regional; Other: Washington metropolitan area
RANGE OF INV./LOAN PER BUSINESS: Min. $1 million; Max. None
PREFERRED TERM FOR LOANS & LEASES: Min. 3 years: Max. 10 years
BUSINESS CHARACTERISTICS DESIRED-REQUIRED: Other: Experienced builders
BRANCHES: 1030 15th St. NW, Washington D.C.; (202) 842-3440; Officer: Brendon McCarthy

COMPANY: **B.F. Saul Company**
ADDRESS: 8401 Connecticut Avenue
Chevy Chase, MD 20815
PHONE: (301) 986-6000
TYPE OF INSTITUTION: Real estate services; mtg. banking
CONTACT OFFICER(S): Payton Fletcher, Senior V.P., Commercial Division
Stephen E. Cox, Senior V.P., Residential Investment Dept.
INVESTMENTS/LOANS MADE: For own account, For managed accounts, Through private placements
INVESTMENTS/LOANS MADE: In securities with a secondary market and in securities without a secondary market
TYPES OF FINANCING: REAL ESTATE LOANS: Long-term senior mtg.; Intermediate-term senior mtg.; Construction; Standbys; Industrial revenue bonds, REAL ESTATE: Acquisitions; Joint ventures; Partnerships/Syndications, OTHER SERVICES PROVIDED: Real estate property management
PREFERRED TYPES OF INDUSTRIES/INVESTMENTS: Real estate: office buildings, shopping centers, warehouses, apartments, land for development
GEOGRAPHIC LIMITS OF INVESTMENTS/LOANS: Regional; Other: Maryland, DC, Virginia, Georgia, Texas, Florida, Arizona
BRANCHES: Barry Field, Robert L. Robinson, 47 Perimeter Center East, N.E., Atlanta, GA; (404) 953-2444

COMPANY: **Hotel Investors Trust**
ADDRESS: 5530 Wisconsin, Suite 1148
Chevy Chase, MD 20815
PHONE: (301) 656-1802
TYPE OF INSTITUTION: REIT
CONTACT OFFICER(S): Dale E. Moulton, V.P., Hotel Development
ASSETS: $94 million
INVESTMENTS/LOANS MADE: For own account
TYPES OF FINANCING: VENTURE CAPITAL: Start-up from developed product stage; First-stage; Buy-outs/Acquisitions, REAL ESTATE: Acquisitions; Joint ventures
PREFERRED TYPES OF INDUSTRIES/INVESTMENTS: Specifically hotels
WILL NOT CONSIDER: Small, budget hotels (but can)
GEOGRAPHIC LIMITS OF INVESTMENTS/LOANS: National
RANGE OF INV/LOAN PER BUSINESS: Min. $1 million; Max. $15 million
PREFERRED TERM FOR LOANS & LEASES: Min. 10; Max. None
BUSINESS CHARACTERISTICS DESIRED-REQUIRED: Minimum number of years in business: 0
REFERRALS ACCEPTED FROM: Investment/Mortgage banker or Borrower/Investee
REMARKS: Shares paired with Hotel Investors Corp.

COMPANY: **Auer Mortgage Co.**
ADDRESS: P.O. Box 12319
Birmingham, MI 48012

COMPANY: **Van Arnem Financial Services, Inc.**
ADDRESS: 870 Bowers
Birmingham, MI 48011
PHONE: (313) 647-3040
TYPE OF INSTITUTION: Financial Services Inc. Specializes in Tax Shelters and income programs
CONTACT OFFICER(S): Mr. H. L. Van Arnem, Chief Executive Officer
ASSETS: $400,400,000
TYPES OF FINANCING: LOANS: Working capital; Equipmment; Equity-related; LEASES: Single-investor; Leveraged; Tax leases; Non-tax leases; Lease syndications; REAL ESTATE: Partnerships/Syndications
PREFERRED TYPES OF INDUSTRIES/INVESTMENTS: Equipment Leases with Fortune 200 Companies; Equipment Lease Syndications
GEOGRAPHIC LIMITS OF INVESTMENTS/LOANS: National
RANGE OF INV./LOAN PER BUSINESS: Min. $1,000,000; Max. $10,000,000
REFERRALS ACCEPTED FROM: Investment/Mortgage banker or Borrower/Investee

COMPANY: **Acquest Capital Management, Inc.**
ADDRESS: 300 E. Long Lake Road
Bloomfield Hills, MI 48013
PHONE: (313) 645-5130
TYPE OF INSTITUTION: SEC Registered Investment Advisor - Real Estate
CONTACT OFFICER(S): David G. Ong, President
ASSETS: $36 million
INVESTMENTS/LOANS MADE: For own account; For managed accounts
TYPES OF FINANCING: REAL ESTATE LOANS: Long-term senior mtg.; Intermediate-term senior mtg. REAL ESTATE: Acquisitions; Joint ventures; Partnerships
PREFERRED TYPES OF INDUSTRIES/INVESTMENTS: Real estate, existing or new, development excluding hotels, motels, apartments, single family residential
WILL NOT CONSIDER: Hotels, motels, apartments, single family residential
GEOGRAPHIC LIMITS OF INVESTMENTS/LOANS: Local; State; Regional; National
RANGE OF INV./LOAN PER BUSINESS: Min. $2 million; Max. $25-30 million
PREFERRED TERM FOR LOANS & LEASES: Min. 7 yrs; Max. 15 yrs.
BUSINESS CHARACTERISTICS DESIRED-REQUIRED: Other: Each real estate project is evaluated on its operating statement and/or proforma future economics

COMPANY: **Taurus Financial Group, Inc.**
ADDRESS: 601 South Norton Road, Suite A-8
Corunna, MI 48817
PHONE: (517) 743-5729
TYPE OF INSTITUTION: A licensed investment advisory and underwriting firm.
CONTACT OFFICER(S): Robert G. Machala, President, Corporate & Real Estate
Cory B. Weston, V.P., Equity and Debt Funding
Robin K. Mitchell, V.P., Offshore Funding
ASSETS: $5 million plus
INVESTMENTS/LOANS MADE: For managed accounts; Through private placements
INVESTMENTS/LOANS MADE: In securities with a secondary market and in securities without a secondary market
TYPES OF FINANCING: SECONDARY-MARKET CORPORATE SECURITIES: Common stock; Bonds, VENTURE CAPITAL: Second-stage (generally 1-3 years); Later-stage expansion; Buy-outs/Acquisitions, LOANS: Working capital (receivables/inventory); Equipment; Equity-related, REAL ESTATE LOANS: Long-term senior mtg.; Wraparounds; Land development, INTERNATIONAL (including import/export), REAL ESTATE: Acquisitions; Joint ventures,
PREFERRED TYPES OF INDUSTRIES/INVESTMENTS: No Preference
GEOGRAPHIC LIMITS OF INVESTMENTS/LOANS: International; Only in the Free World
RANGE OF INV./LOAN PER BUSINESS: Min. $3 million; Max. $50 million or more
PREFERRED TERM FOR LOANS & LEASES: Min. 5; Max. 15 years
BUSINESS CHARACTERISTICS DESIRED-REQUIRED: Minimum number of years in business: 3; Min. annual sales $5 million; Min net worth $4 million; Min. annual net income $1.5 million; Min. annual cash flow $1.5 million
REFERRALS ACCEPTED FROM: Investment/Mortgage banker or Borrower/Investee
REMARKS: Branches are planned for Denver, CO, and Toronto, Canada

COMPANY: **Detroit Mortgage and Realty Company**
ADDRESS: 333 West Fort Street
Detroit, MI 48226
PHONE: (313) 962-0800
TYPE OF INSTITUTION: Mortgage Banker
CONTACT OFFICER(S): Earl I. Heenan, Jr., President
Gordon J. MacNeil, Exec. Vice President - Income Properties
TYPES OF FINANCING: REAL ESTATE LOANS: Long-term senior mtg.; Intermediate-term senior mtg.; Standbys; REAL ESTATE: Acquisitions; Joint ventures
PREFERRED TYPES OF INDUSTRIES/INVESTMENTS: Office, industrials, shopping centers, hotels, apartments.
GEOGRAPHIC LIMITS OF INVESTMENTS/LOANS: State
PREFERRED TERM FOR LOANS & LEASES: Min. 1 year; Max. 10 years

COMPANY: **Midland Mortgage Investment Corp.**
ADDRESS: 72 1st National Bldg.
Detroit, MI 48226
PHONE: (313) 963-4160
TYPE OF INSTITUTION: Mortgage banker
CONTACT OFFICER(S): Walter Olejniczak, Exec. V.P.
ASSETS: Over $100,000,000
TYPES OF FINANCING: LOANS: Equity-related, REAL ESTATE LOANS: Other: Loan guarantees; Interim financing, REAL ESTATE
PREFERRED TYPES OF INDUSTRIES/INVESTMENTS: Multi-family; apartment buildings; townhouses
WILL NOT CONSIDER: Single family
GEOGRAPHIC LIMITS OF INVESTMENTS/LOANS: National
PREFERRED TERM FOR LOANS & LEASES: Min. 1-3 years; Max. 20+ years
BUSINESS CHARACTERISTICS DESIRED-REQUIRED: Other: Determined by insuring and underwriting agency
BRANCES: 600 Cleveland St., Ste. 1090, Clearwater, FL 33515; 800-237-9946, (813) 461-4801 Robert Banks, Pres.

COMPANY: **Manufacturers Hanover Mortgage Corp.**
ADDRESS: 27555 Farmington Rd., P.O. Box 1800
Farmington Hills, MI 48018
PHONE: (313) 661-7000
TYPE OF INSTITUTION: Mortgage Bank
CONTACT OFFICER(S): John C. Fletcher, Assoc. V.P.
Joseph Bourgon, Sr. Com'l. Loan Officer
Susan Laza, Com'l. Loan Officer
TYPES OF FINANCING: REAL ESTATE LOANS: Long-term senior mtg.; Intermediate-term senior mtg.; Wraparounds; Land; Land development; Construction; Standbys, REAL ESTATE: Acquisitions; Joint ventures

PREFERRED TYPES OF INDUSTRIES/INVESTMENTS: Office; Industrial; Retail; Condos
GEOGRAPHIC LIMITS OF INVESTMENTS/LOANS: National
RANGE OF INV./LOAN PER BUSINESS: Min. $2 million
BRANCHES: Stephen J. Emser, Rork Run N, Ste. #250, 5700 Lombardo Centre, Seven Hills, OH 44131

COMPANY: **Edward G. Hacker Co.**
ADDRESS: 225 W. Washtenaw
Lansing, MI 48933
PHONE: (517) 485-2261
CONTACT OFFICER(S): Edward T. Hacker, President
David B. Sharpe, Sr. V.P.
TYPES OF FINANCING: REAL ESTATE LOANS: Long-term senior mtg.; Other: Permanent loans, commercial loans, REAL ESTATE: Acquisitions; Joint ventures; Partnerships/Syndications
PREFERRED TYPES OF INDUSTRIES/INVESTMENTS: Shopping centers; Office and professional buildings; Light industrial
WILL NOT CONSIDER: Apartments
GEOGRAPHIC LIMITS OF INVESTMENTS/LOANS: Regional; So., & Mid-Michigan
RANGE OF INV./LOAN PER BUSINESS: Min. $500,000
BUSINESS CHARACTERISTICS DESIRED-REQUIRED: Other: Only commercial loans
REMARKS: 75% are conventional loans

COMPANY: **Norwest Mortgage, Inc.**
ADDRESS: 744 Northwestern Financial Center, 7900 Xerxes Ave. S.
Bloomington, MN 55431
PHONE: (612) 835-0303
TYPE OF INSTITUTION: Mortgage Banker
CONTACT OFFICER(S): James M. Bifaro, V.P. & Manager
ASSETS: $16,000,000,000
TYPES OF FINANCING: REAL ESTATE LOANS: Long-term senior mtg.; Intermediate-term senior mtg.; Subordinated; Wraparounds; Construction; Gap; Standbys; Industrial revenue bonds, REAL ESTATE: Acquisitions; Joint ventures; Partnerships/Syndications, OTHER SERVICES PROVIDED: Equity sales
PREFERRED TYPES OF INDUSTRIES/INVESTMENTS: Offices, Office warehousing, Shopping centers, Apartments
WILL NOT CONSIDER: Freestanding retail
GEOGRAPHIC LIMITS OF INVESTMENTS/LOANS: National; International
RANGE OF INV./LOAN PER BUSINESS: $2,000,000

COMPANY: **FBS Mortgage Corporation**
ADDRESS: 7201 Ohms Lane
Edina, MN 55435
PHONE: (612) 835-9344
TYPE OF INSTITUTION: Mortgage banker (Member First Bank System)
CONTACT OFFICER(S): Michael Thorsland, V.P.
ASSETS: $500M+
INVESTMENTS/LOANS MADE: For own account, For managed accounts, Through private placements
INVESTMENTS/LOANS MADE: Only in securities without a secondary market
TYPES OF FINANCING: REAL ESTATE LOANS: Long-term senior mtg.; Intermediate-term senior mtg.; Subordinated; Wraparounds; Construction; Gap; Standbys; Industrial revenue bonds; Other: Joint ventures, land sale leasebacks, property sale consultants, LEASES: Tax-oriented lease brokerage, REAL ESTATE: Acquisitions; Joint ventures
PREFERRED TYPES OF INDUSTRIES/INVESTMENTS: Office buildings, shopping centers, retail, hotels-motels, industrial; equipment leasing (Section 38 property).
GEOGRAPHIC LIMITS OF INVESTMENTS/LOANS: National
RANGE OF INV./LOAN PER BUSINESS: Min. $250,000; Max. None
PREFERRED TERM FOR LOANS & LEASES: Min. 1 year; Max. As available
REFERRALS ACCEPTED FROM: Investment/Mortgage banker or Borrower/Investee
BRANCHES: Charles H. Noble, Pres., 4100 Alpha Road, Suite 618, Dallas, TX 75234, (214) 661-3120
REMARKS: Other Branches in Denver, Houston, Kansas City, Miami

COMPANY: **Eberhardt Company**
ADDRESS: 3250 W. 66th St., P.O. Box 1385 (Zip 55440)
Minneapolis, MN 55435
PHONE: (612) 920-9280
TYPE OF INSTITUTION: Mortgage banker, R.E. property management, RE Brokerage
CONTACT OFFICER(S): Jack W. Wilson, Sr. V.P.
INVESTMENTS/LOANS MADE: Through private placements; For managed accounts
TYPES OF FINANCING: REAL ESTATE LOANS: Long-term senior mtg.; Intermediate-term senior mtg.; Subordinated; Wraparounds; Land; Land development; Construction; Gap; Standbys; Industrial revenue bonds, REAL ESTATE: Acquisitions; Joint ventures
PREFERRED TYPES OF INDUSTRIES/INVESTMENTS: Commercial; Residential
GEOGRAPHIC LIMITS OF INVESTMENTS/LOANS: National
REFERRALS ACCEPTED FROM: Investment/Mortgage banker or Borrower/Investee
BRANCHES: Robert A. Morken, Morken-Eberhardt, 2730 E. Broadway, Ste 150, Tucson, AZ 85716; (602) 881-1888

COMPANY: **F&M Marquette National Bank**
ADDRESS: 90 South 6th Street
Minneapolis, MN 55480
PHONE: (612) 341-5700
CONTACT OFFICER(S): M. Ellis Holmen, A.V.P., 341-5788
ASSETS: $1,000,000,000
TYPES OF FINANCING: REAL ESTATE LOANS: Intermediate-term senior mtg.; Land; Land development; Construction, OTHER SERVICES PROVIDED: Long-term senior mtg. and Industrial Revenue bonds not for own portfolio but do brokering
WILL NOT CONSIDER: Secondary housing; Recreation; Land
GEOGRAPHIC LIMITS OF INVESTMENTS/LOANS: Local

RANGE OF INV./LOAN PER BUSINESS: Min. $1,000,000; Max. $4-5,000,000
PREFERRED TERM FOR LOANS & LEASES: Min. 3 years; Max. 5 yearss
REMARKS: Preferred term for construction loans 12 -24 months

COMPANY: **Fidelity Bank & Trust Co.**
ADDRESS: 2338 Central Av., NE
Minneapolis, MN 55418
PHONE: (612) 789-2471
CONTACT OFFICER(S): Michael A. Gronmesh

COMPANY: **First Bank Minneapolis**
ADDRESS: First Bank Place East
Minneapolis, MN 55480
PHONE: (612) 370-4141
CONTACT OFFICER(S): Richard L. Peterson, Vice President
ASSETS: $8,000,000,000
TYPES OF FINANCING: REAL ESTATE LOANS: Long-term senior mtg; Intermediate-term senior mtg.; Wraparounds; Construction; Gap; Standbys; Industrial revenue bonds, REAL ESTATE: Partnerships/ Syndications
GEOGRAPHIC LIMITS OF INVESTMENTS/LOANS: National
RANGE OF INV./LOAN PER BUSINESS: Min. $5,000,000; Max. $40,000,000
PREFERRED TERM FOR LOANS & LEASES: Max. 10 years

COMPANY: **IDS American Express**
ADDRESS: IDS Tower
Minneapolis, MN 55402
PHONE: (612) 372-3131
TYPE OF INSTITUTION: Life Ins. Co.
CONTACT OFFICER(S): Richard Latzer; V.P. Certificate insurance and investments
ASSETS: 18.5 billion
INVESTMENTS/LOANS MADE: SECONDARY-MARKET CORPORATE SECURITIES: Common stock; Preferred stock; Bonds; Other; LOANS: Unsecured; Equipment; REAL ESTATE LOANS: Intermediate-term senior mtg.; Subordinated; Wraparounds; Standbys, Industrial Revenue Bonds; REAL ESTATE: Joint ventures; Partnerships/ Syndications; OTHER SERVICES PROVIDED
RANGE OF INV./LOAN PER BUSINESS: $2 million
REFERRALS ACCEPTED FROM: Investment/Mortgage banker or Borrower/Investee

COMPANY: **Knutson Mortgage and Financial Corporation**
ADDRESS: 17 Washington Avenue North
Minneapolis, MN 55401
PHONE: (612) 371-5888
TYPE OF INSTITUTION: Mortgage Banker
CONTACT OFFICER(S): Gene Hefter, Vice President
Kevin Filter, Comm. loan Officer
ASSETS: $900,000,000
TYPES OF FINANCING: REAL ESTATE LOANS: Long-term senior mtg.; Intermediate-term senior mtg,; Subordinated; Wraparounds; Land; Construction; Standbys; Industrial revenue bonds, REAL ESTATE: Joint ventures
PREFERRED TYPES OF INDUSTRIES/INVESTMENTS: General purpose, Office, etc.
WILL NOT CONSIDER: Special purpose or recreational
GEOGRAPHIC LIMITS OF INVESTMENTS/LOANS: National
RANGE OF INV./LOAN PER BUSINESS: Min. $500,000
PREFERRED TERM FOR LOANS & LEASES: Min. 3 years; Max. 10 years$

COMPANY: **Ministers Life — A Mutual Life Insurance Company**
ADDRESS: 3100 West Lake Street
Minneapolis, MN 55416
PHONE: (612) 927-7131
CONTACT OFFICER(S): Bruce Nicholson, V.P.-Finance Investments
INVESTMENTS/LOANS MADE: For own account
TYPES OF FINANCING: REAL ESTATE LOANS: Intermediate-term senior mtg.
PREFERRED TYPES OF INDUSTRIES/INVESTMENTS: Multi purpose buildings
GEOGRAPHIC LIMITS OF INVESTMENTS/LOANS: National
RANGE OF INV./LOAN PER BUSINESS: Min. $300,000; Max. $800,000
REFERRALS ACCEPTED FROM: Investment/Mortgage banker
REMARKS: Investing is handled through Washington Square Advisors Mike Eidem (612) 372-1820

COMPANY: **National City Bank of Minneapolis**
ADDRESS: 75 S. Fifth Street
Minneapolis, MN 55402
PHONE: (612) 340-3000
CONTACT OFFICER(S): Douglas A. Peterson, V.P.

COMPANY: **Northland Financial Company**
ADDRESS: 3500 West 80th Street, Suite 260
Minneapolis, MN 55431
PHONE: (612) 893-7500
TYPE OF INSTITUION: Real estate financing and sale.
CONTACT OFFICER(S): Ivan S. Kerr, Executive Vice President
INVESTMENTS/LOANS MADE: Through private placements
TYPES OF FINANCING: VENTURE CAPITAL: Buy-outs/Acquisitions; REAL ESTATE LOANS: Long term senior mtg.; Intermediate-term senior mtg.; Wraparound; Land; Construction; Gap; Standbys; Industrial revenue bonds; REAL ESTATE: Acquisitions; Joint Ventures
PREFERRED TYPES OF INDUSTRIES/INVESTMENTS: All types of real estate.
GEOGRAPHIC LIMITS OF INVESTMENTS/LOANS: National
RANGE OF INV./LOAN PER BUSINESS: Min. $500,000; Max. $ none
PREFERRED TERM FOR LOANS & LEASES: Min. none

MINNESOTA

BRANCHES: 12935 North Forty Drive, Suite 201, St. Louis, MO 63141; 314/469-1666; R. Michael O'Brien, Senior Vice President
4370 West 109th - Suite 110, Overland Park, KS 66211; 913/381-5630; Steven R. Duvall, Vice President
3900 East Camelback Road, Suite 406, Phoenix, AZ 85018; 602/955-7100; David C. Frederiksen, Vice President
7535 East Hampden Avenue, Suite 300, Denver, CO 80231; 303/337-2322; Stephen P. Bye, Vice President 375 East Tanque Verde Road, Tucson, AZ 85715; 602/721-0362; Donald Traister

COMPANY: **Towle Real Estate Company**
ADDRESS: 600 2nd Ave. S.
Minneapolis, MN 55402
PHONE: (612) 341-4444
TYPE OF INSTITUTION: Commercial real estate finance
CONTACT OFFICER(S): Gregory S. Miller, Manager, Real Estate Finance
ASSETS: $1,000,000-10,000,000
INVESTMENTS/LOANS MADE: Through private placements
INVESTMENTS/LOANS MADE: Only in securities without a secondary market
TYPES OF FINANCING: REAL ESTATE LOANS: Long-term senior mtg.; Intermediate-term senior mtg.; Subordinated; Wraparounds; Construction; Gap; Standbys; Industrial revenue bonds, REAL ESTATE: Acquisitions;Joint ventures; Partnerships/Syndications
WILL NOT CONSIDER: Restaurants, mini-warehouses, motels, special purpose properties
GEOGRAPHIC LIMITS OF INVESTMENTS/LOANS: National
RANGE OF INV./LOAN PER BUSINESS: Min. $500,000; Max. None
PREFERRED TERM FOR LOANS & LEASES: Min. 1 year; Max. 35 years
BUSINESS CHARACTERISTICS DESIRED-REQUIRED: Minimum number of years in business: 2; Min. net worth $1,000,000; Min. annual net income$100,000; Min. annual cash flow $100,000
REFERRALS ACCEPTED FROM: Investment/Mortgage banker or estee

COMPANY: **Washington Square Capital, Inc.**
ADDRESS: 100 Washington Square, Box 20
Minneapolis, MN 55440
PHONE: (612) 375-7541
TYPE OF INSTITUTION: Investment Advisory Firm
CONTACT OFFICER(S): Donald M. Feroe, V.P., Corporate Securities
Harold W. Leiferman, V.P., Mortgage Loans
Gary J. Kallsen, V.P., Real Estate
ASSETS: $2,800,000,000
INVESTMENTS/LOANS MADE: For managed accounts; Through private placements
INVESTMENTS/LOANS MADE: In securities with a secondary market and in securities without a secondary market
TYPES OF FINANCING: SECONDARY-MARKET CORPORATE SECURITIES: Bonds, VENTURE CAPITAL: Later-stage expansion; Buy-outs/ Acquisitions, LOANS: Unsecured to credits above Baa; Working capital (receivables/inventory); Equipment; Equity-related, REAL ESTATE LOANS: Intermediate-term senior mtg.; Wraparounds; Construction; Standbys; Loan Guarantees, LEASES: Leveraged; Non-tax leases; Vendor financing programs, REAL ESTATE: Acquisitions; Joint ventures
PREFERRED TYPES OF INDUSTRIES/INVESTMENTS: Any
GEOGRAPHIC LIMITS OF INVESTMENTS/LOANS: U.S. and Canada
RANGE OF INV./LOAN PER BUSINESS: Min. $2,000,000; Max. $25,000,000
PREFERRED TERM FOR LOANS & LEASES: Min. 1; Max. 10 years
BUSINESS CHARACTERISTICS DESIRED-REQUIRED: Minimum number of years in business: 5
REFERRALS ACCEPTED FROM: Investment/Mortgage banker or Borrower/Investee

COMPANY:**Minnesota Mutual Fire Casualty Co.**
ADDRESS: 10225 Yellow Cr. Dr.
Minneapolis MN 55343
PHONE: (612) 933-5033
CONTACT OFFICER: Jim Jordan, Exec. V.P.
ASSETS: $35 million
INVESTMENTS/LOANS MADE: In securities with a secondary market or without a secondary market
TYPES OF FINANCING: SECONDARY-MARKET CORPORATE SECURITIES: Common stock; Preferred stock; Bonds; REAL ESTATE LOANS: Other: pools of mortgages—no indv. mtgs.
PREFERRED TYPES OF INDUSTRIES/INVESTMENTS: Gov't. guarantees, municipalities
GEOGRAPHIC LIMITS OF INVESTMENTS/LOANS: National

COMPANY:**First Asset Realty Advisors**
ADDRESS: First Bank Place
Minneapolis MN 55480
PHONE: (612) 370-4729
TYPE OF INSTITUTION: Real Estate Investment Subsidiary of First Bank Minneapolis
CONTACT OFFICER(S): Charles S. Ingwalson, President
ASSETS: $40,000,000
INVESTMENTS/LOANS MADE: For managed accounts
INVESTMENTS/LOANS MADE: Only in securities without a secondary market
TYPES OF FINANCING: REAL ESTATE: Acquisitions
PREFERRED TYPES OF INDUSTRIES/INVESTMENTS: Real Estate - Specifically existing office buildings, shopping centers, and industrials
GEOGRAPHIC LIMITS OF INVESTMENTS/LOANS: National
RANGE OF INV./LOAN PER BUSINESS: Min. $3,000,000; Max. $15,000,000

COMPANY: **Midwest Life Ins. Co.**
ADDRESS: 100 Dain Tower
Minneapolis MN 55402
PHONE: (612) 371-7774
CONTACT OFFICER(S): Bonnie Russ, Sr. V.P. in charge of Administration
ASSETS: $70 million

MINNESOTA

INVESTMENTS/LOANS MADE: In securities with a secondary market and in securities without a secondary market
TYPES OF FINANCING: SECONDARY-MARKET CORPORATE SECURITIES: Bonds; REAL ESTATE LOANS: Long-term senior mtg.; Intermediate-term senior mtg.
GEOGRAPHIC LIMITS OF INVESTMENTS/LOANS: National
RANGE OF INV./LOAN PER BUSINESS: Min. —; Max. $1 mil.
PREFERRED TERM FOR LOANS & LEASES: Min. — years; Max. 30 years
REFERRALS ACCEPTED FROM: Investment/Mortgage banker or Borrower/Investee

COMPANY: **Clapp-Thomssen Company**
ADDRESS: 4 East 4th Street
St. Paul, MN 55101
PHONE: (612) 291-7777
TYPE OF INSTITUTION: Mortgage Banker
CONTACT OFFICER(S): Frederick H. Clapp
Edward Clapp
TYPES OF FINANCING: REAL ESTATE LOANS: Land development, REAL ESTATE: Acquisitions; Joint ventures; Partnerships/Syndications, OTHER SERVCES PROVIDED: Brokerage
PREFERRED TYPES OF INDUSTRIES/INVESTMENTS: Land development, Commercial, Industrial, Residential
GEOGRAPHIC LIMITS OF INVESTMENTS/LOANS: Local; Other: St. Paul and surrounding area

COMPANY:**American Bank and Trust Company**
ADDRESS: Fifth and Minnesota Street
St. Paul, MN 55101
PHONE: (612) 298-6182
TYPE OF INSTITUTION: Real estate Lender
CONTACT OFFICER(S): Michael Kukielka, VP
ASSETS: $450,000,000
TYPES OF FINANCING: REAL ESTATE: Construction; Industrial revenue bonds
WILL NOT CONSIDER: Special use properties
GEOGRAPHIC LIMITS OF INVESTMENTS/LOANS: Local
RANGE OF INV./LOAN PER BUSINESS: Min. $1,000,000; Max. $4,000,000
PREFERRED TERM FOR LOANS & LEASES: Min. 1-2 years
REFERRALS ACCEPTED FROM: Investment/Mortgage banker or Borrower/Investee

COMPANY: **The First National Bank of St. Paul**
ADDRESS: 332 Minnesota Street
St. Paul, MN 55101
PHONE: (612) 291-5000
CONTACT OFFICER(S): Mayer S. Tapper, V.P., 291-5569

COMPANY: **MIMLIC Asset Management Co.**
ADDRESS: 400 North Robert
St. Paul, MN 55101
PHONE: (612) 298-3844
TYPE OF INSTITUTION: Registered investment advisor for MN Mutual Life and its subsidiaries
CONTACT OFFICER(S): Fritz Feuerherm, Sr. Inv. Off., Bonds, Fixed Income
John Clymer, Sr. Inv. Officer, Mortgage & RE
Tim Kasper, Sr. Inv. Officer, Equity
ASSETS: $2.8 billion
INVESTMENTS/LOANS MADE: In securities with a secondary market and in securities without a secondary market
TYPES OF FINANCING: SECONDARY-MARKET CORPORATE SECURITIES: Common stock; Preferred stock; Bonds; Other: Limited partnerships. VENTURE CAPITAL: Later-stage expansion; Oil exploration. LOANS: Unsecured; Working capital; Equipment; Equity-related. REAL ESTATE LOANS: Long-term senior mtg.; Intermediate-term senior mtg.; Subordinated; Wraparounds; Land; Land development. LEASES: Leveraged; Non-tax leases; Operating; Other: equipment. REAL ESTATE: Acquisitions; Joint ventures; Partnerships/Syndications.
PREFERRED TYPES OF INDUSTRIES/INVESTMENTS: Mostly fixed incomes
GEOGRAPHIC LIMITS OF INVESTMENTS/LOANS: National
RANGE OF INV./LOAN PER BUSINESS: Min. $1 million
BUSINESS CHARACTERISTICS DESIRED-REQUIRED: Minimum number of years in business: 5
REFERRALS ACCEPTED FROM: Investment/Mortgage banker or Borrower/Investee

COMPANY: **The Minnesota Mutuual Life Insurance Co.**
ADDRESS: 400 North Robert
St. Paul, MN 55101
PHONE: (612) 298-3500
CONTACT OFFICER(S): Fritz Feuerherm, Inv. Off.
TYPES OF FINANCING: SECONDARY-MARKET CORPORATE SECURITIES: Bonds. LOANS: Equipment, Equity-related. REAL ESTATE LOANS: Long-term senior mtg.; Subordinated
PREFERRED TYPES OF INDUSTRIES/INVESTMENTS: Corporate loans
WILL NO CONSIDER: Banks
GEOGRAPHIC LIMITS OF INVESTMENTS/LOANS: National
RANGE OF INV./LOAN PER BUSINESS: Min. $2 million; Max. $8 million
PREFERRED TERM FOR LOANS & LEASES: Min. 2 years; Max. 15 years
BUSINESS CHARACTERISTICS DESIRED-REQUIRED: Minimum number of years in business: 5; Other: Operating profits within last 5 years
REFERRALS ACCEPTED FROM: Investment/Mortgage banker or Borrower/Investee

COMPANY: **Mutual Service Life Insurance Co.**
ADDRESS: Two Pine Tree Dr.
St. Paul, MN 55112
PHONE: (612) 631-7000
CONTACT OFFICER(S): Loren A. Haugland, VP Investments

INVESTMENTS/LOANS MADE: In securities with a secondary market and in securities without a secondary market
TYPES OF FINANCING: SECONDARY-MARKET CORPORATE SECURITIES: Common stock; Preferred stock; Bonds. VENTURE CAPITAL. REAL ESTATE LOANS: Intermediate-term senior mtg.; Wraparounds; Other: will do second mortgages. LEASES: Single-investor; Leveraged. REAL ESTATE: Acquisitions. OTHER SERVICES PROVIDED: Participate in most phases of venture capital through pooling
GEOGRAPHIC LIMITS OF INVESTMENTS/LOANS: National
RANGE OF INV./LOAN PER BUSINESS: Min. $250,000; Max. $3 million
PREFERRED TERM FOR LOANS & LEASES: Min. 3 years
REFERRALS ACCEPTED FROM: Investment/Mortgage banker or Borrower/Investee

COMPANY: **Rothschild Financial Corporation**
ADDRESS: 410 Degree of Honor Bldg.
St. Paul, MN 55101
PHONE: (612) 224-4651; (612) 835-7511
TYPE OF INSTITUTION: Mortgage Banker
CONTACT OFFICER(S): Gary Gustafson, Sr. V.P.
ASSETS: $10,000,000 - 100,000,000
TYPES OF FINANCING: REAL ESTATE LOANS: Long-term senior mtg.; Intermediate-term senior mtg.; Subordinated; Wraparounds; Construction; Gap; Standbys; Industrial revenue bonds; Other: Sale-Leaseback. REAL ESTATE: Acquisitions; Joint ventures. OTHER SERVICES PROVIDED: RE Acq. for managed accounts (e.g. Ins. Co.'s)
PREFERRED TYPES OF INDUSTRIES/INVESTMENTS: Shopping centers; Office buildings; Industrial
WILL NOT CONSIDER: Some special purpose
RANGE OF INV./LOAN PER BUSINESS: Min. $500,000
BRANCHES: 4140 Broadway, Kansas City, MO 64111, (816) 756-1121, Don Thellman
440 Regency Parkway, Suite 200, Omaha, NE 68114, (402) 391-2110, E.T. (Ding) Daisley

COMPANY: **Clarkson Valley Estates, Inc.**
ADDRESS: 7800 Bonhomme
Clayton, MO 63105
PHONE: (314) 863-0600
TYPE OF INSTITUTION: Independent real estate innvestment company
CONTACT OFFICER(S): Thomas E. Phelps, President
Mark J. Lincoln, Vice President/Chief Investment Officer
INVESTMENTS/LOANS MADE: For own account, For managed accounts
TYPES OF FINANCING: REAL ESTATE: Acquisitions; Joint ventures; Partnerships/Syndications.
GEOGRAPHIC LIMITS OF INVESTMENTS/LOANS: Local
RANGE OF INV./LOAN PER BUSINESS: Min. $100,000

COMPANY: **Business Mens Assurance Co.**
ADDRESS: Box 458
Kansas City, MO 64141
PHONE: (816) 753-8000
TYPE OF INSTITUTION: Life insurance company
CONTACT OFFICER(S): Tony Jacobs, Sr. V.P. & Sr. Sec. Off.
Robert Sawyer, Securities V.P.
Connie Troutman
Charles D. Durbin, Asst. V.P.
TYPES OF FINANCING: SECONDARY-MARKET CORPORATE SECURITIES: Common stock; Preferred stock; Bonds, VENTURE CAPITAL: Research & Development, REAL ESTATE LOANS: Land development, OTHER SERVICES PROVIDED: Purchases through BMA Properties — R.E. & Mortgaging
PREFERRED TYPES OF INDUSTRIES/INVESTMENTS: Diversified
GEOGRAPHIC LIMITS OF INVESTMENTS/LOANS: National
RANGE OF INV./LOAN PER BUSINESS: Min. None; Max. $3 million
PREFERRED TERM FOR LOANS & LEASES: Min. Varies

COMPANY: **Kansas City Life Insurance Company**
ADDRESS: 3520 Broadway, P.O. Box 139
Kansas City, MO 64141-0139
PHONE: (816) 753-7000
CONTACT OFFICER(S): Richard L. Finn, Sr. V.P. Financial
ASSETS: $100 million and up
TYPES OF FINANCING: REAL ESTATE LOANS: Long-term senior mtg.; Intermediate-term senior mtg.
PREFERRED TYPES OF INDUSTRIES/INVESTMENTS: Industrial and Retail
GEOGRAPHIC LIMITS OF INVESTMENTS/LOANS: National; Primarily South, Southwest & West Coast
RANGE OF INV./LOAN PER BUSINESS: Min. $400,000; Max. $4,000,000
PREFERRED TERM FOR LOANS & LEASES: Min. 5; Max. 7-10 years
REFERRALS ACCEPTED FROM: Investment/Mortgage banker or Borrower/Investee

COMPANY: **The Reliable Life Insurance Company**
ADDRESS: 231 W. Lockwood
Webster Groves, MO 63119
PHONE: (314) 968-4900
CONTACT OFFICER(S): Lisa Luehrman, V.P.
ASSETS: $260 million
INVESTMENTS/LOANS MADE: In securities with a secondary market and in securities without a secondary-market
TYPES OF FINANCING: SECONDARY-MARKET CORPORATE SECURITIES: Common stock; Preferred stock; Bonds; VENTURE CAPITAL: First-stage; Second-stage; Buy-outs/Acquisitions; LOANS: Equity-related; REAL ESTATE LOANS: Long-term senior mtg.; Intermediate-term senior mtg.; Land; Land development; Construction; Standbys; REAL ESTATE: Acquisitions; Partnerships/Syndications
GEOGRAPHIC LIMITS OF INVESTMENTS/LOANS: Regional; Midwest; South; Southwest
RANGE OF INV./LOAN PER BUSINESS: Max. 10 years

PREFERRED TERM FOR LOANS & LEASES: Max. 10 years
REFERRALS ACCEPTED FROM: Investment/Mortgage banker only
REMARKS: Have a number of wholly-owned subsidiaries through the Midwest; 50 locations —insurance; all investing done through this office

COMPANY: **Hancock Mortgage Corp**
ADDRESS: P.O. Box 4212
Gulfport, MS 39501
PHONE: (601) 868-4730
TYPE OF INSTITUTION: Mortgage Banker
CONTACT OFFICER(S): Frank Romeo, Sr. V.P.
ASSETS: Servicing Volume over $100,000,000
TYPES OF FINANCING: REAL ESTATE LOANS
PREFERRED TYPES OF INDUSTRIES/INVESTMENTS: Construction & Development; Retailing, Wholesaling & Distribution; Warehousing
GEOGRAPHIC LIMITS OF INVESTMENTS/LOANS: National

COMPANY: **Bailey Mortgage Co.**
ADDRESS: 162 E. Amite St.
Jackson, MS 39205
PHONE: (601) 969-1700
TYPE OF INSTITUTION: Mortgage Banker
CONTACT OFFICER(S): Edward F. O'Connor, V.P.
ASSETS: 250-300 million (Savings & Loan)
TYPES OF FINANCING: REAL ESTATE LOANS: Long-term senior mtg.; Intermediate-term senior mtg.
PREFERRED TYPES OF INDUSTRIES/INVESTMENTS: Retailing, Wholesaling & Distribution; Real Estate; Apartments; Office Bldgs.; Warehouses
CEOCRAPHIC LIMITS OF INVESTMENTS/LOANS: Regional
RANGE OF INV./LOAN PER BUSINESS: Min. $300,000
PREFERRED TERM FOR LOANS & LEASES: Min. 10-15 years; Max. 20+ years

COMPANY: **Deposit Guaranty Mortgage Company**
ADDRESS: P.O. Box 1193
Jackson, MS 39205
PHONE: (601) 968-6855
TYPE OF INSTITUTION: Mortgage banker
CONTACT OFFICER(S): Robert C. Grider, Manager of Income Property Lending
INVESTMENTS/LOANS MADE: For managed accounts, Through private placements
INVESTMENTS/LOANS MADE: In securities with a secondary market and in securities without a secondary market
TYPES OF FINANCING: SECONDARY-MARKET CORPORATE SECURITIES: Other: GNMA Securities, REAL ESTATE LOANS: Long-term senior mtg.; Intermediate-term senior mtg.; Land; Land development; Construction; Gap; Industrial revenue bonds; Other types of tax free financing; Other: Insured project loans
PREFERRED TYPES OF INDUSTRIES/INVESTMENTS: Retailing, wholesaling & distribution; apartments, motels, office & industrial buildings; FHA, VA, FNMA & FHLMC conventional servicing portfolio
GEOGRAPHIC LIMITS OF INVESTMENTS/LOANS: Regional Southeast
RANGE OF INV./LOAN PER BUSINESS: Min. $250,000; Max. $10,000,000 & up
PREFERRED TERM FOR LOANS & LEASES: Min. 5 years; Max. 10 years
REFERRALS ACCEPTED FROM: Investment/Mortgage banker or Borrower/Investee
BRANCHES: Marvin Crabtree, Deposit Guaranty Financial Services, Inc. 201 E. Kennedy, Ste. 914, Tampa, FL 33602; (813) 229-7811

COMPANY: **Southern Farm Bureau Life Insurance Company**
ADDRESS: 1401 Livingston Lane, P.O. Box 78
Jackson, MS 39213
PHONE: (601) 981-7422
CONTACT OFFICER(S): Walter J. Olson, III Portfolio Mgr.
Joel M. Melton, Manager, Mortgage Loans and Real Estate Department
Jerry Betterson, Investment Analyst
ASSETS: $1,300,000,000.00
INVESTMENTS/LOANS MADE: For own account
INVESTMENTS/LOANS MADE: In securities with a secondary market and in securities without a secondary market
TYPES OF FINANCING: LOANS: SECONDARY-MARKET CORPORATE SECURITIES: Common stock; Bonds; VENTURE CAPITAL: Later-stage expansion; Buy-outs/Acquisitions; LOANS: Unsecured to credits above BAA; Equipment; Equity-related; REAL ESTATE LOANS: Intermediate-term senior mtg.; Wraparounds; Construction; Standbys; Industrial revenue bonds; REAL ESTATE: Acquisitions; Joint ventures; OTHER SERVICES PROVIDED: Mortgage Banking
PREFERRED TYPES OF INDUSTRIES/INVESTMENTS: Will consider most types.
WILL NOT CONSIDER: Some S & L and Finance
GEOGRAPHIC LIMITS OF INVESTMENTS/LOANS: National
RANGE OF INV./LOAN PER BUSINESS: Min. $500,000; Max. $5,000,000
PREFERRED TERM FOR LOANS & LEASES: Min. 1; Max. 10 years
BUSINESS CHARACTERISTICS DESIRED-REQUIRED: A rated or equivalent

COMPANY: **Wortman & Mann, Inc., Mortgage Banking Division**
ADDRESS: 525 E. Capitol St., P.O. Box 1571
Jackson, MS 39205
PHONE: (601) 944-3027
TYPE OF INSTITUTION: Mortgage bankers
CONTACT OFFICER(S): W. Don Barkley, President
Jay R. West, V.P.
INVESTMENTS/LOANS MADE: Through private placements
INVESTMENTS/LOANS MADE: Only in securities with a secondary market
TYPES OF FINANCING: REAL ESTATE LOANS: Long-term senior mtg.; Construction, OTHER SERVICES

PROVIDED: Appraisals, insurance, property management
PREFERRED TYPES OF INDUSTRIES/INVESTMENTS: Apartments, office buildings, shopping centers
GEOGRAPHIC LIMITS OF INVESTMENTS/LOANS: Regional; Other: Mississippi and adjacent states
RANGE OF INV./LOAN PER BUSINESS: Min. $1,000,000
PREFERRED TERM FOR LOANS & LEASES: Min. 15 years; Max. 30 years
REFERRALS ACCEPTED FROM: Investment/Mortgage banker or Borrower/Investee

COMPANY: **Cameron-Brown Co.**
ADDRESS: First Union Plaza
Charlotte, NC 28280
PHONE: (704) 374-6787
TYPE OF INSTITUTION: Mortgage Banker
CONTACT OFFICER(S): O. B. Hawkins, Sr. V.P.
ASSETS: Servicing Volume over 7 billion
TYPES OF FINANCING: REAL ESTATE LOANS: All types; REAL ESTATE: Acquisitions; Jooint ventures
PREFERRED TYPES OF INDUSTRIES/INVESTMENTS: Apartments; Office Bldgs.; Manufacturing; Warehousing
GEOGRAPHIC LIMITS OF INVESTMENTS/LOANS: Regional; Other: Southeast, Sunbelt, California, Colorado, Iowa
RANGE OF INV./LOAN PER BUSINESS: Min. $300,000; Max. None
PREFERRED TERM FOR LOANS & LEASES: Max. 20+ years

COMPANY: **North Carolina Mutual Life Insurance Co.**
ADDRESS: Mutual Plaza
Durham, NC 27701
PHONE: (919) 682-9201
CONTACT OFFICER(S): Milan R. Pakaski, R.E.
M. K. Sloan, Treasurer, Equities
ASSETS: $200 million
TYPES OF FINANCING: SECONDARY-MARKET CORPORATE SECURITIES: Bonds, LOANS, REAL ESTATE LOANS
GEOGRAPHIC LIMITS OF INVESTMENTS/LOANS: Regional; Other: East Coast exclusive of NY
RANGE OF INV./LOAN PER BUSINESS: Min. None; Max. $2 mil. for R.E.
PREFERRED TERM FOR LOANS & LEASES: Min. 10-15 years; Max. 15-20 years
BUSINESS CHARACTERISTICS DESIRED-REQUIRED: Other: A, AA, AAA rated on provisional rated; not actively seeking industrial revenues and municipals
REFERRALS ACCEPTED FROM: Investment/Mortgage banker or Borrower/Investee
BRANCHES: 44 branches-district office; 14 states & D.C.

COMPANY: **Jefferson-Pilot Investments, Inc.**
ADDRESS: P.O. Box 20407
Greensboro, NC 27420
PHONE: (919) 378-2387
TYPE OF INSTITUTION: Investment Management Subsidiary of Jefferson-Pilot Corporation
CONTACT OFFICER(S): George Garey, Jr., Senior Vice President-Securities
Hugh B. North, Jr., Senior Vice President-Mortgage Loan
ASSETS: $2.5 Billion
INVESTMENTS/LOANS MADE: For own account; For managed accounts; Through private placements; Through underwriting public offerings
INVESTMENTS/LOANS MADE: In securities with a secondary market and in securities without a secondary market
TYPES OF FINANCING: SECONDARY-MARKET CORPORATE SECURITIES: Common stock; Preferred stock; Bonds; LOANS: Unsecured to credits above BAA; Working capital; Equipment; REAL ESTATE LOANS: Long-term senior mtg.; Intermediate-term senior mtg.; Industrial revenue bonds; LEASES: Single-investor; Leveraged; REAL ESTATE: Acquisitions; Joint Ventures
GEOGRAPHIC LIMITS OF INVESTMENTS/LOANS: National
RANGE OF INV./LOAN PER BUSINESS: Min. $500,000; Max. $10,000,000
PREFERRED TERM FOR LOANS & LEASES: Varies
REFERRALS ACCEPTED FROM: Investment/Mortgage banker or Borrower/Investee

COMPANY: **Southern Life Insurance Company**
ADDRESS: One Southern Life Center, P.O. Box 21887
Greensboro, NC 27420
PHONE: (919) 275-9681
CONTACT OFFICER(S): W. Lee Carter, III, V.P., Investments
ASSETS: $180 million and up
INVESTMENTS/LOANS MADE: In securities with a secondary market and in securities without a secondary market
TYPES OF FINANCING: SECONDARY-MARKET CORPORATE SECURITIES, LOANS:, REAL ESTATE LOANS
GEOGRAPHIC LIMITS OF INVESTMENTS/LOANS: National; Canada
RANGE OF INV./LOAN PER BUSINESS: Min. $100,000; Max. $1,000,000
REFERRALS ACCEPTED FROM: Investment/Mortgage banker or Borrower/Investee

COMPANY: **Durham Life Insurance Company**
ADDRESS: 2610 Wycliff Road, P.O. Box 27807
Raleigh, NC 27611
PHONE: (919) 782-6110
TYPE OF INSTITUTION: Insurance Co.
CONTACT OFFICER(S): F.P. Coley — Executive V.P. & Treasurer-Finance
F. E. Skipper, V.P & Sec.
ASSETS: $400,000,000+
INVESTMENTS/LOANS MADE: For own account; For managed accounts; Through private placements, underwriting public offerings
INVESTMENTS/LOANS MADE: In securities with a secondary market and in securities without a secondary market
TYPES OF FINANCING: SECONDARY-MARKET CORPORATE SECURITIES: Common stock; Preferred

stock; Bonds, LOANS: Unsecured to credits above "A" or better, REAL ESTATE LOANS: Long-term senior mtg.; Intermediate-term senior mtg., REAL ESTATE: Acquisitions
PREFERRED TYPES OF INDUSTRIES/INVESTMENTS: Diversified
GEOGRAPHIC LIMITS OF INVESTMENTS/LOANS: Regional; National; Real Estate — Regional; Securities — National
RANGE OF INV./LOAN PER BUSINESS: Min. $200,000; Max. $3,000,000
BUSINESS CHARACTERISTICS DESIRED-REQUIRED: AAA Paper
REFERRALS ACCEPTED FROM: Investment/Mortgage banker and Borrower/Investee
BRANCHES: NC, SC, VA

COMPANY: **Metropolitan Service Mortgage Corp.**
ADDRESS: 215 No. 5th St., Box 2687
Fargo, ND 58108-2687
PHONE: (701) 293-2600
TYPE OF INSTITUTION: Mortgage Banking Operation
CONTACT OFFICER(S): Ronald L. Hanson, President, Chief Executive Officer
James R. Bokinskie, Vice President
Lyle D. Sustad, Vice President
ASSETS: $55,375,000.00
INVESTMENTS/LOANS MADE: For own account; Through private placements
INVESTMENTS/LOANS MADE: Only in a secondary market
TYPES OF FINANCING: REAL ESTATE LOANS: Long-term senior mtg.; Land: Land development; Construction; Standbys; REAL ESTATE: Joint ventures
PREFERRED TERM FOR LOANS & LEASES: Min. 1 year; Max. 30 years
BRANCHES: Warren Trangsrud, Manager & Vice President, Suite 102, 7353 South Alton Way, P.O. Box 4596, Englewood, CO 80155; (303) 740-7164
Michael H. Downing, Manager & Vice President, 6840 E. Indian School Rd., Scottsdale, AZ 85251; (602) 941-1229
Michael J. Goodman, Manager, 74-399 Highway 111, P.O. Box 897, Plaza Del Sol, Palm Desert, CA 92261; (619) 340-0770

COMPANY: **Bankers Life Insurance Company of Nebraska**
ADDRESS: 5900 "O" St.
Lincoln, NE 68510
PHONE: (402) 467-1122
CONTACT OFFICER(S): Jon C. Headrick, V.P. Securities
ASSETS: $950 million
INVESTMENTS/LOANS MADE: For own account; For managed accounts; Through private placements; Through underwriting public offerings
INVESTMENTS/LOANS MADE: In securities with a secondary market and in securities without a secondary market
TYPES OF FINANCING: SECONDARY-MARKET: Common stock; Preferred stock; Bonds; VENTURE CAPITAL: Start-up from developed product stage; LOANS: Unsecured to credits above BAA; Equipment; Equity related; REAL ESTATE LOANS: Long-term senior mtg.; Intermediate-term senior mtg.; LEASES: Single-Investor; Leveraged; Tax leases; REAL ESTATE: Acquisitions; Joint ventures; Partnerships/Syndications.
GEOGRAPHIC LIMITS OF INVESTMENTS/LOANS: National
RANGE OF INV./LOAN PER BUSINESS: Min. $1,000,000; Max. $5,000,000
PREFERRED TERM FOR LOANS & LEASES: Min. 3 years; Max. 15 years
REFERRALS ACCEPTED FROM: Investment/Mortgage banker; Borrower/Investee

COMPANY: **The Security Mutual Life Insurance Company**
ADDRESS: 200 Centennial Mall N., P.O. Box 82248
Lincoln, NE 68501
PHONE: (402) 477-4141
CONTACT OFFICER(S): Fred Gottchalk, V.P., Investments
ASSETS: $100 million and up
INVESTMENTS/LOANS MADE: In securities with a secondary market and in securities without a secondary market
TYPES OF FINANCING: SECONDARY-MARKET CORPORATE SECURITIES: Bonds, REAL ESTATE LOANS: Long-term senior mtg.
GEOGRAPHIC LIMITS OF INVESTMENTS/LOANS: Regional; Generally West of Mississippi
PREFERRED TERM FOR LOANS & LEASES: Min. 10-15; Max. 20+ years
BUSINESS CHARACTERISTICS DESIRED-REQUIRED: Securities qualify under Nebraska investment statutes
REFERRALS ACCEPTED FROM: Investment/Mortgage banker
REMARKS: Maximum amount is $500,000 for bonds and $850,000 for mortgages.

COMPANY: **Firstier Mortgage Company**
ADDRESS: 8712 Dodd St., 4th Floor, Firstier Pl.
Omaha, NE 68132
PHONE: (402) 390-9100
TYPE OF INSTITUTION: Mortgage Banker
CONTACT OFFICER(S): Delwyn K. Bowden
ASSETS: $850,000,000
TYPES OF FINANCING: REAL ESTATE LOANS: Other: Commercial Construction
PREFERRED TYPES OF INDUSTRIES/INVESTMENTS: Shopping Centers; Industrial
GEOGRAPHIC LIMITS OF INVESTMENTS/LOANS: Regional, Midwest
RANGE OF INV./LOAN PER BUSINESS: Min. varies

COMPANY: **Guarantee Mutual Life Company**
ADDRESS: 8721 Indian Hills Drive
Omaha, NE 68114
PHONE: (402) 391-2121
TYPE OF INSTITUTION: Life Ins. Co.
CONTACT OFFICER(S): Don Schaneberg, V.P. Ass't. Treasurer
ASSETS: $450 million
INVESTMENTS/LOANS MADE: Through private placements; Through underwriting public offerings

INVESTMENTS/LOANS MADE: In securities with a secondary market and in securities without a secondary market
TYPES OF FINANCING: SECONDARY-MARKET CORPORATE SECURITIES: Common stock; Bonds; Other: Govt., Corp., Municipal; REAL ESTATE LOANS: Long-term senior mtg., Intermediate term senior mortgages; Land developments; Other: First mtgs. only; REAL ESTATE: Joint ventures
WILL NOT CONSIDER: Bank holding companies, electric utilities with nuclear exposures
GEOGRAPHIC LIMITS OF INVESTMENTS/LOANS: National; Other: States where the Co. is licensed to sell ins—Real Estate
RANGE OF INV./LOAN PER BUSINESS: Min. $500,000; Max. $2.4 million R.E.
PREFERRED TERM FOR LOANS & LEASES: Min. 5 years; Max. 10 years
BUSINESS CHARACTERISTICS DESIRED-REQUIRED: 5 year track record, flexible
REFERRALS ACCEPTED FROM: Investment/Mortgage banker or Borrower/Investee

COMPANY: **United of Omaha Life Insurance Co.**
ADDRESS: Mutual of Omaha Plaza
Omaha, NE 68175
PHONE: (402) 342-7600
CONTACT OFFICER(S): Bill Arnold, 2nd V.P.
Tom Schmit, 2nd V.P., Securities
ASSETS: $2.25 billion
TYPES OF FINANCING: REAL ESTATE LOANS: Long-term senior mtg.; REAL ESTATE: Joint ventures, Equity Purchase
PREFERRED TYPES OF INDUSTRIES/INVESTMENTS: Diversified
GEOGRAPHIC LIMITS OF INVESTMENTS/LOANS: National
RANGE OF INV./LOAN PER BUSINESS: Min.$500,000; Max. $5,000,000
PREFERRED TERM FOR LOANS & LEASES: Max. 10 years
REFERRALS ACCEPTED FROM: Investment/Mortgage banker

COMPANY: **Western Securities Co.**
ADDRESS: 5060 Dodge St.
Omaha, NE 68132
PHONE: (402) 558-2800
TYPE OF INSTITUTION: Mortgage Banking
CONTACT OFFICER(S): Bob Cowan, V.P.—Residential
INVESTMENTS/LOANS MADE: For managed accounts, Through private placements
INVESTMENTS/LOANS MADE: In securities with a secondary market and in securities without a secondary market
TYPES OF FINANCING: REAL ESTATE LOANS: Long-term senior mtg.; Intermediate-term senior mtg.; Subordinated; Wraparounds, Land development; Construction; Gap; Standbys; Industrial revenue bonds, REAL ESTATE: Acquisitions; Joint ventures; Partnerships/Syndications
WILL NOT CONSIDER: Nursing Homes
GEOGRAPHIC LIMITS OF INVESTMENTS/LOANS: Regional, Midwest

RANGE OF INV./LOAN PER BUSINESS: Min. $500,000
PREFERRED TERM FOR LOANS & LEASES: Max. 10 years
REFERRALS ACCEPTED FROM: Investment/Mortgage banker or Borrower/Investee
BRANCHES: 655 Broadway, Denver, CO, 80203; Ray Cooper, Exec. V.P.

COMPANY: **Woodman of the World Life Insurance Society**
ADDRESS: Woodman Tower, 1700 Farnam Street
Omaha, NE 68102
PHONE: (402) 342-1890
CONTACT OFFICER(S): Stephen W. Mellor, Asst. V.P., Mtg. Loans
Donald Miller, Asst. V.P., Securities
ASSETS: $100 million and up
TYPES OF FINANCING: LOANS: Unsecured; Working Capital; Equipment, REAL ESTATE LOANS: Long-term senior mtg.; Intermediate-term senior mtg.; REAL ESTATE: Joint Ventures
PREFERRED TYPES OF INDUSTRIES/INVESTMENTS: R.E.: Shopping Centers, Office Bldgs., Warehouses, Industrial
GEOGRAPHIC LIMITS OF INVESTMENTS/LOANS: National; Prefer Southeast & Southwest for R.E.
RANGE OF INV./LOAN PER BUSINESS: Min. $1,000,000; Max. $10 million (R.E.), $2 million (other)
PREFERRED TERM FOR LOANS & LEASES: Min. 5-10; Max. 7-15 years
BUSINESS CHARACTERISTICS DESIRED-REQUIRED: Non-Real Estate Loans: BBA, AA Credit Rating
REFERRALS ACCEPTED FROM: Investment/Mortgage banker or Borrower/Investee

COMPANY: **Hampshire Capital Corporation**
ADDRESS: P.O. Box 468
Portsmouth, NH 03801
PHONE: (603) 431-7755wF7CONTACT OFFICER(S): Philip G. Baker, President
Lauren E. Wright, Vice President
ASSETS: $4,300,000
INVESTMENTS/LOANS MADE: For managed accounts, through private placements
INVESTMENTS/LOANS MADE: In securities with a secondary market and in securities without a sencondary market
TYPES OF FINANCING: VENTURE CAPITAL, LOANS: Working capital, Equipment, REAL ESTATE LOANS, INTERNATIONAL (import/export only), REAL ESATE
PREFERRED TYPES OF INDUSTRIES/INVESTMENTS: Open
WILL NOT CONSIDER: Do not prefer hi-tech
GEOGRAPHIC LIMITS OF INVESTMENTS/LOANS: National; East Coast Focus
RANGE OF INV./LOAN PER BUSINESS: Min. 25,000; Max. $100,000
PREFERRED TERM FOR LOANS & LEASES: Min. 5 years; Max. 5 years

COMPANY: **Mortgage Services of America**
ADDRESS: 31 Olney Avenue
Cherry Hill, NJ 08034

PHONE: (609) 424-1300
TYPE OF INSTITUTION: Mortgage Banker
CONTACT OFFICER(S): William T. Schor, President
David A. Lewis Jr., Senior Vice President
James J. Barden, Senior Vice President & Secretary
ASSETS: 8,000,000
INVESTMENTS/LOANS MADE: Through private placements
INVESTMENTS/LOANS MADE: Only in securities with a secondary market
TYPES OF FINANCING: SECONDARY-MARKET CORPORATE SECURITIES: Other: First mortgage loans on residential; income and commercial properties, REAL ESTATE LOANS: Long-term senior mtg; Intermediate-term senior mtg; Construction; Standbys, OTHER SERVICES PROVIDED: Loan Brokerage
PREFERRED TYPES OF INDUSTIRES/INVESTMENTS: Residential real estate
WILL NOT CONSIDER: Anything but real estate loans
GEOGRAPHIC LIMITS OF INVESTMENTS/LOANS: Local, State, Regional
RANGE OF INV./LOAN PER BUSINESS: Min. $35,000; Max. $5,000,000
PREFERRED TERM FOR LOANS & LEASES: Min. 10 years; Max. 30 years
BUSINESS CHARACTERISTIS DESIRED-REQUIRED:Minimum number of years in business: 3; Min. annual sales: no minimum
REFERRALS ACCEPTED FROM: Investment/mortgage banker and borower/investee
BRANCHES: Frederick Hartmann, Senior Vice President, One Broadway, Ste. 403, Elmwood Park, NJ 07407; (201) 794-8000

COMPANY: **Leasetek Funding Group, Inc.**
ADDRESS: 19 Sylvan Avenue
Englewood Cliffs, NJ 07632
PHONE: (201) 224-7700
CONTACT OFFICERS: Anthony Rosato, President
ASSETS: $40,000,000
INVESTMENTS/LOANS MADE: For own account, for managed accounts, through private placements, through underwriting public offerings
INVESTMENTS/LOANS MADE: Only in securities with a secondary market
TYPES OF FINANCING: SECONDARY-MARKET CORPORATE SECURITIES, VENTURE CPAIRAL: Start-up from developed product stage; First-stage; Second-stage; Buyouts/expansions, LOANS: Working capital, equipment, REAL ESTATE LOANS: Long-term senior mtg; intermediate-term senior mtg; wraparounds; construction, FACTORING, LEASES: Single-investor; Leveraged; Tax leases; Operating; Lease syndications; Vendor financing programs
GEOGRAPHIC LIMITS OF INVESTMENTS/LOANS: National
RANGE OF INV./LOAN PER BUSINESS: Min. $50,000; Max. $10,000,000
PREFERRED TERM FOR LOANS & LEASES: Min. 2 years; Max. 20 years

COMPANY: **Financial Resources Group**
ADDRESS: 110 Main Street, P.O. Box 246
Hackensack, NJ 07602
PHONE: (201) 489-6123
TYPE OF INSTITUTION: Financial services (public company)
CONTACT OFFICER(S): M.L. Beer, Manager
ASSETS: $136,744,970
INVESTMENTS/LOANS MADE: For own account, For managed accounts, Through private placements, through underwriting public offerings
INVESTMENTS/LOANS MADE: In securities with a secondary market and in securities without a secondary market
TYPES OF FINANCING: LOANS: Equipment, REAL ESTATE LOANS: Long-term senior mtg.; Intermediate-term senior mtg.; Wraparounds; Construction; Gap; Standbys; Industrial revenue bonds, FACTORING, LEASES: Leveraged: Tax leases, REAL ESTATE: Acquisitions; Joint ventures; Partnerships/Syndications
PREFERRED TYPES OF INDUSTRIES/INVESTMENTS: Real estate loans
WILL NOT CONSIDER: Unsecured
GEOGRAPHIC LIMITS OF INVESTMENTS/LOANS: National
RANGE OF INV./LOAN PER BUSINESS: Min. $500,000; Max. $75,000,000
PREFERRED TERM FOR LOANS & LEASES: Min. 3 years; Max. 30 years
BUSINESS CHARACTERISTICS DESIRED-REQUIRED: Minimum number of years in business: 2; Min. annual sales None; Other: Depends on transaction
REFERRALS ACCEPTED FROM: Investment/Mortgage banker or Borrower/Investee
BRANCHES: Alan Hirsch, 935 White Plains Rd, Trumbull, CT 06611; (203) 261-8308
Ira Shapiro, P.O. Box 1306, White Plains, NY 10602 (914) 997-1976

COMPANY: **Globe Mortgage Company**
ADDRESS: 110 Main Street
Hackensack, NJ 07602
PHONE: (201) 489-6120
TYPE OF INSTITUTION: Mortgage banker
CONTACT OFFICER(S): M. L. Beer, Pres., C.E.O.
ASSETS: Servicing $634,300,000
INVESTMENTS/LOANS MADE: For own account, For managed accounts, Through private placements, Through underwriting public offerings
INVESTMENTS/LOANS MADE: In securities with a secondary mmarket and in securities without a secondary market
TYPES OF FINANCING: REAL ESTATE LOANS: Long-term senior mtg.; Intermediate-term senior mtg.; Subordinated; Wraparounds; Land; Land development; Construction; Gap; Standbys; Industrial revenue bonds, REAL ESTATE: Acquisitions; Joint ventures; Partnerships/Syndications
PREFERRED TYPES OF INDUSTRIES/INVESTMENTS: Commercial, industrial, residential
WILL NOT CONSIDER: Specialties
GEOGRAPHIC LIMITS OF INVESTMENTS/LOANS: National
RANGE OF INV./LOAN PER BUSINESS: Min. $500,000; Max. $30,000,000

PREFERRED TERM FOR LOANS & LEASES: Min. 1 year; Max. 30 years
BUSINESS CHARACTERISTICS DESIRED-REQUIRED: Depends on transaction
REFERRALS ACCEPTED FROM: Investment/Mortgage banker or Borrower/Investee
BRANCHES: Ira Shapiro, P.O. Box 136, White Plains, NY 10602; (914) 997-1976
Alan Hirsch, 935 White Plains Rd., Trumbull, CT, 06611; (203) 261-8308
REMARKS: Prefer Mid-Atlantic State Submission

COMPANY: **WestAmerica Mortgage Company**
ADDRESS: 293 Eisenhower
Irvington, NJ 07039
PHONE: (201)
TYPE OF INSTITUTION: Mortgage banker
CONTACT OFFICER(S): Leslie Johnson, President
MarySue DeMaio, V.P.
ASSETS: Over $1 billion in servicing
INVESTMENTS/LOANS MADE: For own account, Through private placements
TYPES OF FINANCING: REAL ESTATE LOANS: Long-term senior mtg.; Intermediate-term senior mtg.; Subordinated; Wraparounds, Land; Land development; Construction; Gap; Standbys
PREFERRED TYPES OF INDUSTRIES/INVESTMENTS: Residential and commercial income producing properties
WILL NOT CONSIDER: Industrial
GEOGRAPHIC LIMITS OF INVESTMENTS/LOANS: Regional; Other: For residential-national
PREFERRED TERM FOR LOANS & LEASES: Max. 30 years
REFERRALS ACCEPTED FROM: Investment/Mtg. Banker or Borrower/Investee

COMPANY: **The Trust Company of New Jersey**
ADDRESS: 35 Journal Square
Jersey City, NJ 07306
PHONE: (201) 420-2810
TYPE OF INSTITUTION: Commercial bank
CONTACT OFFICER(S): Robert J. Figurski, Sr., V.P.
ASSETS: $1 Billion
INVESTMENTS/LOANS MADE: For own account
TYPES OF FINANCING: VENTURE CAPITAL: Start-up from developed product stage; First-stage; Later-stage expansions; Buy-outs/Acquisitions, LOANS: Unsecured; Working capital (receivables/inventory); Equipment; Equity related, REAL ESTATE LOANS: Long-term senior mtg.; Intermediate-term senior mtg.; Wraparounds; Land; Land development; Construction; Gap; Standbys; Industrial revenue bonds; Other: Economic Development Agency Tax Frees, INTERNATIONAL (including import/export), REAL ESTATE: Acquisitions
PREFERRED TYPES OF INDUSTRIE/INVESTMENTS: Any
RANGE OF IN./LOAN PER BUSINESS: Max. $5 Million
PREFERRED TERM FOR LOANS & LEASES: Miin. Demand; Max. 25 year payout
BUSINESS CHARACTERISTICS DESIRED-REQUIRED: Minimum number of years in business: 0
BRANCHES: 20 branches throughout New Jersey

COMPANY: **C.I.T. Corporation Real Estate Financing Division**
ADDRESS: 650 CIT Drive
Livingston, NJ 07039
PHONE: (201) 740-5449
TYPE OF INSTITUTION: Mortgage lender
CONTACT OFFICER(S): George J. Fiore, Vice President, General Manager
TYPES OF FINANCING: SECONDARY-MARKET CORPORATE SECURITIES: Other: Real Estate Mortgage, REAL ESTATE LOANS: Intermediate-term senior mtg.; Stand-bys
PREFERRED TYPES OF INDUSTRIES/INVESTMENTS: 1st mortgage short term intermediate income producing or owner occupied
WILL NOT CONSIDER: Land, recreation, amusement, spec development
RANGE OF INV./LOAN PER BUSINESS: Min. $1 million; Max. $16 million
PREFERRED TERM FOR LOANS & LEASES: Min. 3 years; Max. 10 years
BUSINESS CHARACTERISTICS DESIRED-REQUIRED: Min. cash fow $1.1 time coverage; Other: cash flow adequate to pay debt service
REFERRALS ACCEPTED FROM Investment/Mortgage banker or Borrower/Investee

COMPANY: **The Morris County Savings Bank**
ADDRESS: 21 South Street
Morristown, NJ 07960
PHONE: (201) 539-0500
TYPE OF INSTITUTION: Savings Bank
CONTACT OFFICER(S): Charles W. Frost, Chief Executive Officer
Jerry F. Smith, Real Estate Financing
Robert W. Freund, Commerical Lending, Leasing
Michael Allison, Investments
ASSETS: $867,500,000
INVESTMENTS/LOANS MADE: For own account
INVESTMENTS/LOANS MADE: Only in securities with a secondary market
TYPES OF FINANCING: SECONDARY-MARKET CORPORATE SECURITIES: Bonds; Other: Commerical Paper, B.A.'s, etc., LOANS: Unsecured; Working capital; Equipment, REAL ESTATE LOANS: Long-term senior mtg; Intermediate-term senior mtg; Subordinated; Construction, LEASES: Operating, REAL ESTATE: Joint Ventures
PREFERRED TYPES OF INDUSTRIES/INVESTMENTS: Not restricted as to industry, interested in developing full relationships with quality credit
GEOGRAPHIC LIMITS OF INVESTMENTS/LOANS: State; National
RANGE OF INV./LOAN PER BUSINESS: Min. $250,000; Max. $4,250,000
PREFERRED TERM FOR LOANS & LEASES: Min. 1/2 year; Max. 3 years
BUSINESS CHARACTERISTICS DESIRED-REQUIRED: Minimum number of years in business: 3; Min. annual sales $1MM; Min. net worth $200M; Min. annual net income $100M; Min. annual cash fow $150M
REFERRALS ACCEPTED FROM Investment/Mortgage banker or Borrower/Investee
REMARKS: All branches within Northwest New Jersey

COMPANY: **The Howard Savings Bank**
ADDRESS: 768 Broad Street
Newark, NJ 07101
PHONE: (201) 430-2000
TYPE OF INSTITUTION: Stockholder-Owned Savings Bank
CONTACT OFFICER(S): Anthony P. Meli, Jr. (201) 533-7721, Vice President - Mortgage Administration
ASSETS: $3.743 billion dollars (8/31/84)
INVESTMENTS/LOANS MADE: For own account
INVESTMENTS/LOANS MADE: Only in securities with a secondary market
TYPES OF FINANCING: SECONDARY-MARKET CORPORATE SECURITIES: Common stock; Preferred stock; Bonds; LOANS: Unsecured; Working capital; Equipment; Equity-related; Other: Warehouse credit lines to mortgage bankers; REAL ESTATE LOANS: Intermediate-term senior mtg.; Land development; Construction; REAL ESTATE
PREFERRED TYPES OF INDUSTRIES/INVESTMENTS: Financial services industries
GEOGRAPHIC LIMITS OF INVESTMENTS/LOANS: National
PREFERRED TERM FOR LOANS & LEASES: Min. 1/4 year; Max. 10 years
REFERRALS ACCEPTED FROM: Investment/Mortgage banker or Borrower/Investee
BRANCHES: We have 58 branches within the State of New Jersey

COMPANY: **The Howard Savings Bank**
ADDRESS: 768 Broad Street
Newark, NJ 07101
PHONE: (201) 430-2000
TYPE OF INSTITUTION: Stockholder-Owned Savings Bank
CONTACT OFFICER(S): Andrew V. Aldi, (201) 430-2806, President - Howco Investment Corp. (a subsidiary)
ASSETS: $3.743 billion dollars (8/31/84)
TYPES OF FINANCING: REAL ESTATE: Acquisitions; Joint ventures; Partnerships/Syndications; OTHER SERVICES PROVIDED: Real estate consulting services related to construction and leasing activities.
PREFERRED TYPES OF INDUSTRIES/INVESTMENTS: Commercial office buildings in excess of 75,000 square feet; Warehouse buildings in excess of 200,000 square feet
BRANCHES: We have 58 branches within the State of New Jersey

COMPANY: **The Howard Savings Bank**
ADDRESS: 768 Broad Street
Newark, NJ 07101
PHONE: (201) 430-2000
TYPE OF INSTITUTION: Stockholder-Owned Savings Bank
CONTACT OFFICER(S): Herbert M. Cannon, (201) 430-2861, Vice President - Mortgage Origination
Scott W. Ashley, (201) 430-2857, Vice President - Mortgage Origination
ASSETS: $3.743 billion dollars (8/31/84)
INVESTMENTS/LOANS MADE: For own account
INVESTMENTS/LOANS MADE: Only in securities without a secondary market
TYPES OF FINANCING:REAL ESTATE LOANS: Long-term senior mtg.; Intermediate-term senior mtg.; Wraparounds; Land development; Construction; Gap; Standbys; REAL ESTATE: Acquisitions; Joint ventures
PREFERRED TYPES OF INDUSTRIES/INVESTMENTS: Office buildings; Apartments; Shopping centers; Hotels/Motels, etc
GEOGRAPHIC LIMITS OF INVESTMENTS/LOANS: National
RANGE OF INV./LOAN PER BUSINESS: Min; $500,000; Max. $30,000,000
PREFERRED TERM FOR LOANS & LEASES: Min. 3 years; Max. 10 years
BUSINESS CHARACTERISTICS DESIRED-REQUIRED: Minimum number of years in business: 3
REFERRALS ACCEPTED FROM: Investment/Mortgage banker or Borrower/Investee
BRANCHES: We have 58 branches within the State of New Jersey

COMPANY: **The Mutual Benefit Life Insurance Co.**
ADDRESS: 520 Broad Street
Newark, NJ 07101
PHONE: (201) 481-8000
CONTACT OFFICER(S): Donald Hagemann, V.P., Fixed income securities
Robert W. Kopchins, Sr. V.P., RE investments
ASSETS: $8.4 billion
INVESTMENTS/LOANS MADE: In securities with a secondary market and in securities without a secondary market
TYPES OF FINANCING: SECONDARY-MARKEET CORPORATE SECURITIES: Common Stock; Preferred stock; Bonds; Fixed income, LOANS: Unsecured; Working capital; Equipment, REAL ESTATE LOANS: Long-term senior mtg.; Intermediate-term senior mtg.; Subordinated; Gap; Standbys, REAL ESTATE: Acquisitions; Joint ventures, OTHER SERVICES PROVIDED: generally do venture capital in partnerships
GEOGRAPHIC LIMITS OF INVESTMENTS/LOANS: National: Mexico, Canada, Europe
RANGE OF INV./LOAN PER BUSINESS: Min. $1 mil.; Max. $35 mil.
PREFERRED TERM FOR LOANS & LEASES: Min. 3-10 years
BUSINESS CHARACTERISTICS DESIRED-REQUIRED: Minimum number of years in business: 5; Other: 3-10 mil. generally
REFFERALS ACCEPTED FROM: Investment/Mortgage banker or Borrower/Investee
BRANCHES: Lots of subsidiaries: do investing for all of them.

COMPANY: **Armco Financial Corporation, Intermediate Term Lending Division**
ADDRESS: 104 Carnegie Center
Princeton, NJ 08540
PHONE: (609) 452-0600
TYPE OF INSTITUTION: Commerical Term Lender
CONTACT OFFICER(S): Richard S. Ballard, President

Susan M. Lamm, Vice President & Senior Loan Officer
ASSETS: $500,000,000
INVESTMENTS/LOANS MADE: For own account
INVESTMENTS/LOANS MADE: In securities with a secondary market and in securities without a secondary market
TYPES OF FINANCING: VENTURE CAPITAL: Later-stage expansion; Buy-outs/Acquisitions, LOANS: Equipment; REAL ESTATE LOANS: Intermediate-term senior mtg.; Subordinated; Wraparounds, LEASES: Non-tax leases
PREFERRED TYPES OF INDUSTRIES/INVESTMENTS: No preferences—will do all types of manufacturing compaies
WILL NOT CONSIDER: Medical Industry; Retail Businesses
GEOGRAPHIC LIMITS OF INVESTMENTS/LOANS: National
RANGE OF INV./LOAN PER BUSINESS: Min. $1,000,000; Max. $10,000,000
PREFERRED TERM FOR LOANS & LEASES: Min. 2 years
BUSINESS CHARACTERISTICS DESIRED-REQUIRED: Minimum number of years in business: 3
REFERRALS ACCEPTED FROM: Investment/Mortgage banker or Borrower/Investee

COMPANY: **Franklin State Bank**
ADDRESS: 630 Franklin Blvd.
Somerset, NJ 08873
PHONE: (201) 745-6044
CONTACT OFFICER(S): John D. Battaglia, Sr. Lending Officer/Exec. V.P.
Harvey A. Mackler, Vice President/Business Development
ASSETS: $650,000,000
INVESTMENTS/LOANS MADE: For own account
INVESTMENTS/LOANS MADE: Only in securities without a secondary market
TYPES OF FINANCING: LOANS: Unsecured; Working capital; REAL ESTATE LOANS: Long-term senior mtg.; Land; Land development; Construction; Industrial revenue bonds, LEASES: Single-investor; Leveraged; Tax leases; Non-tax leases; Vendor financing programs, OTHER SERVICES PROVIDED: Accounts receivable financing
PREFERRED TYPES OF INDUSTRIES/INVESTMENTS: Diversified
GEOGRAPHIC LIMITS OF INVESTMENTS/LOANS: State
RANGE OF INV./LOAN PER BUSINESS: Min. $100,000; Max. $6,000,000
PREFERRED TERM FOR LOANS & LEASES: Min. 1 year; Max. 15-20 years
BUSINESS CHARACTERISTICS DESIRED-REQUIRED: Minimum number of years in business: 1+; Min. annual sales $500,000; Min. net worth $100,000; Min. annual net income $50,000; Min. annual cash flow $50,000

COMPANY: **P. F. Investments Co.**
ADDRESS: 22 Bank Street
Summit, NJ 07901
PHONE: (201) 277-6111
TYPE OF INSTITUTION: Private Venture Capital Fund
CONTACT OFFICER(S): Anthony J. Fennelli, Jr., General Partner
Donald B. Pierson, General Partner
Peter L. Rehm, Associate
ASSETS: $3,200,000
INVESTMENTS/LOANS MADE: For own account
INVESTMENTS/LOANS MADE: Only in securities without a secondary market
TYPES OF FINANCING: VENTURE CAPITAL: Research & Development; Start-up from developed product stage, REAL ESTATE: Acquisitions; Joint ventures; Partnerships/Syndications
PREFERRED TYPES OF INDUSTRIES/INVESTMENTS: High Technology—Start-ups Only; Computer Hardware, Software—Communications; Energy Related
WILL NOT CONSIDER: "Going" Concerns
GEOGRAPHIC LIMITS OF INVESTMENTS/LOANS: Local
RANGE OF INV./LOAN PER BUSINESS: Min. $50,000; Max. $150,000
PREFERRED TERM FOR LOANS & LEASES: Min. 3; Max. 5 years
BUSINESS CHARACTERISTICS DESIRED-REQUIRED: Min. no. of years in business: 0
REFERRALS ACCEPTED FROM: Investment/Mortgage banker or Borrower/Investee

COMPANY: **Ingersoll Rand Financial Corp.**
ADDRESS: 200 Chestnut Ridge Road
Woodcliff Lake, NJ 07675
PHONE: (201) 573-3031
TYPE OF INSTITUTION: Tax Leasing and Secured Financing
CONTACT OFFICER(S): R.A. Layton, Eastern Group Manager
R.J. Rhinesmih, Western Group Manager
J.C. Colbert, National Leasing
ASSETS: $550 million
INVESTMENTS/LOANS MADE: for own account
TYPES OF FINANCING: VENTURE CAPITAL: Later-stage expansion, LOANS: Equipment, REAL ESTATE LOANS: Long-term senior mtg.; Intermediate-term senior mtg.; Standbys; Other, LEASES: Single-investor; Tax leases; Non-tax leases; Vendor financing programs
GEOGRAPHIC LIMITS OF INVESTMENTS/LOANS: National
RANGE OF INV./LOAN PER BUSINESS: Min. $100M; Max. $10,000M
PREFERRED TERM FOR LOANS & LEASES: Min. 1 year; Max. 7 years
BUSINESS CHARACTERISTICS DESIRED-REQUIRED: Minimum number of years in business: 5; Other: Each transaction will stand on merits
REFERRALS ACCEPTED FROM: Investment/Mortgage banker or Borrower/Investee
BRANCHES: Richard A. Layton, Summerfield Commons Office Park, 2585 Washington Rd., Pittsburgh, PA 15241; (412) 854-1810
Robert J. Rhinesmith, 210 Porter Drive, Suite 120, San Ramon, CA 94583; (415) 838-4606

COMPANY:**Goldome Realty Credit Corp. (A subsidiary of Goldome,, FSB)**
ADDRESS: 1 Fountain Plaza
Buffalo, NY 14203
PHONE: (716) 843-6300
CONTACT OFFICER(S): Donald J. Eich, Sr. Vice President—Commercial & Construction Lending
ASSETS: $6 Billion in servicing
INVESTMENTS/LOANS MADE: For own account
INVESTMENTS/LOANS MADE: Only in securities without a secondary market
TYPES OF FINANCING: LOANS: Equity-related. REAL ESTATE LOANS: Intermediate-term senior mtg.; Land; Land development, Construction; Standbys; REAL ESTAE: Acquisitions; Joint ventures; Partnerships/ Syndications
PREFERRED TYPES OF INDUSTRIES/INVESTMENTS: Office parks, Retail industrial (multi tenant)
WILL NOT CONSIDER: Motel/Hotel; Pubs
GEOGRAPHIC LIMITS OF INVESTMENTS/LOANS: National
RANGE OF INV./LOAN PER BUSINESS: Min. $2,000,000 (Construction); Mmax. $20,000,000
PREFERRED TERM FOR LOANS & LEASES: Min. 6 months; Max. 3 years
BUSINESS CHARACTERISTICS DESIRED-REQUIRED: Borrower/Investee
REFERRALS ACCEPTED FROM: Borrower/Investee

COMPANY:**Goldome, FSB**
ADDRESS: One Fountain Plazaa
Buffalo, NY 14203
PHONE: (716) 847-5800
TYPE OF INSTITUTION: Fixed Income Division
CONTACT OFFICER(S): Richard M. Hessinger, Vice President Residential/Commercial Mortgages
ASSETS: $13 billion (Total assets of Goldome, FSB)
INVESTMENTS/LOANS MADE: For own account
INVESTMENTS/LOANS MADE: In securities with a secondary market and in securities without a secondary market
TYPES OF FINANCING: REAL ESTATE LOANS: Intermediate-term senior mtg.; Construction; REAL ESTATE: Joint ventures
GEOGRAPHIC LIMITS OF INVESTMENTS/LOANS: National
RANGE OF INV./LOAN PER BUSINESS: Min. $5 million; Max. 15 million
PREFERRED TERM FOR LOANS & LEASES: Max. Adjustable or 3-5 years

COMPANY: **Coleman Ventures Inc.**
ADDRESS: 5909 Northern Blvd.
East Norwich, NY 11732
PHONE: (516) 626-3642
TYPE OF INSTITUTION: Private firm investing own capital; evaluates and prepares venture proposals
CONTACT OFFICER(S):Gregory S. Coleman, President
ASSETS: $5 million
INVESTMENTS/LOANS MADE: For own account
INVESTMENTS/LOANS MADE: Only in securities without a secondary market
TYPES OF FINANCING: VENTURE CAPITAL: Start-up from developed product stage; First-stage. REAL ESTATE LOANS: Land development. REAL ESTATE: Partnerships/Syndications.
PREFERRED TYPES OF INDUSTRIES/INVESTMENTS: High technology—solid state: lasers, photo-voltaic materials and devices; Hybrid micro circuits
WILL NOT CONSIDER: Propositions not accompanied by at least an informal business plan
GEOGRAPHIC LIMITS OF INVESTMENTS/LOANS: Local; State; Regional
RANGE OF INV./LOAN PER BUSINESS: Min. $100,000; Max. $1,000,000
PREFERRED TERM FOR LOANS & LEASES: Min. Equity only
BUSINESS CHARACTERISTICS DESIRED-REQUIRED: Minimum number of years in business: 0; Min annual sales $ Nominal

COMPANY: **Hotel Investment Group, Inc.**
ADDRESS: 333 Sylvan Av.
Englewood Cliffs NY 07632
PHONE: (201) 568-2525
TYPE OF INSTITUTION: Mortgage bankers, equity investors, development consultants
CONTACT OFFICER(S): Jeffrey D. Wolfert, President
ASSETS: $6,000,000
INVESTMENTS/LOANS MADE: For own account, For managed accounts, Through private placements, Through underwriting public offerings
TYPES OF FINANCING: SECONDARY-MARKET CORPORATE SECURITIES: Hotels and motels, LOANS: Real estate, REAL ESTATE LOANS: Long-term senior mtg.; Intermediate-term senior mtg.; Subordinated; Wraparounds; Construction; Gap; Standbys; Industrial revenue bonds; Other: Any hotel related financing including JVs and acquisitions, REAL ESTATE: Acquisitions; Joint ventures; Partnerships/ Syndications, OTHER SERVICES PROVIDED: Development consulting
PREFERRED TYPES OF INDUSTRIES/INVESTMENTS: Hotels and motels only
GEOGRAPHIC LIMITS OF INVESTMENTS/LOANS: National
RANGE OF INV./LOAN PER BUSINESS: Min. $7.5 million
PREFERRED TERM FOR LOANS & LEASES: Min. 1 year; Max. 30 years
BUSINESS CHARACTERISTICS DESIRED-REQUIRED: Minimum number of years in business: 0
REFERRALS ACCEPTED FROM: Investment/Mortgage banker or Borrower/Investee

COMPANY: **BRT Realty Trust**
ADDRESS: 60 Cutter Mill Rd.
Great Neck, NY 11021
PHONE: (516) 466-3100
TYPE OF INSTITUTION: REIT
CONTACT OFFICER(S): Myron Ginsburg, Treasurer
ASSETS: $25,256,000
TYPES OF FINANCING: REAL ESTATE LOANS: Intermediate-term senior mtg.; Subordinated; Wraparounds; Gap; Standbys.
PREFERRED TYPES OF INDUSTRIES/INVESTMENTS: Existing buildings, occupied, industrial or residential
WILL NOT CONSIDER: Special purpose

GEOGRAPHIC LIMITS OF INVESTMENTS/LOANS: National, east of the Mississippi
RANGE OF INV./LOAN PER BUSINESS: Min. $100,000; Max. $2 million
PREFERRED TERM FOR LOANS & LEASES: Min. 1 year; Max. 5 years

COMPANY: **Gould Investors Trust**
t26ADDRESS: 60 Cutter Mill Rd.
Great Neck, NY 11021
PHONE: (516) 466-3100
TYPE OF INSTITUTION: REIT
CONTACT OFFICER(S): Myron Ginsburg, Treasurer
Frederic H. Gould, President
ASSETS: $75,749,000
TYPES OF FINANCING: REAL ESTATE LOANS: Other: Existing buildings, no construction; Equity-related R.E. loans, REAL ESTATE: Acquisitions
PREFERRED TYPES OF INDUSTRIES/INVESTMENTS: Commercial: Office buildings; Warehouses; Residential apartments
WILL NOT CONSIDER: Specialty
GEOGRAPHIC LIMITS OF INVESTMENTS/LOANS: National; Other: East of Mississippi
RANGE OF INV./LOAN PER BUSINESS: Min. $100,000; Max. $2 million
PREFERRED TERM FOR LOANS & LEASES: Min. 1 year; Max. 5 years

COMPANY: **M. Robert Goldman & Sons**
ADDRESS: 111 Great Neck Rd.
Great Neck, NY 11021
PHONE: (212) 442-1515
TYPE OF INSTITUTION: Mortgage Banker
CONTACT OFFICER(S): S. Howard Goldman
Kenneth M. Goldman
ASSETS: $1,000,000-10,000,000
TYPES OF FINANCING: LOANS: Equity-related, REAL ESTATE LOANS: Long-term senior mtg.; Intermediate-term senior mtg., REAL ESTATE
GEOGRAPHIC LIMITS OF INVESTMENTS/LOANS: International
RANGE OF INV./LOAN PER BUSINESS: Min. $1,000,000
PREFERRED TERM FOR LOANS & LEASES: Min. 5-7; Max. 15-20 years
BUSINESS CHARACTERISTICS DESIRED-REQUIRED: Minimum number of years in business: 5-10; Min. annual sales $10,000,000; Min. net worth $5,000,000; Min. annual net income $1,000,000; Min. annual cash flow $500,000

COMPANY: **U.S. Capital Corporation**
ADDRESS: 525 Northern Boulevard
Great Neck, NY 11021
PHONE: (516) 466-8550
TYPE OF INSTITUTION: Asset based lender, private
CONTACT OFFICER(S): Howard Sommer, Pres.
ASSETS: $10,000,000+
INVESTMENTS/LOANS MADE: For own account
INVESTMENTS/LOANS MADE: In securities with a secondary market and in securities without a secondary market
TYPES OF FINANCING: LOANS: Working capital; Equipment. REAL ESTATE LOANS: Long-term senior mtg.; Intermediate-term senior mtg.; Subordinated; Wraparounds. OTHER SERVICES PROVIDED:: Letter of credit financing
GEOGRAPHIC LIMITS OF INVESTMENTS/LOANS: Regional
RANGE OF INV./LOAN PER BUSINESS: Min. $25,000; Max. $500,000
PREFERRED TERM FOR LOANS & LEASES: Min. 1 year; Max. 4 years
BUSINESS CHARACTERISTICS DESIRED-REQUIRED: Minimum number of years in business: 0
REFERRALS ACCEPTED FROM: Investment/Mortgage banker or Borrower/Investee

COMPANY: **Atlantic Capital Corp.**
ADDRESS: 40 Wall St.
New York, NY 10005
PHONE: (212) 363-5600
CONTACT OFFICER(S): Harold Phaumgarten, Sr. V.P.
TYPES OF FINANCING: VENTURE CAPITAL, REAL ESTATE LOANS, LEASES, REAL ESTATE, OTHER SERVICES PROVIDED: private placements, corporate financing, mergers and acquisitions
RANGE OF INV./LOAN PER BUSINESS: Min. $1 million
REMARKS: Transaction oriented house; no start-ups

COMPANY:**British Land of America**
ADDRESS: 90 Broad St., 12th Floor
New York, NY 10004
PHONE: (212) 509-4840
CONTACT OFFICER(S): John H. Weston Smith, CEO
Frank E. Andersen, V.P. Finance
Edwin F. Heinen, Controller
ASSETS: $67,418,134
TYPES OF FINANCING: REAL ESTATE LOANS: Long-term senior mtg.; Land development; Construction; Other: Mortgage-Lending area; REAL ESTATE: Acquisitions; Joint Ventures; Partnerships/Syndications
PREFERRED TYPES OF INDUSTRIES/INVESTMENTS: Commercial properties
GEOGRAPHIC LIMITS OF INVESTMENTS/LOANS: National; International; England; Puerto Rico; Newfoundland
RANGE OF INV./LOAN PER BUSINESS: Min. $1 million; Max. $20 million

COMPANY: **East River Savings Bank**
ADDRESS: 26 Cortlandt Street
New York, NY 10007
PHONE: (212) 553-9611
TYPE OF INSTITUTION: Savings Bank
CONTACT OFFICER(S): Joseph Charla Jr., E.V.P.
Frank Magilligan, E.V.P.
ASSETS: $1.9 Billion
INVESTMENTS/LOANS MADE: For own account; Through private placements
INVESTMENTS/LOANS MADE: In securities with a secondary market and in securities without a secondary market

TYPES OF FINANCING: REAL ESTATE LOANS: Intermediate-term senior mtg.; Wraparounds; Land; Land development; Construction; Standbys. REAL ESTATE: Joint ventures
GEOGRAPHIC LIMITS OF INVESTMENTS/LOANS: Local; State; Regional; National

COMPANY: **Engle Investment Co.**
ADDRESS: 135 West 50 Street
New York, NY 10020
PHONE: (212) 757-9580
TYPE OF INSTITUTION: Small Business Investment Corp.
CONTACT OFFICER(S): Murray Hendel, President
ASSETS: $2,000,000
INVESTMENTS/LOANS MADE: For own account
INVESTMENTS/LOANS MADE: In securities with a secondary market and in securities without a secondary market
TYPES OF FINANCING: SECONDARY-MARKET CORPORATE SECURITIES: Common stock; Preferred stock; Bonds. VENTURE CAPITAL: Start-up from developed product stage; First-stage; Second-stage; Later-stage expansion; Buy-outs/Acquisitions. LOANS: Working capital; Equipment; Equity-related. REAL ESTATE LOANS: Land development; Construction. OTHER SERVICES PROVIDED: Advisory & Financial Mgt.

COMPANY: **The Equitable Life Assurance Society of the United States**
ADDRESS: 1285 Avenue of the Americas
New York, NY 10019
PHONE: (212) 554-1234
TYPE OF INSTITUTION: Mutual Insurance Company with extensive pension management operations and leasing subsidiary
CONTACT OFFICER(S): John Miller, V.P.
Harold S. Woolley, V.P. — Public Bonds
George R. Peacock, Senior V.P. — Real Estate
Roderic Eaton, Senior V.P. — Equico Lessors
ASSETS: $44 billion
INVESTMENTS/LOANS MADE: For own account; For managed accounts; Through private placements
INVESTMENTS/LOANS MADE: In securities with a secondary market and in securities without a secondary market
TYPES OF FINANCING: SECONDARY-MARKET CORPORATE SECURITIES: Common stock; Preferred stock; Bonds; Private placements, LOANS: Unsecured to credits above mid BA; Equipment; Equity-related, REAL ESTATE LOANS: Long-term senior mtg.; Intermediate-term senior mtg.; Wraparounds; Land; Land development; Construction; Standbys, LEASES: Single-investor; Leveraged; Tax leases; Non-tax leases; Vendor financing programs, REAL ESTATE: Acquisitions; Joint ventures; Partnerships/Syndications
PREFERRED TYPES OF INDUSTRIES/INVESTMENTS: Private Placements — BAA industrial, financial and utility credits; Real Estate — commercial mortgages with kickers or outright purchases of commercial properties.
WILL NOT CONSIDER: Fast-food, start-up venture capital situations
GEOGRAPHIC LIMITS OF INVESTMENTS/LOANS: International
RANGE OF INV./LOAN PER BUSINESS: Min. $3 Million; Max. $100 Million
PREFERRED TERM FOR LOANS & LEASES: Min. 3; Max. 15 years
BUSINESS CHARACTERISTICS DESIRED-REQUIRED: Minimum number of years in business: 5; Min. annual sales $100 million; Min. net worth $20 million; Min. annual net income $3 million; Min. annual cash flow $4 million
REFERRALS ACCEPTED FROM: Investment/Mortgage banker or Borrower/Investee
BRANCHES: National Real Estate Headquarters: Monarch Plaza 3414 Peachtree Road N.E., Atlanta, GA 30326
Field Offices: C.J. Harwood, Regional Vice President, 60 State Street-Suite 1720, Boston, MA 02109, (617) 723-7183
John T. Quartuccio, Regional Vice President, 1350 Avenue of the Americas, 20th Fl., New York, NY 10019, (212) 541-5830
Warren G. Bevan, Regional Vice President, 8 Penn Center-Suite 1900, Philadelphia, PA 19103, (215) 569-0554
Robert L. Blakeman, Regional Vice President, 1875 "Eye" Street, N.W.-Suite 1140, Washington, D.C. 20006, (202) 775-8340
Donald L. Batson, Regional Vice President, Peachtree-Dunwoody Pavillion, 5775-E Peachtree-Dunwoody Road-Suite 500, Atlanta, GA 30342, (404) 256-1020
Joseph W. Kellum, Regional Vice President, 1 Lincoln Place-Suite 451, 1900 Glades Rd., Boca Raton, FL 33431, (305) 392-3902
Edward G. Smith, Regional Vice President, 401 No. Michigan Avenue-Rm. 3350, Chicago, IL 60611, (312) 321-4720
Jerome W. Fruin, Regional Manager, One Centerre Plaza-Suite 2100, St. Louis, MO 63101, (314) 421-5900
Douglas A. Tibbetts, Regional Vice President, Park Central VII-Suite 1100, 12750 Merit Drive, Dallas, TX 75251, (214) 239-1850
Daniel C. Gardner, Regional Vice President, 1140 First National Bank Building, 621 17th St., Denver, CO 80293, (303) 292-3600
Jack Kueneman, Regional Vice President, One Market Plaza, Steuart Street Tower-Suite 1900, San Francisco, CA 94105, (415) 541-5130
John J. Wilhelm III, Regional Vice President, 4100 Wells Fargo Building, 444 South Flower Street, Los Angeles, CA 90071, (213) 689-1900

COMPANY: **FNB Financial Co.**
ADDRESS: Two Penn. Plaza
New York, NY 10001
PHONE: (212) 613-3001
TYPE OF INSTITUTION: Commercial Finance Division—Owned by Bank of Boston
CONTACT OFFICER(S): Gabe Romeo, Senior Vice President
TYPES OF FINANCING: LOANS: Working capital; Equipment; REAL ESTATE LOANS: Land; Land development; FACTORING; INTERNATIONAL
GEOGRAPHIC LIMITS OF INVESTMENTS/LOANS: National

RANGE OF INV./LOAN PER BUSINESS: Min. $750,000
BRANCHES: All over country

COMPANY: **G. A. Thompson Group, Inc.**
ADDRESS: 767 5th Ave.
New York, NY 10153
PHONE: (212) 832-6600
TYPE OF INSTITUTION: Mortgage Broker
CONTACT OFFICER(S): Alan Lawrence, E. V. P. Sales Manager
INVESTMENTS/LOANS MADE: Through private placements
INVESTMENTS/LOANS MADE: Only in securities with a secondary market
TYPES OF FINANCING: REAL ESTATE LOANS: Long-term senior mtg.; Intermediate-term senior mtg.; Wraparounds; Land; Land development; Contruction; Standbys; REAL ESTATE: Acquisitions; Joint ventures; Partnerships/Syndications
GEOGRAPHIC LIMITS OF INVESTMENTS/LOANS: National
RANGE OF INV./LOAN PER BUSINESS: Min. $1,000,000; Max. $ Unlimited
PREFERRED TERM FOR LOANS & LEASES: Max. 15 years
REFERRALS ACCEPTED FROM: Investment/Mortgage banker or Borrower/Investee

COMPANY: **Guardian Life Insurance Co.**
ADDRESS: 201 Park Ave. So.
New York, NY 10003
PHONE: (212) 598-8000
CONTACT OFFICER(S): Charles E. Albers, V.P. Equities & Securities, 598-8420
Henry Spencer, 2nd V.P., Investments
George Keim, Consultant
ASSETS: 2,254,000,000
TYPES OF FINANCING: SECONDARY-MARKET CORPORATE SECURITIES: Common stock; Preferred stock; Bonds, LOANS: Unsecured, REAL ESTATE LOANS: Long-term senior mtg.; Industrial revenue bonds
PREFERRED TYPES OF INDUSTRIES/INVESTMENTS: Real Estate; Commercial properties
GEOGRAPHIC LIMITS OF INVESTMENTS/LOANS: National
RANGE OF INV./LOAN PER BUSINESS: Min. $500,000; Max. $12 million
PREFERRED TERM FOR LOANS & LEASES: Max. 10 years

COMPANY: **Haas Financial Corporation**
ADDRESS: 230 Park Avenue
New York, NY 10169
PHONE: (212) 490-1510
CONTACT OFFICER(S): George C. Haas Jr., President
Robert L. Cummings
Vice President
INVESTMENTS/LOANS MADE: For own account; Through private placements
INVESTMENTS/LOANS MADE: In securities with a secondary market and in securities without a secondary market
TYPES OF FINANCING: SECONDARY-MARKET CORPORATE SECURITIES: Common stock; Bonds; VENTURE CAPITAL: First-stage; Second-stage; Later-stage expansion; Buy-outs/Acquisitions; LOANS: Equipment; REAL ESTATE LOANS: Long-term senior mtg.; Intermediate-term senior mtg.; Subordinated; Wraparounds; LEASES: Single-investor; Operating; Tax-oriented lease brokerage; OTHER SERVICES PROVIDED: Merger Acquisition Divestiture Brokerage; Consulting and Valuation; Acquisition/Divestiture Financing.
PREFERRED TYPES OF INDUSTRIES/INVESTMENTS: Will look at all types of industries, firm has specialty in transportation (planes) consumer products (soft drinks)
GEOGRAPHIC LIMITS OF INVESTMENTS/LOANS: National
RANGE OF INV./LOAN PER BUSINESS: Min. $500,000
PREFERRED TERM FOR LOANS & LEASES: Min. 5 years; Max. 15 years
REFERRALS ACCEPTED FROM: Investment/Mortgage banker or Borrower/Investee

COMPANY: **Hunter, Keith, Marshall & Co., Inc.**
ADDRESS: One Penn Plaza, Ste. 1831
New York, NY 10119
PHONE: (212) 736-6140
TYPE OF INSTITUTION: Private placement investment bank
CONTACT OFFICER(S): Henry C. Marshall, Jr., Managing Director, Equipment & Real Estate
Steven I. Eisenberg, Vice President, Equipment
INVESTMENTS/LOANS MADE: For own account; Through private placements
INVESTMENTS/LOANS MADE: In securities with a secondary market and in securities without a secondary market
TYPES OF FINANCING: LOANS: Equity-related; REAL ESTATE LOANS: Long-term senior mtg.; Intermediate-term senior mtg.; LEASES: Vendor financing programs; Other: debt side of leveraged leases
GEOGRAPHIC LIMITS OF INVESTMENTS/LOANS: National; Other: Will do selected international credits
RANGE OF INV./LOAN PER BUSINESS: Min. $2 MM
PREFERRED TERM FOR LOANS & LEASES: Min. 3 years; Max. 20 years
BUSINESS CHARACTERISTICS DESIRED-REQUIRED: Min. net worth $5 MM; Min. annual net income $ 1.5MM; Min. annual cash flow: $1.5MM; Other: Will do selected startups on secured basis
REFERRALS ACCEPTED FROM: Borrower/Investee
BRANCHES: Andrew M. Hunter III, Robert J. Keith, Jr., 5100 IDS Center, Minneapolis, MN 55402, (612) 338-2799

COMPANY: **Irving Trust Co.—Commercial Finance Dept.**
ADDRESS: 1290 Ave. of the Americas
New York, NY 10015
PHONE: (212) 487-2121
TYPE OF INSTITUTION: Commercial Finance Dept. of Bank
CONTACT OFFICER(S): Robert M. Grosse, V.P. & General Manager

NEW YORK

TYPES OF FINANCING: LOANS: Working capital (receivables/inventory); Equipment, REAL ESTATE LOANS
PREFERRED TYPES OF INDUSTRIES/INVESTMENTS: Receivables
WILL NOT CONSIDER: Computers
GEOGRAPHIC LIMITS OF INVESTMENTS/LOANS: National
RANGE OF INV./LOAN PER BUSINESS: Min. $1 million
BUSINESS CHARACTERISTICS DESIRED-REQUIRED: Minimum number of years in business: 2

COMPANY: **The Manhattan Life Insurance Company**
ADDRESS: 111 W. 57th St.
New York, NY 10019
PHONE: (212) 484-9300
CONTACT OFFICER(S): Tony Miller, Dir. of R&D
James M. Creedon, V.P., Securities
L. John Achenback, II, Sr. V.P., Investments
David Smith, V.P. Mortgages
ASSETS: $1 billion
INVESTMENTS/LOANS MADE: In securities with a secondary market and in securities without a secondary market
TYPES OF FINANCING: SECONDARY-MARKET CORPORATE SECURITIES, LOANS, REAL ESTATE LOANS: Other: Senior mortgages
GEOGRAPHIC LIMITS OF INVESTMENTS/LOANS: National
RANGE OF INV./LOAN PER BUSINESS: Min. $1,000,000; Max. $5,000,000 (R.E.)
BUSINESS CHARACTERISTICS DESIRED-REQUIRED: Min. net worth $20 million
REFERRALS ACCEPTED FROM: Investment/Mortgage banker only
REMARKS: Referrals accepted from brokers

COMPANY: **Metropolitan Life Insurance Company**
ADDRESS: One Madison Avenue
New York, NY 10010
PHONE: (212) 578-2211
TYPE OF INSTITUTION: Real Estate Investments Department of insurance company
CONTACT OFFICER(S): Mr. E. A. Stoudt, V.P.
Mr. T. Bates Westerberg, V.P.
INVESTMENTS/LOANS MADE: For own account, For managed accounts
TYPES OF FINANCING: LOANS: Equity-related, REAL ESTATE: Acquisitions; Joint ventures
PREFERRED TYPES OF INDUSTRIES/INVESTMENTS: Office buildings, hotels, retail, industrial
GEOGRAPHIC LIMITS OF INVESTMENTS/LOANS: National; Other: Canada
RANGE OF INV./LOAN PER BUSINESS: Min. $5,000,000
REFERRALS ACCEPTED FROM: Investment/Mortgage banker or Borrower/Investee
BRANCHES: John Powell, Midwestern Office, Oak Brook, IL; (312) 920-7100
Tom Garesche, Northeastern Office, New York, NY; (212) 578-2211
Charles Sayres, Southeastern Office, Atlanta, GA; (404) 393-0630
Fred Arnholt, Southwestern Office, Houston, TX; (713) 931-4486
William Ripberger, Western Office, Foster City, CA; (415) 574-8181
Andre Vauclair, Canadian Office, Montreal, Canada; (514) 861-0923

COMPANY: **The Mutual Life Insurance Company of New York**
ADDRESS: 1740 Broadway
New York, NY 10019
PHONE: (212) 708-2000
TYPE OF INSTITUTION: Insurance Co.
CONTACT OFFICER(S): Michael J. Drabb, S.V.P.-Securities Invest. Dept.
ASSETS: $10.5 billion
INVESTMENTS/LOANS MADE: For own account, For managed accounts, Through private placements, Through underwriting public offerings
INVESTMENTS/LOANS MADE: In securities with a secondary market and in securities without a secondary market
TYPES OF FINANCING: SECONDARY-MARKET CORPORATE SECURITIES: Bonds. LOANS: Unsecured to credits above Ba. REAL ESTATE LOANS: Intermediate-term senior mtg. INTERNATIONAL. REAL ESTATE: Acquisitions; Joint ventures.
GEOGRAPHIC LIMITS OF INVESTMENTS/LOANS: International
RANGE OF INV./LOAN PER BUSINESS: Min. $3,000,000; Max. $20,000,000
PREFERRED TERM FOR LOANS & LEASES: Min. 3 years; Max. 12 years
BUSINESS CHARACTERISTICS DESIRED-REQUIRED: No startups
REFERRALS ACCEPTED FROM: Investment/Mortgage banker or Borrower/Investee

COMPANY: **Nordic American Bank Corporation**
ADDRESS: 600 Fifth Avenue
New York, NY 10020
PHONE: (212) 315-6500
TYPE OF INSTITUTION: Investment Banking
CONTACT OFFICER(S): Hans Eric Von der Groeben, EVP
Edward Mete, EVP
ASSESTS: $600,000,000
INVESTMENTS/LOANS MADE: For own account; Through private placements
INVESTMENTS/LOANS MADE: In securities with a secondary market and in securities without a secondary market;
TYPES OF FINANCING: SECONDARY-MARKET CORPORATE SECURITIES: Bonds; LOANS: Working Capital (receivables/inventory); Equipment; Equity-related. REAL ESTATE LOANS: Industrial revenue bonds. LEASES: Leveraged; Tax leases; Operating; Lease syndications; Vendor financing programs; INTERNATIONAL (including import/export)
PREFERRED TYPES OF INDUSTRIES/INVESTMENTS: Nordic related business in the U.S. U.S. businesses operating in the Nordic area.

GEOGRAPHIC LIMITS OF INVESTMENTS/LOANS: National; International;
BRANCHES: John A. Redding, SVP, Suite 1963, 135 So. La Salle St., Chicago, IL; (312) 855-1515

COMPANY: **Regulus International Capital Company, Inc.**
ADDRESS: 10 Rockefeller Plaza
New York, NY 10020
PHONE: (212) 582-7715
TYPE OF INSTITUTION: Venture Capital Company
CONTACT OFFICER(S): Lee H. Miller, President
INVESTMENTS/LOANS MADE: For own account, For managed accounts, Through private placements
TYPES OF FINANCING: VENTURE CAPITAL: Research & Development; Start-up from developed product stage; Second-stage (generally 1-3 years); Buy-outs/Acquisitions, FACTORING, INTERNATIONAL (including import/export), REAL ESTATE
PREFERRED TYPES OF INDUSTRIES/INVESTMENTS: Printing, Packaging & Converting, Plastics
GEOGRAPHIC LIMITS OF INVESTMENTS/LOANS: Regional
RANGE OF INV./LOAN PER BUSINESS: Min. $200,000; Max. $2,000,000

COMPANY: **Richard Ellis, Inc.**
ADDRESS: 350 Park Avenue
New York, NY 10022
PHONE: (212) 355-4810
TYPE OF INSTITUTION: International Real Estate Consultants
CONTACT OFFICER(S): Christopher D. Budder, Executive Vice President
Graham J. Bond, Senior Vice President
Terry P. Noyer, Senior Vice President
ASSETS: $700 million approximately
INVESTMENTS/LOANS MADE: For managed accounts
TYPES OF FINANCING: REAL ESTATE: Acquisitions; Joint ventures. OTHER SERVICESS PROVIDED: Portfolio management, Property management, Valvetions, Leasing, Development, International advice.
PREFERRED TYPES OF INDUSTRIES/INVESTMENTS: Major regional shopping centers, at least 300,000 square feet; Office buildings, at least 100,000 square feet; Industrial & business parks
WILL NOT CONSIDER: Hotels, Motels, Apartments, Residential
GEOGRAPHIC LIMITS OF INVESTMENTS/LOANS: National
RANGE OF INV./LOAN PER BUSINESS: Min. $2.5 million
REFERRALS ACCEPTED FROM: Investment/Mortgage banker or Borrower/Investee
BRANCHES: Terry P. Noyer, Senior Vice President, Two Embarcadero Center, San Francisco, CA 94111, (415) 392-1090
Leonard J. Adams, Senior Vice President, 200 E. Randolph Drive, Suite 6545, Chicago, IL 60601, (312) 861-1105
Wm. Jerry Sauls, Senior Vice President, 3414 Peachtree Rd., Suite 852, Atlanta, GA 30326, (404) 231-0400

COMPANY: **Sterling Company**
ADDRESS: 41 East 42nd St., Suite 1510
New York, NY 10017
PHONE: (212) 697-0610
CONTACT OFFICER(S): Martin Lifton, Manager Partner
ASSETS: $10,000,000
INVESTMENTS/LOANS MADE: For own account
INVESTMENTS/LOANS MADE: In securities with a secondary market and in securities without a secondary market
TYPES OF FINANCING: REAL ESTATE LOANS: Intermediate-term senior mtg.;
REFERRALS ACCEPTED FROM: Investment/Mortgage banker or Borrower/Investee

COMPANY: **Sybedon Corporation**
ADDRESS: 1211 Ave. of the Americas
New York, NY 10036
PHONE: (212) 354-5756
TYPE OF INSTITUTION: Mortgage Banking, Real Estate Syndication, Real Estate Venture Capital, Development
CONTACT OFFICER(S): Bertram Lewis, Chmn.
INVESTMENTS/LOANS MADE: For own account; Through private placements
INVESTMENTS/LOANS MADE: Only in securities without a secondary market
TYPES OF FINANCING: REAL ESTATE LOANS: Long-term senior mtg.; Intermediate-term senior mtg.; Subordinated; Wraparounds; Land; Land development; Construction; Gap; Standbys; Industrial revenue bonds, REAL ESTATE: Acquisitions; Joint ventures; Partnerships/ Syndications.
PREFERRED TYPES OF INDUSTRIES/INVESTMENTS: All aspects of Real Estate
GEOGRAPHIC LIMITS OF INVESTMENTS/LOANS: National
RANGE OF INV./LOAN PER BUSINESS: Min. $3 million project
REFERRALS ACCEPTED FROM: Investment/Mortgage banker or Borrower/Investee

COMPANY: **Teachers Insurance & Annuity Association**
ADDRESS: 730 Third Ave.
New York, NY 10017
PHONE: (212) 490-9000
CONTACT OFFICER(S): Frank J. Pados, Securities
John Somers, V.P., Mtg. & R.E.
ASSETS: $100 million and up
TYPES OF FINANCING: SECONDARY-MARKET CORPORATE SECURITIES, LOANS: Equity-related, REAL ESTATE LOANS, LEASES, REAL ESTATE
GEOGRAPHIC LIMITS OF INVESTMENTS/LOANS: National; Other: Canada
RANGE OF INV./LOAN PER BUSINESS: Min. $1,000,000; Max. None
PREFERRED TERM FOR LOANS & LEASES: Min. 7-10 years (Securities); 15-20 years (R.E.); Max. 20+ years
BUSINESS CHARACTERISTICS DESIRED-REQUIRED: Minimum number of years in business: 3-5; Min. annual sales $100 million (Securities)
REFERRALS ACCEPTED FROM: Investment/Mortgage banker or Borrower/Investee

REMARKS: Provide equity; active in buyouts and acquisitions

COMPANY: **Venture Capital Management, Inc. (sub. of Prudential Ins. Co. of America**
ADDRESS: 717 5th Avenue, Suite 1600
New York, NY 10022
PHONE: (201) 877-6000
CONTACT OFFICER(S): William Field, Chairman
John Childs, Sr. V.P.
ASSETS: $100 million and up
INVESTMENTS/LOANS MADE: In securities with a secondary market and in securities without a secondary market
TYPES OF FINANCING: LOANS: Equity-related; Other: Guarantees, REAL ESTATE LOANS: Long-term senior mtg.; Intermediate-term senior mtg.; Subordinated, LEASES, REAL ESTATE: Acquisitions; Joint ventures, OTHER SERVICES PROVIDED: Equity financing
GEOGRAPHIC LIMITS OF INVESTMENTS/LOANS: International
RANGE OF INV./LOAN PER BUSINESS: Min. $500,000; Max. Over $100,000,000
PREFERRED TERM FOR LOANS & LEASES: Min. 10-15 years; Max. 15-20 years

COMPANY: **Avanti Equity, Real Estate**
ADDRESS: Box 402
Woodbury, Long Island, NY 11797
PHONE: (516) 921-6880
TYPE OF INSTITUTION: Agent
CONTACT OFFICER(S): Leonard Sciscio, President & Broker
INVESTMENTS/LOANS MADE: Through private placements
INVESTMENTS/LOANS MADE: In securities with a secondary market and in securities without a secondary market
TYPES OF FINANCING: REAL ESTATE LOANS, LEASES: Tax-oriented lease brokerage; REAL ESTATE: Acquisitions; Joint ventures, OTHER SERVICES PROVIDED: Brokerage in Real Estate mortgage packages
PREFERRED TYPES OF INDUSTRIES/INVESTMENTS: Income producing real estate
WILL NOT CONSIDER: Industrial
GEOGRAPHIC LIMITS OF INVESTMENTS/LOANS: Regional
RANGE OF INV./LOAN PER BUSINESS: Min. $2,500,000; Max. Relative/None
PREFERRED TERM FOR LOANS & LEASES: Min. 1 year; Max. Relative/None
BUSINESS CHARACTERISTICS DESIRED-REQUIRED: Minimum number of years in business: 2; Min. annual sales $250,000; Other: Relative/None
REFERRALS ACCEPTED FROM: Investment/Mortgage banker or Borrower/Investee
REMARKS: Real estate investment liaison to financial institutions & syndicators

COMPANY: **The Union Central Life Insurance Company**
ADDRESS: P.O. Box 179
Cincinnati, OH 45201
PHONE: (513) 595-2200
CONTACT OFFICER(S): Michael Conway, Sr. V.P., CEO
John A. Cooney, V.P., Mortgage
Ronald Killinger, V.P., Corp. Finance Inv.
ASSETS: $1.3 billion
TYPES OF FINANCING: LOANS, REAL ESTATE LOANS: Long-term senior mtg.; Subordinated, LEASES
PREFERRED TYPES OF INDUSTRIES/INVESTMENTS: Diversified
GEOGRAPHIC LIMITS OF INVESTMENTS/LOANS: National
REFERRALS ACCEPTED FROM: Investment/Mortgage banker or Borrower/Investee
REMARKS: Range for R.E.: $500,000-2,500,000; Range for Private Placement: $200,000-5,000,000

COMPANY: **The Western and Southern Life Insurance Company**
ADDRESS: 400 Broadway
Cincinnati, OH 45202
PHONE: (513) 629-1800
CONTACT OFFICER(S): William F. Ledwin, V.P., Finance Department
Richard L. Siegel, V.P., Finance Department
ASSETS: $3.2 Billion
INVESTMENTS/LOANS MADE: For own account
INVESTMENTS/LOANS MADE: In securities with a secondary market and in securities without a secondary market
TYPES OF FINANCING: SECONDARY-MARKET CORPORATE SECURITIES: Common stock; Preferred stock; Bonds; Government Guaranteed Loans, LOANS: Unsecured to credits above A; Equity-related; Equity-Related Mortgage, REAL ESTATE LOANS: Land, LEASES: Leveraged, REAL ESTATE: Joint ventures
PHONE: (213) 278-2102
TYPE OF INSTITUTION: R.E. Company, Management

COMPANY: **Mellon Financial Services**
ADDRESS: 1255 Euclid Ave.
Cleveland, OH 44115
PHONE: (216) 696-5432
TYPE OF INSTITUTION: Mortgage Banker
CONTACT OFFICER(S): Charles E. Keane, Pres.

COMPANY: **Chemical Mortgage Co.**
ADDRESS: 101 E. Town St.
Columbus, OH 43215
PHONE: (614) 460-3000
TYPE OF INSTITUTION: Mortgage banker
CONTACT OFFICER(S): Daniel Goss, President
ASSETS: Servicing volume over $5 billion
TYPES OF FINANCING: REAL ESTATE LOANS: Long-term senior mtg.; Intermediate-term senior mtg.; Subordinated; Other: Sale-leaseback
GEOGRAPHIC LIMITS OF INVESTMENTS/LOANS: National; Other: Canada
RANGE OF INV./LOAN PER BUSINESS: Min. See remarks
PREFERRED TERM FOR LOANS & LEASES: Min. 1-3 years; Max. 20+ years

BRANCHES: Mike Roth, 120 W. 5th St., Suite 1203, Cincinnati, OH 45202; (513) 721-8050
REMARKS: $500,000 in cities with office; $2,000,000 in cities without office

COMPANY: **The Columbus Mutual Life Insurance Company**
ADDRESS: 303 East Broad St.
Columbus, OH 43215
PHONE: (614) 221-5875
CONTACT OFFICER(S): James Barton, V.P. & Chief Investment Officer
J. Gill, Admin. Assistant Mortgage Loans
ASSETS: $500,000,000 & up
INVESTMENTS/LOANS MADE: For own account; Through private placements,underwriting public offerings
INVESTMENTS/LOANS MADE: In securities with a secondary market and in securities without a secondary market
TYPES OF FINANCING: SECONDARY-MARKET CORPORATE SECURITIES, LOANS, REAL ESTATE LOANS, REAL ESTATE: Joint ventures; Partnerships/ Syndications
WILL NOT CONSIDER: Specialty Type Real Estate (Fast Foods, etc.)
GEOGRAPHIC LIMITS OF INVESTMENTS/LOANS: National
RANGE OF INV./LOAN PER BUSINESS: Min. $500,000; Max. $1,500,000
PREFERRED TERM FOR LOANS & LEASES: varies depending on real estate
REFERRALS ACCEPTED FROM: Investment/Mortgage banker

COMPANY: **The Midland Mutual Life Insurance Co.**
ADDRESS: 250 E. Broad St.
Columbus, OH 43215
PHONE: (614) 228-2001
CONTACT OFFICER(S): Mr. Dyer, V.P., Mtg. & Real Estate
ASSETS: $100 million and up
TYPES OF FINANCING: REAL ESTATE LOANS: Long-term senior mtg.; Intermediate-term senior mtg; Wraparounds, REAL ESTATE: Acquisitions; Joint ventures
GEOGRAPHIC LIMITS OF INVESTMENTS/LOANS: National
RANGE OF INV./LOAN PER BUSINESS: Min. $500,000; Max $1,500,000
PREFERRED TERM FOR LOANS & LEASES: Max. 7 years
REMARKS: Referrals accepted from Correspondent. Maximum amounts: $1.5 million for mortgages & $1 million for private placements; amounts in bonds are percent of assets

COMPANY: **Nationwide Life Insurance Company**
ADDRESS: One Nationwide Plaza
Columbus, OH 43216
PHONE: (614) 227-7696
CONTACT OFFICER(S): Robert J. Woodward, V.P., R.E. Investment
ASSETS: $100 million and up
TYPES OF FINANCING: LOANS, REAL ESTATE LOANS: Senior Mortgages
PREFERRED TYPES OF INDUSTRIES/INVESTMENTS: Diversified
GEOGRAPHIC LIMITS OF INVESTMENTS/LOANS: National
RANGE OF INV./LOAN PER BUSINESS: Min. $1,000,000 (R.E.); $2,000,000 (P.P.); Max. $5,000,000
PREFERRED TERM FOR LOANS & LEASES: Min. 15-20; Max. 20+ years
BUSINESS CHARACTERISTICS DESIRED-REQUIRED: Minimum number of years in business: 5
REFERRALS ACCEPTED FROM: Investment/Mortgage banker or Borrower/Investee

COMPANY: **The Kissell Co.**
ADDRESS: 30 Warder St.
Springfield, OH 45501
PHONE: (513) 324-6700
TYPE OF INSTITUTION: Mortgage Banker
CONTACT OFFICER(S): Richard L. Current, Pres.
ASSETS: Servicing Volume over $100,000,000
TYPES OF FINANCING: REAL ESTATE LOANS: Long-term senior mtg.; Intermediate-term senior mtg.
PREFERRED TYPES OF INDUSTRIES/INVESTMENTS: No preference
GEOGRAPHIC LIMITS OF INVESTMENTS/LOANS: National
PREFERRED TERM FOR LOANS & LEASES: Min. 0-1; Max. 20+ years

COMPANY: **Pool Mortgage Co.**
ADDRESS: 227 Chickasha Ave.
Chickasha, OK 73018
PHONE: (405) 224-0551
TYPE OF INSTITUTION: Mortgage Banker
CONTACT OFFICER(S): Fred Smith, Sr. V.P.
ASSETS: $100,000,000 and up
TYPES OF FINANCING: REAL ESTATE LOANS: Long-term senior mtg.; Intermediate-term senior mtg.
GEOGRAPHIC LIMITS OF INVESTMENTS/LOANS: State
PREFERRED TERM FOR LOANS & LEASES: Min. 5-7 years; Max. 20+ years

COMPANY: **American Mortgage and Investment Co.**
ADDRESS: 5th Fl, First National Center East
Oklahoma City, OK 73102
PHONE: (405) 272-4333
TYPE OF INSTITUTION: Mortgage Banker

COMPANY: **Bob L. Cartmill & Associates**
ADDRESS: P.O. Box 19316
Oklahoma City, OK 73144
PHONE: (405) 685-9945
TYPE OF INSTITUTION: Acquisitions/mergers & financing
CONTACT OFFICER(S): Bob L. Cartmill, Pres.
INVESTMENTS/LOANS MADE: Through private placements

INVESTMENTS/LOANS MADE: In securities with a secondary market and in securities without a secondary market
TYPES OF FINANCING: SECONDARY-MARKET CORPORATE SECURITIES, VENTURE CAPITAL: Second-stage; Later-stage expansion; Buy-outs/Acquisitions, LOANS: Equity-related, REAL ESTATE LOANS, LEASES: Single-investor; Leveraged, REAL ESTATE: Acquisitions; Joint ventures; Partnerships/Syndications
PREFERRED TYPES OF INDUSTRIES/INVESTMENTS: All types
WILL NOT CONSIDER: Start up situations
GEOGRAPHIC LIMITS OF INVESTMENTS/LOANS: Local; State; Regional
BUSINESS CHARACTERISTICS DESIRED-REQUIRED: Minimum number of years in business: 5
REFERRALS ACCEPTED FROM: Investment/Mortgage banker or Borrower/Investee
REMARKS: have several associates in several states

COMPANY: **Liberty Mortgage Co.**
ADDRESS: 100 Broadway Liberty Tower, P.O. Box 25757
Oklahoma City, OK 73125
PHONE: (405) 231-6233
TYPE OF INSTITUTION: Mortgage Banker
CONTACT OFFICER(S): Dewane Davidson, Exec. V.P.
ASSETS: Servicing Volume $1,007,000,000
TYPES OF FINANCING: REAL ESTATE LOANS: Long-term senior mtg.; Intermediate-term senior mtg; Industrial Revenue Bonds

COMPANY: **First Security Realty Services Corporation (West)**
ADDRESS: 1336 E. Burnside St.
Portland, OR 97214
PHONE: (503) 231-3400
TYPE OF INSTITUTION: Mortgage banker
CONTACT OFFICER(S): Jack Forell, C.O.O.
K. James Kennedy
ASSETS: Servicing volume over $100,000,000
INVESTMENTS/LOANS MADE: For own account, For managed accounts, Through private placements, underwriting public offerings
TYPES OF FINANCING: REAL ESTATE LOANS: Long-term senior mtg.; Intermediate-term senior mtg.; Subordinated; Wraparounds, Land; Land development; Construction; Gap; Standbys; Industrial revenue bonds, REAL ESTATE: Acquisitions, Joint ventures; Partnerships/Syndications
PREFERRED TYPES OF INDUSTRIES/INVESTMENTS: Office buildings; warehouses; residential apartment buildings; shopping centers
WILL NOT CONSIDER: Churches
GEOGRAPHIC LIMITS OF INVESTMENTS/LOANS: Regional
REFERRALS ACCEPTED FROM: Investment/Mortgage banker or Borrower/Investee
BRANCHES: 1 Union Square, Suite 1920, Seattle, WA 98101;
10415 NE 37th Circle, Kirkland, WA
2025 Gateway Place, Suite 318, San Jose, CA 95110;
1851 Heritage Lane, Suite 223, Sacramento, CA 95815;
3590 Central Ave., Suite 101, Riverside, CA 92506

COMPANY: **General Electric Mortgage Corporation**
ADDRESS: 220 NW Second Ave.
Portland, OR 97209
PHONE: (503) 790-9100
CONTACT OFFICER(S): Lauralee E. Martin, President
Lloyd W. Cahoon, Sr. V.P.
Joseph M. Valdes, Sr. V.P.
Paul F. Bears, Exec. V.P.
TYPES OF FINANCING: REAL ESTATE LOANS: Construction; Other: In-house lender for construction, residential FHA/VA, Income commercial first mortgages; REAL ESTATE: Acquisitions
PREFERRED TYPES OF INDUSTRIES/INVESTMENTS: Office buildings, shopping centers, industrial
GEOGRAPHIC LIMITS OF INVESTMENTS/LOANS: Regional; Other: West of Mississippi
RANGE OF INV./LOAN PER BUSINESS: Min. $500,000
PREFERRED TERM FOR LOANS & LEASES: Min. 6 mos.; Max. 3 years
BRANCHES: 15760 Ventura Blvd., #826, Encino, CA 91463, (818) 995-8863

COMPANY: **Orbanco Real Estate Services Co.**
ADDRESS: 1001 S.W. 5th Ave., P.O. Box 4049
Portland, OR 97208
PHONE: (503) 222-6384
TYPE OF INSTITUTION: Mortgage banker
CONTACT OFFICER(S): John Barnes
Beverly Hanthorn
ASSETS: $10,000,000-100,000,000
TYPES OF FINANCING: REAL ESTATE LOANS: Long-term senior mtg.; Intermediate-term senior mtg.; Other: Commercial 2nd mortgages
GEOGRAPHIC LIMITS OF INVESTMENTS/LOANS: Regional; Other: OR, WA, ID, UT, CA
RANGE OF INV./LOAN PER BUSINESS: Min. $300,000
PREFERRED TERM FOR LOANS & LEASES: Min. 3 years; Max. 10 years
BRANCHES: Ron Thompson, 700 112th NE, Bellevue, WA 98004; (206) 454-2681
Daniel Bradshaw, P.O. Box 873, Boise, ID 83702; (208) 342-4645

COMPANY: **Standard Insurance Co.**
ADDRESS: P.O. Box 711
Portland, OR 97207
PHONE: (503) 248-2836
TYPE OF INSTITUTION: Life insurance company
CONTACT OFFICER(S): Vicky Chase, Asst. V.P.
Wayne Atterberry, V.P., Mortgage Loans
TYPES OF FINANCING: SECONDARY-MARKET CORPORATE SECURITIES: Bonds, LOANS: Equity-related, REAL ESTATE: Acquisitions
PREFERRED TYPES OF INDUSTRIES/INVESTMENTS: Commercial
GEOGRAPHIC LIMITS OF INVESTMENTS/LOANS: Real estate Regional; Bonds : National
RANGE OF INV./LOAN PER BUSINESS: Min. $250,000; Max. $2 million
PREFERRED TERM FOR LOANS & LEASES: Min. 5 years; Max. 12 years

BUSINESS CHARACTERISTICS DESIRED-REQUIRED: Minimum number of years in business: 5 for bonds; Other: Quality Baa or equivalent

COMPANY: **Ward Cook, Inc.**
ADDRESS: 520 S.W. Stark St.
Portland, OR 97204
PHONE: (503) 226-2111
TYPE OF INSTITUTION: Mortgage Banker
CONTACT OFFICER(S): Tom Cornish, V.P.
ASSETS: $10,000,000 - 100,000,000
TYPES OF FINANCING: REAL ESTATE LOANS: Long-term senior mtg.; Intermediate-term senior mtg.; Construction; Sale-Leaseback
GEOGRAPHIC LIMITS OF INVESTMENTS/LOANS: Regional
PREFERRED TERM FOR LOANS & LEASES: Min. 15-20; Max. 20+ years

COMPANY: **Mortgage Bancorporation**
ADDRESS: 167-High St., P.O. Box 230
Salem, OR 97308
PHONE: (503) 363-3151
TYPE OF INSTITUTION: Mortgage Banking
CONTACT OFFICER(S): E. H. Miller, President, Overall
John Coffey, V.P., Const. Loans
Joe W. Bartosz
ASSETS: $10,000,000
INVESTMENTS/LOANS MADE: For own account; For managed accounts; Through private placements, underwriting public offerings
TYPES OF FINANCING: REAL ESTATE LOANS: Land; Land development; Construction, OTHER SERVICES PROVIDED: Real Estate contracts, Mortgages, Trust deeds purchased at a discount on improved and unimproved properties.
PREFERRED TYPES OF INDUSTRIES/INVESTMENTS: Oregon or Washington located Real Estate — Land — Lots — Residential, Commercial
WILL NOT CONSIDER: Projects over 3M
GEOGRAPHIC LIMITS OF INVESTMENTS/LOANS: State
RANGE OF INV./LOAN PER BUSINESS: Min. $5,000; Max. $3,000,000
PREFERRED TERM FOR LOANS & LEASES: Min. 6 mos.; Max. 10 years
BUSINESS CHARACTERISTICS DESIRED-REQUIRED: Minimum number of years in business: 1
REFERRALS ACCEPTED FROM: Investment/Mortgage banker or Borrower/Investee

COMPANY: **Franklin Realty Group**
ADDRESS: 4 Century Parkway
Blue Bell PA 19422
PHONE: (215) 834-1980
TYPE OF INSTITUTION: REIT
CONTACT OFFICER(S): Joseph F. Lebano, Vice President
TYPES OF FINANCING: VENTURE CAPITAL: Research & Development; Start-up from developed product stage, REAL ESTATE LOANS: Land; Land development; Construction; Industrial revenue bonds, REAL ESTATE: Acquisitions; Joint ventures; Partnerships/Syndications, OTHER SERVICES PROVIDED: Specialty-syndicated limited partnerships, land acquisition, planning, R.E.
PREFERRED TYPES OF INDUSTRIES/INVESTMENTS: Diversified; Industrial buildings
WILL NOT CONSIDER: Gas stations, etc., bars, family business
GEOGRAPHIC LIMITS OF INVESTMENTS/LOANS: National
RANGE OF INV./LOAN PER BUSINESS: Min. $1,000,000
BUSINESS CHARACTERISTICS DESIRED-REQUIRED: Other: Prefer developing stages

COMPANY: **Cromwell & Kyle**
ADDRESS: 234 Fountainville Center
Fountainville, PA 18923
PHONE: (215) 249-3583
TYPE OF INSTITUTION: Consulting Investment Bankers
CONTACT OFFICER(S): Alec B. Kyle
Roger J.K. Cromwell
INVESTMENTS/LOANS MADE: Through private placements
INVESTMENTS/LOANS MADE: In securities without a secondary market
TYPES OF FINANCING: SECONDARY-MARKET CORPORATE SECURITIES: Common stock; Preferred stock; Bonds, VENTURE CAPITAL: Research & Development; Start-up from developed product stage; First-stage (less than 1 year); Second-stage (generally 1-3 years); Later-stage expansion; Buy-outs/Acquisitions, LOANS: Unsecured; Working capital (receivables/inventory); Equipment; Equity-related; Other: Mezzanine financing in leveraged buy-outs. Loans against receivables from Mexican government entities, REAL ESTATE LOANS: Long-term senior mtg.; Intermediate-term senior mtg.; Subordinated; Wraparounds; Land; Land development; Construction; Gap; Standbys; Industrial revenue bonds, FACTORING, INTERNATIONAL (including import/export), REAL ESTATE: Acquisitions; Joint ventures; Partnerships/Syndications, OTHER SERVICES PROVIDED: Restructuring financings to command low-interest Swiss funding
PREFERRED TYPES OF INDUSTRIES/INVESTMENTS: No preference
GEOGRAPHIC LIMITS OF INVESTMENTS/LOANS: National; International
RANGE OF INV./LOAN PER BUSINESS: Min. $500,000; Max. $75,000,000
REFERRALS ACCEPTED FROM: Investment/Mortgage banker or Borrower/Investee
BRANCHES: 1960 Bronson Rd., Fairfield, CT 06430; (203) 259-3269

COMPANY: **Mortgage and Realty Trust**
ADDRESS: 7320 Old York Rd.
Melrose Park, PA 19126
PHONE: (215) 782-2055
TYPE OF INSTITUTION: REIT
CONTACT OFFICER(S): James Dalton, Pres. of Advisor
Dan Hennessey, Treasurer of Advisor
Victor H. Schlesinger, V. Chairman, Philadelphia
ASSETS: $211,900,000

TYPES OF FINANCING: REAL ESTATE LOANS: Intermediate-term senior mtg.; Construction; Other: standing and long-term participation loans
PREFERRED TYPES OF INDUSTRIES/INVESTMENTS: General purpose R.E.
WILL NOT CONSIDER: Speciality R.E. — bowling alleys, etc.
GEOGRAPHIC LIMITS OF INVESTMENTS/LOANS: National
RANGE OF INV./LOAN PER BUSINESS: Min. $1.5 million; Max. $10 million
BUSINESS CHARACTERISTICS DESIRED-REQUIRED: Other: Case-dependent
BRANCHES: Victor H. Schlesinger, V.C., PNB Building, 17th foor, Broad & Chestnut Streets, Philadelphia, PA 19107; (215) 864-7324
John Cover, 14724 Ventura Blvd., Ste. 1100, Sherman Oaks, CA 91403; (818) 783-7800

COMPANY: **Central Mortgage Co.**
ADDRESS: Avenue of the Arts Bldg., Broad & Chestnut Streets
Philadelphia, PA 19107
PHONE: (215) 985-6225
TYPE OF INSTITUTION: Mortgage Banking Subsidiary of PSES
CONTACT OFFICER(S): John P. Ferrie, Div. V.P., Commercial Loans
James J. Sheehan, Div. V.P., Commercial Loans
Harold G. Schultz, Sr., Regional Director
John Sheehan, Regional Director
GEOGRAPHIC LIMITS OF INVESTMENTS/LOANS: National
RANGE OF INNV./LOAN PER BUSINESS: Min. $1,000,000; Max. Open
PREFERRED TERM FOR LOANS & LEASES: Min. 1 year; Max. 30 years
BUSINESS CHARACTERISTICS DESIRED-REQUIRED: Minimum number of years in business: Open; Min. annual sales Open; Min. net worth Open; Min. anual net income Open; Min. annual cash fow Open
REFERRALS ACCEPTED FROM: Investment/Mortgage banker and Borrower/Investee
BRANCHES: Miami Regional Office/Miami Branch Office #1, John Bozzuto, Div. V.P., 7220 NW 36th Street, Ste. 103, Miami, FL 33166
Miami Branch Office #2, Thomas J. Lietaert, Branch Mgr., 1501 NW 167th Street, Ste. 448, Miami, FL 33169
Miami Branch Office #3, Paul Saporta, Branch Mgr., 8900 SE 107th Avenue, Ste. 306, Miami, FL 33176
Tampa Branch Office #4, Loyal Walley, Branch Mgr., 5404 Cypress Center Dr., Ste. 260, Tampa, FL 33609
First National Mortgage Corporation, Louis P. Wolfort, III, Div. V.P., 1111 S. Jefferson Davis Parkway, New Orleans, LA 80185
Central Mortgage Co., Marty Saturn, Regional Dir., 4520 E W Hwy, Bethesda, MD 20814

COMPANY: **Fidelity Bond and Mortgage Co.**
ADDRESS: 400 Avenue of the Arts Bldg., Broad & Chestnut Streets
Philadelphia, PA 19107
PHONE: (215) 985-2020
TYPE OF INSTITUTION: Mortgage Banker
CONTACT OFFICER(S): Vincent DiBias, President
ASSETS: Servicing Volume over $100,000,000
TYPES OF FINANCING: REAL ESTATE LOANS: Long-term senior mtg.; Intermediate-term senior mtg.; Subordinated
PREFERRED TYPES OF INDUSTRIES/INVESTMENTS: Apartments; Shopping Centers; Offices; Industrial
GEOGRAPHIC LIMITS OF INVESTMENTS/LOANS: Regional
RANGE OF INV./LOAN PER BUSINESS: Min. $300,000; Max. None
PREFERRED TERM FOR LOANS & LEASES: Max. 20+ years

COMPANY: **Innovest Group, Inc.**
ADDRESS: 1700 Market Street, Ste. 1228
Philadelphia, PA 19103
PHONE: (215) 564-3960
TYPE OF INSTITUTION: Private Venture Capital Company
CONTACT OFFICER(S): Richard E. Woosnam, President
Nila K. Sendzik, V.P.
ASSETS: $10 Million
INVESTMENTS/LOANS MADE: For own account; Through private placements
INVESTMENTS/LOANS MADE: Only in securities without a secondary market
TYPES OF FINANCING: VENTURE CAPITAL: Start-up from developed product stage; First-stage; Second-stage; Later-stage expansion, LEASES: Single-investor; Leveraged; Tax leases; Vendor financing programs, REAL ESTATE
PREFERRED TYPES OF INDUSTRIES/INVESTMENTS: Communications — cable TV, commercial communication, data comm, satellite & miicrowave comm., telephone related; Computer Related — computer graphics & CAD/CAM, computer services, memory devices, micro 7 mini computers, software systems; Electronics Equipment — medical products, laser related, analytical and scientific instrumentation, optics technology, semiconduction; Medical — diagnostic equipment, therapeutic equipment; Other — education related, real estate
GEOGRAPHIC LIMITS OF INVESTMENTS/LOANS: Regional
RANGE OF INV./LOAN PER BUSINESS: Min. $250,000; Max. $1,000,000
BUSINESS CHARACTERISTICS DESIRED-REQUIRED: Minimum number of years in business: 0
REFERRALS ACCEPTED FROM: Investment banker or Borrower/Investee

COMPANY: **Latimer & Buck, Inc.**
ADDRESS: 121 S. Broad St.
Philadelphia, PA 19107
PHONE: (215) 985-3900
TYPE OF INSTITUTION: Mortgage Banker Company
CONTACT OFFICER(S): Thomas Z. Minehart, III, Sr., V.P., Commerical Loan Department
ASSETS: $500,000
INVESTMENTS/LOANS MADE: Through private placements
TYPES OF INVESTMENTS/LOANS MADE: LOANS, REAL ESTATE LOANS: Long-term senior mtg.;

Intermediate-term senior mtg.; Wraparounds; Land; Construction; Gap; Industrial revenue bonds, REAL ESTATE: Acquisitions; Joint ventures; Partnerships/ Syndicates
PREFERRED TYPES OF INDUSTRIES/INVESTMENTS: Office Buildings, Hotels, Industrial, Apartments and Shopping Centers
GEOGRAPHIC LMITS OF INVESTMENTS/LOANS: Other: Eastern Pennsylvania, Southern New Jersey & Deleware concentration
RANGE OF INV./LOAN PER BUSINESS: Min. $500,000; Max. No limit
PREFERRED TERM FOR LOANS & LEASES: Min. 5 years; Max. 20 years
REFERRALS ACCEPTED FROM: Investment/Mortgage banker and Borrower/Investee
BRANCHES: Daniel J. Panichelli, One Carnegie Center, Princeton, NJ 08540; (215) 985-3900

COMPANY: **PSFS**
ADDRESS: 12 South 12th Street
Philadelphia, PA 19107
PHONE: (215) 636-6000
TYPE OF INSTITUTION: Diversified Financial Services
CONTACT OFFICER(S): Philip A. McMunigal III, V.P., Private Placement Unit
ASSETS: $12.5 billion (June 30, 1984)
INVESTMENTS/LOANS MADE: For own account; Through private placements
INVESTMENTS/LOANS MADE: In securities with a secondary market and in securities without a secondary market
TYPES OF FINANCING: SECONDARY-MARKET CORPORATE SECURITIES: Common stock; Preferred stock; Bonds, VENTURE CAPITAL: Start-up from developed product stage, LOANS: Unsecured to credits above Baa; Working capital; Equipment; Equity-related, REAL ESTATE LOANS: Long-term senior mtg.; Intermediate-term senior mtg.; Land development; Construction; Standbys; Industrial revenue bonds, LEASES: Leveraged; Tax leases; Non-tax leases; Operating; Vendor financing programs, REAL ESTATE: Acquisitions; Joint ventures; Partnerships/ Syndications, OTHER SERVICES PROVIDED: pension fund advisory services, trade and stand-by letters of credit
PREFERRED TYPES OF INDUSTRIES/INVESTMENTS: all offerings considered
GEOGRAPHIC LIMITS OF INVESTMENTS/LOANS: Local; State; Regional; National; International
RANGE OF INV./LOAN PER BUSINESS: Min. $1,000,000; Max. depends on quality rating
PREFERRED TERM FOR LOANS & LEASES: Min. one year; Max. 10 years
BUSINESS CHARACTERISTICS DESIRED-REQUIRED: Negotiable

COMPANY: **Strouse Greenberg and Co.**
ADDRESS: 1626 Locust Street
Philadelphia, PA 19103
PHONE: (215) 985-1100
TYPE OF INSTITUTION: Real estate development, investment, and brokerage firm
CONTACT OFFICER(S): Joseph Straus, Jr., Partner/ Senior Management
ASSETS: $100 million
INVESTMENTS/LOANS MADE: For own account, Through private placements, Through underwriting public offerings
TYPES OF FINANCING: SECONDARY-MARKET CORPORATE SECURITIES: Other: Real estate, REAL ESTATE: Acquisitions; Joint ventures; Partnerships/ Syndications
PREFERRED TYPES OF INDUSTRIES/INVESTMENTS: Income producing real estate, minimum size $1.5 million; Office buildings; Shopping centers; Industrial properties; Apartment houses
GEOGRAPHIC LIMITS OF INVESTMENTS/LOANS: Other: East of the Mississippi River
RANGE OF INV./LOAN PER BUSINESS: Min. $1.5 million; Max. No limit
REFERRALS ACCEPTED FROM: Investment/Mortgage banker or Borrower/Investee
BRANCHES: Mr. Robert K. Leste, Mr. James H. Sands, Jr., Suite 408, 4415 West Harrison Street, Hillside, IL 60162; (312) 449-1122

COMPANY: **Dravo Leasing Company**
ADDRESS: One Oliver Plaza
Pittsburgh, PA 15222
PHONE: (412) 566-5186
TYPE OF INSTITUTION: Captive leasing subsidiary
CONTACT OFFICER(S): Patricia M. Rogan, General Manager & Asst. Treasurer
ASSETS: $35,000,000
TYPES OF FINANCING: LOANS: Equipment; Other: Mortgage, LEASES: Single-investor; Tax leases; Non-tax leases; Operating
PREFERRED TYPES OF INDUSTRIES/INVESTMENTS: Finance only Dravo products and services
GEOGRAPHIC LIMITS OF INVESTMENTS/LOANS: National
RANGE OF INV./LOAN PER BUSINESS: Max. $10,000,000
PREFERRED TERM FOR LOANS & LEASES: Min. 1-3 years; Max. 15-20 years
BUSINESS CHARACTERISTICS DESIRED-REQUIRED: Minimum number of years in business: 5

COMPANY: **Twenty-first Century Equity Corp.**
ADDRESS: 150 Beta Dr., P.O. Box 11464
Pittsburgh, PA 15238
PHONE: (412) 963-1100
CONTACT OFFICER(S): Aubrey W. Gladstone
Thomas A. Evans
Gregor Thompson
TYPES OF FINANCING: REAL ESTATE: Acquisitions; Partnerships/Syndications
GEOGRAPHIC LIMITS OF INVESTMENTS/LOANS: National
RANGE OF INV./LOAN PER BUSINESS: Min. $2,000,000; Max. $12,000,000

COMPANY: **Rhode Island Hospital Trust National Bank**
ADDRESS: 1 Hospital Trust Plaza
Providence, RI 02903
PHONE: (401) 278-8000

TYPE OF INSTITUTION: Pension area of a national bank
CONTACT OFFICER(S): Bernard N. Roth, Senior Vice President, Mezzamine financing for corporate buyouts
Celia R. Deluga, Assistant Vice President, Real estate financing, corporate buyout financing & financing for oil & gas properties
ASSETS: $80,000,000
INVESTMENTS/LOANS MADE: For managed accounts, Through private placements
INVESTMENTS/LOANS MADE: In securities with a secondary market and in securities without a secondary market
TYPES OF FINANCING: LOANS: Unsecured to credits above B, Baa; Other: all loans have equity features through the use of warrants, contingent interest, etc. REAL ESTATE LOANS: Intermediate-term senior mtg.; Subordinated; Wraparounds. OTHER SERVICES PROVIDED: Financing for oil & gas transactions
PREFERRED TYPES OF INDUSTRIES/INVESTMENTS: Financing for corporate buyouts: mature smoke stack manufacturing firms; Real estate financing: participating mortgages of office buildings, shopping centers, apartment complexes; Collateralized oil & gas loans, which provide a current return plus on equity sharing
WILL NOT CONSIDER: High tech firms
GEOGRAPHIC LIMITS OF INVESTMENTS/LOANS: National
RANGE OF INV./LOAN PER BUSINESS: Min. $2,000,000; Max. $20,000,000
PREFERRED TERM FOR LOANS & LEASES: Min. 7 years; Max. 12 years
BUSINESS CHARACTERISTICS DESIRED-REQUIRED: Minimum number of years in business: 5; Min. annual sales $25,000,000; Other: firms which have reasonable tangible asset coverage
REFERRALS ACCEPTED FROM: Investment/Mortgage banker or Borrower/Investee

COMPANY: **Textron Inc.**
ADDRESS: 40 Westminster Street
Providence, RI 02903
PHONE: (401) 421-2800
TYPE OF INSTITUTION: Investment Management Department
CONTACT OFFICER(S): John Lemery, Investment Manager, Corporate Private Placements
Laurens W. Goff, Investment Manager, Real Estate Investments
ASSETS: $600,000,000 under management
INVESTMENTS/LOANS MADE: For managed accounts; Through private placements
INVESTMENTS/LOANS MADE: In securities with a secondary market and in securities without a secondary market
TYPES OF FINANCING: VENTURE CAPITAL: Later-stage expansion; Buy-outs/Acquisitions, LOANS: Unsecured; Working capital (receivables/inventory); Equipment; Equity-related, REAL ESTATE LOANS: Intermediate-term senior mtg.; Subordinated; Wraparounds
PREFERRED TYPES OF INDUSTRIES/INVESTMENTS: Generally avoid regulated industries and hospitality real estate projects
WILL NOT CONSIDER: any deal without an equity feature
GEOGRAPHIC LIMITS OF INVESTMENTS/LOANS: National
RANGE OF INV./LOAN PER BUSINESS: Min. $5.0 Million; Max. $20.0 Million
PREFERRED TERM FOR LOANS & LEASES: Min. 3; Max. 12 years
BUSINESS CHARACTERISTICS DESIRED-REQUIRED: Minimum number of years in business: 3-5; Min. annual sales $5.0 Mil; Management in place 3-5 years
REFERRALS ACCEPTED FROM: Investment/Mortgage banker or Borrower/Investee

COMPANY: **Universal Financial Corporation**
ADDRESS: 56 Broad Street, P.O. Box 1014
Charleston, SC 29402
PHONE: (803) 577-4324
TYPE OF INSTITUTION: Business and financial broker
CONTACT OFFICER(S): William E. Craver, Jr., President
INVESTMENTS/LOANS MADE: For own account, Through private placements, Through underwriting public offerings
INVESTMENTS/LOANS MADE: In securities with a secondary market and in securities without a secondary market
TYPES OF FINANCING: VENTURE CAPITAL: Start-up from developed product stage; First-stage (less than 1 year); Second-stage (generally 1-3 years); Later-stage expansion; Buy-outs/Acquisitions, LOANS: Working capital (receivables/inventory); Equipment, Equity-related, REAL ESTATE LOANS: Intermediate-term senior mtg., FACTORING, LEASES: Single-investor; Operating; Tax-oriented lease brokerage; Vendor financing programs, REAL ESTATE: Acquisitions; Joint ventures, OTHER SERVICES PROVIDED: Financial consulting
GEOGRAPHIC LIMITS OF INVESTMENTS/LOANS: Regional; National
RANGE OF INV./LOAN PER BUSINESS: Min. $250,000; Max. Open
PREFERRED TERM FOR LOANS & LEASES: Min. Open; Max. Open
BUSINESS CHARACTERISTICS DESIRED-REQUIRED: Minimum number of years in business: 0
REFERRALS ACCEPTED FROM: Investment/Mortgage banker or Borrower/Investee

COMPANY: **August Kohn and Co., Inc.**
ADDRESS: P.O. Box 225
Columbia, SC 29202
PHONE: (803) 771-3710
TYPE OF INSTITUTION: Mortgage Banker
CONTACT OFFICER(S): Goerge E. Simmons, V.P.
ASSETS: Servicing Volume over $300,000,000
TYPES OF FINANCING: REAL ESTATE LOANS: Long-term senior mtg.; Intermediate-term senior mtg.; Construction
PREFERRED TYPES OF INDUSTRIES/INVESTMENTS: Shopping Centers; Office Bldgs.; Medical Blgds.; Warehouses; Apartments

GEOGRAPHIC LIMITS OF INVESTMENTS/LOANS: Regional
RANGE OF INV./LOAN PER BUSINESS: Min. $500,000
PREFERRED TERM FOR LOANS & LEASES: Min. 5-10; Max. 20+ years

COMPANY: **Bankers Mortgage**
ADDRESS: 324 W. Evans St., P.O. Box 34069
Florence, SC 29501
PHONE: (800) 562-3167
TYPE OF INSTITUTION: Mortgage Banker
CONTACT OFFICER(S): Gary Bettin, Controller
Andy Woodward, Pres.
ASSETS: Servicing Volume over $3.7 billion
TYPES OF FINANCING: REAL ESTATE LOANS: Long-term senior mtg.; Intermediate-term senior mtg.; Construction
PREFERRED TYPES OF INDUSTRIES/INVESTMENTS: No preference
GEOGRAPHIC LIMITS OF INVESTMENTS/LOANS: Regional; Southeast
RANGE OF INV./LOAN PER BUSINESS: Min. $250,000; Max. None

COMPANY: **Provident Life and Accident Insurance Company**
ADDRESS: Fountain Square
Chattanooga, TN 37402
PHONE: (615) 755-1564
CONTACT OFFICER(S): Sam E. Miles, V.P.
John Van Wickler, Sr. V.P.,
A. V. Keyes, V.P., Equity
David Fussell, V.P., Securities & P.P.
Jack R. McNutt V.P. Mtg. Loan & R.E.
ASSETS: $3,194,000,000
TYPES OF FINANCING: LOANS, REAL ESTATE LOANS: Intermediate-term senior mtg., OTHER SERVICES PROVIDED: Equity financing in joint ventures
PREFERRED TYPES OF INDUSTRIES/INVESTMENTS: Shopping centers; medical office buildings
WILL NOT CONSIDER: Farm; Industrial (except distribution); Manufacturing
GEOGRAPHIC LIMITS OF INVESTMENTS/LOANS: National
RANGE OF INV./LOAN PER BUSINESS: Min. $1 million; Max. $24 million
PREFERRED TERM FOR LOANS & LEASES: Max. 10+ years

COMPANY: **Boyle Commercial Mortgage Co.**
ADDRESS: 5900 Poplar Av., P.O. Box 17800
Memphis, TN 38117
PHONE: (901) 767-0100
TYPE OF INSTITUTION: Mortgage Banker
CONTACT OFFICER(S): Richard Nichol, V.P.
ASSETS: Servicing Volume over $100,000,000
TYPES OF FINANCING: REAL ESTATE LOANS
PREFERRED TERM FOR LOANS & LEASES: Max. 20+ years
REMARKS: Strictly Commercial Mortgages Now

COMPANY: **Commerce McGehee Mortgage, Inc.**
ADDRESS: 6055 Primacy Parkway
Memphis, TN 38119
PHONE: (901) 766-8500
TYPE OF INSTITUTION: Mortgage Banker
CONTACT OFFICER(S): J. Davant Latham, Sr. V.P., Income Property Finance, Financing of income producing real estate
INVESTMENTS/LOANS MADE: Through private placements
TYPES OF FINANCING: REAL ESTATE LOANS: Long-term senior mtg.; Intermediate-term senior mtg.; Subordinated; Wraparounds; Construction; Gap; Standbys; Industrial revenue bonds; Other: Sale/Leaseback Transactions. REAL ESTATE: Acquisitions; Joint ventures.
PREFERRED TYPES OF INDUSTRIES/INVESTMENTS: General purpose real estate: Office buildings, Warehouse or Light manufacturing, Combination office/warehouse. Apartments; Retail (shopping centers & free standing); Hotel/Motel
WILL NOT CONSIDER: Raw land, Land development
GEOGRAPHIC LIMITS OF INVESTMENTS/LOANS: National
RANGE OF INV./LOAN PER BUSINESS: Min. $1,000,000 ($500,000 local)
PREFERRED TERM FOR LOANS & LEASES: Max. 10-15 years
BUSINESS CHARACTERISTICS DESIRED-REQUIRED: Other: No fixed requirements—Real Estate Lender
REFERRALS ACCEPTED FROM: Investment/Mortgage banker only

COMPANY: **DeSoto Capital Corporation**
ADDRESS: 60 North Third Street
Memphis, TN
PHONE: (901) 523-6894
TYPE OF INSTITUTION: Financing: Venture capital, loans, equity/debt related
CONTACT OFFICER(S): Damon S. Arney, President
INVESTMENTS/LOANS MADE: For own account, For managed accounts, Through private placements
INVESTMENTS/LOANS MADE: In securities with or without a secondary market
TYPES OF FINANCING: VENTURE CAPITAL: Start-up from developed product stage; First-stage; Second-stage; Later-stage expansion; Buy-outs/Acquisitions. LOANS: Other. REAL ESTATE LOANS. REAL ESTATE: Acquisitions; Joint ventures
GEOGRAPHIC LIMITS OF INVESTMENTS/LOANS: Regional
RANGE OF INV./LOAN PER BUSIINESS: Min. $25,000; Max. $100,000
PREFERRED TERM FOR LOANS & LEASES: Min. 5-7 years; Max. 7-10 years
REFERRALS ACCEPTED FROM: Investment/Mortgage banker or Borrower/Investee

COMPANY: **First Tennessee Bank National Association**
ADDRESS: 165 Madison Avenue
Memphis, TN 38103
PHONE: (901) 523-4632
TYPE OF INSTITUTION: Commercial Finance Division of National Bank

TENNESSEE

CONTACT OFFICER(S): Joseph D. Hardesty, Jr., Senior Vice President, Division Manager
Larry Allen, Vice President, Senior Loan Officer
ASSETS: $5 Billion Approximately
INVESTMENTS/LOANS MADE: For own account
TYPES OF FINANCING: LOANS: Working capital; Equipment; Other: Leveraged buy-outs and acquisitions. REAL ESTATE LOANS: Intermediate-term senior mtg.; Industrial revenue bonds. INTERNATIONAL
PREFERRED TYPES OF INDUSTRIES/INVESTMENTS: Textiles/Apparel; Leisure/Sporting Goods; Chemicals; Automative Aftermarket; Food Processors/Distributors; Industrial Supplies.
GEOGRAPHIC LIMITS OF INVESTMENTS/LOANS: Other: Five hundred mile radius of Memphis, Tennessee.
RANGE OF INV./LOAN PER BUSINESS: Min. $1,000,000; Max. $25,000,000
PREFERRED TERM FOR LOANS & LEASES: Min. 3 years; Max. 7 years
BUSINESS CHARACTERISTICS DESIRED-REQUIRED: Minimum number of years in business: 2; Min. annual sales $5,000,000; Min. net worth $200,000; Min. annual net income $100,000; Min. annual cash flow $100,000.
REFERRALS ACCEPTED FROM: Investment/Mortgage banker or Borrower/Investee

COMPANY: **General Innkeeping Acceptance Corporation**
ADDRESS: P.O. Box 18127
Memphis, TN 38195
PHONE: (901) 362-4426
TYPE OF INSTITUTION: Finance/Leasing, Subsidiary of Holiday Inns, Inc.
CONTACT OFFICER(S): E. Tucker Dickerson, President
Bill Horne, Vice President
ASSETS: $25,000,000
INVESTMENTS/LOANS MADE: For own account
INVESTMENTS/LOANS MADE: Only in securities without a secondary market
TYPES OF FINANCING: LOANS: Equipment. REAL ESTATE LOANS: Subordinated. LEASES: Tax leases; Operating.
PREFERRED TYPES OF INDUSTRIES/INVESTMENTS: Hotel and Restaurant Furniture, Fixtures and Equipment
WILL NOT CONSIDER: Anything except above
GEOGRAPHIC LIMITS OF INVESTMENTS/LOANS: National
RANGE OF INV./LOAN PER BUSINESS: Min. $25,000; Max. $2,800,000
PREFERRED TERM FOR LOANS & LEASES: Min. 5 years; Max. 7 years
BUSINESS CHARACTERISTICS DESIRED-REQUIRED: Minimum number of years in business: 0
REFERRALS ACCEPTED FROM: Investment/Mortgage banker or Borrower/Investee

COMPANY: **Dobson & Johnson, Inc.**
ADDRESS: 1 Commerce Place, Ste. 1800
Nashville, TN 37239
PHONE: (615) 244-8600
CONTACT OFFICER(S): Albert W. Johnson II., Pres.
Brian Johnson, V.P.
ASSETS: $200 million
INVESTMENTS/LOANS MADE: Through private placements
TYPES OF FINANCING: VENTURE CAPITAL: Later-stage expansion; Buy-outs/Acquisitions, REAL ESTATE LOANS: Long-term senior mtg.; Intermediate-term senior mtg.; Subordinated; Wraparounds; Land; Land development; Construction; Gap; Standbys, LEASES: Single-investor; Leveraged; Operating; Tax-oriented lease brokerage, REAL ESTATE: Acquisitions; Joint ventures; Partnerships/Syndications
WILL NOT CONSIDER: Special purpose or industry specific
GEOGRAPHIC LIMITS OF INVESTMENTS/LOANS: International
RANGE OF INV./LOAN PER BUSINESS: Min. $1 million
BUSINESS CHARACTERISTICS DESIRED-REQUIRED: Other: Must have proven track record
REFERRALS ACCEPTED FROM: Investment/Mortgage banker or Borrower/Investee

COMPANY: **Freeman Mortgage Corporation**
ADDRESS: 2517 Lebanon Road
Nashville, TN 37214
PHONE: (615) 889-8250
TYPE OF INSTITUTION: Mortgage Banking Affiliate
CONTACT OFFICER(S): John G. Greer
ASSETS: $20,000,000
INVESTMENTS/LOANS MADE: For own account
INVESTMENTS/LOANS MADE: Only in securities without a secondary market
TYPES OF FINANCING: REAL ESTATE LOANS: Long-term senior mtg.; Intermediate-term senior mtg.; Subordinated; Wraparounds
PREFERRED TYPES OF INDUSTRIES/INVESTMENTS: Investment Real Estate
GEOGRAPHIC LIMITS OF INVESTMENTS/LOANS: Regional
RANGE OF INV./LOAN PER BUSINESS: Min. $100,000; Max. $100,000
PREFERRED TERM FOR LOANS & LEASES: Min. 3 years; Max. 30 years
BUSINESS CHARACTERISTICS DESIRED-REQUIRED: Minimum number of years in business: 3; Min. annual sales $1,000,000
REFERRALS ACCEPTED FROM: Investment/Mortgage banker or Borrower/Investee

COMPANY: **Life and Casualty Insurance Company of Tennessee**
ADDRESS: American General Center
Nashville, TN 37250
PHONE: (615) 749-2000
CONTACT OFFICER(S): J. P. Ellis, Jr., V.P.
ASSETS: $100 million and up
TYPES OF FINANCING: REAL ESTATE LOANS: Long-term senior mtg.; Intermediate-term senior mtg.
PREFERRED TYPES OF INDUSTRIES/INVESTMENTS: Shopping centers; industrial buildings
GEOGRAPHIC LIMITS OF INVESTMENTS/LOANS: Regional

RANGE OF INV./LOAN PER BUSINESS: Min. $500,000; Max. $2,000,000
PREFERRED TERM FOR LOANS & LEASES: Min. 15-20 years; Max. 20+ years
REFERRALS ACCEPTED FROM: Investment/Mortgage banker or Borrower/Investee
REMARKS: Sub. of American General Life, Houston, TX

COMPANY: **Third National Mortgage Co.**
ADDRESS: P.O. Box 2628
Nashville, TN 37219
PHONE: (615) 748-4088
TYPE OF INSTITUTION: Mortgage Banker
CONTACT OFFICER(S): Kenneth E. Reynolds, Pres.

COMPANY: **Lumbermen's Investment Corporation**
ADDRESS: P.O. Box 40
Austin, TX 78767
PHONE: (512) 477-6561
TYPE OF INSTITUTION: Mortgage Banker
CONTACT OFFICER(S): Joseph L. Maverick, Senior V.P., Commercial Loans
ASSETS: Loans serviced: 2.5 billion
TYPES OF FINANCING:REAL ESTATE LOANS: Long-term senior mtg.; Wraparounds; Construction; Gap; Standbys; REAL ESTATE: Joint ventures, OTHER SERVICES PROVIDED: Real estate loans and joint ventures arranged on apartments, office buildings, shopping centers, office/warehouse and free standing retail.
GEOGRAPHIC LIMITS OF INVESTMENTS/LOANS: National
RANGE OF INV./LOANS PER BUSINESS: Min. $1,000,000; Max. $50,000,000
BRANCHES: Texas, Tennesee, Oklahoma, Minnesota

COMPANY: **National Western Life Insurance Co.**
ADDRESS: Hwy. 183 at I.H. 35, 850 E. Anderson
Austin, TX 78776
PHONE: (512) 836-1010
CONTACT OFFICER(S): Lee Posey, V.P., Public Relations
ASSETS: $100 million and up
TYPES OF FINANCING: LOANS: Working capital (receivables/inventory); Equipment; Equity-related; Loan guarantees, REAL ESTATE LOANS
PREFERRED TYPES OF INDUSTRIES/INVESTMENTS: Diversified
GEOGRAPHIC LIMITS OF INVESTMENTS/LOANS: National
PREFERRED TERM FOR LOANS & LEASES: Max. 20 + years
REFERRALS ACCEPTED FROM: Investment/Mortgage banker or Borrower/Investee

COMPANY: **Alliance Investment Corporation**
ADDRESS: 1201 Elm St., Ste. 5200
Dallas, TX 75270
CONTACT OFFICER(S): J. K. Lanyon, Sr. V.P., Securities — (214) 653-4242
Ken Peugh, Assoc. V.P., Mtg. Loans — (214) 653-2753
ASSETS: $100 million and up
INVESTMENTS/LOANS MADE: In securities with a secondary market and in securities without a secondary market
TYPES OF FINANCING: LOANS, REAL ESTATE LOANS: Long-term senior mtg.; Intermediate-term senior mtg.
GEOGRAPHIC LIMITS OF INVESTMENTS/LOANS: National
PREFERRED TERM FOR LOANS & LEASES: Min. 10-15; Max. 20+ years
BUSINESS CHARACTERISTICS DESIRED-REQUIRED: Minimum number of years in business: 5; Min. net worth of $10 million for R.E. loans & $50 million for other loans; No payment default for prior 5 years
REFERRALS ACCEPTED FROM: Investment/Mortgage banker or Borrower/Investee
REMARKS: Range of $1. million — 5 million for Loans; $750,000-3,000,000 for R. E. Loans

COMPANY: **First City Mortgage Company**
ADDRESS: 5999 Summerside Dr., 200
Dallas, TX 75252
PHONE: (214) 733-4500
TYPE OF INSTITUTION: Mortgage Banker
CONTACT OFFICER(S): Jimmy A. Nail, President
Cchristopher G. Griffith, V.P.
TYPES OF FINANCING: REAL ESTATE LOANS: Long-term senior mtg.; Intermediate-term senior mtg.; Subordinated; Wraparounds; Land development; construction; Gap; Standbys; Industrial revenue bonds, REAL ESTATE: Acquisitions; Joint ventures; Partnerships
PREFERRED TYPES OF INDUSTRIES/INVESTMENTS: Commercial
WILL NOT CONSIDER: Residential
GEOGRAPHIC LIMITS OF INVESTMENTS/LOANS: Regional; Other: TX, OK, NM, LA, FL, CO
RANGE OF INV./LOAN PER BUSINESS: Min. $500,000; Max. None
PREFERRED TERM FOR LOANS & LEASES: Max. 15 years

COMPANY: **First Texas Savings Association**
ADDRESS: 14951 Dallas Parkway, P.O. Box 4248
Dallas, TX 75240
PHONE: (214) 960-4500
TYPE OF INSTITUTION: Mortgage Banker
CONTACT OFFICER(S): Robert T. Stafford, Mgr. and VP of Comm. RE
Rita Sesona Juster, Mgr. and VP of Comm. RE
Richard Cacas, Mgr. and VP of Comm. RE
Wiliam David Watson, Mgr. and VP Special Lending
ASSETS: $7,000,000,000
TYPES OF FINANCING: REAL ESTATE LOANS: Wraparounds; Land; Land development; Construction; Gap; Industrial revenue bonds
PREFERRED TYPES OF INDUSTRIES/INVESTMENTS: General income producing properties
WILL NOT CONSIDER: Condominiums
GEOGRAPHIC LIMITS OF INVESTMENTS/LOANS: National
RANGE OF INV./LOAN PER BUSINESS: Min. $500,000; Max. $50,000,000
PREFERRED TERMS FOR LOANS & LEASES: Min. 5 years

COMPANY: **Garvan, Inc.**
ADDRESS: 900 Meadows Bldg.
Dallas, TX 75206
PHONE: (214) 691-0711
TYPE OF INSTITUTION: Real Estate Development Co.
CONTACT OFFICER(S): Guy Griffith, V.P.
ASSETS: $7,000,000
INVESTMENTS/LOANS MADE: For own account
INVESTMENTS/LOANS MADE: In securities with a secondary market; In securities without a secondary market
TYPES OF FINANCING: SECONDARY-MARKET CORPORATE SECURITIES; VENTURE CAPITAL; LOANS: Working capital; Equity-related, REAL ESTATE LOANS: Long-term senior mtg.; Intermediate-term senior mtg.; Subordinated; Land; Land developement, REAL ESTATE: Acquisitions; Joint ventures
GEOGRAPHIC LIMITS OF INVESTMENTS/LOANS: Local
RANGE OF INV./LOAN PER BUSINESS: Min. $250,000; Max. $1,500,000
BUSINESS CHARACTERISTICS DESIRED-REQUIRED: Minimum number of years in business: 0; Other: Good management
REFERRALS ACCEPTED FROM: Investment/Mortgage banker; Borrower/Investee

COMPANY: **Glenn Justice Mortgage Company, Inc.**
ADDRESS: 505 N. Ervay
Dallas, TX 75201
PHONE: (214) 651-1150
CONTACT OFFICER(S): James A. Justice

COMPANY: **Hinton Mortgage and Investment Company**
ADDRESS: 10830 North Central Expressway
Dallas, TX 75231
PHONE: (214) 691-6000
TYPE OF INSTITUTION: Mortgage Banker
CONTACT OFFICER(S): Richard Campbell, VP Secondary Marketing
TYPES OF FINANCING: REAL ESTATE LOANS: Land development; Construction, REAL ESTATE: Joint ventures
PREFERRED TYPES OF INDUSTRIES/INVESTMENTS: Construction, Land development; Communications
GEOGRAPHIC LIMITS OF INVESTMENTS/LOANS: Regional
RANGE OF INV./LOAN PER BUSINESS: Min. $50,000
PREFERRED TERM FOR LOANS & LEASES: Min. 6 months (const); 7 (commercial)

COMPANY: **Jones-Cox Mortgage Corporation**
ADDRESS: 400 North Olive, 3319 Southland Center LB 246
Dallas, TX 75201
PHONE: (214) 754-7000
TYPE OF INSTITUTION: Mortgage Banker
CONTACT OFFICER(S): John C. Cox, Jr., President & CEO
ASSETS: $300,000,000 in servicing volume
TYPES OF FINANCING: REAL ESTATE: Long-term senior mtg.; Subordinated; Standbys; Industrial revenue bonds, REAL ESTATE: Joint ventures
PREFERRED TYPES OF INDUSTRIES/INVESTMENTS: Apartments, Office buildings, Retail, Office showrooms/warehouse, Medical clinics; On case basis: Budget motels, Mini warehouses, Mobile home parks
WILL NOT CONSIDER: Hospitals, Nursing homes
GEOGRAPHIC LIMITS OF INVESTMENTS/LOANS: State; Other: Texas
RANGE OF INV./LOAN PER BUSINESS: Min. $500,000; Max. $50,000,000
PREFERRED TERM FOR LOANS & LEASES: Min. 5 years; Max. 10 years

COMPANY: **Kirby Mortgage & Investments, Inc.**
ADDRESS: 3131 Turtle Creek Boulevard, Suite 1125
Dallas, TX 75219
PHONE: (214) 522-2670
TYPE OF INSTITUTION: Mortgage Banker
CONTACT OFFICER(S): Fred A. Brown, V.P.
Jim F. Kirby, President
TYPES OF FINANCING: REAL ESTATE LOANS: Long-term senior mtg.; Intermediate-term senior mtg.; Wraparounds, Standbys; REAL ESTATE: Acqui sitions; Joint ventures
PREFERRED TYPES OF INDUSTRIES/INVESTMENTS: Commercial income producting properties
GEOGRAPHIC LIMITS OF INVESTMENTS/LOANS: National
RANGE OF INV./LOAN PER BUSINESS: Min. $500,000
PREFERRED TERM FOR LOANS & LEASES: Min. 3 years; Max. 10; 30 years

COMPANY: **L&N Housing Corp.**
ADDRESS: 2001 Bryan Tower 3600
Dallas, TX 75201
PHONE: (214) 746-7111
CONTACT OFFICER(S): Carey B. Wickland
ASSETS: $50,000,000
TYPES OF FINANCING: REAL ESTATE LOANS: Other: Land purchase lease bank and leasehold mtg.
PREFERRED TYPES OF INDUSTRIES/INVESTMENTS: Multi-family land and mtg. participating
GEOGRAPHIC LIMITS OF INVESTMENTS/LOANS: Regional; Other: Sunbelt U.S.
RANGE OF INV./LOAN PER BUSINESS: Min. $5,000,000; Max. $10,000,000
PREFERRED TERM FOR LOANS & LEASES: Min. 5 years

COMPANY: **Lomas & Nettleton Mortgage Investors**
ADDRESS: 2001 Bryan Tower, P.O. Box 225644
Dallas, TX 75265
PHONE: (214) 746-7111
TYPE OF INSTITUTION: REIT
CONTACT OFFICER(S): Ted Enloe, Pres; Carey Wickland, SVP—Underwriting
ASSETS: $315,000,000
INVESTMENTS/LOANS MADE: For own account

TYPES OF FINANCING: REAL ESTATE LOANS: Land; Land development; Construction
PREFERRED TYPES OF INDUSTRIES/INVESTMENTS: Construction Loans - Short term
WILL NOT CONSIDER: Resorts
GEOGRAPHIC LIMITS OF INVESTMENTS/LOANS: Regional; National; Other: Sunbelt
RANGE OF INV./LOAN PER BUSINESS: Min. $1,000,000; Max. $10,000,000
PREFERRED TERM FOR LOANS & LEASES: Min. 6 months; Max. 3 years
BUSINESS CHARACTERISTICS DESIRED-REQUIRED: Other: Quality developers

COMPANY: **The Lomas & Nettleton Co.**
ADDRESS: 2001 Bryan Tower, 36th Floor
Dallas, TX 75201
PHONE: (214) 746-7111
TYPE OF INSTITUTION: Mortgage Banker
CONTACT OFFICER(S): Charles W. Wingo, Ex. V.P.
ASSETS: $19 billion servicing volume
TYPES OF FINANCING: REAL ESTATE LOANS: Other: All types of permanent & interim financing
GEOGRAPHIC LIMITS OF INVESTMENTS/LOANS: National
RANGE OF INV./LOAN PER BUSINESS: Min. $3 million

COMPANY: **MBank Preston**
ADDRESS: 8111 Preston Road
Dallas, TX 75225
PHONE: (214) 363-1511
CONTACT OFFICER(S): Mike Corley, S. VP
Tim Loudermilk,S. VP
ASSETS: $600,000,000
TYPES OF FINANCING: REAL ESTATE LOANS: Intermediate-term senior mtg.; Subordinated; Land; Land development; Construction, REAL ESTATE: Acquisitions; Joint ventures; Partnerships/Syndications
PREFERRED TYPES OF INDUSTRIES/INVESTMENTS: Commercial
GEOGRAPHIC LIMITS OF INVESTMENTS/LOANS: Local
PREFERRED TERM FOR LOANS & LEASES: Min. 3 years

COMPANY: **MBC Financial Services Corporation**
ADDRESS: 2501 Cedar Springs Road, Suite 400, LB 10
Dallas, TX 75201
PHONE: (214) 871-1200
TYPE OF INSTITUTION: Corporate Finance Group of Institutional Lender
CONTACT OFFICER(S): J. Michael McMahon, Senior Vice President
David S. Temin, Vice President
Lynne M. McGanity, Vice President
ASSETS: $500 million
INVESTMENTS/LOANS MADE: For own account
INVESTMENTS/LOANS MADE: In securities with a secondary market and in securities without a secondary market
TYPES OF FINANCING: SECONDARY MARKET CORPORATE SECURITIES: Bonds; Other: Subordinated loans, secured note financing; VENTURE CAPITAL: Later-stage expansion; Buy-outs/Acquisitions; LOANS: Unsecured; Working Capital; Equipment; REAL ESTATE LOANS: Intermediate-term senior mtg.; Wraparounds; Gap; Standbys; LEASES: Single-investor; Leveraged; Tax leases; Non-tax leases
GEOGRAPHIC LIMITS OF INVESTMENTS/LOANS: Regional
RANGE OF INV./LOAN PER BUSINESS: Min. $5 Million; Max. $20 Million
PREFERRED TERM FOR LOANS & LEASES: Min. 3 years; Max. 10 years
BUSINESS CHARACTERISTICS DESIRED-REQUIRED: Minimum number of years in business: 5; Min. annual sales $7 Million; Min. net worth $1 Million; Min. annual net income $1.5 Million; Min. annual cash flow $2 Million
REFERRALS ACCEPTED FROM: Investment/Mortgage banker or Borrower/Investee

COMPANY: **Mercantile National Bank at Dallas**
ADDRESS: 1704 Main Street
Dallas TX 75201
PHONE: (214) 698-6000
CONTACT OFFICER(S): Michael N. Maberry, E. V.P.

COMPANY: **The Murray Investment Company**
ADDRESS: 5550 LBJ Freeway, Suite 950, P.O. Box 809039
Dallas, TX 75240
PHONE: (214) 851-6400
TYPE OF INSTITUTION: Multi Faceted Real Estate - Mortgage Banker
CONTACT OFFICER(S): Ray Rogers, A.V.P.
David Meneek, S.V.P. In Charge of Commercial Lending for Murray Savings
TYPES OF FINANCING: REAL ESTATE LOANS: Long-term senior mtg.; Intermediate-term senior mtg.; Subordinated; Wraparounds; Land; Land development; Construction; Gap, REAL ESTATE: Acquisitions; Joint ventures; Partnerships/Syndications
PREFERRED TYPES OF INDUSTRIES/INVESTMENTS: All types commercial
WILL NOT CONSIDER: Special purpose
GEOGRAPHIC LIMITS OF INVESTMENTS/LOANS: Regional; Other: Sunbelt and Southeast; CO
RANGE OF INV./LOAN PER BUSINESS: Min. $1,000,000; Max. $30,000,000
PREFERRED TERM FOR LOANS & LEASES: Min. Intermediate

COMPANY: **MVenture Corp.**
ADDRESS: P.O. Box 222090
Dallas, TX
PHONE: (214) 741-1469
TYPE OF INSTITUTION: Small Business Investment Company
CONTACT OFFICER(S): Tom Mitchell, Investment Officer
Ted Walker, Investment Officer
ASSETS: $60,000,000.00
INVESTMENTS/LOANS MADE: For own account

INVESTMENTS/LOANS MADE: Only in securities without a secondary market
TYPES OF FINANCING: VENTURE CAPITAL: Later-stage expansion; Buy-outs/Acquisitions; LOANS: Equipment; Equity-related; REAL ESTATE LOANS: Long-term senior mtg.
PREFERRED TYPES OF INDUSTRIES/INVESTMENTS: Basic Manufacturing; Communications; Health Care; Distribution
GEOGRAPHIC LIMITS OF INVESTMENTS/LOANS: State
RANGE OF INV./LOAN PER BUSINESS: Min. $250,000; Max. $3,000,000
PREFERRED TERM FOR LOANS & LEASES: Min. 5; Max. 10 (with 20 amort) years
BUSINESS CHARACTERISTICS DESIRED-REQUIRED: Minimum number of years in business: 3; Min. annual sales $2,000,000
REFERRALS ACCEPTED FROM: Investment/Mortgage banker or Borrower/Investee

COMPANY: **Republic Bank Dallas**
ADDRESS: P.O. Box 225961, Ervay and Pacific Streets
Dallas, TX 75265
PHONE: (214) 653-5000
TYPE OF INSTITUTION: Real Estate Banking Group
CONTACT OFFICER(S): Joe Fortson, Managing Director, (214) 922-5905
Tom Covert, E.V.P., (214) 922-6666
John Hamstra, E.V.P., Houston, (713) 247-6909
Tony Levatino, E.V.P. Austin, (512) 476-6711
ASSETS: $4,000,000,000 (Real Estate)
TYPES OF FINANCING: REAL ESTATE LOANS: Land; Construction, REAL ESTATE: Acquisitions; Joint ventures
WILL NOT CONSIDER: Longterm loans
GEOGRAPHIC LIMITS OF INVESTMENTS/LOANS: National
RANGE OF INV./LOAN PER BUSINESS: Max. $100,000,000
PREFERRED TERM FOR LOANS & LEASES: Max. 36 months
BRANCHES: John Hamstra, Republic Bank Houston, P.O. Box 299001, Houston, TX 77299, (713) 247-6909
Tony Levatino, Republic Bank Austin, P.O. 1328, Austin, TX 78767, (512) 476-6711

COMPANY: **STM Mortgage Co.**
ADDRESS: 2355 Stemmons Frwy.
Dallas, TX 75207
PHONE: (214) 637-4950
TYPE OF INSTITUTION: Mortgage Banker
CONTACT OFFICER(S): William Ross, S.V.P. Commercial
ASSETS: $2.5 billion
TYPES OF FINANCING: REAL ESTATE LOANS: Long-term senior mtg.; Intermediate-term senior mtg.; Other; Residential purchase money seconds
PREFERRED TYPES OF INDUSTRIES/INVESTMENTS: Varied
WILL NOT CONSIDER: Special purpose; Heavy industrial
GEOGRAPHIC LIMITS OF INVESTMENTS/LOANS: National
RANGE OF INV./LOAN PER BUSINESS: Min. $1 million
BRANCHES: Austin, TX

COMPANY: **Teeling Mortgage Company, Inc.**
ADDRESS: 13566 Floyd Circle, Ste D
Dallas, TX 75243
PHONE: (214) 437-1875
CONTACT OFFICER(S): James J. Teeling, President

COMPANY: **Texas American Bank, Dallas North**
ADDRESS: 100 Exchange Park
Dallas, TX 75235
PHONE: (214) 353-8100
TYPE OF INSTITUTION: R. E. Lender
CONTACT OFFICER(S): Ellen Jones

COMPANY: **Texas Commerce Bank - Dallas**
ADDRESS: Commerce Bank Tower (P.O. Box 222265, Zip 75266-0197)
Dallas, TX 75201
PHONE: (214) 922-2300
TYPE OF INSTITUTION: R. E. Lender
CONTACT OFFICER(S): Richard N. Quisenberry, S. V.P.

COMPANY:**Interfirst Bank/Fort Worth, NA**
ADDRESS: One Burnett Plaza, P.O. Box 2260
Fort Worth, TX 76102
PHONE: (817) 390-6161
CONTACT OFFICER(S): James W. Jones, S.V.P.
Lyle E. Mayeaux, V.P.
Michael Henry, V.P.
ASSETS: $2,000,000,000
TYPES OF FINANCING: REAL EASTATE LOANS: Intermediate-term senior mtg; Land; Land development; Construction; Gap; Other: Short-term, REAL ESTATE: Acquisitions
PREFERRED TYPES OF INDUSTRIES/INVESTMENTS: Primarily interim construction lending and development
GEOGRAPHIC LIMITS OF INVESTMENTS/LOANS: State
RANGE OF INV./LOAN PER BUSINESS: Min. $250,000 - $500,000

COMPANY: **Foster Mortgage Corp.**
ADDRESS: 6000 Western Place
Ft. Worth, TX 76107
PHONE: (817) 777-9000
TYPE OF INSTITUTION: Mortgage Corporation
CONTACT OFFICER(S): W.F. McCarver, V.P., Commercial Loans
ASSETS: $2.5 billion
INVESTMENTS/LOANS MADE: For own account; For managed accounts; Through private placements; Through underwriting public offerings
TYPES OF FINANCING: LOANS: Other: Mortgage REAL ESTATE LOANS: Long-term senior mtg.; Construction; Standbys; Industrial revenue bonds; REAL ESTATE: Joint ventures

GEOGRAPHIC LIMITS OF INVESTMENTS/LOANS: State
RANGE OF INV./LOAN PER BUSINESS: Min. $100,000; Max. $ 10,000,000

COMPANY: **Harber - Stephenson, Inc.**
ADDRESS: 1001 Winscott Rd.
Ft. Worth, TX 76126
PHONE: (817) 249-2333
TYPE OF INSTITUTION: Mortgage Bank
CONTACT OFFICER(S): Earl C. Stephenson, Jr., President

COMPANY: **Texas American Bank/Ft. Worth, N.A.**
ADDRESS: 500 Throckmorton Street
Ft. Worth, TX 76113
PHONE: (817) 338-8011
CONTACT OFFICER(S): Royce L. Lee, S. V.P.

COMPANY: **American General Investment Corp.**
ADDRESS: P.O. Box 1375
Houston, TX 77251
PHONE: (713) 522-1111
TYPE OF INSTITUTION: Mortgage banker
CONTACT OFFICER(S): J.J. Gray, Jr., President
Ed James Sr. V.P.
ASSETS: $10,000,000-100,000,000
TYPES OF FINANCING: REAL ESTATE LOANS: Long-term senior mtg.; Intermediate-term senior mtg.; Land; Land development; Construction; Other: Interim financing, REAL ESTATE: Acquisitions; Joint ventures; Partnerships/Syndications
PREFERRED TYPES OF INDUSTRIES/INVESTMENTS: Apartments; Office buildings
GEOGRAPHIC LIMITS OF INVESTMENTS/LOANS: State; Regional
BRANCHES: David Brown, P.O. Drawer 31425, Dallas, TX 75231; (214) 691-4851
Bob Parkinson, 2939 Mossrock Rd., Suite 130, San Antonio, TX 78230; (512) 341-7204

COMPANY: **American Mortgage Co.**
ADDRESS: 2625 Louisiana St.
Houston, TX 77006
PHONE: (713) 525-7600
TYPE OF INSTITUTION: Mortgage Banker
CONTACT OFFICER(S): Frank Gentry, Pres.
TYPES OF FINANCING: REAL ESTATE LOANS: Long-term senior mtg.; Standbys
GEOGRAPHIC LIMITS OF INVESTMENTS/LOANS: Regional; TX & S.W. United States
RANGE OF INV./LOAN PER BUSINESS: Min. $1,000,000
PREFERRED TERM FOR LOANS & LEASES: Max. 20+ years

COMPANY: **Commonwealth Financial Group**
ADDRESS: 2223 W. Loop So., P.O. Box 1529
Houston, TX 77251
PHONE: (7139 439-7200
TYPE OF INSTITUTION: REIT
CONTACT OFFICER(S): W.E. Daniels, Chairman of the Board
Joe Flynch, President
ASSETS: $75,000,000
TYPES OF FINANCING: REAL ESTATE LOANS: Subordinated; Wraparounds; Land; Land development; Construction; Gap; Standbys; Other: Shorter term, REAL ESTATE: Joint ventures
GEOGRAPHIC LIMITS OF INVESTMENTS/LOANS: Principal cities in AZ, NM, TX, OK
RANGE OF INV./LOAN PER BUSINESS: Max. $5,000,000
PREFERRED TERM FOR LOANS & LEASES: Max. 3 years
BUSINESS CHARACTERISTICS DESIRED-REQUIRED: Other: Must have track record

COMPANY: **Commonwealth Financial Group Real Estate Investment Trust**
ADDRESS: 2223 West Loop South, P.O. Box 1529
(Zip-77251)
Houston, TX 77027
PHONE: (713) 439-7200; 626-3870
TYPE OF INSTITUTION: REIT
CONTACT OFFICER(S): Russ Williams, Chief Accountant
W. E. Daniels, Chairman of the Board
Joe F. Lynch, President
ASSETS: $70,500,000
TYPES OF FINANCING: REAL ESTATE LOANS: Land; Land development; Construction; Other: 1st mortgage
PREFERRED TYPES OF INDUSTRIES/INVESTMENTS: Residential; Small commercial projects; Apartments; Shopping centers
WILL NOT CONSIDER: Large projects
GEOGRAPHIC LIMITS OF INVESTMENTS/LOANS: Regional; Other: Southwest
RANGE OF INV./LOAN PER BUSINESS: Min. $500,000; Max. $5 million
PREFERRED TERM FOR LOANS & LEASES: Min. 1 years; Max. 3 years
BUSINESS CHARACTERISTICS DESIRED-REQUIRED: Other: Area preference
BRANCHES: First Continental Mortgage Corp., Dallas, TX; Tulsa, OK ;San Antonio, TX; Albuquerque, NM

COMPANY: **Commonwealth Mortgage Corporation**
ADDRESS: 2223 W. Loop South
Houston TX 77251
PHONE: (713) 439-7200
TYPE OF INSTITUTION: Mortgage Bank
CONTACT OFFICER(S): Tom Frankoviak

COMPANY:**L.J. Melody & Company**
ADDRESS: One Riverway, Suite 1850
Houston, TX 77056
PHONE: (713) 877-1187
TYPE OF INSTITUTION: Mortgage Banking
CONTACT OFFICER(S): Doug Bickser
TYPES OF FINANCING: REAL ESTATE LOANS: Long-term senior mtg.; Intermediate-term senior mtg., REAL ESTATE: Acquisitions; Joint ventures

PREFERRED TYPES OF INDUSTRIES/INVESTMENTS: Office buildings; Industrial; Apartments; Hotels; Shopping centers
GEOGRAPHIC LIMITS OF INVESTMENTS/LOANS: State; Other: Southwest
RANGE OF INV./LOAN PER BUSINESS: Min. $5 million
PREFERRED TERM FOR LOANS & LEASES: Min. 5 years; Max. 10 years

COMPANY:**Kinghorn, Driver & Company**
ADDRESS: 11 Greenway Plaza, Suite 120
Houston, TX 77046
PHONE: (713) 850-8961
TYPE OF INSTITUTION: Mortgage banking
CONTACT OFFICER(S): Ray Driver III, E. V.P.
TYPES OF FINANCING: REAL ESTATE LOANS: Long-term senior mtg.; Intermediate-term senior mtg.; Subordinated; Wraparounds; Land; Construction; Standbys; Industrial revenue bonds, REAL ESATE: Acquisitions; Joint ventures; Partnerships/Syndications
PREFERRED TYPES OF INDUSTRIES/INVESTMENTS: Commercial income producing properties
GEOGRAPHIC LIMITS OF INVESTMENTS/LOANS: National
RANGE OF INV./LOAN PER BUSINESS: Min. None
PREFERRED TERM FOR LOANS & LEASES: Min. 1 year; Max. 15 years

COMPANY:**Johnson-Randolph Mortgage Company**
ADDRESS: 1880 Dairy Ashford, Suite 200
Houston, TX 77077
PHONE: (713) 870-9200
TYPE OF INSTITUTION: Mortgage banker
CONTACT OFFICER(S): John D. Birdwell, V.P.
TYPES OF FINANCING: REAL ESTATE LOANS: Long-term senior mtg.; Intermediate-term senior mtg.; Wraparounds; Land development; Construction, REAL ESTATE: Acquisitions; Joint ventures
PREFERRED TYPES OF INDUSTRIES/INVESTMENTS: Income producing properties
GEOGRAPHIC LIMITS OF INVESTMENTS/LOANS: Regional: Texas and Sunbelt
RANGE OF INV./LOAN PER BUSINESS: Min. $1 million; Max. $10 million

COMPANY:**Holliday, Fenoglio & Company**
ADDRESS: 3003 West Alabama, Ste. 201
Houston, TX 77098
PHONE: (713) 527-9646
TYPE OF INSTITUTION: R.E. Lender
CONTACT OFFICER(S):John T. Fenoglio, President
Harold Holliday, E. V.P.
TYPES OF FINANCING:REAL ESTATE LOANS: Long-term senior mtg.; Intermediate-term senior mtg.; Subordinated; Wraparounds; Land; Land Development; Construction; Gap; Standbys; Industrial revenue bonds, REAL ESTATE: Acquisitions; Joint ventures
PREFERRED TYPES OF INDUSTRIES/INVESTMENTS: Commercial property
GEOGRAPHIC LIMITS OF INVESTMENTS/LOANS: State: Texas
RANGE OF INV./LOAN PER BUSINESS: Min. $1 million
BRANCHES: Robert J. Docherty, S.V.P., 675 American Bank Tower, Austin, TX 78701; (512) 478-3340

COMPANY: **Couch Mortgage Company**
ADDRESS: 6401 Southwest Fwy.
Houston, TX 77074
PHONE: (713) 771-4681
TYPE OF INSTITUTION: Mortgage Bank
CONTACT OFFICER(S): Charley Michalk, Jr.

COMPANY: **Cullen Bank**
ADDRESS: 600 Jefferson
Houston, TX 77002
PHONE: (713) 652-7600
TYPE OF INSTITUTION: R. E. Lender
CONTACT OFFICER(S): Gary M. Olander, S. V.P.

COMPANY: **First City National Bank of Houston**
ADDRESS: Box 2557
Houston, TX 77252
PHONE: (713) 658-6011
TYPE OF INSTITUTION: Real Estate and Mortgage Banking Dept.
CONTACT OFFICER(S): Robert G. Brooks, S.V.P.
Richard G. Armstrong, VP
ASSETS: $9,286,000,000 (bank)
TYPES OF FINANCING: REAL ESTATE LOANS: Land development; Construction; Other: Sort-term interim financing
PREFERRED TYPES OF INDUSTRIES/INVESTMENTS: Income producting properties; Office buildings, Shopping centers; Apartments; Industrial buildings; Hotels
GEOGRAPHIC LIMITS OF INVESTMENTS/LOANS: State; National; Other: Some national or syndicated financing
RANGE OF INV./LOAN PER BUSINESS: Min. $1,000,000; Max. $70,000,000
PREFERRED TERM FOR LOANS & LEASES: Min. 1 year; Max. 3 years

COMPANY: **Gibraltar Savings Association**
ADDRESS: 13401 North Freeway
Houston, TX 77252
PHONE: (713) 537-3100
CONTACT OFFICER(S): Jack Dennis, S.V.P., Inc. Property
Milton Cowden, S.V.P. All Other Land
ASSETS: $4,000,000,000
TYPES OF FINANCING: REAL ESTATE LOANS: Long-term senior mtg.; Intermediate-term senior mtg.; Wraparounds; Land; Land development; Construction; Standbys; Industrial revenue bonds, REAL ESTATE: Acquisitions; Joint ventues; Partnerships/Syndications

COMPANY: **Gulf Coast Investment Corp.**
ADDRESS: P.O. Box 4272
Houston, TX 77210
PHONE: (713) 525-6110

TYPE OF INSTITUTION: Mortgage Banker
CONTACT OFFICER(S): Raymond C. Gamel, Exec. V.P.
ASSETS: $100,000,000 and up
TYPES OF FINANCING: REAL ESTATE LOANS
GEOGRAPHIC LIMITS OF INVESTMENTS/LOANS: Regional
RANGE OF INV./LOAN PER BUSINESS: Min. $1,000,000

COMPANY: **Inter First Bank Houston, N.A.**
ADDRESS: 1100 Louisiana
Houston, TX 77001
PHONE: (713) 652-6211
TYPE OF INSTITUTION: R. E. Lender
CONTACT OFFICER(S): Kenneth E. Pulley, E. V.P.

COMPANY: **North American Mortgage Co.**
ADDRESS: 900 Threadneedle, P.O. Box 19004, (Zip: 77224-9004)
Houston, TX 77027
PHONE: (713) 596-4100
CONTACT OFFICER(S): Jim Lindsey, Exec. V.P.
Bill Reid, V.P. Commercial Loans
ASSETS: $2.3 billion
TYPES OF FINANCING: REAL ESTATE LOANS: Long-term senior mtg.; Intermediate-term senior mtg.
PREFERRED TYPES OF INDUSTRIES/INVESTMENTS: Shopping centers; Apartments; Hotels; Office Buildings; Industrial; Office Warehousing; Medical
GEOGRAPHIC LIMITS OF INVESTMENTS/LOANS: State
RANGE OF INV./LOAN PER BUSINESS: Min. $500,000; Max. None
PREFERRED TERM FOR LOANS & LEASES: Min. 10 years
BRANCHES: Lee Nicol, 1200 Summit, Suite 722, Ft. Worth, TX 76102; (817) 654-2004
Don Wagstaff, Phelps Ct. 350 Phelps, Irving, TX 75038 (214) 257-2600
Bob Waller, 8535 Wurzbach, Ste. 101, San Antonio, TX 78240; (512) 697-0651
Jeff Brinkley, 2499 Loop, 35 South Ste. 107, Austin, TX 78764, (512) 327-9630

COMPANY: **The Robert C. Wilson Company**
ADDRESS: 2217 Welch
Houston, TX 77019
PHONE: (713) 526-8311
TYPE OF INSTITUTION: Mortgage Bank
CONTACT OFFICER(S): Robert C. Wilson Jr., Chairman
Robert C. Wilson, III, President

COMPANY: **Rotan Mosle Mortgage Co.**
ADDRESS: 4100 Republic Bank Center, P.O. Box 3226
Houston, TX 77523
PHONE: (713) 236-3366
TYPE OF INSTITUTION: Mortgage Banker
CONTACT OFFICER(S): Robert Barndollar, Pres.
ASSETS: $2,500,000
TYPES OF FINANCING: REAL ESTATE LOANS: Long-term senior mtg.
PREFERRED TYPES OF INDUSTRIES/INVESTMENTS: Apartments; Office Buildings
GEOGRAPHIC LIMITS OF INVESTMENTS/LOANS: Other: Southwest
RANGE OF INV./LOAN PER BUSINESS: Min. $1,000,000; Max. $50,000,000
PREFERRED TERM FOR LOANS & LEASES: Min. 5-7 years; Max. 20+ years

COMPANY: **American Century Corporation**
ADDRESS: 111 Soledad, Ste. 1300
San Antonio, TX 78205
PHONE: (512) 226-2222
TYPE OF INSTITUTION: Savings and Loan Holding Co.
CONTACT OFFICER(S): John C. Kerr, Pres. & Chairman of the Board
Roger D. Harrison, Exec. V.P. & Treasurer
ASSETS: $809,083,000
INVESTMENTS/LOANS MADE: For own accountt
INVESTMENTS/LOANS MADE: In securities with a secondary market and in securities without a secondary market
TYPES OF FINANCING: LOANS: Unsecured; Working capital; Equipment; Equity-related; REAL ESTATE LOANS; Long-term mtg.; Intermediate-term senior mtg.; Subordinated; Wraparounds; Land; Land development; Construction; Gap; Standbys; Industrial revenue bonds; REAL ESTATE: Acquisitions; Joint ventures; Partnerships/Syndications
PREFERRED TYPES OF INDUSTRIES/INVESTMENTS: Primarily relates to single family dwellings
GEOGRAPHIC LIMITS OF INVESTMENTS/LOANS: Regional
RANGE OF INV./LOAN PER BUSINESS: Min. None; Max. 50 million
PREFERRED TERM FOR LOANS & LEASES: Min. 18 mos; Max. 30 yrs
BUSINESS CHARACTERISTICS DESIRED-REQUIRED: Min. yrs. in business: 3
BRANCHES: 13 branches in Dallas, Houston, Ft. Worth

COMPANY: **Southwestern Venture Capital of Texas, Inc.**
ADDRESS:
1250 N.E. Loop 410, Suite 700
San Antonio, TX 78209
PHONE: (512) 822-9949
TYPE OF INSTITUTION: Venture Capital and SBA Loans
CONTACT OFFICER(S): Kurt Nestman, President
TOTAL ASSETS: $5,000,000
INVESTMENTS/LOANS MADE: For own accout
INVESTMENTS/LOANS MADE: In securities with a secondary market; In securities without a secondary market
TYPES OF FINANCING: VENTURE CAPITAL: First-stage; Second-stage; Later-stage expansion; Buy-outs/Acquisitions, LOANS: Equipment, REAL ESTATE: Long-term senior mtg.; Other: Owner occupied only
GEOGRAPHIC LIMITS OF INVESTMENTS/LOANS: National
RANGE OF INV./LOANS PER BUSINESS: Min. $100,000; Max. $600,000

PREFERRED TERM FOR LOANS & LEASES: Min. 7 years; Max. 25 years
BUSINESS CHARACTERISTICS DESIRED-REQUIRED: Minimum number of years business: 2
REFERRALS: Investment/Mortgage banker; Borrower/investee
BRANCHES: Doug Hatten, Southwestern Commercial Capital, Inc., 100 Chase Stone Center, Suite 440, Colorado, Springs, CO 80903
Joe Justice, SWCC, 444 Executive Center Blvd., Suite 222, El Paso, TX 79902
Ron Kozak, SWCC, 101 Park Ave., Suite 950, Oklahoma City, OK 73102
Kurtis Nestman, SWCC, North Frost Center, 1250 N.E. Loop 410, Suite 700, San Antonio, TX 78209
Bill Murray, SWCC, 1301 Seminole Blvd., Suite 110, Largo, FL 33540
Scott Bobo, SWCC, 1717 Azurite Tr., Plano, TX 75075
REMARKS: Company makes SBA guaranteed loans in addition to venture capital investments

COMPANY: **Surety Life Insurance Company**
ADDRESS: 200 East South Temple
Salt Lake City, UT 84111
PHONE: (801) 355-3000
TYPE OF INSTITUTION: Insurance Company (Mortgage Banking and lending)
CONTACT OFFICER(S): Hoyt S. Wimer, Assistant V.P. — Mortgage Loans
ASSETS: $125,000,000 and up
INVESTMENTS/LOANS MADE: For own account; For managed accounts
INVESTMENTS/LOANS MADE: In securities with a secondary market and in securities without a secondary market
TYPES OF FINANCING: REAL ESTATE LOANS: Long-term senior mtg.; Wraparounds, OTHER SERVICES PROVIDED: Presently originating and servicing mortgages in Utah and other surrounding western states.
PREFERRED TYPES OF INDUSTRIES/INVESTMENTS: Real Estate
WILL NOT CONSIDER: Loan not secured by Real Estate
GEOGRAPHIC LIMITS OF INVESTMENTS/LOANS: Regional; Western Regional and some International on larger loans.
RANGE OF INV./LOAN PER BUSINESS: Min. $500,000.00; Max. open
PREFERRED TERM FOR LOANS & LEASES: Min. 5; Max. 10 years
BUSINESS CHARACTERISTICS DESIRED-REQUIRED: Minimum number of years in business: 5; Prefer 25 to 1 net worth minimum
REFERRALS ACCEPTED FROM: Investment/Mortgage banker or Borrower/Investee

COMPANY: **DeRand Corporation**
ADDRESS: 2201 Wilson Blvd.
Arlington, VA 22201
PHONE: (703) 527-3827
TYPE OF INSTITUTION: Investment Banking, Syndications, Securities Brokerage
CONTACT OFFICER(S): William A. Conway, President-International Stock Brokerage
Randall N. Smith, Chairman of Board-Real Estate
W. David Powell, Vice President-Municipal bonds
ASSETS: $100,000,000+
INVESTMENTS/LOANS MADE: For own account, Through private placements, Through underwriting public offerings
TYPES OF FINANCING: SECONDARY-MARKET CORPORATE SECURITIES: Common stock; Preferred stock; Bonds; Other: Real Estate, Oil and Gas, Telecommunications private placements, municipal bond financing. REAL ESTATE LOANS: Long-term senior mtg.; Intermediate-term senior mtg.; Subordinated; Wraparounds; Industrial revenue bonds. REAL ESTATE: Partnerships/Syndications.
REFERRALS ACCEPTED FROM: Investment/Mortgage banker or Borrower/Investee

COMPANY: **Dominion Bankshares Mortgage Corp.**
ADDRESS: 9900 Main St., Ste. 200, P.O. Box 2786
Fairfax, VA 22031
PHONE: (703) 352-3200
TYPE OF INSTITUTION: Mortgage Banker
CONTACT OFFICER(S): Mr. Zanke, Sr. V.P.
L. Hamilton, EVP
TYPES OF FINANCING: REAL ESTATE LOANS

COMPANY: **Arlington Mortgage Co.**
ADDRESS: 6400 Arlington Blvd.
Falls Church, VA 22042
PHONE: (703) 241-3173
TYPE OF INSTITUTION: Mortgage Banker
CONTACT OFFICER(S): William S. Corish, President
ASSETS: Servicing Volume over $300,000,000
TYPES OF FINANCING: REAL ESTATE LOANS: Long-term senior mtg.; Wraparounds; Construction; Industrial Revenue Bonds
PREFERRED TYPES OF INDUSTRIES/INVESTMENTS: Residential & Commercial; Apartments; Shopping centers; Office buildings
GEOGRAPHIC LIMITS OF INVESTMENTS/LOANS: Regional
RANGE OF INV./LOAN PER BUSINESS: Min. $500,000
PREFERRED TERM FOR LOANS & LEASES: Min. 5 years; Max. 20+ years
BRANCHES: Clinton, MD
Virginia Beach, VA

COMPANY: **Finalco Inc.**
ADDRESS: 8200 Greensboro Drive
McLean, VA 22102
PHONE: (703) 790-0970
CONTACT OFFICER(S): Terry J. Billingsley, President, Finalco, Inc.
ASSETS: $988,000,000
INVESTMENTS/LOANS MADE: For own account, Through private placements, Through private placements
TYPES OF FINANCING: LOANS: Equipment. LEASES: Single-investor; Leveraged; Tax leases; Non-tax leases; Operating; Tax-oriented lease brokerage; Lease syndications; Vendor financing programs. REAL ESTATE: Partnerships/Syndications

VIRGINIA

PREFERRED TYPES OF INDUSTRIES/INVESTMENTS: General equipment
GEOGRAPHIC LIMITS OF INVESTMENTS/LOANS: National
RANGE OF INV./LOAN PER BUSINESS: Min. $200,000; Max. No limit
PREFERRED TERM FOR LOANS & LEASES: Min. 1 year; Max. No limit
BRANCHES: 1553 Little Willeo Road,Marietta, GA 30067
Baldwin Office Park 12 Alfred Street, Woburn, MA 01801
221 N. LaSalle Street, Ste. 1038, Chicago, IL 60601
10999 Reed Highway, Suite 237-239, Cincinnati, OH 45242
Lincoln Center II, 5420 LBJ Freeway, Ste. 1100, Dallas, TX 75240
3333 S. Wadsworth Blvd. Lakewood, CO 80227
30800 Telegraph Road, #3875, Birmingham, MI 48010
12 Greenway Plaza, Ste. 1148, Houston, TX 77046
120 South 6th Street, 1908 First Bank Place West, Minneapolis, MN 55402
4350 Von Karman Ave., Ste. 370, Newport Beach, CA 92660
747 3rd Avenue, 32nd Floor, N.Y.C., NY 10017
5104 N. Orange Blossom Trail, Suite 114, Orlando, FL 32804
1107 Goffle Road, Hawthorne, NJ 07506
8603 E. Royal Palms Rd., Scottsdale, AZ 85258
345 Mt. Lebanon Blvd. Pittsburgh, PA 15234
3470 Mt. Diablo Blvd., Ste. 150, Lafayette, CA 94549
500 Summer Street, Ste. 502, Stamford, CT 06901
5130 Eisenhower Blvd., Tampa. FL 33614

COMPANY: **Fidelity Bankers Life Insurance Company**
ADDRESS: P.O. Box 2368
Richmond, VA 23218
PHONE: (804) 649-8411
CONTACT OFFICER(S): Donald M. Davis, Sr. V.P., Investments
ASSETS: $200 million and up
INVESTMENTS/LOANS MADE: In securities with a secondary market and in securities without a secondary market
TYPES OF FINANCING: REAL ESTATE LOANS: Long-term senior mtg.; Intermediate-term senior mtg.
GEOGRAPHIC LIMITS OF INVESTMENTS/LOANS: National
RANGE OF INV./LOAN PER BUSINESS: Min. $250,000; Max. $1,000,000
PREFERRED TERM FOR LOANS & LEASES: Min. 5-8; Max. 10 years
REFERRALS ACCEPTED FROM: Investment/Mortgage Banker only

COMPANY: **Home Beneficial Life Insurance Company**
ADDRESS: P.O. Box 27572
Richmond, VA 23261
PHONE: (804) 358-8431
CONTACT OFFICER(S): R. W. Wiltshire, Jr., V.P. Securities Dept.
ASSETS: $880,000,000
INVESTMENTS/LOANS MADE: For own account
INVESTMENTS/LOANS MADE: In securities with a secondary market and in securities without a secondary market
TYPES OF FINANCING: SECONDARY-MARKET CORPORATE SECURITIES: Common stock; Preferred stock; Bonds; Other: Mtg. Loans. LOANS: Unsecured to credits above Baa. REAL ESTATE LOANS: Intermediate-term senior mtg.

COMPANY: **The Life Insurance Company of Virginia**
ADDRESS: P.O. Box 27424
Richmond, VA 23235
PHONE: (804) 281-6595
TYPE OF INSTITUTION: Life Insurance Company
CONTACT OFFICER(S): Daniel B. Belcore, Assistant V.P., Private Placement Portfolio Manager
Ron McRoberts V.P., Real Estate & Mtg.
ASSETS: $1.6 Billion
INVESTMENTS/LOANS MADE: For own account; For managed accounts; Through private placements
INVESTMENTS/LOANS MADE: In securities with a secondary market and in securities without a secondary market
TYPES OF FINANCING: SECONDARY-MARKET CORPORATE SECURITIES: Common stock; Preferred stock; Bonds, LOANS: Unsecured; Equipment; Equity-related; REAL ESTATE LOANS: Long-term senior mtg.; Industrial revenue bonds, LEASES: Single-investor; Leveraged; Tax leases, REAL ESTATE: Acquisitions
GEOGRAPHIC LIMITS OF INVESTMENTS/LOANS: National
RANGE OF INV./LOAN PER BUSINESS: Min. $500,000; Max. $5,000,000
PREFERRED TERM FOR LOANS & LEASES: Min. 3; Max. 12 years
BUSINESS CHARACTERISTICS DESIRED-REQUIRED: Minimum number of years in business: 10; Min. annual sales $30 million; Min. net worth $10 million
REFERRALS ACCEPTED FROM: Investment/Mortgage banker or Borrower/Investee

COMPANY: **Old Dominion Real Estate Investment Trust**
ADDRESS: 5 East Franklin Street, Box 12365
Richmond, VA 23241
PHONE: (804) 780-2691
TYPE OF INSTITUTION: Real estate investment trust
CONTACT OFFICER(S): John P. McCann, President & CEO, James Dolphin, Secy. & Controller
ASSETS: $40,000,000
INVESTMENTS/LOANS MADE: For own account
TYPES OF FINANCING: REAL ESTATE: Acquisitions
PREFERRED TYPES OF INDUSTRIES/INVESTMENTS: Purchase apartments; Shopping centers
GEOGRAPHIC LIMITS OF INVESTMENTS/LOANS: Regional (VA, Carolina and neighboring states)
REFERRALS ACCEPTED FROM: Investment/Mortgage banker or Borrower/Investee

COMPANY: **Sorran Mortgage**
ADDRESS: P.O. Box 26388
Richmond, VA 23260
PHONE: (804) 289-3500

TYPE OF INSTITUTION: Mortgage Banker
CONTACT OFFICER(S): Bryant W. Baird, Jr., President
ASSETS: $100,000,000 and up
TYPES OF FINANCING: REAL ESTATE LOANS: Long-term senior mtg.; Intermediate-term senior mtg.
GEOGRAPHIC LIMITS OF INVESTMENTS/LOANS: Regional
PREFERRED TERM FOR LOANS & LEASES: Min. 1-3; Max. 20+ years

COMPANY: **Sovran Mortgage Corporation**
ADDRESS: 1512 Willow Lawn Drive
Richmond, VA 23230
PHONE: (804) 289-3511
TYPE OF INSTITUTION: Mortgage Banker
CONTACT OFFICER(S): John B. Levy, Senior Vice President—Long Term Conventional Financing
Arthur G. Hansen, Asst. Vice Pres.—Long Term Conventional Fiinancing
George H. M. Roper, Comm. Loan Officer—Long Term Conventional Financing
Ronald E. Sweeney, Senior Vice Pres. - HUD - Multi Family
Lester A. Wagner, Vice President - HUD - Multi Family
ASSETS: $143,373,000
INVESTMENTS/LOANS MADE: For managed accounts, Through private placements
INVESTMENTS/LOANS MADE: In securities with or without a secondary market
TYPES OF FINANCING: REAL ESTATE LOANS: Long-term senior mtg.; Wraparounds; Standbbys; Industrial revenue bonds.
PREFERRED TYPES OF INDUSTRIES/INVESTMENTS: Income producing properties such as apartments, shopping centers, office buildings, hotel/motel, retail, industrial
GEOGRAPHIC LIMITS OF INVESTMENTS/LOANS: National
RANGE OF INV./LOAN PER BUSINESS: Min. $1 million
BRANCHES: 3401 Columbia Pike, Arlington, VA 22204, (804) 892-3761, Richard B. Carriker, V.P.
1062 Lancaster Avenue, The Rosemonnt Plaza, Suite 18D, Rosemont, PA 19010, (215) 527-7474, Donald J. Reape, Vice President
4456 Corporation Lane, Suite 134, Virginia Beach, VA 23462 (804) 490-1155, John F. Power, Senior Vice President, Christopher J. Fanney, Asst. Vice President, Gregory P. Marshall, Commercial Loan Officer

COMPANY: **Shenandoah Life Insurance Co.**
ADDRESS: 2301 Brambleton Av., S.W., P.O. Box 12847
Roanoke, VA 24029
PHONE: (703) 345-6711
CONTACT OFFICER(S): William A. Magee, V.P. Investments
ASSETS: $100 million and up
TYPES OF FINANCING: REAL ESTATE LOANS: Long-term senior mtg.; Intermediate-term senior mtg.
PREFERRED TYPES OF INDUSTRIES/INVESTMENTS: Diversified
GEOGRAPHIC LIMITS OF INVESTMENTS/LOANS: Regional
RANGE OF INV./LOAN PER BUSINESS: Min. $150,000; Max. $800,000
PREFERRED TERM FOR LOANS & LEASES: Min. 10-15; Max. 20+ years
REFERRALS ACCEPTED FROM: Investment/Mortgage banker or Borrower/Investee

COMPANY: **Venture Capital Group**
ADDRESS: 401 First St., N.W.
Roanoke, VA 24016
PHONE: (703) 344-6624
TYPE OF INSTITUTION: Investment Division of CDC
CONTACT OFFICER(S): Stanley Hale, Director
ASSETS: Over $3 million
INVESTMENTS/LOANS MADE: For own account; Through private placements
INVESTMENTS/LOANS MADE: In securities with a secondary market and in securities without a secondary market
TYPES OF FINANCING: SECONDARY-MARKET CORPORATE SECURITIES: Common stock; Bonds, VENTURE CAPITAL: Start-up from developed product stage; Later-stage expansion, LOANS: Working capital (receivables/inventory); Equipment; Equity-related, REAL ESTATE LOANS: Land; Land development; Construction, LEASES: Vendor financing programs, REAL ESTATE: Acquisitions; Joint ventures; Partnerships/Syndications, OTHER SERVICES PROVIDED: 501(c)3 Pass Thru of Real Estate
PREFERRED TYPES OF INDUSTRIES/INVESTMENTS: Computer Related Peripheral Equipment, Machine Tools, Material Handling Equipment, Plastics, Medical Diagnostic Equipment, Coal, Minerals, Oil & Gas, Broadcasting, Publishing, Optics
WILL NOT CONSIDER: Long Term Real Estate Mortgages
GEOGRAPHIC LIMITS OF INVESTMENTS/LOANS: Regional
RANGE OF INV./LOAN PER BUSINESS: Min. $100,000; Max. $300,000
PREFERRED TERM FOR LOANS & LEASES: Negotiable
BUSINESS CHARACTERISTICS DESIRED-REQUIRED: Min. no. of years in business: 0; Management Experience; Operational Prototypes
REFERRALS ACCEPTED FROM: Investment/Mortgage banker or Borrower/Investee

COMPANY: **National Life Insurance Co.**
ADDRESS: National Life Drive
Montpelier, VT 05602
PHONE: (802) 229-3333
TYPE OF INSTITUTION: Life insurance company
CONTACT OFFICER(S): Edward S. Blackwell, V.P., Fixed Income
Ralph T. Heath, V.P., R.E. & Mortgages
George C. Coquillard, Exec. V.P., Investment
TYPES OF FINANCING: SECONDARY-MARKET CORPORATE SECURITIES: Common stock; Preferred stock; Bonds, LOANS: Unsecured; Equipment; Equity-related; OTHER: Secured, REAL ESTATE LOANS: Construction, REAL ESTATE: Acquisitions; Joint ventures; Partnerships/Syndications
PREFERRED TYPES OF INDUSTRIES/INVESTMENTS: Bonds; Oil, gas; R.E.; Industrial

WILL NOT CONSIDER: Specialty buildings
GEOGRAPHIC LIMITS OF INVESTMENTS/LOANS: National; International; Other: Canada
RANGE OF INV./LOAN PER BUSINESS: Min. $1 million; Max. $5 million
PREFERRED TERM FOR LOANS & LEASES: Min. 1 year; Max. 10 years
REMARKS: Average investment $2-3 million

COMPANY: **Cable, Howse & Cozadd, Inc.**
ADDRESS: 999 Third Avenue, Suite 4300
Seattle, WA 98104
PHONE: (206) 583-2700
TYPE OF INSTITUTION: Venture Capital Investment Firm
CONTACT OFFICER(S): Wayne C. Wager, General Partner
Michael A. Ellison, General Partner
Bennett A. Cozadd, General Partner
Elwood D. Howse, Jr., General Partner
Thomas J. Cable , General Partner
ASSETS: Over $130 million
INVESTMENTS/LOANS MADE: For own account
TYPES OF FINANCING: VENTURE CAPITAL: Start-up from developed product stage; First-stage; Second-stage; Later-stage expansion; Buy-outs/Acquisitions
GEOGRAPHIC LIMITS OF INVESTMENTS/LOANS: National; Other: Mainly western states.
RANGE OF INV./LOAN PER BUSINESS: Min. $300,000,00; Max. $2,000,00
BUSINESS CHARACTERISTICS DESIRED-REQUIRED: Min. no. of years in business: 0
REFERRALS ACCEPTED FROM: Investment/Mortgage banker or Borrower/Investee

COMPANY: **Continental, Inc.**
ADDRESS: 8th Fl., Pacific Bldg.
Seattle, WA 98104
PHONE: (206) 623-3050
TYPE OF INSTITUTION: Mortgage Banker
CONTACT OFFICER(S): David A. Ballaine, Sr. V.P.
Jack Fisher, Sr. V.P.

COMPANY: **Peoples Mortgage Co.**
ADDRESS: 4th & Battery Bldg.
Seattle, WA 98111
PHONE: (206) 344-4500
TYPE OF INSTITUTION: Mortgage Banker
CONTACT OFFICER(S): Marge Patterson
ASSETS: Servicing volume 2 billion
TYPES OF FINANCING: REAL ESTATE LOANS: Long-term senior mtg.; Intermediate-term senior mtg.; Subordinated, Wraparounds; Construction; Gap; Standbys; Industrial Revenue Bonds
PREFERRED TYPES OF INDUSTRIES/INVESTMENTS: Construction & Development
GEOGRAPHIC LIMITS OF INVESTMENTS/LOANS: Regional
RANGE OF INV./LOAN PER BUSINESS: Min. $500,000
PREFERRED TERM FOR LOANS & LEASES: Min. 1-3 years; Max. 10 years

COMPANY: **Seafirst Capital Corp.**
ADDRESS: Fourth & Blanchard Building
Seattle, WA 98121
PHONE: (206) 583-3278
TYPE OF INSTITUTION: Subsidiary of Seafirst Mortgage Corp. (subsidiary of Seafirst Bank)
CONTACT OFFICER(S): Donald F. Rapp, President & Manager
R. Bruce Harrod, Vice President
Tom C. Doak, Vice President
ASSETS: $7,000,000
INVESTMENTS/LOANS MADE: For own account; Through private placements
INVESTMENTS/LOANS MADE: Only in securities without a secondary market
TYPES OF FINANCING: REAL ESTATE LOANS: Long-term senior mtg.; Subordinated; Land development; Construction; REAL ESTATE: Joint ventures
PREFERRED TYPES OF INDUSTRIES/INVESTMENTS: Owner occupied special purpose Real Estate; JV's in residential or commercial Real Estate.
GEOGRAPHIC LIMITS OF INVESTMENTS/LOANS: Regional; Other: Northwest: Washington, Oregon, Idaho, Montana, Alaska
RANGE OF INV./LOAN PER BUSINESS: Min. $200,000; Max. $600,000
PREFERRED TERM FOR LOANS & LEASES: Min. 10 years; Max. 15 years
BUSINESS CHARACTERISTICS DESIRED-REQUIRED: Other: Depends on characteristics of particular deal.
REFERRALS ACCEPTED FROM: Investment/Mortgage banker or Borrower/Investee

COMPANY: **Seafirst Mortgage Corp.**
ADDRESS: 4th & Blanchard Bldg.
Seattle, WA 98121
PHONE: (206) 583-7070
TYPE OF INSTITUTION: Mortgage Banker
CONTACT OFFICER(S): William Jennings, President
ASSETS: Servicing Volume over $100,000,000
TYPES OF FINANCING: REAL ESTATE LOANS: Long-term senior mtg.; Intermediate-term senior mtg.; Subordinated; Wraparounds; Construction
GEOGRAPHIC LIMITS OF INVESTMENTS/LOANS: National
RANGE OF INV./LOAN PER BUSINESS: Min. $500,000
PREFERRED TERM FOR LOANS & LEASES: Min. 0-1; Max. 20+ years
REMARKS: Minimum amount stated is for out-of-state loans.

COMPANY: **Seattle Mortgage Co.**
ADDRESS: 229 Queen Anne Av. No., (P.O. Box C-19102)
Seattle, WA 98109
PHONE: (206) 281-1500
TYPE OF INSTITUTION: Mortgage Banker
CONTACT OFFICER(S): Robert E. Story, Exec. V.P.
ASSETS: $100,000,000 and up
TYPES OF FINANCING: REAL ESTATE LOANS: Long-term senior mtg.; Intermediate-term senior mtg.; Construction; Other: Land Sale/Leaseback
GEOGRAPHIC LIMITS OF INVESTMENTS/LOANS: Regional

RANGE OF INV./LOAN PER BUSINESS: Min. $250,000; Max. None
PREFERRED TERM FOR LOANS & LEASES: Max. 20 years

COMPANY: **Washington Mutual Savings Bank**
ADDRESS: 1101 2nd Avenue
Seattle, WA 98101
PHONE: (206) 464-4405
TYPE OF INSTITUTION: Commercial; Real Estate Department
CONTACT OFFICER(S): Robert J. Flowers, Director, 464-4444
Marvin Leach, State Program, 464-4471, Greg Skinner, National Program, 464-4896
ASSETS: $3.6 billion
INVESTMENTS/LOANS MADE: For own account
INVESTMENTS/LOANS MADE: In securities with a secondary market and in securities without a secondary market
TYPES OF FINANCING: LOANS; REAL ESTATE LOANS: Long-term senior mtg.; Intermediate-term senior mtg.; Subordinated; Wraparounds; Standbys; Industrial revenue bonds; REAL ESTATE: Joint ventures
PREFERRED TYPES OF INDUSTRIES/INVESTMENTS: Real estate loans on existing and new leased properties, located primarily in the western United States.
WILL NOT CONSIDER: Special purpose real estate loans and construction financing.
GEOGRAPHIC LIMITS OF INVESTMENTS/LOANS: Local; State; Regional; National
RANGE OF INV./LOAN PER BUSINESS: Min. $5 million; Max. $50 million
PREFERRED TERM FOR LOANS & LEASES: Min. 1 year; Max. 10 years
BUSINESS CHARACTERISTICS DESIRED-REQUIRED: Minimum number of years in business: 1
REFERRALS ACCEPTED FROM: Borrower/Investee

COMPANY: **Venture Sum**
ADDRESS: N. 618 Sullivan, #25
Veradale, WA 99037
PHONE: (509) 926-3720
TYPE OF INSTITUTION: Private Venture Capital
CONTACT OFFICER(S): A.T. Zirkle, President
ASSETS: $2,000,000
INVESTMENTS/LOANS MADE: For own account
INVESTMENTS/LOANS MADE: In securities with a secondary market and in securities without a secondary market
TYPES OF FINANCING: VENTURE CAPITAL: Research & Development; Start-up from developed product stage; First-stage (less than 1 year); Buy-outs/Acquisitions; LOANS: Working capital; Equipment; Equity-related; INTERNATIONAL; REAL ESTATE: Acquisitions; Partnerships/Syndications
PREFERRED TYPES OF INDUSTRIES/INVESTMENTS: Industries—High Technology; Real Estate—Commercial & Development
WILL NOT CONSIDER: Those precluded to SBIC's
GEOGRAPHIC LIMITS OF INVESTMENTS/LOANS: Regional

RANGE OF INV./LOAN PER BUSINESS: Min. $10,000; Max. $1,000,000
PREFERRED TERM FOR LOANS & LEASES: Min. 1; Max. 3 years
BUSINESS CHARACTERISTICS DESIRED-REQUIRED: Minimum number of years in business: 0; Min. annual sales $100,000; Min. net worth $100,000; Min. annual net income $0
REFERRALS ACCEPTED FROM: Investment/Mortgage banker or Borrower/Investee

COMPANY: **Aid Association for Lutherans**
ADDRESS: 4321 North Ballard Road
Appleton, WI 54919
PHONE: (414) 734-5721
TYPE OF INSTITUTION: Insurance Co.
CONTACT OFFICER(S): James Abitz, Second V.P.—Securities
Roy B. Glazier, V.P.—Real Estate
ASSETS: $3.3 billion
INVESTMENTS/LOANS MADE: For own account; Through private placements
INVESTMENTS/LOANS MADE: In securities with a secondary market and in securities without a secondary market
TYPES OF FINANCING: SECONDARY-MARKET CORPORATE SECURITIES: Common stock; Bonds; LOANS: Unsecured to credits above Baa; Working capital; Equipment; REAL ESTATE LOANS: Intermediate-term senior mtg.; LEASES: Leveraged
PREFERRED TYPES OF INDUSTRIES/INVESTMENTS: Open to a broad mix
WILL NOT CONSIDER: Bank holding company paper
GEOGRAPHIC LIMITS OF INVESTMENTS/LOANS: National
RANGE OF INV./LOAN PER BUSINESS: Min. 1 million; Max. $10-15 million
PREFERRED TERM FOR LOANS & LEASES: Min. 2½ years; Max. 7-10 years
BUSINESS CHARACTERISTICS DESIRED-REQUIRED: Minimum number of years in business: 0; Other: Min. # years in business—if it is a new subsidiary of a larger, proven company
REFERRALS ACCEPTED FROM: Investment/Mortgage banker or Borrower/Investee

COMPANY: **CUNA Mutual Insurance Co.**
ADDRESS: 5910 Mineral Pointe Road, P.O. 391
Madison, WI 53701
PHONE: (608) 238-5851
CONTACT OFFICER(S): Lyle T. Ibeling, V.P., Secur. Mngr.
William W. Sayles, Sec. Analyst
Alan Hembel, Asst. V.P., R.E. Manager
TYPES OF FINANCING: SECONDARY-MARKET CORPORATE SECURITIES: Common stock; Preferred stock; Bonds, LOANS: Secured, REAL ESTATE LOANS: 3 yr. notes, REAL ESTATE: Acquisitions; Joint Ventures
PREFERRED TYPES OF INDUSTRIES/INVESTMENTS: Diversified
GEOGRAPHIC LIMITS OF INVESTMENTS/LOANS: National

RANGE OF INV./LOAN PER BUSINESS: Min. $2 million; Max. $5 million
PREFERRED TERM FOR LOANS & LEASES: Max. 3 years
BUSINESS CHARACTERISTICS DESIRED-REQUIRED: Other: Credit-union related financial institutions
BRANCHES: Pomona, CA

COMPANY: **Grootemaat Corporation**
ADDRESS: 735 N. Water St., P.O. Box 2030
Milwaukee, WI 53201
PHONE: (414) 271-5690
TYPE OF INSTITUTION: Mortgage Banker
CONTACT OFFICER(S): Robert Richter, V.P.
ASSETS: Servicing Volume over $100,000,000
TYPES OF FINANCING: LOANS: Equity-related, REAL ESTATE LOANS: Long-term senior mtg.; Intermediate-term senior mtg.; Subordinated; Leases, REAL ESTATE: Acquisitions; Joint ventures; Partnerships/ Syndications
GEOGRAPHIC LIMITS OF INVESTMENTS/LOANS: Regional
RANGE OF INV./LOAN PER BUSINESS: Min. $500,000; Max. None
PREFERRED TERM FOR LOANS & LEASES: Min. 0-1; Max. 20+ years

COMPANY: **The Northwestern Mutual Life Insurance Company**
ADDRESS: 720 E. Wisconsin Av.
Milwaukee, WI 53202
PHONE: (414) 271-1444
CONTACT OFFICER(S): James D. Ericson, Sr. V.P., Investments
ASSETS: $14.6 billion
INVESTMENTS/LOANS MADE: In securities with a secondary market and in securities without a secondary market
TYPES OF FINANCING: SECONDARY-MARKET CORPORATE SECURITIES: Common stock; Bonds, LOANS, REAL ESTATE LOANS: Long-term senior mtg.; Intermediate-term senior mtg.
GEOGRAPHIC LIMITS OF INVESTMENTS/LOANS: National
RANGE OF INV./LOAN PER BUSINESS: Min. $10 million; Max. None
PREFERRED TERM FOR LOANS & LEASES: Min. 10; Max. 20 + years
REFERRALS ACCEPTED FROM: Investment/Mortgage banker or Borrower/Investee
REMARKS: 15 Real Estate production offices throughout the country

COMPANY: **Wisconsin National Life Insurance Company**
ADDRESS: 220 Washington Ave., Box 740
Oshkosh, WI 54902
PHONE: (414) 235-0800
CONTACT OFFICER(S): David Diercks, Financial V.P.
ASSETS: $141,000,000
INVESTMENTS/LOANS MADE: In securities with a secondary market and in securities without a secondary market
TYPES OF FINANCING: REAL ESTATE LOANS
GEOGRAPHIC LIMITS OF INVESTMENTS/LOANS: Regional; Midwest
RANGE OF INV./LOAN PER BUSINESS: Min. $200,000; Max. $500,000
REFERRALS ACCEPTED FROM: Investment/Mortgage banker

COMPANY: **Impact Seven, Inc.**
ADDRESS: Box 8, Rt. 2
Turtle Lake, WI
PHONE: (715) 986-4171
TYPE OF INSTITUTION: Community development corporation
CONTACT OFFICER(S): William Bay, President
Mike Schatz, Investment Officer
ASSETS: $5,000,000
INVESTMENTS/LOANS MADE: For own account, For managed accounts, Through private placements
TYPES OF FINANCING: VENTURE CAPITAL: Start-up from developed product stage; First-stage (less than 1 year); Second-stage (generally 1-3 years); Later-stage expansion; Buy-outs/Acquisitions, LOANS: Unsecured; Working capital (receivables/inventory); Equipment; Equity-related; Other, REAL ESTATE LOANS: Land; Land development; Construction; Standbys; Industrial revenue bonds; Other, REAL ESTATE: Acquisitions, OTHER SERVICES PROVIDED: Consulting
PREFERRED TYPES OF INDUSTRIES/INVESTMENTS: Considering any type of industry
GEOGRAPHIC LIMITS OF INVESTMENTS/LOANS: Local; State
RANGE OF INV./LOAN PER BUSINESS: Min. $25,000
PREFERRED TERM FOR LOANS & LEASES: Min. 1 year; Max. 20 years
BUSINESS CHARACTERISTICS DESIRED-REQUIRED: Other: Will look at merits of each investment
REFERRALS ACCEPTED FROM: Investment/Mortgage banker or Borrower/Investee

SAVINGS & LOANS

(Mainly Real Estate Financing)

COLORADO

COMPANY: **Uniwest Financial Corp.**
ADDRESS: 7979 E. Tufts Ave. Parkway, Suite #110
Denver, CO
PHONE: (303) 694-9777
TYPE OF INSTITUTION: Financial Services, Savings and Loan Holdings Co.
CONTACT OFFICER(S): Chuck McKelvey, Executive Vice President Real Estate; James R. Newman, National Credit Manager Leasing; John Holzman, Vice President Securities
ASSETS: $250,000,000
INVESTMENTS/LOANS MADE: For own account; Through private placements
INVESTMENTS/LOANS MADE: In securities with a secondary market and in securities without a secondary market
TYPES OF FINANCING: VENTURE CAPITAL: First-stage (less than 1 year); Second-stage (generally 1-3 years); REAL ESTATE LOANS: Construction; LEASES; REAL ESTATE: Acquisitions; Joint ventures; Partnerships/Syndications
PREFERRED TYPES OF INDUSTRIES/INVESTMENTS: Real Estate, Leasing
GEOGRAPHIC LIMITS OF INVESTMENTS/LOANS: Sun Belt States
RANGE OF INV./LOAN PER BUSINESS: Min. $250,000; Max. $10,000,000
PREFERRED TERM FOR LOANS & LEASES: Min. One-Three years; Max. Thirty years

TEXAS

COMPANY: **American Century Corporation**
ADDRESS: 111 Soledad, Ste. 1300
San Antonio, TX 78205
PHONE: (512) 226-2222
TYPE OF INSTITUTION: Savings and Loan Holding Co.
CONTACT OFFICER(S): John C. Kerr, Pres. & Chairman of the Board
Roger D. Harrison, Exec. V.P. & Treasurer
ASSETS: $809,083,000
INVESTMENTS/LOANS MADE: For own account
INVESTMENTS/LOANS MADE: In securities with a secondary market and in securities without a secondary market
TYPES OF FINANCING: LOANS: Unsecured; Working capital; Equipment; Equity-related; REAL ESTATE LOANS; Long-term mtg.; Intermediate-term senior mtg.; Subordinated; Wraparounds; Land; Land development; Construction; Gap; Standbys; Industrial revenue bonds; REAL ESTATE: Acquisitions; Joint ventures; Partnerships/Syndications
PREFERRED TYPES OF INDUSTRIES/INVESTMENTS: Primarily relates to single family dwellings
GEOGRAPHIC LIMITS OF INVESTMENTS/LOANS: Regional
RANGE OF INV./LOAN PER BUSINESS: Min. None; Max. 50 million
PREFERRED TERM FOR LOANS & LEASES: Min. 18 mos; Max. 30 yrs
BUSINESS CHARACTERISTICS DESIRED-REQUIRED: Min. yrs. in business: 3
BRANCHES: 13 branches in Dallas, Houston, Ft. Worth

SMALL BUSINESS INVESTMENT COMPANIES (SBICs)

(Venture Capital. Also see Minority Enterprise SBICs, Venture Capital Companies and Investment Bankers)

ALASKA

COMPANY: **Alaska Business Investment Corp.**
ADDRESS: 301 West Northern Lights Boulevard
Anchorage, AK 99510
PHONE: (907) 278-2071
CONTACT OFFICER(S): James Cloud, Vice President
REMARKS: Private Capital of $2,500,000

COMPANY: **Alaska Pacific Investment Corp.**
ADDRESS: 101 West Benson Boulevard
Anchorage, AK 99510
PHONE: (907) 276-9661
REMARKS: Private capital of $2,500,000

COMPANY: **Calista Business Investment Corp.**
ADDRESS: 516 Denali Street
Anchorage, AK 99501
PHONE: (907) 277-0425
CONTACT OFFICER(S): Alex Raider, President
REMARKS: Private capital of $750,000

ADDRESS: 406 South Commerce Street
Geneva, AL 36340
PHONE: (205) 684-2824
CONTACT OFFICER(S): William T. Benson, President
REMARKS: Private Capital of $1,000,000

ALABAMA

COMPANY: **First Small Business Investment Company of Alabama**
ADDRESS: 16 Midtown Park East
Mobile, AL 36606
PHONE: (205) 476-0700
TYPE OF INSTITUTION: small business investment company
CONTACT OFFICER(S): David Delaney, President
INVESTMENTS/LOANS MADE: For own account
INVESTMENTS/LOANS MADE OR ARRANGED: only in securities without a secondary market
TYPES OF FINANCING: LOANS: Working capital, Equipment, Equity-relate d; Other, real estate secured; REAL ESTATE LOANS: Long-term senior mtg.; Intermediate-term senior mtg.; Subdordinated, Wraparounds; Land; Land d evelopment; Construction
GEOGRAPHIC LIMITS OF INVESTMENTS/LOANS: Local; State
RANGE OF INV./LOAN PER BUSINESS: Min. $5,000.00; Max. $500,000.00
PREFERRED TERM FOR LOANS & LEASES: Min. 5 years; Max. 10 years
BUSINESS CHARACTERISTICS DESIRED-REQUIRED: Minimum number of years i n business: 0

COMPANY: **Hudson-Thompson Inc.**
ADDRESS: P.O. Drawer Q
Montgomery, AL 36196
PHONE: (205) 288-6250

CONTACT OFFICER(S): Ron Randolph, President
REMARKS: Private Capital of $305,000

COMPANY: **Independence Financial Services, Inc.**
ADDRESS: 103 North 12th St., 3 Town Plaza Office, P.O. Box 3 878
Batesville, AR 72501
PHONE: (501) 793-4533
CONTACT OFFICER(S): Ms. Jeffrey Hance, General Manager
REMARKS: Private capital of $500,100

COMPANY: **First SBIC Of Arkansas, Inc.**
ADDRESS: Worthen Bank Building, Suite 1400
Little Rock, AR 72201
PHONE: (501) 378-1508
CONTACT OFFICER(S): Fred Burns, President
REMARKS: Private Capital of $619,728

COMPANY: **Small Business Inv. Cap. Inc.**
ADDRESS: 10003 New Benton Hwy., P.O. Box 3627
Little Rock, AR 72203
PHONE: (501) 455-3590
CONTACT OFFICER(S): Charles E. Toland, President
REMARKS: Private Capital of $750,000

COMPANY: **American Business Capital Corp.**
ADDRESS: 5331 East Valle Vista
Phoenix, AZ 85018
PHONE: (602) 840-4111
CONTACT OFFICER(S): Leonard A. Frankel, President
REMARKS: Private Capital of $500,000

COMPANY: **FBS Venture Capital Company**
ADDRESS: 6900 E. Camelback Road
Phoenix, AZ 85201
PHONE: (602) 941-2160
TYPE OF INSTITUTION: SBIC
CONTACT OFFICER(S): William B. McKee, President
W. Ray Allen, Exec. Vice President
ASSETS: $20 Million
INVESTMENTS/LOANS MADE: For own account
INVESTMENTS/LOANS MADE: In securities without a secondary market
TYPES OF FINANCING: VENTURE CAPITAL: Start-up from developed product stage; First-stage (less than 1 year); Second-stage (generally 1 -3 years); Later-stage expansion; Buy-outs/Acquisitions
PREFERRED TYPES OF INDUSTRIES/INVESTMENTS: Technology Related Indust ries
WILL NOT CONSIDER: Real Estate
GEOGRAPHIC LIMITS OF INVESTMENTS/LOANS: Local; State; In proximity t o offices located in Arizona, Minnesota and Boulder, Colorado
RANGE OF INV./LOAN PER BUSINESS: Min. $50K; Max. $500K
BUSINESS CHARACTERISTICS DESIRED-REQUIRED: Minimum number of years i n business: 0

COMPANY: **Rocky Mountain Equity Corporation**
ADDRESS: 4530 Central Ave.
Phoenix, AZ 85012
PHONE: (602) 274-7534
CONTACT OFFICER(S): Anthony J. Nicoli, President
REMARKS: Private Capital of $500,000

COMPANY: **VNB Capital Corp.**
ADDRESS: 241 North Central Avenue
Phoenix, AZ 85073
PHONE: (602) 261-2900
CONTACT OFFICER(S): Franklin Greenspan, Vice-President
REMARKS: Private capital of $12,061,000

COMPANY: **Sun Belt Capital Corporation**
ADDRESS: 14255 North 76th Place
Scottsdale, AZ 85260
PHONE: (602) 998-4449
CONTACT OFFICER(S): Bruce L. Vinci, President
REMARKS: Private capital of $500,000

COMPANY: **Ritter Partners**
ADDRESS: 150 Isabella Avenue
Atherton, CA 94025
PHONE: (415) 421-9990
CONTACT OFFICER(S): William C. Edwards, President
REMARKS: Private capital of $1,228,802

COMPANY: **PBC Venture Capital, Incorporated**
ADDRESS: 1408 — 18th Street, (MAIL: P.O. Box 6008, Bakersfi eld 93386)
Bakersfield, CA 93301
PHONE: (805) 395-3555
CONTACT OFFICER(S): Henry L. Wheeler, Manager
REMARKS: Private Capital of $540,000

COMPANY: **San Joaquin Capital Corporation**
ADDRESS: 1675 Chester Ave., P.O. Box 2538
Bakersfield, CA 93303
PHONE: (805) 323-7581
TYPE OF INSTITUTION: SBIC
CONTACT OFFICER(S): Chester Troudy, Executive V.P.
ASSETS: $5,120,722
TYPES OF FINANCING: Equity-related; Convertible debentures
PREFERRED TYPES OF INDUSTRIES/INVESTMENTS: Real Estate, High Tech
WILL NOT CONSIDER: Motion pictures
GEOGRAPHIC LIMITS OF INVESTMENTS/LOANS: Continental U.S.
RANGE OF INV./LOAN PER BUSINESS: Min. $50,000; Max. $200,000
PREFERRED TERM FOR LOANS & LEASES: Min. 5 years; Max. 10 years

COMPANY: **Atalanta Investment Capital Corp.**
ADDRESS: 141 El Camino Drive
Beverly Hills, CA 90212
PHONE: (213) 273-1730
REMARKS: Main Office: New York, NY

SMALL BUSINESS INVESTMENT COMPANIES (SBICs)

(Venture Capital. Also see Minority Enterprise SBICs, Venture Capital Companies and Investment Bankers)

COMPANY: **Developers Equity Capital Corp.**
ADDRESS: 9201 Wilshire Blvd., Suite 204
Beverly Hills, CA 90210
PHONE: (213) 278-3611
CONTACT OFFICER(S): Larry Sade, Chairman of Board
REMARKS: Private Capital of $583,000

COMPANY: **Equilease Capital Corp.**
ADDRESS: 315 So. Beverly Drive
Beverly Hills, CA 90212
PHONE: (213) 445-7211
REMARKS: Main Office: New York, NY

COMPANY: **I.K. Capital Loans, Ltd.**
ADDRESS: 8601 Wilshire Boulevard, Suite 600
Beverly Hills, CA 90211
PHONE: (213) 858-7844
CONTACT OFFICER(S): Iraj Kermanshahchi, President
REMARKS: Private capital of $1,000,000

COMPANY: **Metropolitan Venture Company, Inc.**
ADDRESS: 8383 Wilshire Boulevard, Suite 360
Beverly Hills, CA 90211-2410
PHONE: (213) 651-2171
CONTACT OFFICER(S): Esther Lowy, President
ASSETS: $1,000,000
INVESTMENTS/LOANS MADE: In securities with a secondary market; Secur ities without a secondary market
TYPES OF FINANCING: VENTURE CAPITAL: Second-stage; Buy-outs; Acquisi tions; LOANS; Working capital; Equipment; REAL ESTATE
PREFERRED TYPES OF INDUSTRIES/INVESTMENTS: Real Estate
GEOGRAPHIC LIMITS OF INVESTMENTS/LOANS: State (CA)
RANGE OF INV./LOAN PER BUSINESS: Min. $50,000; Max. $200,000
PREFERRED TERM FOR LOANS & LEASES: Min. 5 years; Max. 10 years
REFERRALS ACCEPTED FROM: Investment/Mortgage Banker or Borrower/Inve stee

COMPANY: **Westamco Investment Co.**
ADDRESS: 8929 Wilshire Blvd., Suite 400
Beverly Hills, CA 90211
PHONE: (213) 652-8288
CONTACT OFFICER(S): Leonard G. Muskin, President
REMARKS: Private Capital of $800,000

COMPANY: **Cornell Capital Corporation**
ADDRESS: 2049 Century Park East, 12th Floor
Century City, CA 90067
PHONE: (213) 277-7793

COMPANY: **Benox, Incorporated**
ADDRESS: 17295 East Railroad Street
City of Industry, CA 91749
PHONE: (818) 965-1541
CONTACT OFFICER(S): Mike Blum
ASSETS: $500,000
TYPES OF FINANCING: LOANS: Equity-related
PREFERRED TYPES OF INDUSTRIES/INVESTMENTS: Truck/trailer retail
GEOGRAPHIC LIMITS OF INVESTMENTS/LOANS: Continental U.S.
RANGE OF INV./LOAN PER BUSINESS: Max. $100,000

COMPANY: **Florists Capital Corporation**
ADDRESS: 11260 Playa Court
Culver City CA 90230
PHONE: (213) 390-9781
CONTACT OFFICER(S): Christopher M. Conroy, Chairman
REMARKS: Private Capital of $1,020,286

COMPANY: **PCF Venture Capital Corporation**
ADDRESS: 3420 East Third Avenue
Foster City, CA 94404
PHONE: (415) 571-5411
CONTACT OFFICER(S): Benedicto Yujuico, Chairman
REMARKS: Private capital of $1,500,000

COMPANY: **Imperial Ventures Incorporated**
ADDRESS: 9920 South La Cienega Blvd.,
Inglewood, CA 90301
PHONE: (213) 417-5600
CONTACT OFFICER(S): Donald B. Prell, President
ASSETS: In excess of $624,000
INVESTMENTS/LOANS MADE: For own account
INVESTMENTS/LOANS MADE: In securities with a secondary market and in securities without a secondary market
TYPES OF FINANCING: SECONDARY-MARKET CORPORATE SECURITIES: Common st ock; Preferred stock; Bonds; VENTURE CAPITAL: Second-stage; Later-stage expansion; Buy-outs/Acquisitions; LOANS: Working capital; Equipment; Equ ity-related
WILL NOT CONSIDER: Start up operations
GEOGRAPHIC LIMITS OF INVESTMENTS/LOANS: State
RANGE OF INV./LOAN PER BUSINESS: Min. $100,000; Max. open as will co -venture
PREFERRED TERM FOR LOANS & LEASES: Max. 5 yrs.
BUSINESS CHARACTERISTICS DESIRED/REQUIRED: Minimum number of years i n business: 3
REFERRALS ACCEPTED FROM: Investment/Mortgage banker or Borrower/Inve stee

COMPANY: **Ivanhoe Venture Capital, L.T.D.**
ADDRESS: 737 Pearl St., Suite 201
La Jolla, CA 92037
PHONE: (619) 454-8882
TYPE OF INSTITUTION: Small Business Investment Co. SBIC (federally l icensed)
CONTACT OFFICER(S): Alan R. Toffler, Managing General Partner
P. Fre derick Wulff, General Partner
ASSETS: $1,100,000
INVESTMENTS/LOANS MADE: For own account

SMALL BUSINESS INVESTMENT COMPANIES (SBICs)

(Venture Capital. Also see Minority Enterprise SBICs, Venture Capital Companies and Investment Bankers)

TYPES OF FINANCING: SECONDARY-MARKET: Common stock; Preferred stock; Convertible Debentures; VENTURE CAPITAL: Second-stage; Later-stage expa nsion; Buy-outs/Acquisitions: LOANS: Equity related
PREFERRED TYPES OF INDUSTRIES/INVESTMENTS: High growth industries
WILL NOT CONSIDER: Start-ups
GEOGRAPHIC LIMITS OF INVESTMENTS/LOANS: National
RANGE OF INV./LOAN PER BUSINESS: Min. $50,000; Max. $200,000
PREFERRED TERM FOR LOANS & LEASES: Min. five years; Max. fifteen yea rs
BUSINESS CHARACTERISTICS DESIRED-REQUIRED: Minimum number of years i n business: 3+
REFERRALS ACCEPTED FROM: Investment/Mortgage Banker and Borrower/Inv estee

COMPANY: **Beverly Glen Venture Capital**
ADDRESS: 1964 Westwood Blvd.
Los Angeles, CA 90025
PHONE: (213) 475-9700
CONTACT OFFICER(S): Herman Jacobs, President
REMARKS: Private capital of $1,000,000

COMPANY: **Brentwood Capital Corporation**
ADDRESS: 11661 San Vincente Blvd.
Los Angeles, CA 90049
PHONE: (213) 826-6581
CONTACT OFFICER(S): T.M. Pennington, Chairman of Board
REMARKS: Private capital of $6,060,510

COMPANY: **Cal Fed Venture Capital Corp.**
ADDRESS: 5670 Wilshire Boulevard, Suite 1875
Los Angeles, CA 90036
PHONE: (213) 932-4051
CONTACT OFFICER(S): James B. Jacobson, Chairman
REMARKS: Private capital of $7,500,000

COMPANY: **California Capital Investors**
ADDRESS: 11812 San Vicente Blvd.
Los Angeles, CA 90049
PHONE: (213) 820-7222
CONTACT OFFICER(S): Harold A. Haytin, Chairman of the Board
REMARKS: Private Capital of $1,162,000

COMPANY: **City Capital Corp.**
ADDRESS: 9080 Santa Monica Boulevard, Suite 201
Los Angeles, CA 90069
PHONE: (213) 273-4080
CONTACT OFFICER(S): Morton Heller, President
REMARKS: Private Capital of $1,000,000

COMPANY: **First Interstate Capital, Inc.**
ADDRESS: 515 South Figueroa Street, Suite 1900
Los Angeles, CA 90071
PHONE: (213) 622-1922
CONTACT OFFICER(S): David B. Jones, President
REMARKS: Private capital of $9,000,000

COMPANY: **Grocers Capital Co.**
ADDRESS: 2601 S. Eastern Avenue
Los Angeles, CA 90040
PHONE: (213) 726-2601
CONTACT OFFICER(S): William Christy, President
REMARKS: Private capital of $1,500,000

COMPANY: **Nelson Capital Corp.**
ADDRESS: 10000 Santa Monica Blvd., Suite 300
Los Angeles, CA 90067
PHONE: (213) 556-1944

COMPANY: **Latigo Ventures**
ADDRESS: 23410 Civic Center Way #E-2
Malibu, CA 90265
PHONE: (213) 456-7024
TYPE OF INSTITUTION: Venture Capital SBIC
CONTACT OFFICER(S): Robert A. Peterson
ASSETS: $15 million
INVESTMENTS/LOANS MADE: For own account
TYPES OF FINANCING: VENTURE CAPITAL: Start-up from developed product stage; First-stage; Second-stage; Later-stage expansion; Buy-outs/Acquisitions
PREFERRED TYPES OF INDUSTRIES/INVESTMENTS: High-technology & Medical; Multi-site Restaurants
GEOGRAPHIC LIMITS OF INVESTMENTS/LOANS: National
RANGE OF INV./LOAN PER BUSINESS: Min. $100,000; Max. $500,000

COMPANY: **California Partners Draper Assoc. CGP**
ADDRESS: 3000 Sand Hill Rd., Bldg. 2, ²60
Menlo Park, CA 94205
PHONE: (415) 493-5600
REMARKS: Private Capital of $500,000

COMPANY: **Crosspoint Investment Corporation**
ADDRESS: 1330 University Dr.
Menlo Park, CA
PHONE: (415) 964-3545
TYPE OF INSTITUTION: Venture Capital
CONTACT OFFICER(S): Max S. Simpson, President
ASSETS: $3.0 million
INVESTMENTS/LOANS MADE: For own account
TYPES OF FINANCING: VENTURE CAPITAL: Later-stage expansion; Buy-outs/Acquisitions
PREFERRED TYPES OF INDUSTRIES/INVESTMENTS: Medical instruments; computer peripherals, instrumentation, automation
WILL NOT CONSIDER: Real estate, movies
GEOGRAPHIC LIMITS OF INVESTMENTS/LOANS: Local, state, regional
RANGE OF INV./LOAN PER BUSINESS: Min. $150,000; Max. $1.0 million
BUSINESS CHARACTERISTICS DESIRED-REQUIRED: Minimum number of years in business 2-3; Min. annual sales $1.0 million; Min. net worth $500,000; Min. annual net income $100,000

REFERRALS ACCEPTED FROM: Borrower/Investee

COMPANY: **Pan American Investment Co.**
ADDRESS: 545 Middlefield Road, Suite 160
Menlo Park, CA 94025
PHONE: (415) 328-4401
CONTACT OFFICER(S): Robert C. Weeks, President
REMARKS: Private Capital of $4,824,484

COMPANY: **First SBIC of California**
ADDRESS: 4000 MacArthur Blvd., Ste. 950
Newport Beach, CA 92660
PHONE: (714) 754-4780
CONTACT OFFICER(S): Tim Hay, President
REMARKS: Private Capital of $25,000,000

COMPANY: **Marwit Capital Corp.**
ADDRESS: 180 Newport Center Drive, Ste. 200
Newport Beach, CA 92660
PHONE: (714) 640-6234
CONTACT OFFICER(S): Martin W. Witte, President
Robert A. Miller, Vice President
ASSETS: $5 million
INVESTMENTS/LOANS MADE: For own account
INVESTMENTS/LOANS MADE: In securities with a secondary market and in securities without a secondary market
TYPES OF FINANCING: VENTURE CAPITAL: Second-stage; Later-stage; Buy-outs/Acquisitions
PREFERRED TYPES OF INDUSTRIES/INVESTMENTS: Diversified
WILL NOT CONSIDER: Restaurants
GEOGRAPHIC LIMITS OF INVESTMENTS/LOANS: National
RANGE OF INV./LOAN PER BUSINESS: Min. $100,000; Max. 2,000,000
PREFERRED TERM FOR LOANS & LEASES: Min. 5 years; Max. 10 years
BUSINESS CHARACTERISTICS DESIRED-REQUIRED: Variable
REFERRALS ACCEPTED FROM: Investment/Mortgage banker or Borrower/Investee

COMPANY: **Wesco Capital, Ltd.**
ADDRESS: 3471 Via Lido, Suite 204
Newport Beach, CA 92663
PHONE: (714) 673-3140
CONTACT OFFICER(S): Peter J. Madigan, General Partner
REMARKS: Private capital of $500,000

COMPANY: **Merrill Pickard Anderson & Eyre I**
ADDRESS: Two Palo Alto Square, Ste. 425
Palo Alto, CA 94306
PHONE: (415) 856-8880
CONTACT OFFICER(S): Steven L. Merrill, President
REMARKS: Private Capital of $28,245,932

COMPANY: **AMF Financial, Inc.**
ADDRESS: 9910-D Mira Mesa Boulevard
San Diego, CA 92123
PHONE: (619) 695-0233
CONTACT OFFICER(S): William Temple, Vice-President
REMARKS: Private capital of $500,000

COMPANY: **Seaport Ventures, Inc.**
ADDRESS: 770 B Street, Suite 420
San Diego, CA 92101
PHONE: (619) 232-4069
TYPE OF INSTITUTION: Small Business Investment Company (SBIC)
CONTACT OFFICER(S): Michael Stolper, President
Carole Luther, Vice President
ASSETS: $Private Capital: $1,500,000; Total funds available for investment $7,500,000
INVESTMENTS/LOANS MADE: Through private placements
TYPES OF FINANCING: SECONDARY MARKET CORPORATE SECURITIES: Common Stock; Preferred stock; Bonds; VENTURE CAPITAL: Second-stage; Later-stage expansion, Buy-outs/Acquisitions; LOANS: Equity related
PREFERRED TYPES OF INDUSTRIES/INVESTMENTS: Will consider any industry
WILL NOT CONSIDER: Real estate, motion pictures, project financings
GEOGRAPHIC LIMITS OF INVESTMENTS/LOANS: National
RANGE OF INV./LOAN PER BUSINESS: Min. $100,000; Max. $300,000
PREFERRED TERM FOR LOANS & LEASES: Min. 5 years; Max. 10 years
BUSINESS CHARACTERISTICS DESIRED-REQUIRED: Minimum number of years in business: 18 mos.; Min. annual sales $500,000; Min. net worth $0; Min. annual net income $0; Min. annual cash flow $0

COMPANY: **Vista Capital Corporation/Vista partners, Inc.**
ADDRESS: 701 "B" Street, Suite 760
San Diego, CA 92101
PHONE: (619) 236-1800
TYPE OF INSTITUTION: Small business Investment Company/Investment Banking
CONTACT OFFICER(S): Fred J. Howden, Jr, Chairman
Leslie S. Buck, President
Gregory D. Howard, Vice President
ASSETS: $5 million
INVESTMENTS/LOANS MADE: For own account, through private placements
INVESTMENTS/LOANS MADE: In securities with a secondary market and securities without a secondary market
TYPES OF FINANCING: SECONDARY MARKET CORPORATE SECURITIES: Common stock; Preferred

stock; Bonds; VENTURE CAPITAL: Research & Development; start-up from developed product stage; Second-stage; Later-stage expans ion; Buy-outs/ Acquisitions, LOANS: Equity-related; LEASES: Leveraged; Tax leases, Non-tax leases, Operating
PREFERRED TYPES OF INDUSTRIES/INVESTMENTS: Diversified; Computer related, Biotechnology
GEOGRAPHIC LIMITS OF INVESTMENTS/LOANS: Regional
RANGE OF INV./LOAN PER BUSINESS: Min. $300,000
BUSINESS CHARACTERISTICS DESIRED-REQUIRED: Minimum number of years in business 3; Min. annual sales $3,000,000

COMPANY: **Bay Venture Group**
ADDRESS: One Embarcadero Center, Suite 3303
San Francisco, CA 94111
PHONE: (415) 989-7680
TYPE OF INSTITUTION: Venture Capital oriented, Unincorporated SBIC
CONTACT OFFICER(S): William R. Chandler, General Partner
ASSETS: $1 million private capital
INVESTMENTS/LOANS MADE: For own account
INVESTMENTS/LOANS MADE: Only in securities without a secondary market
TYPES OF FINANCING: SECONDARY-MARKET CORPORATE SECURITIES: Common stock; Preferred stock, VENTURE CAPITAL: Research & Development; Start-up from developed product stage
PREFERRED TYPES OF INDUSTRIES/INVESTMENTS: Computer Hardware & Software, Electronics, Office Automation, Medical, Optics, Lasers, Analytical Instrumentation, Process Instrumentation, Communications, Robotics, and Related Technologies.
WILL NOT CONSIDER: Real Estate, Food Service, Hotels, Motion Pictures, Oil & Gas
RANGE OF INV./LOAN PER BUSINESS: Max. $200,000
BUSINESS CHARACTERISTICS DESIRED-REQUIRED: Min. no. of years in business: 0
REFERRALS ACCEPTED FROM: Investment/Mortgage banker or Borrower/Investee

COMPANY: **CFB Venture Capital Corporation**
ADDRESS: 350 California Street, Mezzanine
San Francisco, CA 94104
PHONE: (415) 445-0594
REMARKS: Private capital of $1,000,000

COMPANY: **Crocker Capital Corp.**
ADDRESS: 111 Sutter St., Suite 600
San Francisco, CA 94104
PHONE: (415) 399-7889
CONTACT OFFICER(S): Charles Crocker, President
REMARKS: Private Company

COMPANY: **Crocker Ventures Incorporated**
ADDRESS: One Montgomery Street
San Francisco, CA 94104
PHONE: (415) 983-7024
CONTACT OFFICER(S): Jordan V. Burkart, General Manager
REMARKS: Private Capital of $1,000,000

COMPANY: **G C & H Partners**
ADDRESS: One Maritime Plaza, 20th Floor
San Francisco, CA 94110
PHONE: (415) 981-5252
CONTACT OFFICER(S): James C. Gaither, General Partner
REMARKS: Private capital of $1,000,000

COMPANY: **Hamco Capital Corp.**
ADDRESS: 235 Montgomery Street 500
San Francisco, CA 94104
PHONE: (415) 986-5500
CONTACT OFFICER(S): William R. Hambrecht, President
REMARKS: Private capital of $2,000,000

COMPANY: **Jupiter Partners**
ADDRESS: 600 Montgomery Street, 35th Floor
San Francisco, CA 94111
PHONE: (415) 421-9990
CONTACT OFFICER(S): John M. Bryan, President
REMARKS: Private capital of $1,028,720

COMPANY: **Round Table Capital Corporation**
ADDRESS: 601 Montgomery Street
San Francisco, CA 94111
PHONE: (415) 392-7500
CONTACT OFFICER(S): Richard Dumke, President
REMARKS: Private Capital of $700,000

COMPANY: **Small Business Enterprises Co.**
ADDRESS: 555 California St.
San Francisco, CA 94104
PHONE: (415) 953-3001
CONTACT OFFICER(S): Patrick Topolski, President
REMARKS: Private Capital of $12,500,000

COMPANY: **Wells Fargo Equity Corporation**
ADDRESS: 1 Embarcadero Center, Suite 1814
San Francisco, CA 94111
PHONE: (415) 396-3291
TYPE OF INSTITUTION: SBIC Private Venture Capital
CONTACT OFFICER(S): Charles A. Greenberg, President
Michael F. Park, Sr. V.P.
Richard M. Lingua, Sr. V.P.
John H. Mullin, Sr. V.P., Anita M. Trachte V.P.
Paul D. Ardleigh, V.P.

COMPANY: **Enterprise Venture Capital Corp.**
ADDRESS: 1922 The Alameda
San Jose, CA 95126
PHONE: (408) 246-7502
TYPE OF INSTITUTION: Small Business Investment Corp. (SBIC)
CONTACT OFFICER(S): Ernest de la Ossa, President
Michael K. Beauchamp, Operating Manager (contact)
ASSETS: $1,500,000

SMALL BUSINESS INVESTMENT COMPANIES (SBICs)

(Venture Capital. Also see Minority Enterprise SBICs, Venture Capital Companies and Investment Bankers)

INVESTMENTS/LOANS MADE: For own account, Through private placements
INVESTMENTS/LOANS MADE: In securities with a secondary market and in securities without a secondary market
TYPES OF FINANCING: SECONDARY-MARKET CORPORATE SECURITIES: Common stock; Preferred stock; Bonds, VENTURE CAPITAL: Research & Development; Start-up from developed product stage; First-stage; Second-stage; Later-stage expansion, LOANS: Equity-related
PREFERRED TYPES OF INDUSTRIES/INVESTMENTS: Communications, computer service, software, general industry
WILL NOT CONSIDER: Real estate
GEOGRAPHIC LIMITS OF INVESTMENTS/LOANS: Local; State; Regional
RANGE OF INV./LOAN PER BUSINESS: Min. $50,000; Max. $150,000
PREFERRED TERM FOR LOANS & LEASES: Min. 5 years; Max. 10 years
BUSINESS CHARACTERISTICS DESIRED-REQUIRED: Min. number of years in business: 0; Other: Solid management experience - well defined marketing plan
REFERRALS ACCEPTED FROM: Investment/Mortgage banker or Borrower/Investee
REMARKS: We participate with other venture companies

COMPANY: **NSS Investments, Inc.**
ADDRESS: 897 MacArthur Blvd., Suite 103
San Leandro, CA 94577
PHONE: (415) 632-5833
CONTACT OFFICER(S): Bernard N. Nemerov, President
REMARKS: Private capital of $438,162

COMPANY: **Bancorp Venture Capital, Inc.**
ADDRESS: 2633 Cherry Avenue
Signal Hill, CA 90806
PHONE: (213) 595-1177
CONTACT OFFICER(S): Paul R. Blair, President
REMARKS: Private capital of $2,250,000

COMPANY: **Brantman Capital Corp.**
ADDRESS: 2476 Mar East, P.O. Box 877
Tiburon, CA 94920
PHONE: (415) 435-4747
CONTACT OFFICER(S): William T. Brantman, President
REMARKS: Private Capital of $350,100

COMPANY: **HMS Capital, Ltd.**
ADDRESS: 1500 Newell Avenue, Suite 702
Walnut Creek, CA 94596
PHONE: (415) 944-5861
CONTACT OFFICER(S): Michael Hone, President
REMARKS: Private capital of $1,657,000

COMPANY: **Associated Capital Corp.**
ADDRESS: 1983 Tower Road
Aurora, CO 80011
PHONE: (303) 367-7000
CONTACT OFFICER(S): Rodney J. Love, President
REMARKS: Private Capital of $1,842,000

COMPANY: **Colorado Growth Capital, Inc.**
ADDRESS: 1600 Broadway, Suite 2125
Denver, CO 80202
PHONE: (303) 629-0205
TYPE OF INSTITUTION: Small Business Investment Company
CONTACT OFFICER(S): Nicholas H. C. Davis, President
Debra Chavez, Financial Analyst
ASSETS: $1,500,000
INVESTMENTS/LOANS MADE: For own account
INVESTMENTS/LOANS MADE: In securities with a secondary market and in securities without a secondary market
TYPES OF FINANCING: SECONDARY-MARKET CORPORATE SECURITIES: Common stock, VENTURE CAPITAL: Second-stage (generally 1-3 years); Later-stage expansion, Buy-outs
PREFERRED TYPES OF INDUSTRIES/INVESTMENTS: Manufacturing companies with patented or proprietary product, potential national market, managment investment, plan in effect.
WILL NOT CONSIDER: Start-ups, service, retail, real estate, entertainment
GEOGRAPHIC LIMITS OF INVESTMENTS/LOANS: Regional
RANGE OF INV./LOAN PER BUSINESS: Min. $50,000; Max. $200,000
PREFFERED TERM FOR LOANS & LEASES: Min. 5 years; Max. 10 years
BUSINESS CHARACTERISTICS DESIRED-REQUIRED: Minimum number of years in business: 3; Min. annual sales $500,000
REFERRALS ACCEPTED FROM: Investment/Mortgage Banker or Borrower/Invester

COMPANY: **Colorado SBIC**
ADDRESS: 918 Seventeenth Street, P.O. Box 5168
Denver, CO 80217
PHONE: (303) 629-1968
CONTACT OFFICER(S): Frank J. Brainerd, V.P.
REMARKS: Private Capital of $699,800

COMPANY: **E S One Capital Corp.**
ADDRESS: 1700 Broadway, Suite 1510
Denver, CO 80294
PHONE: (303) 861-1066
CONTACT OFFICER(S): Leo Rostermundt, President
REMARKS: Private capital of $3,625,000

COMPANY: **Equilease Capital Corp.**
ADDRESS: 120 Bryant Street
Denver, CO 80219
PHONE: (303) 573-1374
REMARKS: Main Office: New York, NY

COMPANY: **Enterprise Finance Cap Development Corp.**
ADDRESS: 16 Lemond Circle
Snowmass Village, CO 81615
PHONE: (303) 923-4144

CONTACT OFFICER(S): Robert N. Hampton, President
REMARKS: Private capital of $1,000,000

COMPANY: **Capital Resource Company of Connecticut**
ADDRESS: 699 Bloomfield Av.
Bloomfield, CT 06002
PHONE: (203) 243-1114
TYPE OF INSTITUTION: Small Business Investment Company
CONTACT OFFICER(S): I. Martin Fierberg, Gen. Partner
Janice Romanowski, General Partner
ASSETS: $5 million+
TYPES OF FINANCING: VENTURE CAPITAL: Second stage; Later stage
PREFERRED TYPES OF INDUSTRIES/INVESTMENTS: High technology
GEOGRAPHIC LIMITS OF INVESTMENTS/LOANS: Regional
RANGE OF INV./LOAN PER BUSINESS: Min. $25,000; Max. $1,000,000
PREFERRED TERM FOR LOANS & LEASES: Min. 5-7 years
REFERRALS ACCEPTED FROM: Investment/Mortgage Banker or Borrower/Investee
REMARKS: No start-ups

COMPANY: **First Connecticut Small Business Investment Co.**
ADDRESS: 177 State St.
Bridgeport, CT
PHONE: (203) 366-4726
TYPE OF INSTITUTION: Small Business Investment Co.
CONTACT OFFICER(S): Lawrence R. Yurdin, V.P.
Steven A. Breiner, V.P.
ASSETS: $30,000,000
INVESTMENTS/LOANS MADE: For own account
TYPES OF FINANCING: REAL ESTATE LOANS: Long-term senior mtg.; Subordinated; Land; Land development; Construction; Gap, REAL ESTATE: Acquisitions
PREFERRED TYPES OF INDUSTRIES/INVESTMENTS: Diversified
GEOGRAPHIC LIMITS OF INVESTMENTS/LOANS: Regional; Northeast only
RANGE OF INV./LOAN PER BUSINESS: Min. $10,000; Max. $1,000,000
PREFERRED TERM FOR LOANS & LEASES: Min. 5; Max. 20 years
BUSINESS CHARACTERISTICS DESIRED-REQUIRED: Min. no. of years in business: 0
REFERRALS ACCEPTED FROM: Investment/Mortgage banker or Borrower/Investee

COMPANY: **The SBIC of Connecticut**
ADDRESS: 1115 Main St., Rm 610
Bridgeport, CT 06604
PHONE: (203) 367-3282
CONTACT OFFICER(S): Kenneth F. Zarrilli, Pres.
TYPES OF FINANCING: VENTURE CAPITAL, LOANS: Equity-related
RANGE OF INV./LOAN PER BUSINESS: Min. $10,000
PREFERRED TERM FOR LOANS & LEASES: Min. 5 years

COMPANY: **A B SBIC, Inc.**
ADDRESS: School House Road
Cheshire, CT 06410
PHONE: (203) 272-0203
CONTACT OFFICER(S): Adam J. Bozzuto, President
REMARKS: Private Capital of $500,000

COMPANY: **Northeastern Capital Corporation**
ADDRESS: 310 Main Street
East Haven, CT 06512
PHONE: (203) 469-7901
CONTACT OFFICER(S): Frank D'Engenio, President
REMARKS: Private capital of $412,076

COMPANY: **Dewey Investment Corp.**
ADDRESS: 101 Middle Turnpike West
Manchester, CT 06040
PHONE: (203) 649-0654
CONTACT OFFICER(S): George E. Mrosek, President
REMARKS: Private Capital of $510,650

COMPANY: **Nutmeg Capital Corp.**
ADDRESS: 426 East Street
New Haven, CT 06510
PHONE: (203) 776-0643
CONTACT OFFICER(S): Leigh B. Raymond, V.P.
REMARKS: Private Capital of $319,300

COMPANY: **Asset Capital and Management Corp.**
ADDRESS: 608 Ferry Blvd.
Stratford, CT 06497
PHONE: (203) 375-0299
CONTACT OFFICER(S): Ralph Smith, President
REMARKS: Private Capital of $978,787

COMPANY: **All State Venture Capital Corporation**
ADDRESS: 830 Post Road East
Westport, CT 06880
PHONE: (203) 226-9376
CONTACT OFFICER(S): Thomas H. Brown, Jr., President
REMARKS: Private Capital of $338,230

COMPANY: **Marcon Capital Corp.**
ADDRESS: 49 Riverside Ave.
Westport, CT 06880
PHONE: (203) 226-7751
CONTACT OFFICER(S): Martin A. Cohen, President
REMARKS: Private Capital of $550,000

COMPANY: **Capital Investment Co. of Washington**
ADDRESS: 1208 30th Street, N.W.
Washington, DC 20007
PHONE: (202) 342-6304
CONTACT OFFICER(S): John Katkish, President
REMARKS: Private Capital of $502,097

SMALL BUSINESS INVESTMENT COMPANIES (SBICs)

(Venture Capital. Also see Minority Enterprise SBICs, Venture Capital Companies and Investment Bankers)

DISTRICT OF COLUMBIA

COMPANY: **Thompson Venture Group, Inc.**
ADDRESS: 1725 K Street N.W., Suite 200
Washington, DC 20036
PHONE: (202) 872-1766
CONTACT OFFICER(S): Richard E. Thompson, President
REMARKS: Private capital of $504,374

FLORIDA

COMPANY: **First American Investment Corporation**
ADDRESS: 3250 Mary Street, Suite 308
Coconut Grove, FL 33133
PHONE: (305) 441-0881
CONTACT OFFICER(S): Joseph N. Hardin, Jr., President
REMARKS: Private capital of $4,000,000

COMPANY: **Caribank Capital Corp.**
ADDRESS: 255 East Dania Beach Blvd.
Dania, FL 33004
PHONE: (305) 925-2211
CONTACT OFFICER(S): Michael E. Chaney, President
REMARKS: Private capital of $1,000,000

COMPANY: **Allied Investment Corp.**
ADDRESS: One Financial Plaza, Suite 1614
Ft. Lauderdale, FL 33394
PHONE: (305) 763-8484
CONTACT OFFICER(S): G. Cabell Williams III, Asst. V.P.
REMARKS: Main Office: Washington, DC

COMPANY: **Massachusetts Capital Corporation**
ADDRESS: One Financial Plaza, Suite 1614
Ft. Lauderdale, FL 33301
PHONE: (305) 763-8484
REMARKS: Main Office: Boston, MA

COMPANY: **Gold Coast Capital Corporation**
ADDRESS: 3550 Biscayne Blvd., Room 601
Miami, FL 33137
PHONE: (305) 576-2012
TYPE OF INSTITUTION: Small Business Investment Corp. (S.B.I.C)
CONTACT OFFICER(S): William I. Gold, President
ASSETS: $3,000,000
INVESTMENTS/LOANS MADE: For own account
TYPES OF FINANCING: VENTURE CAPITAL: Second-stage; LOANS: Equipment; REAL ESTATE LOANS: Land development; Construction; REAL ESTATE: Acquisitions; Joint ventures OTHER SERVICES PROVIDED: Loans to all businesses secured by property
GEOGRAPHIC LIMITS OF INVESTMENTS/LOANS: Local; State
RANGE OF INV./LOAN PER BUSINESS: Min. $25,000
PREFERRED TERM FOR LOANS & LEASES: 5 yrs.

COMPANY: **Southeast Venture Capital, Inc.**
ADDRESS: 1 Biscayne Tower, 34th Floor
Miami, FL 33131
PHONE: (305) 577-4680
CONTACT OFFICER(S): Clement L. Hofmann, President
REMARKS: Private Capital of $3,001,169

COMPANY: **Western Financial Capital Corp.**
ADDRESS: 1380 N.E. Miami Gardens Drive
North Miami Beach, FL 33179
PHONE: (305) 949-5900
TYPE OF INSTITUTION: SBIC (Small business Investment Corp.)
CONTACT OFFICER(S): Fredric M. Rosemore, President
Lance B. Rosemore, Vice-President
ASSETS: $7,000,000
INVESTMENTS/LOANS MADE: For own account
INVESTMENTS/LOANS MADE: Only in securities without a secondary market
TYPES OF FINANCING: VENTURE CAPITAL: Second-stage; Later-stage, LOANS: Working capital; Equipment; Equity related; purchases of health care practices and business; REAL ESTATE LOANS: Owner occupied-commercial only, LEASES: Vendor financing programs, REAL ESTATE: Acquisitions, OTHER SERVICES PROVIDED: cnnsulting and advisory
PREFERRED TYPES OF INDUSTRIES/INVESTMENTS: Financing doctors, dentists, optometrists, veterinarians, podiatrists for start-ups and business expansion/ modernization
WILL NOT CONSIDER: Equity investments only—Debt and Equity O.K.
GEOGRAPHIC LIMITS OF INVESTMENTS/LOANS: National
RANGE OF INV./LOAN PER BUSINESS: Min. $20,000; Max. $700,000
PREFERRED TERM FOR LOANS & LEASES: Min. 5 years; Max. 20 years

COMPANY: **J & D Capital Corp.**
ADDRESS: 12747 Biscayne Blvd.
North Miami, FL 33181
PHONE: (305) 893-0303
TYPE OF INSTITUTION: SBIC
CONTACT OFFICER(S): Jack Carmel, President
INVESTMENTS/LOANS MADE: For own account
TYPES OF FINANCING: VENTURE CAPITAL: Second-stage. LOANS: Equipment, REAL ESTATE LOANS: Wraparounds; FACTORING. LEASES. INTERNATIONAL
PREFERRED TYPES OF INDUSTRIES/INVESTMENTS: Small Business Investment Company
GEOGRAPHIC LIMITS OF INVESTMENTS/LOANS: Local; State
RANGE OF INV./LOAN PER BUSINESS: Min. $25,000; Max. $500,000
PREFERRED TERM FOR LOANS & LEASES: Min. 5 years; Max. 15/20 years
REFERRALS ACCEPTED FROM: Investment/Mortgage banker or Borrower/Investee

COMPANY: **SBAC of Panama City Florida**
ADDRESS: 2612 W 15th St.
Panama City, FL 32401
PHONE: (904) 785-9577
CONTACT OFFICER(S): Charles Smith, President
TYPES OF FINANCING: VENTURE CAPITAL: Start-up from developed product stage; First-stage (less than 1 year); Second-stage (generally 1-3 years); Later-stage expansion; Buy-outs/Acquisitions, LOANS: Equity-related; Other: Direct lending
PREFERRED TYPES OF INDUSTRIES/INVESTMENTS: Diversified
GEOGRAPHIC LIMITS OF INVESTMENTS/LOANS: State, mainly N.W. Fla.
RANGE OF INV./LOAN PER BUSINESS: Min. None; Max. $500,000
PREFERRED TERM FOR LOANS & LEASES: Min. 5 years; Max. 20 years

COMPANY: **First North Florida SBIC Company**
ADDRESS: 1400 Gadsden St., P.O. Box 1021
Quincy, FL 32351
PHONE: (904) 875-2600
CONTACT OFFICER(S): J.B. Higdon, President
REMARKS: Private Capital of $300,000

COMPANY: **First Tampa Capital Corporation**
ADDRESS: 4600 North Dale Mabry Highway
Tampa, FL 33614
PHONE: (813) 879-4058
CONTACT OFFICER(S): Thomas L. duPont, President
REMARKS: Private capital of $1,950,000

COMPANY: **Market Capital Corp.**
ADDRESS: 1102 North 28th St., P.O. Box 22667
Tampa, FL 33622
PHONE: (813) 247-1357
CONTACT OFFICER(S): E.E. Eads, President
REMARKS: Private Capital of $786,400

COMPANY: **Servico Business Inv. Corporation**
ADDRESS: 1601 Belvedere Rd. Servico Center South, Suite 201
West Palm Beach, FL 33406
PHONE: (305) 689-4906
CONTACT OFFICER(S): Gary O. Marino, President
REMARKS: Private Capital of $500,000

COMPANY: **Equilease Capital Corp.**
ADDRESS: 22-61 Penimeter Pk., Suite 12
Atlanta, GA 30309
PHONE: (404) 457-8278
REMARKS: Main Office: New York, NY

COMPANY: **Investors Equity, Inc.**
ADDRESS: 2629 First Atlanta Tower
Atlanta, GA 30383
PHONE: (404) 523-3999
TYPE OF INSTITUTION: SBIC
CONTACT OFFICER(S): Richard Bell
TYPES OF FINANCING: VENTURE CAPITAL: First-stage; Second-stage; Later-stage expansion; Buy-outs/Acquisitions OTHER SERVICES PROVIDED: All types equity
PREFERRED TYPES OF INDUSTRIES/INVESTMENTS: Light manufacturing
GEOGRAPHIC LIMITS OF INVESTMENTS/LOANS: Regional; Other: Southeast

COMPANY: **Affiliated Investment Fund, Inc.**
ADDRESS: 2225 Shurfine Drive
College Park, GA 30337
PHONE: (404) 766-0221
CONTACT OFFICER(S): Samuel Weissman, President
REMARKS: Private Capital of $742,000

COMPANY: **Mighty Capital Corp.**
ADDRESS: Suite 100, 50 Technology Park/Atlanta
Norcross, GA 30092
PHONE: (404) 448-2232
CONTACT OFFICER(S): Gary Korynoski, General Manager
REMARKS: Private capital of $505,000

COMPANY: **Bancorp Hawaii SBIC, Incorporated**
ADDRESS: 111 South King Street, Suite 1020
Honolulu, HI 96813
PHONE: (808) 536-8357
CONTACT OFFICER(S): James D. Evans, Jr., President
REMARKS: Private capital of $1,000,000

COMPANY: **MorAmerica Capital Corp.**
ADDRESS: 300 American Bldg.
Cedar Rapids, IA 52401
PHONE: (319) 363-8249
TYPE OF INSTITUTION: Small Business Investment Company ("SBIC")
CONTACT OFFICER(S): Jerry Burrows, President
Donald Flynn, Vice President
David Schroder, Vice President
ASSETS: $35,000,000
INVESTMENTS/LOANS MADE: For own account
INVESTMENTS/LOANS MADE: In securities with a secondary market and in securities without a secondary market
TYPES OF FINANCING: VENTURE CAPITAL: First-stage (less than 1 year); Second-stage (generally 1-3 years); Later-stage expansion; Buy-outs/Acquisitions
PREFERRED TYPES OF INDUSTRIES/INVESTMENTS: Diversified
WILL NOT CONSIDER: Real estate, service business, consumer goods

GEOGRAPHIC LIMITS OF INVESTMENTS/LOANS: National
RANGE OF INV./LOAN PER BUSINESS: Min. $200,000; Max. $1,000,000
PREFERRED TERM FOR LOANS & LEASES: Min. 5 years; Max. 10 years
BUSINESS CHARACTERISTICS DESIRED-REQUIRED: Minimum number of years in business: 1; Min. annual sales $500,000
BRANCHES: Kevin Mullane, Suite 2724 Commerce Tower Building, Kansas City, MO 64105, 816-842-0114
Steven Massey, 600 East Mason St., Milwaukee, WI 53202, 414-276-3839

COMPANY: **First Idaho Venture Capital Corp.**
ADDRESS: 900 Washington St.
Boise, ID 83702
PHONE: (208) 345-3460
CONTACT OFFICER(S): Ron Twilegar
REMARKS: Private Capital of $1,000,000

COMPANY: **Alpha Capital Corp.**
ADDRESS: Three First National Plaza, 14th Floor
Chicago, IL 60602
PHONE: (312) 372-1556
CONTACT OFFICER(S): Andrew H. Kalnow, President
REMARKS: Private capital of $1,290,000

COMPANY: **Business Ventures Inc.**
ADDRESS: 20 N. Wacker Dr., Ste. 550
Chicago, IL 60606
PHONE: (312) 346-1580
TYPE OF INSTITUTION: SBIC
CONTACT OFFICER(S): Milton G. Lefton, President
ASSETS: $550,000
INVESTMENTS/LOANS MADE: For own account
TYPES OF FINANCING: VENTURE CAPITAL: Second-stage; Buy-outs/Acquisitions, LOANS: Equity related
PREFERRED TYPES OF INDUSTRIES/INVESTMENTS: No preference
WILL NOT CONSIDER: Real Estate or Start-ups
GEOGRAPHIC LIMITS OF INVESTMENTS/LOANS: Local; State; Regional
RANGE OF INV./LOAN PER BUSINESS: Min. $50,000; Max. 100,000
PREFERRED TERM FOR LOANS & LEASES: Min. 5 years; Max. 7 years
BUSINESS CHARACTERISTICS DESIRED-REQUIRED: Minimum number of years in business: 2
REFERRALS ACCEPTED FROM: Investment/Mortgage Banker or Borrower/Investee

COMPANY: **Certified Grocers Investment Corp.**
ADDRESS: 4800 South Central Avenue
Chicago, IL 60638
PHONE: (312) 585-7000
CONTACT OFFICER(S): Charles D. Nipp, President
REMARKS: Private Capital of $500,000

COMPANY: **Continental Illinois Venture Corp./ Continental Illinois Equity Corp.**
ADDRESS: 231 S. LaSalle St.
Chicago, IL 60693
PHONE: (312) 828-8021
TYPE OF INSTITUTION: SBIC
CONTACT OFFICER(S): William Putze, Sr. V.P.
Judith Bultman Meyer, V.P.
Scott Smith, 2nd V.P.
INVESTMENTS/LOANS MADE: For own account
INVESTMENTS/LOANS MADE: In securities with a secondary market and in securities without a secondary market
TYPES OF FINANCING: SECONDARY-MARKET CORPORATE SECURITIES: Common stock; VENTURE CAPITAL: Start-up from developed product stage; First-stage (less than 1 year); Second-stage (generally 1-3 years); Later-stage expansion; Buy-outs/Acquisitions, LOANS: Equity-related
PREFERRED TYPES OF INDUSTRIES/INVESTMENTS: Computer hardware and software, Electronics, Communications, Retail, Medical, buy-outs/ acquisitions
WILL NOT CONSIDER: Real Estate
GEOGRAPHIC LIMITS OF INVESTMENTS/LOANS: National
RANGE OF INV./LOAN PER BUSINESS: Min. $500,000; Max. $10 million
BUSINESS CHARACTERISTICS DESIRED-REQUIRED: Min. no. of years in business: 0
REFERRALS ACCEPTED FROM: Investment/Mortgage banker or Borrower/Investee

COMPANY: **Mesirow Capital Corp.**
ADDRESS: 135 South LaSalle Street, Suite 3705
Chicago, IL 60603
PHONE: (312) 443-5757
CONTACT OFFICER(S): Lester A. Morris, President
REMARKS: Private capital of $1,250,000

COMPANY: **Equilease Capital Corp.**
ADDRESS: 2400 East Devon
Des Plaines, IL 60018
PHONE: (312) 981-1710
REMARKS: Main Office: New York, NY

COMPANY: **Funds Inc.**
ADDRESS: 1930 George Street
Melrose Park, IL 60160
PHONE: (312) 343-6575
CONTACT OFFICER(S): William R. Breihan, General Manager
REMARKS: Private capital of $500,000

COMPANY: **Abbott Capital Corp.**
ADDRESS: 9933 Lawler Ave.
Skokie, IL 60077
PHONE: (312) 982-0404
CONTACT OFFICER(S): Richard E. Lassar, President
REMARKS: Private Capital of $727,840

COMPANY: **White River Capital Corporation**
ADDRESS: 500 Washington Street, P.O. Box 929

Columbus, IN 47201
PHONE: (812) 372-0111

COMPANY: **First Indiana Equity Group, Inc.**
ADDRESS: 20 North Meridian Street, Room 312
Indianapolis, IN 46204
PHONE: (317) 633-7303
CONTACT OFFICER(S): Thomas R. Creasser, II, Chairman
REMARKS: Private capital of $1,000,000

COMPANY: **Heritage Venture Group Incorporated**
ADDRESS: 2400 One Indiana Square
Indianapolis, IN 46204
PHONE: (317) 635-5696
TYPE OF INSTITUTION: Small Business Investment Company
CONTACT OFFICER(S): Arthur A. Angotti, President
ASSETS: $3,000,000
INVESTMENTS/LOANS MADE: For own account
INVESTMENTS/LOANS MADE: Only in securities without a secondary market
TYPES OF FINANCING: SECONDARY-MARKET CORPORATE SECURITIES: Common stock; Preferred stock; Other: Subordinated Debentures with warrants VENTURE CAPITAL: Second-stage; Later-stage expansion; Buy-outs/Acquisitions; OTHER SERVICES PROVIDED: Management Services
PREFERRED TYPES OF INDUSTRIES/INVESTMENTS: Television; Radio; Cable Television; Cellular Telephone; Satellite and Microwave Communications; Light Manufacturing.
WILL NOT CONSIDER: Real estate
GEOGRAPHIC LIMITS OF INVESTMENTS/LOANS: National
RANGE OF INV./LOAN PER BUSINESS: Min. $100,000; Max. $500,000—$1 million
PREFERRED TERM FOR LOANS & LEASES: Min. 5 years; Max 7 years
BUSINESS CHARACTERISTICS DESIRED-REQUIRED: Min. number of years in business: 3; Min. annual sales: nominal; Min. annual net income: breakeven
REFERRALS ACCEPTED FROM: Investment/Mortgage banker and Borrower/Investee
REMARKS: Long term capital gain and return on investment is of primary concern; we do not charge fees.

COMPANY: **Mount Vernon Venture Capital Company**
ADDRESS: 9102 North Meridian Street
Indianapolis, IN 46260
PHONE: (317) 846-5106
CONTACT OFFICER(S): Thomas J. Grande, General Manager
REMARKS: Private capital of $2,090,500

COMPANY: **Tyler Refrigeration Capital Corp.**
ADDRESS: 2222 East Michigan Blvd.
Michigan City, IN 46360
PHONE: (219) 874-3181
CONTACT OFFICER(S): Gary Slock, President
REMARKS: Private Capital of $303,000

COMPANY: **1st Source Capital Corporation**
ADDRESS: 100 North Michigan Street
South Bend, IN 46601
PHONE: (219) 236-2180
CONTACT OFFICER(S): Eugene L. Cavanaugh, Jr., Vice-President
REMARKS: Private capital of $1,780,000

COMPANY: **Equity Resource Company, Inc.**
ADDRESS: One Plaza Place, 202 South Michigan Street
South Bend, IN 46601
PHONE: (219) 237-5255
CONTACT OFFICER(S): Michael J. Hammes, Vice President
REMARKS: Private capital of $2,000,000

COMPANY: **Kansas Venture Capital Inc.**
ADDRESS: 1030 First National Bank Tower, One Townsite Plaza
Topeka, KS 66603
CONTACT OFFICER(S): George L. Doak, President

COMPANY: **Mountain Ventures, Incorporated**
ADDRESS: P.O. Box 628, 911 North Main,
London, KY 40741
PHONE: (606) 864-5175
TYPE OF INSTITUTION: SBIC
CONTACT OFFICER(S): L. R. Moncrief, President
TYPES OF FINANCING: VENTURE CAPITAL:: Start-up from developed product stage; First-stage; Second-stage; Later-stage expansion; Buy-outs/Acquisitions; LOANS: Equity-related
PREFERRED TYPES OF INDUSTRIES/INVESTMENTS: Manufacturing
GEOGRAPHI LIMITS OF INVESTMENTS/LOANS: State
REFERRALS ACCEPTED FROM: Investment/Mortgage banker or Borrower/Investee

COMPANY: **Blackburn-Sanford Venture Cap. Corp.**
ADDRESS: 3120 First National Tower
Louisville, KY 40202
PHONE: (502) 585-9612
CONTACT OFFICER(S): Mark C. Sanford, President
REMARKS: Private capital of $1,350,000

COMPANY: **Financial Opportunities, Inc.**
ADDRESS: 981 South Third Street
Louisville, KY 40203
PHONE: (502) 584-1281
CONTACT OFFICER(S): Joe P. Peden, President
REMARKS: Private Capital of $900,000

COMPANY: **Capital Equity Corp.**
ADDRESS: 1885 Wooddale Boulevard
Baton Rouge, LA 70806
PHONE: (504) 924-9206

CONTACT OFFICER(S): Arthur J. Mitchell, General Manager
REMARKS: Private capital of $1,100,000

COMPANY: **First Southern Capital Corp.**
ADDRESS: P.O. Box 14205
Baton Rouge, LA 70898
PHONE: (504) 769-3000
CONTACT OFFICER(S): John Crabtree, Pres.
ASSETS: 4-5 million
TYPES OF FINANCING: VENTURE CAPITAL: Start-up from developed product stage; First-stage (less than 1 year); Second-stage (generally 1-3 years); Later-stage expansion; Buy-outs/Acquisitions, LOANS: Equity-related
GEOGRAPHIC LIMITS OF INVESTMENTS/LOANS: Regional; S.E., South
RANGE OF INV./LOAN PER BUSINESS: Min. $100,000; Max. $300,000
PREFERRED TERM FOR LOANS & LEASES: Flexible
BUSINESS CHARACTERISTICS DESIRED-REQUIRED: Minimum number of years in business: 0

COMPANY: **Louisiana Equity Capital Corporation**
ADDRESS: 451 Florida Street
Baton Rouge, LA 70801
PHONE: (504) 389-4421
TYPE OF INSTITUTION: Small Business Investment Company
CONTACT OFFICER(S): Melvin L. Rambin, President
Jack McDonald, Investment Analyst
ASSETS: $7.8 million
INVESTMENTS/LOANS MADE: For own account
INVESTMENTS/LOANS MADE: In securities with a secondary market and in securities without a secondary market
TYPES OF FINANCING: SECONDARY-MARKET CORPORATE SECURITIES: Common stock; Preferred stock, VENTURE CAPITAL: Start-up; First stage; Later-stage expansion, Buy-outs/Acquisitions; LOANS: Unsecured; Working capital; Equipment; Equity-related; REAL ESTATE LOANS: Intermediate-term senior mtg; REAL ESTATE: Acquisitions; Joint ventures; Partnerships/Syndications
PREFERRED TYPES OF INDUSTRIES/INVESTMENTS: Communications, Health Care, Other
GEOGRAPHIC LIMITS OF INVESTMENTS/LOANS: Other: Lead investor only in Louisiana, participating investor throughout U.S.
RANGE OF INV./LOAN PER BUSINESS: Min. $200,000; Max. $500,000
PREFERRED TERM FOR LOANS & LEASES: Min. 5 years; Max. 7 years
BUSINESS CHARACTERISTICS DESIRED-REQUIRED: Minimum number of years in business: 0
REFERRALS ACCEPTED FROM: Investment/Mortgage banker or Borrower/Investee

COMPANY: **Commercial Capital, Inc.**
ADDRESS: P.O. Box 939
Covington, LA 70433
PHONE: (504) 892-4921
CONTACT OFFICER(S): Frederick W. Pierce, President

COMPANY: **Capital for Terrebonne, Inc.**
ADDRESS: 1613 Barrow Street
Houma, LA 70360
PHONE: (504) 868-3930
CONTACT OFFICER(S): Hartwell A. Lewis, President
REMARKS: Private Capital of $750,000

COMPANY: **Dixie Business Investment Company**
ADDRESS: P.O. Box 588
Lake Providence, LA 71254
PHONE: (318) 559-1558
CONTACT OFFICER(S): Wayne Baker; President
James C. Scott, Jr., Manager & Loan Officer
ASSETS: $1,795,366.92
INVESTMENT/LOANS MADE: For own account
INVESTMENT/LOANS MADE: In securities with a secondary market or in securities without secondary market
TYPES OF FINANCING: VENTURE CAPITAL: Start-up; First-stage; Second-stage; Later-stage expansion; LOANS: Unsecured; Working capital (receivables/inventory); Equipment; Equity-related
PREFERRED TYPES OF INDUSTRIES: Open to any
WILL NOT CONSIDER: Any type of Investment or Business Loan
GEOGRAPHIC LIMITS OF INVESTMENTS/LOANS: Regional
RANGE OF INV./LOAN BER BUSINESS: Min. $10,000.00; Max. $100,000.00
PREFERRED TERM FOR LOANS & LEASES: Min. Five years; Max. twenty yearsBUSINESS CHARACTERISTICS DESIRED-REQUIRED: Minimum number of years in business: 0

COMPANY: **Walnut Street Capital Company**
ADDRESS: 231 Carondelet Street, Suite 702
New Orleans, LA 70130
PHONE: (504) 525-2112
CONTACT OFFICER(S): William D. Humphries, Managing G.P.
REMARKS: Private capital of $1,476,000

COMPANY: **CADDO Capital Corp.**
ADDRESS: 3010 Knight Street, Ste. 240
Shreveport, LA 71105
PHONE: (318) 869-1689
CONTACT OFFICER(S): Thomas L. Young, Jr., President
REMARKS: Private Capital of $520,000

COMPANY: **Commercial Venture Capital Corp.**
ADDRESS: 329 Texas Street
Shreveport, LA 71101
PHONE: (318) 226-4638
CONTACT OFFICER(S): William H. Jakson, President
ASSETS: $1,000,000
INVESTMENTS/LOANS MADE: For own account
INVESTMENTS/LOANS MADE: Only in securities without a secondary market
TYPES OF FINANCING: VENTURE CAPITAL: Research & Development; Start-up from developed

product stage; First-stage; Second-stage; Later stage expansion; Buy-outs/Acquisitions; LOANS: Unsecured to credits above; Working capital; REAL ESTATE LOANS: Land; Land development; Construction; Industrial revenue bonds; REAL ESTATE: Acquisitions; Joint ventures
GEOGRAPHIC LIMITS OF INVESTMENTS/LOANS: State
RANGE OF INV./LOAN PER BUSINESS: Min.: $100,000; Max. $198,000
PREFERRED TERM FOR LOANS & LEASES: Min. 5 years; Max. 10 years
BUSINESS CHARACTERISTICS DESIRED-REQUIRED: Min. number of years in business: 0; Min. annual sales $200,000; Min. net worth: $100,000; Min. annual net income $50,000

COMPANY: **First Small Business Investment Co. of Louisiana, Inc.**
ADDRESS: 2852 Carey St., P.O. Box 1336
Slidell, LA 70459
PHONE: (504) 641-2404
CONTACT OFFICER(S): Mrs. N. Gorman Hooper, Exec. V.P.
REMARKS: Private Capital of $161,801

COMPANY: **Advent Atlantic Capital Company L.P.**
ADDRESS: 45 Milk Street
Boston, MA 02109
PHONE: (617) 338-0800
TYPE OF INSTITUTION: Venture Capital
CONTACT OFFICER(S): David D. Croll, Chairman
ASSETS: 2 Billion
INVESTMENTS/LOANS MADE: For own account
INVESTMENTS/LOANS MADE: In securities with a secondary market and in securities without a secondary market
TYPES OF FINANCING: SECONDARY-MARKET: Common stock; Preferred stock, VENTURE CAPITAL: Research & Development; Start-up from developed product stage; First-stage; Second-stage; Later-stage expansion; Buy-Outs/Acquisitions
WILL NOT CONSIDER: Real Estate, Oil & Gas Exploration
RANGE OF INV./LOAN PER BUSINESS: Min. $500,000; Max. $10,000,000
BUSINESS CHARACTERISTICS DESIRED-REQUIRED: Minimum number of years in business: 0
REFERRALS ACCEPTED FROM: Investment/Mortgage banker or Borrower/Investee
REMARKS: Private Capital of $2,517,780

COMPANY: **Advent IV Capital Company**
ADDRESS: 45 Milk Street
Boston, MA 02109
PHONE: (617) 338-0800
CONTACT OFFICER(S): David D. Croll, Chairman
REMARKS: Private capital of $12,050,000

COMPANY: **Alta Capital Corp.**
ADDRESS: P.O. Square, Ste. 3800
Boston, MA 02109
PHONE: (617) 482-8020
CONTACT OFFICER(S): William P. Egan, President
REMARKS: Private Capital of $2,000,000

COMPANY: **Atlantic Energy Capital Corp.**
ADDRESS: One Post Office Square, Suite 1760
Boston, MA 02109
PHONE: (617) 451-6220
CONTACT OFFICER(S): Joost S. Tjaden, President
REMARKS: Private capital of $1,000,000

COMPANY: **Atlas Capital Corp.**
ADDRESS: 55 Court St.
Boston, MA 02108
PHONE: (617) 482-1218
CONTACT OFFICER(S): Herbert Carver, President
REMARKS: Private Capital of $1,254,156

COMPANY: **Bever Capital Corp.**
ADDRESS: One Post Office Square, Suite 1760
Boston, MA 02109
PHONE: (617) 451-9192
CONTACT OFFICER(S): Paul Deiters, President
REMARKS: Private capital of $1,992,000

COMPANY: **Boston Hambro Capital Company**
ADDRESS: One Boston Place
Boston, MA 02106
PHONE: (617) 722-7055
CONTACT OFFICER(S): Edwin Goodman, President of Corp. G.P.
REMARKS: Private Capital of $5,400,000

COMPANY: **Chestnut Capital Corp.**
ADDRESS: 45 Milk St.
Boston, MA 02109
PHONE: (617) 338-0800
CONTACT OFFICER(S): David D. Croll, Chairman & CEO
REMARKS: Private Capital of $2,000,000

COMPANY: **Devonshire Capital Corporation**
ADDRESS: 45 Milk Street
Boston, MA 02109
PHONE: (617) 338-0800
CONTACT OFFICER(S): David D. Croll, Chairman
REMARKS: Private Capital of $2,532,750

COMPANY: **First Capital Corp. of Chicago**
ADDRESS: 200 Clarendon Street, Suite 4901
Boston, MA 02116
PHONE: (617) 247-4040

COMPANY: **International Film Investors (LP)**
ADDRESS: Suite 1400, One Federal Street
Boston, MA 02110
REMARKS: Main Office: New York, NY

COMPANY: **Massachusetts Capital Corporation**
ADDRESS: 75 Federal Street
Boston, MA 02110
PHONE: (617) 426-2488
CONTACT OFFICER(S): Maurice Wiener, President
REMARKS: Private capital of $1,695,445

COMPANY: **New England Capital Corporation**
ADDRESS: One Washington Mall
Boston, MA 02108
PHONE: (617) 722-6400
TYPE OF INSTITUTION: Small Business Investment Co.
CONTACT OFFICER(S): Z. David Patterson, Executive V.P., Leveraged Buyouts and General
Melvin W. Ellis, V.P., General
Thomas C. Tremblay, V.P., High Technology (New England area)
Thomas A. Ballantyne, Assistant Investment Officer
ASSETS: $9 million
INVESTMENTS/LOANS MADE: For own accounts
INVESTMENTS/LOANS MADE: In securities with a secondary market and in securities without a secondary market
TYPES OF FINANCING: SECONDARY-MARKET CORPORATE SECURITIES: Common stock; Preferred stock, VENTURE CAPITAL: First-stage (less than 1 year); Second-stage (generally 1-3 years); Later-stage expansion; Buy-outs/Acquisitions
PREFERRED TYPES OF INDUSTRIES/INVESTMENTS: Communications, Computer Related, Electronic component and Instrumentation, Genetic Engineering, Industrial Products and Equipment, Medical
WILL NOT CONSIDER: Real Estate, Retail
GEOGRAPHIC LIMITS OF INVESTMENTS/LOANS: National
RANGE OF INV./LOAN PER BUSINESS: Min. $200,000; Max. $500,000
PREFERRED TERM FOR LOANS & LEASES: Min. 5; Max. 10 years
BUSINESS CHARACTERISTICS DESIRED-REQUIRED: Min. no. of years in business: 0
REFERRALS ACCEPTED FROM: Investment/Mortgage banker or Borrower/Investee

COMPANY: **Northeast Small Business Investment Corporation**
ADDRESS: 16 Cumberland St.
Boston, MA 02115
PHONE: (617) 267-3983
CONTACT OFFICER(S): Joseph Mindick, Treasurer
REMARKS: Private Capital of $412,076

COMPANY: **T. A. Associates**
ADDRESS: 45 Milk St.
Boston, MA 02109
PHONE: (617) 338-0800
TYPE OF INSTITUTION: Private Venture Capital Firm/SBIC
CONTACT OFFICER(S): C. Kevin Landry, General Partner, Equity
David D. Croll, General Partner, Subordinated Lending
ASSETS: $150,000,000
INVESTMENTS/LOANS MADE: For managed accounts
INVESTMENTS/LOANS MADE: In securities with a secondary market and in securities without a secondary market
TYPES OF FINANCING: SECONDARY-MARKET CORPORATE SECURITIES: Common stock; Preferred stock, VENTURE CAPITAL: Research & Development; Start-up from developed product stage; First-stage (less than 1 year); Second-stage (generally 1-3 years); Later-stage expansion; Buy-outs/Acquisitions, LOANS: Equity-related
PREFERRED TYPES OF INDUSTRIES/INVESTMENTS: Technology: Electronics, Computer, Instrumentation, Medical, Manufacturing Companies, Oil & Gas Service Companies; CATV, Radio, TV; Leveraged Buy-outs
WILL NOT CONSIDER: Most service companies
GEOGRAPHIC LIMITS OF INVESTMENTS/LOANS: National
RANGE OF INV./LOAN PER BUSINESS: Min. $600,000; Max. $5,000,000
PREFERRED TERM FOR LOANS & LEASES: Min. 5; Max. 10 years
REFERRALS ACCEPTED FROM: Investment/Mortgage banker or Borrower/Investee

COMPANY: **Transatlantic Capital Corporation**
ADDRESS: 24 Federal Street, Ste. 400
Boston, MA 02110
PHONE: (617) 482-0015
CONTACT OFFICER(S): Bayard Henry, President
REMARKS: Private Capital of $3,009,000

COMPANY: **UST Capital Corporation**
ADDRESS: 40 Court St.
Boston, MA 02108
PHONE: (617) 726-7000
TYPE OF INSTITUTION: SBIC
CONTACT OFFICER(S): Stephen R. Lewinstein, President
Rick Kohn, V.P.
ASSETS: Approx. $2,000,000
INVESTMENTS/LOANS MADE: For own account; Through private placements
INVESTMENTS/LOANS MADE: In securities with a secondary market and in securities without a secondary market
TYPES OF FINANCING: VENTURE CAPITAL: First-stage (less than 1 year); Second-stage (generally 1-3 years); Later-stage expansion; Buy-outs/Acquisitions, LOANS: Working capital (receivables/inventory); Equipment; Equity-related, REAL ESTATE LOANS: Subordinated; Land; Land development; Construction; Standbys, REAL ESTATE: Acquisitions; Joint ventures; Partnerships/Syndications
PREFERRED TYPES OF INDUSTRIES/INVESTMENTS: General opportunities
WILL NOT CONSIDER: R & D or start-ups
GEOGRAPHIC LIMITS OF INVESTMENTS/LOANS: National
RANGE OF INV./LOAN PER BUSINESS: Our personal SBIC limit is approx. $300,000, but we syndicate up to $5,000,000
PREFERRED TERM FOR LOANS & LEASES: Max. 10 years

BUSINESS CHARACTERISTICS DESIRED-REQUIRED: Minimum number of years in business: 1; Min. annual sales None—prefer positive net worth
REFERRALS ACCEPTED FROM: Investment/Mortgage banker or Borrower/Investee

COMPANY: **Vadus Capital Corp.**
ADDRESS: One Post Office Square, Suite 1760
Boston, MA 02109
PHONE: (617) 451-6220
CONTACT OFFICER(S): Joost S. Tjaden, President
REMARKS: Private capital of $2,000,000

COMPANY: **First United SBIC, Inc.**
ADDRESS: 135 Will Drive
Canton, MA 02021
PHONE: (617) 828-6150
CONTACT OFFICER(S): Alfred W. Ferrara, V.P.
REMARKS: Private Capital of $300,000

COMPANY: **Stevens Capital Corporation**
ADDRESS: 168 Stevens Street
Fall River, MA 02721
CONTACT OFFICER(S): Edward Capuano, Pres.
REMARKS: Private capital of $506,000

COMPANY: **Business Achievement Corporation**
ADDRESS: 1280 Centre Street
Newton Center, MA 02159
PHONE: (617) 965-0550
CONTACT OFFICER(S): Julian H. Katzeff, President
REMARKS: Private Capital of $375,000

COMPANY: **Equilease Capital Corp.**
ADDRESS: 393 Totten Pond Rd., Suite 651
Waltham, MA 02154
PHONE: (617) 826-9056
REMARKS: Main Office: New York, NY

COMPANY: **Worcester Capital Corporation**
ADDRESS: 446 Main Street
Worcester, MA
PHONE: (617) 793-4508
TYPE OF INSTITUTION: Small Business Investment Company—Wholly-owned subidiary of Shawmut Worcester County Bank
CONTACT OFFICER(S): W. Kenneth Kidd, V.P. & General Manager
INVESTMENTS/LOANS MADE: For own account
INVESTMENTS/LOANS MADE: Only in securities without a secondary market
TYPES OF FINANCING: VENTURE CAPITAL: First-stage (less than 1 year); Second-stage (generally 1-3 years)
PREFERRED TYPES OF INDUSTRIES/INVESTMENTS: Manufacturing, Computer, Medical
WILL NOT CONSIDER: Real Estate
GEOGRAPHIC LIMITS OF INVESTMENTS/LOANS: Regional
RANGE OF INV./LOAN PER BUSINESS: Min. $50,000; Max. $200,000

COMPANY: **Suburban Capital Corp.**
ADDRESS: 6610 Rockledge Drive
Bethesda, MD 20817
PHONE: (301) 493-7025
CONTACT OFFICER(S): Henry "Pete" Linsert, Jr., President
REMARKS: Private capital of $5,000,000

COMPANY: **Greater Washington Investors, Inc.**
ADDRESS: 5454 Wisconsin Av.
Chevy Chase, MD 20815
PHONE: (301) 656-0626
CONTACT OFFICER(S): Don Christensen, Pres.
Martin S. Pinson Sr. V.P.
Cyril W. Draffin, V.P.
ASSETS: 28 million
TYPES OF FINANCING: VENTURE CAPITAL: Start-up from developed product stage; First-stage (less than 1 year); Second-stage (generally 1-3 years); Later-stage expansion; Buy-outs/Acquisitions, LOANS: Equity-related
PREFERRED TYPES OF INDUSTRIES/INVESTMENTS: Technology
WILL NOT CONSIDER: Real Estate; Natural Resources; Retailing
GEOGRAPHIC LIMITS OF INVESTMENTS/LOANS: National
RANGE OF INV./LOAN PER BUSINESS: Min. $100,000; Max. $600,000
BUSINESS CHARACTERISTICS DESIRED-REQUIRED: Minimum number of years in business: 0; Other: Rapid growth

COMPANY: **Michigan Capital & Service, Inc.**
ADDRESS: 500 First Nat'l Building
Ann Arbor, MI 48104
PHONE: (313) 663-0702
TYPE OF INSTITUTION: Small Business Investment Company (SBIC)
CONTACT OFFICER(S): Joseph F. Conway, President
James A. Parsons, V. P.
Anthony F. Buffa, V.P.
Carlene D. Dettleff, Asst. Corp. Secretary
ASSETS: $13 million
INVESTMENTS/LOANS MADE: For own account
INVESTMENTS/LOANS MADE: Only in securities without a secondary market
TYPES OF FINANCING: VENTURE CAPITAL: Start-up from developed product stage; First-stage (less than 1 year); Second-stage (generally 1-3 years); Later-stage expansion; Buy-outs/Acquisitions; LOANS: Equity-related

PREFERRED TYPES OF INDUSTRIES/INVESTMENTS: Computer-related; Communications; Medical Devices & Services; Manufacturing; Electronics; Energy-related; Automation, Data Devices
WILL NOT CONSIDER: Real estate; Finance companies; Restaurants
GEOGRAPHIC LIMITS OF INVESTMENTS/LOANS: National
RANGE OF INV./LOAN PER BUSINESS: Min. $250,000; Max. $800,000
PREFERRED TERM FOR LOANS & LEASES: Min. 3-5; Max. 7-10 years
BUSINESS CHARACTERISTICS DESIRED-REQUIRED: Minimum number of years in business: 0
REFERRALS ACCEPTED FROM: Investment/Mortgage banker or Borrower/Investee

COMPANY: **Detroit Metropolitan Small Business Investment Corporation**
ADDRESS: 150 Michigan Avenue
Detroit, MI 48226
PHONE: (313) 963-8190
TYPE OF INSTITUTION: SBIC
CONTACT OFFICERS: Ruby M. Jones, General Manager
ASSETS: $500,000,00
TYPES OF FINANCING: VENTURE CAPITAL: Start-up from developed product stage; First-stage (less than 1 year); Later-stage expansion; Buy-outs/Acquistions; LOANS: Working capital; Equipment; REAL ESTATE LOANS: Subordinated; REAL ESTATE: Acqusition
PREFERRED TYPES OF INDUSTRIES/INVESTMENTS: Negotiable
WILL NOT CONSIDER: Direct Deals
GEOGRAPHIC LIMITS OF INVESTMENTS/LOANS: Local
RANGE OF INV./LOAN PER BUSINESS: Min. $10,000.00; Max. $100,000.000
PREFERRED TERM FOR LOANS & LEASES: Min. 5 years; Max. 10 years
BUSINESS CHARACTERISTICS DESIRED-REQUIRED: Minimum number of years in business; 0
REFERRALS ACCEPTED FROM: Investment/Mortgage banker only; or Borrower/Investee; Referrals accepted from all financial Institutions, accounts, attys and financial consultants.

COMPANY: **Michigan Tech Capital Corp.**
ADDRESS: Technology Park, 1700 Duncan Avenue, P.O. Box 529
Hubbell MI 49934
PHONE: (906) 487-2643
TYPE OF INSTITUTION: Small Business Investment Company (SBIC)
CONTACT OFFICER(S): Edward J. Koepel, President
Clark L. Pellegrini, Vice President and Treasurer
Richard E. Tieder, Vice President and Secretary
ASSETS: $700,000
INVESTMENTS/LOANS MADE: For own account
INVESTMENTS/LOANS MADE: In securities with a secondary market and in securities without a secondary market
TYPES OF FINANCING: VENTURE CAPITAL: First-stage (less than 1 year); LOANS: Unsecured
PREFERRED TYPES OF INDUSTRIES/INVESTMENTS: Software; Processing - Basic Industries; Wood and Minerals
GEOGRAPHIC LIMITS OF INVESTMENTS/LOANS: Regional; Midwest
RANGE OF INV./LOAN PER BUSINESS: Min. $25,000; Max. $150,000
PREFERRED TERM FOR LOANS & LEASES: Min. 5 years; Max. 10 years

COMPANY: **Doan Resources Corp.**
ADDRESS: 333 East Main Street, Third Floor, P.O. Box 1431
Midland, MI 48640
PHONE: (517) 631-2623
CONTACT OFFICER(S): Herbert D. Doan, President
REMARKS: Private capital of $3,300,000

COMPANY: **Tyler Refrigeration Capital Corp.**
ADDRESS: 1329 Lake Street
Niles, MI 49120
PHONE: (616) 683-2000
REMARKS: Main Office: Michigan City, IN

COMPANY: **Federated Capital Corporation**
ADDRESS: 20000 West Twelve Mile Road
Southfield, MI 48076
PHONE: (313) 557-9100
CONTACT OFFICER(S): Louis P. Ferris, Jr., President
REMARKS: Private Capital of $500,000

COMPANY: **United Venture Capital Incorporated**
ADDRESS: 17117 West Nine Mile Road, Suite 910
Southfield, MI 48075
PHONE: (313) 559-7822
CONTACT OFFICER(S): Irving Meklir, President
REMARKS: Private capital of $500,000

COMPANY: **Northland Capital Corporation**
ADDRESS: 613 Missabe Building
Duluth, MN 55802
PHONE: (218) 722-0545
CONTACT OFFICER(S): George G. Barnum, Jr., President
REMARKS: Private capital of $862,750

COMPANY: **Shared Ventures, Inc.**
ADDRESS: 6550 York Ave., S.
Edina, MN 55435
PHONE: (612) 925-3411
CONTACT OFFICER(S): Howard W. Weiner, President
REMARKS: Private Capital of $750,000

COMPANY: **First Midwest Capital Corporation**
ADDRESS: 1010 Plymouth Bldg.
Minneapolis, MN 55402
PHONE: (612) 339-9391
CONTACT OFFICER(S): William Franta, Pres.

COMPANY: **North Star Ventures Inc.**
ADDRESS: 1501 First Bank Place West
Minneapolis, MN 55402
PHONE: (612) 333-1133
CONTACT OFFICER(S): Terrence Glarner, President
INVESTMENTS/LOANS MADE: Through private placements
TYPES OF FINANCING: VENTURE CAPITAL: Research & Development; Start-up from developed product stage; First-stage (less than 1 year); Second-stage (generally 1-3 years); LOANS: Equity-related
PREFERRED TYPES OF INDUSTRIES/INVESTMENTS: Technology; Manufacturing
WILL NOT CONSIDER: Real Estate
GEOGRAPHIC LIMITS OF INVESTMENTS/LOANS: National
RANGE OF INV./LOAN PER BUSINESS: Min. $300,000; Max. $1,000,000

COMPANY: **Retailers Growth Fund, Inc.**
ADDRESS: 2318 Park Ave. S.
Minneapolis, MN 55404
PHONE: (612) 872-4929
CONTACT OFFICER(S): Cornell Moore, Pres.
Rick L. Olson, Treasurer
ASSET: $3,000,000
INVESTMENTS/LOANS MADE: in securities with a secondary market and in securities without a secondary market
TYPES OF FINANCING: LOANS: Working capital; Equipment; Equity-related; LEASES; Single-investor; Vendor financing programs
PREFERRED TYPES OF INDUSTRIES/INVESTMENTS: retailing, transportation, high technology
GEOGRAPHIC LIMITS OF INVESTMENTS/LOANS: National
RANGE OF INV./LOAN PER BUSINESS: Min. $25.000; Max. $125,000
PREFERRED TERM FOR LOANS: Min. 5 years; Max. 10 years
BUSINESS CHARACTERISTICS DESIRED-REQUIRED: Minimum number of years in business: 0

COMPANY: **Threshold Ventures, Inc.**
ADDRESS: 430 Oak Grove Street, Suite #303
Minneapolis, MN 55403
PHONE: (612) 874-7199
TYPE OF INSTITUTION: Venture Capital
CONTACT OFFICER(S): Michael J. Meyer, President
INVESTMENTS/LOANS MADE: For own account
INVESTMENTS/LOANS MADE: Only in securities without a secondary market
TYPES OF FINANCING: VENTURE CAPITAL: First-stage; Second-stage; Later-stage expansion
PREFERRED TYPES OF INDUSTRIES/INVESTMENTS: Communications; Computer Related (Software); Manufacturing (Proprietary Products); Distribution (Computer, Electronics, Industrial and Medical Equipment and Products); Electronic Components and Instrumentation; Genetic Engineering; Medical/Health Related.
GEOGRAPHIC LIMITS OF INVESTMENTS/LOANS: National
RANGE OF INV./LOAN PER BUSINESS: Min. Open; Max. $15,000.00
BUSINESS CHARACTERISTICS DESIRED-REQUIRED: Minimum number of years in business: 0

COMPANY: **Bankers Capital Corp.**
ADDRESS: 4049 Pennsylvania, Suite 304
Kansas City, MO 64111
PHONE: (816) 531-1600
CONTACT OFFICER(S): Raymond E. Glasnapp, President
REMARKS: Private Capital of $502,000

COMPANY: **Capital For Business**
ADDRESS: 911 Main St. Suite 2300
Kansas City, MO 64199
PHONE: (816) 234-2357
TYPE OF INSTITUTION: SBIC
CONTACT OFFICER(S): James B. Hebenstreit, President
Burt Bergman, V.P
ASSETS: $7-10 Million
TYPES OF FINANCING: VENTURE CAPITAL: First-stage (less than 1 year); Second-stage (generally 1-3 years); Later-stage expansion; Buy-outs/Acquisitions, LOANS: Equity-related
GEOGRAPHIC LIMITS OF INVESTMENTS/LOANS: Regional; Other: Will go to other regions
RANGE OF INV./LOAN PER BUSINESS: Min. $200,000; Max. $700,000
PREFERRED TERM FOR LOANS & LEASES: Min. 5 years; Max. 7 years
BUSINESS CHARACTERISTICS DESIRED-REQUIRED: Minimum number of years in business: 0; Other: Startups occasionally (rare) financed
REFERRALS ACCEPTED FROM: Investment/Mortgage banker or Borrower/Investee
REMARKS: 2nd office: 11 S. Meramec, Suite 804, St. Louis, MO 63105, (314) 854-7427, Wm. Cannon

COMPANY: **Moramerica Capital Corp.**
ADDRESS: 911 Main Street, Suite 2724A, Commerce Tower Building
Kansas City, MO 64105
PHONE: (816) 842-0114
REMARKS: Main Office: Cedar Rapids, IA

COMPANY: **Intercapco West, Inc.**
ADDRESS: 7800 Bonhomme Avenue
St. Louis, MO 63105
PHONE: (314) 863-0600
CONTACT OFFICER(S): Thomas E. Phelps, President
REMARKS: Private capital of $525,000

SMALL BUSINESS INVESTMENT COMPANIES (SBICs)

(Venture Capital. Also see Minority Enterprise SBICs, Venture Capital Companies and Investment Bankers)

COMPANY: **Invesat Corporation**
ADDRESS: 162 E. Amite St., Suite 204
Jackson, MS 39201
PHONE: (601) 969-3242
TYPE OF INSTITUTION: Privately held venture capital
CONTACT OFFICER(S): J. Thomas Noojin, Pres.
M. L. McCandle, V.P.
John R. Bise, V.P.
ASSETS: $10,000,000
INVESTMENTS/LOANS MADE: For own account; through private placements
INVESTMENTS/LOANS MADE: In securities with a secondary market and in securities without a secondary market
TYPES OF FINANCING: VENTURE CAPITAL: Start-up from developed product stage; Buy-outs/Acquisitions, LOANS: Unsecured; Equipment; Equity-related, REAL ESTATE LOANS: Subordinated; Wraparounds; Land development
PREFERRED TYPES OF INDUSTRIES/INVESTMENTS: Health Care/Communications
GEOGRAPHIC LIMITS OF INVESTMENTS/LOANS: National
RANGE OF INV./LOAN PER BUSINESS: Min. $200,000; Max. $1,000,000
PREFERRED TERM FOR LOANS & LEASES: Min. 5; Max. 10 years
BUSINESS CHARACTERISTICS DESIRED-REQUIRED: Minimum number of years in business: 0
REFERRALS ACCEPTED FROM: Investment/Mortgage banker or Borrower/Investee

COMPANY: **Vicksburg SBIC**
ADDRESS: 302 First National Bank Building
Vicksburg, MS 39180
PHONE: (601) 636-4762
CONTACT OFFICER(S): David L. May, President
REMARKS: Private Capital of $600,000

COMPANY: **Rocky Mountain Ventures, Ltd.**
ADDRESS: 315 Securities Building
Billings, MT 59101
PHONE: (406) 256-1984
CONTACT OFFICER(S): James H. Koessler, President
REMARKS: Private capital of $525,000

COMPANY: **Delta Capital, Inc.**
ADDRESS: 227 North Tryon Street, Suite 201
Charlotte, NC 28202
PHONE: (704) 372-1410
CONTACT OFFICER(S): Alex B. Wilkins, Jr., President
REMARKS: Private capital of $1,250,000

COMPANY: **Heritage Capital Corp.**
ADDRESS: 2290 First Union Plaza
Charlotte, NC 28282
PHONE: (704) 334-2867
TYPE OF INSTITUTION: Small business investment company
CONTACT OFFICER(S): J. Randolph Gregory, President
William R. Starnes, V.P.
ASSETS: $5,690,000
INVESTMENTS/LOANS MADE: For own account; Through private placements
INVESTMENTS/LOANS MADE: In securities with a secondary market and in securities without a secondary mortgage
TYPES OF FINANCING: SECONDARY-MARKET CORPORATE SECURITIES: Common Stock; Other: Debt securities with equity options; VENTURE CAPITAL: Start-up from developed product stage; First-stage; Second-stage; Later-stage expansion; Buy-outs/Acquisitions; LOANS: Equity-related
PREFERRED TYPES OF INDUSTRIES/INVESTMENTS: No preference
WILL NOT CONSIDER: Straight loans
GEOGRAPHIC LIMITS OF INVESTMENTS/LOANS: National
RANGE OF INV./LOAN PER BUSINESS: Min. $100,000; Max. $500,000
PREFERRED TERM FOR LOANS & LEASES: Min. 5 years; Max. 10 years
BUSINESS CHARACTERISTICS DESIRED-REQUIRED: Minimum number of years in business: 1; Min. annual sales $1,000,000; Min. net worth $250,000
REFERRALS ACCEPTED FROM: Investment/Mortgage banker or Borrower/Investee

COMPANY: **Kitty Hawk Capital**
ADDRESS: One Tryon Center, Ste. 2030
Charlotte, NC 28284
PHONE: (704) 333-3777
TYPE OF INSTITUTION: SBIC
CONTACT OFFICER(S): Walter Wilkinson, President
Chris Hegele, V.P.
ASSETS: 6 million
INVESTMENTS/LOANS MADE: For own account
INVESTMENTS/LOANS MADE: In securities with a secondary market and in securities without a secondary market
TYPES OF FINANCING: VENTURE CAPITAL: Start-up from developed product stage; First-stage; Second-stage; Later-stage expansion; Buy-outs/Acquisitions, LOANS: Equity-related, REAL ESTATE LOANS: Subordinated
PREFERRED TYPES OF INDUSTRIES/INVESTMENTS: Diversified
WILL NOT CONSIDER: Retail
GEOGRAPHIC LIMITS OF INVESTMENTS/LOANS: Regional
RANGE OF INV./LOAN PER BUSINESS: Min. $100,000; Max. None
PREFERRED TERM FOR LOANS & LEASES: Max. 7-8 years
BUSINESS CHARACTERISTICS DESIRED-REQUIRED: Minimum number of years in business: 0; Do start ups
REFERRALS ACCEPTED FROM: Investment/Mortgage banker or Borrower/Investee

COMPANY: **Falcon Capital Corp.**
ADDRESS: 311 South Evans Mall
Greenville, NC 27834
PHONE: (919) 752-5918
REMARKS: Private capital of $504,237

COMPANY: **Lowcountry Investment Corporation**
ADDRESS: Vernon Avenue
Kinston, NC 28659
REMARKS: Main Office: Charleston Heights, SC

COMPANY: **Northwestern Capital Corporation**
ADDRESS: 924 B Street, P.O. Box 310
North Wilkesboro, NC 28674
PHONE: (919) 651-5194
CONTACT OFFICER(S): R. James Maclaren, President
REMARKS: Private capital of $1,363,000

COMPANY: **Dakota First Capital Corporation**
ADDRESS: 51 Broadway, Suite 601
Fargo, ND 58102
PHONE: (701) 237-0450
CONTACT OFFICER(S): Alexander P. MacDonald, President
REMARKS: Private capital of $1,000,000

COMPANY: **United Financial Resources Corp.**
ADDRESS: 7312 Jones Street, P.O. Box 1131
Omaha, NE 68114
PHONE: (402) 393-1272
CONTACT OFFICER(S): Terrence W. Olsen, President
REMARKS: Private capital of $500,000

COMPANY: **Equities Capital Company, Inc.**
ADDRESS: 890 West End Avenue
New York, NY 10025 PHONE: (212) 866-6008
CONTACT OFFICER(S): Leon Scharf, President
REMARKS: Private capital of $502,500

COMPANY: **Granite State Capital, Incorporated**
ADDRESS: 10 Fort Eddy Road
Concord, NH 03301
PHONE: (603) 228-9090
CONTACT OFFICER(S): Stuart D. Pompian, Manager
REMARKS: Private capital of $995,000

COMPANY: **Hampshire Capital Corporation**
ADDRESS: P.O. Box 468
Portsmouth, NH 03801
PHONE: (603) 431-7755wF7CONTACT OFFICER(S):
Philip G. Baker, President
Lauren E. Wright, Vice President
ASSETS: $4,300,000
INVESTMENTS/LOANS MADE: For managed accounts, through private placements
INVESTMENTS/LOANS MADE: In securities with a secondary market and in securities without a secondary market
TYPES OF FINANCING: VENTURE CAPITAL, LOANS: Working capital, Equipment, REAL ESTATE LOANS, INTERNATIONAL (import/export only), REAL ESATE
PREFERRED TYPES OF INDUSTRIES/INVESTMENTS: Open
WILL NOT CONSIDER: Do not prefer hi-tech
GEOGRAPHIC LIMITS OF INVESTMENTS/LOANS: National; East Coast Focus
RANGE OF INV./LOAN PER BUSINESS: Min. 25,000; Max. $100,000
PREFERRED TERM FOR LOANS & LEASES: Min. 5 years; Max. 5 years

COMPANY: **Unicorn Ventures, Ltd.**
ADDRESS: 14 Commerce Drive
Cranford, NJ 07016
PHONE: (201) 276-7880
TYPE OF INSTITUTION: SBIC
CONTACT OFFICER(S): Frak P. Diassi, General Partner
Arthur Bugs Baer,General Partner
ASSETS: $30,000,000
INVESTMENTS/LOANS MADE: For own account
INVESTMENTS/LOANS MADE: In securities with a secondary market and in securities without a secondary market
TYPES OF FINANCING: VENTURE CAPITAL: Start-up from developed product stage; First-stage; Second-stage; Later-stage expansion; Buy-outs/Acquisitions
PREFERRED TYPES OF INDUSTIRES/INVESTMENTS: Communications, Computer Related, Consumer Products & Services, Distribution, Electronics Components & Instrumentation, Energy/Natural Resources, Genetic Engineering, Medical
GEOGRAPHIC LIMITS OF INVESTMENTS/LOANS: National
RANGE OF INV./LOAN PER BUSINESS: Min. $250,000; Max. $1,000,000
PREFERRED TERM FOR LOANS & LEASES: Min. 5 years
BUSINESS CHARACTERISTIS DESIRED-REQUIRED:Minimum number of years in business: 0
REFERRALS ACCEEPTED FROM: Investment/mortgage banker and borower/investee

COMPANY: **Lloyd Capital Corp.**
ADDRESS: 77 State Highway #5
Edgewater, NJ 07020
PHONE: (201) 947-6000
TYPE OF INSTITUTION: SBIC
CONTACT OFFICER(S): Solomon T. Scharf, President
ASSETS: $12,000,000
INVESTMENTS/LOANS MADE: For own account
TYPES OF FINANCING: SECONDARY-MARKET CORPORATE SECURITIES: Other: Loans, VENTURE CAPITAL: Second-stage, LOANS: Equity-related, REAL ESTATE LOANS: Intermediate-term senior mtg.; Subordinated; Wraparounds; Land; Construction, REAL ESTATE: Acquisitions; Joint ventures; Partnerships/Syndications

COMPANY: **Equities Capital Co., Inc.**
ADDRESS: 409 Grand Ave.
Englewood, NJ 07631
PHONE: (201) 567-9655
REMARKS: Man Office: New York, NY

COMPANY: **Engle Investment Co.**
ADDRESS: 35 Essex Street
Hackensack, NJ 07601
PHONE: (201) 489-3583
CONTACT OFFICER(S): Murray Hendel, President
REMARKS: Private Capital of $500,657

COMPANY: **Raybar SBIC**
ADDRESS: 255 West Spring Valley Ave., P.O. Box 1038
Maywood, NJ 07607
PHONE: (201) 368-2663
CONTACT OFFICER(S): Patrick F. McCort, General Manager
REMARKS: Private capital of $554,990

COMPANY: **First Princeton Capital Corp.**
ADDRESS: 227 Hamburg Turnpike
Pompton Lakes, NJ 07442
PHONE: (201) 839-7950
CONTACT OFFICER(S): S. Lawrence Goldstein, President
REMARKS: Private capital of $1,125,00

COMPANY: **Eslo Capital Corp.**
ADDRESS: 485 Morris Avenue
Springfield, NJ 07080
PHONE: (201) 467-2444
CONTACT OFFICER(S): Leo Katz, President
REMARKS: Private Capital of $639,323

COMPANY: **Capital SBIC, Inc.**
ADDRESS: 143 East State Street
Trenton, NJ 08608
PHONE: (609) 394-5221
CONTACT OFFICER(S): Isadore Cohen, President
REMARKS: Private capital of $665,316

COMPANY: **Albuquerque SBIC**
ADDRESS: 501 Tijeras Avenue, N.W., P.O. Box 487
Albuquerque, NM 87103
PHONE: (505) 247-0145
TYPE OF INSTITUTION:privately owned SBIC
CONTACT OFFICER(S): Albert T. Ussery, President
ASSETS: $600,000
INVESTMENTS/LOANS MADE: For own account
INVESTMENTS/LOANS MADE: In securities with a secondary market and in securities without a secondary market
TYPES OF FINANCING: VENTURE CAPITAL: Second-stage, LOANS: Other: Loans with stock warrants
PREFERRED TYPES OF INDUSTRIES/INVESTMENTS: Diversified, usually debt instruments with stock warrants
GEOGRAPHIC LIMITS OF INVESTMENTS/LOANS: Local; Other: with network participants will consider national geographic limits
RANGE OF INVESTMENT/LOAN PER BUSINESS: Min. $75,000; Max. $100,000
PREFERRED TERM FOR LOANS & LEASES: Min. 5 years; Max. 8 years
BUSINESS CHARACTERISTICS DESIRED-REQUIRED: Minimum number of years in business: 2
REFERRALS ACCEPTED FROM: Investment/Mortgage banker or Borrower/Investee

COMPANY: **Fluid Capital Corp.**
ADDRESS: 8421 B Montgomery Blvd., NE
Albuquerque, NM 87111
PHONE: (505) 292-4747
CONTACT OFFICER(S): George T. Slaughter, President
REMARKS: Private Capital of $1,558,680

COMPANY: **New Mexico Capital Corp.**
ADDRESS: 2900 Louisiana Blvd., N.E., Ste. 201
Albuquerque, NM 87110
PHONE: (505) 884-3600
CONTACT OFFICER(S): John C. Evans, Controller
REMARKS: Private Capital of $2,985,001

COMPANY: **Southwest Capital Investments, Inc.**
ADDRESS: The Southwest Building, 3500-E Comanche Road NE
Albuquerque, NM 87107
PHONE: (505) 884-7161
TYPE OF INSTITUTION: Small Business Investment Company
CONTACT OFFICER(S): Martin J. Roe, President/Treasurer
ASSETS: $3,633,503.43
TYPES OF FINANCING: VENTURE CAPITAL: Later-stage expansion, LOANS: Working capital; Equipment; Equity-related, FACTORING
GEOGRAPHIC LIMITS OF LEASES: Regional
RANGE OF LEASE PER BUSINESS: Min. $50,000; Max. $160,000
PREFERRED TERM FOR LOANS & LEASES: Min. 5 years
BUSINESS CHARACTERISTICS DESIRED-REQUIRED: Minimum number of years in business: 3

COMPANY: **Equity Capital Corp.**
ADDRESS: 231 Washington Avenue, Suite 2
Santa Fe, NM 87501
PHONE: (505) 988-4273
CONTACT OFFICER(S): Jerry A. Henson, President
REMARKS: Private capital of $502,000

COMPANY: **Key Venture Capital Corporation**
ADDRESS: 60 State Street
Albany, NY 12207
PHONE: (518) 447-3180
CONTACT OFFICER(S): John M. Lang, President
REMARKS: Private capital of $1,000,000

COMPANY: **NYBDC Capital Corp.**
ADDRESS: 41 State Street
Albany, NY 12207
PHONE: (518) 463-2268
CONTACT OFFICER(S): Marshall R. Lustig, President
REMARKS: Private Capital of $500,000

COMPANY: **Preferential Capital Corporation**
ADDRESS: 16 Court Street
Brooklyn, NY 11241
PHONE: (212) 855-2728
CONTACT OFFICER(S): Bruce Bayroff, Sec.-Treas.
REMARKS: Private Capital of $419,381

COMPANY: **M & T Capital Corp.**
ADDRESS: One M & T Capital Corp.
Buffalo, NY 14240
PHONE: (716) 842-5881
CONTACT OFFICER(S): J. V. Parlato, President
REMARKS: Private capital of $5,007,486

COMPANY: **Peter J. Schmitt SBIC, Incorporated**
ADDRESS: P.O. Box 2
Buffalo, NY 14240
PHONE: (716) 825-1111
CONTACT OFFICER(S): William Wanstedt, President
REMARKS: Private Capital of $500,000

COMPANY: **Venture SBIC, Inc.**
ADDRESS: 249-12 Jericho Turnpike
Floral Park, NY 11001
PHONE: (516) 352-0068
CONTACT OFFICER(S): Arnold Feldman, President
REMARKS: Private Capital of $612,000

COMPANY: **Nelson Capital Corp.**
ADDRESS: 591 Stewart Avenue
Garden City L.I., NY 11530
PHONE: (516) 222-2555
CONTACT OFFICER(S): Irwin Nelson, President
REMARKS: Private Capital of $500,000

COMPANY: **Fundex Capital Corporation**
ADDRESS: 525 Northern Boulevard
Great Neck, NY 11021
PHONE: (516) 466-8550
TYPE OF INSTITUTION: Small Business Investment Corp. (SBIC)
CONTACT OFFICER(S): Howard Sommer, Pres.
INVESTMENTS/LOANS MADE: For own account
INVESTMENTS/LOANS MADE: In securities with a secondary market and in securities without a secondary market
TYPES OF FINANCING: LOANS: Working capital; Equipment; Equity-related. REAL ESTATE LOANS: Long-term senior mtg.; Intermediate-term senior mtg.; Subordinated; Wraparounds.
GEOGRAPHIC LIMITS OF INVESTMENTS/LOANS: Regional
RANGE OF INV./LOAN PER BUSINESS: Min. $50,000; Max. $1,000,000
PREFERRED TERM FOR LOANS & LEASES: Min. 5 years; Max. 10 years
BUSINESS CHARACTERISTICS DESIRED-REQUIRED: Minimum number of years in business: 0
REFERRALS ACCEPTED FROM: Investment/Mortgage banker or Borrower/Investee

COMPANY: **MRN Capital Company**
ADDRESS: 150 Great Neck Road
Great Neck, NY 11021
PHONE: (516) 466-5752
CONTACT OFFICER(S): Robert E. Schulman, President
REMARKS: Private capital of $503,500

COMPANY: **SB Electronics Investment Co.**
ADDRESS: 60 Cuttermill Road
Great Neck, NY 11021
PHONE: (212) 952-7531
CONTACT OFFICER(S): Stanley Meisels, President
REMARKS: Private Capital of $600,000

COMPANY: **TLC Funding Corp.**
ADDRESS: 141 S. Central Avenue
Hartsdale, NY 10530
PHONE: (914) 683-1144
CONTACT OFFICER(S): Philip G. Kass, President
REMARKS: Private capital of $700,000

COMPANY: **Risa Capital Associates**
ADDRESS: 280 Oser Avenue
Hauppauge, NY 11788
PHONE: (516) 231-9319
CONTACT OFFICER(S): Andrew S. Roffe, President
REMARKS: Private capital of $517,050

COMPANY: **Southern Tier Capital Corporation**
ADDRESS: 55 S. Main Street
Liberty, NY 12754
PHONE: (914) 292-3030
CONTACT OFFICER(S): Harold Gold, Secretary-Treasurer
REMARKS: Private Capital of $350,111

COMPANY: **Tappan Zee Capital Corporation**
ADDRESS: 120 North Main St.
New City, NY 10956
PHONE: (914) 634-8890
CONTACT OFFICER(S): Karl Kirchner, President
REMARKS: Private Capital of $659,280

COMPANY: **767 Limited Partnership**
ADDRESS: 767 Third Avenue
New York, NY 10017
PHONE: (212) 838-7776
CONTACT OFFICER(S): H. Wertheim and H. Mallement, G.P.
REMARKS: Private capital of $1,375,333

COMPANY: **American Commercial Capital Corp.**
ADDRESS: 310 Madison Avenue, Suite 1304
New York, NY 10017
PHONE: (212) 986-3305
CONTACT OFFICER(S): Gerald J. Grossman, President
REMARKS: Private capital of $1,000,000

COMPANY: **Amev Capital Corp.**
ADDRESS: Two World Trade Center, Suite 9766
New York, NY 10048
PHONE: (212) 775-1912
CONTACT OFFICER(S): Martin Orland, President
REMARKS: Private capital of $4,500,000

COMPANY: **Atalanta Investment Company, Inc.**
ADDRESS: 450 Park Avenue
New York, NY 10022
PHONE: (212) 832-1104
CONTACT OFFICER(S): L. Mark Newman, Chairman of Board
REMARKS: Private capital of $9,914,945

COMPANY: **Beneficial Capital Corporation**
ADDRESS: 880 Third Ave.
New York, NY 10022
PHONE: (212) 752-1291
CONTACT OFFICER(S): John Hoey, President
REMARKS: Private Capital of $500,000

COMPANY: **Bohlen Capital Corp.**
ADDRESS: 767 Third Avenue
New York, NY 10017
PHONE: (212) 838-7776
CONTACT OFFICER(S): Harvey J. Wertheim, President
REMARKS: Private capital of $1,590,000

COMPANY: **Boston Hambro Capital Company**
ADDRESS: 17 East 71st Street
New York, NY 10021
PHONE: (212) 288-9106

COMPANY: **BT Capital Corp.**
ADDRESS: 280 Park Avenue
New York, NY 10017
PHONE: (212) 850-1916
CONTACT OFFICER(S): James G. Hellmuth, President
REMARKS: Private capital of $15,009,826

COMPANY: **Chase Manhattan Capital Corp.**
ADDRESS: 1 Chase Manhattan Plaza — 4th Floor
New York, NY 10081
PHONE: (212) 552-6275
CONTACT OFFICER(S): Robert Hubbard, President
REMARKS: Private Capital of $24,785,000

COMPANY: **Clinton Capital Corporation**
ADDRESS: 419 Park Avenue South
New York, NY
PHONE: (212) 696-4688
TYPE OF INSTITUTION: Small Business Investment Company
CONTACT OFFICER(S): Alan Leavitt, V.P. Secured Lending
INVESTMENTS/LOANS MADE: For own account
INVESTMENTS/LOANS MADE: In securities with a secondary market and in securities without a secondary market
TYPES OF FINANCING: SECONDARY-MARKET CORPORATE SECURITIES
PREFERRED TYPES OF INDUSTRIES/INVESTMENTS: To businesses secured by real estate
WILL NOT CONSIDER: Start ups
GEOGRAPHIC LIMITS OF INVESTMENTS/LOANS: National
RANGE OF INV./LOAN PER BUSINESS: Min. $50,000; Max. 700,000
PREFERRED TERM FOR LOANS & LEASES: Min. 5 years; Max. 10 years
REFERRALS ACCEPTED FROM: Investment/Mortgage banker or Borrower/Investee

COMPANY: **CMNY Capital Company, Inc.**
ADDRESS: 77 Water Street
New York, NY 10005
PHONE: (212) 437-7078
CONTACT OFFICER(S): Robert Davidoff, Vice President
REMARKS: Private capital of $1,776,480

COMPANY: **Cornell Capital Corp.**
ADDRESS: 230 Park Ave., Ste. 3440
New York, NY 10169
PHONE: (212) 490-9198
CONTACT OFFICER(S): Barry M. Bloom, President
REMARKS: Private Capital of $558,000

COMPANY: **Croyden Capital Corp.**
ADDRESS: 45 Rockefeller Plaza, Suite 2165
New York, NY 10111
PHONE: (212) 974-0184
CONTACT OFFICER(S): Victor L. Hecht, President
REMARKS: Private capital of $1,310,000

COMPANY: **EAB Venture Corp.**
ADDRESS: 90 Park Avenue
New York, NY 10016
PHONE: (212) 437-4182
CONTACT OFFICER(S): Richard C. Burcaw, President
REMARKS: Private Capital of $5,000,000

COMPANY: **Edwards Capital Company**
ADDRESS: 215 Lexington Avenue, Suite 805
New York, NY 10016
PHONE: (212) 686-2568
CONTACT OFFICER(S): Edward H. Teitlebaum, President
REMARKS: Private Capital of $3,000,000

COMPANY: **Engle Investment Co.**
ADDRESS: 135 West 50 Street
New York, NY 10020
PHONE: (212) 757-9580
TYPE OF INSTITUTION: Small Business Investment Corp.
CONTACT OFFICER(S): Murray Hendel, President
ASSETS: $2,000,000
INVESTMENTS/LOANS MADE: For own account
INVESTMENTS/LOANS MADE: In securities with a secondary market and in securities without a secondary market
TYPES OF FINANCING: SECONDARY-MARKET CORPORATE SECURITIES: Common stock; Preferred stock; Bonds. VENTURE CAPITAL: Start-up from developed product stage; First-stage; Second-stage; Later-stage expansion; Buy-outs/Acquisitions. LOANS: Working capital; Equipment; Equity-related. REAL ESTATE LOANS: Land development; Construction. OTHER SERVICES PROVIDED: Advisory & Financial Mgt.

COMPANY: **Equilease Capital Corp.**
ADDRESS: 750 Third Avenue
New York, NY 10017
PHONE: (212) 557-6800
CONTACT OFFICER(S): Norbert Weissberg, President
REMARKS: Private Capital of $3,200,000

COMPANY: **European Development Corp. LP**
ADDRESS: 767 Third Ave.,
New York, NY 10017
PHONE: (212) 867-9709
CONTACT OFFICER(S): Harvey J. Wertheim, President
REMARKS: Private Capital of $3,508 620

COMPANY: **Fairfield Equity Corp.**
ADDRESS: 200 East 42 Street
New York, NY 10017
PHONE: (212) 867-0150
CONTACT OFFICER(S): Matthew A. Berdon, President
REMARKS: Private Capital of $997,109

COMPANY: **Ferranti High Technology, Inc.**
ADDRESS: 505 Park Avenue
New York, NY 10022
PHONE: (212) 688-6667
CONTACT OFFICER(S): Sandford R. Simon, President & Director
REMARKS: Private capital of $3,000,000

COMPANY: **Fifty-Third Street Ventures, Inc.**
ADDRESS: 420 Madison Avenue
New York, NY 10017
PHONE: (212) 319-5740
TYPE OF INSTITUTION: Small Business Investment Company
CONTACT OFFICER(S): Dan Tessler, Chairman
Patricia M. Cloharrety, President
ASSETS: $13 million
INVESTMENTS/LOANS MADE: For own account; Through private placements
TYPES OF FINANCING: VENTURE CAPITAL: Start-up from developed product stage; First-stage; Second-stage; Later-stage expansion; Buy-outs/Acquisitions LOANS: Equity-related
PREFERRED TYPES OF INDUSTRIES/INVESTMENTS: Computers & Allied Fields, Communications; Medical & Health Related; Diversified
GEOGRAPHIC LIMITS OF INVESTMENTS/LOANS: National
RANGE OF INV./LOAN PER BUSINESS: Min. $250,000; Max. $500,000
BUSINESS CHARACTERISTICS DESIRED-REQUIRED: Minimum number of years in business: 0

COMPANY: **First Connecticut SBIC**
ADDRESS: 68 Fifth Avenue
New York, NY 10003
PHONE: (212) 541-6222
REMARKS: Main Office: Bridgeport, CT

COMPANY: **The Franklin Corporation**
ADDRESS: 1185 Avenue of the Americas
New York, NY 10036
PHONE: (212) 719-4844
TYPE OF INSTITUTION: Small business investment company
CONTACT OFFICER(S): Herman E. Goodman, President
Alan L. Farkas, Executive V.P. & Treasurer
ASSETS: $30 million
INVESTMENTS/LOANS MADE: For own account
INVESTMENTS/LOANS MADE: In securities with a secondary market and in securities without a secondary market
TYPES OF FINANCING: SECONDARY-MARKET CORPORATE SECURITIES: Common stock; Preferred stock; Bonds, VENTURE CAPITAL: Second-stage; Later-stage expansion; Buy-outs/Acquisitions, LOANS: Working capital; Equipment, OTHER SERVICES PROVIDED: Management consulting
PREFERRED TYPES OF INDUSTRIES/INVESTMENTS: Manufacturing
WILL NOT CONSIDER: Textiles, real estate, natural resources, agricultural
GEOGRAPHIC LIMITS OF INVESTMENTS/LOANS: National
RANGE OF INV./LOAN PER BUSINESS: Min. $200,000; Max. $2,000,000
PREFERRED TERM FOR LOANS & LEASES: Min. 5 years; Max. 10 years
BUSINESS CHARACTERISTICS DESIRED-REQUIRED: Minimum number of years in business: 2; Min. annual sales $1mm; OTHER: Must be breaking even
REFERRALS ACCEPTED FROM: Investment/Mortgage banker or Borrower/Investee
REMARKS: No start-ups

COMPANY: **The Hanover Capital Corporation**
ADDRESS: 150 E. 58th St., Ste. 2710
New York, NY 10022
PHONE: (212) 532-5173
CONTACT OFFICER(S): Daniel J. Sullivan, President
REMARKS: Private Capital of $847,944

COMPANY: **Heller Capital Services, Inc.**
ADDRESS: 101 Park Avenue
New York, NY 10178
PHONE: (212) 880-7047
TYPE OF INSTITUTION: Venture capital management co., presently managing 5 small business investment companies (SBICs)
CONTACT OFFICER(S): J. Allen Kerr, President
ASSETS: $72,145,000
INVESTMENTS/LOANS MADE: Through private placements
INVESTMENTS/LOANS MADE: In securities with a secondary market and in securities without a secondary market
TYPES OF FINANCING: VENTURE CAPITAL: Start-up from developed product stage; First-stage (less than 1 year); Second-stage (generally 1-3 years); Buy-outs/Acquisitions
PREFERRED TYPES OF INDUSTRIES/INVESTMENTS: Hi-tech
WILL NOT CONSIDER: Real estate
GEOGRAPHIC LIMITS OF INVESTMENTS/LOANS: International
RANGE OF INV./LOAN PER BUSINESS: Min. $500,000; Max. $2,000,000
BUSINESS CHARACTERISTICS DESIRED-REQUIRED: Minimum number of years in business: 0; Min. annual sales 0
REFERRALS ACCEPTED FROM: Investment/Mortgage banker or Borrower/Investee
BRANCHES: Cloyd Marvin, 3000 Sand Hill Rd., Bldg. #1, Ste. 205, Menlo Park, Ca 94025 (415) 854-8400
REMARKS: Private Capital of $2,015,000

COMPANY: **Holding Capital Corp.**
ADDRESS: 685 Fifth Avenue, 14th Floor
New York, NY 10022
PHONE: (212) 486-6670
CONTACT OFFICER(S): Sash A. Spencer, President, Corp. G/P
REMARKS: Private capital of $665,000

COMPANY: **Intercoastal Capital Corporation**
ADDRESS: 380 Madison Ave.
New York, NY 10017
PHONE: (212) 986-0482
CONTACT OFFICER(S): Herbert Krasnow, President
REMARKS: Private Capital of $608,800

COMPANY: **Intergroup Venture Capital Corp.**
ADDRESS: 230 Park Avenue
New York, NY 10017
PHONE: (212) 661-5428
CONTACT OFFICER(S): Ben Hauben, President
REMARKS: Private Capital of $502,500

COMPANY: **Interstate Capital Company, Inc.**
ADDRESS: 655 Third Avenue
New York, NY 1017
PHONE: (212) 986-7333
CONTACT OFFICER(S): David Scharf, President
REMARKS: Private capital of $1,195,848

COMPANY: **J. H. Foster & Co. Ltd.**
ADDRESS: 437 Madison Avenue
New York, NY 10022
PHONE: (212) 753-4810
CONTACT OFFICER(S): John H. Foster, President
REMARKS: Private capital of $2,595,622

COMPANY: **Kwiat Capital Corp.**
ADDRESS: 576 Fifth Avenue
New York, NY 10036
PHONE: (212) 391-2461
CONTACT OFFICER(S): David Kwiat, President

COMPANY: **Lincoln Capital Corporation**
ADDRESS: 41 E. 42nd St., Suite 1510
New York, NY 10017
PHONE: (212) 697-0610
TYPE OF INSTITUTION: Small business investing corporation
CONTACT OFFICER(S): Martin Lifton, President
ASSETS: $1,850,000
INVESTMENTS/LOANS MADE: For own account
TYPES OF FINANCING: LOANS: Working capital; Equipment, REAL ESTATE LOANS: Intermediate-term senior mtg.; Subordinated; Construction
PREFERRED TYPES OF INDUSTRIES/INVESTMENTS: Firm with tangible assets as collateral
WILL NOT CONSIDER: Retail beyond 50 miles of office
GEOGRAPHIC LIMITS OF INVESTMENTS/LOANS: Regional; Other: Northeast region 200 miles of New York City
RANGE OF INV./LOAN PER BUSINESS: Min. $100,000; Max. $2,000,000
REFERRALS ACCEPTED FROM: Investment/Mortgage banker or Borrower/Investee

COMPANY: **Marwit Capital Corp.**
ADDRESS: 6 East 43rd Street
New York, NY 10017
PHONE: (212) 867-3906
REMARKS: Main Office: Newport Beach, CA

COMPANY: **Midland Venture Capital Ltd.**
ADDRESS: 950 Third Avenue
New York, NY 10022
PHONE: (212) 753-7790
CONTACT OFFICER(S): R. Machinist & M. Stanfield, Managers
REMARKS: Private capital of $10,000,100

COMPANY: **N.P.D. Capital, Inc.**
ADDRESS: 375 Park Avenue
New York, NY 10152
PHONE: (212) 826-8500
CONTACT OFFICER(S): Jerome I. Feldman, President
REMARKS: Private capital of $1,010,000

COMPANY: **Noro Capital Corp.**
ADDRESS: 767 Third Avenue
New York, NY 10017
PHONE: (212) 661-5281
CONTACT OFFICER(S): Harvey J. Wertheim, President
REMARKS: Private Capital of $2,000,000

COMPANY: **Pioneer Investors Corp.**
ADDRESS: 113 E. 55th Street
New York, NY 10022
PHONE: (212) 980-9090
CONTACT OFFICER(S): James G. Niven, Pres.
R. Scott Asen
TYPES OF FINANCING: VENTURE CAPITAL: Research & Development; Start- up from developed product stage; First-stage (less than 1 year); Second-stage (generally 1-3 years); Later-stage expansion; Buy-outs/Acquisitions, LOANS: Equity-related
PREFERRED TYPES OF INDUSTRIES/INVESTMENTS: Medical Technology; Communications Technology; Computer Software; Food Products; Natural Resources
GEOGRAPHIC LIMITS OF INVESTMENTS/LOANS: National
BUSINESS CHARACTERISTICS DESIRED REQUIRED: Min. no. of years in business: 0

COMPANY: **Questech Capital Corp.**
ADDRESS: 600 Madison Avenue, 21st floor
New York, NY 10022
PHONE: (212) 758-8522
CONTACT OFFICER(S): Earl W. Brian, M.D., President
REMARKS: Private Capital of $5,000,000

COMPANY: **R&R Financial Corp.**
ADDRESS: 1451 Broadway
New York, NY 10066
PHONE: (212) 564-4500
CONTACT OFFICER(S): Imre Rosenthal, President
REMARKS: Private Capital of $305,000

COMPANY: **Realty Growth Capital Corporation**
ADDRESS: 575 Lexington Avenue
New York, NY
PHONE: (212) 755-9044
TYPE OF INSTITUTION: Small business investment company
CONTACT OFFICER(S): Lawrence A. Benenson, Pres.
ASSETS: $2,000,000
INVESTMENTS/LOANS MADE: For own account
TYPES OF FINANCING: LOANS: Secured loans, REAL ESTATE LOANS: Long-term senior mtg.; Intermediate-term senior mtg.
PREFERRED TYPES OF INDUSTRIES/INVESTMENTS: Collateralized loans on real estate or other collateral
WILL NOT CONSIDER: Straight equity loans
GEOGRAPHIC LIMITS OF INVESTMENTS/LOANS: Local
RANGE OF INV./LOAN PER BUSINESS: Min. $25,000; Max. $100,000
PREFERRED TERM FOR LOANS & LEASES: Min. 5 years; Max. 10 years
REFERRALS ACCEPTED FROM: Investment/Mortgage banker or Borrower/Investee

COMPANY: **Roundhill Capital Corporation**
ADDRESS: 44 Wall Street
New York, NY 10005
PHONE: (212) 747-0144
CONTACT OFFICER(S): Joseph M. Davis, President
REMARKS: Private Capital of $2.500,000

COMPANY: **S & S Venture Associates Ltd.**
ADDRESS: 333 Seventh Avenue
New York, NY 10001
PHONE: (212) 736-4530
CONTACT OFFICER(S): Donald Smith, President
REMARKS: Private Capital of $510,000

COMPANY: **Sprout Capital Corp.**
ADDRESS: 140 Broadway
New York, NY 10005
PHONE: (212) 902-2000
CONTACT OFFICER(S): Lawrence R. Johnson, President
REMARKS: Private capital of $4,115,000

COMPANY: **Telesciences Capital Corporation**
ADDRESS: 26 Broadway, Ste. 841
New York, NY 10004
PHONE: (212) 425-0320
CONTACT OFFICER(S): Mark A. Petrozzo
REMARKS: Private Capital of $1,250,000

COMPANY: **Transworld Ventures, Ltd.**
ADDRESS: 331 West End Avenue
New York, NY 10023
PHONE: (212) 496-1010
CONTACT OFFICER(S): Jack H. Berger, President
REMARKS: Private capital of $517,000

COMPANY: **Walnut Capital Corp.**
ADDRESS: 20 Exchange Place - 31st Floor
New York, NY 10005
PHONE: (212) 425-3144
CONTACT OFFICER(S): Julius Goldfinger, President
REMARKS: Private capital of $2,220,000

COMPANY: **College Venture Equity Corp.**
ADDRESS: 256 Third Street, P.O. Box 135
Niagara Falls, NY 14302
PHONE: (716) 285-8455
TYPE OF INSTITUTION: Small business investment
CONTACT OFFICER(S): Francis M. Williams, President
William J. MacDougal, Secretary, Joseph Williams, V.P.

ASSETS: $620,000
TYPES OF FINANCING: VENTURE CAPITAL, LOANS: Working capital; Equipment

COMPANY: **Sherwood Business Capital Corp.**
ADDRESS: 770 King Street
Port Chester, NY 10573
PHONE: (914) 937-6000
CONTACT OFFICER(S): Louis R. Eisner, President
REMARKS: Private Capital of $504,000

COMPANY: **Vega Capital Corp.**
ADDRESS: 720 White Plains Road
Scarsdale, NY 10583
PHONE: (914) 472-8550
TYPE OF INSTITUTION: Small Business Investment Company (SBIC)
CONTACT OFFICER(S): Ronald A. Linden
Vice President
TOTAL ASSETS: $10,000,000
INVESTMENTS/LOANS MADE: For own account
INVESTMENTS/LOANS MADE: In securities with a secondary market; In securities without a secondary market
TYPES OF FINANCING: VENTURE: Second-stage; Later-stage expansion; Buy-outs/Acquisitions, LOANS: Equity-related, OTHER SERVICES PROVIDED: Specialized in mezzanine financing in leveraged buy-outs
PREFERRED TYPES OF INDUSTRIES/INVESTMENTS: Diversified, but specialize in manufacturing
WILL NOT CONSIDER: Retail, Land Development
GEOGRAPHIC LIMITS OF INV./LOANS: National
RANGE OF INV./LOAN PER BUSINESS: Min. $100,000; Max. $3,000,000
PREFERRED TERM FOR LOANS & LEASES: Min. 5 years; Max. 8 years
REFERRALS ACEPTED FROM: Investment/Mortgage banker; Borrower/Investee

COMPANY: **County Capital Corp.**
ADDRESS: 25 Main Street, P.O. Box 112
Southampton, NY 11968
PHONE: (516) 248-9400
CONTACT OFFICER(S): Myron Joffe, President
REMARKS: Private capital of $500,000

COMPANY: **Central New York SBIC (The)**
ADDRESS: 351 S. Warren Street
Syracuse, NY 13202
PHONE: (315) 478-5026
CONTACT OFFICER(S): Robert E. Romig, President
REMARKS: Private Capital of $150,000

COMPANY: **NIS Capital Corp.**
ADDRESS: 34 S. Broadway
White Plains, NY 10601
PHONE: (914) 428-8600
CONTACT OFFICER(S): Howard Blank, President

COMPANY: **Winfield Capital Corp.**
ADDRESS: 237 Mamaroneck Av.
White Plains, NY 10605
PHONE: (914) 949-2600
TYPE OF INSTITUTION: SBIC
CONTACT OFFICER(S): Stanley Pechman, Pres.
TYPES OF FINANCING: LOANS: Working capital (receivables/inventory); Equipment, LEASES
PREFERRED TYPES OF INDUSTRIES/INVESTMENTS: Manufacturers & Wholesale Trades
GEOGRAPHIC LIMITS OF INVESTMENTS/LOANS: Regional
RANGE OF INV./LOAN PER BUSINESS: Min. $100,000
PREFERRED TERM FOR LOANS & LEASES: Min. 5 years
BUSINESS CHARACTERISTICS DESIRED-REQUIRED: No start-ups

COMPANY: **Multi-Purpose Capital Corporation**
ADDRESS: 31 South Broadway
Yonkers, NY 10701
PHONE: (914) 963-2733
CONTACT OFFICER(S): Eli B. Fine, President
REMARKS: Private Capital of $210,300

COMPANY: **A.T. Capital Corp.**
ADDRESS: 900 Euclid Avenue, T-18
Cleveland, OH 44101
PHONE: (216) 687-4970
CONTACT OFFICER(S): Robert C. Salipante, V.P. & Manager
REMARKS: Private capital of $1,000,000

COMPANY: **Capital Funds Corp.**
ADDRESS: 127 Public Square
Cleveland, OH 44114
PHONE: (216) 622-8628
CONTACT OFFICER(S): Carl Nelson, V.P.
Philip A. Stark, V.P.
ASSETS: $2.4 million
INVESTMENTS/LOANS MADE: For own account
INVESTMENTS/LOANS MADE: In securities with a secondary market or in securities without a secondary market
TYPES OF FINANCING: SECONDARY-MARKET CORPORATE SECURITIES: Prepared Stock; VENTURE CAPITAL: Second-stage; Buy-outs/Acquisitions; LOANS: Equity-related
PREFERRED TYPES OF INDUSTRIES/INVESTMENTS: Communications, Manufacturing
GEOGRAPHIC LIMITS OF INVESTMENTS/LOANS: State
RANGE OF INV./LOAN PER BUSINESS: Min. $100,000; Max. $500,000
REFERRALS ACCEPTED FROM: Investment/Mortgage banker or Borrower/Investee

COMPANY: **Gries Investment Corp.**
ADDRESS: 720 Statler Office Tower
Cleveland, OH 44115
PHONE: (216) 861-1146
TYPE OF INSTITUTION: Venture Capital

CONTACT OFFICER(S): Robert D. Gries, President
Richard F. Brezic, Vice President
INVESTMENTS/LOANS MADE: For own account
INVESTMENTS/LOANS MADE: In securities with a secondary market or in securities without a secondary market
TYPES OF FINANCING: SECONDARY-MARKET CORPORATE SECURITIES: Common stock; Preferred stock; Bonds; Other: Long-term loans; VENTURE CAPITAL: Research & Development; Start-up from developed product stage; First-stage; Second-stage; Later-stage expansion; Buy-outs/Acquisitions; LOANS; OTHER SERVICES PROVIDED: Management Advisory Services
PREFERRED TYPES OF INDUSTRIES/INVESTMENTS: None
WILL NOT CONSIDER: Real Estate Oriented Financing
GEOGRAPHIC LIMITS OF INVESTMENTS/LOANS: National
RANGE OF INV./LOAN PER BUSINESS: Min. $100,000; Max. None
PREFERRED TERM FOR LOANS & LEASES: Min. 5 years; Max. 7-10 years
BUSINESS CHARACTERISTICS DESIRED-REQUIRED: Minimum number of years in business: 0

COMPANY: **Intercapco Inc.**
ADDRESS: One Erieview Plaza
Cleveland, OH 44114
PHONE: (216) 241-7170
CONTACT OFFICER(S): Robert Haas, Pres.
Deborah Rocker, V.P.
TYPES OF FINANCING: VENTURE CAPITAL: Research & Development; Start-up from developed product stage; First-stage (less than 1 year); Second-stage (generally 1-3 years); Later-stage expansion; Buy-outs/Acquisitions, LOANS: Equity-related
PREFERRED TYPES OF INDUSTRIES/INVESTMENTS: Diversified
WILL NOT CONSIDER: Retail
GEOGRAPHIC LIMITS OF INVESTMENTS/LOANS: National
RANGE OF INV./LOAN PER BUSINESS: Min. $300,000
PREFERRED TERM FOR LOANS & LEASES: Min. 5 years

COMPANY: **National City Capital Corporation**
ADDRESS: 623 Euclid Ave.
Cleveland, OH 44114
PHONE: (216) 575-2491
CONTACT OFFICER(S): Michael Sherwin, President
REMARKS: Private Capital of $2,500,000

COMPANY: **RIHT Capital Corp.**
ADDRESS: 796 Union Commerce Building
Cleveland, OH 44114
PHONE: (216) 781-3655

COMPANY: **Tomlinson Capital Corporation**
ADDRESS: 3055 East 63rd Street
Cleveland, OH 44127
PHONE: (216) 271-2103

CONTACT OFFICER(S): John A. Chernak, Vice President
REMARKS: Private capital of $550,000

COMPANY: **Tomlinson Capital Corp.**
ADDRESS: 3055 E. 63rd Street
Cleveland, OH 44127
PHONE: (216) 271-2103
TYPE OF INSTITUTION: Small business investment co.
CONTACT OFFICER(S): Donald R. Calkins, V.P.
INVESTMENTS/LOANS MADE: In securities with a secondary market and in securities without a secondary market
TYPES OF FINANCING: SECONDARY-MARKET CORPORATE SECURITIES: Common stock; Preferred stock; Bonds, VENTURE CAPITAL: Research & Development; Start-up from developed product stage; First-stage; Second-stage; Later-stage expansion, Buy-outs/Acquisitions, LOANS: Working capital; Equipment; Equity-related, INTERNATIONAL

COMPANY: **Miami Valley Capital, Incorporated**
ADDRESS: Talbott Tower, Suite, 315, 131 N. Ludlow Street4Dayton,
OH 45402
PHONE: (513) 222-7222
CONTACT OFFICER(S): W. Walker Lewis, Chairman of the Board
REMARKS: Private capital of $1,446,709

COMPANY: **First Ohio Capital Corporation**
ADDRESS: 606 Madison Avenue
Toledo, OH 43604
PHONE: (419) 259-7146
CONTACT OFFICER(S): John T. Rogers, President
REMARKS: Private capital of $1,000,000

COMPANY: **Tamco Investors (SBIC) Inc.**
ADDRESS: 375 Victoria Road
Youngstown, OH 44515
PHONE: (216) 792-3811
CONTACT OFFICER(S): Nathan H. Monus, President
REMARKS: Private Capital of $300,000

COMPANY: **Bartlesville Investment Corp.**
ADDRESS: P.O. Box 548
Bartlesville, OK 74003
PHONE: (918) 333-3022
CONTACT OFFICER(S): James L. Diamond, President
REMARKS: Private capital of $645,000

COMPANY: **First Venture Corp.**
ADDRESS: Venture Bldg., The Quarters
Bartlesville, OK 74003
PHONE: (918) 333-8820
CONTACT OFFICER(S): J.R.K. Tinkle. Pres.
James G. Thompson, Sr. V.P
Ralph Finkle, V.P.
TYPES OF FINANCING: VENTURE CAPITAL: Start-up frm developed product stage; First-stage, Second-stage; Later-stage expansion; Buy-outs/Acquisitions

PREFERRED TYPES OF INDUSTRIES/INVESTMENTS: High technology; Energy; Medical; Airlines
GEOGRAPHIC LIMITS OF INVESTMENTS/LOANS: National
RANGE OF INV./LOAN PER BUSINESS: Min. $50,000; Max. $350,000
PREFERRED TERM FOR LOANS & LEASES: Min. 5 years; Max. 7 years
BUSINESS CHARACTERISTICS DESIRED-REQUIRED; Minimum number of years in business: 0
Investment/Mortgage banker or Borrower/Investee

COMPANY: **Investment Capital, Inc.**
ADDRESS: 300 N. Harrison
Cushing, OK 74023
PHONE: (918) 225-5850
CONTACT OFFICER(S): James J. Wasson, President
REMARKS: Private Capital of $1,049,981

COMPANY: **First Oklahoma Inv. Capital Corporation**
ADDRESS: 120 North Robinson, Suite 880-C,
Oklahoma City, OK 73102
CONTACT OFFICER(S): Gary Bunch, President
REMARKS: Private capital of $1,005,100

COMPANY: **Alliance Business Investment Co.**
ADDRESS: One Williams Center, Ste. 2000
Tulsa, OK 74172
PHONE: (918) 584-3581
CONTACT OFFICER(S): Barry M. Davis, President
John M. Holliman III, V.P.
INVESTMENTS/LOANS MADE: For own accouont
TYPES OF FINANCING: SECONDARY-MARKET CORPORATE SECURITIES: Other: Debt securities, VENTURE CAPITAL: Second-stage; Later-stage expansion; Buy-outs/Acquisitions
PREFERRED TYPES OF INDUSTRIES/INVESTMENTS: Natural resources (energy related); Broadcast/media; Manufacturing/productivity enhancement/robotics; Health care; Specialty chemicals
WILL NOT CONSIDER: Retailing/wholesaling
GEOGRAPHIC LIMITS OF INVESTMENTS/LOANS: Regional: Southwest United States
RANGE OF INV./LOAN PER BUSINESS: Min. $550,000

COMPANY: **Southwest Venture Capital, Inc.**
ADDRESS: 4120 E. 51st Street, Ste E
Tulsa, OK 74135
PHONE: (918) 742-3031
CONTACT OFFICER(S): Donald J. Rubottom, President
REMARKS: Private Capital of $500,000

COMPANY: **Utica Investment Corp.**
ADDRESS: 1924 South Utica Avenue, Suite 418
Tulsa, OK 74104
PHONE: (918) 747-7581
CONTACT OFFICER(S): David D. Nunneley, President
REMARKS: Private Capital of $505,000

COMPANY: **Western Venture Capital Corp.**
ADDRESS: 4900 South Lewis
Tulsa, OK 74105
PHONE: (918) 749-7981
CONTACT OFFICER(S): Gary L. Smith, President
REMARKS: Private Capital of $2,007,500

COMPANY: **First Interstate Capital, Inc.**
ADDRESS: 1300 South West Fifth Avenue, Suite 2323
Portland, OR 97201
PHONE: (503) 223-4334

COMPANY: **Northern Pacific Capital Corporation**
ADDRESS: P.O. Box 1658
Portland, OR 97207
PHONE: (503) 241-1255
CONTACT OFFICER(S): John J. Tennant, Jr., President
REMARKS: Private Capital of $750,000

COMPANY: **Norwest Growth Fund, Incorporated**
ADDRESS: 1300 S.W. 5th Street, Suite 3108
Portland, OR 97201
PHONE: (503) 223-6622

COMPANY: **American Venture Capital Co.**
ADDRESS: Suite 122, Blue Bell West, 650 Skippack Pike
Blue Bell, PA 19422
PHONE: (215) 278-8907
CONTACT OFFICER(S): Knute C. Albrecht, President
REMARKS: Private Capital of $1,490,000

COMPANY: **Central Capital Corp.**
ADDRESS: 1097 Commercial Avenue
Lancaster, PA 17604
PHONE: (717) 569-9650
CONTACT OFFICER(S): W. D. McElhinny, Chairman of Board
REMARKS: Private capital of $1,000,000

COMPANY: **Capital Corporation of America**
ADDRESS: 225 South 15th Street, Suite 920
Philadelphia, PA 19102
PHONE: (215) 743-1666
CONTACT OFFICER(S): Martin M. Newman, President
REMARKS: Private capital of $1,302,135

COMPANY: **Capital Corporation of America**
ADDRESS: 1521 Walnut Street
Philadelphia, PA 19102
PHONE: (215) 732-1666
CONTACT OFFICER(S): Martin Newman, President
ASSETS: $2.5 million
TYPES OF FINANCING: VENTURE CAPITAL: Second-stage (generally 1-3 years); Buy-outs/Acquisitions, LOANS: Equity-related
PREFERRED TYPES OF INDUSTRIES/INVESTMENTS: Diversified
WILL NOT CONSIDER: Retail
GEOGRAPHIC LIMITS OF INVESTMENTS/LOANS: National
RANGE OF INV./LOAN PER BUSINESS: Min. $50,000; Max. $500,000
PREFERRED TERM FOR LOANS & LEASES: Min. 5 years; Max. 10 years

COMPANY: **PNC Capital Corp.**
ADDRESS: Pittsburgh National Building, Fifth Avenue and Wood Street
Pittsburgh, PA 15222
PHONE: (412) 355-2245
CONTACT OFFICER(S): Gary J. Zentner, President
REMARKS: Private capital of $2,500,000

COMPANY: **First SBIC of California**
ADDRESS: P.O. Box 512
Washington, PA 15301
PHONE: (412) 223-0707
CONTACT OFFICER(S): Daniel A. Dye

COMPANY: **Fleet Venture Resources, Inc.**
ADDRESS: 111 Westminster Street
Providence, RI 02903
PHONE: (401) 278-6770
CONTACT OFFICER(S): Robert M. Van Degna, President
REMARKS: Private capital of $3,000,000

COMPANY: **Charleston Capital Corporation**
ADDRESS: 111 Church St., P.O. Box 328
Charleston, SC 29402
PHONE: (803) 723-6464
CONTACT OFFICER(S): Henry Yaschik, Pres.
REMARKS: Private Capital of $637,000

COMPANY: **Lowcountry Investment Corporation**
ADDRESS: 4444 Daley Street, P.O. Box 10447
Charleston, SC 29411
PHONE: (803) 554-9880
CONTACT OFFICER(S): Joseph T. Newton, Jr., President
REMARKS: Private Capital of $1,908,950

COMPANY: **Reedy River Ventures, Incorporated**
ADDRESS: 400 Haywood Rd. P.O. Box 17526
Greenville, SC 29606
PHONE: (803) 297-9198
CONTACT OFFICER(S): John M. Sterling, President
REMARKS: Private Capital of $1,201,300

COMPANY: **Carolina Venture Capital Corporation**
ADDRESS: 14 Archer Road
Hilton Head Island, SC 29928
PHONE: (803) 842-3101
TYPE OF INSTITUTION: Small Business Investment Company
CONTACT OFFICER(S): Thomas H. Harvey III, President
INVESTMENTS/LOANS MADE: For own account
INVESTMENTS/LOANS MADE: In securities with or without a secondary market
TYPES OF FINANCING: VENTURE CAPITAL: First-stage; Second-stage; Later-stage expansion.
GEOGRAPHIC LIMITS OF INVESTMENTS/LOANS: Regional

COMPANY: **Floco Investment Company, Inc. (The)**
ADDRESS: Hwy. 52 North
Scranton, SC 29561
PHONE: (803) 389-2731
CONTACT OFFICER(S): William H. Johnson, Sr., President
REMARKS: Private Capital of $356,300

COMPANY: **DeSoto Capital Corporation**
ADDRESS: 60 North Third Street
Memphis, TN
PHONE: (901) 523-6894
TYPE OF INSTITUTION: Financing: Venture capital, loans, equity/debt related
CONTACT OFFICER(S): Damon S. Arney, President
INVESTMENTS/LOANS MADE: For own account, For managed accounts, Through private placements
INVESTMENTS/LOANS MADE: In securities with or without a secondary market
TYPES OF FINANCING: VENTURE CAPITAL: Start-up from developed product stage; First-stage; Second-stage; Later-stage expansion; Buy-outs/Acquisitions. LOANS: Other. REAL ESTATE LOANS. REAL ESTATE: Acquisitions; Joint ventures
GEOGRAPHIC LIMITS OF INVESTMENTS/LOANS: Regional
RANGE OF INV./LOAN PER BUSIINESS: Min. $25,000; Max. $100,000
PREFERRED TERM FOR LOANS & LEASES: Min. 5-7 years; Max. 7-10 years
REFERRALS ACCEPTED FROM: Investment/Mortgage banker or Borrower/Investee

COMPANY: **Financial Resources, Incorporated**
ADDRESS: 2800 Sterick Blvd.
Memphis, TN 38103

PHONE: (901) 527-9411
CONTACT OFFICER(S): Milton Picard, Chairman of Board
REMARKS: Private capital of $750,320

COMPANY: **Suwannee Capital Corporation**
ADDRESS: 1991 Corporate Avenue
Memphis, TN 38132
PHONE: (901) 345-4200
CONTACT OFFICER(S): Peter R. Pettit, President
REMARKS: Private capital of $2,005,000

COMPANY: **Business Capital Corp. of Arlington**
ADDRESS: 1112 Copeland Road, Suite 420
Arlington, TX 76011
PHONE: (817) 261-4936
CONTACT OFFICER(S): James E. Sowell, Chairman of the Board
REMARKS: Private capital of $510,000

COMPANY: **Bow Lane Capital Corporation**
ADDRESS: 3305 Graybuck Road
Austin, TX 78748
PHONE: (512) 456-8698

COMPANY: **FSA Capital, Ltd.**
ADDRESS: 301 West Sixth Street
Austin, TX 78701
PHONE: (512) 472-7171
CONTACT OFFICER(S): G. Felder Thornhill, President
REMARKS: Private capital of $1,880,968

COMPANY: **Rust Capital Limited**
ADDRESS: 114 West 7th Street, Suite 1300
Austin, TX 78701
PHONE: (512) 479-0055
CONTACT OFFICER(S): Jeffery Garvey, Partner
REMARKS: Private Capital of $6,872,000

COMPANY: **Omega Capital Corp.**
ADDRESS: 755 So. 11th St., P.O. Box 2173
Beaumont, TX 77704
PHONE: (409) 832-0221
TYPE OF INSTITUTION: S.B.I.C.
CONTACT OFFICER(S): Ted E. Moor Jr., President
Frank J. Ryan Jr., General Manager
TOTAL ASSETS: $500,000
INVESTMENTS/LOANS MADE: For own account
INVESTMENTS/LOANS MADE: In securities with a secondary market; In securities without a secondary market
INVESTMENT/LOANS MADE: TYPES OF FINANCING: VENTURE CAPITAL: Start-up; First-stage
GEOGRAPHIC LIMITS OF INVESTMENTS/LOANS: State; Regional
RANGE OF INV./LOANS PER BUSINESS: Min. $50,000; Max. $100,000
PREFERRED TERM FOR LOANS: Min. 5 years; Max. 5 years
BUSINESS CHARACTERISTICS DESIRED-REQUIRED: Minimum number of years in businss: 0
REFERRRALS ACCEPTED FROM: Investment/Mortgage banker only; Borrower/Investee

COMPANY: **Banctexas Capital, Incorporated**
ADDRESS: 1601 Elm Street, Suite 8000
Dallas, TX 75201
PHONE: (214) 658-6231
CONTACT OFFICER(S): Harold W. McNabb, President
REMARKS: Private capital of $1,003,500

COMPANY: **Brittany Capital Corp.**
ADDRESS: 1525 Elm Street, 2424 LTV Tower
Dallas, TX 75201
PHONE: (214) 742-5810
CONTACT OFFICER(S): Robert E. Clements, President
REMARKS: Private Capital of $500,000

COMPANY: **Capital Southwest Corp.**
ADDRESS: 12900 Preston Rd., Ste. 700
Dallas, TX 75230
PHONE: (214) 233-8242
CONTACT OFFICER(S): William R. Thomas, Pres.
J. Bruce Duty, Secretary-Treasurer
Patrick Hamner, Investment Associate
ASSETS: $50,000,000
INVESTMENTS/LOANS MADE: For own account
INVESTMENTS/LOANS MADE: In securities with/without a secondary market
TYPES OF FINANCING: VENTURE CAPITAL: Research & Development; Start-up from developed product stage; First-stage (less than 1 year); Second-stage (generally 1-3 years); Later-stage expansion; Buy-outs/Acquisitions, LOANS: Equity-related
PREFERRED TYPES OF INDUSTRIES/INVESTMENTS: Diversified
WILL NOT CONSIDER: Construction Cos.
GEOGRAPHIC LIMITS OF INVESTMENTS/LOANS: National
RANGE OF INV./LOAN PER BUSINESS: Min. $250,000; Max. $2,000,000
BUSINESS CHARACTERISTICS DESIRED REQUIRED: Min. no. of years in business: 0

COMPANY: **Interfirst Venture Corporation**
ADDRESS: 1201 Elm St. (P.O. Box 83644; Zip 75283)
Dallas, TX 75270
PHONE: (214) 744-8050
TYPE OF INSTITUTION: SBIC
CONTACT OFFICER(S): Mark C. Masur, A. V.P.

COMPANY: **Mercantile Dallas Corp.**
ADDRESS: 1704 Main St., P.O. Box 222090
Dallas, TX 75222
PHONE: (214) 741-1469
CONTACT OFFICER(S): John G. Farmer, Pres.
REMARKS: Private Capital or $15,000,000

COMPANY: **MVenture Corp.**
ADDRESS: P.O. Box 222090
Dallas, TX
PHONE: (214) 741-1469
TYPE OF INSTITUTION: Small Business Investment Company
CONTACT OFFICER(S): Tom Mitchell, Investment Officer
Ted Walker, Investment Officer
ASSETS: $60,000,000.00
INVESTMENTS/LOANS MADE: For own account
INVESTMENTS/LOANS MADE: Only in securities without a secondary market
TYPES OF FINANCING: VENTURE CAPITAL: Later-stage expansion; Buy-outs/Acquisitions; LOANS: Equipment; Equity-related; REAL ESTATE LOANS: Long-term senior mtg.
PREFERRED TYPES OF INDUSTRIES/INVESTMENTS: Basic Manufacturing; Communications; Health Care; Distribution
GEOGRAPHIC LIMITS OF INVESTMENTS/LOANS: State
RANGE OF INV./LOAN PER BUSINESS: Min. $250,000; Max. $3,000,000
PREFERRED TERM FOR LOANS & LEASES: Min. 5; Max. 10 (with 20 amort) years
BUSINESS CHARACTERISTICS DESIRED-REQUIRED: Minimum number of years in business: 3; Min. annual sales $2,000,000
REFERRALS ACCEPTED FROM: Investment/Mortgage banker or Borrower/Investee

COMPANY: **Republic Venture Group Incorporated**
ADDRESS: P.O. Box 225961
Dallas, TX 75265
PHONE: (214) 653-5078
CONTACT OFFICER(S): Robert H. Wellborn, President & General Mgr.
REMARKS: Private Capital of $11,000,000

COMPANY: **Sunwestern Capital Corporation**
ADDRESS: 2720 Stemmons Freeway, South Tower, Suite 816
Dallas, TX 75207
PHONE: (214) 742-4841
CONTACT OFFICER(S): James F. Leary, President
REMARKS: Private capital of $2,000,000

COMPANY: **Trammell Crow Investment Company**
ADDRESS: 2001 Bryan Tower, Suite 3200
Dallas, TX 75201
PHONE: (214) 747-0643
CONTACT OFFICER(S): Henry W. Billingsley, Pres.
REMARKS: Private Capital of $529,000

COMPANY: **TSM Corporation**
ADDRESS: Box 9938
El Paso, TX 79990
PHONE: (915) 533-6375
CONTACT OFFICER(S): Joe Justice, Gen. Mgr.
REMARKS: Private Capital of $524,242

COMPANY: **Texas State Capital Corporation**
ADDRESS: 900 Austin Avenue
Georgetown, TX 78626
PHONE: (512) 863-2594
CONTACT OFFICER(S): Roger G. Lord, President
REMARKS: Private capital of $500,000

COMPANY: **Allied Bancshares Capital Corp.**
ADDRESS: P.O. Box 3326
Houston, TX 77253
PHONE: (713) 226-1625
TYPE OF INSTITUTION: Small Business Investment Corporation
CONTACT OFFICER(S): Phillip A. Tuttle, President
Mary Bass, Investment Officer
ASSETS: $13 million
TYPES OF FINANCING: VENTURE CAPITAL: Second-stage; Later-stage expansion; Buy-outs/Acquisitions
PREFERRED TYPES OF INDUSTRIES/INVESTMENTS: Industry preference: Communications; Computer Related; Transportation; Manufacturing & Processing; Medical & Other Health Services; Natural Resources; Research & Technology
GEOGRAPHIC LIMITS OF INVESTMENTS/LOANS: Local; State; Regional; National; Other: Prefer Texas & Sunbelt; will consider Continental USA
RANGE OF INV./LOAN PER BUSINESS: Min. $100,000; Max. $2,000,000
BUSINESS CHARACTERISTICS DESIRED-REQUIRED: Other: National market potential: $75 million
REFERRALS ACCEPTED FROM: Investment/Mortgage banker or Borrower/Investee
REMARKS: The product or service must have an understandable economic benefit to its customers. An experienced, competent Management team is a must. If not there, ABCC will help strengthen by identifying others. Type financing: prefer expansion financing and leverage buy-outs. Start-ups and turn-around situations must meet tougher criteria. Company's product/service should have a minimum national annual sales potential of $75,000,000. Company should demonstrate potential to earn $1.5MM after tax in 3 yrs. Investment exit alternatives must be identified prior to investment for early stage deals. Hurdle rate of return is 35-40% pre-tax for expansion financings: 70% for early stage deals. Some current yield is necessary to cover overhead. Comprehensive written business plan should be forwarded prior to initial meeting. Business Plan should include 5 year projections.

COMPANY: **American Energy Investment Corp**
ADDRESS: 1010 Lamar, Suite 1680
Houston, TX 77002
PHONE: (713) 651-0220
CONTACT OFFICER(S): Robert J. Moses, Executive V.P.
REMARKS: Private Capital of $2,500,000

COMPANY:**Americap Corporation**
ADDRESS: 6363 Woodway, #200
Houston, TX 77057
PHONE: (713) 780-8084
TYPE OF INSTITUTION: SBIC
CONTACT OFFICER(S): James L. Hurn, President
ASSETS: $3,000,000
INVESTMENTS/LOANS MADE: For own account; Through private placements
INVESTMENTS/LOANS MADE: In securities with a secondary market; In securities without a secondary market
TYPES OF FINANCING: VENTURE CAPITAL: Research & Development; Start-up from developed product stage; First-stage; Second-stage; Buy-outs/Acquisitions
PREFERRED TYPES OF INDUSTRIES/INVESTMENTS: Oil and gas; Medical technology, computer software; Bio-technology
WILL NOT CONSIDER:Real estate; Retail
GEOGRAPHIC LIMITS OF INVESTMENTS/LOANS: Regional; National
RANGE OF INV./LOAN PER BUSINESS: Min. $200,000
BUSINESS CHARACTERISTICS DESIRED-REQUIRED: Minimum number of years in business: 0, Other: Strong management team

COMPANY: **Bow Lane Capital Corp.**
ADDRESS: 2401 Fountainview, Suite 950
Houston, TX 77057
PHONE: (713) 977-7421
TYPE OF INSTITUTION: Small business investment company
CONTACT OFFICER(S): Stuart Schube, President
Fran Zuieback, Administrative Assistant
ASSETS: $12,000,000
INVESTMENTS/LOANS MADE: For own account, Through private placements
INVESTMENTS/LOANS MADE: In securities with a secondary market and in securities without a secondary market
TYPES OF FINANCING: VENTURE CAPITAL: Second-stage; Later-stage expansion; Buy-outs/Acquisitions
PREFERRED TYPES OF INDUSTRIES/INVESTMENTS: Well managed aggressive companies; businesses which have an outstanding future
GEOGRAPHIC LIMITS OF INVESTMENTS/LOANS: National
RANGE OF INV./LOAN PER BUSINESS: Min. $200,000; Max. $3,000,000
PREFERRED TERM FOR LOANS & LEASES: Min. 5 years; Max. 8 years
BUSINESS CHARACTERISTICS DESIRED-REQUIRED: Minimum number of years in business: 2; Min. annual sales $500,000; Min. net worth $0; Min. annual net income loss; Min. annual cash flow $100,000
REFERRALS ACCEPTED FROM: Investment/Mortgage banker or Borrower/Investee
BRANCHES: Hugh Batey 3305 Graybuck Rd., Austin, TX, 78748 (512) 282-9330

COMPANY: **Charter Venture Group, Inc.**
ADDRESS: 2600 Citadel Plaza Drive, 6th Floor
Houston, TX 77008
PHONE: (713) 699-3588
TYPE OF INSTITUTION: SBIC—Wholly-owned by Charter Bankshares, Inc.
CONTACT OFFICER(S): Kent E. Smith, President
ASSETS: $1.1 million
INVESTMENTS/LOANS MADE: For own account, Through private placements
INVESTMENTS/LOANS MADE: In securities with a secondary market and in securities without a secondary market
TYPES OF FINANCING: VENTURE CAPITAL: Second-stage; Later-stage expansion; Buy-outs/Acquisitions
PREFERRED TYPES OF INDUSTRIES/INVESTMENTS: Diversified
WILL NOT CONSIDER: Real Estate
GEOGRAPHIC LIMITS OF INVESTMENTS/LOANS: Regional; Southwest
RANGE OF INV./LOAN PER BUSINESS: Min. $75,000; Max. $200,000
BUSINESS CHARACTERISTICS DESIRED-REQUIRED: Minimum number of years in business: 1
REFERRALS ACCEPTED FROM: Investment/Mortgage banker or Borrower/Investee

COMPANY: **Energy Assets, Inc.**
ADDRESS: 1800 South Tower, Pennzoil Place
Houston, TX 77002
PHONE: (713) 236-9999
CONTACT OFFICER(S): Laurence E. Simmons, Exec. V.P.
REMARKS: Private Capital of $546,351

COMPANY: **Energy Capital Corporation**
ADDRESS: 953 Esperson Building
Houston, TX 77002
PHONE: (713) 236-0006
CONTACT OFFICER(S): Herbert F. Poyner, President
REMARKS: Private Capital of $11,285,613

COMPANY: **Enterprise Capital Corp.**
ADDRESS: 3401 Allen Parkway
Houston, TX 77019
PHONE: (713) 524-5170
CONTACT OFFICER(S): Fred Zeidman, President
REMARKS: Private Capital of $2,500,000

COMPANY: **First City Capital Corporation**
ADDRESS: One West Loop South, Suite 809
Houston, TX 77027
PHONE: (713) 623-6151
CONTACT OFFICER(S): William E. Ladin, President
REMARKS: Private Capital of $520,005

COMPANY: **Grocers Small Business Investment Corp.**
ADDRESS: 3131 E. Holcombe Blvd., Ste. 101
Houston, TX 77021
PHONE: (713) 747-7913
CONTACT OFFICER(S): Milton H. Levit, President
REMARKS: Private Capital of $1,000,000

COMPANY: **Livingston Capital, Ltd.**
ADDRESS: 5701 Woodway, Suite 332
Houston, TX 77057
PHONE: (713) 977-4040
CONTACT OFFICER(S): J. Livingston Kosberg, General Partner
REMARKS: Private Capital of $1,000,000

COMPANY: **Mapleleaf Capital Corporation**
ADDRESS: 1 West Loop South, Suite 603
Houston, TX 77027
PHONE: (713) 627-0752
TYPE OF INSTITUTION: SBIC
CONTACT OFFICER(S): Edward Fink, President
Bernadette Obermeier, Treasurer
ASSETS: $5,500,000
INVESTMENTS/LOANS MADE: For own account
INVESTMENTS/LOANS MADE: In securities with a secondary market; In securites without a secondary market
TYPES OF FINANCING: SECONDARY-MARKET CORPORATE SECURITIES: Common stock; Preferred stock; Bonds; Convertible debt securities, VENTURE CAPITAL: Start-up from developed product stage; Second-stage; Later-stage expansion; Buy-outs/ Acquisitions, LOANS: Equity-related, OTHER SERVICES PROVIDED: Vent Cap. 75% later stage
PREFERRED TYPES OF INDUSTRIES/INVESTMENTS: Diversified
GEOGRAPHIC LIMITS OF INVESTMENTS/LOANS: Regional; Other: Primarily Southwest
RANGE OF INV./LOAN PER BUSINESS: Min. $150,000; Max. $500,000
PREFERRED TERM FOR LOANS & LEASES: Min. 5 years; Max. 7 years
REFERRALS ACCEPTED FROM: Investment/Mortgage banker; Borrower/Investee

COMPANY: **Retail Capital Corp.**
ADDRESS: 7915 W. FM 1960, Ste. 300
Houston, TX 77070
PHONE: (713) 890-4242
CONTACT OFFICER(S): William J. Boschma, President
REMARKS: Private Capital of $510,000

COMPANY: **Retzloff Capital Corporation**
ADDRESS: 15000 Northwest Freeway, Suite 310A
Houston, TX 77240
PHONE: (713) 466-4690
CONTACT OFFICER(S): James K. Hines, President
REMARKS: Private capital of $2,500,000

COMPANY: **Rice Investment Co.**
ADDRESS: 3350 Rogerdale
Houston, TX 77042
PHONE: (713) 797-1990
CONTACT OFFICER(S): Alvin Diamond, Sec.
REMARKS: Private Capital of $1,770,001

COMPANY: **S.B.I. Capital Corp.**
ADDRESS: P.O. Box 771668
Houston, TX 77215
PHONE: (713) 975-1188
TYPE OF INSTITUTION: SBIC
CONTACT OFFICER(S): William E. Wright, President
ASSETS: $5,000,000
INVESTMENTS/LOANS MADE: For own account
INVESTMENTS/LOANS MADE: In securities with a secondary market; In securities without a secondary market
TYPES OF FINANCING: SECODARY-MARKET CORPORATE SECURITIEES: Preferred stock; Bonds; Other: Warrants and Debt; Warrants and preferred; convertible bonds; VENTURE CAPITAL: First-stage; Second-stage ; Later-stage expansion; Buy-outs/ Acquisitions
PREFERRED TYPES OF INDUSTRIES/INVESTMENTS: Diversified
GEOGRAPHIC LIMITS OF INVESTMENTS/LOANS: State; Other; Major cities in Texas
RANGE OF INV./LOAN PER BUSINESS: $500,000

REFERRALS ACCEPTED FROM: Investment/Mortgage banker; Borrower/Investee
REMARKS: All deals are participating

COMPANY: **Texas Capital Corp.**
ADDRESS: 333 Clay, Suite 2100
Houston, TX 77002
PHONE: (713) 658-9961
CONTACT OFFICER(S): W. Grogan Lord, President
REMARKS: Private capital of $3,050,000

COMPANY: **Texas Commerce Investment Company**
ADDRESS: P.O. Box 2588
Houston TX 77252
PHONE: (713) 236-4719
TYPE OF INSTITUTION: S.B.I.C. Subsidiary of Bank
CONTACT OFFICER(S): Fred Lummis, Manager
Fred Hamilton, Officer
TOTAL ASSETS: $10,000,000
INVESTMENTS/LOANS MADE: For own account
INVESTMENTS/LOANS MADE: In securities with a secondary market; In securities without a secondary market
TYPES OF FINANCING: SECONDARY-MARKET CORPORATE SECURITIES: Common stock; Preferred stock; Bonds, VENTURE CAPITAL: Start-up; First-stage; Second-stage; Later-stage expansion; Buy-outs/Acquisitions
PREFERRED TYPES OF INDUSTRIES/INVESTMENTS: Venture capital; Diversified industries
WILL NOT CONSIDER: Real Estate
GEOGRAPHIC LIMITS OF INVESTMENTS/LOANS: National
RANGE OF INV./LOANS: Min. $300,000; Max. $1,000,000
BUSINESS CHARACTERISTICS DESIRED-REQUIRED: Minimum number of years in business: 1

COMPANY: **Capital Marketing Corporation**
ADDRESS: 1000 Nat Gibbs Drive, P.O. Box 1000
Keller, TX 76248
PHONE: (817) 656-7380
CONTACT OFFICER(S): John Myrick, President
REMARKS: Private capital of $8,915,505

COMPANY: **Pasadena Capital Corporation**
ADDRESS: 1001 East Show
Pasadena, TX 77506
PHONE: (713) 477-1585
CONTACT OFFICER(S): Edward E. Bass, President
REMARKS: Private capital of $2,000,000

COMPANY: **Richardson Capital Corporation**
ADDRESS: 558 South Central Expressway
Richardson, TX 75080
PHONE: (214) 235-4571
CONTACT OFFICER(S): Edward L. Teer, President
REMARKS: Private capital of $1,000,000

COMPANY: **Red River Ventures, Incorporated**
ADDRESS: 2425 N. Central Expressway, Ste. 323
Richardson TX 75080
PHONE: (214) 644-5501
CONTACT OFFICER(S): Delwin W. Morton, President
REMARKS: Private Capital of $751,000

COMPANY: **Southwestern Venture Capital of Texas, Inc.**
ADDRESS:
1250 N.E. Loop 410, Suite 700
San Antonio, TX 78209
PHONE: (512) 822-9949
TYPE OF INSTITUTION: Venture Capital and SBA Loans
CONTACT OFFICER(S): Kurt Nestman, President
TOTAL ASSETS: $5,000,000
INVESTMENTS/LOANS MADE: For own accout
INVESTMENTS/LOANS MADE: In securities with a secondary market; In securities without a secondary market
TYPES OF FINANCING: VENTURE CAPITAL: First-stage; Second-stage; Later-stage expansion; Buy-outs/Acquisitions, LOANS: Equipment, REAL ESTATE: Long-term senior mtg.; Other: Owner occupied only
GEOGRAPHIC LIMITS OF INVESTMENTS/LOANS: National
RANGE OF INV./LOANS PER BUSINESS: Min. $100,000; Max. $600,000
PREFERRED TERM FOR LOANS & LEASES: Min. 7 years; Max. 25 years
BUSINESS CHARACTERISTICS DESIRED-REQUIRED: Minimum number of years business: 2
REFERRALS: Investment/Mortgage banker; Borrower/investee
BRANCHES: Doug Hatten, Southwestern Commercial Capital, Inc., 100 Chase Stone Center, Suite 440, Colorado, Springs, CO 80903
Joe Justice, SWCC, 444 Executive Center Blvd., Suite 222, El Paso, TX 79902
Ron Kozak, SWCC, 101 Park Ave., Suite 950, Oklahoma City, OK 73102
Kurtis Nestman, SWCC, North Frost Center, 1250 N.E. Loop 410, Suite 700, San Antonio, TX 78209
Bill Murray, SWCC, 1301 Seminole Blvd., Suite 110, Largo, FL 33540
Scott Bobo, SWCC, 1717 Azurite Tr., Plano, TX 75075
REMARKS: Company makes SBA guaranteed loans in addition to venture capital investments

COMPANY: **South Texas Small Business Investment Company**
ADDRESS: 120 South Main Place
Victoria, TX 77901
PHONE: (512) 573-5151
CONTACT OFFICER(S): Dave F. Peyton, President
TOTAL ASSETS: $2,500,000
INVESTMENTS/LOANS MADE: For own account

INVESTMENTS/LOANS MADE: Only in securities without a secndary market
TYPES OF FINANCING: VENTURE CAPITAL: Second-stage; Later-stage expansion; Buy-outs/Acquisitions, LOANS: Working capital; Equipment; REAL ESTATE LOANS: Long-term senior mtg.; Intermediate-term senior mtg.; Land development, FACTORING

COMPANY: **Tidewater SBI Corp.**
ADDRESS: 234 Monticello Avenue, 1106 Maritime Tower
Norfolk, VA 23510
PHONE: (804) 627-2315
CONTACT OFFICER(S): Robert H. Schmidt, President
REMARKS: Private capital of $1,000,000

COMPANY: **Vermont Investment Capital, Inc.**
ADDRESS: South Windsor Street, Box 590
South Royalton, VT 05068
PHONE: (802) 763-7716
CONTACT OFFICER(S): Harold Jacobs, President
REMARKS: Private capital of $228,344

COMPANY: **Alaska Pacific Capital Corp.**
ADDRESS: 1309 114th S.E.
Bellevue, WA 98004
PHONE: (206) 455-2662
CONTACT OFFICER(S): Daniel D. Nelson, Manager
REMARKS: Private capital of $500,000

COMPANY: **Old Stone Capital Corporation**
ADDRESS: 1417 Fourth Avenue, P.O. Box 1770
Seattle, WA 98111
PHONE: (206) 682-5400
CONTACT OFFICER(S): Bruce Moger, President
REMARKS: Private capital of $6,996,500

COMPANY: **Peoples Capital Corp.**
ADDRESS: 2411 Fourth Avenue, Suite 400
Seattle, WA 98121
PHONE: (206) 344-5463
CONTACT OFFICER(S): Robert E. Karns, President
REMARKS: Private capital of $1,000,000

COMPANY: **Seattle Trust Capital Corporation**
ADDRESS: 804 Second Avenue
Seattle, WA 98104
PHONE: (206) 223-2281
CONTACT OFFICER(S): Doug McPhee, President
REMARKS: Private capital of $1,005,000

COMPANY: **Clifton Capital Corp.**
ADDRESS: 1408 Washington Building
Tacoma, WA 98402
PHONE: (206) 272-3654
CONTACT OFFICER(S): James H. Wiborg, President
REMARKS: Private capital of $655,710

COMPANY: **Bando-McGlocklin Investment Company, Inc.**
ADDRESS: 13555 Bishops Court, Suite 205
Brookfield, WI 53005
PHONE: (414) 784-9010
TYPE OF INSTITUTION: SBIC (Small business investment company)
CONTACT OFFICER(S): Sal Bando, President
Jon McGlocklin, V.P.
ASSETS: $13 million
INVESTMENTS/LOANS MADE: For own account
INVESTMENTS/LOANS MADE: In securities with a secondary market and in securities without a secondary market
TYPES OF FINANCING: LOANS: Working capital; Equipment, REAL ESTATE LOANS: Long-term senior mtg.; Intermediate-term senior mtg.; Subordinated; Wraparounds; Construction
PREFERRED TYPES OF INDUSTRIES/INVESTMENTS: Diversified. We take no equity position and will go up to 90% on financing.
WILL NOT CONSIDER: Start ups; Turn-arounds
GEOGRAPHIC LIMITS OF INVESTMENTS/LOANS: Local; State; Regional; National
RANGE OF INV./LOAN PER BUSINESS: Min. $100,000; Max. $600,000
PREFERRED TERM FOR LOANS & LEASES: Min. 5 years; Max. 10 years
BUSINESS CHARACTERISTICS DESIRED-REQUIRED: Minimum number of years in business: 1; Other: Must be experienced
REFERRALS ACCEPTED FROM: Investment/Mortgage banker or Borrower/Investee
REMARKS: We are credit lenders who look to real estate as collateral. We are very flexible in meeting the needs of the business.

COMPANY: **Certco Capital Corp.**
ADDRESS: 6150 McKee Road
Madison, WI 53507
PHONE: (608) 271-4500
CONTACT OFFICER(S): Donald G. Watzke, President
REMARKS: Private Capital of $405,000

COMPANY: **Madison Capital Corporation**
ADDRESS: 102 State Street
Madison, WI 53703
PHONE: (608) 256-8185
TYPE OF INSTITUTION: (SBIC) Small business investment corporation
CONTACT OFFICER(S): Mr. Roth Schleck, President, Capital Generation & Investor Liaison
Mr. Roger Ganser, Executive Vice President, Business Development, Investment Analyst, General Operations
ASSETS: $1.28 million
INVESTMENTS/LOANS MADE: For own account
INVESTMENTS/LOANS MADE: In securities with a secondary market and in securities without a secondary market
TYPES OF FINANCING: SECONNDARY-MARKET CORPORATE SECURITIES: Common stock; Preferred stock; Bonds; Other: If not actual stock there are conversion clauses, or convertible debentures; VENTURE CAPITAL: Start-up from developed

product stage; First-stage; Second-stage; Later-stage expansion; Buy-outs/Acquisitions; LOANS: Equity-related; REAL ESTATE LOANS: Intermediate-term senior mtg.; Subordinated
PREFERRED TYPES OF INDUSTRIES/INVESTMENTS: Prefer High Technology Companies or businesses that have potential for substantial growth and profitability.
WILL NOT CONSIDER: Real estate developments, hotel and restaurant.
GEOGRAPHIC LIMITS OF INVESTMENTS/LOANS: Regional; Other: Within 2 hour travel distance to Madison.
RANGE OF INV./LOAN PER BUSINESS: Min. $50,000—prefer 100,000; Max. 20% of Private capital
PREFERRED TERM FOR LOANS & LEASES: Min. 5 years; Max. 20 years
BUSINESS CHARACTERISTICS DESIRED-REQUIRED: Minimum number of years in business: 0
REFERRALS ACCEPTED FROM: Investment/Mortgage banker or Borrower/Investee

COMPANY: **Bankit Financial Corp.**
ADDRESS: 111 E. Wisconsin Ave., Ste 1900
Milwaukee, WI 53202
PHONE: (414) 271-5050
CONTACT OFFICER(S): Roy D. Terracina, Executive V.P.
REMARKS: Private Capital of $350,000

COMPANY: **Capital Investments, Inc.**
ADDRESS: 744 N. 4th St., Ste. 400
Milwaukee, WI 53203
PHONE: (414) 273-6560
CONTACT OFFICER(S): Robert L. Banner, V.P.
ASSETS: $1,000,000—10,000,000
TYPES OF FINANCING: VENTURE CAPITAL: Research & Development; Start-up from developed product stage; First-stage (less than 1 year); Second-stage (generally 1-3 years); Later-stage expansion; Buy-outs/Acquisitions, LOANS: Equity-related
WILL NOT CONSIDER: Real Estate, Nursing Homes, Condos
GEOGRAPHIC LIMITS OF INVESTMENTS/LOANS: National
RANGE OF INV./LOAN PER BUSINESS: Min. $250,000; Max. $6,000,000
PREFERRED TERM FOR LOANS & LEASES: Min. 5; Max. 20 years

COMPANY: **Marine Venture Capital, Inc.**
ADDRESS: 111 East Wisconsin Avenue
Milwaukee, WI 53202
PHONE: (414) 765-2151
CONTACT OFFICER(S): H. Wayne Foreman, President
REMARKS: Private capital of $3,000,000

COMPANY: **Twin Ports Capital Company**
ADDRESS: 1228 Poplar Avenue
Superior, WI 54880
PHONE: (715) 392-8131
CONTACT OFFICER(S): Paul Leonidas, President
REMARKS: Private capital of $510,000

COMPANY: **American Capital, Inc.**
ADDRESS: 300 North Kanawha Street, P.O. Box 1586
Beckley, WV 25801
PHONE: (304) 255-1494
CONTACT OFFICER(S): Gary A. Peck, Investment Advisor & Mgr.
REMARKS: Private capital of $725,000

COMPANY: **Capital Corporation of Wyoming, Inc.**
ADDRESS: P.O. Box 612
Casper, WY 82602
PHONE: (307) 234-5438
CONTACT OFFICER(S): Larry J. McDonald, President
ASSETS: $12,000,000
INVESTMENTS/LOANS MADE: For own account
INVESTMENTS/LOANS MADE: In securities with a secondary market and in securities without a secondary market
TYPES OF FINANCING: SECONDARY-MARKET CORPORATE SECURITIES: Other: Subordinated notes with warrants; VENTURE CAPITAL: First-stage; Second-stage; Later-stage expansion
GEOGRAPHIC LIMITS OF INVESTMENTS/LOANS: State; Other: Wyoming only
RANGE OF INV./LOAN PER BUSINESS: Min. $50,000; Max. $500,000
PREFERRED TERM FOR LOANS & LEASES: Min. 5 years; Max. 20 years
BUSINESS CHARACTERISTICS DESIRED-REQUIRED: Minimum number of years in business: 0

COMPANY: **Capital Resource Corporation**
ADDRESS: 1001 Logan Building
Seattle, WA 98101
PHONE: (206) 623-6550
TYPE OF INSTITUTION: SBIC
CONTACT OFFICER(S): Ted Wight, President
ASSETS: $7,000,000.
INVESTMENTS/LOANS MADE: For own account
INVESTMENTS/LOANS MADE: In securities with a secondary market and in securities without a secondary market
TYPES OF FINANCING: VENTURE CAPITAL; First-stage Second-stage; LOANS: Equity-related
PREFERRED TYPES OF INDUSTRIES/INVESTMENTS: No preference on Industries, Age
WILL NOT CONSIDER: Real Estate; Equipment
GEOGRAPHIC LIMITS OF INVESTMENTS/LOANS: National
RANGE OF INV./LOAN PER BUSINESS: Min. None; Max. $200,000.
BUSINESS CHARACTERISTICS DESIRED-REQUIRED: Min. no. of years in business: 0
REFERRALS ACCEPTED FROM: Investment/Mortgage banker or Borrower/Investee
BRANCHES: Richard H. Drew, Partner, 1 Lincoln Center, Suite 440, 10300 S.W. Greenburg Rd., Portland, OR 97223, (503) 245-5900; Hambrecht & Quist Investment Partners, Partner, 235 Montgomery St., San Francisco, CA 94104; (415) 986-5500

COMPANY: **Central Texas SBI Corp.**
ADDRESS: P.O. Box 829
Waco, TX 76703
PHONE: (817) 753-6461
CONTACT OFFICER(S): David G. Horner, President
REMARKS: Private Capital of $300,000

COMPANY: **Metropolitan Capital Corp.**
ADDRESS: 2550 Huntington Ave.
Alexandria, VA 22303
PHONE: (703) 960-4698
CONTACT OFFICER(S): M. A. Riebe, Pres.
TYPES OF FINANCING: VENTURE CAPITAL: Research & Development; First-stage (less than 1 year); Second-stage (generally 1-3 years); Later-stage expansion; Buy-outs/Acquisitions, LOANS: Equity-related
PREFERRED TYPES OF INDUSTRIES/INVESTMENTS: Diversified
GEOGRAPHIC LIMITS OF INVESTMENTS/LOANS: National
PREFERRED TERM FOR LOANS & LEASES: Min. 5 years
BUSINESS CHARACTERISTICS DESIRED-REQUIRED: proven growth potential

COMPANY: **Tidewater Industrial Capital Corporation**
ADDRESS: Suite 1424, United Va. Bank Bldg.
Norfolk, VA 23510
PHONE: (804) 622-1501
CONTACT OFFICER(S): Armand Caplan, President
REMARKS: Private Capital of $758,200

COMPANY: **Tidewater SBI Corp.**
ADDRESS: 234 Monticello Avenue, 1106 Maritime Tower
Norfolk, VA 23510
PHONE: (804) 627-2315
CONTACT OFFICER(S): Robert H. Schmidt, President
REMARKS: Private Capital of $1,000,000

COMPANY: **Seafirst Capital Corp.**
ADDRESS: Fourth & Blanchard Building
Seattle, WA 98121
PHONE: (206) 583-3278
TYPE OF INSTITUTION: Subsidiary of Seafirst Mortgage Corp. (subsidiary of Seafirst Bank)
CONTACT OFFICER(S): Donald F. Rapp, President & Manager
R. Bruce Harrod, Vice President
Tom C. Doak, Vice President
ASSETS: $7,000,000
INVESTMENTS/LOANS MADE: For own account; Through private placements
INVESTMENTS/LOANS MADE: Only in securities without a secondary market
TYPES OF FINANCING: REAL ESTATE LOANS: Long-term senior mtg.; Subordinated; Land development; Construction; REAL ESTATE: Joint ventures
PREFERRED TYPES OF INDUSTRIES/INVESTMENTS: Owner occupied special purpose Real Estate; JV's in residential or commercial Real Estate.
GEOGRAPHIC LIMITS OF INVESTMENTS/LOANS: Regional; Other: Northwest: Washington, Oregon, Idaho, Montana, Alaska
RANGE OF INV./LOAN PER BUSINESS: Min. $200,000; Max. $600,000
PREFERRED TERM FOR LOANS & LEASES: Min. 10 years; Max. 15 years
BUSINESS CHARACTERISTICS DESIRED-REQUIRED: Other: Depends on characteristics of particular deal.
REFERRALS ACCEPTED FROM: Investment/Mortgage banker or Borrower/Investee

COMPANY: **Northwest Business Investment Corp.**
ADDRESS: 929 West Sprague Avenue
Spokane, WA 99204
PHONE: (509) 838-3111
CONTACT OFFICER(S): C. Paul Sandifur, President
REMARKS: Private Capital of $250,200

VENTURE CAPITAL COMPANIES

(Also see SBICs, MESBICs and Investment Bankers)

COMPANY: **Greyhound Leasing & Financial Corporation**
ADDRESS: 4041 North Center Avenue
Phoenix, AZ 85012
PHONE: (602) 248-4900
CONTACT OFFICER(S): See branches
ASSETS: $1.3 billion
INVESTMENTS/LOANS MADE: In securities with a secondary market and in securities without a secondary market
INVESTMENTS/LOANS MADE: For own account; Through private placements
TYPES OF FINANCING: SECONDARY MARKET CORPORATE SECURITIES: Bonds; VENTURE CAPITAL: Later-stage expansion; LOANS: Equipment; REAL ESTATE LOANS: Long-term senior mtg.; Intermediate-term senior mtg., Land development; Construction; Standbys; Other: Equity Notes Receivables; LEASES: Single-investor; Leveraged; Tax leases; Non-tax leases; Tax-oriented lease brokerage; Lease syndications; Vendor financing programs; INTERNATIONAL; REAL ESTATE: Joint ventures; Partnerships/Syndications
GEOGRAPHIC LIMITS OF INVESTMENTS/LOANS: National
RANGE OF INV./LOAN PER BUSINESS: Min. Leases: $50,000; Loans: $250,000; Max. $—
PREFERRED TERM FOR LOANS & LEASES: Min. Leases: 1; Loans: 3 years; Max. 20 years
BUSINESS CHARACTERISTICS DESIRED-REQUIRED: Minimum number of years in business: 5; Other: Proper operating history upon which to base payment ability projections
REFERRALS ACCEPTED FROM: Investment/Mortgage Banker or Borrower/Investee
BRANCHES: John N. Henning, Donald F. Howell, Jeremiah G. Mahony, Michael J. Naughton, and William H. Vallar (V.P.-Regional Marketing Manager), 445 Park Avenue, New York, NY 10022, (212) 752-2720
Robert E. Marino, John Wm. Salyer, David A. Nielsen (V.P.-Regional Marketing Manager), Centennial Center I, 1900 East Golf Road, Suite 645, Schaumburg, IL 60195, (312) 490-9500
Bruce E. Heine, Mark Lindell, 7801 East Bush Lake Road, Suite 430, Minneapolis, MN 55435, (612) 831-7044
Joseph A. Graffagnini, Canal Place One, Suite 2510, New Orleans, LA 70130, (504) 525-1112
James M. Brown, 12400 Olive Blvd., Suite 200, St. Louis, MO 63141, (314) 469-7373
George C. Baer, 7616 LBJ Freeway , Suite 500, Dallas, TX 75251, (214) 387-3182
Dottie A. Riley, James T. Foley (V.P.-Regional Marketing Manager), 4041 North Central Avenue, Station 3504, Phoenix, AZ 85012, (602) 248-5349
Jeffrey D. Johnson, Scott D. Mayne, 5505 South 900 East, Suite 325, Salt Lake City, UT 84117, (801) 261-1311
Thomas O. Kaluza, 16400 Southcenter Parkway, Suite 203, Seattle, WA 98188, (206) 575-0246
Kenneth B. Giddes, 6400 Powers Ferry Road, Suite 300, Atlanta, GA 30339, (404) 955-3636
Patrick E. Barton, 1776 South Jackson Street, Suite 907, Denver, CO 80210, (303) 757-4973
Jack W. Quinn, Cineco Building, Suite 203, 4401 W. Tradewinds Ave., Lauderdale-by-the-Sea, FL 33308, (305) 493-8322

David C. Phillips, 600 B Street, Suite 2235, San Diego, CA 92101, (619) 231-4751
Ron W. Larson, Neil E. Leddy, Orangegate Plaza, 5455 Garden Grove Blvd., Suite 450, Westminister, CA 92683, (714) 891-2700

COMPANY: **Community First Bank, Mortgage Div.**
ADDRESS: 810 Chester
Bakersfield, CA 93301
PHONE: (805) 395-3270
TYPE OF INSTITUTION: Commercial Bank
CONTACT OFFICER(S): Grady Buck
ASSETS: $100,000,000+
TYPES OF FINANCING: VENTURE CAPITAL: Research & Development; Start-up from developed product stage; First-stage (less than 1 year); Second-stage (generally 1-3 years); Later-stage expansion; Buy-outs/Acquisitions; LOANS: Unsecured; Working capital (receivables/inventory); Equipment; REAL ESTATE LOANS: Long-term senior mtg.; Other: Short-term; REAL ESTATE: Acquisitions
GEOGRAPHIC LIMITS OF INVESTMENTS/LOANS: Local
PREFERRED TERM FOR LOANS & LEASES: Min. 1-3 years; Max. 5 years
REFERALS ACCEPTED FROM: Borrower/Investee
REMARKS: Min. of 2 years in business for loans other than venture capital

COMPANY: **Technology Partners**
ADDRESS: 1550 Tiburon Boulevard, Suite A
Belvedere, CA 94920
PHONE: (415) 435-1935
TYPE OF INSTITUTION: Venture Capital Partnership
CONTACT OFFICER(S): William Hart, Managing Partner
ASSETS: $7+ million
INVESTMENTS/LOANS MADE: For own account
BRANCHES: Peter J. Gillespie, 1910 Surrey Lane, Lake Forest, IL 60045, (312) 234-8440
TYPES OF FINANCING: VENTURE CAPITAL: Research & Development; Start-up from developed product stage; First-stage (less than 1 year); OTHER SERVICES PROVIDED: Active assistance in business development and financing.
PREFERRED TYPES OF INDUSTRIES/INVESTMENTS: Communications, information processing, medical, materials, manufacturing and office automation
WILL NOT CONSIDER: Real estate, oil and gas
GEOGRAPHIC LIMITS OF INVESTMENTS/LOANS: National
RANGE OF INV./LOAN PER BUSINESS: Min. $100,000; Max. $750,000
BUSINESS CHARACTERISTICS DESIRED-REQUIRED: Minimum number of years in business: 0; Long-term growth potential beyond $50 million in sales

COMPANY: **City Ventures, Inc.**
ADDRESS: 404 No. Roxbury Drive, Suite 800
Beverly Hills, CA 90210
PHONE: (213) 550-0416
TYPE OF INSTITUTION: Venture capital subsidiary of commercial bank
CONTACT OFFICER(S): Neill Lawton, President and Investment Manager
Anita Lenz, Investment Analyst
Mimi Shepard, Assistant V.P. and Investment Officer
ASSETS: $2,000,000
INVESTMENTS/LOANS MADE: For own (company's or principals') account
INVESTMENTS/LOANS MADE: only in securities without a secondary market
TYPES OF FINANCING: VENTURE CAPITAL: Second-stage (generally 1-3 years); Later-stage expansion; Buy-outs/Acquisitions; LOANS: Equity-related
PREFERRED TYPES OF INDUSTRIES/INVESTMENTS: Industrial manufacturing firms producing communication products, medical and industrial instrumentation, analytical equipment, computer-related products, chemicals, commercial/industrial products, consumer products and services
WILL NOT CONSIDER: Retailing, wholesale, distribution, transportation, real estate, restaurants
GEOGRAPHIC LIMITS OF INVESTMENTS/LOANS: National
RANGE OF INV./LOAN PER BUSINESS: Min. $100,000; Max. $400,000
PREFERRED TERM FOR LOANS & LEASES: Min. 5 years; Max. 10 years
BUSINESS CHARACTERISTICS DESIRED-REQUIRED: Minimum number of years in business: 2-5; Min. annual sales $1,500,000; Min. net worth $100,000; Min. annual net income $50,000; Min. annual cash flow $100,000
REFERRALS ACCEPTED ROM: Investment/Mortgage banker; Borrower/Investee

COMPANY: **Pacific Lighting Leasing Company (parent)/ Pacific Lighting Commercial Loans, Inc. (subsidiary)**
ADDRESS: 6140 Bristol Parkway
Culver City, CA 90230
PHONE: (213) 642-7595
Wholly owned Leasing and Finance subsidiary of NYSE company
CONTACT OFFICER(S): William M. Hamburg, Vice President—Leasing & Lending
Waldo A. Rodman, Director of Leasing & Remarketing
ASSETS: $76,000,000
INVESTMENTS/LOANS MADE: For own account
INVESTMENTS/LOANS MADE: In securities with a secondary market and in securities without a secondary market
TYPES OF FINANCING: VENTURE CAPITAL; Second-stage; Later-stage; Buy-outs/Acquisitions; LOANS: Equipment; Equity-related; REAL ESTATE LOANS: Intermediateterm senior mtg.; Subordinated; Gap; Standbys; LEASES: Single-investor; Tax leases; Non-tax leases; Operating; Tax-oriented lease brokerage; Vendor financing programs
PREFERRED TYPES OF INDUSTRIES/INVESTMENTS: Office Equipment; Production Equipment; Restaurant; Medical; Air Conditioning; other
WILL NOT CONSIDER: Automobiles
GEOGRAPHIC LIMITS OF INVESTMENTS/LOANS: National
RANGE OF INV./LOAN PER BUSINESS: Min. $2,500; Max. $5,000,000

PREFERRED TERM FOR LOANS & LEASES: Min. 3 yrs; Max. 7 yrs
BUSINESS CHARACTERISTICS DESIRED/REQUIRED: Minimum number of years in business: 0; Min. annual sales $1,000,000
REFERRALS ACCEPTED FROM: Investment/Mortgage banker or Borrower/Investee

COMPANY: **Microtechnology Investments, Ltd.**
ADDRESS: 46 Red Birch Court
Danville, CA 94526
PHONE: (415) 838-9319
TYPE OF INSTITUTION: Corporation
CONTACT OFFICER(S): M. M. Stuckey, Chairman
INVESTMENTS/LOANS MADE: For own account
INVESTMENTS/LOANS MADE: In securities with a secondary market and in securities without a secondary market
TYPES OF FINANCING: Preferred stock; VENTURE CAPITAL; First-stage
PREFERRED TYPES OF INDUSTRIES/INVESTMENTS: Invest solely in "micro software for business" early stage companies
GEOGRAPHIC LIMITS OF INVESTMENTS/LOANS: National
RANGE OF INV./LOAN PER BUSINESS: Min. $100,000;
PREFERRED TERM FOR LOANS & LEASES: Max. 7 yrs
BUSINESS CHARACTERISTICS DESIRED-REQUIRED: Minimum number of years in business: 0
REFERRALS ACCEPTED FROM: Borrower/Investee
BRANCHES: 3400 Comserv Dr., Eagan, MN 55122, 612-681-7581
REMARKS: Investments in affiliation with Control Data Corp. of MN

COMPANY: **Natural Resource Fund**
ADDRESS: 1500 W. Shaw 404
Fresno, CA 93711
PHONE: (209) 226-5513
TYPE OF INSTITUTION: Privately held company
CONTACT OFFICER(S): John Shelburne, Pres.
ASSETS: Over 2.5 million
INVESTMENTS/LOANS MADE: Through private placements
TYPES OF FINANCING: SECONDARY-MARKET CORPORATE SECURITIES: Other: Private syndications and individuals, VENTURE CAPITAL: Research & Development; Start-up from developed product stage; First stage
PREFERRED TYPES OF INDUSTRIES/INVESTMENTS: Oil and gas, mining, laser R&D; product development; wind power R&D to produce electricity. Also, alternate energy equipment
GEOGRAPHIC LIMITS OF INVESTMENTS/LOANS: National; International
RANGE OF INV./LOAN PER BUSINESS: Min. Approximately $500,000
PREFERRED TERM FOR LOANS & LEASES: Min. to be determined
BUSINESS CHARACTERISTICS DESIRED-REQUIRED: Minimum number of years in business: 0
REFERRALS ACCEPTED FROM: Investment/Mortgage banker or Borrower/Investee

COMPANY: **Southern California Ventures**
ADDRESS: 9920 La Cienega Blvd., #510
Inglewood, CA 90301
PHONE: (213) 216-0544
TYPE OF INSTITUTION: Venture Capital
CONTACT OFFICER(S): B. Allen Lay, Gen. Ptnr.
Jay Raskin, Gen. Ptnr.

COMPANY: **Ventana Group, Inc.**
ADDRESS: 19600 Fairchild, Ste. 150
Irvine, CA 92715
PHONE: (714) 476-2204
TYPE OF INSTITUTION: Venture capital, investment banking, syndication
CONTACT OFFICER(S): Thomas O. Gephart, Chairman and Sr. General Partner
ASSETS: $30 million
INVESTMENTS/LOANS MADE: Through private placements
INVESTMENTS/LOANS MADE: In securities with a secondary market and in securities without a secondary market
TYPES OF FINANCING: VENTURE CAPITAL: Research & Development; Later-stage expansion; Buy-outs/Acquisitions
PREFERRED TYPES OF INDUSTRIES/INVESTMENTS: Medical/bio technology; Electronics/computing; energy management and conservation
GEOGRAPHIC LIMITS OF INVESTMENTS/LOANS: International
RANGE OF INV./LOAN PER BUSINESS: Min. $500,000; Max. $5 million
PREFERRED TERM FOR LOANS & LEASES: Min. 2 years; Max. 10 years
BUSINESS CHARACTERISTICS DESIRED-REQUIRED: Min. annual sales $1 million; Min. net worth $200,000; Min. annual cash flow can be negotiated
REFERRALS ACCEPTED FROM: Investment/Mortgage banker or Borrower/Investee
BRACHES: Duane Townsend, 1660 Hotel Circle N., Ste. 502, San Diego, CA 92108; (619) 291-2757
REMARKS: Equity investors

COMPANY: **Wallner & Co.**
ADDRESS: 215 Coast Blvd.
La Jolla, CA 92037
PHONE: (619) 454-3805
TYPE OF INSTITUTION: Private Venture Capital
CONTACT OFFICER(S): Nicholas Wallner, Ph.D
INVESTMENTS/LOANS MADE: For own account
TYPES OF FINANCING: VENTURE CAPITAL: Buy-outs/Acquisitions
GEOGRAPHIC LIMITS OF INVESTMENTS/LOANS: National
BUSINESS CHARACTERISTICS DESIRED-REQUIRED: Minimum number of years in business: 5; Other: 5 yr. income statement, current balance sheet

COMPANY: **Melchor Venture Management, Inc.**
ADDRESS: 170 State Street, Suite 200
Los Altos, CA 94022
PHONE: (415) 941-6565
TYPE OF INSTITUTION: Venture Capital

CONTACT OFFICER(S): Gregory S. Young, V.P.
ASSETS: $17.5 million
TYPES OF FINANCING: VENTURE CAPITAL: Research & Development; Start-up from developed product stage; First-stage
PREFERRED TYPES OF INDUSTRIES/INVESTMENTS: High-technology small cos.
GEOGRAPHIC LIMITS OF INVESTMENTS/LOANS: Local: San Francisco Bay Area
RANGE OF INV./LOAN PER BUSINESS: Min. $350,000

COMPANY: **First Interstate Capital, Inc.**
ADDRESS: 707 Wilshire Blvd. #1850
Los Angeles, CA 90017
PHONE: (213) 614-5903
TYPE OF INSTITUTION: SBIC, subsidiary of bank holding company
CONTACT OFFICER(S): David B. Jones, President
Jonathan E. Funk, V.P.,
Kenneth M. Deemer, V.P.
ASSETS: $52,573,757
INVESTMENTS/LOANS MADE: For own account
TYPES OF FINANCING: VENTURE CAPITAL: Start-up from developed product stage; First-stage; Second-stage; Later-stage expansion; Buy-outs/Acquisitions
PREFERRED TYPES OF INDUSTRIES/INVESTMENTS: High technology, computers, peripherals, electronics, medical instrumentation and devices, biotechnology, software, telecommunication
WILL NOT CONSIDER: Real estate, motion pictures, construction
GEOGRAPHIC LIMITS OF INVESTMENTS/LOANS: National
RANGE OF INV./LOAN PER BUSINESS: Min. $500,000; Max. $1.5 million
PREFERRED TERM FOR LOANS & LEASES: Min. 3 years; Max. 7 years
BUSINESS CHARACTERISTICS DESIRED-REQUIRED: Minimum number of years in business: 0
REFERRALS ACCEPTED FROM: Investment/Mortgage banker or Borrower/Investee
BRANCHES: Wayne Kingsley, V.P., 1300 S.W. Fifth Ave., Ste 2323, Portland, OR 97201; (503) 223-4334

COMPANY: **Julian, Cole, & Stein**
ADDRESS: 11777 San Vicente Boulevard, Suite 522
Los Angeles, CA 90049
PHONE: (213) 826-8002
TYPE OF INSTITUTION: Private Venture Capital firm
CONTACT OFFICER(S): James M. Julian, Gen. Partner
Charles R. Cole, Gen. Partner
David L.R. Stein, Gen. Partner
ASSETS: $35 million
INVESTMENTS/LOANS MADE: For managed accounts
TYPES OF FINANCING: VENTURE CAPITAL: Start-up from developed product stage; First-stage OTHER SERVICES PROVIDED: Seed
PREFERRED TYPES OF INDUSTRIES/INVESTMENTS: Exclusively High-technology
GEOGRAPHIC LIMITS OF INVESTMENTS/LOANS: Other: Prefer Southern CA
RANGE OF INV./LOAN PER BUSINESS: Min. $500,000; 100,000 (seed); Max. $2 million

COMPANY: **SAS Associates**
ADDRESS: 515 So. Figueroa 6th Floor
Los Angeles, CA 90071-3396
PHONE: (213) 624-4232
CONTACT OFFICER(S): Robert W. Campbell, Ass't. Vice President
INVESTMENTS/LOANS MADE: For own account, Through private placements
INVESTMENTS/LOANS MADE: In securities with a secondary market and in securities without a secondary market
TYPES OF FINANCING: VENTURE CAPITAL: Start-up from developed product stage; First stage; Second-stage; Later-stage expansion; Buy-outs/Acquisitions
PREFERRED TYPES OF INDUSTRIES/INVESTMENTS: Diversified
WILL NOT CONSIDER: Real Estate; Entertainment
GEOGRAPHIC LIMITS OF INVESTMENTS/LOANS: Regional; West Coast and Rocky Mountains
BUSINESS CHARACTERISTICS DESIRED-REQUIRED: Flexible
REFERRALS ACCEPTED FROM: Investment/Mortgage banker; Borrower/Investee

COMPANY: **Stanfill, Doig & Co., Inc.**
ADDRESS: 444 S. Flower St. #4650
Los Angeles, CA 90017
PHONE: (213) 689-9235
TYPE OF INSTITUTION: Venture Capital
CONTACT OFFICER(S): Raymond Doig
ASSETS: $25 million
INVESTMENTS/LOANS MADE: For managed accounts
TYPES OF FINANCING: VENTURE CAPITAL: Second-stage; Later-stage expansion; Buy-outs/Acquisitions
PREFERRED TYPES OF INDUSTRIES/INVESTMENTS: Entertainment; Communications & Leisure Industries
GEOGRAPHIC LIMITS OF INVESTMENTS/LOANS: National
BUSINESS CHARACTERISTICS DESIRED-REQUIRED: Minimum number of years in business: 3Other: Financial Statements, 5 year Proformas—general business plan
REMARKS: Preferred range of investment—$500,000 to $1,000,000

COMPANY: **Rothschild, Unterberg, Towbin Ventures**
ADDRESS: 3000 Sand Hill Road, Building 3, Suite 260
Melo Park, CA 94025
PHONE: (415) 854-2576
TYPE OF INSTITUTION: Venture Capital
CONTACT OFFICER(S): J. Michael Gullard, Chairman and General Partner
Thomas A. Tisch, General Partner
ASSETS: $20M
INVESTMENTS/LOANS MADE: Through private placements
INVESTMENTS/LOANS MADE: Only in securities without a secondary market
TYPES OF FINANCING: VENTURE CAPITAL: Start-up from developed product stage; First-stage; Second-stage
PREFERRED TYPES OF INDUSTRIES/INVESTMENTS: Data communications, telephone related, satellite and microwave communications, electronic components

and instrumentation, computer and peripherals, genetic engineering, medical diagnostic equipment, robotics, advanced industrial products and equipment
WILL NOT CONSIDER: Consumer, real estate, retail
GEOGRAPHIC LIMITS OF INVESTMENTS/LOANS: Regional
RANGE OF INV./LOAN PER BUSINESS: Min. 0.5 million; Max. $2.0 million
BUSINESS CHARACTERISTICS DESIRED-REQUIRED:Minimum number of years in business: 0

COMPANY: **Alpha Partners**
ADDRESS: 2200 Sand Hill Rd., #250
Menlo Park, CA 94025
PHONE: (415) 854-7024
TYPE OF INSTITUTION: Venture Capital
CONTACT OFFICER(S): Wallace F. Davis
Ruth Scott

COMPANY: **Commtech International**
ADDRESS: 545 Middlefield Road #180
Menlo Park, CA 94025
PHONE: (415) 328-0190
TYPE OF INSTITUTION: Venture Capital
CONTACT OFFICER(S): Gerald A. Marxman, President
Martin Knestrick, V.P.
ASSETS: $10 million
INVESTMENTS/LOANS MADE: For own account; Through private placements
TYPES OF FINANCING: VENTURE CAPITAL: Research & Development
GEOGRAPHIC LIMITS OF INVESTMENTS/LOANS: State: CA
RANGE OF INV./LOAN PER BUSINESS: Max. $3 million

COMPANY: **Donald L. Lucas**
ADDRESS: 3000 Sand Hill Road #3
Menlo Park, CA 94025
PHONE: (415) 854-4223
TYPE OF INSTITUTION: Private Venture Capital
CONTACT OFFICER(S): Donald L. Lucas, Gen. Partner
INVESTMENTS/LOANS MADE: For own account; Through underwriting public offerings
TYPES OF FINANCING: VENTURE CAPITAL: Start-up from developed product stage; First-stage; Second-stage; Later-stage expansion; Buy-outs/Acquisitions
PREFERRED TYPES OF INDUSTRIES/INVESTMENTS: Computer Software
GEOGRAPHIC LIMITS OF INVESTMENTS/LOANS: National
RANGE OF INV./LOAN PER BUSINESS: Min. $250,000; Max. $1 million
BUSINESS CHARACTERISTICS DESIRED-REQUIRED: Minimum number of years in business: 0

COMPANY: **Glenwood Management**
ADDRESS: 3000 Sand Hill Road, Bldg. 3, Suite 250
Menlo Park, CA 94025
PHONE: (415) 854-8070
TYPE OF INSTITUTION: Venture Capital Investment Manager
CONTACT OFFICER(S): Dag Tellefsen, Partner, Hi-Tech startups
Doug Broyles, Partner, Computer Co's
John Hurrer, Service Companies
ASSETS: $20 million
INVESTMENTS/LOANS MADE: For managed accounts
INVESTMENTS/LOANS MADE: In securities with a secondary market and in securities without a secondary market
TYPES OF FINANCING: SECONDARY-MARKET CORPORATE SECURITIES: Preferred stock, VENTURE CAPITAL: Research & Development; Start-up from developed product stage; First-stage; Second-stage; Buy-outs/Acquisitions
PREFERRED TYPES OF INDUSTRIES/INVESTMENTS: Emerging technologies and services
WILL NOT CONSIDER: Real estate
GEOGRAPHIC LIMITS OF INVESTMENTS/LOANS: National
RANGE OF INV./LOAN PER BUSINESS: Min. $100,000; Max. $1,000,000
BUSINESS CHARACTERISTICS DESIRED-REQUIRED: Minimum number of years in business: 0
REFERRALS: Borrower/Investee only

COMPANY: **Glynn Ventures**
ADDRESS: 3000 Sand Hill Rd. Bldg. 2, Ste. 210
Menlo Park, CA 94025
PHONE: (415) 854-2215
TYPE OF INSTITUTION: Private Venture Capital
CONTACT OFFICER(S): John W. Glynn, Jr.
INVESTMENTS/LOANS MADE: Through private placements
INVESTMENTS/LOANS MADE: Only in securities without a secondary market
TYPES OF FINANCING: VENTURE CAPITAL: Start-up from developed product stage; First-stage; Second-stage; Later-stage expansion
PREFERRED TYPES OF INDUSTRIES/INVESTMENTS: CAE; CAD/CAM; Artificial Intelligence; Networking; Almost all computer related
WILL NOT CONSIDER: R.E. Retailing; Consumer oriented products
GEOGRAPHIC LIMITS OF INVESTMENTS/LOANS: Local
RANGE OF INV./LOAN PER BUSINESS: Min. $250,000; Max. $1 million

COMPANY: **Institutional Venture Partners**
ADDRESS: 3000 Sand Hill, Bldg. 2, Suite 290
Menlo Park, CA 94025
PHONE: (415) 854-0132
TYPE OF INSTITUTION: Private Venture Capital
CONTACT OFFICER(S): John Poitras, Gen. Partner
Mary Jane Elmore, Gen. Partner
Samuel D. Colella, Gen. Partner
ASSETS: $57 million (Capital invested)
INVESTMENTS/LOANS MADE: For own account
INVESTMENTS/LOANS MADE: In securities with a secondary market and in securities without a secondary market
TYPES OF FINANCING: SECONDARY-MARKET CORPORATE SECURITIES: Common stock; Preferred

stock; VENTURE CAPITAL: Start-up from developed product stage; First-stage
PREFERRED TYPES OF INDUSTRIES/INVESTMENTS: Electronics; Computers; Medical
WILL NOT CONSIDER: Retail; Consumer; R.E.
GEOGRAPHIC LIMITS OF INVESTMENTS/LOANS: State
RANGE OF INV./LOAN PER BUSINESS: Min. $750,000; Max. $2,000,000

COMPANY: **Mayfield Fund**
ADDRESS: 2200 Sand Hill Road, Suite 200
Menlo Park, CA 94025
PHONE: (415) 854-5560
TYPE OF INSTITUTION: Venture Capital Partnership
CONTACT OFFICER(S): Thomas J. Davis, Jr., General Partner
F. Gibson Myers, Jr., General Partner
Glenn M. Mueller, General Partner
Norman A. Fogelsong, General Partner
ASSETS: $193 Million
INVESTMENTS/LOANS MADE: For own account
TYPES OF FINANCING: VENTURE CAPITAL: Research & Development; Start-up from developed product stage; First-stage (less than 1 year); Second-stage (generally 1-3 years); Later-stage expansion
PREFERRED TYPES OF INDUSTRIES/INVESTMENTS: COMPUTER RELATED: Computers and minicomputers, Data communications, Peripheral equipment, software, word processing. MANUFACTURING: Automation equipment, chemicals, materials handling equipment. MEDICAL: Clinical laboratories, Diagnostic centers, Drugs and medicines, medical instruments, Microbiology. TECHNOLOGY: Communications, Energy related, Graphic arts, Integrated circuitry, lasers, microfilm and data retrieval, optics technology.
WILL NOT CONSIDER: Real estate; oil and gas
GEOGRAPHIC LIMITS OF INVESTMENTS/LOANS: West Coast
RANGE OF INV./LOAN PER BUSINESS: Min. $100,000; Max. $1,000,000
BUSINESS CHARACTERISTICS DESIRED-REQUIRED: Min. no. of years in business: 0

COMPANY: **Menlo Ventures**
ADDRESS: 3000 Sand Hill Road
Menlo Park, CA 94025
PHONE: (415) 854-8540
TYPE OF INSTITUTION: Venture Capital
CONTACT OFFICER(S): Denise M. O'Leary, Associate
ASSETS: $150,000,000
INVESTMENTS/LOANS MADE: For own account
INVESTMENTS/LOANS MADE: In securities with a secondary market and in securities without a secondary market
TYPES OF FINANCING: SECONDARY-MARKET CORPORATE SECURITIES: Common stock; Preferred stock, VENTURE CAPITAL: Research & Development; Start-up from developed product stage; First-stage; Second-stage; Later-stage expansion; Buy-outs/ Acquisitions
PREFERRED TYPES OF INDUSTRIES/INVESTMENTS: Technology related product or service business
WILL NOT CONSIDER: Real estate, oil and gas, movies
GEOGRAPHIC LIMITS OF INVESTMENTS/LOANS: National
RANGE OF INV./LOAN PER BUSINESS: Min. $100,000; Max. $5,000,000
PREFERRED TERM FOR LOANS & LEASES: Min. 2 years; Max. 7 years
BUSINESS CHARACTERISTICS DESIRED-REQUIRED: Minimum number of years in business: 0; Other: Experienced management
REFERRALS ACCEPTED FROM: Investment/Mortgage banker or Borrower/Investee

COMPANY: **Mohr Venture**
ADDRESS: 3000 Sand Hill Road, Building 4, #240
Menlo Park, CA 94025
PHONE: (415) 854-7236
TYPE OF INSTITUTION: Private Venture Capital
CONTACT OFFICER(S): Larry Mohr, Gen. Partner
Peter Roshko, Associate
INVESTMENTS/LOANS MADE: For own account
INVESTMENTS/LOANS MADE: Only in securities without a secondary market
TYPES OF FINANCING: VENTURE CAPITAL: Research & Development; Start-up from developed product stage; First-stage; Second-stage; Later-stage expansion
PREFERRED TYPES OF INDUSTRIES/INVESTMENTS: High-technology
GEOGRAPHIC LIMITS OF INVESTMENTS/LOANS: Regional; Western
BUSINESS CHARACTERISTICS DESIRED-REQUIRED: Minimum number of years in business: 0
REMARKS: Preferred range of investment $500,000 and up; focus on seed capital

COMPANY: **Oak Grove Ventures**
ADDRESS: 173 Jefferson Drive
Menlo Park, CA 94025
PHONE: (415) 324-2276
TYPE OF INSTITUTION: Venture Capital
CONTACT OFFICER(S): Paul M. Cook, Gen. Partner
Duane C. Montopoli, Gen. Partner
James J. Hornthal, Gen. Partner
INVESTMENTS/LOANS MADE: For own account
INVESTMENTS/LOANS MADE: Only in securities without a secondary market
TYPES OF FINANCING: VENTURE CAPITAL: Seed-capital; Start-up from developed product stage; First-stage
PREFERRED TYPES OF INDUSTRIES/INVESTMENTS: Communications; Computers; Electronics; Genetic Engineering; Industrial; Medical
WILL NOT CONSIDER: Real Estate; Retail; Energy
GEOGRAPHIC LIMITS OF INVESTMENTS/LOANS: Regional; West Coast
RANGE OF INV./LOAN PER BUSINESS: Min. $100,000-300,000
BRANCHES: James J. Hornthal, 2234 Beach St., San Francisco, CA 94123 (415) 563-6336

VENTURE CAPITAL COMPANIES

(Also see SBICs, MESBICs and Investment Bankers)

CALIFORNIA

COMPANY: **Oscco Ventures**
ADDRESS: 3000 Sand Hill Road 4-140
Menlo Park, CA 94025
PHONE: (415) 854-2222
TYPE OF INSTITUTION: Venture Capital Partnership
CONTACT OFFICER(S): Stephen E. Halprin, General Partner
F. Ward Paine, General Partner
James G. Rudolph, General Partner
ASSETS: over $25 million
INVESTMENTS/LOANS MADE: For own account
INVESTMENTS/LOANS MADE: Only in securities without a secondary market
TYPES OF FINANCING: SECONDARY-MARKET CORPORATE SECURITIES: Common stock; Preferred stock; Bonds; Other; VENTURE CAPITAL: Start-up from developed product stage; First-stage; Second-stage; Later-stage expansion;
PREFERRED TYPES OF INDUSTRIES/INVESTMENTS: Preferred equity
WILL NOT CONSIDER: Other
GEOGRAPHIC LIMITS OF INVESTMENTS/LOANS: State; West Coast thru Texas
RANGE OF INV./LOAN PER BUSINESS: Min. $250,000; Max. $1-3 million
BUSINESS CHARACTERISTICS DESIRED-REQUIRED: Minimum number of years in business: 0
REFERRALS: Investment/Mortgage banker and Borrower/Investee

COMPANY: **Pacific Venture Partners**
ADDRESS: 3000 Sand Hill Road, Building 4, #175
Menlo Park, CA 94025
PHONE: (415) 854-2266
TYPE OF INSTITUTION: Venture Capital
CONTACT OFFICER(S): James C. Balderston, Gen. Partner
Rigdon Carrie, Gen. Partner
Anthony T. Ellis, Gen. Partner
ASSETS: $16 million

COMPANY: **Palo Alto Ventures, Inc.**
ADDRESS: 3000 Sand Hill Rd., Bldg. 1, #140
Menlo Park, CA 94025
PHONE: (415) 854-8770
TYPE OF INSTITUTION: Venture Capital
CONTACT OFFICER(S): Daniel L. Larson

COMPANY: **Paragon Partners**
ADDRESS: 3000 Sand Hill Road, Building 2, Suite 190
Menlo Park, CA 94025
PHONE: (415) 854-8000
TYPE OF INSTITUTION: Private Venture Capital
CONTACT OFFICER(S): Jess R. Marzak, Gen. Partner
Robert F. Kibble, Gen. Partner
John S. Lewis, Gen. Partner
ASSETS: $40 million
INVESTMENTS/LOANS MADE: For own account; Through private placements
TYPES OF FINANCING: VENTURE CAPITAL: Start-up from developed product stage; First-stage; Second-stage; Later-stage expansion; Buy-outs/Acquisitions
PREFERRED TYPES OF INDUSTRIES/INVESTMENTS: High-Technology; Computer Related
WILL NOT CONSIDER: Real Estate; Financial Institutions
GEOGRAPHIC LIMITS OF INVESTMENTS/LOANS: National
RANGE OF INV./LOAN PER BUSINESS: Min. $500,000; Max. $3,000,000
BUSINESS CHARACTERISTICS DESIRED-REQUIRED: Minimum number of years in business: 0

COMPANY: **Sequoia Capital**
ADDRESS: 3000 Sand Hill Rd., Bldg. 4, #280
Menlo Park, CA 94025
PHONE: (415) 854-3927
TYPE OF INSTITUTION: Venture Capital
CONTACT OFFICER(S): Don Valentine

COMPANY: **Sierra Ventures**
ADDRESS: 3000 Sand Hill Rd., Bldg. 1, #280
Menlo Park, CA 94025
PHONE: (415) 854-9096
TYPE OF INSTITUTION: Venture Capital
CONTACT OFFICER(S): Peter C. Wendell

COMPANY: **Technology Venture Investors**
ADDRESS: 3000 Sand Hill Rd., Bldg. 4, #210
Menlo Park, CA 94025
PHONE: (415) 854-7472
TYPE OF INSTITUTION: Venture Capital
CONTACT OFFICER(S): James J. Bochnowski, Gen. Ptnr.

COMPANY: **U.S. Venture Partners**
ADDRESS: 2180 Sand Hill Rd., Ste 300
Menlo Park, CA 94025
PHONE: (415) 854-9080
TYPE OF INSTITUTION: Venture Capital
CONTACT OFFICER(S): William K. Bowes, Jr.
Robert Sackman

COMPANY: **Venca Partners**
ADDRESS: 3000 Sand Hill Rd., Bldg. 2, #270
Menlo Park, CA 94025
PHONE: (415) 854-8264
TYPE OF INSTITUTION: Venture Capital
CONTACT OFFICER(S): Carolynn Gandolfo, Gen. Ptnr.

COMPANY: **Happ Ventures**
ADDRESS: 444 Castro Street, Suite 400
Mountain View, CA 94041
PHONE: (415) 961-1115
TYPE OF INSTITUTION: Private Venture Capital Organization
CONTACT OFFICER(S): William D. Happ
INVESTMENTS/LOANS MADE: For managed accounts; through private placements
INVESTMENTS/LOANS MADE: Only in securities without a secondary market
TYPES OF FINANCING: VENTURE CAPITAL: Research & Development; Start-up from developed product stage; First-stage; Second-stage; OTHER SERVICES PROVIDED: R & D Partnerships

PREFERRED TYPES OF INDUSTRIES/INVESTMENTS: Communications, computer related, electronic components & instrumentation, industrial products & equipment, medical/health related
GEOGRAPHIC LIMITS OF INVESTMENTS/LOANS: International
RANGE OF INV./LOAN PER BUSINESS: Min. $100,000; Max. $5,000,000
BUSINESS CHARACTERISTICS DESIRED-REQUIRED:Minimum number of years in business: 0; Min. annual sales: nominal; min. net worth: nominal; Min. annual net income: nominal; Min. annual cash flow: nominal

COMPANY: **First California Business and Industrial Development Corporation**
ADDRESS: 3931 MacArthur Blvd., Suite 212
Newport Beach, CA 92660
PHONE: (714) 851-0855
TYPE OF INSTITUTION: Business Development Company/Small Business Lending
CONTACT OFFICER(S): Leslie R. Brewer, President
INVESTMENTS/LOANS MADE: For own account
TYPES OF FINANCING: VENTURE CAPITAL, First-stage (less than 1 year), Second-stage (generally 1-3 years), Later-stage expansion, Buy-outs/Acquisitions; LOANS, Working capital (receivables/inventory), Equipment; REAL ESTATE LOANS, Long-term senior mtg.; Intermediate-term senior mtg., Subordinated; INTERNATIONAL; OTHER SERVICES PROVIDED, Management consulting, Financial planning, Budgeting, Financing
PREFERRED TYPES OF INDUSTRIES/INVESTMENTS: Manufacturing; Equipment based services; Franchises
WILL NOT CONSIDER: R & D, Films, Publications
GEOGRAPHIC LIMITS OF INVESTMENTS/LOANS: State
RANGE OF INV./LOAN PER BUSINESS: Min. $50,000; Max. $550,000
PREFERRED TERM FOR LOANS & LEASES: Min. 7 years; Max. 25 years
BUSINESS CHARACTERISTICS DESIRED-REQUIRED: Minimum number of years in business: 0; Min. annual sales $500,000 Projected; Min. net worth $50,000; Min. annual net income $60,000; Min. annual cash flow $90,000
REFERRALS ACCEPTED FROM: Investment/Mortgage banker; Borrower/investee
BRANCHES: 130 Montgomery St., San Francisco, CA 94104, (415) 392-5400

COMPANY: **New West Ventures**
ADDRESS: 4600 Campus Dr., #103
Newport Beach, CA 92660
PHONE: (714) 756-8940
TYPE OF INSTITUTION: Venture Capital Fund
CONTACT OFFICER(S): Tim Haidinger, President
ASSETS: $10 million
INVESTMENTS/LOANS MADE: For own account
INVESTMENTS/LOANS MADE: In securities with a secondary market and in securities without a secondary market
TYPES OF FINANCING: VENTURE CAPITAL: Second-stage; Later-stage; Buy-outs/Acquisitions
WILL NOT CONSIDER: Real Estate
GEOGRAPHIC LIMITS OF INVESTMENTS/LOANS: National
RANGE OF INV./LOAN PER BUSINESS: Min. $500,000; Max. 2,500,000
PREFERRED TERM FOR LOANS & LEASES: Min. 5 years; Max. 10 years
BUSINESS CHARACTERISTICS DESIRED-REQUIRED: Minimum number of years in business: 1; Min. annual sales $2,000,000
REFERRALS ACCEPTED FROM: Investment/Mortgage banker or Borrower/Investee

COMPANY: **Security Pacific Venture Capital Group**
ADDRESS: 4000 MacArthur Boulevard
Newport Beach, CA 92660
PHONE: (714) 754-4780
TYPE OF INSTITUTION: Venture Capital subsidiary of a bank holding company
CONTACT OFFICER(S): Brian Jones, Newport Beach, Senior Vice President; (714) 754-4780
Daniel A. Dye, Eastern Office, First Vice President; (412) 223-0707
John Padgett, Los Angeles, Senior Vice President; (213) 613-5215
ASSETS: $140,000,000
INVESTMENTS/LOANS MADE: For own account
INVESTMENTS/LOANS MADE: In securities with a secondary market and in securities without a secondary market
TYPES OF FINANCING: VENTURE CAPITAL: Start-up from developed product stage; First-stage; Second-stage; Later-stage; Buy-outs/Acquisitions
WILL NOT CONSIDER: Movies, tax shelters
GEOGRAPHIC LIMITS OF INVESTMENTS/LOANS: National
RANGE OF INV./LOAN PER BUSINESS: Min. $50,000; Max. 10,000,000
PREFERRED TERM FOR LOANS & LEASES: Max. 12 years
BUSINESS CHARACTERISTICS DESIRED-REQUIRED: Management with a track record of success in its proposed business area
REFERRALS ACCEPTED FROM: Investment/Mortgage banker or Borrower/Investee
BRANCHES: Daniel A. Dye, First Vice Pressident, P.O. Box 512, Washington, PA 15301
Michael Cronin, Vice President, Boston Office, Milk Street, Boston, MA

COMPANY: **Winston Financial Corp**
ADDRESS: 1447 Palisades Drive
Pacific Palisades, CA 90272
PHONE: (213) 454-7030
TYPE OF INSTITUTION: Financial Services, Leasing Specialty
CONTACT OFFICER(S): Paul D. Shlensky, President
Barry G. Morganstern, V.P.
ASSETS: $10,000,000
INVESTMENTS/LOANS MADE: For own account
INVESTMENTS/LOANS MADE: In securities with a secondary market and in securities without a secondary market

TYPES OF FINANCING: SECONDARY-MARKET CORPORATE SECURITIES, VENTURE CAPITAL: Second-stage; Later-stage expansion; Buy-outs/ Acquisitions, LOANS: Working capital; Equipment, LEASES: Single-investor; Leveraged; Tax leases; Operating; Vendor financing programs
PREFERRED TYPES OF INDUSTRIES/INVESTMENTS: Telecommunications, energy
GEOGRAPHIC LIMITS OF INVESTMENTS/LOANS: National
RANGE OF INV./LOAN PER BUSINESS: Min. $250,000; Max. $10,000,000
PREFERRED TERM FOR LOANS & LEASES: Min. 3 years; Max. 5 years
BUSINESS CHARACTERISTICS DESIRED-REQUIRED: Minimum number of years in business: 5 years
REFERRALS ACCEPTED FROM: Investment/Mortgage banker or Borrower/Investee

COMPANY: **Asset Management Co.**
ADDRESS: 1417 Edgewood Drive
Palo Alto, CA 94301
PHONE: (415) 321-3131
TYPE OF INSTITUTION: Venture capital firm
CONTACT OFFICER(S): Daniel Flamen, Partner
ASSETS: $100 million
INVESTMENTS/LOANS MADE: For own account
TYPES OF FINANCING: VENTURE CAPITAL: Research & Development; Start-up from developed product stage; First-stage; Second-stage
PREFERRED TYPES OF INDUSTRIES/INVESTMENTS: Computer hardware, software; Bio Science; Semiconductors
WILL NOT CONSIDER: Real estate, minerals, entertainment, restaurants, agriculture
GEOGRAPHIC LIMITS OF INVESTMENTS/LOANS: National
RANGE OF INV./LOAN PER BUSINESS: Min. $500,000; Max. $1,000,000
BUSINESS CHARACTERISTICS DESIRED-REQUIRED: Minimum number of years in business: 0
REFERRALS ACCEPTED FROM: Borrower/Investee

COMPANY: **Charter Venture Capital**
ADDRESS: 525 University Avenue, Suite 1500
Palo Alto, CA 94301 CA 94301
PHONE: (415) 325-6953
TYPE OF INTITUTION: Venture Capital
CONTACT OFFICER(S): A. Barr Dolan, President
INVESTMENTS/LOANS MADE: For own account
INVESTMENTS/LOANS MADE: Only in securities without a secondary market
TYPES OF FINANCING: VENTURE CAPITAL: Research & Development; Start-up from developed product stage; First-stage; Second-stage; Later-stage expansion
PREFERRED TYPES OF INDUSTRIES/INVESTMENTS: High Technology
GEOGRAPHIC LIMITS OF INVESTMENTS/LOANS: National
RANGE OF INV./LOAN PER BUSINESS: Min. $100,000; Max. $500,000
BUSINESS CHARACTERISTICS DESIRED-REQUIRED: Minimum number of years in business: 0

COMPANY: **Grace Ventures Corporation**
ADDRESS: 630 Hansen Way
Palo Alto, CA 94304
PHONE: (415) 424-1171
TYPE OF INSTITUTION: Venture capital subsidiary of operating company
CONTACT OFFICER(S): Dr. Christian F. Horn
Dr. Charles A. Bauer
Susan Woods
Bill Wittmeyer
INVESTMENTS/LOANS MADE: For own account
INVESTMENTS/LOANS MADE: Only in securities without a secondary market
TYPES OF FINANCING: VENTURE CAPITAL: Research & Development; Start-up from developed product stage; First-stage; Second-stage; Later-stage expansion
PREFERRED TYPES OF INDUSTRIES/INVESTMENTS: Communications; Computers; Electronics; Industrial; Medical
WILL NOT CONSIDER: Consumer; Retail; R.E.
REMARKS: Preferred range of investment $500,000-1,000,000

COMPANY: **Nest Venture Partners**
ADDRESS: 1086 East Meadow Circle
Palo Alto, CA 94303
PHONE: (415) 493-0921
TYPE OF INSTITUTION: Venture Capital
CONTACT OFFICER(S): Gary W. Almond, Ptnr.
INVESTMENTS/LOANS MADE: For own account
INVESTMENTS/LOANS MADE: In securities with a secondary market and in securities without a secondary market
TYPES OF FINANCING: VENTURE CAPITAL: Research & Development; Start-up from developed product stage
WILL NOT CONSIDER: Real Estate; Retail
GEOGRAPHIC LIMITS OF INVESTMENTS/LOANS: Local
REMARKS: Average investment $250,000

COMPANY: **Sutter Hill Ventures**
ADDRESS: 2 Palo Alto Square, Suite 700
Palo Alto, CA 94306
PHONE: (415) 493-5600
TYPE OF INSTITUTION: Venture Capitalists
CONTACT OFFICER(S): Paul M. Wythes, General Partner
G. Leonard Baker, Jr., General Partner
William H. Younger, Jr., General Partner
ASSETS: $500 million
INVESTMENTS/LOANS MADE: For own account
TYPES OF FINANCING: SECONDARY-MARKET CORPORATE SECURITIES: Common stock, VENTURE CAPITAL: Start-up from developed product stage; First-stage; Second-stage; Later-stage expansion, OTHER SERVICES PROVIDED: Board seats
PREFERRED TYPES OF INDUSTRIES/INVESTMENTS: High technology manufacturing

WILL NOT CONSIDER: Asset intensive businesses, real estate, service companies
GEOGRAPHIC LIMITS OF INVESTMENTS/LOANS: National
RANGE OF INV./LOAN PER BUSINESS: Min. $100,000; Max. $3,000,000
BUSINESS CHARACTERISTICS DESIRED-REQUIRED: Minimum number of years in business: 0; Min. annual sales 0; Min. net worth 0; Min. annual net income 0; Min. annual cash flow 0
REFERRALS ACCEPTED FROM: Investment/Mortgage banker or Borrower/Investee

COMPANY: **Vanguard Associates**
ADDRESS: 300 Hamilton Avenue #500
Palo Alto, CA 94301
PHONE: (415) 324-8400
TYPE OF INSTITUTION: Private Venture Capital firm
CONTACT OFFICER(S): Jack M. Gill, Gen. Partner
David H. Rammler, Gen. Partner
Douglas G. Devivo, Gen. Partner
INVESTMENTS/LOANS MADE: For managed accounts
TYPES OF FINANCING: VENTURE CAPITAL: Start-up from developed product stageOTHER SERVICES PROVIDED: Seed
PREFERRED TYPES OF INDUSTRIES/INVESTMENTS: Biotechnology; Computer Hardware & Software; Telecommunications; Medical Instrumentation and other High Technology companies
WILL NOT CONSIDER: CATV, Construction, Consumer Products; Real Estate; Retailing
GEOGRAPHIC LIMITS OF INVESTMENTS/LOANS: Regional; Other: Prefer West Coast but not limited to it
RANGE OF INV./LOAN PER BUSINESS: Min. None; Max. $1,500,000
REMARKS: Average investment $1 million

COMPANY: **Blalack-Loop Inc.**
ADDRESS: 696 E Colorado Blvd, Suite 220
Pasadena, CA 91101
PHONE: (213) 681-2770
TYPE OF INSTITUTION: Investment Advisors
CONTACT OFFICER(S): M. Rosemary Lyons, Vice President
ASSETS: Approx. $100 million
INVESTMENTS/LOANS MADE: Through private placements
INVESTMENTS/LOANS MADE: In securities with a secondary market and in securities without a second market
TYPES OF FINANCING: SECONDARY-MARKET CORPORATE SECURITIES: Common stock, Preferred stock, Bonds; VENTURE CAPITAL: Start-up from developed product stage; First-stage; Later-stage expansion
PREFERRED TYPES OF INDUSTRIES/INVESTMENTS: Venture Capital plays at various stages in a broad variety of industries
WILL NOT CONSIDER: Real Estate, Movies, Mining
GEOGRAPHIC LIMITS OF INVESTMENTS/LOANS: National
RANGE OF INV./LOAN PER BUSINESS: Min. None; Max. $5-10,000,000
BUSINESS CHARACTERISTICS DESIRED-REQUIRED: Minimum number of years in business: 0

COMPANY: **BC & A Enterprises, Inc.**
ADDRESS: 11650 Iberia Place, Ste K
San Diego, CA 92128
PHONE: (619) 693-8081
TYPE OF INSTITUTION: Holding Company for Mergers & Acquisitions
CONTACT OFFICER(S): Dr. William L. Brockhaus, C.E.O.

COMPANY: **CFB Venture Capital Corporation**
ADDRESS: 530 B Street
San Diego, CA 92101
PHONE: (619) 230-3304
TYPE OF INSTITUTION: SBIC. Venture Capital subsidiary of bank
CONTACT OFFICER(S): Piet Westerbeek III, CFO
ASSETS: $1 million & up
INVESTMENTS/LOANS MADE: For own account
INVESTMENTS/LOANS MADE: Only in securities without a secondary market
TYPES OF FINANCING: VENTURE CAPITAL: Start-up from developed product stage; First-stage
PREFERRED TYPES OF INDUSTRIES/INVESTMENTS: High-technology; Bio-technology
GEOGRAPHIC LIMITS OF INVESTMENTS/LOANS: National; Other: Primarily CA
RANGE OF INV./LOAN PER BUSINESS: Min. $100,000-200,000
REMARKS: Total minimum investment—$2 million or more range.

COMPANY: **Gillem Lucas and Associates**
ADDRESS: 311 Camino Del Rio N. #1121
San Diego, CA 92108
PHONE: (619) 280-6201
TYPE OF INSTITUTION: Venture Capital
CONTACT OFFICER(S): R. Gillem Lucas, Gen. Partner
INVESTMENTS/LOANS MADE: For own account
TYPES OF FINANCING: VENTURE CAPITAL: Research & Development; Start-up from developed product stage; First-stage; Second-stage; Later-stage expansion; Buy-outs
WILL NOT CONSIDER: Projects; Magazines; Movies; Art Forms
GEOGRAPHIC LIMITS OF INVESTMENTS/LOANS: Regional; Primarily SW
RANGE OF INV./LOAN PER BUSINESS: Min. $500,000
REMARKS: Preferred range of investment: $500,000-$2,000,000; focus primarily on start-up and early stage

COMPANY: **Girard Capital**
ADDRESS: 9191 Towne Centre Drive, Suite 370
San Diego, CA 92122
PHONE: (619) 457-5114
TYPE OF INSTITUTION: Private Venture Capital
CONTACT OFFICER(S): E. Sam Gudmundson, V.P.
Creighton Gallaway, V.P.
San Jay Subhedar, V.P.

INVESTMENTS/LOANS MADE: For own account; Through private placements
TYPES OF FINANCING: VENTURE CAPITAL: Start-up from developed product stage; First-stage; Second-stage; Buy-outs/Acquisitions OTHER SERVICES PROVIDED: First and second stages usually on own companies; have own saving bank to refer loans
PREFERRED TYPES OF INDUSTRIES/INVESTMENTS: Diversified
GEOGRAPHIC LIMITS OF INVESTMENTS/LOANS: Other: Within 2 hours travel
RANGE OF INV./LOAN PER BUSINESS: Min. $100,000 (seed); $300,000-500,000
BUSINESS CHARACTERISTICS DESIRED-REQUIRED: Other:Complete leverage to cash on buy-outs
REFERRALS ACCEPTED FROM: Investment/Mortgage banker or Borrower/Investee

COMPANY: **Henry & Co.**
ADDRESS: 9191 Towne Centre Drive #230
San Diego, CA 92122
PHONE: (619) 453-1655
CONTACT OFFICER(S): F. David Hare, President
ASSETS: $21 million (fund)
INVESTMENTS/LOANS MADE: For managed accounts; Through private placements; Through underwriting public offerings
TYPES OF FINANCING: VENTURE CAPITAL: Second-stage; Later-stage expansion
PREFERRED TYPES OF INDUSTRIES/INVESTMENTS: Electronics; High Technology; Medical & Health Care
GEOGRAPHIC LIMITS OF INVESTMENTS/LOANS: National
RANGE OF INV./LOAN PER BUSINESS: Min. $500,000
BUSINESS CHARACTERISTICS DESIRED-REQUIRED: Minimum number of years in business: 1

COMPANY: **Arscott, Norton & Associates**
ADDRESS: 369 Pine Street, Ste 506
San Francisco, CA 94104
PHONE: (415) 956-3386
TYPE OF INSTITUTION: Venture Capital
CONTACT OFFICER(S): David G. Arscott
Dean C. Campbell

COMPANY: **Arthur Rock & Co.**
ADDRESS: 1635 Russ Building
San Francisco, CA 94104
PHONE: (415) 981-3921
TYPE OF INSTITUTION: Venture Capital
CONTACT OFFICER(S): Arthur Rock, Principal
INVESTMENTS/LOANS MADE: For own account; Through private placements
INVESTMENTS/LOANS MADE: Only in securities without a secondary market
TYPES OF FINANCING: VENTURE CAPITAL: Research & Development-Partnership; Start-up from developed product stage; First-stage; Second-stage
PREFERRED TYPES OF INDUSTRIES/INVESTMENTS: High-tech w/ Proprietary Product; Computer-related Companies
GEOGRAPHIC LIMITS OF INVESTMENTS/LOANS: Local
RANGE OF INV./LOAN PER BUSINESS: Min. $100,000-300,000
REMARKS: Preferred investment $600,000

COMPANY: **Bank America Capital Corp.**
ADDRESS: 555 California St., 42nd Floor, Dept. 3908
San Francisco, CA 94104
PHONE: (415) 953-3001
TYPE OF INSTITUTION: Venture Capital
CONTACT OFFICER(S): Bob Gibson, Pres.
Phil Gioia, V.P.
Patrick Topolski, V.P.
ASSETS: $100 million
TYPES OF FINANCING: VENTURE CAPITAL: Second-stage, Later-stage expansion; Buyouts/Acquisitions; Other: Equity investments
PREFERRED TYPES OF INDUSTRIES/INVESTMENTS: Mostly manufacturing but open
WILL NOT CONSIDER: Real estate, R & D partnerships, oil & gas
GEOGRAPHIC LIMITS OF INVESTMENTS/LOANS: Regional; Other: West Coast, will do other national
RANGE OF INV./LOAN PER BUSINESS: Max. $2 million
REFERRALS ACCEPTED FROM: Investment/Mortgage banker or Borrower/Investee
REMARKS: No start-ups

COMPANY: **Bruce A. Blinn Associates**
ADDRESS: 220 Sansome St., Suite 1225
San Francisco, CA 94104
PHONE: (415) 391-4194
CONTACT OFFICER(S): Bruce A. Blinn
TYPES OF FINANCING: VENTURE CAPITAL: First-stage; Second-stage; Later-stage expansion; Buy-outs/Acquisitions
PREFERRED TYPES OF INDUSTRIES/INVESTMENTS: Low-medium technology; Consumer services; Manufacturing; Pharmaceuticals
WILL NOT CONSIDER: Chemicals; Plastics; Education; Hotels; Food
GEOGRAPHIC LIMITS OF INVESTMENTS/LOANS: Regional
RANGE OF INV./LOAN PER BUSINESS: Min. $200,000; Max. $1.5 million

COMPANY: **Churchill International**
ADDRESS: 444 Market Street, #2501
San Francisco, CA 94111
PHONE: (415) 398-7677
TYPE OF INSTITUTION: International Venture Capital Company
CONTACT OFFICER(S): Roy G. Helsing, Vice President
ASSETS: $100,000,000
INVESTMENTS/LOANS MADE: For managed accounts
INVESTMENTS/LOANS MADE: In securities with a secondary market and in securities without a secondary market
TYPES OF FINANCING: SECONDARY-MARKET CORPORATE SECURITIES: Common stock; Preferred stock; VENTURE CAPITAL: Start-up from developed product stage; First-stage; Second-stage; Later-stage expansion; Buy-outs/Acquisitions

PREFERRED TYPES OF INDUSTRIES/INVESTMENTS: High technology only: Advanced materials, artificial intelligence, computer & peripherals, computer integrated manufacturing, communications, semmiconductor, software, test & measurement equipment
WILL NOT CONSIDER: Services, Real estate, Films, Energy
GEOGRAPHIC LIMITS OF INVESTMENTS/LOANS: international
RANGE OF INV./LOAN PER BUSINESS: Min. $200,000; Max. $1,500,000
BUSINESS CHARACTERISTICS DESIRED-REQUIRED: Minimum number of years in business: 2; Min. annual sales $2,000,000; Other: recently profitable
REFERRALS ACCEPTED FROM: Investment/Mortgage banker or Borrower/Investee
BRANCHES: R.G. Helsing, 545 Middlefield Road, Menlo Park, CA 94025; (415) 328-4401
David M. Smith, 9 Riverside Road, Weston, MA; (617) 893-6555

COMPANY: **Davis Skaggs Capital**
ADDRESS: 160 Sansome Street
San Francisco, CA 94104
PHONE: (415) 392-7700
TYPE OF INSTITUTION: Venture capital and investment banking
CONTACT OFFICER(S): Charles P. Stetson, Jr., 393-0274, President
Robert S. Miller, Chairman
INVESTMENTS/LOANS MADE: For own account, through private placements
TYPES OF FINANCING: VENTURE CAPITAL: First-stage; Second-stage; Later-stage expansion; Buy-outs/ Acquisitions, OTHER SERVICES PROVIDED: financial consulting service w/investment
REMARKS: Now owned by Shearson-Lehman Am. Express

COMPANY: **Dougery, Jones & Wilder**
ADDRESS: Three Embarcadero Center, Suite 1980
San Francisco, CA 94111
PHONE: (415) 434-1722
TYPE OF INSTITUTION: Private venture capital company
CONTACT OFFICER(S): John R. Dougery, high technology and telecommunications
David A. Jones, oil and gas
Henry L.B. Wilder, bio-medical and health care
ASSETS: $28.4 million for DJW I; $50.0 million for DJW II
INVESTMENTS/LOANS MADE: For own account
INVESTMENTS/LOANS MADE: In securities with a secondary market and in securities without a secondary market
TYPES OF FINANCING: VENTURE CAPITAL: Research & Development; Start-up from developed product stage; First-stage; Second-stage; Later-stage expansion; LOANS: Working capital, equity-related
PREFERRED TYPES OF INDUSTRIES/INVESTMENTS: High technology and telecommunications, bio-medical, health care technology, oil and gas exploration and technology
WILL NOT CONSIDER: Real estate, movies
GEOGRAPHIC LIMITS OF INVESTMENTS/LOANS: Regional, Western and Southwestern U.S.
RANGE OF INV./LOAN PER BUSINESS: Min. $250,000; Max. $2,500,000
BUSINESS CHARACTERISTICS DESIRED-REQUIRED: Minimum number of years in business: 0; Min. annual sales 0; Min. net worth 0; Min. annual net income 0; Min. annual cash flow 0
REFERRALS ACCEPTED FROM: Investment/Mortgage banker or Borrower/Investee
BRANCHES: A. Lawson Howard, Two Lincoln Centre, 5420 LBJ Freeway, Suite 1100, Dallas, TX 75240; (214) 960-0077

COMPANY: **The Early Stages Company**
ADDRESS: 244 California St., Ste. 300
San Francisco, CA 94111
PHONE: (415) 986-5700
TYPE OF INSTITUTION: Venture capital limited partnership
CONTACT OFFICER(S): Michael Berolzheimer, Partner
William P. Lanphear, IV, Partner
Frank W. (Woody) Kuehn, Partner (Initial Screening of Business Plans)
ASSETS: $12.75 million
INVESTMENTS/LOANS MADE: Through private placements
INVESTMENTS/LOANS MADE: In securities with a secondary market and in securities without a secondary market
TYPES OF FINANCING: VENTURE CAPITAL: Start-up from developed product stage; First-stage; Second-stage;
PREFERRED TYPES OF INDUSTRIES/INVESTMENTS: Consumer products and services and transfer of technology to mass markets
WILL NOT CONSIDER: Real estate, motion pictures, oil and gas
GEOGRAPHIC LIMITS OF INVESTMENTS/LOANS: National
RANGE OF INV./LOAN PER BUSINESS: Min. $200,000; Max. $750,000
PREFERRED TERM FOR LOANS & LEASES: Min. 3 years; Max. 5 years
BUSINESS CHARACTERISTICS DESIRED-REQUIRED: Minimum number of years in business: 0; Other: Should have existing product or service and show potential for rapid expansion to minimum sales level of $10-50 MM18REFERRALS ACCEPTED FROM: Investment/Mortgage banker or Borrower/Investee

COMPANY: **The Geneva Group**
ADDRESS: 57 Post Street
San Francisco, CA 94104
PHONE: (415) 781-1313
TYPE OF INSTITUTION: Venture Capital
CONTACT OFFICER(S): Bruce Glaspell

COMPANY: **Green Panther Fund**
ADDRESS: 1255 Post Street #400
San Francisco, CA 94109
PHONE: (415) 441-2600
TYPE OF INSTITUTION: Private Venture Capital

CONTACT OFFICER(S): Hugh Gee, Gen. Partner
INVESTMENTS/LOANS MADE: For own account; For managed accounts
TYPES OF FINANCING: VENTURE CAPITAL: Start-up from developed product stage; First-stage; Second-stage; Buy-outs/Acquisitions
WILL NOT CONSIDER: Agriculture
GEOGRAPHIC LIMITS OF INVESTMENTS/LOANS: State; Other: CA
BUSINESS CHARACTERISTICS DESIRED-REQUIRED: Other: Business Plan

COMPANY: **Hambrecht & Quist**
ADDRESS: 235 Montgomery Street
San Francisco, CA 94104
PHONE: (415) 576-3300
TYPE OF INSTITUTION: Investment banker
CONTACT OFFICER(S): Thomas S. Volpe, Chief Operating Officer
William R. Hambrecht, President
ASSETS: more than $50 million
INVESTMENTS/LOANS MADE: For own account, For managed accounts, Through private placements, underwriting public offerings
INVESTMENTS/LOANS MADE: In securities with a secondary market and in securities without a secondary market
TYPES OF FINANCING: SECONDARY-MARKET CORPORATE SECURITIES: Common stock; Preferred stock; Bonds, VENTURE CAPITAL: Research & Development; Start-up from developed product stage; First-stage; Second-stage; Later-stage expansion; Buy-outs/Acquisitions, OTHER SERVICES PROVIDED: Corporate Partnering/Mergers & Acquisitions
PREFERRED TYPES OF INDUSTRIES/INVESTMENTS: High technology, medical technology, defense electronics
GEOGRAPHIC LIMITS OF INVESTMENTS/LOANS: National
REFERRALS ACCEPTED FROM: Investment/Mortgage banker or Borrower/Investee
BRANCHES: Thomas Greig, 277 Park Avenue, New York, NY 10172; (212) 207-1400
Robert Morrill/Robert Whelan, 45 Milk Street, Boston, MA 02181; (617) 338-4339
Thomas Turney, 700 S. Flower St., #3310, Los Angeles, CA 90017; (213) 617-3101
REMARKS: Hambrecht & Quist does not provide loans to companies.

COMPANY: **Kleiner Perkins Caufield & Byers**
ADDRESS: Four Embarcadero Center, Suite 3520
San Francisco, CA 94111
PHONE: (415) 421-3110
TYPE OF INSTITUTION: Venture capital
CONTACT OFFICER(S): Brook H. Byers, General Partner-Medical Equip., Molecular biology
Tom Perkins, Partner, optics & lasers
Frank J. Caufield, Communications
John Doerr, Computer Hardware & Software
ASSETS: $10,000,000-100,000,000
INVESTMENTS/LOANS MADE: For own account
INVESTMENTS/LOANS MADE: In securities with a secondary market and in securities without a secondary market
TYPES OF FINANCING: SECONDARY-MARKET CORPORATE SECURITIES: Other: Equity, debt and preferred stock convertible into equity, VENTURE CAPITAL: Research & Development; Start-up from developed product stage; First-stage (less than 1 year); Second-stage (generally 1-3 years); Later-stage expansion
PREFERRED TYPES OF INDUSTRIES/INVESTMENTS: Computers and computer peripherals; Medical & other health services; Communications; Manufacturing & processing; Research & technology; Services
GEOGRAPHIC LIMITS OF INVESTMENTS/LOANS: Other: Prefer West Coast, but will invest anywhere with suitable local partners
RANGE OF INV./LOAN PER BUSINESS: Min. $500,000; Max. $2,000,000
BUSINESS CHARACTERISTICS DESIRED-REQUIRED: Minimum number of years in business: 0
REFERRALS ACCEPTED FROM: Investment/Mortgage banker or Borrower/Investee
BRANCHES: James Lally, 2 Embarcadero Pl., 222 Geng Rd., Ste. 205, Palo Alto, CA 94303; (415) 424-1660

COMPANY: **N.C. Berkowitz Co.**
ADDRESS: One Sutter Street
San Francisco, CA 94104
PHONE: (415) 788-4120
TYPE OF INSTITUTION: Venture Capital
CONTACT OFFICER(S): Nathaniel C. Berkowitz

COMPANY: **N.E.A.**
ADDRESS: Suite 1025, Russ Building, 235 Montgomery
San Francisco, CA
PHONE: (415) 956-1579
CONTACT OFFICER(S): Richard Kramlich, General Partner
C. C. Bond, Jr.,
C. Woodrow Rea,
R. John Armor, Associate
ASSETS: $100,000,000
TYPES OF FINANCING: VENTURE CAPITAL: Research & Development; Start-up from developed product stage; First-stage (less than 1 year); Second-stage (generally 1-3 years); Later-stage expansion, OTHER SERVICES PROVIDED: Buy-equity
PREFERRED TYPES OF INDUSTRIES/INVESTMENTS: High-technology: Communications; Life sciences; Computer-related industries; Defense sciences; Robotics; and Specialty retailing
WILL NOT CONSIDER: Cable T.V.
GEOGRAPHIC LIMITS OF INVESTMENTS/LOANS: National
RANGE OF INV./LOAN PER BUSINESS: Min. $500,000; Max. $1,500,000
BUSINESS CHARACTERISTICS DESIRED-REQUIRED: Minimum number of years in business: 0; Other: Active investors, active leads, technical leadership
REFERRALS ACCEPTED FROM: Investment/Mortgage banker or Borrower/Investee
BRANCHES: Charles Newhall, General Partner, Frank Bonsal, General Partner, Nancy Dorman, Director of

Administration, 1119 St. Paul St., Baltimore, MD 21202; (301) 244-0115

COMPANY: **Newtek Ventures**
ADDRESS: 500 Washington Street #720
San Francisco, CA 94111
PHONE: (415) 986-5711
TYPE OF INSTITUTION: Venture Capital
CONTACT OFFICER(S): Peter J. Wardle, Gen. Partner
Barry M. Weinman, Gen. Partner
ASSETS: 19 million
INVESTMENTS/LOANS MADE: For own account
TYPES OF FINANCING: VENTURE CAPITAL: Research & Development; Start-up from developed product stage; First-stage; Second-stage; Buy-outs/Acquisitions
PREFERRED TYPES OF INDUSTRIES/INVESTMENTS: High Technology: Computer; Semiconductors; Capital Equipment; Robotics; Electronic Testing Equipment; Automation; Lasers; Optics; Telecommunications; Medical Instrumentation; Bio-technology
GEOGRAPHIC LIMITS OF INVESTMENTS/LOANS: Other: Prefer local; will go West Coast
RANGE OF INV./LOAN PER BUSINESS: Min. $250,000; Max. $1 million
PREFERRED TERM FOR LOANS & LEASES: Min. 5 years; Max. 25 years
BUSINESS CHARACTERISTICS DESIRED-REQUIRED: Minimum number of years in business: 0

COMPANY: **Pacific Technology Venture Fund**
ADDRESS: 332 Pine Street #610
San Francisco, CA 94104
PHONE: (415) 956-3926
TYPE OF INSTITUTION: Venture Capital
CONTACT OFFICER(S): Ms. Lore Harp, President
ASSETS: $10 million investment portfolio
TYPES OF FINANCING: VENTURE CAPITAL: Start-up from developed product stage; First-stage; Second-stage
PREFERRED TYPES OF INDUSTRIES/INVESTMENTS: Communications; Computer Related; Distribution; Medical Info. related; All Information based companies
WILL NOT CONSIDER: Retail, Real Estate Agriculture
GEOGRAPHIC LIMITS OF INVESTMENTS/LOANS: Regional; Other: Pacific Rim-US & Japan
RANGE OF INV./LOAN PER BUSINESS: Min. $150,000; Max. $700,000
BUSINESS CHARACTERISTICS DESIRED-REQUIRED: Other: Minimum operating data needed—financial resume

COMPANY: **Pacific Technology Venture Fund**
ADDRESS: 332 Pine Street #610
San Francisco, CA 94104
PHONE: (415) 956-3926
TYPE OF INSTITUTION: Venture Capital
CONTACT OFFICER(S): Ms. Lore Harp, President
ASSETS: $10 million investment portfolio
TYPES OF FINANCING: VENTURE CAPITAL: Start-up from developed product stage; First-stage; Second-stage
PREFERRED TYPES OF INDUSTRIES/INVESTMENTS: Communications; Computer Related; Distribution; Medical Info. related; All Information based companies
WILL NOT CONSIDER: Retail, Real Estate Agriculture
GEOGRAPHIC LIMITS OF INVESTMENTS/LOANS: Regional; Other: Pacific Rim-US & Japan
RANGE OF INV./LOAN PER BUSINESS: Min. $150,000; Max. $700,000
BUSINESS CHARACTERISTICS DESIRED-REQUIRED: Other: Minimum operating data needed—financial & resume

COMPANY: **Security Financial Management Corp.**
ADDRESS: 100 Bush St., Ste 1905
San Francisco, CA 94104
PHONE: (415) 981-8060
TYPE OF INSTITUTION: Venture Capital
CONTACT OFFICER(S): Byron Rouda, Pres.

COMPANY: **Sofinnova, Inc.**
ADDRESS: Three Embarcadero #2560
San Francisco, CA 94111
PHONE: (415) 362-4021
TYPE OF INSTITUTION: Venture Capital
CONTACT OFFICER(S): Jean-Bernard Schmidt, President
ASSETS: $16 million
INVESTMENTS/LOANS MADE: Through private placementsIn securities with a secondary market and in securities without a secondary market
TYPES OF FINANCING: SECONDARY-MARKET CORPORATE SECURITIES: Common stock; Preferred stock; VENTURE CAPITAL: Start-up from developed product stage; First-stage; Second-stage
PREFERRED TYPES OF INDUSTRIES/INVESTMENTS: Electronics; Computers; Peripherals; Medical; Genetic Engineering; Automation
WILL NOT CONSIDER: Real Estate
GEOGRAPHIC LIMITS OF INVESTMENTS/LOANS: National
RANGE OF INV./LOAN PER BUSINESS: Min. $200,000; Max. $600,000
BUSINESS CHARACTERISTICS DESIRED-REQUIRED: Minimum number of years in business: 0
REFERRALS ACCEPTED FROM: Investment/Mortgage banker or Borrower/Investee

COMPANY: **T.W. Richardson & Co., Inc.**
ADDRESS: 601 California Street, Suite 301
San Francisco, CA
PHONE: (415) 391-2880
TYPE OF INSTITUTION: Investment manager, real estate developer, investor
CONTACT OFFICER(S):Thomas W. Richardson, President
ASSETS: $10,000,000
INVESTMENTS/LOANS MADE: For own account and for managed accounts
INVESTMENTS/LOANS MADE: In securities with a secondary market and in securities without a secondary market
TYPES OF FINANCING: SECONDARY-MARKET CORPORATE SECURITIES: Common stock; Preferred stock, VENTURE CAPITAL: Buy-outs/Acquisitions,

REAL ESTATE: Acquisitions; Joint ventures; Partnerships/Syndications
PREFERRED TYPES OF INDUSTRIES/INVESTMENTS: Real estate investment companies with office-industrial portfolios and/or undeveloped land assets; operating companies with same.
WILL NOT CONSIDER: Limited partner positions, loans, passive investments, real estate service businesses
GEOGRAPHIC LIMITS OF INVESTMENTS/LOANS: Regional; Western and southern states
RANGE OF INV./LOAN PER BUSINESS: Min. $500,000; Max. $3,000,000
BUSINESS CHARACTERISTICS DESIRED-REQUIRED: Min. number of years in business: 3
REFERRALS ACCEPTED FROM: Investment/Mortgage banker or Investee

COMPANY: **Walden**
ADDRESS: 303 Sacramento St., Suite 400
San Francisco, CA 94111
PHONE: (415) 391-7225
TYPE OF INSTITUTION: Venture Capital
CONTACT OFFICER(S): George S. Sarlo, General Partner
Arthur S. Berliner, General Partner
TOTAL ORGANIZATIONAL ASSETS: $25 million
INVESTMENTS/LOANS MADE: Through private placements
INVESTMENTS/LOANS MADE: In securities with a secondary market and in securities without a secondary market
TYPES OF FINANCING: VENTURE CAPITAL: Start-up from product stage, First-stage; Second-stage; LOANS: Equity related
PREFERRED TYPES OF INDUSTRIES/INVESTMENTS: High technology related companies or any investment where the return on our investment will meet our requirement
RANGE OF INV./LOAN PER BUSINESS: Min. $200,000; Max. $1 million
PREFERRED TERM FOR LOANS & LEASES: Min. 3 to 5 years; Max. 7 years
REFERRALS ACCEPTED FROM: Investment/Mortgage banker and Borrower/Investee

COMPANY: **West Ven**
ADDRESS: 555 California St., Suite 4760
San Francisco, CA 94104
PHONE: (415) 622-6864
CONTACT OFFICER(S): Philip Greer, Managing General Partner
Robert J. Loarie, General Partner
Larry J. Lawrence, General Partner
ASSETS: Over 200 million
TYPES OF FINANCING: VENTURE CAPITAL: Research & Development; Start-up from developed product stage; Buy-outs/Acquisitions
PREFERRED TYPES OF INDUSTRIES/INVESTMENTS: No preference
WILL NOT CONSIDER: R.E.
GEOGRAPHIC LIMITS OF INVESTMENTS/LOANS: National
RANGE OF INV./LOAN PER BUSINESS: Min. $500,000
BUSINESS CHARACTERISTICS DESIRED-REQUIRED: Minimum number of years in business: 0

COMPANY: **R and D Funding Corporation**
ADDRESS: 1290 Ridder Park Drive, Suite 1
San Jose, CA 95131
PHONE: (415) 349-3095
TYPE OF INSTITUTION: Research and Development Funding division of Prudential Bache, Inc.
CONTACT OFFICER(S): John K. Woodman, General Partner
Hugh McClung, General Partner
Devin Weiman, General Partner
ASSETS: $100,000,000
INVESTMENTS/LOANS MADE: For own account
INVESTMENTS/LOANS MADE: In securities with a secondary market and in securities without a secondary market
TYPES OF FINANCING: SECONDARY-MARKET CORPORATE SECURITIES: Common stock, VENTURE CAPITAL: Research & Development
PREFERRED TYPES OF INDUSTRIES/INVESTMENTS: Patentable Technology
WILL NOT CONSIDER: Real estate, movies, leasing
GEOGRAPHIC LIMITS OF INVESTMENTS/LOANS: National
RANGE OF INV./LOAN PER BUSINESS: Min. $400,000; Max. 6 million
PREFERRED TERM FOR LOANS & LEASES: Min. 2 years; Max. 3 years
BUSINESS CHARACTERISTICS DESIRED-REQUIRED: Minimum number of years in business: 2-3; Min. annual sales $1 million
REFERRALS ACCEPTED FROM: Investment/Mortgage banker or Borrower/Investee

COMPANY: **San Jose Capital Corp.**
ADDRESS: 100 Park Center Plaza, Suite 427
San Jose, CA 95113
PHONE: (408) 293-7708
CONTACT OFFICER(S): Robert T. Murphy, General Partner
Daniel Hochman, General Partner
ASSETS: 10,000,000
INVESTMENTS/LOANS MADE: For own account
INVESTMENTS/LOANS MADE: Only in securities without a secondary market
TYPES OF FINANCING: VENTURE CAPITAL: Research & Development; Start-up from deveoped product stage; First-stage (less than 1 year); Second-stage (generally 1-3 years); Later-stage expansion; Buy-outs/Acquisitions
PREFERRED TYPES OF INDUSTRIES/INVESTMENTS: Satellite and microwave communications, Electronic components, Optics tecchnology, Computer grahics and CAD/CAM, Diagnostic medical equipment and Patient Education Systems, Industrial automation, Robotics, Electronic components and instrumentation
WILL NOT CONSIDER: Entertainment Industry, Consumer products, Distribution, Energy/Natural Resources, Genetic Engineering
GEOOGRAPHIC LIMITS OF INVESTMENTS/LOANS: Generally West Coast

RANGE OF INV./LOAN PER BUSINESS: Min. $100,000; Max. $500,000
BUSINESS CHARACTERISTICS DESIRED-REQUIRED: Minimum number of years in business; 0; Min. annual sales $Nominal
REMARKS: San Jose Capital owns San Jose SBIC, Inc., a Small Business Investment Company

COMPANY: **Golden Gate Investments, Inc.**
ADDRESS: 2121 El Camino Real
San Mateo, CA 94403
PHONE: (415) 345-9900
TYPE OF INSTITUTION: Private Venture Capital
CONTACT OFFICER(S): A. Larry Lindsey, President
INVESTMENTS/LOANS MADE: For own account; For managed accounts
TYPES OF FINANCING: VENTURE CAPITAL: Research & Development; Start-up from developed product stage; First-stage; Second-stage; Later-stage expansion; Buy-outs/Acquisitions
PREFERRED TYPES OF INDUSTRIES/INVESTMENTS: All Industries specialize in financially distressed & other troubled companies
WILL NOT CONSIDER: Real Estate; Promotional
GEOGRAPHIC LIMITS OF INVESTMENTS/LOANS: International; Other: Asia & Europe & the Americas
RANGE OF INV./LOAN PER BUSINESS: Min. None; Max. $10 million
REMARKS: Prefers active involvement as lead investors

COMPANY: **Hawaii-Pacific Venture Capital Corporation**
ADDRESS: 2121 El Camino Real
San Mateo, CA 94403
PHONE: (415) 573-0806
TYPE OF INSTITUTION: Venture Capital
CONTACT OFFICER(S): Dr. Michael Yang
INVESTMENTS/LOANS MADE: For own account; For managed accounts
TYPES OF FINANCING: VENTURE CAPITAL: Research & Development; Start-up from developed product stage; First-stage; Second-stage; Later-stage expansion; Buy-outs/Acquisitions
PREFERRED TYPES OF INDUSTRIES/INVESTMENTS: Diversified
GEOGRAPHIC LIMITS OF INVESTMENTS/LOANS: Other: East Asia, Pacific Basin, Hawaii & N. America
BRANCHES: Raymond Y.C. Ho, Chairman, 1164 Bishop Centre, Honolulu, HI 96813

COMPANY: **Health Medical Investments, Inc.**
ADDRESS: 2121 El Camino Real
San Mateo, CA 94403
PHONE: (415) 345-8500
TYPE OF INSTITUTION: Venture Capital
CONTACT OFFICER(S): Dr. L.L. Mak, S.V.P.
INVESTMENTS/LOANS MADE: For own account; For managed accounts
TYPES OF FINANCING: VENTURE CAPITAL: Research & Development; Start-up from developed product stage; First-stage; Second-stage; Later-stage expansion; Buy-outs/Acquisitions
PREFERRED TYPES OF INDUSTRIES/INVESTMENTS: Health; Medical & Biotechnology
GEOGRAPHIC LIMITS OF INVESTMENTS/LOANS: International; Other: Asia, Europe & the Americas
RANGE OF INV./LOAN PER BUSINESS: Min. None; Max. $10 million

COMPANY: **Techno World Investments, Inc.**
ADDRESS: 2121 El Camino Real
San Mateo, CA 94403
PHONE: (415) 573-0800
TYPE OF INSTITUTION: Venture Capital
CONTACT OFFICER(S): Larry Mehl, E.V.P.
INVESTMENTS/LOANS MADE: For own account; For managed accounts
TYPES OF FINANCING: VENTURE CAPITAL: Research & Development; Start-up from developed product stage; First-stage; Second-stage; Later-stage expansion; Buy-outs/Acquisitions
PREFERRED TYPES OF INDUSTRIES/INVESTMENTS: Diversified
GEOGRAPHIC LIMITS OF INVESTMENTS/LOANS: International; Other: Asia, Europe & the Americas
RANGE OF INV./LOAN PER BUSINESS: Min. None; Max. $10 million

COMPANY: **Miller & LaHaye/Peregrine Associates**
ADDRESS: 606 Wilshire Blvd., #602
Santa Monica, CA 90401
PHONE: (213) 458-1441
TYPE OF INSTITUTION: Venture Capital Fund
CONTACT OFFICER(S): Gene Miller, Partner
Frank LaHaye, Partner
ASSETS: Approximately $50 Million
INVESTMENTS/LOANS MADE: For managed accounts
INVESTMENTS/LOANS MADE: In securities with a secondary market and in securities without a secondary market
TYPES OF FINANCING: VENTURE CAPITAL: Start-up from developed product stage; First-stage (less than 1 year); Second-stage (generally 1-3 years); Later-stage expansion; Buy-out/Acquisitions
PREFERRED TYPES OF INDUSTRIES/INVESTMENTS: Rapid Growth Situations
WILL NOT CONSIDER: Real Estate
GEOGRAPHIC LIMITS OF INVESTMENTS/LOANS: National
RANGE ON INV./LOAN PER BUSINESS: Min. $100 Thousand; Max. $1.250 Million
BUSINESS CHARACTERISTICS DESIRED-REQUIRED: Minimum number of years in business: 0
BRANCHES: 20833 Stevens Creek Blvd., Cupertino, CA 95014; (408) 996-7212

COMPANY: **International Business Sponsors, Inc.**
ADDRESS: 765 Bridgeway
Sausalito, CA 94965
PHONE: (415) 331-2262
TYPE OF INSTITUTION: Private Venture Capital Company
CONTACT OFFICER(S): Mel L. Balcharach, President
ASSETS: $6,800,000
INVESTMENTS/LOANS MADE: For own (company's or principals') account

INVESTMENTS/LOANS MADE: In securities with a secondary market and in securities without a secondary market
TYPES OF FINANCING: SECONDARY-MARKET CORPORATE SECURITIES: Common stock; Preferred stock; Bonds; Other; VENTURE CAPITAL: First-stage (less than 1 year); Second-stage (generally 1-3 years); Later-stage expansion; LOANS: Working captial (receivables/inventory); Equipment; INTERNATIONAL: (including import/export)
WILL NOT CONSIDER: Oil, gas, mining, movies, restaurants
GEOGRAPHIC LIMITS OF INVESTMENTS/LOANS: International
RANGE OF INV./LOAN PER BUSINESS: Min. $50,000; Max $ 300,000
PREFERRED TERM FOR LOANS & LEASES: Min. 1 year; Max. 3 years
BUSINESS CHARACTERISTICS DESIRED-REQUIRED: Minimum number of years in business: 1 ('0' if startups financed)
REFERRALS ACCEPTED FROM: Investment/Mortgage banker and Borrower/Investee

COMPANY: **National Investment Management, Inc.**
ADDRESS: 23133 Hawthorne Blvd., Suite 309
Torrance, CA 90505
PHONE: (213) 373-8944
TYPE OF INSTITUTION: Venture Capital
CONTACT OFFICER(S): Richard P. Robins, Pres.

COMPANY: **Woodside Fund**
ADDRESS: 850 Woodside Fund
Woodside, CA 94062
PHONE: (415) 368-5545
TYPE OF INSTITUTION: Venture Capital Firm
CONTACT OFFICER(S): Vincent M. Occhipinti, Ptnr.
Charles E. Greb, Ptnr.
Thomas R. Blakeslee, Ptnr.
William M. Hassebrock, Ptnr.
V. Frank Medicino, Ptnr.
Robert E. Larson, Ptnr.
TYPES OF FINANCING: VENTURE CAPITAL: Research & Development; Start-up from developed product stage; First-stage (less than 1 year), Second-stage (generally 1-3 years); Later-stage expansion; Buy-outs/Acquisitions; LOANS: Working capital (receivables/inventory); Equipment; Equity-related.
PREFERRED TYPES OF INDUSTRIES/INVESTMENTS:
Communications: Commercial communications; Data communications; Satellite and microwave communications; Telephone related
Computer Related: Computer graphics and CAD/CAM; Computer mainframes; Computer services; Memory devices; Micro and mini computers; Office automation; Software-applications; Software-systems; Terminals
Distribution: Electronics equipment
Electronic Components and Instrumentation: Electronic components; Laser-related; Optics technology; Semiconductors
Industrial Products and Equipment: Advanced materials; Equipment machinery; Industrial automation; Plastics; Process control; Robotics
WILL NOT CONSIDER: Cable television; Gas or mineral exploration; Motion pictures; Oil; Real Estate
GEOGRAPHIC LIMITS OF INVESTMENTS/LOANS: National; Early stage prefer West Coast
RANGE OF INV./LOAN PER BUSINESS: Min. $100,000; Max. $500,000
BUSINESS CHARACTERISTICS DESIRED-REQUIRED: Minimum number of years in business: 0
REFERRALS ACCEPTED FROM: Investment/Mortgage banker and Borrower/Investee
BRANCHES: 850 Woodside Drive, Woodside, CA 94062: (415) 368-5545; Partner: Vincent M. Occhipinti
Partner: V. Frank Mendicino; 699 Peters Avenue, Suite A, Pleasanton, CA 94566; (415) 462-0326;

COMPANY: **Boettcher & Company, Inc.**
ADDRESS: 828 17th St.
Denver, CO 80202
PHONE: (303) 628-8000
TYPE OF INSTITUTION: Investment Banker
CONTACT OFFICER(S): Stanley Fallis, Chief Financial Officer, 303-628-8294
Robert Manning, Stephen G. McConahey
ASSETS: $80 million
INVESTMENTS/LOANS MADE: Through private placements, Underwriting public offerings
INVESTMENTS/LOANS MADE: In securities with a secondary market and in securities without a secondary market
TYPES OF FINANCING: SECONDARY-MARKET CORPORATE SECURITIES: Common stock; Preferred stock; Bonds; R. Estate, REAL ESTATE LOANS, REAL ESTATE
PREFERRED TYPES OF INDUSTRIES/INVESTMENTS: Diversified
GEOGRAPHIC LIMITS OF INVESTMENTS/LOANS: Regional; Rocky Mountain region
REFERRALS ACCEPTED FROM: Investment/Mortgage banker or Borrower/Investee

COMPANY: **Cambridge Venture Partners**
ADDRESS: 88 Steele Street, Suite 200
Denver, CO 80206
PHONE: (303) 393-1111
TYPE OF INSTITUTION: Private venture capital fund
CONTACT OFFICER(S): Bruce B. Paul, Managing Partner - all areas
Jack Snyder General Partner - Medical technology
ASSETS: $12,200,000
INVESTMENTS/LOANS MADE: For own account; Through private placements
INVESTMENTS/LOANS MADE: In securities with a secondary market and only in securities without a secondary market
TYPES OF FINANCING: VENTURE CAPITAL: Research & Development; Start-up from developed product stage; First-stage (less than 1 year); Second-stage (generally 1-3 years); Later-stage expansion; Buy-out/Acqusitions; LOANS: Working Capital; REAL ESTATE: Acqusitions
PREFERRED TYPES OF INDUSTRIES/INVESTMENTS: Advanced communications, computer and medical technology

GEOGRAPHIC LIMITS OF INVESTMENTS/LOANS: Regional; prefer Rocky Mountain region and West Coast region
RANGE OF INV./LOAN PER BUSINESS: Min. $100,000; Max. $500,000
BUSINESS CHARACTERISTICS DESIRED-REQUIRED: Minimum number of years in business: 0
BRANCHES: Jack Snyder, 18610 Bernardo Trails Drive, San Diego, CA 92128; (619) 485-9692; Jack Snyder

COMPANY: **Uniwest Financial Corp.**
ADDRESS: 7979 E. Tufts Ave. Parkway, Suite #110
Denver, CO
PHONE: (303) 694-9777
TYPE OF INSTITUTION: Financial Services, Savings and Loan Holdings Co.
CONTACT OFFICER(S): Chuck McKelvey, Executive Vice President Real Estate; James R. Newman, National Credit Manager Leasing; John Holzman, Vice President Securities
ASSETS: $250,000,000
INVESTMENTS/LOANS MADE: For own account; Through private placements
INVESTMENTS/LOANS MADE: In securities with a secondary market and in securities without a secondary market
TYPES OF FINANCING: VENTURE CAPITAL: First-stage (less than 1 year); Second-stage (generally 1-3 years); REAL ESTATE LOANS: Construction; LEASES; REAL ESTATE: Acquisitions; Joint ventures; Partnerships/Syndications
PREFERRED TYPES OF INDUSTRIES/INVESTMENTS: Real Estate, Leasing
GEOGRAPHIC LIMITS OF INVESTMENTS/LOANS: Sun Belt States
RANGE OF INV./LOAN PER BUSINESS: Min. $250,000; Max. $10,000,000
PREFERRED TERM FOR LOANS & LEASES: Min. One-Three years; Max. Thirty years

COMPANY: **Venture Associates Ltd.**
ADDRESS: 1333 18th Street
Denver, CO 80202
PHONE: (303) 297-8670
TYPE OF INSTITUTION: Private venture capital firm
CONTACT OFFICER(S): James B. Arkebauer, President
Peter Thompson, V.P.
ASSETS: N/A
INVESTMENTS/LOANS MADE: For own account; For managed accounts; Through private placements; Through underwriting public offerings
INVESTMENTS/LOANS MADE: In securities with a secondary market and in securities without a secondary market
TYPES OF FINANCING: SECONDARY-MARKET CORPORATE SECURITIES: Common stock; Preferred Stock; VENTURE CAPITAL: Research & Development; Start-up from developed product stage; First-stage (less than 1 year); Second-stage (generally 1-3 years); Buy-outs/Acquisitions
PREFERRED TYPES OF INDUSTRIES/INVESTMENTS: All types
WILL NOT CONSIDER: Real estate

GEOGRAPHIC LIMITS OF INVESTMENTS/LOANS: National; International
RANGE OF INV./LOAN PER BUSINESS: Min. $100K; Max. $ 3 million
BUSINESS CHARACTERISTICS DESIRED-REQUIRED: Minimum number of years in business: 0; Min. annual sales $0; Min. net worth $0; Min. annual net income: $0; Min. annual cash flow $0
REMARKS: Specialize in small public offerings

COMPANY: **Columbine Venture Fund, Ltd.**
ADDRESS: 5613 DTC Parkway #510
Englewood, CO 80111
PHONE: (303) 694-3222
TYPE OF INSTITUTION: Venture Capital Partnership
CONTACT OFFICER(S): Mark Kimmel, General Partner
Sherman Muller, General Partner
Terry Winters, General Partner
ASSETS: $34,500,000
INVESTMENTS/LOANS MADE: For own account
INVESTMENTS/LOANS MADE: Only in securities without a secondary market
TYPES OF FINANCING: VENTURE CAPITAL: Research & Development; Start-up from developed product stage; First-stage (less than 1 year)
PREFERRED TYPES OF INDUSTRIES/INVESTMENTS: High Technology
WILL NOT CONSIDER: Real Estate, Retail, Construction, Natural Resources
GEOGRAPHIC LIMITS OF INVESTMENTS/LOANS: Regional; National
RANGE OF INV./LOAN PER BUSINESS: Min.: $50,000; Max. $3,000,000
PREFERRED TERM FOR LOANS & LEASES: Min. N/A
BUSINESS CHARACTERISTICS DESIRED-REQUIRED: Minimum number of years in business: 0; Min. annual sales $0; Min. net worth $0; Min. annual net income $0; Min. annual cash flow $0
REFERRALS ACCEPTED FROM: Investment/Mortgage Banker or Borrower/Investee

COMPANY: **Advest, Inc.**
ADDRESS: 6 Central Row
Hartford, CT 06103
PHONE: (203) 525-1421
TYPE OF INSTITUTION: Investment banking, mortgage banking, equity syndication
CONTACT OFFICER(S): John Everetts, Corporate Finance
ASSETS: $384,483,000
INVESTMENTS/LOANS MADE: For own account, Through private placements, Through underwriting public offerings
INVESTMENTS/LOANS MADE: In securities with a secondary market and in securities without a secondary market
TYPES OF FINANCING: SECONDARY-MARKET CORPORATE SECURITIES: Common stock; Preferred stock; Bonds, VENTURE CAPITAL: Research & Development; First-stage (less than 1 year), LOANS: Equity-related, REAL ESTATE LOANS: Long-term senior mtg.; Intermediate-term senior mtg.; Subordinated; Wraparounds; Land; Land development; Gap; Standbys; Industrial revenue bonds, LEASES:

Non-tax leases; Operating; Tax-oriented lease brokerage, REAL ESTATE: Acquisitions; Joint ventures; Partnerships/Syndications
GEOGRAPHIC LIMITS OF INVESTMENTS/LOANS: National
RANGE OF INV./LOAN PER BUSINESS: Min. $500,000 Max. $25 million
BRANCHES: 87 offices throughout Northeastern US

COMPANY: **CIGNA Corporation**
ADDRESS: South Bbldg. S-306
Hartford, CT 06152
PHONE: (203) 726-6000
TYPE OF INSTITUTION: Insurance Co.
CONTACT OFFICER(S): Richard W. Maine, Pres.
CIGNA Capital Advisors, 726-6131
David P. Marks, Sr. V.P.
Philip Ward Sr. V.P. RE Production
Thomas J. Watt Sr. V.P. Agricultural RE.
Richard Caupchunos, Sr. V.P. Asset Management
Arthurn C. Reeds, Sr. V.P. Portfolio Management
TYPES OF FINANCING: SECONDARY-MARKET CORPORATE SECURITIES: Common stock; Preferred stock; Bonds, VENTURE CAPITAL, LOANS: Unsecured; Working capital (receivables/inventory); Equipment; Equity-related; REAL ESTATE LOANS: Long-term senior mtg.; Intermediate-term senior mtg.; Subordinated Land; Land development; Standbys; Industrial revenue bonds; Other: Pure development equity, REAL ESTATE: Acquisitions; Joint ventures; Partnerships/Syndications
PREFERRED TYPES OF INDUSTRIES/INVESTMENTS: Mortgage; Communications; Manufacturing and technology; Retail; Foreign
WILL NOT CONSIDER: Gaming industry
RANGE OF INV./LOAN PER BUSINESS: Min. $3 million; Max $40 million
PREFERRED TERM FOR LOANS & LEASES: Min. 1 year; Max. 20 years

COMPANY: **Regional Financial Enterprises**
ADDRESS: 51 Pine
New Canaan, CT 06840
PHONE: (203) 966-2800
TYPE OF INSTITUTION: Venture capital
CONTACT OFFICER(S): Robert M. Williams, Partner
George E. Thomassy, Partner
Howard C. Landis, Partner
ASSETS: $65 million
INVESTMENTS/LOANS MADE: For own account
INVESTMENTS/LOANS MADE: Only in securities without a secondary market
TYPES OF FINANCING: VENTURE CAPITAL: Venture Capital and Buy-outs/Acquisitions
PREFERRED TYPES OF INDUSTRIES/INVESTMENTS: No preference
GEOGRAPHIC LIMITS OF INVESTMENTS/LOANS: National
RANGE OF INV./LOAN PER BUSINESS: Min. $500,000; Max. $2,000,000
PREFERRED TERM FOR LOANS & LEASES: Min. 5 years; Max. 8 years
BUSINESS CHARACTERISTICS DESIRED-REQUIRED: Other: Flexible
REFERRALS ACCEPTED FROM: Investment/Mortgage banker or Borrower/Investee
REMARKS: Will only back a company with a proven management team and a good prospect of going public within a 5-8 year period.

COMPANY: **Vista Ventures**
ADDRESS: 36 Grove Street
New Canaan, CT 06840
PHONE: (203) 972-3400
TYPE OF INSTITUTION: Venture Capital firm investing for own account
CONTACT OFFICER(S): Gerald B. Bay, Managing General Partner
ASSETS: $100 million
INVESTMENTS/LOANS MADE: For own account
TYPES OF FINANCING: VENTURE CAPITAL: Research & Development; Start-up from developed product stage; First-stage (less than 1 year); Second-stage (generally 1-3 years); Later-stage expansion; Buy-outs/Acquisitions
PREFERRED TYPES OF INDUSTRIES/INVESTMENTS: Technology - related
WILL NOT CONSIDER: Real estate, consumer
GEOGRAPHIC LIMITS OF INVESTMENTS/LOANS: National
RANGE OF INV./LOAN PER BUSINESS: Varies widely depending on individual opportunity
BUSINESS CHARACTERISTICS DESIRED-REQUIRED: Minimum number of years in business: 0
REFERRALS ACCEPTED FROM: Investment/Mortgage banker or Borrower/Investee
BRANCHES: Gil Lavasser, 610 Newport Center Drive, Newport Beach, CA 92660; 714-720-3400

COMPANY: **DCS Growth Fund**
ADDRESS: P.O. Box 740
Old Greenwich, CT
PHONE: (203) 637-1704
TYPE OF INSTITUTION: Private Venture Capital Investor
CONTACT OFFICER(S): Donald C. Seibert, Proprietor
ASSETS: $3,000,000 plus
INVESTMENTS/LOANS MADE: For own account
INVESTMENTS/LOANS MADE: In securities with a secondary market and in securities without a secondary market
TYPES OF FINANCING: SECONDARY-MARKET CORPORATE SECURITIES: Common stock; Preferred stock; Bonds; Other: Notes; VENTURE CAPITAL: Research & Development; Start-up from developed product stage; First-stage (less than 1 year); Second-stage (generally 1-3 years); Later-stage expansion; Buy-outs/Acquisitions
PREFERRED TYPES OF INDUSTRIES: Technically based hard product companies, (ie. Test Equipment, Semiconductors, Systems, etc.), Oil & Mineral Resources, Turn-around leverged buy-outs
WILL NOT CONSIDER: Service Companies, Most Commercial Products, Limited Partnerships
GEOGRAPHIC LIMITS OF INVESTMENTS/LOANS: Local; State; Regional; National; International
RANGE OF INV./LOAN PER BUSINESS: Min. $ No Minimum; Max. Usually $100,000

PREFERRED TERM FOR LOANS & LEASES: Min. 1 year; Max. No Max. years
BUSINESS CHARACTERISTICS DESIRED-REQUIRED: Minimum number of years in business: 0 ('0' if startups financed); Min. annual sales $0; Min. net worth $0; Min. annual net income $0; Min. annual cash flow $0;

COMPANY: **Fairchester Associates, Inc.**
ADDRESS: 2777 Summer Street
Stamford, CT 06905
PHONE: (203) 357-0714
TYPE OF INSTITUTION: Venture capital company
CONTACT OFFICER(S): William R. Knobloch, President
ASSETS: $1,000,000-10,000,000
INVESTMENTS/LOANS MADE: For own account
INVESTMENTS/LOANS MADE: In securities with a secondary market and in securities without a secondary market
TYPES OF FINANCING: SECONDARY-MARKET CORPORATE SECURITIES: Common stock; Preferred stock, VENTURE CAPITAL: Second-stage (generally 1-3 years)
PREFERRED TYPES OF INDUSTRIES/INVESTMENTS: Technology; Health care
GEOGRAPHIC LIMITS OF INVESTMENTS/LOANS: Regional; Northeast
RANGE OF INV./LOAN PER BUSINESS: Min. $500,000
BUSINESS CHARACTERISTICS DESIRED-REQUIRED: Minimum number of years in business: 1-3; Min. annual sales $1 million; Min. net worth $500,000; Min. annual net income $50,000
REFERRALS ACCEPTED FROM: Investment/Mortgage banker or Borrower/Investee

COMPANY: **Oxford Venture Corp.**
ADDRESS: 72 Cummings Pt. Rd.
Stamford, CT 06902
PHONE: (203) 964-0592
TYPE OF INSTITUTION: Independent venture capital firm
CONTACT OFFICER(S): Kenneth Rind
Neil Ryan
William R. Lonergan
Stevan A. Birnbaum
ASSETS: $56 million
INVESTMENTS/LOANS MADE: For own account, For managed accounts
INVESTMENTS/LOANS MADE: In securities with a secondary market and in securities without a secondary market
TYPES OF FINANCING: SECONDARY-MARKET CORPORATE SECURITIES: Common stock; Preferred stock, VENTURE CAPITAL: Research & Development; Start-up from developed product stage; First-stage; Second-stage; Later-stage expansion; Buy-outs/Acquisitions, LOANS: Equity-related
PREFERRED TYPES OF INDUSTRIES/INVESTMENTS: Technology
GEOGRAPHIC LIMITS OF INVESTMENTS/LOANS: Other: None
RANGE OF INV./LOAN PER BUSINESS: Min. $100,000; Max. $1.5 million
BUSINESS CHARACTERISTICS DESIRED-REQUIRED: Minimum number of years in business: 0
REFERRALS ACCEPTED FROM: Investment/Mortgage banker or Borrower/Investee

COMPANY: **Saugatuck Capital Co.**
ADDRESS: 999 Summer St.
Stamford, CT 06905
PHONE: (203) 348-6669
TYPE OF INSTITUTION: Venture capital/Leveraged Buyout Partnership
CONTACT OFFICER(S): Frank Hawley, Managing Director
Alex Dunbar, Managing Director
Norman Johnson, Managing Director
ASSETS: $25,000,000 fund
INVESTMENTS/LOANS MADE: For own account
INVESTMENTS/LOANS MADE: In securities with a secondary market and in securities without a secondary market
TYPES OF FINANCING: VENTURE CAPITAL: Second-stage (generally 1-3 years); Later-stage expansion; Buy-outs/Acquisitions; OTHER SERVICES PROVIDED: Leveraged Buyout
PREFERRED TYPES OF INDUSTRIES/INVESTMENTS: Not inclusive: Building Products; Transportation; Energy Service and Products; Health Care Products and Services; Process Control Instrumentation; Industrial Automation; Fasteners; Valves and Pumps
WILL NOT CONSIDER: Real Estate
GEOGRAPHIC LIMITS OF INVESTMENTS/LOANS: National
RANGE OF INV./LOAN PER BUSINESS: Min. $500,000; Max. $4,000,000
BUSINESS CHARACTERISTICS DESIRED-REQUIRED: Minimum number of years in business: 1
REFERRALS ACCEPTED FROM: Investment/Mortgage banker or Borrower/Investee

COMPANY: **Oak Investment Partners, Limited Partnership**
ADDRESS: 257 Riverside Av.
Westport, CT 06880
PHONE: (203) 226-8346
CONTACT OFFICER(S): Edward F. Glassmeyer, General Partner
Jeffrey D. West, General Partner
Stewart H. Greenfield, General Partner
TYPES OF FINANCING: VENTURE CAPITAL: Research & Development; Start-up from developed product stage; First-stage; Second-stage; Later-stage expansion; Buy-outs/Acquisitions
PREFERRED TYPES OF INDUSTRIES/INVESTMENTS: Computers, bio-engineering, office automation, communications, medical instrumentation
WILL NOT CONSIDER: Retail or R.E.
GEOGRAPHIC LIMITS OF INVESTMENTS/LOANS: National
RANGE OF INV./LOAN PER BUSINESS: Min. $750,000 average-1 mil; Max. None
BUSINESS CHARACTERISTICS DESIRED-REQUIRED: Minimum number of years in business: 0; Other: See 5 years projections - cash flow
REMARKS: Average investment $750,000-1,000,000

VENTURE CAPITAL COMPANIES

(Also see SBICs, MESBICs and Investment Bankers)

COMPANY: **Allied Capital Corp.**
ADDRESS: 1625 Eye St., N.W., Ste. 603
Washington, DC 20006
PHONE: (202) 331-1112
TYPE OF INSTITUTION: Venture Capital
CONTACT OFFICER(S): George Williams, Chairman
David Gladstone, President
ASSETS: $54,435,000
INVESTMENTS/LOANS MADE: For own account
INVESTMENTS/LOANS MADE: In securities with a secondary market and in securities without a secondary market
TYPES OF FINANCING: SECONDARY-MARKET CORPORATE SECURITIES: Common Stock; Preferred stock; VENTURE CAPITAL: Second-stage; Buy-outs/Acquisitions; OTHER SERVICES PROVIDED: Loan Packaging, Investment Banking & Corporate Acquisitions
PREFERRED TYPES OF INDUSTRIES/INVESTMENTS: Computers, Communications, Mfg., Retail
WILL NOT CONSIDER: Natural Resources
GEOGRAPHIC LIMITS OF INVESTMENTS/LOANS: National
RANGE OF INV./LOAN PER BUSINESS: Min. $100,000; Max. $3,000,000
PREFERRED TERM FOR LOANS & LEASES: Min. 5 years; Max. 10 years
BUSINESS CHARACTERISTICS DESIRED-REQUIRED: Minimum number of years in business: 1
REFERRALS ACCEPTED FROM: Investment/Mortgage banker or Borrower/Investee
BRANCHES: G. Cabell Williams, III, One Financial Plaza, Suite 1614, Ft. Lauderdale, FL 33394; (305) 763-8484,

COMPANY: **Continental American Life Insurance Co.**
ADDRESS: 300 Continental Dr.
Newark, DE 19713
PHONE: (302) 454-5000
CONTACT OFFICER(S): Michael Greenleaf, V.P.
Thomas Ryan, Asst. V.P.
TYPES OF FINANCING: SECONDARY-MARKET CORPORATE SECURITIES: Common stock; Preferred stock; Bonds, VENTURE CAPITAL: Buy-outs/ Acquisitions, LOANS: Working capital (receivables/ inventory); Equipment; Other: Secured, REAL ESTATE LOANS: Land; Land development; Other: Land purchase lease-back (short-term 5-7 yrs), REAL ESTATE: Joint ventures
PREFERRED TYPES OF INDUSTRIES/INVESTMENTS: Diversified
WILL NOT CONSIDER: Fast foods
GEOGRAPHIC LIMITS OF INVESTMENTS/LOANS: National
RANGE OF INV./LOAN PER BUSINESS: Min. $500,000; Max. $2-3 million
PREFERRED TERM FOR LOANS & LEASES: Min. 3 years; Max. 10 years
BUSINESS CHARACTERISTICS DESIRED-REQUIRED:Minimum number of years in business: 3

COMPANY: **First Western SBLC, Inc.**
ADDRESS: 1380 N.E. Miami Gardens Drive
North Miami Beach, FL 33179
PHONE: (305) 949-5900
TYPE OF INSTITUTION: SBLC (90% SBA Government Guaranteed Loans)
CONTACT OFFICER(S): Lance B. Rosemore, President
Fredric M. Rosemore, Vice-president
ASSETS: $8,000,000; Loan capabilities $26,000,000
INVESTMENTS/LOANS MADE: For own account
INVESTMENTS/LOANS MADE: Only in securities without a secondary market
TYPES OF FINANCING: SECONDARY-MARKET CORPORATE SECURITIES: Business loans-commercial & manufacturing business expansion loans, VENTURE CAPITAL: Second-stage; Later-stage, LOANS: Working capital; equipment, REAL ESTATE LOANS: owner occupied ofice & warehouse condominiums-also purchases of existing businesses, REAL ESTATE: Acquisitions, OTHER SERVICES PROVIDED: Consulting and advisory
PREFERRED TYPES OF INDUSTRIES/INVESTMENTS: any type of business expansion or modernizations loan—limited in real estate to owner-occupied only. Expansion of manufacturing facilities
WILL NOT CONSIDER: Venture capital
GEOGRAPHIC LIMITS OF INVESTMENTS/LOANS: Florida, New Jersey, Georgia, Alabama
RANGE OF INV./LOAN PER BUSINESS: Min. $50,000; Max. $550,000
PREFERRED TERM FOR LOANS & LEASES: Min. 3 years; Max. 20 years
BUSINESS CHARACTERISTICS DESIRED-REQUIRED: Minimum number of years in business: 2; OTHER: all of our loans are 90% SBA guaranteed

COMPANY: **Electro-Science Management Corp.**
ADDRESS: 600 Courtland Street, Suite 490
Orlando, FL 32804
PHONE: (305) 645-1188
TYPE OF INSTITUTION: Private venture capital
CONTACT: G. A. Herbert, Manager
ASSETS: $8.0 million
TYPES OF FINANCING: VENTURE CAPITAL: First-stage
PREFERRED TYPES OF INDUSTRIES/INVESTMENTS: Computers; Computer peripherals; Medical products; Technology
WILL NOT CONSIDER: R.E., services, general loans
GEOGRAPHIC LIMITS OF INVESTMENTS/LOANS: National
RANGE OF INV./LOAN PER BUSINESS: Min. $100,000; Max. $500,000
BUSINESS CHARACTERISTICS DESIRED-REQUIRED: Other: Varies
REFERRALS ACCEPTED FROM: Investment/Mortgage banker or Borrower/Investee

COMPANY: **Business Research Company**
ADDRESS: 205 Worth Ave. P.O. 2137
Palm Beach, FL 33480
PHONE: (305) 832-2155
CONTACT OFFICER(S): George B. Kilborne, Managing Director
A. Donald Grosset, Jr., Managing Director
INVESTMENTS/LOANS MADE: For own account, Through private placements

INVESTMENTS/LOANS MADE: In securities with a secondary market and in securities without a secondary market
TYPES OF FINANCING: VENTURE CAPITAL: Later-stage; Buy-outs/Acquisitions, REAL ESTATE: Acquisitions, OTHER SERVICES PROVIDED: Solutions to ownership problems in private/closely held corporation
PREFERRED TYPES OF INDUSTRIES/INVESTMENTS: Engineered hard goods, General manufacturing, Distribution
WILL NOT CONSIDER: Retailing, High tech, Startups
GEOGRAPHIC LIMITS OF INVESTMENTS/LOANS: Other: Prefer east coast and near midwest
RANGE OF INV./LOAN PER BUSINESS: Min. $500,000
BUSINESS CHARACTERISTICS DESIRED-REQUIRED: Minimum number of years in business: 3; Min. net worth $5,000,000
REMARKS: Specialty is working with family controlled corporations where certain family members are seeking partial or total liquidity.

COMPANY: **Venture Capital Management Corporation**
ADDRESS: P.O. Box 2626
Satellite Beach, FL 32937
TYPE OF INSTITUTION: Private venture capital company
CONTACT OFFICER(S): Dr. Robert A. Adams, President
INVESTMENTS/LOANS MADE: For own account, Through private placements
INVESTMENTS/LOANS MADE: Only in securities without a secondary market
TYPES OF FINANCING: VENTURE CAPITAL: Second-stage; Buy-outs/Acquisitions, LOANS: Equity-related, INTERNATIONAL, REAL ESTATE: Acquisitions; Joint ventures; Partnerships/Syndications, OTHER SERVICES PROVIDED: Financial consulting, Private placement packaging, Chapter 11 bankruptcy reorganization
GEOGRAPHIC LIMITS OF INVESTMENTS/LOANS: State
RANGE OF INV./LOAN PER BUSINESS: Min. $100,000
PREFERRED TERM FOR LOANS & LEASES: Min. 3 years; Max. 5 years
BUSINESS CHARACTERISTICS DESIRED-REQUIRED: Minimum number of years in business: 2; Min. annual sales $500,000; Min. annual net income $Break even
REFERRALS ACCEPTED FROM: Borrower/Investee

COMPANY: **South Atlantic Capital Corporation**
ADDRESS: 220 East Madison, Suite 530
Tampa, FL 33602
PHONE: (813) 229-7400
TYPE OF INSTITUTION: private venture capital firm investing own capital
CONTACT OFFICER(S): Donald W. Burton, Managing General Partner
P. Thomas Vogel, General Partner
ASSETS: 17.5 million
INVESTMENTS/LOANS MADE: For own account
INVESTMENTS/LOANS MADE: In securities with a secondary market and in securities without a secondary market
TYPES OF FINANCING: VENTURE CAPITAL: First-stage; Second-stage; Later-stage expansion; Buy-outs/Acquisitions
PREFERRED TYPES OF INDUSTRIES/INVESTMENTS: Any equity investments other than in real estate.
WILL NOT CONSIDER: Real estate or oil and gas
GEOGRAPHIC LIMITS OF INVESTMENTS/LOANS: Regional, southeastern United States
RANGE OF INV./LOAN PER BUSINESS: Min. $350,000; Max. $1,000,000
BUSINESS CHARACTERISTICS DESIRED-REQUIRED: Min. annual sales $500,000
REMARKS: ROI is of primary concern. We do not charge fees.

COMPANY: **Condor Group Holdings**
ADDRESS: 1601 Belvedere Rd.
West Palm Beach, FL 33406
PHONE: (305) 689-4906
TYPE OF INSTITUTION: Equipment leasing, Venture capital
CONTACT OFFICER(S): James A. Carpinello, Chairman of the Board
ASSETS: $24.5 mil
INVESTMENTS/LOANS MADE: For own account, For managed accounts
TYPES OF FINANCING: SECONDARY-MARKET CORPORATE SECURITIES: Common stock; Bonds, VENTURE CAPITAL: Second-stage; Buy-outs/Acquisitions, LOANS: Equipment; Equity-related, LEASES: Single-investor; Leveraged; Tax leases; Non-tax leases; Operating, Tax-oriented lease brokerage; Lease syndications; Vendor financing programs, REAL ESTATE: Acquisitions; Joint ventures; Partnerships/Syndications
PREFERRED TYPES OF INDUSTRIES/INVESTMENTS: Capital Equipment Manufacturer; Income Producing Real Estate
GEOGRAPHIC LIMITS OF INVESTMENTS/LOANS: National
RANGE OF INV./LOAN PER BUSINESS: Min. $50,000; Max. $5,000,000
PREFERRED TERM FOR LOANS & LEASES: Min. 3 years; Max. 10 years
BUSINESS CHARACTERISTICS DESIRED-REQUIRED: Minimum number of years in business: 1; Min. annual sales $500,000; Min. net worth $150,000; Min. annual net income $50,000; Min. annual cash flow $75,000
REFERRALS ACCEPTED FROM: Investment/Mortgage banker or Borrower/Investee
REMARKS: Start-ups are done

COMPANY: **American Reserves, Inc.**
ADDRESS: 35 Glenlake Parkway, Suite 110
Atlanta, GA 30328
PHONE: (404) 396-4000
TYPE OF INSTITUTION: Venture Capital
CONTACT OFFICER(S): H. Friedman, Treasurer & Director
Alexandre C. Goodwin, President
INVESTMENTS/LOANS MADE: For own account; Through private placements

INVESTMENTS/LOANS MADE: In securities with a secondary market and in securities without a secondary market
TYPES OF FINANCING: VENTURE CAPITAL: Start-up from developed product stage; First-stage; Second-stage; Buy-outs/Acquisitions REAL ESTATE: Joint ventures; Partnerships/Syndications
PREFERRED TYPES OF INDUSTRIES/INVESTMENTS: Consumer Product Co.'s, Real Estate including Resale
WILL NOT CONSIDER: Heavy manufacturing
RANGE OF INV./LOAN PER BUSINESS: Min. $250,000; Max. $1,500,000
BUSINESS CHARACTERISTICS DESIRED-REQUIRED: Minimum number of years in business: 0
BRANCHES: Anthony W. Moro, 21 E. 90th St. Suite 9C, New York, NY 10028, (212) 534-2012

COMPANY: **Anatar Investments, Inc.**
ADDRESS: 235 Peachtree Street NE #2218
Atlanta, GA 30303
PHONE: (404) 588-0770
TYPE OF INSTITUTION: Venture Capital
CONTACT OFFICER(S): Douglas Hamilton, President
Robin Haug, Controller
INVESTMENTS/LOANS MADE: For own account
INVESTMENTS/LOANS MADE: In securities with a secondary market and in securities without a secondary market
TYPES OF FINANCING: VENTURE CAPITAL: Later-stage expansion; Buy-outs/Acquisitions
WILL NOT CONSIDER: Real Estate
GEOGRAPHIC LIMITS OF INVESTMENTS/LOANS: Regional; Other: Southeast
RANGE OF INV./LOAN PER BUSINESS: Min. $200,000
REFERRALS ACCEPTED FROM: Investment/Mortgage banker or Borrower/Investee

COMPANY: **Consumers Ventures/ American Reserves, Inc.**
ADDRESS: 35 Glenlake Parkway, Suite 110
Atlanta, GA 30328
PHONE: (404) 396-4000
TYPE OF INSTITUTION: Private Venture Captial
CONTACT OFFICER(S): H. Friedman, Director
A. Moro, Director
A. Gooodwin, Director
INVESTMENTS/LOANS MADE: For own account; For managed accounts; Through private placments
INVESTMENTS/LOANS MADE: In securities with a secondary market and in securities without a secondary market
TYPES OF FINANCING: SECONDARY-MARKET CORPORATE SECURITIES: Common stock; Preferred stock; VENTURE CAPITAL: Start-up from developed product stage; First-stage (less than 1 year); Second-stage (generally 1-3 years); Later-stage expansion; Buy-outs/Acquisitions; LOANS: Working capital; Equity-related; REAL ESTATE LOANS: Land; Land development; REAL ESTATE: Joint ventures; Partnerships/Syndications
PREFERRED TYPES OF INDUSTRIES/INVESTMENTS: Consumer Product/Service
GEOGRAPHIC LIMITS OF INVESTMENTS/LOANS: Local; State; Regional; National
RANGE OF INV./LOAN PER BUSINESS: Min. $250,000; Max. $1,000,000
PREFERRED TERM FOR LOANS & LEASES: Min. 2 years; Max. 5 years
BUSINESS CHARACTERISITICS DESIRED-REQUIRED: Minimum number of years in business: 0
REFERRALS ACCEPTED FROM: Investment/Mortgage banker or Borrower/Investee

COMPANY: **Lendman Capital Associates**
ADDRESS: 5 Piedmont Center, Suite 320
Atlanta, GA 30305
PHONE: (404) 233-9003
TYPE OF INSTITUTION: Private Venture Capital
CONTACT OFFICER(S): Robert H. Friedman; General Partner
William M. Lendman, General Partner
Loren J. Rivard, General Partner
INVESTMENTS/LOANS MADE: For own account, For managed accounts
INVESTMENTS/LOANS MADE: Only in securities seuritles without a secondary market
TYPES OF FINANCING: VENTURE CAPITAL: Research & Development; Start-up from developed product stage; First-stage; Second-stage; Later-stage expansion; Buy-outs/Acquisitions
PREFERRED TYPES OF INDUSTRIES/INVESTMENTS: Diversified
GEOGRAPHIC LIMITS OF INVESTMENTS/LOANS: National
RANGE OF INV./LOAN PER BUSINESS: Min. $250,000; Max. $500,000

COMPANY: **Noro-Mosely Partners**
ADDRESS: 100 Galleria Parkway, #1240
Atlanta, GA 30339
PHONE: (404) 955-0020
CONTACT OFFICER(S): Charles D. Moseley
Jack R. Kelly, Jr.
ASSETS: $43.5 million
INVESTMENTS/LOANS MADE: For own account
INVESTMENTS/LOANS MADE: Only in securities without a secondary market
TYPES OF FINANCING: VENTURE CAPITAL: Start-up from developed product stage; First-stage; Second-stage; Later-stage expansion; Buy-outs/Acquisitions
WILL NOT CONSIDER: Real Estate
GEOGRAPHIC LIMITS OF INVESTMENTS/LOANS: Regional; Southeast
RANGE OF INV./LOAN PER BUSINESS: Min. $500,000; Max. $4 million
BUSINESS CHARACTERISTICS DESIRED-REQUIRED: Other: Several years of operating profitably—min. annual profit $3-400,000
REMARKS: Prefer later-stage and buyouts

COMPANY: **River Capital, Inc.**
ADDRESS: 235 Peachtree Street NE, #2218
Atlanta, GA 30303
PHONE: (404) 584-7380
TYPE OF INSTITUTION: Venture Capital buyouts
CONTACT OFFICER(S): Larry Mock, Pres.
ASSETS: $10 million

INVESTMENTS/LOANS MADE: For own account
INVESTMENTS/LOANS MADE: Only in securities without a secondary market
TYPES OF FINANCING: VENTURE CAPITOL: Buy-outs/Acquisitions; OTHER SERVICES PROVIDED: Mgmt. and leveraged buyouts
PREFERRED TYPES OF INDUSTRIES/INVESTMENTS: Operating companies manufacturing & distribution
WILL NOT CONSIDER: Start-ups, turn-arounds; High tech.
GEOGRAPHIC LIMITS OF INVESTMENTS/LOANS: Regional; Southern
BUSINESS CHARACTERISTICS DESIRED-REQUIRED: Minimum number of years in business: 5; Min. annual sales $20 million; Min. net worth $10 million; Min.. annual net income $1 million; Other: Operating companies
REMARKS: Range of Investment: Total Price $10-30 million

COMPANY: **Atlanta Financial & Leasing, Inc.**
ADDRESS: 4501 Circle 75 Parkway, Suite A-1240
Atlanta, Georgia 30339
PHONE: (404) 955-2856
TYPE OF INSTITUTION: Financial and leasing brokers, mortgage loans
CONTACT OFFICERS(S): Doug Faust, Owner
Equipment leasing and financing, also act as consultants in the area of equipment purchases. Expertise in the marine (offshore) industry.
INVESTMENTS/LOANS MADE: Through private placements
INVESTMENTS/LOANS MADE: In securities with a secondary market and securities without a secondary market
TYPES OF FINANCING: LOANS: Unsecured; Working capital (receivables/inventory); Equipment; Equity-related; REAL ESTATE LOANS: Long-term senior mtg.; Intermediate-term senior mtg.; Standbys; Industrial revenue bonds; FACTORING; LEASES: Single-investor; Leveraged; Tax leases; Non-tax leases; Operating; Tax-oriented lease brokerage; Lease syndications; Vendor financing programs; REAL ESTATE: Joint ventures. OTHER: Equipment purchases, expertise in the marine industry
PREFERRED TYPES OF INDUSTRIES/INVESTMENTS: Middle market construction, medical, data processing, certain real estate transaction, equipment leasing
GEOGRAPHIC LIMITS OF INVESTMENTS/LOANS: Local; State; Regional; National; International
RANGE OF INV./LOAN PER BUSINESS: Min. $100,000; Max. $ no limit
PREFERRED TERM FOR LOANS & LEASES: Min. 3 years; Max. as pertinent
BUSINESS CHARACTERISTICS DESIRED-REQUIRED: We will look at any situation. It does need to make sense

COMPANY: **R. W. Allsop & Associates**
ADDRESS: Suite 210, 2750 First Avenue, N.E.
Cedar Rapids, IA 52402
PHONE: (319) 363-8971
TYPE OF INSTITUTION: Venture Capital Investment Partnership
CONTACT OFFICER(S): Robert W. Allsop, General Partner
Paul D. Rhines, General Partner
ASSETS: $45,000,000
INVESTMENTS/LOANS MADE: For own account
INVESTMENTS/LOANS MADE: Only in securities without a secondary market
TYPES OF FINANCING: VENTURE CAPITAL: Start-up from developed product stage, First stage; Second-stage (generally 1-3 years); Later-stage expansion; Buy-outs/Acquisitions
PREFERRED TYPES OF INDUSTRIES/INVESTMENTS: Health Care Products and Services, Communications, Industrial Automation, Computer related products and services
WILL NOT CONSIDER: Real Estate
GEOGRAPHIC LIMITS OF INVESTMENTS/LOANS: National
RANGE OF INV./LOAN PER BUSINESS: Min. $300,000; Max. $1,500,000
PREFERRED TERM FOR LOANS & LEASES: Min. 5; Max. 8 years
BUSINESS CHARACTERISTICS DESIRED-REQUIRED: Minimum number of years in business: 1 to 2; Minimum annual sales $1,500,000
REFERRALS ACCEPTED FROM: Investment/Mortgage banker or Borrower/Investee
BRANCHES: Gregory B. Bultman, General Partner, R. W. Allsop & Associates, Suite 1501, 815 E. Mason Street, P.O. Box 1368, Milwaukee, WI 53201; (414) 271-6510
Robert L. Kuk, General Partner, R. W. Allsop & Associates, Suite 600, 111 West Port Plaza, St. Louis, MO 63146; (314) 434-1688
Larry C. Maddox, General Partner, R. W. Allsop & Associates, Suite 244, 35 Corporate Woods, 9101 West 110th Street, Overland Park, KS 66210; (913) 642-4719

COMPANY: **Pappajohn Capital Resources**
ADDRESS: 2116 Financial Center
Des Moines, IA 50309
PHONE: (515) 244-5746
TYPE OF INSTITUTION: Venture Capital Proprietorship
CONTACT OFFICER(S): John Pappajohn, General Partner
ASSETS: $10,000,000
INVESTMENTS/LOANS MADE: For own account; For managed accounts; Thro ugh private placements; Through underwriting public offerings
INVESTMENTS/LOANS MADE: In securities with a secondary market and in securities without a secondary market
TYPES OF FINANCING: SECONDARY-MARKET CORPORATE SECURITIES: Common stock; Preferred stock; Bonds; Other, VENTURE CAPITAL: Research & Development; Start-up from developed product stage; First-stage (less than 1 year); Second-stage (generally 1-3 years); Later-stage expansion; Buy-outs/Acquisitions, LOANS: Unsecured to credits above non-rated; Equity-related; Convertible debentures
PREFERRED TYPES OF INDUSTRIES/INVESTMENTS: State of the Art Medical—High Technology
GEOGRAPHIC LIMITS OF INVESTMENTS/LOANS: National
RANGE OF INV./LOAN PER BUSINESS: Min. $100,000; Max. $1,000,000

BUSINESS CHARACTERISTICS DESIRED-REQUIRED: Min. no. of years in business: 0
REFERRALS ACCEPTED FROM: Borrower/Investee
BRANCHES: Denver, CO
San Diego, CA

COMPANY: **Vanguard Capital Corporation**
ADDRESS: 101 Lions Drive
Barrington, IL 60010
PHONE: (312) 381-2330
CONTACT OFFICER(S): Kenneth M. Arenberg
ASSETS: $150,000-1,000,000
INVESTMENTS/LOANS MADE: In securities with a secondary market and in securities without a secondary market
TYPES OF FINANCING: VENTURE CAPITAL, LOANS: Equity-related
PREFERRED TYPES OF INDUSTRIES/INVESTMENTS: Medical and other health services; research and technology
RANGE OF INV./LOAN PER BUSINESS: Min. $50,000; Max. $250,000
PREFERRED TERM FOR LOANS & LEASES: Min. 1-3 years; Max. 5-7 years
REFERRALS ACCEPTED FROM: Borrower/Investee

COMPANY: **Alpha Capital Corp.**
ADDRESS: 3 First National Plaza, Ste 1400
Chicago, IL 60602
PHONE: (312) 372-1556
TYPE OF INSTITUTION: Venture Capital
CONTACT OFFICER(S): Andrew H. Kalnow

COMPANY: **Associates Commercial Corporation**
ADDRESS: The Associates Center, 150 North Michigan Ave.
Chicago, IL 60601
PHONE: (312) 781-5800
TYPE OF INSTITUTION: Commercial finance subsidiary of Associates Corporation of North America (The Associates), the cornerstone on the Financial Services Group of Gulf & Western Industries, Inc.
CONTACT OFFICER(S): Rocco A. Macri, Executive Vice President, Business Loans Division (Division provides accounts receivable, inventory and fixed asset loans for working capital, refinancings, acquisitions and leveraged buyouts for small annd medium-sized businesses throughout the U.S.).
ASSETS: $6.6 billion (The Associates); $3.5 billion in commerical finance recievables
INVESTMENTS/LOANS MADE: For own account
INVESTMENTS/LOANS MADE: Only in securities without a secondary market
TYPES OF FINANCING: VENTURE CAPITAL: Later-stage expansions; Buy-outs/Acquisitions, LOANS: Working capital; Equipment; Equity-related. Other: Bank participation, REAL ESTATE LOANS: Industrial plants with receivables/inventory, FACTORING, LEASES: Single-investor; Tax leases; Non-tax leases; Operating; Vendor financing programs, REAL ESTATE: Acquisitions, OTHER SERVICES PROVIDED: Retail and wholesale financing of heavy duty trucks and trailers, financing and leasing of construction and mining equipment, machine tools, business aircraft and other capital goods; fleet leasing and management services for cars and trucks
PREFERRED TYPES OF INDUSTRIES/INVESTMENTS: Heavy-duty truck and trailer financing; auto, truck and trailer fleet leasing; communications and industrial equipment financing and leasing; business loans (esp. leveraged buyout financing); and factoring
WILL NOT CONSIDER: Unsecured financing
GEOGRAPHIC LIMITS OF INVESTMENTS/LOANS: National
RANGE OF INV./LOAN PER BUSINESS: Min. $500,000; Max. $100 million or more
PREFERRED TERM FOR LOANS & LEASES: Min. two (2) years; Max. ten (10) years
BUSINESS CHARACTERISTICS DESIRED-REQUIRED: Minimum net worth $500,000
REFERRALS ACCEPTED FROM: Investment/Mortgage banker or Borrower/Investee
BRANCHES: More than 100 regional and branch offices in North America
REMARKS: Associates Commerical has six operting divisions: Business Loans, Communications, Equipment, Factoring , Fleet Leasing and Transportation

COMPANY: **Prince Venture Partners**
ADDRESS: One First National Plaza #4950
Chicago, IL 60603
PHONE: (312) 726-2232
TYPE OF INSTITUTION: Venture Capital
CONTACT OFFICER(S): Angus M. Duthie
James W. Fordyce
INVESTMENTS/LOANS MADE: For own account
TYPES OF FINANCING: VENTURE CAPITAL: Start-up from developed product stage; First-stage (less than 1 year); Second stage
GEOGRAPHIC LIMITS OF INVESTMENTS/LOANS: National
RANGE OF INV./LOAN PER BUSINESS: Min. $300,000; Max $500,000
BRANCHES: 767 Third Ave., New York, NY; (212) 319-6620, James W. Fordyce

COMPANY: **Exchange National Bank of Chicago**
ADDRESS: LaSalle and Monroe Streets
Chicago, IL 60603
PHONE: (312) 781-8000
TYPE OF INSTITUTION: Commercial bank with Venture Capital activity
CONTACT OFFICER(S): Joseph Chevalier
ASSETS: $1.2 million
TYPES OF FINANCING: VENTURE CAPITAL: Later-stage expansion; Buy-outs/Acquisitions
GEOGRAPHIC LIMITS OF INVESTMENTS/LOANS: National
RANGE OF INV./LOAN PER BUSINESS: Min. $500,000
BUSINESS CHARACTERISTICS DESIRED-REQUIRED: Minimum number of years in business: 1

COMPANY: **The December Group, Ltd.**
ADDRESS: Suite 1119, 135 So. La Salle Street
Chicago, IL 60603

PHONE: (312) 372-7733
TYPE OF INSTITUTION: Private Investment Banking
CONTACT OFFICER(S): Gerald K. Neavolls, President
INVESTMENTS/LOANS MADE: For own account; Through private placements
TYPES OF FINANCING: VENTURE CAPITAL: Later-stage expansion; Buy-outs/Acquisitions, LOANS: Equity-related, OTHER SERVICES PROVIDED: Resource Development—Primarily Oil & Gas
PREFERRED TYPES OF INDUSTRIES/INVESTMENTS: Oil & Gas, Coal, Other n atural resources
GEOGRAPHIC LIMITS OF INVESTMENTS/LOANS: National
RANGE OF INV./LOAN PER BUSINESS: Min. $750,000; Max. $3,500,000

COMPANY: **First Chicago Investment Advisors—Institutional V.C. Fund**
ADDRESS: Three First National Plaza, Suite 0140
Chicago, IL 60670
PHONE: (312) 766-4171
CONTACT OFFICER(S): John H. Mahar, V.P.
T. Bondurant French, V.C. Advisor;
Marshall Greenwald, V.C. Advisor
Patrick A. McGivney, V.C. Advisor;
Daniel J. Mitchell, V.C. Advisor
ASSETS: $60,000,000
INVESTMENTS/LOANS MADE: For managed accounts; Through private placements
TYPES OF FINANCING: VENTURE CAPITAL: First-stage; Second-stage; Later-stage expansion, Buy-outs/Acquisitions
PREFERRED TYPES OF INDUSTRIES/INVESTMENTS: Technology, computer, medical, healthcare, telecommunications, manufacturing
WILL NOT CONSIDER: Tax shelters, oil and gas drilling, real estate.
GEOGRAPHIC LIMITS OF INVESTMENTS/LOANS: National
RANGE OF INV./LOAN PER BUSINESS: Min. $500,000; Max. $2,500,000

COMPANY: **Frontenac Venture Company**
ADDRESS: 208 South LaSalle Street
Chicago, IL 60604
PHONE: (312) 368-0044
TYPE OF INSTITUTION: Private partnership (2), SBIC (1)
CONTACT OFFICER(S): Martin J. Koldyke, Medical, Health Sciences
David A.R. Dullum, Computer Related Sciences;
Rodney L. Goldstein, Mature Industry Investments
ASSETS: $75 million
INVESTMENTS/LOANS MADE: For own account; For managed accounts
INVESTMENTS/LOANS MADE: Only in securities without a secondary market
TYPES OF FINANCING: SECONDARY-MARKET CORPORATE SECURITIES: Common stock; Preferred stock; Bonds; VENTURE CAPITAL: Research & Development; Start-up from developed product stage; First-stage (less than 1 year); Second-stage (generally 1-3 years); Later-stage expansion; Buy-outs/Acquistions
PREFERRED TYPES OF INDUSTRIES/INVESTMENTS: Health and Medical science; Computer related; Mature industry investments
GEOGRAPHIC LIMITS OF INVESTMENTS/LOANS: National; Primarily Midwestern
RANGE OF INV./LOAN PER BUSINESS: Min. $300,000; Max. $2,500,000
BUSINESS CHARACTERISTICS DESIRED-REQUIRED: Minimum number of years in business: 0

COMPANY: **Golder, Thoma, Cressey & Co.**
ADDRESS: 120 S. LaSalle St., Ste. 630
Chicago, IL 60603
PHONE: (312) 853-3322
TYPE OF INSTITUTION: Venture Capital Partnership
CONTACT OFFICER(S): Stanley C. Golder, General Partner
Carl D. Thoma, General Partner
Bryan C. Cressey, General Partner
Bruce V. Rauner, General Partner
F. Dan Blanchard, Sr. Associate, (Dallas)
ASSETS: $160 million
INVESTMENTS/LOANS MADE: For own account
INVESTMENTS/LOANS MADE: In securities with a secondary market and in securities without a secondary market
TYPES OF FINANCING: VENTURE CAPITAL: Start-up from developed product stage; First-stage (less than 1 year); Second-stage (generally 1-3 years); Later-stage expansion; Buy-outs/Acquisitions
PREFERRED TYPES OF INDUSTRIES/INVESTMENTS: Telecommunications; heal th care industry; medical products; transportation
WILL NOT CONSIDER: Real Estate
GEOGRAPHIC LIMITS OF INVESTMENTS/LOANS: National
RANGE OF INV./LOAN PER BUSINESS: Min. $500,000; Max. $10 million
PREFERRED TERM FOR LOANS & LEASES: Min. 5; Max. 10 years
BUSINESS CHARACTERISTICS DESIRED-REQUIRED: Min. no. of years in business: 0
REFERRALS ACCEPTED FROM: Investment/Mortgage banker or Borrower/Investee
BRANCHES: 17330 Preston Rd., Dallas, TX 75292; 214-248-7848

COMPANY: **Longworth Ventures**
ADDRESS: 135 S. LaSalle Street, #2712
Chicago, IL 60603
PHONE: (312) 372-3888
TYPE OF INSTITUTION: Venture Capital
CONTACT OFFICER(S): Lawrence Sucsy

COMPANY:**Seidman Jackson Fisher & Co.**
ADDRESS: 233 N. Michigan Avenue, Suite 1812
Chicago IL
PHONE: (312) 856-1812
TYPE OF INSTITUTION: Venture Capital Firm
CONTACT OFFICER(S): Margaret G. Fisher
Douglas L. Jackson
David C. Seidman
ASSETS: $38.4 million

INVESTMENTS/LOANS MADE: For own account
INVESTMENTS/LOANS MADE: In securities with a secondary market and in securities without a secondary market
TYPES OF FINANCING: VENTURE CAPITAL: Start-up from developed product stage; First-stage; Second-stage; Later-stage expansion; Buy-outs/Acquisitions

COMPANY:**North American Capital Group, Ltd.**
ADDRESS: 7250 N. Cicero Ave., Suite 201
Lincolnwood IL 60646
PHONE: (312) 982-1010
TYPE OF INSTITUTION: Subsidiary - financial services holding company, The North American Group, Ltd.
CONTACT OFFICER(S): Gregory I. Kravitt, President
William Andersen, Associate
INVESTMENTS/LOANS MADE: For own account; Through private placements
INVESTMENTS/LOANS MADE: Only in securities without a secondary market
TYPES OF FINANCING: VENTURE CAPITAL: Second-stage; Later-stage; Buy-outs/Acquisitions; LOANS: Working capital; Equipment; Equity-related; Other: Loans with attached warrants; REAL ESTATE LOANS: Long-term senior mtg.; Intermediate-term senior mtg.; Subordinated; Wraparounds; Construction; Standbys; Other: bond guarantees; REAL ESTATE: Acquisitions; Joint ventures; OTHER SERVICES PROVIDED: Financing arranged for both qualified franchisors and qualified franchisees
PREFERRED TYPES OF INDUSTRIES/INVESTMENTS: Franchising, medium to low technology companies, Income property, Real estate (manufacturers, ditributors) leveraged buyouts, profitable service companies
WILL NOT CONSIDER: gambling casinos, entertainment
GEOGRAPHIC LIMITS OF INVESTMENTS/LOANS: Other: Midwest
RANGE OF INV./LOAN PER BUSINESS: Min. $100,000; Max. $3.0 million
PREFERRED TERM FOR LOANS & LEASES: Min. 3 years; Max. 10 years
BUSINESS CHARACTERISTICS DESIRED-REQUIRED: Minimum number of years in business: 1; Min. annual sales $500,000

COMPANY: **Allstate Venture Capital Company - Venture Capital Division**
ADDRESS: Allstate Plaza E-2
Northbrook, IL, 60062
PHONE: (312) 291-5681
TYPE OF INSTITUTION: Venture Capital Div. of Insurance Company
INVESTMENTS/LOANS MADE: For own account
TYPES OF FINANCING: VENTURE CAPITAL: Start-up from developed product stage; First-stage (less than 1 year); Second-stage (generally 1-3 years); Later-stage expansion; Buy-outs; OTHER SERVICES PROVIDED: Leverage Buyouts; mezzanine financing
WILL NOT CONSIDER: Retail
GEOGRAPHIC LIMITS OF INVESTMENTS/LOANS: National
RANGE OF INV./LOAN PER BUSINESS: Min. $500,000

COMPANY: **W. H. Bushing & Co., Inc.**
ADDRESS: 1161 Walnut Lane
Northbrook, IL 60062
PHONE: (312) 272-2578
TYPE OF INSTITUTION: Acquisitions-Mergers, Consulting
CONTACT OFFICER(S): William H. Bushing, President
B.G. Bushing, Sec'y-Treas.
INVESTMENTS/LOANS MADE: For own (company's) account
TYPES OF FINANCING: VENTURE CAPITAL: Research & Development; Start-up from developed product stage; First-stage (less than 1 year); Second-stage (generally 1-3 years); Later-stage expansion; Buy-outs/Acquisitions, OTHER SERVICES PROVIDED: Guaranteed acquisition candidates
GEOGRAPHIC LIMITS OF INVESTMENTS/LOANS: International

COMPANY: **Lang Capital Corporation**
ADDRESS: 1301 West 22nd Street, #601
Oak Brook, IL 60521
PHONE: (312) 920-8000
TYPE OF INSTITUTION: Venture Capital
CONTACT OFFICER(S): Peter D. Lang, Pres.
INVESTMENTS/LOANS MADE: For own account, For managed accounts, Through private placements
TYPES OF FINANCING: VENTURE CAPITAL: Research & Development; Start-up from developed product stage; First-stage (less than 1 year); Buy-outs/ Acqusitions
PREFERRED TYPES OF INDUSTRIES/INVESTMENTS: Information Systems; Electronics; Communications; Computer Hardware & Software; X-Ray Imaging Systems; Lasers
WILL NOT CONSIDER: R.E.; Oil & Gas
GEOGRAPHIC LIMITS OF INVESTMENTS/LOANS: National; International
RANGE OF INV./LOAN PER BUSINESS: Max. $2 million
PREFERRED TERM FOR LOANS & LEASES: Max. 5 years
BUSINESS CHARACTERISTICS DESIRED-REQUIRED: Other; Potential $50 million in sales by 5th year
REMARKS: Loans convertible to equity

COMPANY: **Pivan Management Co.**
ADDRESS: 7840 Lincoln Ave.
Skokie, IL 60077
PHONE: (312) 677-1142
TYPE OF INSTITUTION: Money management
CONTACT OFFICER(S): David B. Pivan, Pres.
Richard Nelson, V.P.
ASSETS: $4 Million
INVESTMENTS/LOANS MADE: For own account, Through private placements
INVESTMENTS/LOANS MADE: In securities with a secondary market and in securities wiithout a secondary market
TYPES OF FINANCING: SECONDARY-MARKET CORPORATE SECURITIES: Common stock. VENTURE CAPITAL: Research & Development; Start-

up from developed product stage; First-stage; Second-stage; Buy-outs/Acquisitions.
PREFERRED TYPES OF INDUSTRIES/INVESTMENTS: High technology companies
WILL NOT CONSIDER: Retail
GEOGRAPHIC LIMITS OF INVESTMENTS/LOANS: Regional; National Other: Regional Preferred
RANGE OF INV./LOAN PER BUSINESS: Min. $100,000; Max. $1,000,000
REFERRALS ACCEPTED FROM: Investment/Mortgage banker or Borrower/Investee

COMPANY: **Irwin Union Corporation**
ADDRESS: 500 Washington St., Box 929
Columbus, IN 47201
PHONE: (812) 372-0111
TYPE OF INSTITUTION: Bank holding company: subsidiaries; Irwin Union Bank, Inland Mortgage, white River Capital
CONTACT OFFICER(S): M. R. Ryan; Commercial Lending, President, Irwin Union Bank
S. K. Kreigh; Mortgage Lending, President, Inland Mortgage
D. J. Blair; Venture Capital, Vice President, White River Capital
ASSETS: $250 million
INVESTMENTS/LOANS MADE: For own account
INVESTMENTS/LOANS MADE: In securities with a secondary market and in securities wiithout a secondary market
TYPES OF FINANCING: SECONDARY MARKET CORPORATE SECURITIES; Industrial Revenue Bond Placements. VENTURE CAPITAL: Second-stage; Later-stage expansion. LOANS: Unsecured to credits Above BBB; Working capital; Equipment; Equity-related. REAL ESTATE LOANS: Long-term senior mtg.; Wraparounds; Construction; Industrial revenue bonds; Other: Primarily single family. OTHER SERVICES PROVIDED: Mortgage servicing, municipal finance, and pension management
PREFERRED TYPES OF INDUSTRIES/INVESTMENTS: Commercial Lending-all forms; Mortgage Banking-Single family, FHA/VA; Venture Capital-no preferences
GEOGRAPHIC LIMITS OF INVESTMENTS/LOANS: State; regional (prefer State)
RANGE OF INV./LOAN PER BUSINESS: Min. $100,000; Max. $2,000,000 (Venture $200,000)
PREFERRED TERM FOR LOANS & LEASES: Min. .25 years; Max. 20 years
BUSINESS CHARACTERISTICS DESIRED-REQUIRED: Minimum number of years in business: 1
REFERRALS ACCEPTED FROM: Investment/Mortgage banker or Borrower/Investee

COMPANY: **Waterfield Mortgage Co., Inc.**
ADDRESS: 333 E. Washington Blvd.
Ft. Wayne, IN 46802
PHONE: (219) 425-8393
TYPE OF INSTITUTION: Mortgage Banker
CONTACT OFFICER(S): Thomas A. Gauldin, V.P., Manager, C.M.B.—Commercial loans
ASSETS: $3 billion
INVESTMENTS/LOANS MADE: For own account; for managed accounts and through private placements
INVESTMENTS/LOANS MADE: In securities with a secondary market and in securities without a secondary market
TYPES OF FINANCING: REAL ESTATE LOANS: SECONDARY-MARKET CORPORATE SECURITIES: Private placements; VENTURE CAPITAL: Start-up from developed product stage; LOANS: Equipment; Equity-related; REAL ESTATE LOANS: Long-term senior mtg.; Intermediate-term senior mtg.; Subordinated; Wraparounds; Land; Land development; Construction; Gap; Standbys; Industrial revenue bonds; LEASES: Single-investor; Leveraged; Tax leases; Non-tax leases; Operating; Tax-oriented lease brokerage; Lease syndications; REAL ESTATE: Acquisitions; Joint ventures; Partnerships/Syndications
PREFERRED TYPES OF INDUSTRIES/INVESTMENTS: Office; Warehouse, Shopping; Retail; Apartments; Motel/hotels
GEOGRAPHIC LIMITS OF INVESTMENTS/LOANS: National
RANGE OF INV./LOAN PER BUSINESS: Min. $200,000; Max. Unlimited
PREFERRED TERM FOR LOANS & LEASES: Min. Flexible
BUSINESS CHARACTERISTICS DESIRED-REQUIRED: Min. yrs. in business: 5
BRANCHES: 35 Nationwide

COMPANY: **Aegis Fund Limited Partnership**
ADDRESS: 171 Milk Street
Boston, MA 02109
PHONE: (617) 338-5655
TYPE OF INSTITUTION: Venture Capital
CONTACT OFFICER(S): John H. Carter, General Partner
Walter J. Levison, General Partner
Clifton C. Smith, General Partner
ASSETS: $15,000,000
INVESTMENTS/LOANS MADE: For own account
INVESTMENTS/LOANS MADE: Only in securities without a secondary market
TYPES OF FINANCING: VENTURE CAPITAL: Start-up from developed product stage; First-stage
PREFERRED TYPES OF INDUSTRIES/INVESTMENTS: Analytical instrumentation; Medical instrumentation; Bio-medical products; Segments of computer electronics; Information technology; Office and factory automation; Some aspects of the specialized energy industry
GEOGRAPHIC LIMITS OF INVESTMENTS/LOANS: Local; Other: Within 75 miles of Boston
RANGE OF INV./LOAN PER BUSINESS: Min. $100,000 - 300,000; Max. $1,000,000

COMPANY: **Ampersand Management Company**
ADDRESS: 100 Federal Street, 31st Floor
Boston, MA 02110
PHONE: (617) 423-8055
TYPE OF INSTITUTION: Private venture firm investing own capital; affiliate of Paine Webber, Inc.
CONTACT OFFICER(S): William C. Mills III
ASSETS: $50 Million
INVESTMENTS/LOANS MADE: For managed accounts

INVESTMENTS/LOANS MADE: Only in securities without a secondary market
TYPES OF FINANCING: VENTURE CAPITAL: Start-up from developed product stage; First-stage (less than 1 year); Second-stage (generally 1-3 years); Later-stage expansion
PREFERRED TYPES OF INDUSTRIES/INVESTMENTS: Diversified; particularly high technology oriented companies
WILL NOT CONSIDER: Real Estate, Oil and Gas
GEOGRAPHIC LIMITS OF INVESTMENTS/LOANS: National; near major metropolitan airports
RANGE OF INV./LOAN PER BUSINESS: Min. $500,000; Max. $1,500,000
BUSINESS CHARACTERISTICS DESIRED-REQUIRED: Min. no. of years in business: 0
REFERRALS ACCEPTED FROM: Investment/Mortgage banker or Borrower/Investee

COMPANY: **Boston Ventures Management, Inc.**
ADDRESS: 45 Milk Street
Boston, MA 02109
PHONE: (617) 292-8125
TYPE OF INSTITUTION: Management Co. of a Limited Partnership Venture Capital Fund
CONTACT OFFICER(S): William F. Thompson, President & Dir.
Richard C. Wallace, Dir.
James M. Wilson, Dir.
Roy F. Coppedge, Dir.
Anthony J. Bolland, Dir.
ASSETS: Capital in excess of $110,000,000
INVESTMENTS/LOANS MADE: For own account
INVESTMENTS/LOANS MADE: Only in securities without a secondary market
TYPES OF FINANCING: VENTURE CAPITAL: Later-stage expansion; Buy-outs/Acquisitions, OTHER SERVICES PROVIDED: Leveraged equities
PREFERRED TYPES OF INDUSTRIES/INVESTMENTS: Communications; Entertainment; and Service industries, Diverse
WILL NOT CONSIDER: High-tech.; Start-ups
GEOGRAPHIC LIMITS OF INVESTMENTS/LOANS: National; International; Other; also UK
RANGE OF INV./LOAN PER BUSINESS: $2-3 Million
BUSINESS CHARACTERISTICS DESIRED-REQUIRED: Minimum number of years in business: 2-3

COMPANY: **Bristol Investment Trust**
ADDRESS: 842A Beacon Street
Boston, MA 02215
PHONE: (617) 556-5212
TYPE OF INSTITUTION: Venture Capital
CONTACT OFFICER(S): Bernard G. Berkman

COMPANY: **Burgess & Leith, Inc.**
ADDRESS: 60 State St.
Boston, MA 02109
PHONE: (617) 742-5900
CONTACT OFFICER(S): V.P., Corp. Finance
TYPES OF FINANCING: VENTURE CAPITAL: Second-stage (generally 1-3 years); Later-stage expansion; Buy-outs/Acquisitions
WILL NOT CONSIDER: R.E., Retail & Wholesale
RANGE OF INV./LOAN PER BUSINESS: Min. $250,000
PREFERRED TERM FOR LOANS & LEASES: Flexible
BUSINESS CHARACTERISTICS DESIRED-REQUIRED: Min. no. of years in business: 0; Strong management
REFERRALS ACCEPTED FROM: Investment/Mortgage bander or Borrower/Investee
REMARKS: Average Investment: $600,000—800,000

COMPANY: **Cabot Corporation**
ADDRESS: 125 High Street
Boston, MA 02110
PHONE: (617) 423-6000
TYPE OF INSTITUTION: Venture Capital Subsidiary
CONTACT OFFICER(S): Nicholas F. Fiore
ASSETS: $2,000,000,000
INVESTMENTS/LOANS MADE: For own account
TYPES OF FINANCING: VENTURE CAPITAL: Research & Development; Start-up from developed product stage; First-stage; Second-stage; Buy-outs/Acquisitions
PREFERRED TYPES OF INDUSTRIES/INVESTMENTS: High technology
GEOGRAPHIC LIMITS OF INVESTMENTS/LOANS: National; Other: Generally prefer regional
BUSINESS CHARACTERISTICS DESIRED-REQUIRED: Other: High growth; Materials intensive
REMARKS: Invest primarily to provide contacts for new business development

COMPANY: **Charles River Partnership**
ADDRESS: 133 Federal Street
Boston, MA 02110
PHONE: (617) 482-9370
TYPE OF INSTITUTION: Venture Capital
CONTACT OFFICER(S): Richard M. Burnes, Jr., General Partner
John T. Neises, General Partner
Donald W. Feddersen, General Partner
Robert F. Higgins, General Partner
Paul A. Maeder, Associate
ASSETS: $140,000,000
INVESTMENTS/LOANS MADE: For own account
INVESTMENTS/LOANS MADE: Only in securities without a secondary market
TYPES OF FINANCING: VENTURE CAPITAL
PREFERRED TYPES OF INDUSTRIES/INVESTMENTS: High Tech - all areas except real estate and oil/gas
GEOGRAPHIC LIMITS OF INVESTMENTS/LOANS: National
RANGE OF INV./LOAN PER BUSINESS: Min. $500,000; Max. $2,500,000
BUSINESS CHARACTERISTICS DESIRED-REQUIRED: Minimum number of years in business: 0

COMPANY: **Claflin Capital Management, Inc.**
ADDRESS: 185 Devonshire Street
Boston, MA 02110
PHONE: (617) 426-6505
TYPE OF INSTITUTION: Venture Capital
CONTACT OFFICER(S): Thomas M. Claflin, II, President & General Partner
Lloyd C. Dahmen, Vice President & General Partner

Joseph Stavenhagen, Vice President & General Partner
INVESTMENTS/LOANS MADE: For own account
INVESTMENTS/LOANS MADE: Only in securities without a secondary market
TYPES OF FINANCING: VENTURE CAPITAL: Start-up from developed product stage; First-stage
WILL NOT CONSIDER: Real Estate
GEOGRAPHIC LIMITS OF INVESTMENTS/LOANS: State
BUSINESS CHARACTERISTICS DESIRED-REQUIRED: Minimum number of years in business: 0

COMPANY: **Eastech Management Company**
ADDRESS: One Liberty Square
Boston, MA 02109
PHONE: (617) 338-0200
TYPE OF INSTITUTION: Venture Capital
CONTACT OFFICER(S): Michael H. Shanahan
ASSETS: $33,000,000
INVESTMENTS/LOANS MADE: Fow own account
INVESTMENTS/LOANS MADE: Only in securities without a secondary market
TYPES OF FINANCING: VENTURE CAPITAL: Research & Development; Start-up from developed product stage; First-stage; Second-stage
PREFERRED TYPES OF INDUSTRIES/INVESTMENTS: Computer-related
GEOGRAPHIC LIMITS OF INVESTMENTS/LOANS: Regional; Other: Prefer New England
RANGE OF INV./LOAN PER BUSINESS: Min. $300,000; Max. $700,000
BUSINESS CHARACTERISTICS DESIRED-REQUIRED: Minimum number of years in business: 0
REFERRALS ACCEPTED FROM: Investment/Mortgage banker; Borrower/Investee

COMPANY: **Faneuil Hall Associates**
ADDRESS: One Boston Place
Boston, MA 02108
PHONE: (617) 723-1955
TYPE OF INSTITUTION: Venture Capital
CONTACT OFFICER(S): David T. Riddiford

COMPANY: **Fidelity Venture Associates, Inc.**
ADDRESS: 82 Devonshire Street
Boston, MA 02109
PHONE: (617) 570-6450
CONTACT OFFICER(S): William Elfers, V.P.
Donald R. Young, Associate
INVESTMENTS/LOANS MADE: For own account
INVESTMENTS/LOANS MADE: In securities with a secondary market and in securities without a secondary market
TYPES OF FINANCING: SECONDARY-MARKET CORPORATE SECURITIES: Common stock, VENTURE CAPITAL: Start-up from developed product stage; First-stage (less than 1 year); Second-stage (generally 1-3 years); Later-stage expansion; Buy-outs/Acquisitions
WILL NOT CONSIDER: Real Estate
GEOGRAPHIC LIMITS OF INVESTMENTS/LOANS: National
RANGE OF INV./LOAN PER BUSINESS: Min. $250,000; Max. $1,000,000
BUSINESS CHARACTERISTICS DESIRED-REQUIRED: Min. no. of years in business: 0

COMPANY: **First Capital Corporation of Boston**
ADDRESS: 100 Federal St.
Boston, MA 02110
PHONE: (617) 434-2442
TYPE OF INSTITUTION: Venture Capital subsidiary of commercial bank
CONTACT OFFICER(S): Jeffery W. Wilson, Vice President & Treasurer
Diana H. Frazier, Assistant Vice President
Edwin M. Kania, Investment Officer
ASSETS: $35,000,000
INVESTMENTS/LOANS MADE: For own account; Through private placement
INVESTMENTS/LOANS MADE: In securities with a secondary market; In securities without a secndary market
TYPES OF FINANCING: SECONDARY-MARKET CORPORATE SECURITIES: common stock, VENTURE CAPITAL: Start-up from developed product stage; First-stage; Second-stage
PREFERRED TYPES OF INDUSTRIES/INVESTMENTS: High technology related, genetic engineering, medical, proprietary manufacturing
GEOGRAPHIC LIMITS OF INVESTMENTS/LOANS: National
RANGE OF INV./LOAN PER BUSINESS: Min. $300,000; Max. $2,000,000
BUSINESS CHARACTERISTICS DESIRED-REQUIRED: Minimum number of years in business: 0

COMPANY: **First Venture Capital Corporation of Boston**
ADDRESS: 100 Federal Street
Boston, MA 02110
PHONE: (617) 434-2200
TYPE OF INSTITUTION: Venture Capital
CONTACT OFFICER(S): Charles Klotz, Pres.

COMPANY: **Greylock Management Corp.**
ADDRESS: 1 Federal Street
Boston, MA 02110
PHONE: (617) 423-5525
CONTACT OFFICER(S): David N. Strohm, V.P.
ASSETS: 50,000,000+ up
TYPES OF FINANCING: VENTURE CAPITAL: Start-up from developed product stage; First-stage; Second-stage; Later-stage expansion; Buy-outs/Acquisitions
PREFERRED TYPES OF INDUSTRIES/INVESTMENTS: Technology-based companies
GEOGRAPHIC LIMITS OF INVESTMENTS/LOANS: National
RANGE OF INV./LOAN PER BUSINESS: Min. $300,000; Max. $1.5 Million
BUSINESS CHARACTERISTICS DESIRED-REQUIRED: Minimum number of years in business: 0; Other: Business should plan to be significant factor in their particular marketplace
REMARKS: Investment in straight equity

COMPANY: **H. C. Wainwright & Co.**
ADDRESS: One Boston Place
Boston, MA 02108
PHONE: (617) 227-3100
TYPE OF INSTITUTION: Venture Capital
CONTACT OFFICER(S): Edward H. Kenerson, Gen. Partner

COMPANY: **Korff Associates, Berman, Lewenberg, Redstone & Korff,**
ADDRESS: 211 Congress Street
Boston, MA 02110
PHONE: (617) 426-9300
TYPE OF INSTITUTION: Private investment of family capital
CONTACT OFFICER(S): Ira A. Korff
INVESTMENTS/LOANS MADE: For own account
TYPES OF FINANCING: VENTURE CAPITAL: Buy-outs/Acquisitions, REAL ESTATE LOANS: Intermediate-term senior mtg.; INTERNATIONAL (including import/export), REAL ESTATE: Acquisitions
WILL NOT CONSIDER: Services

COMPANY: **Massachusetts Community Development Finance Corporation**
ADDRESS: 131 State Street, Suite 600
Boston, MA 02109
PHONE: (617) 742-0366
TYPE OF INSTITUTION: State-owned Venture Capital Company
CONTACT OFFICER(S): Charles T. Grigsby, President
Nancy Nye, Vice President
Judith Cranna, Investment Officer
INVESTMENTS/LOANS MADE: For own account
INVESTMENTS/LOANS MADE: In securities with a secondary market; In securities without a secondary market
TYPES OF FINANCING: VENTURE CAPITAL: Start-up from developed product stage: First-stage: Second-stage: Later-stage expansion; Buy-outs/Acquisitions, LOANS: Equipment, Equity related; REAL ESTATE LOANS: Construction; Gap
PREFERRED TYPES OF INDUSTRIES/INVESTMENTS: Labor intensive, manufacturing or service
GEOGRAPHIC LIMITS OF INVESTMENTS/LOANS: State; Other: Economically distressed areas of Massachusetts
RANGE OF INV./LOAN PER BUSINESS: Min. $75,000; Max. $300,,000
PREFERRED TERM FOR LOANS & LEASES: Min. 1 year; Max. 7 years

COMPANY: **Massachusetts Capital Resource Co.**
ADDRESS: 545 Boylston Street #1100
Boston, MA 02116
PHONE: (617) 536-3900
TYPE OF INSTITUTION: Venture Capital
CONTACT OFFICER(S): William J. Torpey, Jr., President
ASSETS: Invest $20,000,000 a year
INVESTMENTS/LOANS MADE: For own account; For managed accounts; Through private placements; Through underwriting public offerings
INVESTMENTS/LOANS MADE: In securities with a secondary market; In securities without a secondary market
TYPES OF FINANCING: SECONDARY-MARKET CORPORATE SECURITIES: Common Stock; Preferred stock, VENTURE CAPITAL: Start-up from developed product stage: First-stage; Second-stage; Later-stage expansion; Buy-outs/Acquisitions, LOANS: Unsecured to credits; Working capital; Equipment; Equity-related
PREFERRED TYPES OF INDUSTRIES/INVESTMENTS: Diversified
WILL NOT CONSIDER: Retail; Real estate; Construction; Financial services
GEOGRAPHIC LIMITS OF INVESTMENTS/LOANS: State
RANGE OF INV./LOAN PER BUSINESS: Min. $200,000; Max. $7,000,000
REFERRALS ACCEPTED FROM: Investment/Mortgage banker or Borrower/Investee
REMARKS: Amount of start-ups done is small

COMPANY: **Massachusetts Technology Development Corporation (MTDC)**
ADDRESS: 84 State Street
Boston, MA 01209
PHONE: (617) 723-4920
TYPE OF INSTITUTION: Independent public agency providing venture capital financing to early-stage, high-risk technology-based companies located in the Commonwealth of Massachusetts
CONTACT OFFICER(S): John F. Hodgman, President
Robert J. Crowley, Vice President
ASSETS: $8,000,000
TYPES OF FINANCING: SECONDARY-MARKET CORPORATE SECURITIES: Debt & equity investments in early-stage, high-risk technology-based companies located in the Commonwealth of Massachusetts, VENTURE CAPITAL: Start-up from developed product stage; First-stage; Second-stage, LOANS: Unsecured; Working capital; Equity-related
PREFERRED TYPES OF INDUSTRIES/INVESTMENTS: MTDC invests in companies whose product is technology based and sufficiently innovative to give the company a marketing edge. MTDC's current portfolio encompasses, to name just a few, the following industries: computer software & hardware; materials science; fiber optics; automation-factory and publishing; laser technology; medical instrumentation; infra-red technology; and alternative energy
GEOGRAPHIC LIMITS OF INVESTMENTS/LOANS: State
RANGE OF INV./LOAN PER BUSINESS: Min. $100,000; Max. $300,000
BUSINESS CHARACTERISTICS DESIRED-REQUIRED: Minimum number of years in business: 0
REFERRALS ACCEPTED FROM: Investment/Mortgage banker or Borrower/Investee

COMPANY: **Morgan Holland Ventures Corp.**
ADDRESS: 1 Liberty Square, 8th Floor
Boston, MA 02109
PHONE: (617) 423-1765
TYPE OF INSTITUTION: Venture Capital

CONTACT OFFICER(S): Daniel J. Holland, Pres.
Jan Delahanty, V.P.

COMPANY: **Nautilus Fund, Inc.**
ADDRESS: 24 Federal Street
Boston, MA 02110
PHONE: (617) 482-8260
TYPE OF INSTITUTION: Venture Capital
CONTACT OFFICER(S): Richard A. Spillane, Jr.

COMPANY: **New England Mutual Life Insurance Co.**
ADDRESS: 501 Boylston Street
Boston, MA 02117
PHONE: (617) 266-3700
CONTACT OFFICER(S): John Rodgers, Sr. V.P. Securities
Hamilton Coolidge, Sr. V.P. Mortgage
ASSETS: 21,479,000,000 (& subs)
INVESTMENTS/LOANS MADE: For own account
INVESTMENTS/LOANS MADE: In securities with a secondary market and in securities without a secondary market
TYPES OF FINANCING: SECONDARY-MARKET CORPORATE SECURITIES: Common stock; Preferred stock; Bonds; Other: Convertibles. VENTURE CAPITAL: Research & Development; First-stage (less than 1 year); Second-stage (generally 1-3 years) Later-stage expansion; LOANS; Unsecured; Working capital (receivables/inventory); Equipment; Equity-related; REAL ESTATE LOANS: Intermediate-term senior mtg.; Wraparounds; Land; Land development; Construction; Industrial revenue bonds; Other: 2nd mtg. & blanket; LEASES: Single-investor; Leveraged; Tax leases; Non-tax leases; Operating; Lease syndications; REAL ESTATE: Acquisitions; Joint ventures; Partnerships/Syndications; OTHER SERVICES PROVIDED: discount brokerage tax shelter deals thru NESCO
GEOGRAPHIC LIMITS OF INVESTMENTS/LOANS: National
RANGE OF INV./LOAN PER BUSINESS: Min. $1 million; Max. $30 million
BUSINESS CHARACTERISTICS DESIRED-REQUIRED: Min. no. of years in business: 0
REFERRALS ACCEPTED FROM: Investment/Mortgage banker or Borrower/Investee
BRANCHES: Loomis, Sayles, & Co. Inc., 225 Franklin St., Boston, MA 02110; does own investing and all equity for parent

COMPANY: **Orange Nassau**
ADDRESS: One Post Office Square
Boston, MA 02109
PHONE: (617)
TYPE OF INSTITUTION: Venture Capital firm
CONTACT OFFICER(S): Joost E. Tjaden, President
Linda S. Linsalata, Vice President
Richard D. Tadler, Vice President (Dallas)
ASSETS: $85 million
INVESTMENTS/LOANS MADE: For own account; Through private placements; Through underwriting public offerings
TYPES OF FINANCING: SECONDARY-MARKET CORPORATE SECURITIES: Common stock; Preferred stock; VENTURE CAPITAL: Start-up from developed product stage; First-stage (less than 1 year); Second-stage (generally 1-3 years) Later-stage expansion; Buy-outs/Acquisitions; LOANS; Equity-related
PREFERRED TYPES OF INDUSTRIES/INVESTMENTS: Primarily in technology-based and oil and gas service industries. No real estate.
WILL NOT CONSIDER: Real estate
GEOGRAPHIC LIMITS OF INVESTMENTS/LOANS: None
RANGE OF INV./LOAN PER BUSINESS: Min. $500,000; Max. $5 million
BUSINESS CHARACTERISTICS DESIRED-REQUIRED: Min. no. of years in business: 0; Min. annual sales; nominal
REFERRALS ACCEPTED FROM: Investment/Mortgage banker or Borrower/Investee
BRANCHES: Richard D. Tadler, One Galleria Tower, Suite 635, 13355 Noel Road, Dallas, TX 75240, 214/385-9685
John W. Blackburn, Westerly Place, 1500 Quail Street, Suite 540, Newport Beach, CA 92660; 714/752-7811

COMPANY: **Plant Resources Venture Fund**
ADDRESS: 175 Federal Street
Boston, MA 02110
PHONE: (617) 542-5005
TYPE OF INSTITUTION: Venture Capital Fund
CONTACT OFFICER(S): John R. Hesse, Managing General Partner
Richard C. McGinity, General Partner
Richard O. Von Werssowetz, General Partner
INVESTMENTS/LOANS MADE: For own account
TYPES OF FINANCING: VENTURE CAPITAL: Start-up from developed product stage; First-stage; Second-stage; Later-stage expansion; Buy-outs/Acquisitions
PREFERRED TYPES OF INDUSTRIES/INVESTMENTS: Agricultural, Forestry and Fish technology, Biotechnology, Food technology, Water and Waste technology, Consumer Products in Horticulture and Agriculture, Computer Services and Software related to agriculture
GEOGRAPHIC LIMITS OF INVESTMENTS/LOANS: North America and U.K.
RANGE OF INV./LOAN PER BUSINESS: Min. $750,000; Max. $2,500,000
BUSINESS CHARACTERISTICS DESIRED-REQUIRED: Minimum number of years in business: 0; Other: Willing to consider companies experiencing operating losses.
REFERRALS ACCEPTED FROM: Investment/Mortgage banker or Borrower/Investee

COMPANY: **Regent Financial Corp.**
ADDRESS: 10 Commercial Wharf West
Boston, MA 02110
PHONE: (617) 723-4820
CONTACT OFFICER(S): Jason S. Rosenberg

COMPANY: **Schooner Capital Corporation**
ADDRESS: 77 Franklin Street
Boston, MA 02110
PHONE: (617) 357-9031

TYPE OF INSTITUTION: Private Venture Capital
CONTACT OFFICER(S): Bernice E. Bradin
INVESTMENTS/LOANS MADE: For own account
INVESTMENTS/LOANS MADE: Only in securities without a secondary market
TYPES OF FINANCING: VENTURE CAPITAL: First-stage; second-stage; Later-stage; Buy-outs/Acquisitions
PREFERRED TYPES OF INDUSTRIES/INVESTMENTS: Communications; Alternative energy
WILL NOT CONSIDER: Real Estate
GEOGRAPHIC LIMITS OF INVESTMENTS/LOANS: National
RANGE OF INV./LOAN PER BUSINESS: Min. $300,00017Min. annual cash flow positive

COMPANY: **Turner Revis Associates**
ADDRESS: 14 Union Wharf
Boston, MA 02109
PHONE: (617) 227-9734
TYPE OF INSTITUTION: Venture Capital
CONTACT OFFICER(S): John G. Turner, General Partner
Kenneth J. Revis, General Partner
ASSETS: $12,000,000 capacity under management
INVESTMENTS/LOANS MADE: For managed accounts
TYPES OF FINANCING: VENTURE CAPITAL: Start-up from developed product stage; First-stage
PREFERRED TYPES OF INDUSTRIES/INVESTMENTS: Primarily industrial electronics
WILL NOT CONSIDER: Real Estate
GEOGRAPHIC LIMITS OF INVESTMENTS/LOANS: State; Other: MA
RANGE OF INV./LOAN PER BUSINESS: Min. $250,000; Max. $750,000

COMPANY: **Burr, Egan, Deleage & Co.**
ADDRESS: One Post Office Square, Suite 3800
Boston MA 02109
PHONE: (617) 482-8020
CONTACT OFFICER(S): Boston:
William P. Egan
Craig L. Burr
Esther Sharp
Frank Kenny
Jonathan Flint
San Francisco:
Jean Deleage
Thomas Winter
Shirley Cerrudo
Jean-Bernard Schmidt
Brion Applegate
ASSETS: $200,000,000
INVESTMENTS/LOANS MADE: For own account
INVESTMENTS/LOANS MADE: In securities with a secondary market and in securities without a secondary market
TYPES OF FINANCING: SECONDARY-MARKET CORPORATE SECURITIES: Common Stock; Preferred stock; VENTURE CAPITAL: Research & Development; Start-up from developed product stage; First-stage; Second-stage; Later-stage expansion; Buy-outs/Acquisitions
PREFERRED TYPES OF INDUSTRIES/INVESTMENTS: Electronics, Health-related, communications
WILL NOT CONSIDER: Real estate, Oil & Gas
GEOGRAPHIC LIMITS OF INVESTMENTS/LOANS: National
RANGE OF INV./LOAN PER BUSINESS: Min. $750,000; Max. $5,000,000
BUSINESS CHARACTERISTICS DESIRED-REQUIRED: Minimum number of years in business: 0; Min. annual sales 0; Min. net worth 0; Min. annual net income 0; Min. annual cash flow 0; Other: Strong management team
REFERRALS ACCEPTED FROM: Investment/Mortgage banker or Borrower/Investee
BRANCHES: Mr. Jean Deleage, 3 Embarcadero Center, 25th floor, San Francisco, CA 94111; (415) 362-4022

COMPANY: **Applied Technology Partners, L.P.**
ADDRESS: 55 Wheeler St.
Cambridge, MA 02138
PHONE: (617) 354-4107
TYPE OF INSTITUTION: Venture Capital
CONTACT OFFICER(S): Frederick B. Bamber, Managing Director
ASSETS: $5¼ Million
INVESTMENTS/LOANS MADE: For own account
INVESTMENTS/LOANS MADE: In securities with a secondary market and in securities without a secondary market
TYPES OF FINANCING: SECONDARY-MARKET CORPORATE SECURITIES: Preferred stock; Bonds, VENTURE CAPITAL: Research & Development; Start-up from developed product stage; First-stage; Second-stage; Buy-outs/Acquisitions
PREFERRED TYPES OF INDUSTRIES/INVESTMENTS: Information processing industry; Computer hardware, software services; Communications products & services; Industrial Automation companies
WILL NOT CONSIDER: Anything outside the above list
RANGE OF INV./LOAN PER BUSINESS: Min. $200,000; Max. $600,000
REFERRALS ACCEPTED FROM: Investment/Mortgage banker or Borrower/Investee
BRANCHES: Tom Flaherty, Mike Mayers, One New York Plaza, 34th Floor, New York, NY 10004, 21/58-0206

COMPANY: **Arthur D. Little Enterprises, Inc.**
ADDRESS: 20 Acorn Park
Cambridge, MA 02140
PHONE: (617) 864-5700
TYPE OF INSTITUTION: Wholly-owned subsidiary of Arthur D. Little, Inc. - manages venture capital funds for the parent and for selected institutional investors
CONTACT OFFICER(S): Paul J. Ballantine, Senior Investment Analyst
ASSETS: $15,000,000
INVESTMENTS/LOANS MADE: For own account
INVESTMENTS/LOANS MADE: Only in securities without a secondary market
TYPES OF FINANCING: VENTURE CAPITAL: Start-up from developed product stage; First-stage; Second-stage
GEOGRAPHIC LIMITS OF INVESTMENTS/LOANS: East Coast
RANGE OF INV./LOAN PER BUSINESS: Min. $250,000; Max. $600,000

COMPANY: **Memorial Drive Trust**
ADDRESS: 20 Acorn Park
Cambridge, MA 02140
PHONE: (617) 864-5770
TYPE OF INSTITUTION: Diversified investment trust
CONTACT OFFICER(S): Jean deValpine, Chief Exec. Officer-Art, Intelligence, Robotics & Electronics
Jan Senerchia, Telecomm. Computer R.E.
Paul Shanwal, Energy related chem., Gen. mfg., Semiconductors
Schorr Berman, Computers, CadCam, Artificial intelligence, Consumer related, Bio-tech
ASSETS: $280,000,000
INVESTMENTS/LOANS MADE: For own account
INVESTMENTS/LOANS MADE: In securities with a secondary market and in securities without a secondary market
TYPES OF FINANCING: SECONDARY-MARKET CORPORATE SECURITIES: Common stock; Preferred stock; Other: Convertible notes, options, etc., VENTURE CAPITAL: First-stage (less than 1 year); Second-stage (generally 1-3 years); Later-stage expansion; Buy-outs/Acquisitions, REAL ESTATE: Partnerships/Syndications, OTHER SERVICES PROVIDED: Publicly traded bonds, direct investment, parcel developing
PREFERRED TYPES OF INDUSTRIES/INVESTMENTS: Telecommunications, micro-electronics, computer related, advanced materials, other "high-technology", artificial intelligence
GEOGRAPHIC LIMITS OF INVESTMENTS/LOANS: National, prefer regional
REFERRALS ACCEPTED FROM: Investment/Mortgage banker or Borrower/Investee

COMPANY: **Zero Stage Capital Co., Inc.**
ADDRESS: 156 Sixth Street
Cambridge, MA 02142
PHONE: (617) 876-5355
TYPE OF INSTITUTION: Private Venture Capital
CONTACT OFFICER(S): Paul M. Kelly, President
ASSETS: $5,000,000 (fund)
INVESTMENTS/LOANS MADE: For own account
INVESTMENTS/LOANS MADE: Only in securities without a secondary market
TYPES OF FINANCING: VENTURE CAPITAL: Start-up from developed product stage, OTHER SERVICES PROVIDED: Some bridge financing
PREFERRED TYPES OF INDUSTRIES/INVESTMENTS: High Technology
GEOGRAPHIC LIMITS OF INVESTMENTS/LOANS: Local; Other: Prefer 2 hours from Boston
RANGE OF INV./LOAN PER BUSINESS: Min. $50,000; Max. $150,000
PREFERRED TERM FOR LOANS & LEASES: Max. 10 years
BUSINESS CHARACTERISTICS DESIRED-REQUIRED: Other: Some proprietary aspect to the technology

COMPANY: **East Boston Community Development Corp.**
ADDRESS: 73 Marginal Street
East Boston, MA 02128
PHONE: (617) 569-5590
TYPE OF INSTITUTION: Venture Capital
ASSETS: $1,000,000
INVESTMENTS/LOANS MADE: For own account; For managed accounts
INVESTMENTS/LOANS MADE: In securities with a secondary market; In securities without a secondary market
TYPES OF FINANCING: VENTURE CPAITAL: Start-up from developed product stage; First-stage; Second-stage; Later-stage expansion; Buy-outs/Acquisitions, LOANS: Working capital; Equipment; Equity-related, REAL ESTATE LOANS: Subordinated; Land development; Constructions; Gap; Other: Secondary mtg., OTHER SERVICES PROVIDED: SBA financing
PREFERRED TYPES OF INDUSTRIES/INVESTMENTS: Job related, Manufacturing, Electronic assembly
GEOGRAPHIC LIMITS OF INVESTMENTS/LOANS: Local
RANGE OF INV./LOAN PER BUSINESS: Min. $50,000; Max. $1,000,000
BUSINESS CHARACTERISTICS DESIRED-REQUIRED: Investment/Mortgage banker; Borrower/Investee

COMPANY: **Stan Radler Associates, Inc.**
ADDRESS: 78 Pine Hill Road
Framingham, MA 01701
PHONE: (617) 875-1007
CONTACT OFFICER(S): Stan Radler, President
INVESTMENTS/LOANS MADE: For own account
INVESTMENTS/LOANS MADE: In securities with a secondary market and in securities without a secondary market
TYPES OF FINANCING: SECONDARY-MARKET CORPORATE SECURITIES: Common stock, VENTURE CAPITAL: Research & Development; Start-up from developed product stage; First-stage (less than 1 year); Second-stage (generally 1-3 years), INTERNATIONAL (including import/export), OTHER SERVICES PROVIDED: Comprehensive marketing consulting services for young and growth companies involved with high technology
PREFERRED TYPES OF INDUSTRIES/INVESTMENTS: High technology of all types
RANGE OF INV./LOAN PER BUSINESS: Min. $50,000; Max. $500,000
BUSINESS CHARACTERISTICS DESIRED-REQUIRED: Minimum number of years in business: 0; Min. annual sales 0; Min. net worth $50,000
REFERRALS ACCEPTED FROM: Borrower/Investee

COMPANY: **The Boston Venture Fund**
ADDRESS: The Liberties, S. Building 7, 33 Bedford Street
Lexington, MA 02173
PHONE: (617) 862-0269
TYPE OF INSTITUTION: Venture Capital
CONTACT OFFICER(S): Thomas Schinkel, President
INVESTMENTS/LOANS MADE: Through private placements
INVESTMENTS/LOANS MADE: Only in securities without a secondary market
TYPES OF FINANCING: VENTURE CAPITAL: Start-up from developed product stage; First-stage; Second-stage; Later-stage expansion; Buy-outs/Acquisitions
PREFERRED TYPES OF INDUSTRIES/INVESTMENTS: Fiber optics, Medical, Software

GEOGRAPHIC LIMITS OF INVESTMENTS/LOANS: Regional; Other: NE

COMPANY: **Acquivest Group, Inc.**
ADDRESS: One Newton Executive Park, Ste. 204
Newton, MA 02162
PHONE: (617) 527-5757
TYPE OF INSTITUTION: Venture capital and special situation investment firm
CONTACT OFFICER(S): S. John Loscocco, President
Richard L. Baird, Vice President
INVESTMENTS/LOANS MADE: For own account; For managed accounts
INVESTMENTS/LOANS MADE: In securities with a secondary market or in securities without a secondary market
TYPES OF FINANCING: SECONDARY-MARKET CORPORATE SECURITIES: Common stock, VENTURE CAPITAL: Later-stage expansion; Buy-outs/Acquisitions, OTHER SERVICES PROVIDED: Provides total sponsorship and backing for entrepreneurs to acquire businesses.
PREFERRED TYPES OF INDUSTRIES/INVESTMENTS: Will consider any field where new or continuing mangement has relevant know-how and experience.
GEOGRAPHIC LIMITS OF INVESTMENTS/LOANS: National
RANGE OF INV./LOAN PER BUSINESS: Min. $2.0 Million; Max. $20.0 Million
BUSINESS CHARACTERISTICS DESIRED-REQUIRED: Min. annual sales $2.0 million; Min. net worth $1.0 million; Demonstrable projection of at least $500,000 pre-tax, pre-interest income.
REFERRALS ACCEPTED FROM: Borrower/Investee

COMPANY: **Analog Devices Enterprises**
ADDRESS: Two Technology Way
Norwood, MA 02062
PHONE: (617) 329-4700
TYPE OF INSTITUTION: Venture Capital Subsidiary of Operating Company
CONTACT OFFICER(S): Robert A. Book
ASSETS: $28,000,000 (amt. invested)
INVESTMENTS/LOANS MADE: For own acount
INVESTMENTS/LOANS MADE: In securities with a secondary market; In securities without a secondary market
TYPES OF FINANCING: VENTURE CAPITAL: Start-up from developed product stage; First-stage; Second-stage; Later-stage expansion; Buy-outs/Acquisitions
PREFERRED TYPES OF INDUSTRIES/INVESTMENTS: High technology; Electronics, Communications; Industrial
GEOGRAPHIC LIMITS OF INVESTMENTS/LOANS: National; International
RANGE OF INV./LOAN PER BUSINESS: Min. $500,000
BUSINESS CHARACTERISTICS DESIRED-REQUIRED: Other: Look at companies individually
REMARKS: Average range of investment: $1,000,000 - $2,000,000

COMPANY: **Venture Founders Corp.**
ADDRESS: 100 Fifth Ave.
Waltham, MA 02155
PHONE: (617) 890-1000
TYPE OF INSTITUTION: Venture capital company
CONTACT OFFICER(S): Alexander L.M. Dingee, President
Leonard E. Smollen, Executive V.P.
Edward Getchell, V.P.
Ross Yeiter, Treasurer
Joseph M. Frye, Dr., Director European Operations
ASSETS: $80 million (worldwide)
INVESTMENTS/LOANS MADE: For own account
TYPES OF FINANCING: SECONDARY-MARKET CORPORATE SECURITIES: Common stock; Preferred stock, VENTURE CAPITAL: Research & Development; Start-up from developed product stage; First-stage; Second-stage; Later-stage expansion, INTERNATIONAL (including import/export)
PREFERRED TYPES OF INDUSTRIES/INVESTMENTS: High technology only, seed or start-up coupled with entrepreneur who has significant working experience in the proposed field. The entrepreneur team should have previous profit and loss management experience. Product or service must be sold on a national basis.
WILL NOT CONSIDER: Real estate, promotional, general construction, hotels, local retail, gas & oil, restaurants, motion pictures, gambling, finance & lending
GEOGRAPHIC LIMITS OF INVESTMENTS/LOANS: National, International, Other: Canada, U.K., Belgium
RANGE OF INV./LOAN PER BUSINESS: Min. $50,000; Max. $1,000,000
BUSINESS CHARACTERISTICS DESIRED-REQUIRED: Minimum number of years in business: 0
BRANCHES: Venture Founders Ltd., 39 The Green, South Bar St., Banbury, Oxon ENGLAND OX169AE, 011-44-295-65881, Charles Cox

COMPANY: **Plymouth Savings Bank**
ADDRESS: 226 Main Street, P.O. Box 431
Wareham, MA 02571
PHONE: (617) 295-3800
TYPE OF INSTITUTION: Bank—Mortgage banking, commercial lending
CONTACT OFFICER(S): Frank D. Fantasia, Sr. Vice President—Sr. Lending Officer
ASSETS: $270,000,000
TYPES OF FINANCING: VENTURE CAPITAL: Second-stage; Later-stage expansion, LOANS: Working capiital; Equipment; Equity-related, REAL ESTATE LOANS: Long-term senior mtg.; Intermediate-term senior mtg.; Wraparounds; Land; Land development; Construction; Standbys; Industrial revenue bonds, LEASES: Single-investor; Leveraged; Non-tax leases; Operating; Vendor financing programs, REAL ESTATE: Acquisitions; Joint ventures; Partnerships/Syndications
WILL NOT CONSIDER: Restaurants, motels
GEOGRAPHIC LIMITS OF INVESTMENTS/LOANS: Regional
RANGE OF INV./LOAN PER BUSINESS: Min. $25,000; Max. $500,000
REFERRALS ACCEPTED FROM: Investment/Mortgage banker or Borrower/Investee

COMPANY: **EG & G, Inc.**
ADDRESS: 45 William Street
Welleslay, MA 02181
PHONE: (617) 237-5100
TYPE OF INSTITUTION: Venture Capital Susidiary
CONTACT OFFICER(S): Bruce Robinson, Director of New Business Development, L. Dan Valente
INVESTMENT/LOANS MADE: For own account
TYPES OF FINANCING: VENTURE CAPITAL

COMPANY: **Fowler, Anthony & Co.**
ADDRESS: 20 Walnut St.
Wellesley, MA 02181
PHONE: (617) 237-4201
TYPE OF INSTITUTION: Private firm investing own capital and arranging private placements
CONTACT OFFICER(S): John A. Quagliaroli, President
INVESTMENTS/LOANS MADE: For own account; Through private placements; Through underwriting public offerings
INVESTMENTS/LOANS MADE: In securities with a secondary market and in securities without a secondary market
TYPES OF FINANCING: SECONDARY-MARKET CORPORATE SECURITIES, VENTURE CAPITAL: Research & Development; Start-up from developed product stage; First-stage (less than 1 year); Second-stage (generally 1-3 years); Later-stage expansion; Buy-outs/Acquisitions, LOANS, LEASES: Leveraged; Vendor financing programs, OTHER SERVICES PROVIDED: Business Mergers & Acquisitions
PREFERRED TYPES OF INDUSTRIES/INVESTMENTS: High Technology, eg., Computers, Software, Data Communications, Electronics (All Areas), Medical (Including Instrumentations), Technical Services, CATV, Publishing
WILL NOT CONSIDER: Most Real Estate
GEOGRAPHIC LIMITS OF INVESTMENTS/LOANS: Regional, prefer New England
RANGE OF INV./LOANS PER BUSINESS: Min. $25,000 - $200,000
BUSINESS CHARACTERISTICS DESIRED-REQUIRED: Min. no. of years in business: 0
REFERRALS ACCEPTED FROM: Investment/Mortgage banker or Borrower/Investee
REMARKS: Terms on case-by-case basis

COMPANY: **R.C. Berner & Co.**
ADDRESS: 65 William Street
Wellesley, MA 02181
PHONE: (617) 237-9472
TYPE OF INSTITUTION: Management consultants/merger managers/intermediaries in venture capital
CONTACT OFFICER(S): R.C. Berner, President
H.S. Berner, Treasurer
A.M. Albrecht, Asst. to President
ASSETS: Not relevant
TYPES OF FINANCING: VENTURE CAPITAL: Second-stage (generally 1-3 years); Later-stage expansion; Buy-outs/Acquisitions
PREFERRED TYPES OF INDUSTRIES/INVESTMENTS: Industries: computer related; medical; building materials; chemicals; electronics; leisure products; data communications; natural resources; retail; supermarkets; machinery
GEOGRAPHIC LIMITS OF INVESTMENTS/LOANS: National
RANGE OF INV./LOAN PER BUSINESS: Min. $500,000; Max. No maximum
BUSINESS CHARACTERISTICS DESIRED-REQUIRED: Minimum number of years in business: 1; Min. annual sales $500,000; Min. net worth $300,000; Min. annual net income $100,000; Min. annual cash flow $100,000
REFERRALS ACCEPTED FROM: Investment/Mortgage banker or Borrower/Investee
REMARKS: We act as intermediaries only, working on a retainer and success fee

COMPANY: **The Palmer Partners**
ADDRESS: 300 Unicorn Park Dr.
Woburn, MA 01801
PHONE: (617) 933-5445
TYPE OF INSTITUTION: Private Venture Capital Partnership
CONTACT OFFICER(S): Michael T. Fitzgerald, Investment Officer
Karen S. Camp, V.P.
Stephen J. Ricci, General Partner
ASSETS: Approx. $40 Million
INVESTMENTS/LOANS MADE: For own account
INVESTMENTS/LOANS MADE: In securities with a secondary market and in securities without a secondary market
TYPES OF FINANCING: VENTURE CAPITAL: Research & Development; Start-up from developed product stage; First-stage (less than 1 year); Second-stage (generally 1-3 years); Other: Later stage investment
PREFERRED TYPES OF INDUSTRIES/INVESTMENTS: Industrial Services; Manufacturing, particularily technology intensive products
WILL NOT CONSIDER: Turnarounds, Real Estate
GEOGRAPHIC LIMITS OF INVESTMENTS/LOANS: International
RANGE OF INV./LOAN PER BUSINESS: Min. $100,000; Max. $2,000,000
BUSINESS CHARACTERISTICS DESIRED-REQUIRED: Min. no. of years in business: 0

COMPANY: **Broventure Capital Management**
ADDRESS: 16 West Madison Street
Baltimore, MD 21201
PHONE: (301) 727-4520
TYPE OF INSTITUTION: Venture capital limited partnership
CONTACT OFFICER(S): William Gust, Partner
Harvey Branch, Partner
ASSETS: $50 Million
INVESTMENTS/LOANS MADE: For own account; Through private placements
INVESTMENTS/LOANS MADE: Only in securities without a secondary market
TYPES OF FINANCING: VENTURE CAPITAL: Start-up from developed product stage; First-stage (less than 1 year); Second-stage (generally 1-3 years)
PREFERRED TYPES OF INDUSTRIES/INVESTMENTS: Computers, Software, Telecommunications, Medical Products, Peripheral Equipment
WILL NOT CONSIDER: Oil/gas, Real Estate

GEOGRAPHIC LIMITS OF INVESTMENTS/LOANS: National
RANGE OF INV./LOAN PER BUSINESS: Min. $500,000; Max. $1,000,000
BUSINESS CHARACTERISTICS DESIRED-REQUIRED: Minimum number of years in business: 0
REFERRALS ACCEPTED FROM: Investment/Mortgage banker or Borrower/Investee

COMPANY: **Hotel Investors Trust**
ADDRESS: 5530 Wisconsin, Suite 1148
Chevy Chase, MD 20815
PHONE: (301) 656-1802
TYPE OF INSTITUTION: REIT
CONTACT OFFICER(S): Dale E. Moulton, V.P., Hotel Development
ASSETS: $94 million
INVESTMENTS/LOANS MADE: For own account
TYPES OF FINANCING: VENTURE CAPITAL: Start-up from developed product stage; First-stage; Buy-outs/Acquisitions, REAL ESTATE: Acquisitions; Joint ventures
PREFERRED TYPES OF INDUSTRIES/INVESTMENTS: Specifically hotels
WILL NOT CONSIDER: Small, budget hotels (but can)
GEOGRAPHIC LIMITS OF INVESTMENTS/LOANS: National
RANGE OF INV/LOAN PER BUSINESS: Min. $1 million; Max. $15 million
PREFERRED TERM FOR LOANS & LEASES: Min. 10; Max. None
BUSINESS CHARACTERISTICS DESIRED-REQUIRED: Minimum number of years in business: 0
REFERRALS ACCEPTED FROM: Investment/Mortgage banker or Borrower/Investee
REMARKS: Shares paired with Hotel Investors Corp.

COMPANY: **U.S. Venture Development Corp.**
ADDRESS: 2038 Forest Hill Lane
Crofton, MD 21114
PHONE: (301) 858-1164
TYPE OF INSTITUTION: Business Development Company
CONTACT OFFICER(S): Keith S. Richardson, Pres., CEO
C. Stevens Avery II, Chairman
ASSETS: $2,500,000 to $4,500,000 after current public offering
INVESTMENTS/LOANS MADE: For own account
INVESTMENTS/LOANS MADE: In securities with and without a secondary market
TYPES OF FINANCING: SECONDARY-MARKET CORPORATE SECURITIES: Common stock; Other: Units, Generally common stock and warrants; VENTURE CAPITAL: Start-up from developed product stage; First-stage; Second-stage; Buy-outs/Acquisitions; LOANS: Other: Bridge; OTHER SERVICES PROVIDED: Business Managerial & financial public relations
PREFERRED TYPES OF INDUSTRIES/INVESTMENTS: Medical technology companies who appear to be candidates for a public offering within one year. Other industries or technologies: Electronics, semiconductors, data communication, computers, analytical instrumentation, robotics, biotechnology, energy technology and telecommunications
WILL NOT CONSIDER: Brokerage firms, insurance companies, investment banking & investment cos.
GEOGRAPHIC LIMITS OF INVESTMENTS/LOANS: National; Other: Prefer local and/or regional (Mid-Atlantic)
RANGE OF INV./LOAN PER BUSINESS: Min. $50,000; Max. $150,000
PREFERRED TERM FOR LOANS & LEASES: Min. 6-12 mos.-one; Max. 5 years
BUSINESS CHARACTERISTICS DESIRED-REQUIRED: Minimum number of years in business: 0
REFERRALS ACCEPTED FROM: Investment/Mortgage banker or Borrower/Investee
BRANCHES: Mr. C. Stevens Avery-Chairman, 4801 Mass. Ave. N.W., Ste. 400, Washington, D.C., 20016, (202) 364-8890 ;
Mr. Peter W. Gavian, 1326 R. St. N.W., Washington, D.C. 20009, 202-328-9053

COMPANY: **Maine Capital Corp.**
ADDRESS: Seventy Center St.
Portland, ME 04101
PHONE: (207) 772-1001
TYPE OF INSTITUTION: Venture Capital Co.
CONTACT OFFICER(S): David N. Coit, President
ASSETS: $1,000,000
INVESTMENTS/LOANS MADE: For own account
INVESTMENTS/LOANS MADE: Only in securities without a secondary market
TYPES OF FINANCING: VENTURE CAPITAL: Start-up from developed product stage; First-stage; Second-stage; Later-stage expansion; Buy-outs/Acquisitions; LOANS: Equity-related
PREFERRED TYPES OF INDUSTRIES/INVESTMENTS: Growth oriented businesses
GEOGRAPHIC LIMITS OF INVESTMENTS/LOANS: State
RANGE OF INV./LOAN PER BUSINESS: Min. $100,000; Max. $150,000
BUSINESS CHARACTERISTICS DESIRED-REQUIRED: Minimum number of years in business: 0
REFERRALS ACCEPTED FROM: Investment/Mortgage banker or Borrower/Investee

COMPANY: **L. J. Johnson & Co.**
ADDRESS: 2705 Lowell Rd.
Ann Arbor, MI 48103
PHONE: (313) 996-8033
TYPE OF INSTITUTION: Venture Capital
CONTACT OFFICER(S): L. J. Johnson

COMPANY: **Taurus Financial Group, Inc.**
ADDRESS: 601 South Norton Road, Suite A-8
Corunna, MI 48817
PHONE: (517) 743-5729
TYPE OF INSTITUTION: A licensed investment advisory and underwriting firm.
CONTACT OFFICER(S): Robert G. Machala, President, Corporate & Real Estate
Cory B. Weston, V.P., Equity and Debt Funding
Robin K. Mitchell, V.P., Offshore Funding

ASSETS: $5 million plus
INVESTMENTS/LOANS MADE: For managed accounts; Through private placements
INVESTMENTS/LOANS MADE: In securities with a secondary market and in securities without a secondary market
TYPES OF FINANCING: SECONDARY-MARKET CORPORATE SECURITIES: Common stock; Bonds, VENTURE CAPITAL: Second-stage (generally 1-3 years); Later-stage expansion; Buy-outs/Acquisitions, LOANS: Working capital (receivables/inventory); Equipment; Equity-related, REAL ESTATE LOANS: Long-term senior mtg.; Wraparounds; Land development, INTERNATIONAL (including import/export), REAL ESTATE: Acquisitions; Joint ventures,
PREFERRED TYPES OF INDUSTRIES/INVESTMENTS: No Preference
GEOGRAPHIC LIMITS OF INVESTMENTS/LOANS: International; Only in the Free World
RANGE OF INV./LOAN PER BUSINESS: Min. $3 million; Max. $50 million or more
PREFERRED TERM FOR LOANS & LEASES: Min. 5; Max. 15 years
BUSINESS CHARACTERISTICS DESIRED-REQUIRED: Minimum number of years in business: 3; Min. annual sales $5 million; Min net worth $4 million; Min. annual net income $1.5 million; Min. annual cash flow $1.5 million
REFERRALS ACCEPTED FROM: Investment/Mortgage banker or Borrower/Investee
REMARKS: Branches are planned for Denver, CO, and Toronto, Canada

COMPANY: **Michigan Investment Fund, L.P.**
ADDRESS: 333 E. Main St., 3rd Floor
Midland, MI 48640
PHONE: (517) 631-2471
TYPE OF INSTITUTION: Venture Capital
CONTACT OFFICER(S): Ian R. N. Bund

COMPANY: **Cherry Tree Ventures**
ADDRESS: 3600 West 80th Street, Suite 640
Bloomington, MN 55431
PHONE: (612) 893-9012
TYPE OF INSTITUTION: Private Venture Capital Fund
CONTACT OFFICER(S): Gordon F. Stofer, General Partner
Tony J. Christianson, General Partner
Michael K. Butler, Investment Officer
Buzz Benson, Investment Officer
Thomas W. Jackson, Investment Officer
ASSETS: $40,000,000
INVESTMENTS/LOANS MADE: For own account; Through private placement
INVESTMENTS/LOANS MADE: Only in securities without a secondary market
TYPES OF FINANCING: VENTURE CAPITAL: Research & Development; Start-up from developed product stage; First-stage; Second-stage
PREFERRED TYPES OF INDUSTRIES/INVESTMENTS: Health Care, Hardware, Software, Corporate Services, and Consumer Services
WILL NOT CONSIDER: Real Estate
GEOGRAPHIC LIMITS OF INVESTMENTS/LOANS: Other: Prefer upper midwest
RANGE OF INV./LOAN PER BUSINESS: Min. $100,000; Max. $1,500,000
BUSINESS CHARACTERISTICS DESIRED-REQUIRED: Minimum number of years in business: 0
REMARKS: Loans made only in anticipated of conversion to equity

COMPANY: **Microtechnology Investments Ltd.**
ADDRESS: 3400 Comserv Drive
Eagan, MN 55122
PHONE: (612) 681-7581
TYPE OF INSTITUTION: Venture Capital
CONTACT OFFICER(S): M. M. Stuckey, Chairman
ASSETS: $500,000
INVESTMENTS/LOANS MADE: For own account; For managed accounts
TYPES OF FINANCING: VENTURE CAPITAL: Start-up from developed product stage; First-stage; Second-stage; Buy-outs/Acquisitions
PREFERRED TYPES OF INDUSTRIES/INVESTMENTS: Micro marketplace emphasis on software
GEOGRAPHIC LIMITS OF INVESTMENTS/LOANS: National; Other: West Coast, NW
RANGE OF INV./LOAN PER BUSINESS: Min. $250,000; Max. $500,000
BUSINESS CHARACTERISTICS DESIRED-REQUIRED: Other: Start-ups
BRANCHES: M. Stuckey, 46 Red Birch Ct., Danville, CA 94526, (415) 838-9319

COMPANY: **Pathfinder Venture Captial Fund**
ADDRESS: 7300 Metro Blvd., Suite 585
Minneapolis, MN 55435
PHONE: (612) 835-1121
TYPE OF INSTITUTION: Private venture capital fund
CONTACT OFFICER(S): Andrew J. Greenshields, General Partner
Gary A. Stoltz, General Partner
Norman Dann, General Partner
Marvin Bookin, General Partner
Jack K. Ahrens, General Partner
ASSETS: $73 million
INVESTMENTS/LOANS MADE: For own account
INVESTMENTS/LOANS MADE: in securities with or without a secondary market
TYPES OF FINANCING: VENTURE CAPITAL: Research & Development; Start-up from developed product stage; First-stage; Second-stage; Later-stage expansion; Buyouts/Acquisitions; LOANS: Equity - related
PREFERRED TYPES OF INDUSTRIES/INVESTMENTS: Computer; Medical; Communication industries
WILL NOT CONSIDER: Real estate and natural resources
GEOGRAPHIC LIMITS OF INVESTMENTS/LOANS: National
RANGE OF INV./LOAN PER BUSINESS: Min. $100,000; Max. $2,500,000
PREFERRED TERM FOR LOANS & LEASES: Min. 5 years; Max. 10 years
BUSINESS CHARACTERISTICS DESIRED-REQUIRED: Minimum number of years in business: 0

REFERRALS ACCEPTED FROM: Investment/Mortgage banker or Borrower/Investee

COMPANY: **Control Data Capital Corp.**
ADDRESS: 3601 West 77th Street
Minneapolis, MN 55435
PHONE: (612) 921-4118
TYPE OF INSTITUTION: Venture Capital
CONTACT OFFICER(S): Douglas Craig Curtis, Jr., President
INVESTMENTS/LOANS MADE: For own account
TYPES OF FINANCING: VENTURE CAPITAL: Research & Development; Start-up fom developed product stage; First-stage; Second-stage; Later-stage expansion
PREFERRED TYPES OF INDUSTRIES/INVESTMENTS: Electronics, Computer related, Medical, Telecommunications, Artificial Intelligence, Diversified
WILL NOT CONSIDER: Retail, Real estate, Motion pictures, Hospitality services
GEOGRAPHIC LIMITS OF INVESTMENTS/LOANS: National
RANGE OF INV./LOAN PER BUSINESS: Min. $250,000; Max. $1,000,000
BUSINESS CHARACTERISTICS DESIRED-REQUIRED: Minimum number of years in business: 0

COMPANY: **FBS Venture Capital Co.**
ADDRESS: 7515 Wayzata Blvd.
Minneapolis, MN 55426
PHONE: (612) 544-2754
TYPE OF INSTITUTION: Independent, Privately-held Venture Capital Corporation
CONTACT OFFICER(S): William B. McKee, President
W. Ray Allen, Exec. V.P.
Brian Johnson, V.P.
Randy Stolworthy, V.P.
ASSETS: $30,000,000
INVESTMENTS/LOANS MADE: For own account
INVESTMENTS/LOANS MADE: In securities with a secondary market and in securities without a secondary market
TYPES OF FINANCING: VENTURE CAPITAL: Research & Development; Start-up from developed product stage; First-stage (less than 1 year); Second-stage (generally 1-3 years); Later-stage expansion; Buy-outs/Acquisitions
PREFERRED TYPES OF INDUSTRIES/INVESTMENTS: Manufacturing Industries Preferred
WILL NOT CONSIDER: Distributorships, Franchises
GEOGRAPHIC LIMITS OF INVESTMENTS/LOANS: Local; MN, WI, IA, ND, SD
RANGE OF INV./LOAN PER BUSINESS: Min. None; Max. $500,000
BUSINESS CHARACTERISTICS DESIRED-REQUIRED: Min. no. of years in business: 0; Prefer $300-500K of sales and up
REFERRALS ACCEPTED FROM: Investment/Mortgage banker or Borrower/Investee
BRANCHES: 1) Phoenix, AZ;
2) Denver, CO

COMPANY: **Lease Moore Equipment, Inc.**
ADDRESS: 2318 Park Ave. S.
Minneapolis, MN 55404
PHONE: (612) 872-4929
TYPE OF INSTITUTION: Financial services
CONTACT OFFICER(S): C. Moore, President
S. Braatz, Credit Mgr.
ASSETS: $10-20 million
INVESTMENTS/LOANS MADE: For own account
TYPES OF FINANCING: VENTURE CAPITAL: Buy-outs/Acquisitions, LOANS: Equipment, LEASES: Non-tax leases; Vendor financing programs
PREFERRED TYPES OF INDUSTRIES/INVESTMENTS: EDP, medical, construction and hospitality (strong operators)
GEOGRAPHIC LIMITS OF INVESTMENTS/LOANS: National
RANGE OF INV./LOAN PER BUSINESS: Min. $6,000; Max. $1,000,000
PREFERRED TERM FOR LOANS & LEASES: Min. 1 year; Max. 7 years
BUSINESS CHARACTERISTICS DESIRED-REQUIRED: Minimum number of years in business: 3

COMPANY: **Minneapolis Technology Fund**
ADDRESS: 1313 5th St., S.E.
Minneapolis, MN 55414
PHONE: (612) 623-7774
TYPE OF INSTITUTION: Venture Capital
CONTACT OFFICER(S): Terry Hitchcock
ASSETS: $5,000,000

COMPANY: **Minneapolis Technology Enterprise Center**
ADDRESS: 1313 5th St. S.E.
Minneapolis, MN 55414
PHONE: (612) 623-7774
TYPE OF INSTITUTION: Venture Capital; Operating Center for Start-ups
CONTACT OFFICER(S): H. Jan DeZeeuw, President
ASSETS: $3,000,000
INVESTMENTS/LOANS MADE: Through private placements
INVESTMENTS/LOANS MADE: In securities with a secondary market; In securities without a secondary market
TYPES OF FINANCING: VENTURE CAPITAL: Research & Development; Start-ups from developed product stage; First-stage; Second-stage; Later-stage expansion
PREFERRED TYPES OF INDUSTRIES/INVESTMENTS: Medical, Computer
GEOGRAPHIC LIMITS OF INVESTMENTS/LOANS: State; Other: MN
RANGE OF INV./LOAN PER BUSINESS: Min. $25,000; Max. $500,000
BUSINESS CHARACTERISTICS DESIRED-REQUIRED: Other: Growth potential

COMPANY: **Northern Boundary Partners Ltd.**
ADDRESS: 733 Marquette Avenue, Suite 800
Minneapolis, MN 55402
PHONE: (612) 371-8375
TYPE OF INSTITUTION: Venture Capital, Affiliate of Piper Jaffray & Hopwood, Inc.

CONTACT OFFICER(S): R. Hunt Greene, First Vice President
Frank B. Bennett
ASSETS: $10,000,000
INVESTMENTS/LOANS MADE: For own account; For managed accounts; Through private placements; Through underwriting public offerings
INVESTMENTS/LOANS MADE: In securities with a secondary market; In securities without a secondary market
TYPES OF FINANCING: VENTURE CAPITAL: Research & Development; Start-up from developed product stage; First-stage; Second-stage; Later-stage expansion; Buy-outs/Acquisitions
GEOGRAPHIC LIMITS OF INVESTMENTS/LOANS: National
RANGE OF INV./LOAN PER BUSINESS: $200,000
BUSINESS CHARACTERISTICS DESIRED-REQUIRED: Minimum number of years in business: 0; Other: Nominal financial statements, projections & business plan
BRANCHES: Gary Packas, Vice President, 1700 IBM Bldg.; Seattle, WA 98101, (206) 223-3800

COMPANY: **Norwest Venture Capital Management, Inc.**
ADDRESS: 1730 Midwest Plaza Bldg.
Minneapolis, MN 55402
PHONE: (612) 372-8770
TYPE OF INSTITUTION: Venture capital firm
CONTACT OFFICER(S): Robert F.Zicarelli, Chairman
Daniel J. Haggerty, Pres.
Douglas E. Johnson, VP
Leonard J. Brandt, VP
Timothy A. Steponek, VP
John E. Lindahl, VP
John P. Whaley, Treaser
Anthony J. Miadich, VP (Portland)
Dale R. Vogel, VP (Portland)
Larry R. Wonnacott (Denver)
Mark Dubovoy (Denver)
ASSETS: $270 million
INVESTMENTS/LOANS MADE: For own account; For managed accounts
INVESTMENTS/LOANS MADE: only in securities without a secondary market
TYPES OF FINANCING: Other: Private Placements of equity in venture capital and LBO opportunities; VENTURE CAPITAL: Research & Development; Start-up from developed product stage; First-stage (less than 1 year); Second-staged (generally 1-3 years); Buy-outs/ Acquisitions
WILL NOT CONSIDER: Real Estate, Development
GEOGRAPHIC LIMITS OF INVESTMENTS/LOANS: National
RANGE OF INV./LOAN PER BUSINESS: Min. $750,000; Max. $3,000,000
PREFERRED TERM FOR LOANS & LEASES: Min. N/A Max. N/A
BUSINESS CHARACTERISTICS DESIRED-REQUIRED: Min. no. of years in business: 0
BRANCHES: 1801 California St., Suite 585, Denver, CO 80202; 303-297-0537; Larry R. Wonnacott
1300 Southwest 5th Avenue, Suite 3018, Portland, OR 97201; 503-223-6622; Anthony J. Miadich

COMPANY: **Piper Jaffray & Hopwood, Inc.**
ADDRESS: 733 Marquette Ave., Suite 800
Minneapolis, MN 55402
PHONE: (612) 371-6111
TYPE OF INSTITUTION: Investment bank
CONTACT OFFICER(S): Hunt Greene, V.P.
INVESTMENTS/LOANS MADE: For own account, Through private placements, Through underwriting public offerings
INVESTMENTS/LOANS MADE: In securities with a secondary market and in securities without a secondary market
TYPES OF FINANCING: VENTURE CAPITAL: Research & Development; Start-up from developed product stage; First-stage; Second-stage; Later-stage expansion; Buy-outs/Acquisitons, LOANS: Equity-related; Other: Leverage buy-outs, REAL ESTATE LOANS: Long-term senior mtg.; Intermediate-term senior mtg.; Subordinated; Wraparounds; Industrial revenue bonds, OTHER SERVICES PROVIDED: Tax incentives
PREFERRED TYPES OF INDUSTRIES/INVESTMENTS: High-technology; Medical; Electronics
WILL NOT CONSIDER: Land per se
GEOGRAPHIC LIMITS OF INVESTMENTS/LOANS: Regional; National
BUSINESS CHARACTERISTICS DESIRED-REQUIRED: Minimum number of years in business: 0; Min. annual sales 0; Min. net worth 0; Min. annual net income 0; Min. annual cash flow 0
REMARKS: 42 branches (sales offices)

COMPANY: **St. Anthony Holding Co.**
ADDRESS: 529 South Seventh St.
Minneapolis, MN 55415
PHONE: (612) 332-8405
CONTACT OFFICER(S): Robert Andrews, Jr., Vice President
INVESTMENTS/LOANS MADE: For own account
INVESTMENTS/LOANS MADE: In securities without a secondary market
TYPES OF FINANCING: VENTURE CAPITAL: Start-up from developed product stage, LOANS: Equity-related; Other: Secured, REAL ESTATE: Acquisitions, OTHER SERVICES PROVIDED: Purchase-leasebacks
PREFERRED TYPES OF INDUSTRIES/INVESTMENTS: Historically paper and printing industries, Light manufacturing, Will consider others
GEOGRAPHIC LIMITS OF INVESTMENTS/LOANS: Local
RANGE OF INV./LOAN PER BUSINESS: Max. $500,000
BUSINESS CHARACTERISTICS DESIRED-REQUIRED: Minimum number of years in business: 5

COMPANY: **Washington Square Capital, Inc.**
ADDRESS: 100 Washington Square, Box 20
Minneapolis, MN 55440
PHONE: (612) 375-7541
TYPE OF INSTITUTION: Investment Advisory Firm
CONTACT OFFICER(S): Donald M. Feroe, V.P., Corporate Securities
Harold W. Leiferman, V.P., Mortgage Loans
Gary J. Kallsen, V.P., Real Estate

ASSETS: $2,800,000,000
INVESTMENTS/LOANS MADE: For managed accounts; Through private placements
INVESTMENTS/LOANS MADE: In securities with a secondary market and in securities without a secondary market
TYPES OF FINANCING: SECONDARY-MARKET CORPORATE SECURITIES: Bonds, VENTURE CAPITAL: Later-stage expansion; Buy-outs/ Acquisitions, LOANS: Unsecured to credits above Baa; Working capital (receivables/inventory); Equipment; Equity-related, REAL ESTATE LOANS: Intermediate-term senior mtg.; Wraparounds; Construction; Standbys; Loan Guarantees, LEASES: Leveraged; Non-tax leases; Vendor financing programs, REAL ESTATE: Acquisitions; Joint ventures
PREFERRED TYPES OF INDUSTRIES/INVESTMENTS: Any
GEOGRAPHIC LIMITS OF INVESTMENTS/LOANS: U.S. and Canada
RANGE OF INV./LOAN PER BUSINESS: Min. $2,000,000; Max. $25,000,000
PREFERRED TERM FOR LOANS & LEASES: Min. 1; Max. 10 years
BUSINESS CHARACTERISTICS DESIRED-REQUIRED: Minimum number of years in business: 5
REFERRALS ACCEPTED FROM: Investment/Mortgage banker or Borrower/Investee

COMPANY:**Minnesota Seed Capital, Inc.**
ADDRESS: Parkdale Plaza, 1660 South Highway 100, Suite 146
Minneapolis MN 55416
PHONE: (612) 545-5684
TYPE OF INSTITUTION: Independent Venture Capital (Seed Capital) Fund
CONTACT OFFICER(S): Richard C. Gottier, Managing Partner
Thomas M. Neitge, Managing Partner
ASSETS: $7 million
INVESTMENTS/LOANS MADE: For own account
TYPES OF FINANCING: VENTURE CAPITAL: Research & Development; Start-up from developed product stage; First-stage; LOANS: Equity-related
PREFERRED TYPES OF INDUSTRIES/INVESTMENTS: Technology oriented opportunities: Telecommunications, computer and computer related, medical products, electronics, composite materials, process control, manufacturing
GEOGRAPHIC LIMITS OF INVESTMENTS/LOANS: State
RANGE OF INV./LOAN PER BUSINESS: Min. $50,000; Max. $500,000
BUSINESS CHARACTERISTICS DESIRED-REQUIRED: Minimum number of years in business: 0; Other: Start-ups to development stage opportunities
REFERRALS ACCEPTED FROM: Investment/Mortgage banker or Borrower/Investee

COMPANY: **Growth Ventures, Inc.**
ADDRESS: 1550 Norwest Center
St. Paul, MN 55101
PHONE: (612) 292-0199
TYPE OF INSTITUTION: Venture Capital
CONTACT OFFICER(S): Richard W. Mannillo, President
Linda Anderson, Assistant V.P.
INVESTMENTS/LOANS MADE: Through private placements
TYPES OF FINANCING: VENTURE CAPITAL: Research & Development; Start-up from developed product stage; Buy-outs/Acquisitions
PREFERRED TYPES OF INDUSTRIES/INVESTMENTS: Commercial real estate, Food industries
WILL NOT CONSIDER: Computers and technology related
GEOGRAPHIC LIMITS OF INVESTMENTS/LOANS: Local; State; International
RANGE OF INV./LOAN PER BUSINESS: Min. $500,000
BUSINESS CHARACTERISTICS DESIRED-REQUIRED: Other: Compatible with existing projects
REFERRALS ACCEPTED FROM: Investment/Mortgage banker; Borrower/Investee

COMPANY: **MIMLIC Asset Management Co.**
ADDRESS: 400 North Robert
St. Paul, MN 55101
PHONE: (612) 298-3844
TYPE OF INSTITUTION: Registered investment advisor for MN Mutual Life and its subsidiaries
CONTACT OFFICER(S): Fritz Feuerherm, Sr. Inv. Off., Bonds, Fixed Income
John Clymer, Sr. Inv. Officer, Mortgage & RE
Tim Kasper, Sr. Inv. Officer, Equity
ASSETS: $2.8 billion
INVESTMENTS/LOANS MADE: In securities with a secondary market and in securities without a secondary market
TYPES OF FINANCING: SECONDARY-MARKET CORPORATE SECURITIES: Common stock; Preferred stock; Bonds; Other: Limited partnerships. VENTURE CAPITAL: Later-stage expansion; Oil exploration. LOANS: Unsecured; Working capital; Equipment; Equity-related. REAL ESTATE LOANS: Long-term senior mtg.; Intermediate-term senior mtg.; Subordinated; Wraparounds; Land; Land development. LEASES: Leveraged; Non-tax leases; Operating; Other: equipment. REAL ESTATE: Acquisitions; Joint ventures; Partnerships/Syndications.
PREFERRED TYPES OF INDUSTRIES/INVESTMENTS: Mostly fixed incomes
GEOGRAPHIC LIMITS OF INVESTMENTS/LOANS: National
RANGE OF INV./LOAN PER BUSINESS: Min. $1 million
BUSINESS CHARACTERISTICS DESIRED-REQUIRED: Minimum number of years in business: 5
REFERRALS ACCEPTED FROM: Investment/Mortgage banker or Borrower/Investee

COMPANY: **Mutual Service Life Insurance Co.**
ADDRESS: Two Pine Tree Dr.
St. Paul, MN 55112
PHONE: (612) 631-7000
CONTACT OFFICER(S): Loren A. Haugland, VP Investments
INVESTMENTS/LOANS MADE: In securities with a secondary market and in securities without a secondary market

TYPES OF FINANCING: SECONDARY-MARKET CORPORATE SECURITIES: Common stock; Preferred stock; Bonds. VENTURE CAPITAL. REAL ESTATE LOANS: Intermediate-term senior mtg.; Wraparounds; Other: will do second mortgages. LEASES: Single-investor; Leveraged. REAL ESTATE: Acquisitions. OTHER SERVICES PROVIDED: Participate in most phases of venture capital through pooling
GEOGRAPHIC LIMITS OF INVESTMENTS/LOANS: National
RANGE OF INV./LOAN PER BUSINESS: Min. $250,000; Max. $3 million
PREFERRED TERM FOR LOANS & LEASES: Min. 3 years
REFERRALS ACCEPTED FROM: Investment/Mortgage banker or Borrower/Investee

COMPANY: **Donelan, Phelps & Co., Inc.**
ADDRESS: 7800 Bonhomme
Clayton, MO 63105
PHONE: (314) 863-0600
TYPE OF INSTITUTION: Independent investment firm
CONTACT OFFICER(S): Thomas E. Phelps, President
Mark J. Lincoln, Vice President/Chief Financial Officer
INVESTMENTS/LOANS MADE: For own account, For managed accounts, Through private placements
TYPES OF FINANCING: VENTURE CAPITAL: Buy-outs/Acquisitions
GEOGRAPHIC LIMITS OF INVESTMENTS/LOANS: Regional
RANGE OF INV./LOAN PER BUSINESS: Min. $100,000

COMPANY: **Intercapco West, Inc.**
ADDRESS: 7800 Bonhomme
Clayton, MO 63105
PHONE: (314) 863-0600
TYPE OF INSTITUTION: Privately owned Small Business Investment Company
CONTACT OFFICER(S): Thomas E. Phelps, President
Mark J. Lincoln, Vice President/Chief Investment Officer
INVESTMENTS/LOANS MADE: For own account, Through private placements
TYPES OF FINANCING: VENTURE CAPITAL: Second-stage; Later-stage expansion; Buy-outs/Acquisitions
GEOGRAPHIC LIMITS OF INVESTMENTS/LOANS: Regional
RANGE OF INV./LOAN PER BUSINESS: Min. $100,000
BUSINESS CHARACTERISTICS DESIRED-REQUIRED: Minimum number of years in business: 2+; Min. annual net income $ positive.
REFERRALS ACCEPTED FROM: Investment/Mortgage banker or Borrower/Investee

COMPANY:**Harbour Group Investments**
ADDRESS: 7701 Forsyth Boulevard, Suite 550
St. Louis MO 63105
PHONE: (314) 727-5550
TYPE OF INSTITUTION: Private firm investing risk capital of financial institutions
CONTACT OFFICER(S): Douglas J. Von Allmen, Vice President
Peter S. Finley, Director of Corporate Development
ASSETS: $35 million of equity
INVESTMENTS/LOANS MADE: For managed accounts
INVESTMENTS/LOANS MADE: In securities with a secondary market and in securities without a secondary market
TYPES OF FINANCING: VENTURE CAPITAL: Research & Development; Buy-outs/Acquistions
PREFERRED TYPES OF INDUSTRIES/INVESTMENTS: Acquire manufacturing companies with $2 to $20 million of pretax profits and provide equity capital for Management Buyouts
WILL NOT CONSIDER: Anything other than buyouts of profitable companies
GEOGRAPHIC LIMITS OF INVESTMENTS/LOANS: International
RANGE OF INV./LOAN PER BUSINESS: Min. $1 million; Max. $7 million of equity
BUSINESS CHARACTERISTICS DESIRED-REQUIRED: Min. number of years in business: 5; Min. annual sales: $10 million; Min. annual net income: $1 million; Min. annual cash flow: $2 million
REFERRALS ACCEPTED FROM: Investment/Mortgage banker; Borrower/Investee

COMPANY: **The Reliable Life Insurance Company**
ADDRESS: 231 W. Lockwood
Webster Groves, MO 63119
PHONE: (314) 968-4900
CONTACT OFFICER(S): Lisa Luehrman, V.P.
ASSETS: $260 million
INVESTMENTS/LOANS MADE: In securities with a secondary market and in securities without a secondary-market
TYPES OF FINANCING: SECONDARY-MARKET CORPORATE SECURITIES: Common stock; Preferred stock; Bonds; VENTURE CAPITAL: First-stage; Second-stage; Buy-outs/Acquisitions; LOANS: Equity-related; REAL ESTATE LOANS: Long-term senior mtg.; Intermediate-term senior mtg.; Land; Land development; Construction; Standbys; REAL ESTATE: Acquisitions; Partnerships/Syndications
GEOGRAPHIC LIMITS OF INVESTMENTS/LOANS: Regional; Midwest; South; Southwest
RANGE OF INV./LOAN PER BUSINESS: Max. 10 years
PREFERRED TERM FOR LOANS & LEASES: Max. 10 years
REFERRALS ACCEPTED FROM: Investment/Mortgage banker only
REMARKS: Have a number of wholly-owned subsidiaries through the Midwest; 50 locations —insurance; all investing done through this office

COMPANY: **Southern Farm Bureau Life Insurance Company**
ADDRESS: 1401 Livingston Lane, P.O. Box 78
Jackson, MS 39213
PHONE: (601) 981-7422
CONTACT OFFICER(S): Walter J. Olson, III Portfolio Mgr.
Joel M. Melton, Manager, Mortgage Loans and Real Estate Department
Jerry Betterson, Investment Analyst
ASSETS: $1,300,000,000.00

INVESTMENTS/LOANS MADE: For own account
INVESTMENTS/LOANS MADE: In securities with a secondary market and in securities without a secondary market
TYPES OF FINANCING: LOANS: SECONDARY-MARKET CORPORATE SECURITIES: Common stock; Bonds; VENTURE CAPITAL: Later-stage expansion; Buy-outs/Acquisitions; LOANS: Unsecured to credits above BAA; Equipment; Equity-related; REAL ESTATE LOANS: Intermediate-term senior mtg.; Wraparounds; Construction; Standbys; Industrial revenue bonds; REAL ESTATE: Acquisitions; Joint ventures; OTHER SERVICES PROVIDED: Mortgage Banking
PREFERRED TYPES OF INDUSTRIES/INVESTMENTS: Will consider most types.
WILL NOT CONSIDER: Some S & L and Finance
GEOGRAPHIC LIMITS OF INVESTMENTS/LOANS: National
RANGE OF INV./LOAN PER BUSINESS: Min. $500,000; Max. $5,000,000
PREFERRED TERM FOR LOANS & LEASES: Min. 1; Max. 10 years
BUSINESS CHARACTERISTICS DESIRED-REQUIRED: A rated or equivalent

COMPANY: **Bankers Life Insurance Company of Nebraska**
ADDRESS: 5900 "O" St.
Lincoln, NE 68510
PHONE: (402) 467-1122
CONTACT OFFICER(S): Jon C. Headrick, V.P. Securities
ASSETS: $950 million
INVESTMENTS/LOANS MADE: For own account; For managed accounts; Through private placements; Through underwriting public offerings
INVESTMENTS/LOANS MADE: In securities with a secondary market and in securities without a secondary market
TYPES OF FINANCING: SECONDARY-MARKET: Common stock; Preferred stock; Bonds; VENTURE CAPITAL: Start-up from developed product stage; LOANS: Unsecured to credits above BAA; Equipment; Equity related; REAL ESTATE LOANS: Long-term senior mtg.; Intermediate-term senior mtg.; LEASES: Single-Investor; Leveraged; Tax leases; REAL ESTATE: Acquisitions; Joint ventures; Partnerships/ Syndications.
GEOGRAPHIC LIMITS OF INVESTMENTS/LOANS: National
RANGE OF INV./LOAN PER BUSINESS: Min. $1,000,000; Max. $5,000,000
PREFERRED TERM FOR LOANS & LEASES: Min. 3 years; Max. 15 years
REFERRALS ACCEPTED FROM: Investment/Mortgage banker; Borrower/Investee

COMPANY: **Leasetek Funding Group, Inc.**
ADDRESS: 19 Sylvan Avenue
Englewood Cliffs, NJ 07632
PHONE: (201) 224-7700
CONTACT OFFICERS: Anthony Rosato, President
ASSETS: $40,000,000
INVESTMENTS/LOANS MADE: For own account, for managed accounts, through private placements, through underwriting public offerings
INVESTMENTS/LOANS MADE: Only in securities with a secondary market
TYPES OF FINANCING: SECONDARY-MARKET CORPORATE SECURITIES, VENTURE CPAIRAL: Start-up from developed product stage; First-stage; Second-stage; Buyouts/expansions, LOANS: Working capital, equipment, REAL ESTATE LOANS: Long-term senior mtg; intermediate-term senior mtg; wraparounds; construction, FACTORING, LEASES: Single-investor; Leveraged; Tax leases; Operating; Lease syndications; Vendor financing programs
GEOGRAPHIC LIMITS OF INVESTMENTS/LOANS: National
RANGE OF INV./LOAN PER BUSINESS: Min. $50,000; Max. $10,000,000
PREFERRED TERM FOR LOANS & LEASES: Min. 2 years; Max. 20 years

COMPANY: **The Trust Company of New Jersey**
ADDRESS: 35 Journal Square
Jersey City, NJ 07306
PHONE: (201) 420-2810
TYPE OF INSTITUTION: Commercial bank
CONTACT OFFICER(S): Robert J. Figurski, Sr., V.P.
ASSETS: $1 Billion
INVESTMENTS/LOANS MADE: For own account
TYPES OF FINANCING: VENTURE CAPITAL: Start-up from developed product stage; First-stage; Later-stage expansions; Buy-outs/Acquisitions, LOANS: Unsecured; Working capital (receivables/inventory); Equipment; Equity related, REAL ESTATE LOANS: Long-term senior mtg.; Intermediate-term senior mtg.; Wraparounds; Land; Land development; Construction; Gap; Standbys; Industrial revenue bonds; Other: Economic Development Agency Tax Frees, INTERNATIONAL (including import/export), REAL ESTATE: Acquisitions
PREFERRED TYPES OF INDUSTRIE/INVESTMENTS: Any
RANGE OF IN./LOAN PER BUSINESS: Max. $5 Million
PREFERRED TERM FOR LOANS & LEASES: Miin. Demand; Max. 25 year payout
BUSINESS CHARACTERISTICS DESIRED-REQUIRED: Minimum number of years in business: 0
BRANCHES: 20 branches throughout New Jersey

COMPANY: **Investment Partners of America**
ADDRESS: 732 W. 8th Street
Plainfield, NJ 07060
PHONE: (201) 561-3622
TYPE OF INSTITUTION: Limited Partnership specializing in special situation investments
CONTACT OFFICER(S): Frank J. Abella, Jr, Managing Partner
ASSETS: $5,000,000
INVESTMENTS/LOANS MADE: For own account; Through private placements
INVESTMENTS/LOANS MADE: In securities with a secondary market and in securities without a secondary market

TYPES OF FINANCING: SECONDARY-MARKET CORPORATE SECURITIES: Common stock; Preferred stock; Bonds, VENTURE CAPITAL: Research & Development; Start-up from developed product stage, LOANS: Equity related, OTHER SERVIES PROVIDED: Consulting; Investment banking; Research
PREFERRED TYPES OF INDUSTRIES/INVESTMENTS: Natural resources; Consumer products; Publishing; Gift & stationery products; Military electronics, Industrial electronics
WILL NOT CONSIDER: Real estate; Commodities
GEOGRAPHIC LIMITS OF INVESTMENTS/LOANS: Local; State; Regional
BUSINESS CHARACTERISTICS DESIRED-REQUIRED: Minimum number of years in business: 3; Min. annual net income: break even
REFERRALS ACCEPTED FROM: Investment/Mortgage banker or Borrower/Investee

COMPANY: **Armco Financial Corporation, Intermediate Term Lending Division**
ADDRESS: 104 Carnegie Center
Princeton, NJ 08540
PHONE: (609) 452-0600
TYPE OF INSTITUTION: Commerical Term Lender
CONTACT OFFICER(S): Richard S. Ballard, President
Susan M. Lamm, Vice President & Senior Loan Officer
ASSETS: $500,000,000
INVESTMENTS/LOANS MADE: For own account
INVESTMENTS/LOANS MADE: In securities with a secondary market and in securities without a secondary market
TYPES OF FINANCING: VENTURE CAPITAL: Later-stage expansion; Buy-outs/Acquisitions, LOANS: Equipment; REAL ESTATE LOANS: Intermediate-term senior mtg.; Subordinated; Wraparounds, LEASES: Non-tax leases
PREFERRED TYPES OF INDUSTRIES/INVESTMENTS: No preferences—will do all types of manufacturing compaies
WILL NOT CONSIDER: Medical Industry; Retail Businesses
GEOGRAPHIC LIMITS OF INVESTMENTS/LOANS: National
RANGE OF INV./LOAN PER BUSINESS: Min. $1,000,000; Max. $10,000,000
PREFERRED TERM FOR LOANS & LEASES: Min. 2 years
BUSINESS CHARACTERISTICS DESIRED-REQUIRED: Minimum number of years in business: 3
REFERRALS ACCEPTED FROM: Investment/Mortgage banker or Borrower/Investee

COMPANY: **DSV Partners III**
ADDRESS: 221 Nassau St.
Princeton, NJ 08542
PHONE: (609) 924-6420
CONTACT OFFICER(S): Dr. Morton Collins
James Bergman
Robert S. Hillis
John Clarke
ASSETS: $34 million
TYPES OF FINANCING: VENTURE CAPITAL: Research & Development; Start-up from developed product stage; First-stage; Second-stage
PREFERRED TYPES OF INDUSTRIES/INVESTMENTS: Computer-related; High-technology; Medical; Data electronics, Communications, Life Sciences, Energy technology
WILL NOT CONSIDER: Real Estate
GEOGRAPHIC LIMITS OF INVESTMENTS/LOANS: National
RANGE OF INV./LOAN PER BUSINESS: Min. $250,000; Max. $1.5 million
BUSINESS CHARACTERISTICS DESIRED-REQUIRED: Minimum number of years in business: 0
REFERRALS ACCEPTED FROM: Investment/Mortgage banker or Borrower/Investee

COMPANY: **Johnston Associates Inc.**
ADDRESS: 300 Wall Street, Research Park
Princeton, NJ 08540
PHONE: (609) 924-3131
TYPE OF INSTITUTION: Venture Banking
CONTACT OFFICER(S): Robert B. Stockman, Vice President
James F. Mrazek, Managing Director
Harold V. Smith, Managing Director
INVESTMENTS/LOANS MADE: For own account; Through private placements
INVESTMENTS/LOANS MADE: In securities with a secondary market and in securities without a secondary market
TYPES OF FINANCING: VENTURE CAPITAL: Research & Development; Second-stage; Buy-outs/Acquisitions
PREFERRED TYPES OF INDUSTRIES/INVESTMENTS: Health Care, Medical Instrumentation, Biotechnology
GEOGRAPHIC LIMITS OF INVESTMENTS/LOANS: Regional, Northeast
RANGE OF INV./LOAN PER BUSINESS: Min. $500,000; Max. 1.5 million
REFERRALS ACCEPTED FROM: Borrower/Investee

COMPANY: **Princeton/Montrose Partners**
ADDRESS: 1000 Herrontown Road
Princeton, NJ 08540
PHONE: (609) 921-1590
TYPE OF INSTITUTION: Venture Capital Limited Partnership
CONTACT OFFICER(S): Ronald R. Hahn, Managing Partner
Peter R. Rossmassler, General Partner
Donald R. Stroben, Managing Partner
Charles I. Kosmont, General Partner
Richard J. Defieux, Associate
ASSETS: $17,175,000
INVESTMENTS/LOANS MADE: For own account
INVESTMENTS/LOANS MADE: In securities with a secondary market and in securities without a secondary market
TYPES OF FINANCING: VENTURE CAPITAL: Start-up from developed product stage; First-stage; Second-stage; Later-stage expansions; Buy-outs/Acquisitions
PREFERRED TYPES OF INDUSTRIES/INVESTMENTS: Equity or Senior Instruments with equity participation:

Focus—Agribusiness; food chain from biotechnology to packaged foods; Energy; natural resources productivity enhancing technology relating to locating, extracting, processing, and production of energy, forest and mineral resources
GEOGRAPHIC LIMITS OF INVESTMENTS/LOANS: National, International
RANGE OF INV./LOAN PER BUSINESS: Min. $100,000; Max. $850,000BUSINESS CHARACTERISTICS DESIRED-REQUIRED: Minimum Number of years in business; 0
REFERRALS ACCEPTED FROM: Investment/Mortgage banker or Borrower/Investee
BRANCHES: Donald R. Stroben, Managing Partner, 2331 Honolulu Avenue, Suite G, Montrose, CA 91020; (213) 957-3623

COMPANY: **Edelson Technology Partners**
ADDRESS: Park 80 West, Plaza Two
Saddle Brook, NJ 07662
PHONE: (201) 843-4474
TYPE OF INSTITUTION: Venture Capital Fund
CONTACT OFFICER(S): Harry Edelson, General Partner
ASSETS: 44 million
INVESTMENTS/LOANS MADE: For managed accounts
INVESTMENTS/LOANS MADE: In securities with a secondary market and in securities without a secondary market
TYPES OF FINANCING: VENTURE CAPITAL: Start-up from developed product stage; First-stage
PREFERRED TYPES OF INDUSTRIES/INVESTMENTS: Communications, Computer related, Electronic components & instrumentation, Genetic engineering, Industrial products & equipmenut, Entertainment technology
RANGE OF LEASE PER BUSINESS: Max. $1 million
BUSINESS CHARACTERISTICS DESIRED-REQUIRED: Minimum number of years in business: 0; Min. annual sales $500,000
REFERRALS ACCEPTED FROM: Investment/Mortgage banker or Borrower/Investee

COMPANY: **P. F. Investments Co.**
ADDRESS: 22 Bank Street
Summit, NJ 07901
PHONE: (201) 277-6111
TYPE OF INSTITUTION: Private Venture Capital Fund
CONTACT OFFICER(S): Anthony J. Fennelli, Jr., General Partner
Donald B. Pierson, General Partner
Peter L. Rehm, Associate
ASSETS: $3,200,000
INVESTMENTS/LOANS MADE: For own account
INVESTMENTS/LOANS MADE: Only in securities without a secondary market
TYPES OF FINANCING: VENTURE CAPITAL: Research & Development; Start-up from developed product stage, REAL ESTATE: Acquisitions; Joint ventures; Partnerships/Syndications
PREFERRED TYPES OF INDUSTRIES/INVESTMENTS: High Technology—Start-ups Only; Computer Hardware, Software—Communications; Energy Related
WILL NOT CONSIDER: "Going" Concerns

GEOGRAPHIC LIMITS OF INVESTMENTS/LOANS: Local
RANGE OF INV./LOAN PER BUSINESS: Min. $50,000; Max. $150,000
PREFERRED TERM FOR LOANS & LEASES: Min. 3; Max. 5 years
BUSINESS CHARACTERISTICS DESIRED-REQUIRED: Min. no. of years in business: 0
REFERRALS ACCEPTED FROM: Investment/Mortgage banker or Borrower/Investee

COMPANY: **Ingersoll Rand Financial Corp.**
ADDRESS: 200 Chestnut Ridge Road
Woodcliff Lake, NJ 07675
PHONE: (201) 573-3031
TYPE OF INSTITUTION: Tax Leasing and Secured Financing
CONTACT OFFICER(S): R.A. Layton, Eastern Group Manager
R.J. Rhinesmih, Western Group Manager
J.C. Colbert, National Leasing
ASSETS: $550 million
INVESTMENTS/LOANS MADE: for own account
TYPES OF FINANCING: VENTURE CAPITAL: Later-stage expansion, LOANS: Equipment, REAL ESTATE LOANS: Long-term senior mtg.; Intermediate-term senior mtg.; Standbys; Other, LEASES: Single-investor; Tax leases; Non-tax leases; Vendor financing programs
GEOGRAPHIC LIMITS OF INVESTMENTS/LOANS: National
RANGE OF INV./LOAN PER BUSINESS: Min. $100M; Max. $10,000M
PREFERRED TERM FOR LOANS & LEASES: Min. 1 year; Max. 7 years
BUSINESS CHARACTERISTICS DESIRED-REQUIRED: Minimum number of years in business: 5; Other: Each transaction will stand on merits
REFERRALS ACCEPTED FROM: Investment/Mortgage banker or Borrower/Investee
BRANCHES: Richard A. Layton, Summerfield Commons Office Park, 2585 Washington Rd., Pittsburgh, PA 15241; (412) 854-1810
Robert J. Rhinesmith, 210 Porter Drive, Suite 120, San Ramon, CA 94583; (415) 838-4606

COMPANY: **Rand Capital Corporation**
ADDRESS: 1300 Rand Building
Buffalo, NY 14203
PHONE: (716) 853-0803
TYPE OF INSTITUTION: Closed end venture capital fund
CONTACT OFFICER(S): Keith B. Wiley, Vice President
ASSETS: $8,400,000
INVESTMENTS/LOANS MADE: For own account
TYPES OF FINANCING: SECONDARY-MARKET CORPORATE SECURITIES: Common stock. VENTURE CAPITAL: Start-up from developed product stage; First-stage (less than 1 year); Second-stage (generally 1-3 years); Buy-outs/Acquisitions
PREFERRED TYPES OF INDUSTRIES/INVESTMENTS: We have no stated preferences. It should have the potential for substantial growth in a short time, we have tended toward technologically-based situations.

GEOGRAPHIC LIMITS OF INVESTMENTS/LOANS: Regional
RANGE OF INV./LOAN PER BUSINESS: Min. $50,000; Max. $500,000
PREFERRED TERM FOR LOANS & LEASES: Max. 8 years
BUSINESS CHARACTERISTICS DESIRED-REQUIRED: Min. no. of years in business: 0
REFERRALS ACCEPTED FROM: Investment/Mortgage banker or Borrower/Investee

COMPANY: **Coleman Ventures Inc.**
ADDRESS: 5909 Northern Blvd.
East Norwich, NY 11732
PHONE: (516) 626-3642
TYPE OF INSTITUTION: Private firm investing own capital; evaluates and prepares venture proposals
CONTACT OFFICER(S):Gregory S. Coleman, President
ASSETS: $5 million
INVESTMENTS/LOANS MADE: For own account
INVESTMENTS/LOANS MADE: Only in securities without a secondary market
TYPES OF FINANCING: VENTURE CAPITAL: Start-up from developed product stage; First-stage. REAL ESTATE LOANS: Land development. REAL ESTATE: Partnerships/Syndications.
PREFERRED TYPES OF INDUSTRIES/INVESTMENTS: High technology—solid state: lasers, photo-voltaic materials and devices; Hybrid micro circuits
WILL NOT CONSIDER: Propositions not accompanied by at least an informal business plan
GEOGRAPHIC LIMITS OF INVESTMENTS/LOANS: Local; State; Regional
RANGE OF INV./LOAN PER BUSINESS: Min. $100,000; Max. $1,000,000
PREFERRED TERM FOR LOANS & LEASES: Min. Equity only
BUSINESS CHARACTERISTICS DESIRED-REQUIRED: Minimum number of years in business: 0; Min annual sales $ Nominal

COMPANY: **Adler & Company**
ADDRESS: 375 Park Avenue Suite 3303
New York, NY 10152
PHONE: (212) 759-2800
TYPE OF INSTITUTION: Private Venture Capital
CONTACT OFFICER(S): Frederick R. Adler, Managing General Partner
James J. Harrison, General Partner-Manager California Office
Joy London, General Partner
ASSETS: $300,000,000
INVESTMENTS/LOANS MADE: Through private placements
INVESTMENTS/LOANS MADE: In securities with a secondary market and in securities without a secondary market
TYPES OF FINANCING: SECONDARY-MARKET CORPORATE SECURITIES: Primarily private securities. VENTURE CAPITAL: Research & Development; Start-up from developed product stage; First-stage; Second-stage.
PREFERRED TYPES OF INDUSTRIES/INVESTMENTS: Biotechnology; Health Care Delivery Systems; Medical Products & Services; Semiconductors and VSLI Equipment; Storage Devices, Graphic Displays & Printers; Communications; Software; Microcomputers; Automation & Productivity Systems.
WILL NOT CONSIDER: Real Estate
GEOGRAPHIC LIMITS OF INVESTMENTS/LOANS: Local; State; Regional; National; International
RANGE OF INV./LOAN PER BUSINESS: Min. $100,000; Max. $5,000,000
BUSINESS CHARACTERISTICS DESIRED-REQUIRED: Minimum number of years in business: 0
BRANCHES: 1245 Oakmead Parkway, Suite 103, Sunnyvale, CA 94086, (408) 730-8700, James J. Harrison

COMPANY: **Alan Patricof Associates, Inc.**
ADDRESS: 545 Madison Avenue
New York, NY 10022
PHONE: (212) 753-6300
TYPE OF INSTITUTION: Venture Capital Firm
CONTACT OFFICER(S): Alan J. Patricof, Chairman
Robert G. Faris, President
Lewis Solomon, Exec. VP
John Baker, VP
ASSETS: $200 million U.S.; $65 million abroad
INVESTMENTS/LOANS MADE: For managed accounts, Through private placements
INVESTMENTS/LOANS MADE: In securities with a secondary market and in securities without a secondary market
TYPES OF FINANCING: SECONDARY-MARKET CORPORATE SECURITIES: Common stock; Preferred stock; Bonds, VENTURE CAPITAL: Start-up from developed product stage; First stage; Second-stage; Later-stage expansion; Buy-outs/Acquisitions LOANS: Equity-related, INTERNATIONAL (including import/export)
PREFERRED TYPES OF INDUSTRIES/INVESTMENTS: Computers hardware and software; Communications; Electronics; Biotechnology; Consumer & Industrial-related goods & services; Energy
GEOGRAPHIC LIMITS OF INVESTMENTS/LOANS: National; England/France
RANGE OF INV./LOAN PER BUSINESS: Min. $250,000; Max. $2,000,000
BUSINESS CHARACTERISTICS DESIRED-REQUIRED: Minimum number of years in business: 0
REFERRALS ACCEPTED FROM: Investment/Mortgage banker or Borrower/Investee
BRANCHES: Alan Patricof Associates, Inc., 1245 Oakmead Parkway, Sunnyvale, CA 94086, (408) 737-8788, Associate: Barbara J. Lundberg
Alan Patricof Associates Ltd., 24 Upper Brook Street, London W1Y 1PD England, 493-3633, Ronald M. Cohen, Exec. Chairman
Alan Patricof Associates, S.A.R.L., 3. 67 rue de Monceau, Paris 75008 France, 563-4025, Maurice Tchenio, Managing Director

COMPANY: **Atlantic Capital Corp.**
ADDRESS: 40 Wall St.
New York, NY 10005
PHONE: (212) 363-5600
CONTACT OFFICER(S): Harold Phaumgarten, Sr. V.P.

TYPES OF FINANCING: VENTURE CAPITAL, REAL ESTATE LOANS, LEASES, REAL ESTATE, OTHER SERVICES PROVIDED: private placements, corporate financing, mergers and acquisitions
RANGE OF INV./LOAN PER BUSINESS: Min. $1 million
REMARKS: Transaction oriented house; no start-ups

COMPANY: **Bankers Trust New York Corporation**
ADDRESS: 280 Park Avenue
New York, NY 10015
PHONE: (212) 850-1916
TYPE OF INSTITUTION: Venture Capital Group
CONTACT OFFICER(S): James G. Hellmuth, V.P., Group Head
Noel E. Urben, V.P.
Keith R. Fox, V.P.
ASSETS: $70,000,000
INVESTMENTS/LOANS MADE: For own account
TYPES OF FINANCING: VENTURE CAPITAL: Later-stage expansion; Buy-outs/Acquisitions
PREFERRED TYPES OF INDUSTRIES/INVESTMENTS: Manufacturing Industries; Cable Television Industry; Service Industries
WILL NOT CONSIDER: Real Estate, Start-ups, High Technology
GEOGRAPHIC LIMITS OF INVESTMENTS/LOANS: National
RANGE OF INV./LOAN PER BUSINESS: Min. $1,000,000; Max. $5,000,000
PREFERRED TERM FOR LOANS & LEASES: Min. 5; Max. 8 years
BUSINESS CHARACTERISTICS DESIRED-REQUIRED: Min. annual net income $500,000
REFERRALS ACCEPTED FROM: Investment/Mortgage banker or Borrower/Investee

COMPANY: **Charles de Than Group**
ADDRESS: 51 E. 67th Street
New York, NY 10021
PHONE: (212) 988-5108
TYPE OF INSTITUTION: Private capital group and corporate finance broker
CONTACT OFFICER(S): Charles B. de Than, General Partner
INVESTMENTS/LOANS MADE: For own account; Through private placements; Through underwriting public offerings
TYPES OF FINANCING: VENTURE CAPITAL: Start-up from developed product stage; Second-stage; Later-stage expansion; Buy-outs/Acquisitions. LOANS: Equity-related; Other: Acquisitions and mergers, prefer leverageable deals. OTHER SERVICES PROVIDED: Consulting, Evaluations, Financial publicity, Investment advisor.
PREFERRED TYPES OF INDUSTRIES/INVESTMENTS: Invest in or acquire low technology industries with earnings record and reasonable balance sheet; Broker any type acquisitions; Venture placement: any field, prefer computer, medical and other high technology & communcation areas.
GEOGRAPHIC LIMITS OF INVESTMENTS/LOANS: Any area
RANGE OF INV./LOAN PER BUSINESS: Min. $2-300,000; Max. No limit
REFERRALS ACCEPTED FROM: Investment/Mortgage banker or Borrower/Investee

COMPANY: **Citicorp Venture Capital, Ltd.**
ADDRESS: Citicorp Center, 153 E. 53rd St., 28th Floor
New York, NY 10043
PHONE: (212) 559-1127
TYPE OF INSTITUTION: V.C. Subsidiary of Bank
CONTACT OFFICER(S): Peter Gerry, President
ASSETS: $180,000,000 at corp
INVESTMENTS/LOANS MADE: For own account
INVESTMENTS/LOANS MADE: In securities with a secondary market; In securities without a secondary market
TYPES OF FINANCING: SECONDARY-MARKET CORPORATE SECURITIES: Common stock; Preferred stock; Bonds, VENTURE CAPITAL: Start-up fom developed product stage; First-stage; Second-stage; Later-stage expansion; Buy-outs/Acquisitions
PREFERRED TYPES OF INDUSTRIES/INVESTMENTS: Medical, High-tech, Services, Energy, Communication
WILL NOT CONSIDER: Banks, Finance companies, Real estate
GEOGRAPHIC LIMITS OF INVESTMENTS/LOANS: National
RANGE OF INV./LOAN PER BUSINESS: Min. $300,000
BUSINESS CHARACTERISTICS DESIRED-REQUIRED: Other: Business plan
BRANCHES: Thomas F. McWilliams, Diamond Shamrock Tower, 717 Harwood, #2920, Dallas, TX 75221, (214) 880-9670
David A. Wegmann, 220 Geng Rd., 2nd Floor, Palo Alto, CA 94204, (415) 424-8000
J. Mathew Mackowski, 1 Sansome St., San Francisco, CA, (415) 627-6472

COMPANY:**Venture Capital Fund of America**
ADDRESS: 509 Madison Avenue
New York, NY 10022
PHONE: (212) 838-5577
TYPE OF INSTITUTION: Private Venture Capital Partnership
CONTACT OFFICER(S): M. John Sterba, Jr. General Partner
TOTAL ASSETS: $50,000,000
INVESTMENTS/LOANS MADE: For own account
INVESTMENTS/LOANS ARRANGED: Only in securities without a secondary market
TYPES OF FINANCING: VENTURE CAPITAL: Start-up from developed product state; First-stage; Second-stage; Later-stage
PREFERRED TYPES OF INDUSTRIES/INVESTMENTS: Standard Venture Capital
WILL NOT CONSIDER: Real Estate, Movies
GEOGRAPHIC LIMITS OF INVESTMENTS/LOANS: National
RANGE OF INV./LOAN PER BUSINESS: Min. $50,000; Max. $2,500,000
BUSINNESS CHARACTERISTICS DESIRED-REQUIRED: Minimum number of years in business: 0

VENTURE CAPITAL COMPANIES

(Also see SBICs, MESBICs and Investment Bankers)

NEW YORK

COMPANY:**Ventech Partners, L.P.**
ADDRESS: 200 Park Avenue, Suite 2525
New York, NY 10017
PHONE: (22) 692-9177
TYPES OF INSTITUTION: Venture Capital Partnership
CONTACT OFFICER(S): Richard L. King, General Partner
Samuel F. McKay, General Partner
Total ASSETS: $29,000,000
INVESTMENTS/LOANS MADE: For managed accounts
INVESTMENTS/LOANS ARRANGED: Only in securities without a secndary market
TYPES OF FINANCING: VENTURE CAPITAL: Start-up from developed product stage; First-Stage; Second-stage; Later-stage
PREFERRED TYPES OF INDUSTRIES/INVESTMENTS: Technology companies only
GEOGRAPHIC LIMITS OF INVESTMENTS/LOANS: National
RANGE OF INV./LOANS PER BUSINESS: Min.$250,000; Max. $1,000,000
BUSINESS CHARACTERISTICS DESIRED-REQUIRED: Minimum number of years in business: 0

COMPANY: **Euclid Partners Corporation**
ADDRESS: 50 Rockefeller Plaza
New York, NY 10020
PHONE: (212) 489-1770
TYPE OF INSTITUTION: Private venture capital
CONTACT OFFICER(S): Milton J. Pappas
A. Bliss McCrum, Jr., Jeffrey T. Hamilton
ASSETS: Private information
INVESTMENTS/LOANS MADE: For own account
TYPES OF FINANCING: VENTURE CAPITAL: Start-up from developed product stage; First-stage (less than 1 year); Second-stage (generally 1-3 years); Later-stage expansion
PREFERRED TYPES OF INDUSTRIES/INVESTMENTS: High technology in electronics, communication, energy, medical fields
WILL NOT CONSIDER: Publicly-traded companies or leveraged buyouts
RANGE OF INV./LOAN PER BUSINESS: Min. $150,000; Max. $1,500,000
REFERRALS ACCEPTED FROM: Investment/Mortgage banker or Borrower/Investee

COMPANY: **First Century Partnership III**
ADDRESS: 1345 Avenue of the Americas
New York, NY 10105
PHONE: (212) 399-6107
TYPE OF INSTITUTION: Wholly-owned venture capital subsidiary of investment bank.
CONTACT OFFICER(S): John S. Dulaney, Chairman and Partner
Michael J. Myers, President and Partner
Walter C. Johnsen, Vice President and Partner (San Francisco)
Roberto Buaron, Vice President and Partner
David Lobel, Vice President and Partner
Byron K. Adams, Vice President and Partner (San Francisco)
ASSETS: $100 million
INVESTMENTS/LOANS MADE: For own account
INVESTMENTS/LOANS MADE: In securities with a secondary market and in securities without a secondary market
TYPES OF FINANCING: VENTURE CAPITAL: Start-up from developed product stage; First-stage (less than 1 year); Second-stage (generally 1-3 years)
PREFERRED TYPES OF INDUSTRIES/INVESTMENTS: CAD/CAM; Data Communications; Office Automation; Peripheral Equipment/Software; Automation Equipment; Diagnostic Equipment; Medical Disposables; Applied Genetics; Graphic Arts; Integrated Circuitry; Optics Technology; Robotics
WILL NOT CONSIDER: Real Estate; Financial Services; Project Financings
GEOGRAPHIC LIMITS OF INVESTMENTS/LOANS: National; Limited to United States
RANGE OF INV./LOAN PER BUSINESS: Min. $100,000-300,000; Max. $600,000
BUSINESS CHARACTERISTICS DESIRED-REQUIRED: Min. no. of years in business: 0; Min. annual sales Nominal
BRANCHES: Walter C. Johnsen, 350 California Street, San Francisco, CA 94104, (415) 955-1672

COMPANY: **Foster Management Company**
ADDRESS: 437 Madison Ave.
New York, NY 10022
PHONE: (212) 753-4810
TYPE OF INSTITUTION: Private investment firm
CONTACT OFFICER(S): Michael J. Connelly, Executive Vice President
ASSETS: $100 million
INVESTMENTS/LOANS MADE: For own account
INVESTMENTS/LOANS MADE: Only in securities without a secondary market
TYPES OF FINANCING: VENTURE CAPITAL: Start-up from developed product stage; First-stage; Second-stage; Later-stage expansion; Buy-outs/Acquisitions
PREFERRED TYPES OF INDUSTRIES/INVESTMENTS: Health Care; Broadcasting; Home Furnishings; Transportation; Energy; Retail Automation
GEOGRAPHIC LIMITS OF INVESTMENTS/LOANS: National
RANGE OF INV./LOAN PER BUSINESS: Min. $500,000; Max. $8,000,000
BUSINESS CHARACTERISTICS DESIRED-REQUIRED: Minimum number of years in business: 0
REFERRALS ACCEPTED FROM: Investment/Mortgage banker or Borrower/Investee

COMPANY: **Founders Equity Inc.**
ADDRESS: 477 Madison Ave.
New York, NY 10022
PHONE: (212) 319-5900
TYPE OF INSTITUTION: Private investment firm
CONTACT OFFICER(S): Warren H. Haber, Principal
John L. Teeger, Pincipal
Donn L. Hartley, Vice President Corporate Development
INVESTMENTS/LOANS MADE: For own account
INVESTMENTS/LOANS MADE: In securities with a secondary market and in securities without a secondary market

TYPES OF FINANCING: VENTURE CAPITAL: Second-stage; Later-stage expansion; Buy-outs/Acquisitions; REAL ESTATE: Acquisitions; Joint ventures; Partnerships/Syndications
PREFERRED TYPES OF INDUSTRIES/INVESTMENTS: Distributors: Specialty Industrial (Particularly Value Added); Specialty Consumer; Credit Retailers; Catalog/ Mail Order; Food Service/Restaurant Chains; Radio Stations; Franchisors; Manufacturers: Household Goods; Remanufacture/Repair of Industrial Equipment; Industrial Products; Automotive Aftermarket; Vehicle Conversion; Leisure; Apparel
GEOGRAPHIC LIMITS OF INVESTMENTS/LOANS: National
RANGE OF INV./LOAN PER BUSINESS: Min. $2 Million; Max. $50 Million
BUSINESS CHARACTERISTICS DESIRED-REQUIRED: Minimum annual sales; 10 Million; Min. annual net income $1 Million
REFERRALS ACCEPTED FROM: Investment/Mortgage banker or Borrower/Investee

COMPANY: **GeoCapital Venture**
ADDRESS: 655 Madison Ave.
New York, NY 10021
PHONE: (212) 935-0111
TYPE OF INSTITUTION: Venture Capital Investment Limited Partnership
CONTACT OFFICER(S): Stephen J. Clearman, General Partner
Irwin Lieber, General Partner
ASSETS: $20,000,000
INVESTMENTS/LOANS MADE: For own account
INVESTMENTS/LOANS MADE: In securities with a secondary market and in securities without a secondary market
TYPES OF FINANCING: VENTURE CAPITAL: Research & Development; Start-up from developed product stage; First-stage; Second-stage
PREFERRED TYPES OF INDUSTRIES/INVESTMENTS: Software, Data Communications, Information Processing
WILL NOT CONSIDER: Real Estate
GEOGRAPHIC LIMITS OF INVESTMENTS/LOANS: National
RANGE OF INV./LOAN PER BUSINESS: Min. $250,000; Max. $1,000,000
BUSINESS CHARACTERISTICS DESIRED-REQUIRED: Min. no. of years in business: 0
REFERRALS ACCEPTED FROM: Investment/Mortgage banker or Borrower/Investee

COMPANY: **Haas Financial Corporation**
ADDRESS: 230 Park Avenue
New York, NY 10169
PHONE: (212) 490-1510
CONTACT OFFICER(S): George C. Haas Jr., President
Robert L. Cummings
Vice President
INVESTMENTS/LOANS MADE: For own account; Through private placements
INVESTMENTS/LOANS MADE: In securities with a secondary market and in securities without a secondary market

TYPES OF FINANCING: SECONDARY-MARKET CORPORATE SECURITIES: Common stock; Bonds; VENTURE CAPITAL: First-stage; Second-stage; Later-stage expansion; Buy-outs/Acquisitions; LOANS: Equipment; REAL ESTATE LOANS: Long-term senior mtg.; Intermediate-term senior mtg.; Subordinated; Wraparounds; LEASES: Single-investor; Operating; Tax-oriented lease brokerage; OTHER SERVICES PROVIDED: Merger Acquisition Divestiture Brokerage; Consulting and Valuation; Acquisition/Divestiture Financing.
PREFERRED TYPES OF INDUSTRIES/INVESTMENTS: Will look at all types of industries, firm has specialty in transportation (planes) consumer products (soft drinks)
GEOGRAPHIC LIMITS OF INVESTMENTS/LOANS: National
RANGE OF INV./LOAN PER BUSINESS: Min. $500,000
PREFERRED TERM FOR LOANS & LEASES: Min. 5 years; Max. 15 years
REFERRALS ACCEPTED FROM: Investment/Mortgage banker or Borrower/Investee

COMPANY: **Home Life Insurance Company**
ADDRESS: 253 Broadway
New York, NY 10007
PHONE: (212) 306-2060
TYPE OF INSTITUTION: Investment department—Securities section of life insurance company
CONTACT OFFICER(S): Jerry D. Cohen, V.P. , manages Securities Sec.
ASSETS: $2.5 billion and up
INVESTMENTS/LOANS MADE: For own account; Through private placements; Through underwriting public offerings
INVESTMENTS/LOANS MADE: In securities with a secondary market and in securities without a secondary market
TYPES OF FINANCING: SECONDARY-MARKET CORPORATE SECURITIES: Common stock; Preferred stock; Bonds; LOANS: Unsecured; Equipment; Equity-related. LEASES: Other; Debt portion of leveraged lease
WILL NOT CONSIDER: Finance, leasing or foreign companies
GEOGRAPHIC LIMITS OF INVESTMENTS/LOANS: National; Other: Canada
RANGE OF INV./LOAN PER BUSINESS: Min. $1,000,000; Max. $10,000,000
PREFERRED TERM FOR LOANS & LEASES: Min. 7-10 years; Max. 15 years
BUSINESS CHARACTERISTICS DESIRED-REQUIRED: Min. net worth $5,000,000; Min. annual net income Positive

COMPANY: **Investech, L.P.**
ADDRESS: 515 Madison Ave.
New York, NY 10022
PHONE: (212) 308-5811
TYPE OF INSTITUTION: Venture Capital Investments
CONTACT OFFICER(S): Carl S. Hutman, Partner
Tancred V. Schiavoni, Partner
ASSETS: $27.5 Million
INVESTMENTS/LOANS MADE: For own account

TYPES OF FINANCING: VENTURE CAPITAL: Research & Development; Start-up from developed product stage; First-stage (less than 1 year); Second-stage (generally 1-3 years); Later-stage expansion; Buy-outs/Acquisitions
PREFERRED TYPES OF INDUSTRIES/INVESTMENTS: Technology based businesses, Communications, Computer-related, medical and health care, electronics.
GEOGRAPHIC LIMITS OF INVESTMENTS/LOANS: National
RANGE OF INV./LOAN PER BUSINESS: Min. $200,000; Max.$1,000,000
BUSINESS CHARACTERISTICS DESIRED-REQUIRED: Minimum number of years in business: 0; Other: projected profits after 2 years

COMPANY: **Irving Capital Corporation**
ADDRESS: 1290 Avenue of the Americas
New York, NY 10104
PHONE: (212) 487-2121
TYPE OF INSTITUTION: Provide equity oriented capital
CONTACT OFFICER(S): Kathleen Snyder
INVESTMENTS/LOANS MADE: For own account
INVESTMENTS/LOANS MADE: Only in securities without a secondary market
TYPES OF FINANCING: VENTURE CAPITAL: Second-stage (generally 1-3 years); Later-stage expansion; Buy-outs/Acquisitions
PREFERRED TYPES OF INDUSTRIES/INVESTMENTS: Industries—Manufacturing, Distribution
WILL NOT CONSIDER: Real Estate
GEOGRAPHIC LIMITS OF INVESTMENTS/LOANS: National
RANGE OF INV./LOAN PER BUSINESS: Min. $300,000; Max. $10,000,000
BUSINESS CHARACTERISTICS DESIRED-REQUIRED: Minimum number of years in business: 3; Min. annual sales $2,000,000; Min. net worth $100,000; Min. annual net income $100,000
REFERRALS ACCEPTED FROM: Investment/Mortgage banker or Borrower/Investee

COMPANY: **J. H. Whitney & Co.**
ADDRESS: 630 Fifth Avenue
New York, NY 10111
PHONE: (212) 757-0500
CONTACT OFFICERS: Benno C. Schmidt, Management Partner
Don E. Ackerman
Russell E. Planetzer
Edward B. Ryan
TYPES OF FINANCING: VENTURE CAPITAL, LOANS: Equity-related
PREFERRED TYPES OF INDUSTRIES/INVESTMENTS: Manufacturing & Processing; Research & Techology; Data Processing

COMPANY: **Manufacturers Hanover Commercial Corp.**
ADDRESS: 1211 Ave. of the Americas, 12th Floor
New York, NY 10036
PHONE: (212) 382-7000
TYPE OF INSTITUTION: Commercial Finance Co.
CONTACT OFFICER(S): Francis X. Basile, Chairman & CEO
TYPES OF FINANCING: VENTURE CAPITAL: Start-up from developed product stage; First stage (less than 1 year); Second-stage (generally 1-3 years); Later-stage expansion; Buy-outs/Acquisitions; LOANS: Equity-related; FACTORING
GEOGRAHIC LIMITS OF INVESTMENTS/LOANS: International
RANGE OF INV./LOAN PER BUSINESS: Min. $250,000

COMPANY: **Melamede & Co.**
ADDRESS: 655 Madison Ave.
New York, NY 10021
PHONE: (212) 758-4422
TYPE OF INSTITUTION: Private Investment Company
CONTACT OFFICER(S): Amos Melamede, President
Andrew M. Schozer, Treasurer
ASSETS: $15,000,000 and up
INVESTMENTS/LOANS MADE: For own account
TYPES OF FINANCING: VENTURE CAPITAL: Second-stage (generally 1-3 years); Buy-outs/Acquisitions
PREFERRED TYPES OF INDUSTRIES/INVESTMENTS: No Preferences
WILL NOT CONSIDER: Retail
GEOGRAPHIC LIMITS OF INVESTMENTS/LOANS: National
RANGE OF INV./LOAN PER BUSINESS: Min. $1,000,000; Max. $10,000,000
BUSINESS CHARACTERISTICS DESIRED-REQUIRED: Minimum number of years in business: 1-3; Min. annual sales $5,000,000; Min. net worth $1,000,000
REFERRALS ACCEPTED FROM: Investment/Mortgage banker or Borrower/Investee

COMPANY: **N.A.B. Nordic Investors Ltd.**
ADDRESS: C/O Nordic American Banking Corporation,
600 Fifth Ave.
New York, NY 10020
PHONE: (212) 315-6532
TYPE OF INSTITUTION: Venture Capital Fund & Merchant Banking Subsidiary of Commercial Bank
CONTACT OFFICER(S): Jack A. Prizzi, Vice President
Michael Ionata, Assistant Treasurer
ASSETS: $5,000,000
INVESTMENTS/LOANS MADE: For own account; Through private placements
INVESTMENTS/LOANS MADE: only in securities without a secondary market
TYPES OF FINANCING: VENTURE CAPITAL: First-stage (less than 1 year); Second-stage (generally 1-3 years); Later-stage expansion; Buy-outs/Acquisitions
PREFERRED TYPES OF INDUSTRIES/INVESTMENTS: Communications, Computers, Distribution, Electronics, Genetic Engineering, Industrial Products, Medical Products
WILL NOT CONSIDER: Retail, Real Estate, oil & gas, consulting
GEOGRAPHIC LIMITS OF INVESTMENTS/LOANS: National
RANGE OF INV./LOAN PER BUSINESS: Min. $ 500,000; Max. $1,000,000
BUSINESS CHARACTERISTICS DESIRED-REQUIRED: Minimum number of years in business: 1; Min. annual

sales $500,000; Min. annual net income $ losses; Min. annual cash flow $ negative;

COMPANY: **Pennwood Capital Corporation**
ADDRESS: 645 Madison Avenue
New York, NY 10022
PHONE: (212) 753-1600
TYPE OF INSTITUTION: Private investment firm specializing in leveraged buyouts.
CONTACT OFFICER(S): Marc C. Ostrow, President
INVESTMENTS/LOANS MADE: For own account
INVESTMENTS/LOANS MADE: In securities with a secondary market and in securities without a secondary market;
TYPES OF FINANCING: VENTURE CAPITAL: Buy-outs/Acquisitions; LOANS: Equity-related.
PREFERRED TYPES OF OF INDUSTRIES/ INVESTMENTS: Companies that manufacture or distribute industrial or consumer products.
WILL NOT CONSIDER: High-technology
GEOGRAPHIC LIMITS OF INVESTMENTS/LOANS: National;
RANGE OF INV./LOAN PER BUSINESS: Min. $1 million; Max. $40 million
BUSINESS CHARACTERISTICS DESIRED-REQUIRED: Min. annual net income $1.5 million pre-tax
REFERRALS ACCEPTED FROM: Investment/Mortgage banker only; Borrower/Investee;

COMPANY: **Prudential Venture Capital Management, Inc.**
ADDRESS: 717 Fifth Avenue, Suite 1600
New York, NY 10022
PHONE: (212) 753-0901
TYPE OF INSTITUTION: Venture Capital
CONTACT OFFICER(S): William S. Field, Chairman
Robert A. Knox, President
Mark Rossi, V.P.
ASSETS: $350,000,000
INVESTMENTS/LOANS MADE: For own account; For managed accounts
INVESTMENTS/LOANS MADE: In securities with a secondary market; In securities without a secondary market
TYPES OF FINANCING: SECONDARY-MARKET CORPORATE SECURITIES: Common stock; Preferred stock, VENTURE CAPITAL: Second-stage; Later-stage
PREFERRED TYPES OF INDUSTRIES/INVESTMENTS: Open for consideration
GEOGRAPHIC LIMITS OF INVESTMENTS/LOANS: National
RANGE OF INV./LOAN PER BUSINESS: Min. $1,000,000; Max. $5,000,000
BUSINESS CHARACTERISTICS DESIRED-REQUIRED: Open for consideration
REFERRALS ACCEPTED FROM: Investment/Mortgage baker; Borrower/Investee

COMPANY: **Regulus International Capital Company, Inc.**
ADDRESS: 10 Rockefeller Plaza
New York, NY 10020
PHONE: (212) 582-7715
TYPE OF INSTITUTION: Venture Capital Company
CONTACT OFFICER(S): Lee H. Miller, President
INVESTMENTS/LOANS MADE: For own account, For managed accounts, Through private placements
TYPES OF FINANCING: VENTURE CAPITAL: Research & Development; Start-up from developed product stage; Second-stage (generally 1-3 years); Buy-outs/Acquisitions, FACTORING, INTERNATIONAL (including import/export), REAL ESTATE
PREFERRED TYPES OF INDUSTRIES/INVESTMENTS: Printing, Packaging & Converting, Plastics
GEOGRAPHIC LIMITS OF INVESTMENTS/LOANS: Regional
RANGE OF INV./LOAN PER BUSINESS: Min. $200,000; Max. $2,000,000

COMPANY: **Rothchild Ventures, Inc.**
ADDRESS: One Rockefeller Plaza
New York, NY 10020
PHONE: (212) 757-6000
CONTACT OFFICER(S): Archie J. McGill, Pres. & CEO
James C. Blair, Managing Director
ASSETS: $300 million
TYPES OF FINANCING: VENTURE CAPITAL: Research & Development; Start-up from developed product stage; First-stage; Second-stage; Later-stage expansion; Buy-outs/Acquisitions
PREFERRED TYPES OF INDUSTRIES/INVESTMENTS: No preference
GEOGRAPHIC LIMITS OF INVESTMENTS/LOANS: International
RANGE OF INV./LOAN PER BUSINESS: Min. $1 million; Max. $5 million +
BUSINESS CHARACTERISTICS DESIRED-REQUIRED: Minimum number of years in business: 0
REFERRALS ACCEPTED FROM: Investment/Mortgage banker or Borrower/Investee

COMPANY: **Winthrop Ventures**
ADDRESS: 74 Trinity Place
New York, NY 10006
PHONE: (212) 422-0100
TYPE OF INSTITUTION: Private investment bank; registered investment advisor, Computer consultants
CONTACT OFFICER(S): C. Brown
INVESTMENTS/LOANS MADE: For own account, Through private placements
INVESTMENTS/LOANS MADE: In securities with a secondary market and in securities without a secondary market
TYPES OF FINANCING: SECONDARY-MARKET CORPORATE SECURITIES: Common stock; Preferred stock; Bonds; Other: Subordinated debt, VENTURE CAPITAL: Start-up from developed product stage; First-stage (less than 1 year); Second-stage (generally 1-3 years); Later-stage expansion; Buy-outs/ Acquisitions, LOANS: Unsecured; Working capital (receivables/inventory); Equipment; Equity-related, OTHER SERVICES PROVIDED: Portfolio management, computer consulting
PREFERRED TYPES OF INDUSTRIES/INVESTMENTS: Proprietary manufacturing, technology-related, aviation, and other industries with high returns on invested capital

WILL NOT CONSIDER: Real estate, extractive industries
GEOGRAPHIC LIMITS OF INVESTMENTS/LOANS: International
RANGE OF INV./LOAN PER BUSINESS: Min. $500,000; Max. $10,000,000
PREFERRED TERM FOR LOANS & LEASES: Max. 15 years
BUSINESS CHARACTERISTICS DESIRED-REQUIRED: Minimum number of years in business: 0; Other: Track record and financial participation of principals
REFERRALS ACCEPTED FROM: Borrower/Investee

COMPANY: **Wood River Capital Corporation**
ADDRESS: 645 Madison Avenue
New York, NY 10022
PHONE: (212) 750-9420
TYPE OF INSTITUTION: Venture capital fund
CONTACT OFFICER(S): W. Wallace McDowell, President
Elizabeth W. Smith, Executive Vice President
TOTAL ASSETS: $35,000,000,000
INVESTMENTS/LOANS MADE: For own account
INVESTMENTS/LOANS MADE: In securities with a secondary market; In securities without a secondary market
TYPES OF FINANCING: SECONDARY-MARKET CORPORATE SECURITIES: Common stock; Preferred stock; Bonds, VENTURA CAPITAL: Start-up from developed product stage; First-Stage; Second-stage, LOANS: Working capital; Equity-related
PREFERRED TYPES OF INDUSTRIES/INVESTMENTS: Early stage equity investments in a wide diversity of industries
WILL NOT CONSIDER: Retail, Real estate, Entertainment
RANGE OF INV./LOAN PER BUSINESS: Min. $200,000; Max. $1,000,000
PREFERRED TERM FOR LOANS/LEASES: Min. 5 years; Max. 7 years
BUSINESS CHARACTERISTICS DESIRED-REQUIRED: Minimum number of years in business: 0

COMPANY: **The Pittsford Group, Inc.**
ADDRESS: 8 Lodge Pole Road
Pittsford, NY 14534
PHONE: (716) 223-3523
TYPE OF INSTITUTION: Venture Capital
CONTACT OFFICER(S): Logan M. Cheek, Managing Principal
C. C. Hipkins, Jr. Principal
ASSETS: Capital under management: $40,000,000
INVESTMENTS/LOANS MADE: For own account, For managed accounts,
INVESTMENTS/LOANS MADE: In securities with a secondary market and in securities without a secondary market
TYPES OF FINANCING: SECONDARY-MARKET CORPORATE SECURITIES: Common stock, VENTURE CAPITAL, LOANS: Equity-related
PREFERRED TYPES OF INDUSTRIES/INVESTMENTS: Telecommunications; Industrial Process and Controls; Computer Software and Hardware, Life sciences, Office and factory automation, Precision machinery equipment, Information sciences, Medical technology

WILL NOT CONSIDER: Developmental deals, anything with a tax advantage
GEOGRAPHIC LIMITS OF INVESTMENTS/LOANS: National; Some preference to upstate New York
RANGE OF INV./LOAN PER BUSINESS: Min. $100,000; Max. $4,000,000
BUSINESS CHARACTERISTICS DESIRED-REQUIRED: Min. no. of years in business: 0; Projected annual ROI within three years in excess of 40%
REFERRALS ACCEPTED FROM: Investment/Mortgage banker or Borrower/Investee

COMPANY: **Barrett Capital & Leasing Corporation**
ADDRESS: 707 Westchester Avenue
White Plains, NY 10604
PHONE: (914) 682-1960
TYPE OF INSTITUTION: Equipment vehicle leasing and finance company
CONTACT OFFICER(S): Barry P. Korn, President
ASSETS: $60 million
INVESTMENTS/LOANS MADE: For own account, For managed accounts
TYPES OF FINANCING: LEASES: Single-investor; Leveraged; Tax leases; Non-tax leases; Operating; Tax-oriented lease brokerage; Vendor financing programs
PREFERRED TYPES OF INDUSTRIES/INVESTMENTS: For all industries, leases of equipment and vehicles
GEOGRAPHIC LIMITS OF INVESTMENTS/LOANS: International
RANGE OF INV./LOAN PER BUSINESS: Min. $3,000; Max. $100 million
PREFERRED TERM FOR LOANS & LEASES: Min. 2 years; Max. 10 years
BUSINESS CHARACTERISTICS DESIRED-REQUIRED: Minimum number of years in business: 3
REFERRALS: Investment/Mortgage banker;Borrower/Investee

COMPANY: **Harrison Capital Inc.**
ADDRESS: 2000 Westchester Avenue
White Plains, NY 10650
PHONE: (914) 253-7845
TYPE OF INSTITUTION: Corporate Venture Capital Firm
CONTACT OFFICER(S): W. T. Corl, President
E. J. Steigauf, Investment Manager
M. S. Johns, Associate
INVESTMENTS/LOANS MADE: Through private placements
TYPES OF FINANCING: VENTURE CAPITAL: Start-up from developed product stage
PREFERRED TYPES OF INDUSTRIES/INVESTMENTS: Emphasis on High Technology (Including Computers, Communications, Biotechnology, Industrial Processes).
WILL NOT CONSIDER: Real Estate
GEOGRAPHIC LIMITS OF INVESTMENTS/LOANS: National
RANGE OF INV./LOAN PER BUSINESS: Min. $250,000; Max. $2,000,000
BUSINESS CHARACTERISTICS DESIRED-REQUIRED: Min. number of years in business: 0;
REFERRALS ACCEPTED FROM: Investment/Mortgage banker or Borrower/Investee

COMPANY: **Scientific Advances, Inc.**
ADDRESS: 601 W. Fifth Ave.
Columbus, OH 43201
PHONE: (614) 294-5541
TYPE OF INSTITUTION: Venture Capital Subsidiary, Battelle Memorial Institute
CONTACT OFFICER(S): Thomas W. Harvey, V.P.
Daniel J. Shea, V.P.
ASSETS: $20 + Million
INVESTMENTS/LOANS MADE: Only in securities without a secondary mark et
TYPES OF FINANCING: VENTURE CAPITAL: Start-up from developed product stage; First-stage (less than 1 year); Second-stage (generally 1-3 years)
PREFERRED TYPES OF INDUSTRIES/INVESTMENTS: Technically based companies; $0 - 15 million in annual sales.
WILL NOT CONSIDER: Non-technology based companies
GEOGRAPHIC LIMITS OF INVESTMENTS/LOANS: National
RANGE OF INV./LOAN PER BUSINESS: Min. $300,000; Max. $800,000
BUSINESS CHARACTERISTICS DESIRED-REQUIRED: Min. no. of years in business: 0
REFERRALS ACCEPTED FROM: Investment/Mortgage banker or Borrower/Investee

COMPANY:**Basic Search**
ADDRESS: Park Place 10 W. Streetsboro St.
Hudson, OH 44236
PHONE: (216) 656-2442
TYPE OF INSTITUTION: Venture Capital Co.
CONTACT OFFICER(S): Jerry Weisz, President
INVESTMENTS/LOANS MADE: For own account, Through private placements
TYPES OF FINANCING: VENTURE CAPITAL: Start-up from developed product stage
GEOGRAPHIC LIMITS OF INVESTMENTS/LOANS: International
BUSINESS CHARACTERISTICS DESIRED-REQUIRED: OTHER: Potential of $100,000,000 in sales in 5 years

COMPANY: **SDS Biotech Corp. (Joint venture of Diamond Shamrock Corp. and Showa Denko) (216) 357-3000**
ADDRESS: 7528 Auburn Rd., Box 348
Painsville, OH 44077
PHONE: (216) 357-3000
TYPE OF INSTITUTION: Manufacturer and marketer of agricultural and animal health products
CONTACT OFFICER(S): Richard A. DiSanza, V.P., New Ventures
INVESTMENTS/LOANS MADE: In securities with a secondary market and in securities without a secondary market
TYPES OF FINANCING: SECONDARY-MARKET CORPORATE SECURITIES: Common stock; Preferred stock, VENTURE CAPITAL: Research & Deveopment, Start-up from deveoped product stage; First-stage; Second-stage; Later-stage expansion; Buy-outs/ Acquisitions, OTHER SERVICES PROVIDED: R&D Contracts
PREFERRED TYPES OF INDUSTRIES/INVESTMENTS: Agricultural, Biotechnology
GEOGRAPHIC LIMITS OF INVESTMENTS/LOANS: International
RANGE OF INV/LOAN PER BUSINESS: Depends on opportunity assessment
BUSINESS CHARACTERISTICS DESIRED-REQUIRED: Range from start-up to established business
REFERRALS ACCEPTED FROM: Investment/Mortgage banker or Borrower/Investee

COMPANY:**Diamond Venture Capital Corporation**
ADDRESS: 4500 Dorr Street, P.O. Box 1000
Toledo, OH 43697
PHONE: (419) 535-4748
TYPE OF INSTITUTION: Venture capital subisidiary
CONTACT OFFICER(S): Robert C. Richter, President
INVESTMENTS/LOANS MADE: For own account
TYPES OF FINANCING:VENTURE CAPITAL: Start-up from developed product stage; First-stage; Second-stage; Later-stage expansion
PREFERRED TYPES OF INDUSTRIES/INVESTMENTS: Industrial; Communications; Data processing
WILL NOT CONSIDER: Medicial, Biotech
GEOGRAPHIC LIMITS OF INVESTMENTS/LOANS: National
RANGE OF INV./LOAN PER BUSINESS: Min. $250,000
REMARKS: Subsidiary of Dana Corporation

COMPANY:**Shaw Venture Partners**
ADDRESS: 851 S.W. Sixth Avenue, #800
Pportland, OR 97204
PHONE: (503) 228-4884
TYPE OF INSTITUTION: Venture Capital
CONTACT OFFICER(S): Ralph Shaw
Herbert Shaw
Alan Dishlip
ASSETS:$35,000,000
INVESTMENTS/LOANS MADE: For own account
TYPES OF FINANCING: VENTURE CAPITAL: Research & Development; Start-up from developed product stage; First-stage; Second-stage; Later-stage; Buy-outs/Acquisitions
PREFERRED TYPES OF INDUSTRIES/INVESTMENTS: Broad range
WILL NOT CONSIDER: Real Estate
GEOGRAPHIC LIMITS OF INVESTMENTS/LOANS: National
RANGE OF INV./LOAN PER BUSINESS: Max. $1,000,000
BUSINESS CHARACTERISTICS DESIRED-REQUIRED: Other: Experienced management team

COMPANY: **First Valley Capital Corporation**
ADDRESS: One Bethlehem Plaza
Bethlehem, PA 18018
PHONE: (215) 865-8675
TYPE OF INSTITUTION: SBIC of 1.0 billion, bank holding company
CONTACT OFFICER(S): Matthew W. Thomas, President
ASSETS: $550M
INVESTMENTS/LOANS MADE: For own account

INVESTMENTS/LOANS MADE: Only in securities without a secondary market
TYPES OF FINANCING: SECONDARY-MARKET CORPORATE SECURITIES: Preferred stock; Other: Term loans with warrants, VENTURE CAPITAL: Second-stage, LOANS: Other: term loans for all purposes except real estate
PREFERRED TYPES OF INDUSTRIES/INVESTMENTS: No preference
WILL NOT CONSIDER: Real estate
GEOGRAPHIC LIMITS OF INVESTMENTS/LOANS: Local
RANGE OF INV./LOAN PER BUSINESS: Min. $25M; Max. $110M
PREFERRED TERM FOR LOANS & LEASES: Min. 5 years; Max. 10 years
BUSINESS CHARACTERISTICS DESIRED-REQUIRED: Minimum number of years in business: 1-2; Min. annual sales $250M; Min. net worth $0; Min. annual net income $0; Min. annual cash flow $0
REFERRALS ACCEPTED FROM: Investment/Mortgage banker and Borrower/Investee
REMARKS: Aggressive debt oriented with equity features

COMPANY: **NEPA Venture Fund Ltd.**
ADDRESS: 201 Ferry St.
Easton, PA 18042
PHONE: (215) 253-8022
TYPE OF INSTITUTION: Venture Capital Partnership
CONTACT OFFICER(S): Frederick J. Beste III, President
ASSETS: $10 million
TYPE OF INVESTMENTS/LOANS MADE: For own account
TYPES OF FINANCING: VENTURE CAPITAL: Research & Development; Start-up from developed product stage; First-stage; Second-stage; Later-stage expansion; Buy-outs/Acquisitions
PREFERRED TYPES OF INDUSTRIES/INVESTMENTS: Technology based
RANGE OF INV./LOAN PER BUSINESS: Min. $50,000; Max. $3,000,000
REFERRALS ACCEPTED FROM: Investment/Mortgage banker and Borrower/Investee

COMPANY: **Cromwell & Kyle**
ADDRESS: 234 Fountainville Center
Fountainville, PA 18923
PHONE: (215) 249-3583
TYPE OF INSTITUTION: Consulting Investment Bankers
CONTACT OFFICER(S): Alec B. Kyle
Roger J.K. Cromwell
INVESTMENTS/LOANS MADE: Through private placements
INVESTMENTS/LOANS MADE: In securities without a secondary market
TYPES OF FINANCING: SECONDARY-MARKET CORPORATE SECURITIES: Common stock; Preferred stock; Bonds, VENTURE CAPITAL: Research & Development; Start-up from developed product stage; First-stage (less than 1 year); Second-stage (generally 1-3 years); Later-stage expansion; Buy-outs/Acquisitions, LOANS: Unsecured; Working capital (receivables/inventory); Equipment; Equity-related; Other: Mezzanine financing in leveraged buy-outs. Loans against receivables from Mexican government entities, REAL ESTATE LOANS: Long-term senior mtg.; Intermediate-term senior mtg.; Subordinated; Wraparounds; Land; Land development; Construction; Gap; Standbys; Industrial revenue bonds, FACTORING, INTERNATIONAL (including import/export), REAL ESTATE: Acquisitions; Joint ventures; Partnerships/Syndications, OTHER SERVICES PROVIDED: Restructuring financings to command low-interest Swiss funding
PREFERRED TYPES OF INDUSTRIES/INVESTMENTS: No preference
GEOGRAPHIC LIMITS OF INVESTMENTS/LOANS: National; International
RANGE OF INV./LOAN PER BUSINESS: Min. $500,000; Max. $75,000,000
REFERRALS ACCEPTED FROM: Investment/Mortgage banker or Borrower/Investee
BRANCHES: 1960 Bronson Rd., Fairfield, CT 06430; (203) 259-3269

COMPANY: **Century IV Partners**
ADDRESS: 1760 Market Street
Philadelphia, PA
PHONE: (215) 751-9444
CONTACT OFFICER(S): Walter M. Aikman, General Partner
Charles A. Burton, General Partner
Thomas R. Morse, Senior Associate
Michael Radow, Senior Associate
ASSETS$40 million
INVESTMENTS/LOANS MADE: For own account
INVESTMENTS/LOANS MADE: In securities with a secondary market and in securities without a secondary market
TYPES OF FINANCING: VENTURE CAPITAL: Start-up from developed product stage; First-stage; Second-stage; Later-stage expansion; Buy-outs/Acquisitions
PREFERRED TYPES OF INDUSTRIES/INVESTMENTS: Data processing equipment, computer software, communications equipment and services, semiconductor products and equipment, and health care and biotechnical areas
WILL NOT CONSIDER: Real Estate, Oil and Gas
GEOGRAPHIC LIMITS OF INVESTMENTS/LOANS: National
RANGE OF INV./LOAN PER BUSINESS: Min. $500,000; Max. $2,000,000
BUSINESS CHARACTERISTICS DESIRED-REQUIRED: Minimum number of years in business: 0

COMPANY: **Innovest Group, Inc.**
ADDRESS: 1700 Market Street, Ste. 1228
Philadelphia, PA 19103
PHONE: (215) 564-3960
TYPE OF INSTITUTION: Private Venture Capital Company
CONTACT OFFICER(S): Richard E. Woosnam, President
Nila K. Sendzik, V.P.
ASSETS: $10 Million
INVESTMENTS/LOANS MADE: For own account; Through private placements
INVESTMENTS/LOANS MADE: Only in securities without a secondary market

TYPES OF FINANCING: VENTURE CAPITAL: Start-up from developed product stage; First-stage; Second-stage; Later-stage expansion, LEASES: Single-investor; Leveraged; Tax leases; Vendor financing programs, REAL ESTATE
PREFERRED TYPES OF INDUSTRIES/INVESTMENTS: Communications — cable TV, commercial communication, data comm, satellite & miicrowave comm., telephone related; Computer Related —- computer graphics & CAD/CAM, computer services, memory devices, micro 7 mini computers, software systems; Electronics Equipment — medical products, laser related, analytical and scientific instrumentation, optics technology, semiconduction; Medical — diagnostic equipment, therapeutic equipment; Other — education related, real estate
GEOGRAPHIC LIMITS OF INVESTMENTS/LOANS: Regional
RANGE OF INV./LOAN PER BUSINESS: Min. $250,000; Max. $1,000,000
BUSINESS CHARACTERISTICS DESIRED-REQUIRED: Minimum number of years in business: 0
REFERRALS ACCEPTED FROM: Investment banker or Borrower/Investee

COMPANY: **PSFS**
ADDRESS: 12 South 12th Street
Philadelphia, PA 19107
PHONE: (215) 636-6000
TYPE OF INSTITUTION: Diversified Financial Services
CONTACT OFFICER(S): Philip A. McMunigal III, V.P., Private Placement Unit
ASSETS: $12.5 billion (June 30, 1984)
INVESTMENTS/LOANS MADE: For own account; Through private placements
INVESTMENTS/LOANS MADE: In securities with a secondary market and in securities without a secondary market
TYPES OF FINANCING: SECONDARY-MARKET CORPORATE SECURITIES: Common stock; Preferred stock; Bonds, VENTURE CAPITAL: Start-up from developed product stage, LOANS: Unsecured to credits above Baa; Working capital; Equipment; Equity-related, REAL ESTATE LOANS: Long-term senior mtg.; Intermediate-term senior mtg.; Land development; Construction; Standbys; Industrial revenue bonds, LEASES: Leveraged; Tax leases; Non-tax leases; Operating; Vendor financing programs, REAL ESTATE: Acquisitions; Joint ventures; Partnerships/ Syndications, OTHER SERVICES PROVIDED: pension fund advisory services, trade and stand-by letters of credit
PREFERRED TYPES OF INDUSTRIES/INVESTMENTS: all offerings considered
GEOGRAPHIC LIMITS OF INVESTMENTS/LOANS: Local; State; Regional; National; International
RANGE OF INV./LOAN PER BUSINESS: Min. $1,000,000; Max. depends on quality rating
PREFERRED TERM FOR LOANS & LEASES: Min. one year; Max. 10 years
BUSINESS CHARACTERISTICS DESIRED-REQUIRED: Negotiable

COMPANY: **Pennsylvania Financial Development Corporation (Parent)/Pennsylvania Growth Investment Corporation (Wholly-Owned Subsidiary)**
ADDRESS: 1000 RIDC Plaza, Suite 311
Pittsburgh, PA 15238
PHONE: (412) 963-9339
TYPE OF INSTITUTION: Both are Venture Capital Companies
CONTACT OFFICER(S): Mary G. Dell, Executive V.P.
Wm. L. Mosenson, President
INVESTMENTS/LOANS MADE: For own account
INVESTMENTS/LOANS MADE: Only in securities without a secondary market
TYPES OF FINANCING: SECONDARY-MARKET CORPORATE SECURITIES: Tailored to fit, VENTURE CAPITAL: Research & Development; Second-stage (generally 1-3 years); Later-stage expansion; Buy-outs/Acquisitions, REAL ESTATE LOANS: Subordinated
PREFERRED TYPES OF INDUSTRIES/INVESTMENTS: Diversified
WILL NOT CONSIDER: Retail, Franchises
GEOGRAPHIC LIMITS OF INVESTMENTS/LOANS: Regional
RANGE OF INV./LOAN PER BUSINESS: Min. $150,000: Max. $1,000,000
PREFERRED TERM FOR LOANS & LEASES: Min. 3; Max. 6 years
BUSINESS CHARACTERISTICS DESIRED-REQUIRED: No start-ups, significant commitment by principals who must retain control
REFERRALS ACCEPTED FROM: Investment/Mortgage banker or Borrower/Investee

COMPANY: **PNC Venture Capital Group**
ADDRESS: Fifth Avenue & Wood Street
Pittsburgh, PA 15222
PHONE: (412) 355-8882
TYPE OF INSTITUTION: Venture arm of bank holding company
CONTACT OFFICER(S): David Hillman, EVP and General Manager
Jeffrey Schutz, Vice President
TOTAL ASSETS: $7,500,000
INVESTMENTS/LOANS MADE: For own account
INVESTMENTS/LOANS MADE: In securities with a secondary market; In securities without a secndary market
TYPES OF FINANCING: SECONDARY-MARKET COSRPORATE SECURITIES: Prefrred stock; Other: Convertible debt, VENTURE CAPITAL: First-stage; Second-stage; Later-stage expansion; Buy-outs/ Acquisitions, LOANS: Unsecured
PREFERRED TYPES OF INDUSTRIES/INVESTMENTS: Will consider all
WILL NOT CONSIDER: Oil and gas; Real estate
GEOGRAPHIC LIMITS OF INVESTMENTS/LOANS: National
RANGE OF INVESTMENT/LOAN PER BUSINESS: Min. $100,000; Max. $500,000
PREFERRED TERM FOR LOANS & LEASES: Min. 3 years, Max. 7 years
BUSINESS CHARACTERISTICS DESIRED-REQUIRED: Company must have prototype and customer base desired

REFERRALS: Investment/Mortgage banker; Borrower/Investee

COMPANY: **Robinson Venture Partners**
ADDRESS: 6507 Wilkins Avenue
Pittsburgh, PA 15217
PHONE: (412) 661-1200
TYPE OF INSTITUTION: Private venture capital partnership investing own funds
CONTACT OFFICER(S): Stephen G. Robinson, General Partner
TOTAL ASSETS: $2,500,000
INVESTMENTS/LOANS MADE: For own account: Through private placement
INVESTMENTS/LOANS MADE: Only in securities without a secondary market
TYPES OF FINANCING: VENTURE CAPITAL: Start-up from developed product stage; First-stage; Second-stage
PREFERED TYPES OF INDUSTRIES/INVESTMENTS: Technology related industries including communications, computer hardware and software, analytical scientific and medical instrumentation, industrial automation, process control and education related
GEOGRAPHIC LIMITS OF INVESTMENTS/LOANS: National, preference to north east
RANGE OF INV./LOAN PER BUSINESS: Min. $50,000; Max. $300,000
BUSINESS CHARACTERISTICS DESIRED-REQUIRED: Minimum number of years in business: 0
REFERRALS ACCEPTED:Investment/Mortgage banker only; Borrower/Investee

COMPANY: **Maxwell Capital Corporation (MAXCAP)**
ADDRESS: Box 813
Providence, RI 02901
PHONE: (401) 739-3850
TYPE OF INSTITUTION: Corporate Development and Acquisition Consulting
CONTACT OFFICER(S): Dana H. Gaebe, Esq., President
Robert E. Radican, V.P.
INVESTMENTS/LOANS MADE: For own account, Through private placements
INVESTMENTS/LOANS MADE: In securities with a secondary market and in securities without a secondary market
TYPES OF FINANCING: SECONDARY-MARKET CORPORATE SECURITIES: Common stock; Preferred stock, VENTURE CAPITAL: Second-stage (generally 1-3 years): Buy-outs/Acquisitions, LOANS: Equity-related, INTERNATIONAL (including import/export)
PREFERRED TYPES OF INDUSTRIES/INVESTMENTS: Computer Industry; Manufacturing
WILL NOT CONSIDER: Retail; Real Estate Development
GEOGRAPHIC LIMITS OF INVESTMENTS/LOANS: International
RANGE OF INV./LOAN PER BUSINESS: Min. $100,000; Max. $1,500,000
REFERRALS ACCEPTED FROM: Investment/Mortgage banker or Borrower/Investee

COMPANY: **Narragansett Capital Corporation**
ADDRESS: 40 Westminster St.
Providence, RI 02903
PHONE: (401) 751-1000
TYPE OF INSTITUTION: Venture capital firm
CONTACT OFFICER(S): Gregory P. Barber, V.P.
Roger A. Vandenberg, V.P.
ASSETS: $185,000,000
INVESTMENTS/LOANS MADE: For own account, For managed accounts
INVESTMENTS/LOANS MADE: Only in securities without a secondary market
TYPES OF FINANCING: VENTURE CAPITAL: Buy-outs/Acquisitions
GEOGRAPHIC LIMITS OF INVESTMENTS/LOANS: National
RANGE OF INV./LOAN PER BUSINESS: Min. $1,000,000; Max. $7,500,000
BUSINESS CHARACTERISTICS DESIRED-REQUIRED: Min. annual sales $25,000,000
REFERRALS ACCEPTED FROM: Investment/Mortgage banker or Borrower/Investee

COMPANY: **Rhode Island Hospital Trust National Bank**
ADDRESS: 1 Hospital Trust Plaza
Providence, RI 02903
PHONE: (401) 278-8000
TYPE OF INSTITUTION: Pension area of a national bank
CONTACT OFFICER(S): Bernard N. Roth, Senior Vice President, Mezzamine financing for corporate buyouts
Celia R. Deluga, Assistant Vice President, Real estate financing, corporate buyout financing & financing for oil & gas properties
ASSETS: $80,000,000
INVESTMENTS/LOANS MADE: For managed accounts, Through private placements
INVESTMENTS/LOANS MADE: In securities with a secondary market and in securities without a secondary market
TYPES OF FINANCING: LOANS: Unsecured to credits above B, Baa; Other: all loans have equity features through the use of warrants, contingent interest, etc. REAL ESTATE LOANS: Intermediate-term senior mtg.; Subordinated; Wraparounds. OTHER SERVICES PROVIDED: Financing for oil & gas transactions
PREFERRED TYPES OF INDUSTRIES/INVESTMENTS: Financing for corporate buyouts: mature smoke stack manufacturing firms; Real estate financing: participating mortgages of office buildings, shopping centers, apartment complexes; Collateralized oil & gas loans, which provide a current return plus on equity sharing
WILL NOT CONSIDER: High tech firms
GEOGRAPHIC LIMITS OF INVESTMENTS/LOANS: National
RANGE OF INV./LOAN PER BUSINESS: Min. $2,000,000; Max. $20,000,000
PREFERRED TERM FOR LOANS & LEASES: Min. 7 years; Max. 12 years
BUSINESS CHARACTERISTICS DESIRED-REQUIRED: Minimum number of years in business: 5; Min. annual sales $25,000,000; Other: firms which have reasonable tangible asset coverage
REFERRALS ACCEPTED FROM: Investment/Mortgage banker or Borrower/Investee

COMPANY: **Textron Inc.**
ADDRESS: 40 Westminster Street
Providence, RI 02903
PHONE: (401) 421-2800
TYPE OF INSTITUTION: Investment Management Department
CONTACT OFFICER(S): John Lemery, Investment Manager, Corporate Private Placements
Laurens W. Goff, Investment Manager, Real Estate Investments
ASSETS: $600,000,000 under management
INVESTMENTS/LOANS MADE: For managed accounts; Through private placements
INVESTMENTS/LOANS MADE: In securities with a secondary market and in securities without a secondary market
TYPES OF FINANCING: VENTURE CAPITAL: Later-stage expansion; Buy-outs/Acquisitions, LOANS: Unsecured; Working capital (receivables/inventory); Equipment; Equity-related, REAL ESTATE LOANS: Intermediate-term senior mtg.; Subordinated; Wraparounds
PREFERRED TYPES OF INDUSTRIES/INVESTMENTS: Generally avoid regulated industries and hospitality real estate projects
WILL NOT CONSIDER: any deal without an equity feature
GEOGRAPHIC LIMITS OF INVESTMENTS/LOANS: National
RANGE OF INV./LOAN PER BUSINESS: Min. $5.0 Million; Max. $20.0 Million
PREFERRED TERM FOR LOANS & LEASES: Min. 3; Max. 12 years
BUSINESS CHARACTERISTICS DESIRED-REQUIRED: Minimum number of years in business: 3-5; Min. annual sales $5.0 Mil; Management in place 3-5 years
REFERRALS ACCEPTED FROM: Investment/Mortgage banker or Borrower/Investee

COMPANY: **Sterling Capital, Ltd.**
ADDRESS: P.O. Box 17526
Greenville, SC 29606
PHONE: (803) 297-9196
TYPE OF INSTITUTION: Private
CONTACT OFFICER(S): John M. Sterling, Jr., General Partner
Tee Hooper, Jr., General Partner
ASSETS: $5,000,000
INVESTMENTS/LOANS MADE: For own account
INVESTMENTS/LOANS MADE: In securities with or without a secondary market
TYPES OF FINANCING: VENTURE CAPITAL: Research & Development; Start-up from developed product stage; First-stage; Second-staage; Later-stage expansion; Buy-outs/Acquisitions. LOANS: Equity-related.
PREFERRED TYPES OF INDUSTRIES/INVESTMENTS: Diversified industry including manufacturing and distribution
GEOGRAPHIC LIMITS OF INVESTMENTS/LOANS: Regional
RANGE OF INV./LOAN PER BUSINESS: Min. $100,000; Max. $350,000
PREFERRED TERM FOR LOANS & LEASES: Min. 3; Max. 10 years
BUSINESS CHARACTERISTICS DESIRED-REQUIRED: No minimums
REFERRALS ACCEPTED FROM: Investment/Mortgage banker or Borrower/Investee

COMPANY: **Dobson & Johnson, Inc.**
ADDRESS: 1 Commerce Place, Ste. 1800
Nashville, TN 37239
PHONE: (615) 244-8600
CONTACT OFFICER(S): Albert W. Johnson II., Pres.
Brian Johnson, V.P.
ASSETS: $200 million
INVESTMENTS/LOANS MADE: Through private placements
TYPES OF FINANCING: VENTURE CAPITAL: Later-stage expansion; Buy-outs/Acquisitions, REAL ESTATE LOANS: Long-term senior mtg.; Intermediate-term senior mtg.; Subordinated; Wraparounds; Land; Land development; Construction; Gap; Standbys, LEASES: Single-investor; Leveraged; Operating; Tax-oriented lease brokerage, REAL ESTATE: Acquisitions; Joint ventures; Partnerships/Syndications
WILL NOT CONSIDER: Special purpose or industry specific
GEOGRAPHIC LIMITS OF INVESTMENTS/LOANS: International
RANGE OF INV./LOAN PER BUSINESS: Min. $1 million
BUSINESS CHARACTERISTICS DESIRED-REQUIRED: Other: Must have proven track record
REFERRALS ACCEPTED FROM: Investment/Mortgage banker or Borrower/Investee

COMPANY: **Business Capital Corporation Of Arlington**
ADDRESS: 1112 Copeland Rd. Suite 420
Arlington, TX 76011
PHONE: (817) 261-4936
TYPE OF INSTITUTION: SBIC
CONTACT OFFICER(S): Keith Martin, President
ASSETS: $1,010,000
INVESTMENTS/LOANS MADE: For own account
INVESTMENTS/LOANS MADE: In securities with or without a secondary market
TYPES OF FINANCING: SECONDARY-MARKET CORPORATE SECURITIES: Preferred stock; Other: Convertible Debt. VENTURE CAPITAL: Second-stage; Later-stage expansion; Buy-outs/Acquisitions. LOANS: Equity-related
WILL NOT CONSIDER: Startups
GEOGRAPHIC LIMITS OF INVESTMENTS/LOANS: Southwest
RANGE OF INV./LOAN PER BUSINESS: Min. $75,000; Max. $125,000
PREFERRED TERM FOR LOANS & LEASES: Min. 5 years; Max. 7 years
BUSINESS CHARACTERISTICS DESIRED-REQUIRED: Minimum number of years in business: 1.5; Min. annual sales $1,500,000; Min. net worth $150,000
REFERRALS ACCEPTED FROM: Investment/Mortgage banker or Borrower/Investee

VENTURE CAPITAL COMPANIES
(Also see SBICs, MESBICs and Investment Bankers)

COMPANY: **Business Development Partners I & II**
ADDRESS: 10805 Pecan Park Road
Austin, TX 78750
PHONE: (512) 258-1977
TYPE OF INSTITUTION: Private venture capital firm investing own funds
CONTACT OFFICER(S): Robert L. Brueck, General Partner, Austin
Michael E. Faherty, General Partner, Dallas
A.G.W. Biddle III, Associate, Austin
INVESTMENTS/LOANS MADE: For own account
TYPES OF FINANCING: VENTURE CAPITAAL: Research & Development; Start-up from developed product stage; First-Stage; Second-stage.
PREFERRED TYPES OF INDUSTRIES/INVESTMENTS: Technology Based
WILL NOT CONSIDER: Natural resources, Real estate
GEOGRAPHIC LIMITS OF INVESTMENTS/LOANS: Strong but not exclusive interest in Texas investments
RANGE OF INV./LOAN PER BUSINESS: Min. $100,000; Max. $1,500,000
BUSINESS CHARACTERISTICS DESIRED-REQUIRED: Minimum number of years in business: 0
REFERRALS ACCEPTED FROM: Investment/Mortgage banker or Borrower/Investee
BRANCHES: 6133 Highgate Lane, Dallas, TX 75214, Michael E. Faherty
REMARKS: Limited partners: Brentwood Associates, Hambrecht & Quist, Norwest Venture Capital, Rothschild Inc.

COMPANY: **C&G Covert Leasing, Inc.**
ADDRESS: 1700 W. 6th St.
Austin, TX 78703
PHONE: (512) 476-1903
CONTACT OFFICER(S): Clark Covert, General Manager
ASSETS: $2,000,000
INVESTMENTS/LOANS MADE: For own account, Through private placements, Through underwriting public offerings
TYPES OF FINANCING: VENTURE CAPITAL: Resarch & Development; Second-stage (generally 1-3 years); Later-stage expansion, LOANS: Equipment, LEASES: Single-investor; Leveraged; Tax leases; Non-tax leases; Operating; Tax-oriented lease brokerage; Lease syndications
PREFERRED TYPES OF INDUSTRIES/INVESTMENTS: Equipment leases low and middle market
RANGE OF INV./LOAN PER BUSINESS: Min. $7,500; Max. $1,000,000
PREFERRED TERM FOR LOANS & LEASES: Min. 3 years; Max. 7 years
BUSINESS CHARACTERISTICS DESIRED-REQUIRED: Minimum number of years in business: 3; Min. annual sales $1,000,000; Min. net worth $10X annual earnings; Min. annual net income 6 figure; Min. annual cash flow variable
REFERRALS ACCEPTED FROM: Investment/Mortgage banker or Borrower/Investee

COMPANY: **Berry Cash Southwest**
ADDRESS: One Galleria Tower, 13355 Noel Road, #1375; LB 65
Dallas, TX 75240
PHONE: (214) 392-7279
TYPE OF INSTITUTION: Venture Capital
CONTACT OFFICER(S): Berry Cash, General Partner
Glen Norm
Nancy Schuele, Business Manager
ASSETS: $25,000,000
INVESTMENTS/LOANS MADE: For own account
TYPES OF FINANCING: VENTURE CAPITAL: Start-up fom developed product stage; First-stage; Second-stage
PREFERRED TYPES OF INDUSTRIES/INVESTMENTS: Specialize in high technolgy, Bio-medical, Telecommunications
GEOGRAPHIC LIMITS OF INVESTMENTS/LOANS: Regional; Other: Southwest
RANGE OF INV./LOAN PER BUSINESS: Min. $500,000; Max. $1,500,000
BUSINESS CHARACTERISTICS DESIRED-REQUIRED: Other: Do Start-ups and seed
REMARKS: Affiliated with Interwest Partners II

COMPANY: **Capital Southwest Corporation**
ADDRESS: 12900 Preston Road at LBJ Suite 700
Dallas, TX 75230
PHONE: (214) 233-8242
TYPE OF INSTITUTION: Venture Capital
CONTACT OFFICER(S): Pat Hamner, Investment Assoc.
J. Bruce Duty, V.P.
Wiliam R. Thoomas, President
ASSETS: $53,337,670
INVESTMENTS/LOANS MADE: For own account
INVESTMENTS/LOANS MADE: In securities with a secondary market; In securities without a secondary market
TYPES OF FINANCING: VENTURE CAPITAL: Research & Development; Start-up from developed product stage; First-stage; Second-stage; Later-stage; Buy-outs/Acquisitions, LOANS: Equity-related, OTHER SERVICES PROVIDED: Convertible debentures; Convertible preferred stock, Private placements
PREFERRED TYPES OF INDUSTRIES/INVESTMENTS: Communication, Natural resources, Manufacturing and processing, Medical and health services, Transportation, Technology, Diversified
WILL NOT CONSIDER: Constructions or development R.E., Other investments, Retail, Hotels, Motels, Restaraunts, Service companies
GEOGRAPHIC LIMITS OF INVESTMENTS/LOANS: National
RANGE OF INV./LOAN PER BUSINESS: Min. $300,000; Max. $1,200,000
PREFERRED TERM FOR LOANS & LEASES: Min. 5 years; Max. 8 yearss
BUSINESS CHARACTERISTICS DESIRED-REQUIRED: Minimum number of years in business: 0; Other: Quality management, Favorable market, Proprietary product or service; Meaningful financial commitment by management to the venture
REFERRALS ACCEPTED FROM: Investment/Mortgage banker; Borrower/Investee

COMPANY: **The Chairman Corporation**
ADDRESS: 6350 LBJ 183E
Dallas, TX 75240

PHONE: (214) 233-1041
TYPE OF INSTITUTION: Venture Capital
CONTACT OFFICER(S): Sherrill E. Edwards, President
INVESTMENTS/LOANS MADE: For own account; Through private placements
TYPES OF FINANCING: VENTURE CAPITAL: Research & Development; Start-up from developed product stage; First-stage; Buy-outs/Acquisitions, OTHER SERVICES PROVIDED: Consulting
PREFERRED TYPES OF INDUSTRIES/INVESTMENTS: Diversified
WILL NOT CONSIDER: Entertainment
RANGE OF INV./LOAN PER BUSINESS: Min. $1,000,000
BUSINESS CHARACTERISTICS DESIRED-REQUIRED: Minimum number of years in business: 0

COMPANY: **Equity Capital Corporation of Texas**
ADDRESS: 5333 Spring Valley Road
Dallas, TX 75240
PHONE: (214) 991-2961
TYPE OF INSTITUTION: Venture Capital
CONTACT OFFICER(S): John M. Fooshee, President
INVESTMENTS/LOANS MADE: For own account
TYPES OF FINANCING: VENTURE CAPITAL: Start-up from developed product staage; First-stage, LOANS: Working capital; Equity-related
PREFERRED TYPES OF INDUSTRIES/INVESTMENTS: Software, Restaurants; Diversified
GEOGRAPHIC LIMITS OF INVESTMENTS/LOANS: Local; State; Other: Texas

COMPANY: **First Dallas Financial Company**
ADDRESS: 3302 Southland Center
Dallas, TX 75201
PHONE: (214) 922-0070
TYPE OF INSTITUTION: Investment Bank
CONTACT OFFICER(S): John T. McGuire, President
INVESTMENTS/LOANS MADE: Through private placements
TYPES OF FINANCING: VENTURE CAPITAL: Second-stage (generally 1-3 years); Buy-outs/Acquisitions, LOANS: Equity-related
PREFERRED TYPES OF INDUSTRIES/INVESTMENTS: Oil & Gas, Energy Related, High Technology; Industrial
WILL NOT CONSIDER: Real Estate
GEOGRAPHIC LIMITS OF INVESTMENTS/LOANS: Regional (Southwest)

COMPANY: **MBC Financial Services Corporation**
ADDRESS: 2501 Cedar Springs Road, Suite 400, LB 10
Dallas, TX 75201
PHONE: (214) 871-1200
TYPE OF INSTITUTION: Corporate Finance Group of Institutional Lender
CONTACT OFFICER(S): J. Michael McMahon, Senior Vice President
David S. Temin, Vice President
Lynne M. McGanity, Vice President
ASSETS: $500 million
INVESTMENTS/LOANS MADE: For own account
INVESTMENTS/LOANS MADE: In securities with a secondary market and in securities without a secondary market
TYPES OF FINANCING: SECONDARY MARKET CORPORATE SECURITIES: Bonds; Other: Subordinated loans, secured note financing; VENTURE CAPITAL: Later-stage expansion; Buy-outs/Acquisitions; LOANS: Unsecured; Working Capital; Equipment; REAL ESTATE LOANS: Intermediate-term senior mtg.; Wraparounds; Gap; Standbys; LEASES: Single-investor; Leveraged; Tax leases; Non-tax leases
GEOGRAPHIC LIMITS OF INVESTMENTS/LOANS: Regional
RANGE OF INV./LOAN PER BUSINESS: Min. $5 Million; Max. $20 Million
PREFERRED TERM FOR LOANS & LEASES: Min. 3 years; Max. 10 years
BUSINESS CHARACTERISTICS DESIRED-REQUIRED: Minimum number of years in business: 5; Min. annual sales $7 Million; Min. net worth $1 Million; Min. annual net income $1.5 Million; Min. annual cash flow $2 Million
REFERRALS ACCEPTED FROM: Investment/Mortgage banker or Borrower/Investee

COMPANY: **MSI Capital Corporation**
ADDRESS: 6510 Abrams Road, #650
Dallas, TX 75213
PHONE: (214) 341-1553
TYPE OF INSTITUTION: Venture Capital
CONTACT OFFICER(S): Nick Stanfield, President
Richard Wierzbicki, Investement Analyst
INVESTMENTS/LOANS MADE: For own account; Through private placements
TYPES OF FINANCING: VENTURE CAPITAL: Start-up from developed product stage; First-stage
PREFERRED TYPES OF INDUSTRIES/INVESTMENTS: General Industry
GEOGRAPHIC LIMITS OF INVESTMENTS/LOANS: State; Texas
RANGE OF INV./LOAN PER BUSINESS: Min. $100,000
BUSINESS CHARACTERISTICS DESIRED-REQUIRED: Minimum number of years in business: 0; Other: Management team in place; Developed product with benchmark sales
REFERRALS ACCEPTED FROM: Investment/Mortgage banker only; Borrower/Investee
REMARKS: Affiliated with Triad Ventures Ltd.

COMPANY: **Richard R. Jaffe & Company, Inc.**
ADDRESS: 7318 Royal Circle
Dallas, TX 75230
PHONE: (214) 241-6495
TYPE OF INSTITUTION: Venture Capital
CONTACT OFFICER(S): Richard R. Jaffe, President
ASSETS: $1,500,000
INVESTMENTS/LOANS MADE: For own account; Through private placements
INVESTMENTS/LOANS MADE: In securities with a secondary market; In securities without a secondary market
TYPES OF FINANCING: SECONDARY-MARKET CORPORATE SECURITIES: Common stock; Preferred

stock; Other: Subordinated Debentures, VENTURE CAPITAL: Start-up from developed product stage; First-stage, REAL ESTATE LOANS: Land developement, REAL ESTATE: Acquisitions; Joint ventures; Partnerships/Syndications
PREFERRED TYPES OF INDUSTRIES/INVESTMENTS: Computer manufacturing - Automation equipment, Proprietary service business; Real estaate development projects
GEOGRAPHIC LIMITS OF INVESTMENTS/LOANS: State; RegionalMin. $100,000; Max. $300,000
BUSINESS CHARACTERISTICS DESIRED-REQUIRED: Minimum number of years in busness: 0
REFERRALS ACCEPTED FROM: Investment/Mortgage baanker only

COMPANY: **Sevin Rosen Management Company**
ADDRESS: 5050 Quorum Drive 635
Dallas, TX 75240
PHONE: (214) 960-1744
TYPE OF INSTITUTION: Private Venture Capital
CONTACT OFFICER(S): L.J. Sevin
Jon Bayless
ASSETS: $250,000,000
INVESTMENTS/LOANS MADE: For own account; For managed accounts; Through private placements
INVESTMENTS/LOANS MADE: Only in securities without a secondary market
TYPES OF FINANCING: VENTURE CAPITAL: Start-up from developed product stage; First-stage
PREFERRED TYPES OF INDUSTRIES/INVESTMENTS: High technology
GEOGRAPHIC LIMITS OF INVESTMENTS/LOANS: National
RANGE OF INV./LOAN PER BUSINESS: Min. $500,000
BRANCHES: Robin Grossman, 200 Park Avenue, Suite 4503, New York, NY 10166, (212) 687-5115
Roger Borovoy, Stephen Dow, 1245 Oakmead Pkwy, #101, Sunnyvale, CA 94086, (408) 720-8590

COMPANY: **Southwest Enterprise Associates**
ADDRESS: 5420 LBJ Freeway, Suite 1266
Dallas, TX
PHONE: (214) 991-1620
TYPE OF INSTITUTION: Venture Capital Partnership
CONTACT OFFICER(S): Vin Prothro, Managing General Partner
ASSETS: $26 million
INVESTMENTS/LOANS MADE: For own account
TYPES OF FINANCING: VENTURE CAPITAL: Start-up from developed product stage; First-stage
PREFERRED TYPES OF INDUSTRIES/INVESTMENTS: High Technology Computer/Electronics; Biomedical; Telecommunications
WILL NOT CONSIDER: Retail; Real Estate; Oil & Gas; Agriculture
GEOGRAPHIC LIMITS OF INVESTMENTS/LOANS: Regional
RANGE OF INV./LOAN PER BUSINESS: Min. $300,000
BUSINESS CHARACTERISTICS DESIRED-REQUIRED: Minimum number of years in business: 0

COMPANY: **T.V.P. Associates**
ADDRESS: 2777 Stemmons Freeway
Dallas, TX 75207
PHONE: (214) 689-4265
TYPE OF INSTITUTION: Private Venture Capital
CONTACT OFFICER(S): James Silcock
INVESTMENTS/LOANS MADE: For own account; for managed accounts
INVESTMENTS/LOANS MADE: In securities with a secondary market; In securities without a secondary market
TYPES OF FINANCING: SECONDARY-MARKET CORPORATE SECURITIES: Common stock, VENTURE CAPITAL: Research & Development; Start-up from developed product stage; First-stage; Second-stage
PREFERRED TYPES OF INDUSTRIES/INVESTMENTS: Telecommunications, Information processing, Electronics
GEOGRAPHIC LIMITS OF INVESTMENTS/LOANS: Other: Prefer southwest
RANGE OF INV./LOAN PER BUSINESS: Min. $100,000
BUSINESS CHARACTERISTICS DESIRED-REQUIRED: Other: Good management
REMARKS: Affiliated with Bedord Equities

COMPANY: **Idanta Partners**
ADDRESS: 201 Main Street, Suite 3200
Ft. Worth, TX 76102
PHONE: (817) 338-2020
TYPE OF INSTITUTION: Private Venture Capital Firm
CONTACT OFFICER(S): David J. Dunn, Managing Partner
Michael J. Kucha, Partner
Dev Purkayastha, Partner
Harry Lange, Associate
INVESTMENTS/LOANS MADE: For own account
INVESTMENTS/LOANS MADE: In securities with a secondary market and in securities without a secondary market
TYPES OF FINANCING: SECONDARY-MARKET CORPORATE SECURITIES: Common stock; VENTURE CAPITAL: Research & Development; Start-up from developed product stage; First-stage Second-stage
GEOGRAPHIC LIMITS OF INVESTMENTS/LOANS: National
RANGE OF INV./LOAN PER BUSINESS: Min. $250,000
BUSINESS CHARACTERISTICS DESIRED-REQUIRED: Minimum number of years in business: 0
REFERRALS ACCEPTED FROM: Investment/Mortgage banker or Borrower/Investee

COMPANY: **Criterion Venture Partners**
ADDRESS: 333 Clay Street, 4300
Houston, TX 77002
PHONE: (713) 751-2400
TYPE OF INSTITUTION: Venture Capital
CONTACT OFFICER(S): Harvard H. Hill, Jr., General Partner
Crichton W. Brown, Associate
David O. Wicks Jr., General Partner
Gregory A. Rider, General Partner
M. Scott Albert, Associate
ASSETS: $40,000,000 (capital under management)

INVESTMENTS/LOANS MADE: For own account
TYPES OF FINANCING: VENTURE CAPITAL: Start-up fom developed product stage; First-stage; Second-stage; Later-stage expansion; Buy-outs/Acquisitions, OTHER SERVICES PROVIDED: Purchase of secondary positions
PREFERRED TYPES OF INDUSTRIES/INVESTMENTS: Communications, Electronics, Computer-related, Distribution, Energy/natural resurces, Genetic engineering, Medical and health related, Industrial
GEOGRAPHIC LIMITS OF INVESTMENTS/LOANS: Regional; Southwest and Southeast
RANGE OF INV./LOAN PER BUSINESS: Min. $250,000
REMARKS: Preferred size of investment $500,000 - $1,000,000

COMPANY: **Curtin & Co., Inc.**
ADDRESS: 2050 Houston Natural Gas Bldg.
Houston, TX 77002
PHONE: (713) 658-9806
TYPE OF INSTITUTION: Investment Banking & Corporate Finance-Firm
CONTACT OFFICER(S): John D. Curtin, Jr., President
Stewart Cureton, Jr., Vice President
Charles A. Armbrust, Vice President
INVESTMENTS/LOANS MADE: For own account, Through private placements
INVESTMENTS/LOANS MADE: In securities with a secondary market and in securities without a secondary market
TYPES OF FINANCING: VENTURE CAPITAL: Start-up from developed product stage; First-stage; Second-stage; Later-stage expansion; Buy-outs/Acquisitions; LOANS: Unsecured to credits above Baa; Working capital; Equipment; Equity-related
PREFERRED TYPES OF INDUSTRIES/INVESTMENTS: Basic Manufacturing; Industrial Services; Oil & Gas Related; Technology
WILL NOT CONSIDER: Real Estate
GEOGRAPHIC LIMITS OF INVESTMENTS/LOANS: Regional
RANGE OF INV./LOAN PER BUSINESS: Min. $1 million; Max. $30-50 MM
PREFERRED TERM FOR LOANS & LEASES: Min. 3 years; Max. 12-15 years
BUSINESS CHARACTERISTICS DESIRED-REQUIRED: Minimum number of years in business: 0
REFERRALS ACCEPTED FROM: Investment/Mortgage banker or Borrower/Investee

COMPANY: **Taylor and Turner (parent)/Rotan Mosle Technology Partners, Ltd.**
ADDRESS: 3800 Republic Bank Center, 700 Louisiana Street
Houston, TX 77002
PHONE: (713) 236-3180
TYPE OF INSTITUTION: Private Venture Capital
CONTACT OFFICER(S): John Jaggers
ASSETS: $18,500,000 (whole group)
INVESTMENTS/LOANS MADE: For own account
INVESTMENTS/LOANS MADE: Only in securities without a secondary market
TYPES OF FINANCING: VENTURE CAPITAL: Start-up from developed product stage; First-stage; Second-stage; Buy-outs/Acquisitions, OTHER SERVICES PROVIDED: Buy-outs considered but rare
PREFERRED TYPES OF INDUSTRIES/INVESTMENTS: Technology based business: Bio-technolgy, Factory automation, Computer and information processing, Telecommunications, Materials and material science
WILL NOT CONSIDER: Real estate, Natural resurces, Entertainment
GEOGRAPHIC LIMITS OF INVESTMENTS/LOANS: National
RANGE OF INV./LOAN PER BUSINESS: Min. $250,000; Max. $1,500,000
BUSINESS CHARACTERISTICS DESIRED-REQUIRED: Other Major market potential
BRANCHES: William H. Taylor, Marshall C. Turner, Taylor and Turner, 220 Montgomery St. Penthouse 10, San Francisco, CA 94104, (415) 642-3821
J.W. Brock, WestVen Partners (Affiliated), 1506 Westinghouse bldg. Gateway Center, Pittsburgh, PA 15222, (412) 642-5858
REMARKS: Preferred investment range: $400,000 - $750,000

COMPANY: **Texas Capital Corporation/Texas Capital Venture Investments Corporation**
ADDRESS: 333 Clay St., Suite 2100
Houston, TX 77002
PHONE: (713) 658-9961
TYPE OF INSTITUTION: Venture Capital
CONTACT OFFICER(S): Lawrence Schumann, Executive VP
David G. Franklin, VP
Tom Beecroft, Inv. Manager
ASSETS: $16,000,000
INVESTMENTS/LOANS MADE: For own account; Through private placement
INVESTMENTS/LOANS MADE: In securities with a secondary market; In securities without a secondary market
TYPES OF FINANCING: SECONDARY-MARKET CORPORATE SECURITIES: Common stock; Preferred stock, VENTURE CAPITAL: First-stage; Second-stage; Later-stage expansion; Buy-outs/Acquisitions, LOANS: Equity-related
PREFERRED TYPES OF INDUSTRIES/INVESTMENTS: Diversified
WILL NOT CONSIDER: Real estate
GEOGRAPHIC LIMITS OF INVESTMENTS/LOANS: Regional; Other: Southwest
RANGE OF INV./LOAN PER BUSINESS: Min. $300,000; Max. $600,000
BUSINESS CHARACTERISTICS DESIRED-REQUIRED: Other: Strong management
REFERRALS ACCEPTED FROM: Investment/Mortgage banker; Borrower/Investee

COMPANY: **Commercial Equipment Leasing Co.**
ADDRESS: 118 Broadway
San Antonio, TX 78205
PHONE: (512) 223-5525
TYPE OF INSTITUTION: Leasing Co.
CONTACT OFFICER(S): Jim Scott, Vice President
TOTAL ASSETS: $15,000,000
INVESTMENTS/LOANS MADE: For own account

TYPES OF FINANCING: VENTURE CAPITAL: Reasearch & Development; Start-up from developed product stage; First-stage; Second-stage; Later-stage expansion; Buy-outs/Acquisitions, LEASES: Single-investor; Leveraged; Tax leases; Non-tax leases; Vendor financing programs
PREFERRED TYPES OF INDUSTRIES/INVESTMENTS: Equipment leases
GEOGRAPHIC LIMITS OF INVESTMENTS/LOANS: Regional
RANGE OF INV./LOAN PER BUSINESS: Min. $10,000; Max. $250,000
PREFERRED TERMS FOR LOANS & LEASES: Min. 2 years; Max. 7 years
BUSINESS CHARACTERISTICS DESIRED-REQUIRED: Minimum number of years in business: 3

COMPANY: **The Southwest Venture Partnerships**
ADDRESS: 300 Convent, Suite 1400
San Antonio, TX 78205
PHONE: (512) 227-1010
TYPE OF INSTITUTION: Venture Capital
CONTACT OFFICER(S): Michael Bell (San Antonio), General Partner
J. E. McAteer (Dallas), General Partner
C. D. Grojean (San Antonio), General Partner
ASSETS: $100,000,000
INVESTMENTS/LOANS MADE: For own account
INVESTMENTS/LOANS MADE: In securities with a secondary market and in securities without a secondary market
TYPES OF FINANCING: SECONDARY-MARKET CORPORATE SECURITIES: Common stock; Preferred stock, VENTURE CAPITAL: Start-up from developed product stage; First-stage (less than 1 year); Second-stage (generally 1-3 years)
WILL NOT CONSIDER: Loans or Real Estate
GEOGRAPHIC LIMITS OF INVESTMENTS/LOANS: International
RANGE OF INV./LOAN PER BUSINESS: Min. $250,000; Max. $1,000,000
REFERRALS ACCEPTED FROM: Investment/Mortgage banker or Borrower/Investee
BRANCHES: J. E. McAteer, 5080 Spectrum Dr, Suite 610 East, Dallas, TX 75248 (214) 960-0404

COMPANY: **Sunwestern Investment Fund**
ADDRESS: 6750 LBJ Freeway, One Oaks Plaza, Suite 1160
TX 75240
PHONE: (214) 239-5650
TYPE OF INSTITUTION: Venture Capital
CONTACT OFFICER(S): Floyd Collins, VP
ASSETS: 32.6 billion
INVESTMENTS/LOANS MADE: For own account
INVESTMENTS/LOANS MADE: In securities with a secondary market; In securities without a secondary market
TYPES OF FINANCING: SECONDARY-MARKET CORPORATE SECURITIES: Common stock; Preferred stock; convertible debentures, VENTURE CAPITAL: Start-up from developed product stage; First-stage; Second-stage; Later-stage; Buy-outs/Acquisitions

PREFERRED TYPES OF INDUSTRIES/INVESTMENTS: Telecommunications, Medical, Computer hardware and software, Energy, Advance materials
WILL NOT CONSIDER: Restaurants, Real estate
GEOGRAPHIC LIMITS OF INVESTMENTS/LOANS: Regional; Other: Southwest
RANGE OF INV./LOAN PER BUSINESS: Min. $300,000; Max. $5,000,000

COMPANY: **Atlantic Venture Partners**
ADDRESS: 815 Seventh & Franklin Building, P.O. Box 1493
Richmond, VA 23212
PHONE: (804) 644-5496
TYPE OF INSTITUTION: Private Venture Capital Partnership
CONTACT OFFICER(S): Robert H. Pratt, General Partner
Wallace L. Bennett, General Partner
Joseph T. Piemont, Special Partner
ASSETS: $15,000,000
INVESTMENTS/LOANS MADE: For own account
INVESTMENTS/LOANS MADE: In securities with a secondary market and in securities without a secondary market
TYPES OF FINANCING: SECONDARY-MARKET CORPORATE SECURITIES: Common stock, VENTURE CAPITAL: Research & Development; Start-up from developed product state; First-stage (less than 1 year); Second-stage (generally 1-3 years); Later-stage expansion; Buy-outs/Acquisitions, OTHER SERVICES PROVIDED: 1) Will organize and lead equity syndications for larger financings. 2) Will advise on private placements of debt, bank financing, government programs, etc. 3) Will advise on marketing, planning/control, compensation and similar areas.
PREFERRED TYPES OF INDUSTRIES/INVESTMENTS: Interested in any high growth situation
GEOGRAPHIC LIMITS OF INVESTMENTS/LOANS: No limitation
RANGE OF INV./LOAN PER BUSINESS: Min. $100,000; Max. $1,500,000 (pref. $750,000)
BUSINESS CHARACTERISTICS DESIRED-REQUIRED: Min. no. of years in business: 0
REFERRALS ACCEPTED FROM: Investment/Mortgage banker or Borrower/Investee
BRANCHES: Wallace L. Bennett, General Partner, 424 North Washington Street, Alexandria, VA 22314; (703) 548-6026
Joseph T. Piemont, Special Partner, 5950 Fairview Road, Charlotte, NC 28210; (704) 554-7276

COMPANY: **Venture Capital Group**
ADDRESS: 401 First St., N.W.
Roanoke, VA 24016
PHONE: (703) 344-6624
TYPE OF INSTITUTION: Investment Division of CDC
CONTACT OFFICER(S): Stanley Hale, Director
ASSETS: Over $3 million
INVESTMENTS/LOANS MADE: For own account; Through private placements
INVESTMENTS/LOANS MADE: In securities with a secondary market and in securities without a secondary market

TYPES OF FINANCING: SECONDARY-MARKET CORPORATE SECURITIES: Common stock; Bonds, VENTURE CAPITAL: Start-up from developed product stage; Later-stage expansion, LOANS: Working capital (receivables/inventory); Equipment; Equity-related, REAL ESTATE LOANS: Land; Land development; Construction, LEASES: Vendor financing programs, REAL ESTATE: Acquisitions; Joint ventures; Partnerships/Syndications, OTHER SERVICES PROVIDED: 501(c)3 Pass Thru of Real Estate
PREFERRED TYPES OF INDUSTRIES/INVESTMENTS: Computer Related Peripheral Equipment, Machine Tools, Material Handling Equipment, Plastics, Medical Diagnostic Equipment, Coal, Minerals, Oil & Gas, Broadcasting, Publishing, Optics
WILL NOT CONSIDER: Long Term Real Estate Mortgages
GEOGRAPHIC LIMITS OF INVESTMENTS/LOANS: Regional
RANGE OF INV./LOAN PER BUSINESS: Min. $100,000; Max. $300,000
PREFERRED TERM FOR LOANS & LEASES: Negotiable
BUSINESS CHARACTERISTICS DESIRED-REQUIRED: Min. no. of years in business: 0; Management Experience; Operational Prototypes
REFERRALS ACCEPTED FROM: Investment/Mortgage banker or Borrower/Investee

COMPANY: **Cable, Howse & Cozadd, Inc.**
ADDRESS: 999 Third Avenue, Suite 4300
Seattle, WA 98104
PHONE: (206) 583-2700
TYPE OF INSTITUTION: Venture Capital Investment Firm
CONTACT OFFICER(S): Wayne C. Wager, General Partner
Michael A. Ellison, General Partner
Bennett A. Cozadd, General Partner
Elwood D. Howse, Jr., General Partner
Thomas J. Cable , General Partner
ASSETS: Over $130 million
INVESTMENTS/LOANS MADE: For own account
TYPES OF FINANCING: VENTURE CAPITAL: Start-up from developed product stage; First-stage; Second-stage; Later-stage expansion; Buy-outs/Acquisitions
GEOGRAPHIC LIMITS OF INVESTMENTS/LOANS: National; Other: Mainly western states.
RANGE OF INV./LOAN PER BUSINESS: Min. $300,000,00; Max. $2,000,00
BUSINESS CHARACTERISTICS DESIRED-REQUIRED: Min. no. of years in business: 0
REFERRALS ACCEPTED FROM: Investment/Mortgage banker or Borrower/Investee

COMPANY: **Venture Sum**
ADDRESS: N. 618 Sullivan, #25
Veradale, WA 99037
PHONE: (509) 926-3720
TYPE OF INSTITUTION: Private Venture Capital
CONTACT OFFICER(S): A.T. Zirkle, President
ASSETS: $2,000,000
INVESTMENTS/LOANS MADE: For own account
INVESTMENTS/LOANS MADE: In securities with a secondary market and in securities without a secondary market
TYPES OF FINANCING: VENTURE CAPITAL: Research & Development; Start-up from developed product stage; First-stage (less than 1 year); Buy-outs/Acquisitions; LOANS: Working capital; Equipment; Equity-related; INTERNATIONAL; REAL ESTATE: Acquisitions; Partnerships/Syndications
PREFERRED TYPES OF INDUSTRIES/INVESTMENTS: Industries—High Technology; Real Estate—Commercial & Development
WILL NOT CONSIDER: Those precluded to SBIC's
GEOGRAPHIC LIMITS OF INVESTMENTS/LOANS: Regional
RANGE OF INV./LOAN PER BUSINESS: Min. $10,000; Max. $1,000,000
PREFERRED TERM FOR LOANS & LEASES: Min. 1; Max. 3 years
BUSINESS CHARACTERISTICS DESIRED-REQUIRED: Minimum number of years in business: 0; Min. annual sales $100,000; Min. net worth $100,000; Min. annual net income $0
REFERRALS ACCEPTED FROM: Investment/Mortgage banker or Borrower/Investee

OTHER CATEGORIES

ARIZONA

ARIZONA

COMPANY: **Greyhound Leasing & Financial Corporation**
ADDRESS: 4041 North Center Avenue
Phoenix, AZ 85012
PHONE: (602) 248-4900
CONTACT OFFICER(S): See branches
ASSETS: $1.3 billion
INVESTMENTS/LOANS MADE: In securities with a secondary market and in securities without a secondary market
INVESTMENTS/LOANS MADE: For own account; Through private placements
TYPES OF FINANCING: SECONDARY MARKET CORPORATE SECURITIES: Bonds; VENTURE CAPITAL: Later-stage expansion; LOANS: Equipment; REAL ESTATE LOANS: Long-term senior mtg.; Intermediate-term senior mtg., Land development; Construction; Standbys; Other: Equity Notes Receivables; LEASES: Single-investor; Leveraged; Tax leases; Non-tax leases; Tax-oriented lease brokerage; Lease syndications; Vendor financing programs; INTERNATIONAL; REAL ESTATE: Joint ventures; Partnerships/Syndications
GEOGRAPHIC LIMITS OF INVESTMENTS/LOANS: National
RANGE OF INV./LOAN PER BUSINESS: Min. Leases: $50,000; Loans: $250,000; Max. $—
PREFERRED TERM FOR LOANS & LEASES: Min. Leases: 1; Loans: 3 years; Max. 20 years
BUSINESS CHARACTERISTICS DESIRED-REQUIRED: Minimum number of years in business: 5; Other: Proper operating history upon which to base payment ability projections
REFERRALS ACCEPTED FROM: Investment/Mortgage Banker or Borrower/Investee
BRANCHES: John N. Henning, Donald F. Howell, Jeremiah G. Mahony, Michael J. Naughton, and William H. Vallar (V.P.-Regional Marketing Manager), 445 Park Avenue, New York, NY 10022, (212) 752-2720
Robert E. Marino, John Wm. Salyer, David A. Nielsen (V.P.-Regional Marketing Manager), Centennial Center I, 1900 East Golf Road, Suite 645, Schaumburg, IL 60195, (312) 490-9500
Bruce E. Heine, Mark Lindell, 7801 East Bush Lake Road, Suite 430, Minneapolis, MN 55435, (612) 831-7044
Joseph A. Graffagnini, Canal Place One, Suite 2510, New Orleans, LA 70130, (504) 525-1112
James M. Brown, 12400 Olive Blvd., Suite 200, St. Louis, MO 63141, (314) 469-7373
George C. Baer, 7616 LBJ Freeway, Suite 500, Dallas, TX 75251, (214) 387-3182
Dottie A. Riley, James T. Foley (V.P.-Regional Marketing Manager), 4041 North Central Avenue, Station 3504, Phoenix, AZ 85012, (602) 248-5349
Jeffrey D. Johnson, Scott D. Mayne, 5505 South 900 East, Suite 325, Salt Lake City, UT 84117, (801) 261-1311
Thomas O. Kaluza, 16400 Southcenter Parkway, Suite 203, Seattle, WA 98188, (206) 575-0246
Kenneth B. Giddes, 6400 Powers Ferry Road, Suite 300, Atlanta, GA 30339, (404) 955-3636
Patrick E. Barton, 1776 South Jackson Street, Suite 907, Denver, CO 80210, (303) 757-4973
Jack W. Quinn, Cineco Building, Suite 203, 4401 W. Tradewinds Ave., Lauderdale-by-the-Sea, FL 33308, (305) 493-8322

David C. Phillips, 600 B Street, Suite 2235, San Diego, CA 92101, (619) 231-4751
Ron W. Larson, Neil E. Leddy, Orangegate Plaza, 5455 Garden Grove Blvd., Suite 450, Westminister, CA 92683, (714) 891-2700

COMPANY: **Dorf and Associates**
ADDRESS: 760 No. Campus Way
Davis CA 95616
PHONE: (916) 756-5206
TYPE OF INSTITUTION: Venture Capital Consulting
CONTACT OFFICER(S): Barbara Purdy, Partner
INVESTMENTS/LOANS MADE: For own account or through private placements
TYPES OF FINANCING: VENTURE CAPITAL; Research & Development; Start-up from developed product stage; First-stage; Second-stage; Later-stage expansion; Buy-outs/Acquisitions; REAL ESTATE: Acquisitions; Joint ventures; Partnerships/Syndications
PREFERRED TYPES OF INDUSTRIES/INVESTMENTS: Technology and real estate
GEOGRAPHIC LIMITS OF INVESTMENTS/LOANS: Regional
RANGE OF INV./LOAN PER BUSINESS: Open
BUSINESS CHARACTERISTICS DESIRED-REQUIRED: Minimum number of years in business: 0; Min. annual sales: open
REFERRALS ACCEPTED FROM: Investment/Mortgage banker or Borrower/Investee

COMPANY: **EMC II Venture Partners**
ADDRESS: 8950 Villa La Jolla Dr., Suite 2132
La Jolla, CA 92037
PHONE: (619) 455-0362
TYPE OF INSTITUTION: Private venture capital firm affiliated with McKewon Securities, Investment Banker and Broker-Dealer
CONTACT OFFICER(S): Ray W. McKewon, General Partner
Bradley B. Gordon, General Partner- Alan J. Grant, General Partner
Hans W. Schoepflin, General Partner
ASSETS: In excess of $20,000,000
INVESTMENTS/LOANS MADE: For own account and through private placements
INVESTMENTS/LOANS MADE: In securities with a secondary market and in securities without a secondary market
TYPES OF FINANCING: SECONDARY-MARKET CORPORATE SECURITIES; VENTURE CAPITAL: Research & Development; Start-up; First-stage; Second-stage; Buy-outs/Acquisitions; LOANS: Equity-related; INTERNATIONAL; OTHER SERVICES PROVIDED: International joint ventures
PREFERRED TYPES OF INDUSTRIES/INVESTMENTS: Communications; computer related; distribution; manufacturing; medical; energy resources & technologies; retail (specialty) and real estate and financial services
GEOGRAPHIC LIMITS OF INVESTMENTS/LOANS: National, International
RANGE OF INV./LOAN PER BUSINESS: Min. $250,000; Max. $3,000,000
BUSINESS CHARACTERISTICS DESIRED-REQUIRED: Min. number of years in business: 0; Min. annual sales: $15 million by year 5; Other: request business plan detailing product/service concept, market opportunity, qualifications of management team, and 3-5 years projected profit and loss and cash flow
REFERRALS ACCEPTED FROM: Investment/Mortgage banker or Borrower/Investee

COMPANY: **U. S. Bancorp Financial**
ADDRESS: 550 South Hill St. Suite 1200
Los Angeles, CA 90013
PHONE: (213) 622-3820
TYPE OF INSTITUTION: Wholly owned asset based lending institution of U.S. Bancorp, Inc.
CONTACT OFFICER(S): P. A. Yasiello, President/C.E.O.
Owen D. McGreal, Senior V.P.
ASSETS: In excess of $5 billion
INVESTMENTS/LOANS MADE: For own account
TYPES OF FINANCING: LOANS: Working capital; Equipment; Equity-related, INTERNATIONAL, OTHER SERVICES PROVIDED: To support letter of credit and other lines of credit
PREFERRED TYPES OF INDUSTRIES/INVESTMENTS: Manufacturing, distribution and service
GEOGRAPHIC LIMITS OF INVESTMENTS/LOANS: Local; State; Regional; National
RANGE OF INV./LOAN PER BUSINESS: Min. $50,000; Max. $40 million
BUSINESS CHARACTERISTICS DESIRED-REQUIRED: Minimum number of years in business: 0;
REFERRALS ACCEPTED FROM: Investment/Mortgage banker or Borrower/Investee
BRANCHES: Ed Jensen, 555 Southwest Oak, Portland, OR 97205; (503) 225-6270
Gene Drummond, Diamond Shamrock Tower, Suite 2750, 717 North Harwood, Dallas, TX 75201; (214) 651-7101
One Wilshire Building, Suite 2500, Los Angeles, CA 90017; (213) 622-3820
Orange County; (714) 834-0821
One Allen Center, Suite 1000, Houston, TX 77002; (713) 757-0038
City Center Square, 1110 Main Street, 14th Floor, Kansas City, MO 64105; (816) 221-0880

COMPANY: **Rose Investment Co.**
ADDRESS: Transamerica Pyramid, 600 Montgomery St. 35th fl.
San Francisco, CA 94111
PHONE: (415) 398-8222
TYPE OF INSTITUTION: Venture Capital & Consulting firm
CONTACT OFFICER(S): John F. Mangan, Gen. Ptnr.
TYPES OF FINANCING: VENTURE CAPITAL: Research & Development; Start-up from developed product stage; First-stage; Second-stage; Later-stage expansion; Buy-outs/Acquisitions
PREFERRED TYPES OF INDUSTRIES/INVESTMENTS: Diversified
GEOGRAPHIC LIMITS OF INVESTMENTS/LOANS: International

COMPANY: **Leonard Mautner Associates**
ADDRESS: 1434 6th Streeet
Santa Monica, CA 90401
(213) 393-9788
CONTACT OFFICER(S): Leonard Mautner, President
INVESTMENTS/LOANS MADE: For own (company's or principals') account
INVESTMENTS/LOANS MADE: only in securities without a secondary market
TYPES OF FINANCING: VENTURE CAPITAL: Research & Development; Start-up from developed product stage; First-stage (less than 1 year); Second-stage (generally 1-3 years); OTHER SERVICES PROVIDED:Mgmt. consulting, Esp. Technology oriented; corporate finance
PREFERRED TYPES OF INDUSTRIES/INVESTMENTS: Technology oriented — electronics, computers instrumentation, bio-medical
GEOGRAPHIC LIMITS OF INVESTMENTS/LOANS: Local; State
RANGE OF INV./LOAN PER BUSINESS: Min. $100,000; Max. $300,000
BUSINESS CHARACTERISTINC DESIRED-REQUIRED: Minimum number of years in business: 0; Min. annual sales $1MM
REMARKS: Have arranged approx. $50M financing & acquisition & mergers for smaller firms since 1962

COMPANY: **Town of Groton Retirement Fund**
ADDRESS: 45 Fort Hill Road
Groton, CT 06340
PHONE: (203) 445-8551
TYPE OF INSTITUTION: Government, town
CONTACT OFFICER(S): Mel Higgins, Higgins Associates, 24 Federal St, Boston, MA 02110, Account Administrator
ASSETS: $8,845,948 (book value)
TYPES OF FINANCING: SECONDARY-MARKET CORPORATE SECURITIES: Common stock; Bonds; Other: Short term investments

COMPANY: **Anacostia Economic Development Corporation**
ADDRESS: 2041 Martin Luther King Jr. Ave., S.E.
Washington, DC 20020
PHONE: (202) 889-9507
TYPE OF INSTITUTION: Community economic development corporation
CONTACT OFFICER(S): Albert R. Hopkins, Jr., President Augustus Palmer, V.P.ASSETS: $2,000,000
INVESTMENTS/LOANS MADE: For own account; through private placements
INVESTMENTS/LOANS MADE: Only in securities without a secondary market
TYPES OF FINANCING: VENTURE CAPITAL: Second-stage (generally 1-3 years); Buy-outs/Acquisitions, LOANS: Working capital (receivables/inventory); Equipment, REAL ESTATE LOANS: Long-term senior mtg.; Subordinated; Construction; Gap, REAL ESTATE: Acquisitions; Joint ventures; Partnerships/Syndications
PREFERRED TYPES OF INDUSTRIES/INVESTMENTS: Labor intensive, low skill; commercial RE development
WILL NOT CONSIDER: Single family housing
GEOGRAPHIC LIMITS OF INVESTMENTS/LOANS: Local
RANGE OF INV./LOAN PER BUSINESS: Min. $10,000; Max. $150,000
PREFERRED TERM FOR LOANS & LEASES: Min. 2 years
BUSINESS CHARACTERISTICS DESIRED-REQUIRED: Minimum number of years in business: 1
REMARKS: Interested primarily in development projects in S.E. Washington, DC; Terms for loans: can do 5 year amitization

COMPANY: **Corporate Finance of Washington, Inc.**
ADDRESS: 1326 R St. N.W.
Washington, DC 20009
PHONE: (202) 328-9053
TYPE OF INSTITUTION: Investment Banking
CONTACT OFFICER(S): Peter W. Gavian, President
INVESTMENTS/LOANS MADE: Through private placements;
INVESTMENTS/LOANS MADE: In securities with a secondary market and in securities without a secondary market
TYPES OF FINANCING: SECONDARY-MARKET CORPORATE SECURITIES: Common stock; Preferred stock; Bonds; VENTURE CAPITAL: Start-up from developed product stage; First-stage; Second-stage; Later-stage expansion; Buy-outs/Acquisitions; LOANS: Unsecured to credits above Baa; Working capital; Equipment; Equity-related; FACTORING; LEASES: Tax leases; Non-tax leases; Operating; Vendor financing programs
PREFERRED TYPES OF INDUSTRIES/INVESTMENTS: High-tech; Manufacturing; Wholesale
WILL NOT CONSIDER: Publishing, Entertainment
GEOGRAPHIC LIMITS OF INVESTMENTS/LOANS: Regional
RANGE OF INV./LOAN PER BUSINESS: Min. $250,000; Max. No limit
PREFERRED TERM FOR LOANS & LEASES: Min. 5 years; Max. 25 years
BUSINESS CHARACTERISTICS DESIRED-REQUIRED: Minimum number of years in business: 0

COMPANY: **Malcolm Bund & Associates, Inc.**
ADDRESS: 1225 19th Street, N.W., Suite 600
Washington, DC 20036
PHONE: (202) 293-2910
TYPE OF INSTITUTION: Strategic Planning; M&A; Private Placements
CONTACT OFFICER(S): Malcolm B. Bund, President
TYPES OF FINANCING: VENTURE CAPITAL: Second-stage; (generally 1-3 years);

COMPANY: **William H. Hill Associates Inc.**
ADDRESS: 3100 University Blvd. S. S201
Jacksonville, FL 32216
PHONE: (904) 721-8956
TYPE OF INSTITUTION: Mergers Acquisitions, Appraisals & Consulting
CONTACT OFFICER(S): William H. Hill, President
INVESTMENTS/LOANS MADE: For own account

TYPES OF FINANCING: REAL ESTATE: Acquisitions; OTHER SERVICES PROVIDED: Acqquisitions Mergers; Appraisals; Consulting; Divesturers
WILL NOT CONSIDER: Banks, Insurance Co. Franchises
RANGE OF INV./LOAN PER BUSINESS: Min. $500,000; Max. $20,000,000
BUSINESS CHARACTERISTICS DESIRED-REQUIRED: Minimum number of years in business: 5; Min. annual sales $1,000,000; Min. net worth $500,000; Min. annual net income $100,000; Min. annual cash flow $250,000
REFERRALS ACCEPTED FROM: Investment/Mortgage banker or Borrower/Investee

COMPANY: **The Investment Centre, Incorporated**
ADDRESS: 2600 Life of Georgia Tower 600 West Peachtree Street
Atlanta, GA 30365
PHONE: (404) 898-1792
TYPE OF INSTITUTION: Investment advisor for related client companies
CONTACT OFFICER(S): Maurice Moore, V.P. R.E. & Mtg. Loans
Charles B. Morris, V.P. Securities
ASSETS: (managed) 1.5 billion
TYPES OF FINANCING: SECONDARY-MARKET CORPORATE SECURITIES: Common stock; Preferred stock; BondsREAL ESTATE LOANS: Long-term senior mtg.; Intermediate-term senior mtg.; Other: Primarily First mortgages—Longterm REAL ESTATE: Acquisitions
PREFERRED TYPES OF INDUSTRIES/INVESTMENTS: Retail; Medical Office Buildings; Apartments; Offices & Industrial Warehousing
GEOGRAPHIC LIMITS OF INVESTMENTS/LOANS: Other: Southeast—13 states incl. TX & OK—will expand
RANGE OF INV./LOAN PER BUSINESS: Min. $1 million; Max. $5 million
PREFERRED TERM FOR LOANS & LEASES: Min. 5 years; Max. 25-30 years
REMARKS: Operate primarily on Mtg. Correspondent System

COMPANY: **Mid-Southern Financial Corp.**
ADDRESS: One Perimeter Way N.W., #501 P.O. Box 723355
Atlanta, GA 30339
PHONE: (404) 952-2500
TYPE OF INSTITUTION: Financial Consultants
CONTACT OFFICER(S): George H. Naterman, Pres.
INVESTMENTS/LOANS MADE: Through private placements
TYPES OF FINANCING: VENTURE CAPITAL: Research & Development; Start-up from developed product stage; First-stage; Second-stage; Later-stage expansion; Buy-outs/Acquisitions; LOANS: Working capital; Equipment; Equity-related; Other: Asset financing
GEOGRAPHIC LIMITS OF INVESTMENTS/LOANS: Regional; Prefer S.E.
RANGE OF INV./LOAN PER BUSINESS: Min. $250,000
PREFERRED TERM FOR LOANS & LEASES: Flexible
BUSINESS CHARACTERISTICS DESIRED-REQUIRED: Min. net worth $200,000; Minimum capital position—$100,000
REFERRALS ACCEPTED FROM: Investment/Mortgage banker or Borrower/Investee

COMPANY: **Citizens and Southern Commercial Corporation**
ADDRESS: 2059 Cooledge Road, (P.O. Box 4095, Atlanta 30302)
Tucker, GA 30084
PHONE: (404) 491-4839
TYPE OF INSTITUTION: Factoring, commercial finance, equipment leasing & financing (sub. of Commercial Bank)t
CONTACT OFFICER(S): Charles Mitchell, Senior V.P., Commercial Finance
Joel Chasteen, Sr. V.P. & Manager, Equipment Leasing
Bart Smith, Sr. V.P., Factoring
ASSETS: $7,620,000,000
TYPES OF FINANCING: LOANS: Working capital; Equipment, FACTORING, LEASES: Single-investor; Leveraged; Tax leases; Non-tax leases; Operating, INTERNATIONAL
PREFERRED TYPES OF INDUSTRIES/INVESTMENTS: For factoring: apparel, textiles, furniture, carpet, seafood industries; for leasing and commercial finance: manufacturers, distributors
GEOGRAPHIC LIMITS OF INVESTMENTS/LOANS: National; International
RANGE OF INV./LOAN PER BUSINESS: Max. $20,000,000
PREFERRED TERM FOR LOANS & LEASES: Min. 90 days; Max. 7 years
BUSINESS CHARACTERISTICS DESIRED-REQUIRED: Minimum number of years in business: 0; Min. annual sales $1,000,000; Min. net worth $200,000; Min. annual net income $20,000; Min. annual cash flow none; Other: Guaranties of principals with closely-held firms
REFERRALS ACCEPTED FROM: Investment/Mortgage banker or Borrower/Investee
BRANCHES: Claude McEwen, A.V.P., 300 S. Thornton Avenue, Dalton, GA 30720; (404) 278-1929
Fred Gaylord, V.P., 9841 Airport Blvd., Suite 300, Los Angeles, CA 90045; (213) 670-4772; Matthew Creo Jr., Sr. V.P., 1430 Broadway, 19th Floor, New York, NY 10018, 212-719-3700

COMPANY: **Walter E. Heller & Co./Commercial & Industrial Equipment Financing Group**
ADDRESS: 105 West Adams Street
Chicago, IL 60603
PHONE: (312) 621-7600
TYPE OF INSTITUTION: Equipment leasing and financing
CONTACT OFFICER(S): Samuel L. Eichenfield, President
INVESTMENTS/LOANS MADE: For own account
TYPES OF FINANCING: LOANS: Working capital; Equipment, REAL ESTATE LOANS; FACTORING, LEASES: Single-investor; Leveraged; Tax leases; Non-tax leases; Lease syndications; OTHER SERVICES PROVIDED: Floor planning

PREFERRED TYPES OF INDUSTRIES/INVESTMENTS: All types of capital equip. for businesses
GEOGRAPHIC LIMITS OF INVESTMENTS/LOANS: National
RANGE OF INV./LOAN PER BUSINESS: Min. $50,000; Max. No
PREFERRED TERM FOR LOANS & LEASES: Min. 3 years; Max. 10 years
BUSINESS CHARACTERISTICS DESIRED-REQUIRED: Minimum number of years in business: 3
REFERRALS ACCEPTED FROM: Investment/Mortgage banker or Borrower/Investee

COMPANY: **Evanston Community Development Corporation**
ADDRESS: 1817 Church Street
Evanston, IL 60201
PHONE: (312) 869-7651
TYPE OF INSTITUTION: Community development corporation
CONTACT OFFICER(S): Ernestine Jackson, Executive Director
ASSETS: $500,000
INVESTMENTS/LOANS MADE: For own account
TYPES OF FINANCING: REAL ESTATE LOANS: Long-term senior mtg.; Intermediate-term senior mtg.; Subordinated, REAL ESTATE: Acquisitions; Joint ventures
PREFERRED TYPES OF INDUSTRIES/INVESTMENTS: Rehabilitation of single family dwellings, commercial
GEOGRAPHIC LIMITS OF INVESTMENTS/LOANS: Local
RANGE OF INV./LOAN PER BUSINESS: Min. $1,500; Max. $25,000
PREFERRED TERM FOR LOANS & LEASES: Min. 5 years; Max. 20 years
BUSINESS CHARACTERISTICS DESIRED-REQUIRED: Minimum number of years in business: 1
REFERRALS ACCEPTED FROM: Investment/Mortgage banker or Borrower/Investee

COMPANY: **Mellon Financial Services Corporation**
ADDRESS: 1415 West 22nd Street, Suite 1200
Oak Brook, IL 60521
PHONE: (800) 323-7338 outside IL, (312) 986-2950 inside IL
TYPE OF INSTITUTION: Asset based lending affiliate of Mellon Bank, N.A.
CONTACT OFFICER(S): Charles S. Pryce, Senior Vice President
ASSETS: $25 billion
INVESTMENTS/LOANS MADE: For own account
INVESTMENTS/LOANS MADE: In securities with a secondary market and in securities without a secondary market
TYPES OF FINANCING: LOANS: Working capital; Equipment; Equity-related; Other: intermediate term loans; LBO financing. REAL ESTATE LOANS: Intermediate-term senior mtg.; Land; Standbys; Industrial revenue bonds. LEASES: Non-tax leases. INTERNATIONAL
WILL NOT CONSIDER: Building contractors
GEOGRAPHIC LIMITS OF INVESTMENTS/LOANS: National

BUSINESS CHARACTERISTICS DESIRED-REQUIRED: Minimum number of years in business: 0 Min. annual sales $2,000,000; Min. net worth $100,000; Min. annual net income $ positive; Min. annual cash flow $ positive.
REFERRALS ACCEPTED FROM: Investment/Mortgage banker or Borrower/Investee

COMPANY:**Arneson & Company**
ADDRESS: 12715 High Drive
Leawood KS 66209
PHONE: (913) 341-7722*
TYPE OF INSTITUTION: Management Consulting Firm
CONTACT OFFICER(S): George S. Arneson, President
INVESTMENTS/LOANS MADE: Through private placement
TYPES OF FINANCING: VENTURE CAPITAL: Research & Development; Start-up from developed product stage; First-stage; LOANS: Working capital; Equipment; Equity-related
PREFERRED TYPES OF INDUSTRIES/INVESTMENTS: Open—No preference
GEOGRAPHIC LIMITS OF INVESTMENTS/LOANS: Regional
RANGE OF INV./LOAN PER BUSINESS: Min. $2,000,000.00; Max. $10,000,000.00
BUSINESS CHARACTERISTICS DESIRED-REQUIRED: Minimum number of years in business: 0; Min. annual sales $3,000,000
REMARKS: * After April 15, 1985; (913) 491-3171

COMPANY: **Mountain Association for Community Economic Development**
ADDRESS: 210 Center St.
Berea, KY 40403
PHONE: (606) 986-2373
TYPE OF INSTITUTION: Economic development organization operating in central Appalachia
CONTACT OFFICER(S): William A. Duncan, President
ASSETS: $3.5 million
INVESTMENTS/LOANS MADE: For own account, For managed accounts, Through private placements
INVESTMENTS/LOANS MADE: In securities with a secondary market and in securities without a secondary market
TYPES OF FINANCING: SECONDARY-MARKET CORPORATE SECURITIES: Common stock, VENTURE CAPITAL: Start-up from developed product stage; First-stage (less than 1 year); Second-stage (generally 1-3 years); Later-stage expansion, LOANS: Equipment, OTHER SERVICES PROVIDED: Planning assistance
PREFERRED TYPES OF INDUSTRIES/INVESTMENTS: Manufacturing
GEOGRAPHIC LIMITS OF INVESTMENTS/LOANS: Regional
RANGE OF INV./LOAN PER BUSINESS: Min. $50,000; Max. $500,000
PREFERRED TERM FOR LOANS & LEASES: Min. None; Max. 15 years
BUSINESS CHARACTERISTICS DESIRED-REQUIRED: Minimum number of years in business: 0; Min. annual sales $1,000,000
REFERRALS ACCEPTED FROM: Borrower/Investee

COMPANY: **Kentucky Highlands Investment Corp.**
ADDRESS: 911 N. Main St., Box 628
London, KY 40741
PHONE: (606) 864-5175
TYPE OF INSTITUTION: Private economic development corporation
CONTACT OFFICER(S): L. R. Moncrief, President
Steven C. Meng, CEO
ASSETS: $8,000,000
INVESTMENTS/LOANS MADE: For own account
INVESTMENTS/LOANS MADE: In securities with a secondary market and in securities without a secondary market
TYPES OF FINANCING: VENTURE CAPITAL: Research & Development; Start-up from developed product stage; First-stage (less than 1 year); Second-stage (generally 1-3 years); Later-stage expansion, Buy-outs/Acquisitions; LOANS: Working capital; FACTORING
PREFERRED TYPES OF INDUSTRIES/INVESTMENTS: Diversified manufacturing
WILL NOT CONSIDER: Natural resources, retail
GEOGRAPHIC LIMITS OF INVESTMENTS/LOANS: State
RANGE OF INV./LOAN PER BUSINESS: Min. $50,000; Max. $2,000,000
PREFERRED TERM FOR LOANS & LEASES: Min. 5 years; Max. 10 years
REFERRALS ACCEPTED FROM: Investment/Mortgage banker or Borrower/Investee
REMARKS: Will invest in businesses located outside of Kentucky if some operations are (to be) located in the state

COMPANY: **First National Bank of Louisville**
ADDRESS: First National Tower
Louisville, KY 40202
PHONE: (502) 581-4200
TYPE OF INSTITUTION: Bank, full service including commercial finance, leasing, mergers & acquisitions & international
CONTACT OFFICER(S): Max White, S.V.P., Construction Financing
Ed Vittitoe, V.P. Corporate Finance, Mergers & Acquisitions
William Earley, S.V.P., Energy
Charles Williams, S.V.P., International
Jerry Johnston, S.V.P., National Banking
Paul Best, S.V.P., Mortgage Banking
ASSETS: $3.2 billion
INVESTMENTS/LOANS MADE: For own account
TYPES OF FINANCING: LOANS: Unsecured; Working capital (receivables/inventory); Equipment, REAL ESTATE LOANS: Intermediate-term senior mtg.; Wraparounds; Land; Construction; Standbys, LEASES: Leveraged; Tax leases; Non-tax leases; Vendor financing programs, INTERNATIONAL (including import/export)
GEOGRAPHIC LIMITS OF INVESTMENTS/LOANS: Regional; Other: Limited business nationally
RANGE OF INV./LOAN PER BUSINESS: Min. $250,000; Max. $12,000,000
PREFERRED TERM FOR LOANS & LEASES: Min. 2 years; Max. 10 years

BUSINESS CHARACTERISTICS DESIRED-REQUIRED: Minimum number of years in business: 3; Min. annual sales $5,000,000; Min. net worth $3,000,000
REFERRALS ACCEPTED FROM: Investment/Mortgage banker or Borrower/Investee
BRANCHES: Chuck Moeser, V.P., 60 E. 42nd Street, New York, NY; (212) 661-0980
John Hill, V.P., 1945 The Exchange, Suite 104, Atlanta, GA 30339; (404) 953-0930
Jim Sullivan, V.P., 625 N. Michigan Avenue, Suite 1020, Chicago, IL 60611; (312) 642-9779

COMPANY: **Foster Dykema Cabot & Co. Inc.**
ADDRESS: 50 Milk Street
Boston, MA 02109
PHONE: (617) 423-3900
TYPE OF INSTITUTION: Intermediary
CONTACT OFFICER(S): Jere H. DyKema, Chairman
Robert E. Gibbons, President
INVESTMENTS/LOANS MADE: Through private placements
INVESTMENTS/LOANS MADE: Only in securities without a secondary market
TYPES OF FINANCING: VENTURE CAPITAL: Research & Development; Start-up from developed product stage; First-stage; Second-stage; Later-stage expansion; Buy-outs/Acquisitions
GEOGRAPHIC LIMITS OF INVESTMENTS/LOANS: Regional-New England
RANGE OF INV./LOAN PER BUSINESS: Min. $500,000
BUSINESS CHARACTERISTICS DESIRED-REQUIRED: Minimum number of years in business: 0

COMPANY: **R.C. Berner & Co.**
ADDRESS: 65 William Street
Wellesley, MA 02181
PHONE: (617) 237-9472
TYPE OF INSTITUTION: Management consultants/merger managers/intermediaries in venture capital
CONTACT OFFICER(S): R.C. Berner, President
H.S. Berner, Treasurer
A.M. Albrecht, Asst. to President
ASSETS: Not relevant
TYPES OF FINANCING: VENTURE CAPITAL: Second-stage (generally 1-3 years); Later-stage expansion; Buy-outs/Acquisitions
PREFERRED TYPES OF INDUSTRIES/INVESTMENTS: Industries: computer related; medical; building materials; chemicals; electronics; leisure products; data communications; natural resources; retail; supermarkets; machinery
GEOGRAPHIC LIMITS OF INVESTMENTS/LOANS: National
RANGE OF INV./LOAN PER BUSINESS: Min. $500,000; Max. No maximum
BUSINESS CHARACTERISTICS DESIRED-REQUIRED: Minimum number of years in business: 1; Min. annual sales $500,000; Min. net worth $300,000; Min. annual net income $100,000; Min. annual cash flow $100,000
REFERRALS ACCEPTED FROM: Investment/Mortgage banker or Borrower/Investee
REMARKS: We act as intermediaries only, working on a retainer and success fee

COMPANY: **Houston & Associates, Inc.**
ADDRESS: 1625 Woodward Ave., Suite 220
Bloomfield Hills MI 48013
PHONE: (313) 332-1625
TYPE OF INSTITUTION: Private financial consulting firm
CONTACT OFFICER(S): E. James Houston Jr., Pres. (CEO)
INVESTMENTS/LOANS MADE: For own account; Through private placements; Through underwriting public offerings
INVESTMENTS/LOANS MADE: Only in securities without a secondary market
TYPES OF FINANCING: VENTURE CAPITAL: Research & Development; Start-up from developed product stage; First-stage: Second-stage; Later-stage expansion; Buy-outs/Acquisitions; LOANS: Working capital; Equipment; REAL ESTATE LOANS: Land; Industrial revenue bonds; OTHER SERVICES PROVIDED: Internal financial/management consulting
PREFERRED TYPES OF INDUSTRIES/INVESTMENTS: Prefer not to exclude any particular industries
WILL NOT CONSIDER: Pure money-brokerage or "money-finding" deals
GEOGRAPHIC LIMITS OF INVESTMENTS/LOANS: Regional; Other: Midwest
RANGE OF INV./LOAN PER BUSINESS: Min. Nominal; Max. $3,000,000 approx.
BUSINESS CHARACTERISTICS DESIRED-REQUIRED: Minimum number of years in business: 0
REFERRALS ACCEPTED FROM: Investment/Mortgage banker or Borrower/Investee
REMARKS: Alternate Phone: 645-1860

COMPANY: **Western Companies Inc.**
ADDRESS: 1844 Wayzata Blvd.
Long Lake, MN 55356
PHONE: (612) 475-1170
TYPE OF INSTITUTION: Acquisition Consulting firm; Represents companies for sale
CONTACT OFFICER(S): Stephen B. McEachron, Pres.
INVESTMENTS/LOANS MADE: For own account; Through private placements
TYPES OF FINANCING: SECONDARY-MARKET CORPORATE SECURITIES: Common stock; Preferred stock; Other: Conv. Debentures; VENTURE CAPITAL: Second-stage; Later-stage expansion; Buy-outs/Acquisitions; LEASES: Leveraged; Tax leases; Non-tax leases; Operating; Tax-oriented lease brokerage; Lease syndications; Vendor financing programs; Other: We represent leasing companies that require additional equity to grow; INTERNATIONAL; OTHER SERVICES PROVIDED: We sell 100% of closely-held businesses or sell minority interests to larger corporations in order to raise additional growth equity
PREFERRED TYPES OF INDUSTRIES/INVESTMENTS: All industries
GEOGRAPHIC LIMITS OF INVESTMENTS/LOANS: National; International
RANGE OF INV./LOAN PER BUSINESS: Min. $1.0 MM; Max. $100 MM
BUSINESS CHARACTERISTICS DESIRED-REQUIRED: Minimum number of years in business: 2 years; Min. annual sales $1 MM; Min. net worth $100,000; Min. annual net income $200,000; Other; Prefer net investments in $1 MM to $100 MM range.
REFERRALS ACCEPTED FROM: Investment/Mortgage banker only; Borrower/Investee

COMPANY: **The Trust Company of New Jersey**
ADDRESS: 35 Journal Square
Jersey City, NJ 07306
PHONE: (201) 420-2810
TYPE OF INSTITUTION: Commercial bank
CONTACT OFFICER(S): Robert J. Figurski, Sr., V.P.
ASSETS: $1 Billion
INVESTMENTS/LOANS MADE: For own account
TYPES OF FINANCING: VENTURE CAPITAL: Start-up from developed product stage; First-stage; Later-stage expansions; Buy-outs/Acquisitions, LOANS: Unsecured; Working capital (receivables/inventory); Equipment; Equity related, REAL ESTATE LOANS: Long-term senior mtg.; Intermediate-term senior mtg.; Wraparounds; Land; Land development; Construction; Gap; Standbys; Industrial revenue bonds; Other: Economic Development Agency Tax Frees, INTERNATIONAL (including import/export), REAL ESTATE: Acquisitions
PREFERRED TYPES OF INDUSTRIE/INVESTMENTS: Any
RANGE OF IN./LOAN PER BUSINESS: Max. $5 Million
PREFERRED TERM FOR LOANS & LEASES: Miin. Demand; Max. 25 year payout
BUSINESS CHARACTERISTICS DESIRED-REQUIRED: Minimum number of years in business: 0
BRANCHES: 20 branches throughout New Jersey

COMPANY:**Weyhenmeyer and Assoc., Inc.**
ADDRESS: 1280 Terminal Way, Suite #13, (Mailing addess: P.O. Box 21509, Reno, NV 89515)
Reno, NV 89502
PHONE: (702) 329-1442
TYPE OF INSTITUTION: Financial brokers—Aq. & Merger Intermediaries
CONTACT OFFICER(S): E.G. Weyhenmeyer, Ph.D., President
ASSETS: 1.MM+
INVESTMENTS/LOANS MADE: For managed accounts, Through private placements
TYPES OF FINANCING: VENTURE CAPITAL: Research & Development; Start-up from developed product stage; First-stage; Second-stage; Later-stage expansion; Buy-outs/Acquisitions, LOANS: Unsecured; Working capital; Equipment; Equity-related, REAL ESTATE LOANS: Long-term senior mtg.; Intermediate-term senior mtg.; Subordinated; Wraparounds; Land; Land development; Construction; Gap; Standbys; Industrial revenue bonds, FACTORING, LEASES: Single-investor; Leveraged; Vendor financing programs; INTERNATIONAL, REAL ESTATE: Acquisitions; Joint ventures
PREFERRED TYPES OF INDUSTRIES/INVESTMENTS: Dev. of high rise-cond. apts.; Shopping centers; Hotel/casino; raw land for mfg. warehousing; Loans for almost any purpose; Int'l. funding from foreign investors; Business seeking tax shelter in NV Freeport laws

GEOGRAPHIC LIMITS OF INVESTMENTS/LOANS: National; International
PREFERRED TERM FOR LOANS & LEASES: Min. 3-5 years; Max. 30 years
BUSINESS CHARACTERISTICS DESIRED-REQUIRED: Minimum number of years in business: 0
REFERRALS ACCEPTED FROM: Borrower/Investee

COMPANY: **HLC Leasing Co.**
ADDRESS: 7063 So. Virginia Street
Reno, NV 89511
PHONE: (702) 851-3313
TYPE OF INSTITUTION: Financial services
CONTACT OFFICER(S): Tom Gosh, Manager
ASSETS: Approx. $5 million
INVESTMENTS/LOANS MADE: For own account
TYPES OF FINANCING: SECONDARY-MARKET CORPORATE SECURITIES: Other: Equipment & vehicle leases and contracts—real estate financing (commercial and industrial) (residential/discount notes & deeds), LOANS: Equipment, REAL ESTATE LOANS: FACTORING, LEASES: Single-investor; Leveraged; Tax leases; Non-tax leases; Operating; Tax-oriented lease brokerage; Lease syndications; Vendor financing programs; Other: Mini-leases, managers of captives, and consultant underwriters to lending institutions, INTERNATIONAL (including import/export), REAL ESTATE: Acquisitions, Joint ventures, OTHER SERVICES PROVIDED: Real estate, brokerage, business brokerage, vehicle fleet leasing and sales (trucks and passenger cars—all makes and models)
PREFERRED TYPES OF INDUSTRIES/INVESTMENTS: Machinery tools; Construction; Mining; Warehousing; Aircraft; Industrial; Office equipment; Hotel; Motel; Restaurant; Computers; Telephone; Vehicles
GEOGRAPHIC LIMITS OF INVESTMENTS/LOANS: National; International
PREFERRED TERM FOR LOANS & LEASES: Min. 1 year; Max. 10-15 years
BUSINESS CHARACTERISTICS DESIRED-REQUIRED: Minimum number of years in business: 2; Min. annual sales $250,000; Min. net worth $150,000; Min. annual net income $25,000; Min. annual cash flow $25,000
REFERRALS ACCEPTED FROM: Investment/Mortgage banker or Borrower/Investee
REMARKS: We do accept bonafide broker business, and we will pay broker fees if legitimized

COMPANY: **Matthew Stuart & Company, Inc.**
ADDRESS: 308 Main Street
New Rochelle, NY 10802
PHONE: (914) 235-5730
TYPE OF INSTITUTION: Business Consulting, Investment Banking, Financial Consultants
CONTACT OFFICER(S): Robert Pfeffer, President
INVESTMENTS/LOANS MADE: For clients account
TYPES OF FINANCING: VENTURE CAPITAL: Buy-outs/Acquisitions. LOANS: Working capital; Equipment; Equity-related. REAL ESTATE LOANS: Long-term senior mtg. FACTORING. INTERNATIONAL. OTHER SERVICES PROVIDED: Mergers, Acquisitions, Financing Leveraged Buyouts, Management Acquisitions
PREFERRED TYPES OF INDUSTRIES/INVESTMENTS: Industrial/Commercial/All Types
GEOGRAPHIC LIMITS OF INVESTMENTS/LOANS: National; International
RANGE OF INV./LOAN PER BUSINESS: Min. $1 million; Max. $30 million
PREFERRED TERM FOR LOANS & LEASES: Min. 1 year; Max. 20 years
BUSINESS CHARACTERISTICS DESIRED-REQUIRED: Minimum number of years in business: 3; Min. annual sales $3 million; Min. net worth $1 million; Min. annual net income $500 million; Min annual cash flow $500 million
REFERRALS ACCEPTED FROM: Investment/Mortgage banker or Borrower/Investee

COMPANY: **Charles de Than Group**
ADDRESS: 51 E. 67th Street
New York, NY 10021
PHONE: (212) 988-5108
TYPE OF INSTITUTION: Private capital group and corporate finance broker
CONTACT OFFICER(S): Charles B. de Than, General Partner
INVESTMENTS/LOANS MADE: For own account; Through private placements; Through underwriting public offerings
TYPES OF FINANCING: VENTURE CAPITAL: Start-up from developed product stage; Second-stage; Later-stage expansion; Buy-outs/Acquisitions. LOANS: Equity-related; Other: Acquisitions and mergers, prefer leverageable deals. OTHER SERVICES PROVIDED: Consulting, Evaluations, Financial publicity, Investment advisor.
PREFERRED TYPES OF INDUSTRIES/INVESTMENTS: Invest in or acquire low technology industries with earnings record and reasonable balance sheet; Broker any type acquisitions; Venture placement: any field, prefer computer, medical and other high technology & communcation areas.
GEOGRAPHIC LIMITS OF INVESTMENTS/LOANS: Any area
RANGE OF INV./LOAN PER BUSINESS: Min. $2-300,000; Max. No limit
REFERRALS ACCEPTED FROM: Investment/Mortgage banker or Borrower/Investee

COMPANY: **East River Savings Bank**
ADDRESS: 26 Cortlandt Street
New York, NY 10007
PHONE: (212) 553-9611
TYPE OF INSTITUTION: Savings Bank
CONTACT OFFICER(S): Joseph Charla Jr., E.V.P.
Frank Magilligan, E.V.P.
ASSETS: $1.9 Billion
INVESTMENTS/LOANS MADE: For own account; Through private placements
INVESTMENTS/LOANS MADE: In securities with a secondary market and in securities without a secondary market
TYPES OF FINANCING: REAL ESTATE LOANS: Intermediate-term senior mtg.; Wraparounds; Land; Land development; Construction; Standbys. REAL ESTATE: Joint ventures

GEOGRAPHIC LIMITS OF INVESTMENTS/LOANS: Local; State; Regional; National

COMPANY: **Hammond Kennedy & Company, Inc.**
ADDRESS: 230 Park Ave.
New York, NY 10169
PHONE: (212) 867-1010
TYPE OF INSTITUTION: Financial Intermediary
CONTACT OFFICER(S): Douglas A. Worth, V.P. Principal
William F. Moore, V.P. Principal
ASSETS: Substantial
INVESTMENTS/LOANS MADE: For own account
INVESTMENTS/LOANS MADE: Only in securities without a secondary market
TYPES OF FINANCING: VENTURE CAPITAL: Buy-outs/Acquisitions; OTHER SERVICES PROVIDED: Organize, negotiate and participate in management buy-outs
PREFERRED TYPES OF INDUSTRIES/INVESTMENTS: Manufacturing Industries
WILL NOT CONSIDER: Non-manufacturing
GEOGRAPHIC LIMITS OF INVESTMENTS/LOANS: East of the Rockies
RANGE OF INV./LOAN PER BUSINESS: Min. $500,000; Max. $5 million
BUSINESS CHARACTERISTICS DESIRED-REQUIRED: Min. annual sales $30 million
REFERRALS ACCEPTED FROM: Investment/Mortgage banker or Borrower/Investee
REMARKS: The ideal situation is where management of a division or a private company is aware that a sale is likely, would like to buy it themselves and are seeking help to achieve a transaction.

COMPANY: **Hop Chung Capital Investors Inc.**
ADDRESS: 74A Mott Street
New York, NY 10013
PHONE: (212) 219-1777
CONTACT OFFICER(S): You Hon Lee, President
Peter Wong, Secretary-Treasurer
ASSETS: $1,000,000.00
INVESTMENTS/LOANS MADE: For own account; Through private placements
INVESTMENTS/LOANS MADE: In securities with a secondary market and in securities without a secondary market
TYPES OF FINANCING: VENTURE CAPITAL: Start-up from developed product stage; Second-stage; LOANS: Working capital; Equipment; REAL ESTATE: Joint ventures
PREFERRED TYPES OF INDUSTRIES/INVESTMENTS: Restaurant & Garment
GEOGRAPHIC LIMITS OF INVESTMENTS/LOANS: Local; Regional
RANGE OF INV./LOAN PER BUSINESS: Min. $50,000; Max. $150,000
PREFERRED TERM FOR LOANS & LEASES: Min. 4 years
BUSINESS CHARACTERISTICS DESIRED-REQUIRED: Min. no. of years in business: 0;

COMPANY: **James Talcott Inc.; James Talcott Factors Div.**
James Talcott Business Credit, Div.
ADDRESS: 1633 Broadway
New York, NY 10019
PHONE: (212) 484-0300
TYPE OF INSTITUTION: Diversified secured financial institution.
CONTACT OFFICER(S): William R. Gruttemeyer, President
Martin H. Rod, Executive V.P.
David J. Kantes, Executive V.P.
Robert W . Kramer.Executive V.P.
Phillip E. Renle, Jr., Senior V.P.
Anthony Viola, V.P.
ASSETS: Confidential
TYPES OF FINANCING: LOANS: Working capital (receivables/inventory);Equipment; Equity-related; Leveraged buy-outs, acquisition secured by the assets of the acquired co., REAL ESTATE LOANS: Intermediate-term senior mtg.; Wraparounds; Land, FACTORING, LEASES: Single-investor; Operating; Tax-oriented lease brokerage, INTERNATIONAL (including import/export), OTHER SERVICES PROVIDED: "Boot-Strap" Acquisitions
PREFERRED TYPES OF INDUSTRIES/INVESTMENTS: We will consider all types of industries for financing and factoring loans.
WILL NOT CONSIDER: Construction and home improvement loans.
GEOGRAPHIC LIMITS OF INVESTMENTS/LOANS: National; International
RANGE OF INV./LOAN PER BUSINESS: Min. $500,000.00; Max. Unlimited
PREFERRED TERM FOR LOANS & LEASES: Min. One year; Max. Ten years
BUSINESS CHARACTERISTICS DESIRED-REQUIRED: Minimum number of years in business: 0; Min. annual sales $1,500,000; Min. net worth $250,000; Min. annual net income: open; Min. annual cash flow: open
REFERRALS ACCEPTED FROM: Investment/Mortgage banker or Borrower/Investee
BRANCHES: Donald Mintz, One Wilshire Building, Los Angeles, CA, 90017; (213) 620-9200
Vincent Panzera, 717 North Harwood Street, Suite 440, Box 36, Dallas, TX, 75201; (214) 651-8801
REMARKS: Other national offices to be opened in 1982. Parent is The Lloyds Scottish Group in Great Britain which, in turn, is controlled by The Lloyds Bank of England.

COMPANY: **Standard Financial Corporation**
ADDRESS: 540 Madison Avenue
New York, NY 10022
PHONE: (212) 826-8000
TYPE OF INSTITUTION: Banking, financing, leasing and factoring
CONTACT OFFICER(S): Louis J. Cappelli, Executive V.P.
ASSETS: $100,000,000 and up
INVESTMENTS/LOANS MADE: For own account
TYPES OF FINANCING: LOANS, REAL ESTATE LOANS: Long-term senior mtg.; Intermediate-term senior mtg.; Wraparounds; Land; Land development; Construction; Gap; Standbys, FACTORING, LEASES: Single-investor; Leveraged; Tax leases; Non-tax leases;

Operating; Tax-oriented lease brokerage; Lease syndications; Vendor financing programs, INTERNATIONAL (including import/export), REAL ESTATE
GEOGRAPHIC LIMITS OF INVESTMENTS/LOANS: International
RANGE OF INV./LOAN PER BUSINESS: Min. $100,000.00; Max. $15 million
BRANCHES: Kenneth W. Grubbs, V.P., Security Industrial Loan Association, 4th and Main St., Richmond, VA, 23219; (804) 649-1120

COMPANY: **Cromwell & Kyle**
ADDRESS: 234 Fountainville Center
Fountainville, PA 18923
PHONE: (215) 249-3583
TYPE OF INSTITUTION: Consulting Investment Bankers
CONTACT OFFICER(S): Alec B. Kyle
Roger J.K. Cromwell
INVESTMENTS/LOANS MADE: Through private placements
INVESTMENTS/LOANS MADE: In securities without a secondary market
TYPES OF FINANCING: SECONDARY-MARKET CORPORATE SECURITIES: Common stock; Preferred stock; Bonds, VENTURE CAPITAL: Research & Development; Start-up from developed product stage; First-stage (less than 1 year); Second-stage (generally 1-3 years); Later-stage expansion; Buy-outs/Acquisitions, LOANS: Unsecured; Working capital (receivables/inventory); Equipment; Equity-related; Other: Mezzanine financing in leveraged buy-outs. Loans against receivables from Mexican government entities, REAL ESTATE LOANS: Long-term senior mtg.; Intermediate-term senior mtg.; Subordinated; Wraparounds; Land; Land development; Construction; Gap; Standbys; Industrial revenue bonds, FACTORING, INTERNATIONAL (including import/export), REAL ESTATE: Acquisitions; Joint ventures; Partnerships/Syndications, OTHER SERVICES PROVIDED: Restructuring financings to command low-interest Swiss funding
PREFERRED TYPES OF INDUSTRIES/INVESTMENTS: No preference
GEOGRAPHIC LIMITS OF INVESTMENTS/LOANS: National; International
RANGE OF INV./LOAN PER BUSINESS: Min. $500,000; Max. $75,000,000
REFERRALS ACCEPTED FROM: Investment/Mortgage banker or Borrower/Investee
BRANCHES: 1960 Bronson Rd., Fairfield, CT 06430; (203) 259-3269

COMPANY: **MP Ventures, Inc.**
ADDRESS: Suite 227, 5 Great Valley Parkway
Malvern, PA 19355
PHONE: (215) 296-9600
TYPE OF INSTITUTION: Venture consulting firm evaluating and analyzing venture projects and assisting in financing
CONTACT OFFICER(S): Thomas A. Penn, Vice President
INVESTMENTS/LOANS MADE: Through private placements
INVESTMENTS/LOANS MADE: Only in securities without a secondary market
TYPES OF FINANCING: VENTURE CAPITAL: Research & Development; Start-up from deveoped product stage; First-stage; Second-stage; Later-stage expansion; Buy-outs/Acquisitions
PREFERRED TYPES OF INDUSTRIES/INVESTMENTS: Prefer new and small enterprises with high growth potential
WILL NOT CONSIDER: Real estate, oil and gas
GEOGRAPHIC LIMITS OF INVESTMENTS/LOANS: National
RANGE OF INV./LOAN PER BUSINESS: Min. $200,000; Max. varies with circumstances
BUSINESS CHARACTERISTICS DESIRED-REQUIRED: Minimum number of years in business: 0
REFERRALS ACCEPTED FROM: Investment/Mortgage banker and Borrower/Investee

COMPANY: **Howard & Company**
ADDRESS: 1528 Walnut Street
Philadelphia, PA 19102
PHONE: (215) 735-2815
TYPE OF INSTITUTION: VC Financial Consultant
CONTACT OFFICER(S): Michael Cuneo, Director—Venture Associates Div.
INVESTMENTS/LOANS MADE: Through private placements
INVESTMENTS/LOANS MADE: Only in securities without a secondary market
TYPES OF FINANCING: VENTURE CAPITAL: Research & Development; Start-up froom developed product stage; First-stage; Second-stage; Later-stage expansion; Buy-outs/Acquisitions

COMPANY: **Universal Financial Corporation**
ADDRESS: 56 Broad Street, P.O. Box 1014
Charleston, SC 29402
PHONE: (803) 577-4324
TYPE OF INSTITUTION: Business and financial broker
CONTACT OFFICER(S): William E. Craver, Jr., President
INVESTMENTS/LOANS MADE: For own account, Through private placements, Through underwriting public offerings
INVESTMENTS/LOANS MADE: In securities with a secondary market and in securities without a secondary market
TYPES OF FINANCING: VENTURE CAPITAL: Start-up from developed product stage; First-stage (less than 1 year); Second-stage (generally 1-3 years); Later-stage expansion; Buy-outs/Acquisitions, LOANS: Working capital (receivables/inventory); Equipment, Equity-related, REAL ESTATE LOANS: Intermediate-term senior mtg., FACTORING, LEASES: Single-investor; Operating; Tax-oriented lease brokerage; Vendor financing programs, REAL ESTATE: Acquisitions; Joint ventures, OTHER SERVICES PROVIDED: Financial consulting
GEOGRAPHIC LIMITS OF INVESTMENTS/LOANS: Regional; National
RANGE OF INV./LOAN PER BUSINESS: Min. $250,000; Max. Open
PREFERRED TERM FOR LOANS & LEASES: Min. Open; Max. Open

BUSINESS CHARACTERISTICS DESIRED-REQUIRED: Minimum number of years in business: 0
REFERRALS ACCEPTED FROM: Investment/Mortgage banker or Borrower/Investee

COMPANY: **RepublicBank Dallas, N.A.**
ADDRESS: P.O. Box 241
Dallas, TX 75221
PHONE: (214) 922-6139
TYPE OF INSTITUTION: Trust corporate services
CONTACT OFFICER(S): David J. Pittman, Sr. V.P., Trust Corporate Relations, Marketing
ASSETS: $8 billion
INVESTMENTS/LOANS MADE: For own account, For managed accounts
INVESTMENTS/LOANS MADE: Only in securities with a secondary market
TYPES OF FINANCING: SECONDARY-MARKET CORPORATE SECURITIES: Common stock; Preferred stock; Bonds; Other: Real estate equity, oil and gas, guaranteed C D, aggressive stock and bond, REAL ESTATE: Acquisitions

COMPANY: **Mexican American Unity Council**
ADDRESS: 2300 W. Commerce St., Ste 300
San Antonio, TX 78207
PHONE: (512) 225-4275
TYPE OF INSTITUTION: Community development corporation
CONTACT OFFICER(S): Domingo Bueno, President
Ruben M. Saenz, V.P., Business Development
ASSETS: Not available
INVESTMENTS/LOANS MADE: For managed accounts
INVESTMENTS/LOANS MADE: In securities with a secondary market and in securities without a secondary market
TYPES OF FINANCING: SECONDARY-MARKET CORPORATE SECURITIES: Common stock; Preferred stock, VENTURE CAPITAL: Start-up from developed product stage; Later-stage expansion, LOANS: Equity-related, REAL ESTATE: Joint ventures; Partnerships/Syndications
PREFERRED TYPES OF INDUSTRIES/INVESTMENTS: Manufacturing concerns; Real estate development; Housing; Industrial parks; Wholesale distribution; Construction
WILL NOT CONSIDER: R&D, Retail operations
GEOGRAPHIC LIMITS OF INVESTMENTS/LOANS: Other: Will consider certain state, regional or national based on individual deal
RANGE OF INV./LOAN PER BUSINESS: Min. $50,000; Max. $200,000
PREFERRED TERM FOR LOANS & LEASES: Min. 5 years; Max. 7 years
BUSINESS CHARACTERISTICS DESIRED-REQUIRED: Minimum number of years in business: 0; Other: Will consider any company not exceeding $6 million net worth and less than $2 million average income after taxes for the preceeding 2 years
REFERRALS ACCEPTED FROM: Investment/Mortgage banker or Borrower/Investee

COMPANY: **Continental Investment Advisors**
ADDRESS: P.O. Box 27424
Richmond, VA 23261
PHONE: (804) 281-6595
TYPE OF INSTITUTION: Investment Advisor
CONTACT OFFICER(S): Daniel B. Belcore, CFA, Portfolio Manager & Director of Research (private placement bonds & public & private preferred stock)
ASSETS: $2 billion
INVESTMENTS/LOANS MADE: For managed accounts (Public & Private), Through private placements
INVESTMENTS/LOANS MADE: In securities with or without a secondary market
TYPES OF FINANCING: SECONDARY-MARKET CORPORATE SECURITIES: Preferred stock; Bonds. LOANS: Unsecured to credits above Ba; Equipment; Equity-related.
GEOGRAPHIC LIMITS OF INVESTMENTS/LOANS: National
RANGE OF INV./LOAN PER BUSINESS: Min. $500,000; Max. $5,000,000
PREFERRED TERM FOR LOANS & LEASES: Min. 3 years; Max. 20 years
BUSINESS CHARACTERISTICS DESIRED-REQUIRED: Minimum number of years in business: 10; Min. annual sales $50 MM
REFERRALS ACCEPTED FROM: Investment/Mortgage banker or Borrower/Investee

COMPANY: **Impact Seven, Inc.**
ADDRESS: Box 8, Rt. 2
Turtle Lake, WI
PHONE: (715) 986-4171
TYPE OF INSTITUTION: Community development corporation
CONTACT OFFICER(S): William Bay, President
Mike Schatz, Investment Officer
ASSETS: $5,000,000
INVESTMENTS/LOANS MADE: For own account, For managed accounts, Through private placements
TYPES OF FINANCING: VENTURE CAPITAL: Start-up from developed product stage; First-stage (less than 1 year); Second-stage (generally 1-3 years); Later-stage expansion; Buy-outs/Acquisitions, LOANS: Unsecured; Working capital (receivables/inventory); Equipment; Equity-related; Other, REAL ESTATE LOANS: Land; Land development; Construction; Standbys; Industrial revenue bonds; Other, REAL ESTATE: Acquisitions, OTHER SERVICES PROVIDED: Consulting
PREFERRED TYPES OF INDUSTRIES/INVESTMENTS: Considering any type of industry
GEOGRAPHIC LIMITS OF INVESTMENTS/LOANS: Local; State
RANGE OF INV./LOAN PER BUSINESS: Min. $25,000
PREFERRED TERM FOR LOANS & LEASES: Min. 1 year; Max. 20 years
BUSINESS CHARACTERISTICS DESIRED-REQUIRED: Other: Will look at merits of each investment
REFERRALS ACCEPTED FROM: Investment/Mortgage banker or Borrower/Investee

State Institutions and Programs

The format for each state program has been kept constant. Thus, some questions may not be relevant to each program.

The full black square in "Type of Financing" refers to the type of financing offered by the program.

STATE CONTACT OFFICERS

1. Alabama: Jamie Etheredge, Director, Alabama Development Office, State Capitol, Montgomery, AL 36130; (205) 832-6980
2. Alaska: James Weiderman, Development Officer, Dept. of Commerce & Economic Development, Pouch EE, Juneau, Alaska 99811; (907) 465-2018
3. Arizona: Beth Jarman, Executive Director, Office of Economic Planning & Development, 1700 W. Washington, 4th floor, Phoenix, AZ 85007
4. Arkansas: Larry Patrick, Director of Industrial Finance, Arkansas Industrial Development Commission, No. 1, State Capitol Mall, Little Rock, AR 72201; (501) 371-1151
5. California: Christy Campbell, Director, Dept. of Commerce, 1121 L Street, Suite 600, Sacramento, CA 95814; (916) 322-1394
6. Colorado: Steve Schmitz, Director, Div. of Commerce & Development, Room 523, 1313 Sherman Street, Denver, CO 80203; (303) 866-2205
7. Connecticut: John J. Carson, Commissioner, Dept. of Economic Development, 210 Washington Street, Hartford, CT 06106; (203) 566-3787
8. Delaware: Nathan Hayward III, Director, Delaware Development Office, 99 Kings Hwy, P.O. Box 1401, Dover, Delaware 19903; (302) 736-4271
9. Florida: Harold Stone, Supervisor, Office of Business Finance, Dept of Commerce, 107 W. Gaines Street, Collins Bldg, Tallahassee, FL 32301; (904) 488-3104
10. Georgia: George Berry, Commissioner, Department of Industry & Trade, P.O. Box 1776, Atlanta, GA 30301; (404) 656-3556
11. Hawaii: Kent M. Keith, Director, Dept. of Planning & Economic Development, P.O. Box 2359, Honolulu, HI 96804; (808) 548-6914
12. Idaho: Dr. David O. Porter, Administrator, Div. of Economic and Community Affairs, Room 108, Capitol, Boise, ID 83720; (208) 334-2470
13. Illinois: Michael T. Woelffer, Director, Illinois Dept of Commerce and Community Affairs, 620 East Adams Street, Springfield, Il 62701; (217) 782-7500
14. Indiana: Mark Akers, Director, Industrial Development Division, Indiana Dept of Commerce, 1 N. Capitol Street, Suite 700, Indianapolis, IN 46204-2243; (317) 232-8888
15. Iowa: Jack Bailey, Director, Iowa Development Commission, E. 600 Court Street, Ste A, Capitol Center, Des Moines, IA 50309; (515) 281-3619
16. Kansas: Charles J. Schwartz, Secretary, Kansas Dept of Economic Development, 503, Kansas Ave, 6th floor, Topeka, KS 66603; (913) 296-3481
17. Kentucky: James H. Jones, Executive Director, Kentucky Development Finance Authority, 24th floor, Capitol Plaza Tower, Frankfort, KY 40601; (502) 564-4554
18. Louisiana: Neil Myers, Small Business Specialist, Office of Commerce & Industry, LA Dept of Commerce, P.O. Box 44185, Baton Rouge, LA 70804; (504) 342-5382
19. Maine: Les Steven, Acting Director, Finance Authority of Maine, P.O. Box 949, Augusta, ME 04330; (207) 289-3095
20. Maryland: Frank J. De Francis, Secretary, Dept of Economic and Community Development, 45 Calvert Street, Annapolis, MD 21401; (301) 269-2621
21. Massachusetts: Joe Donovan, Director, Office of Financial Development, Dept of Commerce, 100 Cambridge Street, 13th floor, Boston, MA 02202; (617) 727-4521

22. Michigan: Carol Hoffman, Director, Business and Community Development, P.O. Box 30225, Lansing, MI 48909; (517) 373-3530

23. Minnesota: Connie Lewis, Deputy to the Commissioner, Minnesota Dept of Energy and Economic Development, 150 E. Kellogg Blvd, St. Paul, MN 55101; (612) 296-6424

24. Mississippi: Jim Miller, Acting Executive Director, MS Dept of Economic Development, Box 849, Jackson, MS 39205; (601) 359-3449

25. Missouri: Bud Peck, Director, Dept of Economic Development, Harry S. Truman Bldg, 301 W. High Street, 7- South, Jefferson City, MO 65101; (314) 751-2133

26. Montana: William Duffey, Business Location Officer, Business Assistance Division, Montana Dept of Commerce, Capitol Station, Helena, MT 59620; (406) 444-3923

27. Nebraska: Donald M. Dworak, Director, Dept. of Economic Development, 301 Centennial Mall S., P.O. Box 94666, Lincoln, NE 68509; (402) 471-3747

28. Nevada: Jean Towne, Associate Director of The Commission on Economic Development, 600 E. Williams, Ste 203, Capitol Complex, Carson City, NV 89710; (702) 885-4325 or (800) 366-1600

29. New Hampshire: Vasilike Kounas, Executive Secretary, Industrial Development Authority, 4 Park Street, Rm 302, Concord, NH 03301; (603) 271-2391

30. New Jersey: Leonard J. Goldner, Financial Specialist, Office of Industrial Development, Dept of Commerce and Economic Development, CN 823, Trenton, NJ 08625; (609) 292-9727

31. New Mexico: William Weahkee, Assistant Secretary for Economic Development, Economic Development and Tourism Dept, Bataan Memorial Bldg, Santa Fe, NM 87503; (505) 827-6206

32. New York: Robert T. Dormer, President, New York Job Development Authority, 3 Park Avenue, New York, NY 10016; (212) 578-4150

33. North Carolina: Bruce Strickland, Jr., Chief, Industrial Financing Section, North Carolina Dept of Commerce, 430 N. Salisbury St, Room 272, Raleigh, NC 27611; (919)733-5297

34. North Dakota: Sylvan Melroe, Director, ND Economic Development Commission, Bismark, ND 58505; (701) 224-2810

35. Ohio: Howard Wise, Manager, Office of Industrial Development, Business Development Division, Ohio Dept of Development, P.O. Box 1001, Columbus, OH 43216; (614) 466-4551

36. Oklahoma: dustrial Division, Oklahoma Dept of Economic Development, P.O. Box 53424, State Capitol Station, Oklahoma City, OK 73152; (405) 521-2401

37. Oregon: Mark D. Huston, Manager, Financial Services, Oregon Economic Development Department, 595 Cottage Street N.E., Salem, OR 97310; (503) 373-1240

38. Pennsylvania: James O. Pickard, Secretary, Dept of Commerce, Room 433, Forum Bldg, Harrisburg, PA 17120; (717) 787-3003

39. Rhode Island: Norton L. Berman, Director, R.I. Dept of Economic Development, 7 Jackson Walkway, Providence, RI 02903; (401) 277-2601

40. South Carolina: Robert E. Leak, Director, S.C. State Development Board, P.O. Box 927, Columbia, SC 29202; (803) 758-3145

41. South Dakota: Bonnie L Untereiner, Financial Analyst, Dept of State Development, Box 6000, Pierre, SD 57501; (605) 773-5032

42. Tennessee: William H. Long, Commissioner, Dept of Economic and Community Development, 1007 Andrew Jackson Bldg, Nashville, TN 37219; (615) 741-1888

43. Texas: John Kirkley, Business Consultant, Texas Economic Development Commission, P.O. Box 12728, Capitol Station, Austin, TX 78711; (512) 472-5059

44. Utah: Evelyn Lee, Director, Utah Div of Economic Development, 6150 State Office Bldg, Salt Lake City, Utah 84114; (801) 533-5325

45. Vermont: Robert Y. Justice, Jr., Director of Industrial Development, Economic Development Department, Pavilion Office Bldg, Montpelier, VT 05602; (802) 828-3221

46. Virginia: Scott Eubanks, Director, Dept of Economic Development, 1000 Washington Bldg, Richmond, VA 23219; (804) 786-3791

47. Washington: Dennis Matson, Asst Director, Industrial Development Dept, Washington State Dept of Commerce, General Adminstration Bldg, Olympia, WA 98504; (206) 753-3065

48. West Virginia: Patricia H. Keeler, West Virginia Economic Development Authority, Bldg 6, Room 525, State Capitol Complex, Charleston, WV 25305; (304) 348-3650

49. Wisconsin: Phil McGoohan, Administrator, Div of Economic and Community Development, Dept of Development, P.O. Box 7970; 123 W. Washington Ave, Madison, WI 53707; (608) 266-3203

50. Wyoming: John Logan, Chief of Industrial Division, Dept of Economic Planning and Development, Herschler Bldg, Cheyenne, WY 82002; (307) 777-7285

SUMMARY OF STATE PROGRAMS

STATE	STATE DEVELOPMENT CORP. (PRIVATE FUNDS)	STATE INDUSTRIAL DEVELOPMENT AUTHORITY (PUBLIC FUNDS)	REVENUE BONDS (STATE SPONSORED)	REVENUE BONDS (LOCAL GOVT. SPONSORED)	GENERAL OBLIGATION BONDS (STATE SPONSORED)	GENERAL OBLIGATION BONDS (LOCAL GOVT. SPONSORED)	STATE LOANS TO BUSINESSES	STATE LOANS OR LOAN GUARANTEES TO LOCAL DEVELOPMENT ORGANIZATIONS	LOCAL DEVELOPMENT ORGANIZATIONS (INCL. INDUSTRIAL FOUNDATIONS)	INCENTIVES FOR BUSINESS LOCATION IN DESIGNATED AREAS	INCENTIVES FOR RESEARCH & DEVELOPMENT FOR NEW PRODUCTS	OTHER
ALABAMA		●	●	●			●	●	●	●	●	1
ALASKA		●	●	●		●	●		●			2
ARIZONA	●			●			●		●			
ARKANSAS	●		●						●	●		
CALIFORNIA			●	●			●					
COLORADO		●	●	●		●	●	●	●		●	
CONNECTICUT		●	●		●		●			●	●	
DELAWARE			●							●		
FLORIDA				●		●			●	●		
GEORGIA	●		●	●					●	●	●	
HAWAII	●		●				●	●	●	●		
IDAHO				●					●			
ILLINOIS		●	●	●	●		●		●	●	●	3, 4, 5, 6, 7
INDIANA			●	●				●	●	●	●	8
IOWA	●	●	●	●			●		●	●	●	9
KANSAS	●			●					●			
KENTUCKY			●	●	●	●	●		●			
LOUISIANA	●	●	●	●		●	●	●	●	●	●	10
MAINE		●	●	●			●	●	●		●	
MARYLAND	●	●	●	●			●		●	●		11,12,13
MASSACHUSETTS		●	●						●	●	●	
MICHIGAN			●	●			●				●	
MINNESOTA			●	●			●	●	●	●		
MISSISSIPPI	●			●		●	●		●	●		14
MISSOURI		●	●	●		●	●	●	●	●	●	15,16
MONTANA		●	●	●		●	●		●		●	

SUMMARY OF STATE PROGRAMS (CONTINUED)

STATE	STATE DEVELOPMENT CORP. (PRIVATE FUNDS)	STATE INDUSTRIAL DEVELOPMENT AUTHORITY (PUBLIC FUNDS)	REVENUE BONDS (STATE SPONSORED)	REVENUE BONDS (LOCAL GOVT. SPONSORED)	GENERAL OBLIGATION BONDS (STATE SPONSORED)	GENERAL OBLIGATION BONDS (LOCAL GOVT. SPONSORED)	STATE LOANS TO BUSINESSES	STATE LOANS OR LOAN GUARANTEES TO LOCAL DEVELOPMENT ORGANIZATIONS	LOCAL DEVELOPMENT ORGANIZATIONS (INCL. INDUSTRIAL FOUNDATIONS)	INCENTIVES FOR BUSINESS LOCATION IN DESIGNATED AREAS	INCENTIVES FOR RESEARCH & DEVELOPMENT FOR NEW PRODUCTS	OTHER
NEBRASKA	●											
NEVADA	●		●	●			●		●			17
NEW HAMPSHIRE	●	●	●				●		●			
NEW JERSEY		●	●				●		●	●		
NEW MEXICO	●	●	●	●			●		●			
NEW YORK		●		●				●	●			
NORTH CAROLINA				●					●			
NORTH DAKOTA			●	●	●	●	●	●	●	●	●	
OHIO			●	●			●		●	●	●	18
OKLAHOMA	●	●	●	●	●	●		●	●			
OREGON			●	●			●		●	●		19
PENNSYLVANIA		●	●	●			●	●			●	
RHODE ISLAND			●									20
SOUTH CAROLINA	●	●	●				●	●				
SOUTH DAKOTA			●				●					
TENNESSEE				●		●			●	●		
TEXAS			●	●		●		●	●	●	●	
UTAH				●					●		●	21
VERMONT	●	●	●	●			●	●	●			
VIRGINIA				●			●		●	●		
WASHINGTON		●	●	●			●		●		●	
WEST VIRGINIA		●	●	●			●		●			
WISCONSIN	●	●	●	●					●		●	
WYOMING	●	●	●	●		●		●	●		●	22

STATE -- CODED PROGRAMS -- FOOTNOTES

1. ALABAMA: State assisted site preparation grants
2. ALASKA: Tax forgiveness program
3. ILLINOIS: Illinois Development Finance Authority Insured IRBs
4. ILLINOIS: Illinois Farm Development Authority Agribusiness Bond Program
5. ILLINOIS: Illinois Export Development Authority Bond Program
6. ILLINOIS: Illinois Health Facilities Authority Bond Program
7. ILLINOIS: Illinois Development Finance Authority Venture Investment Fund
8. INDIANA: Venture Capital program for manufacturers
9. IOWA: Tax exemptions for industry
10. LOUISIANA: 10 year tax exemptions for industrial expansion
11. MARYLAND: Energy-related Project Financing
12. MARYLAND: Minority and Handicapped Financing
13. MARYLAND: State Loans to Communities for Industrial Land & Shell Buildings
14. MISSISSIPPI: Equity financing for local capital corporations
15. MISSOURI: Loan guarantees to businesses
16. MISSOURI: Economic Development Time Deposit Program
17. NEVADA: State grants to local development authorities
18. OHIO: Loan Guarantees
19. OREGON: Umbrella Revenue Bonds
20. RHODE ISLAND: Guaranteed Industrial Development Revenue Bonds
21. UTAH: State seed-capital program for innovative start-ups
22. WYOMING: Small Business Program -- buys SBA loan guarantees

STATE OF: ALABAMA

NAME OF ORGANIZATION: THE SOUTHERN DEVELOPMENT COUNCIL, INC.

ADDRESS: 135 South Union St. Suite 256, Montgomery,AL 36130

PHONE NO. (205) 264-5441

CONTACT OFFICER: Sam V. Brannon;**TITLE:**President

DESCRIPTION OF PROGRAM: We are a centralized, statewide financial packaging organization which manages the SBA-503 program, the State Economic Development Loan Fund, an EDA funded Revolving Loan Fund, and also utilize other state and federal programs such as UDAG, FmHA, etc.

Organization asset range: $1,000,000 **to $**10,000,000

Range of investment/grant per borrower/grantee: $0 to $250,000

Type of financing: ☐Grants; ■Loans; ■Loan with equity participations or convertibility; ☐Loan Guarantees; ☐Equity; ☐Leases; ☐Sale-leaseback; Other:

Security position: Senior or subordinated

Type of collateral: Cash value of life insurance, Equipment, Real Estate, Guarantees

Term of financing: Maximum: 20 **years; Minimum:** 0-1 **years**

Industry preference (in order of priority, if any): Manufacturing & Processing, Retailing, Wholesaling & Distribution, Research & Technology, Agriculture-Related

Borrower characteristics desired-required:

Min. number of years in business: 1-5

Min. annual sales: $

Min. net worth: $

Min. annual cash flow: $

Min. annual net income: $

Other requirements:

Estimated $ available for investment annually $6,000,000

Annual interest rate for 1985: Max.:12%; **Min.:**8% **Ave.:**10%

Special conditions, if any:

STATE OF: ARIZONA

NAME OF ORGANIZATION: OFFICE OF ECONOMIC PLANNING AND DEVELOPMENT, DEVELOPMENT FINANCE DIVISION

ADDRESS: Executive Tower, Fourth Floor, 1700 West Washington, Phoenix, Arizona 85007

PHONE NO. (602) 255-5705

CONTACT OFFICER: John Lopach; **TITLE:** Director, Development Finance

DESCRIPTION OF PROGRAM: Staffs an SBA 503 Certified Development Company Program ("Arizona Enterprise Development Corporation") for Arizona outside metropolitan Phoenix and Tucson. (Also assists Rural Arizona UDAG-eligible communities in structuring UDAG applications.)

Organization asset range: $10,000,000 **to $**100,000,000

Range of investment/grant per borrower/grantee: $50,000 **to $**500,000

Type of financing: ☐Grants; ■Loans; ☐Loan with equity participations or convertibility; ☐Loan Guarantees; ☐Equity; ☐Leases; ☐Sale-leaseback; Other:

Security position: Senior or subordinated

Type of collateral: Equipment, Real Estate, Personal Guarantee or corporate if Alter Ego financing

Term of financing: Maximum: 20 and up **years; Minimum:** 15-20 **years**

Industry preference (in order of priority, if any): Manufacturing & Processing, Research & Technology, Natural Resources, Agriculture-Related, Diversified

Borrower characteristics desired-required:

Min. number of years in business: 2-3

Min. annual sales: $

Min. net worth: Less than $6000

Min. annual cash flow: Adequate to cover proposed debt service

Min. annual net income: Less than $2000 for preceding two years

Other requirements: Eligible projects are land purchase and improvements, new construction, purchase and/or rehabilitation of exsisting buildings, leasehold improvements, purchase of machinery and equipment, contingency, legal, and professional fees. Inelibile: working capital, debt refinancing or consolidation, or developer projects.

Estimated $ available for investment annually: $No practical limits

Annual interest rate for 1985: Max.: ¾% above long-term treasury issues.

Special conditions, if any: 50% of project financing must be provided from non-federal sources (i.e. bank, savings and loans, or private individuals.)

STATE OF: ARKANSAS

NAME OF ORGANIZATION: ARKANSAS INDUSTRIAL DEVELOPMENT COMMISSION

ADDRESS: No. 1 State Capitol Mall, Little Rock, ARK 72201

PHONE NO. (501) 371-1151

CONTACT OFFICER: Larry Patrick; **TITLE:** Director of Industrial Finance

DESCRIPTION OF PROGRAM: Revenue Bond Guarantee Program — State guarantees loan payments on Revenue Bond issues up to $1,000,000 per project to assist small to medium industrial projects where bonds might not otherwise be marketable.

Organization asset range: $ to $

Range of investment/grant per borrower/grantee: $ to $1,000,000

Type of financing: ☐Grants; ☐Loans; ☐Loan with equity participations or convertibility; ■Loan Guarantees; ☐Equity; ☐Leases; ☐Sale-leaseback; Other:

Security position: Senior or subordinated

Type of collateral: Equipment, Real Estate

Term of financing: Maximum: 10 to 15 **years; Minimum:** 5-7 **years**

Industry preference (in order of priority, if any): Manufacturing & Processing

Borrower characteristics desired-required:

Min. number of years in business: 3

Min. annual sales: $

Min. net worth:

Min. annual cash flow:

Min. annual net income:

Other requirements: Audited financial statements

Estimated $ available for investment annually: $

Annual interest rate for 1985: Max.: %; Min.: % Ave.: %

Special conditions, if any: Interest rate for bonds vary, depending on maturity date of coupon and term of issue and market conditions.

STATE OF: ARKANSAS

NAME OF ORGANIZATION: ARKANSAS INDUSTRIAL DEVELOPMENT COMMISSION

ADDRESS: No. 1 State Capitol Mall, Little Rock, ARK 72201

PHONE NO. (501) 371-1151

CONTACT OFFICER: Larry Patrick; **TITLE:** Director of Industrial Finance

DESCRIPTION OF PROGRAM: The industrial revenue bond program provides: lower interest rates because of the tax-exempt status of bonds.

Organization asset range: $ to $

Range of investment/grant per borrower/grantee: $ to $10,000,000

Type of financing: ☐Grants; ☐Loans; ☐Loan with equity participations or convertibility; ☐Loan Guarantees; ☐Equity; ☐Leases; ☐Sale-leaseback; Other:fixed asset financing (land, machinery and equipment)

Security position:

Type of collateral:

Term of financing: Maximum: 15 to 20 **years; Minimum:** 5-7 **years**

Industry preference (in order of priority, if any): Manufacturing & Processing

Borrower characteristics desired-required:

Min. number of years in business:

Min. annual sales: $

Min. net worth:

Min. annual cash flow:

Min. annual net income:

Other requirements:

Estimated $ available for investment annually: $

Annual interest rate for 1985: Max.: %; Min.: % Ave.: %

Special conditions, if any: Averages 65% to 80% of prime depending upon bond market.

STATE OF: ARKANSAS

NAME OF ORGANIZATION: ARKANSAS INDUSTRIAL DEVELOPMENT COMMISSION

ADDRESS: No. 1 State Capitol Mall, Little Rock, ARK 72201

PHONE NO. (501) 371-5187

CONTACT OFFICER: Anyone in office; **TITLE:**

DESCRIPTION OF PROGRAM: SBA Loan Program - the purpose of this program is to eliminate the gap between the life of asset and the term of the loan for such assets. It is sponsored by the SBA and private lending institutions participation is mandatory.

Organization asset range: $ to $

Range of investment/grant per borrower/grantee: $ to $

Type of financing: ☐Grants; ☐Loans; ☐Loan with equity participations or convertibility; ■Loan Guarantees; ☐Equity; ☐Leases; ☐Sale-leaseback; Other:

Security position: Senoir or subordinated

Type of collateral: Equipment, Real Estate

Term of financing: Maximum: 20 and up **years; Minimum:** 10-15**years**

Industry preference (in order of priority, if any): Manufacturing & Processing, Retailing, Wholesale & Distribution

Borrower characteristics desired-required:

Min. number of years in business: 3

Max. annual sales: $6,000,000

Max. net worth: $2,000,000

Min. annual cash flow:

Min. annual net income:

Other requirements: Audited financial statements

Estimated $ available for investment annually: $

Annual interest rate for 1985: Max.: %; Min.: % Ave.: %

Special conditions, if any: The interest rate for the SBA portion is ¾% above the long-term T-Bill rate; small to medium sized businesses.

STATE OF: CALIFORNIA

NAME OF ORGANIZATION: DEPARTMENT OF COMMERCE

ADDRESS: 1121 L Street, Suite 600, Sacramento, CA 95814

PHONE NO. (916) 322-1394

CONTACT OFFICER: Christy Campbell; **TITLE:** Director

DESCRIPTION OF PROGRAM: Pollution Control Financing is tax exempt financing which can be used by companies needing to comply with air and water quality regulations, having a project for disposal of wastes, or having a project for conversion of wastes to energy. There is no limit on the amount of bond financing per project nor is there any interest rate ceiling. However, one IRS requirement is that the pollution equipment does not improve productivity or generate a valuable by product that would produce a profit to the operator.

Organization asset range: $ to $

Range of investment/grant per borrower/grantee: $ to $

Type of financing: ☐Grants; ☐Loans; ☐Loan with equity participations or convertibility; ☐Loan Guarantees; ☐Equity; ☐Leases; ☐Sale-leaseback; Other: Pollution Control Financing

Security position:

Type of collateral:

Term of financing: Maximum: years; Minimum: years

Industry preference (in order of priority, if any):

Borrower characteristics desired-required:

Min. number of years in business:

Min. annual sales: $

Min. net worth: $

Min. annual cash flow:

Min. annual net income:

Other requirements:

Estimated $ available for investment annually: $

Annual interest rate for 1985: Max.: %; Min.: % Ave.: %

Special conditions, if any:

STATE OF: CALIFORNIA

NAME OF ORGANIZATION: DEPARTMENT OF COMMERCE

ADDRESS: 1121 L Street, Suite 600, Sacramento, CA 95814

PHONE NO. (916) 322-1394

CONTACT OFFICER: Christy Campbell; **TITLE:** Director

DESCRIPTION OF PROGRAM: The industrial development revenue bond financing program allows each California city and county to issue tax-exempt industrial development bonds. The proceeds from these bonds can be used in the financing of an industrial plant's land acquistion, building construction, and equipment. One of the primary advantages of using this method of financing is that, because of its tax-exempt status, the loan bears an interest rate significantly lower than conventional financing. Furthermore under this method, financing would be available for 100 percent of the project cost.

Organization asset range: $ to $

Range of investment/grant per borrower/grantee: $1,000,000 **to $**10,000,000

Type of financing: ☐Grants; ☐Loans; ☐Loan with equity participations or convertibility; ☐Loan Guarantees; ☐Equity; ☐Leases; ☐Sale-leaseback; Other: Industrial Development Bonds

Security position:

Type of collateral:

Term of financing: Maximum: years; Minimum: years

Industry preference (in order of priority, if any): Manufacturing & Processing

Borrower characteristics desired-required:

Min. number of years in business:

Min. annual sales: $

Min. net worth: $

Min. annual cash flow:

Min. annual net income:

Other requirements:

Estimated $ available for investment annually: $

Annual interest rate for 1985: Max.: 12%; Min.: % Ave.: %

Special conditions, if any:

STATE OF: CALIFORNIA

NAME OF ORGANIZATION: DEPARTMENT OF COMMERCE

ADDRESS: 1121 L Street, Suite 600, Sacramento, CA 95814

PHONE NO. (916) 322-1394

CONTACT OFFICER: Christy Campbell; **TITLE:** Director

DESCRIPTION OF PROGRAM: The Employment Training Panel (ETP) will pay for the actual cost of training a company's employees up to $5,000 per employee. The company designs the training program then contracts with the ETP to have them pay for the training costs. The only stipulation is that the workers being trained are either on unemployment insurance, have exhausted their unemployment benefits, or are targeted to be on unemployment insurance.

Organization asset range: $ to $

Range of investment/grant per borrower/grantee: $ to $

Type of financing: ☐Grants; ☐Loans; ☐Loan with equity participations or convertibility; ☐Loan Guarantees; ☐Equity; ☐Leases; ☐Sale-leaseback; Other:

Security position:

Type of collateral:

Term of financing: Maximum: years; Minimum: years

Industry preference (in order of priority, if any):

Borrower characteristics desired-required:

Min. number of years in business:

Min. annual sales: $

Min. net worth: $

Min. annual cash flow:

Min. annual net income:

Other requirements:

Estimated $ available for investment annually: $

Annual interest rate for 1985: Max.: %; Min.: % Ave.: %

Special conditions, if any:

STATE OF: CALIFORNIA

NAME OF ORGANIZATION: DEPARTMENT OF COMMERCE

ADDRESS: 1121 L Street, Suite 600, Sacramento, CA 95814

PHONE NO. (916) 445-6545

CONTACT OFFICER: Patrick Valenzuela; **TITLE:** Chief, Development Finance

DESCRIPTION OF PROGRAM: California Small Business Loan Guarantee Program provides loan guarantees to lending institutions for loans to small businesses not able to obtain financing without loan guarantees.

Organization asset range: $10,000,000 **to $**100,000,000

Range of investment/grant per borrower/grantee: $none **to $**350,000

Type of financing: ☐Grants; ☐Loans; ☐Loan with equity participations or convertibility; ■Loan Guarantees; ☐Equity; ☐Leases; ☐Sale-leaseback; Other:

Security position: Senior or subordinated

Type of collateral: Current Assets (Inventory, Accounts Receivable), Cash value of life insurance, Equipment, Real Estate, Guarantees

Term of financing: Maximum: 5-7 **years; Minimum:** 0-1 **years**

Industry preference (in order of priority, if any): Program funds are available to business and agricultural enterprises without preference to any particular industry.

Borrower characteristics desired-required:

Min. number of years in business:

Min. annual sales: $

Min. net worth: $

Min. annual cash flow:

Min. annual net income:

Other requirements:

Estimated $ available for investment annually: $3,000,000

Annual interest rate for 1985: Bank rate

Special conditions, if any:

STATE OF: CALIFORNIA

NAME OF ORGANIZATION: DEPARTMENT OF COMMERCE

ADDRESS: 1121 L Street, Suite 600, Sacramento, CA 95814

PHONE NO. (916) 445-6545

CONTACT OFFICER: Patrick Valenzuela; **TITLE:** Chief, Development Finance

DESCRIPTION OF PROGRAM: Sudden and Severe Economic Dislocation Program provides direct loans to businesses in certain eligible geographical areas of California. Area must be suffering from unemployment because of plant closures or other sudden dislocation.

Organization asset range: $1,000,000 **to $**10,000,000

Range of investment/grant per borrower/grantee: $100,000 **to $**500,000

Type of financing: ☐Grants; ■Loans; ☐Loan with equity participations or convertibility; ☐Loan Guarantees; ☐Equity; ☐Leases; ☐Sale-leaseback; Other:

Security position: Seniority Mandatory

Type of collateral: Current Assets (Inventory, Accounts Receivable), Cash value of life insurance, Equipment, Real Estate

Term of financing: Maximum: 20 and up **years; Minimum:** 0-1 **years**

Industry preference (in order of priority, if any): Manufacturing & Processing

Borrower characteristics desired-required:

Min. number of years in business:

Min. annual sales: $

Min. net worth: $

Min. annual cash flow:

Min. annual net income:

Other requirements:

Estimated $ available for investment annually: $1,300,000

Annual interest rate for 1985: Based on State investment rate

Special conditions, if any: Business must be willing to train and employ displaced workers. Training funds are available through State assisted programs.

STATE OF: CALIFORNIA

NAME OF ORGANIZATION: DEPARTMENT OF COMMERCE

ADDRESS: 1121 L Street, Suite 600, Sacramento, CA 95814

PHONE NO. (916) 445-6545

CONTACT OFFICER: Patrick Valenzuela; **TITLE:** Chief, Development Finance

DESCRIPTION OF PROGRAM: California Innovation Development Loan Program provides direct loans to high technology and innovative businesses in high unemployment areas of the state.

Organization asset range: $1,000,000 **to** $10,000,000

Range of investment/grant per borrower/grantee: $100,000 **to** $500,000

Type of financing: ☐Grants; ■Loans; ☐Loan with equity participations or convertibility; ☐Loan Guarantees; ☐Equity; ☐Leases; ☐Sale-leaseback; Other:

Security position: Seniority Mandatory

Type of collateral: Current Assets (Inventory, Accounts Receivable), Cash value of life insurance, Equipment, Real Estate, Guarantees

Term of financing: Maximum: 20 and up **years; Minimum:** 0-1 **years**

Industry preference (in order of priority, if any): Manufacturing & Processing

Borrower characteristics desired-required:

Min. number of years in business:

Min. annual sales: $

Min. net worth: $

Min. annual cash flow:

Min. annual net income:

Other requirements:

Estimated $ available for investment annually: $2,000,000

Annual interest rate for 1985: Based on State investment rate

Special conditions, if any:

STATE OF: CALIFORNIA

NAME OF ORGANIZATION: DEPARTMENT OF COMMERCE

ADDRESS: 1121 L Street, Suite 600, Sacramento, CA 95814

PHONE NO. (916) 445-6545

CONTACT OFFICER: Patrick Valenzuela; **TITLE:** Chief, Development Finance

DESCRIPTION OF PROGRAM: Economic Development Loan Program provides direct loans to businesses that create jobs, diversify and enhance the local economy and increases the tax and economic base of communities in California.

Organization asset range: $1,000,000 **to $**10,000,000

Range of investment/grant per borrower/grantee: $100,000 **to $**350,000

Type of financing: ☐Grants; ■Loans; ☐Loan with equity participations or convertibility; ☐Loan Guarantees; ☐Equity; ☐Leases; ☐Sale-leaseback; Other:

Security position: Senior or Subordinated

Type of collateral: Current Assets (Inventory, Accounts Receivable), Cash value of life insurance, Equipment, Real Estate, Guarantees, as required on a case by case basis

Term of financing: Maximum: 20 and up **years; Minimum:** 0-1 **years**

Industry preference (in order of priority, if any): Manufacturing & Processing

Borrower characteristics desired-required:

Min. number of years in business:

Min. annual sales: $

Min. net worth: $

Min. annual cash flow:

Min. annual net income:

Other requirements:

Estimated $ available for investment annually: $1,200,000

Annual interest rate for 1985: Based on State investment rate

Special conditions, if any:

STATE OF: CONNECTICUT

NAME OF ORGANIZATION: CONNECTICUT DEVELOPMENT AUTHORITY

ADDRESS: 217 Washington Street Hartford, Connecticut 06106

PHONE NO. (203) 522-3730

CONTACT OFFICER: Vincent T. Pellegrino; **TITLE:** Program Manager-Mortgage Insurance Program

DESCRIPTION OF PROGRAM: Mortgage Insurance Program; provides insurance for the payment of first mortgage loans made by lending institutions.

Organization asset range: $100,000,000 And up

Range of investment/grant per borrower/grantee: $ to $ 10,000,000

Type of financing: ☐Grants; ☐Loans; ☐Loan with equity participations or convertibility; ■Loan Guarantees; ☐Equity; ☐Leases; ☐Sale-leaseback; Other:

Security position: Senior or Subordinated

Type of collateral: Equipment, Real Estate, Guarantees

Term of financing: Maximum: 20 and up **years; Minimum:** 7-10**years**

Industry preference (in order of priority, if any): Manufacturing & Processing, Research & Technology, Wholesaling & Distribution

Borrower characteristics desired-required:

Min. number of years in business: 3

Min. annual sales: $

Min. net worth: $

Min. annual cash flow:

Min. annual net income:

Other requirements:

Estimated $ available for investment annually: $ 70,000,000

Annual interest rate for 1985: Max.:1%; **Min.: ½% Ave.: %**

Special conditions, if any: 1% premium on land and building loans; ½ premium on machinery and equipment loans.

STATE OF: CONNECTICUT

NAME OF ORGANIZATION: CONNECTICUT DEVELOPMENT AUTHORITY

ADDRESS: 217 Washington Street, Hartford, Connecticut 06106

PHONE NO. (203) 522-3730

CONTACT OFFICER: Paul M. Hughes; **TITLE:** Program Manager-Self Sustaining Program

DESCRIPTION OF PROGRAM: Self Sustaining Revenue Bond Program - provides financial assistance for specific industrial and certain recreational and utility projects through the issuance of special obligation industrial revenue bonds.

Organization asset range: $100,000,000 And up

Range of investment/grant per borrower/grantee: $ to $10,000,000

Type of financing: ☐Grants; ■Loans; ☐Loan with equity participations or convertibility; ☐Loan Guarantees; ☐Equity; ☐Leases; ■Sale-leaseback; Other:

Security position: Senior or subordinated

Type of collateral: Equipment, Real Estate,

Term of financing: Maximum: 15 to 20 **years; Minimum:** 1-3**years**

Industry preference (in order of priority, if any): Hotels, Motels & Restaurants, Manufacturing & Processing, Medical & Other Health Services, Research &Technology, Retailing, Wholesaling & Distribution, Utilities

Borrower characteristics desired-required:

Min. number of years in business:

Min. annual sales: $

Min. net worth: $

Min. annual cash flow:

Min. annual net income:

Other requirements:

Estimated $ available for investment annually: $300,000,000

Annual interest rate for 1985: Varies

Special conditions, if any:

STATE OF: CONNECTICUT

NAME OF ORGANIZATION: CONNECTICUT DEVELOPMENT AUTHORITY

ADDRESS: 217 Washington Street, Hartford, Connecticut 06106

PHONE NO. (203) 522-3730

CONTACT OFFICER: Leonard J. Smart; **TITLE:** Program Manager-Umbrella Loan Program

DESCRIPTION OF PROGRAM: Umbrella Bond Program-provides financial assistance through the issuance of long term Industrial Revenue Bonds.

Organization asset range: $100,000,000 And up

Range of investment/grant per borrower/grantee: $ to $800,000

Type of financing: ☐Grants; ☐Loans; ☐Loan with equity participations or convertibility; ☐Loan Guarantees; ☐Equity; ☐Leases; ☐Sale-leaseback; Other: 50%/40%/10% of private funding, DDC and equity

Security position: Seniority mandatory

Type of collateral: Equipment, Real Estate, Guarantees

Term of financing: Maximum: 15 to 20 **years; Minimum:** 5-7**years**

Industry preference (in order of priority, if any): Manufacturing & Processing, Wholesaling & Distribution, Tranзportation

Borrower characteristics desired-required:

Min. number of years in business: 3

Min. annual sales: $

Min. net worth: $

Min. annual cash flow:

Min. annual net income:

Other requirements: Must pass standard credit analysis based on amount of financing applied for.

Estimated $ available for investment annually: $100,000,000

Annual interest rate for 1985: Max.: 10.75%; **Min.:** 8.75%; **Ave.: %**

Special conditions, if any: Loans are closed under a temporary line or credit subject to interest adjustment at the time of issuance of long term industrial revenue bonds.

STATE OF: CONNECTICUT

NAME OF ORGANIZATION: CONNECTICUT DEVELOPMENT AUTHORITY

ADDRESS: 217 Washington Street, Hartford, Connecticut 06106

PHONE NO. (203) 522-3730

CONTACT OFFICER: Vincent T. Pellegrino; **TITLE:** Program Manager

DESCRIPTION OF PROGRAM: Industrial Mortgage Insurance to insure payment of first mortgages on Industrial Real Estate and Industrial Machinery

Organization asset range: $ to $

Range of investment/grant per borrower/grantee: $ to $

Type of financing:☐Grants; ☐Loans; ☐Loan with equity participations or convertibility; ☐Loan Guarantees; ☐Equity; ☐Leases; ☐Sale-leaseback; Other: Industrial Mortgage Insurance

Security position: Seniority mandatory

Type of collateral: Equipment, Real Estate, Guarantees

Term of financing: Maximum: for machinery & equipment 10 **years;** for Real Estate 25 **years**

Industry preference (in order of priority, if any): Manufacturing & Processing, Assembling, Servicing, Research, Offices, Warehousing & Distribution

Borrower characteristics desired-required:

Min. number of years in business:

Min. annual sales: $

Min. net worth: $

Min. annual cash flow:

Min. annual net income:

Other requirements:

Estimated $ available for investment annually: $

Annual interest rate for 1985: Max.: %; Min.: % Ave.: %

Special conditions, if any:

STATE OF: CONNECTICUT

NAME OF ORGANIZATION: CONNECTICUT DEVELOPMENT AUTHORITY

ADDRESS: 217 Washington, Street Hartford, Connecticut 06106

PHONE NO. (203) 522-3730

CONTACT OFFICER: Richard L. Higgins; **TITLE:** Exec. Director

DESCRIPTION OF PROGRAM: Industrial Revenue Bond Financing for Real Estate, Machinery and Equipment

Organization asset range: $ to $

Range of investment/grant per borrower/grantee: $ to $

Type of financing: ☐Grants; ■Loans; ☐Loan with equity participations or convertibility; ☐Loan Guarantees; ☐Equity; ☐Leases; ☐Sale-leaseback; Other:

Security position: Seniority mandatory

Type of collateral: Machinery and Equipment, Real Estate, Guarantees

Term of financing: Maximum: for M & E 10 **years** and for RE 25 **years**

Industry preference (in order of priority, if any): Manufacturing & Processing, Assembling, Servicing, Research, Offices, Warehousing & Distribution

Borrower characteristics desired-required:

Min. number of years in business:

Min. annual sales: $

Min. net worth: $

Min. annual cash flow:

Min. annual net income:

Other requirements:

Estimated $ available for investment annually: $

Annual interest rate for 1985: Max.: %;Min.: % Ave.: %

Special conditions, if any:

STATE OF: CONNECTICUT

NAME OF ORGANIZATION: DEPT. OF ECONOMIC DEVELOPMENT

ADDRESS: 217 Washington Street Hartford, Connecticut 06106

PHONE NO. (203) 522-3730

CONTACT OFFICER: Vincent T. Pellegrino; **TITLE:** Program Manager

DESCRIPTION OF PROGRAM: State Loans to Small Contractors, Small Home Heating Oil Dealers, and Manufacturing Companies

Organization asset range: $ to $

Range of investment/grant per borrower/grantee: $ to $

Type of financing: ☐Grants; ☐Loans; ☐Loan with equity participations or convertibility; ☐Loan Guarantees; ☐Equity; ☐Leases; ☐Sale-leasedback; Other:

Security position: Senior mandatory

Type of collateral: Current Assets, Equipment, Real Estate, Guarantees

Term of financing: Maximum: 5-7 **years; Minimum** 0-1 **years**

Industry preference (in order of priority, if any): Manufacturing & Processing, Small Contractors, Small Home Heating Oil Dealers

Borrower characteristics desired-required:

Min. number of years in business:

Min. annual sales: $

Min. net worth: $

Min. annual cash flow:

Min. annual net income:

Other requirements:

Estimated $ available for investment annually: $

Annual interest rate for 1985: Max.: ______% **Min.:** __________% **Ave.:**__________%

Special conditions, if any:

STATE OF: DELAWARE

NAME OF ORGANIZATION: DELAWARE ECONOMIC DEVELOPMENT AUTHORITY

ADDRESS: 99 Kings Highway, P.O. Box 1401 Dover Delaware 19903

PHONE NO. (302) 736-4271

CONTACT OFFICER: George E. Hale; **TITLE:** Assistant Director for Business Finance

DESCRIPTION OF PROGRAM: The Delaware Economic Development Authority provides state wide financial assistance to new or expanding business through the issuance of Industrial Revenue Bonds (IRB's). IRB's are purchased by investors at low interest rates since interest from the bonds is exempt from federal income taxes and state income taxes for Delware residents. The business person benefits by obtaining long-term financing at interest rates below the prime rate. IRB's can be especially cost-effective for projects involving over $200,000 in fixed assests.

Organization asset range: $1,000,000 **to $**10,000,000

Range of investment/grant per borrower/grantee: $50,000 **to $**10,000,000

Type of financing: □Grants; □Loans; □Loan with equity participations or convertibility; ■Loan Guarantees; □Equity; □Leases; □Sale-leaseback; Other:

Security position: Seniority mandatory

Type of collateral: Equipment, Real Estate, Guarantees

Term of financing: Maximum: 20 and up **years; Minimum** 5-7 **years**

Industry preference (in order of priority, if any): Agriculture-related, Finance & Insurance, Manufacturing & Processing, Research & Technology, Pharmaceutical

Borrower characteristics desired-required:

Min. number of years in business:

Min. annual sales: $

Min. net worth: $

Min. annual cash flow:

Min. annual net income:

Other requirements:

Estimated $ available for investment annually: $ 120,000,000

Annual interest rate for 1985: Max.: %; Min.: % Ave.: %

Special conditions, if any:

STATE OF: DELAWARE

NAME OF ORGANIZATION: DELAWARE DEVELOPMENT CORPORATION

ADDRESS: 99 Kings Highway, P.O. Box 1401, Dover Delaware 19903

PHONE NO. (302) 736-4408

CONTACT OFFICER: George E. Hale; **TITLE:** Assistant Director for Business Finance

DESCRIPTION OF PROGRAM: The State of Delaware, through the Delaware Development Corporation, became the second state to obtain certification under the U.S. Small Business Administration's Section 503 loan program. This program offers long-term fixed asset financing at fixed rates to the growing small firm.

Organization asset range: $150,000 **to $**1,000,000

Range of investment/grant per borrower/grantee: **$**200,000 **to $**1,500,000

Type of financing: □Grants; □Loans; □Loan with equity participations or convertibility; □Loan Guarantees; □Equity; □Leases; □Sale-leaseback; Other: 50%/40%/10% of private funding, DDC and equity

Security position: First to private lender, second to DDC

Type of collateral: Equipment, Real Estate, Guarantees

Term of financing: Maximum: 15 to 20 **years; Minimum** 10-15**years**

Industry preference (in order of priority, if any): Construction & Development, Manufacturing & Processing, Retailing, Wholesaling & Distribution

Borrower characteristics desired-required:

Min. number of years in business:

Min. annual sales: $

Min. net worth: $

Min. annual cash flow:

Min. annual net income:

Other requirements:

Estimated $ available for investment annually: Unlimited

Annual interest rate for 1985: Max.: %; Min.: % Ave.: %

Special conditions, if any:

STATE OF: DELAWARE

NAME OF ORGANIZATION: DELAWARE DEVELOPMENT OFFICE

ADDRESS: 99 Kings Highway, P.O. Box 1401, Dover Delaware 19903

PHONE NO. (302) 736-4271

CONTACT OFFICER: Bonny Anderson; **TITLE:** Assistant Director for Business Services

DESCRIPTION OF PROGRAM: Blue Collar Jobs Bill - provides significant tax credits and reductions for 10 years on industrial investment of $200,000 and creation of 5 full-time employees. Corporation income tax credits, gross receipts tax, and public utility tax reductions are included. Tax incentives also available for commercial and retail investment and hiring in targeted areas.

Organization asset range: $ to $

Range of investment/grant per borrower/grantee: $ to $

Type of financing: □Grants; □Loans; □Loan with equity participations or convertibility; □Loan Guarantees; □Equity; □Leases; □Sale-leaseback; Other:

Security position:

Type of collateral:

Term of financing: Maximum: years; Minimum years

Industry preference (in order of priority, if any): Agriculture-Related, Communications, Manufacturing & Processing, Medical & Other Health Services, Research & Technology, Retailing, Wholesaling & Distribution, Transportation

Borrower characteristics desired-required:

Min. number of years in business:

Min. annual sales: $

Min. net worth: $

Min. annual cash flow:

Min. annual net income:

Other requirements:

Estimated $ available for investment annually: $

Annual interest rate for 1985: Max.: %;Min.: % Ave.: %

Special conditions, if any:

STATE OF: DELAWARE

NAME OF ORGANIZATION: DELAWARE DEVELOPMENT OFFICE

ADDRESS: 99 Kings Highway, P.O. Box 1401, Dover Delaware 19903

PHONE NO. (302) 736-4271

CONTACT OFFICER: Dorthy Sbriglia; **TITLE:** Business Services Specialist

DESCRIPTION OF PROGRAM: Definition: A Foreign Trade Zone is an enclosed, secured area outside the general customs territory of the United States. While under federal supervision, foreign and domestic merchandise is allowed in and out of this location without being subject to an import tax. The Delaware Foreign Trade Zone will offer local firms many advantages shared by companies utilizing zones in other locations. The Delaware Foreign Trade Zone is unique because it will offer companies the choice of two locations. The FTZ site at the Port of Wilmington will provide the amenities of a deepwater port location, while the FTZ site located at the deepwater location is neither a necessity nor a desire. For further information, please contact: Dorthy Sbriglia

Organization asset range: $ to $

Range of investment/grant per borrower/grantee: $ to $

Type of financing: ☐Grants; ☐Loans; ☐Loan with equity participations or convertibility; ☐Loan Guarantees; ☐Equity; ☐Leases; ☐Sale-leaseback; Other:

Security position:

Type of collateral:

Term of financing: Maximum: years; Minimum years

Industry preference (in order of priority, if any):

Borrower characteristics desired-required:

Min. number of years in business:

Min. annual sales: $

Min. net worth: $

Min. annual cash flow:

Min. annual net income:

Other requirements:

Estimated $ available for investment annually: $

Annual interest rate for 1985: Max.: %;Min.: % Ave.:%

Special conditions, if any:

STATE OF: GEORGIA

NAME OF ORGANIZATION: BUSINESS DEVELOPMENT CORPORATION OF GEORGIA

ADDRESS: 558 South Omni International, Atlanta, GA 30303

PHONE NO. (404) 577-5715

CONTACT OFFICER: ; TITLE:

DESCRIPTION OF PROGRAM:

Organization asset range: $ to $

Range of investment/grant per borrower/grantee: $100,000 to $400,000

Type of financing: ☐Grants; ☐Loans; ☐Loan with equity participations or convertibility; ☐Loan Guarantees; ☐Equity; ☐Leases; ☐Sale-leaseback; Other:

Security position:

Type of collateral:

Term of financing: Maximum: 10-15 **years; Minimum years**

Industry preference (in order of priority, if any):

Borrower characteristics desired-required:

Min. number of years in business:

Min. annual sales: $

Min. net worth: $

Min. annual cash flow:

Min. annual net income:

Other requirements:

Estimated $ available for investment annually: $

Annual interest rate for 1985: Max.: %;Min.: % Ave.: %

Special conditions, if any: SBA and other government guaranteed loans can be for higher amounts.

STATE OF: HAWAII

NAME OF ORGANIZATION: DEPARTMENT OF BUDGET AND FINANCE

ADDRESS: P.O. Box 150, Honolulu, Hawaii 96810

PHONE NO. (808) 548-2325

CONTACT OFFICER: Jensen S. L. Hee; **TITLE:** Director of Finance

DESCRIPTION OF PROGRAM: Provide financial assistance to manufacturing, processing or industrial enterprises and utilities serving the general public through the issuance of industrial development bonds.

Organization asset range: $ to $

Range of investment/grant per borrower/grantee: $ to $

Type of financing: ☐Grants; ■Loans; ☐Loan with equity participations or convertibility; ☐Loan Guarantees; ☐Equity; ☐Leases; ☐Sale-leaseback; Other:

Security position: dependent on credit of applicant

Type of collateral: dependent on credit of applicant

Term of financing: Maximum: 20 and up **years; Minimum** 0-1 **years**

Industry preference (in order of priority, if any): Manufacturing & Processing, Natural Resources, Research & Technology, Diversified

Borrower characteristics desired-required:

Min. number of years in business:

Min. annual sales: $

Min. net worth: $

Min. annual cash flow:

Min. annual net income:

Other requirements: above charateristics examined on a case to case basis.

Estimated $ available for investment annually: prior legislative approval with maximum amount as determined by federal Internal Revenue Code.

Annual interest rate for 1985: Max.: %;Min.: % Ave.: %

Special conditions, if any:

STATE OF: ILLINOIS

NAME OF ORGANIZATION: ILLINOIS DEPARTMENT OF COMMERCE & COMMUNITY AFFAIRS

ADDRESS: 310 South Michigan, Chicago IL 60604

PHONE NO. (312) 793-2086

CONTACT OFFICER: Toni Vasquez; **TITLE:** Export Finance Specialist

DESCRIPTION OF PROGRAM: Illinois is participating in the Bank Credit Insurance Program available through the Exim Bank for exporters who grant short-term credit to foreign buyers. The insurance protects exporters who grant credit for up to 90 % to 100 % of commercial or political losses.

Organization asset range: $100,000,000 and up

Range of investment/grant per borrower/grantee:
$ to $

Type of financing: ☐Grants; ☐Loans; ☐Loan with equity participations or convertibility; ■Loan Guarantees; ☐Equity; ☐Leases; ☐Sale-leaseback; Other:

Security position: Seniority mandatory and Senior or subordinated

Type of collateral: Current Assets (Inventory, Accounts Receivable), Stocks & Bonds, Cash value of life insurance, Equipment, Real Estate, Guarantees

Term of financing: Maximum: 0-1 **years; Minimum** 0-1 **years**

Industry preference (in order of priority, if any): Agriculture-Related, Communications, Construction & Development, Manufacturing & Processing, Medical & Other Health Services, Natural Resources, Recreation & Amusements, Research & Technology, Retailing, Wholesaling & Distribution, Services, Transportation, Diversified: The Export Import Bank does not have a stated industry preference.

Borrower characteristics desired-required:

Min. number of years in business:

Min. annual sales: $

Min. net worth: $

Min. annual cash flow:

Min. annual net income:

Other requirements: No minimums other than enough experience to demonstrate an ability to perform. adequate capital, and ability to repay the debt

Estimated $ available for investment annually:
$

Annual interest rate for 1985: Max.: market %; Min.: %Ave.: %

Special conditions, if any: Interest rates are determined by the market and private commercial banks however eximbank will meet the terms of foreign competition

STATE OF: ILLINOIS

NAME OF ORGANIZATION: ILLINOIS DEPARTMENT OF COMMERCE & COMMUNITY AFFAIRS

ADDRESS: 310 South Michigan, Chicago IL 60604

PHONE NO. (312) 793-2086

CONTACT OFFICER: Toni Vasquez; **TITLE:** Export Finance Specialist

DESCRIPTION OF PROGRAM: Illinois is one of only four states where the Export Import (Exim) Bank Working Capital Guarantee Loan Program is available. Through this program, designated banks may guarantee up to $300,000 in working capital loans for export activity without prior Exim approval.

Organization asset range: $100,000,000 and up Exim Banks Assets

Range of investment/grant per borrower/grantee:
$ to $

Type of financing: ☐Grants; ☐Loans; ☐Loan with equity participations or convertibility; ☐Loan Guarantees; ☐Equity; ☐Leases; ☐Sale-leaseback; Other:

Security position:

Type of collateral:

Term of financing: Maximum: years; Minimum years

Industry preference (in order of priority, if any):

Borrower characteristics desired-required:

Min. number of years in business:

Min. annual sales: $

Min. net worth: $

Min. annual cash flow:

Min. annual net income:

Other requirements:

Estimated $ available for investment annually: $

Annual interest rate for 1985: Max.: %;Min.: % Ave.: %

Special conditions, if any:

STATE OF: ILLINOIS

NAME OF ORGANIZATION: ILLINOIS DEPARTMENT OF COMMERCE & COMMUNITY AFFAIRS

ADDRESS: 310 South Michigan, Chicago IL 60604

PHONE NO. (312) 793-6649

CONTACT OFFICER: Sharon Sharp; **TITLE:** Deputy Director, Marketing

DESCRIPTION OF PROGRAM: The Job Training Partnership Act (JTPA) Program is administered by DCCA through 26 local service delivery areas, which are responsible for training disadvantaged individuals for local jobs. Training is tailored to meet the business' needs, and assistance may include portions of the new employees' salaries as well as other costs of instruction.

Organization asset range: $ to $

Range of investment/grant per borrower/grantee: $ to $

Type of financing: ☐Grants; ☐Loans; ☐Loan with equity participations or convertibility; ☐Loan Guarantees; ☐Equity; ☐Leases; ☐Sale-leaseback; Other:

Security position:

Type of collateral:

Term of financing: Maximum: years; Minimum years

Industry preference (in order of priority, if any):

Borrower characteristics desired-required:

Min. number of years in business:

Min. annual sales: $

Min. net worth: $

Min. annual cash flow:

Min. annual net income:

Other requirements:

Estimated $ available for investment annually: $

Annual interest rate for 1985: Max.: %;Min.: % Ave.: %

Special conditions, if any:

STATE OF: ILLINOIS

NAME OF ORGANIZATION: ILLINOIS FARM DEVELOPMENT AUTHORITY

ADDRESS: Main Ag. Building - State Fairgrounds Springfield, IL 62706

PHONE NO. (217) 782-5792

CONTACT OFFICER: Ron Bailey; **TITLE:** Director

DESCRIPTION OF PROGRAM: The IFDA Agribusiness Development Bond Program provides a mechanism for private lenders to receive tax-exempt interest on loans made to small agribusinesses for purchase of depreciable property or improvements. Applicants may have no more than 100 employees, nor a gross income exceeding $2 million for the previous calendar year. The income ceiling may be waived for businessess locating in Illinois for the first time.

Organization asset range: $150,000 **to $**1,000,000

Range of investment/grant per borrower/grantee: **$ to $**1,000,000

Type of financing: ☐Grants; ☐Loans; ☐Loan with equity participations or convertibility; ☐Loan Guarantees; ☐Equity; ☐Leases; ☐Sale-leaseback; Other: Tax-exempt bond sales

Security position: Lending institution determines its own security and collateral

Type of collateral: Equipment, Real Estate

Term of financing: Maximum: 15-20 **years; Minimum** 5-7 **years**

Industry preference (in order of priority, if any): Agriculture-Related

Borrower characteristics desired-required:

Min. number of years in business: Starting to establised businesses

Min. annual sales: $

Min. net worth: $

Min. annual cash flow:

Min. annual net income:

Other requirements:

Estimated $ available for investment annually: Varies per business

Annual interest rate for 1985: Max.: 12%;**Min.:**8% **Ave.:**9.5%

Special conditions, if any:

STATE OF: ILLINOIS

NAME OF ORGANIZATION: ILLINOIS DEPARTMENT OF COMMERCE & COMMUNITY AFFAIRS

ADDRESS: 310 South Michigan, Chicago IL 60604

PHONE NO. (312) 793-6649

CONTACT OFFICER: Sharon Sharp; **TITLE:** Deputy Director, Marketing

DESCRIPTION OF PROGRAM: The Dislocated Workers Program provides funds, vocational assessment, counseling, job search and placement assistance by working with businesses and civic leaders to serve large concentrations of dislocated workers. This helps cover some of business' training and retraining costs. Service is brokered locally in 15 primary labor market areas within Illinois.

Organization asset range: $ to $

Range of investment/grant per borrower/grantee: **$ to $**

Type of financing: ☐Grants; ☐Loans; ☐Loan with equity participations or convertibility; ☐Loan Guarantees; ☐Equity; ☐Leases; ☐Sale-leaseback; Other:

Security position:

Type of collateral:

Term of financing: Maximum: years; Minimum years

Industry preference (in order of priority, if any):

Borrower characteristics desired-required:

Min. number of years in business:

Min. annual sales: $

Min. net worth: $

Min. annual cash flow:

Min. annual net income:

Other requirements:

Estimated $ available for investment annually: **$**

Annual interest rate for 1985: Max.: %;Min.: % Ave.: %

Special conditions, if any:

STATE OF: ILLINOIS

NAME OF ORGANIZATION: ILLINOIS HEALTH FACILITIES AUTHORITY

ADDRESS: 35 East Wacker Drive, Suite 2188 Chicago, IL 60601

PHONE NO. (312) 782-9447

CONTACT OFFICER: ; **TITLE:**

DESCRIPTION OF PROGRAM: IHFA helps provide high-quality medical care at low-cost by offering tax-exempt revenue bonds for capital financing to not-for-profit health care establishments. physicians' office buildings, and for-profit nursing homes. Financing may be provided through public issues, direct placements, or short-term revenue bonds/tax-exempt commercial paper. In fiscal year 1983, IHFA provided over $367 million in financing.

Organization asset range: $ **to $**

Range of investment/grant per borrower/grantee: $ **to $**

Type of financing: ☐Grants; ☐Loans; ☐Loan with equity participations or convertibility; ☐Loan Guarantees; ☐Equity; ☐Leases; ☐Sale-leaseback; Other:

Security position:

Type of collateral:

Term of financing: Maximum: **years; Minimum** **years**

Industry preference (in order of priority, if any):

Borrower characteristics desired-required:

Min. number of years in business:

Min. annual sales: $

Min. net worth: $

Min. annual cash flow:

Min. annual net income:

Other requirements:

Estimated $ available for investment annually: $

Annual interest rate for 1985: Max.: %;Min.: % Ave.: %

Special conditions, if any:

STATE OF: ILLINOIS

NAME OF ORGANIZATION: ILLINOIS DEPARTMENT OF COMMERCE & COMMUNITY AFFAIRS

ADDRESS: 620 East Adams Springfield, IL 62701

PHONE NO. (217) 785-6162

CONTACT OFFICER: Tom Ticknor; **TITLE:** Business Finance Program Development Manager

DESCRIPTION OF PROGRAM: Innovation Research Grants will be provided to underwrite research or consulting arrangements between Illinois academic institutions and small businesses developing new technology applications. Scheduled to be operational in the spring of 1985, the program will fund approximately $450,000 - $650,000 of such grants in its first year.

Organization asset range: $150,000 **to $**1,000,000

Range of investment/grant per borrower/grantee: $ **to $**100,000

Type of financing: ☐Grants; ☐Loans; ■Loan with equity participations or convertibility; ☐Loan Guarantees; ☐Equity; ☐Leases; ☐Sale-leaseback; Other: Loans with repayment based on new products sales

Security position: Senior or subordinated

Type of collateral: Any of above, depending on circumstances

Term of financing: Maximum: 7-10 **years; Minimum** 3-5 **years**

Industry preference (in order of priority, if any): Research & Technology, Diversified

Borrower characteristics desired-required:

Min. number of years in business: 3

Min. annual sales: $

Min. net worth: $

Min. annual cash flow:

Min. annual net income:

Other requirements:

Estimated $ available for investment annually: $500,000

Annual interest rate for 1985: Max.: %; Min.: %;Ave.: %

Special conditions, if any: Repayment will be based on product sales - term of loan (longer terms will require higher repayment amounts

STATE OF: ILLINOIS

NAME OF ORGANIZATION: ILLINOIS DEPARTMENT OF COMMERCE & COMMUNITY AFFAIRS

ADDRESS: 310 South Michigan, Chicago IL 60604

PHONE NO. (312) 793-6649

CONTACT OFFICER: Sharon Sharp; **TITLE:** Deputy Director, Marketing

DESCRIPTION OF PROGRAM: The Industrial Training Program (ITP) helps new and expanding Illinois industries develop a well-trained labor force by paying directly to the firm a pre-agreed portion of worker/trainee wages. Following a formal request to participate and DDCA approval, the firm chooses the trainees, the methods of training, and the location -on-site, classroom, or both.

Organization asset range: $ to $

Range of investment/grant per borrower/grantee: $ to $

Type of financing: ☐Grants; ☐Loans; ☐Loan with equity participations or convertibility; ☐Loan Guarantees; ☐Equity; ☐Leases; ☐Sale-leaseback; Other:

Security position:

Type of collateral:

Term of financing: Maximum: years; Minimum years

Industry preference (in order of priority, if any):

Borrower characteristics desired-required:

Min. number of years in business:

Min. annual sales: $

Min. net worth: $

Min. annual cash flow:

Min. annual net income:

Other requirements:

Estimated $ available for investment annually: $

Annual interest rate for 1985: Max.: %; Min.: %;Ave.: %

Special conditions, if any:

STATE OF: ILLINOIS

NAME OF ORGANIZATION: ILLINOIS DEPARTMENT OF COMMERCE & COMMUNITY AFFAIRS

ADDRESS: 310 South Michigan, Chicago IL 60604

PHONE NO. (312) 793-6649

CONTACT OFFICER: Sharon Sharp; **TITLE:** Deputy Director, Marketing

DESCRIPTION OF PROGRAM: The High Impact Training Service (HITS) program assists businesses and industries locating in Illinois or expanding in-state operations with short-term employee training needs. Funds are provided project-by-project to public schools for custom-developed training and related costs.

Organization asset range: $ to $

Range of investment/grant per borrower/grantee: $ to $

Type of financing: ☐Grants; ☐Loans; ☐Loan with equity participations or convertibility; ☐Loan Guarantees; ☐Equity; ☐Leases; ☐Sale-leaseback; Other:

Security position:

Type of collateral:

Term of financing: Maximum: years; Minimum years

Industry preference (in order of priority, if any):

Borrower characteristics desired-required:

Min. number of years in business:

Min. annual sales: $

Min. net worth: $

Min. annual cash flow:

Min. annual net income:

Other requirements:

Estimated $ available for investment annually: $

Annual interest rate for 1985: Max.: %;Min.: % Ave.: %

Special conditions, if any:

STATE OF: ILLINOIS

NAME OF ORGANIZATION: ILLINOIS DEVELOPMENT FINANCE AUTHORITY

ADDRESS: Two North LaSalle Street, Suite 780, Chicago, IL 60602

PHONE NO. (312) 793-5586

CONTACT OFFICER: Ron Bean; **TITLE:** Executive Director

DESCRIPTION OF PROGRAM: The IDFA Insured Industrial Revenue Bond Program authorizes IDFA to insure IRB issues for companies otherwise unable to secure financing. IDFA may insure up to 70% of a project, but may not insure more than $2.5 million on any single project. The participating lender must accept a 30% exposure.

Organization asset range: $ to $

Range of investment/grant per borrower/grantee: $ to $

Type of financing: ☐Grants; ☐Loans; ☐Loan with equity participations or convertibility; ☐Loan Guarantees; ☐Equity; ☐Leases; ☐Sale-leaseback; Other:

Security position:

Type of collateral:

Term of financing: Maximum: years; Minimum years

Industry preference (in order of priority, if any):

Borrower characteristics desired-required:

Min. number of years in business:

Min. annual sales: $

Min. net worth: $

Min. annual cash flow:

Min. annual net income:

Other requirements:

Estimated $ available for investment annually: $

Annual interest rate for 1985: Max.: %; Min.: % Ave.: %

Special conditions, if any:

STATE OF: ILLINOIS

NAME OF ORGANIZATION: ILLINOIS DEPARTMENT OF COMMERCE & COMMUNITY AFFAIRS

ADDRESS: 310 South Michigan, Chicago IL 60604

PHONE NO. (312) 793-6649

CONTACT OFFICER: Sharon Sharp; **TITLE:** Deputy Director, Marketing

DESCRIPTION OF PROGRAM: The Energy Conservation Business Loan Program provides 40% of financing small businesses making physical improvements leading up to energy conservation. The limit of State involvement is $6,000, and the remaining 60% of the project must be commercially financed.

Organization asset range: $150,000 **to $**1,000,000

Range of investment/grant per borrower/grantee: $ to $6,000

Type of financing: ☐Grants; ■Loans; ☐Loan with equity participations or convertibility; ☐Loan Guarantees; ☐Equity; ☐Leases; ☐Sale-leaseback; Other: Loans with 60% commercial participation

Security position: As required by bank

Type of collateral: As required by bank

Term of financing: Maximum: 3-5 **years; Minimum** 0-1 **years**

Industry preference (in order of priority, if any): Any small business other than farming operations, residential structure or home operated businesses

Borrower characteristics desired-required:

Min. number of years in business:

Min. annual sales: $

Min. net worth: $

Min. annual cash flow:

Min. annual net income:

Other requirements: As required by bank

Estimated $ available for investment annually: $500,000

Annual interest rate for 1985: Max.: %;Min.: % Ave.: %

Special conditions, if any: 0% interest on state loan; average interest on bank's portion has been 2 points over prime.

STATE OF: ILLINOIS

NAME OF ORGANIZATION: ILLINOIS SMALL BUSINESS GROWTH CORPORATION

ADDRESS: 620 East Adams Springfield, IL 62701

PHONE NO. (217) 782-1998

CONTACT OFFICER: Thomas A. Herring; **TITLE:** President

DESCRIPTION OF PROGRAM: The Small Business Growth Corporation is an SBA 503 Certified Development Company which provides long-term fixed-rate financing for small businesses. Proceeds may be used for fixed assets with at least 15 years of useful life. The loans are funded by debentures issued by the SBA for terms of 15, 20, or 25 years. In addition to the statewide Small Business Growth Corporation, Illinois has 21 local and regional Certified Development Companies.

Organization asset range: $ to $

Range of investment/grant per borrower/grantee: $50,000**to $**500,000

Type of financing: ☐Grants; ☐Loans; ☐Loan with equity participations or convertibility; ☐Loan Guarantees; ☐Equity; ☐Leases; ☐Sale-leaseback; Other:

Security position: Senior or subordinated

Type of collateral:

Term of financing: Maximum: years; Minimum years

Industry preference (in order of priority, if any):

Borrower characteristics desired-required:

Min. number of years in business: 3

Min. annual sales: $

Min. net worth: $

Min. annual cash flow:

Min. annual net income:

Other requirements: Standard SBA requirements

Estimated $ available for investment annually:
$

Annual interest rate for 1985: Max.: %; Min.: %
Ave.: %

Special conditions, if any:

STATE OF: ILLINOIS

NAME OF ORGANIZATION: ILLINOIS DEPARTMENT OF COMMERCE & COMMUNITY AFFAIRS

ADDRESS: 310 South Michigan, Chicago IL 60604

PHONE NO. (312) 793-6649

CONTACT OFFICER: Sharon Sharp; **TITLE:** Deputy Director, Marketing

DESCRIPTION OF PROGRAM: DCCA's Marketing staff will assist small firms to get in touch with the SBA's Small Business Investment Companies, which provide long-term loans, purchase debt securities purchase equity shares to help firms expand or modernize. Illinois currently has eleven SBIC's, and seven Minority Enterprise Small Business Investment Companies (MESBIC's) in the state's metropolitan areas.

Organization asset range: $ to $

Range of investment/grant per borrower/grantee:
$ to $

Type of financing: ☐Grants; ☐Loans; ☐Loan with equity participations or convertibility; ☐Loan Guarantees; ☐Equity; ☐Leases; ☐Sale-leaseback; Other:

Security position:

Type of collateral:

Term of financing: Maximum: years; Minimum years

Industry preference (in order of priority, if any):

Borrower characteristics desired-required:

Min. number of years in business:

Min. annual sales: $

Min. net worth: $

Min. annual cash flow:

Min. annual net income:

Other requirements:

Estimated $ available for investment annually:
$

Annual interest rate for 1985: Max.: %;Min.: %
Ave.: %

Special conditions, if any:

STATE OF: ILLINOIS

NAME OF ORGANIZATION: ILLINOIS DEPARTMENT OF COMMERCE & COMMUNITY AFFAIRS

ADDRESS: 310 South Michigan, Chicago IL 60604

PHONE NO. (312) 793-6649

CONTACT OFFICER: Sharon Sharp; **TITLE:** Deputy Director, Marketing

DESCRIPTION OF PROGRAM: Tax Increment Financing permits local governments to issue bonds to finance development of industrial and commerical projects. The anticipated increase in real estate tax revenue is used to pay off the bond. The advantage to business is that land acquistions and improvements are financed with tax-free borrowing, which reduces interest costs.

Organization asset range: $ to $

Range of investment/grant per borrower/grantee: $ to $

Type of financing: ☐Grants; ☐Loans; ☐Loan with equity participations or convertibility; ☐Loan Guarantees; ☐Equity; ☐Leases; ☐Sale-leaseback; Other:

Security position:

Type of collateral:

Term of financing: Maximum: years; Minimum years

Industry preference (in order of priority, if any):

Borrower characteristics desired-required:

Min. number of years in business:

Min. annual sales: $

Min. net worth: $

Min. annual cash flow:

Min. annual net income:

Other requirements:

Estimated $ available for investment annually: $

Annual interest rate for 1985: Max.: %;Min.: % Ave.: %

Special conditions, if any:

STATE OF: ILLINOIS

NAME OF ORGANIZATION: ILLINOIS DEPARTMENT OF COMMERCE & COMMUNITY AFFAIRS

ADDRESS: 310 South Michigan, Chicago IL 60604

PHONE NO. (312) 793-6649

CONTACT OFFICER: Sharon Sharp; **TITLE:** Deputy Director, Marketing

DESCRIPTION OF PROGRAM: CDAP (Community Development Assistance Program) funds help communities attract or expand local industry. Communities participate in a quarterly competive cycle, or obtain Department funds through a special economic development set-aside fund, and then make loans to local businesses at reduced interest rates. The loans are repaid to the community, and the funds remain in the area to spur local economic development.

Organization asset range: $10,000,000 **to** $100,000,000

Range of investment/grant per borrower/grantee: $10,000**to** $500,000

Type of financing: ☐Grants; ■Loans; ■Loan with equity participations or convertibility; ☐Loan Guarantees; ☐Equity; ☐Leases; ☐Sale-leaseback; Other:

Security position: Senior or subordinated

Type of collateral: Current Assets (Inventory, Accounts Receivable), Stocks and Bonds, Cash value of life insurance, Equipment, Real Estate, Guarantees

Term of financing: Maximum: 20 and up **years; Minimum** 3-5 **years**

Industry preference (in order of priority, if any): Diversifed, High job creation projects

Borrower characteristics desired-required:

Min. number of years in business:

Min. annual sales: $

Min. net worth: $

Min. annual cash flow:

Min. annual net income:

Other requirements: Cash flow equal to or greater than Debt Services

Estimated $ available for investment annually: $18,000,000

Annual interest rate for 1985: Max.: market %; **Min.:** 5%; **Ave.:** bond rate

Special conditions, if any:

STATE OF: ILLINOIS

NAME OF ORGANIZATION: ILLINOIS DEPARTMENT OF COMMERCE & COMMUNITY AFFAIRS

ADDRESS: 310 South Michigan, Chicago IL 60604

PHONE NO. (312) 793-6649

CONTACT OFFICER: Sharon Sharp; **TITLE:** Deputy Director, Marketing

DESCRIPTION OF PROGRAM: UDAG (Urban Development Action Grant) Packaging Assistance is available through DCCA. The UDAG program provides low-interest second-mortgage financing for commercial and industrial projects, including very large projects, when available private financing is insufficient or to make project costs in eligible Illinois cities competitive with those in lower-cost locations.

Organization asset range: $100,000,000 and up

Range of investment/grant per borrower/grantee: $ to $

Type of financing: ☐Grants; ☐Loans; ☐Loan with equity participations or convertibility; ☐Loan Guarantees; ☐Equity; ☐Leases; ☐Sale-leaseback; Other:

Security position:

Type of collateral:

Term of financing: Maximum: years; Minimum years

Industry preference (in order of priority, if any):

Borrower characteristics desired-required:

Min. number of years in business:

Min. annual sales: $

Min. net worth: $

Min. annual cash flow:

Min. annual net income:

Other requirements:

Estimated $ available for investment annually: $

Annual interest rate for 1985: Max.: %; Min.: % Ave.: %

Special conditions, if any:

STATE OF: ILLINOIS

NAME OF ORGANIZATION: ILLINOIS DEPARTMENT OF COMMERCE & COMMUNITY AFFAIRS

ADDRESS: 310 South Michigan, Chicago IL 60604

PHONE NO. (312) 793-6649

CONTACT OFFICER: Sharon Sharp; **TITLE:** Deputy Director, Marketing

DESCRIPTION OF PROGRAM: Local Industrial Revenue Bond Issues have been available in Illinois since 1972. Tax-exempt municipal obligations are issued on behalf of a private business to finance acquistion, construction, expansion or rehabilitation of property for commercial or industrial projects. The company's credit, and in some cases, a mortgage, secure the bonds. Because muni bond interest is not federally taxable, interest rates may be reduced by as much as 25%.

Organization asset range: $ to $

Range of investment/grant per borrower/grantee: $ to $

Type of financing: ☐Grants; ☐Loans; ☐Loan with equity participations or convertibility; ☐Loan Guarantees; ☐Equity; ☐Leases; ☐Sale-leaseback; Other:

Security position:

Type of collateral:

Term of financing: Maximum: years; Minimum years

Industry preference (in order of priority, if any):

Borrower characteristics desired-required:

Min. number of years in business:

Min. annual sales: $

Min. net worth: $

Min. annual cash flow:

Min. annual net income:

Other requirements:

Estimated $ available for investment annually: $

Annual interest rate for 1985: Max.: %; Min.: % Ave.: %

Special conditions, if any:

STATE OF: ILLINOIS

NAME OF ORGANIZATION: ILLINOIS DEPARTMENT OF COMMERCE & COMMUNITY AFFAIRS

ADDRESS: 310 South Michigan, Chicago IL 60604

PHONE NO. (312) 793-6649

CONTACT OFFICER: Sharon Sharp; **TITLE:** Deputy Director, Marketing

DESCRIPTION OF PROGRAM: The Fixed-Rate Financing Fund is a program unique to Illinois which combines the SBA's 7 (a) loans with low-interest state funds to create long-term, fixed-rate financing to Illinois firms providing employment opportunities to low- and moderate-income workers. The program is operated by the Illinois Small Business Growth Corporation, an SBA 503 Certified Development Company.

Organization asset range: $1,000,000 **to $**10,000,000

Range of investment/grant per borrower/grantee: $**75,000 to **$650,000

Type of financing: ☐Grants; ■Loans; ☐Loan with equity participations or convertibility; ☐Loan Guarantees; ☐Equity; ☐Leases; ☐Sale-leaseback; Other:

Security position: Senior or subordinated

Type of collateral:

Term of financing: Maximum: 10-15 **years; Minimum** 3-5 **years**

Industry preference (in order of priority, if any):

Borrower characteristics desired-required:

Min. number of years in business:

Min. annual sales: $

Min. net worth: $

Min. annual cash flow:

Min. annual net income:

Other requirements: SBA lending standards

Estimated $ available for investment annually: $

Annual interest rate for 1985: Max.: Prime; **Min.: % Ave.: %**

Special conditions, if any:

STATE OF: ILLINOIS

NAME OF ORGANIZATION: ILLINOIS DEPARTMENT OF COMMERCE & COMMUNITY AFFAIRS

ADDRESS: 310 South Michigan, Chicago IL 60604

PHONE NO. (312) 793-6649

CONTACT OFFICER: Sharon Sharp; **TITLE:** Deputy Director, Marketing

DESCRIPTION OF PROGRAM: Local Revolving Loan Funds are available throughout the state, providing low-interest direct loans and loan guarantees in conjunction with local financial institutions. Generally, only new industries attracted to a locale and existing industries undertaking expansion are permitted to utilize local RLF funds.

Organization asset range: $1,000,000 **to $**10,000,000

Range of investment/grant per borrower/grantee: $ to $

Type of financing: ☐Grants; ■Loans; ☐Loan with equity participations or convertibility; ☐Loan Guarantees; ☐Equity; ☐Leases; ☐Sale-leaseback; Other:

Security position: Senior or subordinated

Type of collateral: Current Assets (Inventory, Accounts Receivable), Stocks & Bonds, Cash value of life insurance, Equipment, Real Estate, Guarantees

Term of financing: Maximum: 10-15 **years; Minimum** 3-5 **years**

Industry preference (in order of priority, if any): High job creation

Borrower characteristics desired-required:

Min. number of years in business:

Min. annual sales: $

Min. net worth: $

Min. annual cash flow:

Min. annual net income:

Other requirements: Cash flow equal to or greater than debt service

Estimated $ available for investment annually: $

Annual interest rate for 1985: Max.:7%; **Min.:**3% **Ave.:**5%

Special conditions, if any:

STATE OF: ILLINOIS

NAME OF ORGANIZATION: ILLINOIS DEVELOPMENT FINANCE AUTHORITY

ADDRESS: Two North LaSalle Street, Suite 780, Chicago, IL 60602

PHONE NO. (312) 793-5586

CONTACT OFFICER: Ron Bean; **TITLE:** Executive Director

DESCRIPTION OF PROGRAM: The IDFA Direct Loan Program provides fixed-interest loans for 20% to 30% of the cost of fixed-asset projects for small- or medium-sized industrial firms, and is intended to create jobs in areas of high unemployment. The maximum amount of an IDFA Direct Loan is $150,000; maturity ranges from seven to 25 years, matching life of assets.

Organization asset range: $ to $

Range of investment/grant per borrower/grantee: $ to $

Type of financing: ☐Grants; ☐Loans; ☐Loan with equity participations or convertibility; ☐Loan Guarantees; ☐Equity; ☐Leases; ☐Sale-leaseback; Other:

Security position:

Type of collateral:

Term of financing: Maximum: years; Minimum years

Industry preference (in order of priority, if any):

Borrower characteristics desired-required:

Min. number of years in business:

Min. annual sales: $

Min. net worth: $

Min. annual cash flow:

Min. annual net income:

Other requirements:

Estimated $ available for investment annually:
$

Annual interest rate for 1985: Max.: %; Min.: % Ave.: %

Special conditions, if any:

STATE OF: ILLINOIS

NAME OF ORGANIZATION: ILLINOIS DEVELOPMENT FINANCE AUTHORITY

ADDRESS: Two North LaSalle Street, Suite 780, Chicago, IL 60602

PHONE NO. (312) 793-5586

CONTACT OFFICER: Ron Bean; **TITLE:** Executive Director

DESCRIPTION OF PROGRAM: The IDFA Venture Investment Fund is a $10 million pool of venture capital for enterprises developing new technologies, products, processes, or inventions in Illinois. The pool is managed by a private venture capital corporation on behalf of the state.

Organization asset range: $1,000,000 **to $**10,000,000

Range of investment/grant per borrower/grantee:
$ to $

Type of financing: ☐Grants; ☐Loans; ☐Loan with equity participations or convertibility; ☐Loan Guarantees; ☐Equity; ☐Leases; ☐Sale-leaseback; Other:

Security position:

Type of collateral:

Term of financing: Maximum: years; Minimum years

Industry preference (in order of priority, if any):

Borrower characteristics desired-required:

Min. number of years in business:

Min. annual sales: $

Min. net worth: $

Min. annual cash flow:

Min. annual net income:

Other requirements:

Estimated $ available for investment annually:
$

Annual interest rate for 1985: Max.: %;Min.: % Ave.: %

Special conditions, if any:

STATE OF: ILLINOIS

NAME OF ORGANIZATION: ILLINOIS DEVELOPMENT FINANCE AUTHORITY

ADDRESS: Two North LaSalle Street, Suite 780, Chicago, IL 60602

PHONE NO. (312) 793-5586

CONTACT OFFICER: Ron Bean; **TITLE:** Executive Director

DESCRIPTION OF PROGRAM: The IDFA Industrial Revenue Bond Program permits IDFA to issue tax-exempt pollution control equipment bonds and tax-exempt IRB's for small- and medium-sized industrial firms in areas of high unemployment. IDFA has targeted $100 million of its bonding authority for projects in state enterprise zones.

Organization asset range: $ to $

Range of investment/grant per borrower/grantee:
$ to $

Type of financing: ☐Grants; ☐Loans; ☐Loan with equity participations or convertibility; ☐Loan Guarantees; ☐Equity; ☐Leases; ☐Sale-leaseback; Other:

Security position:

Type of collateral:

Term of financing: Maximum: years; Minimum years

Industry preference (in order of priority, if any):

Borrower characteristics desired-required:

Min. number of years in business:

Min. annual sales: $

Min. net worth: $

Min. annual cash flow:

Min. annual net income:

Other requirements:

Estimated $ available for investment annually: $

Annual interest rate for 1985: Max.: %; Min.: % Ave.: %

Special conditions, if any:

STATE OF: IOWA

NAME OF ORGANIZATION: IOWA PRODUCT DEVELOPMENT CORPORATION

ADDRESS: 600 E. Court Ave. Suite C, Des Moines, IA 50309

PHONE NO. (515) 281-3925

CONTACT OFFICER: ; TITLE:

DESCRIPTION OF PROGRAM: The IPDC provides risk capital to companies with an Iowa presence to stimulate and encourage the development of new products within Iowa for invention and innovation in situations in which financial aid would not otherwise be reasonably available from commercial sources.

Organization asset range: $150,000 **to $**1,000,000

Range of investment/grant per borrower/grantee: $ to $

Type of financing: ☐Grants; ☐Loans; ☐Loan with equity participations or convertibility; ☐Loan Guarantees; ☐Equity; ☐Leases; ☐Sale-leaseback; Other:

Security position:

Type of collateral:

Term of financing: Maximum: years; Minimum years

Industry preference (in order of priority, if any):

Borrower characteristics desired-required:

Min. number of years in business:

Min. annual sales: $

Min. net worth: $

Min. annual cash flow:

Min. annual net income:

Other requirements:

Estimated $ available for investment annually: $

Annual interest rate for 1985: Max.: %; Min.: % Ave.: %

Special conditions, if any:

STATE OF: IOWA

NAME OF ORGANIZATION: IOWA BUSINESS DEVELOPMENT CREDIT CORPORATION (IBDCC)

ADDRESS: 901 Insurance Exchange Building, Des, Moines, IA 50309

PHONE NO. ( ) -

CONTACT OFFICER: ; TITLE:

DESCRIPTION OF PROGRAM: IBDCC is a joint effort of banks, insurance companies, savings and loans and other financial institutions to provide a place where firms can borrow at satisfactory rates although collateral and financial backing is less than that accepted by conventional lenders. Loan proceeds may be used to purchase land, purchase or construct buildings, machinery and equipment, inventory or for working capital. A portion may be used to retire debt.

Organization asset range: $ to $

Range of investment/grant per borrower/grantee: $300,000 not including bank participation

Type of financing: ☐Grants; ☐Loans; ☐Loan with equity participations or convertibility; ☐Loan Guarantees; ☐Equity; ☐Leases; ☐Sale-leaseback; Other:

Security position:

Type of collateral:

Term of financing: Maximum: years; Minimum years

Industry preference (in order of priority, if any):

Borrower characteristics desired-required:

Min. number of years in business:

Min. annual sales: $

Min. net worth: $

Min. annual cash flow:

Min. annual net income:

Other requirements:

Estimated $ available for investment annually: $

Annual interest rate for 1985: Max.: %; Min.: % Ave.: %

Special conditions, if any:

STATE OF: KANSAS

NAME OF ORGANIZATION: KANSAS ADVANCED TECHNOLOGY COMMISSION

ADDRESS: 503 Kansas Ave., 6th Floor, Topeka, KS 66603

PHONE NO. (913) 296-5272

CONTACT OFFICER: Phillips Bradford; **TITLE:** Director, Ks. Advanced Tech. Commission

DESCRIPTION OF PROGRAM: Research Matching Grant Program involving cooperative research projects between Kansas institutions of higher education and industry. The intent of the program is to stimulate research and technological innovation in order to create jobs, induce investment, and improve production efficiency of Kansas firms. Each expenditure of state funds under the program must be matched at least 150% by nonstate sources.

Organization asset range: $150,000 **to $**1,000,000

Range of investment/grant per borrower/grantee: $ to $

Type of financing: ☐Grants; ☐Loans; ☐Loan with equity participations or convertibility; ☐Loan Guarantees; ☐Equity; ☐Leases; ☐Sale-leaseback; Other:Grant directly to university to match nonstate resources provided by a firm for specific research.

Security position:

Type of collateral: Guarantee by firm to provide 150% matching funds to university for specific research.

Term of financing: Maximum: 1-3 **years; Minimum** 0-1 **years**

Industry preference (in order of priority, if any): Manufacturing & Processing, Natural Resources

Borrower characteristics desired-required:

Min. number of years in business:

Min. annual sales: $

Min. net worth: $

Min. annual cash flow:

Min. annual net income:

Other requirements:

Estimated $ available for investment annually: $600,000

Annual interest rate for 1985: Max.: %; Min.: % Ave.: %

Special conditions, if any:

STATE OF: KANSAS

NAME OF ORGANIZATION: KANSAS DEPARTMENT OF ECONOMIC DEVELOPMENT

ADDRESS: 503 Kansas Ave., 6th Floor, Topeka, KS 66603

PHONE NO. (913) 296-3004

CONTACT OFFICER: Mary Bogart; **TITLE:** Director of CDBG Program

DESCRIPTION OF PROGRAM: Eligible applicants may use Community Development Block Grant Program funds to provide water, sewer or other infrastructure to aid in locating new firms. Also, direct financial assistance can be provided to include acquisition of land, construction of buildings, purchase of machinery and equipment, and provision of working capital.

Organization asset range: $ to $

Range of investment/grant per borrower/grantee: $ to $

Type of financing: ☐Grants; ☐Loans; ☐Loan with equity participations or convertibility; ☐Loan Guarantees; ☐Equity; ☐Leases; ☐Sale-leaseback; Other:

Security position:

Type of collateral:

Term of financing: Maximum: years; Minimum years

Industry preference (in order of priority, if any):

Borrower characteristics desired-required:

Min. number of years in business:

Min. annual sales: $

Min. net worth: $

Min. annual cash flow:

Min. annual net income:

Other requirements:

Estimated $ available for investment annually: $

Annual interest rate for 1985: Max.: %; Min.: % Ave.: %

Special conditions, if any:

STATE OF: KANSAS

NAME OF ORGANIZATION: "503" CERTIFIED DEVELOPMENT COMPANIES

ADDRESS:

PHONE NO. ( ) -

CONTACT OFFICER: ; TITLE:

DESCRIPTION OF PROGRAM: CDC program offers subordinated mortgage financing to healthy and expanding eligible small commercial and industrial business concerns. The CDCs use SBA "503" loans which are available for fixed asset purchases, such as land, buildings and equipment.

Organization asset range: $ to $

Range of investment/grant per borrower/grantee: $ to $

Type of financing: ☐Grants; ☐Loans; ☐Loan with equity participations or convertibility; ☐Loan Guarantees; ☐Equity; ☐Leases; ☐Sale-leaseback; Other:

Security position:

Type of collateral:

Term of financing: Maximum: years; Minimum years

Industry preference (in order of priority, if any): Manufacturing & Processing, Retailing, Wholesaling & Distribution, Services, Diversified

Borrower characteristics desired-required:

Min. number of years in business:

Min. annual sales: $

Min. net worth: $

Min. annual cash flow:

Min. annual net income:

Other requirements:

Estimated $ available for investment annually: $

Annual interest rate for 1985: Max.: %; Min.: % Ave.: %

Special conditions, if any:

STATE OF: KANSAS

NAME OF ORGANIZATION: LOCAL DEVELOPMENT CORPORATIONS (LDC)

ADDRESS:

PHONE NO. ( )

CONTACT OFFICER: ; TITLE:

DESCRIPTION OF PROGRAM: LDC's are formed at the local level by concerned citizens to provide a vehicle for economic development projects. Projects might include purchase of an industrial site, construction of a "spec" building, or providing start up capital for a new business venture.

Organization asset range: Varies by LDC

Range of investment/grant per borrower/grantee: Variable

Type of financing: ■Grants; ■Loans; ■Loan with equity participations or convertibility; ■Loan Guarantees; ■Equity; ■Leases; ■Sale-leaseback; Other:

Security position:

Type of collateral:

Term of financing: Maximum: years; Minimum years

Industry preference (in order of priority, if any): Manufacturing & Processing, Retailing, Wholesaling & Distribution, Real Estate, Medical & Other Health Services, Agriculture-Related, Transportation, Recreation & Amusements, Hotels, Motels & Restaurants

Borrower characteristics desired-required:

Min. number of years in business:

Min. annual sales: $

Min. net worth: $

Min. annual cash flow:

Min. annual net income:

Other requirements:

Estimated $ available for investment annually: $

Annual interest rate for 1985: Max.: %; Min.: % Ave.: %

Special conditions, if any:

STATE OF: KANSAS

NAME OF ORGANIZATION: KANSAS DEVELOPMENT CREDIT CORPORATION

ADDRESS: First National Bank Towers, Suite 1030, Topeka, KS 66603

PHONE NO. (913) 235-3437

CONTACT OFFICER: George Doak; **TITLE:** President

DESCRIPTION OF PROGRAM: KDCC supplements exsiting sources of credit to foster new or expanding business and industry. Primary orientation is the purchase of SBA guaranteed portion of loans held by Kansas banks so as to release those bank funds for further investment opportunities.

Organization asset range: Varies By LDC

Range of investment/grant per borrower/grantee:
$ to $250,000

Type of financing: ☐Grants; ☐Loans; ☐Loan with equity participations or convertibility; ■Loan Guarantees; ☐Equity; ☐Leases; ☐Sale-leaseback; Other:

Security position:

Type of collateral:

Term of financing: Maximum: years; Minimum years

Industry preference (in order of priority, if any): Manufacturing & Processing, Retailing, Wholesaling & Distribution, Services

Borrower characteristics desired-required:

Min. number of years in business:

Min. annual sales: $

Min. net worth: $

Min. annual cash flow:

Min. annual net income:

Other requirements:

Estimated $ available for investment annually:
$

Annual interest rate for 1985: Max.: %; Min.: % Ave.: %

Special conditions, if any:

STATE OF: KANSAS

NAME OF ORGANIZATION: KANSAS VENTURE CAPITAL, INC.

ADDRESS: First National Bank Towers, Suite 1030, Topeka, KS 66603

PHONE NO. (913) 235-3437

CONTACT OFFICER: George Doak; **TITLE:** President

DESCRIPTION OF PROGRAM: Kansas Venture Capital, Inc. is a SBIC which is a privately owned, for-profit financing device for providing debt-equity capital to small businesses. Funds can be used for working capital, purchase of equipment, debt restructuring, business expansion, and acquisition of shareholder or partner interest.

Organization asset range: Varies by LDC

Range of investment/grant per borrower/grantee:
$ to $200,000

Type of financing: ☐Grants; ☐Loans; ☐Loan with equity participations or convertibility; ☐Loan Guarantees; ☐Equity; ☐Leases; ☐Sale-leaseback; Other:

Security position:

Type of collateral:

Term of financing: Maximum: years; Minimum years

Industry preference (in order of priority, if any): Manufacturing & Processing, Diversified

Borrower characteristics desired-required:

Min. number of years in business:

Min. annual sales: $

Min. net worth: $

Min. annual cash flow:

Min. annual net income:

Other requirements:

Estimated $ available for investment annually: **$**

Annual interest rate for 1985: Max.: %; Min.: % Ave.: %

Special conditions, if any:

STATE OF: KANSAS

NAME OF ORGANIZATION: CITY OR COUNTY GOVERNMENT

ADDRESS:

PHONE NO. ( ) -

CONTACT OFFICER: ; **TITLE:**

DESCRIPTION OF PROGRAM: Industrial Revenue Bonds: Both city and county governments in Kansas can issue industrial revenue bonds for economic development projects.

Organization asset range: $ to $

Range of investment/grant per borrower/grantee: **$**Variable **to $**Variable

Type of financing: ☐Grants; ☐Loans; ☐Loan with equity participations or convertibility; ☐Loan Guarantees; ☐Equity; ■Leases; ☐Sale-leaseback; Other:

Security position:

Type of collateral:

Term of financing: Maximum: 15-20 **years; Minimum** 3-5 **years**

Industry preference (in order of priority, if any): Manufacturing & Processing, Retailing, Wholesaling & Distribution, Medical & Other Health Services, Hotels, Motels & Restaurants, Agriculture-Related, Utilities

Borrower characteristics desired-required:

Min. number of years in business:

Min. annual sales: $

Min. net worth: $

Min. annual cash flow:

Min. annual net income:

Other requirements:

Estimated $ available for investment annually: **$**

Annual interest rate for 1985: Max.: %; Min.: % Ave.: %

Special conditions, if any:

STATE OF: KENTUCKY

NAME OF ORGANIZATION: REVENUE BONDS (STATE SPONSORED)

ADDRESS: Kentucky Development Finance Authority 24th Floor, Capital Plaza Tower, Frankfort, KY 40601

PHONE NO. (502) 564-4554

CONTACT OFFICER: Theresa Middleton; **TITLE:** Loan Officer

DESCRIPTION OF PROGRAM: BOND ISSUES—For companies with sufficient financial strength to obtain conventional financing, KDFA will issue IRB's to allow the company to take advantage of tax-exempt rates of interest.

Organization asset range: $10,000,000 **to $**100,000,000

Range of investment/grant per borrower/grantee: IRS Limit; $10,000,000

Type of financing: □Grants; □Loans; □Loan with equity participations or convertibility; □Loan Guarantees; □Equity; □Leases; □Sale-leaseback; Other:IRB Issues

Security position:

Type of collateral:

Term of financing: Maximum: years; Minimum years

Industry preference (in order of priority, if any):

Borrower characteristics desired-required:

Min. number of years in business:

Min. annual sales: $

Min. net worth: $

Min. annual cash flow:

Min. annual net income:

Other requirements:

Estimated $ available for investment annually: $

Annual interest rate for 1985: varies

Special conditions, if any:

STATE OF: KENTUCKY

NAME OF ORGANIZATION: COMMONWEALTH SMALL BUSINESS DEVELOPMENT CORPORATION

ADDRESS: 24th Floor, Capital Plaza Tower, Frankfort, KY 40601

PHONE NO. (502) 564-2064

CONTACT OFFICER: Theresa Middleton; **TITLE:** Loan Officer

DESCRIPTION OF PROGRAM: Purpose is to stimulate economic growth and small business expansion by providing long term fixed asset financing for periods up to 25 years for the acquisition of land, buildings and heavy machinery, construction, renovation and restoration.

Organization asset range: $ to $

Range of investment/grant per borrower/grantee: $0 to $500,000

Type of financing: □Grants; ■Loans; □Loan with equity participations or convertibility; □Loan Guarantees; □Equity; □Leases; □Sale-leaseback; Other:

Security position: Subordinated. Lien on assets purchased with proceeds of the loan

Type of collateral: Equipment, Real Estate

Term of financing: Maximum: 25 **years; Minimum** 15 **years**

Industry preference (in order of priority, if any): Agriculture-Related, Manufacturing & Processing

Borrower characteristics desired-required:

Min. number of years in business:

Min. annual sales: $

Min. net worth: $

Min. annual cash flow:

Min. annual net income:

Other requirements:

Estimated $ available for investment annually: $

Annual interest rate for 1985: Max.: %; Min.: % Ave.: %

Special conditions, if any: Annual interest rate for 1985: Fixed at long term treasury bond rates, plus fees.

STATE OF: KENTUCKY

NAME OF ORGANIZATION: KDFA

ADDRESS: 24th Floor, Capital Plaza Tower, Frankfort, KY 40601

PHONE NO. (502) 564-4554

CONTACT OFFICER: Theresa Middleton; **TITLE:** Loan Officer

DESCRIPTION OF PROGRAM: Hospital Equipment Lease Program (HELP) Assists hospitals in obtaining equipment at reduced interest rates through tax-exempt financing.

Organization asset range: $10,000,000 **to $**100,000,000

Range of investment/grant per borrower/grantee: $ to $

Type of financing: ☐Grants; ☐Loans; ☐Loan with equity participations or convertibility; ☐Loan Guarantees; ☐Equity; ■Leases; ☐Sale-leaseback;

Security position:

Type of collateral:

Term of financing: Maximum: years; Minimum years

Industry preference (in order of priority, if any):

Borrower characteristics desired-required:

Min. number of years in business:

Min. annual sales: $

Min. net worth: $

Min. annual cash flow:

Min. annual net income:

Other requirements:

Estimated $ available for investment annually: $

Annual interest rate for 1985: Max.: %; Min.: % Ave.: %

Special conditions, if any:

STATE OF: KENTUCKY

NAME OF ORGANIZATION: STATE LOANS TO BUSINESSES

ADDRESS: Kentucky Development Finance Authority 24th Floor, Capital Plaza Tower, Frankfort, KY 40601

PHONE NO. (502) 564-4554

CONTACT OFFICER: James H. Jones; **TITLE:** Executive Director

DESCRIPTION OF PROGRAM: Direct Loans to Businesses - Take approximately 20% of financial package. Must be tourism, agricultural or manufacturing related business. Works side by side with private mortgage financing. Allows small, growth-oriented businesses to obtain long term financing needed to encourage growth.

Organization asset range: $10,000,000 **to $**100,000,000

Range of investment/grant per borrower/grantee: $25,000 **to $**250,000

Type of financing: ☐Grants; ■Loans; ☐Loan with equity participations or convertibility; ☐Loan Guarantees; ☐Equity; ☐Leases; ☐Sale-leaseback; Other:

Security position: Senior or subordinated

Type of collateral: Equipment, Real Estate (Fixed assets), Guarantees (Personal and Corporate)

Term of financing: Maximum: 20 **years; Minimum** 10 **years**

Industry preference (in order of priority, if any): Manufacturing & Processing, Agriculture-Related, Tourism

Borrower characteristics desired-required:

Min. number of years in business:

Min. annual sales: $

Min. net worth: 10% of project

Min. annual cash flow:

Min. annual net income:

Other requirements:

Estimated $ available for investment annually: $

Annual interest rate for 1985: Max.: 7.066%; **Min.:** 5.067%; **Ave.: %**
tied to term

Special conditions, if any:

STATE OF: MARYLAND

NAME OF ORGANIZATION: DEPARTMENT OF ECONOMIC AND COMMUNITY DEVELOPMENT/ MARYLAND INDUSTRIAL AND COMMERCIAL REDEVELOPMENT FUND

ADDRESS: 45 Calvert Street, Annapolis, Maryland 21401

PHONE NO. (301) 269-2064

CONTACT OFFICER: Marion J. McCoy; **TITLE:** Director

DESCRIPTION OF PROGRAM: Provision of loans and grants to Maryland political subdivisions for the undertaking of industrial and commercial redevelopment projects. Loans may be reloaned by the political subdivision to a recipient/developer who commits to undertake the project.

Organization asset range: $10,000,000 **to $**100,000,000

Range of investment/grant per borrower/grantee: $ to $3,000,000

Type of financing: ☐Grants; ■Loans; ☐Loan with equity participations or convertibility; ☐Loan Guarantees; ☐Equity; ☐Leases; ☐Sale-leaseback; Other: Grants for public improvements to local jurisdictions only.

Security position: Pledge of revenues and assets of applying jurisdiction.

Type of collateral: None to MICRF - only to local jurisdiction

Term of financing: Maximum: 10-15 **years; Minimum** none **years**

Industry preference (in order of priority, if any): Any industrial or commercial activity is eligible for consideration.

Borrower characteristics desired-required:

Min. number of years in business:

Min. annual sales: $

Min. net worth: $

Min. annual cash flow:

Min. annual net income:

Other requirements:

Estimated $ available for investment annually: $

Annual interest rate for 1985: Max.: 11.3115%; **Min.: %; Ave.: %**

Special conditions, if any: Projects must leverage private investment, create or retain jobs and have a positive impact on tax revenues received by the applying jurisdiction and the state.

STATE OF: MARYLAND

NAME OF ORGANIZATION: MARYLAND INDUSTRIAL DEVELOPMENT FINANCING AUTHORITY

ADDRESS: Suite 2244 World Trade Center, 401 E. Pratt Street, Baltimore, Maryland 21202

PHONE NO. (301) 659-4262

CONTACT OFFICER: Benjamin L. Hackerman; **TITLE:** Executive Director

DESCRIPTION OF PROGRAM: Provides assistance to businesses moving into the state or existing Maryland firms through the insurance of Industrial Revenue Bonds or conventional, taxable rate financings of all types. The Authority looks closely at the economic impact to be generated through this financial assistance, as well as the credit worthiness of the borrower.

Organization asset range: $10,000,000 **to** $100,000,000

Range of investment/grant per borrower/grantee $25,000 **to** $5,000,000

Type of financing: ☐Grants; ■Loans; ☐Loan with equity participations or convertibility; ■Loan Guarantees*; ☐Equity; ☐Leases; ☐Sale-leaseback; Other: *Tax exempt or conventional loans.

Security position: Senior or subordinated

Type of collateral: Current Assets (Inventory, Accounts Receivable), Stocks & Bonds, Cash value of life insurance, Equipment, Real Estate, Guarantees, (Mainly real estate; equipment and current assets.)

Term of financing: Maximum: 20 and up **years; Minimum** 1-3 **years**

Industry preference (in order of priority, if any): Manufacturing & Processing, Diversified,1983 legislation expanded eligibility to all prospects eligible under Section 103B of the IRS Code for tax exempt financings and all types of conventional loans.

Borrower characteristics desired-required:

Min. number of years in business:

Min. annual sales: $

Min. net worth: $

Min. annual cash flow:

Min. annual net income:

Other requirements:

Estimated $ available for investment annually: $

Annual interest rate for 1985: Max.: %; Min.: % Ave.: %

Special conditions, if any:

STATE OF: MARYLAND

NAME OF ORGANIZATION: MARYLAND SMALL BUSINESS DEVELOP. FINANCING AUTHORITY

ADDRESS: World Trade Center, Suite 1353, Baltimore, Maryland 21201

PHONE NO. (301) 659-4270

CONTACT OFFICER: Stanley Tucker; **TITLE:** Executive Director

DESCRIPTION OF PROGRAM: Financing assistance to socially or economically disadvataged business persons in Maryland.

Organization asset range: $1,000,000 **to** $10,000,000

Range of investment/grant per borrower/grantee: $5,000 **to** $500,000

Type of financing: ☐Grants; ■Loans; ☐Loan with equity participations or convertibility; ■Loan Guarantees; ☐Equity; ☐Leases; ☐Sale-leaseback; Other: Loans for minority government contractors. Loan guarantees for all other businesses.

Security position: Senior or subordinated

Type of collateral: Current Assets (Inventory, Accounts Receivable), Stocks & Bonds, Cash value of life insurance, Equipment, Real Estate

Term of financing: Maximum: 7-10 **years; Minimum** 1-3 **years**

Industry preference (in order of priority, if any):

Borrower characteristics desired-required:

Min. number of years in business: One year or more

Min. annual sales: $

Min. net worth: $

Min. annual cash flow:

Min. annual net income:

Other requirements:

Estimated $ available for investment annually: $5,000,000

Annual interest rate for 1985: Max.: %; Min.: % Ave.: 11.5%

Special conditions, if any: 70% ownership required by minority or disadvantaged persons. Must be U.S. citizens.

STATE OF: MARYLAND

NAME OF ORGANIZATION: DEVELOPMENT CREDIT CORPORATION OF MARYLAND

ADDRESS: 40 West Chesapeake Avenue, P.O. Box 10629 Towson, Maryland 21204

PHONE NO. (301) 828-4711

CONTACT OFFICER: W.G. Brooks Thomas; **TITLE:** President

DESCRIPTION OF PROGRAM: Term loans up to fifteen years from $100,000 to $750,000 when direct bank early maturity paricipations can be obtained for between 15% to 25%. Loans are for working capital, plant construction and purchase of equipment.

Organization asset range: $1,000,000 **to $**10,000,000

Range of investment/grant per borrower/grantee: $100,000 **to $**750,000

Type of financing: ☐Grants; ■Loans; ■Loan with equity participations or convertibility; ☐Loan Guarantees; ☐Equity; ☐Leases; ☐Sale-leaseback; Other:

Security position: Senior or subordinated

Type of collateral: Current Assets (Inventory, Accounts Receivable), Stocks & Bonds, Cash value of life insurance, Equipment, Real Estate, Guarantees

Term of financing: Maximum: 10-15 **years; Minimum** 3-5**years**

Industry preference (in order of priority, if any): Manufacturing & Processing, Diversified

Borrower characteristics desired-required:

Min. number of years in business: Preferred - at least one

Min. annual sales: $300,000

Min. net worth: $10,000

Min. annual cash flow: Must be positive with debt service

Min. annual net income: Must be positive

Other requirements:

Estimated $ available for investment annually: $5,000,000

Annual interest rate for 1985: Max.: 18%; **Min.:** 12% **Ave.:** 15%

Special conditions, if any:

STATE OF: MICHIGAN

NAME OF ORGANIZATION: DEPARTMENT OF COMMERCE

ADDRESS: P.O. Box 30225, Lansing, MI 48909

PHONE NO. (517) 373-0347

CONTACT OFFICER: William Lontz; **TITLE:** Economic Development Specialist

DESCRIPTION OF PROGRAM: Over 200 local units of government have established Economic Development Corporations that provide capital to the private sector through the use of Industrial Revenue Bonds and other financing sources.

Organization asset range: $ to $

Range of investment/grant per borrower/grantee: $450,000**to $**

Type of financing: ☐Grants; ■Loans; ■Loan with equity participations or convertibility; ■Loan Guarantees; ■Equity; ■Leases; ■Sale-leaseback; Other: Industrial Revenue Bonds; federal and local funding programs.

Security position:

Type of collateral: Equipment, Real Estate, Guarantees

Term of financing: Maximum: 20 and up **years; Minimum years**

Industry preference (in order of priority, if any): Manufacturing & Processing, Retailing, Wholesaling & Distribution, Research & Technology, Agriculture-Related

Borrower characteristics desired-required:

Min. number of years in business: 3

Min. annual sales: $

Min. net worth: $

Min. annual cash flow:

Min. annual net income:

Other requirements: Financially secure and can attract bond purchaser

Estimated $ available for investment annually: $

Annual interest rate for 1985: Max.: %; Min.: % Ave.: %

Special conditions, if any: Projects approved at local level and must comply with IRS code.

STATE OF: MICHIGAN

NAME OF ORGANIZATION: MICHIGAN ECONOMIC DEVELOPMENT AUTHORITY

ADDRESS: P.O. Box 30234, Lansing, MI 48909

PHONE NO. (517) 373-6378

CONTACT OFFICER: William Schwartz**; TITLE:** Executive Officer

DESCRIPTION OF PROGRAM: The Private Development Loan Fund makes loans to business to finance industrial projects in participation with loans from other public or private lendors.

Organization asset range: $10,000,000 **to $**100,000,000

Range of investment/grant per borrower/grantee: $150,000 **to $**1,000,000

Type of financing: ☐Grants; ■Loans; ☐Loan with equity participations or convertibility; ☐Loan Guarantees; ☐Equity; ☐Leases; ☐Sale-leaseback; Other: Subordinate to senior lender

Security position: Senior or subordinated; Working capital in distressed citites

Type of collateral: Current Assets (Inventory, Accounts Receivable), Stocks & Bonds, Cash value of life insurance, Equipment, Real Estate, Guarantees

Term of financing: Maximum: 20 and up **years; Minimum** 3-5**years**

Industry preference (in order of priority, if any): Manufacturing & Processing

Borrower characteristics desired-required:

Min. number of years in business:

Min. annual sales: $

Min. net worth: $

Min. annual cash flow:

Min. annual net income:

Other requirements: Variable credit rating and terms

Estimated $ available for investment annually: $

Annual interest rate for 1985: Max.: %; Min.: % Ave.: 9½-10%

Special conditions, if any: Subject to borrower

STATE OF: MICHIGAN

NAME OF ORGANIZATION: MICHIGAN CERTIFIED DEVELOPMENT CORP.

ADDRESS: P.O. Box 30225, Lansing, MI 48909

PHONE NO. (517) 373-0637

CONTACT OFFICER: Harold Hill; **TITLE:** Director

DESCRIPTION OF PROGRAM: A non-profit corporation which provides business loans throughout the state. Funding sources are SBA's 503 program, MCDC, and the business concern.

Organization asset range: $Less than $150,000

Range of investment/grant per borrower/grantee: $50,000 **to** $500,000

Type of financing: □Grants; □Loans; ■Loan with equity participations or convertibility; ■Loan Guarantees; ■Equity; □Leases; □Sale-leaseback; Other:

Security position: Subordinate to private lender, no less than 2nd position

Type of collateral: Current Assets (Inventory, Accounts Receivable), Equipment, Real Estate, Guarantees

Term of financing: Maximum: 20-25 **years; Minimum** 1-3 **years and** 10-15**years**

Industry preference (in order of priority, if any): Manufacturing & Processing, Retailing, Wholesaling & Distribution, Research & Technology, Agriculture-Related, Natural Resources, Services

Borrower characteristics desired-required:

Min. number of years in business: 3

Min. annual sales: $

Min. net worth: $

Min. annual cash flow:

Min. annual net income:

Other requirements: Must have good financing history and business plan for paybacks

Estimated $ available for investment annually: $42,000,000

Annual interest rate for 1985: rates depend on long-term treasury bill rate at time of closing.

Special conditions, if any: Borrower must provide at least 10% of financing. MCDC provides maxium of 40%.

STATE OF: MICHIGAN

NAME OF ORGANIZATION: MICHIGAN JOB DEVELOPMENT AUTHORITY

ADDRESS: P.O. Box 30227, Lansing, MI 48909

PHONE NO. (517) 373-0349

CONTACT OFFICER: William J. Cochran; **TITLE:** Executive Director

DESCRIPTION OF PROGRAM: State level issuer of Industrial Development Revenue Bonds.

Organization asset range: $150,000 **to** $1,000,000

Range of investment/grant per borrower/grantee: $300,000 **to** $10,000,000

Type of financing: □Grants; ■Loans; □Loan with equity participations or convertibility; ■Loan Guarantees; □Equity; ■Leases; □Sale-leaseback; Other:

Security position: Seniority mandatory

Type of collateral: Current Assets (Inventory, Accounts Receivable), Cash value of life insurance Equipment, Real Estate, Guarantees

Term of financing: Maximum: 20 and up **years; Minimum** 1-3 **years**

Industry preference (in order of priority, if any): Manufacturing & Processing, Research & Technology, Agriculture-Related, Diversified

Borrower characteristics desired-required:

Min. number of years in business: 3

Min. annual sales: $

Min. net worth: $

Min. annual cash flow:

Min. annual net income:

Other requirements: Strong financial statements sufficient to attract bond purchaser

Estimated $ available for investment annually:
$

Annual interest rate for 1985: Max.: %; Min.: % Ave.: %

Special conditions, if any: Compliance with Internal Revenue Code

STATE OF: MICHIGAN

NAME OF ORGANIZATION: MDOC, STATE RESEARCH FUND

ADDRESS: P.O. Box 30225, Lansing, MI 48909

PHONE NO. (517) 373-0637

CONTACT OFFICER: David Turner; **TITLE:** Program Manager

DESCRIPTION OF PROGRAM: Matching state grant program for research and development by small companies that can demonstrate the capability to commercially exploit technology developed internally or transferred from college or university. Grants also available to universities directly engaged in research and development with private companies.

Organization asset range: $150,000 **to $**1,000,000

Range of investment/grant per borrower/grantee: $10,000 **to $**200,000

Type of financing: ■Grants; □Loans; □Loan with equity participations or convertibility; □Loan Guarantees; □Equity; □Leases; □Sale-leaseback; Other:

Security position:

Type of collateral:

Term of financing: Maximum years; Minimum years; as negotiated, usually 12-18 months.

Industry preference (in order of priority, if any): Manufacturing & Processing, Research & Technology*, Agriculture-Related. *Target technology has included robotics, genetic engineering, health and medical technology; food processing and forest product technology are current targets.

Borrower characteristics desired-required:

Min. number of years in business:

Min. annual sales: $

Min. net worth: $

Min. annual cash flow:

Min. annual net income:

Other requirements:

Estimated $ available for investment annually:
$

Annual interest rate for 1985: Max.: %; Min.: % Ave.: %

Special conditions, if any:

STATE OF: MICHIGAN

NAME OF ORGANIZATION: OFFICE OF BUSINESS AND COMMUNITY DEVELOPMENT, MICHIGAN DEPT. OF COMMERCE

ADDRESS: P.O. Box 30225, Lansing, MI 48909

PHONE NO. (517) 373-3530

CONTACT OFFICER: Carol Hoffman; **TITLE:** Director

DESCRIPTION OF PROGRAM: Industrial Revenue Bonds

Organization asset range: $ to $

Range of investment/grant per borrower/grantee: **$**0**to $**5,000,000; no limit on pollution control equipment

Type of financing: ☐Grants; ■Loans; ☐Loan with equity participations or convertibility; ☐Loan Guarantees; ☐Equity; ☐Leases; ☐Sale-leaseback; Other:

Security position:

Type of collateral: Machinery and Equipment, Real Estate

Term of financing: Maximum: 40 **years; Minimum** 0 **years**

Industry preference (in order of priority, if any):

Borrower characteristics desired-required:

Min. number of years in business:

Min. annual sales: $

Min. net worth: $

Min. annual cash flow:

Min. annual net income:

Other requirements:

Estimated $ available for investment annually: $

Annual interest rate for 1985: Max.: %; Min.: % Ave.: %

Special conditions, if any:

STATE OF: MICHIGAN

NAME OF ORGANIZATION: JOB DEVELOPMENT AUTHORITY (JDA)

ADDRESS: P.O. Box 30227, Lansing, MI 48909

PHONE NO. (517) 373-0349

CONTACT OFFICER: William J. Cochran, Lawrence R. Schrauben, Roy A. Pentilla;; **TITLE:** Executive Director, Loan Officer, Fiscal Officer

DESCRIPTION OF PROGRAM: JDA is a state level agency that finances industrial projects using Industrial Revenue Bonds. It can finance projects any where in the state.

Organization asset range: $ to $

Range of investment/grant per borrower/grantee: **$**50,000 **to $**10,000,000;

Type of financing: ☐Grants; ■Loans; ☐Loan with equity participations or convertibility; ☐Loan Guarantees; ☐Equity; ☐Leases; ☐Sale-leaseback; Other:

Security position: Mostly Senior

Type of collateral: Equipment, Real Estate, Guarantees

Term of financing: Maximum: 20 and up **years; Minimum** 3-5 **years**

Industry preference (in order of priority, if any): Manufacturing & Processing, Research & Technology

Borrower characteristics desired-required:

Min. number of years in business: Usually 5 years

Min. annual sales: $

Min. net worth: $

Min. annual cash flow:

Min. annual net income:

Other requirements:

Estimated $ available for investment annually: No statutory limit

Annual interest rate for 1985: Max.: %; Min.: % Ave.: %

Special conditions, if any:

STATE OF: MINNESOTA

NAME OF ORGANIZATION: DEPARTMENT OF ENERGY AND ECONOMIC DEV.

ADDRESS: 150 E. Kellogg Blvd, 900 American Center Bldg., St. Paul, MN 55101

PHONE NO. (612) 297-1170

CONTACT OFFICER: Dave Mocol; **TITLE:** Director

DESCRIPTION OF PROGRAM: SBA 503 - OMNI. OMNI is a private corporation certified by the U.S. Small Business Administration. It provides subordinated mortgage financing to industry and manufacturing small businesses through the issuance of debentures.

Organization asset range: $24.3 Million appropriation. $30 Million in bonding authority

Range of investment/grant per borrower/grantee: **$**0 **to $**500,000

Type of financing: ☐Grants; ☐Loans; ☐Loan with equity participations or convertibility; ■Loan Guarantees; ☐Equity; ☐Leases; ☐Sale-leaseback; Other:

Security position: Senior or subordinated

Type of collateral: Equipment, Real Estate

Term of financing: Maximum: 20 and up **years; Minimum** 10-15 **years**

Industry preference (in order of priority, if any): Hotels, Motels & Restaurants, Manufacturing & Processing, Medical & Other Health Services, Retailing, Wholesaling & Distribution, Services, Transportation, Diversified

Borrower characteristics desired-required:

Min. number of years in business:

Min. annual sales: $

Min. net worth: $

Min. annual cash flow:

Min. annual net income:

Other requirements:

Estimated $ available for investment annually: $

Annual interest rate for 1985: Max.: %; Min.: % Ave.: %

Special conditions, if any:

STATE OF: MINNESOTA

NAME OF ORGANIZATION: DEPARTMENT OF ENERGY AND ECONOMIC DEVELOPMENT

ADDRESS: 150 E. Kellogg Blvd, 900 American Center Bldg., St. Paul, MN 55101

PHONE NO. (612) 297-1170

CONTACT OFFICER: Dave Mocol,; **TITLE:** Director

DESCRIPTION OF PROGRAM: Small Business Development Loan. This loan program is dedicated to assisting existing small businesses in their expansion in Minnesota. Applicants deal directly with the Department of Energy and Economic Development.

Organization asset range: $24.3 Million appropriation. $30 Million in bonding authority

Range of investment/grant per borrower/grantee: **$**250,000 **to $**1,000,000

Type of financing: ☐Grants; ■Loans; ☐Loan with equity participations or convertibility; ☐Loan Guarantees; ☐Equity; ☐Leases; ☐Sale-leaseback; Other:

Security position: Seniority mandatory

Type of collateral: Equipment, Real Estate

Term of financing: Maximum: 7-10 **years; Minimum years;** Equipment 10 years maximum, land and building 20 years maximum

Industry preference (in order of priority, if any): Manufacturing & Processing. Our programs are directed to industrial manufacturing and processing finance.

Borrower characteristics desired-required:

Min. number of years in business: 3

Min. annual sales: $

Min. net worth: $

Min. annual cash flow:

Min. annual net income:

Other requirements:

Estimated $ available for investment annually: **$**

Annual interest rate for 1985: Max.:%; Min.: % **Ave.:** 11.73%

Special conditions, if any:

STATE OF: MINNESOTA

NAME OF ORGANIZATION: DEPARTMENT OF ENERGY AND ECONOMIC DEVELOPMENT

ADDRESS: 150 E. Kellogg Blvd, 900 American Center Bldg., St. Paul, MN 55101

PHONE NO. (612) 297-1170

CONTACT OFFICER: Dave Mocol,; **TITLE:** Director

DESCRIPTION OF PROGRAM: Minnesota Fund. This direct loan program of the State of Minnesota provides fixed interest rate, fixed-asset financing for new and existing businesses. Applicants deal directly with the Minnesota Department of Energy and Economic Development.

Organization asset range: $24.3 Million appropriation.

Range of investment/grant per borrower/grantee: **$**0 **to $**250,000

Type of financing: ☐Grants; ■Loans; ☐Loan with equity participations or convertibility; ☐Loan Guarantees; ☐Equity; ☐Leases; ☐Sale-leaseback; Other:

Security position: Senior or subordinated

Type of collateral: Equipment, Real Estate, Guarantees

Term of financing: Maximum: 10-15 **years;** **Minimum** 5-7 **years;**

Industry preference (in order of priority, if any): Manufacturing & Processing, Diversified, Agriculture-Related, Hotels, Motels & Restaurants, Natural Resources, Recreation & Amusements, Services

Borrower characteristics desired-required:

Min. number of years in business: Can assist startups

Min. annual sales: $

Min. net worth: $

Min. annual cash flow:

Min. annual net income:

Other requirements:

Estimated $ available for investment annually: $

Annual interest rate for 1985: Max.: %; Min.: % **Ave.: %**

Special conditions, if any:

STATE OF: MINNESOTA

NAME OF ORGANIZATION: DEPARTMENT OF ENERGY AND ECONOMIC DEVELOPMENT

ADDRESS: 150 E. Kellogg Blvd, St. Paul, MN 55101

PHONE NO. (612) 297-2515

CONTACT OFFICER: Robert Benner; **TITLE:**

DESCRIPTION OF PROGRAM: Small Cities Development Program/Economic Recovery Grants. Provide grants to general purpose local units of government for economic development activities which create or retain private sector jobs, leverage private investments and increase the local tax base.

Organization asset range: $1,000,000 **to $**10,000,000

Range of investment/grant per borrower/grantee: $0 **to $**500,000

Type of financing: □Grants; □Loans; □Loan with equity participations or convertibility; □Loan Guarantees; □Equity; □Leases; □Sale-leaseback; Other: Grants to local governments for loans to businesses or installation of public facilities to support economic development projects.

Security position: Senior or subordinated

Type of collateral: Current Assets (Inventory, Accounts Receivable), Equipment, Real Estate,

Term of financing: Maximum: 20 and up **years; Minimum** 1-3 **years;**

Industry preference (in order of priority, if any): Manufacturing & Processing, Diversified, Agriculture-Related, Construction & Development, Utilities, Real Estate, Recreation & Amusement, Retailing, Wholesaling & Distribution, Communications, Hotels, Motels & Restaurants, Transportation, Finance & Insurance, Medical & Other Health Services, Natural Resources, Services, Research & Technology

Borrower characteristics desired-required:

Min. number of years in business:

Min. annual sales: $

Min. net worth: $

Min. annual cash flow:

Min. annual net income:

Other requirements:

Estimated $ available for investment annually: $6,000,000

Annual interest rate for 1985: Max.: 10%; **Min.:** 0% **Ave.:** 7%

Special conditions, if any: Must be linked to job creation or retention.

STATE OF: MINNESOTA

NAME OF ORGANIZATION: DEPARTMENT OF ENERGY AND ECONOMIC DEVELOPMENT

ADDRESS: 900 American Center Building, St. Paul, MN 55101

PHONE NO. (612) 297-1304

CONTACT OFFICER: Harry Rosefelt; **TITLE:** Director

DESCRIPTION OF PROGRAM: Minnesota Enterprise Zone. An enterprise zone is an economic development tool providing tax reductions over a five year period for business locating in an economically distressed area.

Organization asset range: $ to $

Range of investment/grant per borrower/grantee:

Type of financing: □Grants; □Loans; □Loan with equity participations or convertibility; □Loan Guarantees; □Equity; □Leases; □Sale-leaseback; Other:

Security position:

Type of collateral:

Term of financing: Maximum: years; Minimum years;

Industry preference (in order of priority, if any): locally determined; must be an eligible industial sector defined in Enterprise Zone legistation.

Borrower characteristics desired-required:

Min. number of years in business:

Min. annual sales: $

Min. net worth: $

Min. annual cash flow:

Min. annual net income:

Other requirements:

Estimated $ available for investment annually:
$

Annual interest rate for 1985: Max.: %; Min.: % Ave.: %

Special conditions, if any: 1. General sales-tax exemption for purchases of construction materials or equipment for use in the zone if the purchase was made after the date of application for the zone. 2. A credit against an employer's income tax for additional workers employed in the zone, except construction workers, up to $3,000 per employee per year. 3. An income tax credit for a percentage of the cost of debt financing to construct new or expanded facilities in the zone. 4. A state-paid property-tax credit for a portion of the property taxes paid by the owner of a new commercial or industrial facility, or a portion of the additional property taxes paid by the owner of an exisiting commercial or industrial facility in the zone.

STATE OF: MISSISSIPPI

NAME OF ORGANIZATION: CERTIFIED DEVELOPMENT CORPORATION OF MISSISSIPPI, INC.

ADDRESS: Jackson, MS

PHONE NO. ( ) -

CONTACT OFFICER: ; TITLE:

DESCRIPTION OF PROGRAM: Loan Guaranty Program. CDCM is a 503 Development Corporation (SBA) and also operates a Loan Guaranty Program which is described here. State guarantees loans to small businesses for development and expansion of commercial and industrial enterprises. The maximum loan uder this program is $100,000 and the maximum guaranty is 75% not to exceed $75,000.

Organization asset range: $ to $

Range of investment/grant per borrower/grantee:

Type of financing: ☐Grants; ☐Loans; ☐Loan with equity participations or convertibility; ☐Loan Guarantees; ☐Equity; ☐Leases; ☐Sale-leaseback; Other:

Security position:

Type of collateral:

Term of financing: Maximum: 7-10 **years; Minimum** 0 **years;**

Industry preference (in order of priority, if any): Certian types of businesses ineligible, including Eleemosynary institutions, nonprofit enterprises, publisher, broadcasting cos, film production companies and lenders.

Borrower characteristics desired-required:

Min. number of years in business:

Min. annual sales: $

Min. net worth: $

Min. annual cash flow:

Min. annual net income:

Other requirements:

Estimated $ available for investment annually:
$

Annual interest rate for 1985: Max.: Current Legal rate; Min.: %;**Ave.: %**

Special conditions, if any: Guaranty fee of 1% is charged. The guaranty loan cannot exceed 90% of the fair market value of the collateral pledged to secure the loan. Applicant must have an equity in the business.

STATE OF: MISSOURI

NAME OF ORGANIZATION: MISSOURI INDUSTRIAL DEVELOPMENT BOARD

ADDRESS: Harry S. Truman Bldg.; 301 W. High St., Jefferson City, MO 65101

PHONE NO. (314) 751-4982

CONTACT OFFICER: Tom Monks; **TITLE:**

DESCRIPTION OF PROGRAM: The Industrial Development Funding Act established the Industrial Development Board. This Board is empowered to function as a State Industrial Development Authority utilizing public funds, issue state sponsored revenue bonds, provide state loans to businesses and local development organizations all for the purpose of promoting industrial development.

Organization asset range: $ to $

Range of investment/grant per borrower/grantee: $25,000 **to** $10,000,000

Type of financing: ☐Grants; ■Loans; ☐Loan with equity participations or convertibility; ☐Loan Guarantees; ☐Equity; ☐Leases; ☐Sale-leaseback; Other: Participation loans with conventional lenders.

Security position: Senior or subordinated

Type of collateral: Guarantees, The collateral value must be adequate to support the loan.

Term of financing: Maximum: 20 and up **years; Minimum** 1-3 **years;**

Industry preference (in order of priority, if any): Manufacturing & Processing, Warehousing, Distribution, R & D, Port facilities

Borrower characteristics desired-required:

Min. number of years in business:

Min. annual sales: $

Min. net worth: $

Min. annual cash flow:

Min. annual net income:

Other requirements: Generation of substantial economic impact sound overall financial condition of company.

Estimated $ available for investment annually: $

Annual interest rate for 1985: Max.: %; Min.: % Ave.: %

Special conditions, if any: Must qualify for tax-exempt financing under Section 103 of the IRS Code & fit one of the categories cited under G. Industry Preference.

STATE OF: MISSOURI

NAME OF ORGANIZATION: DEPARTMENT OF ECONOMIC DEV.

ADDRESS: Harry S. Truman Bldg., 301 W. High St. Jefferson City, MO 65101

PHONE NO. (314) 751-3600

CONTACT OFFICER: Cecil Cliburn; **TITLE:** Program Manager, Missouri Community Development Block Grants

DESCRIPTION OF PROGRAM: Provide funding for infrastructure development on public and/or privately owned land deemed necessary to promote economic development in UDAG eligible nonentitlement municipalities or counties.

Organization asset range: $10,000,000 **to** $100,000,000

Range of investment/grant per borrower/grantee:

Type of financing: ☐Grants; ☐Loans; ☐Loan with equity participations or convertibility; ☐Loan Guarantees; ☐Equity; ☐Leases; ☐Sale-leaseback; Other: Direct grants to eligible local governments who in turn provide low interest loans to businesses.

Security position:

Type of collateral:

Term of financing: Maximum: years; Minimum years;

Industry preference (in order of priority, if any): Manufacturing & Processing, Agriculture-Related, Wholesaling & Distribution.

Borrower characteristics desired-required:

Min. number of years in business:

Min. annual sales: $

Min. net worth: $

Min. annual cash flow:

Min. annual net income:

Other requirements:

Estimated $ available for investment annually: **$**

Annual interest rate for 1985: Max.: %; Min.: %;Ave.: %

Special conditions, if any: Firm commitment given by eligible businesses to create or retain full time jobs; 1 job created or retained for each $8,000 of CDBG funds provided; the ratio of private funds to CDGB funds must be $2.5:1 or greater.

STATE OF: MISSOURI

NAME OF ORGANIZATION: DEPARTMENT OF ECONOMIC DEVELOPMENT

ADDRESS: Harry S. Truman Bldg., 301 W. High St. Jefferson City, MO 65101

PHONE NO. (314) 751-4982

CONTACT OFFICER: Bob Simonds; **TITLE:** Program Manager, Enterprise Zone Program

DESCRIPTION OF PROGRAM: Allows substantial state tax credit exemptions and abatements for companies expanding or locating in enterprise zone designated areas.

Organization asset range:

Range of investment/grant per borrower/grantee:

Type of financing: ☐Grants; ☐Loans; ☐Loan with equity participations or convertibility; ☐Loan Guarantees; ☐Equity; ☐Leases; ☐Sale-leaseback; Other: State tax credits, exemptions and abatements.

Security position:

Type of collateral:

Term of financing: Maximum: 20 and up **years; Minimum** 1-3 **years;** credits exemptions and abatements

Industry preference (in order of priority, if any): Any idustrial firm or any commercial business that sells products on leases/rents residential property to low and moderate income persons.

Borrower characteristics desired-required:

Min. number of years in business:

Min. annual sales: $

Min. net worth: $

Min. annual cash flow:

Min. annual net income:

Other requirements:

Estimated $ available for investment annually: **$**

Annual interest rate for 1985: Max.: %; Min.: % Ave.: %

Special conditions, if any: Credits available dependent upon dollar investment and jobs created.

STATE OF: MISSOURI

NAME OF ORGANIZATION: R.M.I. RURAL MISSOURI INC.

ADDRESS: 1014 N.E. Drive, Jefferson City, MO 65101

PHONE NO. (314) 751-4982

CONTACT OFFICER: Eddie Barnett; **TITLE:** Director

DESCRIPTION OF PROGRAM: State-wide Small Business Administration Certified Development Company and 12 regional C.D.C's within Missouri. Provide direct loans in participation with private lenders to qualifying business for fixed assets.

Organization asset range: $ to $

Range of investment/grant per borrower/grantee: **$**10,000 **to $**500,000

Type of financing: ☐Grants; ■Loans; ☐Loan with equity participations or convertibility; ☐Loan Guarantees; ☐Equity; ■Leases; ☐Sale-leaseback; Other:

Security position: Senior or Subordinated

Type of collateral: Current Assets (Inventory, Accounts Receivable), Cash value of life insurance, Equipment, Real Estate, Guarantees, Collateral required must be sufficient to insure repayment

Term of financing: Maximum: 20 and up **years; Minimum** 10-15 **years;**

Industry preference (in order of priority, if any): Any private, for-profit business except regulated media concerns, meeting SBA small business size guidelines is eligible.

Borrower characteristics desired-required:

Min. number of years in business:

Min. annual sales: $

Min. net worth: $ Positive

Min. annual cash flow:

Min. annual net income:

Other requirements: Profitable

Estimated $ available for investment annually: $

Annual interest rate for 1985: Max.: %; Min.: % Ave.: %

Special conditions, if any: Borrower must be a private, for-profit business meeting SBA small business classifications. Any business meeting above criteria, except regulated media concerns is eligible.

STATE OF: MISSOURI

NAME OF ORGANIZATION: MISSOURI ECONOMIC DEVELOPMENT COMMISSION

ADDRESS: Harry S. Truman Bldg.; 301 W. High St., Jefferson City, MO 65101

PHONE NO. (314) 751-4982

CONTACT OFFICER: Tom Monks; **TITLE:** Program Manager, Business Development

DESCRIPTION OF PROGRAM: Guarantee up to 90% of loans made by conventional lenders to qualifying businesses for fixed asset expansions and/or guarantee loans that are reinsured by the U.S. Ex-Im Bank for export trade activities. To guarantee tax-exempt industrial revenue bonds.

Organization asset range: $1,000,000 **to $**10,000,000

Range of investment/grant per borrower/grantee: $25,000 **to $**1,000,000

Type of financing: ☐Grants; ☐Loans; ☐Loan with equity participations or convertibility; ■Loan Guarantees; ☐Equity; ☐Leases; ☐Sale-leaseback; Other: Tax-exempt industrial revenue bonds guarantees

Security position: Subordinated

Type of collateral: Current Assets (Inventory, Accounts Receivable), Equipment, Real Estate, Guarantees, Assignment of sufficient collateral to provide for a reasonable assurance of repayment.

Term of financing: Maximum: 10-15 **years; Minimum** 1-3 **years;**

Industry preference (in order of priority, if any): Manufacturing & Processing, Agriculture-Related, Retailing, Wholesaling & Distribution, Warehousing, Pollution-control Facilities, Reasearch & Technology, R & D only in conjunction with manufacturing, distribution or warehousing.

Borrower characteristics desired-required:

Min. number of years in business:

Min. annual sales: $

Min. net worth: $

Min. annual cash flow:

Min. annual net income:

Other requirements:

Estimated $ available for investment annually: $

Annual interest rate for 1985: Max.: %; Min.: % Ave.: %

Special conditions, if any: Business must be an eligible activity as listed under Section G above.

STATE OF: MISSOURI

NAME OF ORGANIZATION: DEPARTMENT OF ECONOMIC DEV.

ADDRESS: Harry S. Truman Bldg.; 301 W. High St., Jefferson City, MO 65101

PHONE NO. (314) 751-4982

CONTACT OFFICER: Tom Monks; **TITLE:**

DESCRIPTION OF PROGRAM: Missouri municipalities may enter into loan agreements, sell lease or mortgage facilities purchased, constructed or extened to private, for-profit entities for the pupose of manufacturing and industrial development.

Organization asset range: $ to $

Range of investment/grant per borrower/grantee:

Type of financing: ☐Grants; ☐Loans; ☐Loan with equity participations or convertibility; ☐Loan Guarantees; ☐Equity; ■Leases; ☐Sale-leaseback; Other: Tax-exempt industrial revenue bonds

Security position: Seniority mandatory

Type of collateral: Guarantees. Those assets financed by proceeds of the bonds. Collateral offered must be adequate to secure the bonds issued.

Term of financing: Maximum: years; Minimum years;

Industry preference (in order of priority, if any):

Borrower characteristics desired-required:

Min. number of years in business:

Min. annual sales: $

Min. net worth: $

Min. annual cash flow:

Min. annual net income:

Other requirements:

Estimated $ available for investment annually: $

Annual interest rate for 1985: Max.: %; Min.: % Ave.: %

Special conditions, if any:

STATE OF: MISSOURI

NAME OF ORGANIZATION: DEPARTMENT OF ECONMIC DEVELOPMENT

ADDRESS: Harry S. Truman Bldg.; 301 W. High St., Jefferson City, MO 65101

PHONE NO. (314) 751-4982

CONTACT OFFICER: Tom Monks; **TITLE:**

DESCRIPTION OF PROGRAM: Local municipalities and private, locally incorporated Industrial Development Authorities are both empowered to issue tax-exempt revenue bonds for qualifying industrial projects.

Organization asset range: $ to $

Range of investment/grant per borrower/grantee:

Type of financing: ☐Grants; ☐Loans; ☐Loan with equity participations or convertibility; ☐Loan Guarantees; ☐Equity; ■Leases; ☐Sale-leaseback; Other: Tax-exempt industrial revenue bonds

Security position: Seniority mandatory

Type of collateral: Guarantees, Collateral value must be adequete to secure the bonds sold to finance the project

Term of financing: Maximum: years; Minimum years;

Industry preference (in order of priority, if any): Agriculture-Related, Construction & Development, Hotels, Motels & Restaurants, Manufacturing & Processing, Medical & Other Health Services, Retailing, Wholesaling & Distribution, Services, Transportation

Borrower characteristics desired-required:

Min. number of years in business:

Min. annual sales: $

Min. net worth: $

Min. annual cash flow:

Min. annual net income:

Other requirements: Sufficient credit strength of the end use to support the placement of the bonds in the market-place.

Estimated $ available for investment annually: $747,000,000

Annual interest rate for 1985: Max.: %; Min.: % Ave.: %

Special conditions, if any: Eligible activities must qualify under Section 103 of the IRS code, be approved by the chief elected local official and the Dept. of Economic Development.

STATE OF: MISSOURI

NAME OF ORGANIZATION: MISSOURI DEPARTMENT OF ECONOMIC DEVELOPMENT

ADDRESS: Harry S. Truman Bldg.; 301 W. High St., Jefferson City, MO 65101

PHONE NO. (314) 751-4982

CONTACT OFFICER: Tom Monks; **TITLE:**

DESCRIPTION OF PROGRAM: The Economic Development Time Deposit Program authorizes the state to deposit inactive state funds into applying banks who have specifically committed to providing loans to businesses to promote economic development.

Organization asset range:

Range of investment/grant per borrower/grantee: **$**100,000 **to $**5,000,000

Type of financing: ☐Grants; ☐Loans; ☐Loan with equity participations or convertibility; ☐Loan Guarantees; ☐Equity; ☐Leases; ☐Sale-leaseback; Other: Indirect financing mechanism. A deposit (Loan) is placed in banks who have committed to loan to qualifying businesses.

Security position:

Type of collateral:

Term of financing: Maximum: 0-1 **years; Minimum** 0-1 **years;**

Industry preference (in order of priority, if any): Processing, Agriculture-Related, Construction & Development, Manufacturing & Processing, Medical & Other Health Service, Retailing, Wholesaling & Distribution.

Borrower characteristics desired-required:

Min. number of years in business:

Min. annual sales: $

Min. net worth: $

Min. annual cash flow:

Min. annual net income:

Other requirements:

Estimated $ available for investment annually: $

Annual interest rate for 1985: Max.: %; Min.: % Ave.: %

Special conditions, if any:

STATE OF: MONTANA

NAME OF ORGANIZATION: MONTANA ECONOMIC DEVELOPMENT BOARD — COAL TAX LOAN PROGRAM

ADDRESS: 1424 Ninth Ave, Helena, MT 59620

PHONE NO. (406) 444-2090

CONTACT OFFICER: Terry Spalinger; **TITLE:** Loan Officer

DESCRIPTION OF PROGRAM: MEDB makes Coal Tax Loans to basic sector businesses including manufacturing, agriculture and mineral production and processing, transportation, tourism businesses that produce a good or service in Montana that was previously purchased outside the state. and wholesale and retail distribution of Montana-made goods. Give types of loans are offered and are designed to proved fixed-rate, long-term financing at competitive rates.

Organization asset range:

Range of investment/grant per borrower/grantee: **$**0 **to $**1,000,000

Type of financing: ☐Grants; ☐Loans; ☐Loan with equity participations or convertibility; ☐Loan Guarantees; ☐Equity; ☐Leases; ☐Sale-leaseback; Other:

Security position:

Type of collateral:

Term of financing: Maximum: years; Minimum years;

Industry preference (in order of priority, if any):

Borrower characteristics desired-required:

Min. number of years in business:

Min. annual sales: $

Min. net worth: $

Min. annual cash flow:

Min. annual net income:

Other requirements:

Estimated $ available for investment annually: $

Annual interest rate for 1985: Max.: %; Min.: % Ave.: %

Special conditions, if any: Max. loan to value: 75%

STATE OF: MONTANA

NAME OF ORGANIZATION: MONTANA ECONOMIC DEVELOPMENT BOARD

ADDRESS: 1424 Ninth Ave, Helena, MT 59620

PHONE NO. (406) 444-2090

CONTACT OFFICER: Robert M. Pancich **TITLE:** Administrator

DESCRIPTION OF PROGRAM: MEDB operates a series of programs authorized by the State Legislature to increase the availability of long-term fixed-rate financing to Montana small businesses. All programs operate through existing commercial lending institutions.

Organization asset range:

Range of investment/grant per borrower/grantee:

Type of financing: ☐Grants; ☐Loans; ☐Loan with equity participations or convertibility; ☐Loan Guarantees; ☐Equity; ☐Leases; ☐Sale-leaseback; Other:

Security position:

Type of collateral:

Term of financing: Maximum: years; Minimum years;

Industry preference (in order of priority, if any):

Borrower characteristics desired-required:

Min. number of years in business:

Min. annual sales: $

Min. net worth: $

Min. annual cash flow:

Min. annual net income:

Other requirements:

Estimated $ available for investment annually: **$**

Annual interest rate for 1985: Max.: %; Min.: % Ave.: %

Special conditions, if any:

STATE OF: NEBRASKA

NAME OF ORGANIZATION: BUSINESS DEVELOPMENT CORPORATION OF NEBRASKA

ADDRESS: 1044 Stuart Bldg., Lincoln, Nebraska 68502

PHONE NO. (402) 474-3855

CONTACT OFFICER: James H. Childe **TITLE:** Executive Vice President

DESCRIPTION OF PROGRAM: The business Development Corporation of Nebraska is a public corporation backed up by a loan pool provided by member Nebraska financial institutions. The ultimate goal is to help provide jobs for Nebraskans by providing manufacturers and processors a source of funds where these funds are not otherwise available through conventional financial sources.

Organization asset range: $1,000,000 **to $**10,000,000

Range of investment/grant per borrower/grantee: $25,000 **to $**250,000

Type of financing: ☐Grants; ☐Loans; ■Loan with equity participations or convertibility; ☐Loan Guarantees; ☐Equity; ☐Leases; ☐Sale-leaseback; Other: Bank participation loans

Security position: Senior or subordinated

Type of collateral: Current Assets (Inventory, Accounts Receivable), Stocks & Bonds, Cash value of life insurance, Equipment, Real Estate, Guarantees

Term of financing: Maximum: 10-15 **years; Minimum** 3-5 **years;**

Industry preference (in order of priority, if any): Manufacturing & Processing, Retailing, Wholesaling & Distribution, Services, Diversified

Borrower characteristics desired-required:

Min. number of years in business:

Min. annual sales: $

Min. net worth: $

Min. annual cash flow:

Min. annual net income:

Other requirements:

Estimated $ available for investment annually: $500,000to $1,000,000

Annual interest rate for 1985: Max.: 4 over prime; Min.: 2 over prime **Ave.:** 3 over prime

Special conditions, if any:

STATE OF: NEW HAMPSHIRE

NAME OF ORGANIZATION: INDUSTRIAL DEVELOPMENT AUTHORITY

ADDRESS: 4 Park St., Room 302, Concord, N.H. 03301

PHONE NO. (603) 271-2391

CONTACT OFFICER: Vasilike Kounas **TITLE:** Executive Director

DESCRIPTION OF PROGRAM: 100% financing through state guaranty or industrial development revenue bond financing.

Organization asset range: $10,000,000 **to** $100,000,000

Range of investment/grant per borrower/grantee: $75,000**to** $5,000,000

Type of financing: ☐Grants; ■Loans; ☐Loan with equity participations or convertibility; ■Loan Guarantees; ☐Equity; ☐Leases; ■Sale-leasedback; Other:

Security position: Seniority mandatory on guaranteed loan. Can be unsecured on revenue bonds.

Type of collateral: Equipment, Real Estate, Guarantees

Term of financing: Maximum: for quaranty on real estate 25 **years** ;for guaranty on equipment max. 10 **years** Maximum for bonds 40 years; minimum 1 year.

Industry preference (in order of priority, if any): Manufacturing & Processing, Research and Technology; Corporate headquarters

Borrower characteristics desired-required:

Min. number of years in business:

Min. annual sales: $

Min. net worth: $

Min. annual cash flow:

Min. annual net income:

Other requirements:

Estimated $ available for investment annually: $

Annual interest rate for 1985: Max.: %; Min.: % Ave.: %

Special conditions, if any:

STATE OF: NEW YORK

NAME OF ORGANIZATION: NEW YORK JOB DEVELOPMENT AUTHORITY

ADDRESS: 3 Park Avenue, New York, NY 10016

PHONE NO. (212) 578-4168

CONTACT OFFICER: Robert T. Dormer **TITLE:** President

DESCRIPTION OF PROGRAM: JDA functions as a bank, making low-interest cost loans for real estate and for machinery and equipment.

Organization asset range: $100,000,000 and up

Range of investment/grant per borrower/grantee: $25,000 **to** $10,000,000

Type of financing: ☐Grants; ■Loans; ☐Loan with equity participations or convertibility; ■Loan Guarantees; ☐Equity; ☐Leases; ☐Sale-leaseback; Other:

Security position: Senior or subordinated

Type of collateral: Equipment, Real Estate,

Term of financing: Maximum: 10-20 **years Minimum:** 5-7 **years**

Industry preference (in order of priority, if any): Nearly every business in New York State is eligible for JDA assistance, except retail, hotels and apartment buildings.

Borrower characteristics desired-required:

Min. number of years in business:

Min. annual sales: $

Min. net worth: $

Min. annual cash flow:

Min. annual net income:

Other requirements:

Estimated $ available for investment annually: $

Annual interest rate for 1985: Interest rate determined by JDA's cost of borrowing in the tax-exempt market

Special conditions, if any: Projects must be in New York State.

STATE OF: NEW YORK

NAME OF ORGANIZATION: NEW YORK BUSINESS DEVELOPMENT CORPORATION

ADDRESS: 41 State St., Albany,N.Y. 12207

PHONE NO. (518) 463-2268

CONTACT OFFICER: John D. Wasson **TITLE:** V. President

DESCRIPTION OF PROGRAM: Largest business development corporation in the U.S., privately owned taxpaying to both Federal and N.Y. state governments. Program includes wholly owned SBIC-NYBDC Capital Corp.

Organization asset range: $10,000,000 **to $**100,000,000

Range of investment/grant per borrower/grantee: $50,000 **to $**500,000

Type of financing: ☐Grants; ■Loans; ■Loan with equity participations or convertibility; ☐Loan Guarantees; ☐Equity; ■Leases; ■Sale-leaseback; Other:

Security position: Senior or subordinated

Type of collateral: Current Assets, Stocks & Bonds, Cash value of life insurance, Equipment, Real Estate, Guarantees

Term of financing: Maximum: 10-15 **years; Minimum:** 3-5 **years**

Industry preference (in order of priority, if any): Diversified

Borrower characteristics desired-required:

Min. number of years in business:

Min. annual sales: $

Min. net worth: $

Min. annual cash flow:

Min. annual net income:

Other requirements: Each application is reviewed based on its own merits

Estimated $ available for investment annually: $4.5 million to 6.0 million

Annual interest rate for 1985: Prime plus, 2.5%; **Min.:** 1.5%; **Ave.:** 2.25% plus prime

Special conditions, if any: Funds must be used in New York State.

STATE OF: NEW YORK

NAME OF ORGANIZATION: EMPIRE STATE CERTIFIED DEVELOPMENT CORPORATION

ADDRESS: 41 State St., Albany,N.Y. 12207

PHONE NO. (518) 463-2268

CONTACT OFFICER: John D. Wasson **TITLE:** V. President

DESCRIPTION OF PROGRAM: Certified lender under U.S. Small Business Administration's 503 program and can sell debentures, guaranteed 100% by SBA for second mortgages to finance plant construction, conversion or expansion.

Organization asset range: $0 **to $**150,000

Range of investment/grant per borrower/grantee: $100,000 **to $**500,000

Type of financing: ☐Grants; ■Loans; ☐Loan with equity participations or convertibility; ☐Loan Guarantees; ☐Equity; ■Leases; ☐Sale-leaseback; Other:

Security position: Secondary

Type of collateral: Equipment, Real Estate, Guarantees

Term of financing: Maximum: 25 and up **years; Minimum:** 15-20 **years**

Industry preference (in order of priority, if any): Diversified; cannot be single purpose buildings

Borrower characteristics desired-required:

Min. number of years in business:

Min. annual sales: $

Min. net worth: $

Min. annual cash flow:

Min. annual net income:

Other requirements:

Estimated $ available for investment annually: $

Annual interest rate for 1985: Fixed at Federal Financing as of sale date.

Special conditions, if any:

STATE OF: OKLAHOMA

NAME OF ORGANIZATION: OKLAHOMA INDUSTRIAL FINANCE AUTHORITY

ADDRESS: 4024 N. Lincoln Blvd., P.O. Box 53424, Oklahoma City, Oklahoma 73152

PHONE NO. (405) 218-2182

CONTACT OFFICER: John R Baker, Jr.; **TITLE:** Loan Officer

DESCRIPTION OF PROGRAM: State owned institution organized to aid in financing new or expanding industry by making loans to local incorporated industrial development agencies, including public trust authorities (profit and non-profit), for specific industrial projects. Costs incidental to construction and machinery and equipment may be included. Also industrial parks.

Organization asset range: $10,000,000 to $100,000,000

Range of investment/grant per borrower/grantee:

Type of financing: ☐Grants; ■Loans; ☐Loan with equity participations or convertibility; ☐Loan Guarantees; ☐Equity; ☐Leases; ☐Sale-leaseback; Other:

Security position: Senior or subordinated

Type of collateral: Equipment, Real Estate, Guarantees, Key Men Life Insurance, and mortgages on other property

Term of financing: Maximum: 12 **years; Minimum:** 0 **years**

Industry preference (in order of priority, if any): Manufacturing and Processing. Must include Real Estate. Also Industrial Park Development

Borrower characteristics desired-required:

Min. number of years in business:

Min. annual sales: $

Min. net worth: $

Min. annual cash flow:

Min. annual net income:

Other requirements: Land ownership for manufacturing projects

Estimated $ available for investment annually: $5,000,000

Annual interest rate for 1985: Max.: 10%; **Min.:** 10% **Ave.:** 10%

Special conditions, if any: OIFA limits it loans to 25% of the cost of the facility and may be in either first or second mortgage position. It is possible to have a 75% first mortgage followed by OIFA second mortgage for the remaining 25% for 100% total financing.

STATE OF: OKLAHOMA

NAME OF ORGANIZATION: OKLAHOMA BUSINESS DEVELOPMENT CORPORATION

ADDRESS: 1018 United Founders Life Tower, Oklahoma City, Oklahoma 73112

PHONE NO. (405) 840-1674

CONTACT OFFICER: Robert C. Felts; **TITLE:** Executive Vice President

DESCRIPTION OF PROGRAM: Non bank lender. Makes loans to small to medium, size firms who have been denied credit through normal financial channels.

Organization asset range: $1,000,000 **to $**10,000,000

Range of investment/grant per borrower/grantee: $50,000 **to $**500,000

Type of financing: □Grants; ■Loans; □Loan with equity participations or convertibility; □Loan Guarantees; □Equity; □Leases; □Sale-leaseback; Other:

Security position: Senior or subordinated

Type of collateral: Current Assets (Inventory, Accounts Receivable), Stocks & Bonds, Cash value of life insurance, Equipment, Real Estate, Guarantees

Term of financing: Maximum: 7-10 **years; Minimum:** 1-3 **years**

Industry preference (in order of priority, if any): Manufacturing and Processing, Diversified

Borrower characteristics desired-required:

Min. number of years in business:

Min. annual sales: $

Min. net worth: $

Min. annual cash flow:

Min. annual net income:

Other requirements:

Estimated $ available for investment annually: $1,000,000

Annual interest rate for 1985: Max.: %; Min.: % Ave.: %

Special conditions, if any: Loans are made at 2½ to 3½ points above prime, adjusted quarterly.

STATE OF: OREGON

NAME OF ORGANIZATION: OREGON BUSINESS DEVELOPMENT FUND

ADDRESS: 595 Cottage St., N.E., Salem, OR 97310

PHONE NO. (503) 373-1200

CONTACT OFFICER: Mark D. Huston; **TITLE:** Mngr

DESCRIPTION OF PROGRAM: Funds to small business for building, equipment and working capital.

Organization asset range: $500,000 **to $**2,000,000

Range of investment/grant per borrower/grantee: $10,000 **to $**250,000

Type of financing: □Grants; ■Loans; □Loan with equity participations or convertibility; □Loan Guarantees; □Equity; □Leases; □Sale-leaseback; Other: Leveraged — Guarantees from other sources.

Security position: May be subordinated

Type of collateral: Current Assets (Inventory, Accounts Receivable), Stocks & Bonds, Cash value of life insurance, Equipment, Real Estate, Guarantees

Term of financing: Maximum: 25 **years; Minimum:** 3 **years**

Industry preference (in order of priority, if any): Manufacturing and Processing, no retail. Under 50 employees, rural.

Borrower characteristics desired-required:

Min. number of years in business:

Min. annual sales: $

Min. net worth: $

Min. annual cash flow:

Min. annual net income:

Other requirements:

Estimated $ available for investment annually: $

Annual interest rate for 1985: Max.: 11.5%; **Min.:** 9.5% **Ave.:** 10.0%

Special conditions, if any:

STATE OF: OREGON

NAME OF ORGANIZATION: OREGON ECONOMIC DEVELOPMENT DEPT.

ADDRESS: 595 Cottage Street N.E., Salem, OR 97310

PHONE NO. (503) 373-1200

CONTACT OFFICER: Mark D. Huston; **TITLE:** Manager, Financial Services

DESCRIPTION OF PROGRAM: Pool industries revenue bonds into one issue. Ability to finance small projects limited state backing.

Organization asset range: $10,000,000 **to $**100,000,000

Range of investment/grant per borrower/grantee: $50,000 **to $**1,000,000

Type of financing: ☐Grants; ■Loans; ☐Loan with equi ty participations or convertibility; ☐Loan Guarantees; ☐Equity; ☐Leases; ☐Sale-leaseback; Other:

Security position: Senority mandatory

Type of collateral: Real Estate, Guarantees

Term of financing: Maximum: 15-20 **years; Minimum:** 5-7 **years**

Industry preference (in order of priority, if any): Agriculture-Related, Communications, Manufacturing & Processing, Natural Resources, Transportation, Utilites, Diversified

Borrower characteristics desired-required:

Min. number of years in business:

Min. annual sales: $

Min. net worth: $

Min. annual cash flow:

Min. annual net income:

Other requirements:

Estimated $ available for investment annually: $20,000,000

Annual interest rate for 1985: Max.: %; Min.: %; Ave.: 13.5%

Special conditions, if any: Fixed rate

STATE OF: PENNSYLVANIA

NAME OF ORGANIZATION: PENNSYLVANIA INDUSTRIAL DEV. AUTHORITY (PIDA)

ADDRESS: 405 Forum Building, Harrisburg, PA 17120

PHONE NO. (717) 787-6245

CONTACT OFFICER: Gerald W. Kapp; **TITLE:** Executive Director

DESCRIPTION OF PROGRAM: A state financing authority designed to create employment by making long-term, low-interest loans to non-profit community industrial development corporation to pay a portion of the cost of land and buildings to be leased or sold to industrial concerns.

Organization asset range: $100,000,000 and up

Range of investment/grant per borrower/grantee: $0 **to $**500,000 or 1,000,000

Type of financing: ☐Grants; ■Loans; ☐Loan with equi ty participations or convertibility; ☐Loan Guarantees; ☐Equity; ☐Leases; ☐Sale-leaseback; Other:

Security position: Normally second mortgage on real property

Type of collateral: Assignment of leases, and installment sale agreements, Real Estate, Guarantees

Term of financing: Maximum: 15 **years; Minimum:** 0 **years**

Industry preference (in order of priority, if any): Manufacturing & Processing, Research & Technology, Industrial (including warehouse & terminal facilities, national and regional headquarters, and/or computer or clerical operation centers), Agribusiness

Borrower characteristics desired-required:

Min. number of years in business:

Min. annual sales: $

Min. net worth: $

Min. annual cash flow:

Min. annual net income:

Other requirements: Networth equal to the project cost and income at least 10% of project cost. Each case is considered on its own merits.

Estimated $ available for investment annually: **$**50 million

Annual interest rate for 1985: Max.: 10.5%; **Min.:** 4.5%; **Ave.:** 5%

Special conditions, if any: The unemployment rate of the area determines the interest rate of the loan. A minimum of one fourth of PIDA's annual resources are targeted to assist advanced technology companies. PIDA also emphasizes loans for small businesses employing 50 or fewer workers, and for businesses located in counties of high unemployment.

STATE OF: PENNSYLVANIA

NAME OF ORGANIZATION: PENNSYLVANIA ENERGY DEVELOPMENT AUTHORITY

ADDRESS: 462 Forum Building, Harrisburg, PA 17120

PHONE NO. (717) 787-6554

CONTACT OFFICER: William A. Roth, P.E.; **TITLE:** Executive Director

DESCRIPTION OF PROGRAM: Provide loans, loan guarantees, and grants to finance or fund commercial energy development or conservation projects, energy research, feasibility studies and demonstrations of commercially unproven technologies.

Organization asset range: $1,000,000 **to $**10,000,000
Note : Authority became operational in June, 1984. No historical data is available. Program availability announcements are expected in December 1984. Information on Items B-K not available at this time.

Range of investment/grant per borrower/grantee:

Type of financing: ☐Grants; ☐Loans; ☐Loan with equity participations or convertibility; ☐Loan Guarantees; ☐Equity; ☐Leases; ☐Sale-leaseback; Other:

Security position:

Type of collateral:

Term of financing: Maximum: 0 **years; Minimum:** 0 **years**

Industry preference (in order of priority, if any):

Borrower characteristics desired-required:

Min. number of years in business:

Min. annual sales: $

Min. net worth: $

Min. annual cash flow:

Min. annual net income:

Other requirements:

Estimated $ available for investment annually:
$

Annual interest rate for 1985: Max.: %; Min.: %; Ave.: %;

Special conditions, if any:

STATE OF: PENNSYLVANIA

NAME OF ORGANIZATION: BUSINESS INFRASTRUCTURE DEVELOPMENT PROGRAM

ADDRESS: Bureau of Appalachian Development and State Grants, 467 Forum Building, Harrisburg, PA 17120

PHONE NO. (717) 787-7120

CONTACT OFFICER: Thomas Stojek; **TITLE:** Director

DESCRIPTION OF PROGRAM: The BID program provides loans or grants for infrastructure improvements, such as road repair and construction, water and sewer improvements, etc., needed for expansion or location of business and industry.

Organization asset range: $10,000,000 to $100,000,000

Range of investment/grant per borrower/grantee: The matching private funds depends upon the amount of grant/loan funds requested.

Type of financing: ☐Grants; ☐Loans; ☐Loan with equity participations or convertibility; ☐Loan Guarantees; ☐Equity; ☐Leases; ☐Sale-leaseback; Other: Private investment increases as the amount of state investment increases. Example: 1) State $500,000; Private 2-1. 2) State $500,000 - $1,000,000; Private 3-1.

Security position: Senior or subordinated

Type of collateral: Funds loaned are secured by lien positions on the applicant's collateral at the highest level of priority the Department determines to accommodate the project.

Term of financing: Maximum: years; Minimum: years; Variable loans will be a maximum of ten years or the estimated useful life of the equipment or property as established by the IRS.

Industry preference (in order of priority, if any): Agriculture-Related, Manufacturing & Processing, Research & Technology, Commercial and retail enterprises are excluded

Borrower characteristics desired-required: Varies

Min. number of years in business:

Min. annual sales: $

Min. net worth: $

Min. annual cash flow:

Min. annual net income:

Other requirements:

Estimated $ available for investment annually: $16 million

Annual interest rate for 1985: Max.: %; Min.: %; Ave.: %;

Special conditions, if any: The funding for the program is included as part of a $190 million bond issue approved in April 1984 by the voters of PA for economic development purposes.

STATE OF: PENNSYLVANIA

NAME OF ORGANIZATION: INDUSTRIAL REVENUE BOND AND MORTGAGE PROGRAM

ADDRESS: 405 Forum Building, Harrisburg, PA 17120

PHONE NO. (717) 783-1108

CONTACT OFFICER: Shirley J. Dunaway; **TITLE:** Administrator, Revenue Bond and Mortgage Program

DESCRIPTION OF PROGRAM: The low interest Industrial Revenue Bond and Mortgage Program, with bonds issued by local industrial development authorities and mortgage money obtained from local financial institutions, finances land, buildings and equipment for qualified commercial, manufacturing and research and development enterprises.

Organization asset range:

Range of investment/grant per borrower/grantee: $0 to $10 million capital expenditures (federal law)

Type of financing: ☐Grants; ☐Loans; ☐Loan with equity participations or convertibility; ☐Loan

Guarantees; ☐Equity; ☐Leases; ☐Sale-leaseback; Other: Industrial Revenue Bonds

Security position: Security position decided by lender (usually a bank)

Type of collateral: Equipment, Real Estate, Guarantees, Any items required by lender

Term of financing: Maximum: years; Minimum: years; Decided by lender

Industry preference (in order of priority, if any): Maunfacturing & Processing, Research & Technology, All of the above industries may qualify for Industrial Development bond financing and would be given consideration

Borrower characteristics desired-required:

Min. number of years in business:

Min. annual sales: $

Min. net worth: $

Min. annual cash flow:

Min. annual net income:

Other requirements:

Estimated $ available for investment annually: $

Annual interest rate for 1985: Will be set by private sector lender.

Special conditions, if any:

STATE OF: PENNSYLVANIA

NAME OF ORGANIZATION: SMALL BUSINESS RESEARCH SEED GRANTS

ADDRESS: 463 Forum Building, Harrisburg, PA 17120

PHONE NO. (717) 787-4147

CONTACT OFFICER: F. Roger Tellefsen; **TITLE:** Executive Director

DESCRIPTION OF PROGRAM: The seed grant program provides grants for research and development programs to small businesses employing 250 or fewer employees. Preference is given to firms with 50 or fewer employees.

Organization asset range:

Range of investment/grant per borrower/grantee: $0 to $35,000

Type of financing: ■Grants; ☐Loans; ☐Loan with equity participations or convertibility; ☐Loan Guarantees; ☐Equity; ☐Leases; ☐Sale-leaseback; Other:

Security position:

Type of collateral:

Term of financing: Maximum: years; Minimum: years

Industry preference (in order of priority, if any):

Borrower characteristics desired-required:

Min. number of years in business:

Min. annual sales: $

Min. net worth: $

Min. annual cash flow:

Min. annual net income:

Other requirements:

Estimated $ available for investment annually: $

Annual interest rate for 1985: Max.: %; Min.: %; Ave.: %;

Special conditions, if any: Company must be 150 or fewer employees in size.

STATE OF: PENNSYLVANIA

NAME OF ORGANIZATION: BEN FRANKLIN PARTNERSHIP CHALLENGE GRANT PROGRAM FOR TECHNOLOGICAL INNOVATION

ADDRESS: 463 Forum Building, Harrisburg, PA 17120

PHONE NO. (717) 787-4147

CONTACT OFFICER: F. Roger Tellefsen; **TITLE:** Executive Director

DESCRIPTION OF PROGRAM: The challenge grant program operates through four advanced technology centers located throughout the state. Matching grants are available to foster effective partnerships amoung higher education institutions and the private sector to strengthen the technological postition of PA,s industries & to encourage growth, development & nurturing of new enterprises on the leading edge of tech. innovation.

Organization asset range:

Range of investment/grant per borrower/grantee:

Type of financing: ■Grants; □Loans; □Loan with equity participations or convertibility; □Loan Guarantees; □Equity; □Leases; □Sale-leaseback; Other:

Security position:

Type of collateral:

Term of financing: Maximum: years; Minimum: years

Industry preference (in order of priority, if any): Research & Technology

Borrower characteristics desired-required:

Min. number of years in business:

Min. annual sales: $

Min. net worth: $

Min. annual cash flow:

Min. annual net income:

Other requirements:

Estimated $ available for investment annually: $

Annual interest rate for 1985: Max.: %; Min.: %;Ave.: %

Special conditions, if any: For each $1 of state funding a private company must contribute $3

STATE OF: PENNSYLVANIA

NAME OF ORGANIZATION: PENNSYLVANIA CAPITAL LOAN FUND (PCLF)

ADDRESS: 405 Forum Building, Harrisburg, PA 17120

PHONE NO. (717) 783-1786

CONTACT OFFICER: Norman L. Oakes; **TITLE:** Development Finance Specialist

DESCRIPTION OF PROGRAM: The PCLF is a revolving loan fund, both federally (ARC & EDA) and state funded, which makes small loans up to $50,000 or 20% of a project to industrial, manufacturing, or export service businesses. One job must be created for each $15,000.00 loaned. Funds may be used for L & B, M & E, and WC.

Organization asset range: $10,000,000 **to $**100,000,000
$6.6 million ARC; $1.0 million EDA; $5.0 state total $12.6 million

Range of investment/grant per borrower/grantee: $0 to $50,000.00

Type of financing: □Grants; ■Loans; □Loan with equity participations or convertibility; □Loan Guarantees; □Equity; □Leases; □Sale-leaseback; Other:

Security position: Senior or subordinated

Type of collateral: Current Assets (Inventory, Accounts Receivable), Stocks & Bonds, Cash value of life insurance, Equipment, Real Estate, Guarantees

Term of financing: Maximum: 10-15 **years; Minimum:** 3-5 **years**

Industry preference (in order of priority, if any): Maunfacturing & Processing, Services - Export from PA

Borrower characteristics desired-required:

Min. number of years in business:

Min. annual sales: $

Min. net worth: $

Min. annual cash flow:

Min. annual net income:

Other requirements: We require private sector commercial participation; equity injection if at all possible; PCLF will do $50,000 or 20% of project, whichever is less.

Estimated $ available for investment annually: $3 million

Annual interest rate for 1985: Max.: 7.5%; **Min.:** 6%; **Ave.:** 6.5%;

Special conditions, if any:

STATE OF: PENNSYLVANIA

NAME OF ORGANIZATION: SMALL BUSINESS INCUBATORS

ADDRESS: 463 Forum Building, Harrisburg, PA 17120

PHONE NO. (717) 787-4147

CONTACT OFFICER: F. Roger Tellefsen; **TITLE:** Executive Director

DESCRIPTION OF PROGRAM: Loans for the creation and support of small business incubators including building acquisition and renovation costs, operating costs, and management assistance are provided through the Ben Franklin Partnership.

Organization asset range: $1,000,000 **to $**10,000,000

Range of investment/grant per borrower/grantee: $650,000 or 50% of total eligible costs, whichever is less

Type of financing: ☐Grants; ■Loans; ■Loan with equity participations or convertibility; ☐Loan Guarantees; ☐Equity; ☐Leases; ☐Sale-leaseback; Other:

Security position: Ordinarily the Board will accept a second lien position

Type of collateral:

Term of financing: Maximum: years; Minimum: years; Loans may be for 10 years or the useful life of the property as defined in Section 168 (f) (12) of the Internal Revenue Code, but in no case will the term of the loan exceed 120% of the average asset life.

Industry preference (in order of priority, if any): Manufacturing & Processing, Incubator tenants must be engaged in manufacturing or product development. Retail and Wholesale operations are not eligible for incubator tenancy.

Borrower characteristics desired-required:

Min. number of years in business:

Min. annual sales: $

Min. net worth: $

Min. annual cash flow:

Min. annual net income:

Other requirements:

Estimated $ available for investment annually: $5 million

Annual interest rate for 1985: Max.: %; Min.: %; Ave.: %;

Special conditions, if any: Interest rates will be tied to the interest rates on the industrial development bonds used to fund this program.

STATE OF: PENNSYLVANIA

NAME OF ORGANIZATION: EMPLOYEE OWNERSHIP ASSISTANCE PROGRAM

ADDRESS: 405 Forum Building, Harrisburg, PA 17120

PHONE NO. (717) 787-1909

CONTACT OFFICER: Norman L. Oakes; **TITLE:** Development Finance Specialist

DESCRIPTION OF PROGRAM: The Employee Ownership Assistance Program assists community and employee groups attempting to prevent plant shut-downs by providing funds for both (a) feasibility studies (technical assistance) and (b) financing of actual takeovers (financial assistance).

Organization asset range: $1,000,000 **to $**10,000,000
Note: the program first received funding in FY 1984-85. No historical data is available.

Range of investment/grant per borrower/grantee:
(a) Technical assistance - $100,000 or 50% of eligible project costs, whichever is less. (b) Financial assistance - $1.5 million or 25% of eligible project costs, whichever is less.

Type of financing: ☐Grants; ☐Loans; ■Loan with equity participations or convertibility; ☐Loan Guarantees; ☐Equity; ☐Leases; ☐Sale-leaseback; Other:

Security position: Senior or subordinated

Type of collateral: Current Assets (Inventory, Accounts Receivable), Equipment, Real Estate, Guarantees

Term of financing: Maximum: 15-20 **years; Minimum:** 3-5 **years**

Industry preference (in order of priority, if any): (a) industrial or commercial business (b) industrial, manufacturing, agricultural - Preference is given to applicants with estimates of at least 50 jobs created or preserved and/or the firm employs a significant number of employees or represents a significant portion of employment in the community.

Borrower characteristics desired-required:

Min. number of years in business:

Min. annual sales: $

Min. net worth: $

Min. annual cash flow:

Min. annual net income:

Other requirements:

Estimated $ available for investment annually:
$(a) $1 million (b)$4 million

Annual interest rate for 1985: Max.: %; Min.: %; Ave.: %;
Interest rates will be equivalent to bond rates

Special conditions, if any: (b) One job will be created or preserved for every $15,000 in loan proceeds over the next three years.

STATE OF: PENNSYLVANIA

NAME OF ORGANIZATION: PENNSYLVANIA MINORITY BUSINESS DEVELOPMENT AUTHORITY (PMBDA)

ADDRESS: 486 Forum Building, Harrisburg, PA 17120

PHONE NO. (717) 783-1127

CONTACT OFFICER: William F. Peterson; **TITLE:** Executive Director

DESCRIPTION OF PROGRAM: PMBDA provides long-term, low-interest loans to assist in the start-up or expansion of minority owned businesses. Loan recipients must belong to ethnic or minority groups or other groups recognized as disadvantaged. Loans are available primarily for the purpose of providing working capital, purchasing machinery and/or equipment and where such a need is determined by the Board, to defray the costs of acquiring land and buildings or the cost or renovating the same. An additionsl $1.7 million is available in FY 1984-85 as a part of $190 million economic development bond issue to be used as (a) a supplement to the loan program (b) performance bond guarantees to minority businesses on state contract and (c) working capital to be used by minority businesses on state contracts.

Organization asset range: $1,000,000 **to $**10,000,000

Range of investment/grant per borrower/grantee: $100,000 or $200,000 if located in: Ent. Dev. Areas; Adv. Tech.; manufacturing or industrial enterprise.

Type of financing: □Grants; ■Loans; ■Loan with equity participations or convertibility; ■Loan Guarantees; □Equity; □Leases; □Sale-leaseback; Other:

Security position: Senior or subordinated

Type of collateral: Current Assets (Inventory, Accounts Receivable), Stocks & Bonds, Cash value of life insurance, Equipment, Real Estate, Guarantees

Term of financing: Maximum: 15-20 **years; Minimum:** 5-7 **years**

Industry preference (in order of priority, if any): Diversified

Borrower characteristics desired-required:

Min. number of years in business:

Min. annual sales: $

Min. net worth: $

Min. annual cash flow:

Min. annual net income:

Other requirements:

Estimated $ available for investment annually: $2,000,000 appropriation

Annual interest rate for 1985: Max.: ½ prime**; Min.:** 4%; **Ave.: %;**

Special conditions, if any: Minority applicants must own at least 51% of the business; corporate borrowers must be at least 51% controlled by minority stockholders. Also, PMBDA requires at least 25% participation by the owner and/or other lending sources, such as banks, venture capital companies, and other financial institutions.

STATE OF: RHODE ISLAND

NAME OF ORGANIZATION: R.I. INDUSTRIAL FACILITIES CORP.

ADDRESS: 7 Jackson Walkway, Providence, R.I. 02903

PHONE NO. (401) 277-2601

CONTACT OFFICER: Virgil A. Nolan, Jr.; **TITLE:** Treasurer

DESCRIPTION OF PROGRAM: Provides financing to new and exsisting industries to construct, acquire or renovate industrial plants and equipment. It provides 100% financing on industrial projects including feasibility studies and other expenses incidental to the acquisition and financing of capital projects.

Organization asset range:

Range of investment/grant per borrower/grantee:

Type of financing:□Grants; □Loans; □Loan with equity participations or convertibility; □Loan Guarantees; □Equity; □Leases; □Sale-leasedback; Other: Industrial Development Revenue Bonds up to $10,000,000, also may issue Industrial Development Revenue Bonds Guaranteed by the R.I. Industrial Authority for amounts from $100,000 up to 5,000,000

Security position:

Type of collateral:

Term of financing: Maximum: 20 and up **years; Minimum:** 7-10 **years**

Industry preference (in order of priority, if any): Manufacturing & Processing, Diversified, Research & Technology, Warehousing and Distribution, Utilities

Borrower characteristics desired-required:

Min. number of years in business:

Min. annual sales: $

Min. net worth: $

Min. annual cash flow:

Min. annual net income:

Other requirements:

Estimated $ available for investment annually: $

Annual interest rate for 1985: Max.: %; Min.: %; Ave.: %;

Special conditions, if any: Financing should directly increase or save jobs in Rhode Island.

STATE OF: RHODE ISLAND

NAME OF ORGANIZATION: R.I. PORT AUTHORITY AND ECONOMIC DEVELOPMENT CORPORATION

ADDRESS: 7 Jackson Walkway, Providence, R.I. 02903

PHONE NO. (401) 277-2601

CONTACT OFFICER: Virgil A. Nolan, Jr.; **TITLE:** Deputy Director, Finance and Administration

DESCRIPTION OF PROGRAM: Provides financing to new and exsisting industries to construct, acquire or renovate industrial plants and equipment. It provides 100% financing on industrial projects including feasibility studies and other expenses incidental to the acquisition and financing of capital projects.

Organization asset range:

Range of investment/grant per borrower/grantee:

Type of financing: ☐Grants; ☐Loans; ☐Loan with equity participations or convertibility; ☐Loan Guarantees; ☐Equity; ☐Leases; ☐Sale-leaseback; Other: Industrial Development Revenue Bonds

Security position:

Type of collateral:

Term of financing: Maximum: years; Minimum: years

Industry preference (in order of priority, if any): Manufacturing & Processing, Diversified, Research & Technology, Warehousing and Distribution,

Borrower characteristics desired-required:

Min. number of years in business:

Min. annual sales: $

Min. net worth: $

Min. annual cash flow:

Min. annual net income:

Other requirements:

Estimated $ available for investment annually: $

Annual interest rate for 1985: Max.: %; Min.: %; Ave.: %;

Special conditions, if any: Financing should directly increase or save jobs in Rhode Island.

STATE OF: RHODE ISLAND

NAME OF ORGANIZATION: R.I. INDUSTRIAL BUILDING AUTHORITY

ADDRESS: 7 Jackson Walkway, Providence, R.I. 02903

PHONE NO. (401) 277-2601

CONTACT OFFICER: James E. Sullivan Jr.; **TITLE:** Manager

DESCRIPTION OF PROGRAM: Debt insurer of mortgages, security agreements and industrial revenue bonds secured by a first lien. Debt proceeds must be used for new construction or rehabilitation of buildings or for new machinery and equipment. Borrower must be a manufacturing or processing entity.

Organization asset range: $10,000,000 **to** $100,000,000

Range of investment/grant per borrower/grantee: $100,000**to** $5,000,000

Type of financing: □Grants; □Loans; □Loan with equity participations or convertibility; ■Loan Guarantees; □Equity; □Leases; □Sale-leaseback; Other:

Security position: Seniority mandatory

Type of collateral: Equipment, Real Estate, Guarantees

Term of financing: Maximum: 20 and up **years; Minimum:** 7-10 **years**

Industry preference (in order of priority, if any): Manufacturing & Processing,

Borrower characteristics desired-required:

Min. number of years in business: 5

Min. annual sales: $500,000

Min. net worth: $100,000

Min. annual cash flow:

Min. annual net income: $35,000

Other requirements:

Estimated $ available for investment annually: $40,000,000

Annual interest rate for 1985: Max.: %; Min.: %; Ave.: %;

Special conditions, if any:

STATE OF: RHODE ISLAND

NAME OF ORGANIZATION: OCEAN STATE BUS. DEV. AUTH, INC.

ADDRESS: 7 Jackson Walkway, Providence, R.I. 02903

PHONE NO. (401) 277-2601

CONTACT OFFICER: Henry A. Violet; **TITLE:** President

DESCRIPTION OF PROGRAM: Assist small businesses in obtaining financing using a variety of federal programs. Administer the SBA 503 program on a statewide basis.

Organization asset range: $0 to $150,000

Range of investment/grant per borrower/grantee: $20,000 **to $**100,000

Type of financing: □Grants; ■Loans; ■Loan with equity participations or convertibility; ■Loan Guarantees; □Equity; □Leases; □Sale-leaseback; Other:

Security position: Senior or subordinated

Type of collateral: Current Assets (Inventory, Accounts Receivable), Equipment, Real Estate, Guarantees

Term of financing: Maximum: 20 and up **years; Minimum:** 10-15 **years**

Industry preference (in order of priority, if any): Manufacturing & Processing, Diversified

Borrower characteristics desired-required:

Min. number of years in business:

Min. annual sales: $

Min. net worth: $

Min. annual cash flow:

Min. annual net income:

Other requirements:

Estimated $ available for investment annually: $

Annual interest rate for 1985: Max.: %; Min.: %; Ave.: %;

Special Conditions, if any: Interest keyed to long term treasury notes and varies. Current rate is 12.5%

STATE OF: RHODE ISLAND

NAME OF ORGANIZATION: R.I. RECREATIONAL BUILDING AUTHORITY

ADDRESS: 7 Jackson Walkway, Providence, R.I. 02903

PHONE NO. (401) 277-2601

CONTACT OFFICER: James E. Sullivan Jr.; **TITLE:** Manager

DESCRIPTION OF PROGRAM: Debt insurer of mortgages, security agreements and industrial revenue bonds secured by a first lien.

Organization asset range: $10,000,000 **to $**100,000,000

Range of investment/grant per borrower/grantee: $100,000 **to $**5,000,000

Type of financing: ☐Grants; ☐Loans; ☐Loan with equity participations or convertibility; ■Loan Guarantees; ☐Equity; ☐Leases; ☐Sale-leaseback; Other:

Security position: Seniority mandatory

Type of collateral: Equipment, Real Estate, Guarantees

Term of financing: Maximum: 20 and up **years; Minimum:** 7-10 **years**

Industry preference (in order of priority, if any): Hotels, Motels & Restaurants, Recreation & Amusements

Borrower characteristics desired-required:

Min. number of years in business: 5

Min. annual sales: $500,000

Min. net worth: $100,000

Min. annual cash flow:

Min. annual net income: $35,000

Other requirements:

Estimated $ available for investment annually: $15,000,000

Annual interest rate for 1985: Max.: %; Min.: %; Ave.: %;

Special conditions, if any:

STATE OF: SOUTH CAROLINA

NAME OF ORGANIZATION: STATE DEVELOPMENT BOARD

ADDRESS: P.O. Box 927, Columbia, SC 29202

PHONE NO. (803) 758-3145

CONTACT OFFICER: Robert E. Leak; **TITLE:** Director

DESCRIPTION OF PROGRAM: Industrial revenue bonds are obligations issued by the counties or municipalities of the state for any authorized project. Authorized projects include manufacturing, warehousing & distribution, and "research" in connection with any purpose of developing new products or new processes or improving exisiting products or processes.

Organization asset range;

Range of investment/grant per borrower/grantee:

Type of financing: ☐Grants; ☐Loans; ☐Loan with equity participations or convertibility; ☐Loan Guarantees; ☐Equity; ☐Leases; ☐Sale-leaseback; Other: Title may be held by company during the retirement of the bonds

Security position:

Type of collateral: Equipment, Real Estate, Guarantees

Term of financing: Maximum: 20 and up **years; Minimum: years**

Industry preference (in order of priority, if any): Manufacturing & Processing, Agriculture-Related, Research & Technology, Diversified.

Borrower characteristics desired-required:

Min. number of years in business:

Min. annual sales: $

Min. net worth: $

Min. annual cash flow:

Min. annual net income: $

Other requirements:

Estimated $ available for investment annually: **$**

Annual interest rate for 1985: Max.: %; Min.: %; Ave. %;

Special conditions, if any: Dependent upon financial status of company. Rate of interest is typically about ⅔ of prime.

STATE OF: SOUTH CAROLINA

NAME OF ORGANIZATION: BUSINESS DEVELOPMENT CORPORATION OF SOUTH CAROLINA

ADDRESS: P.O. Box 11606 Columbia, SC 29211

PHONE NO. (803) 799-9825

CONTACT OFFICER: William V. Harvey; **TITLE:** Executive Vice President

DESCRIPTION OF PROGRAM: Private corporation organized to attract new industry and create new jobs for the state of South Carolina. Stockholders are banks, insurance companies and S & L's.

Organization asset range; $1,000,000 **to $**10,000,00

Range of investment/grant per borrower/grantee: $25,000 **to $**600,000

Type of financing: ☐Grants; ■Loans; ■Loan with equity participations or convertibility; ■Loan Guarantees; ☐Equity; ☐Leases; ☐Sale-leaseback; Other:

Security position: Senior or subordinated

Type of collateral: Current Assets (Inventory, Accounts Receivable), Stocks & Bonds, Cash value of life insurance, Equipment, Real Estate, Guarantees

Term of financing: Maximum: 7-10 **years; Minimum:** 3-5 **years**

Industry preference (in order of priority, if any): No preference — All businesses acceptable

Borrower characteristics desired-required:

Min. number of years in business:

Min. annual sales: $

Min. net worth: $

Min. annual cash flow:

Min. annual net income: $

Other requirements:

Estimated $ available for investment annually: **$**

Annual interest rate for 1985: Max.: %; Min.: %; Ave.: %;

Special conditions, if any: Interest rate in excess of current prime.

STATE OF: SOUTH CAROLINA

NAME OF ORGANIZATION: SOUTH CAROLINA JOBS—ECONOMIC DEVELOPMENT AUTHORITY

ADDRESS: 1203 Gervais Street, Columbia, South Carolina 29201

PHONE NO. (803) 758-2094

CONTACT OFFICER: Joseph E. Camp; **TITLE:** Chief Executive Officer

DESCRIPTION OF PROGRAM: The South Carloina Jobs-Economic Development Authority is an agency of South Carolina State Government created by the legislature and signed into law by the Governor on June 15, 1983.

Organization asset range; $1,000,000 **to $**10,000,00

Range of investment/grant per borrower/grantee: $0 **to $**250,000

Type of financing: ☐Grants; ■Loans; ☐Loan with equity participations or convertibility; ■Loan Guarantees; ☐Equity; ☐Leases; ☐Sale-leaseback; Other:

Security position: Senior or subordinated

Type of collateral: Current Assets (Inventory, Accounts Receivable), Stocks & Bonds, Cash value of life insurance, Equipment, Real Estate, Guarantees

Term of financing: Maximum: 10-15 **years; Minimum: years**

Industry preference (in order of priority, if any): Manufacturing & Processing, Services, Diversified, Board of Directors policy mandates that loans cannot be made to retail or food establishments.

Borrower characteristics desired-required:

Min. number of years in business:

Min. annual sales: $

Min. net worth: $

Min. annual cash flow:

Min. annual net income: $

Other requirements:

Estimated $ available for investment annually: $6,000,000.00

Annual interest rate for 1985: Max.: %; Min.: %; Ave.: %;

Special conditions, if any: Interest rates will be 85% of the average prime as established by the major South Carolina Banks, but not less than 7.5%. Rates are established at the time of commitment and will remain fixed for the term of the loan.

STATE OF: SOUTH DAKOTA

NAME OF ORGANIZATION: DEPARTMENT OF STATE DEVELOPMENT

ADDRESS: Box 6000, Pierre, SD 57501

PHONE NO. (605) 773-5032

CONTACT OFFICER: Bonnie L. Untereiner; **TITLE:** Financial Analyst

DESCRIPTION OF PROGRAM: Tax-Free Bonds are issued by city and county governments for the financing of fixed assets.

Organization asset range;

Range of investment/grant per borrower/grantee: $0 **to $**40,000,000

Type of financing: ☐Grants; ■Loans; ☐Loan with equity participations or convertibility; ☐Loan Guarantees; ☐Equity; ■Leases; ☐Sale-leaseback; Other: Lease-Purchase

Security position: Seniority mandatory

Type of collateral: Equipment, Real Estate, Guarantees

Term of financing: Maximum: 20 and up **years; Minimum:** 10-15 **years**

Industry preference (in order of priority, if any): Manufacturing & Processing, Diversified, Agriculture-Related, Finance & Insurance, All industries encouraged.

Borrower characteristics desired-required:

Min. number of years in business:

Min. annual sales: $

Min. net worth: $

Min. annual cash flow:

Min. annual net income: $

Other requirements: Credit decisions based on the determination of the buyers of bonds.

Estimated $ available for investment annually: $200 million

Annual interest rate for 1985: Max.: 10.5%; **Min.:** 7%; **Ave.:** 9.75%;

Special conditions, if any: Interest rates determined by the cedit of the borrower.

STATE OF: SOUTH DAKOTA

NAME OF ORGANIZATION: SOUTH DAKOTA DEVELOPMENT CORPORATION

ADDRESS: Box 6000, Pierre, SD 57501

PHONE NO. (605) 773-5032

CONTACT OFFICER: Bonnie L. Untereiner; **TITLE:** Manager

DESCRIPTION OF PROGRAM: Statewide SBA 503 Certified Development Company providing financing for fixed assets of for-profit small business and projects.

Organization asset range;

Range of investment/grant per borrower/grantee: $50,000 **to** $500,000

Type of financing: ☐Grants; ■Loans; ☐Loan with equity participations or convertibility; ☐Loan Guarantees; ☐Equity; ☐Leases; ☐Sale-leaseback; Other: Provide up to 40% of project cost.

Security position: Senior or subordinated generally subordinated.

Type of collateral: Equipment, Real Estate, Guarantees

Term of financing: Maximum: 20 and up **years; Minimum:** 15-10 **years**

Industry preference (in order of priority, if any): Manufacturing & Processing, Agriculture-Related, Retailing, Wholesaling & Distribution, Services, For profit-owner user business.

Borrower characteristics desired-required:

Min. number of years in business:

Min. annual sales: $

Min. net worth:

Min. annual cash flow:

Min. annual net income:

Other requirements:

Estimated $ available for investment annually: $

Annual interest rate for 1985: Max.: 13%; **Min.:** 11%; **Ave.:** 12.5%;

Special conditions, if any: Current Treasury Bond Rate plus ¾%

STATE OF: TEXAS

NAME OF ORGANIZATION: TEXAS ECONOMIC DEVELOPMENT COMMISSION

ADDRESS: 410 East 5th Street, Austin, Texas 78701

PHONE NO. (512) 472-5059

CONTACT OFFICER: John Kirkley; **TITLE:** Business Development Consultant

DESCRIPTION OF PROGRAM: Rural Loan Program: A State Revolving Loan Fund Channeled to Approved Texas Non Porfit Corp. -(Econ Dev. Foundations) and then passed on to the borrower/.private business. The fund is Limited up to 40% of the total project costs and only to approved rural communities.

Organization asset range;

Range of investment/grant per borrower/grantee:

Type of financing: ☐Grants; ■Loans; ☐Loan with equity participations or convertibility; ☐Loan Guarantees; ☐Equity; ☐Leases; ☐Sale-leaseback; Other:

Security Position: Senior or subordinated
The security position is dictated by the amount of funds made available in proportion to the other lenders

Type of collateral: Equipment, Real Estate, Fixed Assets only.

Term of financing: Maximum: 20 **years; Minimum:** 0-1 **years**

Industry preference (in order of priority, if any):
Manufacturing & Processing, Manufacturing and Industrial Projects

Borrower characteristics desired-required:

Min. number of years in business:

Min. annual sales: $

Min. net worth: $

Min. annual cash flow:

Min. annual net income: $

Other requirements: (Feasible) ability to repay debt., and the creation of jobs; and minimum of 10% injection.

Estimated $ available for investment annually:
not to exceed balance of Revenue Fund

Annual interest rate for 1985: Max.: %; Min.: %; Ave.: %;

Special conditions, if any: 75% of Prime Rate (New York) for a 3 year period, and to be renegotiated there after.

STATE OF: TEXAS

NAME OF ORGANIZATION: TEXAS ECONOMIC DEVELOPMENT COMMISSION

ADDRESS: 410 East 5th Street, Austin, Texas 78701

PHONE NO. (512) 472-5059

CONTACT OFFICER: John Kirkley; **TITLE:** Business Development Consultant

DESCRIPTION OF PROGRAM: (TX Small Bus. Ind. Dev. Corp.) A statewide issuer of industrial revenue bonds for small business only. Both the state and federal defination are accepted for small businesses. The program has a dollar limitation of $750,000 including bond issuance costs.

Organization asset range:

Range of investment/grant per borrower/grantee: $200,000 **to $**750,000

Type of financing: ☐Grants; ☐Loans; ☐Loan with equity participations or convertibility; ☐Loan Guarantees; ☐Equity; ☐Leases; ☐Sale-leaseback; Other: Fixed assets - (Industrial Revenue Bonds)

Security position: Seniority mandatory

Type of collateral: Equipment, Real Estate, Fixed Assets and eligible project costs approved by federal status concerning I.R.B.'s.

Term of financing: Maximum: 20 max **years; Minimum:** 0-1 **years**

Industry preference (in order of priority, if any):
Manufacturing & Processing, Industrial (Commercial with certain provisions)

Borrower characteristics desired-required:

Min. number of years in business: new venturer permissible

Min. annual sales:

Min. net worth: $

Min. annual cash flow:

Min. annual net income:$

Other requirements: (Feasible) ability to repay debt service, an annual sales do not exceed small business guidelines for definition of small businesses.

Estimated $ available for investment annually: not to exceed state allocation for I.R.Bs

Annual interest rate for 1985: Max.: %; Min.: %; Ave.: %;

Special conditions, if any: Interest rate will be at a percentage of the Prime Rate.

STATE OF: UTAH

NAME OF ORGANIZATION: DESERET CERTIFIED DEVELOPMENT COMPANY

ADDRESS: 4885 South 900 East, Salt Lake City, Utah 84117

PHONE NO. (801) 266-0443

CONTACT OFFICER: Scott G. Davis; **TITLE:** Executive Director

DESCRIPTION OF PROGRAM: Certified by SBA for "502" and "503" loans statewide. Orginated subordinated financing for long-term fixed assets (owner user only).

Organization asset range; $0 **to $**150,000

Range of investment/grant per borrower/grantee: $100,000 **to $**2 million

Type of financing: ☐Grants; ■Loans; ☐Loan with equity participations or convertibility; ■Loan Guarantees; ☐Equity; ☐Leases; ☐Sale-leaseback; Other:

Security position: Senior or subordinated

Type of collateral: Equipment, Real Estate, Guarantees

Term of financing: Maximum: 20 and up **years; Minimum:** 10-15 **years**

Industry preference (in order of priority, if any): Manufacturing & Processing, Research & Technology, Retailing, Wholesaling & Distribution, Services, Hotels, Motels & Restaurants, Diversified

Borrower characteristics desired-required:

Min. number of years in business: 3

Min. annual sales: $

Min. net worth: $

Min. annual cash flow: Sufficient to meet projected debt service

Min. annual net income: $

Other requirements: Business must have net worth of less that $6 million and profits after-taxes of less than $2 million.

Estimated $ available for investment annually: $

Annual interest rate for 1985: Max.: 14%; **Min.:** 11%; **Ave.:** 13%;

Special conditions, if any:

STATE OF: UTAH

NAME OF ORGANIZATION: UTAH DIVISION OF ECONOMIC DEVELOPMENT

ADDRESS: 6150 State Office Bldg., Salt Lake City, UT 84114

PHONE NO. (801) 533-5325

CONTACT OFFICER: Evelyn Lee; **TITLE:** Director

DESCRIPTION OF PROGRAM: Personal Income Tax Credit for up to 25% of cash contributions as a partner in a qualifying R & D partnership.

Organization asset range;

Range of investment/grant per borrower/grantee:

Type of financing: ☐Grants; ☐Loans; ☐Loan with equity participations or convertibility; ☐Loan Guarantees; ☐Equity; ☐Leases; ☐Sale-leaseback; Other: Tax credit

Security position:

Type of collateral:

Term of financing: Maximum: years; Minimum: years

Industry preference (in order of priority, if any): Research & Technology, R & D Partnerships

Borrower characteristics desired-required:

Min. number of years in business:

Min. annual sales: $

Min. net worth: $

Min. annual cash flow:

Min. annual net income: $

Other requirements:

Estimated $ available for investment annually: **$**

Annual interest rate for 1985: Max.: %; Min.: %; Ave.:%;

Special conditions, if any: Must be organized under laws of state of Utah, securities must be filed with state Division of Securities, must be technology based business, must be a small business concern per federal Small Business Innovation Development Act of 1982

STATE OF: UTAH

NAME OF ORGANIZATION: UTAH DIVISION OF ECONOMIC DEVELOPMENT

ADDRESS: 6150 State Office Bldg., Salt Lake City, UT 84114

PHONE NO. (801) 533-5325

CONTACT OFFICER: Evelyn Lee; **TITLE:** Director

DESCRIPTION OF PROGRAM: Industrial Development Revenue Bonds.

Organization asset range;

Range of investment/grant per borrower/grantee: **$**500,000 **to $**10 million

Type of financing: ☐Grants; ☐Loans; ☐Loan with equity participations or convertibility; ☐Loan Guarantees; ☐Equity; ☐Leases; ☐Sale-leaseback; Other: City or county-issued revenue bonds.

Security position: Seniority mandatory

Type of collateral: Equipment, Real Estate

Term of financing: Maximum: 20 and up **years; Minimum:** 5-7 **years**

Industry preference (in order of priority, if any): Manufacturing & Processing, Research & Technology, Services, Natural Resources

Borrower characteristics desired-required:

Min. number of years in business:

Min, annual sales: $

Min. net worth: $

Min. annual cash flow:

Min. annual net income: $

Other requirements: Varies

Estimated $ available for investment annually: **$**234 million

Annual interest rate for 1985: Varies

Special conditions, if any:

STATE OF: VIRGINIA

NAME OF ORGANIZATION: VIRGINIA SMALL BUSINESS FINANCING AUTHORITY

ADDRESS: 1000 Washingtion Bldg. Richmond VA 23219

PHONE NO. (804) 786-3791

CONTACT OFFICER: Nic Walker; **TITLE:** Executive Director

DESCRIPTION OF PROGRAM: See Attached Brochure

Organization asset range; $100,000,000 and up

Range of investment/grant per borrower/grantee: $0 **to $**10 million

Type of financing: ☐Grants; ☐Loans; ☐Loan with equity participations or convertibility; ■Loan Guarantees; ☐Equity; ☐Leases; ☐Sale-leaseback; Other: Industrial Development Bonds (Tax-exempt)

Security position: Currently only IDB program in effect. Other programs to be developed in 1985

Type of collateral:

Term of financing: Maximum: years; Minimum: years

Industry preference (in order of priority, if any): Diversified; The Authority's primary concern is providing access for small businesses to capital resources, independent of business type.

Borrower characteristics desired-required:

Min. number of years in business:

Min. annual sales: $

Min. net worth: $

Min. annual cash flow:

Min. annual net income: $

Other requirements:

Estimated $ available for investment annually: $400,000 reserve fund

Annual interest rate for 1985: Max.: %; Min.: %; Ave.: %;

Special conditions, if any: Authority will be developing certian lending paramiters for working capital loan quarentee fund and taxable bond financing program to enhance SBA 7a guaranteed loans.

STATE OF: VIRGINIA

NAME OF ORGANIZATION: URBAN ENTERPRISE ZONE PROGRAM

ADDRESS: VA DPT of Housing and Community Development

PHONE NO. ( ) -

CONTACT OFFICER: ; **TITLE:**

DESCRIPTION OF PROGRAM: Six zones have been designated in VA for a period of 20 years. These are in Norfolk/Portsmouth, Newport News, Roanoke, Lynchburg, Danville and Saltville. Qualified businesses locating in zones will be eligible to receive state tax incentives for a period of up to five years.

Organization asset range;

Range of investment/grant per borrower/grantee:

Type of financing: ☐Grants; ☐Loans; ☐Loan with equity participations or convertibility; ☐Loan Guarantees; ☐Equity; ☐Leases; ☐Sale-leaseback; Other:

Security position:

Type of collateral:

Term of financing: Maximum: years; Minimum: years

Industry preference (in order of priority, if any):

Borrower characteristics desired-required:

Min. number of years in business:

Min. annual sales: $

Min. net worth: $

Min. annual cash flow:

Min. annual net income: $

Other requirements:

Estimated $ available for investment annually: $

Annual interest rate for 1985: Max.: %; Min.: %; Ave.: %;

Special conditions, if any:

STATE OF: WASHINGTON

NAME OF ORGANIZATION: COMMUNITY ECONOMIC REVITALIZATION BOARD

ADDRESS: c/o Dept. of Commerce & Economic Development, 101 General Admin. Bldg. Olympia, WA 98504 (AX-13)

PHONE NO. (206) 753-3065

CONTACT OFFICER: Beth J. Davis; **TITLE:** Administrator

DESCRIPTION OF PROGRAM: A loan/grant funding assistance program to local governments for public facilities construction to facilitate economic development activity and job creation in the private sector. Also functions as a statewide issuing authority for industrial revenue bonds with ability to issue both single (under certain circumstances) and umbrella/composite issues.

Organization asset range; $1,000,000 **to $**10,000,000

Range of investment/grant per borrower/grantee: $46,000 **to $**3.1 million

Type of financing: ■Grants; ■Loans; □Loan with equity participations or convertibility; □Loan Guarantees; □Equity; □Leases; □Sale-leaseback; Other: Loan/grant combination

Security position: Senior or subordinated, Unsecured, usually subordinated

Type of collateral: local government borrowers; either general obligation (backed by general taxes, ect.) or revenue-type obligations (backed by revenues generated by project)

Term of financing: Maximum: 15-20 **years; Minimum:** 0-1 **years**

Industry preference (in order of priority, if any): Manufacturing & Processing, Wholesaling & Distribution, others may be allowed if a significant portion of the revenues are generated by the project will be from out-of-state

Borrower characteristics desired-required:

Min. number of years in business:

Min. annual sales: $

Min. net worth: $

Min. annual cash flow:

Min. annual net income: $

Other requirements:

Estimated $ available for investment annually: $10 million dependent on legislative action/budget approval, ect.

Annual interest rate for 1985: Max.: 10%; **Min.: %; Ave.:** 7%;

Special conditions, if any: Compliance with applicable permits; demonstration of convincing evidence that a specific private development will occur if the project is funded; others as might be required for each individual project

STATE OF: WASHINGTON

NAME OF ORGANIZATION: INDUSTRIAL REVENUE BOND PROGRAM

ADDRESS: c/o Dept. of Commerce & Economic Development 101 General Admin. Bldg. Olympia, WA 98504 (AX-13)

PHONE NO. (206) 753-3065

CONTACT OFFICER: Beth J. Davis; **TITLE:** Administrator, Economic Development Assistance

DESCRIPTION OF PROGRAM: Industrial Revenue Bond Program

Organization asset range;

Range of investment/grant per borrower/grantee:

Type of financing: ☐Grants; ☐Loans; ☐Loan with equity participations or convertibility; ☐Loan Guarantees; ☐Equity; ☐Leases; ☐Sale-leaseback; Other: IRB tax-exempt financings

Security position: Varies; determined by parties to transactions

Type of collateral: Varies

Term of financing: Maximum: years; Minimum: years

Industry preference (in order of priority, if any): Manufacturing & Processing, Research & Technology, Retailing, Wholesaling & Distribution Transportation, Utilities, pollution control, solid waste disposal, energy facilities, industrial parks

Borrower characteristics desired-required:

Min. number of years in business:

Min. annual sales: $

Min. net worth: $

Min. annual cash flow:

Min. annual net income: $

Other requirements: Varies; determined by parties to transactions

Estimated $ available for investment annually: $

Annual interest rate for 1985: Max.: %; Min.: %; Ave.: %;

Special conditions, if any: Subject to volume allocation under The Federal Deficit Reduction Act of 1984

STATE OF: WEST VIRGINIA

NAME OF ORGANIZATION: WEST VIRGINIA ECONOMIC DEVELOPMENT AUTHORITY

ADDRESS: Building 6, Room 525, State Capitol Complex, Charleston, West Virginia 25305

PHONE NO. (304) 348-3650

CONTACT OFFICER: Patricia H. Keeler; **TITLE:** Executive Director

DESCRIPTION OF PROGRAM: (1) Low cost direct loans for land, building & equipment; up to 50 % of project; based on job creation. (2) Issues Industrial Revenue Bonds (3) Also lends through statewide SBA 503 industrial development program.

Organization asset range; $10,000,000 to $100,000,000

Range of investment/grant per borrower/grantee:

Type of financing: ☐Grants; ■Loans; ☐Loan with equity participations or convertibility; ☐Loan Guarantees; ☐Equity; ☐Leases; ☐Sale-leaseback; Other:

Security position: Shared lien postitions with private sector lenders

Type of collateral: Equipment, Real Estate, Guarantees

Term of financing: Maximum: 20 and up **years; Minimum: years**

Industry preference (in order of priority, if any): Diversified

Borrower characteristics desired-required:

Min. number of years in business:

Min. annual sales: $

Min. net worth: $

Min. annual cash flow:

Min. annual net income: $

Other requirements: Open

Estimated $ available for investment annually: $6 Million plus SBA 503 funding & State Industrial Development pool ($50 million)

Annual interest rate for 1985: Max.: %; Min.: %; Ave.: 6%;

Special conditions, if any: Each financial package is tailored for a specific project.

STATE OF: WYOMING

NAME OF ORGANIZATION: WYOMING INDUSTRIAL DEVELOPMENT CORPORATION

ADDRESS: P.O. Box 612 Casper, WY 82062

PHONE NO. (307) 234-5351

CONTACT OFFICER: Larry McDonald; **TITLE:** Executive Director

DESCRIPTION OF PROGRAM: Make loans and investments and provide management counseling services to promising industries in the State of Wyoming

Organization asset range; $1,000,000 **to $**10,000,000

Range of investment/grant per borrower/grantee:

Type of financing: □Grants; ■Loans; ■Loan with equity participations or convertibility; □Loan Guarantees; ■Equity; ■Leases; ■Sale-leaseback; Other:

Security position: Seniority mandatory, Senior or subordinated

Type of collateral: Current Assets (Inventory, Accounts Receivable), Stocks & Bonds, Cash value of life insurance, Equipment, Real Estate, Guarantees

Term of financing: Maximum: years; Minimum: years

Industry preference (in order of priority, if any): Agriculture-Related, Communications, Construction & Development, Finance & Insurance, Hotels, Motels & Restaurants, Manufacturing & Processing, Medical & Other Health Services, Natural Resources, Real Estate, Recreation & Amusement, Research & Technology, Retailing, Wholesaling, Distribution, Services, Transportation, Utilities, Diversified

Borrower characteristics desired-required:

Min. number of years in business:

Min. annual sales: $

Min. net worth: $

Min. annual cash flow:

Min. annual net income: $

Other requirements:

Estimated $ available for investment annually: $

Annual interest rate for 1985: Max.: %; Min.: %; Ave.: %;

Special conditions, if any:

STATE OF: WYOMING

NAME OF ORGANIZATION: WYOMING COMMUNITY DEVELOPMENT AUTHORITY

ADDRESS: P.O. Box 612 Casper, WY 82062

PHONE NO. (307) 265-0603

CONTACT OFFICER: George Axlund; **TITLE:** Executive Director

DESCRIPTION OF PROGRAM: IRB's; AAA-rated letter of credit to secure bond issue, Direct loans by WCDA to bank borrowers; Requires letter of credit issued in support of WCDA's bonds by Texas Commercial Bank.

Organization asset range;

Range of investment/grant per borrower/grantee: **$**0 **to $**400,000

Type of financing: ☐Grants; ☐Loans; ☐Loan with equity participations or convertibility; ☐Loan Guarantees; ☐Equity; ☐Leases; ☐Sale-leaseback; Other: Bonds

Security position:

Type of collateral:

Term of financing: Maximum: 15-20 **years; Minimum: years**

Industry preference (in order of priority, if any): Agriculture-Related, Communications, Construction & Development, Finance & Insurance, Hotels, Motels & Restaurants, Manufacturing & Processing, Medical & Other Health Services, Natural Resources, Real Estate, Retailing, Wholesaling, Distribution, Services, Transportation, Utilities, Diversified

Borrower characteristics desired-required:

Min. number of years in business:

Min. annual sales: $

Min. net worth: $

Min. annual cash flow:

Min. annual net income: $

Other requirements:

Estimated $ available for investment annually: $

Annual interest rate for 1985: Max.: %; Min.: %; Ave.: %;

Special conditions, if any:

STATE OF: WYOMING

NAME OF ORGANIZATION: DEPT. OF ECONOMIC PLANNING & DEVELOPMENT

ADDRESS: Herschler Bldg, Cheyenne, WY 82002

PHONE NO. (307) 777-7285

CONTACT OFFICER: William (Butch) Keadle; **TITLE:** Financing Specialist

DESCRIPTION OF PROGRAM: Set aside programs for gap financing for small existing business in the State of Wyoming. Set aside is $1 million from Community Development Block Grant.

Organization asset range; $150,000 **to $**1,000,000

Range of investment/grant per borrower/grantee:

Type of financing: ☐Grants; ■Loans; ☐Loan with equity participations or convertibility; ☐Loan Guarantees; ☐Equity; ☐Leases; ☐Sale-leaseback; Other:

Security position: Senior or subordinated

Type of collateral: Equipment, Real Estate, Guarantees

Term of financing: Maximum: 15-20 **years; Minimum:** 0-1 **years**

Industry preference (in order of priority, if any): Agriculture-Related, Construction & Development, Hotels, Motels & Restaurants, Manufacturing & Processing, Real Estate,

Borrower characteristics desired-required:

Min. number of years in business: 3

Min. annual sales: $

Min. net worth: $

Min. annual cash flow:

Min. annual net income: $

Other requirements:

Estimated $ available for investment annually: **$**1 million

Federal Programs

Guide to Federal Programs

Agriculture-Related Programs

10.051 Commodity Loans & Purchases
(Price Supports)
10.052 Cotton Production Stabilization
(Cotton Direct Payments)
10.053 Dairy Indemnity Payments
(Milk and Dairy Cow Indemnity Payments)
10.055 Feed Grain Stabilization
(Feed Grain Direct Payments)
10.056 Storage Facilities and Equipment Loans
(Farm Storage and Drying Equipment Loans)
10.058 Wheat Production Stabilizaton
(Wheat Direct Payments)
10.059 National Wool Act Payments
(Wool and Mohair Payments)
10.065 Rice Production Stabilization
(Rice Direct Payments)
10.067 Grain Reserve Program
(Farmer-held and Owned Grain Reserve)
10.068 Rural Clean Water Program
10.404 Emergency Loans
10.406 Farm Operating Loans
10.407 Farm Ownership Loans

Business/Industry-Related Programs

10.850 Rural Electrification Loans and
Loan Guarantees
10.851 Rural Telephone Loans and Loan Guarantees
10.852 Rural Telephone Bank Loans
11.408 Fishermen's Contingency Fund
11.409 Fishing Vessel and Gear—
Damage Compensation Fund
11.415 Fishing Vessel Obligation Guarantees
59.002 Economic Injury Disaster Loans
59.003 Economic Opportunity Loans for
Small Businesses (EOLs)
59.008 Physical Disaster Loans (7(b)loans)
59.011 Small Business Investment Companies
(SBICs and MESBICs)
59.012 Small Business Loans (7(a))
59.013 State and Local Development Company
Loans
59.016 Bond Guarantees for Surety Companies
(Surety Bond Guarantees)
59.021 Handicapped Assistance Loans
(HAL-1 and HAL-2 loans)
59.030 Small Business Energy Loans
59.031 Small Business Pollution Control
Financing Guarantee
70.002 Foreign Investment Guarantees
(Extended-Risk Guarantees)
70.003 Foreign Investment Insurance
(Political Risk Insurance)

Conservation-Related Programs

10.064 Forestry Incentives Program
10.416 Soil and Water Loans

Indian Tribes and Tribal Corporations

15.124 Indian Loans-Economic Development

FEDERAL PROGRAMS

NOTE: The number before each program refers to the number in the 1984 Catalog of Federal Domestic Assistance. These summaries have omitted some details which information can be obtained from the contacts named. Housing and Community Economic Development-type programs have not been included in this listing. Programs which can directly benefit a businessman or farmer have been included.

AGENCY: DEPARTMENT OF AGRICULTURE AGRICULTURAL STABILIZATION & CONSERVATION SERVICE

PROGRAM NO. AND NAME:
10.051 Commodity Loans & Purchases (Price Supports)

TYPE OF ASSISTANCE:
Direct purchases and loans to support minimum prices

WHO IS ELIGIBLE:
Producers of eligible commodities, which are feed grains, rice, wheat, rye, soybeans, upland and extra-long staple cotton, dairy products, peanuts, tobacco, honey and sugar.

RESTRICTIONS/CONDITIONS:
Nonrecourse loans and direct purchases of commodities; available through March 31, May 31 or June 30 of the year following harvest, depending on commodity

MAXIMUM $ LIMITS*:
Purchase—Range not available; Loans—Range: $50 to $33,000,000; Average: $13,771

TERM:
Generally for 9 months or less

COLLATERAL:
Commodity

CONTACT:
Agricultural Stabilization and Conservation Service (ASCS) County or State Office

*Maximum $ limits (range and average) shown are figures for past and current fiscal years from "The 1984 Catalog of Federal Domestic Assistance."

AGENCY: DEPARTMENT OF AGRICULTURE AGRICULTURAL STABILIZATION & CONSERVATION SERVICE

PROGRAM NO. AND NAME:
10.052 Cotton Production Stabilization (Cotton Direct Payments)

TYPE OF ASSISTANCE:
Direct payments to support minimum price, and assistance if natural disaster prevents planting or reduces harvest, under certain conditions. Payment-in-kind offers payment in commodities.

WHO IS ELIGIBLE:
Cotton producer

RESTRICTIONS/CONDITIONS:
Applicant must have a record as a cotton producer; there are deadlines for application

MAXIMUM $ LIMITS:
Range: $3-$50,000;

TERM:
N/A

COLLATERAL:
N/A

CONTACT:
Agricultural Stabilization and Conservation Service (ASCS) County or State Office

AGENCY: DEPARTMENT OF AGRICULTURE
AGRICULTURAL STABILIZATION & CONSERVATION SERVICE

PROGRAM NO. AND NAME:
10.055 Feed Grain Production Stabilization (Feed grain direct payments)

TYPE OF ASSISTANCE:
Direct payments

WHO IS ELIGIBLE:
Producer of feed grains

RESTRICTIONS/CONDITIONS:
Used to guarantee a minimum price; and payments if natural disasters prevent planting or reduce harvest under certain conditions. Deadlines on applications have to be met. Payment-in-kind offers payment in commodity

MAXIMUM $ LIMITS:
Actual range: $3-$50,000

TERM:
N/A

COLLATERAL:
N/A

CONTACT:
ASCS County or State Office

AGENCY: DEPARTMENT OF AGRICULTURE
AGRICULTURAL STABILIZATION & CONSERVATION SERVICE

PROGRAM NO. & NAME:
10.056 Storage Facilities and Equipment Loans (Farm facility loans)

TYPE OF ASSISTANCE:
Direct loans to finance on-farm storage structures.

WHO IS ELIGIBLE:
Producer of one or more of 12 eligible commodities (barley, corn, grain sorghum, oats, wheat and rice; and soybeans under certain conditions)

RESTRICTIONS/CONDITIONS:
To finance the purchase of storage structures and to remodel existing grain storage facilities.

MAXIMUM $ LIMITS:
Maxmium loan amount is $25,000; aggregate outstanding loan balance cannot exceed $25,000 and $50,000 if the producer is participating in the grain reserve program at the time of application

TERM:
Maximum of 4 equal annual installments over 5 years

COLLATERAL:
Varies

CONTACT:
ASCS County or State Office

AGENCY: DEPARTMENT OF AGRICULTURE
AGRICULTURAL STABILIZATION & CONSERVATION SERVICE

PROGRAM NO. & NAME:
10.058 Wheat Production Stabilization (Wheat direct payments)

TYPE OF ASSISTANCE:
Direct payments

WHO IS ELIGIBLE:
Producer of wheat

RESTRICTIONS/CONDITIONS:
Used to guarantee a minimum price; and payments if natural disasters prevent planting or reduce harvest in qualified areas. Payment-in-kind program offers payment in commodity.

MAXIMUM $ LIMITS:
Actual range: $3-$50,000

TERM:
N/A

COLLATERAL:
N/A

CONTACT:
ASCS County or State Office

AGENCY: DEPARTMENT OF AGRICULTURE
AGRICULTURAL STABILIZATION & CONSERVATION SERVICE

PROGRAM NO. & NAME:
10.059 National Wool Act payments (Wool and Mohair payments)

TYPE OF ASSISTANCE:
Direct payments

WHO IS ELIGIBLE:
Owner of sheep, lambs or angora goats who sells wool or mohair from the animals

RESTRICTIONS/CONDITIONS:
Used to supplement farm income

MAXIMUM $ LIMITS:
Wool: Actual range: $5-$327,464; Average: $749; Mohair: Actual range: $5-$289,338; Average: $2,061

TERM:
N/A

COLLATERAL:
N/A

CONTACT:
ASCS County or State Office

AGENCY: DEPARTMENT OF AGRICULTURE
AGRICULTURAL STABILIZATION &
CONSERVATION SERVICE

PROGRAM NO. AND NAME:
10.063 Agricultural Conservation Program

TYPE OF ASSISTANCE:
Direct payments for specified use

WHO IS ELIGIBLE:
Owners, tenants, or groups who wish to share costs (ranging up to 75%) for conservation of soil, water, woodland, and energy, and pollution abatement

RESTRICTIONS/CONDITIONS:
Conservation on agricultural land, to conserve soil and water

MAXIMUM $ LIMITS:
Individual agreement: $3 - 3,500; $900 average
Pooling agreements: $3 - 10,000; $1800 average

TERM:
As specified in approvals

COLLATERAL:
N/A

CONTACT:
ASCS County or State Office

AGENCY: DEPARTMENT OF AGRICULTURE
AGRICULTURAL STABILIZATION &
CONSERVATION SERVICE

PROGRAM NO. & NAME:
10.064 Forestry Incentives Program

TYPE OF ASSISTANCE:
Direct payments for specified use

WHO IS ELIGIBLE:
Owner of "Non-industrial" private forest lands of 1,000 acre or less who is willing to share costs —usually 35%

RESTRICTIONS/CONDITIONS:
Used for tree planting and timber stand improvement. County should be designated as forestry incentives program county. Forest management plan needs to be developed by state forester and landowner

MAXIMUM $ LIMITS:
$3 - 10,000; $1,600 average

TERM:
10 years maximum; 1 year minimum

COLLATERAL:
N/A

CONTACT:
ASCS County or State Office

AGENCY: DEPARTMENT OF AGRICULTURE
AGRICULTURAL STABILIZATION & CONSERVATION SERVICE

PROGRAM NO. AND NAME:
10.065 Rice Production Stabilization (Rice Direct Payments)

TYPE OF ASSISTANCE:
Direct payments

WHO IS ELIGIBLE:
Producer of rice

RESTRICTIONS/CONDITIONS:
Used to guarantee a minimum price; and payments if natural disasters prevent planting or reduce harvest in qualified counties. Payment-in-kind offers payment in commodity.

MAXIMUM $ LIMITS:
Actual range: $3 - $50,000

TERM:
N/A

COLLATERAL:
N/A

CONTACT:
ASCS County or State Office

AGENCY: DEPARTMENT OF AGRICULTURE
AGRICULTURAL STABILIZATION & CONSERVATION SERVICE

PROGRAM NO. AND NAME:
10.067 Grain Reserve Program (Farmer-held and owned grain reserve)

TYPE OF ASSISTANCE:
Direct payments with unrestricted use

WHO IS ELIGIBLE:
Producers or approved cooperatives having a CCC loan on grain from an authorized crop year

RESTRICTIONS/CONDITIONS:
Producers must have a loan on the grain and provide storage

MAXIMUM $ LIMITS:
$25 - $50,000; Average: $1,300

TERM:
N/A

COLLATERAL:
N/A

CONTACT:
ASCS County or State Office

AGENCY: DEPARTMENT OF AGRICULTURE
AGRICULTURAL STABILIZATION & CONSERVATION SERVICE

PROGRAM NO. AND NAME:
10.068 Rural Clean Water Program (RCWP)

TYPE OF ASSISTANCE:
Direct payments to solve critical water quality problems resulting from agricultural nonpoint source pollution

WHO IS ELIGIBLE:
Landowner or operator (except governments and publicly traded corporations) in an approved project area whose land or activity contributes to the area's water quality problems and who has an approved water quality plan

RESTRICTIONS/CONDITIONS:
Project areas must be approved, and must reflect the water quality priority concerns

MAXIMUM $ LIMITS:
$50,000 per individual for life of contract

TERM:
3 - 10 years

COLLATERAL:
N/A

CONTACT:
ASCS County or State Office

AGENCY: DEPARTMENT OF AGRICULTURE
FARMERS HOME ADMINISTRATION

PROGRAM NO. AND NAME:
10.404 Emergency Loans

TYPE OF ASSISTANCE:
Guaranteed/insured loans

WHO IS ELIGIBLE:
Farmers, ranchers, and aquaculture operators affected by a disaster or emergency

RESTRICTIONS/CONDITIONS:
Loans to assist recovery from a natural and/or major disaster; no other sources of credit should be available; loans to cover losses and expenses for damaged or destroyed farm property and working capital; loans for actual dollar losses at varying below-market annual interest rates

MAXIMUM $ LIMITS:
$500 - $6,000,000

TERM:
Varies according to individual needs, type of losses and type of security available

COLLATERAL:

CONTACT:
FmHA County or State Office

AGENCY: DEPARTMENT OF AGRICULTURE
FARMERS HOME ADMINISTRATION

PROGRAM NO. AND NAME:
10.406 Farm Operating Loans

TYPE OF ASSISTANCE:
Guaranteed/insured loans

WHO IS ELIGIBLE:
U.S. citizen with farming background and family size farm

RESTRICTIONS/CONDITIONS:
Used for most farm operating expenses and refinance existing debt; no other sources of credit

MAXIMUM $ LIMITS:
Insured up to $100,000; Average: $30,050
Guaranteed up to $200,000; Average: $103,600

TERM:
7 years; renewals up to 7 years

COLLATERAL:

CONTACT:
FmHA County or State Office

AGENCY: DEPARTMENT OF AGRICULTURE
FARMERS HOME ADMINISTRATION

PROGRAM NO. AND NAME:
10.407 Farm Ownership Loans

TYPE OF ASSISTANCE:
Guaranteed/insured loans

WHO IS ELIGIBLE:
U.S. citizen with ability to manage a family farm or nonfarm enterprise

RESTRICTIONS/CONDITIONS:
Used for most farm real estate expenses, or starting nonfarm enterprise on farm property; no other sources of credit; limits on maximum amount of debt to FmHA

MAXIMUM $ LIMITS:
Actual range: $16,000 - $200,000;
Average: $73,680

TERM:
40 years

COLLATERAL:
Real estate

CONTACT:
FmHA County or State Office

AGENCY: DEPARTMENT OF AGRICULTURE
FARMERS HOME ADMINISTRATION

PROGRAM NO. AND NAME:
10.416 Soil and water loans

TYPE OF ASSISTANCE:
Guaranteed/insured loans

WHO IS ELIGIBLE:
Individual farmer, partnership, cooperatives or corporation or tenants who have no other sources of credit

RESTRICTIONS/CONDITIONS:
Used for soil conservation; water development; conservation and use; forestation; drainage of farmland; pasture expenses and related measures; pollution abatement and control facilities on farms; energy conserving measures

MAXIMUM $ LIMITS:
Actual range: $3,300 - $100,000;
Average: $18,000

TERM:
40 years

COLLATERAL:
Real estate and fixed assets

CONTACT:
FmHA County or State Office

AGENCY: DEPARTMENT OF AGRICULTURE
FARMERS HOME ADMINISTRATION

PROGRAM NO. AND NAME:
10.421 Indian Tribes and Tribal Corporation Loans

TYPE OF ASSISTANCE:
Guaranteed/Insured Loans

WHO IS ELIGIBLE:
Any Indian tribe recognized by the Secretary of the Interior or tribal corporation established pursuant to the Indian Reorganization Act without adequate uncommitted funds. Must be unable to obtain adequate credit elsewhere and must be able to show reasonable prospects of success.

RESTRICTIONS/CONDITIONS:
Loan funds may be used to acquire additional land within the reservation and for incidental costs associated with land purchase. Land may be used for development, equipment, or operating costs.

MAXIMUM $ LIMITS:
Range: $750,000 to $3,000,000; Average: $1,490,000

TERM:
Term may be up to 40 years

COLLATERAL:
Land

CONTACT:
Regional or Local Farmers Home Administration Office

AGENCY: DEPARTMENT OF AGRICULTURE
FARMERS HOME ADMINISTRATION

PROGRAM NO. AND NAME:
10.422 Business and Industrial Loans

TYPE OF ASSISTANCE:
Guaranteed/Insured Loans

WHO IS ELIGIBLE:
Public, private or cooperative organizations (profit or nonprofit), Indian tribes or individuals in rural areas

MAXIMUM $ LIMITS:
Guarantee to the lender cannot exceed 90 percent of the loss on principal advanced, including protective advances and accrued interest. Range: $11,000 to $50,000,000; Average: $1,277,000

TERM:
Maximum term is: 30 years for land and buildings, the usable life of machinery and equipment purchased with loan funds, not to exceed 15 years, and 7 years for working capital.

COLLATERAL:
All assets

CONTACT:
Regional or Local office, Farmers Home Administration, or Administrator, Farmers Home Administration, Department of Agriculture, Washington, D.C. 20250. Phone: (202) 447-7967

AGENCY: DEPARTMENT OF AGRICULTURE
RURAL ELECTRIFICATION
ADMINISTRATION

PROGRAM NO. AND NAME:
10.850 Rural Electrification Loans and Loan Guarantees

TYPE OF ASSISTANCE:
Guaranteed/insured loans

WHO IS ELIGIBLE:
Rural electric coops, public utility districts, power companies, municipalities, and other qualified power suppliers

RESTRICTIONS/CONDITIONS:
To facilitate central station electric service on a continuing basis in rural areas; may require obtaining a concurrent loan from a supplemental financing source

MAXIMUM $ LIMITS:
Insured loans: $250,000 - $25,000,000; Average: $2,700,000
Guaranteed loans: $5,000,000 - $1,500,000,000; Average: $170,000,000

TERM:
35 years

COLLATERAL:

CONTACT:
Administrator, Rural Electrification Administration, Department of Agriculture, Washington, D.C. 20250; (202)382-9540

AGENCY: DEPARTMENT OF AGRICULTURE
RURAL ELECTRIFICATION
ADMINISTRATION

PROGRAM NO. AND NAME:
10.851 Rural Telephone Loans and Loan Guarantees

TYPE OF ASSISTANCE:
Guaranteed/insured loans

WHO IS ELIGIBLE:
Telephone companies or cooperatives; non-profit, limited dividend, mutual associations or public bodies serving rural customers

RESTRICTIONS/CONDITIONS:
To supply and improve telephone service in rural areas; may require obtaining a concurrent loan from a supplemental financing source

MAXIMUM $ LIMITS:
Insured loans: $200,000 - $10,000,000; Average: $3,000,000
Guaranteed loans: $10,000,000 - $40,000,000; Average: $15,000,000

TERM:
35 years

COLLATERAL:

CONTACT:
Administrator, Rural Electrification Administration, Department of Agriculture, Washington, D.C. 20250; (202)382-9540

AGENCY: DEPARTMENT OF AGRICULTURE
RURAL ELECTRIFICATION
ADMINISTRATION

PROGRAM NO. AND NAME:
10.852 Rural Telephone Bank Loans

TYPE OF ASSISTANCE:
Direct loans

WHO IS ELIGIBLE:
Borrowers who have received a loan or loan commitment under Sec. 201 of the Rural Electrification Act; or certified by the administrator

RESTRICTIONS/CONDITIONS:
Supplemental financing to supply and improve telephone service in rural areas; sometimes will require obtaining a concurrent REA telephone loan

MAXIMUM $ LIMITS:
$250,000 - $15,000,000;Average: $2,500,000

TERM:
35 years

COLLATERAL:

CONTACT:
Governor, Rural Telephone Bank, Department of Agriculture, Washington, D.C. 20250; (202)382-9540

AGENCY: DEPARTMENT OF COMMERCE
NATIONAL OCEANIC AND
ATMOSPHERIC ADMINISTRATION

PROGRAM NO. AND NAME:
11.408 Fishermen's Contingency Fund

TYPE OF ASSISTANCE:
Direct payments for damage/loss of fishing gear and resulting economic loss due to oil and gas related activities in any area of the Outer Continental Shelf

WHO IS ELIGIBLE:
U.S. commercial fisherman

RESTRICTIONS/CONDITIONS:
Loss must be documented

MAXIMUM $ LIMITS:
Range: $500 - $25,000; Average:$4,939

TERM:
N/A

COLLATERAL:
N/A

CONTACT:
Chief, Financial Services Division, National Marine Fisheries Service, 3300 Whitehaven St. N.W., Washington, D.C. 20235. Telephone (202) 634-4688

AGENCY: DEPARTMENT OF COMMERCE
NATIONAL OCEANIC AND
ATMOSPHERIC ADMINISTRATION

PROGRAM NO. AND NAME:
11.409 Fishing Vessel and Gear Damage Compensation Fund

TYPE OF ASSISTANCE:
Direct Payments for loss, damage or destruction of U.S. fishermen's vessels by foreign fishing vessels and their gear by any vessel

WHO IS ELIGIBLE:
U.S fisherman (citizen)

RESTRICTIONS/CONDITIONS:
Incident causing claim must have occurred within the U.S. Fishery Conservation Zone or in an area where the U.S. has exclusive management authority

MAXIMUM $ LIMITS:
Claims are paid for depreciated replacement cost of gear and economic loss based on 25% of gross income lost.
Range: $600 - $150,000; Average: $6,000

TERM:
N/A

COLLATERAL:
N/A

CONTACT:
Michael Grable, National Marine Fisheries Service, Dept. of Commerce, 3300 Whitehaven St, NW, Washington, D.C. 20235; Phone: (202)634-7496

AGENCY: DEPARTMENT OF COMMERCE
NATIONAL OCEANIC AND
ATMOSPHERIC ADMINISTRATION

PROGRAM NO. AND NAME:
11.415 Fishing Vessel Obligation Guarantees

TYPE OF ASSISTANCE:
Guaranteed/insured loans

WHO IS ELIGIBLE:
Obligee able to service the obligation; obligor able to operate and maintain the mortgaged property

RESTRICTIONS/CONDITIONS:
Guarantee private loans to construct or upgrade U.S. fishing fleet or shoreside facilities; limited to 87.5% of actual costs

MAXIMUM $ LIMITS:
$15,000 - $9,000,000; Average:$500,000

TERM:
25 years

COLLATERAL:

CONTACT:
Chief, Financial Services Division, National Marine Fisheries Service, Department of Commerce, 3300 Whitehaven St. N.W., Washington, D.C. 20235
(202)634-7496 (Michael Grable)

AGENCY: DEPARTMENT OF THE INTERIOR
BUREAU OF INDIAN AFFAIRS (BIA)

PROGRAM NO. AND NAME:
15.124 Indian Loans — Economic Development

TYPE OF ASSISTANCE:
Direct loans, Guaranteed/insured loans; Technical assistance

WHO IS ELIGIBLE:
Individual Indians or Alaska natives from federally recognized tribes, tribes or organizations satisfactory to the Commissioner of Indian Affairs, who need funds to obtain financing for economic development projects from other government or private sources; no other source of credit must be available

RESTRICTIONS/CONDITIONS:
Except education, funds must be used on or near a reservation; uses can be for business, industry, agriculture, rehabilitation, housing, education; guaranty limited to 90% of outstanding principal and interest

MAXIMUM $ LIMITS:
$1,000 - over $1,000,000; Average: $100,000

TERM:
N/A

COLLATERAL:
N/A

CONTACT:
Local Bureau Office, or HQ: Director, Office of Indian Services, BIA, 18th and C Streets, N.W., Room 4600, Washington, D.C. 20245
(202)343-3657

AGENCY: DEPARTMENT OF TRANSPORTATION
MARITIME ADMINISTRATION

PROGRAM NO. AND NAME:
20.802 Federal Ship Financing Guarantees (Title XI)

TYPE OF ASSISTANCE:
Guaranteed/insured loans to promote construction and reconstruction of ships in the foreign and domestic commerce of the United States by providing Government guarantees of obligations so as to make commercial credits more readily available.

WHO IS ELIGIBLE:
Any U.S. citizen with the ability, experience, financial resources, and other qualifications necessary to the adequate operation and maintenance of the vessel.

RESTRICTIONS/CONDITIONS:
Aid available for vessels which are designed for research or for commercial use. Any vessel of not less than 5 net tons, and any vessel (other than a towboat, barge, scow, lighter, car float, canal boat or tank vessel of less than 25 gross tons) is eligible. There are deadlines for obtaining financial aid.

MAXIMUM $ LIMITS:
Shipowner must provide 12.5% or 25% of the total "actual cost" depending on the proposed construction. Range: $1,716,000 to $94,833,000

TERM:
Not to exceed the time period for which the obligation is guaranteed but in any case not to exceed 25 years.

COLLATERAL:

CONTACT:
Associate Administrator for Maritime Aids, Maritime Administration, Department of Transportation, Washington, D.C. 20590. Phone: (202)382-0364

SMALL BUSINESS ADMINISTRATION (SBA)

Practically all SBA programs exclude assistance to speculation businesses, publishing, nonprofit enterprises, and real property held for investment or speculation.

For business loan purposes, SBA defines a small business as one that is not dominant in its field and meets employment or sales standards developed by the Agency. For most industries, these standards are as follows:

Manufacturing: Maximum number of employees may range from 500 - 1,500 depending on the applicant's industry.

Wholesaling: Maximum number of employees not to exceed 500.

Services: annual receipts not over $3,500,00 $14,500,000 depending on the applicant's industry

Retailing: annual receipts not over $3,500,000-$13,500,00 depending on the industry.

Construction: average annual receipts not over $17,000,000 for three most recently completed fiscal years for general construction; and average annual receipts not exceeding $7,000,000 for special trade construction.

Agriculture: annual receipts not over 0.1 to 3. million.

AGENCY: SMALL BUSINESS ADMINISTRATION

PROGRAM NO. AND NAME:
59.002 Economic Injury Disaster Loans

TYPE OF ASSISTANCE:
Direct loans; Guaranteed/insured loans

WHO IS ELIGIBLE:
Small businesses suffering economic injury as a result of certain presidential, SBA and Department of Agriculture disaster designations

RESTRICTIONS/CONDITIONS:
Funds to be used for working capital, not real estate, equipment repair and acquisition

MAXIMUM $ LIMITS:
Range: $5,000 to $500,000; Average: $76,000

TERM:
30 years

COLLATERAL:

MAXIMUM PERCENT LOANED OR GUARANTEED:

AGENCY: SMALL BUSINESS ADMINISTRATION

PROGRAM NO. AND NAME:
59.003 Loans for Small Businesses (Business Loans 7 (a) (11))

TYPE OF ASSISTANCE:
Direct loans; Guaranteed/insured loans; Technical assistance

WHO IS ELIGIBLE:
Small businesses owned by low-income persons or located in areas of high unemployment

RESTRICTIONS/CONDITIONS:
Eligible businesses exclude publishing media, nonprofit enterprises, speculators in property, lending or investment enterprises, and financing real property held for investment; no other funds must be available on reasonable terms

MAXIMUM $ LIMITS:
Direct Loans: $1,000 to $100,000;
Guaranteed Loans: $2,250 to $315,600

TERM:

COLLATERAL:

MAXIMUM PERCENT LOANED OR GUARANTEED:

AGENCY: SMALL BUSINESS ADMINISTRATION

PROGRAM NO. AND NAME:
59.008 Physical Disaster Loans (7 (b) loans)

TYPE OF ASSISTANCE:
Direct loans; Guaranteed/insured loans

WHO IS ELIGIBLE:
Individuals, businesses, churches, private schools, colleges, universities and hospitals who have suffered physical property loss in an area designated as eligible for assistance by the Administration

RESTRICTIONS/CONDITIONS:
May be used to repair or replace damaged or destroyed realty, machinery and equipment, household and other personal property

MAXIMUM $ LIMITS:
Direct loans
Homes: $55,000 plus $50,000 in special cases
Businesses: $500,000
Additional amounts available as guaranteed loans made by financial institutions

TERM:
30 years

COLLATERAL:

MAXIMUM PERCENT LOANED OR GUARANTEED:

AGENCY: SMALL BUSINESS ADMINISTRATION

PROGRAM NO. AND NAME:
59.011 Small Business Investment Companies (SBICs & MESBICs)

TYPE OF ASSISTANCE:
Direct loans; Guaranteed/insured loans; Technical assistance

WHO IS ELIGIBLE:
Chartered SBIC or minority enterprise SBIC (MESBIC); and who provide equity and venture capital to small business

RESTRICTIONS/CONDITIONS:
SBICs and MESBICs to provide long-term loans or equity to small businesses; MESBICs invest only in businesses controlled by socially or economically disadvantaged persons; investment company cannot invest more than 20% of equity in any one small concern

MAXIMUM $ LIMITS:
Loan limits are based on equity, i.e., $3 or $4 for each $1 in equity
Actual: Guaranteed loans: $50,000 - $35,000,000; Average: $1,000,000

TERM:
15 years; MESBICs can also sell preferred stock to SBA

COLLATERAL:

MAXIMUM PERCENT LOANED OR GUARANTEED:
100%

AGENCY: SMALL BUSINESS ADMINISTRATION

PROGRAM NO. AND NAME:
59.012 Small Business Loans (7 (a))

TYPE OF ASSISTANCE:
Direct loans; Guaranteed/insured loans

WHO IS ELIGIBLE:
Small businesses excluding gambling establishments, publishing media, nonprofit enterprises, property speculators, lending or investment companies, property held for investment; no other sources of funds must be available; not to be used to pay unsecured creditor who is likely to sustain loss

RESTRICTIONS/CONDITIONS:
Funds not to be used for business relocation; used for working capital, equipment or building to be used for the business

MAXIMUM $ LIMITS:
$500,000 for Guaranteed/insured loans;
Actual:
Direct loans: $1,000 - $350,000; Average: $54,782
Guaranteed/insured loans: $1,800 - $500,000; Average: $113,589

TERM:
N/A

COLLATERAL:
Real estate, equipment, current assets, personal guarantees, etc.

MAXIMUM PERCENT LOANED OR GUARANTEED:
90%

AGENCY: SMALL BUSINESS ADMINISTRATION

PROGRAM NO. AND NAME:
59.013 State and Local Development Company Loans

TYPE OF ASSISTANCE:
Guaranteed/insured loans

WHO IS ELIGIBLE:
State or local development corporations organized to lend funds to small business in a designated geographic area; may be profit or nonprofit; state development corporations must be incorporated under a special state law

RESTRICTIONS/CONDITIONS:
Loans to state development corporation are to assist in form of long-term financing; loans to local development corporations (LDCs) are for real estate and machinery and equipment — not for working capital or for refinancing; some businesses ineligible (see 59.012)

MAXIMUM $ LIMITS:
Actual:
Direct loans: $13,000 - $500,000; Average: $32,258
Guaranteed loans: $15,840 - $500,000; Average: $186,206
Max. to LDC per borrower: $500,000

TERM:
Up to 25 years

COLLATERAL:
Real estate, machinery and equipment

MAXIMUM PERCENT LOANED OR GUARANTEED:

AGENCY: SMALL BUSINESS ADMINISTRATION

PROGRAM NO. AND NAME:
59.016 Bond Guarantees for Surety Companies (Surety Bond Guarantee)

TYPE OF ASSISTANCE:
Guaranteed/insured loans

WHO IS ELIGIBLE:
Surety companies who can meet the SBA's requirements or holding certificates of authority from the Secretary of the Treasury as acceptable sureties for bonds on Federal contracts.

RESTRICTIONS/CONDITIONS:
Applies to contracts of $1,000,000 or less on which bonding is required; guarantee is limited to performance of a specific contract; beneficiaries should be small general construction contractors with gross annual sales of less than $3,500,000

MAXIMUM $ LIMITS:
$1,000,000 contracts

TERM:
N/A

COLLATERAL:

MAXIMUM PERCENT LOANED OR GUARANTEED:
90% of a surety's losses on a contract

AGENCY: SMALL BUSINESS ADMINISTRATION

PROGRAM NO. AND NAME:
59.021 Handicapped Assistance Loans (HAL-1 and HAL-2 loans)

TYPE OF ASSISTANCE:
Direct loans; Guaranteed/insured loans

WHO IS ELIGIBLE:
Nonprofit sheltered workshops and similar organizations; and small business owned solely by handicapped individuals

RESTRICTIONS/CONDITIONS:
Used for working capital, equipment or facilities; not for training, education, housing or other supportive services

MAXIMUM $ LIMITS:
Direct loans: $500 - $350,000; Average: $88,944
Guaranteed loans: $15,000 - $346,500
Average: $175,000

TERM:

COLLATERAL:

MAXIMUM PERCENT LOANED OR GUARANTEED:

AGENCY: SMALL BUSINESS ADMINISTRATION

PROGRAM NO. AND NAME:
59.030 Small Business Energy Loans

TYPE OF ASSISTANCE:
Direct Loans; Guaranteed/Insured Loans (including Immediate Participation Loans)

WHO IS ELIGIBLE:
Small business involved in specific energy measures to finance equipment, real estate and materials

RESTRICTIONS/CONDITIONS:
Manufacture, design, market, install or service specific energy measures. Research and development expenses limited to 30 percent of loan outlay.

MAXIMUM $ LIMITS:
Direct: $350,000 (statutory), $150,000 (administration)
Guarantee: $500,000 or 90%

TERM:
25 years

COLLATERAL:
All, including personal guaranty, may be necessary

MAXIMUM PERCENT GUARANTEED:
90%

AGENCY: SMALL BUSINESS ADMINISTRATION

PROGRAM NO. AND NAME:
59.031 Small Business Pollution Control Financing Guarantee

TYPE OF ASSISTANCE:
Guaranteed/Insured Loans

WHO IS ELIGIBLE:
Small business to meet pollution control requirements and remain competitive. Applicant has minimum five years in business, profitable three of last five years

RESTRICTIONS/CONDITIONS:
Small concern requiring pollution control facilities/equipment, but have operational or financing disadvantage for obtaining such. Need willing lender to provide funds with SBA's guarantee

MAXIMUM $ LIMITS:
Average: approximately $1,300,000

TERM:
30 years

COLLATERAL:
N/A

CONTACT:
Chief, Pollution Control Financing Div., Office of Special Guarantees, SBA, 4040 N. Fairfax Drive, Ste 500, Arlington, VA 22203; Phone: (703) 235-2902

AGENCY: SMALL BUSINESS ADMINISTRATION

PROGRAM NO. AND NAME:
59.036 Certified Development Company Loans (503 Loans)

TYPE OF ASSISTANCE:
Guaranteed/insured loans to assist small businesses in the acquisition of land and buildings, construction, expansion, renovation and modernization, machinery and equipment.

WHO IS ELIGIBLE:
Certified Development Companies must be incorporated under general State corporation statute and certified by the SBA. Small businesses must be independently owned and operated for a profit, and satisfying additional SBA criteria.

RESTRICTIONS/CONDITIONS:
SBA criteria, and satisfying financial feasibility requirements. SBA acts as a conduit for funds raised through the Federal Financing Bank, and loaned to the small business through the CDC. SBA restricts its participation to 40% of the loan amount, and the loans are subordinated to the bank loan (which is normally 50%). The loans are fixed rate loans.

MAXIMUM $ LIMITS:
SBA participation ranges up to $500,000

TERM:
Loans may not exceed 25 years

COLLATERAL:
Assets financed and guarantees

CONTACT:
Local or regional office of the SBA; or Office of Economic Development, Small Business Administration, Room 720, 1441 L Street, NW, Washington, DC 20416

AGENCY: SMALL BUSINESS ADMINISTRATION

PROGRAM NO. AND NAME:
59.038 Veterans Loan Program

TYPE OF ASSISTANCE:
Direct Loans

WHO IS ELIGIBLE:
Small business as described by the SBA, and owned (minimum of 51 percent) by an eligible veteran(s). Management and daily operation of the business must be directed by one or more of the veteran owners of the applicant whose veteran status is used to qualify for the loan.

RESTRICTIONS/CONDITIONS:
To construct, expand, or convert facilities; to purchase building equipment or materials; for working capital. Funds must not be otherwise available on reasonable terms, or used for paying off a loan to an unsecured creditor who is in a position to sustain a loss. Guaranty loans must be used if available before a direct loan can be considered.

MAXIUM $ LIMITS:
Direct loans $1,000 to $350,000; $62,745

TERM:
N/A

COLLATERAL:
Varies

CONTACT:
Local or regional office of the Small Business Administration, or Director, Office of Business Loans, Small Business Administration, 1441 L Street, NW, Washington, D.C. 20416; Phone (202)653-6570

AGENCY: OVERSEAS PRIVATE INVESTMENT CORPORATION (OPIC)

PROGRAM NO. AND NAME:
70.002 Foreign Investment Guarantees

TYPE OF ASSISTANCE:
Guaranteed/insured loans by eligible U.S. investors in less-developed friendly countries and areas

WHO IS ELIGIBLE:
Guaranteed lender or investor must be U.S. citizen or U.S. corporation, partnership, etc. controlled by U.S. citizens, or 95% owned foreign subsidiary of such corporation

RESTRICTIONS/CONDITIONS:
Guarantee loans and investments against loss

MAXIMUM $ LIMITS:

TERM:
5-15 years

COLLATERAL:

CONTACT:
Robert L. Jordan, Information Officer, OPIC, Washington, D.C. 20527, Telephone: (202) 653-2800

AGENCY: OVERSEAS PRIVATE INVESTMENT CORPORATION (OPIC)

PROGRAM NO. AND NAME:
70.003 Foreign Investment Insurance (Political Risk Insurance)

TYPE OF ASSISTANCE:
Insurance (political risk) against risks of inconvertibility, expropriation, and war, revolution and insurrection in less developed friendly countries

WHO IS ELIGIBLE:
U.S. citizen or U.S. corporation, partnership or other association substantially owned by U.S. citizens, or wholly-owned foreign subsidiary of such corporation

RESTRICTIONS/CONDITIONS:
To encourage long-term private U.S. investment in developing countries; should contribute to developing the economy; insurance must be obtained prior to investment; should obtain host country's governmental approval;

MAXIMUM $ LIMITS:
$4,000 - $100,000,000; Average: $2,500,000

TERM:
20 years for equity investment, term of loan or contract

COLLATERAL:
N/A

CONTACT:
Same as Program 70.002

Index — Business Finance